PETERSON'S®

MASTER THE™ ACT®

About Peterson's®

Peterson's has been your trusted educational publisher for more than 50 years. It's a milestone we're quite proud of as we continue to offer the most accurate, dependable, high-quality educational content in the field, providing you with everything you need to succeed. No matter where you are on your academic or professional path, you can rely on Peterson's for its books, videos, online information, expert test-prep tools, the most up-to-date education exploration data, and the highest quality career success resources—everything you need to achieve your education goals. For our complete line of products, visit **www.petersons.com**.

For more information, contact Peterson's, 4380 S. Syracuse St., Suite 200, Denver, CO 80237; 800-338-3282 Ext. 54229; or visit us online at **www.petersons.com**.

Peter Giebel, Editorial Manager; Lacey N. Smith, Content Editor; Michelle Galins, Book Designer; Jeff Bellomi, Editor; Chrissy Frye, Editor; Kelsie McWilliams, Editor; Colleen Luckett, Editor

Peterson's Master the ACT

ISBN-13: 978-0-7689-4596-6

Printed in the United States of America

10 9 8 7 6 5 4 3 2 1   25 24 23

Fifth Edition

CONTENTS

BEFORE YOU BEGIN . . . . **X**

Why You Should Use This Book x

How This Book Is Organized xi

How to Use This Book xii

Special Study Features xiii

Eight Ways to Raise Your Score xiv

Peterson's® Publications xv

Give Us Your Feedback xv

You're Well on Your Way to Success xv

Part I: Preparing for the ACT®

CHAPTER 1: ALL ABOUT THE ACT® **4**

An Overview of the ACT® 6

What to Expect on the ACT® 8

How the ACT® is Scored 13

When to Take the ACT® 15

Registering for the ACT® 15

Getting Ready for Test Day 16

Next Steps 17

Summing It Up 18

CHAPTER 2: ACT® DIAGNOSTIC TEST **20**

Diagnostic Test Answer Sheet 23

Section 1: English Test 27

Section 2: Mathematics Test 47

Section 3: Reading Test 58

Section 4: Science Test 72

Section 5: Writing Test 86

Answer Key and Explanations: English Test 94

Answer Key and Explanations: Mathematics Test 102

Answer Key and Explanations: Reading Test 109

Answer Key and Explanations: Science Test 114

Answer Key and Explanations: Writing Test 119

Scoring Charts 128

CHAPTER 3: USING YOUR DIAGNOSTIC TEST RESULTS **130**

Reflecting on Your Diagnostic Test Experience 133

Forming a Study Plan 134

General Study Strategies 140

Mindsets to Improve Performance 142

ACT® Performance Tasks and Targets 143

Summing It Up 146

CONTENTS

Part II: The English Test on the ACT®

CHAPTER 4: INTRODUCTION TO ACT® ENGLISH **150**
How to Study with Part II 153
All about the English Test 153
Scoring Table 154
Sample Questions 155
Common Challenges 157
Summing It Up 158

CHAPTER 5: PRODUCTION OF WRITING AND KNOWLEDGE OF LANGUAGE **160**
Production of Writing Questions 163
Knowledge of Language Questions 173
Summing It Up 178
Test Yourself: Production of Writing and Knowledge of Language 179

CHAPTER 6: CONVENTIONS OF STANDARD ENGLISH **186**
Grammar 189
Sentence Structure and Formation 194
Punctuation 203
Verbs, Usage, and Agreement 211
Summing It Up 227
Test Yourself: Conventions of Standard English 229

CHAPTER 7: STRATEGIES FOR APPROACHING THE ENGLISH SECTION **234**
Reflecting on Your Diagnostic Test Score 237
Overall Section Strategies 238
Question Type Strategies 241
Test Yourself: English Strategies 248
General Reminders and Advice 253
Strategy Roundup 254
Summing It Up 255
Knowledge Check: English 257

Part III: the Mathematics Test on the ACT®

CHAPTER 8: INTRODUCTION TO ACT® MATH **282**
How to Study with Part III 285
All about the Math Section 285
Scoring Table 287

Sample Questions 288
Common Challenges. 289
Summing It Up 291

CHAPTER 9: ESSENTIAL SKILLS IN MATH. 292
Numbers and Operations 295
Ratios, Proportions, Rates, Decimals, and Percentages. 309
Basic Algebra 316
Basic Geometry. 320
Basic Statistics and Probability 335
Summing It Up 338
Test Yourself: Integrating Essential Skills 341

CHAPTER 10: PREPARING FOR HIGHER MATH: NUMBER & QUANTITY. 348
Number Properties. 351
Radical and Rational Exponents 352
Imaginary and Complex Numbers 356
Matrices 360
Vectors 362
Summing It Up 364
Test Yourself: PHM—Number & Quantity 365

CHAPTER 11: PREPARING FOR HIGHER MATH: ALGEBRA 370
Scientific Notation 372
Polynomials and Factoring 375
Rational Expressions 379
Systems of Linear Equations 382
Quadratics 384
Literal Equations 387
Inequalities 388
Summing It Up 394
Test Yourself: PHM—Algebra 395

CHAPTER 12: PREPARING FOR HIGHER MATH: FUNCTIONS 404
Logarithms 407
Functions 409
Operations and Functions 410
Graphing Functions 411
Types of Functions 411
Sequences 422
Summing It Up 424
Test Yourself: PHM—Functions 426

CONTENTS

CHAPTER 13: PREPARING FOR HIGHER MATH: GEOMETRY **430**

   2D Shapes 433

   Right Triangle Trigonometry 443

   Coordinate Geometry 447

   Summing It Up 460

   Test Yourself: PHM—Geometry 462

CHAPTER 14: PREPARING FOR HIGHER MATH: STATISTICS & PROBABILITY **468**

   Statistics 471

   Probability 475

   Summing It Up 480

   Test Yourself: PHM—Statistics & Probability 481

CHAPTER 15: STRATEGIES FOR APPROACHING THE MATHEMATICS SECTION **484**

   Reflecting on Your Diagnostic Test Score 487

   Overall Section Strategies 488

   Question Strategies 490

   Test Yourself: Math Strategies 496

   General Reminders and Advice 500

   Strategy Roundup 501

   Summing It Up 502

   Knowledge Check: Mathematics 503

Part IV: The Reading Test on the ACT®

CHAPTER 16: INTRODUCTION TO ACT® READING **524**

   How to Study with Part IV 527

   All about the Reading Section 528

   Scoring Table 528

   Types of Reading Passages 529

   Sample Questions 530

   Common Challenges 533

   Summing It Up 534

CHAPTER 17: KEY CONCEPTS IN READING COMPREHENSION **536**

   Understanding the ACT® Reading Section 539

   ACT® Reading Question Types (with Practice!) 541

   Building Vocabulary to Increase Comprehension 576

   Summing It Up 579

   Test Yourself: Reading Comprehension 580

CHAPTER 18: STRATEGIES FOR APPROACHING THE READING SECTION............**584**

Reflecting on Your Diagnostic Test Score 587
Overall Section Strategies.....................................588
Passage Strategies..593
Test Yourself: Reading Strategies..............................603
General Reminders and Advice 608
Strategy Roundup 609
Summing It Up 610
Knowledge Check: Reading.....................................612

Part V: The Science Test on the ACT®

CHAPTER 19: INTRODUCTION TO ACT® SCIENCE............................**632**

How to Study with Part V 635
All about the Science Section 635
Scoring Table 636
Types of Passages 637
Sample Questions 637
Common Challenges...642
Summing It Up 643

CHAPTER 20: KEY CONCEPTS IN SCIENCE **644**

Science Passages and Question Types 647
Research Summaries 648
Data Representation...658
Conflicting Viewpoints 664
Summing It Up 672
Test Yourself: Science 674

CHAPTER 21: STRATEGIES FOR APPROACHING THE SCIENCE SECTION............**682**

Reflecting on Your Diagnostic Test Score 685
Overall Section Strategies....................................686
Question and Passage Strategies...............................689
Test Yourself: Science Strategies..............................699
General Advice and Reminders 702
Strategy Roundup 702
Summing It Up 704
Knowledge Check: Science 706

CONTENTS

Part VI: The Writing Test on the ACT®

CHAPTER 22: INTRODUCTION TO ACT® WRITING.............................**726**
How to Study with Part VI.......................729
All about the Writing Test......................729
Rubric for the Writing Test.....................730
Sample Prompt................................734
Common Challenges..........................735
Summing It Up................................737

CHAPTER 23: WRITING SKILLS AND STRATEGIES.........................**738**
Traits of a Strong Argumentative Essay..........741
Improving Your Writing Skills...................742
Strategies for the ACT® Writing Test.............754
Summing It Up................................761
Sample Essay and Practice Writing Prompts.......762

Part VII: Practice Test

CHAPTER 24: ACT® PRACTICE TEST...................................**770**
Practice Test Answer Sheet.....................773
Section 1: English Test.........................777
Section 2: Mathematics Test.....................793
Section 3: Reading Test.........................805
Section 4: Science Test.........................818
Section 5: Writing Test.........................833
Answer Key and Explanations: English Test........841
Answer Key and Explanations: Mathematics Test....848
Answer Key and Explanations: Reading Test........855
Answer Key and Explanations: Science Test........860
Answer Key and Explanations: Writing Test........866
Scoring Charts................................870

Credits

Excerpt from "The Sculptor's Funeral" by Willa Cather (1905)

Excerpt from "European Invasion: DNA Reveals the Origins of Modern Europeans" by Alan Cooper and Wolfgang Haak, published by *The Conversation* (March 2015)

Excerpt from *The Autobiography of Charles Darwin* by Charles Darwin (1887)

Excerpt from *The French Impressionists* by Camille Mauclair (1903)

Excerpt from *The Science of Human Nature: A Psychology for Beginners* by William Henry Pyle (1917)

Excerpt from *A Daughter of the Samurai* by Etsu Inagaki Sugimoto (1925)

Excerpt from *The Outline of Science, Vol. 1* by J. Arthur Thomson (1921)

Excerpt from "When modern Eurasia was born" from University of Copenhagen – Faculty of Science, published by *ScienceDaily* (June 2015)

Excerpt from *Twilight Sleep* by Edith Wharton (1927)

Review of "Overview – SSRI Antidepressants" by UK National Health Service (February 2021)

Peterson's Updates and Corrections:

Check out our website at **www.petersonsbooks.com/updates-and-corrections/** to see if there is any new information regarding the test and any revisions or corrections to the content of this book. We've made sure the information in this book is accurate and up to date; however, the test format or content may have changed since the time of publication.

BEFORE YOU BEGIN

OVERVIEW

Why You Should Use This Book

How This Book Is Organized

How to Use This Book

Special Study Features

Eight Ways to Raise Your Score

Peterson's® Publications

Give Us Your Feedback

You're Well on Your Way
to Success

WHY YOU SHOULD USE THIS BOOK

Peterson's *Master the*™ *ACT*® is designed by test experts and educators to fully prepare you for test-day success. From the start of your test prep journey to your final review, this book includes an array of tools and tips to help you shine on the ACT. This helpful guide includes the following:

ESSENTIAL TEST INFORMATION

We take the stress out of planning for the ACT by providing all the information you'll need to know before the big day in one place—including how to register, where to go, and even what to bring on the day of the exam. We've got you covered!

COMPREHENSIVE COVERAGE OF ACT TEST FORMAT

After using this book, you'll know the structure and format of the ACT from start to finish and have all the information you'll need for success on test day.

THOROUGH TEST TOPIC REVIEW

You'll get a thorough review of every topic tested on the ACT and help with creating an effective study plan for reaching your goal score. Not only will there be no surprises on test day, but you'll also have the confidence that comes with being thoroughly prepared.

PLENTY OF REALISTIC TEST QUESTION PRACTICE

This book has parts to cover each of the four core subjects tested on the ACT (English, Mathematics, Reading, and Science) as well as the optional Writing test. Within each part, you'll find abundant opportunities for realistic practice with questions just like those you'll encounter during the actual test.

PRE- AND POST-TESTING TO SUPPORT ANY STUDY PLAN

Take a full-length diagnostic exam to help you determine your strengths and weaknesses and target your study time effectively. Then, build your confidence with practice test sections at the end of each part. When you're close to exam day, take a practice test to see your progress and find places to target last minute review. And if you need more practice, there are additional practice tests available through **www.petersons.com!**

EXPERT TIPS, ADVICE, AND STRATEGIES

Our test prep professionals are veteran educators who know what it takes to get a top score on the ACT—you'll get the expert tools that have proven to be effective on exam day, putting you a step ahead of the test-taking competition. Consider this your inside edge as you prepare to conquer the ACT!

We know that doing well on the ACT is important, both to you and your family—we're here to help you through every step of your journey. Consider this book your all-in-one test preparation package to get you through the ACT and on your way to the school of your choice.

HOW THIS BOOK IS ORGANIZED

This book has all the answers to your questions about the ACT. It contains up-to-date information, hundreds of practice questions, and solid test-taking advice. Here's how you can use it to optimize your ACT prep journey.

Familiarize Yourself with the ACT

Part I contains answers to all your questions about the ACT. You'll learn what kinds of questions to expect and how they look, how the different tests that comprise the ACT are scored, and numerous learning strategies and study skills to help you make the most of your prep time.

It also contains the diagnostic test and a chapter on how to analyze your diagnostic test results so you can use that information to make an effective study plan.

Study by ACT Subject

Each of the following parts will contain information on each individual test within the ACT, how many questions it contains, how long test takers will have to complete it, the different scoring categories, and extensive review of the skills and strategies necessary to perform well on that test.

- **Part II** covers the English test.
- **Part III** covers the Mathematics test.
- **Part IV** covers the Reading test.
- **Part V** covers the Science test.
- **Part VI** covers the optional Writing test. You'll only need to look at this section if you are planning on taking the optional test, which some may choose to do if they believe it will help them stand out. Check with your schools of choice to see if they require it or talk with a guidance counselor or admissions officer to determine if taking the optional Writing test might be an appropriate move for you.

Evaluate Progress and Review

- **Part VII** contains a practice test. While you can take this test at any time in your study journey, we recommend taking it towards the end of your studying by using it as a post-test. Doing so allows you to evaluate your overall progress since the diagnostic test. Furthermore, if you analyze your post-test the same way we suggest you do with the diagnostic test in Chapter 3, you'll receive useful feedback on any subjects you can target during your final test prep review sessions.

HOW TO USE THIS BOOK

The way this book is set up lends itself to two primary paths of study. Choose the one that works the best for your study goals.

Diagnostic Test Method

One way to use this book is to start with the diagnostic test in Chapter 2. A diagnostic test is a type of pre-test that helps you understand your strengths and weaknesses before you begin studying. It "diagnoses" the skills that need the most improvement.

In this method, you start with Part I and familiarize yourself with the specifications of the ACT before taking a diagnostic test. This test will give you a sampling of the kinds of questions you are likely to see on the ACT, and it will show you where you might need to focus your test-prep efforts.

Once you've taken your diagnostic test, turn to Chapter 3 for help understanding your results and using them to form a cohesive study plan. From there, you'll be prepared to work through the rest of the book in an order that suits your performance goals. You don't have to follow the book in the order it was written in this case; instead, you can feel free to jump around between the different parts based on the personalized study plan you created from your diagnostic test results.

Front-to-Back Method

Another way to use this book is the front-to-back method. In this method, you work through the book the way it is organized.

Start at Part I of the book and carefully read through the introductory section on the ACT. This will help you understand the exam and how it's scored. Next, take a diagnostic test and analyze your results in Part II. Then, study the content sections in Parts II–VI. If you know your stronger and weaker skills, you might devote extra time to sections where you need the most improvement.

After you've reviewed the content, take a practice test in Part VII. Taking a practice test will help you be more prepared on exam day. Even if you somehow don't improve your score between the diagnostic test and

TIP

Test takers who want extra practice can find additional practice exams online. For more information, go to www.petersons.com/testprep/act/

practice test, the process of taking each can itself help increase your score. This is because you become more familiar with the test format each time you try, which increases your confidence.

SPECIAL STUDY FEATURES

Peterson's *Master the*™ ACT® was designed to be easy to use so that you can locate the information you need. It includes several features to make your preparation easier.

Overview

Each chapter begins with a bulleted overview listing the topics that will be covered in the chapter. You know immediately where to look for a topic that you need to work on.

Summing It Up

Each chapter ends with a point-by-point summary that captures the most important topics covered.

Practice Sets

In some chapters, you'll find Practice Sets that are designed to help you practice question types or specific concepts as you learn them. Use these practice exercises to ensure that you understand key concepts as they are introduced.

Test Yourself Exercises

In addition to Practice Sets, you'll notice that some chapters include Test Yourself exercises. These are similar to practice sets but they are longer and offer you the opportunity to practice multiple new strategies or skills simultaneously. Each

time you encounter a Test Yourself is an opportunity to check your progress so far and play with different strategies you've been considering for exam day.

Knowledge Checks

At the end of each of the parts that covers one of the four core subjects on the ACT, you'll find a Knowledge Check, which is a test-length practice section designed to evaluate your understanding of the concepts presented throughout the chapter. When you add the Knowledge Checks in the book together, they create a complete practice test. At the end of Part VI, you'll find multiple practice prompts for the optional Writing test. You only need to complete one of these practice essays as an official Knowledge Check for it to "count" towards taking a full practice test, but the additional prompts are included to facilitate extra writing practice.

What makes the Knowledge Checks different from the practice test in Chapter 24 is that they are separated out so that you'll only practice for one subject test at a time. This means you can practice under test conditions without having to set aside the time for a full practice test run. Set a timer and try to complete the Knowledge Check in the time allotted so that you can see how you might perform on the full-length practice test you'll take later. Doing so allows you to evaluate how your mastery of a given subject is coming along midway through your studies.

Bonus Information

In addition, be sure to look in the page margins of your book for the following test prep tools:

- **FYI:** FYI notes highlight critical information about the format of the ACT.

- **TIPS:** Tips draw your attention to valuable concepts, advice, and shortcuts for tackling the tests or your study time.

- **ALERT:** Whenever you need to be careful of a common pitfall or test-taker trap, you'll find an *Alert*. This information reveals and helps eliminate the wrong turns many people take on the exam.

EIGHT WAYS TO RAISE YOUR SCORE

When it comes to taking the ACT, some test-taking skills will help you more than others. There are concepts you can learn, techniques you can follow, and tricks you can use that will help you to perform your very best. Those strategies and tricks can be found throughout this book, but generally speaking, here are our picks for the eight best ways to raise your score:

Regardless of your study plan, get started by reading Part I to familiarize yourself with the test formats. Understanding the ins and outs of the ACT will make it easier to strategize when studying.

Use your diagnostic test analysis in Chapter 3 to understand yourself better as a test taker. Your results provide you with key information about how you perform on timed tests. Use your reflections on your diagnostic test experience to optimize your study plan.

Use your diagnostic test to plan your study time. Spend the most time studying concepts you struggled with, but save time for review of each section type, as well.

Make sure to complete the exercises in each chapter you read. You can do so as you go along to practice concepts right after you review them.

Revisit challenging chapters and their summaries. Try and summarize each chapter like you were teaching the concepts to someone else. If there's one you are struggling to "teach," that's a good clue you need to review it. Making your own notes or study guides is a helpful way to reinforce concepts.

After you have completed all the study sections, take your practice test. When you go to take your practice test, make sure you are applying new test-taking strategies you've picked up, as well.

During the last phase of your study, review your practice test. Can you readily identify why questions you got wrong were wrong and how you'd solve them now? Can you spot any old mistakes you used to make and imagine what you'd do differently now that you've studied hard? This is a good way to refresh your knowledge of all the concepts you've learned and pinpoint where you can focus during any last-minute review.

The night before your exam, RELAX. You'll be prepared—you've already put in the work, so get some rest and go into your exam feeling awake and refreshed.

PETERSON'S® PUBLICATIONS

Peterson's publishes a full line of books—career preparation, education exploration, test prep, and financial aid. Peterson's books are available for purchase online at **www.petersons.com**. Sign up for one of our online subscription plans and you'll have access to our entire test prep catalog of more than 150 exams *plus* instructional videos, flashcards, interactive quizzes, and more! Our subscription plans allow you to study as quickly as you can or as slowly as you'd like.

GIVE US YOUR FEEDBACK

Peterson's publications can be found at your local bookstore and library, high school guidance offices, college libraries and career centers, and at www.petersonsbooks. com. Peterson's books are now also available as ebooks.

We welcome any comments or suggestions you may have about this publication. Your feedback will help us make educational dreams possible for you—and others like you.

YOU'RE WELL ON YOUR WAY TO SUCCESS

Remember that knowledge is power. By using this book, you will be studying the most comprehensive guide available. We *know* you're eager to get to the test practice and review but taking the time to develop a thorough understanding of the exam from top to bottom will give you a real advantage—and put you ahead of the test-taking competition. We'll go carefully through each section of the ACT so you'll be confident and prepared for test day success. Let's get started!

PART I
PREPARING FOR THE ACT®

1 | All about the ACT®

2 | ACT® Diagnostic Test

3 | Using Your Diagnostic Test Results

CHAPTER

All about the ACT®

ALL ABOUT THE ACT®

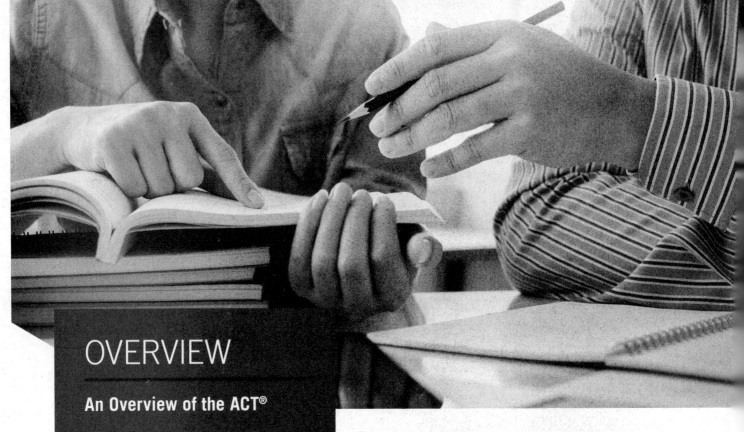

OVERVIEW

An Overview of the ACT®

What to Expect on the ACT®

How the ACT® is Scored

When to Take the ACT®

Registering for the ACT®

Getting Ready for Test Day

Next Steps

Summing It Up

AN OVERVIEW OF THE ACT®

Before you jump straight into the review sections and test practice in the chapters that follow, it's worth your time and attention to get to know some of the ACT fundamentals first. The more you know about the exam and its different components, the more prepared you'll be on the big day, and the greater your advantage will be over other test takers.

Why Does the ACT Matter?

Your academic record includes your GPA, extra-curricular activities, and any awards, distinctions, and letters of recommendation written on your behalf. College admissions staff use your ACT scores alongside your academic record to determine whether you're a good fit for their school and are ready to handle college-level subject material.

If college is in your long-term plans and the schools you're planning on applying to require the ACT, then it's certainly in your best interest to take the exam seriously.

Should I Take the ACT?

Each college and university has a unique set of requirements to be considered for admission—know the rules of the schools to which you plan to apply so you can determine if you need to take the ACT exam. As a result of the COVID-19 pandemic, fewer institutions require students to submit ACT scores as part of their college applications. Even if the school you're applying to doesn't require the ACT exam, it might be worth taking the exam as a supplement to your other application materials. The ACT can help college admissions departments gauge your academic proficiency in several key subject areas and help you demonstrate that you're ready to handle the rigors of college-level coursework.

How Has the COVID-19 Pandemic Affected ACT Scores?

The average score for the high school class of 2022 was 19.8, which is the first time since 1991 that the average ACT composite score fell below 20.0. While scores have been trending downward for years, this decline was exacerbated by the COVID-19 pandemic. Due to the disruptions caused by the pandemic, many students postponed taking the ACT exam or took it under circumstances that were less than ideal. As a result, some test takers may have been unable to prepare as thoroughly as they would have liked while others may have faced additional stress and anxiety related to the pandemic. Moreover, the shift to remote learning and the closure of schools significantly impacted students' educational experiences, which in turn likely affected their ACT scores. Some students may have contracted COVID-19, which could have limited their ability to participate fully in remote learning. Others may have experienced different obstacles, such as limited internet access, the pressure caused by financial or caretaking responsibilities, or other sources of stress and distractions. These factors, among many others, led some colleges and universities to drop the requirement for prospective students to submit ACT scores as part of their applications. However, many institutions still require applicants to submit their ACT scores to be eligible for admission. They may also require ACT scores to qualify students for certain types of scholarships or other aid.

As you review the concepts covered in this book, consider how the pandemic affected your own education. Did you thrive or struggle with the shift to remote learning? Were there certain concepts or ideas that you weren't able to fully grasp? Are there any content areas that would be helpful for you to brush up on prior to taking the ACT exam? Throughout this book, we encourage you to reflect on your own learning and to identify opportunities to learn or relearn concepts that you might have missed during your education. Because the COVID-19 pandemic was such an unprecedented disruption to education and society at large, there's no shame in acknowledging areas where you could benefit from additional review time. This book is intended to be a valuable tool and reference guide to help you every step of the way.

 FYI -

If at any point you feel like you could benefit from more focused instruction on a given topic or if you would like additional opportunities for practice, visit Petersons.com/testprep/act to learn more. Use the coupon code ACTJUST4U to save 15%.

WHAT TO EXPECT ON THE ACT®

The ACT exam is designed to test your knowledge and abilities in the following core subjects: English, Mathematics, Reading, Science, and Writing. Here's the official exam breakdown:

ACT® EXAM BREAKDOWN

Test Section	Number of Questions	Time to Complete
English	75 multiple-choice questions	45 minutes
Mathematics	60 multiple-choice questions	60 minutes
Reading	40 multiple-choice questions	35 minutes
Science	40 multiple-choice questions	35 minutes
Writing*	1 essay	40 minutes

* Optional

The English Test

The ACT English test consists of a set of five essays accompanied by 75 multiple-choice questions. The essays you'll encounter on the exam will span a variety of genres and rhetorical situations, each designed to test your language and writing skills. Each essay will contain underlined portions that are numbered to correspond with a numbered set of questions that offer alternatives to how the text is currently written. It is your job to determine if each underlined portion is correct as written or requires a revision to accomplish one of the following goals:

- Improve clarity or cohesion
- Promote consistency in the author's style or tone
- Correct an error in standard English grammar, usage, or mechanics

For each question, if there is an error or multiple errors, you'll select the best correction offered from among the available answer choices. If there are no errors, you'll select the choice that reads NO CHANGE.

You'll also encounter questions that target the following:

- Specific sections of the essay
- Ideas covered in or based on the essay
- Structure and organization of the essay

These questions will typically ask you about the best way to think about, organize, or style a specific portion of each essay or perhaps an entire essay. The relevant portion in each passage will be numbered, and those numbers will refer to the corresponding questions that address those portions. These questions test your ability to analyze and comprehend a piece of writing, determine if the author was effective in achieving their goals, recognize the key effects of making text revisions, and make determinations regarding potential improvements.

Your scores on the English test will include a total test score, which is based on how well you answer the entire set of 75 questions, as well as scores for the following three individual reporting categories.

CONVENTIONS OF STANDARD ENGLISH
(51–56% of English test questions)

These questions will test your ability to demonstrate your understanding and mastery of standard English grammar conventions, usage, and mechanics. You'll make determinations regarding revising, editing, and improving the essays presented in the following key areas:
- Punctuation
- Usage
- Sentence structure and formation

PRODUCTION OF WRITING
(29–32% of English test questions)

These questions will test your understanding and mastery regarding the focus and purpose of a given piece of writing in the following key areas:

- **Organization, cohesion, and unity:** Does the text utilize a coherent and consistent structure and flow? You will be asked to evaluate the logic and organization of the piece among the various elements and in its entirety (including an appropriate introduction, body, and conclusion).
- **Topic development:** Are the rhetorical elements of the text sound? You'll be tasked with recognizing if the author has achieved their intended goal for the piece, analyzing the author's purpose for various parts of the text, and evaluating the relevance of the material presented within the larger text's focus.

KNOWLEDGE OF LANGUAGE
(13–19% of English test questions)

These questions will test your understanding and mastery of appropriate language use, effective concision and precision regarding an author's word choice, and how well an author maintains a consistent tone and style within a given piece of writing.

The Mathematics Test

The Mathematics test on the ACT exam is a 60-minute test consisting of 60 multiple-choice questions that span five key math subcategories, which you'll have likely encountered during high school and are typically covered in entry-level college mathematics courses. Your scores on the Mathematics test will include a total test score, which is based on how well you answer the entire set of 60 questions, as well as scores for three individual reporting categories.

PREPARING FOR HIGHER MATHEMATICS
(57–60% of Mathematics test questions)

These questions will include the following math subcategories:

- **Algebra (12–15% of questions):** For these questions, you will be asked to use and interpret equations including polynomial, linear, radical, and exponential relationships; graph, model, and solve various types of expressions; solve systems of equations; and apply various results to real-world contexts.
- **Geometry (12–15% of questions):** These questions will test your understanding of various solids and shapes; your ability to apply such concepts as surface area, congruence, similarity relationships, and volume measurement; your knowledge of composite objects, solving for missing values in circles, triangles, and other figures; trigonometric ratios; and equations of conic sections.
- **Functions (12–15% of questions):** These questions focus on the application, notation, definition, manipulation, translation, and representation of functions including linear, radical, polynomial, logarithmic, and piecewise functions. Your ability to interpret and utilize key features of graphs will also be tested.
- **Statistics and probability (8–12% of questions):** For these questions, you will be evaluated on your understanding of various data collection methods and center and spread of distributions, as well as your ability to model bivariate data relationships and calculate probabilities that require you to recognize related sample spaces.
- **Number and quantity (7–10% of questions):** These questions will test your understanding and knowledge of numerical quantities, including expressions with integers and rational exponents; real and complex number systems; and vectors and matrices.

INTEGRATING ESSENTIAL SKILLS
(40–43% of Mathematics test questions)

Your ability to apply and synthesize your aggregate mathematical knowledge and skills to solve more complex problems will be tested here. You'll be tasked with addressing such concepts as:
- Proportional relationships
- Area, volume, and surface area
- Percentages and rates
- Average and median
- Expressing numbers
- Solving multistep, nonroutine problems that require combining skills
- Applying skills in varied contexts
- Demonstrating fluency
- Understanding important mathematical connections

MODELING
(~47% of Mathematics test questions)

Questions in this category overlap with the other question categories and are designed to measure your ability to work with models and apply concepts of modeling across the math topics presented on the ACT exam. You will be asked to evaluate, understand, produce, interpret, and improve models.

While you will have to know basic formulas and computations for the Mathematics test, you will *not* be expected to remember more complex ones—they'll be provided for you along with the questions. Although most of the questions on the ACT Math test will be self-contained, there will be some that may be part of a set of questions. Be sure to read each question and its associated instructions carefully to earn your best possible score.

You'll be permitted to use certain calculators on the Math test, though a calculator is not required and may not always be the best approach to solving a problem.

When tackling a math question, use your best judgment and the skills you've developed to determine the best route to the correct answer. For more information, review the ACT calculator policy.

The Reading Test

The Reading test of the ACT exam is a 35-minute test consisting of 40 multiple-choice questions that assess your ability to read critically, integrate information from multiple text sources, and apply logical reasoning skills using evidence from the passage.

The passages you encounter on exam day represent those typically found in a student's first-year college coursework and will span a variety of subject areas. Of the four sections on the ACT Reading test, one will contain two short prose passages and three will include one longer prose passage each. For each passage, you'll be provided with key supporting information, including the type of passage it is, the author and source, and any other relevant supporting information required to help you answer the associated questions correctly.

Your scores on the Reading test will include a total test score, which is based on how well you answer the entire set of 40 questions, an Understanding Complex Texts indicator, and scores for three individual reporting categories.

KEY IDEAS AND DETAILS
(55–60% of Reading test questions)

Questions in this category are designed to measure your ability to do the following:
- Accurately summarize key information and ideas
- Draw logical inferences and conclusions
- Understand relationships (including sequential, comparative, and cause-effect relationships)
- Read texts critically
- Determine central themes and ideas

CRAFT AND STRUCTURE
(25–30% of Reading test questions)

Questions in this category will assess your ability to do the following:
- Determine the meanings of words and phrases
- Analyze text structure
- Analyze an author's decisions regarding word choice
- Understand an author's perspective and purpose
- Analyze various points of view and perspectives
- Determine the effectiveness of an author's rhetorical decisions
- Differentiate and analyze sources of information

INTEGRATION OF KNOWLEDGE AND IDEAS
(13–18% of Reading test questions)

Questions in this category will assess your ability to do the following:
- Differentiate between opinion and fact
- Make key connections between different yet related facts using evidence
- Understand author claims
- Analyze how authors construct their arguments
- Evaluate reasoning and evidence from a variety of sources

Make sure you carefully read each passage, its supporting documentation, and all instructions, as the questions on the ACT Reading test require you to think critically about the texts, determine meanings that are stated both explicitly and implicitly, recognize main ideas, and identify the meanings of words as they are used in context. You'll also have to locate and interpret significant details, understand the correct sequence of events, comprehend cause-effect relationships, analyze tone and mood, and draw generalizations.

The Science Test

The ACT Science test is a 35-minute test consisting of 40 multiple-choice questions. The test includes various authentic scientific scenarios and is designed to measure your ability to reason, evaluate, analyze, problem solve, and interpret key college-level scientific information. The science skills tested cover the following core topic areas: biology, chemistry, physics, and Earth/space science (meteorology, astronomy, geology, etc.).

The scientific information you'll encounter on test day will appear in three distinct formats.

RESEARCH SUMMARY
(45–55% of Science test passages)

This format requires you to read about experiments and draw conclusions about their designs and results.

DATA REPRESENTATION
(30–40% of Science test passages)

This format requires you to read and interpret information on graphs, scatterplots, and tables.

CONFLICTING VIEWPOINTS
(15–20% of Science test passages)

This format features pairs of contrasting hypotheses about data or premises and requires you to understand, analyze, compare, and contrast those viewpoints.

Your scores on the Science test will include a total test score, which is based on how well you answer the entire set of 40 questions, as well as scores for three individual reporting categories.

INTERPRETATION OF DATA
(45–55% of Science test questions)

Questions in this category will assess your ability to do the following:
- Recognize key trends when analyzing scientific data
- Manipulate scientific data in diagram, graphical, and tabular forms
- Apply reasoning skills to understanding scientific data and drawing conclusions

EVALUATION OF MODELS, INFERENCES, AND EXPERIMENTAL RESULTS
(25–35% of Science test questions)

Questions in this category will assess your ability to do the following:
- Judge the validity of scientific information
- Draw conclusions and make predictions based on scientific information
- Determine the validity of explanations for scientific phenomena based on information provided

SCIENTIFIC INVESTIGATION
(20–30% of Science test questions):

Questions in this category will assess your ability to do the following:
- Analyze and understand experimental design, procedures, and tools
- Identify variables and controls within a scientific experiment
- Modify, compare, and extend experiments as needed, including predicting the results of additional experimental trials

The Optional Writing Test

The optional Writing test of the ACT exam is a 40-minute test consisting of a single essay writing task. Administered after the four mandatory multiple-choice sections, the Writing test is designed to assess your current writing skills and abilities that are typically taught at the high school and college entry levels. Your score on the Writing test will be based on a point scale derived from combined scores in four writing domains.

LANGUAGE USE AND CONVENTIONS

Your ability to communicate a clear and effective written argument will be tested here. This includes your ability to use standard written English language conventions such as word usage, grammar, syntax, and mechanics. Your ability to develop and deploy an appropriate, consistent, and compelling style and tone will also be assessed.

DEVELOPMENT AND SUPPORT

Your ability to develop cogent ideas, support your point of view, and offer clear reasoning will be measured here. This includes offering evidence, demonstrating clear and sound logic and reasoning, exploring ideas, illustrating through examples, and discussing potential impacts and implications.

ORGANIZATION

Your ability to galvanize and deploy your thoughts and ideas in a cohesive, consistent, and effective manner will be assessed here. This includes your adherence to sound essay format and structure as well as your ability to develop and present your thoughts on the issue provided in a clear and logical fashion, to maximum effect.

IDEAS AND ANALYSIS

Your ability to effectively generate ideas on the topic provided and to engage critically and thoughtfully with multiple perspectives will be measured here. This includes your ability to understand the topic and its relevance and purpose, as well as the audience, and to generate and develop ideas accordingly.

Again, this is an optional exam section and not every college requires that you take it. You can find the Writing test requirements for your target college(s) on the official ACT website: **www.act.org**.

FYI

Your score on the optional Writing test will not affect your composite score or your scores on the individual multiple-choice tests.

Your Target ACT Score and Test Goals

Don't forget that you're a unique individual with unique goals for the ACT exam. Do not feel pressured to compete with other students—determine what your goals are for the ACT and then work toward achieving them. Depending on which colleges and universities you're applying to, you might need to aim for the best score you can get while other schools might only require scores that fall in the middle or lower range. No matter what score you're aiming for, we'll provide tips and tricks throughout this book to help you get the score you want on the ACT exam.

The best path to hitting your target score on the ACT exam is to fully understand and become comfortable with the structure, timing, and format of the test and to make sure your skills on each test are razor sharp. The most effective approach for ACT exam success is thorough practice and review with your individual strengths and weaknesses in mind. Make the most of the material presented in this book between now and test day to make your test goals a reality!

HOW THE ACT® IS SCORED

For each of the four multiple-choice tests—English, Mathematics, Reading, and Science—the number of questions you answered correctly are tabulated and that number becomes your raw score for each test. Your raw scores are then converted into scale scores to give you a test score for each subject test that ranges from 1 (low) to 36 (high). Your total score, also known as your composite score, is the average score of these four tests.

You'll also receive a score in each reporting category (covered previously), which will include the total number of questions in the category and the number of questions you answered correctly, as well as the percentage of questions in that category that you answered correctly.

FYI

On the ACT exam, you are not penalized for incorrect answers. However, a blank answer will be marked as incorrect. Therefore, it's important to answer every question on the test, even if you need to guess. Never leave a question blank!

The optional Writing section is scored a bit differently. Two official essay readers will score your essay independently on a scale from 1 to 6 in each of the following four writing domains:

- Development and Support
- Ideas and Analysis
- Language Use and Conventions
- Organization

If you choose to take the ACT Writing test, you will receive a total of five scores—four domain scores, which will range from 2–12, and a subject-level writing score, which will also range from 2–12 and will be the rounded average of your four domain scores.

The official ACT test administrators prepare three types of score reports for students.

The high school report, which is delivered to your high school, includes your ACT scores and college and career planning information. Scores for the multiple-choice tests are generally available for online viewing approximately two weeks after your test date but can take up to eight weeks. If you've decided to take the optional Writing test, your scores (including your writing score) will typically be released approximately two weeks after your multiple-choice scores.

The student report, which includes your ACT scores and college and career planning information, is delivered to your online web account. Scores for the multiple-choice tests are generally available for online viewing approximately two weeks after your test date but can take up to eight weeks. If you've decided to take the optional Writing test, your scores (with writing score) will typically be released approximately two weeks after your multiple-choice scores.

The college report, which is delivered to the colleges you selected prior to taking the ACT exam, includes your ACT scores and college and career planning information, as well as your reported high school course grades. Delivery varies based on the colleges you selected.

For a complete breakdown of scoring on the ACT exam and what it all means, visit the ACT website.

 FYI

You may need to be patient when waiting for your scores. Just keep checking back once a week since scores are posted on a weekly basis.

WHEN TO TAKE THE ACT®

In the United States, the ACT is given several times a year—in September, October, December, February, April, June, and July. Select the test date that works best for you and your specific goals. Generally, it is recommended that you choose a test date at least two months ahead of the application deadlines for the institutions to which you plan to apply.

If you are preparing to take the ACT for the first time, try setting a goal for yourself after reading through this book and making your way through the practice quizzes, practice tests, and benchmark questions. This should give you an idea of how well you will do on the actual test. If you reach that goal the first time you take the ACT, you may not want to take it again, but it's good to have the option to retest if you need it.

Visit the ACT website for a complete list of key dates, registration requirements and deadlines, and options regarding special circumstances.

REGISTERING FOR THE ACT®

Now that you have a better understanding of the structure, format, timing, and scoring of the ACT exam—and have determined that taking the ACT is right for you—the next important step is signing up for the exam.

Online Registration

Registering online for the ACT exam is the quickest method—go to the ACT website and follow the instructions to create an online account to get started and register. Once you've created your MyACT account, you can make any necessary test changes and updates.

Registration will take approximately 30 minutes to complete, and here's what you'll need to have handy to finish the process:

- [ ] A valid credit card or other form of payment
- [ ] A computer with internet accessibility
- [ ] School codes (for sending your score to your high school and potential colleges; a code lookup is available on the ACT website)
- [ ] A headshot photo, for test security purposes (see the official ACT website for photo file requirements and upload deadlines); please note that you'll also need to bring a valid photo ID with you on test day, along with your printed test ticket, which will contain your uploaded photo
- [ ] Information regarding any special accommodations, including English Learner (EL) supports
- [ ] Your decision regarding whether or not you're taking the optional Writing test
- [ ] Your parent's or guardian's email address (an optional but helpful tool for communicating information regarding the ACT exam)

You can also use the official ACT website to locate a convenient test center near you to take the exam or to find out more information about arranged testing (if you're located at a significant distance from an ACT test center) and standby testing.

Registration Fees

The fee for taking the ACT exam without the optional Writing test is $63, which includes having your score report sent to you, your high school, and as many as four colleges of your choice. If you're taking the optional Writing test, the total fee is $88. If you decide to add or remove the Writing test, you'll pay a $25 fee, and if you change your test date or test center, you'll pay a $42 change fee.

If you decide to have your score report sent to more than four colleges, there is a $16 fee for each additional school (this must be requested online before your test date).

Other options and fees include:

- Standby testing: $63
- Late registration (available only in the United States and Canada): $36
- Requesting a copy of your test and answers (Test Information Release): $32

You may be eligible for a fee waiver or a state voucher to help cover the cost of the exam. To find out if you're eligible, and for additional fee information, check out the official ACT website.

GETTING READY FOR TEST DAY

In addition to thoroughly preparing for each of the subject tests on the ACT exam, be sure to brush up on test day fundamentals and focus on getting ready for the big day—including selecting a test day and location, and determining what to expect when you arrive at your test center, what to bring, and what to leave at home. Taking these steps will help you avoid surprises, reduce anxiety, and stay ahead of the competition.

Getting ready for the ACT exam is essential, but getting ready for what you'll encounter on exam day is just as important to your success.

What to Expect, What to Bring, and What to Leave at Home

Test time always begins at 8:00 a.m., and by this time, you should be present and in your seat. Plan to arrive a little early, giving you time to relax, get comfortable, and get settled into test-taking mode; you definitely don't want to have to deal with the stress of racing the clock to avoid missing the start of the test, and you will not be admitted to take the test if you arrive late. Consider making a practice run to the test center in advance of test day so that you'll know just how long you'll need the morning of the exam.

When you arrive at your test center, the staff will check your photo ID and ticket, admit you into the room, bring you to your seat, and provide you with the required test materials.

 FYI

All students need to be present at their test centers no later than 8:00 a.m. Individuals taking the ACT exam without the optional Writing test are generally dismissed at 12:35 p.m. Those taking the Writing test are generally dismissed at 1:35 p.m.

Your Test Day Checklist

Make absolutely certain that you bring the following items with you on test day:

☐ A printed copy of your test admission ticket

☐ Acceptable photo ID (visit the official ACT website for what constitutes acceptable ID)

☐ Sharpened No. 2 pencils with erasers

Consider bringing the following optional items to help maximize your test-taking experience:

☐ A watch (without an alarm) to help you pace yourself through each test section

☐ A permitted calculator for use on the Math test (see the ACT website for details on which calculators are allowed)

☐ Comfortable clothing that will allow you to adapt to the test center temperature—whatever it may be

☐ Snacks, which can be consumed only outside of the test room during the break

☐ A face mask to reduce the spread of COVID-19

Do not **bring the following items with you to the test room, or keep them completely silent and out of sight while taking the exam—you will absolutely not be able to use them:**

✗ The following electronic devices: smartphone, cell phone, mobile digital device (e.g., iPad or tablet), camera, headphones, smart watches, and fitness bands

✗ Reading material, textbooks, reference materials (including dictionaries and other study aids), scratch paper, and any other outside notes

✗ Highlighters, colored pens and pencils, or correction tape/fluid

✗ Tobacco in any form

✗ Outside reading material

The makers of the ACT like to test out their questions when developing future versions of the test. Plan on completing an additional, shorter multiple-choice test following your standard scored test in one of the four subject areas to help shape future ACT exams. This additional test will not count toward your score.

NEXT STEPS

You now have a better understanding of the ACT fundamentals, including the structure, format, and timing of the exam, how it's all scored, what you need to do to register, and what you should expect on the day of the exam—this is powerful information that will help set you up for success on test day.

Now it's time to move on to building your ACT study plan and making the most of the time you have between now and test day to study, practice, and review each test section as you work toward achieving your best possible scores. And remember—we'll be with you every step of the way. Let's begin!

SUMMING IT UP

- The ACT consists of four multiple-choice tests on English, Mathematics, Reading, and Science with a total of 215 questions. You will have 3 hours and 30 minutes to complete the tests. There is also an optional Writing test that takes an additional 40 minutes to complete. Some colleges do not require the Writing test.

- The English test consists of a set of 5 essays accompanied by 75 multiple-choice questions that test your skills in conventions of standard English, production of writing, and knowledge of language. Questions focus on testing your ability to do the following:

    o Analyze and comprehend a piece of writing

    o Determine if the author was effective in achieving their goals

    o Recognize the key effects of making text revisions

    o Make determinations regarding potential improvements

- The Mathematics test consists of 60 multiple-choice questions that test your knowledge of higher mathematics (algebra, number and quantity, geometry, functions, and statistics and probability), integrating essential skills (solving complex problems with mathematical knowledge), and modeling.

- The Reading test consists of four reading passages and 40 multiple-choice questions that test your ability to read critically, integrate information from multiple text sources, and apply logical reasoning skills regarding the texts using evidence.

- The Science test consists of 40 questions assessing your reasoning and problem-solving skills and your ability to interpret, analyze, and evaluate data representation, research summaries, and conflicting viewpoints. These questions are derived from information taught in the natural sciences: biology, chemistry, physics, and Earth/space science (meteorology, astronomy, geology, etc.).

- The optional Writing test consists of an essay that requires you to evaluate three perspectives on an issue, create your own perspective on that issue, and explain how your perspective relates to the ones provided. There are no multiple-choice questions. Scoring is based on the following:

    o Language use and conventions

    o Development and support

    o Organization

    o Ideas and analysis

- The ACT is given several times a year—in September, October, December, February, April, June, and July. Select the test date that works best for you.

- Register for the test online through the ACT website. During registration, you will choose where and when you will take the test. You will also receive a registration ticket that you MUST bring with you on test day. Registration fees apply.

- Your scores on the ACT exam will be an important variable that college admissions staff will use to help determine whether or not you're a good fit for their school and are ready to handle college-level subject material. For each of the four multiple-choice tests—English, Mathematics, Reading, and Science—the number of questions you answer correctly will be tabulated, becoming your raw score for each test.

- Your raw scores are then converted into scale scores to give you a test score for each subject test that ranges from 1 (low) to 36 (high).

- Your total score, also known as your composite score, is the average score of the four tests. The maximum score you can get on the ACT is 36.

- The maximum score you can get on the Writing test is 12, and that score is determined from the average of the four domain scores awarded by two essay readers. The optional Writing test does not impact your composite score.

- Scores are posted online for you to view within two to eight weeks after the test date. Reports for the multiple-choice scores are released and mailed within three to eight weeks after the test dates. If you take the Writing test, your score reports will be released approximately two weeks after the multiple-choice scores.

CHAPTER

ACT® Diagnostic Test

ACT® DIAGNOSTIC TEST

DIAGNOSTIC TEST

This diagnostic test is designed to help you recognize your strengths and weaknesses at the start of your preparation for the ACT. It covers every section of the ACT. In Chapter 3, we'll discuss how you can use your results to help guide your study time.

DIAGNOSTIC TEST ANSWER SHEET

Section 1: English Test

1. Ⓐ Ⓑ Ⓒ Ⓓ	16. Ⓕ Ⓖ Ⓗ Ⓙ	31. Ⓐ Ⓑ Ⓒ Ⓓ	46. Ⓕ Ⓖ Ⓗ Ⓙ	61. Ⓐ Ⓑ Ⓒ Ⓓ
2. Ⓕ Ⓖ Ⓗ Ⓙ	17. Ⓐ Ⓑ Ⓒ Ⓓ	32. Ⓕ Ⓖ Ⓗ Ⓙ	47. Ⓐ Ⓑ Ⓒ Ⓓ	62. Ⓕ Ⓖ Ⓗ Ⓙ
3. Ⓐ Ⓑ Ⓒ Ⓓ	18. Ⓕ Ⓖ Ⓗ Ⓙ	33. Ⓐ Ⓑ Ⓒ Ⓓ	48. Ⓕ Ⓖ Ⓗ Ⓙ	63. Ⓐ Ⓑ Ⓒ Ⓓ
4. Ⓕ Ⓖ Ⓗ Ⓙ	19. Ⓐ Ⓑ Ⓒ Ⓓ	34. Ⓕ Ⓖ Ⓗ Ⓙ	49. Ⓐ Ⓑ Ⓒ Ⓓ	64. Ⓕ Ⓖ Ⓗ Ⓙ
5. Ⓐ Ⓑ Ⓒ Ⓓ	20. Ⓕ Ⓖ Ⓗ Ⓙ	35. Ⓐ Ⓑ Ⓒ Ⓓ	50. Ⓕ Ⓖ Ⓗ Ⓙ	65. Ⓐ Ⓑ Ⓒ Ⓓ
6. Ⓕ Ⓖ Ⓗ Ⓙ	21. Ⓐ Ⓑ Ⓒ Ⓓ	36. Ⓕ Ⓖ Ⓗ Ⓙ	51. Ⓐ Ⓑ Ⓒ Ⓓ	66. Ⓕ Ⓖ Ⓗ Ⓙ
7. Ⓐ Ⓑ Ⓒ Ⓓ	22. Ⓕ Ⓖ Ⓗ Ⓙ	37. Ⓐ Ⓑ Ⓒ Ⓓ	52. Ⓕ Ⓖ Ⓗ Ⓙ	67. Ⓐ Ⓑ Ⓒ Ⓓ
8. Ⓕ Ⓖ Ⓗ Ⓙ	23. Ⓐ Ⓑ Ⓒ Ⓓ	38. Ⓕ Ⓖ Ⓗ Ⓙ	53. Ⓐ Ⓑ Ⓒ Ⓓ	68. Ⓕ Ⓖ Ⓗ Ⓙ
9. Ⓐ Ⓑ Ⓒ Ⓓ	24. Ⓕ Ⓖ Ⓗ Ⓙ	39. Ⓐ Ⓑ Ⓒ Ⓓ	54. Ⓕ Ⓖ Ⓗ Ⓙ	69. Ⓐ Ⓑ Ⓒ Ⓓ
10. Ⓕ Ⓖ Ⓗ Ⓙ	25. Ⓐ Ⓑ Ⓒ Ⓓ	40. Ⓕ Ⓖ Ⓗ Ⓙ	55. Ⓐ Ⓑ Ⓒ Ⓓ	70. Ⓕ Ⓖ Ⓗ Ⓙ
11. Ⓐ Ⓑ Ⓒ Ⓓ	26. Ⓕ Ⓖ Ⓗ Ⓙ	41. Ⓐ Ⓑ Ⓒ Ⓓ	56. Ⓕ Ⓖ Ⓗ Ⓙ	71. Ⓐ Ⓑ Ⓒ Ⓓ
12. Ⓕ Ⓖ Ⓗ Ⓙ	27. Ⓐ Ⓑ Ⓒ Ⓓ	42. Ⓕ Ⓖ Ⓗ Ⓙ	57. Ⓐ Ⓑ Ⓒ Ⓓ	72. Ⓕ Ⓖ Ⓗ Ⓙ
13. Ⓐ Ⓑ Ⓒ Ⓓ	28. Ⓕ Ⓖ Ⓗ Ⓙ	43. Ⓐ Ⓑ Ⓒ Ⓓ	58. Ⓕ Ⓖ Ⓗ Ⓙ	73. Ⓐ Ⓑ Ⓒ Ⓓ
14. Ⓕ Ⓖ Ⓗ Ⓙ	29. Ⓐ Ⓑ Ⓒ Ⓓ	44. Ⓕ Ⓖ Ⓗ Ⓙ	59. Ⓐ Ⓑ Ⓒ Ⓓ	74. Ⓕ Ⓖ Ⓗ Ⓙ
15. Ⓐ Ⓑ Ⓒ Ⓓ	30. Ⓕ Ⓖ Ⓗ Ⓙ	45. Ⓐ Ⓑ Ⓒ Ⓓ	60. Ⓕ Ⓖ Ⓗ Ⓙ	75. Ⓐ Ⓑ Ⓒ Ⓓ

ANSWER SHEET: ACT® DIAGNOSTIC TEST

Section 2: Mathematics Test

1. Ⓐ Ⓑ Ⓒ Ⓓ Ⓔ
2. Ⓕ Ⓖ Ⓗ Ⓙ Ⓚ
3. Ⓐ Ⓑ Ⓒ Ⓓ Ⓔ
4. Ⓕ Ⓖ Ⓗ Ⓙ Ⓚ
5. Ⓐ Ⓑ Ⓒ Ⓓ Ⓔ
6. Ⓕ Ⓖ Ⓗ Ⓙ Ⓚ
7. Ⓐ Ⓑ Ⓒ Ⓓ Ⓔ
8. Ⓕ Ⓖ Ⓗ Ⓙ Ⓚ
9. Ⓐ Ⓑ Ⓒ Ⓓ Ⓔ
10. Ⓕ Ⓖ Ⓗ Ⓙ Ⓚ
11. Ⓐ Ⓑ Ⓒ Ⓓ Ⓔ
12. Ⓕ Ⓖ Ⓗ Ⓙ Ⓚ

13. Ⓐ Ⓑ Ⓒ Ⓓ Ⓔ
14. Ⓕ Ⓖ Ⓗ Ⓙ Ⓚ
15. Ⓐ Ⓑ Ⓒ Ⓓ Ⓔ
16. Ⓕ Ⓖ Ⓗ Ⓙ Ⓚ
17. Ⓐ Ⓑ Ⓒ Ⓓ Ⓔ
18. Ⓕ Ⓖ Ⓗ Ⓙ Ⓚ
19. Ⓐ Ⓑ Ⓒ Ⓓ Ⓔ
20. Ⓕ Ⓖ Ⓗ Ⓙ Ⓚ
21. Ⓐ Ⓑ Ⓒ Ⓓ Ⓔ
22. Ⓕ Ⓖ Ⓗ Ⓙ Ⓚ
23. Ⓐ Ⓑ Ⓒ Ⓓ Ⓔ
24. Ⓕ Ⓖ Ⓗ Ⓙ Ⓚ

25. Ⓐ Ⓑ Ⓒ Ⓓ Ⓔ
26. Ⓕ Ⓖ Ⓗ Ⓙ Ⓚ
27. Ⓐ Ⓑ Ⓒ Ⓓ Ⓔ
28. Ⓕ Ⓖ Ⓗ Ⓙ Ⓚ
29. Ⓐ Ⓑ Ⓒ Ⓓ Ⓔ
30. Ⓕ Ⓖ Ⓗ Ⓙ Ⓚ
31. Ⓐ Ⓑ Ⓒ Ⓓ Ⓔ
32. Ⓕ Ⓖ Ⓗ Ⓙ Ⓚ
33. Ⓐ Ⓑ Ⓒ Ⓓ Ⓔ
34. Ⓕ Ⓖ Ⓗ Ⓙ Ⓚ
35. Ⓐ Ⓑ Ⓒ Ⓓ Ⓔ
36. Ⓕ Ⓖ Ⓗ Ⓙ Ⓚ

37. Ⓐ Ⓑ Ⓒ Ⓓ Ⓔ
38. Ⓕ Ⓖ Ⓗ Ⓙ Ⓚ
39. Ⓐ Ⓑ Ⓒ Ⓓ Ⓔ
40. Ⓕ Ⓖ Ⓗ Ⓙ Ⓚ
41. Ⓐ Ⓑ Ⓒ Ⓓ Ⓔ
42. Ⓕ Ⓖ Ⓗ Ⓙ Ⓚ
43. Ⓐ Ⓑ Ⓒ Ⓓ Ⓔ
44. Ⓕ Ⓖ Ⓗ Ⓙ Ⓚ
45. Ⓐ Ⓑ Ⓒ Ⓓ Ⓔ
46. Ⓕ Ⓖ Ⓗ Ⓙ Ⓚ
47. Ⓐ Ⓑ Ⓒ Ⓓ Ⓔ
48. Ⓕ Ⓖ Ⓗ Ⓙ Ⓚ

49. Ⓐ Ⓑ Ⓒ Ⓓ Ⓔ
50. Ⓕ Ⓖ Ⓗ Ⓙ Ⓚ
51. Ⓐ Ⓑ Ⓒ Ⓓ Ⓔ
52. Ⓕ Ⓖ Ⓗ Ⓙ Ⓚ
53. Ⓐ Ⓑ Ⓒ Ⓓ Ⓔ
54. Ⓕ Ⓖ Ⓗ Ⓙ Ⓚ
55. Ⓐ Ⓑ Ⓒ Ⓓ Ⓔ
56. Ⓕ Ⓖ Ⓗ Ⓙ Ⓚ
57. Ⓐ Ⓑ Ⓒ Ⓓ Ⓔ
58. Ⓕ Ⓖ Ⓗ Ⓙ Ⓚ
59. Ⓐ Ⓑ Ⓒ Ⓓ Ⓔ
60. Ⓕ Ⓖ Ⓗ Ⓙ Ⓚ

Section 3: Reading Test

1. Ⓐ Ⓑ Ⓒ Ⓓ
2. Ⓕ Ⓖ Ⓗ Ⓙ
3. Ⓐ Ⓑ Ⓒ Ⓓ
4. Ⓕ Ⓖ Ⓗ Ⓙ
5. Ⓐ Ⓑ Ⓒ Ⓓ
6. Ⓕ Ⓖ Ⓗ Ⓙ
7. Ⓐ Ⓑ Ⓒ Ⓓ
8. Ⓕ Ⓖ Ⓗ Ⓙ

9. Ⓐ Ⓑ Ⓒ Ⓓ
10. Ⓕ Ⓖ Ⓗ Ⓙ
11. Ⓐ Ⓑ Ⓒ Ⓓ
12. Ⓕ Ⓖ Ⓗ Ⓙ
13. Ⓐ Ⓑ Ⓒ Ⓓ
14. Ⓕ Ⓖ Ⓗ Ⓙ
15. Ⓐ Ⓑ Ⓒ Ⓓ
16. Ⓕ Ⓖ Ⓗ Ⓙ

17. Ⓐ Ⓑ Ⓒ Ⓓ
18. Ⓕ Ⓖ Ⓗ Ⓙ
19. Ⓐ Ⓑ Ⓒ Ⓓ
20. Ⓕ Ⓖ Ⓗ Ⓙ
21. Ⓐ Ⓑ Ⓒ Ⓓ
22. Ⓕ Ⓖ Ⓗ Ⓙ
23. Ⓐ Ⓑ Ⓒ Ⓓ
24. Ⓕ Ⓖ Ⓗ Ⓙ

25. Ⓐ Ⓑ Ⓒ Ⓓ
26. Ⓕ Ⓖ Ⓗ Ⓙ
27. Ⓐ Ⓑ Ⓒ Ⓓ
28. Ⓕ Ⓖ Ⓗ Ⓙ
29. Ⓐ Ⓑ Ⓒ Ⓓ
30. Ⓕ Ⓖ Ⓗ Ⓙ
31. Ⓐ Ⓑ Ⓒ Ⓓ
32. Ⓕ Ⓖ Ⓗ Ⓙ

33. Ⓐ Ⓑ Ⓒ Ⓓ
34. Ⓕ Ⓖ Ⓗ Ⓙ
35. Ⓐ Ⓑ Ⓒ Ⓓ
36. Ⓕ Ⓖ Ⓗ Ⓙ
37. Ⓐ Ⓑ Ⓒ Ⓓ
38. Ⓕ Ⓖ Ⓗ Ⓙ
39. Ⓐ Ⓑ Ⓒ Ⓓ
40. Ⓕ Ⓖ Ⓗ Ⓙ

Section 4: Science Test

1. Ⓐ Ⓑ Ⓒ Ⓓ	9. Ⓐ Ⓑ Ⓒ Ⓓ	17. Ⓐ Ⓑ Ⓒ Ⓓ	25. Ⓐ Ⓑ Ⓒ Ⓓ	33. Ⓐ Ⓑ Ⓒ Ⓓ
2. Ⓕ Ⓖ Ⓗ Ⓙ	10. Ⓕ Ⓖ Ⓗ Ⓙ	18. Ⓕ Ⓖ Ⓗ Ⓙ	26. Ⓕ Ⓖ Ⓗ Ⓙ	34. Ⓕ Ⓖ Ⓗ Ⓙ
3. Ⓐ Ⓑ Ⓒ Ⓓ	11. Ⓐ Ⓑ Ⓒ Ⓓ	19. Ⓐ Ⓑ Ⓒ Ⓓ	27. Ⓐ Ⓑ Ⓒ Ⓓ	35. Ⓐ Ⓑ Ⓒ Ⓓ
4. Ⓕ Ⓖ Ⓗ Ⓙ	12. Ⓕ Ⓖ Ⓗ Ⓙ	20. Ⓕ Ⓖ Ⓗ Ⓙ	28. Ⓕ Ⓖ Ⓗ Ⓙ	36. Ⓕ Ⓖ Ⓗ Ⓙ
5. Ⓐ Ⓑ Ⓒ Ⓓ	13. Ⓐ Ⓑ Ⓒ Ⓓ	21. Ⓐ Ⓑ Ⓒ Ⓓ	29. Ⓐ Ⓑ Ⓒ Ⓓ	37. Ⓐ Ⓑ Ⓒ Ⓓ
6. Ⓕ Ⓖ Ⓗ Ⓙ	14. Ⓕ Ⓖ Ⓗ Ⓙ	22. Ⓕ Ⓖ Ⓗ Ⓙ	30. Ⓕ Ⓖ Ⓗ Ⓙ	38. Ⓕ Ⓖ Ⓗ Ⓙ
7. Ⓐ Ⓑ Ⓒ Ⓓ	15. Ⓐ Ⓑ Ⓒ Ⓓ	23. Ⓐ Ⓑ Ⓒ Ⓓ	31. Ⓐ Ⓑ Ⓒ Ⓓ	39. Ⓐ Ⓑ Ⓒ Ⓓ
8. Ⓕ Ⓖ Ⓗ Ⓙ	16. Ⓕ Ⓖ Ⓗ Ⓙ	24. Ⓕ Ⓖ Ⓗ Ⓙ	32. Ⓕ Ⓖ Ⓗ Ⓙ	40. Ⓕ Ⓖ Ⓗ Ⓙ

Section 5: Writing Test (optional)

Essay Instructions for Self-Scoring on page 119

ANSWER SHEET: ACT® DIAGNOSTIC TEST

SECTION 1: ENGLISH TEST

75 Questions—45 Minutes

Directions: In the following five passages, certain words and phrases are underlined and numbered. In the right-hand column, you will find alternatives for the part that is underlined. In most cases, you are to choose which alternative best expresses the idea, makes the statement appropriate in standard written English, or is worded to best reflect the style and tone of the whole passage. If you think the original version is best, choose "NO CHANGE." Sometimes, you may also find a question in the right-hand column about the underlined part. Here, you should choose the best answer to the question.

You may also find questions about a section of a passage, or a passage in its entirety. These questions do not refer to specific underlined portions of the passage, but rather are identified by a number or numbers in a box.

For each question, choose the answer you consider best. Read each passage through once before you begin to answer the questions that accompany it. For many of the questions, you must read several sentences beyond the questions to determine the answer. Be sure that you have read far enough ahead each time you choose an alternative.

PASSAGE I

Vaudeville

[1]

Ask people if they have ever heard of vaudeville, and most of them will have no idea what the word even means. However, around 100 years ago, vaudeville was <u>the most popular form, of entertainment</u> in the United States.

1. **A.** NO CHANGE
   B. the most popular form of entertainment
   C. the most popular, form of entertainment
   D. the most popular form. Of entertainment

Between the years 1875 and 1932, <u>it was vaudeville bringing laughter and joy throughout the country to millions of people.</u>

2. **F.** NO CHANGE
   G. vaudeville brought laughter and joy to millions of people throughout the country.
   H. it was vaudeville that brought laughter and joy throughout the country to millions of people.
   J. vaudeville was bringing laughter and joy to people throughout the country in the millions.

GO ON TO THE NEXT PAGE.

[2]

Vaudeville's <u>significant popularity</u> stemmed from
                  ₃
the fact that it had something for everyone.

Each show featured <u>jugglers horseback riders; musicians</u>
                                 ₄
<u>and puppeteers</u> to entertain the crowd.
    ₄

<u>The audience would laugh at the clowns and comedians,</u>
                        ₅
<u>joining the singers in song, and in amazement of the</u>
                        ₅
<u>magic tricks and acrobats.</u>
       ₅

Since acts like magic, mime, and dancing required little

to no <u>verbal communication or speaking</u>, many of the
               ₆
new immigrants to this country did not need to speak

English to join in the fun.

In addition, tickets to vaudeville shows were relatively

<u>inexpensive. Making</u> it possible for people with limited
    ₇
means to purchase them.

3. Which choice most effectively continues the discussion of the ideas from the preceding sentence?

  A. NO CHANGE

  B. wonderful applause

  C. minor appeal

  D. broad enthusiasm

4. **F.** NO CHANGE

  G. jugglers horseback; riders musicians; and puppeteers

  H. jugglers, horseback riders, musicians, and puppeteers

  J. jugglers, horseback; riders; musicians, and puppeteers

5. **A.** NO CHANGE

  B. The audience would laugh at the clowns and comedians, join the singers in song, and watch the magic tricks and acrobats in amazement.

  C. The audience would laugh at the clowns and comedians, join the singers in song, and being amazed by the magic tricks and acrobats.

  D. The audience would have laughed at the clowns and comedians, joining the singers in song, and be amazed by the magic tricks and acrobats.

6. **F.** NO CHANGE

  G. verbal communication, or speaking

  H. verbal communication or speech,

  J. verbal communication,

7. **A.** NO CHANGE

  B. inexpensive, this made

  C. inexpensive, making

  D. inexpensive, yet making

Another reason for vaudeville's popularity <u>will be</u> the
₈
family-oriented nature of the acts.

Vulgarity was not allowed, so when parents took their
children, <u>we could</u> enjoy the show without worrying
₉
about exposing them to improper language or behavior.

[3]

[10] The word vaudeville comes from the French
phrase *voix de ville*, or "voices of the town." In France,
people would gather in the valleys to amuse each other
with song and dance. Gradually, vaudeville spread
to America, into the saloons of the wild west. There,
performers delighted the audience with acts like singing
and rope spinning.

As the acts became <u>mostly creative</u> and diverse,
₁₁

they <u>attracted a wider audience, and businesspeople</u>
₁₂
began opening theaters all over the country. When
vaudeville reached its peak in the 1920s, there were over
600 theaters showcasing 60,000 acts.

8. **F.** NO CHANGE
   G. was
   H. is
   J. will never be

9. **A.** NO CHANGE
   B. he or she could
   C. they could
   D. one could

10. Which of the following sentences offers the best
    introduction to Paragraph 3?

    F. The French language has given us many words
    commonly used in English.

    G. People have always enjoyed singing and
    dancing.

    H. The origins of vaudeville can be traced to
    Europe.

    J. Historians have different theories about the
    origins of vaudeville.

11. **A.** NO CHANGE
    B. mostly, creative
    C. more creative
    D. overly creative

12. If the writer were to delete the underlined
    portion, the sentence would primarily lose an
    explanation of:

    F. who was attending the vaudeville shows.

    G. why businesspeople began opening more
    vaudeville theaters.

    H. why the vaudeville shows were attracting
    wider audiences.

    J. how much the audience for vaudeville shows
    grew.

GO ON TO THE NEXT PAGE.

[4]

[1] W. C. Fields, Ethel Merman, and Will Rogers are just a few examples of performers who achieved celebrity status. [2]Some performers gained fame and stardom on the vaudeville stage. [3] Other famous vaudevillians include the Marx Brothers and Sarah Bernhardt. 13

[5]

Despite its immense success, vaudeville would not last forever. The Great Depression as well as techno-logical advances like the radio and movies contributed to the demise of a great form of entertainment.

13. Which of the following sequences of sentences makes Paragraph 4 most logical?

A. NO CHANGE

B. 3, 1, 2

C. 2, 3, 1

D. 2, 1, 3

Questions 14 and 15 ask about the passage as a whole.

---

14. For the sake of the unity and coherence of this essay, Paragraph 3 should be placed:

F. where it is now.

G. after Paragraph 4.

H. before Paragraph 1.

J. after Paragraph 1.

15. Suppose the author wanted to write an essay to convince readers that modern movie theaters should be replaced by vaudeville theaters. Which paragraph would offer the best support for this argument? Follow the original order of the paragraphs.

A. Paragraph 1

B. Paragraph 2

C. Paragraph 3

D. Paragraph 4

PASSAGE II

THE HUANG HE FLOOD

[1]

Rivers are an essential natural resource to human
life. They provide fish, water for drinking and farming,
16
and a means of transportation. Unfortunately, rivers can
also be a source of destruction.

The Huang He, which flows through China has brought
17   17
both life and death to the people of the region.

[2]

The Huang He cuts a meandering path across the
North China Plain. Also known as the Yellow River,
it gets its name from the yellow mud that coats the
18
riverbed.

For centuries it is being a vital part of Chinese life.
19

16. **F.** NO CHANGE
    G. Rivers are to human life an essential natural
    resource.
    H. Rivers are an essential resource natural to
    human life.
    J. Rivers are a natural resource essential to
    human life.

17. **A.** NO CHANGE
    B. The Huang He which flows through
    China, has
    C. The Huang He that flows through China has
    D. The Huang He, which flows through
    China, has

18. **F.** NO CHANGE
    G. get's it's
    H. get's its
    J. gets it's

19. **A.** NO CHANGE
    B. it be
    C. it has been
    D. it is

GO ON TO THE NEXT PAGE.

[20] The Huang He has an unfortunate propensity for flooding, bursting its banks an average of two years in every three and washing away entire villages with <u>their</u> [21] raging floodwaters.

The flood in the summer of 1935 was <u>devastating,</u> [22] <u>which caused</u> enormous suffering for the villagers [22] flooded out of their homes.

[3]

In that tragic summer, the villagers and farmers <u>who</u> resided along the river had endured a long drought. [23] Their crops, which included sweet potatoes, corn, wheat, and cucumbers, were in serious need of rain.

With their crops and lives in jeopardy, they were <u>content</u> [24] when the long-awaited rain finally arrived. However, the rain turned into a torrential downpour.

20. At this point, the writer would like to add a sentence to Paragraph 2. Which of the following choices would provide the best transition between the sentences before and after?

F. It has helped to sustain the people, but it has demanded a heavy price.

G. The river deposits fertile mud each time it floods the nearby lowlands.

H. It has been a valuable natural resource for the Chinese people.

J. It is about 3,000 miles long, and its receding floodwaters have caused it to change course numerous times in the last few thousand years.

21. A. NO CHANGE
B. they're
C. them
D. its

22. F. NO CHANGE
G. devastating and caused
H. devastating that caused
J. devastating, and which caused

23. A. NO CHANGE
B. whom
C. which
D. whose

24. F. NO CHANGE
G. satisfied
H. pleased
J. elated

Some areas received 20 inches of rain in two days, more than some parts of the world receive for <u>the period of</u> an entire year. The river swelled to dangerously high levels, threatening to overflow the dikes along the riverbank.

[4]

<u>The villagers working desperately to raise the dikes,</u>
<u>the farms and houses in the fields below were on the</u>
<u>verge of disaster.</u>

They reinforced the dikes with rocks and kaoling stalks. [27] Sadly, this did not prevent the Huang He from bursting its banks and rushing down with explosive and deadly power. The valley below was washed away in <u>floodwaters that like Niagara Falls</u>
<u>swelled to six times the volume.</u> The river flooded 6,000 square miles of land. The results were disastrous.

GO ON TO THE NEXT PAGE.

25. A. NO CHANGE

B. the duration of

C. the length of

D. OMIT the underlined portion.

26. F. NO CHANGE

G. The villagers were working desperately to raise the dikes, the farms and houses in the fields below were on the verge of disaster.

H. The villagers worked desperately to raise the dikes and save the farms and houses in the fields below.

J. The villagers worked desperately to raise the dikes and the farms and houses in the fields below.

27. Kaoling is a plant similar to sugarcane. Should the writer define this word in the passage?

A. Yes, because the writer defines other unfamiliar words in the passage.

B. Yes, because defining a word unfamiliar to most readers would enhance the readers' understanding of the sentence.

C. No, because this passage is not about kaoling or sugarcane.

D. No, because most readers will know what kaoling means.

28. F. NO CHANGE

G. floodwaters, which like Niagara Falls swelled to six times the volume.

H. floodwaters that swelled to six times the volume of Niagara Falls.

J. floodwaters that swelled to six times the volume, like Niagara Falls.

[5]

Thousands of people drowned. Some were lucky and were able to flee in small boats. Others managed to climb to the roofs of the more stable buildings and wait for possible rescue. They suffered great hunger and thirst. Surrounded by floodwater, they were unable to drink from it because it contained sewage and the corpses of people who had been unable to escape. The situation turned even more tragic, as hundreds of thousands died from the famine that followed. The villagers were also beset by outbreaks of cholera and the bubonic plague. An earlier catastrophic flood occurred when the Huang He burst its banks in 1887, resulting in the deaths of possibly a million people. [29]

[6]

It is little wonder that the Huang He has earned the nickname "China's Sorrow." It is a river of life, but it is also a river of tears.

29. In Paragraph 5, should the final sentence be kept or eliminated?

   A. Kept, because the passage is about floods.
   B. Kept, because it is an interesting detail.
   C. Eliminated, because the flood of 1887 is not a focus of this paragraph or the passage.
   D. Eliminated, because it happened too long ago to be historically important or relevant.

Question 30 asks about the passage as a whole.

---

30. Which of the following statements most effectively summarizes the passage as a whole?

   F. The Huang He floods the river valley along its banks every two out of three years.
   G. The Huang He Flood of 1935 caused massive devastation throughout the river valley.
   H. The villagers' failure to build stronger dikes left them vulnerable to the disastrous flood of 1935.
   J. The Huang He has brought both life and death to villagers of the river valley.

PASSAGE III

BUYER BEWARE

[1]

We buy lots of things for many different reasons.
Some items are <u>insignificant</u>, and these are the things
₃₁

we need to have, like <u>groceries' or clothing</u>. Others are
₃₂
indulgences, like movie tickets, hot fudge sundaes, and
sports cars. There are also investments, what—

we hope—accrues value over time; <u>stocks, bonds and
₃₃
precious metals</u> all fall into this category.
₃₃

[2]

Then there's a fourth category of purchases that I
recently had experience with, one that I have affectionately dubbed "mistakes." If <u>you will be lucky</u>, you have
₃₄
little or no experience with throwing your money away
on these useless, dangerous, or just plain dumb items. If
you have, though, I hope it was a real learning experience for you!

[3]

35 I was lying in bed but just couldn't fall asleep
for some reason, despite being tired, which, in retro-
spect, might have led to my lapse in judgment and my
poor decision making. I thought that watching a little
television might lull me to sleep, so I turned it on and
started flipping through the channels.

31. A. NO CHANGE
   B. essential
   C. inconsequential
   D. delicious

32. F. NO CHANGE
   G. grocery or clothing
   H. groceries or clothing
   J. groceries' or clothing's

33. A. NO CHANGE
   B. stocks bonds, and precious metals
   C. stocks bonds and precious metals
   D. stocks, bonds, and precious metals

34. F. NO CHANGE
   G. you're lucky
   H. you'll be lucky
   J. your lucky

35. The author of the passage would like to add an
introductory sentence to Paragraph 3. Which of
the following sentences would serve as an effective introductory sentence here?

   A. I quickly fell into a blissful sleep.
   B. I had horrible nightmares that I couldn't forget.
   C. I remember the night clearly.
   D. I prefer to sleep with a window open.

GO ON TO THE NEXT PAGE.

[4]

<u>My attention on one channel in particular got</u>
<u>caught</u>—it showed a lively fellow with a distinctive
36
Scottish accent talking enthusiastically about a new

miracle product that I'd never heard of—and couldn't

even believe existed. Confidence in a Can, he said, was

an easy, effective, and ebullient way to build your per-

sonal confidence with just a few quick sprays. Amazing!

[5]

Admittedly, I was skeptical, but the charisma and

energy of the man was hard to resist. As he exclaimed

again and again, he himself used a full can every day.

While attentive, I was tired, and in that state, I was every

infomercial's dream customer. I wanted sleep but also

to hear more, so I kept watching. Before long, a parade

of happy and satisfied customers began <u>endorsing</u>
37
Confidence in a Can with stories of how the product

completely changed their lives for the better. How could

I argue with that?

[6]

After everything I heard and saw, I was interested,

but I still couldn't decide whether I was going to make

a purchase. I wanted to be more confident, of course,

and I knew that if this can actually worked, my life could

change (they said it themselves). Why wouldn't I want

that? The man continued, saying that all I had to do was

call the toll-free number on the bottom of the screen

36. F. NO CHANGE
  G. One channel in particular caught my attention
  H. My attention in particular caught one channel
  J. In particular, one channel got caught on my attention

37. A. NO CHANGE
  B. entering
  C. enraging
  D. enveloping

and I would get not one but two full cans of Confidence in a Can for one low discount price—that was all <u>I'm needing</u> to hear! [39]
38

38

[7]

I raced to my door, flung it wide, and without even looking at the mailperson, I snatched the box from their hands and tore off the packaging as fast as I could. I felt a hint of impropriety, realizing that I must have looked insane, but such thoughts vanished from my mind when I was struck by the hypnotizing gleam of the cans. I juggled them into my arms. The cans were pure chrome, cool and light. On one side, a large label read "Instructions."

[8]

The next several days were an agonizing waiting game. Confidence was coming in the mail, but time dragged on. Each day at work was pure drudgery until I could slip out and race home to my mailbox. For days, though, nothing came. Just as I was about to give up hope, willing to admit I had been swindled by some late night snake oil salesman when I should have been asleep, the doorbell rang.

[9]

"Hold 6 inches away from your body and spray liberally for 5 seconds." I happily complied, even going so far as to use both cans at the same time.

[10]

Admittedly, the smell was strong, even, some would say, a little strange. But that didn't matter—as long

38. **F.** NO CHANGE
   G. I need
   H. I will be needing
   J. I needed

39. Which of the following true statements would provide the best concluding sentence for paragraph 6?
   A. I was impressed by how convincing the host was.
   B. The whole concept of Confidence in a Can seemed ridiculous.
   C. I grabbed out my phone and made an order.
   D. The offer could only have been better if it was for three cans.

GO ON TO THE NEXT PAGE.

as it worked! The directions told me that I needed to wait 10 minutes before I did anything else. "The confidence," as the can stated, "needed to cauterize with the skin," whatever that meant. I sat there, itching with anticipation. I could feel it working. I was tingling with boldness and tenacity. When the clock hand hit that last second, I sprinted out of my front door and down the street, eager to share my newfound self-assurance with anyone I could. I passed people on the sidewalk and smiled brightly. At first, they smiled too, but then, as I got closer, their expressions soured. What could I be doing wrong? My newfound confidence was fading fast. <u>However</u>, when I saw my friend Jackie's house,
40
I made for the door. I knew I could count on him to recognize the new and improved me. When the door opened, Jackie's face donned a wide smile, but just like the others, it quickly sagged into a frown. I began pacing and babbling about everything until Jackie stopped me and <u>said "You're acting weird and you smell terrible!"</u> 42
41

40. F. NO CHANGE
  G. So
  H. Nevertheless
  J. In other words

41. A. NO CHANGE
  B. said "You're acting weird and smell terrible!"
  C. said, "You're acting weird, you smell terrible!"
  D. said, "You're acting weird, and you smell terrible!"

42. For essay clarity, the most effective organizational flow for paragraphs 7, 8, 9, and 10 should be which of the following?
  F. 7, 8, 9, 10
  G. 8, 7, 9, 10
  H. 9, 8, 7, 10
  J. 10, 9, 8, 7

[11]

In that moment, I had a pungent epiphany. Somewhat deflated, I walked home. Without hesitation, I tossed my Confidence in a Can into the garbage and learned a very valuable lesson. 43

43. The author would like to add a final sentence to this essay that captures what he's learned from this experience. Based on the information provided in the passage, which of the following would be the most effective concluding sentence?

A. You should never make any risky purchasing decisions when you're tired!

B. Nothing that's sold in a can ever works!

C. You should never rely too much on confidence to help you achieve your goals!

D. Some products take more than just a few days to start working properly!

Questions 44 and 45 ask about the passage as a whole.

---

44. The writer is thinking of deleting the first paragraph in an effort to make the piece shorter and meet their assignment guidelines. Should the writer make this change?

F. Yes, because the passage is definitely too long as it currently is.

G. Yes, because readers don't need the information presented in this paragraph.

H. No, because paragraph 3 would be a better choice to cut from the passage.

J. No, because the first paragraph contains information essential for following the story.

45. Suppose the writer's primary purpose had been to offer a well-supported critique of the predatory nature of advertisements in modern media. Would this essay accomplish that purpose?

A. Yes, because it demonstrates a situation in which people are particularly vulnerable to the claims of commercials.

B. Yes, because the writer builds a chronological narrative that recounts a humorous experience related to an impulse purchase from late-night television.

C. No, because the informal tone of the essay is used to convey a personal revelation rather than explicit claims about the nature of advertising.

D. No, because the beginning of the essay spends too much time discussing the kinds of products that people purchase and their reasons for doing so.

GO ON TO THE NEXT PAGE.

PASSAGE IV

THE SPORT OF ROWING

[1]

Have you ever wondered what it would be like to glide silently across the water, <u>using only your muscles but not an engine or sail to power your travel?</u>
₄₆
Thousands, in fact millions, of rowers worldwide experience this feeling every day as they train on their local rivers.

<u>Rowing is such a popular sport that there are now clubs</u>
₄₇
<u>in cities and towns across the globe.</u>
₄₇

[2]

It's not <u>what it looks like.</u> The best athletes make it
₄₈
look easy, but in reality it takes an intense coordinated effort of <u>body or mind</u> to propel a rowing shell over the
₄₉
surface of the water.

<u>When rowing in a team boat, the athletes must mimic</u>
₅₀   ₅₀
the exact movements of their teammates, right down to their breathing at times.

46. F. NO CHANGE
   G. using only your muscles, not an engine or sail, to power your travel
   H. using only your muscles, and not an engine or sail to power your travel
   J. using only your muscles, but not an engine, or sail to power your travel

47. A. NO CHANGE
   B. Rowing is such a popular sport, because there are now clubs in countless cities and towns across the globe.
   C. Rowing is such a popular sport, that there are now, rowing clubs in cities and towns across the globe.
   D. Rowing is such a popular sport. There are now rowing clubs in cities and towns across the globe.

48. F. NO CHANGE
   G. very hard
   H. as effortless as you might think
   J. something you can do

49. A. NO CHANGE
   B. body, not mind,
   C. body but mind
   D. body and mind

50. F. NO CHANGE
   G. When rowing together in a team boat; rowers must mimic
   H. When rowing together in a team boat. Rowers must mimic
   J. When rowing together in a team boat and rowers must mimic

If they become unsynchronized, you see, even for a
                                                    51
moment, the boat will lose crucial speed necessary to

thrust the boat through the water.

[3]

Lost speed is not something rowers want to happen
                                                52
to their boat, especially when racing.
  52

Sometimes, races are won or lost by thousandths
        53
of a second, which can be devastating for a team that

trains as hard as elite rowers usually do. They often train

on the water two times a day (morning and night) and

spend hours in the weight room additionally the time
                                              54
they spend on the water.

[4]

Races, which are usually 2,000 meters in length,

only last for about 6 to 8 minutes, depending on the size

of the boat and wind conditions. Often rowers will train

thousands of hours a year for one inconsequential race,
                                              55
such as the World Championships.

These are a lot of training for such a short race!
  56

51. **A.** NO CHANGE
- **B.** If they become unsynchronized, consequently, even for a moment
- **C.** If they become briefly unsynchronized, even for a moment
- **D.** If they become unsynchronized, even for a moment

52. **F.** NO CHANGE
- **G.** Losing speed is not something rowers want happening to their boat
- **H.** Losing speed (is not something rowers want) happening to their boat
- **J.** To lose speed is not something that should have happened to their boat

53. **A.** NO CHANGE
- **B.** Conversely,
- **C.** Instead,
- **D.** However,

54. **F.** NO CHANGE
- **G.** in addition to
- **H.** because of
- **J.** since

55. **A.** NO CHANGE
- **B.** important
- **C.** imperfect
- **D.** illegitimate

56. **F.** NO CHANGE
- **G.** That
- **H.** That been
- **J.** That is

GO ON TO THE NEXT PAGE.

[57] Dedicated rowers, however, will tell you that the sacrifice is well worth having the chance to win a national or even Olympic medal one day.

[5]

You may be watching a past, present, or future Olympian. Or perhaps you will see someone who just
58
loves to spend his or her morning on the river, enjoying the sport of rowing.

57. At this point in the essay, the author is considering the addition of the following sentence:

> There are a few long-distance races that measure approximately 3.5 miles and are raced in a "chase" fashion with each boat starting in 10-second intervals.

Would this be a logical and relevant addition to the essay?

A. Yes, because it serves to further explain the types of races in which rowers participate.
B. Yes, because it serves to establish the main point of this paragraph.
C. No, because this paragraph is discussing only the World Championships for which rowers train many hours.
D. No, because it does not serve to emphasize the difference in the amount of training relative to the length of the races.

58. How can the author best combine these two sentences?

F. future Olympian, or perhaps
G. future Olympian: or perhaps
H. future Olympian and perhaps
J. future Olympian so perhaps

Questions 59 and 60 ask about the passage as a whole.

59. The writer wants to add the following sentence to the essay:

> The next time you travel near a river, be sure to notice any long, skinny boats skimming lightly atop the water, silently propelled by these well-trained athletes.

The sentence would most logically be placed at the beginning of:

A. Paragraph 1
B. Paragraph 2
C. Paragraph 3
D. Paragraph 5

60. Suppose the author had been assigned to write a brief essay detailing the technical aspects of the training and performance of elite rowers. Would this essay accomplish that purpose?

F. Yes, because the essay describes the length and time of rowing races.
G. Yes, because the essay tells us in great detail about the weight-room training schedule of elite rowers.
H. No, because the essay does not discuss any training or performance techniques in detail.
J. No, because the essay suggests that rowing is not a sport that requires much training or technique.

PASSAGE V

A New Link Between Saturated Fats and Alzheimer's Disease

[1]

Recent studies seem to indicate <u>that</u> a diet high in fat is somehow linked to the onset of Alzheimer's disease and dementia.

61. A. NO CHANGE
    B. for
    C. in
    D. how

A recent article in the *Archives of Neurology* <u>cite</u> experiments that show how sticking to a diet rich in "good fats"—fats found in nuts, fatty fish, and vegetable oils—seems to lower the risk of mental disease.

62. F. NO CHANGE
    G. citation
    H. citing
    J. cites

GO ON TO THE NEXT PAGE.

"Bad fats" otherwise known as saturated fats seem to
63
increase the risk. Interestingly, the new studies point
63
out that antioxidant vitamins, once touted as possessing

curative effects for Alzheimer's and dementia, now seem

to be ineffective.

[2]

The studies claim a profound discovery saturated
64
fats and cholesterol are detrimental to overall brain
64
functions. In one study, scientists assembled a group of

815 senior citizens who reported no signs of deterio-

rated mental condition.

Each member of the group was asked to list the foods it
65
ate regularly. Two years later, each was asked again to list

the foods eaten on a regular basis.

Then, for a period of four years followed the second test,
66
the research team tracked the health of each member

of the group. By the end of the observation period, 131

seniors had developed Alzheimer's.

[3]

The data collected from this experiment showed

that the seniors who had reported eating more saturated

and hydrogenated fats from foods such as red meat,
67

fried foods, and packaged goods such as cookies, chips,

and cakes were more than double as likely to develop
68
Alzheimer's. Those who had recorded salmon, tuna,

fruits, avocados, nuts, and grains as their favorite foods

63. A. NO CHANGE

B. "Bad fats" otherwise known as saturated fats, seem to increase the risk.

C. "Bad fats," otherwise known as saturated fats, seem to increase the risk.

D. "Bad fats," otherwise known as saturated fats seem to increase the risk.

64. F. NO CHANGE

G. a profound discovery: saturated fats and cholesterol

H. a profound discovery with saturated fats and cholesterol

J. a profound discovery saturating fats and cholesterol

65. A. NO CHANGE

B. he or she

C. that they

D. that was

66. F. NO CHANGE

G. that following the second

H. following the second

J. follow did the second

67. A. NO CHANGE

B. like

C. with

D. because

68. F. NO CHANGE

G. over double

H. more than twice

J. half

carried less of a risk for dementia. These foods are rich in polyunsaturated and monounsaturated fats.

[4]

A second experiment <u>attacks</u> a very popular and
₆₉
long-upheld medical theory. Many researchers have

gone on record in order <u>in supporting the notion that</u>
₇₀
unstable compounds in the bloodstream, called "free radicals," are responsible for damaging nerve cells and causing the onset of dementia. Traditionally, vitamins such as C, E, and beta carotene <u>has</u> been singled out as
₇₁
agents that can reduce the risk of free-radical damage within the human system.

[5]

[1] During that time, 242 people developed Alzheimer's. [2] <u>Researchers tracked the eating habits of</u>
₇₂
<u>980 elderly people —none of whom displayed dementia</u>
₇₂
<u>symptoms—for four years.</u> [3] Lead researcher Jose A.
₇₂
Luchsinger, an associate at Columbia University in New York City, wrote: "Neither dietary, supplemental, nor intake of carotenes and vitamins C and E was associated with a decreased risk." [4] No link could be found between the afflicted people's dietary supplement intake and the prevention of disease. [73]

69. **A.** NO CHANGE
 B. launches an attack on
 C. will attack
 D. did attack

70. **F.** NO CHANGE
 G. to supporting the notion that
 H. to support the notion that
 J. with support for the notion which

71. **A.** NO CHANGE
 B. have
 C. are
 D. will be

72. In the sentence, the clause "none of whom displayed dementia symptoms" primarily serves to indicate:
 F. a consequential detail about the people in the study.
 G. why researchers were concerned about the people in the study.
 H. how dementia develops in people with no previous symptoms.
 J. when it is important to begin treatment for dementia.

73. Of the following, which sentence order will make Paragraph 5 most logical?
 A. NO CHANGE
 B. 3, 4, 1, 2
 C. 1, 2, 4, 3
 D. 2, 1, 4, 3

GO ON TO THE NEXT PAGE.

Questions 74 and 75 ask about the passage as a whole.

74. The writer's main purpose was to provide an overview of a recent scientific discovery. Would this essay accomplish that purpose?

F. Yes, because the author outlines the findings of two new experiments, providing illustrations and details only as needed.

G. Yes, because the author wisely references the work of Jose A. Luchsinger, a researcher from Columbia University.

H. No, because the author does not offer valuable details concerning food sources for antioxidant vitamins.

J. No, because the author makes no attempt to provide counterpoints to the information supposedly gleaned by the experiments.

75. After reading this article, readers could infer that in order to reduce their own risk of contracting Alzheimer's disease or dementia, they could:

A. increase their dosage of antioxidant vitamins.

B. maintain a diet rich in saturated fats rather than polyunsaturated and monounsaturated fats.

C. maintain a diet rich in polyunsaturated and monounsaturated fats rather than saturated fats.

D. remove antioxidant vitamins from their diet.

STOP.

If you finish before time is up, you may check your work on this section only.
Do not turn to any other section in the test.

SECTION 2: MATHEMATICS TEST

60 Questions—60 Minutes

Directions: Solve each problem, choose the correct answer, and then fill in the corresponding oval on your answer sheet.

Do not dwell on problems that take too long. First, solve as many as you can; then, you can return to others you have left.

You are permitted to use a calculator on this test. You may use your calculator for any problem you like, but some of the problems may best be completed without a calculator.

Note: Unless otherwise stated, all of the following should be assumed:

1. Illustrative figures are NOT necessarily drawn to scale.

2. Geometric figures lie in a plane.

3. The word line indicates a straight line.

4. The word average indicates arithmetic mean

---

1. A cat food company conducted a poll of people who bought its product. When the marketing director asked 400 people to select one of three colors for new packaging, 150 people chose blue, 200 people chose red, and the rest chose green. Of the people questioned, what percentage chose green?

   A. 12.50%

   B. 25%

   C. 37.50%

   D. 50%

   E. 87.50%

2. A hand is a unit of length equivalent to 4 inches. If the height of a horse's back is 57 inches, what is the height of the horse's back in hands?

   F. 10

   G. 14.25

   H. 53

   J. 142.5

   K. 228

3. What is the midpoint of the line segment with endpoints (2, –8) and (–6, 2)?

   A. (–3, –2)

   B. (4, –5)

   C. (–5, 4)

   D. (–2, –3)

   E. (–4, –6)

4. What value of z makes the following proportion true?

   $$\frac{15}{3z} = \frac{10}{4}$$

   F. 2

   G. $2\frac{1}{2}$

   H. 5

   J. 6

   K. 30

GO ON TO THE NEXT PAGE.

5. Airplane A travels at a constant speed of 540 miles per hour for 3 hours. Airplane B travels at a constant speed of 400 miles per hour for 3 hours and 30 minutes. What is the total number of miles traveled by the two airplanes?

   A. 1,400

   B. 1,620

   C. 3,020

   D. 3,090

   E. 6,110

6. The upload speed offered by an internet provider is x megabits per second. If running several wi-fi devices in a house decreases this speed by 12%, what is the upload speed in this case?

   F. $0.12x$

   G. $x - 0.12$

   H. $0.88 + x$

   J. $0.88x$

   K. $\dfrac{12x}{88}$

7. What is the value of $-a^2 (1 - 3a)$ when $a = -2$?

   A. −28

   B. −20

   C. −16

   D. 20

   E. 28

8. If $f(x) = 2x^2 - 3x + 6$, what is the value of $f(3)$?

   F. 5

   G. 6

   H. 9

   J. 15

   K. 33

9. Suppose the point $M(-3,1)$ is the midpoint of the line segment AB, where A has coordinates $(7, -9)$. What are the coordinates of the other endpoint B?

   A. $(11, -13)$

   B. $(1, -7)$

   C. $(-7, 1)$

   D. $(-13, 11)$

   E. $(2, -4)$

10. For $i = \sqrt{-1}$, compute $-i(2 - 5i)^2$.

    F. $20 - 21i$

    G. $-20 + 21i$

    H. $-20 + 29i$

    J. $-21 - 20i$

    K. $-29i$

11. Mike listened to a radio station for eight separate half-hour sessions. He counted the number of songs played during each session and listed the results in the table below.

Number of songs	6	8	9	12
Number of sessions	1	3	2	2

    What is the average number of songs played per half-hour?

    A. 4.375

    B. 8.5

    C. 8.75

    D. 9

    E. 18

12. If $(m + 4)(m - 2) = 0$, which of the following is a possible value of m?

    F. 0

    G. 2

    H. 4

    J. 6

    K. 8

13. What is the value of $||-7 + 9| - |4 - 12||$?

    A. -111

    B. -6

    C. 6

    D. 32

    E. 111

14. In the figure below, UV is perpendicular to both PQ and ST. What is the measure of angle VRW?

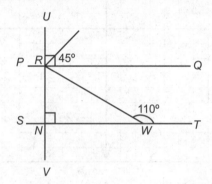

    F. $20°$

    G. $45°$

    H. $70°$

    J. $90°$

    K. $110°$

15. A solution of the equation $2x^2 = 310$ lies between which two consecutive negative integers?

    A. -15 and -16

    B. -14 and -15

    C. -13 and -14

    D. -12 and -13

    E. -11 and -12

16. What is the least common multiple for the set of whole numbers 12, 18, 24?

    F. 2

    G. 6

    H. 48

    J. 72

    K. 144

17. The equation $y = x^2 + 4x - 21$ would have how many roots?

    A. 0

    B. 1

    C. 2

    D. 3

    E. 4

18. In a group of 40 students, each student is asked to identify math, history, or art as their favorite class. The probability that a student chosen randomly from this group did NOT say math is their favorite is $\frac{1}{5}$. How many students said math is their favorite?

    F. 8

    G. 10

    H. 20

    J. 32

    K. 36

19. What are the solutions of the equation $3|x| + 2 = 9|x|$?

    A. $x = -\dfrac{1}{\sqrt{3}}$

    B. $x = -3, 3$

    C. $x = -2, 2$

    D. $x = -\dfrac{1}{3}, \dfrac{1}{3}$

    E. No solution

20. What is the equation of the line passing through the points $(4, -4)$ and $(-4, 8)$?

    F. $3x + 2y = 4$

    G. $-3x + 2y = 4$

    H. $2x + 3y = -4$

    J. $2x - 3y = 4$

    K. $3x + 2y = -8$

GO ON TO THE NEXT PAGE.

21. What is the greatest common factor of 12, 32, and 96?

    A. 2

    B. 4

    C. 16

    D. 18

    E. 24

22. The sale price of an OLED television is $2,250. If this is the price after a 15% discount has been applied, which expression represents the original price of the television?

    F. 0.85(2,250) dollars

    G. 2,250 + 0.85 dollars

    H. $\dfrac{2,250}{1.15}$ dollars

    J. 1.15(2,250) dollars

    K. $\dfrac{2,250}{0.85}$ dollars

23. If $4x^2 - 25 = 0$ and $x > 0$, what is the value of x?

    A. $-\dfrac{5}{2}$

    B. $\dfrac{2}{5}$

    C. $\dfrac{5}{4}$

    D. $\dfrac{5}{2}$

    E. $\dfrac{25}{4}$

24. If rectangle ABCD is rotated 180°, centered at point A, what are the new coordinates of point C?

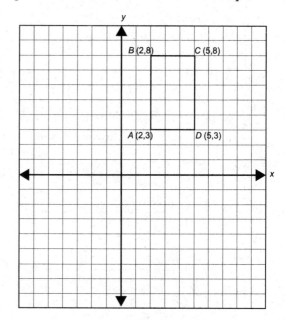

    F. (7, 0)

    G. (−3, 6)

    H. (2, −2)

    J. (−1, 3)

    K. (−1, −2)

25. Which of the following is the graph of $j(x) = 3^x - 2$?

A.

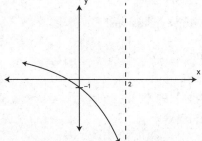

B.

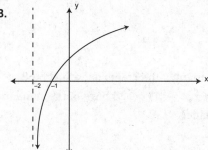

C.

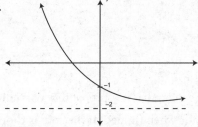

D.

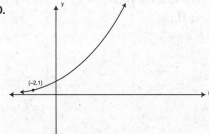

E.

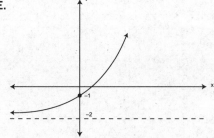

26. What is the slope of a line perpendicular to the line whose equation is $2x - 5y - 1 = 0$?

F. $-\dfrac{5}{2}$

G. $-\dfrac{1}{2}$

H. $\dfrac{2}{5}$

J. $\dfrac{1}{2}$

K. 2

27. The length of a rectangle is 6 inches greater than the width. If the perimeter of the rectangle is 44 inches, what is the area of the rectangle, in square inches?

A. 55

B. 112

C. 121

D. 187

E. 475

28. What is the x-intercept of the line whose equation is $2y = 1 - 4x$?

F. $\dfrac{1}{4}$

G. $\dfrac{1}{2}$

H. 2

J. 4

K. 8

29. A broadcasting network shows 5 commercial segments during a 30-minute sitcom. The lengths of four of these segments are 85 seconds, 125 seconds, 95 seconds, and 145 seconds. For the average length of the five segments to be 130 seconds, what must be the length of the fifth segment?

A. 70 seconds

B. 100 seconds

C. 130 seconds

D. 200 seconds

E. 650 seconds

GO ON TO THE NEXT PAGE.

30. What is the area of the rectangle shown below in the standard (x, y) coordinate plane?

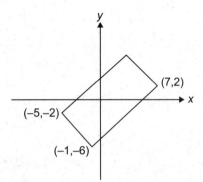

F. $32\sqrt{2}$

G. 64

H. $24\sqrt{2}$

J. 128

K. 144

31. Maria bought some vinyl record albums for her club. She bought 2 single albums and 1 double album, all on sale for 30% off. The single albums regularly cost $16 each, and the double albums regularly cost $24. Assuming no sales tax, how much in total did Maria pay for her albums?

A. $16.80

B. $28

C. $39.20

D. $46.40

E. $48.80

32. The average of a set of 7 integers is 13. When an eighth number is included in the set, the average of the set decreases to 12. What is the eighth number?

F. 4

G. 5

H. 8

J. 13

K. 25

33. For all nonzero values of a, b, and c, $\dfrac{-a^4(b^2)^4 c^6}{(-a)^3 b^3 c^8}$ is equivalent to which of the following expressions?

A. $-\dfrac{ab^3}{c^2}$

B. $a^7 b^{11} c^{14}$

C. $-a^{12} b^{24} c^{48}$

D. $\dfrac{ab^3}{c^2}$

E. $\dfrac{ab^5}{c^2}$

34. How many x-intercepts does the graph of $f(x) = x(x^2 - 4)(x^2 + 9)$ have in the standard xy-plane?

F. 1

G. 2

H. 3

J. 5

K. 6

35. A biased coin has a $\dfrac{3}{5}$ probability of landing on heads when flipped. If the coin is flipped 250 times, which expression represents the expected value of the number of heads obtained in these flips?

A. $\left(\dfrac{2}{5}\right)^{250}$

B. $\left(\dfrac{3}{5}\right)^{250}$

C. $\dfrac{3}{5}$

D. $250 \cdot \dfrac{2}{5}$

E. $250 \cdot \dfrac{3}{5}$

36. For what value of a, if any, does the system $\begin{cases} y = 5x - 1 \\ x = ay - 1 \end{cases}$ have infinitely many solutions?

F. -5

G. $-\dfrac{1}{5}$

H. $\dfrac{1}{5}$

J. 5

K. No such value of a

37. A small pump can remove water from a pool at the rate of 8.25 gallons per minute. How many minutes would it take to remove g gallons at this rate?

A. $8.25g$

B. $8.25g + g$

C. $\dfrac{8.25}{g}$

D. $g - 8.25$

E. $\dfrac{g}{8.25}$

38. If $\log_3 \left(\dfrac{1}{81} \right) = y$, what is y?

F. -27

G. -4

H. $\dfrac{1}{243}$

J. $\dfrac{1}{27}$

K. 4

39. From the top of an airport control tower, the angle between a horizontal line and an approaching airplane is 27°, as shown below. If the distance between the control tower and the airplane is 35,000 meters, what is the difference, in meters, between the altitude of the plane and the top of the control tower?

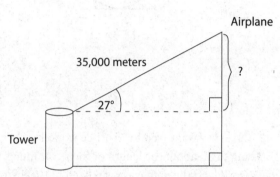

A. $35,000 \times \sin 63°$

B. $35,000 \times \sin 27°$

C. $35,000 \times \cos 27°$

D. $\dfrac{35,000}{\sin 27°}$

E. $\dfrac{35,000}{\cos 27°}$

40. For real numbers a, b, and c, $a > b$ and $c < 0$. Which of the following inequalities must be true?

F. $ab > 0$

G. $ac < 0$

H. $\dfrac{a}{b} > \dfrac{c}{b}$

J. $\dfrac{a}{c} > \dfrac{b}{c}$

K. $\dfrac{a}{c} < \dfrac{b}{c}$

GO ON TO THE NEXT PAGE.

41. In the diagram below, a circle is inscribed in a square. If the radius of the circle is 3 units, what is the area of the square, in square units?

   A. 9

   B. 24

   C. 28

   D. 36

   E. 113

42. A survey was given to 75 office workers asking them about the length of their commutes to work, and the data was visualized in the histogram below. What is the approximate relative frequency of the number of people whose commute is greater than 2 hours?

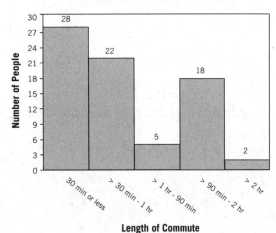

   F. 0.02

   G. 0.03

   H. 0.27

   J. 0.47

   K. 0.97

43. A balanced six-sided die with faces 1, 2, 3, 4, 5, and 6 is rolled twice. What is the probability of getting one 5 and one 6?

   A. $\dfrac{17}{18}$

   B. $\dfrac{5}{9}$

   C. $\dfrac{1}{3}$

   D. $\dfrac{1}{6}$

   E. $\dfrac{1}{18}$

44. If $A = \begin{bmatrix} -2 & -3 \\ 1 & -1 \end{bmatrix}$ and $B = \begin{bmatrix} 4 & -2 \\ -3 & -1 \end{bmatrix}$, what is $2B - 3A$?

   F. $\begin{bmatrix} 14 & 1 \\ -4 & 0 \end{bmatrix}$

   G. $\begin{bmatrix} 2 & -13 \\ -3 & -5 \end{bmatrix}$

   H. $\begin{bmatrix} 8 & -4 \\ -6 & -2 \end{bmatrix}$

   J. $\begin{bmatrix} 14 & 5 \\ -9 & 1 \end{bmatrix}$

   K. $\begin{bmatrix} -6 & -9 \\ 3 & -3 \end{bmatrix}$

45. What is the equation of the line passing through the point (–2, –1) that is parallel to the line whose equation is $x = -\dfrac{1}{3}y + 4$?

   A. $3x - y + 5 = 0$

   B. $3x + y - 1 = 0$

   C. $3x - y - 1 = 0$

   D. $x + 3y + 5 = 0$

   E. $3x + y + 7 = 0$

46. A right triangle has a hypotenuse of 17 and a leg of 15. What is the length of the other leg?

F. 4

G. $\sqrt{32}$

H. 8

J. $\sqrt{514}$

K. 64

47. Suppose $(a, -b)$ and $(b, -a)$ are points in the xy-plane. Which of these expressions represents the distance between these two points?

A. 2a

B. $\sqrt{2}|a-b|$

C. $\sqrt{2}|a|+\sqrt{2}|b|$

D. $\sqrt{2\left(a^2+b^2\right)}$

E. $2(a-b)^2$

48. The temperature at 9 a.m. is –15.5°C. The temperature at 10 a.m. is –13.0°C. If the temperature changes by the same amount each hour, what will the temperature be at 1 p.m.?

F. –20.5°C

G. –8.0°C

H. –5.5°C

J. 2.5°C

K. 7.5°C

49. A line passes through the points $\left(-\dfrac{4}{5},\dfrac{1}{2}\right)$ and $\left(\dfrac{3}{10},-\dfrac{5}{6}\right)$. What is the slope of a line perpendicular to this line?

A. $-\dfrac{22}{15}$

B. $-\dfrac{40}{33}$

C. $-\dfrac{33}{40}$

D. $\dfrac{33}{40}$

E. $\dfrac{40}{33}$

50. If the graph of $g(x) = (x + 3)^2 - 2$ is translated 2 units to the right, what is the range of the resulting function?

F. $(-\infty, \infty)$

G. $(-\infty, -1]$

H. $[-2, \infty)$

J. $[-1, \infty)$

K. $(-\infty, -2]$

51. In a game at the county fair, Inez has a 25% chance of winning $1, a 50% chance of winning $2, and a 25% chance of losing $4. What is the expected value of the game?

A. –$1

B. $0.25

C. $1.25

D. $1.50

E. $2.50

GO ON TO THE NEXT PAGE.

52. If m is a negative integer and n is a positive integer, which of the following must be true?

F. $|m - n| = |m| - |n|$

G. $|m - n| = |m + n|$

H. $|m - n| \leq |m| - |n|$

J. $|m - n| = -|m + n|$

K. $|m - n| \neq 0$

53. During the winter months, the thermostat in a sunroom is programmed to increase the temperature by 25% at 6 a.m. to warm it up. Once it reaches this temperature, it decreases the temperature by 10% and keeps it there for the duration of the day. If the starting temperature in the sunroom is 60° F, what is the final temperature?

A. 62.5° F

B. 65° F

C. 67.5° F

D. 75° F

E. 76.5° F

54. What is the inverse of the function $g(x) = \dfrac{2x}{x-1}$?

F. $g^{-1}(x) = \dfrac{x-1}{2x}$

G. $g^{-1}(x) = \dfrac{1}{x-2}$

H. $g^{-1}(x) = \dfrac{x-2}{x}$

J. $g^{-1}(x) = \dfrac{x}{x-2}$

K. $g^{-1}(x) = \dfrac{x(x-1)}{2x}$

55. A bucket contains 10 red balls, 5 blue balls, 3 green balls, and 2 yellow balls. What is the probability of randomly selecting a ball that is neither blue nor yellow?

A. 0.25

B. 0.35

C. 0.65

D. 0.75

E. 0.9

56. If $f(x) = \dfrac{1}{x+2}$ and $g(x) = \dfrac{1}{2x}$, compute $(f \circ g)(-4)$.

F. -3

G. $-\dfrac{3}{8}$

H. $-\dfrac{1}{2}$

J. $\dfrac{3}{16}$

K. $\dfrac{8}{13}$

57. Kaia can row 300 meters in 80 seconds. If she maintained this pace, how many kilometers would she row in one hour?

A. 9.6

B. 10.8

C. 13.5

D. 18

E. 45

58. The formula for the volume of a right circular cone is $V = \frac{1}{3}\pi r^2 h$, where r is the radius of the base and h is the height. If the radius is tripled and the height is doubled, by what factor is the volume increased?

    F. 2

    G. 3

    H. 6

    J. 9

    K. 18

59. What is the maximum value of $y = 4\sin(3x) - 1$?

    A. 0

    B. 1

    C. 3

    D. 4

    E. 5

60. What are the solutions of the quadratic equation $2x^2 - x + 3 = 0$?

    F. $x = \frac{1}{4} \pm i\frac{\sqrt{5}}{4}$

    G. $x = \frac{1}{4} \pm i\frac{\sqrt{23}}{4}$

    H. $x = \frac{1}{4} \pm \frac{23}{4}$

    J. $x = -\frac{3}{2}, 1$

    K. $x = -1, \frac{3}{2}$

STOP.

If you finish before time is up, you may check your work on this section only.
Do not turn to any other section in the test.

SECTION 3: READING TEST

40 Questions—35 Minutes

Directions: There are multiple passages in this test. Each passage is accompanied by multiple questions. After you finish reading a passage, choose the best answer to each question and fill in the corresponding oval on your answer sheet. You may refer to the passages as often as necessary.

PASSAGE I

LITERARY NARRATIVE: This excerpt is taken from *The Autobiography of Charles Darwin* (1887). Note that the HMS *Beagle* is a ship on which Darwin worked as a naturalist.

The voyage of the "Beagle" has been by far the most important event in my life, and has determined my whole career; yet it depended on so small a circumstance as my uncle offering to
5 drive me thirty miles to Shrewsbury, which few uncles would have done, and on such a trifle as the shape of my nose. I have always felt that I owe to the voyage the first real training or education of my mind; I was led to attend closely to several
10 branches of natural history, and thus my powers of observation were improved, though they were always fairly developed.

The investigation of the geology of all the places visited was far more important, as reason-
15 ing here comes into play. On first examining a new district nothing can appear more hopeless than the chaos of rocks; but by recording the stratification and nature of the rocks and fossils at many points, always reasoning and predict-
20 ing what will be found elsewhere, light soon begins to dawn on the district, and the structure of the whole becomes more or less intelligible. I had brought with me the first volume of Lyell's 'Principles of Geology,' which I studied atten-
25 tively; and the book was of the highest service to me in many ways. The very first place which I examined, namely St. Jago in the Cape de Verde islands, showed me clearly the wonderful superiority of Lyell's manner of treating geology,

30 compared with that of any other author, whose works I had with me or ever afterwards read.

Another of my occupations was collecting animals of all classes, briefly describing and roughly dissecting many of the marine ones; but
35 from not being able to draw, and from not having sufficient anatomical knowledge, a great pile of [manuscripts] which I made during the voyage has proved almost useless. I thus lost much time, with the exception of that spent in acquir-
40 ing some knowledge of the Crustaceans, as this was of service when in after years I undertook a monograph of the Cirripedia.

During some part of the day I wrote my Journal, and took much pains in describing care-
45 fully and vividly all that I had seen; and this was good practice. My Journal served also, in part, as letters to my home, and portions were sent to England whenever there was an opportunity.

The above various special studies were,
50 however, of no importance compared with the habit of energetic industry and of concentrated attention to whatever I was engaged in, which I then acquired. Everything about which I thought or read was made to bear directly on what I had
55 seen or was likely to see; and this habit of mind was continued during the five years of the voyage. I feel sure that it was this training which has enabled me to do whatever I have done in science.
60 Looking backwards, I can now perceive how my love for science gradually preponderated over every other taste. During the first two years my old passion for shooting survived in nearly full force, and I shot myself all the birds and animals

65 for my collection; but gradually I gave up my
gun more and more, and finally altogether, to
my servant, as shooting interfered with my work,
more especially with making out the geological structure of a country. I discovered, though
70 unconsciously and insensibly, that the pleasure of
observing and reasoning was a much higher one
than that of skill and sport. That my mind became developed through my pursuits during the
voyage is rendered probable by a remark made
75 by my father, who was the most acute observer
whom I ever saw, of a sceptical disposition, and
far from being a believer in phrenology*; for on
first seeing me after the voyage, he turned round
to my sisters, and exclaimed, "Why, the shape of
80 his head is quite altered."

*The historical study of the shape of the head as a supposed indicator of
mental capacity and character.

1. The narrator of the passage characterizes his
   voyage on the HMS *Beagle* as a:

   A. time-consuming journey during which his
      explicit role as a naturalist was not clearly
      defined for him.

   B. thought-provoking sojourn into his later focus
      on geology above all other pursuits.

   C. turning point in his development as a scientist,
      during which he developed important faculties
      for observation and analysis.

   D. risk, since he did not know what he would find
      in the various destinations he encountered
      while traveling with the ship's crew.

2. Which of these events from the passage happened first chronologically?

   F. The narrator gave up his gun to his servant.

   G. The narrator's father noticed that he'd devel-
      oped his mind and altered his demeanor.

   H. The narrator recorded the stratification and
      nature of rocks and fossils.

   J. The narrator's uncle drove him 30 miles to
      Shrewsbury to see about a job.

3. The narrator describes Lyell's "Principles of
   Geology" as being "of the highest service"
   (line 25–26) to him in order to:

   A. thank Lyell for letting him publish his findings
      on the geology of St. Jago in the "Principles of
      Geology."

   B. emphasize how useful Lyell's work was in
      helping him with the massive task of stratify-
      ing and classifying chaotic piles of rocks.

   C. demonstrate that it required energetic indus-
      try and concentrated attention to study Lyell's
      work effectively.

   D. critique Lyell's work for containing factual
      inaccuracies that hindered his own pursuits as
      a scientist.

4. The narrator indicated that when he looked back
   on his experiences aboard the HMS *Beagle*, he
   realized that:

   F. his abilities as a scientist developed consider-
      ably during this time, setting up the entire rest
      of his career as a scientist.

   G. it was a job he was reluctant to undertake but
      nonetheless happy to have had.

   H. being a naturalist on a ship wasn't exactly the
      best way to use his considerably developed
      scientific qualities.

   J. it would not be his last voyage on the HMS
      Beagle, for he wanted to get right back to work
      on his geological pursuits.

5. The passage indicates that when the narrator
   wrote in his journal, he did so to:

   A. record his scientific observations in detail
      somewhere no one would find them.

   B. make detailed notes about his work as well as
      write letters he wished to send home.

   C. keep a diary of his feelings and thoughts so
      that he could show his family later.

   D. make notes for his future autobiography.

GO ON TO THE NEXT PAGE.

6. Based on the passage, when the narrator describes his father as an "acute observer" (line 75), this most likely refers to his father's:

   F. scientific mind.

   G. ability to discern traits and shifts that others might miss.

   H. tendency to miss obvious social cues.

   J. reliance on reasoning and analysis to make sense of the world.

7. The narrator describes his work dissecting and classifying marine creatures as:

   A. a time-consuming process that nonetheless proved useful.

   B. a compulsory requirement of his job as naturalist that he eventually resented.

   C. indispensable to his understanding of the marine life in the places he visited.

   D. mostly a waste of time, beyond the help it provided in some of his later research.

8. The statement "everything about which I thought or read was made to bear directly on what I had seen or was likely to see" (lines 53–55) can most directly be attributed to:

   F. the way the narrator continued to expand his thoughts on geology and biology in the five years after the journey.

   G. the narrator's recognition of how the research he did in preparation for his journey proved beneficial.

   H. the narrator's recollection of how his understanding and faculties of reason grew gradually over the course of his five year journey.

   J. the narrator's experience of classifying marine life and geological anomalies in the different locales he visited.

9. For the narrator, compared to shooting or engaging in feats of skill, pursuing scientific work is:

   A. more fulfilling.

   B. more tedious.

   C. less appealing.

   D. less adventurous.

10. When the narrator's father said "Why, the shape of his head is quite altered" (lines 79–80), he was most likely referring to the:

   F. physical changes the narrator had undergone while working on a ship.

   G. mental developments the narrator exhibited upon returning.

   H. literal shape of the narrator's head, in accordance with the tenets of phrenology.

   J. emotional changes that were apparent in the narrator's behavior.

PASSAGE II

SOCIAL SCIENCE: The following passage is adapted from an article on the relationship between grief and the brain.

Grief is a universal human condition in that virtually all people will experience it at some point; nonetheless, it is a unique experience for each individual. Until you find yourself in the
5 midst of grief, you don't know what to expect, and even those enveloped in it may struggle to predict the forms it could take going forward. Those deep in grief often report taking things day by day because of how often the experience
10 shifts and changes. Increasingly, psychologists and neuroscientists alike recognize this as a result of how the grieving process affects the human brain.

Psychologically speaking, grief represents
15 an array of emotional responses that can occur following any number of traumatic or deeply sorrowful events but is most often associated with the death of someone close. It is also common following a divorce, job loss, or end of a friend-
20 ship and can happen after recent revelations of abuse, in the wake of a medical event, or due to numerous other deeply sorrowful experiences. The thing that makes grief what it is is loss and, quite often, the twin experience of yearning for
25 what was, what might have been, or what one cannot change.

Though the ins and outs of grief are difficult to quantify, our collective understanding of the experience has expanded as the study of neuro-
30 science has grown in the last few decades. Today, we are learning more all the time about how grief affects the body and mind; the hope is to one day turn this newfound knowledge toward developing comprehensive approaches to grief that help
35 people better deal with its effects.

At the forefront of new discoveries is the recognition that the brain experiences grief as a form of emotional trauma, meaning that significant grief experiences are akin to post-traumatic
40 stress disorder (PTSD). Like PTSD, grief experiences can activate the fight or flight mechanism, causing people to behave in ways that may seem irrational, unprompted, or confusing to onlookers. This is because when the fight or flight
45 mechanism is activated in a person, their heart rate and blood pressure tend to increase and their body releases specific hormones, like cortisol and adrenaline, that affect how they behave.

We also know that, like PTSD, grief tends to
50 rewire the brain enough that a grieving person can experience cognitive effects, such as so-called "brain fog," as well as changes in memory and behavior. There is a high correlation between grief and sleep deprivation as well, so one often
55 sees reduced immune function and sometimes heart issues as a result of grief. When grief activates defense mechanisms like the fight or flight response, the body switches gears to focus exclusively on survival. This is why so many grievers
60 report being unable to do more than "function" on a day-to-day level; as far as their bodies are concerned, those deep in grief truly can't do more than survive.

Another discovery psychologists and neuro-
65 scientists point to is the growing recognition that grief must be considered a process. Most have heard of Elisabeth Kübler-Ross's theory on the five stages of grief—denial, anger, bargaining, depression, and acceptance—but beyond that one
70 particular theory, it's helpful to recognize that grief changes over time and involves a learning curve. Rather than following a specific linear process, as is sometimes implied by the Kübler-Ross model, grief tends to circle back on itself,
75 feeling at times easier and at other times harder. Certain habits or faculties may come back quicker than others while unknown triggers may cause waves of grief to come on. The individual adapts over time, and this journey is itself what
80 we often call "the grieving process."

If one considers grief a learning process, it's easier to recognize the link between

GO ON TO THE NEXT PAGE.

neuroplasticity, or the brain's ability to rewire itself and change in light of new information

85 and experiences, and the grieving process. As we grieve, our brains rewire to account for the new reality. For instance, some neuroscientists believe that one of our common brain functions involves creating maps of loved ones' daily activities so we

90 can better locate those close to us when we need them. As one grieves, say, the loss of a spouse, the neural pathways involved in this mapping must adjust to the new information that the significant other who was once there is no longer there; in

95 other words, as the brain learns its new reality, the individual experiences the waves of grief anew each time they note the absence of what was once predictably there.

This experience of grief is emotional, yes,
100 and affects us cognitively, but it's also evidence of how the brain learns and rewires over the course of time. The adage that the only thing that heals grief is time proves quite true, for the brain indeed requires time to make sense of its new

105 paradigm after a significant loss or emotional trauma.

11. Which of the following statements best expresses the main idea of the passage?

   A. Grief is primarily a learning process, so dealing with how we collectively address it means teaching people how to learn more effectively.

   B. Grief is so amorphous that it is hard for scientists to nail down exactly what it looks like, especially since every individual responds to it differently.

   C. Neuroscience has helped psychology researchers better understand grief in recent decades, particularly the idea that grief is a process that can mimic the effects of PTSD.

   D. Because of the unique neural pathways each individual creates, there is no way to predict how a given individual will react to a grief experience.

12. It can reasonably be inferred that the "brain fog" the author mentions in line 52 refers to:

   F. a cognitive sense of fogginess that many feel when faced with grief.

   G. an emotional sense of deep loneliness that many feel when faced with grief.

   H. the isolation one feels from the rest of the world when grieving.

   J. how grief can cause lapses in short- and long-term memory.

13. It can reasonably be inferred from the passage that:

   A. PTSD can cause a fight or flight response.

   B. grief is more intense in those who have already experienced PTSD.

   C. grief is less intense each time you encounter a new grief experience.

   D. by a certain age, most people can predict how a grief event will affect them.

14. Based on the passage, which of the following statements best describes the author's summation of Kübler-Ross's theory as it relates to the grieving process?

   F. Kübler-Ross ineffectively describes the way trauma interacts with the grieving process.

   G. Kübler-Ross's five stages of grief theory has widely been dismissed at this point.

   H. Kübler-Ross asserts that acceptance is the most prolonged stage of grief, but neuroscientists don't necessarily agree.

   J. Kübler-Ross asserts that there are five stages of grief that one must go through to process grief, but we now know that the grieving process isn't always as linear as her model might suggest.

15. According to the passage, the end of a significant romantic relationship can trigger grief:

   A. only if the relationship was exceptionally close, as grief only happens as a result of close relationships.

   B. because a breakup or divorce is an experience of great sorrow combined with loss and yearning.

   C. only after one has begun the first of five stages of the grieving process.

   D. because people generally get PTSD from major losses like a breakup or divorce.

16. According to the passage, the term *neuroplasticity* describes:

   F. a person's ability to bounce back from grief experiences.

   G. the brain's ability to create new social routines as a result of a significant loss.

   H. the brain's ability to change and make sense of new information it receives over time.

   J. a scientist's ability to measure how much a subject's brain has changed as the result of a grief event.

17. In Paragraph 7 (lines 81–98), the author provides the example of a person who is grieving the death of a spouse primarily in order to:

   A. explain why this type of grief would be easier to manage if one understands neuroplasticity.

   B. prompt an emotional response in the reader, who might consider the example in terms of their own loved ones.

   C. force the reader to consider how intense one's grief would be following the death of a spouse.

   D. demonstrate the relationship between neuroplasticity and the grieving process using a common grief experience.

18. In lines 78 and 96, the author compares grief to "waves" to show that:

   F. grief comes in cycles with high points and low points of differing intensities that can't always be predicted.

   G. grief is rhythmic, coming in predictable patterns that one can reliably anticipate with time.

   H. no one can do anything to avoid their grief, for it is as immense as the ocean's tides.

   J. grief changes with a person's emotional state, just like the ocean's tides change the nature of waves.

19. According to the passage, which of the following statements best describes the fight or flight response as relates to the grieving process?

   A. When grief triggers the fight or flight response, the body releases hormones and shifts to focus primarily on survival.

   B. When grief triggers the fight or flight response, individuals always become erratic and unpredictable.

   C. It will be obvious if the fight or flight response has been triggered in a grieving individual because they will exhibit physical symptoms of their condition.

   D. It will be obvious if the fight or flight response has been triggered in a grieving individual since they will appear agitated and confused.

20. The author mentions the adage that "the only thing that heals grief is time" (lines 102–103) primarily in order to:

   F. explain why it's a false adage.

   G. point out that there is some truth to it.

   H. summarize the grief experience.

   J. warn people against listening to old sayings over science.

GO ON TO THE NEXT PAGE.

PASSAGE III

HUMANITIES: This passage is adapted from a scholarly article that investigates the transformations Berlin underwent in the decades following the fall of the Berlin Wall in November 1989.

At the beginning of 1990, the Berlin Wall had just been demolished. In its wake, the cities formerly dubbed East and West Berlin were tasked with knitting themselves back together
5 into a unified urban space. During this period, decrepit ruins at what was now the city's center became a playground for students, artists, and activists working in commune-style collectives who shared a common drive. These groups
10 wished to remake Berlin in their own image by squatting deserted spaces along the Wall's former path and transforming them to match their vision for the New Berlin. Though the main activity by squatting groups took place through-
15 out 1990, the impact of the post-Wall squatters is still visible in Berlin more than three decades after the fact.

The locus of squatting activity was Mitte, a formerly eastern neighborhood featuring pyra-
20 mids of rubble, ruins of bombed-out buildings, and urban infrastructure in utter disrepair. In the decades of reconstruction that followed WWII, East German leadership had neither the resources nor the interest to repair all buildings
25 in their zone. The border, especially along the Wall, made undesirable real estate, so many of the decaying structures there remained unintentional monuments to the destruction of war until the post-Wall squatters took up residence within
30 them.

Friedrichshain, another neighborhood that had once sat along the eastern path of the Berlin Wall, now lay adjacent to bustling western border neighborhoods like Kreuzberg and Schöneberg.
35 Its newfound proximity to these neighborhoods helped make Friedrichshain a satellite to the primary occupations in Mitte. From at least the 1960s onward, large enclaves of immigrants, students, and artists had called Kreuzberg home.

40 They favored the neighborhood due to its cheap rents and bustling nightlife. Less constrained than their Eastern counterparts, these Kreuzberg groups challenged traditional modes of urban living and the logic of the Wall itself, including
45 by scrawling graffiti on the western side of the Wall and squatting abandoned buildings; when the Wall fell at the end of 1989, these activities extended to neighborhoods (like Friedrichshain) that had once laid unreachably close on the other
50 side of the Berlin Wall, as well as to the strips of now-abandoned "no-man's land" that had once sat between its two borders.

The post-Wall squatters were innovative, artistically inclined, and group-oriented. They
55 erected artistic monuments and remade the space to reflect a different, gentler Germany they hoped to bring to fruition. Some collectives utilized the bombed-out buildings themselves, creating diorama-like art installations where
60 missing facades exposed the inner workings of the building. Others used rubble and other raw materials to create sculptures and rebuild new structures for both artistic and practical purposes as the occupation was not merely for
65 show—the squatters were truly living there and needed to make it habitable.

They staged performances, held dance parties, organized political demonstrations, and put on concerts but also created daycares, makeshift
70 medical clinics, and cafes. Do-it-yourself (DIY) repairs became not just a necessity (to get potable water, to find places to dispose of waste, to have safe shelter) but a unifying ethos among the disparate groups. If the space was to be occupied,
75 it needed to also serve the needs of those who inhabited it, so the varied squatters' factions made sure it could.

Some groups commandeered relics of the former eastern regime and turned them into art,
80 such as by moving abandoned military equipment and transforming it into sculptures or making makeshift play structures and interactive sculptures. Graffiti was a common form of

artistic and political expression among post-Wall
85 squatters as it allowed them to both "tag" the
space as their own and share messages, such as
"Nie wieder Krieg" ("Never again war"), a statement emblazoned next to a sculpture of a real
east German fighter jet posed as if it were about
90 to take off. Similarly, banners emblazoned with
messages were often hung from buildings.

Within the squatters' collective actions,
historians observe the democratization of public
space as private and private space as public,
95 which is itself a unifying principle for the range
of occupying groups—all challenged the established rules of who owned the city space and how
it could be used. This was echoed in the demographics of those who came to the space, for it
100 brought together not just east and west Berliners
but also immigrants, the unhoused, and other
groups who had often been relegated to the edges
of German society by the city's former regimes.

A very small number of post-Wall groups
105 still occupy houses in the city. The commune at
Rigaerstrasse 94 in Friedrichshain still exists, as
does the punk-rock squatter's commune lovingly dubbed "Köpi" at Köpenickerstrasse 137 at
the edge of Mitte; this space is known for being
110 welcoming and artistic. However, the powers that
be continue to target post-Wall squatters groups
for evictions; for instance, Liebig 34, which had
occupied Liebigstraße 34, was not successfully
evicted until 2020 after a series of high-profile
115 attempts to forcefully resist their mandated
removal.

While a vast majority of the squatters' collectives have long since disbanded or been evicted
from the now highly gentrified neighborhoods
120 of Mitte and Friedrichshain, their legacy lives on
in Berlin. For instance, the graffiti dotting the
city is a reminder of these groups' artistic drive
to claim ownership of public space. Squatting is
also now a common form of resistance in Berlin,
125 most notably in recent years as used by refugees
seeking recognition from the German government in the 2010s.

21. Based on the passage, why was Friedrichshain a
logical "satellite" for the squatting occupations in
the once-eastern neighborhood of Mitte?

A. As a former western neighborhood, Friedrichshain helped provide a logical linking
point between former east Berliners and west
Berliners.

B. As a border neighborhood, Friedrichshain
boasted cheap rents and was seen as a center of
nightlife for West Berliners in the years leading up to the fall of the Wall.

C. Like Mitte, Friedrichshain was located along
the heavily-guarded East Berlin border, so it
wasn't possible for anyone to live in the neighborhood before that.

D. Friedrichshain was next to Mitte in the East,
but it was also geographically close to former
western neighborhoods with artists and activists who likely moved those activities eastward
after the Wall fell.

22. The author mentions a piece of graffiti that reads
"Nie wieder Krieg" (lines 86–87) in order to:

F. highlight that German was the primary language spoken among the squatting groups at
that time.

G. provide a contextual example of a real graffiti
message made by members of the squatting
community in 1990.

H. illustrate the political message that united all
of the groups that squatted in Mitte.

J. show how people reacted to the graffiti messages the squatting community created in the
early 1990s.

GO ON TO THE NEXT PAGE.

23. The author mentions that the post-WWII reconstruction of East Berlin took decades in order to:

    A. provide clarity as to why there might still have been so many buildings in the city that hadn't been rebuilt yet, especially within neighborhoods bordering the Berlin Wall.

    B. demonstrate that the Berlin Wall had been a necessary evil for the East German government to limit interference with reconstruction.

    C. criticize the East German government for not repairing the buildings sooner since it was dangerous to have them in such a state for so long.

    D. explain why the assorted groups of squatters shared different values and belief systems beyond their vision for squatting the city.

24. According to the author, the squatting community used DIY efforts primarily to:

    F. make the space they were occupying habitable since they were living in it consistently.

    G. make the space uninhabitable so others would not want to take it back.

    H. create environments that were solely meant to be understood as artwork.

    J. highlight the array of different crafts and skills represented in the squatting collectives.

25. The author indicates that the path of the former Berlin Wall was also important to the squatting community's collective goals because:

    A. it had formerly been a "no-man's-land," so when the Berlin Wall came down, it was uninhabited space.

    B. many groups of squatters saw it as politically advantageous to use those areas.

    C. it was more habitable than the decaying infrastructure in bombed-out parts of Mitte and Friedrichshain.

    D. it helped them remember where the border division used to be.

26. As it is used in line 57, the phrase "to bring to fruition" most nearly means to:

    F. prevent.

    G. make happen.

    H. imagine in detail.

    J. analyze closely.

27. In Paragraph 7 (lines 93–103), the author mentions that immigrants and the unhoused were included in the greater squatting community in order to:

    A. emphasize that all of the squatters had come from the edges of "proper" society.

    B. highlight how more than just students, activists, and artists from Berlin were among the squatting factions.

    C. question the validity of the squatters' political views.

    D. praise the squatters for being open-minded and inclusive.

28. The author describes the commune known as "Köpi" as being:

F. political, creative, and a center of nightlife.

G. decrepit, bombed-out, and in ruins.

H. punk-rock, welcoming, and artistic.

J. innovative, artistically inclined, and group-oriented.

29. From the last two paragraphs of the passage, you can infer that:

A. there are no longer any squatters in Mitte.

B. most squatters in Berlin are occupying houses legally.

C. most Berliners in 1990 agreed with what the squatters were doing.

D. some squatters' groups may have used violence to resist their evictions.

30. The author provides the examples in the final two paragraphs most likely to support their claim that:

F. the eviction of groups from buildings that are unlawfully squatted is justified.

G. the eviction of groups from buildings that are unlawfully squatted is not justified.

H. the question of whether to evict squatting tenants is still politically relevant in Berlin.

J. refugee groups are treated very differently by the government when they use squatting as political resistance.

DIAGNOSTIC TEST

GO ON TO THE NEXT PAGE.

PASSAGE IV

NATURAL SCIENCE: Passage A is adapted from an entry in a biology textbook. Passage B is adapted from an article in a science journal.

PASSAGE A

Unless completely deprived of a source of carbon, soil is packed full of microorganisms. Of the six types of microorganisms found in soil, fungi account for the largest amount of relative
5　biomass in soil, followed by bacteria and actinomycetes. Algae, protozoa, and nematodes are also present in soil to varying, much smaller degrees of relative biomass. Scientists collectively refer to these six microbial species as the "living" portion
10　of soil organic matter (SOM). SOM also includes "dead" matter, like fresh residues from decaying organic material, and "very dead" matter, such as humus, which is a type of soil compound that forms only after organic matter has com-
15　pletely finished decaying. Humus is generally many centuries old and is not susceptible to decomposition.

RELATIVE BIOMASS OF MICROBIAL SPECIES AT 0–6 INCHES SOIL DEPTH	
Microorganisms	**Biomass (g/m²)**
Actinomycetes	40–500
Algae	1–50
Bacteria	40–500
Fungi	100–1500
Nematodes	Varies
Protozoa	Varies

Source: https://ohioline.osu.edu/factsheet/SAG-16

SOM can be divided into active and passive components, where the oldest matter comprises
20　the majority of the passive component that is not as susceptible to decomposition. Passive SOM only has a marginal effect on the presence of microorganisms. Active SOM, by contrast, is instrumental if microbial species in soil are to thrive.
25　　Certain behaviors, like tilling, tend to disrupt the development of active SOM, making it difficult for microorganisms to develop in volumes that support healthy soil. Evidence from numerous studies supports the idea that the more
30　often soil is tilled, the less rich it is in microorganism health and diversity. Tilling disrupts decomposition processes and effectively starves microorganisms, meaning that there are fewer individual microbes and less flourishing diver-
35　sity among microorganisms within the greater soil microbiome. The longer soil is left untilled, the more effectively it builds up active SOM and, in turn, develops a healthy, diverse, and life-enriching microbiome. This effect is the driving
40　force behind farmers leaving some fields fallow (meaning organic material is not removed and is instead left to decompose) for a season or more to restore soil health.

　　We know that the presence of dead and
45　decaying matter is crucial to the long-term health and efficacy of soil because the microorganisms in active SOM make both the decomposition and growth of organic matter possible in the first place. When organic matter is not left to decay in
50　soil, microorganisms have nothing to feed on and in turn, cannot convert that decaying biomass into nutrients and compounds necessary for vegetation to grow. If you think of active SOM as a storehouse for nutrients a plant needs to thrive,
55　you can see why creating an optimal environment for both the growth and the decomposition of organic matter might be a chief pursuit of agricultural scientists; when it comes to good soil, to a certain extent, life cannot exist without death.

PASSAGE B

60   Agricultural scientists generally agree that the diversity of a soil's microbiome is the key to its health. Given that soil is the most biodiverse environment on Earth, a healthy soil microbiome is one where myriad forms of microorganisms
65 flourish. Like all other living things, microbial species in soil are deeply affected by the way climate change is reshaping the earth, but questions remain as to just how soil might be affected as the climate changes.

70   Today, farmers are increasingly urgent about tackling a set of interlocking questions regarding the relationship between soil microbiomes and climate change, particularly in an economic environment where healthy soil is the bedrock
75 of many farmers' livelihoods. These questions include but are not limited to the following: how will increasing drought, flooding, or other weather shifts affect the soil? Will these changes cause less beneficial microbes to take over the
80 beneficial ones, throwing soil balance off in the process? Will farmers have to change the kinds of crops they produce as growing conditions change? What are the best ways to protect soil health from climate change's effects? How will
85 different types of soil environments respond to climate change?

    Answering these questions is not simple, but agricultural scientists are beginning to deepen their understanding of how climate change
90 might affect soil conditions. For instance, one thing many microbiologists note is that soil microorganisms are some of the most adaptable life forms on earth, so it is unlikely that shifts in soil health will be extreme; instead, these microbial
95 species will adapt over time to new conditions. It's possible that in the short term, the benefits of certain types of soil microorganisms may become less efficacious, but on a long-term scale, these life forms will tend to survive.

100   However, while scientists can predict that soil microbiomes are likely to survive the effects of climate change, the frustration comes in their inability to predict how. Take carbon dioxide (CO_2) for example. As they break down decaying
105 organic matter, soil microbiomes tend to either store carbon in soil or release it as CO_2. There is no way to determine in advance if climate change will cause soil to release more CO_2 into the atmosphere, exacerbating existing climate
110 effects, or, conversely, if soil microbiomes might play a key role in combating these effects by adapting to store more carbon underground.

    There is also uncertainty that stems from the complexity of soil microbiomes themselves. The
115 intricate threads of life that exist between fungi, protozoa, bacteria, and other elements of active soil organic matter are so dense and complex that scientists have only just begun to unravel them. Since there is so much that is still unknown
120 about how soil microbiomes operate, many scientists worry that our relevant understanding is too elementary to effectively make predictions about or respond to how climate change will affect them.

31. According to Passage A, the microbial species with the largest relative biomass in the top six inches of soil is:

    A. algae.

    B. bacteria

    C. fungi

    D. protozoa

GO ON TO THE NEXT PAGE.

32. The author of Passage A most likely states that there are both active and passive components of SOM in order to:

   F. compare and contrast both components in relation to humus development.

   G. set up their discussion of why the active component of SOM is much more critical to soil health than the passive component.

   H. illustrate that SOM is complex, which makes it difficult to know how climate change will affect it.

   J. illustrate the difference between growth and decay as it affects microorganisms in soil.

33. Which of the following represents a fact from Passage A that supports the author's claim that farmers often leave some fields fallow to support soil health?

   A. Farmers are interested in using natural methods to promote soil health instead of pesticides.

   B. Evidence shows that tilling soil too often makes it difficult for active SOM to grow and diversify.

   C. SOM includes "dead" matter and "very dead" matter, like humus, and it needs these components to flourish.

   D. Farmers are increasingly concerned about the effects of climate change on soil health.

34. Passage B most strongly suggests that agricultural scientists who study climate change are eager to quickly learn more about soil microbiomes because:

   F. doing so will help them grow more robust vegetation if there are global food shortages.

   G. it is highly likely that healthy soil microbiomes won't survive the effects of climate change.

   H. very little, if anything, is known about what kind of microorganisms are found in soil.

   J. the more they learn about the connections between microorganisms in the soil microbiome, the better equipped they will be to address the ways climate change affects soil.

35. The author of Passage B most likely uses the phrase "soil is the bedrock of many farmers' livelihoods" (lines 74–75) to emphasize that:

   A. if soil health suffers due to climate change, it is likely to have serious economic consequences for many farmers.

   B. if farmers don't take climate change seriously, there is no way their soil will survive climate change.

   C. many farms are affected by rocky soil conditions that make it difficult to maintain soil health.

   D. farmers are passionate about solving issues that affect their crops.

36. As it is used in line 109, the word *exacerbating* most nearly means:

   F. impacting.

   G. reversing.

   H. intensifying.

   J. soothing.

37. In Passage B, it can most reasonably be inferred from Paragraph 4 (lines 100–113) that if rising atmospheric CO_2 levels increasingly become an issue as the climate changes, then:

   A. soil will make the issue worse by releasing more carbon dioxide into the atmosphere.

   B. soil will improve the issue by holding more carbon underground.

   C. soil could potentially make the problem better or worse, depending on how robust and diverse a given plot of soil's initial microbiome is.

   D. soil could potentially make the problem better or worse, depending on how soil microbiomes adapt to climate change.

38. Which of the following statements best describes the difference in the author's purpose for each of the two passages?

   F. The author of Passage A is primarily interested in informing the reader about climate change while the author of Passage B seeks to explain how climate change will affect soil microbiomes.

   G. The author of Passage A is primarily interested in informing the reader about how microorganisms affect SOM while the author of Passage B discusses how soil microbiomes in general could be affected by climate change.

   H. The author of Passage A presents factual information while the author of Passage B focuses on their own argument for how to address soil microbiome concerns.

   J. The author of Passage A analyzes the importance of soil microorganisms while the author of Passage B is skeptical about their necessity for long-term soil health.

39. Compared to the author of Passage A, the author of Passage B provides more information about the:

   A. questions agricultural scientists face when trying to address how climate change will affect microorganisms in the soil.

   B. seven types of microorganisms found in SOM and their relative sizes in terms of biomass.

   C. effect that rising carbon dioxide is likely to have on the development of soil organic matter.

   D. types of measures agricultural scientists are already taking to combat climate change.

40. How does Passage B expand on Passage A's discussion of soil microorganisms?

   F. Passage A considers how adaptable soil microorganisms are, and Passage B suggests that scientists are unconcerned with what will happen to active SOM during climate change since soil microbiomes are adaptable.

   G. Passage B adds nuance to Passage A by considering how different climate issues could affect the conditions that allow the healthy, active SOM described in Passage A to develop.

   H. Passage B spends more time explaining the economic consequences of what occurs when active SOM can't develop than Passage A does, since it is focused only on definitions.

   J. Passage B explains how climate change could cause more passive components of SOM, like humus, to develop while Passage A mostly explains what those components are.

STOP.

If you finish before time is up, you may check your work on this section only.
Do not turn to any other section in the test.

SECTION 4: SCIENCE TEST

40 Questions—35 Minutes

> **Directions:** There are multiple passages in this test. Each passage is followed by several questions. After you read a passage, choose the best answer for each question and fill in the corresponding oval on your answer sheet. You may refer to the passages as often as necessary. Calculators are NOT permitted for this test.

PASSAGE I

According to quantum theory, light consists of individual particles called photons. When photons with enough energy strike a bare metal surface, they can eject negatively charged electrons from that surface. The energy of a single photon is transferred to a single electron, called a photoelectron, in a phenomenon known as the photoelectric effect.

The photoelectric effect, one of the first important tests of quantum theory, can be observed with the use of an apparatus similar to the one shown in Figure 1. A metal plate and a small electrode are placed within a glass tube called a photocell. The photocell is connected to a circuit through which electric current can flow. The circuit contains an ammeter, a device that measures electric current. When the photocell is in the dark, the ammeter shows a reading of zero; when light shines on the photocell, the ammeter indicates a current flowing in the circuit. This current is produced by the photoelectrons emitted from the metal plate.

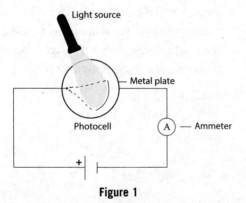

Figure 1

In 1986, at a physics workshop in Boulder, Colorado, a group of high school teachers studied the photoelectric effect in a two-part experiment.

Study 1

In the first part of the experiment, the teachers placed a light source at different distances from the photocell and measured the photocurrent, which is proportional to the number of photoelectrons being ejected from the surface. The experiment was conducted with two different color filters, blue and green, as different colors of light have different wavelengths. A filter transmits only one wavelength of light—a green filter, for example, allows only green light to pass through it. The results of this part of the experiment are shown in Table 1. (Current is being measured in microamperes, μA.)

Table 1			
Distance to light source with green filter (m)	Photocurrent in μA (a)	Distance to light source with blue light filter (m)	Photocurrent in μA (a)
0.10	430	0.10	350
0.20	100	0.20	90
0.30	50	0.30	45
0.40	25	0.40	20

Study 2

A voltage can be applied to a circuit to either speed up or stop the flow of photoelectrons. The voltage required to stop the flow of photoelectrons is known as the stopping potential. In the second part of the experiment, the teachers measured the stopping potential.

They used four different colors for the filters, and the stopping voltage was measured three times for each color filter as well as for no filter at all. The distance to the light source was held constant. Table 2 is a summary of the data from this part of the experiment.

Table 2			
Stopping Potential (Volts)			
Color of filter	Trial 1	Trial 2	Trial 3
Red	0.0	0.0	0.0
Yellow	0.4	0.4	0.4
Green	0.65	0.65	0.65
Blue	1.0	1.1	1.1
No filter (white)	1.2	1.1	1.0

1. Which of the following graphs best represents the relationship between light source distance (m) and photocurrent (a) in Study 1?

A.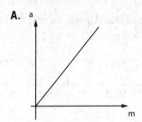

B.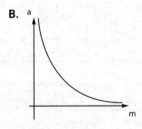

C.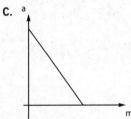

D.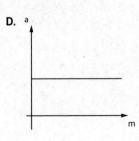

2. The data in Table 2 suggest that stopping potential:

    F. depends on the intensity of light.

    G. depends on the wavelength of light.

    H. depends on the characteristics of the metal plate.

    J. is constant for all wavelengths of light.

3. What is the dependent variable in Study 2?

    A. The stopping potential

    B. The photocurrent measured in microamperes (μA)

    C. The color filter

    D. The absence of color filter

4. Study 1 and Study 2 differed from each other in which of the following ways?

    F. The distance to the light source measured was changed in Study 2.

    G. Study 1 measured the photocurrent, while Study 2 measured the stopping potential.

    H. Study 1 was experimenting with the principles behind photoelectrons, while Study 2 was experimenting with the principles behind photoelectron flow speed.

    J. Study 2 did not use a photocell.

5. Which of the following was an independent variable in both Study 1 and Study 2?

    A. Distance to light source

    B. Photocurrent magnitude

    C. Stopping potential

    D. Filter color

6. Suppose the teachers were to use an orange filter in Study 2. One would expect the stopping potential with this filter to be:

    F. between 0 and 0.4 volts.

    G. between 0.4 and 0.65 volts.

    H. between 0.65 and 1.1 volts.

    J. greater than 1.1 volts.

GO ON TO THE NEXT PAGE.

PASSAGE II

Although different regions of Earth's surface are assigned specific names, it is dominated by a single ocean that covers about 70 percent of the surface. The continents and oceans are not evenly distributed around Earth. If you look at Earth from a viewpoint in the South Pacific, as shown in Figure 1, you can see that almost one-half of the planet has no land masses larger than small islands. In fact, in the Southern Hemisphere, between the latitudes of 50°S and 65°S, there are essentially no land masses at all.

Figure 1

Figure 2 considers various elevations and depths and indicates the percentage of Earth's surface that lies at each level.

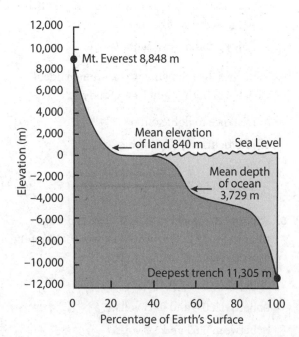

Figure 2

Ocean water is saltwater, which means that the water contains dissolved salts and other minerals. The most abundant salt found in ocean water is sodium chloride. Sodium chloride is the most soluble of all the common minerals, so it readily dissolves out of rocks and soil and washes into the ocean.

The amount of dissolved salts and minerals in ocean water contributes to ocean water's density. The density of a substance is the mass of the substance per unit of volume. The greater the mass of dissolved salts, the greater the density of the ocean water. The percentage of dissolved salts is known as salinity.

Density is also affected by temperature. Pure water, which freezes at 0°C, reaches its maximum density at around 4°C. Adding salt and other minerals to water lowers both the freezing point and the temperature at which maximum density occurs. Figure 3 shows the relationship among the salinity of water, its freezing point, and its temperature of maximum density.

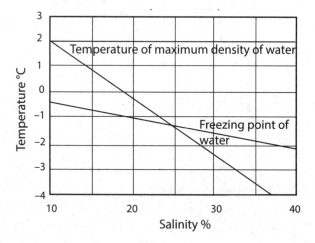

Figure 3

7. Based on the information in Figure 2, what is the approximate median elevation of Earth's surface?

    A. 4,500 m

    B. 0 m

    C. –1,000 m

    D. –5,500 m

8. Large mountain ranges disrupt air flow in a way that reduces storms. Consequently, one would expect to find less extreme weather in the:

    F. Northern Hemisphere, because of the presence of large land masses.

    G. Southern Hemisphere, because of the presence of large oceans.

    H. Northern Hemisphere, because of the presence of large oceans.

    J. Southern Hemisphere, because of the presence of large land masses.

9. According to Figure 2, about what percentage of Earth's surface lies above the mean land elevation of 840 m?

    A. 10%

    B. 20%

    C. 30%

    D. 40%

10. In Figure 3, at what salinity does the temperature of maximum density drop below the freezing point?

    F. 15%

    G. 20%

    H. 25%

    J. 30%

11. Assuming that the relationship between temperature of maximum density and salinity is constant, what would be the expected temperature of maximum density for ocean water with 40% salinity?

    A. 4°C

    B. –2.1°C

    C. –4°C

    D. –4.8°C

GO ON TO THE NEXT PAGE.

PASSAGE III

Bone loss in astronauts is a serious concern during long-term spaceflights. The gravity on a space station is much less than the gravity on Earth, a condition called microgravity. In microgravity, astronauts' bones do not support the weight that they normally do on Earth, so they begin to lose mass. Weight-bearing bones experience the greatest change in weight load in space, so they experience the greatest bone loss. To counteract bone loss, astronauts exercise all parts of the body on specially designed resistance machines that simulate the weights that their bones support on Earth.

To test the effectiveness of different types of exercise machines on preventing bone loss, researchers measured the bone mineral density (BMD) of astronauts before and after they spent several months on the *Mir* space station or the International Space Station (ISS). The astronauts on the *Mir* did not have specially designed resistance machines, only aerobic exercise and muscular endurance machines. Some ISS astronauts used a resistance machine called an interim Resistive Exercise Device (iRED) that could simulate weights up to 297 pounds. Other ISS astronauts used a newer resistance machine called the Advanced Resistive Exercise Device (ARED) that could simulate weights up to 600 pounds. Astronauts exercised for the same amount of time per day on these different machines. The typical change in BMD for the pelvis and average change in BMD for the whole body of these astronauts are shown in Figure 1.

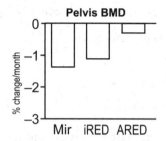

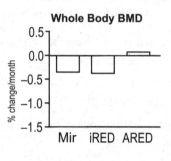

Figure 1

Researchers also tested whether diet could help prevent bone loss. Astronauts on the ISS logged how much protein they ate every day, and the average number of grams of protein they ate per kilogram of their body weight was calculated. Their pelvis bone mineral content (BMC) was measured before and after their time on the ISS. These results are shown in Figure 2.

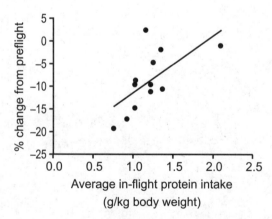

Figure 2

12. Based on the data from Figure 1, which type of exercise machine is most effective in preventing bone loss?

    F. ARED
    G. iRED
    H. Aerobic exercise machine
    J. Muscular endurance machine

13. Based on the information in the passage, which of the following best explains why the change in BMD for the pelvis is different from that for the whole body?

    A. The astronauts exercise only certain parts of their bodies on the exercise machines.
    B. The weight-bearing parts of the body like the pelvis will have greater bone loss than the average bone loss for the entire body.
    C. The pelvis is a non-weight-bearing part of the body, so it experiences less bone loss than the average bone loss for the entire body.
    D. The different types of exercise machines result in different degrees of bone loss.

14. The control group in the first experiment was the astronauts who:

    F. used the iRED.
    G. used aerobic exercise and muscular endurance machines.
    H. used the ARED.
    J. were tested for their BMC.

15. Based on the results shown in Figures 1 and 2, the researchers would most likely recommend which regimen to keep bone loss in astronauts as low as possible?

    A. Low-protein diet and low-resistance exercise
    B. High-protein diet and low-resistance exercise
    C. Low-protein diet and high-resistance exercise
    D. High-protein diet and high-resistance exercise

16. According to Figure 1, what is the difference in the change in BMD in the pelvis between the astronauts using ARED and the astronauts on the *Mir* space station?

    F. *Mir* astronauts lost 0.2% less BMD than astronauts using ARED.
    G. *Mir* astronauts lost 0.2% more BMD than astronauts using ARED.
    H. *Mir* astronauts lost 1.0% more BMD than astronauts using ARED.
    J. *Mir* astronauts lost 1.4% more BMD than astronauts using ARED.

17. If the researchers had not tested for diet, how might that have changed the results of the experiment?

    A. The results may have shown that the resistance machines were not effective in reducing bone loss.
    B. The astronauts would have been low on energy if they didn't have enough protein and would not perform well on the machines.
    C. The researchers may not have been able to draw a conclusion about the overall effectiveness of the machines.
    D. This wouldn't change the results.

GO ON TO THE NEXT PAGE.

PASSAGE IV

All matter is composed of atoms. An atom consists of a positively charged nucleus surrounded by negatively charged particles called electrons. Some atoms join together, or bond, by transferring or sharing electrons.

The nature of the electron bonds between two atoms is largely determined by the electronegativity of each atom. Electronegativity is the ability of an atom to attract the electrons of other atoms. A greater electronegativity value signifies a superior ability to attract electrons. Figure 1 shows the electronegativities of selected groups of elements in the periodic table.

1A			3A	4A	5A	6A	7A
H 2.2	2A						
Li 1.0	Be 1.6		B 1.8	C 2.5	N 3.0	O 3.4	F 4.0
Na 0.93	Mg 1.3		Al 1.6	Si 1.9	P 2.2	S 2.6	Cl 3.2
K 0.82	Ca 1.0		Ga 1.8	Ge 2.0	As 2.2	Se 2.6	Br
Rb 0.82	Sr 0.9		In 1.8	Sn 1.8	Sb 2.0	Te 2.1	I 2.7
Cs 0.79	Ba 0.9		Tl 2.0	Pb 2.3	Bi 2.0	Po 2.0	At 2.2

Figure 1

Atoms with very similar electronegativities form molecules that are nonpolar. The electrons of these atoms are shared equally, and their molecules are said to be electrically symmetrical. The electron bond is equidistant between the nuclei of each atom.

Atoms with moderately different electronegativities form polar covalent bonds. In this case, one atom attracts electrons more than the other atom does; these molecules are said to be electrically asymmetrical. The electron bond between such atoms is closer to the more electronegative atom. Molecules that contain such atoms have a relative concentration of negativity at the end that is closer to the more electronegative atom.

The greater the difference in electronegativity, the more polar the molecule is.

18. In Figure 1, elements are arranged in vertical columns called groups, or families, and in horizontal rows called periods. Based on the patterns of electronegativity values among the families and periods, one would predict that the approximate electronegativity of bromine (Br) is:

F. 2.6
G. 3
H. 3.6
J. 4

19. Which element has the least ability to attract electrons?

A. Li (lithium)
B. Na (sodium)
C. Al (aluminum)
D. Ti (titanium)

20. Which of the following molecules is most likely to be nonpolar?

F. NaCl
G. MgO
H. Cl_2
J. BeO

21. Which of the following bonds is likely to be the most polar?

A. K–Cl
B. Ba–Se
C. Na–S
D. Be–O

22. Based on Figure 1, what is the most highly polar bond that can be generated from the presented elements?

F. O-F
G. H-At
H. Cs-F
J. K-Cl

PASSAGE V

In 2001, members of a national health foundation who were interested in examining possible links between cigarette smoking and cancer in the United States gathered relevant data from ten selected states.

First, they surveyed residents in each state to determine what percentage of the state's residents were cigarette smokers. For consistency, smokers were defined as those who smoked every day or most days and who had smoked at least 100 cigarettes in their lifetime. Smokers were further asked whether they had ever attempted to quit smoking. For the purpose of consistency, a quit attempt was defined as having gone one day or longer without a cigarette in a deliberate effort to stop smoking. In both cases, percentages were weighted to reflect population characteristics.

The foundation's members then collected information from medical facilities, disease control centers, and other health organizations to reflect numbers of cancer-related deaths. They compared these numbers with the population figures in each state.

The members separated each state's data by gender and reported their findings. Table 1 summarizes the data.

State	Cigarette Smoking Rate		Number of Cancer Deaths per 100,000 Population		Percent of Smokers Who Attempt to Quit	
	Females	Males	Females	Males	Females	Males
California	13.3%	19.6%	156.7	212.8	63.6%	62.9%
Colorado	19.4%	21.4%	150.7	200.4	57.7%	52.7%
Florida	20.6%	23.4%	155.3	229.8	55.3%	48.4%
Indiana	25.7%	29.7%	172.9	271.9	61.0%	51.6%
Kentucky	30.3%	34.7%	182.0	297.6	53.6%	42.9%
Maine	21.0%	26.4%	170.5	262.7	62.2%	60.2%
Ohio	25.0%	28.3%	173.5	261.4	53.8%	49.5%
Rhode Island	20.9%	24.0%	167.7	253.9	64.4%	66.6%
Utah	11.4%	14.1%	117.2	181.0	72.1%	64.6%
West Virginia	27.2%	29.7%	186.0	267.9	48.9%	47.3%

Table 1

GO ON TO THE NEXT PAGE.

Figure 1 plots these same ten states' cancer mortality rates against the percentage of their residents who smoke. Data in this graph is not separated by gender.

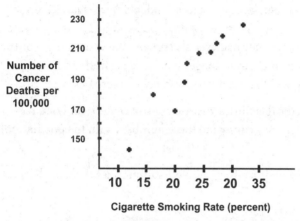

Figure 1

23. Based on the data in Figure 1, which of the following rates best approximates the trend for cancer deaths for every 5% increase in the number of people who smoke?

    A. The rate increases by 10 per 100,000.

    B. The rate increases by 18 per 100,000.

    C. The rate increases by 40 per 100,000.

    D. The rate decreases by 10 per 100,000.

24. Which of the following statements is NOT supported by Table 1?

    F. Kentucky has a higher percentage of smokers than any other listed state.

    G. Within each listed state, the percentage of males who smoke is higher than the percentage of females who smoke.

    H. Rhode Island has the highest listed percentage of males who attempt to quit smoking.

    J. Within each listed state, the percentage of females who attempt to quit smoking is higher than the percentage of males who attempt to quit smoking.

25. Taken together, the data indicate that there is a relationship between higher rates of smoking and increased risk of death from cancer. What could the researchers do to try and prove that smoking increases death rates in the study region?

    A. Limit the study to those cancers known to be associated with smoking.

    B. Add more states that have even higher rates of smoking.

    C. Examine cancer rates in those who successfully quit smoking.

    D. Find a comparison population made up only of non-smokers.

26. In New Jersey in 2001, nearly 177 out of every 100,000 females died from cancer. Based on the information in Table 1, out of every 100,000 males in New Jersey in 2001, a likely estimate of the number who died from cancer would be:

    F. 246

    G. 177

    H. 150

    J. 118

27. A separate study of social networks in these states determined that women in every state but Rhode Island have an average of 2.4 more social connections than men. Which of the following is a plausible statement based on that information and Table 1?

    A. Most smoking occurs in social settings.

    B. Friendships help patients survive cancer.

    C. Friends encourage each other to quit smoking.

    D. Friends encourage each other to start smoking.

PASSAGE VI

One hallmark of the modern world is the ease of travel for both people and goods. For most of human history, travel was difficult and time consuming. Except for certain seafaring peoples, until the invention of sailing ships, moving between continents was virtually impossible. Sailing ships made travel across the oceans possible, but still slow and not that widespread.

But as technology improved so too did travel and shipping. Steamships could cross the oceans in weeks or days, and ships grew larger, carrying greater and greater loads between more and more places. Air travel eased connections between far-flung areas even more. And it isn't only people taking advantage of greater connectivity between places: plants, animals, and marine life are moving around as well. Plants and animals from Asia or Europe that previously would have been confined to their native range can now easily establish populations in the Americas. When a species settles in a place far from its native range, it is said to be introduced. Examples include house sparrows, zebra mussels, and rats.

Frequently, when a species from one area ends up in another, it does well. These species often flourish, reproducing rapidly and spreading out into the new habitat. They can be especially damaging in isolated areas or areas with low species diversity, where local species are more specialized and less likely to have encountered new risks.

Perspective 1

The mere presence of an introduced species is an invasion, a disruptive change caused by humans. The ecosystems and species already present, called natives, cannot compete with the newcomers. The new species are threats, killing or replacing native species and permanently destroying unique environments. They may also present an economic nuisance. The newcomers often have an edge over native species, as the natives are not familiar with the newcomers. These species often have few or no predators or parasites, and the natives have no defense against them. Introduced species can be fish, snakes, mammals, plants, insects, aquatic invertebrates, or even diseases. Native forests get replaced with invasive trees, invasive grasses replace native grasslands, and soon the original native environment is unrecognizable.

Managers must do everything in their power to eradicate introduced species. It's especially important to find and eradicate new infestations before a new species can take hold, but otherwise all steps must be taken to fight the spread of new species and remove or kill them where they are established. Introduced species must be removed even if some damage occurs to native species in the process. Otherwise, unique native ecosystems will be destroyed or forever changed.

Perspective 2

Some of these species can now be considered part of the new environment. Restoring or preserving the "original" ecosystem is impossible because, after hundreds of years of human impact, nobody knows for sure what the original ecosystem is, and that's assuming introduced species can even be removed, given that removal is not always successful. Many introduced species become established in new territories and experience rapid population growth, but it is not always clear if they are actually harming native species or simply coexisting alongside them. Some introduced species provide food or habitat for native species, even rare or important native species. Introduced species are part of a global ecosystem, and introduced populations are simply another population. There may even be economic benefits if an invasive species can be commercially exploited. It is not always worth making intensive efforts to fight against introduced species and remove them wherever they are found.

Perspective 3

While some introduced species are an immediate threat to native ecosystems, most problems are temporary. Many introduced species follow a pattern of initial population growth and ecosystem disruption, followed by a decline in the introduced population. Eventually, native and introduced species adjust to one another, and the populations of both native and introduced species stabilize at an acceptable level. Regardless of that condition, it is always necessary to monitor introduced populations.

GO ON TO THE NEXT PAGE.

28. Given the information about each perspective, what names would be appropriate for Perspective 1 and Perspective 2, respectively?

   F. The introduction perspective and the acceptance perspective

   G. The eradication perspective and the invasion perspective

   H. The unacceptable perspective and the beneficial perspective

   J. The invasion perspective and the assessment perspective

29. A population of wattle-necked turtles from Asia has been found on the Hawaiian island of Kauai. Which of the following statements reflects information provided in the passage?

   A. Perspective 1 would support leaving the turtles alone.

   B. Perspective 2 would support eradicating the turtles.

   C. Perspective 2 would leave the turtles alone if they were endangered in their native range.

   D. Perspective 1 would wait to assess the turtles' impact before recommending removal.

30. The resources available for conservation work are limited. This would factor into:

   F. only Perspective 2, because funds need to be reserved only for harmful species.

   G. only Perspective 1, because eradicating species is more expensive than acting on a case-by-case basis.

   H. only Perspective 2, because resources should be used exclusively for other purposes besides introduced species.

   J. both Perspectives 1 and 2, since there is not enough money to eradicate everything, regardless of whether it is desirable to do so.

31. Rats are a species that have been introduced all over the world. Based on the passage, in which area are they likely to disrupt the local ecosystem the most?

   A. A small, isolated island

   B. A large rainforest

   C. A different continent

   D. A coastal island

32. With which of the following would all three perspectives agree?

   F. Introduced species should be managed according to the actual risk.

   G. Some introduced species are very harmful.

   H. Introduced species become less harmful over time.

   J. All species introductions present a risk.

33. Which of the following is a strategy for the management of introduced species that all three perspectives would utilize?

   A. Divert all resources to eradicating introduced species.

   B. Wait a few years, then eradicate all non-helpful species.

   C. Eliminate harmful species and ignore the others.

   D. Prevent species from traveling on planes and ships.

34. What would a graph of introduced and native species populations over time look like according to Perspective 3?

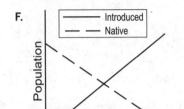

F.

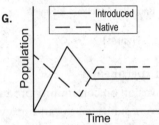

G.

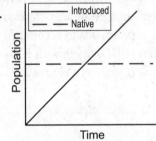

H.

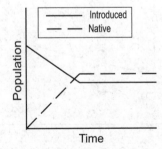

J.

PASSAGE VII

Microorganisms are critical components of virtually any ecosystem, and how these microorganisms react to changes in the biotic and abiotic environment affects interactions within the ecosystem. A group of scientists wanted to study the importance of bacterial diversity in maintaining stability of community productivity. In particular, the scientists decided to focus on the effect of genotypic richness of bacterial communities. The scientists opted to focus on *Pseudomonas fluorescens* communities, subjecting the bacteria to various resource environments and related invaders to test community stability. For varied genotypic richness, the scientists constructed resident bacterial communities from eight *P. fluorescens* strains with similar body sizes and growth rates. Varying bacterial communities were assembled by randomly assorting strains; a diversity level of 1 consisted of each strain on its own, while increasing diversity levels increased the number of genome types present. Each genotype occurred in the same number of communities at each richness level. As such, a genotypic richness of 8 represents the highest level of bacterial diversity tested, with each genotype equally represented throughout all levels.

Experiment 1

The first stressor added to the community was varied resource richness. Five different carbon sources were used to set up a resource richness gradient: glucose, mannose, fructose, and citrate. As with the genotypic richness gradient, the lowest level of richness involved each individual carbon source on its own, while the highest level of richness combined all five carbon sources together. All other necessary minerals required for bacterial growth were included in the media. Stability of community productivity was measured using the inverse coefficient of variation (CV - 1). The data is shown in Figure 1.

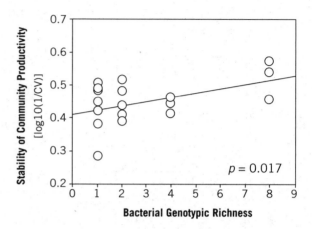

Figure 1

Experiment 2

To test the effect of invasion on community productivity, the communities were subjected to varying levels of invasion by *Serratia fliquefaciens* MG1 or *Pseudomonas putida* IsoF, invaders that occupy the same niche as *P. fluorescens*. An intermediate resource richness level was chosen for this set of experiments to account for the fact that these invaders will compete with *P. fluorescens* for resources. The data is shown in Figure 2.

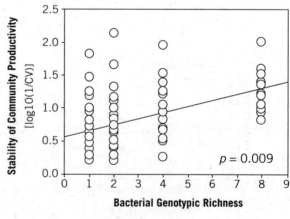

Figure 2

35. Which of the following hypotheses is most appropriate for this set of experiments?

   A. If bacterial genotypic richness is a major driver of community performance and stability, then community stability should decrease as genotypic richness increases.

   B. If bacterial genotypic richness is a major driver of community performance and stability, then community stability should increase as genotypic richness increases.

   C. If community stability is a major driver of bacterial genotypic richness, then genotypic richness should decrease as community stability increases.

   D. If community stability is a major driver of bacterial genotypic richness, then genotypic richness should increase as community stability increases.

36. A constant among every trial throughout these experiments is:

   F. bacterial genotypic richness.

   G. stability of community productivity.

   H. the use of glucose as the primary carbon source.

   J. the use of *P. fluorescens* as the measured bacterial species.

37. *Serratia fliquefaciens* MG1 or *Pseudomonas putida* IsoF were chosen as invaders in the varied invader experiments because:

   A. they are the most common invaders in most natural ecosystems.

   B. these species thrive on the specific carbon sources used in the experiments.

   C. they are invaders typically found where *P. fluorescens* is found.

   D. these species can survive under extreme temperature and pH conditions.

38. Based on the best-fit curves determined for community stability as a function of bacterial genotypic richness, the scientists determined that the relationship between the variables:

   F. increases linearly.

   G. increases exponentially.

   H. decreases linearly.

   J. decreases exponentially.

39. Which of the following conditions induced a more dramatic change in stability of community productivity as a function of bacterial genotypic richness?

   A. Varied carbon sources

   B. Varied nitrogen sources

   C. Varied invader presence

   D. Varied P. fluorescens genomic diversity

40. Based on the results obtained in this experiment, communities of low bacterial diversity are:

   F. more likely to increase productivity in response to environmental changes.

   G. more sensitive to environmental changes relative to diverse communities.

   H. buffered against changes in resource composition and invader presence.

   J. decimated by limitations in resource composition and invader presence.

STOP.

If you finish before time is up, you may check your work on this section only.
Do not turn to any other section in the test.

SECTION 5: WRITING TEST

1 Essay—40 Minutes

Directions: This is a test of your writing skills. You have forty (40) minutes to read the prompt, plan out how you'll respond, and write an essay in English. Before you start, read all material in the prompt carefully to make sure you know exactly what you are being asked to do.

You will write your essay on the lined pages provided with your answer sheet. On the official ACT exam, any work on the lined pages of your test booklet will be scored. You will also be permitted to use the unlined pages in your test booklet to plan your essay. Your work on the unlined pages will not be scored.

Your essay will be evaluated based on the evidence it provides of your ability to:

- clearly state your own perspective on a complex issue and analyze the relationship between your perspective and at least one other perspective

- develop and support your ideas with reasoning and examples

- organize your ideas clearly and logically

- communicate your ideas effectively in standard written English.

On test day, you are expected to lay your pencil down immediately when time is called.

A Dangerous Sport

Is American football too dangerous a sport to keep playing? Media coverage regarding the increasing number of football-related injuries and brain damage at every level—from youth football leagues to the NFL—has placed this issue in the national spotlight and subjected the sport to more scrutiny than ever before. Primarily out of concerns for player safety, the number of people calling for a ban altogether is on the rise. What are your thoughts regarding the future of football? How should we address the growing concerns regarding the safety of this sport? Should football be banned? Should serious reform, which might alter the way the game is currently played but would make the game safer to play, be considered?

Read and carefully consider these perspectives. Each suggests a particular way of thinking about how the dangers of American football should be addressed.

DIAGNOSTIC TEST

Perspective One

Football is simply too dangerous a sport to play, and people's lives should not be put at risk for a game. Those who love the sport should choose a safer one.

Perspective Two

Generations have grown up with football, and it cannot simply be taken away or changed. Most approach the game responsibly and carefully. We can't just ban every activity that contains some level of risk, especially when the activity in question is such a big part of our cultural experience.

Perspective Three

Football players put themselves at risk, even if they play carefully with proper safety equipment. However, this doesn't mean football should be banned. People should mostly be free to make their own choices and assess their own risk; however, there should be safety limits placed on youth football.

Essay Task

Write a unified, cohesive essay about the potential pros and cons of banning the sport of American football for safety reasons. In your essay, be sure to:

- clearly state your personal perspective on the issue and analyze the relationship between your own and at least one other perspective

- develop and support your ideas with examples and reasoning

- organize your ideas clearly and logically

- use standard written English to effectively communicate your ideas

Your perspective may be in full or partial agreement with any of those given, or it may be completely different.

Planning Your Essay

To mimic the ACT, we have provided you with some blank prewriting pages. On the ACT exam, your work on these prewriting pages will not be scored.

Use the indicated prewriting space to generate ideas and plan your essay. You may wish to consider the following as you think critically about the task:

- Strengths and weaknesses of different perspective on the issue

- What insights do they offer, and what have they failed to consider?

- Why might they successfully persuade others, or why might they fail to be persuasive?

- Your own knowledge, experience, and values

- What is your perspective on the issue, and what are its strengths and weaknesses?

- How will you support your perspective in your essay?

NOTES

Prewriting Page

On the ACT exam, you will be graded on anything you write into the lined pages of your booklet. Please write your essay on the lined pages provided.

 NOTES

GO ON TO THE NEXT PAGE.

ANSWER KEY AND EXPLANATIONS
Section 1: English Test

1. B	16. J	31. B	46. G	61. A
2. G	17. D	32. H	47. A	62. J
3. A	18. F	33. D	48. H	63. C
4. H	19. C	34. G	49. D	64. G
5. B	20. F	35. C	50. F	65. B
6. J	21. D	36. G	51. D	66. H
7. C	22. G	37. A	52. G	67. A
8. G	23. A	38. J	53. A	68. H
9. C	24. J	39. C	54. G	69. A
10. H	25. D	40. G	55. B	70. H
11. C	26. H	41. D	56. J	71. B
12. G	27. B	42. G	57. D	72. F
13. D	28. H	43. A	58. F	73. D
14. J	29. C	44. J	59. D	74. F
15. B	30. G	45. C	60. H	75. C

1. **The correct answer is B.** As written, the sentence contains unnecessary commas and creates confusion. No commas or internal punctuation are needed here, so choice B is correct.

2. **The correct answer is G.** The sentence is written awkwardly, so look for a better construction, one in which *vaudeville* is the subject. Choice G is best because "It was vaudeville" is simplified to just the subject, *vaudeville*; the simple past tense of the verb, *brought*, is more concise and effective in this sentence; and reordering the words in the second half is also a stylistic improvement. Choice H is awkward, and choice J is unclear, using a modifier ("in the millions") that is far from the subject it modifies (*people*).

3. **The correct answer is A.** The last sentence of Paragraph 1 emphasizes that vaudeville entertained a significant number of people in the United States from 1875 to 1932. Since Paragraph 2 explains how vaudeville came to appeal to many people through the diversity of its acts and its reliance on both family-friendly and language-free entertainment, the first sentence of the paragraph should offer a strong transition between these ideas. The use of "significant popularity" (choice A) does this effectively. The phrase "wonderful applause" (choice B) alludes to the response of an audience but does not connect to the previous sentence. The phrase "minor appeal" (choice C) contradicts the previous sentence and the information contained in Paragraph 2. The phrase "broad enthusiasm" (choice D) perhaps captures the spirit around vaudeville but does not connect to the previous sentence or accurately reference something that vaudeville itself possessed.

4. **The correct answer is H.** The listed items in this sentence need to be separated by commas, which choice H does correctly. The other choices use incorrect internal punctuation to separate the items in this list.

5. **The correct answer is B.** The original sentence suffers from poor construction in that it lacks parallelism. The audience takes three basic actions in the sentence: laugh, join, and watch. In a correctly

structured sentence, the form of each verb is parallel to the form of the other verbs. The verbs in the correct answer are all in the same tense, controlled by the helping verb *would*. Choices C and D do not solve the parallelism problem.

6. **The correct answer is J.** Speaking is a form of verbal communication, so the phrase is redundant as written. The only way to correct the redundancy is to take out either "verbal communication" or "speaking."

7. **The correct answer is C.** As written, the sentence ending in *inexpensive* is grammatically correct. However, the sentence beginning with *Making* is a fragment, not a complete sentence, and therefore needs to be changed. Choice C corrects the fragment by joining it to the other sentence with a comma. Choice B is incorrect because it creates a comma splice (two complete sentences separated by a comma). Choice D is incorrect because the conjunction *yet* indicates contrast, which would be illogical in this sentence.

8. **The correct answer is G.** The appropriate verb tense here is the past tense, since it refers to vaudeville's popularity, which is in the past. Therefore, *was* (choice G) is the correct choice. The other answer choices utilize incorrect verb forms, given the context of the sentence.

9. **The correct answer is C.** There is an error in this sentence as written. The word *we* refers to the parents who took their children to vaudeville shows. Because *parents* is in the third person and *we* is in the first person, the sentence needs a different pronoun. *Parents* is plural, so it cannot be referred to with the singular *he* or *she* (choice B) or *one* (choice D). The only word that works is *they*.

10. **The correct answer is H.** While choice F is a true statement, it is not the main idea of the paragraph, which is the origin of vaudeville. Choice G, too, might be true, but it is too general and does not introduce the main idea of the paragraph. Choice H is correct because it is about the origins of vaudeville and leads logically into the sentence that currently begins Paragraph 3. Choice J would work if the paragraph presented various theories on the origin of vaudeville, but it does not.

11. **The correct answer is C.** It makes logical sense that as acts became more creative, they would attract larger audiences, so choice C is correct. As the sentence stands, the phrase "mostly creative" (choice A) makes little sense; an act is by definition creative or not. Choice B merely adds a misplaced comma, and choice D is illogical: how could the acts be overly creative, and if they were, why would that attract a wider audience?

12. **The correct answer is G.** The underlined portion of the sentence explains that the increasing popularity of vaudeville is the reason businesspeople began opening more theaters. Therefore, choice G is the best answer.

13. **The correct answer is D.** It doesn't make sense for the paragraph to begin with examples, so eliminate choice A. Logically, examples should go after a statement of some kind. Since Sentence 3 begins by referring to other famous vaudevillians, this means that some vaudevillians were already mentioned. You can guess that Sentence 3 goes after Sentence 1. Sentence 2 is the topic sentence, referring in general to the performers who gained fame. It should be followed by Sentence 1, which lists several specific examples. Sentence 3 should end the paragraph by providing some additional examples. This is the most logical sequence. Choices B and C do not improve the logical flow of Paragraph 4.

14. **The correct answer is J.** This paragraph should be placed early in the essay because it gives introductory information, such as the origin and meaning of the word *vaudeville*. Nonetheless, the first paragraph should remain where it is because it is most effective as the introduction, so you can eliminate choice H. Therefore, Paragraph 3 should come directly after Paragraph 1. Choice G would place the introductory information at the end of the essay.

15. **The correct answer is B.** Paragraph 1 (choice A) mentions the laughter and joy that vaudeville brought to millions, but Paragraph 2 makes the author's argument more convincing. It provides many details—the diversity of the acts, vaudeville's appeal to non-English speakers, and its focus on family fun—to make the author's argument

more convincing. Paragraph 3 (choice C) does not advance the author's argument because it is mostly background information on the roots of vaudeville. Paragraph 4 (choice D) would not help the author's argument because it focuses on performers who became famous on the vaudeville stage.

16. **The correct answer is J.** Although the meaning of this sentence is clear, it is awkwardly constructed, so eliminate choice F. Word order is crucial to the meaning of a sentence, so the sentence reads most effectively when *essential* is not separated from the phrase "to human life," as it is in the other answer choices. Only choice J expresses the meaning clearly and smoothly.

17. **The correct answer is D.** This sentence contains a nonrestrictive element. Think of a nonrestrictive element as a little bit of extra information in a sentence. When it appears in the middle, it must be set off by two commas, not one (as shown in choices A and B). Using *that* and no commas (choice C) makes the phrase suggest that there is more than one Huang He, one of which flows through China, which is incorrect.

18. **The correct answer is F.** The sentence is correct as written. As a verb, *gets* should have no apostrophe, so choices G and H are incorrect. Additionally, *its* is correctly used here as a possessive; *it's* is a contraction for *it is* and is, therefore, used incorrectly in choices G and J.

19. **The correct answer is C.** The verb in the sentence is in present progressive tense, which indicates that the action is currently ongoing. In this sentence, *it* creates an awkward, confusing sense of time and ignores that the river has been vital both presently and in the past. *It be* is simply incorrect, so eliminate choice B. Saying *it is* (choice D) ignores the role the river has played throughout history—for centuries, according to the passage. The only choice that works is choice C, which describes something that began in the past but still has an effect at the time of the writing.

20. **The correct answer is F.** The correct answer should provide a logical transition between the sentence about the river's importance to Chinese life and the

sentence about the devastation caused by its flooding, as it includes and relates both topics. Eliminate choice G because the river's propensity for flooding is not mentioned until the sentence that follows, so this answer choice creates an illogical sequence. Choice H just rephrases the idea in the previous sentence, that the river is crucial to life in China. It is a needless repetition and doesn't introduce the idea of the river's devastation. Eliminate choice J because a description of the river's physical characteristics does nothing to provide the needed transition between sentences. Only choice F makes sense.

21. **The correct answer is D.** The antecedent to the pronoun *their* is the Huang He. Since Huang He is a singular antecedent, *their* must be replaced with a singular possessive pronoun. The contraction *they're* means "they are." It makes no sense to say "with they are raging waters," so eliminate choice B. *Them* is not possessive, so eliminate choice C. *Its* is the correct possessive to use here.

22. **The correct answer is G.** This sentence reads as if *caused* is modifying (or referring to) *devastating*, when it should refer to *flood*. In choice G, both *devastating* and *caused* correctly and clearly modify the noun *flood*. Choices F, H, and J are awkward and create confusion over which noun *caused* modifies.

23. **The correct answer is A.** The pronouns *who* and *whom* are frequently confused. *Who* is in the subjective case, which means that it functions as a subject. *Whom* (choice B) is in the objective case, which means that it functions as an object. Since *who* refers to villagers and farmers, which is the subject of the sentence, the pronoun must be in the subjective case. The sentence is correct as written. The pronoun *which* is not used to refer to people, so eliminate choice C. The pronoun *whose* shows possession, or ownership, which is not needed here, so eliminate choice D.

24. **The correct answer is J.** As written, the use of the word *content* indicates a sense of satisfaction, but it does not convey the stronger emotion that the villagers would have felt. Neither does *satisfied* (choice G) nor *pleased* (choice H). The word *elated*, which means "overjoyed," expresses the extreme happiness

that the villagers would have felt. The sentence tells you that their crops and lives were in jeopardy, so they would have felt more than just contentment or satisfaction at the end of the long drought.

25. **The correct answer is D.** The original sentence is wordy. This is a problem with style, not grammar, which is why wordiness can be easy to miss. A year is a period, so there is no need to state the obvious. Choices B and C simply reword the original unnecessary phrase; they do not correct the problem.

26. **The correct answer is H.** The original sentence is confusing and awkward. It sounds as though "the villagers working desperately to raise the dikes" modifies the second part of the sentence, which doesn't make sense. Choice G incorrectly uses a comma splice, and choice J needlessly alters the meaning of the sentence. Choice H correctly shows the cause-and-effect relationship between the two parts of the sentence.

27. **The correct answer is B.** Eliminate choice A because the writer does not define other unfamiliar words in the passage. While it is true that the word is not the focus of the passage, writers do often define words and terms in their works, even if not crucial to the passage as a whole (choice C). It is unlikely that most readers will know the word, so eliminate choice D.

28. **The correct answer is H.** Choice H provides specifics about the magnitude of the floodwaters and emphasizes their intensity since Niagara Falls is a well-known and very large waterfall. Choice F would be a fine answer if it did not repeat information already provided in the sentence. Choice G simply isn't specific enough. Choice J repeats information already given in the paragraph and fails to emphasize the floodwaters' magnitude or intensity.

29. **The correct answer is C.** The passage focuses on the flood of 1935. Paragraph 5 gives details of the tragic consequences of that particular flood. Throwing in one sentence about an earlier flood detracts from the unity of the paragraph and the passage, so choices A and B are incorrect. Choice D misidentifies the reason the sentence should be eliminated.

30. **The correct answer is G.** Choice G mentions the specific flood that the passage describes. It is the best summary of the passage as a whole. Choices F and H are too narrow, and choice J is too broad.

31. **The correct answer is B.** In order to determine the correct word choice, we need to examine its context within the sentence. This part of the sentence is discussing the "things we need to have" in life, so *essential* (choice B) is the best fit. The other answer choices are inappropriate, given the context of the sentence.

32. **The correct answer is H.** As written, the sentence contains an incorrect possessive plural form of the underlined phrase. There is no possession, so choice H, "groceries or clothing," is correct.

33. **The correct answer is D.** The underlined portion of the sentence contains a list of items, so they should all be separated by commas, as choice D correctly does. Choice A is incorrect as a comma is required before the coordinating conjunction *and* (called a serial or Oxford comma).

34. **The correct answer is G.** The underlined portion of the sentence contains the future tense phrase "you will be lucky," which is inappropriate given the context of the sentence and the present tense in the following independent clause. The correct word given the context is *you're*, which is a contraction of *you are*. Choice H is the contracted form of *you will be lucky*, which maintains the improper future tense. Choice J uses the possessive pronoun *your* rather than the subject pronoun *you* and corresponding present tense verb *are*.

35. **The correct answer is C.** Paragraph 3 contains a recollection of a memory about one night in the life of the author. Choice C would serve as the best opening for this paragraph.

36. **The correct answer is G.** As written, the words in the clause are jumbled, creating improper modification, which affects the clarity of the thought expressed. Choice G fixes this issue and makes the text clear and comprehensible. The other answer choices contain awkwardly worded passive constructions (choice F) or reverse the relationship

between the channel and the speaker's attention (choices H and J).

37. **The correct answer is A.** This question is asking you to examine the author's word choice in the underlined portion of the sentence. Scanning the sentence, we can see that the customers provided "stories of how the product completely changed their lives for the better," so the correct word choice should indicate that they approved of or recommended the product. The sentence is correct as written—the customers endorsed the product. The other choices don't fit, given the context of the sentence.

38. **The correct answer is J.** As written, the sentence contains an inappropriate contraction, *I'm*, and the incorrect form of the verb *to need*. As written, the sentence requires the pronoun *I* and the past tense, *needed*, so Choice J fixes the issue.

39. **The correct answer is C.** Without the statement in choice C, it would not be clear that the author actually decided to place the order.

40. **The correct answer is G.** The sentence needs to begin with a transitional word indicating that the author went to Jackie's house as a consequence of needing to see if the Confidence in a Can was working. *So* is a transitional word indicating a consequence. The transitional words *however* (choice F) and *nevertheless* (choice H) indicate contrast, not consequence. "In other words" (choice J) indicates a clarification.

41. **The correct answer is D.** The underlined portion of the sentence contains a piece of dialogue spoken by a person in the story—a quote—so it should be set off with a comma from the rest of the sentence. In the quote, there are two independent clauses that should be separated by a comma and a coordinating conjunction. Choices A and B omit the comma after *said*. Choice C creates a comma splice by omitting a conjunction before "you smell terrible!"

42. **The correct answer is G.** Carefully analyzing the paragraphs in question, it seems that there's some disorganization. Paragraph 7 discusses opening the package, while Paragraph 8 mentions waiting for the package to arrive. Logically, this information is out of

sequence; reversing these two paragraphs, as choice G suggests, fixes the issue.

43. **The correct answer is A.** An effective concluding sentence should tie up the themes and/or purpose of the written piece. This passage is all about the author learning that a purchase they made late at night while sleepy was a bad decision; choice A effectively captures the author's learned lesson.

44. **The correct answer is J.** Deleting the first paragraph would delete essential details for understanding the passage, so it is not a good idea.

45. **The correct answer is C.** A critique of a topic as expansive as advertising in the modern media landscape would be best served by a formal tone and a focus on key facts and statistics related to an average person's behaviors in response to advertising. This essay describes a situation in which the writer was susceptible to the claims of the late-night commercials (choice A), but this point alone does not turn the essay into a critique of advertisements. And while it is true that the narrative is a recounting of the writer making an impulse purchase (choice B), that does not make it "well-supported critique" of advertising. Spending significant time discussing the different kinds of products (choice D) would actually offer an effective segue into a discussion of the things that consumers purchase because of modern advertising, thus acting as a useful setup for a critique of advertising practices.

46. **The correct answer is G.** This sentence requires two commas to set apart the two separate ideas of muscle power versus engine or sail power, and the original sentence is missing both. Choice G places the commas between the two ideas correctly.

47. **The correct answer is A.** The sentence is correct as written. The conjunction *because* in choice B is incorrect since it changes the meaning of the original sentence, creating a statement that incorrectly indicates that rowing is popular due to the number of clubs. Choice C contains two unnecessary commas that splice and interrupt the flow of the sentence. Choice D should be eliminated (although it is not grammatically incorrect) because separating

the original sentence into two does not convey the meaning that the author intends.

48. **The correct answer is H.** As written, the first sentence of the paragraph lacks clear indication of the subject of the paragraph. Only choice H indicates that the paragraph will discuss the significant amount of effort required to row well. Choice G contradicts the following sentences. Choice J makes a remark regarding the abilities of the reader, thus working against the purpose of the paragraph and the passage.

49. **The correct answer is D.** As written, there's an internal error in logic in this sentence: a "coordinated effort" is mentioned, but then an uncoordinated effort—body or mind—is referenced. Choice D corrects the error by showing that the coordinated effort mentioned refers to body and mind.

50. **The correct answer is F.** The sentence is correct as written. Choice G is incorrect because the semicolon divides the independent and dependent clauses. The period in choice H creates the sentence fragment "When rowing together in a team boat." Choice J is also a sentence fragment and can be eliminated.

51. **The correct answer is D.** Choice D is the only option that does not add unnecessary modifiers. Choice A is incorrect because it contains an unnecessary phrase: "you see." Choice B can be eliminated because adding *consequently* does not make sense; the author has not given a possible reason for the rowers getting out of sync, so there is no consequence to discuss. Choice C is incorrect because it is redundant, since *briefly* repeats the idea behind "even for a moment."

52. **The correct answer is G.** The present participles of the verbs *to lose* and *to happen* are in agreement in choice G.

53. **The correct answer is A.** Context is essential when determining the appropriate conjunctive adverb to begin this sentence. Choices B, C, and D reference a contrast between the sentence or independent clause it appears in and the previous sentence or independent clause—and are not appropriate here.

54. **The correct answer is G.** This is the appropriate compound preposition for this sentence. Choice F is incorrect because *additionally* is an adverb that is not modifying a verb in its current location. Choice H should be eliminated; the rowers do not spend time in the weight room as a result of training on the water. Choice J is incorrect because *since* is also an adverb and is grammatically incorrect.

55. **The correct answer is B.** The sentence as written doesn't make sense—who would train thousands of hours a year for a race that was inconsequential? Only a race that was significant would make sense for rowers to devote that much effort to it. Therefore, *important* (choice B) makes the most sense here and is the correct answer.

56. **The correct answer is J.** *Is* provides the proper tense and agreement for the verb *to be* for this sentence.

57. **The correct answer is D.** The mention of longer races does not support the point the author is making about training time versus time spent racing. Choice A is incorrect because the placement of this sentence would be at the end of the paragraph where it would not help to further explain races themselves, a concept introduced in the very beginning of the paragraph. Choice B can be eliminated because the main point of this paragraph is that time spent racing is far less than the time spent training. Choice C is incorrect due to the fact that the World Championships are not the sole focus of this paragraph.

58. **The correct answer is F.** The comma precedes *or* and serves to join the two independent clauses. The colon in choice G is incorrect because it does not join the clauses. Choices H and J can be eliminated; they do not express the author's original intention of comparing one type of rower to another.

59. **The correct answer is D.** Without choice D at the beginning of Paragraph 5, the statement about watching possible Olympian rowers would not make any sense. The statement would make no sense if placed at the beginning of Paragraphs 2 (choice A), 3 (choice B), or 4 (choice C).

60. **The correct answer is H.** While the essay does mention that rowers train many hours, it is not

composed entirely of specific details about racing and training.

61. **The correct answer is A.** The sentence is correct as written. It is most common in English to say: "…studies indicate that." You would be highly unlikely to hear "…studies indicate for" (choice B) or "…studies indicate in" (choice C). While it might pass in casual spoken conversation to say "…studies indicate how," this is not a proper construction in standard written English, so choice D is incorrect.

62. **The correct answer is J.** Choice J pairs the singular verb *cites* with the singular subject *article*. Eliminate choice F since it offers a plural verb to match with the singular subject: "A recent article …cite experiments …." Eliminate choice G since it offers a noun instead of a verb, and a verb is most definitely required for this spot. Choice H proposes the gerund (*-ing*) form of the verb, which is inappropriate for this situation because the underlined word bears the responsibility of being the operative verb for the sentence. *Citing* could only be used if another verb bears the brunt of that work, as in: "A recent article citing several noted neurobiologists stated that …." In this example, *stated* becomes the operative verb.

63. **The correct answer is C.** As written, the original lacks commas to separate the nonessential phrase "otherwise known as saturated fats." Choices B and D fail to properly enclose the phrase between commas. Choice C properly encloses the phrase between commas.

64. **The correct answer is G.** Choice G proposes the best combination of proper punctuation and grammar to convey the meaning of the sentence because it appropriately uses a colon to signal that information on the new discovery is forthcoming.

65. **The correct answer is B.** This question primarily tests your command of pronouns. "Each member" is the operative subject of the sentence and is a singular construction. Singular pronouns must be used in reference to singular nouns. Although it is a singular pronoun, *it* is not used to refer to people, the antecedent in the sentence being "Each member of the group," so choice A is incorrect. While in recent years *they* is increasingly seen as a plausible singular

pronoun, the ACT still tests on the assumption that it is a plural pronoun only; consequently, choice C is incorrect because it uses a plural pronoun. Choice D can be eliminated since it suggests no pronoun at all.

66. **The correct answer is H.** Choice H provides a grammatically correct descriptive phrase for the sentence. The underlined portion is essentially a phrase modifying "a period of four years." Each option attempts to convey the idea that the referenced period occurred after the second research test was administered. A gerund (the *-ing* form of a word) is the most commonly used construction for this grammatical situation, so choices F and J are incorrect. We frequently hear "a period following" in English. There is no need to insert *that* as offered by choice G—it only interrupts the flow of the sentence.

67. **The correct answer is A.** The studies show that eating foods rich in saturated and hydrogenated fats can increase a person's chance of developing Alzheimer's disease. For clarification, the author chooses to list examples of these foods. The correct phrase for listing examples is "such as." *Like* is often used incorrectly for this purpose. *Like* should be used when you are ascribing similar qualities to two things. Eliminate choices C and D since *with* and *because* are inappropriate words for listing examples of a concept.

68. **The correct answer is H.** This question asks you to find the most idiomatically acceptable expression of quantity. According to the author's information, a diet rich in saturated and hydrogenated fats will increase a person's chances of developing Alzheimer's disease. How much will it increase the chances? "More than twice." Why? Because *double* is either a verb or an adjective. It cannot stand in for "two times" like the word *twice* does. So, eliminate choices F and G. Eliminate choice J as *half*, while grammatically correct and concise, contradicts the passage.

69. **The correct answer is A.** The sentence is correct as written because *attacks* offers the correct verb tense and agreement. Choice B offers appropriate

verb tense and agreement but is less concise than the original. Choice C proposes that the study will attack a theory in the future, but this doesn't hold up to the information contained in the rest of the essay: the study is currently being considered. Choice D's construction incorrectly references the past tense.

70. **The correct answer is H.** The passage says, "Many researchers have gone on record," followed by the phrase "in order." This construction requires you to choose an underlined portion that describes their stance. Choice H offers a grammatically correct predicate phrase. Choice F disrupts the syntax of the sentence by incorrectly pairing *in* with the gerund *supporting* creating awkward phrasing with the preceding "in order." Choice G, "to supporting the notion *that*," offers an improper form for the infinitive *to support*. Choice J switches *that* to *which*. *Which* is used to establish a modifying clause, which does not exist in this case.

71. **The correct answer is B.** The subject of the sentence is *vitamins*, a plural noun. It must be coupled with a plural verb. Choice A offers *has*, which is a singular verb and can be eliminated. Choice C proposes *are*, which does not fit with the rest of the sentence—"are been singled out" is never a proper construction in English. Choice D proposes a repetition of forms of the verb to be: "will be been." The best option is choice B, which notes that vitamins have been singled out as agents that can reduce the risk of free radical damage. This answer choice has the correct subject-verb agreement.

72. **The correct answer is F.** Without the clause it would not be clear that the research subjects were being tracked to learn whether or not they developed dementia symptoms, so choice F is the best answer.

73. **The correct answer is D.** Choices A and C can be eliminated immediately. They propose to begin the paragraph with "during that time" without previously establishing a point of reference. In fact, Sentence 2 contains the increment of time to which Sentence 1 refers. Therefore, any correct ordering of the paragraph must put Sentence 2 before Sentence 1, which choice B does not do. The only option that does this is choice D.

74. **The correct answer is F.** Eliminate choice H since it focuses only on antioxidant vitamins. Antioxidants are merely a point of reference in the author's narrative, which provides readers with an outline of these new scientific studies. Delving into more detail concerning antioxidants would only harm the author's mission to provide an overview of the studies. Eliminate choice J since there is no need to provide counterpoints in order to offer an overview of the studies. Eliminate choice G on the basis that the author's inclusion of a quote from Jose A. Luchsinger in no way validates his success of creating an overview of the studies cited. Only choice F explains how the essay fulfills the assignment accurately.

75. **The correct answer is C.** Eliminate choices A and D since the second study mentioned by the author maintains that despite widely held beliefs concerning antioxidants, they are apparently ineffectual for decreasing the risk of contracting Alzheimer's disease or dementia. Eliminate choice B since it maintains the exact opposite of what the cited studies show. Saturated fats have been linked to an increased chance of contracting Alzheimer's disease or dementia. Increasing your dosage of saturated fats will only increase your chances of contracting these two ailments. Therefore, choice C is the best answer.

ANSWER KEY AND EXPLANATIONS

Section 2: Mathematics Test

1. A	11. D	21. B	31. C	41. D	51. B
2. G	12. G	22. K	32. G	42. G	52. K
3. D	13. C	23. D	33. E	43. E	53. C
4. F	14. F	24. K	34. H	44. J	54. J
5. C	15. D	25. E	35. E	45. E	55. C
6. J	16. J	26. F	36. K	46. H	56. K
7. A	17. C	27. B	37. E	47. B	57. C
8. J	18. J	28. F	38. G	48. H	58. K
9. D	19. D	29. D	39. B	49. D	59. C
10. G	20. F	30. G	40. K	50. H	60. G

1. **The correct answer is A.** To figure out what percentage chose green, first determine how many chose green. Out of 400 total people, 150 chose blue and 200 chose red, leaving 400 – (150 + 200) = 50 people. So, 50 out of 400 chose green. Now calculate the percentage:

$$\text{Percent} = \frac{\text{part}}{\text{whole}}$$
$$\frac{x}{100} = \frac{50}{400}$$
$$400x = 5{,}000$$
$$x = \frac{50}{4} = 12.5$$

2. **The correct answer is G.** You're given that 1 hand equals 4 inches, and you want to find out how many hands are in 57 inches. This can best be solved by setting up a proportion:

$$\frac{1}{4} = \frac{x}{57}$$
$$4x = 57$$
$$x = \frac{57}{4} = 14.25$$

3. **The correct answer is D.** The x-coordinate of the midpoint of a line segment is the average of the x-coordinates of its endpoints; the same goes for the

y-coordinate of the midpoint. So, the midpoint of this segment is $\left(\dfrac{2-6}{2}, \dfrac{-8+2}{2}\right) = (-2, -3)$.

4. **The correct answer is F.** You're already given the properly laid out proportion, so cross-multiply to solve for z:

$$\frac{15}{3z} = \frac{10}{4}$$
$$30z = 60$$
$$z = 2$$

Beware of choice J (6), which is the equivalent of $3z$, the unknown denominator, but doesn't correctly answer the question. If you plug the values of z in choices G, H, and K into the proportion, you do not get equality.

5. **The correct answer is C.** To find the total number of miles traveled by the two airplanes, first find the distance traveled by each, remembering that distance = rate × time.

For Airplane A: distance = (540 mph)(3 hours) = 1,620 miles.

For Airplane B: distance = (400 mph)(3.5 hours) = 1,400 miles.

The total distance, therefore, is 1,620 miles + 1,400 miles = 3,020 miles.

6. **The correct answer is J.** Twelve percent of x is $0.12x$. Reducing the speed by this amount is represented by subtracting it from x: $x - 0.12x = 0.88x$.

7. **The correct answer is A.** Substitute $a = -2$ into the expression and simplify:

$$-(-2)^2 (1 - 3(-2)) = -4(1 + 6) = -4(7) = -28$$

8. **The correct answer is J.** To find $f(3)$, plug in 3 for every instance of x in the function and remember to follow PEMDAS.

$$f(3) = 2(3)^2 - 3(3) + 6$$
$$= 18 - 9 + 6$$
$$= 15$$

9. **The correct answer is D.** Call the coordinates of endpoint B (x, y). Using the midpoint formula yields:

$$(-3, 1) = \left(\frac{x+7}{2}, \frac{y-9}{2} \right)$$

Therefore,

$$\frac{x+7}{2} = -3 \qquad \frac{y-9}{2} = 1$$
$$x + 7 = -6 \qquad y - 9 = 2$$
$$x = -13 \qquad y = 11$$

Endpoint B has coordinates (–13, 11).

10. **The correct answer is G.** FOIL the squared binomial, then distribute the $-i$ and simplify:

$$-i(2-5i)^2 = -i(2-5i)(2-5i)$$
$$= -i(4 - 20i + 25i^2)$$
$$= -i(4 - 20i - 25)$$
$$= -i(-21 - 20i)$$
$$= 21i + 20i^2$$
$$= 21i - 20$$
$$= -20 + 21i$$

11. **The correct answer is D.** To find the average, divide the total number of songs played by the number of half-hour sessions. To find the total number of songs played, add up all the numbers of songs and divide by 8. Remember that some of the numbers of songs occur more than once, as indicated in the bottom row of the table.

$$\frac{6 + 8 + 8 + 8 + 9 + 9 + 12 + 12}{8} = \frac{72}{8} = 9$$

Therefore, the average was 9 songs per half-hour session.

12. **The correct answer is G.** If the product of two expressions is zero, then one of those expressions must equal zero. So, either $m + 4 = 0$ or $m - 2 = 0$.

$$m + 4 = 0$$
$$m = -4$$
$$\text{or}$$
$$m - 2 = 0$$
$$m = 2$$

Only 2 is among the answer choices, so it must be correct. If you substitute any of the values in choices F, H, J, and K in for m, you do not get zero.

13. **The correct answer is C.** Remember that absolute value is always the positive distance from zero on a number line, so addition or subtraction within absolute value brackets can never result in a negative. Eliminate choices A and B.

Work from the interior absolute value expressions outward:

$$\big\| -7 + 9 \big| - \big| 4 - 12 \big\| =$$
$$= \big\| 2 \big| - \big| -8 \big\|$$
$$= \big| 2 - 8 \big|$$
$$= \big| -6 \big|$$
$$= 6$$

14. **The correct answer is F.** There are multiple ways to find this solution using angle properties. One possibility is as follows. The measure of angle RWS is 70° because it is supplementary to angle RWT. The angle measures in triangle RNW must add up to 180°, so 180° – 70° – 90° = 20°. Another method is to consider that angles PRW and RWT are alternate interior angles between parallel lines and therefore have the same measure. Since PRV is a right angle, the measure of angle VRW is 110° – 90° = 20°. The measures of all angles are shown in this figure.

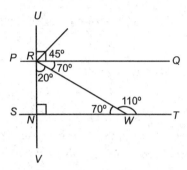

Choices G, H, J, and K are all measures of angles in the figure, but they are not the measure of angle VRW.

15. **The correct answer is D.** First, divide both sides of the equation by 2 to simplify it:

$$\frac{2x^2}{2} = \frac{310}{2}$$
$$x^2 = 155$$

The two nearest consecutive perfect squares between which 155 lies are 144 and 169; that is, $144 < 155 < 169$. Taking the square root of all terms of the inequality yields $12 < \sqrt{155} < 13$. Multiplying by –1 then gives $-13 < -\sqrt{155} < -12$. All other choices have pairs of integers for which 155 does not lie between their squares.

16. **The correct answer is J.** Compute the least common multiple of 12, 18, and 24 as follows:

$$\begin{array}{r|ccc} 6 & 12 & 18 & 24 \\ 2 & 2 & 3 & 4 \\ \hline & 1 & 3 & 2 \end{array}$$

So the least common multiple is $6 \cdot 2 \cdot 3 \cdot 2 = 72$. Choice F is a common factor, but not the least common multiple. Choice G is the greatest common factor. Choice H is incorrect because 48 is not a multiple of 18. Choice K is a common multiple of these numbers, but it is not the least common multiple.

17. **The correct answer is C.** You should recognize that $y = x^2 + 4x - 21$ is the equation of a parabola that opens upward. One of the characteristics of such a parabola is that it will always intersect the x-axis 0, 1, or 2 times, but never more. These x-intercepts are also known as the roots of a quadratic

equation. This means that you can eliminate choices D and E right away. Remember that the graph will intersect the x-axis only when y equals zero. To find the number of x-intercepts of a quadratic equation, $ax^2 + bx + c = 0$, evaluate the discriminant, $b^2 - 4ac$. If the discriminant is positive, there are two x-intercepts; if it's zero, there is one x-intercept; if it's negative, there are none. In this case:

$$b^2 - 4ac = (4)^2 - 4(1)(-21)$$
$$= 16 - (-84)$$
$$= 100$$

18. **The correct answer is J.** If the probability of NOT saying math is the favorite is $\frac{1}{5}$, then the probability of saying math IS the favorite is $1 - \frac{1}{5} = \frac{4}{5}$. Therefore, we have the following proportion:

$$\frac{4}{5} = \frac{\text{number of students who say math is their favorite}}{40}$$

Cross-multiplying yields $4(40) = 5 \times$ number of students who say math is their favorite, and then dividing both sides by 5 yields that the number of students who say math is their favorite is 32.

19. **The correct answer is D.** Gather the $|x|$-terms on one side and the constants on the other, and then divide by the coefficient of $|x|$. Then, use the definition of absolute value to conclude what the values of x must be:

$$3|x| + 2 = 9|x|$$
$$2 = 6|x|$$
$$\frac{1}{3} = |x|$$

So, $x = -\frac{1}{3}, \frac{1}{3}$.

20. **The correct answer is F.** The slope of the line containing these two points is $m = \frac{8 - (-4)}{-4 - 4} = \frac{12}{-8} = -\frac{3}{2}$. Using the point-slope form of the equation of a line with the point (4, –4) and then simplifying yields the following.

$$y + 4 = -\frac{3}{2}(x - 4)$$

$$y + 4 = -\frac{3}{2}x + 6$$

$$y = -\frac{3}{2}x + 2$$

$$2y = -3x + 4$$

$$3x + 2y = 4$$

21. **The correct answer is B.** When listing out the factors of each number, you arrive at the following set of lists:

    Factors of 12: 1, 2, 3, 4, 6, 12

    Factors of 32: 1, 2, 4, 8, 16, 32

    Factors of 96: 1, 2, 3, 4, 6, 8, 12, 16, 24, 32, 48, 96

    Within these groups, the greatest common factor is 4.

22. **The correct answer is K.** Let x be the original price. Then, $0.85x = \$2{,}250$. So $x = \dfrac{\$2{,}250}{0.85}$.

23. **The correct answer is D.** Factor the quadratic expression, which is a difference of squares, then use the zero-product property to find the solutions:

    $$4x^2 - 25 = 0$$

    $$(2x + 5)(2x - 5) = 0$$

    $$(2x + 5) = 0 \text{ or } (2x - 5) = 0$$

    Thus, $x = -\dfrac{5}{2}$ or $x = \dfrac{5}{2}$.

    Since $x > 0$, $x = \dfrac{5}{2}$ is the only acceptable solution.

24. **The correct answer is K.** The final rectangle after a 180° rotation, centered at A, is shown below.

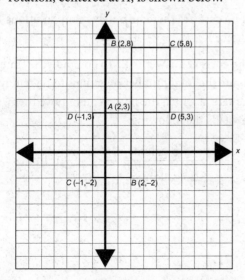

25. **The correct answer is E.** This is the graph of $y = 3^x$ shifted down 2 units. The shape remains the same, and the horizontal asymptote goes from $y = 0$ to $y = -2$. This results in the graph of choice E.

26. **The correct answer is F.** Rewrite the equation in slope-intercept form:

    $$2x - 5y - 1 = 0$$

    $$2x - 1 = 5y$$

    $$y = \frac{2}{5}x - \frac{1}{5}$$

    The slope of the given line is $\dfrac{2}{5}$. Thus, a line perpendicular to it must have slope $-\dfrac{5}{2}$.

27. **The correct answer is B.** The perimeter of a rectangle is $P = 2(l + w)$. Since the length is 6 inches greater than the width, we can substitute $l = w + 6$ and $P = 44$ and solve:

    $$P = 2(l + w)$$

    $$44 = 2\big[(w + 6) + w\big]$$

    $$22 = (w + 6) + w$$

    $$22 = 2w + 6$$

    $$16 = 2w$$

    $$8 = w$$

    Since the width is 8 inches, the length is 8 + 6 = 14 inches, and the area is $A = l \times w = 8 \times 14 = 112$.

28. **The correct answer is F.** Set $y = 0$ in $2y = 1 - 4x$ and solve for x:

    $$1 - 4x = 0$$

    $$1 = 4x$$

    $$x = \frac{1}{4}$$

29. **The correct answer is D.** Let x be the length of the fifth commercial segment. For the average to be 130 seconds, x must satisfy the equation $\dfrac{85 + 125 + 95 + 145 + x}{5} = 130$. Solving for x yields the following.

The final position of point C is (–1, –2).

$$\frac{85+125+95+145+x}{5}=130$$

$$\frac{450+x}{5}=130$$

$$450+x=650$$

$$x=200$$

30. **The correct answer is G.** Solve for the width (w) and length (l) of the rectangle using the distance formula:

$$w=\sqrt{(-5-(-1))^2+(-2-(-6))^2}$$

$$=\sqrt{16+16}$$

$$=4\sqrt{2}$$

$$l=\sqrt{(-1-7)^2+(-6-2)^2}$$

$$=\sqrt{64+64}$$

$$=\sqrt{128}$$

$$=8\sqrt{2}$$

The area of the rectangle is $(4\sqrt{2})(8\sqrt{2})=64$.

31. **The correct answer is C.** The total price for the albums at regular price is $16 + $16 + $24 = $56. To find the discounted price, you can find 30% of the total price and subtract it from $56, or find 70% of $56, since Maria paid 70% of the regular price (100% − 30% = 70%):

$$70\% \text{ of } \$56 = \frac{70}{100} \times \$56 = \$39.20$$

32. **The correct answer is G.** Since average is equal to $\frac{\text{sum of values}}{\text{number of values}}$, the sum is the product of the average and the number of values. The average of the first 7 integers is 13, so their sum is $7 \times 13 = 91$. The average of all 8 integers is 12, so their sum is $8 \times 12 = 96$. The value of the eighth number must be equal to the difference between the two sums: $96 − 91 = 5$.

33. **The correct answer is E.** Use the exponent rules to simplify the expression:

$$\frac{-a^4(b^2)^4c^6}{(-a)^3b^3c^8}=\frac{-a^4b^8c^6}{-a^3b^3c^8}=\frac{a^{4-3}b^{8-3}}{c^{8-6}}=\frac{ab^5}{c^2}$$

34. **The correct answer is H.** Factor the expression as $f(x) = x(x − 2)(x + 2)(x^2 + 9)$. The x-intercepts of a function are the real x-values for which the function equals 0. This only occurs when $x = −2$, 0 and 2. The other two values that make $x^2 + 9 = 0$ are imaginary ($3i$ and $−3i$); a graph does not have an x-intercept at an imaginary value. Thus, there are three x-intercepts.

35. **The correct answer is E.** This situation is modeled by a binomial distribution, where $n = 250$ and $p = \frac{3}{5}$. The expected value of a binomial distribution is simply $np = 250 \cdot \frac{3}{5}$.

36. **The correct answer is K.** Solve both equations for y and equate the resulting expressions. The second equation can be written as $y = \frac{1}{a}x + \frac{1}{a}$. Equating the expressions yields the equation $5x − 1 = \frac{1}{a}x + \frac{1}{a}$. Solve for x, as follows:

$$5x-1=\frac{1}{a}x+\frac{1}{a}$$

$$5x-\frac{1}{a}x=1+\frac{1}{a}$$

$$\left(5-\frac{1}{a}\right)x=1+\frac{1}{a}$$

If $a = \frac{1}{5}$ (choice H), then this equation becomes $0 = 6$, which means there is no solution. Otherwise, there is a unique solution:

$$x=\frac{1+\dfrac{1}{a}}{5-\dfrac{1}{a}}$$

In no case are there infinitely many solutions (choice K).

37. **The correct answer is E.** To compute the time, divide the total number of gallons to be removed by the rate at which the pump can remove them. Doing so yields the following:

$$\frac{g \text{ gallons}}{8.25 \text{ gallons}\big/\text{minute}}=\frac{g}{8.25}\text{minutes}$$

38. The correct answer is G. Rewrite the equation in exponential form: $3^y = \dfrac{1}{81}$. Since $81 = 3^4$, it follows that $\dfrac{1}{81} = \dfrac{1}{3^4} = 3^{-4}$. So $y = -4$.

39. The correct answer is B. The distances in the diagram form a right triangle. To find the height difference, h, between the altitude of the plane and the top of the control tower, use the sine function:

$$\sin = \frac{\text{opposite}}{\text{hypotenuse}}$$

$$\sin 27° = \frac{h}{35,000}$$
$$h = 35,000 \times \sin 27°$$

40. The correct answer is K. Plug in numbers to solve this problem. Let $a = 0$ because this will quickly get rid of answer choices that might otherwise remain with "easier" numbers. Since $b < a$, we can use -3 to replace b. And since $c < 0$, let's pick -1. So $a = 0$, $b = -3$, and $c = -1$. If you plug these numbers into each answer choice, you'll see that only choice K yields a valid result:

$$\frac{a}{c} < \frac{b}{c}$$
$$\frac{0}{-1} < \frac{-3}{-1}$$
$$0 < 3$$

41. The correct answer is D. If the radius of the circle is 3, then the diameter is 6. Since a diameter of the circle is congruent to one side of the square, as shown below, the side length of the square is 6 units, and the area of the square is $6 \times 6 = 36$ square units.

$d = 6$ units

42. The correct answer is G. To calculate relative frequency, divide the number of people whose commute is greater than 2 hours by the total number of people:

$$\frac{2}{75} \approx 0.03$$

The answer rounds up to 0.03.

43. The correct answer is E. Rolling a fair six-sided die twice gives $6^2 = 36$ outcomes. You must determine how many of these outcomes yield one 5 and one 6. The only rolls that can result in this scenario are (5, 6) or (6, 5). Since all rolls are equally likely, the probability of this occurring is $\dfrac{2}{36} = \dfrac{1}{18}$.

44. The correct answer is J. Since $2B = \begin{bmatrix} 8 & -4 \\ -6 & -2 \end{bmatrix}$ and $3A = \begin{bmatrix} -6 & -9 \\ 3 & -3 \end{bmatrix}$, it follows that

$$2B - 3A = \begin{bmatrix} 8-(-6) & -4-(-9) \\ -6-3 & -2-(-3) \end{bmatrix} = \begin{bmatrix} 14 & 5 \\ -9 & 1 \end{bmatrix}.$$

45. The correct answer is E. The line $x = -\dfrac{1}{3}y + 4$ can be written equivalently as $y = -3x + 12$, so its slope is -3. Using the point-slope form of a line with slope -3 and the point $(-2, -1)$ gives the following equation:

$$y + 1 = -3(x + 2)$$
$$y + 1 = -3x - 6$$
$$y = -3x - 7$$

46. The correct answer is H. Use the Pythagorean theorem to solve for the missing length:

$$a^2 + b^2 = c^2$$
$$15^2 + b^2 = 17^2$$
$$b = \sqrt{17^2 - 15^2}$$
$$= \sqrt{289 - 225}$$
$$= \sqrt{64}$$
$$= 8$$

47. The correct answer is B. Use the distance formula:

$$\sqrt{(a-b)^2 + (-b-(-a))^2} = \sqrt{(a-b)^2 + (-b+a)^2}$$
$$= \sqrt{(a-b)^2 + (a-b)^2}$$
$$= \sqrt{2(a-b)^2}$$
$$= \sqrt{2}|a-b|$$

48. The correct answer is H. The temperature at 9 a.m. is –15.5°C, and at 10 a.m., it is –13.0°C. This is a difference of –13.0°C – (–15.5°C) = 2.5°C. If the temperature increases by 2.5°C each hour, then 3 hours later at 1 p.m., it will be –13.0°C + 3(2.5°C) = –13.0°C + 7.5°C = –5.5°C.

49. The correct answer is D. The slope of the line passing through these two points is

$$\frac{\frac{1}{2}-\left(-\frac{5}{6}\right)}{-\frac{4}{5}-\frac{3}{10}}=\frac{\frac{3}{6}+\frac{5}{6}}{-\frac{8}{10}-\frac{3}{10}}=\frac{\frac{8}{6}}{-\frac{11}{10}}=\frac{8}{6}\cdot\left(-\frac{10}{11}\right)=-\frac{40}{33}$$

A line perpendicular to this line must have slope $\frac{33}{40}$.

50. The correct answer is H. The translation of $g(x)$ two units to the right is given by $g(x - 2)$. Computing this yields $g(x - 2) = (x - 2 + 3)^2 - 2 = (x + 1)^2 - 2$. This is a parabola opening upward with vertex $(-1, -2)$. As such, the range is $[-2, \infty)$.

51. The correct answer is B. The expected value is obtained by multiplying each outcome by its probability, and then summing these products. Here we have $(0.25 \cdot 1) + (0.5 \cdot 2) + (0.25 \cdot -4) = 0.25$.

52. The correct answer is K. The only way $|m - n|$ could equal zero is for m to equal n. But m and n have opposite signs and so cannot be equal.

53. The correct answer is C. The initial 25% increase is given by $60° + 0.25(60°) = 75°$. The subsequent 10% decrease is then given by $75° - 0.10(75°) = 67.5°$.

54. The correct answer is J. Write $g(x)$ as $y = \frac{2x}{x-1}$. To find the inverse, switch the x and y and solve for y:

$$y = \frac{2x}{x-1}$$
$$x = \frac{2y}{y-1}$$
$$x(y-1) = 2y$$
$$xy - x = 2y$$
$$xy - 2y = x$$
$$y(x-2) = x$$
$$y = \frac{x}{x-2}$$

so, $g^{-1}(x) = \frac{x}{x-2}$

55. The correct answer is C. All balls are equally likely to be chosen. So, the probability of selecting a red ball or a green ball is $\frac{10+3}{20} = \frac{13}{20} = 0.65$.

56. The correct answer is K. First, $g(-4) = \frac{3}{2(-4)} = -\frac{3}{8}$. Compute as follows:

$$(f \circ g)(-4) = f(g(-4))$$
$$= f\left(-\frac{3}{8}\right)$$
$$= \frac{1}{-\frac{3}{8}+2}$$
$$= \frac{1}{\frac{13}{8}}$$
$$= \frac{8}{13}$$

57. The correct answer is C. Since 1 hour = 60 minutes and 1 minute = 60 seconds, it follows that 1 hour = 3,600 seconds. Also, 300 m = 0.3 km. Let x be the number of kilometers rowed in one hour. Set up and solve the following proportion:

$$\frac{0.3 \text{ km}}{80 \text{ sec}} = \frac{x \text{ km}}{3,600 \text{ sec}}$$
$$(3,600)(0.3) = 80x$$
$$x = \frac{(3,600)(0.3)}{80}$$
$$x = 13.5 \text{ km}$$

58. The correct answer is K. Substitute $3r$ in for the radius and $2h$ in for the height in the volume formula to get $V = \frac{1}{3}\pi(3r)^2(2h) = 18 \cdot \left(\frac{1}{3}\pi r^2 h\right)$. Thus, the volume increases by a factor of 18.

59. The correct answer is C. The maximum value of $y = 4\sin(3x)$ is 4. Subtracting 1 from this shifts the entire graph down 1 unit. The new maximum is 3.

60. The correct answer is G. Use the quadratic formula directly to get:

$$x = \frac{-(-1)\pm\sqrt{(-1)^2-4(2)(3)}}{2(2)} = \frac{1\pm\sqrt{-23}}{4} = \frac{1\pm i\sqrt{23}}{4} = \frac{1}{4}\pm\frac{i\sqrt{23}}{4}$$

$$\sqrt{-23} = \sqrt{-1}\cdot\sqrt{23} = i\sqrt{23}$$

ANSWER KEY AND EXPLANATIONS

Section 3: Reading Test

1. C	9. A	17. D	25. A	33. B
2. J	10. G	18. F	26. G	34. J
3. B	11. C	19. A	27. B	35. A
4. F	12. F	20. G	28. H	36. H
5. B	13. A	21. D	29. D	37. D
6. G	14. J	22. G	30. H	38. G
7. D	15. B	23. A	31. C	39. A
8. H	16. H	24. F	32. G	40. G

1. **The correct answer is C.** In both the first and final paragraphs, the narrator emphasizes how his time on the *Beagle* helped shape him as a scientist.

2. **The correct answer is J.** In this case, you need only recognize two things to determine the correct answer. First, you need to recognize that the passage as a whole is in chronological order. Then, you must identify which of the answer options appears first in the narrative, which is the one that refers to the narrator's uncle driving him to see about a job (lines 3–6).

3. **The correct answer is B.** Contextually, the narrator explains that this particular book was "of the highest service [to him]" (lines 25–26) because studying it attentively and then applying Lyell's theories when he analyzed places like the Cape Verde islands "showed [him]" clearly the wonderful superiority of Lyell's manner of treating geology, compared with that of any other author" (lines 28–30).

4. **The correct answer is F.** In the first and final paragraphs, the narrator reflects on his time as a naturalist and sees that it helped grow his love for science and his abilities as a scientist. For example, this answer is supported by lines 7–9, which read "I have always felt that I owe to the voyage the first real training or education of my mind," as well as lines 57–59, which read, "I feel sure that it was this training which has enabled me to do whatever I have done in science."

5. **The correct answer is B.** Some of these answers (choices A and C) are partially correct, but only choice B accurately summarizes the full explanation the narrator gives for why he wrote in his journal. As he indicates in the fourth paragraph (lines 43–48), it served as a place for both detailed notes on his scientific observations and personal thoughts intended for future family correspondence. Note also that choice A adds the unnecessary assertion that the narrator was trying to keep the notes away from others and that there is no support for choice D.

6. **The correct answer is G.** In this context, the word *acute* means something like "shrewd" or "insightful." If someone is an acute observer, they can discern traits and shifts that others might miss. The narrator is implying that while not everyone might have noticed how much he'd changed, his father noticed the shift in him because of his acute observation skills.

7. **The correct answer is D.** If context clues from the third paragraph (lines 32–42) weren't enough to recognize the answer right away, you could use a process of elimination. At no point does the narrator mention resenting his work (choice B). His assertion that he "lost much time" (lines 38–39) supports either choice A or choice D, but his admission that it was "almost useless" (line 38) eliminates choice C and supports choice D. Furthermore, choice D provides an extra detail that is supported by the last sentence of the paragraph, which reads "I thus

lost much time, with the exception of that spent in acquiring some knowledge of the Crustaceans, as this was of service when in after years I undertook a monograph of the Cirripedia" (lines 38–42).

8. **The correct answer is H.** Essentially, this is a main idea question since the quotation you are given has to do with the main idea of the passage. Here, the narrator is trying to say that each time he had a new experience on his journey, the things he learned helped him for the next endeavor he undertook. Consequently, the best answer is the one that discusses the growth of the narrator's abilities and understanding over the five years he spent on the ship.

9. **The correct answer is A.** The narrator says "my love for science gradually preponderated over every other taste" (lines 61–62) and that "the pleasure of observing and reasoning was a much higher one than that of skill and sport" (lines 70–72). Given these two observations, you can reasonably infer that the narrator finds scientific pursuits more fulfilling than hobbies involving skill or sport.

10. **The correct answer is G.** You don't have any evidence that the narrator was talking about physical changes (choice F) or emotional changes (choice J), so you can eliminate those options right away. Of the two that remain, the narrator explicitly states that his father was not a believer in phrenology, so it's unlikely that he was implying that the narrator's literal head shape had changed as a result of his learning (choice H), which is what phrenologists believe.

11. **The correct answer is C.** The main idea of the passage is that neuroscience has helped psychology researchers better understand grief in recent decades, particularly the idea that grief is a process that involves the brain learning and rewiring to account for new information as a result of a grief event. The passage notes that grief can mimic PTSD in the fourth paragraph. Choice A only addresses one idea within the passage, not the main idea of the whole text. There is nothing in the passage to support choice B. While choice D may technically be correct, it is not the main idea of the passage nor is it stated directly in the passage.

12. **The correct answer is F.** As the author states in lines 50–53, "a grieving person can experience cognitive effects, such as so-called 'brain fog,' as well as changes in memory and behavior." This supports choice F because you know that brain fog is an example of a cognitive effect caused by grief. Note that this sentence also helps eliminate choice J, since memory issues are mentioned in addition to other cognitive effects—it is unlikely that the author would differentiate memory changes from brain fog if they were the same. There is nothing in the passage to support choices G and H.

13. **The correct answer is A.** Lines 40–41 assert that "Like PTSD, grief experiences can activate the fight or flight mechanism." This question is asking you to make an inference, but this inference isn't a stretch since the author states that PTSD experiences can activate the fight or flight mechanism, just not in those exact words. This question is testing your ability to draw a conclusion from the statement that *is* given.

14. **The correct answer is J.** The author first introduces Kübler-Ross's five stages of grief as one theory that is widely accepted about the grieving process. The author goes on to say in lines 72–74 that "rather than following a specific linear process, as is sometimes implied by the Kübler-Ross model, grief tends to circle back on itself." Therefore, the statement that best describes the author's summation is the one that states "Kübler-Ross asserts that there are five stages of grief that one must go through to process grief, but we now know that the grieving process isn't always as linear as her model might suggest."

15. **The correct answer is B.** Here, you are tasked with determining the context in which "divorce" is given as an example of a grief-triggering event in line 19 as well as the general definition the author gives in saying "The thing that makes grief what it is is loss and, quite often, the twin experience of yearning" (lines 23–24). From there, you can reasonably infer that the end of a significant romantic relationship (such as a divorce) causes grief because it represents a sorrowful experience characterized by loss and yearning.

16. **The correct answer is H.** As the author states in lines 83–85, *neuroplasticity* is defined as "the brain's ability to rewire itself and change in light of new information and experiences." Your task is to choose the response that most effectively summarizes this definition in different words, which is "the brain's ability to change and make sense of new information it receives over time."

17. **The correct answer is D.** Notice that the question asks you for the primary reason the example was provided. The context of the example in paragraph 7 suggests it is provided in order to situate the claim that "If one considers grief a learning process, it's easier to recognize the link between neuroplasticity, or the brain's ability to rewire itself and change in light of new information and experiences, and the grieving process" (lines 81–85). This is exemplified by how a recently widowed person might experience grief over time (the grieving process) as their brain relearns new patterns in the absence of the predictable patterns it had formerly deeply wired to map the deceased spouse's daily habits (neuroplasticity).

18. **The correct answer is F.** Here, you must look at the lines identified for you. Both the idea of "unknown triggers" causing "waves of grief to come on" (lines 77–78) and the recognition that "the individual experiences the waves of grief anew each time they recognize the absence of what was once predictably there" (lines 96–98) point to the unpredictability of grief and the idea that it is sometimes more intense and heightened than at other times. This is supported by the author's assertion in lines 74–75 that "grief tends to circle back on itself, feeling at times easier and at other times harder."

19. **The correct answer is A.** While the passage does mention that some of the effects of grief include unpredictable or erratic behavior (choice B), physical symptoms (choice C), and confused or agitated behavior (choice D), only choice A effectively summarizes how the fight or flight response relates to the grieving process.

20. **The correct answer is G.** The author's intention with this line is to point out how the findings from neuroscientists and psychologists alike suggest that this adage about grief has some truth to it.

21. **The correct answer is D.** First, to answer this question, you need to know that the word *satellite* in this case is defined as "an extension of something else that is more central." By calling Friedrichshain a satellite to the squatting actions in Mitte, the author is saying that Friedrichshain was a second neighborhood to which these actions extended. Lines 32–34 state that, like Mitte, Friedrichshain "had once sat along the eastern path of the Berlin Wall, [but] now lay adjacent to bustling western border neighborhoods like Kreuzberg and Schöneberg." That paragraph goes on to say that "when the Wall fell at the end of 1989, these modes of resistance extended to neighborhoods (like Friedrichshain) that had once laid unreachably close on the other side of the Berlin Wall," so you can infer that choice D most accurately summarizes the passage. You could also use a process of elimination by recognizing that choices A and B falsely identify Friedrichshain as a former western neighborhood and that choice C asserts that it wasn't possible to live in border neighborhoods like Friedrichshain at all, which is neither correct nor stated in the passage.

22. **The correct answer is G.** Since the author gives the context for this phrase both by translating it for an English-speaking audience and explaining where the graffiti message was situated (on a building next to an art piece made from an abandoned east German fighter jet), you can conclude that the author mentions the quote "Nie wieder Krieg" to provide a contextual example of a genuine piece of graffiti that originated with the squatting community.

23. **The correct answer is A.** This question requires you to read the author's tone and intentions alike. In this passage, the author mentions that reconstruction after WWII took decades in order to provide clarity as to why repairing buildings in border areas like Mitte and Friedrichshain might have been a low priority for East German leadership. You don't have enough information to infer that the author considers the Berlin Wall a necessary evil for the East German government (choice B). The author's tone

toward the East German government's failure to reconstruct the buildings is neutral, so it's unlikely an attempt to criticize (choice C). At no point in the passage does the author explain why the groups of squatters had differing beliefs and values (choice D), though it is implied that they did.

24. **The correct answer is F.** As the author states in lines 70–74, "Do-it-yourself (DIY) repairs became not just a necessity (to get potable water, to find places to dispose of waste, to have safe shelter) but a unifying ethos among the disparate groups." You can infer from this sentence that their DIY efforts involved making the buildings they occupied habitable. This observation supports choice F being correct and eliminates choices G and H. There is nothing in the passage to support choice J.

25. **The correct answer is A.** This is the only answer that can be directly supported by what the author states in lines 50–52, which is that activities like graffiti and squatting extended into "the strips of now-abandoned 'no-man's land' that had once sat between its two borders."

26. **The correct answer is G.** The phrase "to bring to fruition" refers to making something happen; the term *fruition* is defined as "the point at which a project or plan is finally realized."

27. **The correct answer is B.** The author spends most of their discussion of the squatting community focusing on students, activists, and artists. However, when talking about how historians see the 1990 post-Wall squatters, the author adds that immigrants and those who had been unhoused before the fall of the Wall were included in their numbers. You can infer that the author does so to highlight that it was not solely students, activists, and artists from Berlin who participated but also anyone else who was drawn to the squatters' cause.

28. **The correct answer is H.** In the section in question (lines 105–110), the author writes "The commune at Rigaerstrasse 94 in Friedrichshain still exists, as does the punk-rock squatter's commune lovingly dubbed 'Köpi' at Köpenickerstrasse 137 at the edge of Mitte; this space is still known for being welcoming and artistic." This question essentially tests your ability

to scan for the keyword "Köpi" and then accurately relay the information the author said about it rather than guessing based on words that came up in the passage when describing other things.

29. **The correct answer is D.** The key to answering this question lies in the last sentence of the second to last paragraph (lines 114–116), which states that Liebig 34 engaged in "a series of high-profile attempts to forcefully resist their mandated removal." Since the terms *series* and *forcefully* suggest that at least this one group used force to resist on two or more occasions, you can reasonably infer that some squatters' groups may have used violence to resist their evictions.

30. **The correct answer is H.** The last two paragraphs taken together focus on why discussions of the post-Wall squatters are still relevant to understanding how Berlin has evolved in the decades since the Berlin Wall fell. The section in question specifically offers examples of groups that are still in operation and one that was recently evicted despite forcefully resisting in 2020. Therefore, you can infer from these supporting details that the author is claiming that the question of whether to evict squatting tenants is still politically relevant in Berlin.

31. **The correct answer is C.** You can find the answer to this question in two different places. First, the chart included with Passage A indicates that fungi have the largest relative biomass. Second, the author mentions it in lines 4–5.

32. **The correct answer is G.** Understanding the main idea of Passage A is key to answering this question. If you know that the primary purpose of this passage is to explain what SOM is and how the active and passive components function differently, then it's clear that this distinction is made early on in the passage to set up the continued discussion of why active SOM is so critical to soil health.

33. **The correct answer is B.** If you noted the quotation from lines 36–39 that reads "The longer soil is left untilled, the more effectively it builds up active SOM and, in turn, develops a healthy, diverse, and life-enriching microbiome," then you probably picked out the correct answer easily. Otherwise,

you could eliminate incorrect answers by recognizing that choice A is not mentioned in the passage, choice C refers to a different part of the passage, and choice D is too vague to answer the question.

34. **The correct answer is J.** You can infer this answer from the last sentence of the final paragraph, which states "Since there is so much that is still unknown about how soil microbiomes operate, many scientists worry that our understanding of them is too elementary to effectively make predictions about or respond to how climate change will affect them" (lines 119–124).

35. **The correct answer is A.** This question relies both on your understanding of the word *livelihood* as meaning "financial and other resources necessary for living" as well as your ability to read between the lines of what is said and make inferences. Here, the author includes this statement about soil being the bedrock (meaning "foundation") of farmers' livelihoods to emphasize that if climate change negatively affects soil health, then farmers could suffer economic consequences as a result.

36. **The correct answer is H.** To exacerbate something means to intensify, inflame, or worsen it.

37. **The correct answer is D.** The entire paragraph is focused on the fact that if rising CO_2 levels become a bigger problem in climate change, scientists don't yet know if soil microbiomes will help calm these effects or worsen them. Here, test makers want you to recognize that choices A and B are only partially correct since they each represent a potential outcome mentioned in the paragraph, but neither summarizes the correct answer in its entirety. Choice C incorrectly identifies the nature of a given soil microbiome as the determining factor in how soil will respond to climate change, which is not supported by the passage.

38. **The correct answer is G.** Remember that for an answer to be correct, both parts of the answer must be correct. Only choice G correctly summarizes both passages. Choice F correctly summarizes the author's purpose in Passage B but inaccurately represents Passage A. Conversely, choices H and J correctly summarize Passage A but inaccurately summarize the author's purpose in Passage B.

39. **The correct answer is A.** To answer this question, you need a good understanding of what is covered by each passage. Having a basic summary of each in mind helps you eliminate incorrect answers. For instance, you know that SOM and biomass were primarily discussed in Passage A, so you can eliminate choice B. You also know that while Passage B mentions carbon dioxide, it does not do so to discuss the development of SOM, so you can eliminate choice C. You can then eliminate D by recognizing that neither passage talks about the measures agricultural scientists are already taking to combat climate change. You can then confirm your answer by recognizing that lines 77–86 concern different questions farmers and agricultural scientists must consider regarding soil health and climate change.

40. **The correct answer is G.** As with other questions requiring synthesis of more than one passage, having a working understanding of how each passage could be summarized will help you greatly. Start by eliminating answers you know are wrong; for instance, Passage B doesn't spend much time focusing on economic consequences, so you can eliminate choice H. Eliminate choice J because it suggests that Passage B discusses humus, a topic that you know only came up in Passage A. Of your two remaining options, note that the summary of Passage A as a discussion on the adaptability of soil microorganisms is inaccurate, so you are left with choice G. Confirm your answer by recognizing that the summary of Passage A as being about what makes for "healthy, active SOM" and Passage B being about how climate change could affect those conditions is accurate.

ANSWER KEY AND EXPLANATIONS
Section 4: Science Test

1. B	9. B	17. C	25. A	33. D
2. G	10. H	18. G	26. F	34. G
3. A	11. D	19. B	27. C	35. B
4. G	12. F	20. H	28. J	36. J
5. D	13. B	21. A	29. C	37. C
6. F	14. G	22. H	30. J	38. G
7. C	15. D	23. B	31. A	39. C
8. F	16. H	24. J	32. G	40. G

1. **The correct answer is B.** Both sets of data in Table 1 show inverse relationships between distance to light source (m) and the photocurrent in μA (a), meaning that they change in opposite directions. The change, however, is not linear; they do not necessarily change by the same amount. Choice B is the best choice because it depicts nonlinear, inverse variation.

2. **The correct answer is G.** According to Table 2, the stopping potential varies with the color of light. The color of light is determined by its wavelength. Therefore, the stopping potential must depend on the wavelength.

3. **The correct answer is A.** The dependent variable in Study 2 is the stopping potential, which is the voltage required to stop the flow of photoelectrons. It is affected by the color filters and/or the absence of a filter, but the distance to the light source is held constant.

4. **The correct answer is G.** The first sentence of Study 1 states, "[the teachers] measured the photocurrent." The last sentence of the first paragraph of Study 2 states, "the teachers measured the stopping potential." These measurements can also be seen in Table 1 and Table 2, respectively.

5. **The correct answer is D.** The question is asking you which independent variable is common to both studies. An independent variable is one that the researchers control and can change as they wish.

In Study 1, the researchers changed the color of the filter and the distance to the light source. In Study 2, the researchers changed the color of the filter. Thus, the only independent variable that the two studies have in common is the filter color. Don't be fooled by choice A; while the distance to the light source was an independent variable in Study 1, it was held constant in Study 2, meaning it was not a variable. Choice B is incorrect because photocurrent magnitude was the dependent variable—the experimental variable not controlled by the researchers—in Study 1. Choice C is incorrect because stopping potential was the dependent variable in Study 2.

6. **The correct answer is F.** Orange is a color between red and yellow, so use the stopping potential values from Table 2 to interpolate the approximate stopping potential of an orange filter. Since the three red trials yielded 0.0 volts and the three yellow trials yielded 0.4 volts, you can assume that a typical trial with an orange filter would yield a stopping potential between 0.0 and 0.4 volts.

7. **The correct answer is C.** The median elevation of Earth's surface, because it is the midpoint between the highest and lowest elevations on that surface, will be the elevation that 50% of Earth's surface lies above. Luckily, you do not have to make any calculations to find the answer—you can just read the graph. Going up from 50% on the horizontal axis to the curve, and then going across to the vertical axis, we see that the corresponding elevation is about

−1,000 m. So, 50% of Earth's surface is above (or below) −1,000 m, the median elevation. If you did not figure out that you could read the graph to find the median elevation, you likely noticed that you can calculate it. We can estimate the highest elevation on Earth to be about 9,000 m ($\approx$ 8,848 m, the elevation of Mt. Everest) and the lowest elevation to be about −11,000 m ($\approx$ −11,305 m, the elevation of the deepest trench). Therefore, the total range of elevation on Earth is 9,000 m − (−11,000 m) $\approx$ 9,000 m + 11,000 m = 20,000 m. The midpoint of this range is half of the range either added to the lowest point or subtracted from the highest point: (20,000 m ÷ 2) + (−11,000 m) = 10,000 m − 11,000m = −1,000 m.

8. **The correct answer is F.** If the presence of mountains can reduce storms, one would expect to find the mildest or least extreme weather in areas dominated by land. According to the passage, the Southern Hemisphere is dominated by oceans while the Northern Hemisphere is dominated by land, so one would expect less extreme weather in the Northern Hemisphere.

9. **The correct answer is B.** In Figure 2, read down from the arrow pointing to the mean elevation of land at 840 m to the horizontal axis to find the percentage of land above this elevation. The value on the horizontal axis associated with 840 m is approximately 20%.

10. **The correct answer is H.** Look for the point at which the lines representing the temperature of maximum density and the freezing point of water intersect. This happens at the point corresponding to 25 percent on the horizontal axis, so above 25 percent salinity, the temperature of maximum density of water is below the freezing point of water, as opposed to below 25 percent salinity, where it is above the freezing point.

11. **The correct answer is D.** Looking at Figure 3, the temperature of maximum density drops by about 2.3°C for every 10% increase in salinity. Using this estimate, since the temperature of maximum density at 30% salinity is about −2.5°C, then at 40% salinity it should be 2.3°C less, or about −4.8°C. If you trace the line for temperature of maximum density to 40% salinity and extend the temperature

axis down to −5°C, then you will see when reading across that this estimate is correct.

12. **The correct answer is F.** From Figure 1, you can see that bone loss is the least with the ARED, in both the pelvis and the whole body. With the ARED, there is a slight average gain in bone density for the whole body. Notice when reading the graphs in Figure 1 that the x-axis is at or near the top of the y-axis rather than at the bottom, so a larger bar below the x-axis means a greater negative change, or greater loss of bone density. A bar above the x-axis indicates a gain in bone density.

13. **The correct answer is B.** The introduction explains that bone loss occurs in space because bones do not have to bear as much weight as usual. From Figure 1, for all exercise machines, the pelvis experiences more bone loss than the whole-body average. It is also stated in the introduction that bones that bear the most weight will experience the largest change in weight load and so experience the largest change in bone density. The pelvis is a weight-bearing part of the body, as it supports the upper body and anchors the legs.

14. **The correct answer is G.** The control in the first experiment is the group of astronauts who did not have access to the resistance machines, only the aerobic exercise and muscular endurance machines.

15. **The correct answer is D.** Figure 1 demonstrates that exercising on ARED leads to the least amount of bone loss. The passage states that ARED offers the highest resistance of all the exercise machines, up to 600 pounds, so high-resistance exercise should be one of the recommendations. In Figure 2, the higher the protein intake, the lower the amount of bone loss. Therefore, a high-protein diet should be the other recommendation. Therefore, you are looking for the only option that pairs a high protein diet with high-resistance exercise, which is choice D.

16. **The correct answer is H.** In Figure 1, the change in BMD in the pelvis for an astronaut on the Mir is about −1.4%, while for an astronaut exercising with ARED the loss is about −0.4%. The difference between these two values is −1.4% − (−0.4%) = −1.4% + 0.4% = −1.0%. Thus, Mir astronauts lost 1.0% more BMD than ARED-using astronauts.

17. **The correct answer is C.** The astronaut's diet could significantly affect their physical performance, so without testing for diet, the researchers likely wouldn't have been able to draw as clear a conclusion about the overall effectiveness of the machines in reducing bone loss. Choice A is incorrect because, even without diet, the researchers may have been able to draw some conclusions about the effectiveness of one resistance machine over the other. Choice B is incorrect because there would be no way of knowing which astronauts were low on protein without testing for diet.

18. **The correct answer is G.** Notice that electronegativity increases from left to right in a given period, and it decreases from top to bottom in a given family. Therefore, the electronegativity of Br should be greater than that of Se (2.6) and between that of Cl (3.2) and I (2.7). In other words, it should be in the range of 2.8 – 3.1.

19. **The correct answer is B.** Higher electronegativity means a greater ability to attract electrons, so an atom with higher electronegativity attracts electrons more easily. The element with the lowest electronegativity will have the lowest ability to attract electrons. Of the choices, the lowest electronegativity rating belongs to Na, sodium, at 0.93. This is lower than lithium (choice A) by a small amount and aluminum (choice C) by a larger margin. Titanium (choice D) is a very unreactive element, but it still has a relatively high electronegativity compared to sodium.

20. **The correct answer is H.** The polarity of a molecule is determined by the difference in electronegativity between its atoms. A smaller difference in electronegativity means less polarity. In a nonpolar molecule, therefore, if you subtract the value of the smaller electronegativity from that of the larger electronegativity, you should get a result near zero. Since two atoms of the same element, such as Cl_2, have identical values for electronegativity, the result of subtracting one electronegativity from the other is exactly 0, making the molecule nonpolar.

21. **The correct answer is A.** In this case, use the reverse reasoning from that used to find the answer to 20. Look for the greatest difference between the electronegativities of the bonded atoms. The difference for K–Cl (choice A) is 2.38, and none of the other differences are as great.

22. **The correct answer is H.** The most highly polar bond would be generated from a bond between the element with the highest polarity and the element with the lowest polarity, which would be F and Cs, respectively.

23. **The correct answer is B.** The recorded range of smoking rates in the study population is 10% on the low end and 35% on the highest end. That is 5 increments of 5% over the entire range of the study. As the smoking rate increases from 10% to 35%, the rate increases from about 140 deaths per 100,000 people when 10% of the population smokes to 230 deaths per 100,000 people when 35% of the population smokes, a difference of 90 deaths per 100,000 people. Over the range of the study there is some variation from point to point, but overall, 90 deaths per 100,000 people divided by 5 increments of 5% gives approximately 18 more deaths per 100,000 people per 5% increase in the smoking rate. Choices A, C, and D are all changes that occur between particular data points in the study, but only choice B reflects the entire range of smoking rates examined.

24. **The correct answer is J.** This is an EXCEPT/NOT question, meaning that three of the four answer choices will be supported by Table 1. The correct answer will be the one that is false. Choices F, G, and H are all supported by the numbers in the table. Choice J, however, is not supported by the data because the percentage of Rhode Island females who attempt to quit smoking is actually lower than the percentage of Rhode Island males.

25. **The correct answer is A.** The study is examining all cancer mortality, but cancer has a variety of causes. Some cancers are not associated with smoking and may be affiliated with other health or environmental problems in the study area. The study would be much stronger if cancers not caused by smoking were eliminated from the findings.

26. **The correct answer is F.** This question relates to the second data group in Table 1, the number of cancer deaths. In all ten listed states, the number of males who died from cancer was significantly higher than the number of females who died from cancer. Having only these data to consult, it's reasonable to conclude that New Jersey would be likely to have a similar result. The only answer greater than 177, the number of females, is 246 (choice F).

27. **The correct answer is C.** In every state but Rhode Island, women are more likely to attempt to quit smoking than men are; that is the only major difference between Rhode Island and the rest of the study. Without any other additional information, it is conceivable that the larger social networks mean women have more people to support them as they try to quit. Choice A has no information to support it; the nature of smoking is not discussed, only how often it occurs. Choice B might possibly be true but the study does not provide any information about people who have cancer but survive. Choice D is unlikely to be correct as women in every state smoke at lower rates than men do.

28. **The correct answer is J.** Perspective 1 focuses on the negative aspects of introduced species, viewing these introductions as unwelcome invasions. Perspective 2 takes a more nuanced view, assessing what the actual impact of an introduced species is and how the introduction fits into the global conservation picture.

29. **The correct answer is C.** Advocates of Perspective 2 regard introduced members of a species as part of the global population of that species. If a species is endangered, and if an introduced population elsewhere can help the species as a whole survive, then Perspective 2 supports allowing the turtles to establish their new population.

30. **The correct answer is J.** The passage makes it clear that limited resources will play a role in both perspectives, making choice J the only possible correct answer.

31. **The correct answer is A.** The passage states that introduced species are most harmful in isolated or low-diversity areas. A small, remote island meets these criteria as small areas usually have lower diversity, resulting from the limited space.

32. **The correct answer is G.** While each view of introduced species disagrees in part about how to manage introduced populations and the degree of risk they pose, all three perspectives agree that some species introductions do pose a serious risk to native ecosystems. All three perspectives agree that, if at all possible, some of these introductions must be eliminated.

33. **The correct answer is D.** All three perspectives differ in their assessment of the degree of risk and how to handle introduced species, but none of the perspectives fully embraces introduced species as a benefit. All three perspectives assess costs, no matter how serious they consider the threat of invasive species to be, and those costs will be minimized if species are never introduced in the first place.

34. **The correct answer is G.** According to Perspective 3, the population of an introduced species typically increases at first, then decreases, and then the populations of both introduced and native species stabilize. Only choice G shows the initial population increase and decrease prior to stabilization for introduced species.

35. **The correct answer is B.** Choice B indicates the correct independent variable, genotypic richness, and the correct dependent variable, community stability. The "effect" of the second half of choice B correctly makes sense in light of the "cause" in the first half of the hypothesis statement.

36. **The correct answer is J.** Choice F is incorrect because it represents the independent variable throughout the experiments. Choice G is incorrect because it represents the dependent variable throughout the experiments. Choice H is incorrect because not all of the varied resource experiments used glucose as the primary carbon source; in fact, most of the trials used a variety of carbon sources. By a process of elimination, choice J must be correct.

37. **The correct answer is C.** Choice A is incorrect because the passage indicates that these bacterial species are common invaders specifically in the niche of *P. fluorescens*, not necessarily in most

natural ecosystems. Choice B is incorrect because there is no indication that these bacteria are any more successful under the given carbon source conditions. Choice D is incorrect because the passage does not indicate that these bacteria are extremophiles or can survive under extreme conditions. The passage does state that these invaders occupy the same niche as *P. fluorescens*, and choice C correctly states this relationship.

38. **The correct answer is G.** The best-fit curve for both figures is a straight line; however, the key here is that the units of the *y*-axis are log10(1/CV). This is important because logarithm calculations are used to convert exponential graphs to linear graphs.

39. **The correct answer is C.** The slope of the line in Figure 2 is significantly steeper than the slope of the line in Figure 1. The primary difference between the two experiments is the presence of the invaders in Experiment 2.

40. **The correct answer is G.** Low-diversity communities were, for both tested environmental changes in resource composition and invader presence, more sensitive to the environmental changes than the high-diversity populations, as indicated by the positive slope of the best-fit lines in Figures 1 and 2.

ANSWER KEY AND EXPLANATIONS
Section 5: Writing Test

Essay Instructions for Self-Scoring

Now that you have completed your exam, it's time to figure out your score. On the actual exam, your essay will be scored across four different domains by two unique graders, on a scale from 1–6. The scores from each domain and each grader will then be added together for a final domain score. All domain final scores are then averaged together to give you your final ACT score, which will range from 2 to 12.

Because this is a practice exam, we have provided you with tools to evaluate and score your own writing. This should help you approximate where you stand according to the ACT's grading standards. The elements you should be considering when deciding your score areas are categorized as follows:

Ideas and Analysis: Did you build an argument that engages with the multiple perspectives given, reflecting precision in thought and purpose? Did you take a clear position on the issue while establishing insightful analysis of the issue and its perspectives?

Development and Support: Did you use sound reasoning and illustration to convey fully developed ideas and support for your perspective? Does your reasoning enhance your analysis of the issue and the perspectives while strengthening your own perspective?

Organization: Does the structure of your essay make sense? Is it logical, does it communicate a purpose, and does it increase the effectiveness of your argument? Is it in paragraphs made up of complete sentences? Do the transitions between paragraphs strengthen the relationships among ideas?

Language Use: Did you write in Standard English? Did you use a variety of words, including more difficult vocabulary? Was your grammar and syntax correct; e.g., do your subjects agree with your verbs, and did you use proper punctuation?

Essay Scoring Rubric

As with most standardized essay exams, the ACT test makers use a rubric to score your writing. Scoring is done by two different raters on a holistic basis, meaning they take the entire essay into account when considering your scores within each band of the rubric. Because the criteria by which your essay is graded are set in stone by the rubric, you can also evaluate your own writing using the same rubric. Familiarizing yourself with the scoring rubric will give you a better sense of what raters must consider when evaluating your writing. If you know what they look for when assigning the highest score, then there's a better chance that you can replicate those expectations in your own essay.

THE ACT® WRITING TEST SCORING RUBRIC

	Ideas and Analysis	Development and Support	Organization	Language Use
Score 6: **Responses at this scorepoint demonstrate effective skill in writing an argumentative essay.**	The writer generates an argument that critically engages with multiple perspectives on the given issue. The argument's thesis reflects nuance and precision in thought and purpose. The argument establishes and employs an insightful context for analysis of the issue and its perspectives. The analysis examines implications, complexities and tensions, and/or underlying values and assumptions.	Development of ideas and support for claims deepen insight and broaden context. An integrated line of skillful reasoning and illustration effectively conveys the significance of the argument. Qualifications and complications enrich and bolster ideas and analysis.	The response exhibits a skillful organizational strategy. The response is unified by a controlling idea or purpose, and a logical progression of ideas increases the effectiveness of the writer's argument. Transitions between and within paragraphs strengthen the relationships among ideas.	The use of language enhances the argument. Word choice is skillful and precise. Sentence structures are consistently varied and clear. Stylistic and register choices, including voice and tone, are strategic and effective. While a few minor errors in grammar, usage, and mechanics may be present, they do not impede understanding.
Score 5: **Responses at this scorepoint demonstrate well-developed skill in writing an argumentative essay.**	The writer generates an argument that productively engages with multiple perspectives on the given issue. The argument's thesis reflects precision in thought and purpose. The argument establishes and employs a thoughtful context for analysis of the issue and its perspectives. The analysis addresses implications, complexities and tensions, and/or underlying values and assumptions.	Development of ideas and support for claims deepen understanding. A mostly integrated line of purposeful reasoning and illustration capably conveys the significance of the argument. Qualifications and complications enrich ideas and analysis.	The response exhibits a productive organizational strategy. The response is mostly unified by a controlling idea or purpose, and a logical sequencing of ideas contributes to the effectiveness of the argument. Transitions between and within paragraphs consistently clarify the relationships among ideas.	The use of language works in service of the argument. Word choice is precise. Sentence structures are clear and varied often. Stylistic and register choices, including voice and tone, are purposeful and productive. While minor errors in grammar, usage, and mechanics may be present, they do not impede understanding.

THE ACT® WRITING TEST SCORING RUBRIC

	Ideas and Analysis	Development and Support	Organization	Language Use
Score 4: **Responses at this scorepoint demonstrate adequate skill in writing an argumentative essay.**	The writer generates an argument that engages with multiple perspectives on the given issue. The argument's thesis reflects clarity in thought and purpose. The argument establishes and employs a relevant context for analysis of the issue and its perspectives. The analysis recognizes implications, complexities and tensions, and/or underlying values and assumptions.	Development of ideas and support for claims clarify meaning and purpose. Lines of clear reasoning and illustration adequately convey the significance of the argument. Qualifications and complications extend ideas and analysis.	The response exhibits a clear organizational strategy. The overall shape of the response reflects an emergent controlling idea or purpose. Ideas are logically grouped and sequenced. Transitions between and within paragraphs clarify the relationships among ideas.	The use of language conveys the argument with clarity. Word choice is adequate and sometimes precise. Sentence structures are clear and demonstrate some variety. Stylistic and register choices, including voice and tone, are appropriate for the rhetorical purpose. While errors in grammar, usage, and mechanics are present, they rarely impede understanding.
Score 3: **Responses at this scorepoint demonstrate some developing skill in writing an argumentative essay.**	The writer generates an argument that responds to multiple perspectives on the given issue. The argument's thesis reflects some clarity in thought and purpose. The argument establishes a limited or tangential context for analysis of the issue and its perspectives. Analysis is simplistic or somewhat unclear.	Development of ideas and support for claims are mostly relevant but are overly general or simplistic. Reasoning and illustration largely clarify the argument but may be somewhat repetitious or imprecise.	The response exhibits a basic organizational structure. The response largely coheres, with most ideas logically grouped. Transitions between and within paragraphs sometimes clarify the relationships among ideas.	The use of language is basic and only somewhat clear. Word choice is general and occasionally imprecise. Sentence structures are usually clear but show little variety. Stylistic and register choices, including voice and tone, are not always appropriate for the rhetorical purpose. Distracting errors in grammar, usage, and mechanics may be present, but they generally do not impede understanding.

THE ACT® WRITING TEST SCORING RUBRIC

	Ideas and Analysis	Development and Support	Organization	Language Use
Score 2: **Responses at this scorepoint demonstrate weak or inconsistent skill in writing an argumentative essay.**	The writer generates an argument that weakly responds to multiple perspectives on the given issue. The argument's thesis, if evident, reflects little clarity in thought and purpose. Attempts at analysis are incomplete, largely irrelevant, or consist primarily of restatement of the issue and its perspectives.	Development of ideas and support for claims are weak, confused, or disjointed. Reasoning and illustration are inadequate, illogical, or circular, and fail to fully clarify the argument.	The response exhibits a rudimentary organizational structure. Grouping of ideas is inconsistent and often unclear. Transitions between and within paragraphs are misleading or poorly formed.	The use of language is inconsistent and often unclear. Word choice is rudimentary and frequently imprecise. Sentence structures are sometimes unclear. Stylistic and register choices, including voice and tone, are inconsistent and are not always appropriate for the rhetorical purpose. Distracting errors in grammar, usage, and mechanics are present, and they sometimes impede understanding.
Score 1: **Responses at this scorepoint demonstrate little or no skill in writing an argumentative essay.**	The writer fails to generate an argument that responds intelligibly to the task. The writer's intentions are difficult to discern. Attempts at analysis are unclear or irrelevant.	Ideas lack development, and claims lack support. Reasoning and illustration are unclear, incoherent, or largely absent.	The response does not exhibit an organizational structure. There is little grouping of ideas. When present, transitional devices fail to connect ideas.	The use of language fails to demonstrate skill in responding to the task. Word choice is imprecise and often difficult to comprehend. Sentence structures are often unclear. Stylistic and register choices are difficult to identify. Errors in grammar, usage, and mechanics are pervasive and often impede understanding.

As you read through the rubric, you'll notice that the language describing each score tends to repeat itself but change degree. For instance, a score of 6 in organization describes a "skillful organizational strategy," while the same skill is described as a "clear organizational strategy" at the score 4 level and a "rudimentary organizational structure" at the score 2 level. At the level 1 score, the rubric describes an essay that does not have an organizational strategy at all.

The takeaway is that each of these scoring bands describes a spectrum of capability. In other words, there is not so much a wrong way to do things and a right way to do things so much as a set of skills to display and a spectrum upon which those skills are evaluated. If you succeed in displaying each of those four specific skills as effectively as you're able throughout the course of your essay, you can rest assured that a higher score will be the result. Note also that some parts of the rubric aren't as strict as you might expect. For instance, even at the level 6 scoring band, the description in Language Use suggests that you won't be marked down for a few minor spelling errors or grammar issues as long as they don't hinder your ability to communicate with your reader. In other words, the test isn't looking for perfection at the highest level, only exceptionally effective written communication.

While scoring your own diagnostic essay, start by considering each of the four scoring bands individually. Using reflection questions can be a good way to do this since you can first consider your essay holistically (like your graders will) and then compare it to the descriptions from the rubric after. Here is a table of questions you might want to consider when evaluating each scoring band.

Self-Reflection Questions for Essay Self Scoring

Ideas and Analysis

- Did you express your own argument on the topic clearly and with specific details for support?

- Did you include a thesis statement that expresses your argument concisely, specifically, and argumentatively?

- Did you address other perspectives in your writing and, if so, how many?

- Did you provide your reader with enough context to understand your argument?

- How effectively did you explore any underlying implications, complexities, or tensions that exist within the issue your essay was supposed to evaluate?

- Did you explore the issue deeply or were you vague and more non-specific?

- Did you bring up unique ideas throughout your writing or did you tend to repeat the same ideas over and over?

Development and Support

- How clearly and effectively did you communicate details and examples to support your claims?

- Did you develop responses and counterclaims to other perspectives, or did you simply mention them?

- Is your purpose as author clear throughout the entire essay?

- Do the details and examples you provide deepen your reader's understanding or distract from your main point?

- Did you illustrate the reasoning that supports your argument(s)?

- Did you engage in analysis by looking at the issue from multiple angles, or did you merely summarize your thoughts?

- Did you express ideas in your own words rather than copying from the given prompt?

Organization

- Did you choose a strategy for how to organize your essay and stick to it? If so, is that organizational pattern clear to the reader?

- Do you have a "connective thread" throughout your essay that unifies the ideas you discuss?

- Do you follow a progressive, linear train of thought that develops throughout the essay?

- How effectively did you use transitions, topic sentences, thesis statements, and other organizational tools to guide your reader?

- Did you divide up your thoughts by paragraph?

- Did you have an introduction and a conclusion?

- Is there a clear progression in your paragraphs so that each increases the effectiveness of your essay?

- Does your essay stay "on task" or did you tend to go on tangents and jump around?

Language Use

- How rich and varied is your word choice? Do you use a wide range of vocabulary words, or do you tend to repeat the same terms and phrases?

- How precisely did you use vocabulary, syntax, and sentence structure to express your ideas skillfully?

- Did you use effective and varied sentence structure?

- Do the stylistic choices you made, such as those regarding tone and voice, effectively convey your argument?

- How frequently did you make grammatical errors, and how often did they get in the way of a reader understanding what you meant?

Once you have taken the time to consider each of these questions, it should be a lot easier to recognize where you fall on the rubric for each of these skills. Give yourself a 0 only if you absolutely did not complete the assignment: you left it blank, you wrote about something completely unrelated to the question, or you just complained about the assignment. Give yourself a 6 only if you really think your essay met or exceeded every criterion listed in the rubric. For everything in between, interpret the rubric based on the self-reflection you engaged in. Try to give yourself a fair and honest evaluation. If you're having trouble deciding, you might ask a trusted friend or mentor to help you evaluate.

Sample Essays

While interpreting a rubric is the most effective way to engage in scoring, it can also be helpful to measure your own writing against samples. These samples may not look exactly like every essay for the score levels they represent, but most essays that score at these levels will exhibit traits similar to the samples given. Figure out how close or far from either model you might be when judging your own essay.

Sample Essay: Score 1

Ideas and Analysis	Score = 1
Development and Support	Score = 1
Organization	Score = 1
Language Use and Conventions	Score = 1

The question is complicated because there are some good reasons and some bad reasons to ban football, so it's compleks. I think my opinion is somewhere in the middle of the other opinions. Because it's simply too dangerous a sport to play, and people's lives should not be put at risk for a game. As such, we can't just ban every activity that contains some level of risk. Many people do football. I have done football: mostly in middle school. I was on a team called the Sheridan Sharks. Football taught me a lot disipline and also working hard. I am glad I plaid football because it made me learn a lot of new things. So it's complicated because, there are some good reasons and bad reasons. And it seems like the answer is in the middle. I think that. Also, don't forget that people have doctors who can tell them if its a problem or not so they can talk to their doctors and decide.

Scoring Explanation

Ideas and Analysis: Score = 1

The writer of this essay attempts to address the question provided by saying that their opinion is "somewhere in the middle," but they do not clarify exactly what their viewpoint is. It's difficult to figure out what, exactly, the writer wanted to communicate, and many sentences are lifted word for word from the perspectives given in the essay prompt, meaning they don't reflect the writer's own thoughts in their own words. While there is an attempt to engage in analysis, such as by reflecting on their own experiences playing football, the writer fails to connect those attempts to a clear argument for the reader. Additionally, little to no discussion takes place of competing perspectives on the issue.

Development and Support: Score = 1

There is almost enough support when the writer talks about what they learned from football to push this score to a 2. However, since they don't connect that analysis to developing a specific argument, it comes off as disconnected or irrelevant. The length of the essay also shows very little development of ideas and does not give the writer much opportunity to build up proper support for the limited claims they do make.

Organization: Score = 1

There is little attempt to organize thoughts in this brief essay. The writer makes a claim in the first sentence, but it's weak and non-specific. Additionally, the only way they address the competing perspectives is by restating one perspective from the prompt. The sentence about doctors at the end is disconnected from the other thoughts and not integrated well into the existing writing and seems to end the paragraph on a vague tangent. There is no clear conclusion to the essay.

Language Use and Conventions: Score = 1

While the basic grammar of the essay is sound, many of the errors made hinder understanding. There are a few spelling errors, some of which are easier to interpret (*compleks*, *disipline*) than others (*plaid*). There are also choices in diction that do not serve the relationship between ideas, such as the choice to use "As such" when transitioning to a point that is unrelated to the one directly before. The sentence structure lacks variation, using lots of short sentences that could be made more complex by adding relevant details. Sentence fragments are also present. Words are occasionally missing, as is seen with the missing preposition *of* in the statement "Football taught me a lot disipline." Another issue is improper use of punctuation marks, such as misplaced commas and a needless colon.

Sample Essay: Score 6

Ideas and Analysis	Score = 6
Development and Support	Score = 6
Organization	Score = 6
Language Use and Conventions	Score = 6

On and off the athletic fields of America, the debate regarding the dangers of full-contact sports such as football rages on. Professional players, both active and retired, are more vocal about the physical perils and toll the game takes on players during their comparatively brief careers. Concerned parents across the country are thinking twice before allowing their children to play football, for fear of serious injury. Media outlets large and small are giving increased attention to the issue, asking questions to help shape the national debate: Is football too dangerous as played? And, as such, should it be banned? Once posed, we have an obligation to answer these questions. In short, football is inexorably woven into the fabric of American culture, and attempting to ban the game would be an unfair and rash decision.

It can be argued that football is now our primary national pastime, as evidenced by massive TV ratings and revenue generated by the game. Attempting to strip it from our collective hands would only demonstrate our inability to take a measured, careful approach to this issue. A blind, blanket ban on anything deemed somewhat dangerous, including football, stands in opposition to the tenets of a free and democratic society.

Yes, football is a dangerous sport. Injuries both major and minor, from sprains and concussions, to broken bones and life-altering catastrophic trauma, occur at all levels of the game—from the NFL down to pee-wee football and everything in between. We should adopt a careful, phased approach to address this issue. Initially, there should be a collective acknowledgement of the sport's inherent dangers and a strict adherence to all accepted and available safety precautions. The game should simply not be played without the use of appropriate safety equipment. A thorough information campaign should be deployed, so anyone playing the game or interested in playing, could be made aware of the possible risks. Furthermore, I think a significant portion of the enormous profits generated by football at the professional and college levels should be invested into the exploration and development of enhanced safety equipment for players. We have come far from the days of leather helmets, but there is always room for improvement.

Does the game itself need to change? This question needs to stay at the forefront of our national discussion, and a serious review and exploration of ways to make the game safer needs to occur—even if this entails an alteration of the game's core structure in some way. Perhaps if there's a way to reduce the bone-crunching tackles and brutal pile-ups that occur in defense of a team's end zone, they should be considered and tested.

Anyone who defends football can no longer do so in ignorance. The tragic suicide of former NFL player Junior Seau brought media attention to chronic traumatic encephalopathy (CTE), a disease that occurs from repeated head trauma, which has affected numerous NFL players. We're all aware of the risks. Mature and realistic adults should accept the notion that football, like many facets of modern life, contains risks, and it is our responsibility to address them and do our best to minimize these risks whenever possible.

Take airplane flying for example. It is a mode of transportation with inherent risk, including loss of life, but that doesn't mean we should abandon it altogether. We approach it responsibly and carefully, we follow strict, evolving safety protocols, and we always look for ways to make flying even safer, even if it comes at a cost—whether it be money, time, or convenience. We should approach the sport of football in much the same way.

Informed compromise is often the best approach to any debate, and we cannot let blind devotion to tradition keep us from making progress. Restructuring of football will not only make the game safer but it may also make it more enjoyable and accessible to everyone. We shouldn't ban the sport altogether, but its high time to innovate new ways to make the game safer.

Scoring Explanation

Ideas and Analysis: Score = 6

The writer provides a clear thesis statement and addresses the concerns of other perspectives. This argument goes on to offer considerable insight and analysis regarding the dangers of football and how the debate regarding the safety and future of the game should be handled. The writer calls for a "measured, careful approach" to address the issue, but clearly has considered both sides of the argument—those that defend the sport (arguably "our primary national pastime") and those who demand it to change or be banned ("a serious review and exploration of ways to make the game safer needs to occur")—resulting in a nuanced, effective essay that thoughtfully addresses the essay task.

Development and Support: Score = 6

The essay acknowledges cogent points on both sides of the football debate (football is dangerous but is "inexorably woven into the fabric of American culture"), develops a clear perspective on the topic (a stricter adherence to all safety protocols and a review of the game, with an eye towards making it safer), and makes a compelling argument for a considered yet aggressive march forward to make football safer. Support is provided to lend credence to the writer's argument, and knowledge of the field of football-related injuries (chronic traumatic encephalopathy) is mentioned. The in-depth examination of both sides and skillful development and support of the writer's viewpoint leads to an essay that successfully tackles the task at hand.

Organization: Score = 6

This written response displays a strong command of effective essay structure and organization. It begins with a compelling call for action that asserts the seriousness of the topic, but wisely offers fair coverage of both sides of the debate in a clear, streamlined fashion. The writer's point-of-view on the topic is evident, and a sufficient level of support is provided. The writer uses paragraphs for specific purposes, choosing to weave in examples of other dangerous activities (flying) that aren't banned, but rather are carefully regulated, to help assert their concluding plea for a "careful, phased approach" and "informed compromise" to make the sport of football safer for everyone involved.

Language Use and Conventions: Score = 6

The writer displays a firm command of standard English language use and conventions. Sentences are well constructed and grammatically sound. The writer uses varied syntax, transitions, and word choice throughout. The resulting essay is both compelling and effective and capably addresses the task provided. Note that there are a few minor grammar errors throughout, such as misplaced commas, but since these do not hinder the writer's communication, they do not count against them.

Determining Your Final Score

Once you've engaged in self-reflection, evaluated your essay against the rubric, and compared it to the benchmark samples given, it's time to assign yourself a score. To self-score your essay, assign yourself a 1–6 for each domain based on the rubric. Next, double each score to represent the two unique graders' scores. Lastly, find the average by adding all four scores together and dividing by 4. Record the values on the scoring chart at the end of this section. While this number is no guarantee of your ACT score, it can help you determine your strengths and weaknesses and predict where your skills are to target improvement before exam day.

SCORING CHARTS

Mark missed questions and calculate your total for each question category and each test as a whole. Then convert your individual test scores to scaled scores and calculate your composite score.

ENGLISH		
Question Types	**Question Numbers**	**Score**
Conventions of Standard English (CSE)	1, 4, 5, 7, 8, 9, 11, 17, 18, 19, 21, 22, 23, 26, 28, 32, 33, 34, 38, 41, 46, 47, 49, 50, 52, 56, 58, 61, 62, 63, 64, 65, 66, 67, 68, 69, 70, 71	_____ /38
Production of Writing (POW)	3, 10, 12, 13, 14, 15, 20, 27, 29, 30, 35, 39, 40, 42, 43, 44, 45, 53, 54, 57, 59, 60, 72, 73, 74, 75	_____ /26
Knowledge of Language (KLA)	2, 6, 16, 24, 25, 31, 36, 37, 48, 51, 55	_____ /11
		Raw Score: _____ /75

MATHEMATICS		
Question Types	**Question Numbers**	**Score**
Integrating Essential Skills (IES)	1, 3, 4, 5, 6, 7, 11, 12, 13, 14, 16, 19, 21, 22, 24, 26, 29, 31, 32, 33, 34, 41, 46, 48, 53, 57	_____ /26
Preparing for Higher Math (PHM)*		_____ /34
Number and Quantity	2, 10, 15, 36	_____ /4
Algebra	20, 23, 28, 43, 44, 45, 49, 60	_____ /8
Functions	8, 25, 37, 38, 39, 54, 56, 59	_____ /8
Geometry	9, 17, 18, 27, 30, 40, 47, 50, 58	_____ /9
Statistics and Probability	35, 42, 51, 52, 55	_____ /5
Modeling**	1, 5, 6, 11, 18, 20, 22, 25, 27, 29, 31, 35, 37, 39, 42, 45, 47, 49, 50, 51, 53, 57, 58	_____ /23**
		Raw Score: _____ /60

*Combine all subcategories of PHM questions for this score and add to your IES total to find your Raw Score.

**Modeling overlaps other scoring categories and is not added to your raw score.

READING

Question Types	Question Numbers	Score
Key Ideas and Details (KID)	1, 2, 4, 5, 7, 8, 9, 10, 11, 12, 13, 14, 15, 16, 19, 21, 24, 25, 28, 29, 30, 31, 33, 34, 37	_____/25
Craft and Structure (CS)	3, 6, 17, 18, 20, 22, 23, 26, 27, 32, 35, 36	_____/12
Integration of Knowledge and Ideas (IKI)	38, 39, 40	_____/3
		Raw Score: _____ **/40**

SCIENCE

Question Types	Question Numbers	Score
Interpretation of Data (IOD)	1, 2, 6, 7, 9, 10, 11, 12, 13, 16, 18, 19, 20, 21, 22, 23, 24, 26, 38, 39	_____/20
Scientific Investigation (SIN)	3, 4, 5, 14, 17, 25, 35, 36, 37	_____/9
Evaluation of Models, Inferences, and Experimental Results (EMI)	8, 15, 27, 28, 29, 30, 31, 32, 33, 34, 40	_____/11
		Raw Score: _____ **/40**

WRITING

Domain	Rubric Score	Domain Score*
Ideas and Analysis	_____/6	
Development and Support	_____/6	
Organization	_____/6	
Language Use	_____/6	
	Writing Score**:_____ /12	

*Multiply Rubric Score by 2

**Sum Domain Scores and divide by 4; round to nearest whole number

Section	Raw Score	Scaled Score*
English	_____/75	
Mathematics	_____/60	
Reading	_____/40	
Science	_____/40	
	Composite Score**: _____	

*See p. 154 for English Score Conversion, p. 287 for Math Score Conversion, p. 529 for Reading Score Conversion, p. 636 for Science Score Conversion.

**Sum Scaled Scores and divide by 4; round to nearest whole number.

CHAPTER

Using Your Diagnostic Test Results

USING YOUR DIAGNOSTIC TEST RESULTS

OVERVIEW

Reflecting on Your Diagnostic Test Experience

Forming a Study Plan

General Study Strategies

Mindsets to Improve Performance

ACT® Performance Tasks and Targets

Summing It Up

In the last chapter, you took a diagnostic test to establish a baseline measurement of your preparedness for the ACT. The purpose of a diagnostic test is exactly what it sounds like—it diagnoses your strengths and weaknesses so you can make informed decisions about how you want to study going forward. In this chapter, we'll help you reflect on your performance in the diagnostic test so you can make the most of your study time while prepping for the ACT. We'll offer reflection questions to help you analyze your diagnostic test scores, discuss how to create a study plan as well as some tips to make the most of your studying, and talk about overall test strategies and mindsets that can help you optimize your performance.

REFLECTING ON YOUR DIAGNOSTIC TEST EXPERIENCE

The ACT is not just about what you know. It's also about how well you apply what you know. The test places constraints on you, the test taker, and your responses to those constraints can impact your score, for better or worse. Familiarizing yourself with the test format by taking a diagnostic test is one of the first steps towards internalizing those constraints and learning how to respond to them in ways that positively impact your score. The experience of taking a diagnostic test like the one we included in Chapter 2 provides you useful feedback that can help shape your ACT prep journey. Before we break down how to make a study plan based on your performance in individual test sections, take a moment to reflect on your overall experience during your diagnostic test.

DIAGNOSTIC TEST REFLECTION: OVERALL

Diagnostic Test Composite Score: _____

Reflection Question	Notes
What went well for you during the diagnostic test, and which skills were easiest for you to use?	
What did you struggle with during the diagnostic test, or which skills were harder for you to use?	
After your experience, what are some things you might like to keep in mind as you study?	
What are some aspects of approaching the ACT for which you are most hoping to build strategies?	
What do you think are the 1–2 things you do best as a test taker?	
What 1–2 improvements could you make as a test taker that would help you most?	
Where did you run out of time?	
Where did you end up with extra time?	
Are there any parts of the different sections that took you longer? Any parts that you know you did quickly?	
Did you answer all the questions? If not, how many did you leave blank?	

Now that you've reflected on your prior experience, think about your ACT goals. For many test takers, the goal may simply be to get the best score possible in every section. However, some might prioritize improving their score in one subject that matters more for their college goals than another. Or, perhaps, there might be a minimum score a test taker is hoping to achieve to stand out to their school of choice. Maybe they've taken the ACT once before and simply want to improve upon a prior section score. No matter what goals you have, it's important to keep them in mind as you study so that you can make decisions and choose strategies that will help you achieve them.

FORMING A STUDY PLAN

Just as people will have different scoring goals, test takers will have different goals for how they spend their study time. For example, if you are a math whiz who aces every algebra II test you take but you struggle a lot with reading comprehension, you may be planning to devote significantly more of your time to studying for the Reading and Science sections, which both rely heavily on reading comprehension skills. Different test takers also have differing amounts of time to allot to studying for the ACT. If you have an hour a day for several months to devote to preparation, you'll probably approach things differently than someone who is trying to study as comprehensively as they can in the two weeks leading up to their registered test date.

Using Data to Inform Your Goals

Recent ACT data can help guide some of the basic decisions you need to make regarding your target score and study time. Let's start with average scores. As you'll see in the following table, the average ACT composite score is 20.3 and each of the average section scores falls within one point of that score.

AVERAGE ACT SCORES (2020–2022)	
English	19.5
Math	19.9
Reading	20.9
Science	20.3
Composite	**20.3**

Source: Official ACT data, https://www.act.org/content/dam/act/unsecured/documents/MultipleChoiceStemComposite.pdf

While the ACT doesn't track average scores for the optional Writing test as closely, the average is close to 6 (out of 12). These average scores reflect all who take the ACT. However, they may be lower (or higher) than the typical minimum score for a given school. It's always worth investigating admissions materials for the colleges you're considering to determine what a minimum score goal should be for you.

Another piece of data that can help you determine your personal target involves ACT score percentiles. Consider the chart that follows.

ACT SCORE PERCENTILES (2020–2022)	
Composite Score	**Percentile**
30+	90th percentile and higher
25+	75th percentile and higher
20+	50th percentile and higher

Source: Official ACT data, https://www.act.org/content/dam/act/unsecured/documents/MultipleChoiceStemComposite.pdf

This means that a test taker who scores a 30 can assume that they performed better than 90% of test takers. If you are applying to highly competitive schools where you need to stand out, then you can assume that 30 is the minimum composite score you'd want to achieve. Those applying to slightly less competitive schools might consider aiming for 25 or higher, as that will still ensure they outperform 75% or more of test takers.

Take a moment to ask yourself the following questions:

- What are my score goals? Is there a minimum score I want to achieve?
- Given what I know about average scores and percentiles, are my score goals realistic and appropriate for the types of schools to which I am applying?
- Are my score goals even across test subjects, or am I aiming to perform better on a particular section (or sections) of the ACT?
- How can I best divide my study time to address my score goals?

Once you've considered these questions, you're ready to start analyzing your diagnostic test scores in service of creating a personalized study plan.

Analyzing Your Diagnostic Test Scores

At the beginning of this chapter, we asked you to reflect on your diagnostic test as a whole. Now that you've done so and learned a bit about ACT average scores and percentiles, it's time to think about your performance on each of the individual sections of your diagnostic test. Jot down some thoughts in the following chart or take notes independently to help you reflect.

MY DIAGNOSTIC TEST SCORES

Minimum Composite Score Goal: _____

Test	Scaled Score	Strengths	Opportunities
English			
Math			
Reading			
Science			
Composite			
Writing (optional)			

If you decided to take the ACT tomorrow without any further preparation, and you did things the exact same way, you would likely score the same as how you performed on the diagnostic test. Since you are working with this book, you likely have some amount of time to prepare for the ACT, which means you have ample opportunity to improve upon that score. Your task is, therefore, to mentally divide the amount of preparation time you have according to your study priorities. Only you can determine what the best way to do this might be. However, your diagnostic test offers helpful clues about how to do this most effectively. Let's look at the box you completed before using a sample test taker's diagnostic test scores as a guide.

SAMPLE DIAGNOSTIC TEST SCORES

Minimum Composite Score Goal: 25

Test	Score	Strengths	Opportunities
English	23	Finished with extra time, did well on grammar questions	Got confused on questions that asked about purpose and writing skills instead of grammar Didn't revisit questions with remaining time
Math	21	Geometry questions were all correct Did fine with pre-algebra questions	Algebra and Functions were lowest scores Just guessed on later questions Didn't have time to review anything
Reading	24	Did very well on Social Science and Humanities passages	Took a long time with Literary Narrative passage and didn't score that well, read slowly, ran out of time on the last passage (Natural Sciences)
Science	18	Did well with Scientific Investigation questions	Struggled with interpreting graphs and charts Ran out of time on section with two passages remaining
Composite	**22**	**Reading comprehension in general, not spending too long per question**	**Eliminating wrong answers, time management when there is a lot to read, guessing effectively**
Writing (optional)	6	I developed a clear argument of my own with a thesis statement	Not enough pre-planning, didn't address perspectives enough, ran out of time to edit my essay

Our example test taker achieved a composite score of 22 on their diagnostic test, but they are hoping to achieve a minimum score of 25. The test taker's goal now is to use this information to plan their study time.

Let's start by looking at the section in which they performed best: Reading. It might seem like this test taker doesn't need to spend any time studying for the Reading test since their score in that section is already close to their goal. However, that high score means that Reading is one of their strongest subjects, so it might be an easy place for them to pick up extra points to pad the other scores. In this case, the test taker should consider what space for improvement exists in that subject: they said that time management and addressing the Literary Narrative passage were the two places they struggled most during the Reading test. As such, their best bet would be to review reading strategies in Chapter 18 and adapt their approach to the section accordingly. They may not spend as much time studying reading skills (Chapter 17) as they might for, say, science skills (Chapter 20), but they're going to devote at least some study time to beefing up their reading techniques so they can improve their score.

Next, the test taker is going to consider the section in which they had the lowest performance. In this case, that was Science. Right away, we can assume that they will want to spend a bit more time studying science skills since this is where they have the greatest room for improvement. Looking at their reflections, they note that dealing with charts and graphs was more confusing for them than handling questions that required reading skills, so when they are working through the part of the book that covers the Science section (Part V), they should devote extra time to practicing interpreting charts and graphs. They should also be extra mindful of strategies in Chapter 21 that might help them overcome those weak spots, such as time management techniques to help them complete the section quickly.

The test taker is going to apply this same analytical process to the remaining sections as well as their composite score. As they do, they should consider how much space for improvement exists and how they can target the strategies that will help them most. For instance, this test taker noted that during the English test, they excelled at questions that tested grammar and the conventions of standard English but struggled with those that required them to analyze writing skills and the purpose of a given passage. Consequently, they

know that any time they spend studying for the English test should focus most of their time on the types of questions that address writing and purpose (Chapter 5). Depending on how well they did with grammar questions, they might be able to review grammar concepts (Chapter 6) and net some additional points. At the same time, they can develop some English strategies (Chapter 7). In doing so, they may be able to work through grammar questions faster and find more time for the purpose and style questions.

For Mathematics, this test taker knows that they need to focus their time on Algebra and Functions questions. They should also review content for the other higher-math questions, with the exception of Geometry (Chapter 13), which they may only need to skim as review. Because they scored a 21, they answered only about half of the questions correctly. That leaves them some big opportunities for higher-math question categories. Apart from reviewing math topics, some work with math strategies (Chapter 15) might lead to better guessing or better time management to allow time to review and check guesses.

Remember, the Writing test is optional, so you only need to include it in your study time if you are planning to take it. The best way to do so involves writing practice essays and engaging in self-scoring, which we covered extensively following the writing exam in Chapter 2. You'll also find tips and strategies for the optional Writing test as well as multiple practice prompts in Chapter 23. For the purposes of our sample test taker, they decided they are going to allot themselves a small portion of their total study time for reviewing writing skills and doing some practice essays to net at least a couple of points for the section.

Create an Informed Study Schedule

Now that our sample test taker has analyzed their diagnostic test results, they are ready to create a study plan. Let's say our sample test taker has an hour a day after school for 5 weeks to study for their exam. At the end of the 5 weeks, they plan to take their practice test on a Saturday to see how they improved, leaving them a week before their official exam for any last-minute review based on the results of their practice test. This means the test taker has 25 total hours to devote to studying (not including the practice test they'll take towards the end) before their practice test and 5 more for post-practice test review. Accordingly, they might plan their time as follows:

8 Hours – Science

6 Hours – Math

4 Hours – English

3 Hours – Writing

3 Hours – Reading

1 Hour – Pre-practice test review

5 Hours – Post-practice test review

Of course, the actual breakdown depends on the individual test taker. Moreover, they can approach this plan flexibly and adjust as they go along; for instance, if the test taker feels like they've reviewed Science pretty thoroughly after seven hours of study and decides to spend a spare hour on English instead, that would still be perfectly suitable for their overarching goals. To be even more organized, they may break down their study plan by day, as in the following chart.

Of course, the test tasker could allot the hours however makes sense for them. Not everyone will be able to plan their studying in this orderly of a fashion. Some test takers will also benefit from focusing on more than

one subject in a given study session, so it doesn't always have to be divided this neatly. Nonetheless, creating a specific study calendar helps remind you that organized studying correlates with a better chance of meeting your score goals. Here, the test taker has planned in such a way as to include variety (so they don't get too bored with one subject) and ample chances to review skills they practiced earlier. By the time they take their practice test at the end of their studying, they will be thoroughly prepared and will almost undoubtedly improve their score.

Take a moment to ask yourself the following questions. Then, come up with a study plan that works for you and your goals.

- How much total time can I commit to studying for the ACT?

- How do I want to divide that study time, based on my diagnostic performance?

- What are some of the most important skills I want to work on overall?

- What are some of the most important skills I want to work on for each individual test within the exam?

- When would it be most useful for me to take a practice test, given my study style?

Once you have a study plan in place, you are ready to consider how to make the most of your study time.

SAMPLE TEST TAKER'S ACT STUDY PLAN					
	Monday	**Tuesday**	**Wednesday**	**Thursday**	**Friday**
Week 1	Science	Math	Science	English	Reading
Week 2	Science	English	Science	Math	Writing
Week 3	Science	Math	Reading	Writing	Math
Week 4	Science	English	Science	Math	Writing
Week 5	Science	Math	English	Reading	Review
Week 6	Review concepts missed on the practice test taken over the weekend				

FYI

You don't have to wait to take the practice test included in this book until the end of your study time if you think it would be more beneficial to you to take it at a midpoint to check your progress. It's up to you! Remember, there are additional practice tests available through our ACT course at **www.petersons.com/testprep/act/** for those who want extra review.

Setting an Environment

How and where you prep for the ACT matters. Creating optimal study conditions will help keep you focused and motivated. How you do so is largely dictated by what has worked for you in the past as well as your current life and schedule. The earlier you start preparing for the ACT, the more likely you are to have wiggle room in your study schedule and to create a routine and environment for study that suits your needs.

When you're designing your perfect study environment, keep the following in mind.

- **Keep distractions to a minimum.** Your study space should be free of anything that will distract you from the task at hand. This means that cell phones, tablets, TVs, and other items that make it difficult to focus should be kept elsewhere. Most people should avoid listening to music with lyrics as they can make it hard to focus.

- **Get comfortable—but not too comfortable.** Your study space should be comfortable, so you can relax and focus on practice and review without fidgeting, but it shouldn't be so comfortable that you find yourself napping whenever you sit down to study. A good chair and uncluttered desk are often a better choice than lying down in bed.

- **Find a location that works for you.** Do you prepare better alone in your bedroom or in a bustling coffee shop or library? This choice is totally up to you and should be based on what has worked for you in the past. A bit of background noise can be helpful to some and distracting to

others, so if you're not sure what works best for you, then experiment.

- **Adjust your lighting.** Make sure your study space has the perfect level of sound that will help you stay focused and alert. Then, make sure your study environment contains the right level of light to keep you engaged. Whatever lighting matches your preferences is fine—just be sure not to study in a dark place that will make you sleepy.

- **Decide if you'd rather prep alone or in a group.** Studying alone may help you stay focused, but if you're struggling in a certain area, then working with others whose strengths and weaknesses complement each other may be a great way to help you improve. Studying in a group may be distracting for some while others find it difficult to avoid distractions when studying alone and need others to keep them on task. Decide for yourself which individual approach (or combination of both) works for you.

- **Find your ideal time of day.** The time of day during which you study best is an important part of your study environment. Do you work best first thing in the morning, or are you a nighttime study owl? Can you focus right after school, or do you need a bit of downtime before studying in the early evening? If possible, schedule your study sessions at the time of day that matches what naturally works best for you.

- **Fuel up.** Don't try to study on an empty tank. Make sure to approach each study session well rested, energized, and fueled. Keep in mind that nutritious foods tend to keep your energy levels higher for longer while things like sugary snacks, sodas, and caffeine tend to create spikes in energy levels that will eventually send you crashing back down.

- **Gather your tools.** Make sure you have all of your most effective study tools at hand in your workspace, including this book, paper and pens/pencils, a calculator, a highlighter, and a watch or clock if you're taking a timed practice test. The last thing you want to do every time you sit down to study is waste time searching for your study tools. Also, staying organized will help keep you focused, serious, and motivated.

- **Pay attention to your mental environment.** Just as important as having the perfect physical study environment is having the right mindset during each study session. Try to leave external worries, stressors, or anxieties outside of your ACT prep since they will only drain your energy and focus. A great way to do this is to take a few minutes before each study session to relax, breathe, and clear your mind and thoughts. Sometimes, just a minute or two is enough and can make a big difference. When your mind is clear and free from distractions, you'll be much more likely to devote yourself to effective ACT test preparation. Remember also that you can schedule rest days into your study calendar to give your brain time to recharge as necessary.

GENERAL STUDY STRATEGIES

Once you've made a schedule and set your environment, there are some general study strategies that can help you make the most of your prep time.

- **Don't wait until the last minute—start early!** It takes time to move things you review into long-term memory, and the more time you give yourself to learn and review different concepts, the better you'll be able to recall them on exam day. Don't cram all of your studying into the last minute; instead, come up with a reasonable study calendar early in your test prep process and stick to it.

- **Spread out your study sessions over time.** Few people are served better by a multi-hour cram session than they are a couple different shorter study sessions spread out over time. Your brain needs time to process what you've learned and then time to recall it later, so spreading your studying out across multiple sessions is the best way to allow this to happen.

- **Study regularly.** People need to periodically return to information to ensure that it sticks around in memory, so studying new materials demands that learners complete a periodic review of what they've already learned. Studying regularly leading up to the date of an assessment is the best way to do this and is far more effective than cramming, which offers few opportunities to recall information learned earlier.

- **Study intensely rather than passively.** There is a documented relationship between stress and performance. Low-stress situations tend to result in lower performance. High-stress situations do the same. But there's a sweet spot where just the right amount of pressure and intensity can improve performance on tasks, especially when learning. For studying, this means that you are far better served by short, intense intervals of studying. Languidly skimming over notes for hours on end will do significantly less than an hour of active retrieval combined with paraphrasing, timed practice questions, or intentional mind mapping.

Studying is a question of efficiency, and the most efficient and effective way to study usually involves real effort.

- **Develop active learning practices.** Active learning involves planning, monitoring, and reflecting on your learning process. Here are some tips for active learning:

  - Plan out your work time
  - Read strategically
  - Take some form of notes
  - Regularly self-assess
  - Spread out your study time
  - Keep a regular schedule
  - Create something while studying (diagrams, flowcharts, lists, etc.)
  - Use metacognitive techniques (such as reflective questions) to think about what you've learned so far and how well you learned it

- **Eliminate distractions.** Humans can multitask, just not well. Your divided attention is often the weakest of your attentive modes. To truly attend to a task, you need to be able to isolate what you're trying to learn from other stimuli; this is how you ensure that what you learn can be registered properly. One of the most significant distractors for most people is language, whether that's lyrics to a song or a TV playing in the background. Our brains often struggle to not pay attention to another person speaking. Turn off TVs, pause streaming, and put your phone far away so that you can't even see it. Of course, there are certain people for whom this is not an issue at all, so consider which type of person you are.

- **Encode new information meaningfully.** Whenever we talk about memory, we're talking about a process called encoding, wherein information moves through your senses to be stored for later use. There are any number of tricks and tips for getting information to stick around, but one of the most effective ways is what's called elaborative encoding. When you make information

meaningful by connecting it to your own life and interests, the brain more easily stores that information for later use. For example, if you practice a new math concept by thinking about a real-life situation in which you are likely to need it, you are more likely to retain the concept for later retrieval because you've encoded it in a way that holds meaning for you.

- **Divide tasks and information into chunks.** Divide topics into digestible chunks of information rather than larger blocks so you can deal with one chunk at a time. Resources (like this book) have organizational structures that may or may not suit your learning objectives. A chapter may cover a vast swath of topics that makes your studying load too great while also not necessarily aligning with what you need to know to suit your personalized goals. In this case, it might be useful to focus on a given section, chart, or exercise at a time. Use different study strategies for different chunks of information to prevent getting overwhelmed. Reorganize resources in your notes and study materials based on relationships that you see, not necessarily what is prescribed by the resource itself. Consider what you can cover in the time you have for a given study session and focus only on that.

- **Vary topics and weave them together as you learn.** Alternate between topics while studying rather than dedicating time to just one topic at a time. This applies to both what you review and self-quiz in your notes as well as practice questions. When you encounter different kinds of questions in sequence (say, multiplication, division, addition, and subtraction), you have to retrieve different kinds of information and strategies to answer accurately. That cross-talk will increase connections between different topics and processes, ultimately improving your learning. While you're at it, look for connections between different fields of study. For instance, how does working on reading comprehension for the Reading test also help you with the English and Science tests? Can studying for the English test provide you insights on how to approach the Writing test? Reflecting on these connections as you study helps solidify concepts in your mind.

- **Create new materials as you study.** To retain and understand information, you need to recall and process as well as apply topics and concepts. Learning about something isn't enough. You need exposure in different forms and in different ways. That usually means doing something with the information you're trying to learn. Often, practice tests are one of the best ways to study, but mixing your methods can have positive results. You can do this in some of the following ways:

  - Creating something using the new information, such as forming your own example questions or mini practice test

  - Developing a visual aid that helps you make sense of new information

  - Using different modes (auditory, visual, physical) to study

  - Seeking outside sources to expand your research and understanding

  - Creating materials that help you engage in repetitive learning (such as flashcards)

- **Regularly assess your retention and understanding.** In this book, we've included Test Yourselfs in chapters and Knowledge Checks at the end of each part to assist you with assessing your retention and understanding as you develop new skills, but there are lots of other ways to do

this as well. Periodically check in with yourself and look for ways to test or elaborate on what you've learned so far. Then, reflect on what skills you've developed well and which may still need some improvement.

- **At the end of each study session, review and summarize what you learned.** This is yet another form of metacognition that helps you make the most of your study time. By reflecting on what you learned and summarizing new information, you are encoding that new information to give you a better chance of recalling it later. If you can't summarize a concept that you've just learned, then it's a good indicator that you should devote more time to it during a future study session.

MINDSETS TO IMPROVE PERFORMANCE

Up to this point, we've discussed what it takes to create a study plan that will help you prepare for the ACT. Now, we'll pivot to some of the overarching mindsets and strategies that can help you maximize your study time and exam performance.

Every Strategy Can Be Personalized

Each of the strategy chapters throughout this book will offer you a basic point of reference for how to approach each section of the test, but the good news is that you can alter your approach to suit your needs. Part of the reason we previously had you consider your strengths

and weaknesses in each test section was so that as you work through this book, you'll be on the lookout for the tips and strategies that will help you most. While you practice with the Knowledge Checks in this book (which added together make up one full practice test in addition to the practice test in Chapter 24), play with these techniques and figure out which work best for you. Remember, you can personalize your approach for every individual subject test, not just the ACT as a whole.

Time Management Is Paramount

One thing that makes the ACT the ACT is the absurdly rigorous time constraints. For many test takers, time management is the biggest obstacle to their success. However, if you practice with these time constraints in mind and recreate test conditions by timing yourself whenever possible, you'll find it much easier to develop techniques that help you manage your time. Wherever possible, look for ways to save yourself time without reducing accuracy. Each of the strategies chapters in this book also includes subject-specific tips for how to make the most of your time, so keep an eye out!

Keep the Stakes in Mind

You need to approach the ACT as the high-stakes test that it is since it has important long-term consequences. Don't let that awareness spike your anxiety so much that you can't cope, but do be aware that each time you take the ACT matters a great deal. Depending on when your college applications are due, you may be able to take the ACT multiple times, but each time you take it is important, so you need to be thorough and focused. This is especially true if you only get one shot at it.

Build Confidence by Building Strategies

Your goal is to be as certain as possible when you answer a question. There are numerous strategies that can help you get there, many of which are in this book, but you need to know them and practice them to be able to use them. The good news is that as you become more adept at using these strategies, so too will you become more confident in your ability to perform well on the ACT. Confidence correlates positively with test performance, so the act of building confidence in yourself is worthwhile in its own right as a test prep technique.

ACT® PERFORMANCE TASKS AND TARGETS

Here are some things you can do across all sections on the ACT to improve your overall performance.

Keys to Success

1. **Know the directions for each test.** Keep in mind that the ACT test directions can be found throughout this book, so it's okay to save time by familiarizing yourself with them each time you do a Knowledge Check or Practice Test. On the actual test, they're not going to tell you anything you don't already know.

2. **Know the question types for each test.** We will cover these in the first chapter of each part of this book that focuses on a test section. Understanding and recognizing the different question types will help you make choices that improve your performance.

3. **Use all the time you're allotted.** There is no such thing as "finishing early" with the ACT—use every minute you're given! Every extra second is an opportunity to review guesses, double-check math, and make sure that you did as well as you possibly could have.

4. **Answer every single question.** You are not penalized for guessing on the ACT, and whenever you guess, you raise your chances of guessing correctly—especially if you eliminate obviously wrong options first. Always guess rather than leave a question blank since you can always

note and review guesses later anyhow. If you're running out of time, guess on all the questions that remain. Don't worry about selecting different letter options for each guess. Statistically, there is an equal likelihood of each choice being right, so for blind guesses select a letter pair (A/F, B/G, C/H, D/J, E/K) and use it each time.

5. **Know how many questions you can guess on based on your goal.** For example, if you know that to get a 25 or better on the Reading section, you could guess on around 10 questions (an entire passage), then you could divide your time for that section accordingly by saving the passage type you struggle with most for last. Recognize what your score goals are compared with your prior performance, then use available scoring charts to see how many questions you can get away with guessing on. That way, you'll be able to prioritize doing well on the questions you're likely to perform better with rather than spending time on questions you may not get right anyway.

6. **Have a strategy for every single section.** Don't just go in blindly—plan how you want to approach each of the individual tests that comprise the ACT. The chapters in this book are designed to help you make such a plan. You'll know exactly how you'll move through and spend your time on each section of the test.

7. **Have strategies for approaching different kinds of questions or passages.** Just like the chapters in this book can help you craft a strategy for each test section, they also can help you craft strategies for approaching different types of questions or passages. Make sure you familiarize yourself with different question or passage strategies, especially if you struggle with a given type. Even if you perform well with a question type, using and refining a specific strategy can increase your performance, improving both your accuracy and speed—helping you get more time for your scoring weaknesses.

8. **Be certain of your answers.** Don't just select an answer that seems right and call it a day. Instead, always make sure you review all the answer options and eliminate incorrect options as best you can so you can be certain of the answer you do select. When guessing, if you have the time, take the time to eliminate answers you're pretty sure are incorrect first. This will dramatically increase your chances of a correct guess.

9. **Time your practice.** Other than when you are encouraged to experiment on a given practice section, you should always time your practice for a Test Yourself, Knowledge Check, or Practice Test. These sections are designed to recreate test conditions and should be used as simulations. If you do them timed, you will have much more information about how well you perform within the time constraints of the ACT. Then, you can develop strategies to help you meet the time constraints while also familiarizing yourself with how long a given length of time feels to you when testing. When applying strategies, if something is improving your accuracy but pushing you over on time, you need to evaluate whether it can still serve your goals or if it needs to be changed to help you work faster. It's important to note that certain strategies will take longer initially but will be faster the more you practice.

Test Performance Targets

Just as there are certain mindsets you can practice on exam day and while studying, there are also certain things you can do on exam day to improve your performance. The following represent the targets you're trying to hit when taking the ACT, including when recreating test conditions for a practice test.

1 **Answer every question before time is called.** Remember, there is no penalty for guessing, so always guess rather than leave a question blank. If you are running out of time on a section, spend the last 1–2 minutes filling in an answer choice for any questions that remain.

2 **Have time for review.** One of your primary goals as you develop exam strategies should be to find places you can save time so that you have time to review any guesses you did make. On tests, make it a goal to use your time as efficiently as possible so you have at least a few moments to review guesses.

3 **Guess on as few questions as possible.** While it is better to guess than leave a question blank, your goal should still be to maximize the number of questions for which you give a well-considered answer. The more you work on time management, the better equipped you'll be to answer every question with careful consideration.

4 **Prioritize the questions you can answer with confidence.** When deciding the order in which to approach questions, prioritize the questions you feel confident about first (the easier questions), then move on to harder questions. That way, you can maximize the number of questions you're more likely to get right rather than focusing on questions that will take more time and that you may still get wrong.

5 **Use strategies for handling different kinds of passages and questions.** You'll spend plenty of your study time developing strategies for how to handle certain types of passages and questions, so remember to use those strategies when the time comes!

Once you've analyzed your diagnostic test scores, determined a study plan, set up an optimal study environment and routine, and familiarized yourself with the mindsets and performance goals that are critical for the ACT, you'll be well prepared to jump into studying for your exam.

SUMMING IT UP

- Use the charts provided at the beginning of this chapter to reflect on your performance during the diagnostic test in Chapter 2. These self-reflection questions are designed to help you plan your study time to more effectively address your testing goals.

- Consider the total amount of time you have to study for the ACT, then create a study calendar (or other form of study plan) that accounts for your study needs as based on your analysis of your diagnostic test results.

- Studying is most effective when done in a conducive environment. Make your environment more optimal for studying by doing the following:

  - Minimizing distractions
  - Working somewhere comfortable (but not so cozy you fall asleep)
  - Finding a location that suits your learning habits
  - Adjusting background noise and lighting to increase focus
  - Making individual determinations regarding group vs. solo study
  - Studying on a "full tank" by making sure to eat and get rest ahead of studying
  - Ensuring you have all the tools you need to study ahead of time
  - Paying attention to your mental environment in addition to your physical environment

- Start early rather than waiting until the last minute and spread study sessions out over time rather than trying to engage in long cramming sessions.

- Study regularly, actively, and with enough intensity to encode information meaningfully. When you can apply new concepts to your own life and experiences, you tend to retain them better.

- Divide tasks and information into chunks so you can address one piece of the overall puzzle at a time.

- Create new materials as you study to concretize new concepts and terms.

- Engage in regular metacognition (thinking about what you've learned and how well you learned it) and regularly assess how much information you've retained and which techniques helped you develop understanding.

- Summarize what you've learned at the end of each study session to help you encode new information and check understanding.

- Adopt mindsets that help you improve performance by remembering to personalize your strategies, recognizing the importance of time management, keeping the high stakes of the test in mind (without letting anxiety take over), and building your exam confidence through strategic learning.

- When taking the ACT exam or any practice tests, remember the following Must-Do Items:

    o Know the directions for each test.

    o Know the question types for each test.

    o Use all the time you're allotted.

    o Answer every single question.

    o Know how many questions you can guess on based on your goal.

    o Have a strategy for each test section.

    o Have strategies for approaching different kinds of questions or passages.

    o Be certain of your answers.

    o Time your practice.

- When taking the ACT exam or any practice tests, remember the following test performance targets:

    o Answer every question before time is called.

    o Save time for review whenever possible.

    o Guess on as few questions as possible.

    o Prioritize questions you can answer with confidence.

    o Use strategies for different types of passages and questions.

- Take the practice test in Chapter 24 at any time that makes sense for your study schedule. When you do, feel free to return to this chapter and analyze your results the same way you did for the diagnostic test. You can also find additional practice tests at www.petersons.com through our online ACT course.

PART II

THE ENGLISH TEST ON THE ACT®

4 | Introduction to ACT® English

5 | Production of Writing and Knowledge of Language

6 | Conventions of Standard English

7 | Strategies for Approaching the English Section

CHAPTER

Introduction to ACT® English

INTRODUCTION TO ACT® ENGLISH

OVERVIEW

How to Study with Part II

All about the English Test

Scoring Table

Sample Questions

Common Challenges

Summing It Up

As you prepare for the ACT English test, it's essential for you to be aware of the section's layout, the nature of the questions you'll be asked to answer, and the typical challenges that test takers face. You'll find a brief summary of the English test in this chapter. The chapters that follow include information on essential concepts you'll need to master in order to do well on the test. We'll also delve into specific techniques you can employ to approach questions and sample texts on the English test.

HOW TO STUDY WITH PART II

Before you get into the details about the ACT English test, take some time to reflect on your experience with English. What kind of English classes did you take over the course of your high school career? At which English skills do you excel? With which ones do you struggle? For example, do you enjoy researching and developing an argument, or are you an expert at grammar and mechanics? Are you a native speaker of English, or is English a second or third language for you? Knowing your strengths and weaknesses when it comes to English will help you narrow down how to prepare and where to focus your energy as you study for the English test on the ACT.

This chapter covers the structure of the English test and provides information on the types of questions you'll be given. In Chapter 5, we'll talk about the major skills necessary for success in answering the Production of Writing and Knowledge of Language questions and give you an opportunity to brush up on your rhetorical knowledge and skills. In Chapter 6, we'll provide in-depth explanations and examples of important concepts in English grammar, usage, and mechanics that will help you address the bulk of questions in the English test. If you already have a strong grasp of English, both when it comes to the organization, structure, and overall development of ideas and the intricacies of English grammar and mechanics, then feel free to just skim Chapters 5 and 6. If you'd like to focus on improving your English skills, then Chapters 5 and 6 will be helpful resources for you. In Chapter 7, we'll discuss strategies to implement on the ACT English test to help you do your best. You can put these strategies to the test with the Knowledge Check at the end of Chapter 7.

Self-Reflection: English

- Which English courses did you take in high school, and which have you not taken (yet)?

- Which English concepts have historically been easier for you to understand?

- Which English concepts have historically been harder for you to understand?

- What grammatical errors do you often find in your writing?

- Did you experience any conditions during your high school experience (remote learning, recovering from surgery, etc.) that could have created gaps in your English learning? If so, what topics were covered during those gaps?

- Which English skills require more effort for you?

- Is English your native language? If not, how has this impacted your experience learning key concepts in English?

ALL ABOUT THE ENGLISH TEST

The English test on the ACT is designed to assess a test taker's ability to understand and apply strong writing practices and the conventions of standard written English in a variety of contexts. This includes the ability to analyze and evaluate written passages, identify errors in writing, and make effective choices in revising and editing texts. The English test contains 75 multiple-choice questions that must be completed within 45 minutes. There are five passages, each with 15 questions.

Types of English Questions

You can expect to see three categories of questions on the ACT English test.

CONVENTIONS OF STANDARD ENGLISH (51–56% OF QUESTIONS)

You'll be asked to apply the conventions of standard English, including grammar, usage, and mechanics, as you edit and revise sample texts. Within this category, you'll see questions on sentence structure and formation, punctuation, and usage, covering essential aspects of English conventions.

PRODUCTION OF WRITING (20–30% OF QUESTIONS)

You'll be asked to apply rhetorical skills in revising sample texts. These questions test your ability to make revisions pertaining to the development of a topic by identifying a text's purpose, determining whether a text has accomplished its purpose, and evaluating the relevance of certain information to a text's overall organization and structure. You'll also be asked to make revisions that enhance the organization, unity, and cohesion of a text, including the rearrangement of sentences and paragraphs and the selection of appropriate transition words.

KNOWLEDGE OF LANGUAGE (13–19% OF QUESTIONS)

You'll be tasked with making revisions that are consistent with a text's style and tone while also ensuring both precision and concision in word choice and expression.

SCORING TABLE

The diagnostic test in Chapter 2 was designed to help you anticipate how you might perform on the ACT before you take advantage of the strategies and concepts covered in this book. While working through this part of the book, consider what type of score you're aiming for in light of your goals for college—what types of schools you want to attend and how their applicants typically score on the ACT. Although the raw-to-scaled score conversion is different for every ACT subject test, here we've provided a table that can help you translate your raw score (0–75 questions) on the English test to your desired scaled score (1–36). Remember that this information is an estimate and not an exact reflection of official ACT scoring metrics.

SCORING TABLE—ENGLISH

Raw Score	Scaled Score
75–74	36
72–73	35
70–71	34
69	33
68	32
67	31
66	30
65	29
63–64	28
61–62	27
59–60	26
57–58	25
54–56	24
52–53	23

SCORING TABLE—ENGLISH

Raw Score	Scaled Score
49–51	22
45–48	21
42–44	20
40–41	19
38–39	18
36–37	17
33–35	16
30–32	15
27–29	14
25–26	13
23–24	12
20–22	11
17–19	10
15–16	9
12–14	8
10–11	7
8–9	6
7	5
6	4
4–5	3
2–3	2
0–1	1

SAMPLE QUESTIONS

Questions on the ACT English test will fall into one of three categories: Conventions of Standard English, Production of Writing, and Knowledge of Language. Throughout Part II, we'll cover these question categories in more depth along with innovative strategies you can use on test day.

Here, we've provided three examples of questions you might encounter on the exam: The first is a Conventions of Standard English question; the second is a Knowledge of Language question; and the third is a Production of Writing question. You'll be given a passage with certain words or phrases underlined, each of which corresponds to a question number. Sometimes, there will be a question stem, such as "Which choice would most effectively introduce the rest of this paragraph?" Other times, there will be no question stem. In that scenario, you are expected to choose the best version of the underlined portion of the text, and the first answer option will always be "NO CHANGE," which you should choose if the underlined portion does not need any revisions or corrections that align with the ACT's standards and goals.

EXAMPLE

THE DECORATING GENE

My mother is an <u>interior designer: someone</u>
₁
<u>who</u> decorates and arranges the interiors of houses.
₁
Usually, a designer works in homes of other people,
but from the first moments I can remember, she was
always redesigning our own house as well. I guess
<u>the huge multitudes of clients</u> who hired her did not
₂
keep her busy enough!

At least once a month, Mom would rearrange
our living room furniture, repaint a bathroom, or
make new curtains for a bedroom. Her efforts were
not limited to just the inside walls and rooms of our
home; she repainted our front door so often that my
father would call home from work to ask us what
color the door was that day, <u>consequently he didn't</u>
₃
<u>recognize</u> his own house.
₃

1. **A.** NO CHANGE
   B. interior designer someone who
   C. interior designer; someone who
   D. interior designer, that is: someone who

2. **F.** NO CHANGE
   G. the multitude of clients
   H. the huge multitude of clients
   J. the huge multitudes in terms of clients

3. **A.** NO CHANGE
   B. because he didn't recognize
   C. in case he didn't recognize
   D. as a result he didn't recognize

1. The correct answer is A. The sentence is correct as it stands. The writer uses a colon after an independent clause to elaborate on the idea of what an interior designer does. Choice B is missing a comma after *designer*. Choice C uses a semicolon, but semicolons must connect two independent clauses. The phrase "someone who decorates and arranges the interior of houses" is not an independent clause because it is not a complete idea. Choice D incorrectly uses a colon after the phrase "that is."

2. The correct answer is G. The words *huge* and *multitude* are redundant when used together; therefore, you can eliminate choices F, H, and J. Choice J also creates the phrase, "I guess the huge multitudes in terms of clients who hired her," which does not make sense. Only choice G is clearly written and devoid of redundancies.

3. The correct answer is C. There is a problem with logic if we leave the sentence as it stands. If the author's father is calling home to find out what color the door is, he hasn't seen it yet. The only logical answer is choice C. Choices A, B, and D only make sense if the father had already come home.

Common Challenges

There are some common challenges that test takers encounter on the ACT English test.

Time pressure

The English test is timed, and you will have to answer 75 questions in 45 minutes. This means you'll be answering each question in less than a minute. The time pressure can make it difficult to carefully read and analyze the given passages and questions. We'll cover strategies for how to beat the clock while carefully approaching each question.

Complex sentence structure

Sample passages and texts on the English test may include complex sentence structures and vocabulary. We'll walk through strategies for how to approach a question where you're unsure of the correct answer. Remember that you're not penalized for incorrect answers on the ACT, so guessing is always an option if you're stuck.

Plausible but misleading answer options

The ACT English test includes answer choices that can seem grammatically correct and relevant but may not be the best choice in the context of the passage or question. This can be confusing, but we'll discuss important criteria to consider as you weigh the answer choices presented to you.

Applying rhetorical skills

The ACT English test can include questions that require you to carefully analyze the author's tone or the passage's purpose. These questions may require more time and more critical thinking than those focused on grammar or punctuation. If you struggle with concepts pertaining to rhetorical analysis, then Chapter 5 will be a valuable resource for you.

Specific grammar knowledge

There are a lot of grammar rules and conventions in the English language. You don't need to know all of them to do well on the ACT English test, but there are specific rules and concepts the ACT considers imperative for every English user to know when entering college. Chapter 6 will discuss those essential concepts to provide exactly what you need to know to succeed. Additionally, Chapter 7 will provide you with specific strategies for approaching English questions to improve both your speed and accuracy.

Consider the self-reflection exercise that was introduced at the beginning of this chapter. Have you experienced any of the challenges presented here as a high school student? In light of your own strengths and weaknesses, how might you need to approach studying for the English test? As you progress through the remaining chapters of this section, be mindful of the challenges we've presented here and identify any that you feel apply to you. Afterwards, review the strategies provided and assess which ones may be most effective for your unique skills, goals, and experiences.

SUMMING IT UP

- The English test contains 75 multiple-choice questions that must be completed within 45 minutes.

- There are five passages, each with 15 questions.

- The questions fit into three categories: Conventions of Standard English, Production of Writing, and Knowledge of Language.

- You'll be given a passage with certain words or phrases underlined, each of which corresponds to a question number. You'll be asked to revise the underlined portion in some fashion, depending on which category of question you're answering. Other questions may, instead of providing possible revisions, include a question stem that asks about the writer's rhetorical choices or the passage as a whole.

- Some challenges you might encounter on the ACT English test include time management, navigating complex vocabulary and syntax, choosing the correct and most effective answer option, applying rhetorical skills to revise the sample text, and maintaining knowledge of diverse, but specific, grammar concepts. As you go through the next three chapters in Part II, be sure to pay attention to where you struggle the most and focus on the strategies that will help you compensate for any areas where you feel less prepared or confident.

CHAPTER

Production of Writing and Knowledge of Language

PRODUCTION OF WRITING AND

OVERVIEW

Production of Writing Questions

Knowledge of Language Questions

Summing It Up

Test Yourself: Production of Writing and Knowledge of Language

In Chapter 4, we outlined what to expect on the English section of the ACT. In this chapter, we'll focus on two types of questions you'll encounter on the English test: Production of Writing questions and Knowledge of Language questions. Then, in the next chapter, we'll focus on the Standards of English Conventions questions. When you're finished with the chapters on English skills, you'll have the opportunity in Chapter 7 to practice more as you build a strategy toolkit that can help you make the most of the ACT's expectations on the English test.

PRODUCTION OF WRITING QUESTIONS

Production of Writing questions constitute 20–30% of the questions you'll encounter on the English test. For these questions, you'll be given a sample text and asked to make changes and revisions as needed to improve its overall development. As such, questions in this category will ask you to identify a text's purpose, evaluate whether a text has been successful in achieving its purpose, and determine whether certain information is relevant to a text given its organization and structure. You may also be asked to make changes that improve the sample text's organization, unity, and cohesion.

Topic Development Questions

Topic development questions require you to clearly understand rhetorical aspects of the passage, including the main idea or purpose as well as the details, examples, and analysis deployed in service of both. These questions will ask you to make revisions in accordance with the author's rhetorical goals, so you'll need to make decisions related to a text's argument, structure, or focus. As such, you may be asked to incorporate information that clarifies the meaning or purpose of the text, delete information that detracts from the text's purpose, or select evidence that best supports an argument.

A common type of topic development question asks test takers what type of evidence or example would be most persuasive as support. You may also be presented with additional evidence and asked to determine whether it would be advantageous to incorporate it into a specific sentence or paragraph. Additionally, you may encounter questions where you'll be given a sentence and asked where it would work best in a paragraph or passage. Finally, you may be given a question in which your task is to determine that a sentence is unrelated or does not really fit within the paragraph.

Take a look at the sample passage we've provided, which we will use to illustrate different types of Production of Writing questions. Note that Production

of Writing questions are often about the passage or a given paragraph as a whole, so they will not always be connected to an underlined portion of text.

Example Passage

CITIES ON THE SEA

[1]

Hunger has long plagued millions of the world's people, especially in the vast cities of the world's underdeveloped nations. The food to feed the world's growing population may come largely from ocean resources. [1]

[2]

Three quarters of the earth's surface is covered with water. Many scientists are now looking at these vast watery regions for solutions to some pressing human dilemmas. The impact of climate change makes the need to make the most of the ocean's resources all the more pressing.

[3]

Minerals such as iron, nickel, copper, aluminum, and tin are in limited supply on the earth. Undersea mines are expected to yield fresh supplies of many of these resources. Oil and gas deposits have been discovered under the ocean floor. [2]

[4]

To take advantage of these ocean-based resources, some scientists foresee entire cities on the ocean. At first, they will be built close to the shore. Later, floating cities might be located hundreds of miles at sea. These cities could serve many functions. Some of the people living there could harvest fish and sea plants, like farmers of the ocean. Others could operate oil and gas wells or work in undersea enclosures mining the ocean floors. Additionally, the floating cities could serve as terminals or stations for international travel, where ships could stop for refueling or repairs.

[5]

Much of the technology needed to build such cities has already been developed. Oil drilling on a large scale is already conducted at sea. Rigs as large as small towns built on floating platforms or on platforms anchored into the seabed serve as homes to scores of workers for months at a time. 3

[6]

The cities would have to be virtually self-sufficient since shipping supplies from the mainland would be quite costly. [A] Each city would be a multi-story structure with room for all inhabitants. [B] The ocean itself could provide much of the needed food and other raw materials, while solar panels and generators running on waterpower could provide energy. [C] Many thousands of men, women, and children might inhabit such a city. [D] Over time, entire new cultures might even flourish as a result of this futuristic way of living, changing the way we think about human inhabitance on the earth. 4

Example Topic Development Questions

Now, let's isolate a portion of our example passage to examine how it relates to topic development. Try answering the question for yourself first, then read our analysis.

EXAMPLE

Hunger has long plagued millions of the world's people, especially in the vast cities of the world's underdeveloped nations. The food to feed the world's growing population may come largely from ocean resources. 1

1. Which of the following sentences, if added here, would most effectively support the assertion made in the previous sentence?

    A. Fish, sea-grown plants, and even food-stuffs synthesized from algae are all examples.

    B. If population growth can be brought under control, the problem of hunger may well be alleviated.

    C. Pollution of the seas has not yet reached a level where it endangers the use of salt-water fish by humans.

    D. For thousands of years, humans have drawn nourishment from the seas around us.

In this type of topic development question, you need to identify which sentence should be added in at the indicated location. The context of the paragraph reveals that you're looking for a sentence that will provide evidence or analysis to support the idea that the hungry people of the world may be fed from ocean resources.

The sentence in choice A does this by giving several concrete examples of foods derived from the oceans. An inverse version of this same type of topic development question may ask you which information is NOT suitable in a given paragraph. The principles there are the same: first determine the context, then identify the situations that do (or in this case, do not) suit the paragraph.

In other topic development questions, you'll be told what the writer hopes to accomplish and then asked to determine the answer that best accomplishes that rhetorical task. Consider the following excerpt and question from the same example passage.

EXAMPLE

[3]

Minerals such as iron, nickel, copper, aluminum, and tin are in limited supply on the earth. Undersea mines are expected to yield fresh supplies of many of these resources. Oil and gas deposits have been discovered under the ocean floor. [2]

2. The writer wishes to add another relevant example to Paragraph 3. Which of the following sentences does that best?

   F. Exploration of the deepest reaches of the ocean floors has only recently begun.

   G. And the tides and thermal currents—water movements caused by temperature variations—may be future energy sources.

   H. Solar energy, too, is expected to become a major supplier of the world's future energy needs.

   J. The sea, after all, is the ultimate source of all life on the earth.

Though the question is phrased slightly differently, you will still answer it by determining the context provided for the given section as well as the author's rhetorical aims, meaning what they are trying to accomplish with their writing. Here, the correct answer is G. To find it, you'd first determine the context (the purpose of Paragraph 3, which is to list some of the resources that exist in oceans). The question informs you that the rhetorical purpose of the new addition would be to provide "another relevant example," so you are looking for the sentence that provides another relevant example of resources that can be found in the ocean. Since the sentence in choice G identifies how tides and thermal currents could potentially be future energy sources, it accomplishes that rhetorical purpose.

As you take this opportunity to practice with topic development questions, remember to consider the context given and the author's rhetorical purpose. After that, we'll continue with our example passage and discuss questions related to organization, unity, and cohesion.

Practice Set 1: Topic Development (Production of Writing)

AN OBOIST'S QUEST

[1]

I started playing the oboe because I'd heard it was a challenging instrument. That was four years ago, and I've enjoyed learning to play the oboe as much as I expected I would. However, it was not until recently that I realized what an oboist's real challenge is: finding good oboe reeds.

[2]

Though the reed is a small part of the instrument, it determines the quality of the oboe's sound. Professional oboists make their own reeds, but students like me must buy reeds either from their teachers or from mail-order companies.

[3]

My troubles began when my teacher stopped making reeds, sending all of her students on a wild goose chase for the perfect reed. The problem is that there is no such thing as a perfect reed, though oboists like to daydream about it. There is also no such thing as a perfect reed supplier. Reed makers are much in demand, and the reeds are often very expensive —typically $15 to $30 each for something which, in my opinion, is only worth $7.

[4]

Also, the reed makers tend to take their time in sending reeds to you; I usually have to wait three to six weeks after they've received my check in the mail. This wouldn't be a problem if I always ordered my reeds

1. Which choice most effectively provides readers with a specific detail to substantiate the writer's claim about the expense of oboe reeds?

   A. NO CHANGE

   B. something that I, a student with limited funds to spend, am highly concerned about.

   C. with an additional $3 to $5 charged for shipping and handling on every order sent.

   D. although professional oboe players could probably afford to pay a relatively high price for their reeds.

ahead of time, but oboe reeds are temperamental and often crack or break without warning. Thus, I need to have several back-up reeds available at all times.

[5]

I first tried buying reeds from a reed maker in Massachusetts. They were pretty good at first, but they became progressively worse the longer I bought them from him. It got to the point where none of the reeds he supplied worked, so I had to move on.

[6]

My next source was a company in California. However, their reeds sounded like ducks quacking, so I dropped them from my list. Desperate, I called an oboist friend of my parents. She helped me fix a few salvageable reeds I owned, and soon I had several which played in tune and had good tone. It seemed my reed troubles were over. However, within two weeks, those precious reeds were all played out, and I needed more.

[7]

Recently, a friend suggested a reed maker from New York City whose reeds, she said, were rather good. I called him up immediately and he asked me questions about my playing so that he could cater to my oboe needs. He promised to send out a supply of reeds within a week. Imagine my disappointment when the reeds he sent turned out to be poorly made, with unstable tones and a thin, unpleasant sound. My search for the perfect reed continues and it may never come to an end until I learn to make reeds myself.

Questions 2 and 3 refer to the passage as a whole.

2. The writer is considering adding the following sentence into the essay:

> Oboe reeds are made from two pieces of cane tied together with string and supported by a cylindrical piece of metal with some cork wrapped around at the base.

If the writer were to add this sentence, it would fit most smoothly and logically into Paragraph:

F. 2, before the first sentence.

G. 2, after the last sentence.

H. 3, after the last sentence.

J. 4, before the first sentence.

3. Suppose the writer were to eliminate Paragraph 4. This omission would cause the essay as a whole to lose primarily:

A. a relevant anecdote about the unreliability of many makers of oboe reeds.

B. irrelevant details about the technicalities of ordering oboe reeds through the mail.

C. relevant details about some of the difficulties oboists encounter in maintaining an adequate supply of reeds.

D. an irrelevant anecdote about the slowness of mail-order oboe reed suppliers.

Answers

1. **The correct answer is A.** The original phrase substantiates the writer's complaint about the high price of oboe reeds. Choices B, C, and D introduce ideas that are either completely irrelevant or slightly off the point.

2. **The correct answer is F.** This basic introductory information about what oboe reeds are needs to appear early in the essay.

3. **The correct answer is C.** The information in Paragraph 4 is relevant to the overall content and theme of the essay, since it contributes to the explanation of why oboists have so much difficulty in getting enough good reeds for their instruments, or why it might be hard to replace them quickly enough to be useful.

To answer these questions effectively, you'll need a solid understanding of how a thesis statement establishes the argument in a text's introduction and then reinforces that argument throughout the entirety of the text using claims supported by evidence and analysis. In these questions, you'll need to make sure that claims and evidence are closely aligned, that thesis statements are well-supported and developed by body paragraphs, and that every piece of information is purposeful, relevant to the text, and incorporated at a logical point in the passage.

Organization, Unity, and Cohesion Questions

Another category under the Production of Writing heading refers to questions that ask readers about the organization, unity, and cohesion of a passage. These questions are similar to those on topic development, since they concern the choices that a writer makes when developing an argument; however, they specifically focus on the organizational choices a writer makes to bring elements of an argument together, particularly as concerns both introducing the argument and concluding it. You might be asked about paragraph or sentence sequencing, the relevance of certain details or sentences to a given section of the text, or the logical placement of sentences or paragraphs within the context of the passage as a whole. You may also be asked about the effectiveness of a given transition, or tasked with choosing a new transition that better defines the relationship between given parts of the passage. In all cases, your goal is to ensure the text is logically organized, that the essay has an effective introduction and conclusion, and that the writer's words flow smoothly.

Like topic development questions, questions regarding organization, unity, and cohesion will sometimes ask you to determine which answer option represents a sentence that should be added or subtracted from the argument. Where these questions differ is that they will do so to test your ability to identify the option that makes the argument seem clearer and more cohesive. Returning to our example passage from before, consider the following excerpt and related question.

 TIP

If you find yourself struggling to identify the structure, organization, or other rhetorical elements of an argument when practicing for the English test, review writing strategies in Chapter 22.

EXAMPLE

[5]

Much of the technology needed to build such cities has already been developed. Oil drilling on a large scale is already conducted at sea. Rigs as large as small towns built on floating platforms or on platforms anchored into the seabed serve as homes to scores of workers for months at a time. ③

[6]

The cities would have to be virtually self-sufficient since shipping supplies from the mainland would be quite costly.

3. Suppose the writer wants to add a sentence to conclude Paragraph 5. If added, which option would most suitably conclude the paragraph while appropriately setting up a transition to Paragraph 6?

A. What does this leave one but questions about the efficacy of such a program?

B. Consequently, there are many who do not see the point in pursuing the development of ocean-going cities.

C. Yet no one bothers to question whether improvements like these can be done at suitably low enough costs to be efficient.

D. The same principles, on a larger scale, could be used to create ocean-going cities.

A keen eye may notice that this question is very similar to one on topic development, but it differs in that it is asking the test taker to determine which option creates a smooth transition that preserves the flow and cohesion of the argument. Your goal is to determine the answer that maintains proper contextual relationships and helps unify the two paragraphs within the argument in the most organized way.

If the answer wasn't apparent, this question is also a good example of how you can isolate the answer by eliminating options that do not fulfill the task. For instance, the rhetorical question in choice A is too vague to connect the two paragraphs. The use of the transition word *consequently* in choice B illogically links Paragraph 5, which is about different ways people have already found to live at sea, to a cause-and-effect relationship between the existence of these examples and the rise of those who critique the idea of building ocean-going cities. Similarly, the transition word *yet* in choice C needlessly sets up an oppositional relationship between the two paragraphs that does not make contextual sense. Choice D, by contrast, effectively connects the two paragraphs using repetition of the key term *cities* as well as a logical relationship between the context of Paragraph 5 and the new topic introduced in Paragraph 6 (the difficulties of establishing such a city).

Other questions on organization, unity, and cohesion may ask you to determine where within a given paragraph an addition would best contribute to improvements along these lines, or in what order sentences within a paragraph might best be presented to maintain clarity. Consider the following excerpt from our example passage.

EXAMPLE

[6]

The cities would have to be virtually self-sufficient since shipping supplies from the mainland would be quite costly. [A] Each city would be a multi-story structure with room for all inhabitants. [B] The ocean itself could provide much of the needed food and other raw materials, while solar panels and generators running on waterpower could provide energy. [C] Many thousands of men, women, and children might inhabit such a city. [D] Over time, entire new cultures might even flourish as a result of this futuristic way of living, changing the way we think about human inhabitance on the earth. [4]

4. Suppose the writer wanted to include the following sentence in Paragraph 6:

   They would probably visit the mainland from time to time, but otherwise would spend their lives at sea as ocean-dwelling pioneers.

   At what point in the paragraph would this sentence most logically fit?

   F. Point A
   G. Point B
   H. Point C
   J. Point D

The sentence that the writer wants to add uses the pronoun *they*, so your first step is to determine to which antecedent the pronoun refers. Here, context clues reveal that *they* likely refers to potential inhabitants of these cities at sea; therefore, you know that you want to place the additional sentence after a sentence that mentions inhabitants to keep the paragraph organized and linear. The sentence that precedes point D is the only one that mentions inhabitants, so you can logically assume that the best spot for the new sentence is point D (choice J).

Now that you've looked at some samples, take a moment to practice with another passage that addresses questions on organization, unity, and cohesion. As with other Production of Writing questions, not all organization, unity, and cohesion questions will be linked to a specific underlined portion of text; instead, some will address the passage or a given paragraph as a whole.

To answer these questions effectively, you need a solid understanding of what the main idea of the essay is, what purpose the author hopes to accomplish by writing it, and how the different pieces of the argument need to fit together to make sense for a reader and build on the argument over time.

Practice Set 2: Organization, Unity, and Cohesion (Production of Writing)

SHAKESPEARE'S *KING LEAR*

[1]

In the world of literature, there are many texts that are considered classics and studied in schools throughout the world. One of these works is William Shakespeare's play *King Lear*, a tragedy about a man who undergoes great suffering on the path to self-knowledge.

[2]

[1] There were a number of sources for Shakespeare's version of the Lear story, although there is debate over which ones Shakespeare had actually read. [2] However, there are records that indicate that the play was first staged around 1604. [3] Shakespeare was undoubtedly familiar with the basic story—a folk tale about a daughter who tells her father that she loves him as much as salt, then must prove that this means he is indispensable to her. [4] As with many old texts, the exact date of composition is uncertain. [5] Other sources included the anonymous play *King Leir*, Spencer's *The Faerie Queene*, and Higgins's *A Mirror for Magistrates*. ⬚1

1. Which of the following sequences of sentences makes this paragraph most logical?

   A. NO CHANGE
   B. 4, 2, 5, 3, 1
   C. 1, 3, 4, 2, 5
   D. 4, 2, 1, 3, 5

[3]

Shakespeare's play extracted details and ideas from various sources, but he made the play his own. He added characters, changed their nature, created a subplot, and altered the fate of the central characters dramatically. In *King Lear*, the evil nature of the wicked characters is magnified, and the suffering of the good is immeasurable. The two evil sisters, Regan and Goneril, kill each other in a jealous rage. The Earl of Gloucester is betrayed by one of his sons and violently blinded. And what some people have considered most heartbreaking of all, both Lear and his one true daughter, Cordelia, die at the end of the play. ☐2

[4]

Over the centuries, scholars have disagreed about the greatness of the play. One writer even deemed the anonymous *King Leir* to be of superior quality to Shakespeare's *King Lear*. There was even a production of *King Lear* that changed Shakespeare's ending, allowing Lear and Cordelia to live. ☐3

2. Which of the following sentences would be the best closing statement for Paragraph 3?

F. Shakespeare transformed King Lear into an exploration of raw human emotions.

G. These were all very sad events.

H. Shakespeare's sources proved to be quite useful.

J. Shakespeare was an imaginative playwright.

3. At this point, the writer would like to add a sentence to the paragraph. Given the context of the paragraph and the placement of the new sentence, which of the following statements would be the most logical addition?

A. This was a notable improvement to Shakespeare's play.

B. This was not a significant deviation from Shakespeare's play.

C. In the first place, not too many people are aware that this happened.

D. As such, the fact that the play could now scarcely be called a tragedy does not seem to matter.

Answers

1. The correct answer is D. Sentences 2 and 4 refer to the play's date of composition. Sentences 1, 3, and 5 deal with the play's sources, as does the first sentence of the next paragraph. So, as the passage is written, it does not follow a logical order, which means choice A is wrong. Similarly, choice C shuffles the two main themes illogically. Choice B groups the sentences about the two themes (date of composition and sources) but places them in an illogical order. Choice D groups the sentences about the two themes (date of composition and sources) while also placing them in a logical order; it thus represents the most logical sequence of sentences.

2. The correct answer is F. The paragraph states that Shakespeare modified the Lear story in significant

ways and gives examples of the evil and suffering in the play. Choice F emphasizes the transformation, and its reference to raw human emotions logically follows the examples of human suffering in the paragraph. Choices G, H, and J all might be true, but they do not reflect the theme of the paragraph.

3. The correct answer is D. The point of the paragraph is that the change was NOT an improvement to the play, so eliminate choice A. Choice B is also the opposite of the truth. Choice C might be true, but it does not serve well as a transition to the following sentence, particularly since the transition phrase "in the first place" does not suit the relationships represented in the passage. Choice D refers back to the other information in the paragraph and is a logical addition that uses a suitable transition phrase ("as such").

KNOWLEDGE OF LANGUAGE QUESTIONS

Knowledge of Language questions constitute 13–19% of questions you'll encounter on the English section of the ACT. For these questions, you'll be tasked with making revisions that are consistent with a text's style and tone while also ensuring both precision and concision in word choice. Where Production of Writing questions focus on the craft of writing in terms of an argument's development and organization, Knowledge of Language questions focus on the craft of writing as concerns thoughtful, logical, and precise use of standard written English to convey style and tone. For instance, you may be asked to eliminate redundant words, make wordy sections more concise, reduce the ambiguity of pronoun usage, or change words to better reflect the author's tone.

Concision and Precision

Questions addressing precision will ask you to choose the language that is most concise. Language is concise if it expresses an idea without using unnecessary or repetitive words. The wordier a sentence is, the less likely it is to be concise. When evaluating precision, look for ways to eliminate redundant or unnecessary words.

Consider the example sentences below:

- **Not Concise:** Athletes and those who play sports should thoughtfully consider and keep in mind how important it is to regularly hydrate by drinking water frequently.

- **Concise Revision:** Athletes should keep in mind how important it is to hydrate frequently.

Here, the writer has gone through and eliminated any redundant terms, making the sentence clearer for the reader. Similarly, you may be asked to identify the redundancy in underlined portions of a sentence rather than a sentence as a whole. Consider the following example question based on an excerpt from an ACT passage.

As written, the sentence contains a redundancy, since the phrases "eating well" and "consuming nutritious

EXAMPLE

Nonetheless, Collins believes that if injured athletes <u>eat well, stay hydrated, and consume nutritious meals</u>, they will heal faster. [5]

5. **A.** NO CHANGE
   B. eat well, stay hydrated, and consume a lot of water
   C. eat, hydrate, and consume nutritious meals
   D. eat nutritious meals and stay hydrated

meals" both describe the same activity. The only answer option that eliminates this redundancy is choice D.

The use of pronouns may also come up for Knowledge of Language questions, even though it they may seem like a topic that would be restricted to Conventions of Standard English. That's because when the connection between a pronoun and its antecedent (the noun it replaces) is unclear, it can cause a breakdown in the clarity and cohesion of an idea. Consider the following example.

- **Ambiguous Pronoun:** Olive and Lucy decided to go to the mall after she had finished her homework.

- **Unambiguous Pronoun:** Olive and Lucy decided to go to the mall after Olive had finished her homework.

As you can see, *she* and *her* in the first sentence are ambiguous since a reader cannot tell if the pronouns refer to Olive or Lucy. In the second sentence, the writer replaces *she* with *Olive,* so it's clear that *her* refers to Olive rather than Lucy. Your goal with questions related to ambiguous pronouns is to identify revisions that ensure that any pronouns used are clearly connected to their antecedent. You may also need to revise a sentence so that a missing noun or pronoun is replaced.

Consider the following example question from an excerpted ACT passage.

EXAMPLE

Given that teaching requires a great deal of personal sacrifice, <u>they</u> really ought to be making more money.
6

6. **F.** NO CHANGE
   G. teachers
   H. people
   J. we

Here, the pronoun *they* is ambiguous because its antecedent is only implied. To correct the sentence, one must replace the pronoun with a noun that matches the context of the sentence. You can eliminate *we* (choice J) because the original sentence is not meant to be in first person. Choice H does replace *they* with a plural noun (*people*), but that noun is too vague to make contextual sense. The noun *teachers*, however, makes it very clear that those who should be better compensated because of the personal sacrifices required by teaching are, in fact, teachers.

Tone

In an essay, *tone* refers to the character or attitude of the piece of writing. *Style*, in turn, is the way an author arranges their words to communicate tone. Most often, if you have a question that addresses tone or style, it is asking you to choose an answer that increases the accuracy of word choices to better reflect the author's intended meaning. Words and phrases need to agree with the meaning of the given sentence or paragraph, as well as the passage as a whole. An example ACT question on tone might look like the following, which is based on an excerpt pulled from a longer passage.

EXAMPLE

The world of fungi goes far beyond the portobello and shiitake mushrooms that most of us are more likely to encounter on a dinner plate than growing wild in the woods. The term *mushroom* describes fungus which has fruited and can release spores. There are roughly 14,000 species of mushrooms, also known as toadstools, described in nature so far, though some scientists suspect there could be millions more as of yet undiscovered. Of those thousands, as many as 20 are potentially lethal to humans while hundreds more are known to be poisonous. Still others are known to have medicinal qualities. [7]

7. Which choice for a concluding sentence to Paragraph 1 best maintains the essay's informative but lighthearted tone and most successfully mimics the author's style in the rest of the paragraph?

   A. Have you ever had a mushroom? They're pretty delicious!
   B. The incredible variety represented in the weird, wide world of mushrooms makes them fascinating fodder for scientific investigation.
   C. Mushrooms are overrated; there isn't much to learn about them that scientists don't already know.
   D. The North American Mycological Society is an organization of like-minded individuals who appreciate mushrooms in all their forms.

For a question like this one, you may notice that there is some overlap with questions on Production of Writing since the correct answer needs to also make contextual sense with the rest of the paragraph; this recognition would allow you to eliminate choice D right away since it veers off topic. However, to land on the correct answer, you'd still need to recognize which of the remaining options adopts the correct style and tone. Choice A is lighthearted, as indicated in the question, but it does not match the informative, academic style the writer uses in the rest of the paragraph. Choice C uses a critical tone, which does not match the existing paragraph either. The correct answer (choice B) adopts the informative and lighthearted tone of the rest of the paragraph, contextually makes sense, and matches the author's style.

Tone and style questions will often also take the form of questions about word choice since your task is to determine which replacement word better suits the tone and style of a given sentence or paragraph. Observe how this plays out with the following sample question from our previously excerpted passage on mushrooms.

EXAMPLE

This <u>kooky</u> fungus also lets off a stench of
                8
death in hopes of attracting insects to help it

spread spores.

8. **F.** NO CHANGE
   G. freakish
   H. strange
   J. icky

As we previously established, the author for the essay on mushrooms is using an informative but lighthearted tone. If we consider tone alone, all of these words might fit. However, we also noted that they are using a straightforward, academic style. In that context, words like *kooky, freakish,* and *icky* all seem too informal for the given style, particularly since they pass judgment on the mushroom's traits rather than reporting about them factually. The more straightforward term *strange* is thus a better word choice.

You now have the opportunity to practice working with a passage devoted to Knowledge of Language questions. In the next chapter, we'll also discuss the conventions of standard English, which will help you recognize the ways grammar and usage play into a writer's development of style and tone by informing word choices.

Practice Set 3: Knowledge of Language

ADDICTED TO TV

Do you pick up the TV remote control before you brush your teeth in the morning? Is your favorite reading material the *TV Guide*? ☐1 If there were a fire and you could save either your kitten or your TV set, would you hesitate before reaching for the cat? If you answered "yes" to any of these questions, you may be a TV addict.

Most people have favorite TV <u>programs that they prefer to others</u>. They watch these shows every week and talk about them with their friends or coworkers. This behavior does not necessarily indicate a TV addiction, but some people watch TV even if there is nothing on they really want to see. They will spend hours flipping through channels, searching in vain for something to watch, failing to consider other ways to pass the time, and the TV set is rarely turned off. Drop by a TV addict's home, and you will discover that their TV stays on throughout your entire visit.

It can be difficult, but there are ways that TV addicts can gradually spend fewer hours in front of the television set. They could keep a written record of the number of hours spent watching TV each week. The shock of seeing the total hours might <u>jolt</u> them off the couch and into action. TV addicts could also make a list of activities to fill in the time they would have spent watching TV. Before they know it, they could be enjoying more of what life has to offer.

1. At this point, the writer would like to add a sentence. Given the content and style of the introduction, which of the following sentences is the best choice?

   A. Maybe you name your fish after your favorite TV stars!

   B. Do you plan your daily activities around your favorite TV programs?

   C. What is your favorite TV show?

   D. Some people would rather read the *TV Guide* than a good book.

2. F. NO CHANGE

   G. programs, which they prefer to others.

   H. programs.

   J. programs, preferring them to others.

3. Which verb choice most effectively matches the tone and context of the text?

   A. NO CHANGE

   B. nudge

   C. find

   D. keep

Answers

1. The correct answer is B. The writer has made the stylistic choice to begin the introduction with a series of questions that directly address the reader. The sentences immediately before and after the new sentence are questions. To maintain parallelism and match the style in this section of the paragraph, the new sentence should also be a question. Choice A doesn't work because it is an exclamation, not a question, and it is an irrelevant tangent. Choice D is relevant, but it is not a question. Choice C doesn't work because all of the other sentences are specifically about arranging one's life around television.

2. The correct answer is H. The sentence is redundant as written—something that you "prefer to others" is by definition your favorite, so choice F is wrong. Only choice H eliminates the extra phrase and fixes the problem. Choices G and J are incorrect because they retain the redundant information.

3. The correct answer is A. The verb *jolt* (choice A) best carries the image of shock that begins the sentence. If one is jolted into action, it is an act of abruptness, often caused by shock. A *nudge* (choice B) is a slight or gentle push. This hardly conveys the image of shock that begins the sentence. *Find* (choice C) and *keep* (choice D) don't make sense in context.

To do well with Knowledge of Language questions, you should pay close attention to how word choice and sentence structure interact with the meaning of what is said. You should also have a strong sense of what the argument is so you can recognize sentences that are repetitive or which become overly wordy and thus unclear.

SUMMING IT UP

- Production of Writing questions involve making revisions to improve the development of a text. They account for 20–30% of the questions on the English test and are divided into two main categories:

  - Topic Development Questions: These questions task you with making revisions to support the development and structure of an argument, including use of evidence, paragraph and essay structure (in terms of developing ideas), and relevance of information.

  - Organization, Unity, and Cohesion Questions: These questions task you with making revisions to improve the organization, cohesion, and unity of the passage. These questions will ask you to determine if words, sentences, or paragraphs are logically placed within the passage and if paragraphs are constructed reasonably.

- Knowledge of Language questions involve determining whether the language used in a passage is produced precisely and logically to further the writer's purpose and argument. They account for 13–19% of the questions on the English test and may include questions on redundancy, concision, word choice, and clarity of pronouns. Test takers will also be expected to identify responses that align with the tone and style of the passage.

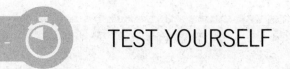
PRODUCTION OF WRITING AND KNOWLEDGE OF LANGUAGE

15 Questions—9 Minutes

Directions: In the following passage, certain words and phrases are underlined and numbered. In the right-hand column, you will find alternatives for the part that is underlined. In most cases, you are to choose which alternative best makes the statement appropriate in standard written English. If you think the original version is best, choose "NO CHANGE." Sometimes, you may also find a question in the right-hand column about the underlined part. Here, you should choose the best answer to the question.

You may also find questions about a section of a passage, or a passage in its entirety. These questions do not refer to specific underlined portions of the passage, but rather are identified by a number or numbers in a box.

For each question, choose the answer you consider best. Read the passage through once before you begin to answer the questions that accompany it. For many questions, you must read several sentences beyond the question to determine the answer. Be sure that you have read far enough ahead each time you choose an alternative.

Note: In this particular practice section, all of the questions fall under the Production of Writing and Knowledge of Language categories. Passages on the ACT English Test will also have questions addressing Conventions of Standard English (covered in Chapter 6) accompanying each passage. The passage and questions have been modified from the classic ACT format to give you greater opportunity to practice the specific skills covered in this chapter.

THE MAGIC OF SPECIAL EFFECTS

[1]

The movies are one place where magic can come true. You can see sights you might never <u>under any circumstances</u> hope to see in real life—ocean liners sinking, earthquakes swallowing cities, planets exploding.

1. **A.** NO CHANGE
   B. normally
   C. in daily life
   D. OMIT the underlined portion.

You can also see sights that might never exist at <u>all, as</u>
<u>such rampaging monsters</u>, battles in outer space, sky-
high cities of the future.

[2]

All these are examples of the movie magic known as
special effects. <u>It's the hard work and dedicated labor of</u>
amazingly clever and skilled effects artists.

<u>Moreover</u> the real magic lies in how they're able to
make a man in a gorilla suit into King Kong, tiny plastic
models into huge space ships, and instructions in a
computer into images of a world that no one has ever
imagined before.

[3]

Effects artists have developed many tricks and
techniques <u>over the years and they are always evolving</u>.
Working closely with movie directors, producers, and
actors, special effects artists are responsible for much of
what we call movie magic.

2. **F.** NO CHANGE
   G. all, such as rampaging monsters
   H. as rampaging monsters
   J. all, rampaging monsters as such

3. **A.** NO CHANGE
   B. It's the hard work of
   C. It's the dedicated and hard labor and work of
   D. It's the hard work, which requires a lot of dedi-
   cated labor, of

4. **F.** NO CHANGE
   G. Nonetheless,
   H. However,
   J. Because

5. **A.** NO CHANGE
   B. over the years, which are always evolving
   C. over the years and it is always evolving
   D. over the years, always evolving

The movies as we know them have changed since the advent of special effects, <u>so they are</u> important members of the movie industry. 7

6

[4]

[1] They can be used to save money, as some movie scenes would be impossibly costly to produce using ordinary methods. [2] Special effects techniques are useful to moviemakers in several ways. [3] Clever use of special effects can cut those costs dramatically. [4] For example, to show an imaginary city, it would cost millions of dollars to build real buildings, roads, and so on. 8

6. **F.** NO CHANGE

   G. so directors are

   H. so special effects artists are

   J. so special effects are

7. The writer is considering adding the following sentence to the end of Paragraph 3.

   > For instance, top visual effects companies like Industrial Light & Magic and Pixar have become prominent players in the film industry as a result of the expert effects artists they employ.

   Would this be a logical and relevant addition to the paragraph?

   A. Yes, because it is unclear why the paragraph mentions effects artists otherwise.

   B. Yes, because it provides a concrete example showing that effects artists are becoming more important to filmmaking.

   C. No, because it is irrelevant to the paragraph and would be better placed elsewhere.

   D. No, because it is needlessly wordy and does not help develop the topic.

8. Which of the following sequences of sentences will make Paragraph 4 most logical?

   F. 2, 1, 4, 3

   G. 3, 1, 4, 2

   H. 2, 4, 3, 1

   J. 1, 4, 3, 2

[5]

⑨ Battle or disaster scenes involving explosions, floods, or avalanches can be very dangerous to film.

Effects artists can simulate <u>such</u> in ways that give audi-
10
ences the thrill of witnessing a dangerous event without

<u>the exposing of actors</u> to real hazards.
11

[6]

<u>Most importantly,</u> special effects allow movie
12
makers to film scenes that would otherwise be

impossible.

9. Which of the following sentences would pro-
    vide the best transition here linking the topic of
    the previous paragraph to the new topic of this
    paragraph?

    A. Today's moviemakers are highly budget
       conscious.

    B. Some of the most exciting special effects
       involve computer-simulated imagery.

    C. There is a long history to the use of special
       effects in movies.

    D. Special effects can also make moviemaking safer.

10. F. NO CHANGE
    G. these events
    H. those
    J. it

11. A. NO CHANGE
    B. exposing actors
    C. actors being exposed
    D. actors having to be exposed

12. F. NO CHANGE
    G. By contrast,
    H. On the other hand,
    J. Nevertheless,

They let movies show non-existent, even impossible worlds. [13] Special effects are a moviemaker's tool for communicating a unique imaginative experience.

Well, aren't the movies something else?
14

13. At this point, the writer is considering the addition of the following sentence:

> Visions of unknown, unseen worlds have long stimulated the imaginations of human beings the world over.

Would this be a logical and relevant addition to the essay?

A. Yes, because it emphasizes the important role that special effects play in the movies.

B. Yes, because it underscores the universal appeal of works of the imagination.

C. No, because it does not directly relate to the topic of movie special effects.

D. No, because most of the world's most popular movies are produced in the United States, not "the world over."

14. Which option best suits the tone and style of the essay?

F. NO CHANGE

G. Can you believe what effects artists can do?

H. And, after all, isn't that exactly why we go to the movies?

J. Movies were better before they had so many visual effects, but what can you do?

Question 15 refers to the passage as a whole.

15. Imagine the author's purpose in writing this essay was to critique the film industry's use of special effects in modern filmmaking. Would this essay accomplish that task?

A. Yes, because the author provides many different examples of what can be done with special effects.

B. Yes, because the author provides multiple criticisms of the way effects artists tend to be disregarded by the industry as a whole.

C. No, because the author does not think that special effects have much impact on the moviegoing experience.

D. No, because the author praises special effects and their impact on modern films rather than critiquing them.

ANSWER KEY AND EXPLANATIONS

1. D	**4.** H	**7.** B	**10.** G	**13.** C
2. G	**5.** B	**8.** F	**11.** B	**14.** H
3. B	**6.** H	**9.** D	**12.** F	**15.** D

1. The correct answer is D. The underlined phrase is redundant, since the words "under no circumstances" add nothing to the meaning conveyed by the word *never*. It can be omitted with no loss of meaning, making the sentence more concise.

2. The correct answer is G. The correct phrase to connect the two parts of the sentence is "such as," which should follow the comma after the word *all* from the previous clause.

3. The correct answer is B. The only option that eliminates the redundancy and wordiness of the original sentence is choice B.

4. The correct answer is H. *However* followed by a comma is the most logical transition among the answer choices for connecting this sentence with the previous one. The other answer choices all imply a shift in meaning or a different relationship between clauses.

5. The correct answer is B. The sentence as written (choice A) contains an ambiguous pronoun, since it is unclear if the antecedent for *they* is *effects artists*, *tricks*, *techniques*, or a combination of these terms. The phrasing in choice B eliminates the ambiguous pronoun entirely, using a dependent clause starting with *which* to indicate that what is always evolving are the tricks and techniques that effects artists use. Choice C incorrectly replaces "they are" with "it is," which does not solve the pronoun ambiguity. Choice D eliminates any reference to what is evolving altogether, making the sentence unclear.

6. The correct answer is H. As written (choice F), the pronoun *they* is used ambiguously and needs to be replaced with a noun that makes contextual sense for the paragraph as a whole. The term *members* in the sentence denotes that the noun replacing *they* must refer to people, so you can eliminate choice

J. After that, context makes it clear that the term *members* should be referring to "special effects artists" (choice H) rather than *directors* (choice G).

7. The correct answer is B. The topic of the third paragraph is the importance of effects artists in the filmmaking industry, so you can assume that a new sentence that provides a concrete example of how is neither irrelevant to the paragraph (choice C) nor unnecessary for topic development (choice D). Since the existing paragraph does make it clear why the author is discussing effects artists, you can eliminate choice A.

8. The correct answer is F. It makes sense to start with sentence 2, which makes the general point (about the usefulness of special effects) that the rest of the paragraph then explains in more detail. And it makes sense for sentence 3 to follow sentence 4, since it refers to "those costs" described in that sentence.

9. The correct answer is D. This sentence introduces the topic around which the other sentences in the paragraph are organized.

10. The correct answer is G. In the original sentence (choice A), the pronoun *such* is vague, leaving the reader slightly uncertain of what its antecedent might be. Additionally, the sentence as a whole is awkward and non-idiomatic; in other words, it's "weird sounding." The phrase "these events" is a suitable replacement because it refers to the previous sentence clearly and understandably. Neither choice H nor choice J suitably replaces the vague pronoun.

11. The correct answer is B. This wording is the simplest and most concise of the answer choices.

12. The correct answer is F. The words "Most importantly" introduce the point made in the final paragraph in a logical fashion: The idea that special effects give movie makers the freedom to depict impossible worlds is, arguably, the "most important" or at least most remarkable idea in the passage. The other alternative connecting words or phrases don't make as much sense in context.

13. The correct answer is C. Since this sentence adds nothing to our understanding of movie special effects or how they are used, it can be omitted without losing anything.

14. The correct answer is H. Every option ends the essay with a rhetorical question, but only choice H matches both the tone and style of the passage and connects logically to the sentiments from the sentence before and the passage as a whole. The remaining options either take too informal of a tone or do not contextually make sense as concluding sentences for this passage.

15. The correct answer is D. The author's purpose in this passage is to discuss the role special effects play in modern filmmaking, and the tone is fairly laudatory throughout. There is no attempt to critique, so you can eliminate choices A and B right away. Choice C is incorrect because it contradicts the content of the passage—the author makes it abundantly clear that they believe special effects have an impact on the moviegoing experience.

CHAPTER

Conventions of Standard English

CONVENTIONS OF STANDARD ENGLISH

OVERVIEW

Grammar

Sentence Structure
and Formation

Punctuation

Verbs, Usage, and
Agreement

Summing It Up

Test Yourself:
Conventions of
Standard English

The ACT English section is a test of your editing skills. Most of the 75 questions fall into a category called Conventions of Standard English (CSE). These questions, as their name implies, ask you to find errors in written English according to standard conventions. To perform well, you need a thorough (but not comprehensive) understanding of English grammar, sentence structure, punctuation, verb tense, usage, and agreement. While the topics and applications are diverse, the scope of English conventions on the ACT is focused on what contributes to strong, clear writing—with sentence structure and punctuation receiving most of the emphasis. This chapter will provide you with a refresher on the essential conventions of standard written English the ACT commonly assesses. You'll find multiple opportunities throughout the chapter to practice the conventions as you review them. The concepts here are also critical if you opt to take the optional Writing test, which we discuss at length in Chapters 22 and 23.

GRAMMAR

The rules of grammar govern the ways in which parts of speech are organized in a sentence. There are rules concerning word endings, word order, and which words may be used together. You must know the parts of speech to follow the rules of grammar.

PARTS OF SPEECH		
Type	**Definition**	**Examples**
Noun	A person, place, thing, or idea	teacher, city, desk, democracy
Pronoun	Substitute for a noun	he, they, ours, those
Adjective	Describes a noun	warm, quick, tall, blue
Verb	Expresses action or a state of being	yell, interpret, feel, are
Adverb	Modifies a verb, an adjective, or another adverb	fast, slowly, friendly, well
Conjunction	Joins words, sentences, and phrases	for, and, nor, but, or, yet, so
Preposition	Shows position in time or space	in, during, after, behind

Nouns

A noun is a person, place, thing, or idea. There are different kinds of nouns:

- **Common nouns** are general, such as *house*, *person*, *street*, or *city*.
- **Proper nouns** are specific, such as *White House*, *Fernando*, *Main Street*, or *New York*.
- **Collective nouns** name groups like *team*, *crowd*, *organization*, or *Congress*.

Nouns have cases:

- A noun is in the **nominative case** when it is the subject of the sentence.

> **EXAMPLE**
>
> *Roberto* joined the band.

- A noun is in the **objective case** when it is the direct object, indirect object, or object of the preposition.

> **EXAMPLES**
>
> **Direct object:** She built a *treehouse*.
>
> **Indirect object:** Joel sent *Marco* a message.
>
> **Object of the preposition:** The fairies danced around *Jasmine*.

- **Possessive case** is the form that shows possession or ownership.

> **EXAMPLE**
>
> The *queen's* crown was filled with rubies.

Pronouns

A pronoun is a substitute for a noun. The antecedent of the pronoun is the noun that the pronoun replaces. A pronoun must agree with its antecedent in gender, person, and number. There are several kinds of pronouns:

- **Demonstrative pronoun:** this, that, these, those
- **Indefinite pronoun:** anyone, anybody, everyone, nobody, several, some, someone, somebody
- **Interrogative pronoun:** who, which, what
- **Personal pronoun:** I, you, we, me, him, her, us, they

Verbs

A verb expresses action or a state of being. There are four major kinds of verbs: transitive, intransitive, linking, and auxiliary or helping verbs.

- **Transitive verbs** are action verbs and always have a direct object. In other words, there's something receiving the action of a transitive verb.

EXAMPLES

The dog *broke* her tooth.

The teacher *discussed* the effects of nuclear radiation.

- **Intransitive verbs** are action verbs with no direct object. Some verbs can be either transitive or intransitive depending on their usage.

EXAMPLES

The vase *broke*.

Misha *cried*.

- **Linking verbs** indicate a state of being and have no action. These verbs serve to link the subject to additional descriptive information. Examples include *is, are, was, were, be, been, am, smell, taste, feel, look, seem, become,* and *appear*. Sometimes, the verbs listed here can be linking, auxiliary, or action verbs depending on their usage.

EXAMPLES

I *am* here.

He *looks* nervous.

She *is* sick.

The food *tasted* delicious.

- **Auxiliary verbs** or **helping verbs** are used with an infinitive or participle to create a verb phrase. Auxiliary verbs always need a primary verb to function. Examples of auxiliary verbs include all forms of the verbs *to be, to have, to do,* and *to keep,* as well as *can, could, may, might, must, ought to, shall, will, would,* and *should.*

EXAMPLES

I *am having* a glass of water.

She *might go* to the store.

Alex *should study* harder.

Adjectives

An adjective describes a noun. Adjectives can answer questions like:

- "Which one?"
- "What kind?"
- "How many?"

There are three uses of adjectives:

- A **noun modifier** is usually placed directly before the noun it describes.

> **EXAMPLE**
>
> He is a *tall* man.

- A **predicate adjective** follows a linking verb and modifies the subject.

> **EXAMPLES**
>
> She is *happy*.
>
> I feel *terrible*.

- An **article** or **noun marker** points to a noun. The articles are *the*, *a*, and *an*.

> **EXAMPLE**
>
> *The* teacher took *a* vacation to *an* island.

Adverbs

An adverb modifies a verb, an adjective, or another adverb and can answer questions like:

- "Why?"
- "How?"
- "Where?"
- "When?"
- "To what degree?"

Adverbs should not be used to modify nouns. Many adverbs are easy to identify because they end in *-ly*. But there are other adverbs that do not have this ending.

> **EXAMPLES**
>
> He *quickly* jumped over the hole.
>
> I am doing *well*.
>
> The water swirled *clockwise* down the drain.

Adverbs can also operate like conjunctions. **Conjunctive adverbs** act as transitions, indicating relationships between clauses. They are used to begin complete sentences or independent clauses.

> **EXAMPLE**
>
> The motorcyclist lost control and collided with a tree; *however*, he was able to stand and walk away from the crash.

In the preceding example, the word *however* is used at the beginning of the second half of the sentence to establish the contrasting relationship with the first half of the sentence. Other examples of conjunctive adverbs include the following: *additionally, alternatively, certainly, consequently, meanwhile,* and *furthermore.*

Conjunctions

A conjunction joins words, sentences, and phrases. There are multiple kinds of conjunctions: coordinating conjunctions, subordinating conjunctions, and correlative conjunctions.

Coordinating conjunctions link together things that are of equal importance. The best way to remember the coordinating conjunctions is with the acronym FANBOYS. This stands for: <u>f</u>or, <u>a</u>nd, <u>n</u>or, <u>b</u>ut, <u>o</u>r, <u>y</u>et, <u>s</u>o.

EXAMPLES

She *and* I went to the park.

I wanted to play video games, *but* my mom said it was time to leave.

Subordinating conjunctions link together a dependent clause and an independent clause. Common subordinating conjunctions include the following: *after, although, because, before, despite, since, though, until, whether,* and *while.*

Correlative conjunctions are pairs of conjunctions. When the first of the pair appears in a sentence, so too then must the second. For instance, *neither/nor* is a correlative pair.

EXAMPLE

Neither John *nor* his children wanted to move to the new city.

Other correlative conjunctions you may see on the ACT include the following: *either/or, such/that, not only/but also, both/and, whether/or.*

 TIP

For coordinating conjunctions, remember the acronym **FANBOYS:**

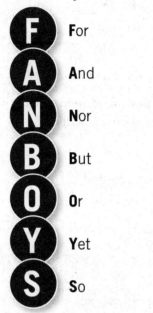

For

And

Nor

But

Or

Yet

So

Conjunctions connect ideas together. If you're using a comma to separate two complete sentences, you also need one of the FANBOYS.

Prepositions

A preposition shows position in time or space. Common prepositions are words like *around, in, over, under, during, after,* and *behind.* A preposition starts a prepositional phrase that usually shows the relationship between a noun or pronoun and the rest of the information in the sentence.

EXAMPLES

The dog sleeps *under the bed.*

She stood up *during the presentation.*

After the meeting, Dr. Williams changed her policy.

Practice Set 1: Grammar

LAST MONTANA WINTER

The thing about winter in the Beartooth Range is that it <u>had recent become difficult</u> for Bo, espe-cially since he had turned 70. These days, he felt the

weather changes first <u>toward</u> his joints, and the wet, cold air made him red in the cheeks and hoarse in the throat, even when he was bundled up inside. It's no secret that his children had been bothering him to move out of that tiny cabin in the woods and into one of their homes, but he was <u>a stubborn man</u> and wouldn't hear of it.

No, Bo had built that cabin with his own two hands, <u>yet</u> he wasn't about to

abandon <u>it</u> just because the snowstorms were getting harder to navigate with each passing year.

1. **A.** NO CHANGE
   B. had recent become difficultly
   C. had recently become difficult
   D. had recently become difficultly

2. **F.** NO CHANGE
   G. against
   H. in
   J. near to

3. **A.** NO CHANGE
   B. a stubbornly man
   C. stubbornly man
   D. stubborn man

4. **F.** NO CHANGE
   G. for
   H. nor
   J. and

5. **A.** NO CHANGE
   B. them
   C. us
   D. they

Answer Explanations

1. The correct answer is C. *Recent* is incorrect because the verb *become* must be modified by an adverb rather than an adjective—you can elimi-nate choices A and B. Choice D incorrectly turns *difficult* into an adverb by adding *-ly*, so the cor-

rect answer is choice C, which changes *recent* to *recently* but leaves the term *difficult* as is.

2. The correct answer is H. The key to answering this preposition question is recognizing that in standard English, one would refer to a sensation in the joints, rather than toward, against, or near to the joints.

3. The correct answer is A. The sentence is correct as written. All of the other options either incorrectly change the adjective *stubborn* to an *-ly* adverb (choices B and C) or needlessly omit the article *a* (choices C and D).

4. The correct answer is J. Here, you must locate the conjunction that best connects the two parts of the last sentence. *Yet* (choice A) is incorrect because what comes after the conjunction doesn't contradict what came before it. *For* (choice B) illogically implies that not abandoning the cabin is the reason Bo built said cabin. *Nor* (choice C) is only used to introduce a second element after *neither* or a construction with *not* introduces the first. the first.

5. The correct answer is A. The sentence is correct as written since *it* is the proper singular pronoun to refer to the antecedent *cabin*.

SENTENCE STRUCTURE AND FORMATION

Understanding the parts of speech is fundamental to good writing and editing, but so is understanding how to combine the parts of speech to form effective sentences. Sentence structure and formation plays a key role in the English section of the ACT. Understanding sentence structure in English requires you to be an expert on two related concepts: complete sentences and sentence fragments.

Independent Clauses

A complete sentence is called an independent clause. An independent clause possesses a subject (something that completes an action) and a verb (the action), and the clause expresses a complete thought; for example, "My ACT English score will improve." That's a complete sentence—an independent clause. It has a subject ("My ACT English score") and a verb ("will improve.") It also expresses a complete thought.

Dependent Clauses

Sentence fragments are missing one or more of the key ingredients for a sentence: a subject, a verb, or the expression of a complete thought.

A kind of sentence fragment you'll encounter regularly on the ACT is a dependent clause. Dependent clauses are used to add information to independent clauses, often expanding on the conditions under which the action of the independent clause will occur. A dependent clause has a subject and a verb, but it doesn't express a complete thought. For instance, "When I learn the conventions of standard English" is not a complete sentence—it's a dependent clause. It has a subject ("I") and a verb ("learn"), but it doesn't express a complete thought. "When I learn the conventions of standard English" . . .what happens then? It can't stand on its own, but we can address the error by combining it with an independent clause to produce a complete sentence: "When I learn the conventions of standard English, my ACT English score will improve."

Adding the dependent clause to the independent clause not only creates a complete sentence for the dependent clause but it also adds information to the independent clause, creating a more sophisticated sentence structure and specific idea. That's just one possible sentence type in English.

On the ACT English section, you will need to be able to recognize, restructure, and engineer four different kinds of sentences:

Four Types of Sentences

SIMPLE SENTENCE (an independent clause)	**COMPOUND SENTENCE** (two independent clauses joined together)	**COMPLEX SENTENCE** (an independent and at least one dependent clause)	**COMPOUND-COMPLEX SENTENCE** (at least two independent clauses and one dependent clause)

Sentence Fragments

Every sentence must have a subject (something to do the action) and a verb or predicate (the action) and express a complete idea. You know that when all those items are present, you get an independent clause. If a group of words is missing one of these elements, it is called a sentence fragment or an incomplete sentence. If the group of words has a subject and verb but doesn't express a complete thought, it's a dependent clause. If a sentence fragment appears on the ACT, you'll need to address the error.

There are two ways to correct incomplete sentences.

1 Add a subject and/or verb to the fragment.

Incorrect: Considerable time studying animals in their natural habitats.

Correct: Wildlife biologists may spend considerable time studying animals in their natural habitats.

Explanation: A subject (*wildlife biologists*) and verb (*may spend*) are added to the fragment.

2 Add the fragment to the sentence that precedes it or the sentence that follows.

Incorrect: Zoologists and wildlife biologists study animals and other wildlife. Including how they interact with their ecosystems.

Correct: Zoologists and wildlife biologists study animals and other wildlife, including how they interact with their ecosystems.

Explanation: The fragment is added to the sentence that precedes it by inserting a comma.

Incorrect: By studying animal behaviors. Wildlife biologists seek to understand how animals interact with their ecosystems.

Correct: By studying animal behaviors, wildlife biologists seek to understand how animals interact with their ecosystems.

Explanation: The fragment is added to the sentence that follows it by inserting a comma. (The fragment now serves as a prepositional phrase that modifies the rest of the sentence.)

Run-Ons and Comma Splices

Complete sentences must be separated by a period, a comma and a coordinating conjunction, or a semicolon. A run-on sentence occurs when a writer fails to use either end-stop punctuation to divide complete thoughts or suitable conjunctions to join two ideas. When two independent clauses are joined only by a comma, it creates an error called a comma splice.

The following rules will help you avoid and fix run-on sentences and comma splices.

1 Divide the sentence using periods.

❌ **Incorrect:** Zoologists need a bachelor's degree for entry-level positions a master's degree or Ph.D. is often needed for advancement.

✔ **Correct:** Zoologists need a bachelor's degree for entry-level positions. A master's degree or Ph.D. is often needed for advancement.

ℹ **Explanation:** Inserting a period between *positions* and *A* corrects the run-on sentence by creating two independent clauses.

2 Create a compound sentence by joining independent clauses using a coordinating conjunction such as *and*, *but*, or *so*.

❌ **Incorrect:** Zoologists need a bachelor's degree for entry-level positions, a master's degree is often needed for advancement.

✔ **Correct:** Zoologists need a bachelor's degree for entry-level positions, but a master's degree is often needed for advancement. (Remember that a comma is required when you use a coordinating conjunction to join two independent clauses.)

ℹ **Explanation:** Adding a comma and the coordinating conjunction *but* eliminates the comma splice and connects the two independent clauses correctly.

3 Create a complex sentence by adding a subordinating conjunction—such as *because*, *although*, or *while*—making one of the independent clauses a dependent clause.

❌ **Incorrect:** Zoologists need only a bachelor's degree for entry-level positions a master's degree is often needed for advancement.

✔ **Correct (option 1):** Zoologists need only a bachelor's degree for entry-level positions although a master's degree is often needed for advancement.

ℹ **Explanation:** Adding the conjunction *although* between the two independent clauses corrects the run-on sentence by changing the second clause to a dependent clause and creating a complex sentence. (In general, commas are not required when the dependent clause follows the independent clause.)

Correct (option 2): Although a master's degree is often needed for advancement, zoologists need only a bachelor's degree for entry-level positions.

Explanation: Adding the conjunction *although* before the first independent clause corrects the run-on sentence by changing the first clause to a dependent clause and creating a complex sentence. (A comma is required when the dependent clause precedes the independent clause.)

4

Use a semicolon when ideas in two independent clauses are closely related in meaning.

Incorrect: Zoologists and wildlife biologists study how animals and other wildlife interact with their ecosystems, these scientists work outdoors or in offices or laboratories.

Correct: Zoologists and wildlife biologists study how animals and other wildlife interact with their ecosystems; these scientists work outdoors or in offices or laboratories.

Explanation: Inserting a semicolon between the two independent clauses corrects the comma splice and creates a compound sentence.

Coordination and Subordination

Coordinating and subordinating conjunctions are used to join phrases and clauses and form compound and complex sentences.

COMMON CONJUNCTIONS	
Coordinating conjunctions	**Subordinating conjunctions**
and, but, for, nor, or, so, yet	after, although, as, as if, because, before, even if, even though, if, if only, rather than, since, that, though, unless, until, when, where, whereas, wherever, whether, which, while

Basic Rule of Coordinating Conjunctions

Coordinating conjunctions are used to add items to a list and join independent clauses to make compound sentences. With items in a list, the last item in the list should be preceded by a coordinating conjunction.

Independent clauses: There was a Treaty of Paris signed in 1763. There was also one signed in 1783. There was another signed in 1919.

Joined: There were Treaties of Paris signed in 1763, 1783, and 1919.

When two clauses are joined, if the second remains an independent clause, a comma must be used before the coordinating conjunction. The coordinating conjunction signals that each clause carries the same weight while also creating a relationship between the ideas (additive, contrasting, or causal).

Independent clauses: There was a Treaty of Paris signed in 1763. There was also one signed in 1783.

Joined: There was a Treaty of Paris signed in 1763, but there was another Treaty of Paris signed in 1783.

TIP

Remember that an independent clause is just a complete sentence. It has a subject and a verb and expresses a complete thought.

Basic Rule of Subordinating Conjunctions

Subordinating conjunctions are added to an independent clause to make it a dependent clause.

A dependent clause establishes a place, time, reason, condition, concession, or comparison for the independent clause—some form of extra information that clarifies the action of the independent clause. Dependent clauses have a subject and a verb but don't express a complete thought, usually as indicated by a subordinating conjunction. A subordinating conjunction signals that the clause needs (or *depends* on) an independent clause to be grammatically correct. This also means that dependent clauses are subordinate to the information in the independent clause—meaning they're less important (offering extra information) and preceded by a subordinating conjunction. Dependent clauses can come before or after an independent clause, but if they're before, they must be separated from the independent clause by a comma. Review the list of subordinating conjunctions to identify dependent clauses more quickly. Let's look at some examples of subordinating conjunctions used to create dependent clauses.

 Independent clauses: A tax on imported goods from another country is called a tariff. A tax on imported goods from another country to protect a home industry is called a protective tariff.

 Joined: A tax on imported goods from another country is called a tariff while a tax on imported goods from another country to protect a home industry is called a protective tariff.

Here, the subordinating conjunction *while* was added to the second independent clause. The resulting dependent clause is then joined to the end of the first independent clause without using any punctuation.

A subordinating conjunction can also be used at the beginning of a sentence. The resulting dependent clause must be joined to an independent clause and separated by a comma.

Independent clauses: A tax on imported goods from another country is called a tariff. A tax on imported goods from another country to protect a home industry is called a protective tariff.

Joined: While a tax on imported goods from another country is called a tariff, a tax on imported goods from another country to protect a home industry is called a protective tariff.

Modifier Placement

A modifier is a word, phrase, or clause that adds detail to a sentence. To avoid confusion, modifiers should be placed as close as possible to the things they modify. Examples of different modifiers are underlined in the sentences below.

1

Example 1: Within the field of marine biology, employment is highly competitive.

Explanation: The phrase "within the field of marine biology" modifies the subject of the sentence, which is *employment*. The word *highly* modifies our understanding of the competitive nature of finding employment.

2

Example 2: The abundant supply of marine scientists far exceeds the demands, and the number of government jobs is limited.

Explanation: *Abundant* modifies *supply*. *Marine* modifies *scientists*. *Limited* modifies our understanding of the number of jobs. *Government* modifies *jobs*.

When the subject of a modifier is unclear or is not included in the sentence, it is considered a dangling modifier.

Incorrect: Not realizing that the job title "marine biologist" rarely exists in the real world, *marine biology* is a term recognized by most people. (What is the first phrase modifying?)

Possible revision: Not realizing that the job title "marine biologist" rarely exists in the real world, most people recognize the term *marine biology*.

Misplaced modifiers occur when a modifier is poorly placed and doesn't express the writer's intent accurately.

Incorrect: The term *marine biologist* is used to almost describe all of the disciplines and jobs that deal with the study of marine life, not just those that deal with the physical properties of the sea.

Possible revision: The term *marine biologist* is used to describe almost all of the disciplines and jobs that deal with the study of marine life, not just those that deal with the physical properties of the sea.

Parallel Structure

Parallel structure is the repetition of a grammatical form within a sentence. When things are parallel, they are moving in the same direction. Parallel structure is a hallmark of effective writing and is often used to emphasize ideas and present compared items in an equal light. Coordinating conjunctions are often used in parallel constructions.

 Nonparallel structure: As a child, George Washington Carver enjoyed reading, learned about plants, and he made art.

 Parallel structure: As a child, George Washington Carver enjoyed reading, learning about plants, and making art.

In the first sentence, "George Washington Carver enjoyed reading" leads the reader to expect that the next items in the list will also be gerunds (verbs that end in -*ing* and function as nouns). However, the next items in the list are not in the same form: "learned about plants" is in the past tense, while "he made art" is an independent clause. To resolve the issue with parallel structure, we need to pick one form of the word and stick to it. The easiest and most concise fix is to change the last two items to gerunds to match the first item, *reading.*

Issues with parallel structure are most noticeable in lists of things. It's important to remember that parallel structure applies to other parts of speech as well. To be grammatically correct, items that are being compared should be the same part of speech and used correctly in the structure of the sentence. When writing, parallel structure is especially effective in divided thesis statements, wherein the author expresses their primary argument in a single statement at the end of their first paragraph, using parallel structure to present the elements of their argument.

Active Vs. Passive Voice

Voice, as related to sentence structure, tells us whether the subject of a sentence is the actor (active) or is acted upon (passive). In formal writing, active voice is generally preferred because it is more immediate and places the reader closer to the action. Passive voice can be the better choice when you want to emphasize what received the action (e.g. "I was hit by a car" vs. "A car hit me."). The ACT will almost always prefer active voice to passive construction, unless the active construction is not grammatically correct, concise, or relevant to the passage.

 Passive voice example: According to legend, the cherry tree was chopped down by George Washington.

 Active voice example: According to legend, George Washington chopped down the cherry tree.

Practice Set 2: Sentence Structure

THE HUNT FOR A HOBBY

After everything that happened last year, I decided that I needed a hobby. I wanted something I could do easily in my spare <u>time nor</u> I also wanted
₁
something that I enjoyed.

To figure out what my new hobby <u>could be. I spent</u>
₂
<u>time researching</u> and discovered that the local
₂
Parks and Recreation Department offered a dozen different programs. So, I set out to get a taste of each. <u>A vegan cooking course was the first thing</u>
₃
<u>I tried.</u>
₃

Day one, our instructor taught us how to make <u>a curried sweet potato soup. And a kind of cream</u>
₄
<u>made from cashews to garnish the soup. Plus vegan</u>
₄
<u>cupcakes for dessert.</u>
₄

1. **A.** NO CHANGE
   B. time, but
   C. time yet
   D. time; and

2. **F.** NO CHANGE
   G. could be I spent time researching
   H. could be and spent time researching
   J. could be, I spent time researching

3. **A.** NO CHANGE
   B. The first thing I tried was a vegan cooking course.
   C. A vegan cooking course I tried was the first thing.
   D. First, I tried a vegan cooking course.

4. **F.** NO CHANGE
   G. a curried sweet potato soup; a kind of cream made from cashews to garnish the soup; vegan cupcakes for dessert.
   H. a curried sweet potato soup and vegan cupcakes for dessert, plus: a kind of cream made from cashews to garnish the soup.
   J. a curried sweet potato soup, a kind of cream made from cashews to garnish the soup, and vegan cupcakes for dessert.

Unfortunately, my soup turned out okay, but I
            5
almost made my station partner cry because I put
                    5
in too much cayenne pepper!
            5

5. **A.** NO CHANGE

B. My soup turned out okay. Unfortunately, I almost made my station partner cry because I put in too much cayenne pepper!

C. My soup turned out unfortunately okay, but I almost made my station partner cry because I put in too much cayenne pepper!

D. My soup turned out okay, but I almost made my station partner cry unfortunately because I put in too much cayenne pepper!

Answer Explanations

1. The correct answer is B. This is a run-on sentence as there are two independent clauses without proper punctuation. They need to be separated with a period, a semicolon, or a comma with a coordinating conjunction. While choices A, C, and D all have one of the FANBOYS, they each lack a comma. While a semicolon can be used to separate independent clauses (choice D), no coordinating conjunction is necessary.

2. The correct answer is J. The clause before the period is a sentence fragment. It's an infinitive clause that provides context for the ensuing independent clause. To join them together, the period should be replaced with a comma.

3. The correct answer is D. This sentence uses passive voice, wherein the subject of the sentence (a vegan cooking course) is receiving the action. It should be rephrased into active voice. Choice C is a passive construction. Choice B uses the linking verb *was* to state that "The first thing I tried" equals "a vegan cooking course." That construction is acceptable; however, it is less concise than choice D.

4. The correct answer is J. Choice J takes the related sentence and two fragments and combines them effectively into a list. Choice F is incorrect because "And a kind of cream made from cashews to garnish the soup" and "Plus vegan cupcakes for dessert" are both fragments. Choice G is incorrect because it creates three equal clauses instead of a list. Choice H is incorrect because it needlessly changes the order and deploys a colon in the middle of the list.

5. The correct answer is B. The adverb *unfortunately* should be as close to what it modifies as possible. Only the placement and punctuation in choice B has it properly modify the action of "almost [making] the station partner cry."

PUNCTUATION

Like the other conventions of good writing, punctuation helps you communicate more effectively. Punctuation includes commas, semicolons, em dashes, parentheses, colons, and apostrophes, among other punctuation marks. Here, we'll prioritize the most important punctuation to remember for your English test.

The Comma

We use commas for a lot of things, but focus on using them to separate the following:

- Independent clauses that are connected by a coordinating conjunction
- Introductory clauses and phrases
- Dependent and independent clauses
- Items in a series
- Nonessential and parenthetical elements
- Coordinate adjectives

Let's look at some examples:

- To separate independent clauses connected by a coordinating conjunction

> **EXAMPLE**
>
> Toni Morrison's first novel was published in 1970, and it received a rave review from *The New York Times*.

- To set off introductory clauses and phrases

> **EXAMPLE**
>
> The year after winning her Nobel Prize, Toni Morrison published the novel *Jazz*.

- To separate a leading dependent clause from an independent clause

> **EXAMPLE**
>
> While she was praised for her writing style and range of emotion, Toni Morrison was also celebrated for the attention she drew to racial tension in the past and present of the United States.

- To separate three or more items in a list

> **EXAMPLE**
>
> In a span of 15 years, Toni Morrison won a National Book Critics Circle Award, the Pulitzer Prize, and the Nobel Prize for Literature.

If you pay attention to punctuation, it's likely you've noticed that not everyone puts the serial or Oxford comma before the *and* when separating three or more items in a list. In recent years, a lot of writing (especially online) has ignored the serial comma, but its absence or presence can affect what a sentence means. In 2018, a missing Oxford comma in a Maine labor law cost a dairy company in the state $5 million dollars in a lawsuit with its employees. Increasingly, using the Oxford comma is considered preferable punctuation, and you will see it (or see it missing) in questions in the ACT English section.

- To separate nonessential and parenthetical elements from the main clause

> **EXAMPLE**
>
> Toni Morrison, who won the Nobel Prize in Literature in 1993, was a Professor Emeritus at Princeton University.

EXAMPLE

Last night, Toni Morrison began her lecture, titled "The Future of Time: Literature and Diminished Expectations," with a meditation on the nature of time and the human perception of progress.

- To separate coordinate adjectives that precede the noun they describe

EXAMPLE

Toni Morrison was described as a fun, entertaining speaker.

When you have at least two adjectives describing a noun (e.g., "The tall, funny man" or "The cold and windy weather"), you can separate the adjectives with a comma when their order can be reversed or when the conjunction *and* can be placed between them while still preserving the meaning of the phrase. If reversing the order or adding *and* disrupts the meaning of the phrase (e.g., "The giant hockey players" as "The hockey giant players" or "The giant and hockey players"), no comma is needed.

The Semicolon

A semicolon may be used to separate two complete ideas (independent clauses) in a sentence when the two ideas have a close relationship and are *not* connected with a coordinating conjunction.

EXAMPLE

"Inalienable rights" are basic human rights that many believe cannot and should not be given up or taken away; life, liberty, and the pursuit of happiness are some of those rights.

The semicolon is often used between independent clauses connected by conjunctive adverbs such as *consequently, therefore, also, furthermore, for example, however, nevertheless, still, yet, moreover,* and *otherwise*.

EXAMPLE

In 1867, critics thought William H. Seward foolish for buying the largely unexplored territory of Alaska for the astronomical price of $7 million; however, history has proven that it was an inspired purchase.

TIP

Nonessential and parenthetical elements provide extra information that is not necessary for the meaning or grammatical correctness of a sentence. Commas, parentheses, and em dashes serve similar purposes; the difference between them is one of emphasis. On the ACT, you will not be asked to choose between these three marks as that is often a stylistic decision. If a question presents them in different answer choices, there are likely other errors present to help you eliminate choices.

A word of caution: Do not use the semicolon between an independent clause and a phrase or subordinate clause.

 Incorrect: While eating ice cream for dessert; Clarence and Undine discussed their next business venture.

 Correct: While eating ice cream for dessert, Clarence and Undine discussed their next business venture.

Similar to serial commas, semicolons are used to separate items in a list but only when the items themselves contain commas.

Some kinds of biologists study specific species of animals. For example, cetologists study marine mammals, such as whales and dolphins; entomologists study insects, such as beetles and butterflies; and ichthyologists study wild fish, such as sharks and lungfish.

The Em Dash

Em dashes are used to set off parenthetical material that you want to emphasize. Dashes interrupt the flow of your sentence, thereby calling attention to the information they contain. An em dash always precedes the nonessential information, so the aside must start later in the sentence.

Many consider Toni Morrison—winner of both the Pulitzer and Nobel Prizes in Literature—to be one of the greatest writers of her generation.

Benjamin Franklin's many intellectual pursuits—from printmaking to politics—exemplify his eclectic personality.

Em dashes can also be used to rename a nearby noun. Typically, a comma would be used to set off this information, but since it includes commas already, use an em dash.

Benjamin Franklin—a printer, writer, inventor, and statesman—was the son of a soap maker.

An em dash also indicates a list, a restatement, an amplification, or a dramatic shift in tone or thought.

Eager to write for his brother's newspaper, young Benjamin began submitting letters to the editor under the pseudonym Silence Dogood—they were a hit!

The Colon

The colon is used to precede a list, a long quotation, or a statement that illustrates or clarifies the earlier information. A colon can be used only after an independent clause.

EXAMPLES

There are only three nations that have successfully landed spacecraft on the moon: the Soviet Union, the United States, and China.

In the United States, there are three branches of government: the Executive, the Legislative, and the Judicial.

Use colons only after independent clauses. Most commonly, that means that you won't use colons after a verb. Further, no introductory or connecting information should occur before or after a colon, such as *and* or *including*.

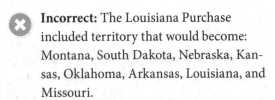 **Incorrect:** The Louisiana Purchase included territory that would become: Montana, South Dakota, Nebraska, Kansas, Oklahoma, Arkansas, Louisiana, and Missouri.

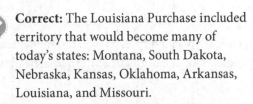 **Correct:** The Louisiana Purchase included territory that would become many of today's states: Montana, South Dakota, Nebraska, Kansas, Oklahoma, Arkansas, Louisiana, and Missouri.

The Apostrophe

Apostrophes usually serve one of two purposes.

To indicate a contraction—the omission of one or more letters: Place the apostrophe exactly where the missing letters occur.

 Examples:

can't = cannot

it's = it is

we're = we are

To indicate the possessive case of nouns: If the noun does not end in *s*—whether singular or plural—add an *'s*; if the noun ends in *s* simply add the *'*. Some writers like to add *'s* to all nouns, even those that already end in *s*, but the ACT will default to *s'*.

 Example 1: The impact of Allen Ginsberg's poem "Howl" on the cultural landscape of the United States cannot be overstated.

Example 2: A car's headlights are typically wired in parallel so that if one burns out the other will keep functioning.

Example 3: The women's club sponsored many charity events.

Example 4: Charles Mingus' skill as a jazz musician is widely recognized.

ALERT

Do not use apostrophes with possessive pronouns such as *yours, hers, ours, theirs,* and *whose*, which indicate possession already.

Example 4 represents an interesting grammatical point. Some people and style guides prefer to place a lone apostrophe after words that end in *s* (Example: Silas' cat) while others add *'s* (Example: Silas's cat). On the ACT English test, you are more likely to see a single apostrophe used to show possession when a term ends in *s*, whether the term is plural (Example: teachers' salaries) or if it just ends in an *s* (Example: dress' hem). However, you may see –*'s* used when a word ends in an *s* and is also a proper noun (Example: Cass's dog).

End-of-Sentence Punctuation

There are three types of punctuation used to end a sentence: the period, the question mark, and the exclamation mark.

1

A period is used at the end of a sentence that makes a statement.

Example: In 1620, the Pilgrims in Plymouth signed the Mayflower Compact.

2

A question mark is used after a direct question. A period is used after an indirect question.

Direct Question: Were *The Federalist Papers* written by James Madison, John Jay, or Alexander Hamilton?

Indirect Question: Profession Mahin wanted to know if you knew who wrote *The Federalist Papers.*

3

An exclamation mark is used after an expression that shows strong emotion or issues a command. It may follow a word, a phrase, or a sentence.

Example: Koko the gorilla knew more than 1,000 sign-language signs and could communicate with humans. Amazing!

Unnecessary Punctuation

Unnecessary punctuation can break a sentence into confusing and illogical fragments. Here are some common mistakes to look out for.

- Don't use a comma alone to connect independent clauses. This is called a comma splice.

❌ **Incorrect:** Toni Morrison grew up in an integrated neighborhood, she did not become fully aware of racial divisions until she was in her teens.

✅ **Possible revision:** Toni Morrison grew up in an integrated neighborhood and did not become fully aware of racial divisions until she was in her teens.

- Don't use a comma between compound elements that are not independent clauses.

❌ **Incorrect:** In 1998, Oprah Winfrey, and Danny Glover starred in a film adaptation of Morrison's novel *Beloved*.

✅ **Possible revision:** In 1998, Oprah Winfrey and Danny Glover starred in a film adaptation of Morrison's novel *Beloved*.

- Do not use an apostrophe when making a noun plural.

❌ **Incorrect:** In 2006, *The New York Times Book Review* named *Beloved* the best American novel published in the last 25 year's.

✅ **Possible revision:** In 2006, *The New York Times Book Review* named *Beloved* the best American novel published in the last 25 years.

Practice Set 3: Punctuation

BARNARD STREET'S TRANSFORMATION

Barnard Street looked like a lost cause just thirty years ago. Walking or driving through, you might have seen <u>burned-out cars feral animals hunting for scraps of food and piles of garbage littering the cracked and deserted sidewalks.</u> No one ₁ wanted to spend much time there, let alone make it their home.

<u>Neighbors would say: it was a spot best left alone.</u> ₂ Since then, things have changed dramatically on Barnard Street.

<u>A community volunteer group, Barnard SWEEP,</u> ₃ came together

<u>in 1996 and organized a massive effort</u> to clean up ₄ the lots and sidewalks.

1. **A.** NO CHANGE
   B. burned-out cars feral, animals, hunting for scraps of food, and piles of garbage, littering the cracked and, deserted, sidewalks.
   C. burned-out cars feral animals hunting, for scraps of food. And piles of garbage littering the cracked and deserted sidewalks.
   D. burned-out cars, feral animals hunting for scraps of food, and piles of garbage littering the cracked and deserted sidewalks.

2. **F.** NO CHANGE
   G. Neighbors would say it was a spot best left alone.
   H. Neighbors would say, it was a spot best left alone.
   J. Neighbors would say "it was a spot best left alone."

3. **A.** NO CHANGE
   B. A community volunteer group Barnard SWEEP
   C. A community volunteer, group Barnard SWEEP,
   D. A community volunteer group Barnard SWEEP,

4. **F.** NO CHANGE
   G. in 1996, and organized a massive effort
   H. in 1996 and organized, a massive effort
   J. in 1996, and organized, a massive effort

It took months over the summer to do the initial

<u>clean-up tasks: however, at the end of a few years, it</u>
                                    5

<u>was looking</u> like a completely different street.
        5

5. **A.** NO CHANGE

   B. clean-up tasks: however at the end of a
   few years it was looking

   C. clean-up tasks; however, at the end of a
   few years, it was looking

   D. clean-up tasks; however at the end of a
   few years it was looking

Answer Explanations

1. The correct answer is D. The sentence is not correct as stands (choice A) because it is missing the commas that are necessary to separate the items into a list. However, choice B adds multiple unnecessary commas. Choice C also adds an unnecessary comma before "for scraps of food" but also needlessly breaks the statement into two fragments by introducing an unnecessary period.

2. The correct answer is G. As it stands, the sentence adds an unnecessary colon, so eliminate choice A. There is no need to add punctuation to separate "Neighbors would say" from "it was a spot best left alone," so choice G is correct. Choice H needlessly adds a comma, and choice J incorrectly uses quotation marks—while these may seem correct since the sentence references something that was said, they should only be used if what is within the quotation marks is a direct quotation of something said, rather than a general statement like the one used here.

3. The correct answer is A. The sentence is correct as it stands, since the commas are used to clarify the additional information that the community volunteer group mentioned is called Barnard SWEEP. None of the other options convey this information or use commas correctly.

4. The correct answer is F. There is no need to separate any part of this phrase with commas, so the sentence is correct as it stands.

5. The correct answer is C. The commas in the original sentence are placed correctly, but the sentence erroneously uses a colon instead of a semicolon to separate the initial clause from the one that starts with *however*. Therefore, you need only find the answer that replaces the colon with a semicolon without removing the existing commas.

VERBS, USAGE, AND AGREEMENT

In addition to English grammar, sentence structure, and punctuation, you will encounter questions in the English section that focus on the ways in which English is used conventionally to convey meaning. There are any number of things that are done in English not because they follow a strict grammatical rule but because they are how we use English on a day-to-day basis that makes sense to most people. Alongside those concepts, we'll spend more time looking at proper use of verbs, especially as tested by the ACT, as well as agreement—which describes how how both verbs and pronouns are used to match the meaning of phrases and sentences.

Verb Tense

Use the same verb tense whenever possible within a sentence or paragraph. Do not shift from one tense to another unless there is a valid reason for doing so.

> ❌ **Incorrect:** The Magna Carta *was* signed in 1215 by King John of England and *has been* the first document of its kind to limit the power of the British monarchy.
>
> ✅ **Correct:** The Magna Carta *was* signed in 1215 by King John of England and *was* the first document of its kind to limit the power of the British monarchy.

Naturally, different verb tenses have different forms, but you will see some overlap. For example, even though the sentences "He was tall" and "He was running" both use the verb *was*, the former is a simple past tense verb while the latter is called the past progressive and has a helping verb attached to the word *running*. Complete verbs can be individual words or consist of a helping verb (often a form of "to be," "to have," or "to do") and a main verb or a participle. Look out for those small verbs to decide which choice is best for the passage.

When to Use the Perfect Tenses

Knowing when to choose between the simple (past, present, and future) and perfect tenses can be challenging, as those choices often depend on the author's intended meaning. However, information presented in the sentence, like prepositional phrases or other modifiers, can help you decide which tense makes the most sense.

- Use *present perfect* for an action begun in the past and extended to the present.

> 🔍 **Example:** Scientists at NASA *have seen* an alarming increase in the accumulation of greenhouse gases.
>
> ℹ️ **Explanation:** In this case, *scientists at NASA saw* would be incorrect. What they *have seen* (present perfect) began in the past and extends to the present.

 ALERT

Different verb tenses have different forms, and there may be some overlap. It's important to select the choice that is the best for the passage.

- Use *past perfect* for an action begun and completed in the past before some other past action.

> **Example:** Despite their preparations, Lewis and Clark *had never encountered* the kinds of challenges that awaited them before their expedition.
>
> **Explanation:** In this case, *never encountered* would be incorrect. The action *had never encountered* (past perfect) is used because it is referring to events prior to their expedition.

- Use *future perfect* for an action begun at any time and completed in the future.

> **Example:** When the American astronauts arrive, the Russian cosmonauts *will have been* on the International Space Station for six months.
>
> **Explanation:** In this case, although both actions occur in the future, the Russian cosmonauts *will have been* on the space station before the American astronauts *arrive*. When there are two future actions, the action completed first is expressed in the future perfect tense.

Common Verbs and Their Tenses

Refer to the following chart to familiarize yourself with some common verbs and their tenses.

COMMON VERBS AND THEIR TENSES*						
Infinitive	Present	Past	Future	Present Perfect	Past Perfect	Future Perfect
to ask	ask	asked	will ask	have asked	had asked	will have asked
to be	am	was	will be	have been	had been	will have been
to become	become	became	will become	have become	had become	will have become
to begin	begin	began	will begin	have begun	had begun	will have begun
to come	come	came	will come	have come	had come	will have come
to do	do	did	will do	have done	had done	will have done
to eat	eat	ate	will eat	have eaten	had eaten	will have eaten
to feel	feel	felt	will feel	have felt	had felt	will have felt
to find	find	found	will find	have found	had found	will have found
to get	get	got	will get	have gotten	had gotten	will have gotten
to give	give	gave	will give	have given	had given	will have given
to go	go	went	will go	have gone	had gone	will have gone
to grow	grow	grew	will grow	have grown	had grown	will have grown
to have	have	had	will have	have had	had had	will have had
to hear	hear	heard	will hear	have heard	had heard	will have heard

			COMMON VERBS AND THEIR TENSES*			
Infinitive	Present	Past	Future	Present Perfect	Past Perfect	Future Perfect
to hide	hide	hid	will hide	have hidden	had hidden	will have hidden
to keep	keep	kept	will keep	have kept	had kept	will have kept
to know	know	knew	will know	have known	had known	will have known
to leave	leave	left	will leave	have left	had left	will have left
to like	like	liked	will like	have liked	had liked	will have liked
to look	look	looked	will look	have looked	had looked	will have looked
to make	make	made	will make	have made	had made	will have made
to meet	meet	met	will meet	have met	had met	will have met
to put	put	put	will put	have put	had put	will have put
to say	say	said	will say	have said	had said	will have said
to see	see	saw	will see	have seen	had seen	will have seen
to sleep	sleep	slept	will sleep	have slept	had slept	will have slept
to speak	speak	spoke	will speak	have spoken	had spoken	will have spoken
to study	study	studied	will study	have studied	had studied	will have studied
to take	take	took	will take	have taken	had taken	will have taken
to think	think	thought	will think	have thought	had thought	will have thought
to walk	walk	walked	will walk	have walked	had walked	will have walked
to want	want	wanted	will want	have wanted	had wanted	will have wanted
to work	work	worked	will work	have worked	had worked	will have worked
to write	write	wrote	will write	have written	had written	will have written

*Note: For consistency, all verbs are conjugated in the first-person singular.

Pronoun Case

Pronouns substitute for nouns in sentences. Every pronoun must have a clear antecedent (the noun that it replaces), have the same number as the antecedent (singular or plural), share the same perspective or person (1st, 2nd, or 3rd), and be in the proper pronoun case for its use in the sentence (subjective, objective, possessive).

EXAMPLES

George Washington was born on February 22, 1732, in Pope's Creek, Virginia; *he* was the first American president.

Did you know that Besty Ross and George Washington both went to the same church? *It* was called Christ Church, and *it* was located in Philadelphia.

The following pronoun chart may prove useful.

PRONOUNS				
Number	Person	Subjective Case	Objective Case	Possessive Case
Singular	1st person	I	me	mine
	2nd person	you	you	yours
	3rd person	he, she, it, who	him, her, it, whom	his, hers, whose
Plural	1st person	we	us	ours
	2nd person	you	you	yours
	3rd person	they, who	them, whom	theirs, whose

A pronoun must agree in number with its antecedent, using a singular or plural pronoun of the correct person and case. In recent years, it, it has increasingly become grammatically acceptable to use *they* or *them* as a singular pronoun; however, the ACT does not yet recognize this use.

> ❌ **Incorrect:** George Washington was among the seven figures that were key to the formation of the United States government, the Founding Fathers, because *they* shaped and served the country's executive branch. (What is the antecedent for the marked pronoun? George Washington or Founding Fathers?)
>
> ✅ **Correct:** George Washington was among the seven figures that were key to the formation of the United States government, the Founding Fathers, because *he* shaped and served the country's executive branch. (The pronoun needs to be in the third-person singular in the subjective case in order to agree with the antecedent *George Washington*.)
>
> ❌ **Incorrect:** George Washington issued two vetoes successfully during his two presidential terms. One was issued in his first term, and the other was issued after he left office. Congress was unable to overturn *it*. (What was Congress unable to overturn?)
>
> ✅ **Correct:** George Washington issued two vetoes successfully during his two presidential terms. One was issued in his first term, and the other was issued after he left office. Congress was unable to overturn *them*. (The pronoun needs to be third-person plural in the objective case to agree with the antecedent *two vetoes* and work with the grammar of the sentence.)

A pronoun uses the *subjective* case when it is the subject of the sentence or when it renames the subject as a subject complement.

Incorrect: One story of the American flag's creation says George Ross, Robert Morris, and *him* asked Betsy Ross to sew the first flag.

Correct: One story of the American flag's creation says George Ross, Robert Morris, and *he* asked Betsy Ross to sew the first flag. (*He* is part of the compound subject of the sentence and stands in for George Washington.)

Incorrect: *Him* is George Washington.

Correct: *He* is George Washington. (*He* renames the subject.)

If a pronoun is the object of a verb or preposition, it is placed in the *objective* case.

Incorrect: Washington placed a lot of trust in Benedict Arnold. In 1780, George Washington gave command of West Point to *he*.

Correct: Washington placed a lot of trust in Benedict Arnold. In 1780, George Washington gave command of West Point to *him*.

Incorrect: Despite the fact that *us* turned in our American history paper late, our teacher gave Franklin and *I* an A grade.

Correct: Despite the fact that *we* turned in our American history paper late, our teacher gave Franklin and *me* an A grade. (*We* is the subject of the dependent clause, and *me* is an object of the verb *gave*.)

Avoid ambiguity and confusion by making sure that the antecedent of the pronoun is clear. The presence of multiple nouns that share the same gender and number means that the sentence must clarify which antecedent is being referred to. Sometimes, modifying the sentence may mean removing the pronoun, as in the second example below.

Incorrect: At the height of his career, Frank Lloyd Wright told an architectural scholar that *he* thought *his* work was improving. (Is Wright talking about his own work or the work of the scholar?)

Correct: At the height of his career, Frank Lloyd Wright told an architectural scholar that he thought *his own* work was improving.

Incorrect: Frank Lloyd Wright and his wife Olgivanna founded a school for aspiring artists in Spring Green, Wisconsin, where *they* could "learn by doing." (Does *they* refer to the Wrights or the artists?)

Correct: Frank Lloyd Wright and his wife Olgivanna founded a school in Spring Green, Wisconsin, where aspiring artists could "learn by doing."

Possessive Determiners

When a pronoun expresses ownership, it is placed in the possessive case. An absolute possessive pronoun can stand on its own without needing a noun to follow it to be clear. Absolute possessive pronouns are *mine*, *yours*, *his*, *hers*, *its*, *ours*, and *theirs*.

EXAMPLES

The watch is *mine*.

That one is *his*.

Theirs are broken.

A possessive pronoun that identifies, specifies, or quantifies the noun it precedes is called a possessive determiner. Possessive determiners are *my, your, his, her, its, our,* and *their.*

It's *my* watch.

That's *his* watch.

Their watches are broken.

either, and *neither.* Some indefinite pronouns—*any, more, most, some*—will be singular or plural as dependent on usage. The pronouns *both, many, others,* and *several* will always need a plural verb for agreement.

Pronoun-Antecedent Agreement

A pronoun agrees with its antecedent in both person and number.

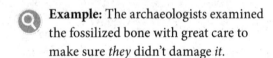 **Example:** The archaeologists examined the fossilized bone with great care to make sure *they* didn't damage *it.*

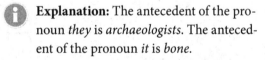 **Explanation:** The antecedent of the pronoun *they* is *archaeologists.* The antecedent of the pronoun *it* is *bone.*

Remember to use a singular verb when you refer to indefinite pronouns such as *everyone, everybody, each, every, anyone, anybody, nobody, none, no one, one,*

EXAMPLES

Although Union High School's male lacrosse players operate as a team, each knows it's *his* (not *their*) responsibility to arrive on time and in uniform.

Despite the fact that many of the women came from wealthy families, everyone who attended the Seneca Falls conference on women's rights risked *her* (not *their*) life and reputation.

When the programmers were questioned, none could be certain if it was *his* or *her* (not *their*) mistake that caused the computer network to crash.

 TIP

Increasingly in everyday English usage, the word *their* is considered an acceptable substitute for *his* or *her* when the gender of an individual is unknown (also *them* for *him* or *her* and *they* for *he* or *she*). However, the ACT is all about formal English usage, so stick with the phrases *his or her, he or she,* or *him or her* when the antecedent for a pronoun is singular and gender is unclear.

Subject-Verb Agreement

A verb agrees in number with its subject. A singular subject takes a singular verb. A plural subject takes a plural verb.

> **EXAMPLES**
>
> *Coral reefs are* an important part of the marine ecosystem.
>
> *My teacher believes* that *coral reefs are* an important part of the marine ecosystem.

Let's take a look at an example.

> **Example:** Choose the correct verb (is, am, are):
>
> Booker T. Washington, Frederick Douglass, and W.E.B. DuBois _____ all important historical figures.
>
> **Explanation:** Remember that the verb must agree with the subject. Since the subject is plural—subjects joined by *and* are plural—a plural verb is needed. The correct response is:
>
> Booker T. Washington, Frederick Douglass, and W.E.B. DuBois *are* all important historical figures.

Sometimes, the subject comes after the verb, but the rule still applies.

> **Example:** Choose the correct verb (is, are):
>
> While the lecture has lasted two hours already, there _____ still three more speakers.
>
> **Explanation:** The correct choice is *are* since the subject *speakers* is plural and requires a plural verb.

There is one major exception to this rule. When the sentence is introduced by the word *there* and the verb is followed by a compound (double) subject, the first part of the subject dictates whether the verb should be singular or plural.

> **EXAMPLE**
>
> There is one American astronaut and four Russian astronauts in the space station.

When compound subjects are joined by *either-or* or *neither-nor*, the verb agrees with the subject closest to the verb.

> **Examples:**
>
> Neither the violinist nor *the other musicians have had* much experience performing for an audience.
>
> Neither you nor *I am* willing to make the sacrifices required of a professional musician.
>
> **Explanation:** In the first example, *musicians* (plural) is closest to the verb; in the second example, *I* (singular) is closest to the verb.

 TIP

> Indefinite pronouns—such as *anyone, everyone, someone, no one,* and *nobody*—are singular and require singular verbs. Others are plural—such as *both, few, many,* and *several.* The number of some indefinite pronouns will depend on context.

Sometimes, a word or a group of words may come between the subject and the verb. The verb still must agree with the simple subject, and the simple subject is never part of a prepositional phrase.

> **Example:** Stephen King, the author of hundreds of best-selling novels, novellas, and short stories, *is* also a guitarist and singer in a band.
>
> **Explanation:** The simple subject is *Stephen King*, a singular noun. The verb must be *is*.

When a question in the English section underlines a verb, the choice is either correct or contains an error related to tense or agreement. The ACT will often select verbs that are next to plural nouns but agree with a singular noun located earlier in the sentence. Work to identify which noun is performing the action, not just what's nearby.

> **Example:** Choose the correct verb (was, were):
>
> The causes of the deterioration of the coral reef _____ not known until recently.
>
> **Explanation:** The simple subject is *causes*; "of the deterioration of the coral reef" is a prepositional phrase. Since the subject is plural, the plural verb *were* is required. The correct answer is *were*.

Collective Nouns

Collective nouns present special problems. A collective noun names a group of people or things. Although usually singular in form, it is treated as either singular or plural according to the sense of the sentence:

- A *collective noun* is treated as singular when members of the group act, or are considered, as a unit.

EXAMPLE

The citizens' *assembly is drafting* a petition that would seek to protect local aquifers from chemical run-off and hazardous waste.

- A *collective noun* is treated as plural when the members act, or are considered, as multiple individuals.

EXAMPLE

Because of an outbreak of flu at the court house, the jury were all wearing masks.

TIP

The third person singular of most present-tense verbs ends in –*s*. For other forms, consider the following: I, we speak (first person); you speak (second person); he, she, it speaks (third person singular). Examples: He runs. She jogs. It jumps. The man sees. Eric laughs. The child walks. They run.

COMMON COLLECTIVE NOUNS			
assembly	commission	crowd	minority
association	committee	department	number
audience	company	family	pair
band	corporation	firm	press
board	council	group	public
cabinet	counsel	jury	staff
class	couple	majority	United States

Idiomatic Prepositional Usage

Like many languages, English is full of idioms. Idioms are phrases that are peculiar to not only a particular language but also to a time and place. There's no strict logic or rule behind their usage; just know that they are used. For ACT Conventions of Standard English questions, you'll likely encounter idioms as related to the use of prepositions. In English, there are prepositions that are used in some ways and not others. Often, prepositions, through everyday usage, are attached to other words, creating some stock phrases. This is called idiomatic prepositional usage.

Consider the following: You wait *for* a bus, and when it arrives, you get *on* the bus. You may have had to stand *in* the rain (not *under* it). If you had decided to call a taxi or get a Lyft instead of waiting, when it arrives, you would get *in*. Those are largely idiomatic usages of prepositions. Why you get *on* a bus versus getting *in* is very much up for debate. You'll simply find that certain words in English always take a certain preposition. For more examples, one may look *at*, look *in*, look *through*, etc. However, one always disagrees *with* rather than disagrees *against*, or has scorn *for* rather than scorn *at*.

> The quarterback assured the waterboy that he had no intention to encroach against the latter's interest in the captain of the cheerleaders.

According to idiomatic usage, the word *intention* should be followed by the preposition *of*. Because the preposition *of*, like all prepositions, must have an object, and the object must be a noun or pronoun, the verb *encroach* must also be changed to a noun

form—the gerund (the *-ing* construction) *encroaching*. The fully corrected sentence then reads as follows:

> The quarterback assured the waterboy that he had no intention of encroaching on the latter's interest in the captain of the cheerleaders.

Encroaching *on* rather than encroach *against*—yet another idiom.

These questions can be challenging as they depend on your sense of English, not necessarily how well you understand it. The more immersed you are in English via reading, writing, and other media, the more natural these questions will feel and the harsher improper prepositional usage will be on your ear.

Commonly Confused Words

Many English words are easily confused and misused because they have similar spellings, sounds, or meanings. Using the wrong word can have a negative effect on the clarity of your writing, so it's important to know some of the most commonly confused words and how to use them correctly. It's also important to build your vocabulary, such as by using the techniques discussed in Chapter 17. Doing so affords you a wider variety of words from which to choose when writing.

Words that are pronounced the same but mean different things are known as homophones. For example, I might be *bored* in class, but I'm not *board* in class. *Bored* means to be dissatisfied with a tedious task while *board* means a piece of wood. Even though these words sound alike, their meanings are quite different.

There are also some words that don't have similar spellings or pronunciations, but it can still be difficult to decide which word to use. For example, when do you use *good* and when do you use *well*? *Good* is an adjective and describes a noun while *well* is an adverb that describes a verb. For example, I did *well* on the exam, but this pizza is *good*!

Confusing words can lead to a variety of problems in usage, so we've included a list of commonly misused words and examples of how to use them correctly. Some of these words have been found in official ACT questions, so make sure you have a good grasp of the differences in order to better prepare for conventions questions.

- -

a is used before words that start with a consonant sound

an is used before words that start with a vowel sound

> Please give the baby *a* toy.
>
> He is *an* only child. We put up *a* united front. (*United* begins with a consonant sound—*y*.)
>
> We spent *an* hour together. (*Hour* begins with a vowel sound, since the *h* is silent.)

- -

accept means to receive or to agree to something

except means to exclude or excluding

> I'll *accept* the gift from you.
>
> Everyone *except* my uncle went home.
>
> My uncle was *excepted* from the group of losers.

- -

advice means counsel (noun), opinion

advise means to offer advice (verb)

> Let me give you some free *advice*.
>
> I'd *advise* you to see your doctor.

- -

affect means to influence (verb)

effect means to cause or bring about (verb) or a result (noun)

> The pollution can *affect* your health.
>
> The landmark decision will *effect* a change in the law.
>
> The *effect* of the storm could not be measured.

- -

all ready means everybody or everything ready

already means previously

> They were *all ready* to write when the test began.
>
> They had *already* written the letter.

- -

all together means everybody or everything together

altogether means completely

> The boys and girls stood *all together* in line.
>
> His action was *altogether* strange for a person of his type.

- -

among is used when selecting from a group of three or more things

between is used when selecting from a group of two things

> The students could choose from among five different types of cuisines for lunch.
>
> The man couldn't decide between going for a jog or a bike ride.

- -

amount applies to quantities that cannot be counted one by one

number applies to quantities that can be counted one by one

> The review provided a vast *amount* of data.
>
> The farmer delivered a *number* of fruits.

- -

in is used to indicate inclusion, location, or motion within limits

into is used for motion toward one place from another

> The spoons are *in* the drawer.
>
> We were walking *in* the room.
>
> I put the spoons *into* the drawer.
>
> She walked *into* the room.

- -

it's is the contraction of *it is* or *it has*

its is a possessive pronoun meaning belonging to it

> *It's* a very difficult assignment.
>
> We tried to analyze *its* meaning.

- -

lay means to put (a transitive verb)

lie means to recline (an intransitive verb) or tell a falsehood

LAY VS. LIE		
Tense	*To lay*	*To lie*
(present)	I lay my bag down.	I lie.
(past)	I laid the gift on the table.	I lay on my blanket at the beach.
(present perfect)	I have laid my keys somewhere.	I have lain.

- -

less and *more* are used for uncountable quantities, signifying how *much* of something

fewer is used for countable quantities, signifying how *many* of something

> After looking at his bank statement, he didn't understand why he had so *much less* money. He should have *more*.
>
> For lunch, he spent five *fewer* dollars than yesterday. He didn't get as *many* sides.

- -

lets is third person singular present of *let*

let's is a contraction for *let us*

> He *lets* me park my car in his garage.
>
> *Let's* go home early today.

- -

loose means not fastened or restrained, or not tight-fitting

lose means to mislay, to be unable to keep, to be defeated

> The dog got *loose* from the leash.
>
> Try not to *lose* your umbrella.

- -

passed is the past tense of *to pass*

past means just preceding or an earlier time

> The week *passed* very quickly.
>
> The *past* week was a very exciting one.

- -

principal means chief or main (adjective), or a leader, or a sum of money (noun)

principle means a fundamental truth or belief

> His *principal* support comes from the real estate industry.
>
> The *principal* of the school called a meeting of the faculty.
>
> He earned 10 percent interest on the *principal* he invested last year.
>
> As a matter *of principle*, he refused to register for the draft.

- -

raise means to lift, to erect

raze means to tear down

rise means to get up, to move from a lower to a higher position, to increase in value

> The neighbors helped him *raise* a new barn.

> The demolition crew *razed* the old building.

> The price of silver will *rise* again this month.

- -

set means to place something down (mainly)

sit means to seat oneself (mainly)

SET VS. SIT		
Tense	*To set*	*To sit*
(present)	He sets his stuff down.	He sits.
(past)	He set the lamp on the table.	He sat on the chair.
(present perfect)	He has set the groceries in his trunk.	He has sat.

- -

stationary means standing still

stationery means writing material

> In ancient times, people thought that the earth was *stationary*.

> We bought our school supplies at the *stationery* store.

- -

than is used to express comparison

then is used to express time or a result or consequence

> Jim ate more *than* we could put on the large plate.

> I knocked on the door, and *then* I entered.

> If you go, *then* I will go too.

- -

their means belonging to them

there means in that place

they're is the contraction for *they are*

> We took *their* books home with us.

> Your books are over *there* on the desk.

> *They're* coming over for dinner.

- -

though means although or as if

thought is the past tense of *to think*, or an idea (noun)

through means in one side and out another, by way of, finished

> *Though* he is my friend, I can't recommend him for this job.

> I *thought* you were serious!

> We enjoyed running *through* the snow.

- -

to means in the direction of (preposition); it is also used before a verb to indicate the infinitive

too means very, also

two is the numeral 2

> We shall go *to* school.

> It is *too* hot today.

> We shall go *too*.

> I ate *two* sandwiches for lunch.

- -

weather refers to atmospheric conditions

whether introduces a choice; it should not be preceded by *of* or *as to*

> I don't like the *weather* in San Francisco.

> He inquired *whether* we were going to the dance.

- -

well is an adverb (modifies a verb, adverb, or adjective) meaning in a good or proper manner

good is an adjective (modifies a noun) meaning favorable, pleasant, suitable, etc.

> I did *well* on my test.

> I received a *good* score on my test.

- -

were is a past tense of *to be*

we're is a contraction of *we are*

where refers to place or location

> They *were* there yesterday.

> *We're* in charge of the decorations.

> *Where* are we meeting your brother?

- -

who is a pronoun in the subjective case

whom is a pronoun in the objective case

> The man *who* stole my car was just seen at the supermarket.

> *Who* is at the door?

> For *whom* are you calling?

> To *whom* should I speak about scheduling an appointment?

- -

who's is the contraction for *who is* (or *who has*)

whose means of whom, implying ownership

> *Who's* the next batter?

> *Whose* notebook is on the desk?

- -

your is a possessive, showing ownership

you're is a contraction for *you are*

> Please give him *your* notebook.

> *You're* very sweet.

- -

 TIP -

While the difference between *who* and *whom* has a minimal effect on your day-to-day life, it will more than likely come up on the ACT. Try substituting *he* or *she* and *him* or *her* for the pronoun in the sentence. You may have to rearrange the sentence a bit to make this work. If *he* or *she* fits in place of the pronoun, you should use *who*. If *him* or *her* fits, you should use *whom*.

Practice Set 4: Verbs, Usage, and Agreement

THE POETRY OF ECONOMICS

"The poetry of economics?" you might ask. "How can 'the dismal science' be associated with the subtlety and creativity of poetry?" You're skepticism¹ is understandable, and perhaps a story from an economist's life can sketch the poetry of economics at work.

1. A. NO CHANGE
   B. Your
   C. Their
   D. A reader's

Shortly after the Second World War, the agricultural economist Theodore Schultz, later to win a Nobel prize, spent a term based at Auburn University in Alabama. He is interviewing² farmers in the neighborhood. One day, he interviewed an old and poor farm couple and was struck by how contented they seemed.

2. F. NO CHANGE
   G. He interviews
   H. He interviewed
   J. He was interviewed

"Why are you so contented," he asked, "though very poor?" They answered: "You're wrong, Professor. We're not poor. We've used up our farm to educate four children through college, remaking fertile land and well-stocked pens into knowledge of law and Latin. We are rich."

The parents told Schultz that the physical capital, which economists think they understand, is of³ some senses just like the human capital of education. The children now owned it, and so the parents did too.

3. A. NO CHANGE
   B. on
   C. over
   D. in

Once, the capital had been rail fences and hog pens, and also their mules. Now <u>they were</u> in the children's brains, this human capital. The farm couple was rich.

4

The average economist was willing to accept the discovery of human capital as soon as they understood it, which is in fact how <u>many scientific and scholarly discoveries are received</u>. It was an argument in a metaphor (or, if you like, an analogy, a simile, a model). A hog pen, Schultz would say to another economist, is "just like" Latin 101.

5

The other economist would have to admit that there was something to it. Both the hog pen and the Latin instruction are paid for by saving. Both are valuable assets for earning income, understanding "income" to mean, as economists put it, "a stream of satisfaction." Year after year, the hog pen and the Latin <u>causes</u> satisfaction to stream out like water from a dam.

6

4. **F.** NO CHANGE

   G. it was

   H. they are

   J. it is

5. **A.** NO CHANGE

   B. a scientific and scholarly discovery are received

   C. many scientific and scholarly discoveries is received

   D. a scientific and scholarly discoveries are received

6. **F.** NO CHANGE

   G. cause

   H. produce

   J. effect

Answer Explanations

1. The correct answer is B. *You're* is a contraction meaning "you are." While the second person pronoun is appropriate, *You're* does not match the syntax of the sentence, nor does it meet the need for the possessive pronoun *your*. Choices C and D represent pronoun shifts away from the antecedent of the first sentence of the passage, *you*.

2. The correct answer is H. While choices F, G, and J all represent proper subject-verb agreement, the context of the paragraph indicates that the verb should be in the past tense. Only choice H accomplishes this. Choice J creates a passive construction that changes the meaning of the sentence, stating that Schultz was interviewed instead of being the one conducting the interviews.

3. The correct answer is D. The idiomatic phrase is "in some senses." The prepositions in choices A, B, and C do not fit the common expression.

4. The correct answer is G. Capital, not "rail fences and hog pens, and also their mules," is the antecedent of the correct pronoun in the underlined portion of the sentence. This narrows the possible correct answers to choices G and J. The verbs around this sentence are in some form of the past tense, thus allowing you to eliminate choice J.

5. The correct answer is A. As written, the phrase demonstrates proper agreement within the phrases in the subject, "many scientific and scholarly discoveries," as well as between the subject and the verb phrase, "are received." Choices B, C, and D all contain mismatches between the modifiers *a* and *many* and *discovery* and *discoveries* as well as the auxiliary verbs *is* and *are*.

6. The correct answer is G. The verb *causes* needs to agree with the plural subject "the hog pen and the Latin." As written, *causes* only agrees with a singular subject, "the Latin." Choices H and J represent words with similar meanings but that don't fit the expression in the sentence.

SUMMING IT UP

- Knowing the parts of speech is critical for understanding the conventions and rules of grammar:

  - A **noun** is a person, place, thing, or idea.
  - A **pronoun** is a substitute for a noun.
  - An **adjective** describes a noun.
  - A **verb** expresses action or a state of being.
  - An **adverb** modifies a verb, an adjective, or another adverb.
  - A **conjunction** joins words, sentences, and phrases.
  - A **preposition** shows position in time or space.

- The following list summarizes the key conventions you need to remember to edit ACT English questions effectively:

  - **Sentence Structure and Formation**

    - **Fragments:** Every sentence must have a subject and a verb and express a complete idea.
    - **Run-Ons and Comma Splices:** Connect complete sentences with proper punctuation.
    - **Combining Independent Clauses:** Use periods, a comma + FANBOYS, or a semicolon; you can also make an independent clause dependent with a subordinating conjunction to link sentences.
    - **Combining Dependent and Independent Clauses:** Place a comma after a dependent clause at the beginning of a sentence.
    - **Misplaced Modifiers:** Place modifiers (adjectives, adverbs, prepositional phrases) as close to the word they're modifying as possible.
    - **Parallel Structure:** Keep verbs and phrases in the same grammatical form when writing sentences.

  - **Punctuation**

    - **Commas:** Separate independent clauses with a comma and FANBOYS; add a comma after an introductory phrase or leading subordinate clause; separate items in lists of three or more (including before the *and* before the final item); place commas around nonessential information to separate it from the main clause of a sentence.
    - **Em dashes:** Indicate nonrestrictive or nonessential information with em dashes; these tangents, asides, and parenthetical statements follow em dashes and must be closed by another em dash—unless they finish the sentence.

- **Semicolons:** Separate related independent clauses and items in a list where the items have commas with a semicolon.

- **Colons:** Indicate the start of a list, a quotation, or emphasis with a colon; colons must be preceded by an independent clause.

- **Apostrophes:** Indicate possession with an *'s* (or just an apostrophe after a noun that ends in an *–'s*), or signal the contraction of two words into one (*they + are = they're*).

- **End-Stop Punctuation:** End statements and indirect questions with periods; use question marks to end direct questions; end statements that indicate strong emotion or commands with an exclamation point.

○ **Verbs, Usage, and Agreement**

- **Verb Tense:** Keep consistent verb tense within sentences and paragraphs unless otherwise justified.

- **Perfect Tense Verbs:** The perfect tenses are used for actions begun and completed at different times. Whether the tense is past, present, or future perfect will depend on when the action is completed.

- **Common Verbs and Their Tenses:** In English, most verbs change in predictable ways when shifted from tense to tense; however, there are also irregular verbs (such as *eat, get, give, go*, etc.) that will have more significant changes in the past and perfect tenses.

- **Pronoun Case:** The pronoun you choose depends on the situation in which the pronoun is used. Personal pronouns change case depending on whether they are the subject or object of an action. Determine first if the pronoun is performing (subject) or receiving the action (object).

- **Possessive Determiners:** An absolute possessive pronoun (*mine, yours, his, hers*) can stand on its own without a noun preceding it. A possessive pronoun (*my, your, his her, its, our, their*) that quantifies the noun it precedes is a possessive determiner.

- **Pronoun-Antecedent Agreement:** A pronoun must agree with its antecedent (the word it replaces) in number, person, and gender (where applicable).

- **Subject-Verb Agreement:** Verbs must agree in number with their subjects.

- **Collective Nouns:** Collective nouns describe a group of things but are treated as singular when it comes to subject-verb and pronoun agreement.

- **Idiomatic Prepositional Usage:** In English, certain situations will demand the use of certain prepositions. These are not fixed grammar rules so much as conventions of everyday English usage.

- **Commonly Confused Words:** The ACT will have Conventions of Standard English questions that offer answer choices with words that have similar meanings, sounds, or spellings. You need to determine which word is most appropriate given the context of the sentence and passage.

CONVENTIONS OF STANDARD ENGLISH

15 Questions—9 Minutes

Directions: In the following passage, certain words and phrases are underlined and numbered. In the right-hand column, you will find alternatives for the part that is underlined. In most cases, you are to choose which alternative best makes the statement appropriate in standard written English. If you think the original version is best, choose "NO CHANGE."

Note: In this practice section, all of the questions relate to conventions of standard English. Passages on the ACT English test will usually also include questions about the content of the passage and will not typically focus solely on conventions as this passage's questions do.

SWIMMING WITH SHARKS

It was a beautiful Sunday morning but I was at the beach.
1

1. **A.** NO CHANGE
   B. It was a beautiful Sunday morning, and I was at the beach.
   C. It was a beautiful Sunday morning at the beach.
   D. I was at the beach, it was a beautiful Sunday morning.

I barely had been in the water for ten minutes when
2

2. **F.** NO CHANGE
   G. In the water for ten minutes, I had been barely
   H. I had in the water for ten minutes been barely
   J. Barely in the water for ten minutes, I had been

I saw the fins, jumping out, in the surf. Dark triangles
3
surfaced briefly before disappearing back under the waves. My first thought: sharks!

3. **A.** NO CHANGE
   B. I saw the fins jumping out in the surf.
   C. I saw the fins jumping out, in the surf.
   D. I saw, the fins jumping out in, the surf.

There were sharks right off the coast for Southern Point
4
Beach!

4. **F.** NO CHANGE
   G. from
   H. of
   J. above

The beach was crowded with people, so I had another thought: <u>Everyone are in danger!</u> I yelled at the
<u>5</u>
top of my voice, "Shark!"

The lifeguard, who was texting, <u>didn't look up from</u>
<u>6</u>
<u>their phone.</u> People around me heard, though.
<u>6</u>

<u>Parents started to pull their kids out of the water</u>
<u>7</u>
<u>children began to scream.</u> It was pure chaos.
<u>7</u>

Eventually, the lifeguard noticed the noise and
looked up. <u>Blew the whistle, then waved everyone out</u>
<u>8</u>
<u>of the water.</u> By then I had made it back to my blanket.
<u>8</u>
There were four young men playing volleyball nearby.

I could still see those deadly fins <u>lurking, coming dan-</u>
<u>9</u>
<u>gerously close</u> to a paddle boarder who was still out on
<u>9</u>
the water. Worried, I trotted over to the lifeguard to let
him know.

Surely, he had noticed <u>he</u> was in danger.
<u>10</u>

5. **A.** NO CHANGE
   B. Everyone is in danger
   C. Anyone are in danger
   D. No one is in danger

6. **F.** NO CHANGE
   G. doesn't look up from their phone
   H. didn't look up from his phone
   J. didn't look up from my phone

7. **A.** NO CHANGE
   B. Parents started pulling their kids out of the water, but children began screaming
   C. Parents started to pull their kids. Out of the water children began to scream
   D. Parents started to pull their kids out of the water; children began to scream

8. **F.** NO CHANGE
   G. I blew the whistle, and waved everyone out of the water.
   H. The lifeguard blew his whistle, then waved everyone out of the water.
   J. They blew the whistle, then waved everyone out of the water.

9. **A.** NO CHANGE
   B. lurking, though coming dangerously close
   C. lurking
   D. lurking or coming dangerously close

10. **F.** NO CHANGE
    G. the lifeguard
    H. I
    J. the paddle boarder

Before I could reach <u>the lifeguard's stand, he</u>
¹¹
<u>lowered his binoculars and hopped down</u> to the sand.
¹¹
"Everyone back in the water," the lifeguard shouted.
"It's safe."

Safe? Had he not seen *Jaws*? <u>I asked he how him</u>
¹²
<u>could possibly let people back into the water with the</u>
¹²
<u>sharks just off the shore?</u>
¹²

"You mean the dolphins?" he replied. "Those are
dolphin fins. They're out here every day. <u>Their</u> haven't
¹³
been any sharks around here in at least 50 years."

<u>After he explained this: I felt pretty foolish.</u> I walked
¹⁴
back to my towel, but I could see the lifeguard shooting
annoyed looks at me as other beachgoers continued
peppering him with questions about the "sharks."

So, to recap, my big adventure of swimming
<u>with the sea's deadliest creatures were</u> really just an
¹⁵
embarrassing mistake. At least I now know where I can
go to watch friendly dolphins frolicking in the surf!

11. **A.** NO CHANGE

   B. the lifeguard's stand he lowered his binoculars, and hopped down

   C. it, he lowered them and hopped down

   D. the lifeguard's stand, he subtly lowered his binoculars, and hopped down sudden

12. **F.** NO CHANGE

   G. I asked he how he could possibly let people go back into the water with the sharks just off the shore!

   H. I asked him how he could possible let people go back into the water with the sharks just off the shore?

   J. I asked him how he could possibly let people go back into the water with the sharks just off the shore.

13. **A.** NO CHANGE

   B. There

   C. They're

   D. Theirs

14. **F.** NO CHANGE

   G. After he explained this, I felt pretty foolish.

   H. After he explained this; I felt pretty foolish.

   J. After he explained this I felt pretty foolish.

15. **A.** NO CHANGE

   B. with the sea's deadliest creatures was

   C. with the seas' deadliest creatures were

   D. with the seas deadliest creatures was

ANSWER KEY AND EXPLANATIONS

1. C	**4.** H	**7.** D	**10.** J	**13.** B
2. F	**5.** B	**8.** H	**11.** A	**14.** G
3. B	**6.** H	**9.** A	**12.** J	**15.** B

1. **The correct answer is C.** As written, a comma is missing between the two independent clauses and an improper coordinating conjunction, *but*, is used. Choice D creates a comma splice. Choices B and C avoid grammatical errors. However, when compared, choice C is more concise.

2. **The correct answer is F.** As written, the adverb *barely* modifies the phrase "had been in the water for ten minutes." For proper modification, and to maintain the syntax of the sentence (continuing with *when*), the modifier should be as close to the thing it modifies as possible. That would require the *barely* to precede the verb *had been*. At the same time, the adverbial prepositional phrase "in the water for ten minutes" needs to follow the verb. Only the original accomplishes this modification without hampering the clarity of the sentence.

3. **The correct answer is B.** There are no commas necessary in this sentence, so choice B is correct.

4. **The correct answer is H.** Here, you are looking for the preposition that most appropriately fills the blank in the phrase "off the coast _____ Southern Point Beach." The only contextually appropriate preposition among the choices is *of*.

5. **The correct answer is B.** The indefinite pronoun *everyone* is singular in number. Thus, it requires a singular verb for agreement. This eliminates choice F. The indefinite pronoun *anyone* in choice C is also singular, not plural, thus creating disagreement with the plural verb *are*. Both choices B and C demonstrate proper subject-verb agreement; however, only choice B is relevant to the passage—as according to the circumstances described by the narrator, there are people in danger.

6. **The correct answer is H.** As written, the possessive pronoun *their* does not agree with the antecedent *lifeguard*. Choice G repeats this error and changes the verb tense. Choice J incorrectly asserts that the phone belongs to the narrator. Choice H has the proper verb tense (simple past tense) and an appropriate singular possessive pronoun, *his*.

7. **The correct answer is D.** The original sentence is a run-on. The second independent clause, "children began to scream," needs to be separated from the first with either a comma and an appropriate coordinating conjunction, a semicolon, or a period. Choices B, C, and D explore these options; however, the use of the conjunction *but* (choice B) establishes a contrasting relationship between the clauses, which is not the case. Choice C uses a period but separates the prepositional phrase "out of the water" from what it modifies.

8. **The correct answer is H.** The underlined text is incorrect because it is an unclear fragment. The sentence fails to establish who blew the whistle, so there is no subject. Choice G is incorrect because, based on the context, it is much likelier that the lifeguard and not the narrator blew the whistle. Choice J is incorrect because the pronoun *they* does not agree in number in this context and makes it unclear as to who is actually blowing the whistle.

9. **The correct answer is A.** The sentence from which the underlined portion is taken has two parts: a main clause ("I could still see those deadly fins lurking") and a subordinate clause that gives more detail ("coming dangerously close to a paddle boarder who was still out on the water"). These are connected appropriately by a comma, so choice A is correct. Choice B is incorrect because the conjunction *though*

suggests that the fins are coming dangerously close despite the lurking, which doesn't make sense given the context. Choice C is incorrect because "lurking to a paddle boarder . . ." is improper use of the verb. Choice D is incorrect because it sets up the two clauses as a choice between one or the other.

10. **The correct answer is J.** Given the context of the rest of the paragraph, the pronoun *he* (choice F) creates an unclear antecedent—does *he* refer to the lifeguard or the paddle boarder? Choice B is incorrect because the lifeguard is on the beach, out of danger, and cannot be the person to whom the original pronoun referred. Choice H is incorrect because the narrator is not worried for their own safety but rather for that of the paddle boarder. Choice J is correct because it logically fits the context and removes the ambiguity created by using the unclear pronoun instead.

11. **The correct answer is A.** As written, the sentence includes a dependent clause ("Before I could reach the lifeguard's stand") that is correctly connected to an independent clause ("he lowered his binoculars and hopped down to the sand"). The other options either misplace the comma (choices B and D) or make the sentence confusing, such as by needlessly replacing nouns with pronouns (choice C) or adding extraneous and unclear adverbs and modifiers (choice D).

12. **The correct answer is J.** The underlined sentence contains several errors: it swaps the pronouns *he* and *him* and includes a question mark for an indirect question. Choice H maintains the question mark and can thus be eliminated. Choice G switches the object pronoun *him* to *he* but keeps the first subject pronoun use of *he* instead of using the correct objective case, *him*. Only choice J uses the correct pronouns and removes the question mark.

13. **The correct answer is B.** *Their* (choice A) is a possessive determiner and therefore does not function properly. *Theirs* (choice D) is a possessive pronoun and incorrectly serves as the subject of the sentence.

14. **The correct answer is G.** Punctuation is necessary to separate the dependent clause "After he explained this" from the independent clause "I felt pretty foolish," so you can eliminate choice J. The type of punctuation needed is a comma, so only choice G is correct.

15. **The correct answer is B.** The underlined phrase contains an error in subject-verb agreement. The verb in the underlined portion needs to agree with the singular *adventure* mentioned earlier in the sentence, not the plural *creatures* located next to the verb. Choice C repeats the error from the underlined portion and also changes the apostrophe on *sea's*, making it plural possessive. Choices B and D correct the verb, but choice D removes the apostrophe, creating a punctuation error.

CHAPTER

**Strategies for Approaching
the English Section**

STRATEGIES FOR APPROACHING THE

OVERVIEW

Reflecting on Your Diagnostic Test Score

Overall Section Strategies

Question Type Strategies

Test Yourself: English Strategies

General Reminders and Advice

Strategy Roundup

Summing It Up

Knowledge Check: English

While the last two chapters focused on helping you review skills you'll need for the ACT English test, this chapter offers you some tools and strategies to apply what you know in the context of the test. The goal of the material in this chapter is to help you make the most of your time to maximize your score. That process is all about understanding how the English test asks questions and what it sees as necessary for strong written English. Throughout this chapter, we'll cover some of the different ways you can use the specifications of the ACT English test for your own benefit, ensuring your best performance come exam day. We'll give you opportunities to practice these strategies along the way before rounding things out with a test-length Knowledge Check at the end of the chapter.

ENGLISH SECTION

REFLECTING ON YOUR DIAGNOSTIC TEST SCORE

As you work through the strategies for each section of the ACT, you'll notice us frequently asking you to flip back to Chapter 2: Diagnostic Test and your analysis of it in Chapter 3. That's because studies have proven that metacognition—the act of reflecting on and analyzing one's own learning and thought processes—can help with overall learning. Take a few moments to reflect on your performance when you started studying for the English test. You can do so in your head, take notes on your own, or use this table to jot down some ideas.

DIAGNOSTIC TEST REFLECTION: ENGLISH	
Diagnostic Test Score (English): _____	**Scoring Goal (English):** _____
Reflection Question	**Notes**
What went well for you during the diagnostic test and which skills were easiest for you to use?	
What did you struggle with during the diagnostic test or which skills were harder for you to use?	
Did you feel rushed? Did you have left over time?	
How close were you to your goal?	
After reviewing grammar and writing skills in the last two chapters, what are some things you might like to keep in mind as you study further?	
What are some aspects of approaching the English test for which you are hoping to build strategies?	

Now, consider your goals for the English section. If there are large gaps in your understanding that you identified with diagnostic testing, then your primary goal while studying for the English test should be developing strategies that help you close those gaps. Whatever your goals may be, keep them in mind as you start building your strategy toolkit for the test.

Each point for your scaled score for the ACT English section is roughly equivalent to two correct answers—though that estimate can fall apart at certain points on the scale. On average, then, answering two more questions correctly will yield an additional point for your scaled score. Acing 15 questions for one passage then would put you below a 10. Two perfect passages would yield around a 15. Three passages would put you around the national average of 20. Four passages would be in the 25-28 range. And all five passages (75 questions) get you a perfect 36. Rather than filling out three passages and putting your pencil down, though, try to answer as many questions as you can. Eliminating answers will improve your chances of guessing, and you may find that your goal (short of a perfect score) can be accomplished without having to spend equal time and energy on every single question.

What's important is that you start to understand that the choices you make within a section should be informed by what you're trying to achieve, not just how the section is presented to you. Your goal can and should evolve as you build competency with ACT English skills and strategies since you should be able to do more with the time you're given as you improve.

OVERALL SECTION STRATEGIES

The following strategies can help you approach the ACT English test as a whole. They have been carefully considered by experts to make sure they are beneficial to test takers like you. As you study for your ACT English test, make sure to experiment with these strategies until you can combine them in a way

that creates an effective overall approach that matches your section goals.

As with the other sections of the ACT, for English, your goal is to make choices that improve your time management and accuracy.

You have 45 minutes to answer 75 questions. The answers to those 75 questions are contingent, on the context of the underlined material and information contained within 5 passages. Your greatest challenge is figuring out how to extract the information you need from the passages to answer each of those 75 questions in the time you have.

As you'll see later on with the strategies for the ACT Reading section, you can make choices for how you approach the English section to overcome some of the challenges created by its format and time constraints. Just like in Reading, you only earn points for answering questions correctly, not reading the passage. As such, your primary goal is to minimize reading time (but still read enough so that you can answer questions effectively). From there, you can learn to approach certain question types in specific ways. How you decide to invest your time and energy into reading and breaking down questions, though, will vary depending on your goals.

Divide Your Time According to Your Goals

Not all test-takers have the same goals. If you're aiming for a perfect score, then you'll likely need to divide your time evenly across passages. Since you have 45 minutes and five passages with 15 questions each, this would mean devoting no more than 9 minutes to each passage and question set. However, someone who really only needs to perform well on three of the five passages

TIP

If you find yourself spending more than 30–45 seconds on a given ACT English question, and you're trying to work through every single question, it's time to make your best guess and move on. Remember, you're trying to answer as many questions as you can as quickly and accurately as you can. No one question, unless you need it for your goal, is worth sacrificing time with others.

in order to achieve their target score (around 20) can consider focusing more time on only three passages and then plan to work quickly through the remaining passages (perhaps making educated guesses) with whatever time remains. Neither solution is right or wrong—it all depends on your goals, the progress you make through practice, and your reading and editing abilities. Think about what your score goals are and then divide your time to match those goals. As you improve, evaluate your time and accuracy and adjust your goals accordingly. The goal for every test taker should be to have worked through all the passages and questions well before time expires. It's absolutely possible, but build up to that point rather than requiring yourself to hit that mark from the very beginning.

Recognize the Different Question Types

We covered the different question types for the English test extensively in Chapter 5 and Chapter 6. However, here is a basic breakdown to refresh your memory. For our purposes, "NO CHANGE" questions are those that do not indicate a specific question but rather offer a few options to revise the underlined portion, with NO CHANGE being the first choice.

The better you become at recognizing the different question types, the more you'll be able to approach questions strategically for a given passage. For instance, if you know you can handle grammar questions quickly, one strategy might be to go through and answer all the CSE questions for a passage before addressing those that relate to POW and KLA, which can be more time-consuming or abstract. This strategy also proves useful since CSE questions comprise the majority of questions in the ACT English section, and building recognition can help you more quickly apply the question-specific strategies we discuss in the next section.

Read Strategically

Almost every question will be linked to either an underlined segment of the passage or a particular position within a given paragraph. The exception to this rule would be any of the questions (usually one to three per passage) that address the passage as a whole. Because most questions are largely dependent on only pieces of the passage, you shouldn't read the entire passage before answering questions, even if the ACT directions tell you to do so. Instead, you can prioritize reading only the information you need to answer the questions.

ACT ENGLISH QUESTION TYPES		
Question Type	**Purpose**	**Example Question(s)**
Production of Writing (POW)	Tests your ability to recognize the focus and purpose of a piece of writing, as well as how it's organized	• Which choice most effectively introduces the paragraph? • "NO CHANGE" questions: The change you'll need to identify likely concerns transitions or organization, specifically identifying transitions the suit the passage's organizational strategy.
Knowledge of Language (KLA)	Tests your ability to use language effectively and precisely	• Which choice most effectively emphasizes the complexity of the narrator's task? • "NO CHANGE" questions: The change you'll need to identify likely concerns word choice or addresses style and tone.
Conventions of Standard English (CSE)	Tests your ability to apply conventions of standard English	• Which choice correctly places the commas in the sentence? • "NO CHANGE" questions: The change you'll need to identify likely concerns errors in grammar, usage, or mechanics—most "NO CHANGE" questions on the test fall under this category.

The challenge with such a strategy, you may be thinking, is that you don't know exactly what information is valuable for answering a question until you've thought about the question. But that's not exactly true. We know certain things about how the ACT writes questions and selects passages. Keep in mind the following:

1 Most questions are questions that underline part of the passage. The answers to those questions will most often depend on the full sentence in which the underlining appears (and sometimes require a little context before and after).

2 Even if a question asks about a paragraph or the passage as a whole, you can grasp the purpose of a passage (or its part) without reading the whole thing. The title and first and last paragraphs of a passage (or first and last sentences of a paragraph) can offer you great insight into the key ideas, often enough to assist you with broader scope questions.

Because you don't have much time, you need to use what you know about how the ACT English test is written and how passages work to prioritize the information that can solve most of your problems. That means minimizing what you read until you know (because of the question or any uncertainty on your part) that you need to read more.

When you turn to a passage, glance at the first question in the right-hand column. If there's no question stem and you see NO CHANGE, you can jump to the passage, starting at the beginning of the sentence in which the underlining appears. If you glance at the question and see a full written question, read the question, and decide if you need to just read a sentence (because there's underlining), a paragraph with the question marker, or think about the whole passage. Then, read what you need. If the answer is still unclear (and you're within your allotted time for a question), read more around the question marker for additional context.

Then, repeat this process, only reading what you know has the best chance of helping you answer the next question and skipping everything else in between. Only read more if you discover that you need additional information.

To generalize, your reading can be strategic scanning and searching for information that is relevant to your question. It can also mean only reading the sentences that are indicated by the questions (or sometimes the paragraph). In situations where a question refers to the whole passage, more often than not, it can be addressed by reading the first and last paragraphs of a passage alone.

Depending on how quickly you move through the passage, you may consider reading the passage title and the first and last sentence of the first and last paragraph when you start a passage to get a general sense of the

TIP

Don't waste your time reading through the parts that don't matter for your questions unless it is necessary to do so to answer a question about the passage as a whole. Focus on picking up necessary context clues without reading too thoroughly, as this costs you time. Few questions require an understanding of the entire passage, let alone all the details.

passage's purpose. Additionally, when answering questions, by default, you could read the sentence before and after any underlined segment in question in addition to the underlined material. That all depends on your time, abilities, needs, and progress through practice. With all that said, remember that in most cases, you will not need to read the full passage. Doing so is rarely necessary and can cost you valuable time.

Complete All Questions for a Passage before Moving On

It will take you time to revisit passages and remind yourself of the passage topics, so rather than skipping around from passage to passage, make a habit of answering all the questions for one passage before moving on. You can always mark those you guess on to review later. Use your section goal to determine how much time you have for each passage and work within that constraint. Recall that you have no more than 9 minutes per passage if your intention is to get to every question. That number can change if you're aiming for a score that's less than 36.

Make Notes to Review Guesses

The goal of these time-saving strategies is to net you time to review answers you weren't certain about before time expires. That certainty needs to be there for you to feel confident that you're achieving your goals, and that certainty can only come from having a clear reason for why the answer you selected is correct and why all the other

TIP

Don't forget that you can make notes on the passage in your test booklet if doing so helps you.

answers are wrong. If you don't have those reasons, you're guessing. And, in accordance with your goals, you want to have the time to revisit guesses to maximize your score.

If you've used a notation system to remember the questions you've guessed on, then you'll be able to spend any extra time revisiting them. You can even use multiple notation marks for different types of guesses so you can prioritize reviewing questions you might be able to figure out over those for which you are taking a complete guess. Remember, if you eliminate any incorrect answers that you can identify first, your chances of guessing correctly go up.

QUESTION TYPE STRATEGIES

So far, the strategies we've covered provide you with a general approach to the ACT English test, but there are a couple methods that can also help you with specific types of questions. The expectations of the ACT English test mean that you can make specific choices with different kinds of questions that help you cut away distracting answers and focus on what the test prioritizes.

Strategy #1: Use a Process of Elimination for CSE Questions

The English test's parameters for what makes an answer correct are fairly rigid. As a result, the different kinds of answer choices you'll see can be somewhat predictable. That means you can deploy strategies that use the parameters of the test to your advantage. Conventions of Standard English (CSE) questions, as you saw in Chapter 6, are all about grammar, usage, and mechanics. But that doesn't mean that the only difference between a right answer and a wrong answer will always be grammatical. Wordiness and meaning also act as differentiators between answer choices. A correct answer to a CSE question will always be grammatically correct; however, if multiple answers are grammatically correct, then the best choice will also be well written and connected to the passage.

The following strategy works to balance the different concerns of the CSE questions. Each step can help you eliminate answers to narrow down your choices to the correct answer.

How to Do It

1. Glance at the question. If you see NO CHANGE without a question, read the sentence with the underlining. Otherwise, read the question and use Strategy #2.

2. If there is a grammatical error in the sentence, eliminate NO CHANGE and proceed with steps 3-5. If you don't see an error, you'll need to check the other answer options to see what changes. (If grammar is changing between choices, it's a CSE question. Otherwise, it is a KLA or POW: Organization question. In that case, use Strategy #2.)

3. Look through the answer choices. Eliminate those that repeat the original error (if there is one) or create grammatical errors in the context of the sentence.

4. If multiple answer choices still remain, find the answer that uses proper grammar, supports the meaning of the passage, and is succinct—without sacrificing grammar or connections to the passage.

5. If no answer choices remain and you have time, reread the sentence and reevaluate what you eliminated. Otherwise, select an answer you know is grammatically correct, and move on.

The nice thing about this strategy is that it's useful for all test takers. For instance, if on step 2 you cannot identify a problem, proceeding to step 3 will help ensure you still consider all answer choices before choosing NO CHANGE to indicate that the sentence is already correct as written.

Take a look at this process in action using the following excerpted paragraph and question.

But this wasn't the first time I'd messed up, and it wouldn't be the last. In fact, before I finally made the dance team, <u>I had to audition, 12 times</u> <u>but I only got callbacks three, of those times</u>. I was persistent, yes, but my efforts didn't pay off until my lucky 13th audition where I finally nailed my callback routine.

11. **A.** NO CHANGE

B. I had to audition 12 times, but I only got callbacks, three of those times

C. I had to audition 12 times, but I only got callbacks three times

D. I had to audition 12 times, but only three of those times did I get a callback

Question 11

Following the CSE process, your first step is to glance at the question. Since you see NO CHANGE, read the entire sentence with the underlining. Then, determine if there is a problem in the underlined text. When reading the sentence in question, it becomes clear that the placement of commas in the sentence is incorrect as written. The commas improperly separate phrases and clauses in the sentence, demonstrating improper sentence structure and hampering clarity. As such, choice A can be eliminated, and you can proceed through the rest of the steps for the CSE process.

Next, we must consider the following questions:

- **Do any of the remaining answer choices have grammatical errors?** Choice B moves both commas. The placement of the first comma correctly joins the independent clauses present, but the second comma still breaks up the phrase "got a callback three of those times," just in a different way. This maintains one of the original errors, allowing you to eliminate choice B. Choice C removes one comma and moves another before the contraction *but*, correctly separating two independent clauses with a comma and a conjunction. Choice D also creates a grammatical compound sentence.

- **Are any of the remaining options disconnected from the passage or less concise than other grammatically correct answer choices?** You've been able to eliminate two choices because of their misused punctuation. Now you have to consider the other elements of strong written English. The correct answer will be grammatically correct, maintain the meaning of the passage, and be written as concisely as possible without the meaning suffering. Both choices C and D make it clear the number of times the speaker got audition callbacks, which transitions well into the next sentence. When compared for word count, though, choice C uses fewer words to express the same idea as D. It seems you've found the correct answer: choice C.

Now, you can re-read the sentence with the new answer inserted to see if it reads correctly according to the priorities of the Conventions of Standard English questions:

In fact, before I finally made the dance team, I had to audition 12 times, but I only got callbacks three times.

This sentence is grammatically sound, concise (when compared to other choices), and maintains the meaning of the text. With all of those factors in check, we know that we have landed on the correct answer. Sometimes, the answer to a CSE question will be obvious to you right away and you might not feel you need to go through all these steps. However, this process can help focus your attention and ensure that you've take all the steps necessary to feel certain in your answers.

Strategy #2: Use Contextual Information for POW and KLA Questions

For Production of Writing (POW) and Knowledge of Language (KLA) questions, you can follow a similar strategy as the process of elimination for CSE questions, but rather than trying to decipher grammatical concerns, you'll need to think about the specific question being asked (when there is one) and the context provided to assist you with an answer.

How to Do It

1. Glance at the question. If you see NO CHANGE without a question, read the sentence with the underlining. Otherwise, read the question. The question wording will tell you whether it is focused on KLA or POW (proceed to step 3 or 4, respectively).

2. If there's no question and you see issues in the underlining and answer choices with, as the ACT states, "precision or concision in word choice" or "consistency in style and tone," it's a KLA question (proceed to step 3). If the underlining and answer choices point to transitions, it's a type of POW question (proceed to step 4).

3. For KLA questions, eliminate answers that are redundant or inconsistent with the passage, as well as those that are disconnected from the meaning, style, and tone of the sentence, paragraph, and passage. Read more of the sentences around the question marker to make those determinations.

4. For POW questions, identify whether the focus is on the passage's topic or organization.

   ○ For Topic Development, read for the passage's or paragraph's purpose using things like the passage's title and first and last paragraphs and sentences. Read as much as you need to answer the question with confidence. You can eliminate any answer that does not match the purpose of the passage or the question's goal.

   ○ For Organization, choose answers that create a logical flow of ideas. If a transitional word or phrase is indicated, read the preceding and following sentences to identify the relationship to be represented. If a sentence or whole paragraph is marked, it needs to stay where it is or be moved so long as it connects to the sentences before and after its placement.

This may seem like a complicated flow of steps but the more you practice with it, the more it will become second nature. The key is to determine why the test makers have given you a particular type of question. This way, you can figure out what kind of answer you are expected to give. When more than one answer choice seems plausible, rely on this flow of steps to help you eliminate choices.

As an example, let's look at the following excerpted paragraphs and some questions that relate to them. These paragraphs are excerpted from a full-length ACT English passage entitled "The Art of Gerhard Richter."

FYI

Notice that the first steps for both the CSE process and the approach for KLA and POW questions is the same. Look at the question, and use what you see there to guide you to what you should read. If you see a grammatical error in the underlined text or in the answers, you know it's a CSE question. If the question is focused on organization, purpose, or has changes that affect style and tone, you're dealing with a POW or KLA question.

GUIDED PRACTICE

THE ART OF GERHARD RICHTER

After acquiring formal training in painting through his teen years and early adulthood, Richter became interested in blurring the lines between photographs and paintings—what would it mean if you could make a painting that looked just like a photograph? How would people know it was a painting? Would it matter that it was a painting and not a photograph if people couldn't tell the difference? Questions like these drove Richter to experiment. He was hoping that his experiments [13] would force viewers to grapple with the same questions that drove him to experiment with abstracted [13] but realistic oil paintings meant to look exactly like [13] motion-blurred or unfocused photographs and [13] question the division between the two forms. Such [13] avant-garde undertakings have characterized much of Richter's career.

13. **A.** NO CHANGE

B. He created abstracted but realistic oil paintings meant to look exactly like motion-blurred or unfocused photographs in hopes that viewers would grapple with these same questions.

C. Abstracted oil paintings of realistic photographs made people grapple with these questions.

D. To grapple with these questions, Richter made abstracted oil paintings that were realistic like photographs, asking viewers to grapple with the question of what separated hyperreal painting and photography.

Nevertheless, Richter is regarded as one of
14
Germany's finest contemporary artists. He has
been celebrated by museums all over the world,
including the Museum of Modern Art in New York
City, which in 2002 hosted a major retrospective of
Richter's work entitled "Forty Years of Painting." 15

14. F. NO CHANGE

   G. Today

   H. However

   J. Conversely

15. Which of the following sentences would most effectively conclude the paragraph?

   A. Another famous German artist who is considered one of Richter's contemporaries is Georg Baselitz.

   B. Many people don't think Richter's works are that interesting, while others think he is a visionary.

   C. Gerhard Richter has also made glass sculptures, but they aren't as famous as his paintings.

   D. Richter is still making art to this day, continuously expanding his body of work to include new forms of experimentation.

Following the context location strategy we outlined, you identified each question type: Question 13 is a KLA question, while Question 14 is an Organization POW question and Question 15 is a Topic Development POW question. You can then tackle each question individually according to the kind of context you need to locate for each. In the following paragraphs we'll break down the application of the relevant strategies.

Question 13

You can see that NO CHANGE is an answer option, so you'll start by reading the sentence with the underlined word or phrase. In this case, the entire sentence is underlined. In comparing the answer choices, you can see that there are no apparent grammatical errors. The changes made affect wording, style, and clarity. You know then that you need to evaluate the sentences for concision, consistency, and relevance to the text. Choice A is wordy (repeating *experiment* and *question*) and redundant ("grapple with the same questions" and "question the division"). Choice B is relatively concise. Choice C is concise but lacks precision. It is unclear whether Richter is the one responsible for the paintings. Choice D possesses similar issues of wordiness and redundancy as choice A. Seemingly, we've found good reasons to eliminate all answers but choice B. It is concise, specific and consistent with the information around it, and is connected to the purpose of the paragraph. You can then place the sentence in the paragraph and verify that it fits. You can see how the preceding sentence tells us that the subject of the next sentence should probably be Richter's experiments. Choice B supports that purpose well.

Question 14

After glancing at the question and reading the underlined sentence, you see the focus is on a transition. Therefore, your task is to determine which transition fits both the paragraph that contains it and the one that comes before it. In other words, which transition word or phrase effectively guides the reader from one paragraph to the next? The existing transition *Nevertheless* signals a pivot away from the previous discussion of Richter's work, perhaps preparing to offer contrasting ideas. In reading further into the second paragraph, there is nothing that contradicts statements made in the first paragraph. Instead, paragraph 2 continues the discussion of Richter's career, discussing his current place in the art world and a retrospective show in 2002. As such, any choices that present contrasting transitions can be eliminated (choices F, H, and J). This leaves you with choice G, *Today*. To check that answer, examine the structure of the paragraphs. Such a transition signals a temporal relationship, which works well with the apparent chronological order of the text.

Question 15

When you see the question box, you refer to the question first. From there, you know that you need to read the entire paragraph and determine its purpose. For a full-length passage, you may also want to scan the first and last sentences of the first and last paragraph to ensure you have a sense of the overall purpose. For our example, given the provided title, you can infer that the overall purpose is to provide the reader with an overview of the life and art of artist Gerhard Richter. Scanning the paragraph in question as well as the question itself, you'll recognize that this is a

concluding paragraph that requires an adequate concluding sentence. Only choice D fulfills this task. Choice A introduces a new topic entirely, and choices B and C bring up topics that would be better suited for placement elsewhere in the passage (if included at all).

In all three cases, you had to rely on locating and interpreting contextual information in order to draw a conclusion. POW and KLA questions are alike in that both require you to make sense of the provided context. While practicing this strategy, you may have noticed that these questions can take more time than CSE questions either because of the thinking involved or the reading required. Luckily, there are fewer of them on your test than CSE questions. Whether you tackle all the CSE questions first within a passage to leave yourself more time for KLA and POW at the end or start with the KLA and POW questions knowing you can work through CSE questions quickly and easily is up to you and what works for your test taking style. Keep in mind a few things: all questions are worth the same number of points, so your goal is to answer accurately for as many questions as possible. Similarly, be mindful of the time you spend per passage. Your goal is to get through all the questions for a passage within the time frame that will help you meet your goal.

TEST YOURSELF

ENGLISH STRATEGIES

Now that you've had a chance to review strategies, take some time to test out combining these strategies with a sample passage. In the Knowledge Check at the end of this chapter, you'll have the opportunity to practice under timed test conditions. Here, while you may opt to time yourself, the goal is more to practice the different strategies we've introduced rather than replicate test conditions exactly. See how the different strategies affect your ability to work quickly and eliminate answers. It's okay if it takes you a little longer than normal to complete since your goal is to try out the strategies and see which help you.

GLORIA STEINEM, FEMINIST HEROINE

[1]

Gloria Steinem is a political writer and activist, <u>mostly famous</u> for her work as a leading figure in the
1
women's rights movement. Growing up with the lasting effects of the Great Depression on her once-wealthy family, Steinem became an independent young woman, working her way through the elite Smith College with minimal aid from the school or her family. While in college, she became engaged, but her fiancé called off the <u>wedding; because his</u> parents felt that Steinem was
2
not wealthy enough to marry into their family. It was one of Steinem's first encounters with the social and economic aspects of relations between men and women.

[2]

After graduating in 1956, Steinem became a Chester Bowles Asian Fellow and made plans to attend the

1. **A.** NO CHANGE
   B. most famous
   C. more famous
   D. famousest

2. **F.** NO CHANGE
   G. wedding because his
   H. wedding, because his
   J. wedding because, his

universities of Delhi and Calcutta. <u>The Chester Bowles</u>
<u>Asian Fellowship commemorated the American dip-</u>
₃
<u>lomat and Indian ambassador by the same name.</u>
₃

She spent two years <u>in India studying, writing, and</u>
₄
<u>learning the grassroots organizing skills used by</u>
₄
<u>Mahatma Gandhi.</u>
₄

Beyond her studies, she traveled throughout the country and witnessed local women combatting some of the ills rankling <u>the young nation; the affronts</u> of the caste
₅
system, disparities in education, and sectarian violence. During this time, Steinem began writing articles for Indian newspapers, effectively launching her career in journalism.

[3]

<u>As</u> Steinem was back in America, finding steady
₆
work as a writer was quite difficult, especially for a young woman. However, she was given the opportunity to write one of her most enduring articles while free-lancing for the now-defunct magazine *Show*. Steinem worked undercover as a "bunny" hostess in a Playboy

3. The author is considering deleting the under-lined phrase. Should the author make this change?

   A. Yes, because it fails to explain the process of applying for the fellowship.
   B. Yes, because it distracts from the discussion of Steinem's time in India.
   C. No, because it provides background for an important event in Steinem's academic career.
   D. No, because it offers political context for the time period.

4. F. NO CHANGE
   G. in India to study, write, and learning the grassroots organizing skills used by Mahatma Gandhi.
   H. in India studying, writing, and to learn the grassroots organizing skills used by Mahatma Gandhi.
   J. in India to spend two years learning to study, writing, and the grassroots organizing skills used by Mahatma Gandhi.

5. A. NO CHANGE
   B. the young nation the affronts
   C. the young nation, the affronts:
   D. the young nation: the affronts

6. F. NO CHANGE
   G. Whenever
   H. Once
   J. While

<u>club. And</u> wrote
7

a <u>ground-breaking</u> first-person account of the joyless
8
lives the bunnies led.

[4]

☐9☐ She soon enjoyed regular assignments writing for

<u>such magazines like</u> *Vogue* and *Cosmopolitan*. However,
10
she was limited to writing about "women's topics," such

as hairstyles and weight loss. Eventually, Steinem landed

a job with *New York* magazine, writing about politics.

She also took part in many activist causes and joined

<u>the Redstockings; a feminist group</u>.
11

7. **A.** NO CHANGE

   B. club; and

   C. club and

   D. club. And she

8. Which of the alternatives best emphasizes the impact of Steinem's article?

   F. NO CHANGE

   G. fascinating

   H. colorful

   J. vivid

9. Which of the following sentences provides the best transition from the previous paragraph to this one?

   A. Steinem was now 30 years old.

   B. This famous story helped to boost Steinem's career.

   C. Undercover reporting was not Steinem's major interest, however.

   D. The article has been widely reprinted and is still well known to this day.

10. **F.** NO CHANGE

   K. magazines, that included

   L. such magazines including

   J. such magazines as

11. **A.** NO CHANGE

   B. the Redstockings a feminist group

   C. the Redstockings, a feminist group.

   D. the Redstockings—a radical feminist group established in the 1960s.

[5]

In 1963, Steinem attended a rally for reproductive rights, and this issue; she says, helped her make the
12

transition to feminism. Reproductive rights remain a
13
controversial topic in many parts of the world. Steinem
13
also supported causes such as the unionization of Chicano farm workers and peace in Vietnam.

Steinem soon stepped to the forefront of the women's
14
rights movement, a tireless worker and advocate. In
14
1972, she co-founded the most successful feminist publication, *Ms.* Although the magazine was popular and influential, it lost money due to lack of advertising, and within fifteen years, the magazine was sold.

[6]

After the sale of the magazine, Steinem was able to concentrate on writing for herself. She wrote many famous articles, the likes of which included "Marilyn,"
15
about the actress Marilyn Monroe, and published several books, including a psychological memoir called *Revolution from Within*, a collection of essays titled *Beyond Words*, and an autobiography.

12. F. NO CHANGE

  G. rights, and this issue, she says, helped

  H. rights; and this issue she says helped

  J. rights—and this issue, she says—helped

13. Which of the alternatives would most effectively support the assertion made in the previous sentence?

  A. NO CHANGE

  B. Reproductive rights were only one of the many causes feminists espoused during the 1960s.

  C. Many people have been critical of her stance on those issues.

  D. She wanted women to have true freedom when it came to their reproductive rights.

14. F. NO CHANGE

  G. Steinem soon stepped, tirelessly working and advocating, to the forefront of the women's rights movement.

  H. A tireless worker and advocate, Steinem soon stepped to the forefront of the women's rights movement.

  J. Soon stepping to the forefront of the women's rights movement, Steinem was a tireless worker and advocate.

15. A. NO CHANGE

  B. they included

  C. inclusive of

  D. including

Answer Explanations

1. **The correct answer is B.** The correct superlative form of the adjective *famous* is "most famous."

2. **The correct answer is G.** The word *because* signals a dependent clause which, when following an independent clause, does not require additional punctuation. The semicolon is wrong because what follows the punctuation mark is not an independent clause. Choice H uses a comma to separate the independent clause from the dependent clause. Such a comma is only necessary when the clauses offer an extreme contrast, which is not apparent here. Choices J incorrectly inserts an intrusive comma after the word *because*, which instead should flow directly into what follows.

3. **The correct answer is B.** The focus of the paragraph is Steinem's time in India. Any sentences present should contribute to the narrative of how her experience was formative for her career and political activities.

4. **The correct answer is F.** As written, the underlined text uses proper parallel structure for all verbs. The other choices present errors in this regard.

5. **The correct answer is D.** A colon must follow an independent clause and can be used to set off a point of emphasis or short list. This is a case of the latter with the information following the word *nation* being a list of three items.

6. **The correct answer is H.** *Once* makes a better introductory word as it clarifies the logical relationship between the two clauses while also proscribing the appropriate chronology to the sentence. Choices G and J imply that Steinem was back in the United States periodically without any context from the passage suggesting as much. Choice F would suffice if the ending of the previous paragraph had stated that Steinem was returning to America; otherwise, it stands as an abrupt transition.

7. **The correct answer is C.** As it stands, the phrase after the period lacks a subject and is not a complete sentence. The two statements can be joined by *and* or with a comma, coordinating conjunction, and a subject for the second phrase ("she"). Choice D takes the latter approach but instead uses a period. That is grammatically acceptable but not as concise as choice C.

8. **The correct answer is F.** Since the writer wants to stress the unusual nature of the article, "groundbreaking" seems to be the appropriate adjective.

9. **The correct answer is B.** In paragraph 3, Steinem was struggling to find work; in paragraph 4, she is a successful writer. The sentence given in choice B explains the transition logically.

10. **The correct answer is J.** This choice makes appropriate formal usage of the "such as" construction, used when the examples are specific and do not merely resemble (or appear like) the objects referenced.

11. **The correct answer is C.** A semi-colon is used to separate two independent clauses or items in a list in which the items contain commas. Choices C and D offer solutions that properly offsets the appositive phrases from the sentence; however, choice C is more concise while still being relevant to the passage.

12. **The correct answer is G.** A semicolon isn't needed here; the independent clauses are joined by *and*, which calls for a comma instead. Choice G appropriately sets off the parenthetical phrase "she says" with a pair of commas.

13. **The correct answer is D.** This sentence is the only one that explains and demonstrates how concern over reproductive rights motivated Steinem to become a committed feminist.

14. **The correct answer is H.** The modifying phrase "a tireless worker and advocate" must be placed next to "Steinem" for proper modification. Choices F, G, and J create improper modification.

15. **The correct answer is D.** *Including* is grammatically correct and the most concise choice in this context.

Now that you have practiced with a full passage, reflect on the strategies you used to complete it. Answer the following questions for yourself:

- Which strategies seemed to help you most?
- Did any strategy prove to be unhelpful for you? If so, could you modify it to make it helpful?
- After practicing, how might you like to change your overall approach to the English section? What would you like to keep the same about your approach?

Engaging in this kind of reflection is useful in its own right, as it helps you make sense of what to expect on exam day and how best to plan for it.

GENERAL REMINDERS AND ADVICE

Here are a few other things to keep in mind as you prepare for the ACT English test. Please also refer back to Chapter 3 for additional test-taking advice.

Read All Your Answer Choices

Don't just automatically mark down the first answer that seems correct. Instead, make sure you read each answer choice and eliminate those you know are wrong before choosing the *best* answer. The strategies for CSE and POW/KLA questions will guide you through how to evaluate each answer choice.

Don't Worry If You Don't Know the Passage Topic

The passages used in the English section will come from any number of subjects and cover any number of topics. Luckily, you're not being tested on your reading comprehension in this section so much as your ability to spot errors in and effectively correct standard written English. No matter what the topic of a given passage is, you only need to focus on the grammar, phrasing, and construction of the writing.

Trust Yourself

Don't spend too long going back and forth about a correct answer simply because two different answers seem plausibly correct. When in doubt, save time and go with your gut instinct. You can always mark it as a guess and come back to think about it harder when reviewing.

Personalize Your Approach

Everything we've laid out here is a basic template for how to approach the English test, but you might need to adapt these strategies to suit your own needs as a test taker. Practicing like you are now is the best way to develop a personalized strategy, so you're already halfway there! In the next section, we'll lay out a base level approach that can help you bring all these skills together but remember that you can adapt it to account for your own strengths, weaknesses, and score goals.

STRATEGY ROUNDUP

It's important to personalize your approach to ensure you are using the strategies that make the most sense for your performance (your timing, your accuracy, and your goals). As a starting point for all test takers, we recommend the following path to success. From here, you can make adjustments that suit your needs.

STEP 1: USE THE QUESTIONS TO GUIDE YOUR READING

You're in a race against the clock to answer all 75 questions accurately and efficiently. To do that and have time to check answers, you need to minimize how much of the passage you read. That is not only going to save you time but also keep you focused on what counts for the questions. You know that most of the questions don't require you to read much of the passage. At minimum, you need to read the sentence with the underlined text. At any one time, the maximum you'll be reading is a little before and after the question marker, or perhaps a paragraph or two—for those whole-passage questions.

STEP 2: PRIORITIZE EASIER QUESTION TYPES

Work through the passage and prioritize the question type that is easier for you to complete accurately and quickly. For the vast majority of test takers, this will be the CSE or "NO CHANGE" questions. You can also start by answering any questions that are connected to underlined segments of text and then move on to those that are boxed or that address the passage as a whole later. Whatever order, aim to knock out the questions that are easiest for you first to save time for those that take more effort.

STEP 3: APPLY YOUR QUESTION STRATEGIES

Use what you know about the priorities of the ACT English questions to guide how you work through each question. We gave you an in-depth look at the priorities and processes of all three English question types. It's up to you to apply those and modify them based on how your English knowledge and skills progress. Some questions will require the full strategies while others can be answered in a few seconds. Those step-by-step processes are there to help you work quickly and avoid some of the common mistakes test takers make. You may find that you're able to trim or combine certain steps as you improve.

STEP 4: ANSWER ALL QUESTIONS FOR A GIVEN PASSAGE

Even if you have to guess for some, answer all the questions for a given passage first. Mark any for which you make guesses in case you have time to review them later. Remember to use the strategies you practiced in this chapter as you approach questions.

STEP 5: REPEAT THE PROCESS FOR THE NEXT PASSAGE

Once you are completely done with one passage, you can move on to another. Remember, if you are dividing your time evenly between the five passages, you don't want to spend more than 8–9 minutes on a given passage and question set.

SUMMING IT UP

- Use your diagnostic score to determine the best way to practice for your ACT exam. As you learn different English strategies that work for you, look for opportunities to practice editing your writing in other contexts outside of test prep too. The more you think about how writing is constructed and how the different rules of standard English come together, the better equipped you'll be on exam day.

- Since you have 45 minutes to complete 75 questions across 5 passages, you should plan to spend no more than 9 minutes per passage and question set if you are splitting time evenly between passages.

- Avoid spending more than 30–45 seconds on any one question. If you can't find the answer in that time, eliminate the distractors you can and guess. Mark guesses to review later if time allows.

- Use overall section strategies to help with the ACT English test:

  ○ Divide your time according to your personal score goals.

  ○ Familiarize yourself with the different question types so you can spot them and react when you see them.

  ○ Restrict your reading to what you definitely need for the questions.

  ○ Complete all the questions for a given passage before moving on to another.

  ○ Use a notation system to mark guesses so you can review them if you have time.

- Engage in strategies that are specific to a given question type:

  ○ Approach Conventions of Standard English (CSE) questions using a step-by-step process:

    1. Use the question to guide your reading. When you see NO CHANGE, read the sentence with underlining.

    2. If there is a grammatical error, eliminate choice A/F NO CHANGE.

    3. Look at each answer choice and eliminate all answers with grammatical errors.

    4. If multiple choices remain, eliminate answers that change the meaning of the text and/or are wordier than other grammatical choices.

    5. 5. If no answer choices remain, reread the sentence and reevaluate answer choices. If you're low on time, choose a grammatically correct answer and move on.

- Approach Knowledge of Language (KLA) and Production of Writing (POW) questions with a mind for the context necessary to answer them.

  - For KLA questions, determine which answer is most concise, precise, and consistent with the style, tone, and meaning of the passage.

  - For POW questions that deal with topic development, choices will be relevant to the text in question. For whole-passage questions, review the passage title and the first and last sentences of the first and last paragraph. Questions related to paragraphs need you to understand the purpose of the paragraph, which can be done using the first and last sentence of the paragraph that contains the question.

  - For POW questions that deal with organization, determine if you are looking at a transition, a full sentence, or a full paragraph, then make sure your selection matches the context that comes before and after the underlined text or question marker. Any choice you make should create a smooth transition that accurately reflects the relationship of the ideas.

- As a basic strategy for bringing all these skills together, consider the following approach:

  1. Use the questions to guide your reading.

  2. Start with easier question types.

  3. Apply your question-specific strategies for speed and accuracy.

  4. Answer all questions for a given passage.

  5. Repeat the process for the next passage.

- Remember that you can personalize your approach to reflect your own strengths, weaknesses, and score goals, and that you should refine your approach based on how you improve as you practice.

KNOWLEDGE CHECK: ENGLISH

75 Questions—45 Minutes

Directions: In the following five passages, certain words and phrases are underlined and numbered. In the right-hand column, you will find alternatives for the part that is underlined. In most cases, you are to choose which alternative best expresses the idea, makes the statement appropriate in standard written English, or is worded to best reflect the style and tone of the whole passage. If you think the original version is best, choose "NO CHANGE." Sometimes, you may also find a question in the right-hand column about the underlined part. Here, you should choose the best answer to the question.

You may also find questions about a section of a passage, or a passage in its entirety. These questions do not refer to specific underlined portions of the passage, but rather are identified by a number or numbers in a box.

For each question, choose the answer you consider best. Read each passage through once before you begin to answer the questions that accompany it. For many of the questions, you must read several sentences beyond the questions to determine the answer. Be sure that you have read far enough each time you choose an alternative.

PASSAGE I

THE NAMES OF FLOWERS

[1]

I look and staring at the first green shoots sprouting
up through the dead leaves.

1. **A.** NO CHANGE
   B. I look and stare
   C. I looking and staring
   D. I looking and stare

The sight sets me trembling with anticipation, and I

2. **F.** NO CHANGE
   G. to anticipate
   H. and anticipating
   J. OMIT the underlined portion.

kneel toward the earth to make sure I'd seen correctly.

3. **A.** NO CHANGE
   B. I've seen
   C. I can see
   D. I will see

Yes, the daffodils have already begun pushing toward
the sun. Like in a fever, I forget my work and wander
about the garden inspecting the mulched beds. Winter

4. **F.** NO CHANGE
   G. have beginning
   H. will soon began
   J. soon beginning to

is almost <u>over, I</u> can taste the coming delirium of
                5
flowers.

[2]

Gardening is something new to me, a delight this
city boy never imagined. As a child growing up in an
apartment in New York, it <u>seems</u> enough to know that
                                        6

there were flowers and trees. <u>Culture marked even more</u>
                                                    7
<u>than the seasons were by nature.</u> Autumn was when we
        7
played football in the street, or when I was older, tried to
pick the peak foliage weekend to go camping. We were
familiar with the highlights that marked each season,

though not the subtle particulars, <u>like the gradual</u>
                                                8
<u>way one transformed into another.</u> Such intimacy was
        8
reserved for buildings, crowds, and subway trains. ⑨

5. **A.** NO CHANGE
   B. over and I
   C. over, and I
   D. over, yet I

6. **F.** NO CHANGE
   E. does seem
   F. did seem
   J. seemed

7. **A.** NO CHANGE
   B. Even culture was marked more than the seasons than nature.
   C. Even the seasons were marked more by culture than by nature.
   D. Seasons were marked more even by culture than by nature.

8. If the writer were to delete the underlined portion, the paragraph would primarily lose:
   F. proof that the author did not understand the seasons.
   G. an example of a particular with which the author was not familiar.
   H. a poetic turn of phrase that makes the essay more appealing to read.
   J. a key transition between two different yet related ideas.

9. The author is considering deleting Paragraph 2. If the author made this change, the passage would primarily lose:
   A. background that helps to explain the significance of the garden to the writer.
   B. background that explains why the writer feels lucky to have escaped the city.
   C. a description of the writer's childhood as vivid as the description of the writer's garden.
   D. evidence of the writer's sensitive personality and ability to appreciate flowers.

[3]

Now the twilight of summer is marked for me by budding chrysanthemums spilling over the retaining wall at the side of the house. In <u>too seasons</u>, they've
10
grown huge and sprawling. At the height of autumn,

they are as <u>bright yellow and red and purple</u> as any
11
foliage, and the season ends when they turn brown and the last rose buds on the climbers leaning up the porch fail to open.

[4]

Daffodils along the front walk <u>mark</u> the beginning
12
of a long Missouri spring that unfolds with crocuses and tulips, irises and peonies under my study window, and forsythia and spirea around the edges of the lawn. Summer means daisies swaying on the hill, and later, black-eyed Susans jostling along the fence.

[5]

At thirty-five, I'm beginning to learn the names of flowers, and more than just the names. Names are our entry into the world, and I feel a fresh side of myself come alive as I become familiar with the words standing for all those vivid scents and colors springing from the ground. It's nice to know that one can keep on <u>growing.</u>
13
<u>Finding</u> enough space inside for gardens and for subway
13
trains.

10. **F.** NO CHANGE
   G. too season's
   H. to seasons
   J. two seasons

11. **A.** NO CHANGE
   B. bright yellow red and purple
   C. bright, yellow, and red, and purple
   D. bright yellow, and red, and purple

12. **F.** NO CHANGE
   G. have marked
   H. marks
   J. marked

13. **A.** NO CHANGE
   B. growing finding
   C. growing, finding
   D. growing; finding

Questions 14 and 15 ask about the passage as a whole.

14. Suppose the writer's main purpose had been to provide a timeline of care for chrysanthemums during their lifecycle. Would this essay accomplish that purpose?

   F. Yes, because it describes how chrysanthemums look at different points in their life cycle.

   G. Yes, because it explains when to plant chrysanthemums, when they bloom, and when they die.

   H. No, because the author spends more time discussing personal and sensory experiences with flowers than gardening tips.

   J. No, because the author describes the history of chrysanthemums cultivation.

15. The writer wishes to insert the following detail into the essay:

   I could tell you there were pines, but not distinguish them from cedar.

   This sentence would most logically be inserted into which paragraph?

   A. Paragraph 1

   B. Paragraph 2

   C. Paragraph 3

   D. Paragraph 4

PASSAGE II

PASTA AND TOMATOES

[1]

As trade goes, <u>so also goes</u> the world. In these days
of global markets where people and goods crisscross the
world, the idea that a development in Asia can have

a major <u>affect on</u> America is taken for granted.

Less widely understood <u>was</u> the fact that exchange has
always been a major force in world affairs.

16. F. NO CHANGE

   G. so therefore,

   H. also goes

   J. so goes

17. A. NO CHANGE

   B. effect on

   C. effect over

   D. affect over

18. F. NO CHANGE

   G. is

   H. had been

   J. could be

[2]

[19] Agricultural techniques developed in the Near East spread deeper into Asia, as well as Europe and Africa, evolving into new forms as they went.

Goods, religion, knowledge, all of these things have moved about through the ages, adopted here by one people, forced on another people there, and every wealth of interchange also witnessed a wealth of transformation.

[3]

That is why Herodotus could marvel at the different practices he found upon his tour, of the ancient

Mediterranean, and why too his impressions had been passed on to generations born two millennia later.

In fact, the ancient Greeks, whom were well aware of the influences of Egypt on their civilization, did not pass their wealth of knowledge directly on to the rest of Europe, which claims Greece as its root. Greek thought

19. Which of the following sentences, if inserted at this point, would provide the most effective transition to the second paragraph?

  A. Throughout history, agriculture has always played a major role in the development of civilizations.

  B. Throughout history, the movement of people and goods has been a major factor in changing human societies.

  C. Many examples of this can be found by studying the history of trade over the past 100 years.

  D. However, this phenomenon was never as important as it is in the modern world.

20. **F.** NO CHANGE

  G. Goods, religion, knowledge: all of these things have moved

  H. Movement has occurred in goods, religion, and knowledge

  J. Goods, religion, and knowledge have all moved

21. **A.** NO CHANGE

  B. tour—of

  C. tour; of

  D. tour of

22. **F.** NO CHANGE

  G. have been

  H. are

  J. will be

23. **A.** NO CHANGE

  B. that

  C. who

  D. which

was kept alive by Arab scholars at the height of Islam's
<u>power and Greek</u> texts had to be translated from Arabic
₂₄
into Latin before the likes of Thomas Aquinas could
open the intellectual door to the European Renaissance.

[4]

But perhaps the clearest examples of this exchange
and transformation lay in a realm less heady and much
closer to the stomach. <u>How would modern Italy be</u>
₂₅
without pasta and tomatoes?

<u>Imagine</u> Switzerland without chocolate or Ireland and
₂₆
Eastern Europe without potatoes. ⎡27⎤

[5]

Marco Polo brought pasta back to Europe from
China. Tomatoes, potatoes, and <u>cacao,</u> they were all
₂₈
brought back from the Americas and transformed into
something else.

24. **F.** NO CHANGE
    G. power, and Greek
    H. power, but Greek
    J. power, therefore Greek

25. **A.** NO CHANGE
    B. What would modern Italy be like
    C. Where would modern Italy be
    D. Would modern Italy be

26. **F.** NO CHANGE
    G. Can you imagine
    H. It's like imagining
    J. Isn't it strange to imagine

27. Which of these sentences provides the most
    logical conclusion for Paragraph 4?

    A. Yet none of these familiar staples were known
    in the Europe of the Middle Ages.

    B. These staples have become part of the very
    identity of these nations.

    C. They would not be the same countries that
    they are today.

    D. Cuisine is an important element of every
    culture.

28. **F.** NO CHANGE
    G. cacao,
    H. cacao
    J. cacao, which

29. **A.** NO CHANGE
    B. Because
    C. Since
    D. Yet

Therefore, while neither tomatoes nor pasta is originally
<u>29</u>
Italian, <u>one cannot think of pasta and tomato sauce in</u>
<u>30</u>
<u>all their glorious forms without thinking of Italy.</u>
30

30. F. NO CHANGE

G. they have been adapted by Italians.

H. they are now important in Italian cooking.

J. one cannot forget that they were once unknown in Italy.

PASSAGE III

THE LIFE OF ASPIRIN

[1]

There are so many innovations and inventions in our lives that we take for <u>granted there</u> are even things
31
that are a part of our daily lives that we have little or no idea about, including where they came from or how they developed, although we're happy that they exist and that we have access to them. 32

31. A. NO CHANGE

B. granted; there

C. granted there;

D. Granted there

32. The author of this passage would like to add a sentence to the end of Paragraph 1, which would help transition to Paragraph 2. Which of the following sentences would best serve that purpose?

F. Take, for instance, aspirin.

G. Perhaps that means we're ignorant.

H. The truth is, some things are better unknown.

J. The Internet is a good place to research new things.

[2]

Little serious thought is <u>given; to</u> these humble,
33
unassuming little pills by the average person, although billions are bought and sold each year and you'd be hard pressed to find someone who doesn't have some in his or her house. These simple-looking little discs have been responsible for easing <u>countless and innumerable</u> head-
34
aches, aches, and pains around the world,

33. A. NO CHANGE

B. given to

C. given, to

D. given. To

34. F. NO CHANGE

G. countless

H. innumerable or countless

J. many and several

yet most of us don't know much more about <u>it</u> beyond
                                           35
the fact that there's likely a bottle full of them somewhere in our medicine cabinets. Let's give aspirin the

respect its due by taking a <u>closer—look!</u>
                                    36

[3]

Aspirin has taken on different forms over its long
and illustrious history, dating back over 2,400 years to
salicin extracts from the bark of the <u>willow tree; which</u>
                                              37
<u>are</u> metabolized by the human body into salicylic acid
37

<u>active ingredient of aspirin</u>. Evidence of this has been
                      38
recorded in ancient Egyptian, Assyrian, and Sumerian texts.

[4]

Through the centuries that followed, chemists
sought to improve the effectiveness of salicylic acid,
reduce its side effects, and make it easier to mass
produce as a medicine for widespread public use. In the
late nineteenth century, acetylsalicylic acid was studied
as a possible replacement for salicylic acid and, in 1899,
the modern aspirin was born and named by the phar-
maceutical company Bayer.

[5]

Today, aspirin is perhaps the most widely used
medicine on the planet, and <u>exceeds 50 billion pills</u>
                                            39
<u>estimates the consumption, globally and annually.</u> This
                            39
nonsteroidal anti-inflammatory drug (NSAID) is used
to treat a wide array of symptoms, inflammatory conditions, and illnesses. These include fevers, blood clots,

35. A. NO CHANGE
B. him
C. us
D. them

36. F. NO CHANGE
G. closer—look.
H. closer; look.
J. closer look.

37. A. NO CHANGE
B. willow tree which is
C. willow tree, which are
D. willow tree, which is

38. F. NO CHANGE
G. (an active ingredient of aspirin)
H. an active ingredient of aspirin
J. "an active ingredient of aspirin"

39. A. NO CHANGE
B. 50 billion estimates the globe—annual consumption of excess pills
C. the globe annually consumes 50 billion estimated pill excesses
D. estimates of global annual consumption exceed 50 billion pills

headaches, rheumatoid arthritis, and everyday aches and pains. In specific low doses, aspirin has also been suggested as a preventative medicine to reduce the risk of strokes and certain types of cancer.

[6]

Despite its impressive array of beneficial effects, over the years <u>we were learned</u>, largely through
40

<u>trail and error</u>, that there are some common unwanted
41
side effects connected with aspirin consumption. These include stomach pain and bleeding, worsening of asthma symptoms, and ulcers. Aspirin can also be haz-ardous for women who are pregnant or those who drink excessive amounts of alcohol. 42

[7]

Here's an interesting bit of aspirin trivia: Humans aren't the only creatures who benefit from the medicinal effects of aspirin. Veterinarians sometimes administer aspirin to a wide array of animals, including dogs and horses, as an anticoagulant and pain reliever. 43 44

40. **F.** NO CHANGE
    G. we could have learned
    H. we've learned
    J. we will be learning

41. **A.** NO CHANGE
    B. trial and error
    C. trail and era
    D. try all and error

42. In Paragraph 6, the author is considering deleting the final sentence. Should the author make this change?

    F. Yes, because it repeats information stated earlier in the paragraph.

    G. Yes, because the paragraph has already provided sufficient evidence that aspirin can have dangerous side effects.

    H. No, because it is the paragraph's most convincing evidence that aspirin can be dangerous.

    J. No, because it adds relevant information.

43. The author of this passage has just discovered that aspirin, when taken at regular low doses, can help reduce the risk of heart attacks. To which of the following paragraphs should the author add this information?

    A. Paragraph 3
    B. Paragraph 4
    C. Paragraph 5
    D. Paragraph 6

44. The author of this passage has decided to add a concluding sentence to this passage. Which of the following would be the most effective choice?

   F. The next time you reach for an aspirin, remember that you're about to have a tiny bit of medicinal history and innovation!

   G. There are lots of other things you can take if you're feeling ill; aspirin is not your only option!

   H. Aspirin is among the most easy-to-purchase medicines, and you'll find it in most small grocery stores, supermarkets, and pharmacies!

   J. Can you think of any other significant medical innovations that have changed our daily lives?

> Question 45 asks about the passage as a whole.

45. The author of this essay was recently given an assignment to research the history of medicines in the ancient world. Does this essay fulfill this requirement?

   A. Yes, because this essay discusses a medicine that has existed for a long time.

   B. Yes, because aspirin was used by the ancient Egyptians, Assyrians, and Sumerians.

   C. No, because this essay isn't comprehensive enough to fulfill the scope of the assignment.

   D. No, because aspirin wasn't invented until the twentieth century.

PASSAGE IV

A PROFESSIONAL LESSON

[1]

When I first began working as a journalist in the 1970s, <u>there are few women in the field who are taken</u> <u>seriously</u>. I had no illusions; I would have to

46. F. NO CHANGE

   G. there are few women in the field who is taken seriously.

   H. there were few women in the field who are taken seriously.

   J. there were few women in the field who were taken seriously.

<u>prove, myself</u> again and again.

47. A. NO CHANGE

   B. prove myself

   C. prove, myself,

   D. prove—myself

[2]

Editors were surprised when my work turned out to be first rate. It took me a long time to understand that the reason had to do with the way I carried myself, not to mention the fact that I was making no attempt with which to conceal my anxieties. I had not yet learned to put on a professional face.

[3]

Editors who would try to hand me the softer stories, or the stories with a "woman angle."

"Maybe you could do a piece on the charity work of the First Lady." I was undaunted by these incidents, and by the inevitable sexist jokes and innuendoes. After all, I had chosen a career that meant not breaking ground in a traditional male bastion. Determination and a thick skin were mandatory.

[4]

There was, however, an aspect of professional life for whom many of us were not prepared. I remember

48. **F.** NO CHANGE
    G. not to mention the fact I was making no attempt to conceal my anxieties
    H. with the fact that I made no attempt to conceal my anxieties
    J. I made no attempt to conceal my anxieties

49. **A.** NO CHANGE
    B. Editors would try to hand me the softer stories,
    C. The softer stories were the ones editors would try to hand me,
    D. Editors who tried to hand me the softer stories,

50. **F.** NO CHANGE
    G. could do the charity work of
    H. could be doing it on the charity work of
    J. could do a piece on charity work for

51. **A.** NO CHANGE
    B. breaking ground in
    C. it broke ground in
    D. broken ground in

52. **F.** NO CHANGE
    G. for which
    H. for what
    J. for why

that when <u>I will be working</u> on a difficult assignment
                    53
and I checked in with the editor, I would tell him about
my worries, describe the obstacles I had yet to sur-
mount, or sometimes even complain about the minor
frustrations that had made for a bad day. I thought of
it as communication, being honest in my work. I never
doubted that I would get past these problems. They
merely represented the moment-to-moment process of
doing my job. After all, life was like that too—full of difficulties that I discussed with friends as a way of getting
through them. ⁵⁴

[5]

I noticed, therefore, that when my male colleagues
spoke to editors, no matter what doubts they had, they
always said that everything was under control. It seemed
like lying. What were these men <u>afraid of, I</u> didn't realize
                                        55
that <u>by behaving the way in which I'd been acting,</u> my
                    56
honesty was creating a negative impression with my
editors. Editors assumed that if I was speaking about
my difficulties, then I must really be in trouble. Like
all managers, they wanted to know that everything was
under control. By <u>sharing the struggles</u> that are part of
                        57
the process of all work, I made my editors worry and
at the same time reinforced all those stereotypes about
women who can't stand the pressure.

53. A. NO CHANGE
  B. I was working
  C. I will have worked
  D. I will work

54. The author is considering adding a paragraph at
this point describing the way in which she discussed problems with a close friend. Should she
make this change?

  F. No, because the writer's description of how she
  interacted with her editor is already clear.

  G. No, because such a description belongs just
  before this paragraph.

  H. Yes, because the writer needs to more fully
  illustrate how she interacts with other people.

  J. Yes, because the writer needs to show why she
  wanted the "softer stories" she was assigned.

55. A. NO CHANGE
  B. afraid of I
  C. afraid of? I
  D. afraid of—I

56. F. NO CHANGE
  G. my behavior and
  H. my behaving in that way and
  J. OMIT the underlined portion.

57. A. NO CHANGE
  B. share the struggles
  C. shared the struggles
  D. will share the struggle

Questions 58–60 ask about the passage as a whole.

58. For the sake of unity and coherence, Paragraph 2 should be placed:

   F. where it is now.

   G. before Paragraph 1.

   H. after Paragraph 4.

   J. after Paragraph 5.

59. The writer is considering eliminating Paragraph 4. If the writer removed this paragraph, the essay would primarily lose:

   A. relevant details about the mistakes the writer made that led to their ultimate realization.

   B. historical information regarding women in the workplace.

   C. relevant details regarding the writer's male colleagues' behavior.

   D. a revealing anecdote about the writer's experience with their friends.

60. Which of the following assignments would this essay most clearly fulfill?

   F. Write a persuasive essay about the benefits of holding a job.

   G. Write an essay comparing current and past business environments for women.

   H. Write an essay about a lesson you learned from a professional experience.

   J. Write an essay about an experience in which your personal integrity was challenged.

PASSAGE V

Edwidge Danticat, A Born Writer

[1]

Those who live in countries where a large proportion of the population is illegible share their stories orally.

61. A. NO CHANGE

   B. are ineligible

   C. is illiterate

   D. are illiterate

In Haiti, one of the world's smaller countries, when someone has a tale to tell, he or she will call out Krik?

62. F. NO CHANGE

   G. a small country

   H. a particularly small country

   J. DELETE the underlined portion

<u>Neighbors:</u> friends, and relatives will then gather around
63

with an answering call of Krak!, signaling <u>there</u> will-
64
ingness to listen.

[2]

[1] The Haitian-born writer Edwidge Danticat
<u>would have been</u> only twenty-six when she took these
65
two words and made them the title for her collection of
stories. 66 [2] The nine stories in *Krik? Krak!* focus on
the hardships of living under a dictatorship.

[3] Families are forced to flee Haiti and seek new <u>lives, in</u>
67
the United States.

[4] The book received <u>much critical</u> acclaim and even
68
became a finalist for the National Book Award.

[3]

Born in Port-au-Prince in 1969, <u>her family moved</u>
69
<u>to New York City when Danticat was twelve.</u> She spoke
69
little as a new immigrant, because when she did speak,
other children made fun of her heavily accented English.

63. A. NO CHANGE
   B. Neighbors—
   C. Neighbors
   D. Neighbors,

64. F. NO CHANGE
   G. they're
   H. their
   J. they are

65. A. NO CHANGE
   B. having been
   C. was being
   D. was

66. For the sake of the logic and coherence of this
   paragraph, Sentence 2 of the paragraph should be
   placed:
   F. where it is now.
   G. before Sentence 1.
   H. after Sentence 3.
   J. after Sentence 4.

67. A. NO CHANGE
   B. lives' in
   C. lives in
   D. life in

68. F. NO CHANGE
   G. many critically
   H. too critical
   J. much criticism

69. A. NO CHANGE
   B. Danticat moved to New York City when she
      was twelve.
   C. New York City is where Danticat moved when
      she was twelve.
   D. when she was twelve Danticat moved to New
      York City.

[70] Her thesis in graduate school later became the novel *Breath, Eyes, Memory*. That novel, which was subsequently chosen by Oprah Winfrey for her book club,

featured a heroine who, <u>like the author</u>, moved from
71
Haiti to New York City at the age of twelve. Danticat's third book, *The Farming of Bones*, is also set in Haiti.

[4]

This young <u>authors</u> chosen subject matter, as well as
72
the Creole-accented language she uses to tell her stories, demonstrate that while Danticat may have left Haiti for her adopted country of America, she hasn't forgotten <u>both the land of her birth and its brave people</u>.
73

70. Which of the following sentences, if added here, would best provide a transition from the description of Danticat as a young girl to that of Danticat as an author?

   F. Danticat refrained from criticizing them in return, however, and was successful in the end.

   G. Most Haitians speak Creole, and the language is quite different from American English.

   H. Many writers have had difficult childhoods.

   J. Although she was silent much of the time, Danticat watched and remembered, as if already thinking like a writer.

71. A. NO CHANGE

   B. not unlike the author

   C. just as the author did

   D. in much the same manner as the author

72. F. NO CHANGE

   G. authors'

   H. author's

   J. author

73. A. NO CHANGE

   B. either the land of her birth or its

   C. neither the land of her birth or its

   D. neither the land of her birth nor its

Questions 74 and 75 ask about the passage as a whole.

74. The writer wishes to open the essay with a sentence that will set the theme and tone of the essay. Which of the following would most effectively accomplish this goal?

    F. Whether or not they can read, people all over the world love stories.

    G. One of my favorite books is a collection of stories set in Haiti.

    H. The problem of illiteracy results in a variety of consequences for people all over the world.

    J. Have you ever wondered what it feels like not to be able to read?

75. Suppose the writer's goal had been to provide a detailed history of the hardships the people of Haiti have endured. Would this essay accomplish that goal?

    A. Yes, because the essay mentions that the plot of *Krik? Krak!* involves such hardships.

    B. Yes, because the essay is about Edwidge Danticat, who fled Haiti because of the hardships she endured while living there.

    C. No, because the essay does not provide nearly enough information about Haiti to serve as a detailed history.

    D. No, because the essay does not imply that the people of Haiti ever suffered hardships.

ANSWER KEY AND EXPLANATIONS

1. B	14. H	27. A	40. H	53. B	66. F
2. F	15. B	28. H	41. B	54. F	67. C
3. B	16. J	29. D	42. J	55. C	68. F
4. F	17. B	30. F	43. C	56. J	69. B
5. C	18. G	31. B	44. F	57. A	70. J
6. J	19. B	32. F	45. C	58. J	71. A
7. C	20. J	33. B	46. J	59. A	72. H
8. G	21. D	34. G	47. B	60. H	73. D
9. A	22. G	35. D	48. H	61. C	74. F
10. J	23. C	36. J	49. B	62. J	75. C
11. A	24. G	37. C	50. F	63. D	
12. F	25. B	38. G	51. B	64. H	
13. C	26. F	39. D	52. G	65. D	

1. **The correct answer is B.** As written, the verbs in the sentence are not in proper parallel form. Both of the verbs in the underlined portion of the sentence need to be in the present tense.

2. **The correct answer is F.** *With* is the appropriate preposition in this common phrase. Choice G introduces a grammatical error, and choice H changes the meaning of the sentence. The phrase should not be omitted because it adds detail by modifying the verb *trembling*.

3. **The correct answer is B.** The verb here refers to an action (staring at the green shoots) that began in the immediate past and continues into the present; therefore, the present perfect tense is appropriate. The original sentence mistakenly uses the past perfect tense, so choice A is incorrect. Choice C reflects the simple present tense, and choice D reflects the simple future tense.

4. **The correct answer is F.** The verb tense of the underlined portion of this sentence is correct as written. The other answer choices contain incorrect verb forms for this sentence.

5. **The correct answer is C.** The conjunction *and* is needed to correct the comma splice in the original sentence. A comma is also necessary before *and*

because this conjunction is being used to coordinate two independent clauses with two separate subjects, so choice B is incorrect. The conjunction *yet* (choice D) is inappropriate because there is no change in direction between the two clauses.

6. **The correct answer is J.** The past tense is appropriate because the writer is describing his childhood. Choices F, G, and H are all written in the present tense.

7. **The correct answer is C.** This option most clearly states the writer's point that in New York, culture was the dominating element, even when it came to marking the passage of the seasons. Choices A, B, and D all contain confusing wording.

8. **The correct answer is G.** In the full sentence, the phrase "like the gradual way one transformed into another" functions as an example of one of the "particulars" with which the narrator was not familiar. Removing the underlined portion would mean losing this example.

9. **The correct answer is A.** Paragraph 2 tells us that the writer grew up knowing little about nature. This fact is essential to understanding the garden's effect on the writer. The writer's current environment is quite different from a city, but they never suggest the

city was something they felt lucky to have escaped, so choice B is incorrect. Paragraph 2 may be a vivid recollection (choice C) or an indication of the writer's sensitivity (choice D), but neither of these describes the paragraph's main purpose.

10. **The correct answer is J.** As written, the underlined portion of the sentence contains an incorrect, commonly confused word—*too*. Its homonym, *two*, is the appropriate word choice here as, contextually, the writer requires the word that indicates a number. Choice G contains the incorrect homonym *too* and an inappropriate possessive form of *season*. Choice H contains another incorrect homonym, *to*.

11. **The correct answer is A.** No comma should be used before *yellow* because *bright* modifies *yellow* and all the other color adjectives used. No commas are needed to separate the colors (choices C and D) because the writer has chosen to link them with the conjunction *and*. Choice B fails to link *yellow* and *red* with either a comma or *and*, so it is incorrect.

12. **The correct answer is F.** The present tense is appropriate for a general situation that is repeated year after year. *Daffodils* signals the necessity for the third-person plural form of the verb. Choices G and J are in the past tense. Choice H is a singular verb when a plural is required.

13. **The correct answer is C.** As written, this sentence creates a sentence fragment. There is a need for internal sentence punctuation to join the fragment to the prior sentence, so choice B is incorrect. Choice D recreates the issue with choice A by using a semi-colon. Choice C correctly uses a comma to connect the fragment.

14. **The correct answer is H.** Throughout the passage, the author describes a changing relationship to flowers and gardening over the course of their life. While chrysanthemums are described in terms of their seasonal behaviors in the third paragraph, the discussion does not provide a timeline of care, nor does the discussion of chrysanthemums represent a primary point of emphasis in the passage. Choices F and G speak to the life cycle of the flower, not care. Choice J is not representative of the content of the passage.

15. **The correct answer is B.** This detail is an example of how little the writer knew about nature; therefore, it belongs in the paragraph that discusses growing up in New York. Paragraphs 1 (choice A), 3 (choice C), and 4 (choice D) all take place in the present.

16. **The correct answer is J.** The idiomatic expression is: as *x* goes, so goes *y*, so choice J is correct. Choices F and G add unnecessary words. Choice H fails to complete the idiom.

17. **The correct answer is B.** As these words are most commonly used, *affect* is the proper verb form, while *effect* is the noun form. Here the word is a noun and the proper word to use is *effect*, so eliminate choices A and D. The preposition that properly follows *effect* is *on*, so choice B is correct and choice C is incorrect.

18. **The correct answer is G.** The writer is speaking about our present understanding of historical trade, so you can eliminate choices F and H, which are in the past tense. The assertion is not conditional, so choice J is incorrect.

19. **The correct answer is B.** This is the only sentence that stresses the historical importance of exchange and thereby links the previous paragraph to the examples of this phenomenon presented in Paragraph 2.

20. **The correct answer is J.** The clearest construction lists the subjects and proceeds directly to the verb without punctuation or unnecessary words. As originally written, the list lacks the conjunction *and* between the last two items in the list and misuses a comma to separate the list from the rest of the sentence. Choice G correctly uses a colon but still omits the conjunction *and*. Choice H changes the meaning of the sentence.

21. **The correct answer is D.** No punctuation should separate the noun *tour* from the prepositional phrase (beginning with *of*) that modifies it. Choices A, B, and C all contain unnecessary punctuation.

22. **The correct answer is G.** The present perfect tense indicates the connection between the past and the present, between antiquity and today.

23. **The correct answer is C.** *Greeks* is the subject of the relative clause, so the relative pronoun *who* is appropriate. *Whom* is a personal pronoun, so the original sentence is incorrect. Choices B and D are inappropriate because they refer to non-human subjects.

24. **The correct answer is G.** A comma is required before a coordinating conjunction when linking two independent clauses. *And* is the best conjunction choice because it indicates the non-contrasting relationship between the clauses, so choices F and H are incorrect. *Therefore* also expresses this relationship but cannot be used to link two independent clauses with only a comma; a semicolon would be required instead, so you can eliminate choice J.

25. **The correct answer is B.** This phrasing properly indicates that the question is about the character of modern Italy.

26. **The correct answer is F.** The imperative form of *imagine* avoids unnecessary words and maintains the authoritative tone of the sentence. Choices B and D ask questions and would be appropriate only if the sentence ended with a question mark. Choice C changes the meaning of the sentence.

27. **The correct answer is A.** This sentence makes the point that these foods are not indigenous to the nations that rely on them, and this point is crucial to the main idea of the essay. Choice C makes this point awkwardly, while choices B and D do not make this point at all.

28. **The correct answer is H.** The sentence begins with a series of subjects and should proceed to the verb without punctuation (choices F, G, and J) or unnecessary words (choices F and J).

29. **The correct answer is D.** *Yet* creates a smooth transition from the previous sentence without changing the meaning and appropriately indicates that the sentiment is a contrast since these items that are now associated with Italy did not originate there. *Therefore* (choice A) wrongly indicates that the way we think of Italy is a direct consequence of the way exchanged goods were transformed. Choices B and C do not make grammatical sense in the context of this sentence.

30. **The correct answer is F.** As is, the sentence emphasizes the author's point about how popular the Italian transformations of these food goods became, so there is no need to change it. Choices B, C, and D do not express this crucial idea effectively.

31. **The correct answer is B.** As written, the sentence is a run-on and needs to be fixed. Choice B correctly combines the two independent clauses with a semicolon while eliminating the run-on sentence. Choice C places the semicolon in the wrong place in the sentence. Choice D incorrectly creates a fragment by inserting a period.

32. **The correct answer is F.** Paragraph 1 discusses everyday innovations that we take for granted and Paragraph 2 jumps into discussing aspirins. Choice F would make an effective transition sentence from Paragraph 1 to Paragraph 2 since it introduces aspirin as a topic. The other choices are off-target and would not serve as effective transitions.

33. **The correct answer is B.** No punctuation is required at this position in the sentence, so choice B is correct.

34. **The correct answer is G.** Since *countless* and *innumerable* have the same meaning, including both words in this sentence is redundant. Choice G eliminates redundancy.

35. **The correct answer is D.** A plural pronoun is required to replace the antecedent *discs*, so *them* (choice D) is correct.

36. **The correct answer is J.** This simple declarative statement should end in a period, and no internal punctuation is needed between *closer* and *look*.

37. **The correct answer is C.** The semi-colon (choice A) is unnecessary as the information that follows is not a complete sentence. Choices B and D use the verb *is*, but agreement is with "salicin extracts," not "willow tree."

38. **The correct answer is G.** The underlined portion of the sentence contains an aside regarding salicylic acid and belongs in parentheses. Choice F incorrectly omits *an*. The other answer choices are inappropriate treatments for this information.

39. **The correct answer is D.** As written, the flow of information in the underlined portion of the sentence is confusing and awkward. Choice D avoids confusion by adjusting the word order to position the subject *estimates of global annual consumption* first, followed by the verb *exceed*.

40. **The correct answer is H.** Each option makes changes to the verb tense, affecting grammar and the phrase's relevance to the passage. Choice F creates an illogical relationship between researchers and the side effects of aspirin. Choice G creates the beginning of a conditional statement. Choice J places the action in the future, though context suggests the observations have happened over a period of time that began in the past.

41. **The correct answer is B.** Recognizing commonly used phrases is a helpful skill to have when editing for effective use of language. The correct idiomatic phrase for this sentence is "trial and error."

42. **The correct answer is J.** The final sentence adds relevant additional evidence supporting the paragraph's topic that aspirin can have dangerous side effects, so choice J is the best answer. The sentence provides additional evidence; it does not repeat evidence already provided earlier in the paragraph as choice F suggests. While the paragraph has already provided some evidence that aspirin can have dangerous side effects, additional evidence just strengthens the paragraph's thesis, so choice G is not the best answer. However, the fact that aspirin can be hazardous to pregnant people or those who drink excessive amounts of alcohol is not necessarily more convincing evidence than any evidence previously given in the paragraph, so choice H is not as strong an answer as choice J is.

43. **The correct answer is C.** Additional information about aspirin reducing the risk of heart attacks would best fit in Paragraph 5, which covers the wide array of symptoms, inflammatory conditions, and illnesses that aspirins are used to help treat.

44. **The correct answer is F.** An effective concluding sentence ties up the ideas presented in the written piece. The passage is about how aspirin, an everyday object often taken for granted, is actually an interesting bit of medicinal history and innovation, and choice F effectively captures this notion. Choices G and J take the focus off aspirin. Choice H focuses on a minor detail and is too narrow in scope for a concluding sentence.

45. **The correct answer is C.** This essay focuses solely on aspirin and no other medicines, so it isn't comprehensive enough to fulfill the requirements of an assignment to research the history of medicines in the ancient world.

46. **The correct answer is J.** The phrase refers to the past, so the verbs must be in the past tense. Choices F and G are in the present tense and choice G contains a singular verb (*is*) that does not agree with its plural antecedent (*women*). Choice H incorrectly combines the present and past tenses.

47. **The correct answer is B.** As written, the comma in the underlined portion of the sentence creates an awkward pause and is incorrect. Choice B correctly fixes the sentence by removing the comma. Choices C and D simply replace one incorrect punctuation mark with another.

48. **The correct answer is H.** This option maintains the parallel structure set up by the preposition *with*, thus indicating that the factors mentioned are two sides of the same problem. As originally written, the phrase "not to mention the fact" suggests an incidental piece of information and not the explanatory information that actually follows the phrase. Choices G and J are phrased awkwardly.

49. **The correct answer is B.** As written, the underlined portion is a fragment and contains the superfluous word *who* after *editors*, which eliminates choices A and D. Choice B turns the fragment into a complete sentence and avoids the needless use of the passive voice in choice C.

50. **The correct answer is F.** This option makes it clear that the writer is being asked to write a piece about the First Lady's charity work. Choices G and J change the sentence's meaning. Choice H is unnecessarily wordy.

51. **The correct answer is B.** The gerund phrase acts as a noun—in this case the object of the verb *meant*,

creating a correct sentence. The verbs in choices C and D are in the wrong form. The form should be positive because the essay makes it clear that the author did, indeed, break ground. As originally written, the sentence contradicts its own meaning by including the word *not*.

52. **The correct answer is G.** As written, the sentence contains an incorrect word choice, the pronoun *whom*. Choice G appropriately corrects the improper word choice.

53. **The correct answer is B.** The phrase "I remember" signals that the action in the sentence is a memory of something that has already happened, so the past tense should be used. Choice B is the only option that uses the past tense.

54. **The correct answer is F.** The suggested paragraph would add unnecessary details and distract from the writer's point. Since the suggested paragraph does not belong at any point in this essay, you need only select the answer that indicates that the paragraph is unnecessary.

55. **The correct answer is C.** As written, the comma creates a run-on sentence. This first clause is a question and should end in a question mark; the question word *what* at the beginning of the sentence serves as a clue.

56. **The correct answer is J.** This option avoids unnecessary wording and correctly conveys the writer's feeling that her complete honesty was inappropriate for her workplace. Choices F, G, and H would all leave the sentence wordy and unclear.

57. **The correct answer is A.** The sentence is correct as written and utilizes the correct form of the verb "to share." The other answer choices utilize incorrect verb forms for the context of the sentence.

58. **The correct answer is J.** The opening sentence of the paragraph indicates that the writer has set up some kind of expectation that their work will not be first rate. Therefore, in order for this paragraph to be most effective, it should come at the end of the passage, after the writer has shown us what they have done to set up such an expectation. In addition, the last line of the paragraph serves to point out the lesson that has

been learned, concluding the essay. The paragraph would disrupt the flow of the essay if placed anywhere else, so choices F, G, and H are incorrect.

59. **The correct answer is A.** In Paragraph 4, the writer sets up important, relevant information regarding their own behavior that ultimately helped them to understand why they needed to put on a professional face.

60. **The correct answer is H.** The writer is conveying an experience from their professional life that led to a personal revelation. The paragraph is a personal essay, not a persuasive (choice F) or comparative (choice G) one. The writer's personal integrity is not challenged in the essay, so choice J does not make sense.

61. **The correct answer is C.** *Illiterate* means unable to read, and *population* is a singular noun, so choice C is the correct answer, and choice D, which uses the plural verb *are*, can be eliminated. The original sentence is incorrect because *illegible* means "unreadable." Choice B uses the wrong verb form and the wrong word; *ineligible* means "not entitled."

62. **The correct answer is J.** The size of Haiti is completely irrelevant to the topic being discussed, so this underlined information should be deleted.

63. **The correct answer is D.** The word *Neighbors* is part of a list and should be separated from the next item by a comma. Choices A and B use incorrect punctuation, and choice C uses no punctuation at all.

64. **The correct answer is H.** In this sentence, *willingness* refers to that of the neighbors, friends, and relatives, so the possessive pronoun *their* is appropriate. Choices F and G both use homonyms mistakenly: *there* means a particular spot, and *they're* is a contraction of *they* and *are*. Since *they are* does not make sense in this context under any circumstances, choice J is incorrect.

65. **The correct answer is D.** The sentence describes the age of the author at the specified time, requiring the simple past tense of the verb "to be."

66. **The correct answer is F.** Because it logically follows the first sentence, the second sentence would not be as effective if moved elsewhere in the paragraph.

67. The correct answer is C. No punctuation is needed before the prepositional phrase that begins with *in*, so choice C is correct and choice A can be eliminated. The sentence discusses plural families, which eliminates choice D due to its use of the singular *life*. An apostrophe is used to show possession (choice B), which is not necessary in this sentence.

68. The correct answer is F. Since *acclaim* is a noun, it should be modified by the adjective *critical*, not the adverb *critically* (choice G) or the noun *criticism* (choice J). Adding *too* in front of this adjective changes the connotation, so choice C is not as strong an answer as choice F.

69. The correct answer is B. The first word that follows the comma should be the subject of the modifying phrase "born in Port-au-Prince in 1969." That would be *Danticat*, which is not the first word in choices A, C, or D. Choice C is also too wordy.

70. The correct answer is J. This option links Danticat's childhood behavior with her development as a writer. Choices A and B do not create such a link. Choice C is too vague.

71. The correct answer is A. This option notes the similarity between Danticat and the heroine in the clearest language. *Like* is the appropriate preposition to use when comparing nouns. The wordiness of choices B and D leaves the sentence unclear. Choice C suggests a comparison between actions, not people.

72. The correct answer is H. Only one author is being discussed, and the possessive form is used to indicate that the subject matter belongs to the author. Choices F and G indicate more than one author. Choice J lacks the elements needed to show possession.

73. The correct answer is D. This option is the most logical, given the author's subject matter. The proper negative construction is *neither . . . nor*. The constructions in choices A and B create sentences that contradict their own intended meanings. Choice C disrupts the proper negative construction by following *neither* with *or*.

74. The correct answer is F. This option introduces the informative, impersonal tone of the essay and provides an introduction to the theme of storytelling. Choice G is too personal. Choice H is too vague. Choice J is too informal and suggests the main theme of the essay is illiteracy, not storytelling.

75. The correct answer is C. The essay does not provide nearly enough information about Haiti to serve as a detailed history, so choice C is the best answer. Choices A and B may be true in themselves, but neither makes a convincing argument that this essay could serve as a detailed history of the hardships the people of Haiti have endured. Choice D is simply untrue.

Scoring Chart

Mark missed questions and calculate your total for each question category and the test as a whole. Then convert your raw score to a scaled score using the chart on page 154 in Chapter 4.

Question Types	Question Numbers	Score
Conventions of Standard English (CSE)	1, 2, 3, 4, 5, 6, 10, 11, 12, 13, 17, 18, 20, 21, 22, 23, 24, 28, 31, 33, 35, 36, 37, 38, 40, 41, 46, 47, 48, 49, 51, 52, 53, 55, 57, 61, 63, 64, 65, 67, 68, 69, 72, 73	_____ /44
Production of Writing (POW)	8, 9, 14, 15, 19, 27, 29, 32, 42, 43, 44, 45, 54, 58, 59, 60, 66, 70, 74, 75	_____ /20
Knowledge of Language (KLA)	7, 16, 25, 26, 30, 34, 39, 50, 56, 62, 71	_____ /11

Raw Score: _____ /75

Scaled Score:

PART III

THE MATHEMATICS TEST ON THE ACT®

8 | Introduction to ACT® Math

9 | Essential Skills in Math

10 | Preparing for Higher Math:
Number and Quantity

11 | Preparing for Higher Math: Algebra

12 | Preparing for Higher Math: Functions

13 | Preparing for Higher Math: Geometry

14 | Preparing for Higher Math:
Statistics and Probability

15 | Strategies for Approaching
the Math Section

CHAPTER

Introduction to ACT® Math

INTRODUCTION TO ACT® MATH

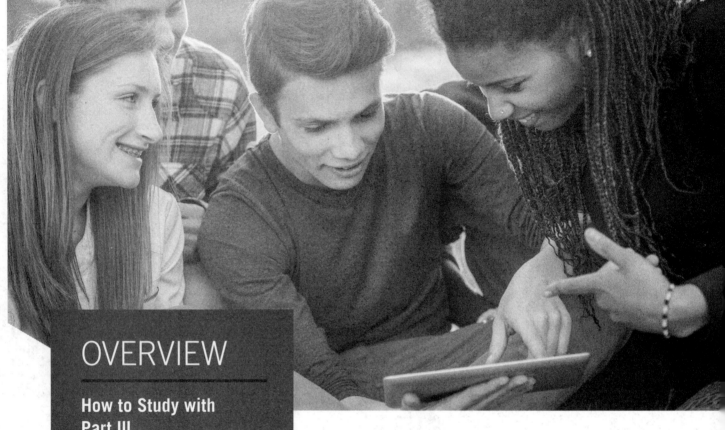

OVERVIEW

- **How to Study with Part III**
- **All about the Math Section**
- **Scoring Table**
- **Sample Questions**
- **Common Challenges**
- **Summing It Up**

To adequately prepare for the Math section of the ACT exam, you'll want to familiarize yourself with the structure of the ACT Mathematics test, the types of questions you'll be presented with, the skills you'll be tested on, and some common challenges test takers face. In this chapter, we'll go over the basic information about the test, including what's on it and how it's structured, along with some example questions.

HOW TO STUDY WITH PART III

Before delving into the details about the test itself, reflect on your experiences as a student of math. What sort of math classes have you taken throughout your high school career? Which kinds of math skills do you enjoy using, and which skills do you struggle with? For example, have you excelled at working with equations in algebra but struggled with trigonometric ratios in geometry? Before getting started with this part of the book, it's important for you to know your own strengths and weaknesses when it comes to math. That way, you can focus your energy on the math concepts that are challenging for you or the concepts that will make the biggest difference in your score.

Self-Reflection: Math

- Which math courses did you take in high school, and which have you not taken (yet)?

- Which math concepts have historically been easier for you to understand?

- Which math concepts have historically been harder for you to understand?

- Did you experience any conditions during your high school experience (remote learning, recovering from surgery, etc.) that could have created gaps in your math learning? If so, what topics were covered during those gaps?

- Which math skills require more effort for you, and how does this inform your studying and learning?

- What math skills can make the biggest difference for your ACT score?

This chapter provides an overview of the ACT Math test and what you can expect. In Chapter 9, we'll talk about essential skills in math to help remind you of the mathematical basics that serve test takers across the different math question categories. In Chapter 10, we'll discuss key concepts in math, especially those pertaining to number and quantity, and build on the skills we reviewed in Chapter 9. In Chapter 11, we'll focus on algebraic concepts. In Chapter 12, we'll start preparing for higher math, specifically functions. In Chapter 13, we'll cover concepts and skills in geometry. In Chapter 14, we'll discuss both probability and statistics. If you feel pretty confident in your math skills and have already taken a lot of advanced math classes, you might find yourself skimming through these skill chapters. Otherwise, you'll want to review each chapter closely, focusing first on skills you've already learned before building new skills. You can also use your diagnostic test results to guide you to essential areas of improvement. Finally, in Chapter 15, we'll cover some skills and strategies to help you do your best on the ACT Mathematics test. At the end of Chapter 15 is a Knowledge Check that you can use to practice strategies you learned and pinpoint any further areas for study.

ALL ABOUT THE MATH SECTION

The ACT Mathematics test is designed to measure a student's understanding of basic mathematical concepts and skills, as well as high-school level mathematical content applied to a variety of different scenarios. It consists of 60 multiple-choice questions, and students have 60 minutes to complete the section, meaning you have about a minute for each question. Questions on the Math section of the ACT exam will fall into one of two major categories: Preparing for Higher Math and Integrating Essential Skills. In addition to these categories, some questions will also count as Modeling questions, which are designed to evaluate a test taker's ability to model effectively across mathematical topics. Unlike the other sections on the ACT, questions in the Math section of the ACT will have five answer options instead of four.

FYI -

Calculators are permitted only on the Mathematics section of the ACT exam. Please see the calculator policy on the ACT website to make sure your calculator meets the required specifications. In general, as long as your calculator does not have internet or print-out capabilities, it will be valid for use. Standard accepted models include the Texas Instruments TI-83 and TI-84 graphing calculators.

The question categories are explained as follows.

PREPARING FOR HIGHER MATH (PHM) (57–60% OF QUESTIONS)

These questions are designed to focus on your skills and knowledge pertaining to higher math concepts.

Number and Quantity (7–10%): For these questions, you'll need to demonstrate your knowledge of real and complex number systems, exponent rules, vectors, and matrices.

Algebra (12–15%): For these questions, you'll work with algebraic expressions, equations, polynomials, and systems of equations, in addition to other algebraic topics.

Functions (12–15%): These questions test your knowledge of function definition, notation, representation, and application.

Geometry (12–15%): These questions require you to apply your knowledge of solids and shapes and solve for missing values as needed as related to volume, area, and other geometric measures.

Statistics and Probability (8–12%): Questions in this category involve understanding measures of central tendency and variability, as well as evaluating data collection techniques and computation of probabilities in complex scenarios.

INTEGRATING ESSENTIAL SKILLS (IES) (40–43% OF QUESTIONS)

These questions will require you to work with ratios and proportions; percentage calculations; surface area, volume, and area; mean and median; and expressing numbers in diverse formats.

MODELING

This category applies to all questions that require working with models. It accounts for questions within the PHM and IES categories that require the use of modeling skills.

Throughout Part III, we'll cover these question categories in more depth along with targeted strategies you can use when approaching the Math section.

SCORING TABLE

In Chapter 2, you completed a diagnostic test to help gauge your current skills and knowledge when it comes to what's covered on the ACT. As you work through this part of the book, consider the score you're aiming for, especially if you're applying to colleges whose applicants tend to receive certain score ranges on the ACT. While the raw-to-scaled score conversion is different for every ACT test, we've created a table that can help you anticipate how your raw score (0–60 questions) might translate into a scaled score (1–36). Please note that this is an estimate and not an exact reflection of official ACT scoring metrics.

SCORING TABLE – MATH	
Raw Score	Scaled Score
60	36
58–59	35
56–57	34
54–55	33
53	32
51–52	31
49–50	30
47–48	29
45–46	28
42–44	27

SCORING TABLE – MATH	
Raw Score	Scaled Score
39–41	26
37–38	25
35–36	24
33–34	23
31–32	22
29–30	21
28	20
26–27	19
23–25	18
21–22	17
17–20	16
13–16	15
10–12	14
8–9	13
7	12
5–6	11
4	10
–	9
3	8
–	7
2	6
–	5
1	4
–	3
–	2
0	1

SAMPLE QUESTIONS

Here we've presented three sample questions. The first is a Preparing for Higher Math: Functions question, the second is a Preparing for Higher Math: Statistics and Probability question that is also a Modeling question, and the third is an Integrating Essential Skills question.

EXAMPLE

1. Let $h(x) = 1 - \dfrac{2}{3x}$. Compute $h\left(-\dfrac{4}{x}\right)$.

   A. x

   B. $\dfrac{x + 24}{x}$

   C. $\dfrac{2x + 1}{12}$

   D. $\dfrac{8 - 12x}{3x^2}$

   E. $\dfrac{x + 6}{6}$

The correct answer is E. Calculate as follows:

$$h\left(-\frac{4}{x}\right) = 1 - \frac{2}{3\left(-\dfrac{4}{x}\right)}$$

$$= 1 - \frac{2}{-\dfrac{12}{x}} = 1 + 2\left(\frac{x}{12}\right)$$

$$= 1 + \frac{x}{6} = \frac{x + 6}{6}$$

Choice A is incorrect because $\dfrac{x+6}{6} \neq \dfrac{x + \cancel{6}}{\cancel{6}}$.
Choice B is incorrect because you did not simplify the complex fraction correctly. Choice C is incorrect because $\dfrac{2x}{12} + 1 \neq \dfrac{2x+1}{12}$; you must first get a common denominator. Choice D is incorrect because it is the product of $h(x)$ and $-\dfrac{4}{x}$.

2. Maddie plays a carnival game that consists of having 200 rubber ducks labeled on the bottom with one of four markings (S, M, L, XL) floating randomly in a pool; these markings indicate the size of the prize. She selects a rubber duck and receives the size of the prize indicated on the bottom of the duck. There are 110 rubber ducks labeled S, 60 labeled M, 25 labeled L, and 5 labeled XL. What is the probability of Maddie getting either an M or L prize?

   F. 0.3

   G. 0.125

   H. 0.425

   J. 0.45

   K. 0.55

The correct answer is H. Because you're looking for the probability of selecting either an M or L duck, you can combine the numbers of medium and large prizes. Then, divide the sum of the number of medium prizes and number of large prizes by the total number of rubber ducks to get the probability:

$$\frac{60 + 25}{200} = \frac{85}{200} = \frac{17}{40} = 0.425$$

3. If the length of the hypotenuse of a right triangle is 5 and the length of one of the legs is 4, what is the length of the other leg?

   A. 1

   B. 3

   C. $\sqrt{41}$

   D. 9

   E. 41

The correct answer is B. If you recognized that the sides given fit the ratio of a 3-4-5 right triangle, you would immediately know that the length of the remaining leg is 3. If you did not realize this, you could use the Pythagorean theorem to solve for the length of the unknown side. The Pythagorean theorem says that for right triangles, $(\text{hypotenuse})^2 = (\text{leg1})^2 + (\text{leg2})^2$. In this case, $5^2 = 4^2 + x^2$, which simplifies to $25 = 16 + x^2$. Thus, $9 = x^2$, and $x = 3$.

Common Challenges

Some common challenges test takers experience on the ACT Mathematics test include the following.

Time pressure	Because you only have 60 minutes to answer 60 questions, you'll need to work quickly and not get bogged down on any one problem. As such, you must be aware of your own skills and what math concepts you haven't encountered yet in your education. This will help you recognize when you might need to guess on a specific question.
Understanding the problem	Some test takers may struggle to understand the wording of the questions, identify the important information needed to solve the problem, or determine the goal of the question. This can lead to errors and frustration. We'll provide helpful strategies for how to navigate complex problems later on in this part of the book.
Selecting the appropriate method	There are often multiple ways to solve a problem on the Mathematics test, and test takers may struggle to choose the most efficient or effective method. This can result in lost time and incorrect answers. We'll discuss tools for how to solve problems in simple and efficient ways in Chapter 15.

Common Challenges

Some common challenges test takers experience on the ACT Mathematics test include the following.

Algebraic manipulation	Algebraic manipulation is a key component of the Math section of the ACT, and many students struggle with this concept. This can make it difficult to solve certain types of problems, especially those that involve equations or systems of equations. If you struggle with algebraic equations, focus your studies on Chapter 11.
Geometry	Geometry is another area that can be challenging for some students. This is especially true for students who have not taken a geometry course recently or who struggle with spatial reasoning. If this is one area you struggle with, pay close attention to Chapter 13.

Look back at your responses to the self-reflection exercise at the beginning of this chapter. Do any of your responses overlap with the common challenges we've covered here? If so, how might you focus your time and energy knowing where you excel and where you struggle with math? Remember, use this part of the book in the way that makes the most sense for you. Be mindful of where you can simply brush up on your existing skills, where you should focus your time and attention to improve, and which concepts or skills are too advanced for where you are currently in your math education.

SUMMING IT UP

- The ACT Mathematics Test contains 60 multiple-choice questions that must be completed within 60 minutes. There are five answer options for questions on the Math section. See the ACT website for guidelines on what kind of calculator you can use on test day.

- Questions on the Math section of the ACT exam will fall into one of two major categories: Preparing for Higher Math and Integrating Essential Skills. In addition to these categories, some questions will also count as Modeling questions, which are designed to evaluate a test taker's ability to model effectively across mathematical topics.

- Some challenges you might encounter on the ACT Mathematics Test include managing to answer all 60 questions in 60 minutes, navigating complex problems, approaching certain math concepts like algebra or geometry, and using the most effective method for solving a problem. As you go through the next seven chapters in this part, don't feel obligated to read every chapter word for word. Be sure to focus your attention where you struggle the most and master the strategies that will help you compensate for any areas where you feel less prepared or confident.

CHAPTER

Essential Skills in Math

ESSENTIAL SKILLS IN MATH

OVERVIEW

Numbers and Operations

Ratios, Proportions, Rates, Decimals, and Percentages

Basic Algebra

Basic Geometry

Basic Statistics and Probability

Summing It Up

Test Yourself: Integrating Essential Skills

The following concepts represent fundamental math knowledge that students typically acquire throughout middle school and their high school careers. These concepts also appear as standalone concepts or in combination in the Integrating Essential Skills (IES) questions on the ACT Mathematics section. At the same time, these topics also form the foundation of knowledge for each subcategory of the Preparing for Higher Math (PHM) questions. In some way or another, you will need to use the information that follows to be able to accurately and efficiently answer the 60 questions on the ACT Mathematics test. Mastery of this information is essential to improving your performance and achieving high scores (with roughly 25 questions directly assessing these concepts for IES questions).

In conjunction with the results from your Ch. 2 Diagnostic Test, determine which concepts you need to review. Use the practice questions throughout the chapter to assess your understanding and use the Test Yourself at the end of the chapter to identify any areas for further review.

NUMBERS AND OPERATIONS

To perform well with math questions, you need to develop (or just review) the vocabulary and basic operations that will come to play a role in most of the questions on the test in some way or another. The following section will discuss different types of numbers, mathematical properties, order of operations, factors and multiples, prime numbers, exponents, fractions, and more.

Number Types

In math, various terms exist to describe the array of numbers used for counting and calculations. The ability to distinguish whole numbers, integers, and rational and irrational numbers can keep you from selecting incorrect answer choices on your exam.

TYPES OF NUMBERS		
Number Type	**Definition**	**Examples**
Whole Numbers	Positive numbers, including 0	0, 1, 2, 73, 546
Integers	All whole numbers and negative numbers—excluding decimals and fractions	−54, −6, 0, 9, 43
Rational Numbers	Numbers that result from dividing two integers	$\frac{1}{3}, \frac{3}{5}, \frac{7}{3}$
Irrational Numbers	All real numbers that are not rational numbers; have nonterminating, nonrepeating decimals	pi (π) $\sqrt{2} = 1.41421356237...$ $\sqrt{3} = 1.73205080756...$

Properties and Identities

When studying math, it's important to understand how properties describe the behavior of numbers in certain situations. Properties and identities in math are rules that have been proven over time to be consistent. Knowing these can help simplify the process of solving problems because you can count on the fact that certain things will always function in predictable ways. To add to your confidence on your exam, become thoroughly familiar with the rules in this section, and commit to memory as many properties and rules as possible.

Here's a list of properties and identities along with definitions and examples. You may need to refer to this section as we get into more advanced math in the next two chapters, such as when solving algebraic equations.

PROPERTIES AND IDENTITIES

Name	Definition	Example
Commutative Property	In addition and multiplication, order does not affect outcome	$7 + 8 = 8 + 7$ $3 \times 5 = 5 \times 3$
Distributive Property	Given an equation, $a(b + c)$, you can distribute the value of a to the value inside the parentheses	$7(2 + 8) = 7 \times 2 + 7 \times 8 = 14 + 56 = 70$
Associative Property	In addition and multiplication, changing how numbers are grouped will not change the result	$2(5 \times 4) = 5(2 \times 4) = 4(2 \times 5)$ $3 + (5 + 2) = 2 + (3 + 5) = 5 + (2 + 3)$
Identity Property	Any number added to zero will not change; any number multiplied by 1 will not change	$15 + 0 = 15$ $15 \times 1 = 15$
Reflexive Property	A number is always equal to itself	$a = a$
Symmetric Property	If $a = b$, then $b = a$	If $x = 10$, then $10 = x$
Transitive Property	If $a = b$ and $b = c$, then $a = c$	If $a = b$ and $b = 3 + 4$, then $a = 3 + 4$
Substitution Property	If $a = b$, then a can be substituted for b	If $a = 7$ and $b = 7$, then $a + 3 = 10$ and $b + 3 = 10$
Additive Identity	Any variable added to zero will remain unchanged	$x + 0 = x$
Multiplicative Property of Zero	Any number multiplied by zero equals zero	$1 \times 0 = 0$ $4{,}962 \times 0 = 0$
Multiplicative Inverse	Any number multiplied by its reciprocal will equal 1	$2 \times \dfrac{1}{2} = 1$ $12 \times \dfrac{1}{12} = 1$

Operations with Signed Numbers

Signed numbers are multiplied as any other numbers would be, with the following exceptions:

 The product of two negative numbers is positive.

$$(-3) \times (-6) = +18$$

 The product of two positive numbers is positive.

$$(+3.05) \times (+6) = +18.30$$

 The product of a negative and positive number is negative.

$$\left(+4\tfrac{1}{2}\right) \times (-3) = -13\tfrac{1}{2}$$

$$(+1) \times (-1) \times (+1) = -1$$

As with multiplication, the division of signed numbers requires you to observe three simple rules.

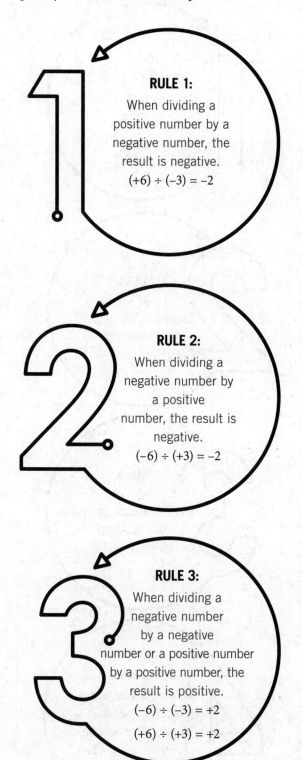

RULE 1:

When dividing a positive number by a negative number, the result is negative.
$(+6) \div (-3) = -2$

RULE 2:

When dividing a negative number by a positive number, the result is negative.
$(-6) \div (+3) = -2$

RULE 3:

When dividing a negative number by a negative number or a positive number by a positive number, the result is positive.
$(-6) \div (-3) = +2$
$(+6) \div (+3) = +2$

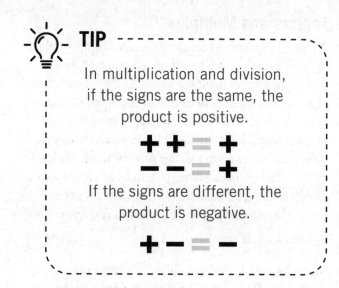

TIP

In multiplication and division, if the signs are the same, the product is positive.

$$+ \; + = +$$
$$- \; - = +$$

If the signs are different, the product is negative.

$$+ \; - = -$$

Order of Operations

One of the most important things to know when solving math problems is where to start. You will often encounter problems that have a series of operations to perform. Fortunately, there are rules to explain what goes first. We call these rules the order of operations. The order of operations ensures that, by solving operations in this order, you'll always be able to arrive at the same correct solution. At this stage of mathematics, there are only four rules to know. They are as follows:

1. Solve operations within parentheses first.

2. Solve operations with exponents and square roots next.

3. Solve multiplication and division from left to right.

4. Solve addition and subtraction from left to right.

These rules inform where you should start when solving a math problem. In short, solve anything in parentheses first, going from hardest to easiest. As you go through problems using the order of operations, note each step carefully to make sure that you don't skip a step or forget anything along the way.

Factors and Multiples

A factor is a number that can be divided into a whole number evenly without leaving a remainder. The factors of any integer include 1 as well as the integer itself. Figuring out whether one number is a factor of another requires you to divide that number by another whole number that is less than itself. For example, to determine what numbers are factors of 4, we would divide 4 by the numbers in question: 1, 2, and 4 all divide into 4 evenly, without a remainder. In contrast, 3 is not a factor of 4 because when you divide 4 by 3 you do not end up with a whole number: $4 \div 3 = 1\frac{1}{3}$.

Multiples are the result of multiplying a number by an integer. Finding a list of multiples can be as simple as selecting a number and working through a series of multiplication equations.

EXAMPLE

What are the first four multiples of the number 2, starting with the integer 1?

Solution

$$1 \times 2 = \mathbf{2}$$
$$2 \times 2 = \mathbf{4}$$
$$3 \times 2 = \mathbf{6}$$
$$4 \times 2 = \mathbf{8}$$

Starting with the integer 1, the first four multiples of the number 2 are **2, 4, 6, 8.**

Note that multiples **must** be the result of multiplying a number by an integer. For instance, this means that a number multiplied by a fraction would **not** result in a multiple for that number. Since 0 is in fact an integer, this does mean that you can use it to find a multiple of any number. The result simply is always 0.

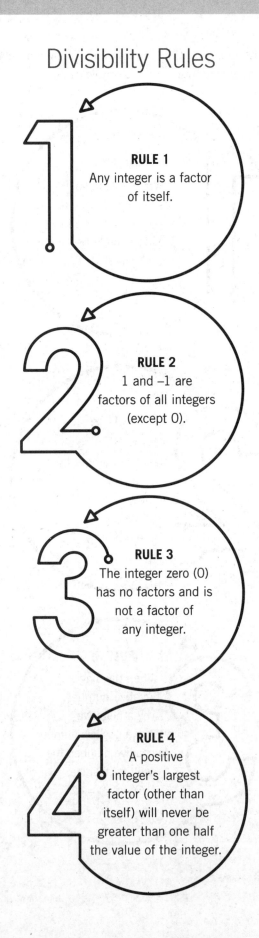

Divisibility Rules

RULE 1
Any integer is a factor of itself.

RULE 2
1 and −1 are factors of all integers (except 0).

RULE 3
The integer zero (0) has no factors and is not a factor of any integer.

RULE 4
A positive integer's largest factor (other than itself) will never be greater than one half the value of the integer.

Keep in mind the following two basic rules about factors.

Rules about Factors

1. Complementing factors are multiples. If *f* is a factor of *n*, then *n* is a multiple of *f*. For example, 8 is a multiple of 2 for the same reason that 2 is a factor of 8: because $8 \div 2 = 4$, which is an integer.

2. A prime number is a positive integer that is divisible by only two positive integers: itself and 1. Zero (0) and 1 are not considered prime numbers; 2 is the first prime number. Here are all the prime numbers less than 50:

   2 3 5 7

   11 13 17 19

   23 29

   31 37

   41 43 47

As you can see, factors, multiples, and divisibility are different aspects of the same concept.

Greatest Common Factor

To solve problems with fractions, you'll need to be able to determine the greatest common factor. The term *greatest common factor* (GCF) refers to the largest number that can be factored into two numbers cleanly (that is, without a remainder). For example, the greatest common factor of 10 and 15 is 5. For 10 and 20, the GCF is 10. How did we get those answers? Let's look at a pair of numbers.

If you are asked to find the greatest common factor of 16 and 32, you can start by listing out the factors of each.

16: 1, 2, 4, 8 **16**

32: 1, 2, 4, 8, **16**, 32

Here, we can easily see that the greatest common factor is the number 16.

There may be number pairs, like (7, 13), that don't have anything other than 1 in common. When this happens, the numbers can be described as "relatively prime." Remember that a prime number is a number that is only divisible by itself and 1.

 TIP

> Don't be confused by the term Greatest Common Divisor as the terms *divisor* and *factor* have the same meaning. They are both numbers that can divide into something.

Least Common Multiple

In addition to using the greatest common factor, solving problems with fractions will also require you to find the least common multiple. The term *least common multiple* (LCM) refers to the smallest whole number into which each number in a list divides evenly. For example, the GCF of {18, 36, 63} is 9, and the LCM of {18, 36, 63} is 252.

You'll need to find the least common multiple when you need to add or subtract fractions with different denominators, as you'll need each to have the same denominator to be able to add them together. However, you will likely use greatest common factor to reduce or simplify the result. To find a common multiple, you can multiply the listed values together. But to find the least common multiple, you'll need to make a list of the different multiples for each number in the set or use prime factorization, which is discussed in the next section.

It is a good idea to be familiar with the smaller prime numbers, because you might need them at your fingertips for a problem. Here are the first ten: 2, 3, 5, 7, 11, 13, 17, 19, 23, and 29.

PRACTICE

Which of the following sets contains two elements with a greatest common factor of 6 and a least common multiple of 72?

    A. {6, 30}

    B. {12, 18}

    C. {18, 24}

    D. {24, 72}

    E. {6, 144}

The correct answer is C. You should use the answer choices provided to you and test them all out to find the pair of numbers with a greatest common factor of 6 and a least common multiple of 72. If a choice does not meet one of the two conditions, stop and move on—do not bother testing for the other condition. Choices A, B, C, and E all have a GCF of 6. Choice D has a GCF of 12, thus it is incorrect. You can think of the factors of 72 and see which values match that list. Choice E cannot have an LCM of 72, so it can be eliminated. In choice A, 30 is not a factor of 72. For choices B and C, the LCM needs to be 72. Choice B has an LCM of 36, thus choice C is correct.

Prime Numbers and Factorization

As referenced earlier, prime numbers are divisible by only two integers, themselves and 1. Another way of saying this is to state that a prime number only has two multiples: itself and 1. 11 is a prime number since the only integers that evenly divide into 11 are 11 and 1. Notice that 1 is not a prime number since it has one multiple (1×1) and not two.

PRACTICE

If n equals the number of prime numbers greater than 10 and less than 20, then $3n =$

    A. 3

    B. 6

    C. 9

    D. 12

    E. 15

The correct answer is D. Before you can find $3n$, you must figure out what n is. There are four prime numbers between 10 and 20: 11, 13, 17, 19. If $n = 4$, then $3n$ will be $(3)(4) = 12$. Therefore, (D) is the correct answer.

Any integer that is not prime can be written as a product of prime numbers in only one way. This product is known as the *prime factorization* of the integer. In order to factor an integer into primes, we take the integer and write it as a product of two smaller integers. If either or both of these smaller integers is not prime, write it as a product of smaller integers. Keep going until there are only prime numbers in the product. Note that sometimes you will have a choice as to how to factor a number. For example, if you are trying to factor 30 into primes, you can begin by writing $30 = 2 \times 15$ or $30 = 5 \times 6$. Regardless of the choices that you make, you will always end up with the same prime factorization.

Suppose we began by writing $30 = 2 \times 15$. The factor 2 is prime, but 15 is not. Therefore, we must break 15 down into $15 = 3 \times 5$. Thus, the prime factorization of 30 is $2 \times 3 \times 5$. We say that 30 has three distinct prime factors: 2, 3, and 5.

9

Consider the prime factorization of 48. Note that 48 = 6 × 8. The integer 6 can be further broken down into 2 × 3, while 8 can be broken down into 2 × 2 × 2. Thus, the prime factorization of 48 is 2 × 2 × 2 × 2 × 3; i.e., 48 = 2^4 × 3. The number 48 has two distinct prime factors, 2 and 3. The factor 2 appears four times, and the factor 3 appears only once.

Which of the following is the prime factorization of 3,780?

- **A.** $2^2 \times 3^3 \times 35$
- **B.** $2 \times 3 \times 5 \times 7$
- **C.** $2^2 \times 3^3 \times 5 \times 7$
- **D.** $2 \times 3^3 \times 5 \times 6 \times 7$
- **E.** $2^2 \times 3^4 \times 5 \times 7$

The correct answer is C. A prime factorization is the product of the powers of the prime factors of a whole number. The prime factorization of 3,780 is $2^2 \times 3^3 \times 5 \times 7$. The best way to get the prime factorization is by using the divisibility rules. In choice B, although 2, 3, 5, and 7 are the prime factors of 3,780, both 2 and 3 occur more than once in the correct factorization. You can try to eliminate as many of the remaining choices as possible. Choices A and D involve non-prime numbers, and so they can be eliminated immediately. Choice E contains one too many factors of 3.

Prime factorization can be used to find the least common multiple in a group of numbers. Consider the LCM of 40 and 75. You can multiply them together to find a common multiple of 3,000. But they have a lower common multiple, their LCM. It can be found by taking the numbers through prime factorization. The number 40 has as its prime factors 2 × 2 × 2 × 5. The number 75 has prime factors of 3 × 2 × 5 × 5. Write those factors in

their exponent forms. So, the factors of 40 become $2^3 \times 5^1$, and the factors of 75 become $3^1 \times 2^1 \times 5^2$. Then take the unique factors with the highest powers and multiply them together. In this case, you would multiply $2^3 \times 5^2 \times 3^1$. That equals 600, the LCM of 40 and 75. If you wanted to find the LCM of 40, 75, and 540, you would use the same process. You would end up with the following: $3^3 \times 2^3 \times 5^2$, or 5,400.

Exponents

An exponent represents the number of times that a number (referred to as the "base number") is multiplied by itself. In the exponential number 2^4, the base number is 2 and the exponent is 4. To calculate the value of 2^4 means to multiply 2 by itself 4 times: $2^4 = 2 \times 2 \times 2 \times 2 = 16$. An exponent is also referred to as a power, meaning you can express the exponential number 2^4 as "2 to the 4th power."

A variety of rules exist for working with exponents with different operations. Use the following table as a guide:

RULES FOR EXPONENTS	
Product	$a^m a^n = a^{m+n}$
Product of a power	$(a^m)^n = a^{mn}$
Quotient to a power	$\left(\dfrac{a}{b}\right)^n = \dfrac{a^n}{b^n}$
Quotient	$\dfrac{a^m}{a^n} = a^{m-n}$
Zero exponent	$a^0 = 1$
Negative exponent	$a^{-n} = \dfrac{1}{a^n}$
Inversion	$\left(\dfrac{a}{b}\right)^{-n} = \left(\dfrac{b}{a}\right)^n$
Fractional powers	$a^{\frac{m}{n}} = \sqrt[n]{a^m}$

If $\dfrac{x^3 y^2}{z}$ is negative, then which of the following could be true?

    I. x and z are both negative.

    II. x is negative and z is positive.

    III. x is zero.

    A. I only

    B. II only

    C. I and II

    D. II and III

    E. I, II, and III

The correct answer is B. In order for the expression to be negative, you must have an odd number of negative signs. Since y is squared, the term y^2 cannot be negative. However, both x^3 and z are negative whenever x and z are negative, respectively. Statement I is false because if x and z are both negative, then x^3 and z are both negative, making the quotient positive. Statement II is true because if x is negative, then so is x^3. So you have a quotient with one negative term all told; therefore, it must be negative. Statement III is false because if $x = 0$, the entire quotient is zero and thus not negative. Using this information, you can conclude that choice B is the correct answer and that all other choices are incorrect.

Roots

The square root of a number n is a number that you "square" (multiply it by itself, or raise to the power of 2), to obtain n. The radical sign signifies square root and looks like this: $\sqrt{}$. A simple example of a square root is $2 = \sqrt{4}$ (the square root of 4) because 2×2 (or 2^2) = 4.

The cube root of a number n is a number that you raise to the power of 3 (multiply by itself twice) to obtain n. You determine higher roots (for example, the "fourth root") in the same way. Except for square roots, the radical sign will indicate the root to be taken. For example:

$$2 = \sqrt[3]{8} \text{ (the cube root of 8) because } 2 \times 2 \times 2 \text{ (or } 2^3) = 8$$

$$2 = \sqrt[4]{16} \text{ (the fourth root of 16)}$$
$$\text{because } 2 \times 2 \times 2 \times 2 \text{ (or } 2^4) = 16$$

Square roots, cube roots, etc. can be expressed using fractional exponents. The following notation is used:

$$\sqrt{a} = a^{\frac{1}{2}}$$
$$\sqrt[3]{a} = a^{\frac{1}{3}}$$
$$\vdots$$
$$\sqrt[n]{a} = a^{\frac{1}{n}}$$

Using the exponent rules, we have the more general definition:

$$\sqrt[n]{a^m} = (a^m)^{\frac{1}{n}} = a^{\left(m \cdot \frac{1}{n}\right)} = \left(a^{\frac{1}{n}}\right)^m = a^{\frac{m}{n}}$$

For instance:

$$8^{\frac{2}{3}} = \left(8^{\frac{1}{3}}\right)^2 = (2)^2 = 4$$

$$16^{\frac{3}{2}} = \left(16^{\frac{1}{2}}\right)^3 = 4^3 = 64$$

Solve the following equation: $\dfrac{\sqrt{25}+\sqrt[3]{64}}{\sqrt[4]{81}} =$

A. $\sqrt{2}$

B. 2

C. $\sqrt{5}$

D. 3

E. 5

The correct answer is D. First, simplify each of the roots to arrive at a more easily divisible set of numbers:

$$\frac{\sqrt{25}+\sqrt[3]{64}}{\sqrt[4]{81}} = \frac{5+4}{3} = \frac{9}{3} = 3$$

Since each of the roots can be fully reduced down to whole numbers, the resulting fraction can be simply reduced to 3.

Fractions

A fraction is a part of a whole. For instance, there are 10 dimes in a dollar, so one dime is one-tenth of a dollar—one of ten equal parts. The fraction to represent one-tenth is written $\frac{1}{10}$. The top number of a fraction is called the numerator, and the bottom number is called the denominator. The denominator tells you how many equal parts the object or number is divided into, and the numerator tells you how many parts are represented.

$$\frac{3}{4} \begin{matrix} \leftarrow \text{ numerator} \\ \leftarrow \text{ denominator} \end{matrix} \begin{matrix} \rightarrow \\ \rightarrow \end{matrix} \frac{7}{8}$$

A proper fraction is one in which the numerator is less than the denominator. An improper fraction is one in which the numerator is the same as or greater than the denominator. $\frac{3}{5}$ is a proper fraction, but $\frac{5}{3}$ is an improper fraction. Sometimes, you will see an integer and a fraction together. This is called a mixed number, such as $2\frac{3}{5}$.

Here is a quick reference chart that shows how to handle arithmetic operations involving fractions. You can bookmark this page and come back to it if you get caught on a fraction problem and are unsure of the rules and how to apply them.

 TIP

Need an easy way to remember which part of a fraction is which? Use alliteration to remember that the **d**enominator goes **d**own at the bottom.

OPERATIONS WITH FRACTIONS

Arithmetic Operation	Rule (in Symbols)	Interpretation
Adding/ Subtracting	$\dfrac{a}{b} \pm \dfrac{c}{d} = \dfrac{ad \pm cb}{bd}$	When fractions have different denominators, first find a common denominator. Apply it to the fractions and then add or subtract the numerators.
Simplifying/ Reducing	$\dfrac{a \cdot c}{b \cdot c} = \dfrac{a}{b}$	You can cancel like factors in the numerator and denominator of a fraction to reduce it to lowest terms.
Multiplying by –1	$-\dfrac{a}{b} = \dfrac{-a}{b} = \dfrac{a}{-b}$	When multiplying a fraction by –1, you can multiply either the numerator or the denominator by –1, but NOT both.
Multiplying	$\dfrac{a}{b} \cdot \dfrac{c}{d} = \dfrac{ac}{bd}$	When multiplying two fractions, you can simply multiply their numerators and their denominators.
Dividing	$\dfrac{a}{b} \div \dfrac{c}{d} = \dfrac{a}{b} \cdot \dfrac{d}{c} = \dfrac{ad}{bc}$ $\dfrac{\frac{a}{b}}{\frac{c}{d}}$ means $\dfrac{a}{b} \div \dfrac{c}{d}$	When dividing two fractions, start by converting the quotient into a multiplication problem.

There are several errors test-takers often make when working with fractions. You can prevent yourself from choosing incorrect answers when working with fractions on the ACT exam by observing the following rules.

COMMON ERRORS WITH FRACTIONS

Error	Comment
$\dfrac{a}{b+c} \neq \dfrac{a}{b} + \dfrac{a}{c}$	You cannot pull a fraction apart as a sum of two fractions when the sum occurs in the denominator.
$\dfrac{a}{b} + \dfrac{c}{d} \neq \dfrac{a+c}{b+d}$	When adding fractions, do not simply add the numerators and denominators. First, get a common denominator.
$\dfrac{a}{a+b} \neq \dfrac{\cancel{a}}{\cancel{a}+b}$	You cannot cancel terms that are the same in the numerator and denominator. You can only cancel factors common to both.

Reciprocals

When working with fractions (or any numbers), you may need to find a fraction's reciprocal. Reciprocals can be boiled down to flipping something over. Defined, a reciprocal is $\frac{1}{x}$ where x is the number in question. For example, the reciprocal of $5 = \frac{1}{5}$ or 0.2 as a decimal. The following are numbers and their reciprocals:

$$17 = \frac{1}{17}$$

$$100 = \frac{1}{100}$$

$$42 = \frac{1}{42}$$

One thing to think about with a whole number is that 17 is the same as $\frac{17}{1}$. Keep that in mind not only with reciprocals but any time you have a mix of whole numbers and fractions. Finding the reciprocal of a fraction requires flipping the numerator and denominator. For example, to find the reciprocal of $\frac{4}{5}$, you flip the fraction over to get $\frac{5}{4}$. Here are a few other examples of reciprocal fractions:

$$\frac{1}{8} = \frac{8}{1} = 8$$

$$\frac{2}{10} = \frac{10}{2} = 5$$

$$\frac{1}{0.25} = \frac{0.25}{1} = 0.25$$

Equivalent Fractions

Fractions having different denominators and numerators might represent the same amount. These are equivalent fractions.

$$\frac{20}{10} = \frac{10}{5} = \frac{2}{1}$$

$$\frac{1}{4} = \frac{2}{8} = \frac{3}{12} = \frac{4}{16}$$

$$\frac{3}{5} = \frac{9}{15} = \frac{27}{45}$$

The fractions $\frac{1}{2}$, $\frac{2}{4}$, and $\frac{4}{8}$ are equivalent fractions because they all represent the same amount. Notice that the denominator is twice as large as the numerator in every case. Any fraction you write that has a denominator that is exactly twice as large as the numerator will be equivalent to $\frac{1}{2}$.

When you cannot divide the numerator and denominator of a fraction evenly by the same whole number (other than 1), the fraction is in its simplest form.

To write equivalent fractions where the numerator is not 1 requires one more step. The quickest way to find an equivalent fraction is to divide the denominator of the fraction you want by the denominator of the fraction that you currently have. Take the result and multiply it by the numerator of the original fraction. This becomes the numerator of the equivalent fraction.

Consider the following example: you have the fraction $\frac{1}{2}$ and want to find an equivalent with a denominator of 16. Dividing the target denominator (16) by the current one (2) will result in the number 8. Multiplying this number by the original numerator will complete the target fraction as follows:

$$8 \times \frac{1}{16} = \frac{8}{1} \times \frac{1}{16} = \frac{8}{16}$$

$$\frac{1}{2} = \frac{8}{16}$$

Simplifying Fractions

A fraction can be simplified to its lowest terms if its numerator and denominator share a common factor. Here are a few simple examples:

$$\frac{6}{9} = \frac{(3)(2)}{(3)(3)} = \frac{2}{3}$$

(you can "cancel" or factor out the common factor 3)

$$\frac{21}{35} = \frac{(7)(3)}{(7)(5)} = \frac{3}{5}$$

(you can factor out the common factor 7)

Before you perform any operation with a fraction, always check to see if you can simplify it first. By reducing a fraction to its lowest terms, you will also simplify whatever operation you perform on it.

Adding and Subtracting Fractions

To add or subtract fractions with the same denominators, combine the numerators and keep the common denominator.

EXAMPLES

Find the difference between $\dfrac{7}{8}$ and $\dfrac{3}{8}$.

Solution

$\dfrac{7}{8} - \dfrac{3}{8} = \dfrac{4}{8}$ and simplified, $\dfrac{4}{8} = \dfrac{1}{2}$.

To add or subtract fractions with different denominators, you must first find the lowest common denominator, also known as the least common multiple. A common denominator is a number that can be divided by the denominators of all the fractions in the problem without a remainder. Finding the lowest common denominator is important to ensure that you have the simplest fraction.

Add the fractions $\dfrac{1}{4}$ and $\dfrac{1}{3}$.

Solution

Multiply the denominators to get $4 \times 3 = 12$. 12 can be divided by both 4 and 3:

$$\dfrac{1}{4} \text{ is equivalent to } \dfrac{3}{12}$$

$$\dfrac{1}{3} \text{ is equivalent to } \dfrac{4}{12}$$

To maintain equivalence, each numerator must be multiplied by the value used to reach the common denominator. We can now add the fractions because we have written equivalent fractions with a common denominator.

$$\dfrac{3}{12} + \dfrac{4}{12} = \dfrac{7}{12}$$

Therefore:

$$\dfrac{1}{4} + \dfrac{1}{3} = \dfrac{7}{12}$$

Seven-twelfths is in its simplest form because 7 and 12 do not have a whole number (other than 1) by which they are both divisible.

Multiplying and Dividing Fractions

When multiplying fractions, multiply numerators by numerators and denominators by denominators.

$$\dfrac{3}{5} \times \dfrac{4}{7} \times \dfrac{1}{5} = \dfrac{3 \times 4 \times 1}{5 \times 7 \times 5} = \dfrac{12}{175}$$

Try to work with numbers that are as small as possible. You can make numbers smaller by dividing out common factors. Do this by dividing the numerator of any one fraction and the denominator of any one fraction by the same number.

$$\dfrac{\overset{1}{\cancel{3}}}{\underset{2}{\cancel{4}}} \times \dfrac{\overset{1}{\cancel{2}}}{\underset{3}{\cancel{9}}} = \dfrac{1 \times 1}{2 \times 3} = \dfrac{1}{6}$$

In this case, we divided the numerator of the first fraction and the denominator of the second fraction by 3, while the denominator of the first fraction and the numerator of the second fraction were divided by 2.

To divide by a fraction, multiply by the reciprocal of the divisor.

$$\dfrac{3}{16} \div \dfrac{1}{8} = \dfrac{3}{\underset{2}{\cancel{16}}} \times \dfrac{\overset{1}{\cancel{8}}}{1} = \dfrac{3}{2} = 1\dfrac{1}{2}$$

Mixed Numbers and Improper Fractions

As noted earlier, a mixed number consists of a whole number along with a fraction. The number $4\dfrac{2}{3}$ is an example of a mixed number. Before combining fractions, you might need to convert mixed numbers to improper fractions (a fraction where the numerator is larger than the denominator). To convert, follow these three steps:

 01 Multiply the denominator of the fraction by the whole number.

 02 Add the product to the numerator of the fraction.

 03 Place the sum over the denominator of the fraction.

For example, here's how to convert the mixed number $4\frac{2}{3}$ to an improper fraction:

$$4\frac{2}{3} = \frac{(3)(4)+2}{3} = \frac{14}{3}$$

To add or subtract mixed numbers, you can convert each one to an improper fraction, then find their lowest common denominator and combine them. Alternatively, you can add together the whole numbers, and add together the fractions separately.

A fraction that has a numerator greater than the denominator is an improper fraction. Examples of improper fractions include $\frac{3}{2}$, $\frac{12}{7}$, and $\frac{9}{5}$. Improper fractions can also be in their simplest forms when the numerator and denominator cannot be divided evenly by a number other than 1.

Improper fractions can be represented as mixed numbers and vice versa. Below are a few examples of how to rename a mixed number as an improper fraction.

Examine the following examples:

Rename $2\frac{1}{4}$ as an improper fraction.

The whole number 2 contains 8 fourths, or $\frac{8}{4}$. Add $\frac{1}{4}$ to it to write the equivalent fraction $\frac{9}{4}$.

To rename an improper fraction as a mixed number, proceed backward.

Rename $\frac{9}{4}$ as a mixed number.

Divide the numerator by the denominator and use the remainder (R) as the fraction numerator:

$$9 \div 4 = 2\ \text{R}1 \text{ or } 9 \div 4 = 2\frac{1}{4}$$

Now try the following question.

Compute: $\dfrac{4+\frac{3}{8}}{2+\frac{3}{8}}$

- **A.** $\frac{35}{64}$
- **B.** $\frac{7}{5}$
- **C.** $\frac{35}{19}$
- **D.** 2
- **E.** $\frac{565}{64}$

The correct answer is C. This problem is a combination of order of operations in disguise and properties of fractions. The most common error committed when trying to simplify an expression like this is to cancel like terms in the numerator and denominator rather than like factors. The former are separated by plus and minus signs, whereas the latter are separated by multiplication signs.

For example, the following calculation is incorrect: $\dfrac{4+\frac{3}{8}}{2+\frac{3}{8}} \neq \dfrac{\cancel{4}\ 2+\frac{\cancel{3}}{\cancel{8}}}{\cancel{2}+\frac{\cancel{3}}{\cancel{8}}}$.

Instead, the given expression can be written equivalently as $\dfrac{4+\frac{3}{8}}{2+\frac{3}{8}} = \left(4+\frac{3}{8}\right) \div \left(2+\frac{3}{8}\right)$.

Simplifying this expression requires the use of the order of operations: simplify each of the two sums enclosed in parentheses first by getting a common denominator, then divide the resulting fractions.

The correct steps are as follows:

$$\left(4 + \frac{3}{8}\right) \div \left(2 + \frac{3}{8}\right) = \left(\frac{32}{8} + \frac{3}{8}\right) \div \left(\frac{16}{8} + \frac{3}{8}\right)$$

$$= \frac{35}{8} \div \frac{19}{8}$$

$$= \frac{35}{\cancel{8}} \cdot \frac{\cancel{8}}{19}$$

$$= \frac{35}{19}$$

Ordering Real Numbers by Value

A real number p is less than another real number q, written $p < q$, if q lies further to the right along the real number line than p. We also say that q is greater than p. The same process can be used to compare whole numbers, decimals, and fractions—you can compare two fractions by first converting them to decimal numbers and using the same process.

For instance, $-2 < -\frac{7}{5}$, $3 \leq 4.102$, $\pi \geq 3.14$, and $0 > -0.001$.

The questions related to ordering on the ACT Mathematics test can be a bit tricky, primarily because they are often asked in a more abstract manner. That is, they usually involve variables rather than numbers.

The following properties will be helpful to know when handling these types of questions.

TIP

When dealing with problems involving variables and inequalities, it is always a good idea to plug in actual numbers to eliminate choices. Always try to find a way to make the problem less abstract!

ORDERING REAL NUMBERS

Rule	Explanation
If $0 < a < b$, then $a^n < b^n$, for any positive exponent n.	If a is less than b, then you can raise both sides of the inequality to a positive exponent without reversing the inequality sign. (Note: You reverse the inequality sign whenever you multiply or divide both sides by a negative number.)
If $0 < a < b$, then $-b < -a < 0$.	If a and b are both positive, and a is less than b, then the reverse inequality is true for the negatives of a and b.
If $a < b$ and $c < d$, then $a + c < b + d$.	You can add the left sides and right sides of inequalities that have the same signs; the resulting sums satisfy the same inequality.
If $0 < a < 1$, then $a^2 < a$.	Squaring a real number between 0 and 1 produces a smaller real number.
If $a > 1$, then $a^2 > a$.	Squaring a real number greater than 1 produces a larger real number.
If $0 < a < b$, then $\frac{1}{b} < \frac{1}{a}$.	If a and b are both positive, and a is less than b, then the reverse inequality is true for the reciprocals of a and b.

PRACTICE

If $x > y$ and $z > y$, which of the following MUST be true?

    A. $z^2 > y^2$

    B. $x^2 > y^2$

    C. $x > z$

    D. $x + z > 2y$

    E. $z > x$

The correct answer is D. You know that both x and z are greater than y, but you are not given any information about how they relate to one another. This means that you cannot tell which, if either of them, is greater than the other, so you can eliminate choices C and E. You might assume that since $x > y$, $x^2 > y^2$, but this is not necessarily true. If $x = 2$ and $y = -3$, for example, then $2^2 < (-3)^2$, making $x^2 < y^2$. This allows you to eliminate choices A and B, leaving choice D as correct. It must be true that $x + z > 2y$; since both x and z are greater than y, their sum must be greater than $2y$.

RATIOS, PROPORTIONS, RATES, DECIMALS, AND PERCENTAGES

Ratios

On the ACT exam, ratios, proportions, and percentages are tested under the category of Integrating Essential Skills. A ratio is a comparison of one quantity x to another quantity y, expressed as a fraction $\frac{x}{y}$, or sometimes using the notation $x:y$ (read "x to y"). In plain English, this is interpreted as, "For every x of one type, there are y of the second type."

For example, if there are 3 girls to every 1 boy in a class, we say that the ratio of girls to boys is 3:1, or 3 to 1, and write the fraction $\frac{3}{1}$. Similarly, if there are 5 dogs for every 2 cats in an animal shelter, we say that the ratio of dogs to cats is 5:2, or 5 to 2, and write the fraction $\frac{5}{2}$. We could have instead described the ratio as 2 cats for every 5 dogs and said the ratio of cats to dogs is 2:5, writing the fraction as $\frac{2}{5}$. This conveys the same information. However, since $\frac{2}{5} \neq \frac{5}{2}$, the two ratios are not equal. The order in which the quantities appear in a ratio is important because we represent the ratio as a fraction.

The ratio of butter to chocolate chips in a cookie recipe is 2:3. If $2\frac{1}{4}$ cups of butter are used, how many cups of chocolate chips are used?

- **A.** $\frac{2}{3}$
- **B.** $1\frac{1}{2}$
- **C.** 3
- **D.** $3\frac{3}{8}$
- **E.** 5

The correct answer is D. Set up a proportion to determine the number of cups of chocolate chips needed for the recipe, setting this unknown equal to x. Cross-multiply to solve for x:

$$\frac{2}{3} = \frac{2\frac{1}{4}}{x}$$

$$\frac{2}{3} = \frac{\frac{9}{4}}{x}$$

$$2x = 3\left(\frac{9}{4}\right)$$

$$2x = \frac{27}{4}$$

$$x = \frac{27}{8} = 3\frac{3}{8}$$

Proportions

A proportion is an equation relating two ratios. In symbols, a proportion is expressed by setting two fractions equal to each other, say $\frac{a}{b} = \frac{c}{d}$. This establishes a relationship between the two fractions or ratios. Proportions arise when solving many different types of problems—for example, you'll use them in problems that ask you to change units of measurement and find side lengths of similar triangles.

Proportion problems are formulated when one ratio is known and one of the two quantities in an equivalent ratio is unknown. They arise when changing units of measurement or scaling up a ratio, like when preparing a recipe, among other applications. Since you can express any ratio as a fraction, you can set two equivalent ratios (also called proportionate ratios) equal to each other as fractions. For instance, the ratio 16:28 is proportionate to the ratio 4:7 because $\frac{16}{28} = \frac{4}{7}$.

If one of the four terms is missing from the equation (the proportion), you can solve for the missing term using the following method:

01 Simplify the known fraction, if possible.

02 Cross multiply the numbers you know.

03 Divide the product by the third number you know.

For example, if the ratio 10:15 is proportionate to 14:x, you can find the missing number by first setting up the following proportion:

$$\frac{10}{15} = \frac{14}{x}$$

Reading the ratio 10:15 as a fraction, simplify it to $\frac{2}{3}$.

$$\frac{2}{3} = \frac{14}{x}$$

Then, cross multiply both sides:

$$3 \times 14 = 2x$$

$$42 = 2x$$

Finally, divide both sides by the coefficient of x, which is 2 in this case:

$$\frac{2x}{2} = \frac{41}{2}$$

$$x = 21$$

Therefore, the ratio 10:15 is equivalent to the ratio 14:21. You'll often encounter proportion problems as word problems. Word problems will require you to parse out the numbers and then set up the ratios so that they are proportionate in order to solve for the missing term.

Suppose there are 2 hockey sticks for every 5 pucks in the storage room. If the last count was 60 pucks, how many hockey sticks are in the storage room?

    A. 8

    B. 12

    C. 6

    D. 18

    E. 24

The correct answer is E. Let h denote the number of hockey sticks in the storage room. Here, we know that there are 2 hockey sticks for every 5 pucks. We know that there's a total of 60 pucks, but we don't know how many hockey sticks there are. However, because the number of hockey sticks is proportional to the number of pucks, we can scale up the ratio we do know to solve for the number of hockey sticks. Set up the proportion as follows:

$$\frac{2}{5} = \frac{h}{60}$$

$$5h = 120$$

$$h = 24$$

Rates of Speed, Time, and Distance

The basic formula used in solving problems for distance is:

$$D = RT \text{ (Distance = Rate} \times \text{Time)}$$

You can use this same formula to find rate (speed) and time.

To find rate, use $R = \dfrac{D}{T}$ (Rate = Distance ÷ Time).

To find time, use $T = \dfrac{D}{R}$ (Time = Distance ÷ Rate).

Let's look at two examples.

PRACTICE

An aircraft flies 600 miles in 5 hours. At what rate did it complete the trip?

- **A.** 80 mph
- **B.** 90 mph
- **C.** 120 mph
- **D.** 200 mph
- **E.** 220 mph

The correct answer is C. Here you're provided distance and time, and you're asked to determine the rate at which the distance of 600 miles can be covered in 5 hours. With the formula for calculating rate, you can see that distance will be divided by time. This creates a unit rate with the unit label of miles per hour, specifying how much distance can be covered per unit of time (every hour). Dividing the total distance by the total travel time $\left(\dfrac{600 \text{ miles}}{5 \text{ hours}} \right)$ yields a rate of 120 miles per hour (mph), communicating that for every hour of flight time, the aircraft will travel 120 miles.

We can look at another example to see how possessing the unit rate allows you to determine the different rate components.

PRACTICE

A driver is traveling from Denver, CO, to Laramie, WY. The distance between these two cities is 128 miles. If the driver goes straight there without stopping and drives at a rate of 60 mph the entire time, about how long will it take them to get to Laramie?

- **F.** 2 hours
- **G.** 2.5 hours
- **H.** 3 hours
- **J.** 3.5 hours
- **K.** 4 hours

The correct answer is F. Here, we are given two of the variables we need: rate and distance. This means we need to solve for time. To solve for time, we'll use the $T = \dfrac{D}{R}$ and plug in the values we know.

Here, we know that the driver is traveling at a rate of 60 mph. We also know that the drive is 128 miles total. If we plug the values into our formula, we get:

$$T = \frac{128 \text{ miles}}{60 \text{ miles per hour}}$$

If we divide 128 miles by 60 mph, we get 2.13 hours (notice how the shared units—miles—cancel). Note that this is **not** the same as 2 hours and 13 minutes, but we generally know that it will take the driver a little over 2 hours to make the drive.

Rates Involving Other Units

Not all rates are related to speed. Rates can involve any kind of units. You may see a question related to money. For example, if you earn $30.00 in 2 hours, your rate is $15.00 per hour. The rate in a money problem represents a unit amount—such as a salary (dollars per hour) or an individual price (cost per item).

When you solve these questions, your rate formula will look like this:

$$\text{Rate (unit amount)} = \frac{\text{Total amount}}{\text{Number of units}}$$

This calculation will yield the unit rate. If you find the unit rate first, you'll be able to scale it easily to find whatever equivalent you need. Try out the sample question we've provided here.

PRACTICE

If a 20-ounce bottle of juice costs $1.80, what is the cost for three ounces of juice?

    A. $0.09

    B. $0.11

    C. $0.18

    D. $0.27

    E. $0.33

The correct answer is choice D. To solve this problem, you must first identify the three pieces of the problem:

$$\text{Number of units} = 20 \text{ ounces}$$
$$\text{Total amount} = \$1.80$$
$$\text{Unit amount (cost per ounce)} = ?$$

Then, plug the known values into the rate formula and use it to solve for the unit amount.

$$\begin{aligned}\text{Rate (unit amount)} &= \frac{\text{Total amount}}{\text{Number of units}}\\[4pt] &= \frac{\$1.80}{20 \text{ ounces of juice}}\\[4pt] &= \$0.09 \text{ per ounce of juice}\end{aligned}$$

The cost per ounce of juice is $0.09, which is choice A. This dollar-to-ounce value is the unit rate. However, you've been asked to find the cost of 3 ounces of juice, not just one. You'll need to multiply the unit rate by the total number of units you need. That total will be $0.27, choice D.

Decimals

A fraction that has a denominator that is either 10 or a power of 10 is called a *decimal fraction*, or simply a *decimal*. You are already familiar with the shorthand notation used to express decimal fractions:

$$\frac{7}{10} = 0.7, \frac{37}{100} = 0.37, \frac{59}{1,000} = 0.059, \frac{4,139}{10,000} = 0.4139$$

As noted in the previous section, when a problem involves fractions, it is sometimes easier to change each fraction into a decimal.

Comparing Decimals

The simplest way to compare a group of decimal numbers is to add zeros to the end of each decimal number, until all of the numbers have the same number of digits to the right of the decimal point. Then, ignore the decimal point, and directly compare the resulting numbers.

Suppose you need to put the decimals 0.73, 0.737, and 0.7314 in order from smallest to largest. The number 0.7314 contains four digits to the right of the decimal point, and this is more digits than any of the other numbers. Therefore, add zeros to each of the other numbers until they also have four digits to the right of the decimal point. The numbers become 0.7300, 0.7370, and 0.7314. From this, we can see that 0.737 is the largest of the numbers, followed by 0.7314. Lastly, 0.7300 is the smallest.

Percentages

A percentage (%) is a fraction or decimal number written in a different form, specifically as a number out of 100. A percentage expressed as a fraction is the number divided by 100. As an example, there are 100 cents in a dollar. One percent of $1.00, then, is one cent. Using decimal notation, we can write one cent as $0.01, five cents as $0.05, twenty-five cents as $0.25, and so forth. Instead of saying that 25 cents equal 25 hundredths of a dollar, though, we use the word percent and the form 25%. The decimal number 0.25 as a percentage, then, can be written as 25% as well.

The information in this section will help you understand the relationship between decimals, fractions, and percentages and to convert numbers from one form to another.

Converting between Decimals, Fractions, and Percentages

You can find a percentage with the following equation: $\text{percentage} = \left(\dfrac{\text{part}}{\text{whole}} \right) \times 100$. That equation can be flipped around algebraically to find that $\text{part} = \text{whole} \times \left(\dfrac{\text{percentage}}{100} \right)$ or $\text{whole} = \text{part} \div \left(\dfrac{\text{percentage}}{100} \right)$

 TIP

There's a shortcut for finding a certain percentage of a number. Here are some examples: 5% of 50 is the same as 50% of 5: 2.5. 3% of 150 is the same as 150% of 3: 4.5. 10% of 60 is the same as 60% of 10: 6. You can use this trick to flip around some percentage problems if it makes the math easier.

Here are some examples that demonstrate how to convert between decimals, fractions, and percentages.

 To change a decimal to a percentage, multiply by 100 and add the % sign.

$$0.25 = 0.25 \times 100 = 25\%$$

 The fraction bar in a fraction means "divided by." To change a fraction to a decimal, follow through on the division.

$$\frac{4}{5} = 4 \div 5 = 0.8$$

 To change a fraction to a percentage, multiply by 100, simplify, and add the percent sign (%).

$$\frac{1}{4} \times 100 = \frac{100}{4} = 25\%$$

 To change a percentage to a decimal, remove the percent sign (%) and divide the number by 100.

$$25\% = \frac{25}{100} = 0.25$$

 To change a percentage to a fraction, remove the % sign and use that number as your numerator, with 100 as your denominator, and simplify.

$$25\% = \frac{25}{100} = \frac{1}{4}$$

Percentage is not limited to comparing other numbers to 100. You can divide any number into hundredths and talk about percentage. Similarly, we can find a percentage of any number we choose by multiplying it by the correct decimal notation. For example:

Five percent of 50: $0.05 \times 50 = 2.5$

Three percent of 150: $0.03 \times 150 = 4.5$

Ten percent of 60: $0.10 \times 60 = 6$

Solving Percentage Problems

A question involving percentages might involve one of these three tasks:

 Finding the percentage of a number

 Finding a number when a percentage is given

Finding what percentage one number is of another

Regardless of the task, three distinct values are involved: the part, the whole, and the percentage. Often, the problem will give you two of the three numbers, and your job is to find the missing value. To work with percentages, use the following formula:

$$\text{percentage} = \frac{\text{part}}{\text{whole}} \times 100$$

Once again, to know any two of those values allows you to determine the third.

Finding the Percentage

30 is what percent of 50?

In this question, 50 is the whole, and 30 is the part. Your task is to find the missing percent:

$$\text{percentage} = \frac{30}{50} \times 100$$
$$= 60\%$$

Finding the Part

What number is 25% of 80?

In this question, 80 is the whole, and 25 is the percentage. Your task is to find the part:

$$25\% = \frac{\text{part}}{80} \times 100$$

In this situation, it can be helpful to change the percentage into its decimal form (.25), which then lets you drop the 100 from the equation so you can represent the percentage as a fraction, in this case $\frac{25}{100}$. That gives us a new form of the equation:

$$\frac{25}{100} = \frac{\text{part}}{80}$$

To solve for the missing part, cross multiply 25 and 80 and 100 with the missing part. That yields the following:

$$100(\text{part}) = 25(80)$$
$$100(\text{part}) = 2,000$$
$$\text{part} = \frac{2,000}{100}$$
$$\text{part} = 20$$

25% of 80 is 20. Because of the values used, there are any number of ways you could have come to that solution faster, such as by simplifying the left fraction to $\frac{1}{4}$, or calculating $80 \div 4$ or $80 \times .25$, but it's important that you see the full process. Let's look at how you can streamline your work in the next example.

Finding the Whole

An example of a question that requires you to find the whole might be something like "75% of what number is 150?"

In this question, 150 is the part, and 75 is the percentage. Your task is to find the whole. Here's the streamlined equation:

$$\frac{75}{100} = \frac{150}{\text{whole}}$$

Here, you can simplify the fraction on the left to $\frac{3}{4}$ and then cross multiply:

$$\frac{3}{4} = \frac{150}{\text{whole}}$$
$$\text{whole}(3) = 150(4)$$

Then, multiply the two diagonally situated numbers you know:

$$150 \times 4 = 600$$

Finally, divide 600 by 3, which equals 200.

$$75\% \text{ of } 200 \text{ is } 150$$

1% of 200 is what percentage of 40?

    A. 0.2

    B. 2

    C. 5

    D. 10

    E. 40

The correct answer is C. 1% of 200 is 1/100, or 0.01, of 200. Multiply 200 by 0.01. That is equivalent to 2. Then divide 2 by 40, which yields 5%.

Percent Increase and Decrease

You've likely encountered the concept of percent change with investment interest, sales tax, and discount pricing. Percent change always relates to the value before the change. Here are a few simple examples to explain the concept.

1. 10 increased by what percent is 12? First, note that the numerical amount of the increase is 2. Compare the change (2) to the original number (10), and you'll find that the change in percent is $\frac{2}{10}$, or 20%.

2. 12 decreased by what percent is 10? In this example, the amount of the numerical decrease is 2. Compare the change (2) to the original number (12). The change is $\frac{2}{12}$, or $\frac{1}{6}$ (or 16.66%).

Notice that the percent increase from 10 to 12 (20%) is not the same as the percent decrease from 12 to 10 (16.66%). That's because the original number (before the change) is different in the two questions.

Percent-change problems typically involve tax, interest, profit, discount, or weight. In handling these problems, you might need to calculate more than one percent change.

A computer originally priced at $500 is discounted by 10%, then by another 10%. What is the price of the computer after the second discount, to the nearest dollar?

    A. $400

    B. $405

    C. $425

    D. $450

    E. $475

The correct answer is B. After the first 10% discount, the price was $450 ($500 minus 10% of $500). After the second discount, which is calculated based on the $450 price, the price of the computer is $405 ($450 minus 10% of $450).

A positive number x is increased by 20 percent, and the result is then decreased by 30 percent. The final result is equal to which of the following?

    F. x decreased by 50 percent

    G. x decreased by 16 percent

    H. x decreased by 10 percent

    J. x increased by 10 percent

    K. x increased by 24 percent

The correct answer is G. Begin by plugging in 100 for x. If 100 is increased by 20 percent, the result is 120. This number is then decreased by 30 percent. Thirty percent of 120 is 36, so the final result is 120 − 36 = 84. This is the same as decreasing 100 by 16 percent. Choice F is incorrect because the percentages are actually acting in different directions, so you cannot simply add them in this manner. Choices H and J are incorrect because you cannot just add percentages; they must be applied to a whole. For choice K, you assumed that x was initially decreased by 20% and then applied 30% to $0.80x$.

Absolute Value

A number line is a convenient way of illustrating the position of real numbers with respect to zero. The integers 7 and –7 are both 7 units away from 0, even though they exist on either side of 0. For any real number a, we use the absolute value of a, denoted $|a|$, to measure the distance between a and 0. Since distance is a nonnegative quantity, the definition has two parts:

$$|a| = \begin{cases} a, & \text{if } a \geq 0 \\ -a, & \text{if } a < 0 \end{cases}$$

For instance, $|8| = 8$ and $|-8| = -(-8) = 8$. This definition works for any type of real number: integers, fractions, decimal numbers, or irrational numbers.

The following are some useful properties of absolute value you should master before taking the ACT exam:

ABSOLUTE VALUE PROPERTIES	
Property (in symbols)	**Property (in words)**
$|a| = b$ whenever $a = b$ or $a = -b$	The real numbers b and $-b$ are both $|b|$ units from the origin.
$|a \cdot b| = |a| \cdot |b|$	The absolute value of a product is the product of the absolute values.
$\left|\dfrac{a}{b}\right| = \dfrac{|a|}{|b|}$, whenever $b \neq 0$	The absolute value of a quotient is the quotient of the absolute values.

Remember, when a and b have opposite signs, $|a + b| \neq |a| + |b|$. For example, $|-5 + 4| \neq |-5| + |4|$. The correct way of simplifying $|-5 + 4|$ is by first simplifying the whole expression inside the absolute value bars (much like parentheses). Then, when there is a single number enclosed by the absolute value bars, compute the absolute value. So $|-5 + 4| = |-1| = 1$. This is not equivalent to $|-5| + |4|$, which equals 9.

BASIC ALGEBRA

Fundamentally, algebra is the manipulation of mathematical symbols. More than likely, your familiarity with the topic stems from solving for unknowns by applying various rules and procedures. Algebraic expressions, linear equations, and inequalities are useful in helping you break down and solve complex equations in algebra.

Expressions and Equations

So far, you've already seen plenty of mathematical expressions, defined as containing at least two values with some math operator used between them. Algebraic expressions, however, are usually used to form equations—the goal is to set two expressions equal to one another. When we're talking about algebraic expressions, know that a term is any coefficient, variable, or combination of a coefficient and a variable. In equations, at least one of the terms will be a variable—a letter such as x or y that represents a number that can vary. It does not need an exponent, but if it has one, it must be a non-negative exponent. A coefficient is the number that multiplies with a variable, such as the 2 in $2y$.

Standard Form

Standard form is something you've been using since you learned how to write numbers. Write the number one hundred: 100. That is standard form—the usual way you'd write a number. In addition to being the way you've written numbers all your life, standard form is also an agreed upon method of writing an equation. The standard form for equations has a couple of rules you need to know.

Always set an equation equal to 0. Example: $x = 7$ should have everything on the left of the equal sign, and 0 on the right: $x - 7 = 0$ is standard form.

 Work down from the highest exponent. Example: $7x^3 + 3x^6 - 5 + 4x^2$ should start with the highest exponent: $3x^6 + 7x^3 + 4x^2 - 5$.

Writing equations in standard form makes it easier to locate information because it is presented in a consistent order. When an equation is in standard form, you'll know what to expect and how to proceed with isolating and solving for the variable.

Evaluating Expressions through Substitution

You know that expressions can have terms, coefficients, variables, and exponents. When putting expressions into standard form, you'll often be simplifying the expression. Expressions can be simplified by combining like terms. Like terms must have the same variable (or lack thereof) and the same power (e.g., 3 and 4, $3x$ and x, $4y^7$ and $253y^7$). Sometimes, though, you'll not only be given an expression but also a value that can be substituted in for a variable to evaluate the expression. For instance, if you were told to evaluate the expression $4x^2 + 3x$ when $x = 3$, you would substitute 3 for each instance of x.

PRACTICE

Evaluate the equation $y = 4x + 5$ when $x = -3$.

- **A.** -7
- **B.** -3
- **C.** -1
- **D.** 9
- **E.** 17

The correct solution is A. Plug -3 in for x and then find the resulting value for y:

$$y = 4x + 5$$
$$y = 4(-3) + 5$$
$$y = -7$$

The answer is $y = -7$.

Expressions in Word Problems

One of the most challenging parts of algebra, and a major part of the ACT Mathematics test, is translating words that describe a math scenario into symbols.

When creating an algebraic expression, equation, or inequality that describes a relationship between one or more quantities, you must first identify what the unknowns are and how many of them you have. Use a different letter for each unknown. Then, identify common words and phrases (*is, of, less than, greater than,* etc.) and translate them, piece by piece, into algebraic expressions.

Let's look at some examples:

 A number is three less than two times another number: $x = 2y - 3$

 The square of the sum of two numbers is greater than 4: $(x + y)^2 > 4$

 The sum of two numbers is twice the product of two other numbers: $x + y = 2wz$

Linear Equations in One Variable

As we've mentioned, algebraic expressions are usually used to form equations with two expressions that are set equal to each other. Equations contain at least one variable, most often x or y (though variables can be represented by any letter). Most equations you'll see on the test are linear equations. In linear equations, the variables x and y don't come with exponents, and they can be graphed along the x- and y-axis of a coordinate plane.

To find the value of a linear equation's variable is to solve the equation. To solve any linear equation containing only one variable, your goal is always the same: isolate the variable on one side of the equation. To accomplish this, you may need to perform one or more operations on both sides, depending on the equation.

Whatever operation you perform on one side of an equation you must also perform on the other side; otherwise, the two sides won't be equal. Performing any of the operations on both sides does not change the equality; it merely restates the equation in a different form.

Simplifying Equations

Sometimes, you need to simplify one or both sides of an equation before you can undo what's been done to the variable. This can be done through various means depending on the nature of the expression. In general, you'll combine like terms and then isolate the target variable to one side of the equation, using standard order of operations, to reach its solution.

Simplify $3(x - 2) - 2x = 8$.

    A. -14

    B. -6

    C. 2

    D. 8

    E. 14

The correct answer is E. Simplify any parts of the equation, remembering to follow the order of operations (PEMDAS). First, multiply the expression in parentheses by 3.

$$3x - 6 - 2x = 8$$

Then, combine like terms containing the variable x.

$$3x - 6 - 2x = 8$$
$$x - 6 = 8$$

To undo the subtraction of 6, add 6 to both sides.

$$x - 6(+6) = 8(+6)$$
$$x = 14$$

Simplification Methods

Here is a more detailed rundown of several simplification methods.

Performing Operations to Isolate the Variable

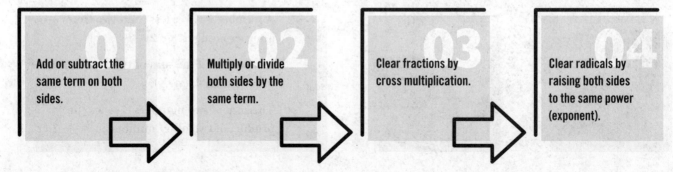

01	02	03	04
Add or subtract the same term on both sides.	Multiply or divide both sides by the same term.	Clear fractions by cross multiplication.	Clear radicals by raising both sides to the same power (exponent).

To find the value of the variable (to solve for *x*, *y*, or any other variable), you may need to either add a term to both sides of the equation or subtract a term from both sides. What follows are examples for each operation.

Adding the same number to both sides:

$$x - 2 = 5$$
$$x - 2 + 2 = 5 + 2$$
$$x = 7$$

Subtracting the same number from both sides:

$$y + 3 = 7$$
$$y + 3 - 3 = 7 - 3$$
$$y = 4$$

The first system isolates *x* by adding 2 to both sides. The second system isolates *y* by removing 3 from both sides.

The objective is to isolate the variable. To do this, like terms must be combined until the variable stands alone on one side of the equation. The following example isolates *x* by subtracting $\frac{3}{2}$ from both sides, then combining like terms and dividing by –1 to make the variable positive:

$$\frac{3}{2} - x = 12$$
$$\frac{3}{2} - \frac{3}{2} - x = 12 - \frac{3}{2}$$
$$-x = 10\frac{1}{2}$$
$$x = -10\frac{1}{2}$$

In some cases, solving for *x* (or *y*) requires that you either multiply or divide both sides of the equation by the same term. What follows are two examples.

Multiplying both sides by the same number:

$$\frac{x}{2} = 14$$
$$2 \cdot \frac{x}{2} = 14 \cdot 2$$
$$x = 28$$

Dividing both sides by the same number:

$$3y = 18$$
$$\frac{3y}{3} = \frac{18}{3}$$
$$y = 6$$

The first system isolates *x* by multiplying both sides by 2. The second system isolates *y* by dividing both sides by 3. If the variable appears on both sides of the equation, first perform whatever operation is required to position the variable on just one side—either the left or the right. The next system positions both *x*-terms on the left side by subtracting 2*x* from both sides:

$$16 - x = 9 + 2x$$
$$16 - x - 2x = 9 + 2x - 2x$$
$$16 - 3x = 9$$

Now that *x* appears on just one side, the next step is to isolate it by subtracting 16 from both sides, and then divide both sides by –3:

$$16 - 3x = 9$$
$$16 - 3x - 16 = 9 - 16$$
$$-3x = -7$$
$$\frac{-3x}{-3} = \frac{-7}{-3}$$
$$x = \frac{7}{3}$$

Solve $2(x + 1) = -10$.

    A. -11

    B. -6

    C. -5

    D. 5

    E. 11

The correct answer is B. First use the distributive property to eliminate the parentheses:

$$2(x+1)=-10$$
$$2x+2=-10$$

Next, subtract 2 from each side:

$$2x+2-2=-10-2$$
$$2x=-12$$

Now simplify by dividing each side by 2:

$$\frac{2x}{2}=\frac{-12}{2}$$
$$x=-6$$

BASIC GEOMETRY

You have likely already encountered the terms *point*, *line*, *line segment*, *ray*, and *angle* throughout your education. Those terms form the foundation of geometry. In this section, we will explore those terms in the context of ACT IES questions and examine key concepts around basic geometric shapes, as well as the fundamental principles of coordinate geometry.

Points and Lines

A *point* is defined as having no size of its own, and only a position. On the ACT, a point is typically represented by a dot and named by using a capital letter. The graphic below depicts point A.

        •A

A *line* is a continuous set of points. It only has one dimension—length—and has no width of its own. Lines can be named in several ways. Sometimes, a letter is placed next to a drawing of the line, and the line is named using this letter. For example, the following figure is a picture of line l.

Lines are also commonly named by putting a double-headed arrow over any two of the points on the line. For example, the figure below is a picture of line $\overleftrightarrow{AB}$.

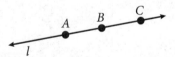

Note that, since the point C is also on this line, the line could just as well have been called line $\overleftrightarrow{AC}$ or line $\overleftrightarrow{BC}$. Also note that it is standard to put arrowheads on the ends of lines to indicate that the line "keeps going" in both directions forever.

A *line segment* is the portion of line between two of its points, which are called the *endpoints* of the line segment. A line segment is named by placing a bar over its endpoints. For example, the figure below depicts line segment $\overline{PQ}$.

Note that, while $\overleftrightarrow{AB}$ and $\overleftrightarrow{AC}$ refer to the same line, $\overline{AB}$ and $\overline{AC}$ refer to different line segments. Line segment $\overline{AB}$ runs between points A and B, while line segment $\overline{AC}$ runs between points A and C.

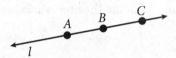

Unlike a line, which is of infinite length, a line segment is of finite length. The length of a line segment is indicated by writing its two endpoints next to each other. For example, based on the figure below, $\overline{EF} = 12$.

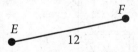

If two line segments have the same length, they are said to be *congruent*. There is a special symbol for congruence, which may be used on the ACT. The symbol is ≅. Thus, if $\overline{BC}$ and $\overline{EF}$ have the same length, that is, if $\overline{BC} = \overline{EF}$, we write $\overline{BC} \cong \overline{EF}$.

A ray is a portion of a line, beginning at one point on the line, called the endpoint, and extending infinitely in one direction. A ray is indicated by writing the endpoint of the ray next to another point on the ray and placing a one-headed arrow over it. For example, the figure below depicts $\overrightarrow{AB}$.

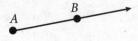

Graphing Basics

To start, let's familiarize you with the coordinate plane. The coordinate plane (or grid) is divided into four sections. Each section is called a quadrant. The two number lines that divide the grid into quadrants are called the *x*-axis (the horizontal axis) and the *y*-axis (the vertical axis). The center of the grid, where the two axes meet, is called the origin. Any point on the plane has two coordinates that indicate its location relative to the axes. The points that are drawn on the grid are identified by ordered pairs. In ordered pairs, the *x*-coordinate is always written first. The ordered pair for the origin, in the middle of the grid, is (0, 0).

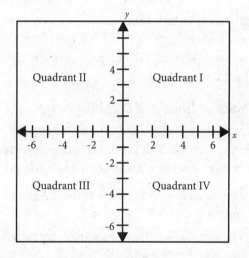

The quadrants of a grid are named in counter-clockwise order, beginning with the first quadrant in the upper right corner. For any point in the first quadrant, the coordinates are positive. The quadrant in the top left is called the second quadrant. For any point in the second quadrant, the *x*-coordinate is negative, but the *y*-coordinate is positive. The quadrant in the lower left is called the third quadrant. In the third quadrant, both coordinates are negative. The quadrant in the lower right is called the fourth quadrant, and in the fourth quadrant, the *x*-coordinate is positive, and the *y*-coordinate is negative.

On the following graph, the *x*-coordinate of point A is 3. The *y*-coordinate of point A is 2. The coordinates of point A are given by the ordered pair (3, 2). Point B has coordinates (–1, 4). Point C has coordinates (–4, –3). Point D has coordinates (2, –3).

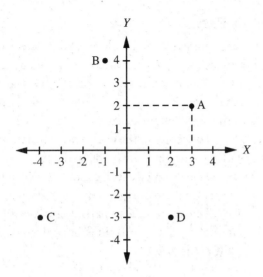

To graph a point whose coordinates are given, first locate the *x*-coordinate on the *x*-axis, then from that position, move vertically the number of spaces indicated by the *y*-coordinate.

Equations of Lines and Graphing

In a coordinate plane, a line can be defined by the equation $y = mx + b$. This is called the slope-intercept form. In this equation, you can see the following:

- The variable *m* as the slope of the line (its steepness).
- The variable *b* as the line's *y*-intercept (where the line crosses the *y*-axis).
- The variables *x* and *y*, which are the coordinates of any point on the line. Any (x, y) pair defining a point on the line can substitute for the variables *x* and *y*.

For a line with an equation of $y = 3x + 2$, the line has a positive slope of 3 and a *y*-intercept of 2. Let's review these terms and learn more about working with the slope-intercept equation.

Slope

Slope is a ratio that describes the steepness of a line.

$$\text{slope } (m) = \frac{\text{rise}}{\text{run}}$$
$$= \frac{\text{vertical change}}{\text{horizontal change}}$$
$$= \frac{\text{change in } y}{\text{change in } x}$$

To find the slope of a line from a graph, count the spaces from one point on the line to another.

PRACTICE

Determine the slope of the line below:

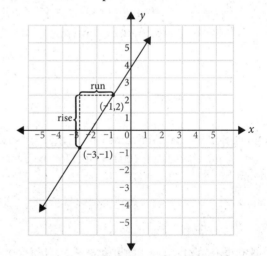

A. $\frac{1}{3}$

B. $\frac{1}{2}$

C. $\frac{2}{3}$

D. $\frac{3}{2}$

E. $\frac{3}{1}$

The correct answer is D. On the graph shown,

count the vertical spaces and the horizontal spaces from (−3, −1) to (−1, 2).

$$\text{Slope} = \frac{\text{vertical change}}{\text{horizontal change}} = \frac{3}{2}$$

The slope of the line is $\frac{3}{2}$.

You can also calculate slope without a graph if you know two points on a line. You can find the slope of the line using the formula for slope (m):

$$m = \frac{y_2 - y_1}{x_2 - x_1}$$

If a line passes through points (−3, −1) and (−1, 2), let (x_1, y_1) be (−3, −1) and (x_2, y_2) be (−1, 2). Plug these values into the slope formula:

$$m = \frac{y_2 - y_1}{x_2 - x_1}$$
$$= \frac{2 - (-1)}{-1 - (-3)}$$
$$= \frac{2 + 1}{-1 + 3}$$
$$= \frac{3}{2}$$

Therefore, the slope of the line is $\frac{3}{2}$.

Keep in mind that when you plug points into the slope formula, it doesn't matter which point you name (x_1, y_1) and (x_2, y_2). The slope will be the same either way as long as you place your values appropriately in the formula.

Y-Intercepts

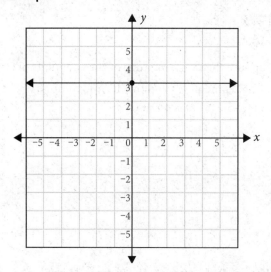

The y-intercept of a line is the y-coordinate of the point where the line crosses the y-axis. The coordinates of the y-intercept are (0, y). The y-intercept of the line shown is 3, since the line crosses the y-axis at (0, 3).

In any set of points on a line, you can find the y-intercept by looking for the point with an x-coordinate of 0. Each straight line crosses the y-axis only one time, so there can only be one point with an x-coordinate of 0. This point is the y-intercept.

Distance and Midpoint Formulas

You can quickly compute the length of any vertical or horizontal line segment by simply subtracting its y- or x-coordinates, respectively, and taking the absolute value of the result (since length cannot be negative). For diagonal segments, the distance formula comes in handy:

The distance between two points $P(x_1, y_1)$ and $Q(x_2, y_2)$ is $\sqrt{(x_2 - x_1)^2 + (y_2 - y_1)^2}$.

Likewise, the midpoint of the line segment with endpoints $P(x_1, y_1)$ and $Q(x_2, y_2)$ is the point with coordinates $\left(\frac{x_1 + x_2}{2}, \frac{y_1 + y_2}{2} \right)$.

Often, the problems on the ACT Mathematics test that involve the distance and midpoint formulas are word problems, such as the following questions.

Suppose that $P(-1, 6)$ is one of the endpoints of a line segment $\overline{PQ}$ and that its midpoint is $M(4, -5)$. What is point Q?

A. $\left(\dfrac{3}{2}, \dfrac{1}{2}\right)$

B. $(-5, 11)$

C. $(5, -11)$

D. $(9, -16)$

E. $(-9, 16)$

The correct answer is D. Since we do not know the coordinates of Q, let's call that point (x, y); we must determine the values of both x and y. Using the midpoint formula, we can express the midpoint of $\overline{PQ}$ as $\left(\dfrac{-1+x}{2}, \dfrac{6+y}{2}\right)$. Since we are given that the midpoint is $(4, -5)$, we know that $\dfrac{-1+x}{2} = 4$ and $\dfrac{6+y}{2} = -5$. Solving each of these yields $x = 9$ and $y = -16$. Hence, the coordinates of Q are $(9, -16)$.

A map is laid out in the standard (x, y) coordinate plane. How long in units is the path from City A located at $(4, 11)$ to City B located at $(8, 9)$, given that the path is a straight line between the cities?

F. 2 units

G. $\sqrt{6}$ units

H. $2\sqrt{5}$ units

J. 6 units

K. 20 units

The correct answer is H. You can use the

distance formula to find the straight-line distance between any two points in the (x, y) plane.

$$
\begin{aligned}
d &= \sqrt{(x_1 - x_2)^2 + (y_1 - y_2)^2} \\
&= \sqrt{(4-8)^2 + (11-9)^2} \\
&= \sqrt{-4^2 + 2^2} \\
&= \sqrt{16 + 4} \\
&= \sqrt{20} \\
&= 2\sqrt{5}
\end{aligned}
$$

Angles

Angles are classified according to their measure. Angle units are expressed in degrees (and often radians when studying trigonometry), and the notation $m\angle$ (name of angle) is used to denote the measure of a given angle.

These are the various angle characterizations you should know—these terms will likely come up somewhere on the ACT exam.

ANGLE TYPES

Term	Illustration	Definition
Acute Angle		An angle with a measure between 0 and 90 degrees
Right Angle		An angle with a measure of 90 degrees
Obtuse Angle		An angle with a measure between 90 and 180 degrees
Straight Angle		An angle with a measure of 180 degrees
Complementary Angles	$A + B = 90°$	Two angles with measures that sum to 90 degrees
Supplementary Angles	$A + B = 180°$	Two angles with measures that sum to 180 degrees
Congruent Angles		Two angles that have the same measure

It's not only important that you understand individual angle classifications but also how pairs of angles relate to each other. Knowing these relationships will help you determine angle values in figures and perform more complex calculations.

Take a look at the following image and the table that follows. You will likely be presented with a figure on the ACT exam that has some angle values provided and then will ask you to determine some missing values in order to solve a problem. We suggest that you review and memorize these angle relationships until they're second nature to you—they are sure to come in handy when you take the test.

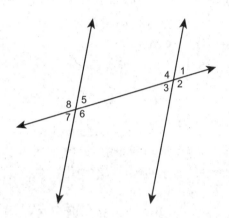

Term	Examples from Diagram
Corresponding Angles	∠1 and ∠5, ∠3 and ∠7 In a diagram such as the one above, if the lines are parallel then corresponding angles are congruent.
Adjacent Angles	∠1 and ∠2, ∠6 and ∠7
Vertical Angles	∠1 and ∠3, ∠6 and ∠8 Vertical angles are always congruent.
Alternate Interior Angles	∠4 and ∠5, ∠3 and ∠6 In a diagram such as the one above, if the lines are parallel, then alternate interior angles are congruent.

Remember: typically, parallel lines are denoted by two vertical hash marks, like 1∥2. Congruence is generally denoted by a single hash mark.

If two lines cut by a transversal are NOT parallel, then pairs of corresponding angles and pairs of alternate interior angles are *not* necessarily congruent.

Let's look at an example dealing with lines and angles.

Points A, D, and E lie on the same line in the figure below. What is the $m\angle BEC$?

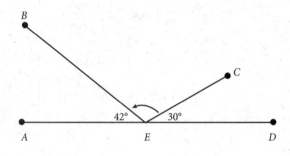

A. 60°

B. 48°

C. 90°

D. 108°

E. 150°

The correct answer is D. In the diagram, the three angles form a straight line and therefore, their measures must sum to 180°.

$$m\angle AEB + m\angle BEC + m\angle CED = 180°$$
$$42° + m\angle BEC + 30° = 180°$$
$$m\angle BEC = 180° - 42° - 30°$$
$$= 108$$

Polygons

Polygons include all two-dimensional figures formed only by line segments. Remember these two reciprocal rules about polygons:

 If all angles of a polygon are congruent (equal in degree measure), then all sides are congruent (equal in length).

 If all sides of a polygon are congruent (equal in length), then all angles are congruent (equal in degree measure).

A polygon in which all sides are congruent and all angles are congruent is called a regular polygon.

You can use the following formula to determine the sum of all interior angles of *any* polygon with angles that each measure less than 180° (n = number of sides):

$(n - 2)(180°)$ = sum of interior angles

For regular polygons, the average angle size is also the size of every angle. But for *any* polygon (except for those with an angle exceeding 180°), you can find the average angle size by dividing the sum of the angles by the number of sides. One way to shortcut the math is to memorize the angle sums and averages for polygons with three to eight sides:

3 sides: $(3 - 2)(180°) = 180° ÷ 3 = 60°$

4 sides: $(4 - 2)(180°) = 360° ÷ 4 = 90°$

5 sides: $(5 - 2)(180°) = 540° ÷ 5 = 108°$

6 sides: $(6 - 2)(180°) = 720° ÷ 6 = 120°$

7 sides: $(7 - 2)(180°) = 900° ÷ 7 = 129°$

8 sides: $(8 - 2)(180°) = 1,080° ÷ 8 = 135°$

Triangles

A triangle is a three-sided shape. All triangles, regardless of shape or size, share the following properties:

- **Length of the sides:** Each side is shorter than the sum of the lengths of the other two sides.
- **Angle measures:** The measures of the three interior angles total 180°.
- **Angles and opposite sides:** Comparative angle sizes correspond to the comparative lengths of the sides opposite those angles. For example, a triangle's largest angle is opposite its longest side. (The sides opposite two congruent angles are also congruent.)

The next figure shows three particular types of triangles.

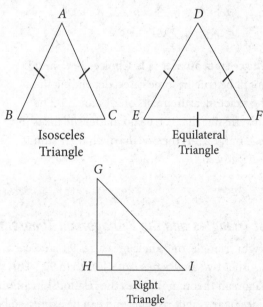

An isosceles triangle is one in which two sides (and two angles) are congruent. In the figure shown, angle *B* and angle *C* are congruent, and the sides opposite those two angles, *AB* and *AC*, are congruent. In an equilateral triangle, all three angles are congruent, and all three sides are congruent. In a right triangle, one angle is a right angle, and the other two angles are acute angles. The longest side of a right triangle (in this case, *GI*) is called the hypotenuse.

PRACTICE

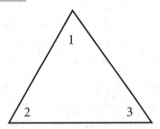

Given that $m\angle 2 = 60°$, which of the following is true?

    A. $m\angle 1 + \angle 3 > 180°$

    B. $m\angle 1 > m\angle 3$

    C. $m\angle 1 = \angle 3$

    D. $m\angle 1 - m\angle 3 > m\angle 2$

    E. $m\angle 1 + \angle 3 = 120°$

The correct answer is E. Choices B, C, and D might be true in some cases, depending upon the exact measurements of $\angle 1$ and $\angle 3$. The only answer that is true no matter the measures of $\angle 1$ and $\angle 3$ is the one in which their sum is equal to 120°.

Right Triangles and the Pythagorean Theorem

In a right triangle, one angle measures 90° and each of the other two angles measures less than 90°. The Pythagorean theorem involves the relationship among the sides of any right triangle and can be expressed by

the equation $a^2 + b^2 = c^2$. As shown in the next figure, the letters a and b represent the lengths of the two legs

(the two shortest sides) that form the right angle, and c is the length of the hypotenuse (the longest side, opposite the right angle).

Pythagorean theorem: $a^2 + b^2 = c^2$

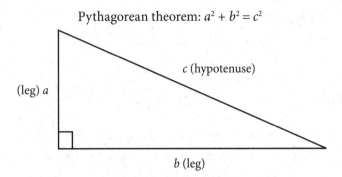

For any right triangle, if you know the length of two sides, you can determine the length of the third side by applying the Pythagorean theorem.

Quadrilaterals

A quadrilateral is a figure in a plane with four sides, each of which is a line segment. There are several common quadrilaterals (e.g., square, rectangle, parallelogram, rhombus, trapezoid) that arise in solving practical problems. As four-sided shapes, each has internal angle measures of 360 degrees. See the following table for a comparison of properties of common quadrilaterals.

COMMON QUADRILATERALS

Property	Rectangle	Square	Parallelogram	Rhombus	Trapezoid
All sides are equal length		✔		✔	
Opposite sides are equal length	✔	✔	✔	✔	(nonparallel sides in isosceles trapezoids)
Opposite sides are parallel	✔	✔	✔	✔	(only the bases)
All angles are equal	✔	✔			
Opposite angles are equal	✔	✔	✔	✔	
Sum of two adjacent angles is 180 degrees	✔	✔	✔	✔	(base and leg angles)
Diagonals bisect	✔	✔	✔	✔	
Diagonals are perpendicular		✔		✔	

Congruency and Similarity

Two geometric figures that have the same size and shape are said to be congruent. The symbol for congruency is ≅. Two angles are congruent if their degree measure (size) is the same. Two line segments are congruent if they are equal in length. Two triangles are congruent if the angle measures and sides are all identical in size. (The same applies to figures with more than three sides.)

If a two-dimensional geometric figure, such as a triangle or rectangle, has exactly the same shape as another one, then the two figures are similar. Similar figures share the same angle measures, and their sides are proportionate (though not the same length).

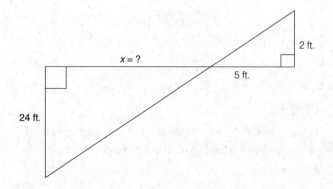

These two triangles are similar. They share an angle and both have right angles. Thus, their third angles must be equal. Because their angles are equal, their sides must be proportional. The ratio 2:5 is the same as 24:x. By creating a proportion, you can solve for x and find the missing side length as 60 ft.

In the figure below, triangles BCA and DEF are similar. What is the length of segment EF?

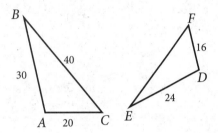

A. 28

B. 30

C. 32

D. 36

E. 40

The correct answer is C. Set up a proportion between similar sides:

$$\frac{24}{30} = \frac{x}{40}$$
$$30x = 960$$
$$x = 32$$

Circles

Let's review some key terms related to the geometry of circles before exploring some additional characteristics of the shape.

- **Circumference:** The distance around the circle (the same as *perimeter*, but the word *circumference* applies only to circles, ovals, and other curved figures)

- **Radius:** The distance from a circle's center to any point along the circle's circumference, often represented by *r*

- **Diameter:** The greatest distance from one point to another on the circle's circumference (twice the length of the radius) through the center point of the circle, often represented by *d*

- **Chord:** A line segment connecting two points on the circle's circumference (a circle's longest possible chord is its diameter, passing through the circle's center)

- **Pi (π):** This Greek letter represents the ratio between a circle's circumference and its diameter; for all circles, the circumference divided by the diameter is π, approximated as 3.14 or $\frac{22}{7}$.

As previously noted, a circle's diameter is twice the length of its radius. The next figure shows a circle with radius 6 and diameter 12.

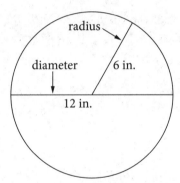

For most questions related to circles, you'll apply one, or possibly both, of two basic formulas involving circles (*r* = radius, *d* = diameter):

Circumference = $2\pi r$, or πd

Area = πr^2

With the circumference and area formulas, all you need is one value—area, circumference, diameter, or radius—and you can determine all the others. Based on the circle shown, which has a diameter of 12:

Radius = 6

Circumference = 12π

Area = $\pi(6)^2 = 36\pi$

Perimeter and Area of Planar Regions

The perimeter of a region in the plane is the "distance around." The area of a region in the plane is the number of unit squares needed to cover the shape. The following are some standard perimeter and area formulas with which you should be familiar.

PERIMETER AND AREA FORMULAS			
Region	**Illustration**	**Perimeter Formula**	**Area Formula**
Square		$P = 4s$	$A = s^2$
Rectangle		$P = 2l + 2w$	$A = l \times w$
Triangle		Sum the three lengths of the triangle.	$A = \frac{1}{2}b \cdot h$
Circle		The perimeter of a circle is called the circumference; it's found with two common expressions: $C = 2\pi r = \pi d$	$A = \pi r^2$
Arcs and Sectors of Circles		Arc length: $P = \left(\dfrac{\theta}{360°}\right) \cdot 2\pi r$	Sector area: $A = \left(\dfrac{\theta}{360°}\right) \cdot \pi r^2$

PRACTICE

What is the area of right triangle ABC below, in square centimeters?

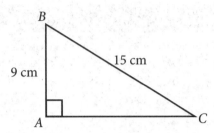

A. 12

B. 36

C. 54

D. 108

E. 135

The correct answer is C. The area of a triangle is $\frac{1}{2}bh$. We already know the height of the triangle, 9 centimeters. To find the base, use the Pythagorean theorem, or recognize this as similar to a 3-4-5 right triangle:

$$9^2 + AC^2 = 15^2$$

$$81 + AC^2 = 225$$

$$AC^2 = 144$$

$$AC = 12$$

Since the base of the triangle is 12, the area of the triangle is $\frac{1}{2}(12)(9) = 54$ square centimeters.

Which of the following answers represents the area of a circle with diameter 20 inches?

F. 16π in²

G. 64π in²

H. 100π in²

J. 400π in²

K. 1600π in²

The correct answer is H. The formula for the area of a circle is A = πr², where r is the radius of the circle. Since the diameter of the circle is given as 20 inches, we can find the radius by dividing the diameter by 2: r = 20/2 = 10 inches. So, the area of the circle is A = π(10)² = 100π in². Choice F is the area of a circle with a radius of 4 inches, not 10 inches. Choice G is the area if the circle had a radius of 8 inches, meaning the diameter would have to be 16 inches. Choice H indicates a circle with a diameter of 40 inches, and choice J indicates a diameter of 80 inches.

Surface Area and Volume of Solids

Two measures of interest for three-dimensional solids are surface area and volume. Conceptually, to compute the surface area of a solid, the solid is dissected and flattened out so that it can be visualized as a combination of recognizable figures whose areas can be computed using known formulas. The volume of a solid in space is the number of unit cubes needed to fill it. The following table details formulas for the surface area and volume of some common solids.

SURFACE AREA AND VOLUME FORMULAS

Solid	Illustration	Surface Area Formula	Volume Formula
Cube		$SA = 6e^2$	$V = e^3$
Rectangular Prism		$SA = 2(lw + lh + wh)$	$V = lwh$
Circular Cone		$SA = \pi r^2 + \pi r\sqrt{r^2 + h^2}$	$V = \dfrac{1}{3}\pi r^2 h$
Circular Cylinder		$SA = 2\pi r^2 + 2\pi rh$	$V = \pi r^2 h$
Sphere		$SA = 4\pi r^2$	$V = \dfrac{4}{3}\pi r^3$

PRACTICE

Find the volume of a right rectangular prism with dimensions 5 in., 9 in., and 6 in.

    A. 39 in³

    B. 49 in³

    C. 59 in³

    D. 240 in³

    E. 270 in³

The correct answer is E. The volume formula for a rectangular prism is $V = l \times w \times h$. After plugging in the given values, the volume of this rectangular prism is 270. Choice C is the result of multiplying the length and width then adding the height. Choice D is the result of finding the surface area. Choice A is the result of multiplying the width and height then adding the length.

If the surface area of a cube is 150 square inches, what is the length of the diagonal of one of its faces?

    F. 5 inches

    G. $\sqrt{10}$ inches

    H. $2\sqrt{5}$ inches

    J. $5\sqrt{2}$ inches

    K. 50 inches

The correct answer is J. Think about what a cube looks like and what you are being asked to find. The diagonal of a face of a cube is the hypotenuse of a right triangle whose legs are both edges, e, of the cube. So it can be found using the Pythagorean theorem if you know e. You must use the given information about the surface area to find e. The surface area of a cube with edge e is $6e^2$. Setting that equal to 150 and solving for e yields the following:

$$6e^2 = 150$$
$$e^2 = 25$$
$$e = 5$$

As such, a face of the cube looks like this:

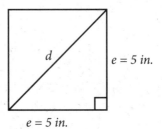

$e = 5$ in.

$e = 5$ in.

Use the Pythagorean theorem to find d:

$$d^2 = 5^2 + 5^2 = 50$$
$$d = \sqrt{50}$$
$$d = 5\sqrt{2}$$

BASIC STATISTICS AND PROBABILITY

Statistics is the analysis of data to determine patterns and trends. You'll need to demonstrate basic knowledge of statistics by finding measures of center and spread (mean, median, and mode). Additionally, you'll also need to be familiar with basic probability calculations—the ability to determine the likelihood of an event occurring (or not occurring). Both topics not only arise in IES questions but are also foundational for the PHM: Statistics and Probability questions (discussed more in Chapter 14).

Calculating Measures of Center and Spread

A set of data values may be summarized using measures of center and/or measures of spread. Measures of center include mean, median, and mode and represent the center of the data. Measures of spread include range and standard deviation and represent how spread out the data values are within a data set.

Arithmetic Mean

An average or arithmetic mean is a value that is computed by dividing the sum of a set of terms by the number of terms in the collection. To find the average (arithmetic mean) of a group of n numbers, simply add the numbers and divide by n. Try the following question.

> **PRACTICE**
>
> Find the average (arithmetic mean) of 32, 50, and 47.
>
> **A.** 26
> **B.** 32
> **C.** 33
> **D.** 43
> **E.** 65
>
> **The correct answer is D.**
>
> $$\frac{32+50+47}{3} = 43$$

Median and Mode

In order to find the median of a group of numbers, list the numbers in numerical order from smallest to largest. The median is the number in the middle. For example, the median of the numbers 3, 3, 5, 9, and 10 is 5. The median and the arithmetic mean are not the same. For those numbers, for example, the arithmetic mean is $30 \div 5 = 6$.

If there is an even number of numbers, the median is equal to the arithmetic mean of the two numbers in the middle. For example, to find the median of 3, 3, 5, 7, 9, and 10, note that the two middle numbers are 5 and 7. The median, then, is $\frac{5+7}{2} = 6$.

The mode of a group of numbers is simply the number that occurs most frequently. Therefore, the mode of the group of numbers 3, 3, 5, 7, 9, and 10 is 3. If all of the numbers in a group only appear once, then there is no mode. A data set can have more than one mode.

> **PRACTICE**
>
> What is the median of the following group of eight numbers?
>
> 2, 7, 8, 9, 9, 9, 10, and 10
>
> **A.** 2
> **B.** 7
> **C.** 8
> **D.** 9
> **E.** 10
>
> **The correct answer is D.** Since this data set has an even number of data values, the median is the arithmetic mean of the two numbers in the middle. These numbers are both 9, so the median is $\frac{9+9}{2} = 9$. Note that the mode is the number that occurs most often, which is also 9.

Probability

Probability refers to the likelihood of an event occurring (or not occurring). By definition, probability ranges from 0 to 1. Probability is never negative, and it is never greater than 1. Here's the basic formula for determining probability:

$$\text{Probability} = \frac{\text{desired outcomes}}{\text{total number of possible occurrences}}$$

Probability can be expressed as a fraction, a percent, or a decimal number. The greater the probability, the greater the fraction, percent, or decimal number.

Determining Probability (Single Event)

Probability plays an integral role in games of chance, including many casino games. In the throw of a single die, for example, the probability of rolling a 5 is "one in six," or $\frac{1}{6}$, or $16\frac{2}{3}$%. Of course, the probability of rolling a certain other number is the same. A standard deck of 52 playing cards contains 12 face cards. The probability of selecting a face card from a full deck is $\frac{12}{52}$, or $\frac{3}{13}$. The probability of selecting a queen from a full deck is $\frac{4}{52}$, or $\frac{1}{13}$, as a full card deck would contain four queen cards. To calculate the probability of an event NOT occurring, just subtract the probability of the event occurring from 1.

A bag contains only white, yellow, and purple cubes. There are a total of 40 cubes in the bag, and the probability of NOT selecting a yellow cube is $\frac{3}{4}$. How many yellow cubes are in the bag?

- **A.** 4
- **B.** 5
- **C.** 8
- **D.** 10
- **E.** 30

The correct answer is D. If the probability of NOT selecting a yellow cube is $\frac{3}{4}$, then the probability of selecting a yellow cube is $1 - \frac{3}{4} = \frac{1}{4}$. Let x represent the number of yellow cubes in the bag. Set up the following proportion to solve for x:

$$\frac{1}{4} = \frac{x}{40}$$
$$40 = 4x$$
$$10 = x$$

Therefore, there are 10 yellow cubes in the bag.

Determining Probability (Two Events)

To determine probability involving two or more events, it is important to distinguish probabilities involving independent events from an event that is dependent on another one.

Two events are independent if neither event affects the probability that the other will occur. The events may involve the random selection of one object from *each of two or more groups*. Alternatively, they may involve randomly selecting one object from a group, then *replacing* it and selecting again (as in a "second round" or "another turn" of a game).

In either scenario, to find the probability of two events BOTH occurring, multiply their individual probabilities together:

probability of event 1 occurring × probability of event 2 occurring

=

probability of both events occurring

For example, assume that you randomly select one letter from each of two sets: {A, B} and {C, D, E}. The probability of selecting A and C = $\frac{1}{2} \times \frac{1}{3} = \frac{1}{6}$.

To calculate the probability that two events will not both occur, subtract the probability of both events occurring from 1.

Now let's look at dependent probability. Two distinct events might be related in that one event affects the probability of the other one occurring—for example, randomly selecting one object from a group, then selecting a second object from the same group without replacing the first selection. Removing one object from the group increases the odds of selecting any particular object from those that remain.

For example, assume that you randomly select one letter from the set {A, B, C, D}. Then, from the remaining three letters, you select another letter. What is the probability of selecting both A and B? To answer this question, you need to consider each of the two selections separately.

In the first selection, the probability of selecting either A or B is $\frac{2}{4}$. But the probability of selecting the second of the two is $\frac{1}{3}$. Why? Because after the first selection, only *three* letters remain from which to select. Since the question asks for the odds of selecting both A and B (as opposed to either one), multiply the two individual probabilities: $\frac{2}{4} \times \frac{1}{3} = \frac{2}{12}$, or $\frac{1}{6}$.

SUMMING IT UP

- Both the Integrating Essential Skills and Preparing for Higher Math questions rely on keen understanding of numbers and operations; ratios, proportions, and percentages; algebra; geometry; and probability and statistics. IES questions will test these concepts individually or combine them to increase question complexity. The different sub-categories of PHM questions will draw on these concepts but also explore higher-level, related topics. Improving your score for ACT Mathematics requires a firm grasp of these fundamental mathematical concepts.

- Numbers and Operations topics represent fundamental math vocabulary and calculation procedures for performing basic operations—whether for working with basic calculations, fractions, exponents, absolute value, and more.

  - The greatest common factor (GCF) of two whole numbers n and m is the largest whole number that divides into both n and m evenly. The least common multiple (LCM) of two whole numbers n and m is the smallest whole number into which both n and m divide.

  - The order of operations when simplifying an expression is first parentheses, then exponents, then multiplication and division from left to right, and finally addition and subtraction from left to right.

  - If b and n are natural numbers, then $b^n = \underbrace{b \times \ldots \times b}_{n \text{ times}}$. Here, b is called the base and n is the exponent.

  - The square root of a nonnegative real number a is another number b whose square is a, that is $b^3 = a$. In such case, we write $\sqrt{a} = b$. A cube root of a real number a is another number b whose cube is a, that is $b^3 = a$. In such case, we write $\sqrt[3]{a} = b$.

  - The absolute value of a, denoted $|a|$, measures the distance between a and 0.

- Ratios, Decimals, Proportions, Rates, and Percentages represent ways of thinking about part-to-whole relationships. These concepts are all related and can be found together in some ACT IES questions.

  - A ratio is a comparison of one quantity x to another quantity y, expressed as a fraction $\dfrac{x}{y}$, or sometimes using the notation $x:y$. In words, this is interpreted as, "for every x of one type, there are y of the second type."

  - A proportion is an equation relating two ratios. In symbols, a proportion is expressed by setting two fractions equal to each other, say $\dfrac{a}{b} = \dfrac{c}{d}$.

  - The word percent means "per hundred." A percentage is used to express the number of parts of a whole.

- Basic Algebra questions will appear in the ACT Mathematics section to assess your understanding of how to manipulate basic expressions and equations.

- An algebraic expression is an arithmetic combination of terms. All of the rules (exponent rules, order of operations, etc.) and properties of arithmetic (commutative property, associative property, etc.) apply to algebraic expressions.

- Linear equations are equations in which the variable is raised to the first power. The process of solving linear equations involves simplifying various expressions by clearing fractions and using the order of operations and the distributive property of multiplication in order to get the variable on one side of the equation.

- A variable is an unknown quantity represented by a letter, like x, y, or z; a constant is a real number whose value does not change.

- Like terms are two or more terms that have the same variables.

• Basic Geometry problems will appear in IES questions to assess your knowledge of points, lines, angles, polygons (properties as well as calculations for perimeter, area, and volume), in addition to some essential knowledge of coordinate geometry.

- Points are defined positions on a plane, and they are often seen in both coordinate grids and planar figures.

- Lines are sequences of points that have indefinite lengths. Line segments have definite end points.

- Coordinate grids are divided into four quadrants, and points placed in these quadrants are given x and y coordinates.

- Quadrant I assigns positive x and y coordinates. Quadrant II assigns negative x and positive y coordinates. Quadrant III assigns negative x and y coordinates. Quadrant IV assigns positive x and negative y coordinates.

- The distance and midpoint formulas can be used to determine the distance between two points and the exact middle point of a line/line segment, respectively.

- The slope of a line is its steepness, calculated by dividing the rise (vertical change) over the run (horizontal change).

- Angles are classified according to their "size" or measure; the units in which this is expressed are degrees or radians.

- An angle with a measure between 0 and 90 degrees is acute.

- An angle with a measure of 90 degrees is a right angle.

- An angle with a measure between 90 and 180 degrees is obtuse.

- An angle with a measure of 180 degrees is a straight angle.

- Two angles with measures that sum to 90 degrees are complementary; two angles with measures that sum to 180 degrees are supplementary.

- Two angles that have the same measure are congruent. Vertical angles are always congruent.

- A right triangle is one that has a right angle; an acute triangle is one in which all three angles are acute; an obtuse triangle has one obtuse angle.

- An equilateral triangle is one in which all three sides have the same length; an isosceles triangle has at least two sides with the same length; a scalene triangle has three sides of different lengths.

- The triangle sum rule says that the sum of the measures of the three angles in any triangle must be 180. The triangle inequality says that the sum of the lengths of any two sides of a triangle must be strictly larger than the length of the third side.

- The Pythagorean theorem states that for a right triangle with legs a and b and hypotenuse c, $a^2 + b^2 = c^2$.

- Two triangles $\triangle ABC$ and $\triangle DEF$ are congruent if all three corresponding pairs of angles are congruent AND all three corresponding sides are congruent. Two triangles $\triangle ABC$ and $\triangle DEF$ are similar if the ratios of the three pairs of corresponding sides are the same; that is, $\dfrac{AB}{DE} = \dfrac{BC}{EF} = \dfrac{AC}{DF} = k$, where k is a positive number.

- The area formula for a triangle with base b and height h is $A = \dfrac{1}{2} b \cdot h$.

- Two quadrilaterals of the same type are congruent if their corresponding sides are all congruent, and they are called similar if the four ratios of their corresponding sides are equal.

- The perimeter of a square with side length s is $P = 4s$. The area of a square with side length s is $A = s^2$.

- The perimeter of a rectangle with length l and width w is $P = 2l + 2w$. The area of a rectangle with length l and width w is $A = lw$.

- The circumference of a circle with radius r (or diameter $d = 2r$) is $C = 2\pi r = \pi d$. The area of a circle with radius r is $A = \pi r^2$.

- The volume of a cube with side length s is $V = s^3$.

- The volume of a rectangular box with side lengths l, w, and h is $V = lwh$.

- The volume of a cylinder with base radius r and height h is $V = \pi r^2 h$.

- Basic Statistics and Probability topics will appear to check your understanding of basic measures of center (mean, median, and mode) and your grasp of how to calculate simple probability.

  - An outcome is the result of a single trial of a probability experiment.

  - The probability of an event A, denoted by $P(A)$, is a number between 0 and 1, inclusive, that describes the percent chance that event A has of occurring.

  - If each outcome in the sample space is equally likely and the sample space contains N outcomes, then the probability of any one of them occurring is $\dfrac{1}{N}$.

  - This can be extended to events in the sense that if A contains k elements, then $$P(A) = \frac{\text{Number of outcomes in } A}{\text{Number of possible outcomes}} = \frac{k}{N}.$$

  - To compute the mean of a list of numbers, simply add the numbers and divide by how many numbers are added: $\text{mean} = \dfrac{\text{sum of values}}{\text{number of values}}$.

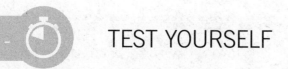

TEST YOURSELF

INTEGRATING ESSENTIAL SKILLS

20 Questions—20 Minutes

Directions: Solve each problem and choose the correct answer.

Do not dwell on problems that take too long. First, solve as many as you can; then, you can return to others you have left.

You are permitted to use a calculator. You may use your calculator for any problem you like, but some of the problems may best be completed without a calculator.

Note: Unless otherwise states, all of the following should be assumed.

1. Illustrative figures are NOT necessarily drawn to scale.
2. Geometric figures lie in a plane.
3. The word *line* indicates a straight line.
4. The word *average* indicates arithmetic mean.

---

1. If $\dfrac{n}{4}$ and $\dfrac{n}{14}$ are both integers, all of the following could be n EXCEPT:

   A. 56
   B. 70
   C. 112
   D. 168
   E. 224

2. In order to set up the internet connection in a computer lab, the following amounts of cable are needed for each computer in the lab:

   2 cables, each measuring 3 feet

   3 cables, each measuring 9 inches

   1 wire, measuring 5 feet

   If the room requires 25 computers and cable costs $0.15 per inch, approximately how much will it cost to set up the computers for the lab?

   F. $23.85
   G. $72
   H. $159
   J. $596.25
   K. $3,975

3. A board game involves a spinner with congruent sections numbered 1 through 25. On a given spin, the spinner has an equal chance of landing on any number. What is the probability that the spinner will land on a number that is divisible by 3?

   A. $\dfrac{17}{25}$

   B. $\dfrac{14}{25}$

   C. $\dfrac{8}{25}$

   D. $\dfrac{7}{25}$

   E. $\dfrac{3}{25}$

4. If x is a real number such that $x^3 = 160$, between which two consecutive integers does x lie on the number line?

   F. 2 and 3

   G. 3 and 4

   H. 4 and 5

   J. 5 and 6

   K. 6 and 7

5. Phillip answered 4 of the 35 questions on his driving exam incorrectly. What percentage of the questions did Phillip answer correctly?

   A. $\dfrac{4}{35} \times 100\%$

   B. $\dfrac{31}{35} \times 100\%$

   C. $\dfrac{4}{35 \times 100}\%$

   D. $\dfrac{31}{35 \times 100}\%$

   E. $\dfrac{31}{100\%} \times 35$

6. Increasing a positive number by 40% and then decreasing the result by 30% is the same as which of the following?

   F. Increasing the original number by 10%

   G. Increasing the original number by 12%

   H. Decreasing the original number by 12%

   J. Increasing the original number by 2%

   K. Decreasing the original number by 2%

7. If $3x + 2 = 9x + 14$, then $4x^3 =$

   A. −108

   B. −32

   C. −24

   D. −2

   E. 32

8. For real numbers a, b, and c, $a < b$ and $c < 0$. Which of the following inequalities MUST be true?

   F. $ab > 0$

   G. $ac < 0$

   H. $a + c < 0$

   J. $\dfrac{a}{c} > \dfrac{b}{c}$

   K. $\dfrac{a}{c} < \dfrac{b}{c}$

9. What is the value of $m^2 - 6mn^3 + n$ when $m = -2$ and $n = -1$?

   A. −17

   B. −13

   C. −9

   D. 9

   E. 17

10. A lab technician took a measurement of new rainfall once a day during a five-day work week. The table below indicates how many inches of new rainfall were recorded on each day.

Day	Inches of New Rainfall
Monday	1.0
Tuesday	1.5
Wednesday	0
Thursday	1.0
Friday	0.5

What is the average number of inches per day for this work week?

F. 4

G. 1

H. 0.8

J. 0.4

K. 0

11. Suppose $m < n < 0$. Which of these ordered pairs cannot be in Quadrant III of the xy-plane?

A. $(n, m + n)$

B. $(m - n, m - n)$

C. $(n, m - 1)$

D. (n^{-1}, m^{-1})

E. $\left(\dfrac{m}{n}, m \right)$

12. Assume $a > 0$. Which of these expressions represents the distance between the points $P(-a, 2a)$ and $Q(-3a, -2a)$?

F. $2a$ units

G. $a\sqrt{2}$ units

H. $2a\sqrt{5}$ units

J. $2a^2$ units

K. $20a^2$ units

13. The measure of angle A is 6 degrees less than twice the measure of angle B. If angles A and B are complementary, what is the measure of angle A?

A. 32°

B. 58°

C. 28°

D. 62°

E. 118°

14. Assume lines l and m are parallel in the diagram below. Determine the value of $y + x$.

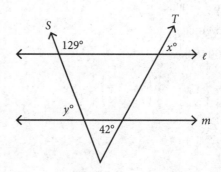

F. 42

G. 51

H. 93

J. 171

K. 189

15. Which expression represents the length of CD in the rectangle ABCD?

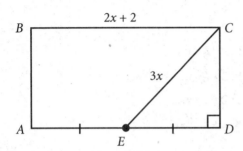

A. $2x - 1$

B. $4x + 1$

C. $8x^2 - 2x - 1$

D. $\sqrt{8x^2 - 2x - 1}$

E. $\sqrt{10x^2 + 2x + 1}$

16. The area of a square is 80 square inches. What is its perimeter?

F. $4\sqrt{5}$ inches

G. $4\sqrt{10}$ inches

H. $16\sqrt{5}$ inches

J. 160 inches

K. 400 inches

17. Solve for x: $-\dfrac{1}{3}\left(3 - \dfrac{4}{3}x\right) = -3x$

A. $-\dfrac{9}{23}$

B. $\dfrac{9}{31}$

C. $\dfrac{9}{23}$

D. $\dfrac{9}{13}$

E. $\dfrac{9}{7}$

18. Suppose x is a negative integer. Which of these has the greatest value?

F. $2x$

G. $\dfrac{1}{2}x$

H. $|x|$

J. $|1 - x|$

K. $|x^{-1}|$

19. Compute: $\left(1 - \big|8 - 3\big| - 4\big|\right)^2$

A. -6

B. -15

C. 9

D. 25

E. 361

20. What is the sum of the polynomials $4ab^3 + 3a^2b^3$ and $-a^2b - 2a^2b^3$?

F. $4ab^3 - a^2b + 5a^2b^3$

G. $3ab^3 + a^2b^3$

H. $3ab^3 + 5a^2b^3$

J. $4ab^3 - a^2b + a^2b^3$

K. $4ab^3 + a^3b + 5a^3b^3$

ANSWER KEY AND EXPLANATIONS

1. B	5. B	9. C	13. B	17. B
2. J	6. K	10. H	14. H	18. J
3. C	7. B	11. E	15. D	19. C
4. J	8. J	12. H	16. H	20. J

1. **The correct answer is B.** Since $\dfrac{n}{4}$ and $\dfrac{n}{14}$ are both integers, then n must be divisible by both 4 and 14. The question asks for the one value that does not satisfy this condition, so you are looking for the one choice that is not divisible by both 4 and 14. Since it is difficult to do this by inspection, start with the first answer choice and move through the list until you find the correct number.

2. **The correct answer is J.** First, get the total inches for each type of cable. Two 3-foot cables are 2 × 3 = 6 feet, which converts to 6 × 12 = 72 inches. Three 9-inch cables are 3 × 9 = 27 inches. And the last cable is 5 × 12 = 60 inches. Adding together the inches for all cables gives 72 + 27 + 60 = 159 inches of cable needed to connect one computer to the internet. At a cost of $0.15 per inch, the cost of connecting one computer in the lab to the internet is 159($0.15) = $23.85. Hence, the cost of connecting all 25 computers to the internet is 25($23.85) = $596.25.

3. **The correct answer is C.** There are a total of 25 numbers on the wheel, so we must determine how many of these 25 numbers are divisible by 3. Writing them down, we see that 3, 6, 9, 12, 15, 18, 21, and 24 are precisely the numbers from 1 to 25 that are divisible by 3. Since there are 8 of them and 25 numbers in all, the probability that the number on which the spinner lands is divisible by 3 is $\dfrac{8}{25}$.

4. **The correct answer is J.** The problem is asking you to find two consecutive integers, the first of which has a cube less than 160, and the second of which has a cube greater than 160. Use the answer choices to help you. The cubes of 2, 3, 4, 5, and 6 are, respectively: 8, 27, 64, 125, and 216. Since 160 falls between 125 and 216, you know that x is between 5 and 6,

and you do not need to go any further. As such, the other choices are not possible.

5. **The correct answer is B.** If Phillip answered 4 of the 35 questions incorrectly, then he answered 35 − 4 = 31 correctly. By definition, the percentage is equal to $\dfrac{\text{part}}{\text{whole}} \times 100\%$. So Phillip answered $\dfrac{31}{35} \times 100\%$ of the questions correctly.

6. **The correct answer is K.** Let x represent some number. Increasing the number by 40% produces the new number $(1 + 0.40)x = 1.40x$. Now, decreasing this result by 30% means to subtract 30% of $1.40x$ from $1.40x$: $(0.30)(1.40x) = 0.42x$, and subtracting this from $1.40x$ yields $0.98x$. So, comparing this to the original number x shows that the end result is $0.02x$ less than x. You could have decreased the number by 2% to arrive at the same result.

7. **The correct answer is B.** First, solve the given equation for x:

$$3x + 2 = 9x + 14$$
$$2 = 6x + 14$$
$$-12 = 6x$$
$$-2 = x$$

Now, evaluate $4x^3$ at $x = -2$ to get $4(-2)^3 = 4(-8) = -32$.

8. **The correct answer is J.** If you divide both sides of the inequality $a < b$ by c, since c is negative, you must reverse the inequality sign when doing so. This yields the inequality $\dfrac{a}{c} > \dfrac{b}{c}$.

9. **The correct answer is C.** Plug the given values of m and n into the expression and evaluate:

$$m^2 - 6mn^3 + n = (-2)^2 - 6(-2)(-1)^3 + (-1)$$
$$= 4 - 6(-2)(-1) - 1$$
$$= 4 - 12 - 1$$
$$= -8 - 1$$
$$= -9$$

10. **The correct answer is H.** Remember that
average $= \dfrac{\text{sum of values}}{\text{number of values}}$. To find the average number of inches of rainfall per day for this data, divide the total number of inches of rainfall for the week by the number of days, 5:

$$\frac{(1.0+1.5+0+1.0+0.5)}{5} = \frac{4.0}{5} = 0.8$$

So the mean daily rainfall is 0.8 inches.

11. **The correct answer is E.** To be in Quadrant III, both the x- and y-coordinates must be negative. In choice E, $\dfrac{m}{n}$ is positive because it is the quotient of two negative real numbers. Since $m < 0$, the points are always in Quadrant IV.

12. **The correct answer is H.** You must use the distance formula to solve this question. Many of the distractors are the results of either forgetting part of the formula (like the radical sign, as in choice K), subtracting the wrong coordinates (as in choice G), or making a combination of those errors (as in choice J).

Applying the formula and simplifying yields the following:

$$\sqrt{\left(-a-(-3a)\right)^2 + \left(2a-(-2a)\right)^2} = \sqrt{\left(-a+3a\right)^2 + \left(2a+2a\right)^2}$$

$$= \sqrt{\left(2a\right)^2 + \left(4a\right)^2}$$

$$= \sqrt{4a^2 + 16a^2}$$

$$= \sqrt{20a^2}$$

$$= 2a\sqrt{5}$$

13. **The correct answer is B.** Since you are given how two angles are related but do not know the measure of either one, you need to call one of them x. Since angle A is defined in terms of angle B, the better choice is to give the name x to the measure of angle B. Then, the measure of angle A is $2x - 6$.

Being complementary angles, the sum of their measures is 90°. This gives the equation $x + (2x - 6) = 90$. Solve for x, as follows:

$$x + (2x - 6) = 90$$
$$3x - 6 = 90$$
$$3x = 96$$
$$x = 32$$

The measure of angle A is $2(32) - 6 = 58°$.

14. **The correct answer is H.** The strategy here is to fill in several of the missing angles using various facts about how corresponding angles and vertical angles are related, as well as supplementary angles. Do so in the order shown in the following diagram, starting with the circled number 1 and proceeding to circled number 4:

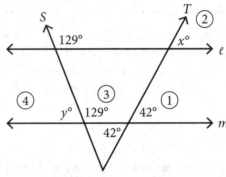

Step 1: Vertical angles are always congruent. So this angle measures 42°.

Step 2: Since lines l and m are parallel, you can use line T as a transversal. Then, corresponding angles are congruent, so that the angle has a measure of 42°.

Step 3: Since lines l and m are parallel, you can use line S as a transversal. Then, corresponding angles are congruent, so that the angle has a measure of 129°.

Step 4: This angle is supplementary to angle 3, so that it measures 180° − 129° = 51°.

Thus, $x = 42$ and $y = 51$. So $x + y = 93$.

15. **The correct answer is D.** This problem can be intimidating at first glance. But if you break it down into small steps, it is not so difficult. Here is the thought process. If you had the length of ED, then you could use the Pythagorean theorem to find CD. Segments AE and ED have the same number of hash marks, which means they are congruent. Since $ABCD$ is a rectangle, AD and BC are congruent. So ED must be half the length of BC, or $\dfrac{1}{2}(2x+2) = x+1$. Now you can use the Pythagorean theorem to find ED:

$$(EC)^2 = (CD)^2 + (ED)^2$$
$$(3x)^2 = (CD)^2 + (x+1)^2$$
$$(CD)^2 = (3x)^2 - (x+1)^2$$
$$(CD)^2 = 9x^2 - (x^2 + 2x + 1)$$
$$(CD)^2 = 8x^2 - 2x - 1$$
$$CD = \sqrt{8x^2 - 2x - 1}$$

16. **The correct answer is H.** To find the perimeter of the square, all you need is the length of a side, s. You are given the area is 80 square inches. Since the area of a square is s^2, this gives the equation $s^2 = 80$. Taking the square root of both sides yields $s = \sqrt{80} = 4\sqrt{5}$ inches, so the perimeter is $4(4\sqrt{5}) = 16\sqrt{5}$ inches.

17. **The correct answer is B.** Generally, getting rid of fractions in an equation as soon as possible is preferable. Here, multiply both sides by –3 to get rid of the leftmost fraction on the left side:

$$(-3) \cdot -\frac{1}{3}\left(3 - \frac{4}{3}x\right) = (-3) \cdot (-3x)$$
$$3 - \frac{4}{3}x = 9x$$

Now, multiply both sides by 3 again to get rid of the remaining fraction:

$$3 \cdot \left(3 - \frac{4}{3}x\right) = 3 \cdot (9x)$$
$$9 - 4x = 27x$$

Now add $4x$ to both sides to gather the x terms on one side of the equation $9 = 31x$; make sure you do not subtract it, or you will get choice B. Finally, divide both sides by the coefficient of x to get $x = \frac{9}{31}$.

18. **The correct answer is J.** Try to eliminate as many choices as possible right off the bat. Since we know that x is negative, we can eliminate choices A and B because both $2x$ and $\frac{1}{2}x$ are negative. The remaining three choices (H, J, and K) are all positive. We can eliminate choice K because $\left|x^{-1}\right| = \left|\frac{1}{x}\right|$, and since x is an integer, it follows that this is no greater than 1 no matter what x-value is chosen, while $|x|$ is at least equal to 1. But

how do you choose between choices H and J? Plug in some values of x to help guide your thinking:

x	$|x|$	$|1 - x|$
–2	2	$|1 - (-2)| = |3| = 3$
–4	4	$|1 - (-4)| = |1 + 4| = 5$
–9	9	$|1 - (-9)| = |1 + 9| = 10$

While you might have instinctively thought that $|x|$ (choice H) was larger because you were subtracting inside $|1 - x|$, it turns out that $|1 - x|$ (choice J) gives the largest value.

19. **The correct answer is C.** Before computing anything, realize that the whole quantity is the square of an expression. Therefore, it cannot be negative. You can eliminate choices A and B right away. You must use the order of operations when simplifying arithmetic expressions, but where does the absolute value fit into the hierarchy? Treat this as you would any other grouping symbol. Start from the innermost grouping symbol and work your way outward:

$$\left(1 - \left|8 - 3\underbrace{\left|-4\right|}_{\substack{\text{Compute} \\ \text{this first}}}\right|\right)^2 = \left(1 - \left|\underbrace{8 - 3 \cdot 4}_{\substack{\text{Now, compute this} \\ \text{following the order} \\ \text{of operations}}}\right|\right)^2$$

$$= \left(1 - |8 - 12|\right)^2$$
$$= \left(1 - \underbrace{\left|-4\right|}_{\text{Now this}}\right)^2$$
$$= (1 - 4)^2$$
$$= (-3)^2$$
$$= 9$$

20. **The correct answer is J.** Do not be thrown by the variables—simply combine like terms. In the expression $(4ab^3 + 3a^2b^3) + (-a^2b - 2a^2b^3)$, there are two multiples of a^2b^3. Since $3a^2b^3 + (-2a^2b^3) = a^2b^3$, the entire expression simplifies to $4ab^3 - a^2b + a^2b^3$.

CHAPTER

**Preparing for Higher Math:
Number & Quantity**

PREPARING FOR HIGHER MATH:

OVERVIEW

Number Properties

Radical and Rational Exponents

Imaginary and Complex Numbers

Matrices

Vectors

Summing It Up

Test Yourself: PHM – Number & Quantity

Preparing for Higher Math: Number & Quantity questions represent the smallest portion of the PHM category on the ACT, comprising approximately five questions per test. These questions draw on some fundamental math knowledge related to numbers and number systems (like types of numbers and exponent rules) but can also probe into less common numerical quantities. You may see questions about unit conversions, imaginary and complex numbers, vectors, and matrices. The chapter will reintroduce some concepts from Chapter 9 while also expanding upon them. At the end of the chapter, you'll find a Test Yourself that will assess your understanding of Number & Quantity question topics.

NUMBER & QUANTITY

NUMBER PROPERTIES

Because of the terminology that is used for some questions on the ACT, it is important to understand the differences between different number types in mathematics, as well as key terms in standard math vocabulary.

Real Numbers

Real numbers represent all rational and irrational numbers. Rational numbers also encompass natural numbers and integers (what can be described as whole numbers).

Natural Numbers

The set of natural numbers consists of the numbers 1, 2, 3, 4... The result when at least two natural numbers are multiplied is called a product and each number in the list being multiplied is a factor or divisor. A natural number is a multiple of each of its factors. For instance, in the expression $2 \times 5 \times 7 = 70$, 70 is the product; 2, 5, and 7 are factors of 70; and 70 is a multiple of 2, 5, and 7.

A natural number other than 1 is prime if it can only be written as a product of itself and 1; otherwise, it is composite.

Every composite number can be written as a product of prime numbers; the product is the prime factorization of the number. For instance, $56 = 2 \times 2 \times 2 \times 7$, or more succinctly, $56 = 2^3 \times 7$.

The following divisibility rules are useful when determining factors of a natural number.

NATURAL NUMBERS AND DIVISION	
Natural Number	A natural number n is divisible by the number in the left column if...
2	The number n ends in 0, 2, 4, 6, or 8.
3	The digit sum of n (i.e., the sum of all digits in the numeral n) is divisible by 3.
4	The last two numbers of n, taken as a number in and of itself, is divisible by 4.
5	The number n ends in 0 or 5.
6	The number n is divisible by both 2 and 3.
9	The digit sum of n is divisible by 9.
10	The number n ends in 0.

For instance, 459 is divisible by 3 because the digit sum ($4 + 5 + 9 = 18$) is divisible by 3. The greatest common factor (GCF) of two natural numbers x and y is the *largest* natural number that is a factor of both x and y, while the least common multiple (LCM) of x and y is the *smallest* natural number that is a multiple of both x and y. For instance, the GCF of 32 and 56 is 8. The LCM is 224.

Integers

The set of integers is comprised of the natural numbers, their negatives, and 0: $\{\ldots, -3, -2, -1, 0, 1, 2, 3 \ldots\}$.

The following rules and terminology are useful when working with integers:

- $-(-a) = a$, for any integer a.
- $a - (-b) = a + b$, for any integers a, b.
- A product of two negative integers is positive.
- A product of one positive and one negative integer is negative.
- An integer is *even* if it is a multiple of 2, while it is *odd* if it is not a multiple of 2. Any even number can be written as $2n$, where n is an integer, and an odd number can be written as $2n + 1$, where n is an integer.

Rational Numbers and Irrational Numbers

Real numbers encompass both rational and irrational numbers. A rational number is a quotient of two integers, denoted by $\frac{a}{b}$, where $b \neq 0$. Such a fraction is simplified if a and b do not share common factors. If $a \neq 0$, the reciprocal of $\frac{a}{b}$ can be computed by flipping the fraction over to get $\frac{b}{a}$. To get the reciprocal of a mixed number, first convert it to an improper fraction (one with a numerator greater than its denominator) and flip *that* fraction over. As the name implies, an irrational number is a real number that is not rational. An irrational number is a real number that cannot be written as a simple fraction. Some common examples are square roots of prime numbers, π, and e. Irrational numbers can be formed by performing arithmetic combinations of pairs of rational and irrational numbers:

- The sum of two positive irrational numbers is a positive irrational number.
- The sum of two negative irrational numbers is a negative irrational number.
- The product of a nonzero rational number and an irrational number is an irrational number.
- The sum or difference of a rational number and an irrational number is an irrational number.

RADICAL AND RATIONAL EXPONENTS

Number & Quantity questions will make use of fundamental rules for exponents. At the same time, you'll also need to understand how to work with radicals and rational exponents in increasingly complex scenarios.

Positive and Negative Exponents

You know that an exponent represents the number of times that a number (referred to as the "base number") is multiplied by itself. Working with exponent problems requires knowing a few rules, as shown in the following table.

RULES FOR EXPONENTS	
Product	$a^m a^n = a^{m+n}$
Product of a power	$(a^m)^n = a^{mn}$
Quotient to a power	$\left(\dfrac{a}{b}\right)^n = \dfrac{a^n}{b^n}$
Quotient	$\dfrac{a^m}{a^n} = a^{m-n}$
Zero exponent	$a^0 = 1$
Negative exponent	$a^{-n} = \dfrac{1}{a^n}$
Inversion	$\left(\dfrac{a}{b}\right)^{-n} = \left(\dfrac{b}{a}\right)^n$
Fractional powers	$a^{\frac{m}{n}} = \sqrt[n]{a^m}$

Here is an example that demonstrates several of these rules:

Simplify the expression: $\left(\dfrac{x^2 y^4}{x^{-1} y}\right)^{-2}$

Here, apply the rules for exponents within the parentheses and then apply the -2 power. Note that a variable with no exponent is assumed to have an exponent of 1:

$$\left(\frac{x^2 y^4}{x^{-1} y}\right)^{-2} = \left(x^{2-(-1)} y^{4-1}\right)^{-2}$$

$$= \left(x^3 y^3\right)^{-2}$$

$$= x^{-6} y^{-6}$$

$$= \frac{1}{x^6 y^6}$$

COMMON ERRORS WHEN WORKING WITH EXPONENTS

Error	Interpretation
$-a^2 \neq -(a)^2$ $(-1)a^2 \neq (-a)(-a)$	If the negative sign is inside the parentheses of a quantity being squared, then the square applies to it. Otherwise, it does not.
$(a + b)^n \neq a^n + b^n$	The power of a sum is not equal to the sum of the powers.
$\dfrac{a^n}{b^m} \neq \left(\dfrac{a}{b}\right)^{n-m}$	You cannot write the quotient of terms with different bases raised to different powers as a single quotient raised to a power.
$a^n \cdot b^n \neq (a \cdot b)^{n+m}$	You cannot write the product of terms with different bases raised to different powers as a single product raised to a power.

PRACTICE

Which of the following is equivalent to $(-4x^3)^2$?

A. $-4x^5$

B. $-3x^6$

C. $-16x^6$

D. $8x^6$

E. $16x^6$

The correct answer is E. For this problem, it is important to remember the rules of exponents. When a product is raised to a power, each of the terms must be raised to that power. So $(-4x^3)^2$ is equal to $(-4)^2 \times (x^3)^2$. When a power is raised to another power, you multiply the exponents. So $(-4)^2 \times (x^3)^2$ is equal to $(-4)^2 \times (x^6)$. Now evaluate: $(-4)^2 \times (x^6) = 16 \times (x^6) = 16x^6$. In choice A, note that $(a^b)^c \neq a^{b+c}$; you must apply the exponent to the coefficient, -4, as well. Choice B is incorrect because you must apply the exponent to the coefficient, -4. In choice C, you forgot to square the -1. In choice D, $(-4)^2 = (-4)(-4)$, you do not multiply the base times the exponent.

Roots and Radicals

You know that a radical sign signifies square root and looks like this: $\sqrt{}$. The following are useful properties of radicals to master before you take the ACT.

PROPERTIES OF RADICALS

Radical Rule (in symbols)	Interpretation
$\left(\sqrt{a}\right)^2 = a, \left(\sqrt[3]{a}\right)^3 = a$	Raising an nth root to the nth power gives back the original radicand.
$\sqrt{a \cdot b} = \sqrt{a} \cdot \sqrt{b}$, when a ≥ 0 and b ≥ 0.	The square root of a product is the product of the square roots.
$\sqrt{\dfrac{a}{b}} = \dfrac{\sqrt{a}}{\sqrt{b}}$, when a ≥ 0 and b > 0.	The square root of a quotient is the quotient of the square roots.
$\dfrac{1}{\sqrt{a}} = \dfrac{1}{\sqrt{a}} \cdot \dfrac{\sqrt{a}}{\sqrt{a}} = \dfrac{\sqrt{a}}{a}$, when a > 0.	You can clear a square root from the denominator of a fraction by multiplying the numerator and denominator of the fraction by the square root. (This is often called "multiplying by the conjugate" or "rationalizing the denominator.")
If $0 < a < b$, then $\sqrt{a} < \sqrt{b}$.	If a is less than b, then you can take the square root on both sides of the inequality without having to reverse the sign.

Adding and Subtracting Radical Expressions

To simplify an integer under a radical, you can break it into its factors. The initial factors you choose will affect how many steps you need in order to reach a simplified form. Observe the following example factored in different ways.

$$\sqrt{72} = \sqrt{2\cdot36} = \sqrt{2\cdot2\cdot18} = \sqrt{2\cdot2\cdot2\cdot9} = 2\sqrt{2\cdot9} = 2\cdot3\sqrt{2} = 6\sqrt{2}$$
$$\sqrt{72} = \sqrt{2\cdot4\cdot9} = \sqrt{2}\cdot\sqrt{4}\cdot\sqrt{9} = \sqrt{2}\cdot2\cdot3 = 6\sqrt{2}$$
$$\sqrt{72} = \sqrt{3\cdot24} = \sqrt{3\cdot3\cdot8} = 3\sqrt{2\cdot4} = 3\cdot2\sqrt{2} = 6\sqrt{2}$$
$$\sqrt{72} = \sqrt{9}\cdot\sqrt{8} = 3\sqrt{4\cdot2} = 3\cdot2\sqrt{2} = 6\sqrt{2}$$
$$\sqrt{72} = \sqrt{2\cdot36} = 6\sqrt{2}$$

Note that selecting a factor that is a perfect square will allow you to reduce the amount of work you need to perform. In the first example, if we had not continued the prime factorization, we would have been able to simplify to $6\sqrt{2}$ after the first step (36 is a perfect square).

If the terms you want to add have the same radical parts, just add or subtract the coefficients:

$$2\sqrt{5} - 6\sqrt{5} =$$
$$(2-6)\sqrt{5} = -4\sqrt{5}$$

However, terms that have different radical parts cannot be combined:

$$3\sqrt{5} + 4\sqrt{7} - 9\sqrt{5} =$$
$$(3-9)\sqrt{5} + 4\sqrt{7} = -6\sqrt{5} + 4\sqrt{7}$$

Here is another example that involves a rational expression:

Simplify $\dfrac{56\sqrt{7}}{28\sqrt{42}}$.

For this example, you can apply the rules of multiplying fractions to simplify this expression:

$$\frac{56\sqrt{7}}{28\sqrt{42}} = \frac{2\cdot28\sqrt{7}}{28\sqrt{7\cdot6}} = \frac{2\sqrt{7}}{\sqrt{7}\cdot\sqrt{6}} = \frac{2}{\sqrt{6}}$$

Then, you can rationalize the denominator (removing its root symbol) by multiplying the numerator and denominator by $\sqrt{6}$:

$$\underbrace{\frac{56\sqrt{7}}{28\sqrt{42}} = \frac{2}{\sqrt{6}}}_{\text{From above}} = \underbrace{\frac{2}{\sqrt{6}}\cdot\frac{\sqrt{6}}{\sqrt{6}}}_{\substack{\text{Rationalizing the}\\\text{denominator}}} = \frac{2\sqrt{6}}{6} = \frac{\sqrt{6}}{3}$$

Estimating roots, such as $\sqrt{47}$ and $\sqrt[3]{11}$, can be tricky. For instance, it's not easy to compute $\sqrt{47}$. In a case like this, you can determine numbers with more obvious square roots on either side of 47.

You know that $6^2 = 36$ and tha $7^2 = 49$. Further, you know that $36 < 47 < 49$. Therefore, you know $\underset{=6}{\sqrt{36}} < \sqrt{47} < \underset{=7}{\sqrt{49}}$, so that $6 < \sqrt{47} < 7$. The answer to $\sqrt{47}$ must lie somewhere between 6 and 7.

Fractional Exponents

Recall that for fractional exponents the following notation is used:

$$\sqrt{a} = a^{\frac{1}{2}}$$
$$\sqrt[3]{a} = a^{\frac{1}{3}}$$
$$\vdots$$
$$\sqrt[n]{a} = a^{\frac{1}{n}}$$

 TIP

A common error is to apply the radical to each individual term of a sum. Note that the square root of a sum is not the sum of the square roots. In this example, note that $-6\sqrt{5} + 4\sqrt{7} \neq (-6+4)\sqrt{5+7}$! The same goes for cube roots.

We also have a more general definition:

$$\sqrt[n]{a^m} = (a^m)^{\frac{1}{n}} = a^{\left(m \cdot \frac{1}{n}\right)} = \left(a^{\frac{1}{n}}\right)^m = a^{\frac{m}{n}}$$

Let's look at a more complex example of fractional exponents in action.

Simplify the expression $\dfrac{x^{\frac{1}{2}} y^2}{x^{\frac{2}{3}} y^{\frac{1}{2}}}$.

Write your answer as a radical expression.

First, apply the rules for exponents. Then apply the rule that $x^{\frac{m}{n}} = \sqrt[n]{x^m}$:

$$\frac{x^{\frac{1}{2}} y^2}{x^{\frac{2}{3}} y^{\frac{1}{2}}} = x^{\frac{1}{2} - \frac{2}{3}} y^{2 - \frac{1}{2}} = x^{-\frac{1}{6}} y^{\frac{3}{2}} = \frac{y^{\frac{3}{2}}}{x^{\frac{1}{6}}} = \frac{\sqrt{y^3}}{\sqrt[6]{x}}$$

This expression can be simplified further.

Since $y^3 = y \cdot y^2$ and $\sqrt{y^2} = y$, we can write:

$$\frac{\sqrt{y^3}}{\sqrt[6]{x}} = \frac{\sqrt{y \cdot y^2}}{\sqrt[6]{x}} = \frac{y\sqrt{y}}{\sqrt[6]{x}}$$

The following table provides useful rules for working with radical expressions:

Radical Expression Laws

$$\sqrt[n]{a} = a^{\frac{1}{n}}$$

$$a^{\frac{m}{n}} = \sqrt[n]{a^m}$$

$$\sqrt[n]{a} \cdot \sqrt[n]{b} = \sqrt[n]{ab}$$

$$\sqrt[n]{\frac{a}{b}} = \frac{\sqrt[n]{a}}{\sqrt[n]{b}}$$

$$\sqrt[nm]{a} = \sqrt[m]{\sqrt[n]{a}}$$

$$\sqrt[n]{a^n} = a$$

Now, look at the following examples of arithmetic expressions involving radicals:

1. $\left(3\sqrt{5}\right)^2 = $ _____

$$\left(3\sqrt{5}\right)^2 = 3^2 \cdot \left(\sqrt{5}\right)^2$$
$$= 9 \cdot 5$$
$$= 45$$

2. $\left(4 + \sqrt{3}\right)\left(5 - \sqrt{3}\right) = $ _____

$$\left(4 + \sqrt{3}\right)\left(5 - \sqrt{3}\right) = (4 \cdot 5) - (4 \cdot \sqrt{3}) + (5 \cdot \sqrt{3}) - \left(\sqrt{3}\right)\left(\sqrt{3}\right)$$
$$= 20 - 4\sqrt{3} + 5\sqrt{3} - 3$$
$$= 20 + \sqrt{3} - 3$$
$$= 17 + \sqrt{3}$$

The same rules used in the previous examples can also be used to simplify more complicated algebraic expressions involving radicals.

Try your hand at the following examples:

EXAMPLE

Suppose that x, y, and z are positive real numbers. Simplify the following radical expression:

$$\sqrt{8x^8 y^2 z^3} = $$ _____

Solution

Two properties are at play here, namely $\sqrt{a \cdot b} = \sqrt{a} \cdot \sqrt{b}$ and $\sqrt{a^2} = a$ whenever a > 0. The idea is to express the radicand as a product of squared terms and everything that is left over. Employing that strategy, we see that:

$$\sqrt{8x^8 y^2 z^3} = \sqrt{2} \cdot \sqrt{4} \cdot \sqrt{\left(x^4\right)^2} \cdot \sqrt{y^2} \cdot \sqrt{z^2} \cdot \sqrt{z}$$
$$= \sqrt{2} \cdot 2 \cdot \left(x^4\right) \cdot y \cdot z \cdot \sqrt{z}$$
$$= 2 \cdot x^4 \cdot y \cdot z \cdot \sqrt{2} \cdot \sqrt{z}$$
$$= 2 \cdot x^4 \cdot y \cdot z \cdot \sqrt{2z}$$
$$= 2x^4 yz\sqrt{2z}$$

Suppose that x, y, and z are positive real numbers. Simplify the following radical expression:

$$\frac{\sqrt{64x^3y^5}}{xy\sqrt{y}} = \underline{\hspace{2cm}}$$

Solution

This problem is similar to the previous example, but now we need to simplify a rational expression. We have:

$$\frac{\sqrt{64x^{3y^5}}}{xy\sqrt{y}} = \frac{\sqrt{8^2 x^2 \cdot x \cdot y^4 \cdot y}}{xy\sqrt{y}}$$

$$= \frac{8x \cdot y^2 \cdot \sqrt{xy}}{x \cdot y \cdot \sqrt{y}}$$

$$= \frac{8\cancel{x} \cdot y^{\cancel{2}}\sqrt{x} \cdot \cancel{\sqrt{y}}}{\cancel{x} \cdot \cancel{y} \cdot \cancel{\sqrt{y}}}$$

$$= 8y\sqrt{x}$$

Simplify the following algebraic expression involving radicals:

$$2\sqrt{a^5b^3c} \cdot \sqrt{abc^2} = \underline{\hspace{2cm}}$$

Solution

Use the following steps for each expression:

$$2\sqrt{a^5b^3c} \cdot \sqrt{abc^2} = 2\sqrt{\left(a^5b^3c\right)\cdot\left(abc^2\right)}$$

$$= 2\sqrt{a^6b^4c^3}$$

$$= 2a^3b^2c\sqrt{c}$$

IMAGINARY AND COMPLEX NUMBERS

Number & Quantity questions are interested in assessing your ability to work with a variety of different number forms, including complex numbers, which have both real and imaginary components.

Powers of *i*

The imaginary number *i* is a variable that stands in for the value $\sqrt{-1}$. In turn, we can conclude that $i^2 = -1$. This means that other powers of *i* follow a cyclical pattern.

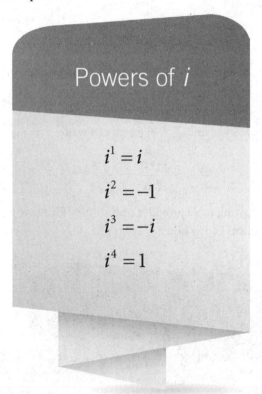

Powers of *i*

$$i^1 = i$$
$$i^2 = -1$$
$$i^3 = -i$$
$$i^4 = 1$$

This pattern repeats as you go into higher powers. For example, $i^5 = \sqrt{-1}$ or *i*, and $i^{24} = 1$.

When simplifying a power of *i*, always use the pattern. Write the exponents using rules of exponents in terms of one of these four powers.

Look at the following example:

Find i^{52}.

$$i^{52} = i^{4 \cdot 13} = (1)^{13} = 1$$

Complex Numbers

A complex number is a number made up of a real number and an imaginary number. It can be written in standard form $a + bi$, where a and b are real numbers and i is an imaginary unit. For example, in the complex number $2 + 3i$ the real number is 2 and the imaginary number is $3i$. Complex numbers can be added, subtracted, multiplied, and divided.

Remember that the square root of a negative real number is not a real number. However, it is imaginary, meaning that it involves i, where $i^2 = -1$. We can use this to further simplify some radicals. For instance:

$$\sqrt{-36} = \sqrt{-1} \cdot \sqrt{36} = i \cdot 6 = 6i$$
$$\sqrt{81} - \sqrt{-125} = 9 - \sqrt{-1} \cdot \sqrt{125} = 9 - i \cdot 5\sqrt{5} = 9 - 5i\sqrt{5}$$

The following are the basic rules of arithmetic and some important computations involving complex numbers:

Which of the following is equivalent to i^{28}?

- **A.** -1
- **B.** 1
- **C.** i
- **D.** $-i$
- **E.** 0

The correct answer is B. If you follow the cyclical pattern outlined above, you will reach the conclusion that i^{28} is equal to 1. Another way of solving this is to note that the number 28 is divisible by 4. Any exponent of i that is divisible by 4 will result in a value of 1.

COMPLEX NUMBER PROPERTIES	
Definition (in Symbols)	**Definition (in Words)**
Sum $(a + bi) + (c + di) = (a + c) + (b + d)i$	When adding complex numbers, add the real parts and the imaginary parts separately, and form the complex number using those sums.
Difference $(a + bi) - (c + di) = (ac) + (adi) + (bci) + (bd)i^2$	When subtracting complex numbers, subtract the real parts and the imaginary parts separately, and form the complex number using those differences.
Product $(a + bi) \cdot (c + di) = (a + c) + (b + d)i$	To multiply two complex numbers, apply the FOIL technique and use the fact that $i^2 = -i$.
Complex Conjugate The *complex conjugate* of $z = a + bi$ is $a - bi$	To form the complex conjugate of a complex number, change the sign of the imaginary part, but leave the real part the same. To divide two complex numbers, multiply top and bottom by the conjugate of the denominator and simplify.
Quotient $\dfrac{a+bi}{c+di} = \dfrac{a+bi}{c+di} \cdot \dfrac{c-di}{c-di}$ $= \dfrac{(ac+bd)+(bc-ad)i}{c^2+d^2}$	To divide two complex numbers, multiply top and bottom by the conjugate of the denominator and simplify

Adding Complex Numbers

To add complex numbers, add the real numbers and the imaginary numbers separately.

Sum: $(a + bi) + (c + di) = (a + c) + (b + d)i$

Look at this example:

Add: $(2 + 3i) + (8 + 4i)$

Add the real numbers and then the imaginary numbers.

$$(2 + 8) + (3i + 4i) = 10 + 7i$$

Subtracting Complex Numbers

To subtract complex numbers, subtract the real numbers and the imaginary numbers separately.

Difference: $(a + bi) - (c + di) = (a - c) + (b - d)i$

Here's an example:

Subtract: $(2 + 3i) - (8 + 4i)$

Subtract the real numbers and then the imaginary numbers.

$$(2 + 3i) - (8 + 4i) = (2 - 8) + (3i - 4i) = -6 - i$$

Multiplying Complex Numbers

Multiplying complex numbers is like multiplying polynomials by using the distributive property or the FOIL method.

Product: $(a + bi)(c + di) = (ac) + (adi) + (bci) + (bd)i^2$

An example:

Multiply: $3i(-2 + 9i)$

Distribute $3i$ to all of the terms in the parentheses.

$$3i(-2 + 9i) = (3i)(-2) + (3i)(9i)$$
$$= (3i)(-2) + 27i^2$$
$$i^2 = (\sqrt{-1})(\sqrt{-1}) = -1$$
$$= -6i + 27(-1)$$
$$= -27 - 6i$$

Another example:

Multiply: $(2 + 3i)(8 + 4i)$

Find the sum of the products of the **First** terms, the **Outer** terms, the **Inner** terms, and the **Last** terms of the binomials. The acronym FOIL stands for First Outer Inner Last and will help you to remember how to multiply two binomials.

When simplifying an expression that involves complex numbers, simplify i^2 to -1.

Simplify and write in standard form $a + bi$.

$$(2 + 3i)(8 + 4i) = (2 \cdot 8) + (2 \cdot 4i) + (8 \cdot 3i) + (3i \cdot 4i)$$
$$= 16 + 8i + 24i + 12i^2$$
$$= 16 + 32i + 12(-1)$$
$$= 4 + 32i$$

Dividing Complex Numbers

Dividing complex numbers is more complicated because the denominator cannot contain a radical. This process is called rationalizing the denominator. In order to make the denominator rational, you must use its complex conjugate. The product of two complex conjugates is always a real number $a^2 + b^2$. The numbers $2 + 8i$ and $2 - 8i$ are examples of complex conjugates, and their product is the real number $2^2 + 8^2 = 4 + 64 = 68$.

Complex conjugates: $(a + bi)$ and $(a - bi)$

Product of complex conjugates: $(a + bi)(a - bi) = a^2 + b^2$

Check out this example:

Simplify: $\dfrac{8}{7i}$

Rationalize the denominator by multiplying the numerator and denominator by i.

$$\frac{8}{7i} = \frac{8}{7i} \cdot \frac{i}{i} = \frac{8i}{7i^2} = \frac{8i}{7(-1)} = \frac{8i}{-7}$$

Another example:

Simplify: $\dfrac{4+2i}{-3+5i}$

Rationalize the denominator by multiplying the numerator and denominator by the conjugate for the denominator. Then simplify by combining like terms.

$$\frac{4+2i}{-3+5i} = \frac{4+2i}{-3+5i} \cdot \frac{-3-5i}{-3-5i}$$

$$= \frac{-12-20i-6i-10i^2}{9+15i-15i-25i^2}$$

$$= \frac{-12-20i-6i-10(-1)}{9+15i-15i-25(-1)} \quad \text{(Recall that } i^2 = -1\text{)}$$

$$= \frac{-12-20i-6i+10}{9+15i-15i+25}$$

$$= \frac{-2-26i}{9+25}$$

$$= \frac{-2-26i}{34}$$

$$= \frac{-2}{34} - \frac{26i}{34}$$

$$= \frac{-1}{17} - \frac{13i}{17}$$

$$= -\frac{1}{17} - \frac{13}{17}i$$

Which of the following is equivalent to $-\sqrt{-48} + 2\sqrt{27} - \sqrt{-75}$?

- **A.** $9\sqrt{3} - 6i\sqrt{3}$
- **B.** $6\sqrt{3} + 9i\sqrt{3}$
- **C.** $6\sqrt{3} - 6i\sqrt{3}$
- **D.** $6\sqrt{3} - 9i\sqrt{3}$
- **E.** $9\sqrt{3} + 6i\sqrt{3}$

The correct answer is D. Simplify each radical term and then combine those with the same radical part:

$$-\sqrt{-48} + 2\sqrt{27} - \sqrt{-75} = -\sqrt{-4^2 \cdot 3} + 2\sqrt{3^2 \cdot 3} - \sqrt{-5^2 \cdot 3}$$

$$= -4i\sqrt{3} + 6\sqrt{3} - 5i\sqrt{3}$$

$$= (-4-5)i\sqrt{3} + 6\sqrt{3}$$

$$= 6\sqrt{3} - 9i\sqrt{3}$$

Assume that a is a positive real number. What is the real part of $\left(\dfrac{1}{a-i}\right)^2$?

- **F.** $\dfrac{2a}{\left(a^2+1\right)^2}$
- **G.** $\dfrac{a^2-1}{\left(a^2+1\right)^2}$
- **H.** $\dfrac{1}{a^2+1}$
- **J.** $\dfrac{1}{a^2}$
- **K.** $\dfrac{a}{a^2+1}$

The correct answer is G. Before squaring the given expression, it is helpful to get the i out of the denominator. To do this, multiply inside by

1 in the form of $\dfrac{a+i}{a+i}$; here, $a + i$ is the conjugate of the denominator. Multiplying by this expression generates a difference of squares in reverse which amounts to squaring the a and the i and not leaving a middle term.

And since $i^2 = -1$, this gets rid of the i in the bottom:

$$\frac{1}{a-i} = \frac{1}{a-i} \cdot \frac{a+i}{a+i} = \frac{a+i}{a^2-i^2} = \frac{a+i}{a^2+1}$$

If you incorrectly assume that $i^2 = 1$, you will get choice H. If you stopped here and did not square the expression, the real part corresponds to choice K.

Now, square the expression by squaring the top and bottom separately:

$$\left(\frac{1}{a-i}\right)^2 = \left(\frac{a+i}{a^2+1}\right)^2 = \frac{(a+i)^2}{(a^2+1)^2} = \frac{a^2+2ai+i^2}{(a^2+1)^2} = \frac{(a^2-1)+2ai}{(a^2+1)^2}$$

When squaring the numerator, remember to FOIL. Now, separate this into two parts:

$$\frac{(a^2-1)+2ai}{(a^2+1)^2} = \frac{a^2-1}{(a^2+1)^2} + \left(\frac{2a}{(a^2+1)^2}\right)i$$

The real part is the portion not multiplied by i, namely $\dfrac{a^2-1}{(a^2+1)^2}$. Choice F is the imaginary part.

MATRICES

A matrix is an array of real numbers. If a matrix A has r rows and c columns, we say A is an $r \times c$ (read "r by c") matrix. A matrix is written by listing all of its entries in an array, enclosed by brackets. Here are some examples:

$$\underbrace{\begin{bmatrix} a & b \\ c & d \end{bmatrix}}_{2 \cdot 2 \text{ matrix}} \quad \underbrace{\begin{bmatrix} 1 & -2 & 3 \\ 1 & 0 & 2 \\ 5 & 2 & 1 \end{bmatrix}}_{3 \cdot 3 \text{ matrix}} \quad \underbrace{\begin{bmatrix} 1 \\ 3 \\ 2 \\ 1 \end{bmatrix}}_{4 \cdot 1 \text{ matrix}}$$

The basic arithmetic operations involving matrices are performed "component-wise," which means you need to pay attention to each entry's position in a matrix.

PRACTICE

Determine the value of x that makes the following equation true:

$$3\begin{bmatrix} x & -1 \\ 1 & 1 \end{bmatrix} - \begin{bmatrix} 3 & 1 \\ 0 & -1 \end{bmatrix} = \begin{bmatrix} 9 & -4 \\ 3 & 4 \end{bmatrix}$$

   A. −6

   B. 1

   C. 3

   D. 4

   E. 12

The correct answer is D. First, simplify the left side of the equation using the rules for multiplying a matrix by a scalar and subtracting matrices. Then, equate corresponding entries to get an equation to solve for x:

$$3\begin{bmatrix} x & -1 \\ 1 & 1 \end{bmatrix} - \begin{bmatrix} 3 & 1 \\ 0 & -1 \end{bmatrix} = \begin{bmatrix} 9 & -4 \\ 3 & 4 \end{bmatrix}$$

$$\begin{bmatrix} 3x & -3 \\ 3 & 3 \end{bmatrix} - \begin{bmatrix} 3 & 1 \\ 0 & -1 \end{bmatrix} = \begin{bmatrix} 9 & -4 \\ 3 & 4 \end{bmatrix}$$

$$\begin{bmatrix} 3x-3 & -4 \\ 3 & 4 \end{bmatrix} = \begin{bmatrix} 9 & -4 \\ 3 & 4 \end{bmatrix}$$

Since two matrices are equal only when their corresponding entries are the same, then $3x - 3$ must equal 9. Solving this equation yields $x = 4$.

MATRIX PROPERTIES	
Term/Operation	**Definition**
Equality: $\begin{bmatrix} a & b \\ c & d \end{bmatrix} = \begin{bmatrix} e & f \\ g & h \end{bmatrix}$	$\begin{bmatrix} a & b \\ c & d \end{bmatrix} = \begin{bmatrix} e & f \\ g & h \end{bmatrix}$ whenever $\underbrace{a = e,\ b = f,\ c = g,\ d = h}_{\text{corresponding entries are equal}}$
Sum: $\begin{bmatrix} a & b \\ c & d \end{bmatrix} + \begin{bmatrix} e & f \\ g & h \end{bmatrix}$	$\begin{bmatrix} a & b \\ c & d \end{bmatrix} + \begin{bmatrix} e & f \\ g & h \end{bmatrix} = \begin{bmatrix} a+e & b+f \\ c+g & d+h \end{bmatrix}$ In words, add corresponding entries to get the sum.
Difference: $\begin{bmatrix} a & b \\ c & d \end{bmatrix} - \begin{bmatrix} e & f \\ g & h \end{bmatrix}$	$\begin{bmatrix} a & b \\ c & d \end{bmatrix} - \begin{bmatrix} e & f \\ g & h \end{bmatrix} = \begin{bmatrix} a-e & b-f \\ c-g & d-h \end{bmatrix}$ In words, subtract corresponding entries to get the difference.
Scalar Multiplication: $k\begin{bmatrix} a & b \\ c & d \end{bmatrix}$	$k\begin{bmatrix} a & b \\ c & d \end{bmatrix} = \begin{bmatrix} ka & kb \\ kc & kd \end{bmatrix}$ In words, multiply all entries by the constant k.

Matrix Multiplication

Matrix multiplication is much more involved than scalar multiplication. To multiply matrices, you will need to match up the 1st, 2nd, nth rows of the first matrix with the corresponding 1st, 2nd, nth columns of the second matrix. Then, you must multiply each entry in the nth row of the first matrix by each corresponding entry in the nth column of the second matrix. Then, the sum of these products will be the entry for the product in the resulting matrix.

Matrices can only be multiplied if the number of columns in the first matrix is the same as the number of rows in the second matrix. For instance, a 2 by 3 matrix could be multiplied by a 3 by 5 matrix but not another 2 by 3 matrix.

Look at the example here:

$$\begin{bmatrix} A & B & C \\ W & X & Y \end{bmatrix} \begin{bmatrix} 1 & 4 \\ 2 & 5 \\ 3 & 6 \end{bmatrix} = \begin{bmatrix} (1A+2B+3C) & (4A+5B+6C) \\ (1W+2X+3Y) & (4W+5X+6Y) \end{bmatrix}$$

Notice that the top entry in the first column of the product matrix is $(1A + 2B + 3C)$. This was the result of mapping the first row of the first matrix $\begin{bmatrix} A & B & C \end{bmatrix}$ onto the first column of the second matrix $\begin{bmatrix} 1 \\ 2 \\ 3 \end{bmatrix}$. The entries matched up as follows: A corresponded with 1, B corresponded with 2, and C corresponded with 3.

Therefore, to find the product of $\begin{bmatrix} A & B & C \end{bmatrix}$ and $\begin{bmatrix} 1 \\ 2 \\ 3 \end{bmatrix}$, we multiplied A by 1, B by 2, and C by 3, and the sum of these products was $(1A + 2B + 3C)$.

If $A = \begin{pmatrix} 2 & 6 \\ 3 & -1 \end{pmatrix}$ and $B = \begin{pmatrix} 4 & 3 & -2 \\ 2 & 1 & 5 \end{pmatrix}$, then the entry in the second row, third column of AB will be:

    A. –11

    B. –1

    C. 1

    D. 11

    E. 20

The correct answer is A. We need to find the product of the second row of A and the third column of B, that is:

$$(3 \; -2) \begin{pmatrix} -2 \\ 5 \end{pmatrix} = (3)(-2) + (-1)(5) = -11$$

VECTORS

A vector is a quantity that has both magnitude and direction. Examples of such quantities are the velocity or acceleration of a moving object, or the force exerted by an object. A vector is represented by an arrow whose direction indicates the vector's direction, and whose length indicates the vector's magnitude.

There are several ways to notate the following vector, such as $\overrightarrow{AB}, \overline{AB}$, or a.

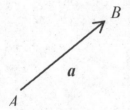

Two vectors are equal to each other if they have the same magnitude and direction. Two vectors are negatives of each other if they have the same magnitude, but opposite directions.

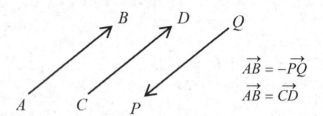

$$\overrightarrow{AB} = -\overrightarrow{PQ}$$
$$\overrightarrow{AB} = \overrightarrow{CD}$$

Vectors can be manipulated in a variety of ways, including the following six methods. They are provided below with images to help when applicable.

In order to add vectors graphically, connect them head-to-tail.

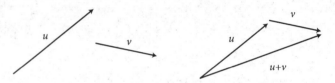

In order to subtract vector v from vector u graphically, first reverse the direction of v, and then add this new vector head-to-tail with vector u (add the negative of v):

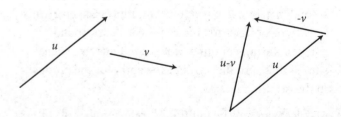

Vectors may also be broken down into horizontal and vertical components:

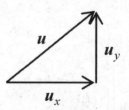

The above vector may be expressed as the ordered pair (x, y), where x is the magnitude of the vector's horizontal component and y is the magnitude of its vertical component.

In order to add vectors expressed using components algebraically, add the first components together and the second components together:

If $a = (x, y)$ and $b = (u, v)$,
then $a + b = (x + u, y + u)$.

In order to multiply a vector by a scalar—that is, a quantity with magnitude only and no direction—multiply each component of the vector by the scalar. Thus, the product of vector $a = (x, y)$ by the scalar c equals (cx, cy).

Here is an example of such a situation:

Given vectors $a = (-3, 5)$ and $b = (1, 2)$, what is $a - 2b$?

$$a - 2b = (-3, 5) - 2(1, 2)$$
$$= (-3, 5) - (2, 4)$$
$$= (-3 - 2, 5 - 4)$$
$$= (-5, 1)$$

Consider vectors plotted in the rectangular coordinate system, with the unit vector (that is, the vector of magnitude 1) along the x-axis called i, and the unit vector along the y-axis called j. In terms of these unit vectors, the vector $a = (x, y)$ may be written as $a = xi + yj$, with x and y being the vector's coordinates.

Here is an example of this process:

Given vectors $a = -3i + 5j$ and $b = i + 2j$, what is $a - 2b$?

$$a - 2b = (-3i + 5j) - 2(i + 2j)$$
$$= (-3i + 5j) - (2i + 4j)$$
$$= -3i + 5j - 2i - 4j$$
$$= -5i + j$$

If a and b are vectors such that $a = (-3, 1)$ and $b = 2i$, what is $a - b$?

    A. $-i + j$

    B. $-5i - j$

    C. $-5i + j$

    D. $5 + j$

    E. $-i - 3j$

The correct answer is C. Convert the two vectors to the same notation and calculate:

$$a - b = (-3i + j) - 2i = -5i + j$$

SUMMING IT UP

- Real numbers encompass all rational and irrational numbers. Rational numbers include integers and natural numbers.

- An exponent represents the number of times that a number (referred to as the "base number") is multiplied by itself.

- The square root of a number n is a number that you "square" (multiply it by itself, or raise to the power of 2), to obtain n.

- The cube root of a number n is a number that you raise to the power of 3 (multiply by itself twice) to obtain n. You determine higher roots (for example, the "fourth root") in the same way.

- Exponents and radicals follow a series of properties and rules, all of which can be used to simplify expressions.

- The imaginary number i means $\sqrt{-1}$.

- When raised to different powers, i follows a cyclical pattern of results based on the value of the exponent, with the pattern repeating every 4 powers.

- Complex numbers are combinations of real and imaginary numbers, and they follow their own set of properties and rules.

- Matrices are arrays of numbers arranged within brackets, and they are subject to particular operations when working with them.

  o Adding and subtracting numbers within two matrices requires pairing each number of the first matrix with its corresponding position in the second, then adding and subtracting these pairs respectively.

  o Multiplying a matrix by a constant requires multiplying each number within the matrix by the constant individually.

  o Multiplying matrices by each other is a complicated procedure. To multiply matrices, you will need to match up the 1st, 2nd, nth rows of the first matrix with the corresponding 1st, 2nd, nth columns of the second matrix. Then, you must multiply each entry in the nth row of the first matrix by each corresponding entry in the nth column of the second matrix. Then, the sum of these products will be the entry for the product in the resulting matrix.

- Vectors are quantities with both magnitude and direction. Scalar quantities only have magnitude.

- There are six principal methods of working with and manipulating vectors, several of which can be represented graphically for greater ease.

TEST YOURSELF

PREPARING FOR HIGHER MATH – NUMBER & QUANTITY

10 Questions—10 Minutes

Directions: Solve each problem and choose the correct answer.

Do not dwell on problems that take too long. First, solve as many as you can; then, you can return to others you have left.

You are permitted to use a calculator. You may use your calculator for any problem you like, but some of the problems may best be completed without a calculator.

1. If $\frac{1}{4} < z < \frac{1}{2}$, which of the following must be greater than 1?

   A. $2z$

   B. z^2

   C. $z - 1$

   D. $z + \frac{3}{4}$

   E. $\sqrt{z}$

2. Simplify: $(2^{-1} + 3^{-1})^{-2}$

   F. $\frac{25}{36}$

   G. $\frac{36}{25}$

   H. $\frac{36}{5}$

   J. 13

   K. 25

3. Simplify the following expression:

   $$\sqrt{91} \cdot \left(\frac{\sqrt{13}}{\sqrt{7}} - \frac{\sqrt{7}}{\sqrt{13}} \right)$$

   A. $-\sqrt{91}$

   B. $\frac{6}{91}$

   C. 6

   D. $\frac{3}{\sqrt{91}}$

   E. 20

4. Assume x, y, and z are positive real numbers.

   Simplify: $\sqrt{32x^{-9}y^{16}z^{-4}} \cdot \frac{\sqrt{xz^2}}{y^2}$

   F. $\frac{4y^2\sqrt{2x}}{x^3z}$

   G. $\frac{4y^7\sqrt{2}}{x^5z^3}$

   H. $\frac{4y^8\sqrt{2}}{x^4z^2\sqrt{x}}$

   J. $\frac{4y^6\sqrt{2}}{x^4z}$

   K. $\frac{4x^4z\sqrt{2}}{y^6}$

5. Assume that $x > 1$. Simplify: $\left(\sqrt{x} - \sqrt{x-1}\right)^2$

A. $2x - 1 - 2\sqrt{x^2 - x}$

B. 1

C. $1 - 2\sqrt{x^2 - x}$

D. $2x - \sqrt{x^2 - x - 1}$

E. $2x - 1 - \sqrt{2x^2 - 2x}$

6. Assume a and b are positive real numbers. If $x = 3\sqrt{ab}$ and $y = b\sqrt{3a}$, then which of these expressions is equivalent to $x^4 y^{-2}$?

F. $\dfrac{a}{b^2}$

G. $27a$

H. $\dfrac{6}{\sqrt{3b}}$

J. $\dfrac{1}{27a}$

K. $24a^3 b^4$

7. Compute and simplify the following expression:

$$\dfrac{i}{1+3i} - \dfrac{3}{1-3i}$$

A. i

B. $i - 3$

C. $\dfrac{8i}{6i - 1}$

D. $-\dfrac{4}{5}i$

E. $\dfrac{i - 3}{10}$

8. Assume that a and b are positive real numbers. What is the imaginary part of $\dfrac{bi}{a} - \dfrac{a}{bi}$?

F. 0

G. $\dfrac{a^2 + b^2}{ab}$

H. $\dfrac{b^2 - a^2}{ab}$

J. $a + b$

K. $\dfrac{a^2 + b^2}{ab}$

9. For what value(s) of a, if any, is this equation satisfied?

$$a\begin{bmatrix} -1 & a+1 \\ 2 & 4 \end{bmatrix} - \begin{bmatrix} a & 0 \\ 2a & 4a \end{bmatrix} = \begin{bmatrix} 0 & 0 \\ 0 & 0 \end{bmatrix}$$

A. -1 and 0

B. -1 only

C. 0 only

D. 0 and 1

E. There is no such value of a.

10. Vector $\overrightarrow{AB}$ has coordinates $(-5, 8)$. Vector $\overrightarrow{CD}$ is a scalar multiple of $\overrightarrow{AB}$, and the sum of the coordinates of $\overrightarrow{CD}$ is -21. What is the second coordinate of $\overrightarrow{CD}$?

F. -56

G. -35

H. -7

J. 7

K. 56

ANSWER KEY AND EXPLANATIONS

1. D	3. C	5. A	7. D	9. C
2. G	4. J	6. F	8. K	10. F

1. **The correct answer is D.** First, the question asks which of the expressions must be greater than 1. This means no matter what value of z between $\frac{1}{4}$ and $\frac{1}{2}$ is plugged in, the resulting value must be greater than 1.

   To begin, eliminate choice C. This involves subtracting 1 from a positive fraction less than 1, which makes it smaller than 1, not greater.

   Next, choices B and E can be eliminated using the following rules:

   - If $0 < a < b$, then $a^2 < b^2$.
   - If $0 < a < b$, then $\sqrt{a} < \sqrt{b}$.

   With $\frac{1}{4} < z < \frac{1}{2}$, squaring all parts yields the following:

   $$\left(\frac{1}{4}\right)^2 < z^2 < \left(\frac{1}{2}\right)^2 = \frac{1}{6} < z^2 < \frac{1}{4}$$

   So z^2 must be less than 1.

   Finding the square roots of all parts yields the following:

   $$\sqrt{\frac{1}{4}} < z < \sqrt{\frac{1}{2}} = \frac{1}{2} < \sqrt{z} < \frac{1}{\sqrt{2}}$$

   So $\sqrt{z}$ must be less than 1.

   This problem comes down to deciding between choices A and D. At this point, it is often helpful to plug in values for z to aid in the decision process. But do not do so sporadically. Choosing values of z close to the endpoints of its range (that is, close to $\frac{1}{4}$ and $\frac{1}{2}$) is often the way to go.

   To make the value as big as possible when multiplying (as in choice A), choose values at the upper end of the range. No matter what value of z you choose between $\frac{1}{4}$ and $\frac{1}{2}$, it will always be less than 1; it only equals 1 when z is chosen to be $\frac{1}{2}$, and that is

   not in the range. Therefore, the correct answer cannot be choice A; it must be choice D.

2. **The correct answer is G.** Dealing with exponents in the context of order of operations can be tricky. For this problem, the most common error involves incorrectly applying the –2 exponent. A common mistake is to distribute the –2 power to both terms, but $(2^{-1} + 3^{-1})^{-2} \neq (2^{-1})^{-2} + (3^{-1})^{-2}$. Making this incorrect assumption leads to choice J.

   Following the order of operations requires that you simplify the expression inside the parentheses first. To do this, convert the terms to fractions (since they each involve a negative power) and then combine the fractions by getting a least common denominator:

   $$\left(2^{-1} + 3^{-1}\right)^{-2} = \left(\frac{1}{2} + \frac{1}{3}\right)^{-2} + \left(\frac{3}{6} + \frac{2}{6}\right)^{-2} = \left(\frac{5}{6}\right)^{-2}$$

   So how do you handle the negative power? In the simplified form above, the effect of the negative power is to flip the fraction inside to obtain $\left(\frac{5}{6}\right)^{-2} = \left(\frac{6}{5}\right)^2$. A common error is to apply the negative power too early and flip the fractions in the second step above; that is, $\left(\frac{1}{2} + \frac{1}{3}\right)^{-2} \neq \left(2 + 3\right)^2$.

   Doing this results in choice K. Another common error is to forget to flip the fraction entirely and square it; this results in choice F. Complete the simplification by squaring both the numerator and denominator to get $\left(\frac{6}{5}\right)^2 = \frac{36}{25}$. If you only square the numerator, you get choice H.

3. **The correct answer is C.** Using the order of operations, you need to simplify the expression inside the parentheses first. To do so, you must combine the fractions into a single fraction. To do this, you need a common denominator. (If you just subtract

the numerators and denominators, you will get choice A). The common denominator is the product $\sqrt{7} \cdot \sqrt{13}$, applied as follows:

$$\sqrt{91} \cdot \left(\frac{\sqrt{13}}{\sqrt{7}} - \frac{\sqrt{7}}{\sqrt{13}} \right) = \sqrt{91} \cdot \left(\frac{\sqrt{13} \cdot \sqrt{13}}{\sqrt{7} \cdot \sqrt{13}} - \frac{\sqrt{7} \cdot \sqrt{7}}{\sqrt{13} \cdot \sqrt{7}} \right)$$

$$= \sqrt{91} \cdot \left(\frac{\sqrt{13} \cdot \sqrt{13} - \sqrt{7} \cdot \sqrt{7}}{\sqrt{7} \cdot \sqrt{13}} \right)$$

Now, use the fact that $\sqrt{a} \cdot \sqrt{a} = a$ to simplify the numerator as follows:

$$\sqrt{91} \cdot \left(\frac{\sqrt{13} \cdot \sqrt{13} - \sqrt{7} \cdot \sqrt{7}}{\sqrt{7} \cdot \sqrt{13}} \right) = \sqrt{91} \cdot \left(\frac{13 - 7}{\sqrt{7} \cdot \sqrt{13}} \right)$$

$$= \sqrt{91} \cdot \left(\frac{6}{\sqrt{7} \cdot \sqrt{13}} \right)$$

Next, simplify the denominator using the property $\sqrt{a} \cdot \sqrt{b} = \sqrt{a \cdot b}$:

$$\sqrt{91} \cdot \left(\frac{6}{\sqrt{7} \cdot \sqrt{13}} \right) = \sqrt{91} \cdot \left(\frac{6}{\sqrt{91}} \right) = 6$$

The incorrect answer choices will often be the results of some arithmetic error. For example, choice J is the result of saying $\sqrt{a} \cdot \sqrt{a} = 2a$, while choice K is the result of adding inside the parentheses instead of subtracting.

4. **The correct answer is J.** This is a combination of an exponent rule problem and a radical problem. First, take care of the negative exponents inside the first radical:

$$\sqrt{32x^{-9} y^{16} z^{-4}} \cdot \frac{\sqrt{xz^2}}{y^2} = \sqrt{\frac{32 y^{16}}{x^9 z^4}} \cdot \frac{\sqrt{xz^2}}{y^2}$$

Next, use the radical properties $\sqrt{\frac{a}{b}} = \frac{\sqrt{a}}{\sqrt{b}}$ and $\sqrt{ab} = \sqrt{a}\sqrt{b}$ to simplify:

$$\sqrt{\frac{32 y^{16}}{x^9 z^4}} \cdot \frac{\sqrt{xz^2}}{y^2} = \frac{\sqrt{32}\sqrt{y^{16}}}{\sqrt{x^9}\sqrt{x^4}} \cdot \frac{\sqrt{x}\sqrt{z^2}}{y^2}$$

Use the fact that if $a > 0$, then $\sqrt{a^2} = a$ to further simplify the individual radicals. For instance:

$$\sqrt{y^{16}} = \sqrt{\left(y^8\right)^2} = y^8$$

$$\sqrt{x^9} = \sqrt{x^8 \cdot x} = \sqrt{\left(x^4\right)^2 \cdot x} = \sqrt{\left(x^4\right)^2} \cdot \sqrt{x} = x^4 \sqrt{x}$$

Doing this for all the radical terms yields the following:

$$\frac{\sqrt{32}\sqrt{y^{16}}}{\sqrt{x^9}\sqrt{z^4}} \cdot \frac{\sqrt{x}\sqrt{z^2}}{y^2} = \frac{4\sqrt{2} \cdot y^8}{x^4 \cdot z^2 \sqrt{x}} \cdot \frac{z\sqrt{x}}{y^2}$$

Finally, cancel pair of factors common to the top and bottom of the product to get the final expression:

$$\frac{4\sqrt{2} \cdot y^8}{x^4 \cdot z^2 \sqrt{x}} \cdot \frac{z\sqrt{x}}{y^2} = \frac{4\sqrt{2} \cdot y^6 \cdot \cancel{y^2}}{x^4 \cdot z \cdot \cancel{z} \cdot \cancel{\sqrt{x}}} \cdot \frac{\cancel{z} \cancel{\sqrt{x}}}{\cancel{y^2}} = \frac{4 y^6 \sqrt{2}}{x^4 z}$$

The incorrect answer choices are the results of mis-applying exponent and radical rules. Choice F is the result of saying $\sqrt{x^n} = x^{\sqrt{n}}$.

5. **The correct answer is A.** The most typical error here is to distribute the exponent to the two terms to get $\left(\sqrt{x}\right)^2 - \left(\sqrt{x-1}\right)^2 = x - (x-1) = 1$ (choice B). However, you cannot do this. Rather, you must FOIL:

$$\left(\sqrt{x} - \sqrt{x-1}\right)^2 = \left(\sqrt{x} - \sqrt{x-1}\right) \cdot \left(\sqrt{x} - \sqrt{x-1}\right)$$

$$= \left(\sqrt{x}\right)^2 - 2\sqrt{x} \cdot \sqrt{x-1} + \left(\sqrt{x-1}\right)^2$$

$$= x - 2\sqrt{x} \cdot \sqrt{x-1} + (x-1)$$

Choice C is the result of getting $-\left(\sqrt{x-1}\right)^2$ instead of $+\left(\sqrt{x-1}\right)^2$. Choice D is the result of not doubling the middle term; that is, using $-\sqrt{x} \cdot \sqrt{x-1}$ instead of $-2\sqrt{x} \cdot \sqrt{x-1}$.

Finally, use the fact that $\sqrt{ab} = \sqrt{a}\sqrt{b}$ to write $2\sqrt{x} \cdot \sqrt{x-1}$ as $2\sqrt{x(x-1)} = 2\sqrt{x^2 - x}$. This yields the final expression $2x - 1 - 2\sqrt{x^2 - x}$. Choice E is the result of bringing the 2 in $2\sqrt{x^2 - x}$ inside the radical incorrectly.

6. **The correct answer is F.** Substitute the expressions for x and y into $x^4 y^{-2}$ to get the following:

$$x^4 y^{-2} = \left(3\sqrt{ab}\right)^4 \cdot \left(b\sqrt{3a}\right)^{-2}$$

Then get rid of the negative power as follows:

$$\left(3\sqrt{ab}\right)^4 \cdot \left(b\sqrt{3a}\right)^{-2} = \left(3\sqrt{ab}\right)^4 \cdot \frac{1}{\left(b\sqrt{3a}\right)^2} = \frac{\left(3\sqrt{ab}\right)^4}{\left(b\sqrt{3a}\right)^2}$$

Choice E is the result of ignoring the negative in the power $^{-2}$.

Next, use the fact that $(c \cdot d)^m = c^m \cdot d^m$ to obtain the following:

$$\frac{\left(3\sqrt{ab}\right)^4}{\left(b\sqrt{3a}\right)^2} = \frac{3^4 \cdot \left(\sqrt{ab}\right)^4}{b^2 \cdot \left(\sqrt{3a}\right)^2}$$

Use the properties $\sqrt{c} = c^{\frac{1}{2}}$ and $(cm)^n = c^{m \cdot n}$ to further simplify:

$$\frac{3^4 \cdot \left(\sqrt{ab}\right)^4}{b^2 \cdot \left(\sqrt{3a}\right)^2} = \frac{3^4 \cdot \left((ab)^{\frac{1}{2}}\right)^4}{b^2 \cdot \left((3a)^{\frac{1}{2}}\right)^2} = \frac{3^4 \cdot (ab)^2}{b^2 \cdot (3a)} = \frac{81a^2b^2}{3ab^2}$$

Finally, cancel pairs of factors common to the numerator and denominator:

$$\frac{81a^2b^2}{3ab^2} = \frac{\cancel{3} \cdot 27 \cdot a \cdot a \cdot b^2}{\cancel{3} \cdot a \cdot b^2} = 27a$$

7. **The correct answer is D.** Treat this as you would any difference of fractions. Find the least common denominator, which is $(1 + 3i)(1 - 3i)$. If you simply subtract numerators and denominators, you will get choice B.

$$\frac{i}{1+3i} - \frac{3}{1-3i} = \frac{i}{1+3i} \cdot \frac{1-3i}{1-3i} - \frac{3}{1-3i} \cdot \frac{1+3i}{1+3i} = \frac{i(1-3i)-3(1+3i)}{(1+3i)(1-3i)}$$

Simplify the numerator using the distributive property and then FOIL the denominator, combining like terms afterwards:

$$\frac{i(1-3i)-3(1+3i)}{(1+3i)(1-3i)} = \frac{i-3i^2-3-9i}{1-9i^2} = \frac{-3(-1)-3-8i}{1-9(-1)} = \frac{3-3-8i}{1+9} = \frac{-8i}{10} = -\frac{4}{5}i$$

If you do not use the distributive property correctly, you will get choice E. Simplifying the denominator incorrectly yields choices A and C.

8. **The correct answer is K.** The goal is to rewrite this expression in the form of $a + bi$, where a and b are real numbers (that will be in terms of a and b). Doing this requires that you first combine the fractions into a single fraction with the least common denominator abi. Once you do this, simplify the numerator using the fact that $i^2 = -1$:

$$\frac{bi}{a} - \frac{a}{bi} = \frac{bi}{a} \cdot \frac{bi}{bi} - \frac{a}{bi} \cdot \frac{a}{a}$$

$$= \frac{b^2i^2 - a^2}{abi}$$

$$= \frac{b^2(-1) - a^2}{abi}$$

$$= -\frac{a^2 + b^2}{abi}$$

A common error here is to identify the imaginary part at this point as $-\dfrac{a^2+b^2}{ab}$, but you cannot do this because the i is in the denominator. You must first multiply the top and bottom of the fraction by i to get the following:

$$-\frac{a^2+b^2}{abi} = -\frac{a^2+b^2}{abi} \cdot \frac{i}{i} = \left(-\frac{a^2+b^2}{abi^2}\right)i = \left(-\frac{a^2+b^2}{ab(-1)}\right)i = \left(\frac{a^2+b^2}{ab}\right)i$$

So, the imaginary part is $\dfrac{a^2+b^2}{ab}$.

9. **The correct answer is C.** The strategy is to simplify the expression on the left side first. Then, equate corresponding entries of matrices on both sides of the equation to determine the condition(s) of a that must hold true:

$$a\begin{bmatrix} -1 & a+1 \\ 2 & 4 \end{bmatrix} - \begin{bmatrix} a & 0 \\ 2a & 4a \end{bmatrix} = \begin{bmatrix} -a & a^2+a \\ 2a & 4a \end{bmatrix} - \begin{bmatrix} a & 0 \\ 2a & 4a \end{bmatrix} = \begin{bmatrix} -a-a & a^2+a \\ 2a-2a & 4a-4a \end{bmatrix} = -\begin{bmatrix} -2a & a^2+a \\ 0 & 0 \end{bmatrix}$$

Now, equate corresponding entries of the matrices in the equation:

$$\begin{bmatrix} -2a & a^2+a \\ 0 & 0 \end{bmatrix} = \begin{bmatrix} 0 & 0 \\ 0 & 0 \end{bmatrix}$$

This yields the equations $-2a = 0$ and $a^2 + a = 0$. The first equation implies $a = 0$. If this value of a satisfies the second equation, then the two matrices will be equal. Certainly, it satisfies the equation $a^2 + a = 0$. Note that $a = -1$ also satisfies this equation, but not the first one. The lower left entries of the two matrices would not be equal, so it is not a value that satisfies the original matrix equation. Hence, the answer is choice C.

10. **The correct answer is F.** Let c be the scalar by which $\overrightarrow{AB}$ is multiplied to produce $\overrightarrow{CD}$. Then, the coordinates of $\overrightarrow{CD}$ are $(-5c, 8c)$, and their sum is $-5c + 8c$. Set this equal to -21 and solve for c.

$$-5c + 8c = -21$$
$$3c = -21$$
$$c = -7$$

CHAPTER

**Preparing for Higher
Math: Algebra**

PREPARING FOR HIGHER MATH:

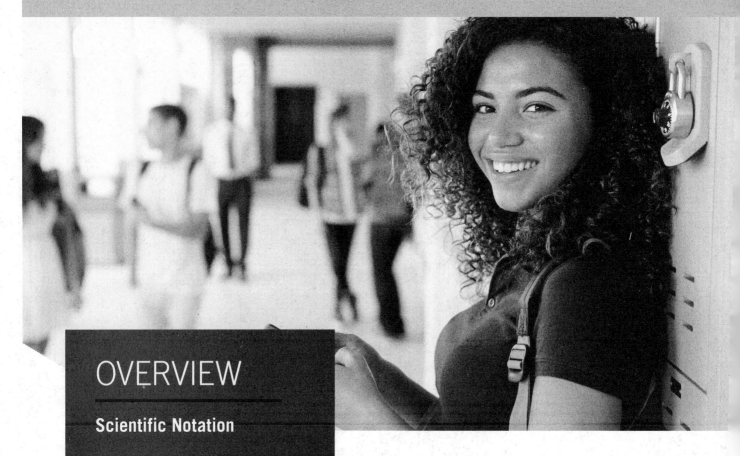

OVERVIEW

Scientific Notation

Polynomials and Factoring

Rational Expressions

Systems of Linear Equations

Quadratics

Literal Equations

Inequalities

Summing It Up

Test Yourself: PHM—Algebra

Algebra questions represent more than 20% of the Preparing for Higher Math questions on the Mathematics section of the ACT. The questions largely center on topics you would have likely covered in your algebra class. This chapter will discuss each of the topics you're likely to encounter while providing various examples, practice opportunities, and a longer Test Yourself section at the end.

SCIENTIFIC NOTATION

Scientific notation is a system for writing extremely large or extremely small numbers. In scientific notation, an integer or decimal number between 1 and 10 is written to a power of 10. For example, the number 380,000,000 can be written as 3.8×10^8. The number between 1 and 10 that you are working with is 3.8.

When you count the number of zeros plus the number to the right of the decimal point, you can see that there are 8 digits. That means that the exponent is 8. A negative exponent signifies a fractional number.

To illustrate further, here's a list of related decimal numbers and their equivalents in scientific notation:

$$837,000 = 8.37 \times 10^5 \text{ (decimal point shifts 5 places to the left)}$$

$$8,370 = 8.37 \times 10^3 \text{ (decimal point shifts 3 places to the left)}$$

$$837 = 8.37 \times 10^2 \text{ (decimal point shifts 1 place to the left)}$$

$$8.37 = 8.37 \times 10^0 \text{ (decimal point unchanged in position)}$$

$$0.837 = 8.37 \times 10^{-1} \text{ (decimal point shifts 1 place to the right)}$$

$$0.0837 = 8.37 \times 10^{-2} \text{ (decimal point shifts 2 places to the right)}$$

$$0.000837 = 8.37 \times 10^{-4} \text{ (decimal point shifts 4 places to the right)}$$

Addition and Subtraction with Scientific Notation

When adding and subtracting values in scientific notation, the first step is to make sure that each instance of scientific notation is of the same power. We can start with addition:

$$(4.5 \times 10^2) + (6.7 \times 10^3) = ?$$

Since the first value is raised to the power of 2 and the second to the power of 3, these cannot be easily added together. In order to modify the power in scientific notation, you can shift the decimal point left or right to change the power. If you shift the decimal to the left, you raise the power. If you shift it to the right, you lower it.

So, in this situation, we would want to move the decimal point of the first integer to the left to raise the power of the scientific notation as a whole, seen below:

$$(0.45 \times 10^3) + (6.7 \times 10^3) = ?$$

With this done, we can now add the two values together, combining the two integers with decimals and maintaining the same exponential expression at the end:

$$(0.45 + 6.7) \times 10^3 = 7.15 \times 10^3$$

Subtraction requires the same steps of raising or lowering the power accordingly, and we can switch around some values of the prior equation to arrive at a straightforward example:

$$(4.5 \times 10^3) - (6.7 \times 10^2) = ?$$

First, we shift the decimal to the left as we did before, but this time we do so with the second value:

$$(4.5 \times 10^3) - (0.67 \times 10^3) = ?$$

Then, we group and subtract the decimal values to find our solution:

$$(4.5 - 0.67) \times 10^3 = 3.83 \times 10^3$$

Multiplication and Division with Scientific Notation

Multiplying and dividing with scientific notation is a simpler process, as it relies upon exponent rules that we already know. Remember that when multiplying exponents, you add the exponents together to arrive at the correct value. In contrast, when dividing exponents, you subtract the exponents from one another.

As such, when multiplying and dividing with scientific notation, you multiply or divide the integers in the first part of the notation, and then add or subtract the exponents accordingly. We will start with an example of multiplication:

$$(3 \times 10^5) \times (6 \times 10^7) = ?$$

In this case, we would multiply the integers by each other, and then subsequently add the two exponents together, as follows:

$$(3)(6) \times 10^{5+7} = 18 \times 10^{12}$$

Remember, scientific notation requires that the integer must be a number between 1 and 10. So, to find the proper answer to this equation, we shift the decimal point one space to the left, raising the exponent's power by 1 in turn:

$$18 \times 10^{12} = 1.8 \times 10^{13}$$

We can use the same values to practice division:

$$\frac{6 \times 10^7}{3 \times 10^5}$$

In this situation, we would divide the two integers and then subtract the exponent in the denominator from the one in the numerator:

$$\frac{6}{3} \times 10^{7-5} = 2 \times 10^2$$

Simplify: $\dfrac{(2.5 \times 10^5) + (8 \times 10^6)}{(5.1 \times 10^3) - (1 \times 10^2)}$

- **A.** 0.55×10^3
- **B.** 1.65×10^3
- **C.** 6.6×10^3
- **D.** 1.65×10^9
- **E.** 6.6×10^9

The correct answer is B. To arrive at the correct answer, first simplify the numerator and denominator following the operations for addition and subtraction. To do so, we must make sure that they both are using the same exponent power in order to successfully add and subtract them, respectively. We achieve this by shifting the decimal of both values with a lower power one space to the left, raising their respective powers by 1:

$$\frac{(0.25 \times 10^6) + (8 \times 10^6)}{(5.1 \times 10^3) - (.1 \times 10^3)}$$

Next, we add and subtract the integer values on the numerator and denominator to arrive at a simplified case of division:

$$\frac{(0.25 + 8) \times 10^6}{(5.1 - .1) \times 10^3}$$
$$= \frac{8.25 \times 10^6}{5 \times 10^3}$$

Finally, we divide the two integers and subtract the exponent in the denominator from that of the numerator:

$$\frac{8.25}{5} \times 10^{6-3} = 1.65 \times 10^3$$

POLYNOMIALS AND FACTORING

Polynomials and factoring represent key concepts for working with algebraic expressions, equations, and inequalities. These concepts will appear in many of the Preparing for Higher Math: Algebra questions. The following section will focus on key terms and methods involved in combining and separating, or factoring, terms in algebra.

Polynomials

A polynomial is one or more terms, each having a variable with a whole number (0, 1, 2, ...) as an exponent. A term is:

- a number (such as 2 or 4.99 or $\frac{2}{3}$ or $\sqrt{20}$)
- a variable (such as x or k)
- any combination of numbers and variables without an operation symbol (such as $5x$, $k\sqrt{3}$, abc, $\frac{h}{2}$, or $15mn^2$)

Terms make up expressions (such as $5x + 3$) and equations (such as $5x + 3 = 23$), and they also are the building blocks of polynomials, as seen here:

- $4x^6$
- $m^2 - 5m + 7$
- $9 - 2t^3$
- 17

Even the number 17 counts as a polynomial due to the implied existence of a variable and exponent. From the laws of exponents, a number with an exponent of zero is equal to 1. So, you could look at 17 in the following way: $17x^0$. This would be equivalent to $17(1)$ and therefore equals 17.

The following are some examples of sequences that may appear to be polynomials but are in fact in violation of some central rules.

- $\frac{3}{c}$ (This is a rational expression and not a polynomial.)
- $\sqrt{5x}$ (This is a radical expression and not a polynomial.)

- $6y^{-3}$ (This expression contains a negative exponent, equivalent to a rational expression.)
- $3x^2 - 7x^{\frac{1}{2}}$ (This expression likewise contains a non-whole number exponent.)

For now, let's look at an example of a more complex polynomial.

$$x^4 + 14x^3 + 15x - 7$$

This polynomial has four terms: x^4, $14x^3$, $15x$, and -7. If we focused on the second term, we have a coefficient (14), a variable (x), and an exponent (3). If you wanted to read this out loud, you'd say, "fourteen x to the third power" or "fourteen x cubed."

Simplifying Polynomials

We remember that there are several methods to consider when simplifying linear equations, and these rules still apply to polynomials of varying lengths. One of the most important aspects is combining like terms, and this can become quite complex when dealing with polynomials. However, there are clear steps and techniques that you can memorize.

In short, simplifying polynomials means organizing and combining like terms to make a polynomial as easy to read as possible. This includes putting a polynomial into standard form. Let's look at a sample polynomial that has not been simplified:

$$2x + 4x^2 - 13 + 7x - x^2 + x - 3$$

To simplify, first gather like terms:

$$4x^2 - x^2 + 2x + 7x + x - 13 - 3$$

Then, combine like terms:

$$4x^2 - x^2 = 3x^2$$

$$2x + 7x + x = 10x$$

$$-13 - 3 = -16$$

Finally, write out the expression in standard form:

$$3x^2 + 10x - 16$$

This is much easier to read—and make sense of—than the original expression.

Adding and Subtracting Polynomials

If you have two polynomials and you want to combine them through addition or subtraction, the steps are similar to what you've done already. Let's take a look:

$$(11x^2 + 14 + 3x) + (-3x^2 + 2x + 6)$$

Since you have two polynomials inside of parentheses connected by addition, the first step is to remove the parentheses:

$$11x^2 + 14 + 3x + -3x^2 + 2x + 6$$

From here, gather terms and simplify:

$$11x^2 - 3x^2 + 3x + 2x + 14 + 6$$

The resulting polynomial is:

$$8x^2 + 5x + 20$$

Let's look at the same set of polynomials when we subtract one from the other. The process is essentially the same, except that you need to pay careful attention to number signs.

$$(11x^2 + 14 + 3x) - (-3x^2 + 2x + 6)$$

Now that you're subtracting one polynomial from the other, remove the parentheses and distribute the negative sign to the terms inside the second set of parentheses:

$$(11x^2 + 14 + 3x) + (3x^2 - 2x - 6)$$

Remove the parentheses, gather like terms, and combine to simplify:

$$11x^2 + 14 + 3x + 3x^2 - 2x - 6$$

$$11x^2 + 3x^2 + 3x - 2x + 14 - 6$$

$$14x^2 + x + 8$$

Multiplying Monomials

Remember that a monomial is a polynomial with only one term. For example, $7x$ is a monomial. $2y^2$ and $1{,}784{,}921t^{45}$ are also monomials. Multiplying monomials gives us the chance to combine two terms that are not alike, such as $3x^2$ and $6x^4$. First, let's review the operation of multiplying exponents.

$$3x^2 (6x^4)$$

As with any polynomial equation, it's easier to solve after simplifying. With two monomials, break each monomial into its component parts:

$$3 \times 6 \text{ and } x^2 \cdot x^4$$

The first portion requires standard multiplication:

$$3 \times 6 = 18$$

As for the exponents, when you are asked to multiply, remember that if they have the same base, you will add the exponents. Therefore, $3x^2 \cdot 6x^4 = 18x^6$.

Multiplying a Polynomial and a Monomial

When multiplying a polynomial and a monomial, distribution is the key. Here is a sample problem:

$$2(x^2 + 7x + 4)$$

The first step is to distribute the 2 to the terms in the trinomial (a polynomial with three terms):

$$(2 \cdot x^2) + (2 \cdot 7x) + (2 \cdot 4)$$

Finish multiplying and then add the terms together to present the polynomial in standard form:

$$2x^2 + 14x + 8$$

Note that even though you can factor 2 out of each term, $2x^2 + 14x + 8$ is the simplified answer. Factoring out the 2 would bring us back to the original monomial and polynomial of $2(x^2 + 7x + 4)$.

Multiplying Binomials (FOIL)

Let's start with a problem involving two binomials:

$$(4x + 3)(2x + 9)$$

These binomials need to be multiplied together. To multiply binomials, you'll use a process called FOIL. FOIL is a mnemonic that stands for First, Outer, Inner, Last. It describes the order in which you multiply terms.

Start with the first terms: $4x$ and $2x$, and multiply them together:

$$4x \cdot 2x = 8x^2$$

Then, multiply the outer terms, $4x$ and 9:

$$4x \cdot 9 = 36x$$

Continue following FOIL. Next, multiply the inner terms:

$$3 \cdot 2x = 6x$$

Then, multiply the last terms:

$$3 \cdot 9 = 27$$

Combine:

$$8x^2 + 36x + 6x + 27$$

$$= 8x^2 + 42x + 27$$

While you could have also used standard distribution to multiply the polynomial, tracking what you've multiplied can become challenging, especially as the number of terms in your polynomials grows. The mnemonic FOIL serves to remind you of the distributive property of multiplication.

There are cases wherein you can factor a trinomial (seen in the previous example) to produce two binomials. Here are some examples of algebraic expressions that can also be factored:

$$4x + 2y = 2 \cdot (2x + y)$$

$$xz - bz = z \cdot (x - b)$$

Factoring Numbers and Variables Out of Expressions

In some cases, all of the numbers in a polynomial can be factored out. Here is a simple example:

$$4x - 4z$$

There are two terms: $4x$ and $4z$. Each of these terms has a 4 in it, so each of these terms is divisible by 4. It also is the case that 4 is the largest possible term that is factorable. Dividing $4x$ by 4 leaves x, and dividing $4z$ by 4 leaves z. So, factoring out the 4 produces the following:

$$4x - 4z = 4(x) - 4(z)$$
$$= 4 \cdot (x - z)$$
$$= 4(x - z)$$

For some expressions, a number can be factored out, but not the entire number. In these instances, you have to first pull out a factor of the number in question. Consider the following example:

$$9xy - 6ab$$

The number 6 can't be factored out because 6 doesn't divide evenly into 9. Similarly, 9 can't be factored out as 9 doesn't divide evenly into 6. However, both numbers have a common factor: 3. This means that you can factor 3 out of both terms:

$$9xy = 3(3xy)$$
$$6ab = 3(2ab)$$

As a result, the whole expression becomes:

$$9xy - 6ab = 3(3xy - 2ab)$$

In addition to numbers, variables can also be factored out of expressions. If the same variable occurs in every term, it can be factored out. Look at the following expression:

$$11a - 5ab$$

There are no common factors for 11 and 5. However, both $11a$ and $5ab$ contain a factor of a. Therefore, you can factor out the variable, leaving the numbers as they are:

$$11a - 5ab = a(11 - 5b)$$

Sometimes, both a number and a variable can be factored out of an expression. Since the process for factoring out variables is essentially the same as it is for factoring out numbers, these operations can be done together under certain circumstances—as in the following example.

$$8xyz - 4yb$$

Factor out the number first. Both 8 and 4 are divisible by 4, so:

$$8xyz - 4yb = 4(2xyz - yb)$$

Now, look at the variables in the parentheses. Since there is a y in both terms inside the parentheses, it can be factored out. Pull the y outside the parentheses:

$$4(2xyz - yb) = 4y(2xz - b)$$

Sometimes, you can factor an entire term from an expression. There are situations in which this might result in an unexpected change, as the following example illustrates.

$$4x + x$$

In this expression, an x can be factored out of both terms. Note that factoring an x away from the second term leaves a 1. It does not simply remove the x entirely.

$$4x + x = x(4 + 1)$$

Factoring Trinomials

Factoring a trinomial is essentially the same as multiplying binomials but in reverse. Let's look at the standard form of a trinomial and an example:

$$Ax^2 + Bx + C$$

$$x^2 + 5x + 6$$

When factoring a trinomial, the goal is to build two binomials that, when you use FOIL, recreate the trinomial.

Here's what you will see:

$$x^2 + 5x + 6 = (x + a)(x + b)$$

Let's expand the right side of this equation:

$$x^2 + 5x + 6 = (x + a)(x + b)$$
$$= x^2 + ax + bx + ab$$
$$= x^2 + (a + b)x + ab$$

What you see here is true for any trinomials that can be factored. You're looking for the values of a and b that multiply to make the C term of the standard form but also add up to the B term. In the example, ab must equal 6 and $a + b$ must equal 5.

We start by factoring the constant, 6.

$$6 \times 1$$
$$3 \times 2$$

Now, $6 \times 1 = 6$ but $6 + 1 = 7$. Try another pair of factors.

What about 3×2?

$$3 \times 2 = 6$$
$$3 + 2 = 5$$

The numbers look correct, but test them in the expression to be sure.

$$a = 3, \ b = 2$$
$$x^2 + 5x + 6 = (x + a)(x + b)$$
$$= (x + 3)(x + 2)$$
$$= (x)(x) + (x)(2) + (3)(x) + (3)(2)$$
$$= x^2 + 2x + 3x + 6$$
$$= x^2 + 5x + 6$$

Our original trinomial was $x^2 + 5x + 6$, so $(x + 2)(x + 3)$ would suffice as an answer. If the trinomial was set equal to 0 (as an equation), you would then solve for the roots (where the trinomial would intersect the x-axis if graphed) and the algebra would yield –2 and –3.

Let's look at another example. What if you are told to factor the following trinomial?

$$5x^2 + 35x + 50$$

To start, look to see if there are any common factors among 5, 35, and 50. The greatest common factor of these three numbers is 5. So, factor out a 5 from each term:

$$5(x^2 + 7x + 10)$$

From here, factor the trinomial like you did in the first example:

$$5\left(x^2 + 7x + 10\right) = (x + a)(x + b)$$

$$a + b = 7$$

$$ab = 10$$

We can factor 10 as 10 and 1 or 5 and 2. Since we need the factors to add to 7, the factors of the C term, only 5 and 2 add to 7. Substitute 5 and 2 for the a and b terms and you have your answer:

$$5(x + 5)(x + 2)$$

PRACTICE

Compute: $-2(2 - x^2) + x^2(x - 4) - 2x(1 - 4x)$.

A. $x^3 - x^2 - 6x - 8$

B. $x^3 + 4x^2 - 2x - 4$

C. $x^3 - 6x^2 + 2x + 4$

D. $x^3 + 6x^2 - 2x - 4$

E. $x^3 + 4x^2 + 2x - 4$

The correct answer is D. This problem is all about making proper use of the distributive property and keeping track of negative signs. All distractor choices are the results of making an error in one or both. To begin, apply the distributive property on all three products to get the following:

$$-2(2 - x^2) + x^2(x - 4) - 2x(1 - 4x) = -4 + 2x^2 + x^3 - 4x^2 - 2x = 8x^2$$

Make certain to multiply each term in the parentheses by the factor outside.

Next, gather like terms (meaning terms with the exact same variable parts) and add their coefficients. It's convenient to underline like terms using the same marking to ensure you do not miss any:

$$-4 + \underline{2x^2} + x^3 \underline{\underline{- 4x^2}} - 2x + 8x^2 = x^3 + \underline{6x^2} - 2x - 4$$

RATIONAL EXPRESSIONS

Rational expressions employ many of the rules that govern working with fractions. The math here is similar to what you have already seen—you simply add, subtract, multiply, and divide polynomials like you did before and cancel like factors in the top and bottom as you would when simplifying a fraction involving only numbers.

Here are a few examples that you can use to practice these techniques.

Examples

Simplify: $\dfrac{8x^2 + 2x - 3}{1 - 2x}$

Solution

First, factor the numerator and see if anything can be canceled in the top and bottom:

$$\frac{8x^2 + 2x - 3}{1 - 2x} = \frac{(4x + 3)(2x - 1)}{-(2x - 1)} \quad \text{Factor.}$$

$$= \frac{(4x + 3)\cancel{(2x - 1)}}{-\cancel{(2x - 1)}} \quad \text{Cancel like factors}$$

Note that we factored a -1 out of the denominator. Always be on the lookout for negatives when factoring—a common error (and likely one of the incorrect answer choices) is a final expression that drops the -1.

Add and simplify: $\dfrac{2x - 4}{x^2 - 1} + \dfrac{3 - x}{x^2 - 1}$

Solution

In this case, we can simply add the numerators while keeping the denominator the same because the two fractions already have the same denominator. Then, we simplify the result as much as possible:

$$\frac{2x-4}{x^2-1}+\frac{3-x}{x^2-1}=\frac{2x-4+3-x}{x^2-1} \quad \text{Combine the fractions.}$$

$$=\frac{x-1}{x^2-1} \quad \text{Simplify.}$$

$$=\frac{\cancel{x-1}}{\cancel{(x-1)}(x+1)} \quad \text{Factor and cancel like factors in top and bottom.}$$

$$=\frac{1}{x+1}$$

Subtract and simplify: $\dfrac{x}{5-2x}-\dfrac{1}{2+x}$

Solution

First, find a common denominator—remember, you can't add or subtract without one. You can simply multiply the denominators already present: $(5 - 2x)(2 + x)$. Express both fractions using this denominator, and then combine and simplify:

$$\frac{x}{5-2x}-\frac{1}{2+x}=\frac{x(2+x)}{(5-2x)(2+x)}-\frac{5-2x}{(5-2x)(2+x)}$$

$$=\frac{x^2+2x}{(5-2x)(2+x)}-\frac{5-2x}{(5-2x)(2+x)}$$

$$=\frac{x^2+2x-5+2x}{(5-2x)(2+x)}$$

$$=\frac{x^2+4x-5}{(5-2x)(2+x)}$$

$$=\frac{(x+5)(x-1)}{(5-2x)(2+x)}$$

Note that the final expression cannot be simplified further since there are no factors common to the top and the bottom.

Multiply and simplify: $\dfrac{2x^2+2x}{x^2-4}\cdot\dfrac{x+2}{x^2-1}$

Solution

First, factor all expressions and then cancel those common to the top and bottom:

$$\frac{2x^2+2x}{x^2-4}\cdot\frac{x+2}{x^2-1}=\frac{2x\cancel{(x+1)}}{(x-2)\cancel{(x+2)}}\cdot\frac{\cancel{x+2}}{\cancel{(x+1)}(x-1)}=\frac{2x}{(x-2)(x-1)}$$

Do not multiply the numerators and the denominators before factoring. Doing so can create a huge mess that is much more difficult to simplify.

TIP

If you are asked to divide two rational expressions, the process is practically identical to multiplication, with the additional step of first rewriting the division problem as a multiplication problem, just as with division of numerical fractions.

PRACTICE

Simplify the following rational expression: $\dfrac{x^2 - y^2}{5x - 5y}$.

A. $\dfrac{x-y}{5}$

B. $\dfrac{5}{x+y}$

C. $\dfrac{x+y}{5}$

D. $\dfrac{1}{5}$

E. $\dfrac{x^2 - 5x}{y^2 - 5y}$

The correct answer is C. First, factor both the numerator and denominator of the fraction, and then cancel any common factors:

$$\frac{x^2 - y^2}{5x - 5y} = \frac{\cancel{(x-y)}(x+y)}{5\cancel{(x-y)}} = \frac{x+y}{5}$$

If x and y are positive numbers, $\dfrac{x}{5} - \dfrac{2}{y} =$

F. $\dfrac{xy - 2}{5y}$

G. $\dfrac{xy - 10}{5 + y}$

H. $\dfrac{2x}{5y}$

J. $\dfrac{xy - 10}{5y}$

K. $\dfrac{x - 2}{5 - y}$

The correct answer is F. To solve, you need a common denominator. The common denominator is $5y$. Write the first fraction, $\dfrac{x}{5}$, as an equivalent one with a denominator of $5y$: $\dfrac{y}{y} \cdot \dfrac{x}{5} = \dfrac{xy}{5y}$. Likewise, rewrite the fraction after the minus sign as one with a denominator of $\dfrac{5}{5} \times \dfrac{2}{y} = \dfrac{10}{5y}$. Since the denominators are now the same, you can subtract:

$$\frac{xy}{5y} - \frac{10}{5y} = \frac{xy - 10}{5y}$$

SYSTEMS OF LINEAR EQUATIONS

A system of equations is a set of two or more (usually just two) equations that share a set of variables.

Here's an example of a system of equations:

$$2y + 7x = 24$$
$$y + 3x = 12$$

The solution to a system of equations with two variables is an ordered pair of numbers. The ordered pair is a solution to both equations in the system, representing the intersection point between the two equations if they were graphed in a coordinate plane.

For example, the solution to the system of equations above is (0, 12). With ordered pairs, the first number is the value for x and the second is the value for y. By substituting these numbers for the variables into both equations, you can check to make sure they work:

$$2(12) + 7(0) \rightarrow 24 + 0 = 24$$
$$12 + 3(0) \rightarrow 12 + 0 = 12$$

Given a system of equations, there are two different methods for finding the values of the two variables: the substitution method and the elimination method.

There are only three possibilities that can occur when trying to find the solution to a system:

NUMBER OF SOLUTIONS	
Number of Solutions	**Geometric Interpretation**
0	The graphs of the lines in the system are parallel. Hence, there is no point that is on both lines simultaneously.
1	The graphs of the lines in the system intersect in a single point. The intersection point is the solution of the system.
Infinitely many	The graphs of the lines in the system are exactly the same. Every point on the line is a solution of the system.

The Substitution Method

To solve a system of two equations using the substitution method, follow these steps (we'll use x and y here):

1. In *either* equation, isolate one variable (x) on one side.
2. Substitute the expression that equals x in place of x in the other equation.
3. Solve that equation for y.
4. Now that you know the value of y, plug it into either equation to find the value of x.

Consider these two equations:

Equation A: $x = 4y$

Equation B: $x - y = 1$

In equation B, substitute $4y$ for x, and then solve for y:

$$4y - y = 1$$
$$3y = 1$$
$$y = \frac{1}{3}$$

To find x, substitute $\frac{1}{3}$ for y into either equation. The value of x will be the same for both.

Equation A:
$$x = 4\left(\frac{1}{3}\right) = \frac{4}{3}$$

Equation B: $x - \frac{1}{3} = 1$; $x = \frac{4}{3}$

The Elimination Method

Another way to solve for two variables in a system of two equations is with the elimination method, sometimes also referred to as the addition-subtraction method. Here are the steps:

1. "Line up" the two equations by listing the same variables and other terms in the same order. Place one equation above the other.

2. Make the coefficient of *either* variable the same in both equations (you can disregard the sign) by multiplying every term in one of the equations.

3. Add the two equations (work down to a sum for each term), or subtract one equation from the other, to eliminate one variable.

Consider these two equations:

Equation A: $x = 3 + 3y$

Equation B: $2x + y = 4$

In equation A, subtract $3y$ from both sides, so that all terms in the two equations "line up":

Equation A: $x - 3y = 3$

Equation B: $2x + y = 4$

To solve for y, multiply each term in Equation A by 2, so that the x-coefficient is the same in both equations:

Equation A: $2x - 6y = 6$

Equation B: $2x + y = 4$

Subtract Equation B from Equation A, thereby eliminating x, and then isolate y on one side of the equation:

$$\begin{array}{r} 2x - 6y = 6 \\ -2x - y = -4 \\ \hline 0x - 7y = 2 \\ -7y = 2 \\ y = -\dfrac{2}{7} \end{array}$$

Then, substitute that solution into one of the equations and solve for the value of the other variable.

If $x - 4y = -2$ and $2x + y = 23$, what is the value of $5xy$?

    A. 10

    B. 13

    C. 30

    D. 50

    E. 150

The correct answer is E. The two methods are equally convenient to use, so let's apply the substitution method. Solve the first equation for x to get $x = 4y - 2$ and substitute this in for x in the second equation to get $2(4y - 2) + y = 23$. Solving for y yields $8y - 4 + y = 23$, which is equivalent to $9y = 27$, so $y = 3$. Plugging this value back into the substitution expression yields $x = 4(3) - 2 = 10$.

The final step here is to evaluate the expression $5xy$ using $x = 10$ and $y = 3$ (since these are the only values of x and y for which both equations hold simultaneously). Doing so yields $5(10)(3) = 150$.

Suppose the system $\begin{cases} x + ky + 1 = 4x \\ -3x = 5 - 2y \end{cases}$

has no solution.

What must be the value of k?

    F. -2

    G. 2

    H. $\dfrac{1}{2}$

    J. $-\dfrac{1}{2}$

    K. 4

The correct answer is G. The only way a linear system can have no solution is for the two lines to be parallel, which means they have the same slope. In order to determine the value of k, put each of the lines into slope-intercept form and equate the slopes:

$$x + ky + 1 = 4x \Rightarrow ky = 3x - 1 \Rightarrow y = \frac{3}{k}x - \frac{1}{k}$$

$$-3x = 5 - 2y \Rightarrow -5 - 3x = -2y \Rightarrow y = \frac{3}{2}k + \frac{5}{2}$$

In this form, the slopes of the lines are $\dfrac{3}{k}$ and $\dfrac{3}{2}$. Setting them equal and solving for k yields $k = 2$. This is the only value for which these two lines are parallel.

QUADRATICS

Quadratics take their name from *quad*, meaning "square," because in quadratics, the variable is squared. These sorts of equations come up in many real-life scenarios including those related to designing spaces or objects, calculating area, determining an object's speed, evaluating profits and loss, and much more. For this reason, quadratics are especially common in word problems and represent a key topic for PHM: Algebra questions.

What Is a Quadratic Equation?

In the prior section, you learned how to go about multiplying two binomials together. The resulting expression of such an operation is a special type of polynomial (often a trinomial) called a quadratic function. Simply put, a quadratic function includes one or more variables that are squared (x^2) and contains no exponents greater than this.

When set in standard form, a quadratic equation looks like the following:

$$ax^2 + bx + c = 0$$

In this particular equation type, *a* must be any real number other than 0. Likewise, when applicable, *b* and *c* are also real numbers. Not all quadratic equations contain a constant at the end (*c*), and they do not necessarily need a second *x* variable attached to a *b* coefficient. What is important is the presence of a squared variable, and these sets of restrictions allow for unique mathematical operations and graphs. We will cover them throughout this section.

Here are some examples of quadratic equations (trinomials):

$$x^2 + 2x + 3 = 0$$
$$3x^2 - 5x = -6$$
$$x^2 + 6x = 0$$
$$2x^2 - 8 = 0$$

The Quadratic Formula

In the Polynomials and Factoring section earlier in this chapter, we looked at how to factor trinomials (a form that quadratic functions often take). Not all quadratics can be factored, though. There is another method of solving for the roots of quadratic equations that can always be used: the quadratic formula.

Once again, a quadratic can be expressed in standard form as follows:

$$ax^2 + bx + c = 0$$

Remember that *x* is the variable, *a* and *b* are coefficients, and *c* is a constant. Those values can be arranged in the quadratic formula as follows:

$$x = \frac{-b \pm \sqrt{b^2 - 4ac}}{2a}$$

Notice that this formula uses a sign for plus or minus in the numerator, and this is because quadratics have two solutions, as we've previously seen. By plugging in all known values for a general quadratic into this formula, you can solve for both solutions. When graphing a quadratic, the result will be a parabola, which is a u-shaped graph that opens upwards or downwards. The two solutions to the quadratic formula will always mark

the two locations where the arms of the parabola cross the *x*-axis—the roots of the equation.

Let's take the following general quadratic as an example:

$$x^2 + 6x - 8 = 0$$

In this case, *a* = 1 (as the coefficient is assumed to be 1), *b* = 6, and *c* = –8. Plugging what we have into the quadratic formula will result in this equation:

$$x = \frac{-6 \pm \sqrt{6^2 - 4(1)(8)}}{2(1)}$$
$$x = \frac{-6 \pm \sqrt{36 - 32}}{2}$$
$$x = \frac{-6 \pm \sqrt{4}}{2}$$
$$x = \frac{-6 \pm 2}{2}$$
$$x_1 = \frac{-8}{2} = -4$$
$$x_2 = \frac{-4}{2} = -2$$

Since we have to both add and subtract 2 from –6 before dividing by 2, we are left with two solutions:

$$-4 \text{ and } -2$$

These will be the points where the resultant parabola crosses the *x*-axis.

What are the solutions of the quadratic
equation $2x^2 - x + 3 = 0$?

A. $x = \dfrac{1}{4} \pm i\dfrac{\sqrt{5}}{4}$

B. $x = \dfrac{1}{4} \pm i\dfrac{\sqrt{23}}{4}$

C. $x = \dfrac{1}{4} \pm \dfrac{23}{4}$

D. $x = -\dfrac{3}{2}, 1$

E. $x = -1, \dfrac{3}{2}$

The correct answer is B. Use the quadratic formula to get the following:

$$x = \frac{-(-1) \pm \sqrt{(-1)^2 - 4(2)(3)}}{2(2)} = \frac{1 \pm \sqrt{-23}}{4} = \frac{1 \pm i\sqrt{23}}{4} = \frac{1}{4} \pm \frac{i\sqrt{23}}{4}$$

Choice A is incorrect because the radical portion of the quadratic formula is $\sqrt{b^2 - 4ac}$, not
$\sqrt{b^2 - ac}$. Choice C is incorrect because you
forgot i; note that $\sqrt{-23} = \sqrt{-1} \cdot \sqrt{23} = i\sqrt{23}$.
Choice D is incorrect because you computed the
radicand portion of the quadratic formula incorrectly since it should have been negative. Choice
E is incorrect because the radical portion of the
quadratic formula is $\sqrt{b^2 - 4ac}$, not $\sqrt{b^2 + 4ac}$.

The Discriminant

The part of the quadratic formula that is underneath
the square root symbol is called the discriminant
($b^2 - 4ac$). Evaluating the discriminant tells you
whether a quadratic equation has two real roots, one
real root, or no real roots. Let's look at some examples
of how the discriminant changes for each scenario.

Positive Discriminant

If the discriminant is positive, the equation has two real
roots. In other words, the equation has two different
solutions.

The discriminant of the equation $2x^2 + x - 1 = 0$ is:

$$b^2 - 4ac = 1^2 - 4(2)(-1)$$
$$b^2 - 4ac = 1 + 8$$
$$b^2 - 4ac = 9$$

Since 9 is positive, the equation has two real roots. (If
you looked at the whole quadratic formula, not just the
discriminant, you'd see that the roots are -1 and $\dfrac{1}{2}$.)

Discriminant Is Zero

If the discriminant is zero, the equation has one real
root.

The discriminant of the equation $x^2 - 2x + 1 = 0$ is:

$$b^2 - 4ac = 1^2 - 4(2)(1)$$
$$b^2 - 4ac = 1 - 8$$
$$b^2 - 4ac = -7$$

The discriminant is zero, so this equation has one real
root.

Negative Discriminant

If the discriminant is negative, the equation has no
real roots. This is because the discriminant is under a
square root symbol, and the square root of a negative
number is an imaginary number, not a real number.

The discriminant of the equation $2x^2 + x + 1 = 0$ is:

$$b^2 - 4ac = 1^2 - 4(2)(1)$$
$$b^2 - 4ac = 1 - 8$$
$$b^2 - 4ac = -7$$

Since -7 is negative, the equation has no real roots, only
imaginary roots.

Assume $m > 0$. Which of the following conditions on m guarantees that the equation $2m^2 - \sqrt{m}x + (m-1) = 0$ has two imaginary solutions?

    A. $m > 1$

    B. $m > \dfrac{9}{8}$

    C. $m < \dfrac{9}{8}$

    D. $-8m^2 - 1 < 0$

    E. $m < \dfrac{7}{8}$

The correct answer is B. The sign of the discriminant, or the radicand of the radical part of the quadratic formula, is all you need to determine the nature of the solutions of a quadratic equation. The discriminant for a quadratic equation of the form $ax^2 + bx + c = 0$ is $b^2 - 4ac$.

Applying this to the given equation yields the expression and simplifying yields:

$$\left(-\sqrt{m}\right)^2 - 4(2m)(m-1) = m - 8m(m-1)$$
$$= m - 8m^2 + 8m = -8m^2 + 9m$$

Choices A, D, and E are all results of making errors by not identifying the discriminant formula correctly, or not applying the distributive property when simplifying. If the discriminant is negative, then the equation has imaginary solutions. This yields the condition $-8m^2 + 9m = m(9 - 8m) < 0$.

Since m is assumed to be positive, this expression will be negative only if the other factor, $9 - 8m$, is negative. That is, $9 - 8m < 0$, which is equivalent to $m > \dfrac{9}{8}$. Choice C will guarantee two distinct real solutions.

LITERAL EQUATIONS

An equation that contains more than one variable is known as a literal equation. For example, $xy + z = t$ is a literal equation, as it contains four variables: x, y, z, and t. It is not possible to "solve" this equation and find the actual values of these variables. However, it is possible to rewrite the equation in a number of different ways. In its present form, the equation is said to be "solved" for t, since the variable t appears by itself on one side of the equation only, and all other terms appear on the other side.

If you were asked to solve this equation for z, you would need to rewrite the equation in such a way that z appeared by itself on one side of the equation only, and the other variables appeared on the other side. Solving for z is quite straightforward. You simply need to treat all of the other variables as if they were constants and apply the rules for manipulating equations discussed in the previous section. Thus, starting with $xy + z = t$, simply remove the term xy from the left by subtracting it from the right. The equation solved for z would be $z = t - xy$.

Suppose you were asked to solve the equation $xy + z = t$ for x. It takes two steps to do this. Starting with $xy + z = t$, begin by moving z from the left by subtracting it from the right. This would give you $xy = t - z$. Remove the y from the left by dividing the right by y. This gives you $x = \dfrac{t - z}{y}$, and you have successfully solved the equation for x.

If $5p = xy^2$, which of the following is equal to $5px$?

A. xy

B. y^2

C. $(xy)^2$

D. x^2y

E. $\dfrac{5p}{y^2}$

The correct answer is C. Recall that we are allowed to "do the same thing" to both sides of an equation at any time. Perhaps the quickest way to solve this problem is to multiply both sides by x. This would give us the $5px$ we want. In fact, starting with $5p = xy^2$, if we multiply both sides by x, the result is $5px = xy^2(x)$. This means that $5px = x^2y^2$. Thus, $5px = (xy)^2$.

If $p = \dfrac{q^4}{r^2}$, what is the value of $\dfrac{1}{q^4}$?

F. $\dfrac{p}{r^2}$

G. $\dfrac{r^2}{p}$

H. pr^2

J. 1

K. $\dfrac{1}{pr^2}$

The correct answer is K. In this problem, we are given a literal equation and asked to solve it for $\dfrac{1}{q^4}$. Note that the expression q^4 appears on the top of the fraction on the right. An efficient way to solve this problem is to rewrite the equation by inverting both sides to get $\dfrac{1}{p} = \dfrac{r^2}{q^4}$. We can now divide both sides by r^2 to get $\dfrac{1}{r^2p} = \dfrac{1}{q^4}$.

INEQUALITIES

An equation is a mathematical statement that contains an equal sign. In turn, an inequality is a mathematical statement that contains an inequality sign. Recall that the inequality signs are ">" which means "greater than," "<" which means "less than," "≥" which means "greater than or equal to," and "≤" which means "less than or equal to."

The procedure for solving an inequality is identical to the procedure for solving an equation, with one crucial difference. When solving an inequality, whenever you divide or multiply both sides by a negative number, you must "reverse" the inequality sign. If the sign was originally "less than," <, it will become "greater than," >, after dividing or multiplying by a negative number. Similarly, if the sign was ≤, it will become ≥.

Problems involving inequalities come in different varieties on the ACT. The table on the following page provides typical forms in which these questions are frequently asked, along with some suggestions for how to approach them.

When 2 times a number x is decreased by 8, the result is less than 20. Which of the following represents the solution set of this relationship?

A. $x < 2$

B. $x < 6$

C. $x < 14$

D. $x < 20$

E. $x < 28$

The correct answer is C. First, translate the given information into an inequality: $2x - 8 < 20$. Now solve the inequality for x:

$$2x - 8 < 20$$
$$2x < 28$$
$$x < 14$$

STRATEGIES FOR INEQUALITIES

Problem Type	Method of Attack
Solve a given inequality, where the answer choices are given symbolically.	Solve the inequality as you would a linear equation, being careful with the inequality sign. The final step will have the variable on one side and a number on the other. This should be one of the choices.
Solve a given inequality, where the choices are given graphically on the number line.	Solve the inequality as you would a linear equation, being careful with the inequality sign. Once you have the variable on one side and a number on the other, match that to the correct picture. Double-check whether each circle over its correct numerical value is open or closed.
You are given a ray on the number line and are asked to identify which of the inequalities listed is its solution set.	If the pictured ray has a closed circle at its endpoint, you can discard any of the choices involving a strict inequality (that is, one with < or >). Likewise, if there is an open circle on the endpoint of the ray, discard any of the choices involving a ≤ or ≥ sign. To distinguish among the remaining choices, choose an extreme x-value (very large or very small) that is in the graphed ray, plug it into the inequalities, and see the one it satisfies. That is the solution.
You are given a verbal description whose translation into symbols results in an inequality, and you are asked for the solution set.	Translate the verbal scenario into an inequality, and solve as above.

Sometimes, you will be asked to solve a double inequality, as in the following example.

Determine the solution set for the double inequality $-4 < 8 - 3x < 20$.

The strategy behind solving such inequalities is to get the variable in the middle by itself. To do that here, simply subtract 8 from all parts of the inequality, and then divide all parts by −3. When you perform this division, make certain to switch both signs since you are working with a negative number:

$$-4 < 8 - 3x < 20$$
$$-12 < -3x < 12$$
$$4 > x > -4$$

The last line is the solution set and can be written equivalently as $-4 < x < 4$.

Consider the following problem.

Solve for x: $\dfrac{-5x}{9} \le -15$

The best first step to solve this equation would be to multiply both sides by 9. Since 9 is a positive number, the inequality sign remains as it is.

$$-5x \le -15(9)$$
$$-5x \le -135$$

The next step is to divide both sides by -5 and since this number is negative, the inequality sign must be reversed.

$$\frac{-5x}{-5} \ge \frac{-135}{-5}$$

This becomes $x \ge 27$, which is the solution to the inequality. The value of x, therefore, can be 27 or any number larger.

PRACTICE

Given $4y \leq 84 \leq 5y$, how many different possible integers values for y are there?

    A. 1

    B. 2

    C. 3

    D. 4

    E. 5

The correct answer is E. The key to this problem is being able to interpret the "compound inequality" given in the problem statement: $4y \leq 84 \leq 5y$. This inequality is telling us that 84 is somewhere between the value of $4y$ and $5y$. In other words, we are being told that both $4y \leq 84$ and $84 \leq 5y$ must be true. In order to determine the biggest value y can have, solve the inequality $4y \leq 84$. If we divide both sides by 4, we determine that $y \leq 21$. Therefore, y can be no larger than 21. To determine the smallest value that y can have, solve $84 \leq 5y$. Dividing both sides by 5 gives us the inequality $16.8 \leq y$, which means that the smallest y can be is 17. Since y must be an integer, the possible values for y are 17, 18, 19, 20, and 21. There are 5 possible values for y.

If $q > 6$, which of the following is *not* true?

    F. $-q < -6$

    G. $q + 5 > 11$

    H. $2q > 12$

    J. $q - 4 < 2$

    K. $q^2 > 3$

The correct answer is J. One way to solve this problem is to solve each of the answer choice inequalities for q. Note that multiplying both sides of choice F by -1 yields $q > 6$, since multiplying by a negative reverses the inequality. Subtracting 5 from both sides of choice G yields $q > 6$. Dividing both sides of choice H by 2 yields $q > 6$. However, adding 4 to both sides of choice J yields $q < 6$.

Graphing Inequalities on a Number Line

The solutions of an inequality with one variable can be graphed on a number line.

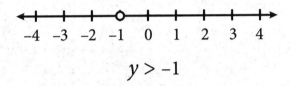

$$y > -1$$

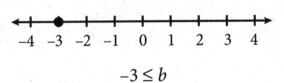

$$-3 \leq b$$

The solutions of the inequality $y > -1$ are all the real numbers that are greater than -1. Since -1 is not greater than -1, the graph of $y > -1$ contains an open dot to show that -1 is not a solution. The bold portion of the number line to the right of the open dot shows that all real numbers to the right of -1 are solutions.

Since -3 is included in the set of solutions for the inequality, $-3 \leq b$, the graph of $-3 \leq b$ contains a closed dot to show that -3 is a solution. Since $-3 \leq b$ is the same as $b \geq -3$, the bold portion of the number line to the right of the closed dot shows that -3 and all real numbers to the right of -3 are solutions.

Another distinguishing factor of linear inequalities in contrast to linear equations is that the solution set of an inequality (that is, the set of real numbers that satisfies the inequality) contains infinitely many values. The solution set is often depicted on a number line, as seen in the following table.

PLOTTING LINEAR INEQUALITIES

Linear Inequality	Picture on Number Line
$x < a$	← — — — ○ —— (open at a)
$x \leq a$	← — — — ● —— (closed at a)
$x > a$	○ — — — → (open at a)
$x \geq a$	● — — — → (closed at a)
$a \leq x \leq b$	●———● (closed at a and b)
$a < x < b$	○———○ (open at a and b)
$-\infty < x < \infty$	←————————→ (through 0)

Quadratic Inequalities

A quadratic inequality is any inequality that can be arranged so that there is a quadratic expression on one side and a zero on the other.

$$x^2 - 7x + 10 \leq 0$$
$$x^2 + 7 \leq 7x - 3$$

Just as you can solve for the solution set to a linear inequality, you can solve for the solution set of a quadratic inequality.

The method is a little more involved than solving a linear inequality. To solve quadratic inequalities, follow these steps:

- **Step 1:** Rewrite the inequality so that one side equals zero.

- **Step 2:** Factor the resulting quadratic expression, if possible, to determine its roots (that is, where the expression equals zero). If you cannot factor it, use the quadratic formula to find the roots.

- **Step 3:** Draw a number line and label the roots. Choose any number in each interval of the number line before, between, or after the roots. Plug this number into the quadratic expression and note its sign.

- **Step 4:** The solution set is those intervals where the sign determined in step 3 satisfies the inequality. If the inequality is strict (that is, either < or >), then do NOT include the roots in the solution set; if the inequality includes equals (that is, either ≤ or ≥), DO include the roots in the solution set.

The following example demonstrates these steps.

Find the solution to $x^2 + 2x > 3$.

Use the steps for solving quadratic inequalities.

Step 1: Rewrite the inequality so that one side equals zero and factor the quadratic:

$$x^2 + 2x > 3$$
$$x^2 + 2x - 3 > 0$$
$$x^2 + 2x - 3 = 0$$
$$(x + 3)(x - 1) = 0$$

Step 2: Solve the corresponding equation (i.e., find solutions for $x^2 + 2x - 3 = 0$):

$$(x + 3)(x - 1) = 0$$

$$x + 3 = 0$$
$$x - 1 = 0$$

Step 3: Thus $x = -3$ and 1, so any regions that make the inequality true will have strict boundaries at -3 and 1.

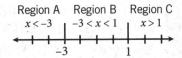

Region A   Region B   Region C
$x < -3$ $-3 < x < 1$ $x > 1$

-3 1

Step 4: Test each region with a value from that region and determine if the original inequality is true or false.

Pick any value from each region and test the value in the original inequality written in terms of zero ($x^2 + 2x - 3 > 0$) and determine if the solution is positive or negative. Any value that satisfies the original inequality is part of the solution set.

Region A: Test value $x = -4$

$$(-4)^2 + 2(-4) - 3 = 16 - 8 - 3$$
$$= 5 \text{ positive}$$

Region B: Test value $x = 0$

$$(0)^2 = 2(0) - 3 = -3 \text{ negative}$$

Region C: Test value $x = 2$

$$(2)^2 = 2(2) - 3 = 1 \text{ positive}$$

We find that the solution is positive for region A and C, where $x < -3$ and $x > 1$ or $(-\infty, -3) \cup (1, \infty)$.

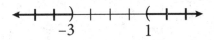

-3 1

Absolute Value Equations and Inequalities

You should also be comfortable working with linear equations and inequalities involving absolute values. Solve these problems by writing them in equivalent forms involving plain linear equations and inequalities without absolute values, as follows:

ABSOLUTE VALUE INEQUALITIES	
Absolute Value Equation/ Inequality	**Solution**
$|x| = a$	$x = a$ or $x = -a$
$|x| \geq a$	$x \geq a$ or $x \leq -a$
$|x| > a$	$x > a$ or $x < -a$
$|x| \leq a$	$-a \leq x \leq a$
$|x| < a$	$-a < x < a$

Use these definitions when x is replaced by some linear expression in x, and then solve the resulting equation(s) or inequality in the same manner that you would solve other more standard linear equations and inequalities. Work through the following examples.

Which of the following inequalities gives the complete solution set for the inequality $|2x - 3| < 8$?

A. $x < -\dfrac{5}{2}$ or $x > \dfrac{11}{2}$

B. $x < \dfrac{11}{2}$

C. $x > -\dfrac{5}{2}$

D. $-5 < x < 11$

E. $-\dfrac{5}{2} < x < \dfrac{11}{2}$

The correct answer is E. Express the absolute value inequality as the equivalent double inequality $-8 < 2x - 3 < 8$. Then add 3 to all parts of the inequality to get $-5 < 2x < 11$. Finally, divide all parts by 2 to get the solution set $-\dfrac{5}{2} < x < \dfrac{11}{2}$.

Zane earns an annual salary of Z dollars, and Wendi earns an annual salary of W dollars. If the difference between Zane's and Wendi's average monthly salaries is \$450, which of the following represents the relationship between Z and W?

F. $|Z - W| = 5{,}400$

G. $\left|\dfrac{Z + W}{2}\right| = 5{,}400$

H. $|Z + W| = 5{,}400$

J. $|Z + W| = 450$

K. $|Z - W| = 4$

The correct answer is F. The difference between Zane's and Wendi's average monthly salaries is \$450, so the difference between their annual salaries is $\$450 \times 12 = \$5{,}400$. We do not know who earns more, but the difference between their annual salaries is $|Z - W|$ dollars. Thus, $|Z + W| = 5{,}400$.

SUMMING IT UP

- Scientific notation is a system for writing extremely large or extremely small numbers. In scientific notation, an integer or decimal number between 1 and 10 is written to a power of 10. For example, the number 380,000,000 can be written as 3.8×10^8.

- There are a series of operations you can use with scientific notation, governing the addition, subtraction, multiplication, and division thereof. When using these operations, remember that moving the decimal to the left raises the power, while moving it to the right lowers the power.

- A polynomial is one or more terms, each having a variable with a whole number (0, 1, 2, ...) as an exponent.

- Terms make up expressions (such as $5x + 3$) and equations (such as $5x + 3 = 23$), and they also are the building blocks of polynomials.

- Polynomials can be simplified by gathering like terms, combining them as needed to put them into standard form. This method is also used when adding and subtracting polynomials.

- When multiplying a polynomial by a monomial (a polynomial with only one term), you can often distribute the monomial throughout the polynomial, putting it into standard form.

- When multiplying two binomials (polynomials with two terms), you can use the FOIL operation (first, outer, inner, last) to multiply each term by each other. This will similarly result in an expression in standard form.

- A rational expression is a quotient of polynomials. You can add, subtract, multiply, and divide rational expressions in the same manner as fractions—you're now just combining algebraic expressions.

- A system of linear equations is a pair of linear equations involving x and y that must be satisfied at the same time. To solve a system means to identify ordered pairs (x, y) that satisfy both equations—not just one, but both! A linear system can have 0, 1, or infinitely many solutions, which can be determined using the elimination method or substitution method.

- The solutions of $ax^2 + bx + c = 0$ are given by the quadratic formula: $x = \dfrac{-b \pm \sqrt{b^2 - 4ac}}{2a}$.

- The discriminant of $ax^2 + bx + c = 0$ is $b^2 - 4ac$. The sign of the discriminant determines the number and nature of the quadratic equation's solutions.

- Linear inequalities can be solved by using the same basic strategy used to solve linear equations, with the additional step of switching the inequality sign whenever both sides of the inequality are multiplied by a negative real number.

PREPARING FOR HIGHER MATH: ALGEBRA

14 Questions—14 Minutes

Directions: Solve each problem and choose the correct answer.

Do not dwell on problems that take too long. First, solve as many as you can; then, you can return to others you have left.

You are permitted to use a calculator. You may use your calculator for any problem you like, but some of the problems may best be completed without a calculator.

---

1. Suppose a and b are nonzero real numbers.

Simplify: $\dfrac{a}{ax-b} - \dfrac{b}{bx+a}$

A. $\dfrac{ax-b}{(ax-b)(bx+a)}$

B. $\dfrac{a-b}{(a-b)x-(b+a)}$

C. $\dfrac{1}{(x-1)(x+1)}$

D. $\dfrac{\left(a^2-b^2\right)x-2ab}{(ax-b)(bx+a)}$

E. $\dfrac{a^2+b^2}{(ax-b)(bx+a)}$

2. Divide and simplify:

$$\dfrac{4x^2-12x+9}{3x^2-2x} \div \dfrac{3x-2x^2}{9x^2-12x+4}$$

F. $-\left(\dfrac{2x-3}{3x-2}\right)^3$

G. $\dfrac{4x^2-12x+9}{9x^2-12x+4}$

H. $\dfrac{6x^2-13x+6}{-x^2}$

J. $(2x-3)(3-2x)$

K. $12-13x$

3. Simplify: $\dfrac{\dfrac{m}{n}-\dfrac{n}{m}}{\dfrac{m}{n}+\dfrac{n}{m}}$

A. 0

B. $\dfrac{m^2-n^2}{m^2+n^2}$

C. $\dfrac{m^4-n^4}{m^2n^2}$

D. $\dfrac{m-n}{m+n}$

E. $\left(\dfrac{m-n}{m+n}\right)^2$

4. If (x, y) satisfies the following system, what is the value of x^y?

$$\begin{cases} x - 2y = -1 \\ y - 2x = 5 \end{cases}$$

F. -1

G. $\dfrac{1}{9}$

H. $\dfrac{1}{3}$

J. 3

K. 6

5. For what real numbers a, if any, does the following system have no solution?

$$\begin{cases} \dfrac{x}{3} = ay \\ \dfrac{y}{a} = 3x \end{cases}$$

A. $-\dfrac{1}{3}$ and $\dfrac{1}{3}$

B. -3 and 3

C. -1 and 1

D. 0 only

E. There is no such value of a.

6. For what real number a, if any, does the following system have infinitely many solutions?

$$\begin{cases} a(x + y) = 3 \\ y + x = -2 \end{cases}$$

F. There is no such value of a.

G. -2

H. $-\dfrac{3}{2}$

J. $-\dfrac{2}{3}$

K. 1

7. If $\dfrac{1}{4}y - \dfrac{1}{12} = \dfrac{5}{8}y + \dfrac{3}{4}$, then what is the value of $\dfrac{1}{y}$?

A. 20

B. 11

C. $-\dfrac{9}{20}$

D. $-\dfrac{20}{9}$

E. -11

8. Solve for x: $81 - x^2 = 0$

F. -81 and 81

G. 9

H. 81

J. -9 and 9

K. 0 and 9

9. Solve for x: $(2x - 3)^2 - (3x - 2)^2 = 0$

A. -1 and 1

B. $\dfrac{3}{2}$ and $\dfrac{2}{3}$

C. $-\sqrt{5}$ and $\sqrt{5}$

D. $-\dfrac{3}{2}$ and $-\dfrac{2}{3}$

E. No real solutions

10. There is only one real solution for x for the equation $4x^2 + 12x = k$. Which of the following could be k?

F. -18

G. -9

H. 0

J. 4

K. 9

11. Assume $a > 0$. What are the solutions of the equation $a^2x^2 + ax - 1 = 0$?

   A. $\dfrac{-1 \pm \sqrt{5}}{2a}$

   B. $\dfrac{-a \pm \sqrt{a^2 + 4a}}{2a^2}$

   C. $\dfrac{-1 \pm \sqrt{5}}{2a}$

   D. $\dfrac{-1 \pm \sqrt{a^2 + 4a}}{2a}$

   E. $-a \pm \dfrac{\sqrt{5}}{2a}$

12.

   F. $|x - 2| > 3$

   G. $|x + 2| < 3$

   H. $|x - 3| \geq 2$

   J. $|x - 2| \geq 3$

   K. $|x + 2| > 3$

13. Which of the following is the completely factored form of $6d^4e^2 - 18de^3$?

   A. $6(d^4e^2 - 18de^3)$

   B. $6de^2(d^3 - 3e)$

   C. $6(d^4e^2 - 3de^3)$

   D. $6d(d^3e^2 - 3e^3)$

   E. $-12de^{-3}$

14. Simplify: $\dfrac{\dfrac{x}{x-1} - \dfrac{x}{x+1}}{\dfrac{x}{x-1} + \dfrac{x}{x+1}}$

   F. 0

   G. $\dfrac{4x^3}{(x-1)^2(x+1)^2}$

   H. $-\dfrac{1}{x}$

   J. x

   K. $\dfrac{1}{x}$

ANSWER KEY AND EXPLANATIONS

1. E	**4.** F	**7.** C	**10.** G	**13.** C
2. H	**5.** A	**8.** J	**11.** C	**14.** K
3. B	**6.** H	**9.** A	**12.** K	

1. The correct answer is E. All choices are written as single rational expressions, which suggests that to simplify the given expression, you must start by getting a least common denominator, which is $(ax - b)(bx + a)$. If you simply subtract numerators and denominators rather than getting a least common denominator, you will get choice B.

Rewrite each fraction as an equivalent one with this denominator, then subtract:

$$\frac{a}{ax-b} - \frac{b}{bx+a} = \frac{a}{ax-b} \cdot \frac{bx+a}{bx+a} - \frac{b}{bx+a} \cdot \frac{ax-b}{ax-b}$$
$$= \frac{a(bx+a)-b(ax-b)}{(ax-b)(bx+a)}$$

Remember, you multiply the top and bottom of a fraction by the portion of the least common denominator that is NOT already present; if you multiply by the portion that is there, you will get choice D. Next, simplify the numerator using the distributive property; if you misapply this property and only multiply the first term within the parentheses by the one outside, you will get choice A. Then, combine like terms:

$$\frac{a(bx+a)-b(ax-b)}{(ax-b)(bx+a)} = \frac{abx+a^2-bax+b^2}{(ax-b)(bx+a)} = \frac{\cancel{abx}+a^2-\cancel{bax}+b^2}{(ax-b)(bx+a)} = \frac{a^2+b^2}{(ax-b)(bx+a)}$$

You cannot cancel the a and b in this expression since they are not factors; doing so will yield choice C.

2. The correct answer is H. When faced with the division or multiplication of rational expressions, your first step should be to factor the numerators and denominators as much as possible. Doing so here yields the following:

$$\frac{4x^2-12x+9}{3x^2-2x} \div \frac{3x-2x^2}{9x^2-12x+4} = \frac{(2x-3)(2x-3)}{x(3x-2)} \div \frac{x(3-2x)}{(3x-2)(3x-2)}$$

Since this is a division problem, before you cancel any factors, rewrite it as an equivalent product by flipping over the rational expression that is after the division sign:

$$\frac{(2x-3)(2x-3)}{x(3x-2)} \div \frac{x(3-2x)}{(3x-2)(3x-2)} = \frac{(2x-3)(2x-3)}{x(3x-2)} \cdot \frac{(3x-2)(3x-2)}{x(3-2x)}$$

If you forget to do so, you will get choice F, assuming you simplify correctly.

Next, cancel any factor that is identical in the numerator and denominator, with emphasis on identical. That is especially important here because the factors $(2x - 3)$ in the top and $(3 - 2x)$ in the bottom look very similar. However, they are not the same—they are off by a factor of -1. So before you cancel that pair, you must factor out -1 from one of them.

Let's try $(3 - 2x)$:

$$\frac{(2x-3)(2x-3)}{x(3x-2)} \cdot \frac{(3x-2)(3x-2)}{x(3-2x)} = \frac{(2x-3)(2x-3)}{x(3x-2)} \cdot \frac{(3x-2)(3x-2)}{-x(2x-3)}$$

$$= \frac{(2x-3)(2x-3)}{x(3x-2)} \cdot \frac{(3x-2)(3x-2)}{-x(2x-3)}$$

$$= \frac{(2x-3)(3x-2)}{-x^2}$$

Amidst the canceling, you must make certain that you are canceling pairs of common factors such that one is in the top and the other is in the bottom; if you mistakenly cancel the x's in the denominators, you will get choice J. Finally, FOIL the numerator to get $\dfrac{6x^2 - 13x + 6}{-x^2}$. At this point, if you incorrectly cancel the x^2 term, you get choice K.

3. The correct answer is B. The most common error committed in this type of problem is canceling the two fractions in the top with the same ones in the denominator. However, you cannot do this because they are being subtracted or added, not multiplied. Doing so results in choice A.

The first step is to rewrite the numerator and denominator as single fractions by getting the least common denominators, both of which are mn. Doing so yields the following:

$$\frac{\dfrac{m}{n} - \dfrac{n}{m}}{\dfrac{m}{n} + \dfrac{n}{m}} = \frac{\dfrac{m}{n} \cdot \dfrac{m}{m} - \dfrac{n}{m} \cdot \dfrac{n}{n}}{\dfrac{m}{n} \cdot \dfrac{m}{m} + \dfrac{n}{m} \cdot \dfrac{n}{n}} = \frac{\dfrac{m^2 - n^2}{mn}}{\dfrac{m^2 + n^2}{mn}}$$

None of the choices are expressions containing fractions within fractions, so you must go further. Using the definition of division of fractions, this is equivalent to the following:

$$\frac{\dfrac{m^2 - n^2}{mn}}{\dfrac{m^2 + n^2}{mn}} = \frac{m^2 - n^2}{mn} \div \frac{m^2 + n^2}{mn} = \frac{m^2 - n^2}{mn} \cdot \frac{mn}{m^2 + n^2}$$

If you mistakenly do not flip over the fraction after the division sign, you will get choice C. Now, cancel the common factor of mn in the top and bottom to get the final expression $\dfrac{m^2 - n^2}{m^2 + n^2}$. If you arrived at choice D, you made a mistake in factoring; the denominator is the sum of squares and does not factor.

4. The correct answer is F. When solving a linear system, you often have your choice of method to use. Whenever at least one of the equations has a variable with coefficient 1, a good strategy is to solve that equation for the variable and substitute it into the other equation. That is the method we will proceed with to solve this system.

Solve the first equation for x to get $x = 2y - 1$. Then, substitute this expression in for x in the second equation to get the following equation involving only y: $y - 2(2y - 1) = 5$.

Solve this equation for y:

$$y - 2(2y - 1) = 5$$
$$y - 4y + 2 = 5$$
$$-3y + 2 = 5$$
$$-3y = 3$$
$$y = -1$$

Be careful to use the distributive property when solving the linear equation, otherwise you will get choice K.

Plug −1 in for y in your initial substitution to get the corresponding value of x:

$$x = 2(-1) - 1 = -2 - 1 = -3$$

Finally, the value of $x^y = (-3)^{-1} = \dfrac{1}{-3} = -\dfrac{1}{3}$

5. The correct answer is A. Without knowing how to attack the problem, choice D can be eliminated off the bat because the second equation is not defined when $a = 0$.

The key to this problem is knowing that two lines that are parallel do not intersect; so a linear system comprised of such lines has no solution. Lines are parallel if they have the same slope.

Using these facts, the strategy is to write the two equations in the form $y = mx$. Then, equate the slopes and solve for a. The equations in this system can be written as follows:

$$\frac{x}{3} = ay \Rightarrow x = 3ay \Rightarrow y = \left(\frac{1}{3a}\right)x$$

$$\frac{y}{a} = 3x \Rightarrow y = (3a)x$$

Equating the slopes yields the equation $\dfrac{1}{3a} = 3a$. Solve for a, as follows:

$$\frac{1}{3a} = 3a$$
$$9a^2 = 1$$
$$a^2 = \frac{1}{9}$$
$$a = -\sqrt{\frac{1}{9}}$$
$$a = -\frac{1}{3}$$

So $-\dfrac{1}{3}$ and $\dfrac{1}{3}$ (choice A) is the correct answer. Choices B and C are the results of not solving this equation correctly.

6. The correct answer is H. For a linear system to have infinitely many solutions, the equations must be multiples of each other. Dividing both sides of the first equation by a yields the equivalent system:

$$\begin{cases} x + y = \dfrac{3}{a} \\ y + x = -2 \end{cases}$$

Since the left sides are identical, the only way these two equations are multiples of each other is if the right sides are equal. That is, $\dfrac{3}{a} = -2$. Solving for a yields $a = -\dfrac{3}{2}$.

7. The correct answer is C. Multiply both sides of the equation by the LCD, 24, to eliminate the fractions. Then solve the equation for y:

$$\frac{1}{4}y - \frac{1}{12} = \frac{5}{8}y + \frac{3}{4}$$
$$24 \cdot \left(\frac{1}{4}y - \frac{1}{12}\right) = 24 \cdot \left(\frac{5}{8}y + \frac{3}{4}\right)$$
$$6y - 2 = 15y + 18$$
$$-20 = 9y$$
$$-\frac{20}{9} = y$$

Therefore, $\dfrac{1}{y} = -\dfrac{9}{20}$.

8. The correct answer is J. You could substitute the values into the equation directly and see which result in true statements, but there is a faster way. Recognize that the left side factors because it is a so-called difference of squares. Remember, $a^2 - b^2 = (a - b)(a + b)$ is a form frequently tested on the ACT Math test; it will enable you to avoid cumbersome calculations.

Factoring the left side of $81 - x^2 = 0$ yields $(9 - x)(9 + x) = 0$. Since the only way a product of two expressions can be zero is for one of the expressions itself to be zero, simply set each factor equal to zero and solve for x to see that $x = 9$ or $x = -9$.

9. The correct answer is A. A common approach is to move the second squared term to the right side and take the square root of both sides. But students often forget to affix $\pm$ to one side, resulting in missing a solution. The safer approach is to expand both squared terms (by FOILing), simplifying the left side by combining like terms, and then refactoring the entire quadratic expression:

$$(2x-3)^2 - (3x-2)^2 = 0$$
$$(4x^2 - 12x + 9) - (9x^2 - 12x + 4) = 0$$
$$4x^2 - 12x + 9 - 9x^2 + 12x - 4 = 0$$
$$-5x^2 + 5 = 0$$
$$-5(x^2 - 1) = 0$$
$$-5(x - 1)(x + 1) = 0$$

Now set each factor on the left-side equal to zero and solve for x to get $x = -1$ and $x = 1$.

10. The correct answer is G. If a quadratic equation of the form $ax^2 + bx + c = 0$ has only one solution, or root, it means that the expression on the left can be factored as a binomial squared, or $(Mx + N)^2$. First, put the given equation in standard form:

$$4x^2 + 12x - k = -0$$

If you substitute $k = -9$, you get the expression $4x^2 + 12x + 9 = 0$ on the left side, which factors as $(2x + 3)$, which implies the equation has only one real solution: $-\dfrac{3}{2}$.

All other choices of k lead to an expression that cannot be written in the form $(Mx + N)^2$, so the equations corresponding to the other choices of k either have two real solutions or no real solutions.

11. The correct answer is C. Use the quadratic formula to find the solutions to this equation and then simplify the result:

$$x = \frac{-a \pm \sqrt{a^2 - 4(a^2)(-1)}}{2(a^2)} = \frac{-a \pm \sqrt{a^2 + 4a^2}}{2a^2} = \frac{-a \pm \sqrt{5a^2}}{2a^2} = \frac{-a \pm a\sqrt{5}}{2a^2} = \frac{a(-1 \pm \sqrt{5})}{2a \cdot a} = \frac{-1 \pm \sqrt{5}}{2a}$$

The errors typically made when using the quadratic formula are misidentifying the parameters to use in the formula (choices B and D) and getting the formula wrong by not dividing the entire numerator by the denominator (choice E). Other errors are usually related to arithmetic problems, usually involving signs (choice A).

12. The correct answer is K. One approach would be to choose a solution value from the graph. Select a value from the ">1" ray, like 2, that can be substituted into the equation in each of the distractor choices. In this case, it is true only for choice K. Be careful with this method. In other problems, more than one equation could be true, and you would have to choose another solution to check.

You could also solve each of the inequalities to determine its solution set to find the correct solution (assuming you made no errors along the way), but this method is not the most efficient way to approach this type of problem. Rather, it is much better to understand a bit about the nature of absolute value inequalities. Since the solution set consists of two rays rather than a finite segment between two endpoints, and the ends of the rays are not included in the solution, the absolute value inequality to which this is the solution set must be of the form $|x - a| > b$ for some real numbers a and b. So you can eliminate choices G, H, and J.

This leaves choices F and K. Here, it is helpful to analyze the inequality geometrically. The solution set of $|x - a| > b$ consists of all real numbers x that are at least b units away from a on either side. So a serves as a center, and b serves as a radius, of sorts. The center for the inequality in choice F would be 2, which is inside the ray extending to the right, while the center for the inequality in choice K is −2, which is halfway between the two ray endpoints. The latter is the correct choice.

13. The correct answer is B. To factor the expression, look for terms that are common to both quantities. For example, 6 can be divided out of both terms, as can d and e^2. Thus, you can factor out $6de^2$, leaving $(d^3 - 3e)$. So the completely factored form is: $6de^2(d^3 - 3e)$.

14. The correct answer is K. By far, the most common error made here is canceling common terms, not factors, in the numerator and denominator. This error would cause you to select zero (choice A). Specifically:

$$\dfrac{\dfrac{x}{x-1} - \dfrac{x}{x+1}}{\dfrac{x}{x-1} + \dfrac{x}{x+1}} \neq \dfrac{\dfrac{\cancel{x}}{\cancel{x}-1} - \dfrac{\cancel{x}}{x+1}}{\dfrac{\cancel{x}}{\cancel{x}-1} + \dfrac{\cancel{x}}{x+1}} \neq 0$$

Complex fractions can look intimidating, but remember they are just notation for division. The given expression can be written equivalently as follows:

$$\dfrac{\dfrac{x}{x-1} - \dfrac{x}{x+1}}{\dfrac{x}{x-1} + \dfrac{x}{x+1}} = \left(\dfrac{x}{x-1} - \dfrac{x}{x+1}\right) \div \left(\dfrac{x}{x-1} + \dfrac{x}{x+1}\right)$$

It is more apparent in this form how the order of operations applies. Simplify the expressions in each set of parentheses first, then divide the results. To simplify these expressions, you must get a common denominator, which is $(x - 1)(x + 1)$:

$$\dfrac{x}{x-1} - \dfrac{x}{x+1} = \dfrac{x}{x-1} \cdot \dfrac{x+1}{x+1} - \dfrac{x}{x+1} \cdot \dfrac{x-1}{x-1} = \dfrac{x(x+1) - x(x-1)}{(x+1)(x-1)} = \dfrac{x^2 + x - x^2 + x}{(x+1)(x-1)} = \dfrac{2x}{(x+1)(x-1)}$$

$$\dfrac{x}{x-1} + \dfrac{x}{x+1} = \dfrac{x}{x-1} \cdot \dfrac{x+1}{x+1} + \dfrac{x}{x+1} \cdot \dfrac{x-1}{x-1} = \dfrac{x(x+1) + x(x-1)}{(x+1)(x-1)} = \dfrac{x^2 + x + x^2 - x}{(x+1)(x-1)} = \dfrac{2x^2}{(x+1)(x-1)}$$

So $\left(\dfrac{x}{x-1}-\dfrac{x}{x+1}\right)\div\left(\dfrac{x}{x-1}+\dfrac{x}{x+1}\right)=\dfrac{2x}{(x+1)(x-1)}\cdot\dfrac{2x^2}{(x+1)(x-1)}.$

Now you must convert this to an equivalent product by flipping the fraction after the division sign:

$$\dfrac{2x}{(x+1)(x-1)}\div\dfrac{2x^2}{(x+1)(x-1)}=\dfrac{2x}{(x+1)(x-1)}\cdot\dfrac{(x+1)(x-1)}{2x^2}$$

Finally, cancel like factors in the numerators and denominators and simplify:

$$\dfrac{\cancel{2x}}{\cancel{(x+1)(x-1)}}\cdot\dfrac{\cancel{(x+1)(x-1)}}{\cancel{2x^2}\,x}=\dfrac{1}{x}$$

CHAPTER

**Preparing for Higher Math:
Functions**

PREPARING FOR HIGHER MATH:

OVERVIEW

Logarithms

Functions

Operations and Functions

Graphing Functions

Types of Functions

Sequences

Summing It Up

**Test Yourself:
PHM—Functions**

Understanding functions is a critical step in the development of higher math skills. From working with basic logarithms to trigonometric equations, functions serve a variety of mathematic purposes aimed towards myriad real-world applications, particularly in engineering and the natural sciences. Moreover, functions questions also represent more than 20% of the Preparing for Higher Math questions on the ACT, having the same weight as algebra and geometry questions. In this section, we'll cover the basics you'll need to address functions in the ACT Mathematics section. Keep in mind that depending on the courses you've taken up to this point in your math studies, these concepts may or may not be new for you.

Some topics, like the unit circle and trig functions, will likely be the highest-level math you've seen thus far and will require more rigorous study on your part to master.

LOGARITHMS

Logarithms are not tested heavily on the ACT Mathematics test, but they do arise occasionally under the category of Preparing for Higher Math (and the subcategory of Functions), so it's best to be prepared. A logarithm is simply an exponent. The key formula to remember is $y = \log_a x$, which means the same thing as $x = a^y$. So, for instance, $\log_4 64 = x$ can be written as $4^x = 64$, making the answer $x = 3$. Therefore, $\log_4 64 = 3$, meaning the quantity $\log_4 64$, is the exponent to which you raise 4 in order to get 64.

This also works for fractional exponents. For example, $\log_9 27 = \frac{3}{2}$ because $9^{\frac{3}{2}} = \left(\sqrt{9}\right)^3 = 27$.

There are three main properties used to simplify logarithmic expressions.

These properties are used to combine arithmetic expressions involving logarithms with the same base into a single logarithm. The following illustrates how these properties are used:

$$\log_7 \frac{2}{49} - \log_7 \frac{2}{7} = \log_7 \left(\frac{2}{49} \div \frac{2}{7}\right)$$
$$= \log_7 \left(\frac{2}{49} \cdot \frac{7}{2}\right)$$
$$= \log_7 \frac{1}{7}$$
$$= -1$$

$$3\log_4 \frac{2}{3} + \log_4 27 = \log_4 \left(\frac{2}{3}\right)^3 + \log_4 27$$
$$= \log_4 \frac{8}{27} + \log_4 27$$
$$= \log_4 \left(\frac{8}{27} \cdot 27\right)$$
$$= \log_4 8$$
$$= \frac{3}{2}$$

LOGARITHM PROPERTIES

Logarithmic Property (in symbols)	Explanation
$\log_a M \cdot N = \log_a M + \log_a N$	The logarithm of a product is the sum of the logarithms of the individual factors.
$\log_a \frac{M}{N} = \log_a M - \log_a N$	The logarithm of a quotient is the difference of the logarithms of the dividend and divisor (i.e., numerator and denominator).
$\log_a (M^n) = n \log_a M + \log_a N$	The logarithm of the power of a quantity is the power times the logarithm of just the quantity (without the power).

TIP

If a log does not have a visible base, it is assumed to be base 10, what is called the common logarithm. The natural logarithm (represented by ln) has base *e*.

PRACTICE

$\log_2 128 =$

    A. 5

    B. 6

    C. 7

    D. 9

    E. 11

The correct answer is C. Remember that $\log_2 128$ can be written in equivalent form as $2^x = 128$. This means that in order to solve the logarithm, we need to find the exponent value that would result in an amount of 128. Since $2^7 = 128$, our answer is 7 (choice C).

Simplify: $\log_5 \left(\dfrac{1}{125} \right)$

    F. −3

    G. 3

    H. $\dfrac{1}{625}$

    J. $\dfrac{1}{25}$

    K. 25

The correct answer is F. The logarithms you will be asked to compute on the ACT will result in integers or fractions. Even so, students are often alarmed by logarithms, but it is mainly due to the intimidating notation. To overcome this mental block, let's change the way it looks by calling the expression *x*:

$$\log_5 \left(\dfrac{1}{125} \right) = x$$

Once we have done so, we can write an equivalent exponential equation by raising the base to the right side and setting it equal to the quantity from which we are taking the logarithm. Here, that equation is

$$5^x = \dfrac{1}{125}.$$

In other words, the equation requires you to find the value of *x* for which, when it is expressed as an exponent of 5, you get $\dfrac{1}{125}$. Rewriting the right side of the equation as a power of 5 is helpful in this regard. Observe that $\dfrac{1}{125} = \dfrac{1}{5^3} = 5^{-3}$. Therefore, *x* must be −3.

Simplify: $\log \left(\dfrac{z}{1000} \right)$

    A. $3\log z$

    B. $\log (z - 1{,}000)$

    C. $3 + \log z$

    D. $-3 + \log z$

    E. $\log (z + 1{,}000)$

The correct answer is D. Use the logarithm property governing quotients and simplify to get $\log \left(\dfrac{z}{1000} \right) =$ $\log z - \log 1{,}000 = \log z - 3 = -3 + \log z$.

FUNCTIONS

Functions are used to discuss and evaluate how one variable, known as an independent variable, relates to another variable, known as a dependent variable.

Let D and R be any two sets of numbers, where the set D is called the domain of the function, and the set R is called the range. A function is a rule that assigns to each element of D one and only one element of R. It can be specified by listing all of the elements in the first set next to the corresponding elements in the second set or by giving a rule or a formula by which elements from the first set can be associated with elements from the second set.

As an example, let set $D = \{1, 2, 3, 4\}$ and set $R = \{5, 6, 7, 8\}$. The diagram below indicates a particular function, f, by showing how each element of D is associated with an element of R.

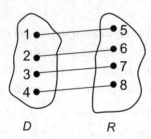

This diagram shows that the domain value of 1 is associated with the range value of 5. Similarly, 2 is associated with 6, 3 is associated with 7, and 4 is associated with 8. To express the function f in words, one might say that f is the function that assigns to each domain value x the range value $x + 4$.

Typically, the letter x is used to represent the elements of the domain and the letter y is used to represent the elements of the range. This convention enables us to write the equation $y = x + 4$ to express the rule of association for the function above. Note that as soon as a domain value x is selected, a range value y is determined by this rule. For this reason, x is referred to as the independent variable, and y is called the dependent variable (since it is determined by the independent variable).

Often, the rule of association for a function is written in function notation. In function notation, the symbol $f(x)$, which is read "f of x," is used in place of y to represent the range value. Therefore, the rule for our example function can be written $f(x) = x + 4$. For example, if you were asked to determine which range value was associated with the domain value of 3, you would compute $f(x) = f(3) = 3 + 4 = 7$. Note that, in this notation, the letter f is typically used to stand for "function," although any other letter could be used in its place. So, for instance, this rule could also be written as $g(x) = x + 4$.

Consider the notation of functions in the following examples.

Examples

 Using function notation, write the rule for a function that associates, to each number in the domain, a range value that is 7 less than 5 times the domain value.

Solution

$$f(x) = 5x - 7$$

 Use $f(x) = 5x - 7$ to determine the range value that is associated with a domain value of -12.

Solution

$$f(-12) = 5(-12) - 7 = -60 - 7 = -67$$

 If $f(x) = 8x + 9$, determine the value of $f(5), f(q), f(p^2)$, and $f(r + 3)$.

Solution

$$f(5) = 8(5) + 9 = 40 + 9 = 49$$

In the same way, to determine the value of $f(q)$, simply substitute q for the value of x in the rule for $f(x)$.

Therefore, $f(q) = 8q + 9$.

Similarly, $f(p^2) = 8(p^2) + 9 = 8p^2 + 9$.

Similarly, $f(r + 3) = 8(r + 3) + 9 = 8r + 24 + 9 = 8r + 33$.

If $f(x) = x^2 - \sqrt{x}$, what is $f(x+4)$?

A. $x^2 - \sqrt{x} + 4$

B. $x^2 + 16 - \sqrt{x+4}$

C. $x^2 + 8x + 14 - \sqrt{x}$

D. $x^2 + 8x + 16 - \sqrt{x+4}$

E. $x^2 + 14 - \sqrt{x}$

The correct answer is D. Some test takers confuse the variable used to define the function, namely x, and the expression by which they are to compute the function, namely $x + 4$. To remove this confusion, replace the x in the definition of the function with a box (or a place holder). In other words, $f(x) = x^2 - \sqrt{x}$ really means:

$$f(\square) = \square^2 - \sqrt{\square}$$

Whatever is inside the parentheses is what goes into each of those boxes. So:

$$f(\boxed{x+4}) = \boxed{x+4}^2 - \sqrt{\boxed{x+4}}$$

This will help you to avoid the common error of just "adding 4" to the function as in choice A.

Now, simplify the expression:

$$f(x+4) = (x+4)^2 - \sqrt{x+4}$$
$$= (x+4)(x+4) - \sqrt{x+4}$$
$$= x^2 + 8x + 16 - \sqrt{x+4}$$

Two critical errors that often occur here are (1) not FOILing $(x + 4)^2$, as in choice B, and (2) distributing the radical to both terms of the sum, as in choices C and E.

OPERATIONS AND FUNCTIONS

Functions can be added, subtracted, multiplied, and divided. Function operations work just like operations on expressions. The notation for these operations can be found in the following table.

FUNCTION OPERATIONS	
Sum of f and g	$(f+g)(x) = f(x) + g(x)$
Difference of f and g	$(f-g)(x) = f(x) - g(x)$
Product of f and g	$(f \cdot g)(x) = f(x) \cdot g(x)$
Quotient of f and g	$\left(\dfrac{f}{g}\right)(x) = \dfrac{f(x)}{g(x)}$
Composite function	$(f \circ g)(x) = f(g(x))$

The composite function is an important operation to remember because it allows you to find the function of another function. In this case, the input becomes the function as a whole instead of a value for x, demonstrated as follows:

- $h(f(x))$
- $f(g(x))$
- $g(h(x))$

Examples

Find $(f \circ g)(x)$ for $f(x) = 2x - x^2$ and $g(x) = x + 1$.

Solution

Replace each x in $f(x)$ with $g(x)$, then replace $g(x)$ with $x + 1$ and simplify.

$$(f \circ g)(x) = f(g(x)) = 2(g(x)) - (g(x))^2$$
$$= 2(x+1) - (x+1)^2$$
$$= 2x + 2 - (x^2 + 2x + 1)$$
$$= 2x + 2 - x^2 - 2x - 1$$
$$= -x^2 + 1$$

Find $(f \circ g)(x)$ for $f(x) = 4x^2 - 6$ and $g(x) = x + 4$?

Solution

Replace each x in $f(x)$ with $g(x)$, then replace $g(x)$ with $x + 1$ and simplify.

$$
\begin{aligned}
(f \circ g)(x) &= f(g(x)) = 4(g(x))^2 - 6 \\
&= 4(x + 4)^2 - 6 \\
&= 4((x + 4)(x + 4)) - 6 \\
&= 4(x^2 + 4x + 4x + 16) - 6 \\
&= 4(x^2 + 8x + 16) - 6 \\
&= 4x^2 + 32x + 64 - 6 \\
&= 4x^2 + 32x + 58
\end{aligned}
$$

GRAPHING FUNCTIONS

When you have a graph of a function, you can figure out if an x-value belongs to the domain of f by simply determining if an ordered pair with that x-value belongs to the graph of f. You should be familiar with the following features of the graph of a function $y = f(x)$:

- The minimum of f is the smallest y-value in the range of f; it is the y-value of the lowest point on the graph of f.

- The maximum of f is the largest y-value in the range of f; it is the y-value of the highest point on the graph of f.

- f is decreasing if its graph falls from left to right as you progress through the interval from left to right.

- f is increasing on an interval if its graph rises from left to right as you progress through the interval from left to right.

- An x-intercept of f is a point of the form $(x, 0)$. You determine the x-intercepts of a function by solving the equation $f(x) = 0$.

- A y-intercept of f is the point $(0, f(0))$.

See the next page for graphs of the most common functions on the ACT.

Functions can be moved within the coordinate plane using horizontal and vertical translations and reflections, defined as follows. Here, let h and k stand for positive real numbers.

FUNCTION TRANSFORMATIONS	
New Function	**Graphing the Function By Translation or Reflecting the Graph of $y = f(x)$**
$F(x) = f(x) + k$	Translate the graph of $y = f(x)$ k units vertically upward.
$F(x) = f(x) - k$	Translate the graph of $y = f(x)$ k units vertically downward.
$F(x) = f(x - h)$	Translate the graph of $y = f(x)$ h units to the right.
$F(x) = f(x + h)$	Translate the graph of $y = f(x)$ h units to the left.
$F(x) = -f(x)$	Reflect the graph of $y = f(x)$ over the x-axis.

TYPES OF FUNCTIONS

There are numerous types of functions that you may be asked to work with in either their original or inverse forms for PHM: Functions questions.

Linear Functions

Linear functions are functions of the form $y = f(x) = mx + b$. When graphed as a line, they will have a slope (steepness) m and y-intercept (the point that crosses the y-axis) of b.

FUNCTIONS AND THEIR GRAPHS

Function	Typical Graphs
Linear Functions $f(x) = mx + b$	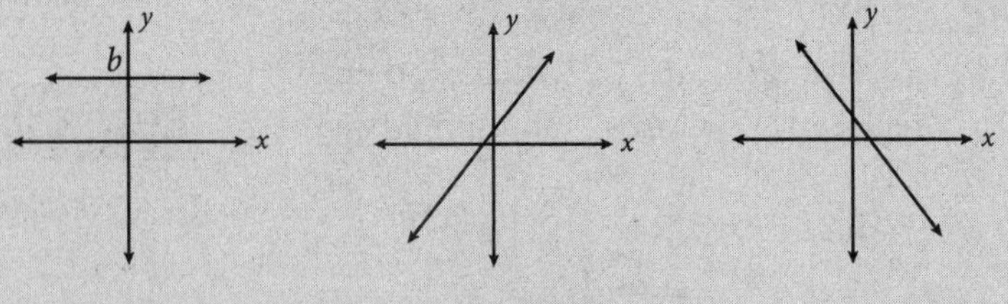 $m = 0$ $\quad$ $m > 0$ $\quad$ $m < 0$
Quadratic Functions $f(x) = a(x - h)^2 + k$	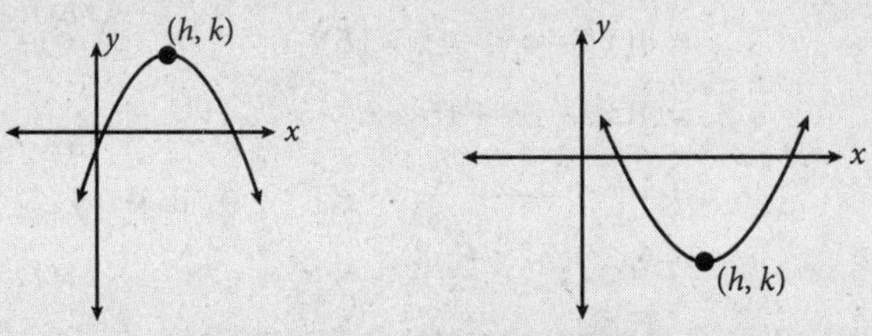 $a < 0$ $\quad$ $a > 0$ The graph is called a parabola. The vertex is the point (h, k). Note that the maximum or minimum value of a parabola occurs at the vertex
Cubic Function $f(x) = x^3$	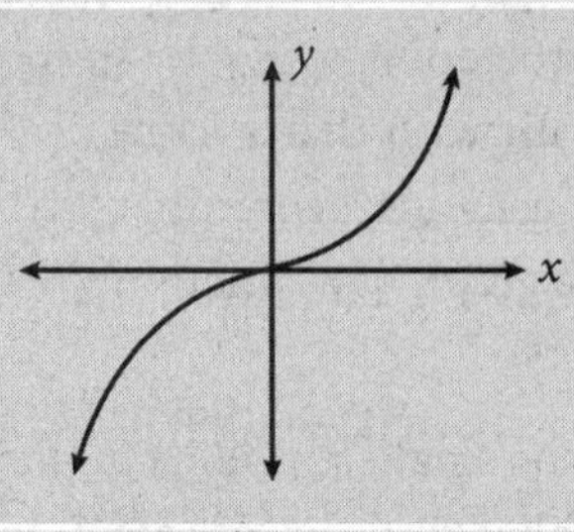
Absolute Value Function $f(x) = |x|$	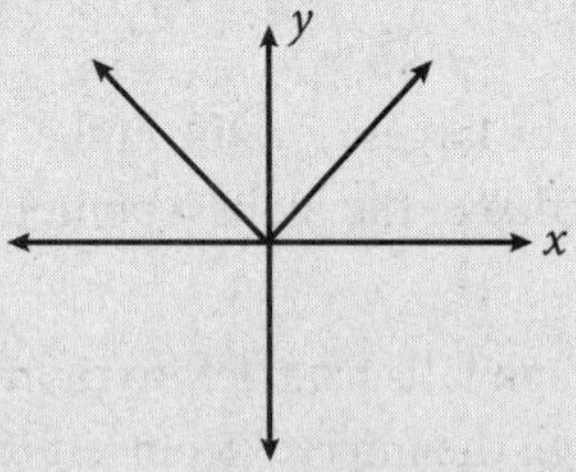 More generally, if h and k are positive numbers, then the graph of $g(x) = |x - h| + k$ is obtained by moving the shown graph to the right h units and up k units.
Square Root Function $f(x) = \sqrt{x}$	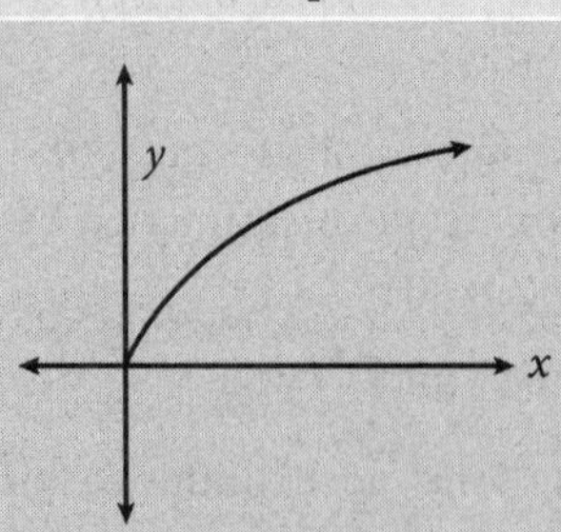

Example of Two Different Lines:

$$f(x) = -2x + 2 \text{ and } f(x) = 3x - 2$$

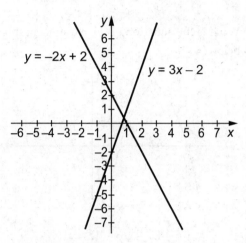

Quadratic Functions

A quadratic function is any function of the form $f(x) = ax^2 + bx + c$ where a, b, and c are real numbers. The shape of the graph of a quadratic function is called a parabola. It reaches a maximum or minimum height called the vertex.

Example of a Quadrtic:

$$f(x) = x^2 + 3$$

When $a > 0$, the graph opens up. When $a < 0$, the graph opens down. The x-coordinate of the vertex can be found using the formula $-\dfrac{b}{2a}$. The resulting value can then be substituted into the function to find the y-coordinate.

Example

Find the minimum value reached by the function $f(x) = x^2 - 6x + 1$.

Solution

The minimum value is reached when:

$$x = -\frac{b}{2a} = -\left(\frac{-6}{2}\right) = 3$$

Evaluate the function for 3 to find the minimum value:

$$f(3) = 3^2 - 6(3) + 1 = 9 - 18 + 1 = -8$$

Thus, the vertex is at (3, −8), and the minimum value reached by the function is −8.

Quadratic functions can be written in different forms. The *vertex form* is the most useful for determining the vertex, which will also show either the maximum or minimum value of the function.

The vertex form of a quadratic function is $y = a(x - h)^2 + k$, where the x-coordinate of the vertex is h and the y-coordinate of the vertex is k.

For example, in the function $y = (x - 3)^2 - 2$, the vertex is located at (3, −2). This also means that the axis of symmetry is $x = 3$ and the minimum value of the function is −2.

$$y = (x - 3)^2 - 2$$

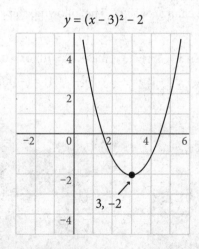

The *factored form* of a quadratic function is the most useful for identifying the roots of the function. The factored form of a quadratic function is

$y = a(x - r_1)(x - r_2)$, where r_1 and r_2 are the roots of the function. The roots may also be referred to as the x-intercepts of the graph or the zeros of the function.

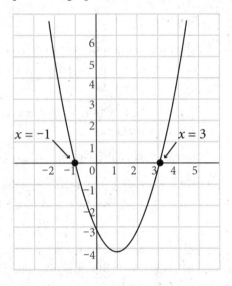

In the example shown, the quadratic function $y = x^2 - 2x - 3$ can be rewritten as $y = (x - 3)(x + 1)$, because:

$$(x - 3)(x + 1) = x^2 + x - 3x - 3$$
$$= x^2 - 2x - 3$$

The roots of the function are then $x = 3$ and $x = -1$ (notice the change of sign). The following steps show why this works:

- When $x = 3$, $y = (3 - 3)(3 + 1) = (0)(4) = 0$
- When $x = -1$, $y = (-1 - 3)(-1 + 1) = (-4)(0) = 0$

PRACTICE

What is the equation of the parabola graphed below?

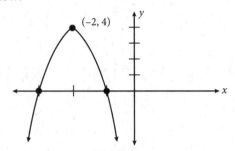

A. $y = -4x^2 - 16x - 12$

B. $y = -x^2 - 2x + 3$

C. $y = -x^2 + 4x + 3$

D. $y = 4x^2 - 16x - 12$

E. $y = 4x^2 + 16x + 12$

The correct answer is A. Factor the expression:

$-4x^2 - 16x - 12 = -4(x^2 + 4x + 3) = -4(x + 3)(x + 1)$.

This equals zero at $x = -3$ and $x = -1$; as shown, the y-intercept is -12; the parabola opens downward because the coefficient of x^2 is negative. Therefore, this is the equation of the graph shown.

Polynomial Functions

Polynomial functions have the same form as polynomial expressions. Polynomial functions have variables taken to a power, are multiplied by some coefficient, and then are added together. For example, $f(x) = -x^3 + 4x^2 - x$. Technically, both linear functions and quadratic functions are polynomial functions. But they have special properties, as shown in the previous sections. We will focus on polynomials where the degree (highest power) is 3 or greater.

The graphs of polynomial functions are curves with turning points where they change direction.

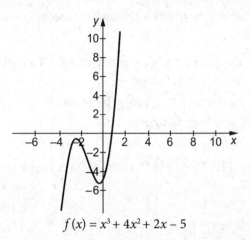

$$f(x) = x^3 + 4x^2 + 2x - 5$$

The number of turning points is equal to the degree minus 1. The polynomial function shown in the figure has a degree of 3 and two turning points.

The end behavior of a polynomial function can be determined by the degree of the polynomial and the coefficient of the highest degree term. The following table explains these properties.

POLYNOMIAL FUNCTION PROPERTIES

Degree	Sign of the Highest Degree Term	End Behavior
Even	Positive	Rises on both left and right
Even	Negative	Falls on both left and right
Odd	Positive	Falls on left, rises on right
Odd	Negative	Rises on left, falls on right

In the previous example, the polynomial function has an odd degree and a positive coefficient for the highest degree term.

Rational Functions

Rational functions are similar to rational expressions. Their domain is determined by the denominator. When the denominator is zero, the value is not included in the domain. Further, rational functions have asymptotes. The function approaches these lines but never crosses them.

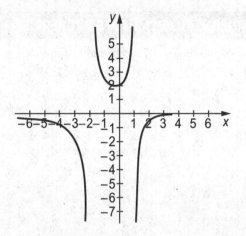

To find the vertical asymptotes of a rational function, find all values where the denominator is 0 but the numerator is not 0.

Example

Find all vertical asymptotes of the function $f(x) = \dfrac{x^2 - x - 2}{x^2 - 2x - 3}$.

Solution

$$f(x) = \frac{x^2 - x - 2}{x^2 - 2x - 3} = \frac{(x+1)(x-2)}{(x+1)(x-3)}$$

The denominator is 0 whenever $x = -1$ or 3. However, -1 also makes the numerator 0, so the only vertical asymptote is $x = 3$.

Horizontal asymptotes are found by looking at the degrees of the highest degree terms. The following table shows the rules for this.

HORIZONTAL ASYMPTOTE PROPERTIES	
Degrees of the terms	**Horizontal asymptote**
The same	y = the ratio of the coefficients Ex: $y = \dfrac{2x^3 - 4}{5x^3}$ has the horizontal asymptote $y = \dfrac{2}{5}$
Higher degree in the numerator	No horizontal asymptote
Lower degree in numerator	$y = 0$ is the horizontal asymptote

The function $f(x) = \dfrac{x^2 - x - 2}{x^2 - 2x - 3}$ has a horizontal asymptote of $y = 1$ since the degrees are the same and the coefficients are both 1.

Radical Functions

Radical functions $\left(\text{e.g., } y = \sqrt{x}\right)$ are easily recognized thanks to the presence of the radical sign. Since the x in $y = \sqrt{x}$ cannot be negative, the graph of $y = \sqrt{x}$ only appears in the first quadrant.

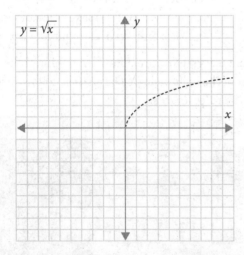

The image shows the graph $y = \sqrt{x}$. The graphs of all square root functions have this general appearance.

Some other characteristics of square root functions are as follows:

- The graph of $y = \sqrt{x}$ is the top half of a parabola that opens sideways.
- As you travel out along the graph of $y = \sqrt{x}$, the graph keeps going higher.
- The domain and range of $y = \sqrt{x}$ are both numbers greater than or equal to zero.

Which of the following represents the parent function for the graph below?

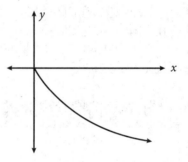

A. $y = Ax$

B. $y = Ax^2$

C. $y = Ax^3$

D. $y = Ax^4$

E. $y = A\sqrt{x}$

The correct answer is E. Even if you didn't immediately recognize that this graph of $y = \sqrt{x}$ is reflected over the x-axis, you can still answer this question using the process of elimination. Choice A can be immediately eliminated because it is a linear equation, and its graph would therefore be a straight line. Choices B, C, and D can be eliminated because to yield a right opening graph, the x and y variables would need to be switched.

Absolute Value Functions

Absolute value functions ($y = |x|$) are easily recognizable due to the presence of the absolute value sign. The graphs of these functions are also distinctive due to their V shape.

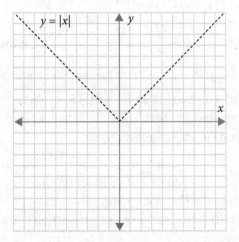

The image shows the graph $y = |x|$. The graphs of all absolute value functions have this general appearance.

Some other characteristics about absolute value functions are as follows:

- The graph of $y = |x|$ is symmetric over the y-axis.
- The domain of $y = |x|$ is all real numbers.
- The range of $y = |x|$ is limited to numbers greater than or equal to zero.

Exponential Functions

The graph of an exponential function $f(x) = b^x$ has a horizonal asymptote of the x-axis—that is, $y = 0$. If the base is a whole number, the graph rises rapidly on the right. If the base is a fraction or decimal, the graph falls quickly from left to right.

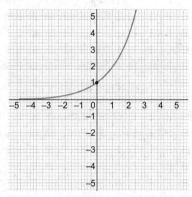

Graph of $y = 2^x$

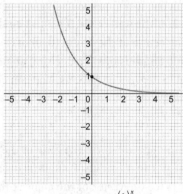

Graph of $y = \left(\dfrac{1}{2}\right)^x$

Logarithmic Functions

Logarithmic functions are inverse functions to exponential functions. Their graphs are a reflection across $y = x$ of the graph of the corresponding exponential function. The graph of a logarithmic function $f(x) = \log_b(x)$ has a vertical asymptote of the y-axis—that is, $x = 0$. The graph rises from left to right, but not as quickly as with an exponential function.

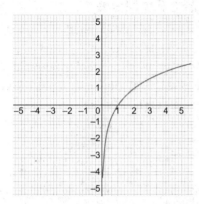

Graph of $y = \log_2(x)$

Note that if a function like that shown is translated (rewritten by adding or subtracting within or outside the function), the locations of the asymptotes may change.

Trigonometric Functions

For trigonometric functions, such as $f(x) = \sin(x)$, you need to consider the unit circle. The unit circle is a circle with the center at the origin $(0, 0)$ of the coordinate plane and a radius of 1. The central angle θ can be expressed in degrees or radians. You can convert degrees to radians by using the following formula:

$$\text{Radians} = \frac{\text{Degrees}}{180°} \cdot \pi.$$

To find radian measure, form the ratio of the arc length of a circle's sector to its radius. As shown in the figure that follows, place the vertex of the angle at the center of a circle of radius r and denote the length of the arc of the circle formed by the two rays of this angle by s:

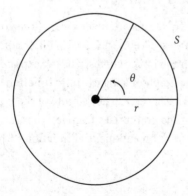

The radian measure of the angle θ is given by $\theta = \dfrac{s}{r}$.

Let's say that $\theta = 90°$. Since the circumference of the entire circle is $2\pi r$, and the central angle of an entire circle is $360°$, it follows that an angle with measure $\theta = 90°$ cuts off an arc with a length that is $\dfrac{1}{4}$ of the entire circle; that is, $s = \dfrac{1}{4}(2\pi r)$. As such, the measure of angle θ in radians is $\theta = \dfrac{s}{r} = \dfrac{\frac{1}{4}(2\pi r)}{r} = \dfrac{\pi}{2}$ radians.

So $90° = \dfrac{\pi}{2}$ radians. And that means that an entire $360°$ circle has a measure of 2π radians. The same type of reasoning works to determine the radian measure corresponding to any degree measure.

If an angle θ is drawn in the standard position, the terminal side of the angle will intersect the unit circle. The x-coordinate of the intersection point will be the cosine of θ and the y-coordinate of the intersection point will be the sine of θ.

In the first quadrant (0 radians to $\dfrac{\pi}{2}$ radians), both the cosine and the sine are positive. As angles rotate into quadrants II, III, and IV, the signs of the cosine and sine change accordingly.

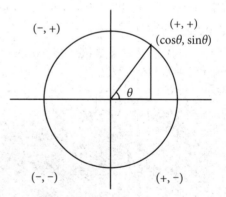

Graphing Trigonometric Functions

Sine and cosine are periodic functions since their patterns of y-values repeat every $360°$ (or every 2π radians). The graphs for $f(x) = \sin x$ and $f(x) = \cos x$ can be seen here. Note that the x-axis is measured in radians, marked with the key values $\dfrac{\pi}{2}$ (or $90°$), π (or $180°$), $\dfrac{3\pi}{2}$ (or $270°$), and 2π (or $360°$).

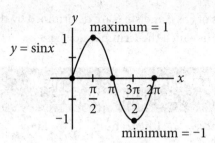

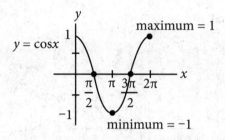

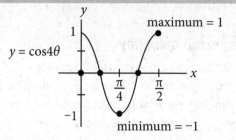

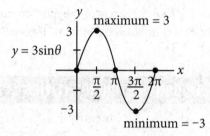

For the equation $y = 3 \sin \theta$, the amplitude is 3 and the period is $\dfrac{2\pi}{1} = 2\pi$.

The period of both of these graphs is 2π since that is the interval of x-values over which the function completes one cycle. The points on the waves represent the changing values of sine and cosine around the circumference of the unit circle. Over 2π radians, both a basic sine and cosine wave will oscillate between 1 and -1, just with different starting points at $x = 0$.

The amplitude is one-half the positive difference of the maximum and minimum values of the functions. For both these graphs, the amplitude is:

$$\frac{1}{2}\left(1 - (-1)\right) = \frac{1}{2}(2) = 1$$

Note that the sine function is positive between 0 and π, and negative between π and 2π. The cosine function is positive between 0 and $\dfrac{\pi}{2}$ and between $\dfrac{3\pi}{2}$ and 2π, and negative between $\dfrac{\pi}{2}$ and $\dfrac{3\pi}{2}$.

Amplitude and Period

You can use the equation and/or the graph of a trigonometric function to identify its amplitude and period. For an equation in the form $y = a \sin b\,\theta$ or $y = a \cos b\,\theta$, the amplitude is a and period is $\dfrac{2\pi}{b}$.

For the equation $y = \cos 4\,\theta$, the amplitude is 1 and the period is $\dfrac{2\pi}{4} = \dfrac{\pi}{2}$.

How many cycles does the function $y = 3 \cos(8x)$ complete when $0 \le x \le 2\pi$?

- **A.** $\dfrac{1}{8}$
- **B.** $\dfrac{1}{2}$
- **C.** 1
- **D.** 3
- **E.** 8

The correct answer is E. The coefficient of x determines the period of a cosine function, while the coefficient in front (in this case, 3) determines the amplitude and has no effect on the period. Since we know the period of $g(x) = \cos(bx)$ is $\dfrac{2\pi}{b}$ and the same is true for $g(x) = a \cos(bx)$ for any non-zero number a, we can conclude that, with a period of $\dfrac{\pi}{4}$, the graph of $y = 3 \cos(8x)$ completes 8 full cycles in the interval $0 \le x \le 2\pi$.

Trigonometric Identities

Trigonometric identities are useful equalities that are always true—you can use them on questions that ask you to simplify expressions involving trigonometric functions or to determine the sine or cosine of an angle when the cosine or sine of that angle is known. The following table features just a few of the most commonly used identities you might see on the ACT exam.

TRIGONOMETRIC IDENTITIES	
Name	**Identity**
Pythagorean Identity	$\cos^2\theta + \sin^2\theta = 1$
Periodicity Identities	$\sin(2n\pi + \theta) = \sin(\theta)$, where n is an integer
	$\cos(2n\pi + \theta) = \cos(\theta)$, where n is an integer
Symmetry Identities	$\sin(-\theta) = -\sin(\theta)$
	$\cos(-\theta) = \cos(\theta)$
Complementary Angle Identities	$\cos\dfrac{\pi}{2} - \theta = \sin\theta$
	$\sin\dfrac{\pi}{2} - \theta = \cos\theta$
Double-Angle Identities	$\sin(2\theta) = 2\sin\theta\cos\theta$
	$\cos(2\theta) = \cos2\theta - \sin2\theta$

One term that you might see on the ACT exam is the "terminal side of an angle." The terminal side of an angle that is swept out from the positive *x*-axis in the counterclockwise direction is the radial segment that forms the angle, along with the positive *x*-axis:

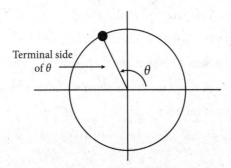

The signs of cos θ and sin θ are determined by the quadrant in which the terminal side lies.

TERMINAL SIDES AND SIGNS OF COSINE AND SINE			
Quadrant in which the Terminal Side Lies	**Illustration**	**Sign of cos θ**	**Sign of sin θ**
I		+	+
II		–	+
III		–	–
IV		+	–

Example

Suppose $\cos\theta = -\dfrac{1}{5}$ and the terminal side of θ intersects the unit circle in Quadrant II. Compute $\sin\theta$.

Solution

To solve, use the Pythagorean identity $\sin^2\theta + \cos^2\theta = 1$ to find two possible values for $\sin\theta$. Then, use the fact that the sine of an angle whose terminal side is in Quadrant II must be positive to choose the correct value:

$$\sin^2\theta + \cos^2\theta = 1$$
$$\sin^2\theta + \left(-\frac{1}{5}\right)^2 = 1$$
$$\sin^2\theta + \frac{1}{25} = 1$$
$$\sin^2\theta = \frac{24}{25}$$
$$\sin\theta = \pm\frac{\sqrt{24}}{5} = \pm\frac{2\sqrt{6}}{5}$$

Since the terminal side is in Quadrant II, we conclude that the correct value is $\dfrac{2\sqrt{6}}{5}$.

PRACTICE

Suppose that $\sin\theta = \dfrac{3}{5}$ and that the terminal side of θ is in Quadrant II. Which of the following equals $\cos 2\theta$?

A. $-\dfrac{4}{5}$

B. $-\dfrac{3}{5}$

C. $\dfrac{7}{25}$

D. $\dfrac{4}{5}$

E. $\dfrac{9}{5}$

The correct answer is C. First, use the Pythagorean identity $\sin^2\theta + \cos^2\theta = 1$ to find two possible values for $\cos\theta$. Then, choose the correct value in light of the fact that the cosine of an angle whose terminal side is in Quadrant II must be negative. Finally, use the double-angle formula $\cos^2\theta = \cos^2\theta - \sin^2\theta$:

$$\sin^2\theta + \cos^2\theta = 1$$
$$\left(\frac{3}{5}\right)^2 + \cos^2\theta = 1$$
$$\cos^2\theta = 1 - \frac{9}{25}$$
$$\cos\theta = \pm\frac{4}{5}$$

Since the terminal side is in Quadrant II, we conclude that $\cos\theta = -\dfrac{4}{5}$. Therefore,

$$\cos 2\theta = \cos^2\theta - \sin^2\theta = \left(-\frac{4}{5}\right)^2 - \left(\frac{3}{5}\right)^2 = \frac{16}{25} - \frac{9}{25} = \frac{7}{25}$$

Solving Trigonometric Equations

Just as there are linear equations, quadratic equations, and equations involving radicals of an unknown, there are equations involving the trigonometric functions. The general aim is the same—you need to find values of the input that will make the equation true.

In the case of trigonometric equations, it will be very helpful for you to remember these common values of trigonometric functions. If you can recall these, you will be able to save several steps if faced with a trigonometric equation on the ACT exam. These problems will not turn up frequently on the test—but if they do, there's a good chance that they will include one or more of the values from the following table:

COMMON TRIGONOMETRIC VALUES

x	$\sin(x)$	$\cos(x)$
0	0	1
$\dfrac{\pi}{6}$	$\dfrac{1}{2}$	$\dfrac{\sqrt{3}}{2}$
$\dfrac{\pi}{4}$	$\dfrac{\sqrt{2}}{2}$	$\dfrac{\sqrt{2}}{2}$
$\dfrac{\pi}{3}$	$\dfrac{\sqrt{3}}{2}$	$\dfrac{1}{2}$
$\dfrac{\pi}{2}$	1	0
π	0	−1
$\dfrac{3\pi}{2}$	− 2	0
2π	0	1

PRACTICE

Which of the following is a solution of the equation $\cos(3x) = 1$?

- **A.** π
- **B.** $\dfrac{2\pi}{3}$
- **C.** 2π
- **D.** $\dfrac{\pi}{6}$
- **E.** $\dfrac{\pi}{4}$

The correct answer is B. Looking at the table, you can see any value of x for which $3x = 0$ or 2π is a solution of this equation (it will lead to a value of 1, which is what you are seeking). So $x = 0$ and $x = \dfrac{2\pi}{3}$ are both solutions. Of these, only the latter is a choice, so the answer is B.

SEQUENCES

Some ACT exam questions will ask you to find the value of an unknown term if given a sequence of terms. There are two special types of sequences for which we can find explicit formulas for the nth term rather easily.

An arithmetic sequence is a sequence with terms obtained by adding a fixed constant to the previous term. For instance, the sequence 8, 12, 16, 20, 24, … is an arithmetic sequence because the constant 4 is added to one term to get the next term. Likewise, the sequence 5, 1, –3, –7, –11, … is an arithmetic sequence because the constant –4 is added to one term to get the next term. However, the sequence 3, 6, 10, 15, 21, … is not an arithmetic sequence because the same constant is not added to each term to get the next. To get the second term, you add 3 to the first one; but, to get the third term, you must add 4 to the second term, and to get the fourth term, you must add 5 to the third one, and so on.

In general, if a sequence is arithmetic (and you add d to a term to get the next term), then the formula for its nth term is given by $a_n = (\text{first term}) + (n - 1)d$.

A geometric sequence is a sequence with terms obtained by multiplying the previous term by a fixed constant r. For instance, the sequence $\frac{1}{3}, \frac{1}{9}, \frac{1}{27}, \frac{1}{81}, \ldots$ is a geometric sequence because each term is multiplied by $\frac{1}{3}$ to get the next term. However, the sequence 8, 4, 0, −4, −8, … is not geometric because there is no single number by which you can multiply each term to get the next term.

In general, if a sequence is geometric (and you multiply a term by r to get the next term), then the formula for the nth term a_n is given by $a_n = r^{n-1} \times a_1$.

PRACTICE

What is the seventh term of the sequence 6, 12, 18, …?

- **A.** 24
- **B.** 30
- **C.** 36
- **D.** 42
- **E.** 108

The correct answer is D. To answer this question, we must determine a pattern that the numbers of the sequence follows. Here the pattern is to add 6 to the previous term to get the next one. So, the next term in the sequence is 24, but that's not the answer, as that is only the fourth term. We need the seventh term, so we continue to expand, getting 30, 36, and 42. Therefore, the seventh term is 42.

SUMMING IT UP

- A function is a rule that associates to each input x a corresponding y-value. They are typically named using letters, like f or g. The notation $f(x)$ represents the functional value at x.

- The domain of a function is the set of all values of x that can be substituted into the expression and yield a meaningful output. The range of a function is the set of all possible y-values attained at some member of the domain.

- The sum $(f + g)(x)$ is defined as $f(x) + g(x)$. Likewise, the difference function $(f - g)(x)$ is defined as $f(x) - g(x)$, the product function $(f \cdot g)(x)$ is defined as $f(x) \cdot g(x)$, and the quotient function $\left(\dfrac{f}{g}\right)(x)$ is defined as $\dfrac{f(x)}{g(x)}$.

- The composition of f and g, denoted by $(f \circ g)$, is defined by $(f \circ g)(x) = f(g(x))$.

- The minimum of f is the smallest y-value in the range of f; it is the y-value of the lowest point on the graph of f. Likewise, the maximum of f is the largest y-value in the range of f; it is the y-value of the highest point on the graph of f.

- f is decreasing on an interval if its graph falls from left to right as you progress through the interval from left to right; f is increasing on an interval if its graph rises from left to right as you progress through the interval from left to right.

- An x-intercept of f is a point of the form $(x, 0)$. You determine the x-intercepts of a function by solving the equation $f(x) = 0$.

- A y-intercept of f is the point $(0, f(0))$.

- Trigonometric identities are useful equalities that are always true that can help you to simplify expressions involving trigonometric functions or to determine the sine or cosine of an angle when the cosine or sine of that angle is known. The most commonly used identities are as follows:

  - Pythagorean identity: $\cos^2\theta + \sin^2\theta = 1$
  - Periodicity identities: $\sin(2n\pi + \theta) = \sin(\theta)$, $\cos(2n\pi + \theta) = \cos(\theta)$, where n is an integer
  - Symmetry identities: $\sin(-\theta) = -\sin(\theta)$, $\cos(-\theta) = \cos(\theta)$
  - Complementary angle identities: $\cos\dfrac{\pi}{2} - \theta = \sin\theta$, $\sin\dfrac{\pi}{2} - \theta = \cos\theta$
  - Double-angle identities: $\sin(2\theta) = 2\sin\theta\cos\theta$, $\cos(2\theta) = \cos^2\theta - \sin^2\theta$

- An arithmetic sequence is a sequence whose terms are obtained by adding a fixed constant to the previous term. A formula for its nth term is $a_n = (\text{first term}) + (n-1)d$.

- A geometric sequence is a sequence whose terms obtained by multiplying the previous term by a fixed constant r. A formula for the nth term an is $a_n = r^{n-1} \times a_1$.

TEST YOURSELF

PREPARING FOR HIGHER MATH — FUNCTIONS

10 Questions—10 Minutes

> **Directions:** Solve each problem and choose the correct answer.
>
> Do not dwell on problems that take too long. First, solve as many as you can; then, you can return to others you have left.
>
> You are permitted to use a calculator. You may use your calculator for any problem you like, but some of the problems may best be completed without a calculator.

1. Compute: $\log_2\left(\dfrac{2^2 \cdot 2^{-3}}{2^3}\right)$

   A. -3

   B. -4

   C. 2

   D. 4

   E. Undefined

2. If $f(g) = \sqrt[3]{g-7}$, what is $f(-20)$?

   F. $-\sqrt{27}$

   G. -3

   H. 3

   J. 9

   K. Undefined

3. If $\log_6 216 = x$, then $x =$

   A. $\dfrac{\log 216}{6}$

   B. $\sqrt[6]{216}$

   C. 36

   D. 3

   E. 6^{216}

4. Consider the function $H(x) = \dfrac{x}{4-x}$ where $x > 0$. For which pairs of functions $f(x)$ and $g(x)$ does $H(x) = (f \circ g)(x)$?

   F. $f(x) = x$ and $g(x) = \dfrac{1}{4-x}$

   G. $f(x) = \sqrt{\dfrac{x}{16-x}}$ and $g(x) = x^2$

   H. $f(x) = \left(\dfrac{x}{4-x}\right)^2$ and $g(x) = \sqrt{x}$

   J. $f(x) = \dfrac{x^2}{4-x^2}$ and $g(x) = \sqrt{x}$

   K. $f(x) = \sqrt{x}$ and $g(x) = \dfrac{x^2}{4-x^2}$

5. What is the domain of $f(x) = \sqrt[4]{6-2x}$?

   A. $x < 6$

   B. $x > -3$

   C. $x < 3$

   D. $x \leq 3$

   E. $x > 6$

6. Which of the following is the set of all values of θ in the interval $[0, 2\pi]$ for which $\cot \theta = -1$?

   F. $\left\{ \dfrac{\pi}{4}, \dfrac{5\pi}{4} \right\}$

   G. $\left\{ \dfrac{\pi}{2}, \dfrac{3\pi}{2} \right\}$

   H. $\left\{ \dfrac{3\pi}{4}, \dfrac{7\pi}{4} \right\}$

   J. $\left\{ \dfrac{\pi}{4}, \dfrac{3\pi}{4}, \dfrac{5\pi}{4}, \dfrac{7\pi}{4} \right\}$

   K. $\left\{ 0, \pi, 2\pi \right\}$

7. The graph of which of these functions is as follows:

   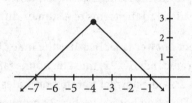

   A. $f(x) = 3 - |x - 4|$
   B. $f(x) = 3 + |x + 4|$
   C. $f(x) = 3 - |x + 4|$
   D. $f(x) = |x - 4| - 3$
   E. $f(x) = -|x - 4| - 3$

8. Which of these formulas gives the 111th term of the geometric series $27, -9, 3, -1, \dots$?

   F. $\left(-\dfrac{27}{3} \right)^{110}$

   G. $-27(3)^{110}$

   H. $-27 \left(\dfrac{1}{3} \right)^{110}$

   J. $27 \left(-\dfrac{1}{3} \right)^{110}$

   K. $27(-3)^{111}$

9. Which of these formulas gives the 58th term of the arithmetic sequence $-6, 1, 8, 15, \dots$?

   A. $-6 + (58 - 1)(7)$
   B. $-6 + 58(7)$
   C. $-6 + (58 - 1)(-7)$
   D. $-6 + 58(-7)$
   E. $-6(58)$

10. Which of the following is the set of all values of θ in the interval $[0, 2\pi]$ for which $\sin^2 \theta - \dfrac{3}{4} = 0$?

   F. $\left\{ \dfrac{\pi}{4}, \dfrac{3\pi}{4} \right\}$

   G. $\left\{ \dfrac{\pi}{3}, \dfrac{2\pi}{3} \right\}$

   H. $\left\{ \dfrac{\pi}{6}, \dfrac{5\pi}{6} \right\}$

   J. $\left\{ \dfrac{\pi}{6}, \dfrac{5\pi}{6}, \dfrac{7\pi}{6}, \dfrac{11\pi}{6} \right\}$

   K. $\left\{ \dfrac{\pi}{3}, \dfrac{2\pi}{3}, \dfrac{4\pi}{3}, \dfrac{5\pi}{3} \right\}$

ANSWER KEY AND EXPLANATIONS

1. B	3. D	5. D	7. C	9. A
2. G	4. J	6. H	8. J	10. K

1. **The correct answer is B.** The key to this problem lies in using the property $\log_a(a^x) = x$. Since the base $a = 2$, you need to express the quantity in the parentheses as a power of 2. This requires the use of the exponent rules:

$$\frac{2^2 \cdot 2^{-3}}{2^3} = \frac{2^2}{2^3 \cdot 2^3} = \frac{2^2}{\left(2^3\right)^2} = \frac{2^2}{2^6} = 2^{2-6} = 2^{-4}$$

So $\log_2\left(\frac{2^2 \cdot 2^{-3}}{2^3}\right) = \log_2\left(2^{-4}\right) = -4$.
The errors often made in this type of problem stem from trouble with computing with exponents and using exponent rules. For instance, $\frac{2^{-3}}{2^3} \neq 1$; choice C is a result of making this error. Similarly, $2^{-3} \neq -2^3$; this error leads to $\log_2(-4)$, which is undefined (choice E). Making the error $\log_2\left(\frac{1}{2^4}\right) \neq 4$ results in choosing choice D. In this case, you must bring the 2 to the numerator before applying the property $\log_a(a^x) = x$. Finally, $2^3 \cdot 2^3 = (2^3)^2 = 2^6$, not $2^{3+2} = 2^5$; this error is represented by choice A.

2. **The correct answer is G.** Substitute for the variable g to get $f(-20) = \sqrt[3]{-20-7} = \sqrt[3]{-27} = -3$.

3. **The correct answer is D.** The equation $\log_6 216 = x$ is the same as saying $6^x = 216$. Note that $6^3 = 216$, so that the answer is 3. Choice A is incorrect because the denominator should be $\log_6$, not just 6. Choice B is incorrect because $\log_6 216 = x$ is equivalent to $6^x = 216$, not $216^{\frac{1}{6}} = \sqrt[6]{216} = x$. For choice C, $6^2 = 36$, not 216. Choice E is incorrect because $\log_6 216 = x$ is equivalent to $6^x = 216$, not $6^{216} = x$.

4. **The correct answer is J.** The most direct approach is to compute $(f \circ g)(x)$ which is $f(g(x))$ for the given

pairs to see which one works. Keep in mind that the order of this composition matters.

Using the pairs in choice J yields $\frac{\left(\sqrt{x}\right)^2}{4-\left(\sqrt{x}\right)^2} = \frac{x}{4-x}$, as desired.

Choice F is the result of misinterpreting the composition as a product. Choice K is equal to the reverse composition $g(f(x))$. Choices G and H involve errors with computing the radical term; you cannot distribute a radical to the terms of a sum or difference.

5. **The correct answer is D.** Because the index, 4, is even, the radicand, $6 - 2x$, must be nonnegative. Hence $6 - 2x \geq 0$. Subtract 6 from both sides to get $-2x \geq -6$. Dividing both sides by -2 and reversing the inequality (because of division by a negative number) yields $x \leq 3$. Choices A, B, and E are not correct because all three domains include values greater than 3 that result in a negative number under the radical. Choice C is incorrect because it excludes $x = 3$, which is an allowable value in $f(x)$
$f(x) : \sqrt[4]{6-2(3)} = \sqrt[4]{0} = 0$.

6. **The correct answer is H.** Write the equation in terms of $\sin\theta$ and $\cos\theta$:

$$\cot\theta = -1$$
$$\frac{\cos\theta}{\sin\theta} = -1$$
$$\cos\theta = -\sin\theta$$

The only values of θ for which this is true are $\frac{3\pi}{4}, \frac{7\pi}{4}$.
Choice F is the set of values where $\cot\theta = 1$, while choice G is where it equals 0. Choice J includes the values that make $\cot\theta = 1$ as well. Choice K is the set where $\cot\theta$ is undefined.

7. **The correct answer is C.** The idea is to use the translation results with the basic absolute value graph, as follows:

Step	Action	Equation
1.	Start with basic absolute value graph.	$y = \lvert x \rvert$
2.	Reflect over the x-axis.	$y = -\lvert x \rvert$
3.	Move the graph left 4 units.	$y = -\lvert x + 4 \rvert$
4.	Move the graph up 3 units.	$y = -\lvert x + 4 \rvert + 3$

This equation can be written equivalently as $y = 3 - \lvert x + 4 \rvert$. All the distractor choices involve sign changes on the constant terms, which change the direction of the translation or if the original graph is reflected over the x-axis. While it is recommended to be familiar with the function translation facts stated above, sometimes the "trial and error" method may be quicker or your only alternative if you forget the facts. In this case, any point on a graph must make the equation true. Choosing either x-intercept $(-7, 0)$ or $(-1, 0)$ proves true for choice C alone.

8. **The correct answer is J.** You must know the formula for a geometric sequence, which is $a_n = a_1 \cdot r^{n-1}$, $n \geq 1$, where r is the number you multiply a term to get the next term and a_1 is the first term of the sequence. Here, $a_1 = 27 =$ and $27r = -9$ so that $r = -\dfrac{1}{3}$. Since you want the 111th term, use $n = 111$ with these two values in the formula to get $a_{111} = 27\left(-\dfrac{1}{3}\right)^{111-1} = 27\left(-\dfrac{1}{3}\right)^{110}$. The incorrect answer

choices are variations of mistakes made in the formula itself. For instance, choice F should have the 27 outside the parentheses, while choice H should have the negative sign inside the parentheses. Choices G and K use the wrong value for r; this would require the terms to increase in size, and choice K also has the wrong power—it should be reduced by 1.

9. **The correct answer is A.** You must know the formula for an arithmetic sequence, which is $a_n = a_1 + (n - 1)d$, $n \geq 1$, where d is the number you add or subtract from a term to get the next term, and a_1 is the first term of the sequence. Here, $a_1 = -6$ and $d = 1 - (-6) = 7$. Since you want the 58th term, use $n = 58$ with these two values in the formula to $a_{58} = -6 + (58 - 1)(7)$. The incorrect answer choices are variations of mistakes made in the formula itself.

10. **The correct answer is K.** First, isolate $\sin\theta$ on one side of the equation:

$$\sin^2\theta - \frac{3}{4} = 0$$

$$\sin^2\theta = \frac{3}{4}$$

$$\sin\theta = -\sqrt{\frac{3}{4}}$$

$$\sin\theta = -\frac{\sqrt{3}}{2}$$

Now, use the known values of sin to conclude that the solution set is $\left\{ \dfrac{\pi}{3}, \dfrac{2\pi}{3}, \dfrac{4\pi}{3}, \dfrac{5\pi}{3} \right\}$.

Choice B is the result of not putting "±" when taking the square root of both sides. The other choices simply identify the wrong values of θ.

CHAPTER

**Preparing for Higher Math:
Geometry**

PREPARING FOR HIGHER MATH:

OVERVIEW

2D Shapes

Right Triangle Trigonometry

Coordinate Geometry

Summing It Up

Test Yourself: PHM—Geometry

ACT questions that fall under the domain of Preparing for Higher Math: Geometry will test a deeper understanding of geometric principles. PHM: Geometry questions will build off of the basic core concepts typical of Integrating Essential Skills (IES) questions (as seen in Chapter 9), tapping into more in-depth subjects such as higher-level understanding of polygons and circles, introductory trigonometry, and more detailed engagement with coordinate geometry. While many PHM: Geometry questions will typically present you with equations and formulas on their own, some will also take the form of real-world scenarios. This is crucial to remember, as a sizeable portion of math questions on the ACT are categorized as "Modeling." Since this category addresses, in part, the ability to construct models and figures as a means of engaging with practical mathematics, it is no surprise that many of these questions could very well be geometric in scope.

GEOMETRY

2D SHAPES

In Chapter 9, you saw some basic geometry concepts regarding polygons, specifically related to determining area and perimeter. Here, we'll review those ideas and also look at some more specialized concepts related to polygons (including triangles) and circles.

Triangles

Recall that all triangles obey the triangle sum and triangle inequality rules. The triangle sum rule says that the sum of the measures of the three angles in any triangle must be 180°. The triangle inequality says that the sum of the lengths of any two sides of a triangle must be strictly larger than the length of the third side.

Triangles come in all different sizes and are classified using their angles and sides. The following tables provide some essential terms and examples.

CLASSIFIED BY ANGLES		
Term	**Definition**	**Illustration**
Right	One of the angles is a right angle (the other two, therefore, must be acute)	
Acute	All three angles are acute	
Obtuse	One of the angles is obtuse (the other two, therefore, must be acute)	

CLASSIFIED BY SIDES		
Term	**Definition**	**Illustration**
Equilateral	All three sides have the same length; that is, all three sides are congruent	
Isosceles	At least two sides have the same length; that is, at least two sides are congruent	
Scalene	All three sides have different lengths	

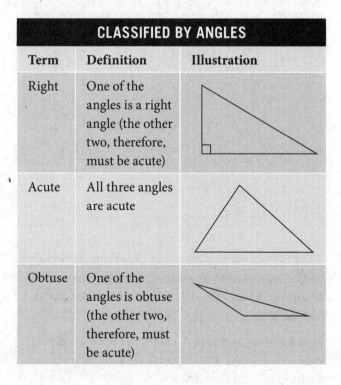

Let's put some of these rules into practice with this sample problem.

PRACTICE

What is the measure of angle *DEF*?

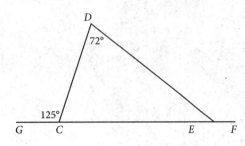

A. 127°

B. 125°

C. 108°

D. 90°

E. 53°

The correct answer is A. Angle *DCE* is supplementary to angle *DCG*, so its measure is 180° – 125° = 55°. The interior angles of a triangle sum to 180°, so the measure of angle *DEC* is 180° – 55° – 72° = 53°. Finally, angle *DEF* is supplementary to angle *DEC*, so its measure is 180° – 53° = 127°.

Congruent and Similar Triangles

We say two triangles *ABC* and *DEF* are congruent if all three corresponding pairs of angles are congruent and all three corresponding sides are congruent. Always identify corresponding sides of two triangles using the order in which their vertices (i.e., points where two sides meet) are written. As noted here in our description, vertex *A* corresponds to vertex *D*, *B* to *E*, and *C* to *F*.

Congruent triangles have the same perimeter and area.

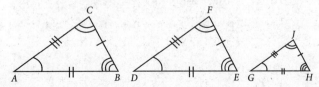

△*ABC* is congruent to △*DEF* and similar to △*GHJ*.

Two triangles *ABC* and *DEF* that are not congruent can still be proportional to each other in the sense that the ratios of the three pairs of corresponding sides are the same—that is, $\frac{AB}{GH} = \frac{BC}{HJ} = \frac{AC}{GJ} = k$, where *k* is a positive number.

In such cases, we say triangles *ABC* and *GHJ* are similar. Note that corresponding angles in two similar triangles must be congruent.

Perimeter and Area of Triangles

The perimeter of a triangle is the sum of the lengths of its three sides. Often, a question will require you to compute the perimeter of a right triangle, but you will not explicitly be given the lengths of all the sides. In such a case, do not forget that you have the Pythagorean theorem.

The area of a two-dimensional plane figure is the number of unit squares needed to cover it. The standard units of measure of area are square inches, square feet, square yards, etc.; the metric system is also commonly used (square centimeters, square meters, etc.). The area formula for a triangle with base *b* and height *h*, as illustrated below, is $A = \frac{1}{2}b \cdot h$.

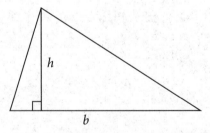

The height of a triangle must be perpendicular to its base. That means there are three possible pairings of heights with bases for any triangle—each base has its own height.

Take a look at some problems similar to what you may see on the ACT exam that deal with the area and perimeter of right triangles.

The open area in front of a museum is a square lawn bordered by footpaths 250 feet long on each side. The museum plans to create a diagonal footpath that would connect the northwest corner of the lawn to the southeast corner of the lawn. Approximately how many feet shorter would the new path be than the shortest possible route on the existing footpaths?

    A. 500

    B. 354

    C. 250

    D. 146

    E. 125

The correct answer is D. The current paths require a trip of 500 feet (250 feet for each of the two sides one must travel along to get from one corner to the other). A diagonal path would form a 45°–45°–90° isosceles right triangle with the existing paths being its legs. As such, the length of the diagonal path would be $250\sqrt{2}$ feet, or approximately 354 feet. The new path would shorten the route by approximately 500 − 354 = 146 feet.

A certain triangle has sides of lengths 50, 120, and 130 centimeters. If a similar triangle has a perimeter of 1,500 centimeters, what is the length (in centimeters) of the triangle's shortest side?

    F. 50

    G. 130

    H. 250

    J. 600

    K. 650

The correct answer is H. The two triangles are similar, so their sides are in proportion. The first triangle has a perimeter of 50 + 120 + 130 = 300 centimeters. The second triangle has a perimeter that is 5 times this: 1,500 centimeters. Thus, the sides of the second triangle are exactly 5 times as long as the sides of the first triangle: 250, 600, and 650 centimeters. So, the length of the shortest side is 250 centimeters.

Right Triangles and the Pythagorean Theorem

The lengths of the sides of right triangles are always related by the Pythagorean theorem. Consider the right triangle shown here:

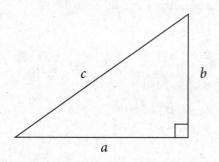

The sides with lengths a and b are called legs, and the side opposite the right angle is the hypotenuse. The hypotenuse is the longest side of a right triangle. The Pythagorean theorem says that $a^2 + b^2 = c^2$.

This relationship between the legs and hypotenuse can take on specific forms for triangles of specific side lengths and angle measures. Two common right triangles have sides that measure 3-4-5 and 5-12-13, or multiples thereof. Be on the lookout for these Pythagorean triples—recognizing them within a problem can make calculating a missing side easier. You'll also want to be on the lookout for two special right triangles: 30-60-90 and 45-45-90 triangles; the numbers indicate the triangles' angle measures.

45-45-90 Triangle

A 45-45-90 right triangle, also called an isosceles right triangle, because of its interior angle measures, has a specific relationship between its side lengths, as seen in the following diagram.

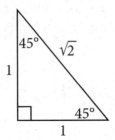

The hypotenuse of a 45-45-90 triangle will always be the length of the short leg multiplied by $\sqrt{2}$. Whether the leg opposite one of the 45° angles is 1 or x or 27, the hypotenuse will always have the same relationship. You can see this using the Pythagorean theorem with a triangle with a right angle and 45° angle with a leg length of x:

$$x^2 + x^2 = c^2$$
$$2x^2 = c^2$$
$$x\sqrt{2} = c$$

30-60-90 Triangle

Similar to an isosceles right triangle, the 30-60-90 right triangle also has specific relationships among its side lengths.

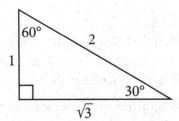

The side length relationships in a 30-60-90 triangle can also be generalized since all triangles of that type are geometrically similar and thus have the same ratio between sides. The hypotenuse's length will always be twice as much as the side length opposite the 30° angle. The side opposite the 60° angle will always be the shortest leg multiplied by $\sqrt{3}$.

Memorizing these relationships can bring some added proficiency to your work with geometry questions in the ACT Mathematics section. You may find that recognizing these kinds of special right triangles helps you answer some complex triangle questions with exceptional speed.

What is the area in square inches of a right triangle with one side length of 27 inches and a hypotenuse of 45 inches?

    A. 972

    B. 486

    C. 192

    D. 96

    E. Cannot be determined from the given information

The correct answer is B. To find the area of a right triangle, you'll need to find the length of both legs. You can use the Pythagorean theorem, but you may also notice that this triangle is a multiple of a 3-4-5 right triangle: 3(9) = 27 and 5(9) = 45. Thus the missing leg length is 4(9) = 36. Since it is a right triangle, the legs serve as the base and height. The area is half the product of its legs: $\frac{1}{2}(27)(36) = 486$ square inches.

Which of the following sets of triangle side lengths represents a right triangle?

    F. 4-5-6

    G. 5-12-14

    H. $\sqrt{2}, \sqrt{2}, 1$

    J. $\sqrt{3}, 3, 2\sqrt{3}$

    K. 1, 3, 2

13

The correct answer is J. Without access to angle measures, you can use the Pythagorean theorem to determine whether the side lengths of a triangle result in a right triangle. However, in this situation, instead of using the Pythagorean theorem to check each answer choice, you can first look for side length relationships that may indicate the presence of a special right triangle or Pythagorean triple. Choices F and G are close to the 3-4-5 and 5-12-13 right triangles, but have some sides increased to a value that doesn't result in satisfaction of the Pythagorean theorem. Choices H and K resemble some of the relationships of the special right triangles but have switched the lengths of the legs and the hypotenuse (choice H) or forgotten a radical (choice K). This leaves choice J. When examined, you can see that this is a 30-60-90 right triangle with the shortest leg being $\sqrt{3}$ (opposite the 30° angle), the second leg being $\sqrt{3} \cdot \sqrt{3} = 3$, and the hypotenuse as twice the length of the shortest leg, $2\sqrt{3}$.

Rectangles, Parallelograms, and Other Polygons

Any geometric figure with straight line segments for sides is called a polygon (including triangles, quadrilaterals, and more). It is possible to draw a polygon with one or more interior angles greater than 180°, as illustrated in the figure below.

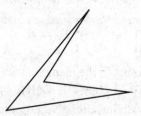

However, if all the interior angles in the polygon are less than 180°, we have a convex polygon. The sum of the angle measurements in any convex polygon is

$180(n - 2)$, where n is the number of vertices. Thus, for a triangle, $n = 3$, and the sum is 180°. For a quadrilateral (a four-sided figure), $n = 4$, and the sum is 360°. For a pentagon (a five-sided figure), $n = 5$, and the angle sum is 540°, and so on.

To find the perimeter of a polygon (the distance around the figure), simply add together the lengths of all the sides. To find its area, connect the vertices by line segments to divide the polygon into triangles; then sum the areas of the triangles. See the following example.

Example

Find the area of figure *ABCDE*.

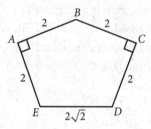

Solution

Drawing *BE* and *BD* divides the region into three triangles as shown. Triangles *ABE* and *BCD* are both 45°-45°-90° right triangles, making $BE = BD = 2\sqrt{2}$.

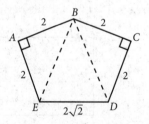

This makes the central triangle an equilateral triangle. The area of each of the two outer triangles is 2. Together, the outside triangles have an area of 4. The center triangle has a base whose length is $2\sqrt{2}$. If you draw the altitude from *B* to the midpoint of *ED*, you create two 30°-60°-90° right triangles with a shorter leg whose length is $\sqrt{2}$. This makes the height $\sqrt{6}$ (recall that the side opposite the 60° angle in this type of special right triangle is the shorter leg multiplied by $\sqrt{3}$). This yields an area of $\frac{\sqrt{2}\sqrt{6}}{2} = \frac{\sqrt{12}}{2} = \frac{2\sqrt{3}}{2} = \sqrt{3}$. Because that area represents only half the area of the central triangle, you must multiply it by 2, resulting in $2\sqrt{3}$. Adding together the areas of all of the triangles in the polygon, the total area is then $4 + 2\sqrt{3}$, or approximately 7.46.

A parallelogram is a quadrilateral in which the pairs of opposite sides are parallel. The opposite angles in a parallelogram are equal, and the opposite sides are of equal length (see the figure below).

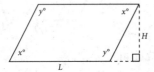

The area of a parallelogram is determined by its length times its height; that is, $A = LW$, as labeled in the diagram.

If the angles in the parallelogram are right angles, we have a rectangle. For a rectangle of length L and width W, the area is $A = LW$, and the perimeter is $P = 2L + 2W$.

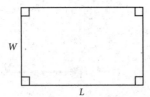

For example, the area of a rectangular garden that is 20 yards long and 10 yards deep is $(20)(10) = 200$ square yards. However, to put a fence around the same garden (that is, around its perimeter) requires $2(20) + 2(10) = 60$ running yards of fencing. These relatively easy formulas can be used to get you to think about more complex situations using compound shapes, as seen in the following example.

Example

If sod comes in 4 × 4 foot squares costing $3.50 per square, how much will it cost to sod the lawn shown on the following page (all distances indicated in feet)? You may assume that all angles that appear to be right angles are right angles.

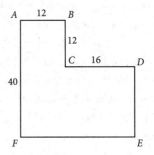

Solution

Completing the rectangle as shown in the figure below, we see that the large rectangle $AGEF$ is $40 \times 28 = 1,120$ square feet.

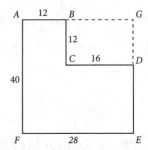

The lesser rectangle $BGDC$ is $12 \times 16 = 192$ square feet. Hence, the area that must be sodded is $1,120 - 192 = 928$ square feet. Now, each 4 × 4 foot piece of sod is 16 square feet. Therefore, we need $928 \div 16 = 58$ squares of sod at $3.50 each. The total cost is $(58)(3.50) = \$203$.

Circles

The set of all points in the plane that are a given distance r from a fixed-point P is a circle. Here is the basic terminology involving circles you should know before you take the ACT exam. Most of these are sure to surface on the exam, so you should absolutely memorize these definitions.

You will use these terms when configuring values of circles, as in the following formulas. Circumference and area of circles are the formulas that come up most frequently on the ACT exam.

CIRCLE TERMINOLOGY

Term	Definition	Illustration
Center	The point P equidistant from all points on the circle	
Radius	The common distance r that points on the circle are from the center	
Diameter	A line segment that passes through the center of the circle and has endpoints on the circle (its length is twice the radius)	
Central Angle	An angle formed between two radial segments	
Arc	A portion of the circle that lies between two points	
Sector	The portion of the inside of a circle that lies between two radial segments	

CIRCLE FORMULAS

Term	Definition	Illustration
Circumference of a Circle	Since the diameter d is $2r$, there are two expressions for this formula: $P = 2\pi r = \pi d$	
Length of an Arc of a Circle	$P = \dfrac{\theta}{360°} \cdot 2\pi r$	
Area of a Circle	$A = \pi r^2$	
Area of a Sector of a Circle	$A = \dfrac{\theta}{360°} \cdot \pi r^2$	

TIP

Notice that the formulae for arc length and sector area actually represent two proportional relationships. If you were to make each side of the equations a ratio, $\dfrac{P}{2\pi r} = \dfrac{\theta}{360°}$ and $\dfrac{A}{\pi r^2} = \dfrac{\theta}{360°}$, you would see that you have two part-to-whole relationships (the arc length or sector area compared to the circumference or total area, respectively, and the angle measure of the arc or sector and the total angle measure of the circle).

Problems involving circles come in different varieties, but they all involve using the same formulas. Sometimes, you will be given a diameter instead of a radius, or you will be given an area of a sector or the perimeter of an arc and then be asked to identify the radius or diameter. The key is to be flexible with using the formulas in various ways, depending on what information is provided.

Sector Area

The area of a sector of a circle is the product of the ratio $\dfrac{\text{measure of the arc}}{360°}$ and the area of the circle. For example, if the radius of a circle is 3 cm and the measure of the arc is 60°, then the area of the sector is $\dfrac{60°}{360°} \cdot \pi (3)^2 = \dfrac{9\pi}{6} = \dfrac{3\pi}{2}\ \text{cm}^2$.

$$\text{Area of sector } AOB = \frac{m\widehat{AB}}{360} \cdot \pi r^2$$

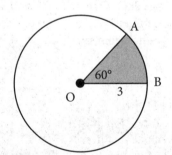

PRACTICE

The length of the radius of circle *A* is 4 times as long as the radius of circle *B*. If the radius of circle *B* is *x* units, what is the area (in square units) of circle *A*?

F. $16x$

G. $\dfrac{x}{16}$

H. $\dfrac{x}{4}$

J. $16\pi x^2$

K. $\dfrac{\pi x^2}{16}$

The correct answer is J. The radius of circle *A* is $4x$. So its area is $\pi(4x)^2 = 16\pi x^2$.

PRACTICE

What is the area of the shaded region in the circle shown below?

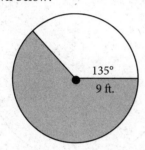

135°
9 ft.

A. 27π square feet

B. 81π square feet

C. $\dfrac{243}{8}$ square feet

D. $\dfrac{405\pi}{8}$ square feet

E. $\dfrac{605\pi}{8}$ square feet

The correct answer is D. The central angle corresponding to the shaded region is 360 – 135 = 225 degrees. So the area of the shaded region is $\dfrac{225}{360} \cdot \pi \cdot (9)^2 = \dfrac{405\pi}{8}$ square feet.

Arc Length

An arc is a portion of the circumference of a circle, as indicated by the shading in the example shown. Recall that the circumference of a circle, C, is the distance around the circle, which is found by multiplying the length of the radius, r, by 2π: $C = 2\pi r$. The length of an arc is determined by the central angle which creates the arc. Arc length is typically represented by the variable s. The measure of the central angle of a circle is typically represented by the Greek letter theta, which is θ. You can create a proportion as follows to solve for the arc length: $\dfrac{s}{C} = \dfrac{\theta}{360}$, where s represents the arc length and

C represents the circumference of the circle. However, if the measure of the central angle is given in radians (or a question is looking for you to convert degrees to radians, as seen later in this chapter), you can simplify the formula for finding the arc length.

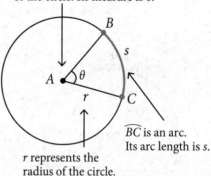

∠ BAC is a central angle of the circle. Its measure is θ.

$\overarc{BC}$ is an arc. Its arc length is s.

r represents the radius of the circle.

The radian measure θ of a central angle of a circle is defined as the ratio of the length of the arc, s, opposite of the central angle, to the radius r of the circle:

$$\theta = \frac{s}{r}$$

To find the arc length, multiply the radius of the circle by the measure of the central angle in radians:

$$s = r\theta$$

When given an angle in radian measure, substitute the angle in radians for θ, and multiply it by the radius of the circle.

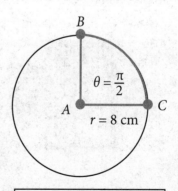

$$s = \frac{\pi}{2} \cdot 8 = 4\pi \approx 4(3.14)$$
$$= 12.56 \text{ cm}$$

If the central angle measure is given in degrees, change the angle to radians first, and then use the arc length formula.

The formula for finding the arc length, when an angle is given in degrees, is:

$$s = r\theta \cdot \frac{\pi}{180°}$$

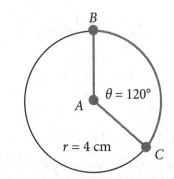

$$s = 4 \cdot 120° \cdot \frac{\pi}{180°} = \frac{8}{3}\pi = \frac{8}{3}(3.14)$$
$$\approx 8.38 \text{ cm}$$

In this situation, you may also notice that the central angle is one third of the total angle measure of the circle. Thus, the arc length will be one third of the circumference of the circle. Circumference is $2\pi r$ or πd, so the arc length can quickly be determined to be $\frac{8\pi}{3}$. If answer choices are provided in terms of π, one method for determining arc length may be faster than the other.

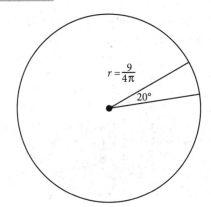

Note: Figure not drawn to scale.

Given the circle shown above, what is the length of the arc formed by the 20° angle?

A. $\dfrac{45}{\pi}$

B. $\dfrac{\pi}{2}$

C. $\dfrac{\pi}{4}$

D. $\dfrac{1}{2}$

E. $\dfrac{1}{4}$

The correct answer is D. First, we convert 20° to radians:

$$\frac{\pi \text{ radians}}{180°} \cdot 20° = \frac{\pi}{9} \text{ radians}$$

Then, we use the formula for the length of an arc, s, formed by an angle of θ radians on a circle of radius, r: $s = r\theta$. Evaluating this formula for the given radius and central angle measure, in radians, gives:

$$\frac{9}{4\pi} \cdot \frac{\pi}{9} = \frac{1}{4}$$

The length of the arc that intercepts the given central angle is $\frac{1}{4}$.

TRIGONOMETRIC FUNCTIONS

Trigonometric Function	Abbreviation
Cosine	cos
Sine	sin
Tangent	tan
Secant	sec
Cosecant	csc
Cotangent	cot

If given on the ACT exam, you will likely see the abbreviated form of the name. All trigonometry questions fall under the category Preparing for Higher Math but could be related to either the Geometry or Functions subdomain.

The Three Basic Trigonometric Ratios

The three basic trigonometric ratios are sine, cosine, and tangent. You can find the sine, cosine, or tangent of an acute angle (θ) in a right triangle with the following ratios.

$$\text{Sin } \theta = \frac{\text{Opposite}}{\text{Hypotenuse}}$$

$$\text{Cos } \theta = \frac{\text{Adjacent}}{\text{Hypotenuse}}$$

$$\text{Tan } \theta = \frac{\text{Opposite}}{\text{Adjacent}}$$

RIGHT TRIANGLE TRIGONOMETRY

You saw information on trigonometric functions in Chapter 12. Here, we'll look more specifically at trigonometric ratios and their application to right triangles in geometry. Trigonometric ratios were defined, in part, to identify the lengths of sides of a right triangle when one side and one angle (instead of two sides) are known. The names of these six ratios, with their abbreviations, are as follows:

There are, in fact, three more ratios that are also used with trigonometric calculations: secant, cosecant, and cotangent.

Finding Trigonometric Ratios

Use SOH, CAH, TOA to remember how to find each ratio.

Consider $\angle B$:

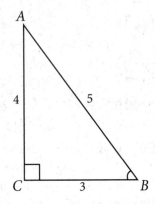

The side opposite or across from $\angle B$ is $\overline{AC}$.

The side adjacent or next to $\angle B$ is $\overline{CB}$.

The hypotenuse of the right triangle is $\overline{AB}$.

Find the trigonometric ratios.

Sine of $\angle B$

To find the sine of $\angle B$ think SOH:

$$\sin B = \frac{\text{Opposite}}{\text{Hypotenuse}} = \frac{AC}{AB} = \frac{4}{5}$$

Cosine of $\angle B$

To find the cosine of $\angle B$ think CAH:

$$\cos B = \frac{\text{Adjacent}}{\text{Hypotenuse}} = \frac{CB}{AB} = \frac{3}{5}$$

Tangent of $\angle B$

To find the tangent of $\angle B$ think TOA:

$$\tan B = \frac{\text{Opposite}}{\text{Adjacent}} = \frac{AC}{CB} = \frac{4}{3}$$

The measure of angle B will correspond to each of those ratios. If you were to use a calculator to find the inverse

of $\sin B = \frac{4}{5} \left(\sin^{-1} \left(\frac{4}{5} \right) \right)$ or the inverses of $\cos B = \frac{3}{5}$ or $\tan B = \frac{4}{3}$, they would all reveal that angle B measures 53.13 degrees. If you input $\sin 53.13$, you would get a ratio of 0.8, or $\frac{4}{5}$, the relationship between the opposite side and the hypotenuse.

SOH, CAH, TOA is an easy way to remember how to use the three basic trigonometric functions. In the case that you are asked about the remaining three functions on the ACT, there are also simple formulas to memorize. See the following for all six trigonometric ratios and their related formulas:

$$\sin \theta = \frac{\text{opposite}}{\text{hypotenuse}}$$

$$\cos \theta = \frac{\text{adjacent}}{\text{hypotenuse}}$$

$$\tan \theta = \frac{\text{opposite}}{\text{adjacent}} = \frac{\sin \theta}{\cos \theta}$$

$$\cot \theta = \frac{\text{adjacent}}{\text{opposite}} = \frac{\cos \theta}{\sin \theta} = \frac{1}{\tan \theta}$$

$$\sec \theta = \frac{\text{hypotenuse}}{\text{adjacent}} = \frac{1}{\cos \theta}$$

$$\csc \theta = \frac{\text{hypotenuse}}{\text{opposite}} = \frac{1}{\sin \theta}$$

Unknown Lengths

If one side length and one angle measurement of a right triangle are known, all remaining sides and angle measurements can be found. Since the trigonometric ratios of most angles are irrational, a calculator (in degree mode) can be used.

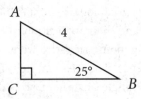

In right triangle ABC, $AB = 4$ and $\angle B$ measures $25°$.

Side *AC* is opposite to angle *B* and we know the hypotenuse, so use the sine ratio:

$$\frac{AC}{4} = \sin 25 \rightarrow AC = 4\sin 25° \approx 1.7$$

Side *BC* is adjacent to angle *B* and we know the hypotenuse, so use the cosine ratio:

$$\frac{BC}{4} = \cos 25° \rightarrow BC = 4\cos 25° \approx 3.6$$

If the hypotenuse is unknown but the measure of a leg and one angle is known, the solution process is very similar. The only difference is the ratio that is used and the location of the unknown in the equation.

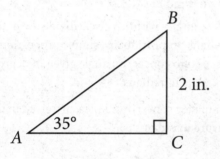

In triangle *ABC*, *BC* = 2 in. and angle *A* measures 35°.

Side *AC* is adjacent to angle *A* and we know the opposite side, so use the tangent ratio:

$$\frac{\text{opp}}{\text{adj}} : \frac{2}{AC} = \tan 35° \rightarrow AC = \frac{2}{\tan 35°} \approx 2.9 \text{ in.}$$

Side *AB* is the hypotenuse and side *BC* is opposite angle *A*, so use the sine ratio:

$$\frac{\text{opp}}{\text{hyp}} : \frac{2}{AB} = \sin 35° \rightarrow AB = \frac{2}{\sin 35°} \approx 3.5 \text{ in.}$$

The problems related to trigonometry on the ACT Mathematics test come in two main varieties:

1. Compute a trigonometric function or determine a side of a triangle using given information.
2. Solve a word problem that can be modeled using a right triangle.

Let's take a look at two sample ACT–type trigonometry problems.

A 95-foot cable attached to the top of a telephone pole is anchored to the ground. If the wire rises at a 64° angle from the ground, how tall is the telephone pole (in feet)?

    A. 5 tan 64°

    B. 64 cos 95°

    C. 95 cos 64°

    D. 95 sin 64°

    E. 64 sin 95°

The correct answer is D. As shown in the diagram below, the height of the telephone pole, *x*, is opposite a 64° angle, and the hypotenuse of the triangle is 95 feet.

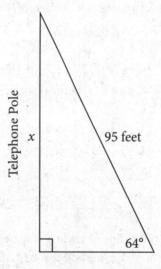

Since sine equals $\frac{\text{opposite}}{\text{hypotenuse}}$, we get the formula $\frac{x}{95} = \sin 64°$; $x = 95\sin 64°$.

Degrees and Radians

There are two ways in which angles can be measured: degrees and radians.

Converting Degrees to Radians

While degree measures are frequently used, a radian measure is helpful in that it relates to the circumference of a circle and trigonometric functions.

- One entire revolution of a circle is equivalent to 360°. In terms of radians, one entire revolution is equivalent to 2π radians. Therefore, 2π radians = 360°.

- Half of a circle measures 180°, so half of 2π radians is π radians.

- Since angles within a circle divide the entire 2π radians proportionally, simple proportions can be used to convert an angle given in degrees to an angle in radians.

The formula for converting a measure given in degrees to a measure in radians is:

$$\text{Radians} = \frac{\text{Degrees}}{180°} \cdot \pi$$

Example

Convert 240° to radians.

Solution

$$\text{Radians} = \frac{240°}{180°} \cdot \pi$$
$$= \frac{4}{3}\pi$$
$$240° = \frac{4}{3}\pi \text{ radians}$$

Converting Radians to Degrees

Just as an angle measure given in degrees can be converted into an equivalent angle measure in radians, an angle measure in radians can be converted into an equivalent degree measure. The formula for converting radians to degrees is:

$$\text{Degrees} = \frac{180°}{\pi} \cdot \text{Radians}$$

PRACTICE

In right triangle ABC, $\sin A = \frac{1}{2}$. What is the value of $\cos A$?

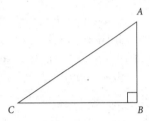

- **F.** $\sqrt{3}$
- **G.** 2
- **H.** $\frac{\sqrt{3}}{3}$
- **J.** $\frac{1}{2}$
- **K.** $\frac{\sqrt{3}}{2}$

The correct answer is K. Remember that sine is $\frac{\text{opposite}}{\text{hypotenuse}}$ and that cosine is $\frac{\text{adjacent}}{\text{hypotenuse}}$. From what is given, $\frac{CB}{AC} = \frac{1}{2}$. We label the lengths of CB and AC in the triangle:

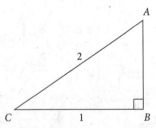

To find the cosine of angle A, you need to know the length of the side adjacent to it, namely segment AB. Since the length of a leg of this triangle is related to the length of its hypotenuse in the ratio of 1:2, remember from earlier in this chapter that this is a 30-60-90 right triangle, whose three sides are related in the ratio of $1 : \sqrt{3} : 2$. Therefore, $AB = \sqrt{3}$, so $\cos A = \frac{\sqrt{3}}{2}$.

Example

1 Convert $\dfrac{5\pi}{6}$ radians to degrees.

Solution

$$\frac{180°}{\pi} \cdot \frac{5\pi}{6} = 150°$$

$$\frac{5\pi}{6} \text{ radians} = 150°$$

x	y
0	1
1	3
2	5
3	7
4	9

When those points are plotted, you see the following graph.

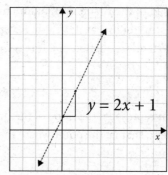

COORDINATE GEOMETRY

You saw elements of coordinate geometry in Chapters 9 and 10, dealing with distances between points, the basics of lines, and other fundamental concepts. Now, let's examine some higher-level coordinate geometry concepts that are likely to arise on the ACT, specifically related to graphing lines, inequalities, circles, ellipses, and transformations in the coordinate plane.

Lines and Their Equations

The ability to work with lines and their equations, points, and forms is critical to success with a significant number of the Preparing for Higher Math questions. The following section revisits some topics discussed in Chapters 9 and 10.

Graphing a Line in Slope-Intercept Form

Take a look at the following equation:

$$y = 2x + 1$$

If you were to create a table to represent the points on that line, you can start with $x = 0$ as you know the corresponding y value will be 1 (since it is the y-intercept). From there, you can use the slope value in the equation to determine each successive y value. With a slope of two, each successive point on the line will rise 2 and run 1, resulting in the following table.

Graphing a Linear Equation

The slope of a straight line is a number that measures how steep the line is. Traditionally, the variable m is used to stand for the slope of a line. A line that increases from left to right has a positive slope, and a line that decreases from left to right has a negative slope. A horizontal line has a slope of 0 since it is "flat," and a vertical line has an undefined slope.

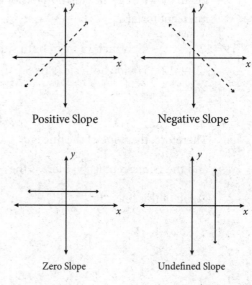

If (x_1, y_1) and (x_2, y_2) are any two points on a line, the slope is given by the formula:

$$m = \frac{(y_2 - y_1)}{(x_2 - x_1)}$$

For example, if a line contains the points (5, 7) and (3, 4), the slope would be $m = \frac{7-4}{5-3} = \frac{3}{2}$. A slope of $\frac{3}{2}$ represents the fact that for every 2 units moved horizontally along the x-axis, the line rises vertically 3 units.

An equation of degree one that contains the variables x and/or y raised to the first power, but no higher, will always have a straight line as its graph. A very convenient way to write the equation of a line is in the slope-intercept form:

$$y = mx + b$$

In this form, m represents the slope of the line, and b is the y-intercept, that is, the point where the graph crosses the y-axis.

Let's look at a series of examples demonstrating different methods for graphing linear equations as dependent on the initial information provided.

Example

Consider the line represented by the equation $2x + 5y = 12$.

Solution

Begin by writing this equation in slope-intercept form.

$2x + 5y = 12$ Subtract 2x from both sides.

$5y = -2x + 12$ Divide both sides by 5.

$$y = -\frac{2}{5}x + \frac{12}{5}$$

Therefore, the slope of the line is $-\frac{2}{5}$, and the y-intercept is $\frac{12}{5}$. Here is the graph of this line.

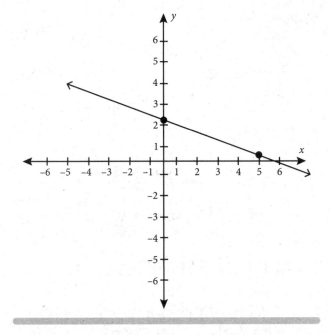

Write the equation of the line containing the point (2, 1) and having slope 5.

Solution

Begin by taking the slope-intercept form $y = mx + b$, and substituting $m = 5$ to obtain $y = 5x + b$. To determine the value of the y-intercept b, substitute the coordinates of the point (2, 1) into the equation.

$y = 5x + b$ Substitute (2, 1).

$1 = 5(2) + b$ Solve for b.

$1 = 10 + b$

$-9 = b$

Therefore, the equation of the line is $y = 5x - 9$.

Graph the function $f(x) = 2x + 5$.

Solution

Begin by recognizing that the slope is 2 and the y-intercept is (0, 5). To graph this function, first graph the point (0, 5). Then move up 2 units and then to the right 1 unit. This location is (1, 7). Starting at

(0, 5) again, go down 2 units and then to the left 1 unit. This location is (–1, 3). Connect these points to form the graph of the function $f(x) = 2x + 5$.

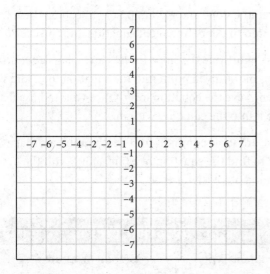

You can write an equation of a line from a graph given any two points on the line. First, use the two points to find the slope. Then use the point–slope form of an equation of a line: $y - y_1 = m(x - x_1)$. As an example, consider the following graph.

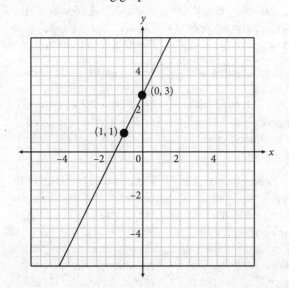

You need to first find the slope using two points on the line.

The slope formula is $m = \dfrac{y_2 - y_1}{x_2 - x_1}$. Use the points (0, 3) and (–1, 1) to find the slope.

$$m = \frac{y_2 - y_1}{x_2 - x_1} = \frac{1-3}{-1-0} = \frac{-2}{-1} = 2$$

Use the point-slope form and either given point.

$$y - y_1 = m(x - x_1)$$
$$y - 1 = 2(x - (-1))$$
$$y - 1 = 2(x + 1)$$

To write this equation in slope-intercept form, solve for y.

$$y - 1 = 2(x + 1)$$
$$y = 2(x + 1) + 1$$
$$y = 2x + 2 + 1$$
$$y = 2x + 3$$

Here's an example of how to write an equation of a line from a word problem and then graph the equation using the intercepts.

Example

You decide to purchase holiday gift cards for your family. You have $300 to spend on the cards, and you purchase cards for either $20 or $30. What are three combinations of cards that you can purchase?

Solution

To write an equation that represents this situation, first define your variables.

Let x = number of $20 gift cards purchased and y = number of $30 gift cards purchased.

Now write an equation to represent the situation.

$$20x + 30y = 300$$

Use the intercepts to draw the graph.

$$20x + 30y = 300$$
$$20(0) + 30y = 300$$
$$30y = 300$$
$$y = 10$$

$$20x + 30y = 300$$
$$20x + 30(0) = 300$$
$$20x = 300$$
$$x = 15$$

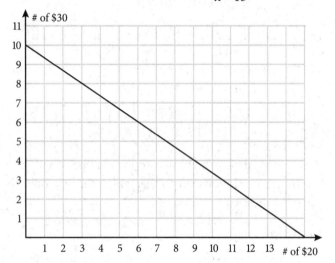

You cannot purchase a fraction of a card, so only the integer combinations can be solutions. You can purchase fifteen $20 cards and zero $30 cards, six $20 cards and six $30 cards, or zero $20 cards and ten $30 cards.

Although the question only asked for three answers, the other possible combinations are twelve $20 gift cards and two $30 gift cards, nine $20 gift cards and four $30 gift cards, and three $20 gift cards and eight $30 gift cards.

Determining Linear Equations from Slope and Points

To write the slope-intercept equation of a line when slope (*m*) and one point are given, you need to find the *y*-intercept (*b*).

Given the slope and a point on the line, plug these values into the slope-intercept equation and solve for *b*.

First, substitute the slope for *m*. Next, plug the coordinates of the given point into the equation for *x* and *y*. Then, solve the equation for *b*. Once you find *b*, substitute it into the equation with *m*.

Here are some common ACT math problems that ask you to find the equation of a line, along with the best method of attack for each

QUESTION TYPES	
Problem Type	**Method of Attack**
1. Given a point and a slope (either written or by way of a graph), determine the equation of the line.	Use the point-slope formula immediately.
2. Given two points on a line (either written or by way of a graph), determine the slope or the equation of the line.	First, find the slope of the line. (If this is what the question asks for, you are done.) Use the point-slope formula to find its equation.
3. Given a table of points that describe a linear relationship between variables x and y, determine the equation of the line.	Use any two of the points to find the slope. Then, use any of the points from the table with the slope to find the equation of the line.
4. Given a scenario in which two quantities are related linearly, find the equation of the line, or determine the value of one of the variables given the value of the other.	Identify one quantity as the input (*x*) and the other as the output (*y*). Typically, the input variable *x* is the quantity you change; the output variable *y* is the quantity you observe. Extract information from the description—either two points or a point and slope. Proceed as above.

For all of the problem types listed in the table, depending on the way the choices are listed, you might then need to put the equation into slope-intercept form or standard form.

PRACTICE

What is the equation of a line that has a slope of −2 and passes through point (1, 5)?

A. $y = -2x - 1$

B. $y = -2x - 5$

C. $y = -2x + 7$

D. $y = 5x + 1$

E. $y = 5x + 7$

The correct answer is C. Start with the slope-intercept equation, and substitute in the values $m = -2$, $x = 1$, and $y = 5$. Then, solve for b.

$$y = mx + b$$
$$5 = -2(1) + b$$
$$5 = -2 + b$$
$$5 + 2 = b$$
$$7 = b$$

The slope-intercept form of the equation of the line is $y = -2x + 7$.

If given two points on a line, you'll use the same process, but first you'll need to find the slope using the slope formula. From there, you'll substitute in coordinates for one point and the slope into the slope-intercept form to find the y-intercept.

Suppose that the points (1, −5) and (2, −1) lie on a line. Which of the following is the equation of this line?

F. $y = x - 8$

G. $y = 4x - 9$

H. $y = 4x + 9$

J. $y = x + 8$

K. $y = \dfrac{1}{4}x - 9$

The correct answer is G. First, determine the slope:

$$\text{slope} = m = \frac{-5 - (-1)}{1 - 2} = 4$$

Using the point (2, −1) with the point-slope formula, the equation of the line passing through these two points is $y - (-1) = 4(x - 2)$. This is equivalent to $y = 4x - 9$.

Parallel Lines

Two lines in the same plane are parallel if they do not intersect. The slopes of lines can be used to determine whether two lines are parallel. Two lines are parallel if they have the same slope, m.

Let's look at an example. The following graph displays the equations $y = \dfrac{1}{2}x + 2$ and $y = \dfrac{1}{2}x - 3$.

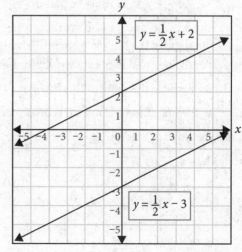

Both equations are written in the slope-intercept form, $y = mx + b$. The slope, m, of both lines is $\frac{1}{2}$. Because these two lines have the same slope, they are parallel lines.

The graph of which of the following equations is parallel to the line shown?

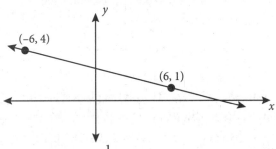

A. $y = 4x - \frac{1}{4}$

B. $4x - y = -2$

C. $4y + x = 2$

D. $2x - 8y = 1$

E. $5x + 10y = 20$

The correct answer is C. The slope of the line shown is $m = \frac{4-1}{-6-6} = -\frac{1}{4}$. Any line with this same slope must be parallel to the one shown. Note that the equation in choice C can be written as $y = -\frac{1}{4}x + \frac{1}{2}$ and so must be parallel to the one shown. Choices A and B are incorrect because the slope of the lines is 4, making the lines perpendicular to the line shown. Choice D is incorrect because the slope of this line is $\frac{1}{4}$, not $-\frac{1}{4}$ as the one shown. Choice E is incorrect because the slope of this line is $-\frac{1}{2}$, not $-\frac{1}{4}$ as the one shown.

Perpendicular Lines

Two lines are perpendicular if they intersect to form right angles. The slopes of perpendicular lines are negative reciprocals of each other. This means that the product of the slopes equals –1.

For example, look at the graphs of equations $y = -2x + 2$ and $y = \frac{1}{2}x - 3$:

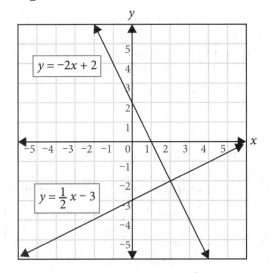

These two lines have slopes of –2 and $\frac{1}{2}$. The slopes are negative reciprocals of each other because –2 multiplied by $\frac{1}{2}$ equals –1. Therefore, these two lines are perpendicular.

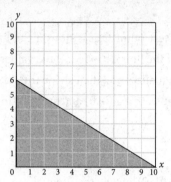

PRACTICE

A line passing through the point (–1, 4) is perpendicular to the line passing through (–3, 2) and (–3, –5). What is the equation of the line passing through (–1, 4)?

A. $y = x + 5$

B. $y = 4$

C. $9x + 2y = 5$

D. $x = -1$

E. $y = -x - 5$

The correct answer is B. The given line is vertical since it passes through two points having the same x-coordinate. As such, a line that is perpendicular must be horizontal. Since it passes through the point (–1, 4), its equation must be $y = 4$. In choices A, C, and E, you used the point (–1, 4) when computing the slope of the given line, but it does not pass through this point. Choice D is parallel to the given line.

Graphing Inequalities in a Coordinate Plane

Graphing linear inequalities requires that you determine points on the line and what side of the line should be shaded to indicate what other points satisfy the inequality. Consider this example word problem.

Example

Charlene, a professional landscaper, purchased x small plants for $3 each and y large plants for $5 each. She spent no more than $30.

Solution

The inequality $3x + 5y \leq 30$ represents this situation. The following graph displays the inequality.

Since Charlene cannot purchase a negative number of plants, only positive values for x and y are shown. Any point in the shaded area or on the line represents a reasonable solution for the inequality.

Here's a review of how to graph inequalities with two variables, using $3x + 5y \leq 30$ as an example.

1. Graph the line for the equation $3x + 5y = 30$. Find the y-intercept by substituting 0 for x in the equation:

$$3(0) + 5y = 30$$
$$5y = 30$$
$$y = 6$$

Now find the x-intercept:

$$3x + 5(0) = 30$$
$$3x = 30$$
$$x = 10$$

2. Plot (0, 6) and (10, 0), and the line connecting them. Use a solid line as points along the line still satisfy the inequality (less than or equal to). If the inequality sign were less than or greater than, the line would be dashed.

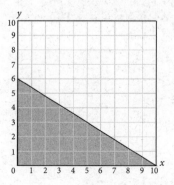

3. Choose a test point that is not on the line to decide which side of the line is shaded. If the values of the point make the inequality true, then shade the side the point is on. For example, using (0, 0) and substituting:

$$3(0) + 5(0) \leq 30$$
$$0 \leq 30$$

4. The point (0, 0) makes the inequality true. So, shade the side of the line containing this point.

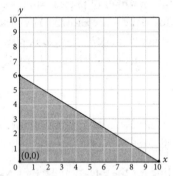

5. The points (3, 2), (5, 3), and (4, 5) are plotted on the graph. The point (3, 2) is in the shaded region and the point (5, 3) is on the line. These points represent a reasonable number of small and large plants that the landscaper could have purchased. The point (4, 5) is not in the shaded region. It does not represent a reasonable solution.

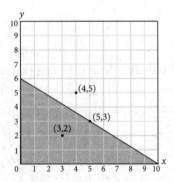

PRACTICE

What is the solution set for the inequality $y \geq 4x - 2$?

A.

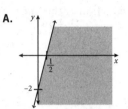

B.

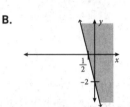

C.

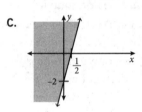

D.

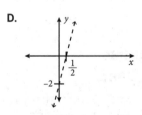

E.

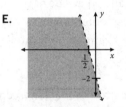

The correct answer is C. The line must be solid, not dashed, since the inequality sign includes "equals"; so, you can discard choices D and E. You must shade above the line since the inequality is of the form "$y \geq$"; so, you can discard choice A. Now, it's between choices B and C. Note that the slope of the line in choice B is −4, not 4. So, it can be discarded, leaving choice C as the answer.

Graphing Circles

More often than not, the ACT will have at least one question requiring you to apply the formula for graphing circles in the standard (x, y) coordinate plane. All you need to know to represent a circle in this form is the length of the radius and the coordinates of the center of the circle:

Circle-radius form of a circle with center (h, k) and radius r:

$$(x - h)^2 + (y - k)^2 = r^2$$

Example

What is the equation for a circle that has a center at $(-1, -3)$ and passes through the point $(2, 1)$?

Solution

We are given the center coordinates, but not the radius. Find the radius by using the distance formula with the center point and the point on the circumference:

$$d = \sqrt{(x_2 - x_2)^2 + (y_2 - y_1)^2} = \sqrt{(-1-2)^2 + (-3-1)^2} = \sqrt{25} = 5$$

The radius equals 5, so the equation for the circle is $(x + 1)^2 + (y + 3)^2 = 25$.

PRACTICE

The circle drawn below in the standard (x, y) coordinate plane has its center at (a, b), passes through the point (c, d), and is tangent to the y-axis. Which of the following is an equation for this circle?

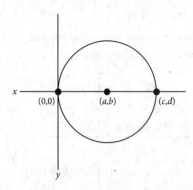

A. $(x + a)^2 + (y + b)^2 = c^2$

B. $(x - a)^2 + (y - b)^2 = c^2$

C. $(x - a)^2 + (y - b)^2 = \left(\dfrac{1}{2}c^2\right)$

D. $(x + a)^2 + (y + b)^2 = \left(\dfrac{1}{2}c^2\right)$

E. $(x - a)^2 + (y - b)^2 = \left(\dfrac{1}{2}c\right)^2$

The correct answer is E. The center, (h, k), for the circle illustrated is (a, b) and the radius is $\dfrac{1}{2}c$. Putting this information into the center-radius form, $(x - h)^2 + (y - k)^2 = r^2$, yields $(x - a)^2 + (y - b)^2 = \left(\dfrac{1}{2}c\right)^2$.

Graphs of Ellipses

Very rarely, you will see an ellipse question on the ACT. Whether you commit the equation of an ellipse to memory or forget it, you should be able to answer the question by working backward and plugging points from the graph into the given equations. Before we spring the formulas on you, let's review a few things about ellipses:

- An ellipse has two lines of symmetry: a vertical and a horizontal line that would each cut the ellipse in half.

- The major axis is the longer line segment that cuts the ellipse in half.

- The minor axis is the short line segment that cuts the ellipse in half.
- The center, (h, k), sits at the intersection of the major axis and the minor axis.

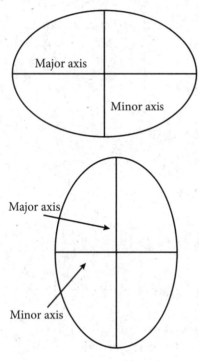

The distance from the center of the ellipse to the endpoint of the major axis is called a. Similarly, the distance from the center of the ellipse to the endpoint of the minor axis is called b. In other words, a is half the length of the major axis and b is half the length of the minor axis. In the formula for an ellipse, the placement of a and b changes, depending on whether the ellipse is wide or tall. Notice below that a is paired with the x-coordinate when the ellipse is wide, and conversely, a is paired with the y-coordinate when the ellipse is tall (and the b-value changes accordingly).

Formula for a *wide* ellipse: $\dfrac{(x-h)^2}{a^2} + \dfrac{(y-k)^2}{b^2} = 1$

Formula for a *tall* ellipse: $\dfrac{(y-k)^2}{a^2} + \dfrac{(x-h)^2}{b^2} = 1$

Aside from the placement of a and b previously, it is also important to notice that both of these values are squared. So, remember that after you cut the lengths of the minor and major axes in half, you must square those values before using them in the formula for the ellipse.

Transformations

A transformation is a sequence of steps that moves a planar figure around in the xy-plane without changing its actual size or shape. The result of applying a transformation to a figure creates an image of that figure. If P is a point on the original figure, then the image of P is typically denoted by P'.

A transformation is a change in the position, shape, or size of a figure. The transformed figure is called the image of the original figure. Transformations include the following:

- Translations (slides)
- Reflections (flips)
- Rotations (turns)
- Dilations (enlargement or reduction)

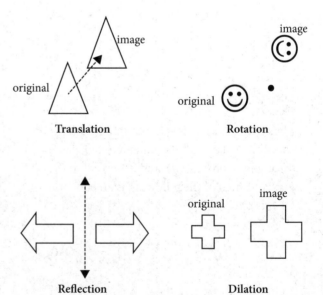

There are various movements that can be performed to transform figures.

TYPES OF TRANSFORMATIONS

Transformation	Description	Illustration
Translation	All points on a figure are moved in the same direction and distance.	Here, each point on *PQR* was moved two units to the right and one unit up.
Rotation	All points on a figure are connected to a common point (called the center of rotation) and are rotated clockwise or counterclockwise by the same angle.	This illustrates a 180-degree rotation counterclockwise of figure *PQR* about the center marked *O*.
Reflection	All points on a figure are reflected over a given line in the plane. To do so, a line segment is drawn from a point on the figure perpendicularly to the line over which it is being reflected. The image of that point is obtained by going the same distance on the opposite side of the reflection line.	This illustrates quadrilateral *PQRS* being reflected over the line $x = 3$.

Translations in the Coordinate Plane

When a translation is applied to a figure in the coordinate plane, the x- and y-coordinates of every point in the figure each change by a fixed number of units. The resulting figure is congruent with the original.

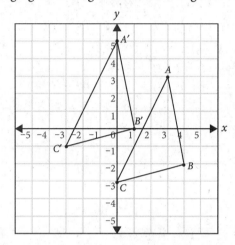

The notation $(x, y) \rightarrow (x + h, y + k)$ describes a translation of h units along the x-axis and k units along the y-axis. When h and k are positive, the figure moves h units to the right in the x-direction and k units up in the y-direction.

The figure shows a translation of $\triangle ABC$ to its image $\triangle A'B'C'$ according to the rule $(x, y) \rightarrow (x - 3, y + 2)$. Note that each point in the triangle moves 3 units to the left and 2 units up.

Reflections in the Coordinate Plane: Y-Axis

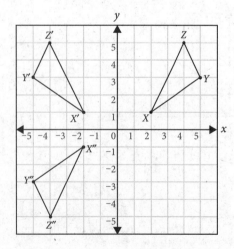

A figure in the coordinate plane can be reflected across any line.

A reflection across the y-axis is represented by the rule:

$$(x, y) \rightarrow (-x, y)$$

$\triangle X'Y'Z'$ is the image of $\triangle XYZ$ after a reflection across the y-axis. The y-coordinate of each point in the image is the same as the y-coordinate of each point in the original figure. The x-coordinates are opposites.

Note that the changes in the coordinates of the vertices of $\triangle XYZ$ follow the rule above:

$$X\,(2, 1) \rightarrow X'\,(-2, 1)$$

$$Y\,(5, 3) \rightarrow Y'\,(-5, 3)$$

$$Z\,(4, 5) \rightarrow Z'\,(-4, 5)$$

Reflections in the Coordinate Plane: X-Axis

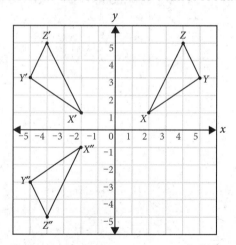

A reflection across the x-axis is represented by the rule:

$$(x, y) \rightarrow (x, -y)$$

$\triangle X''Y''Z''$ is the image of $\triangle X'Y'Z'$ after a reflection across the x-axis.

The x-coordinate of each point in $\triangle X''Y''Z''$ is the same as the x-coordinate of each point in $\triangle X'Y'Z'$.

The y-coordinates are opposites.

Rotations

A rotation, or turn, is a congruent transformation in which every point of an object rotates the same number of degrees about a fixed center point. The center point may be a point in the figure or a point outside the figure and is called the center of rotation.

A rotation is defined by the following:

- its center of rotation.
- the number of degrees the figure is turned.
- the direction of the turn (clockwise or counterclockwise).

Example

The heart in the figure shown is rotated 60° counterclockwise about point C. The moon could be described by a 180° rotation, either clockwise or counterclockwise, about point D.

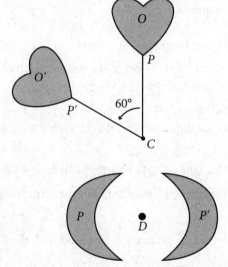

Dilations

A dilation is a nonrigid transformation, meaning that it is not congruent. However, the figures in a dilation will be similar. In a dilation, a figure will either stretch (grow larger) or shrink (grow smaller) proportionally, meaning it maintains its existing shape and proportions. A dilation requires the following:

- a scale factor
- a fixed point called a center of dilation

The center of dilation determines the fixed point around which shrinking or stretching occurs, and the scale factor indicates the degree of stretching or shrinking. The three square figures that follow show the same figure stretching by 100% each time it dilates from left to right, which is the scale factor. Each dilation happens around the center of dilation in the middle of the figure.

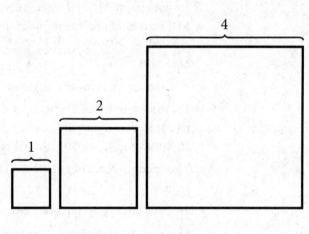

SUMMING IT UP

- Any geometric figure with straight line segments for sides is called a polygon.
- A right triangle is one that has a right angle; an acute triangle is one in which all three angles are acute; an obtuse triangle has one obtuse angle.
- An equilateral triangle is one in which all three sides have the same length; an isosceles triangle has at least two sides with the same length; a scalene triangle has three sides of different lengths.
- The triangle sum rule says that the sum of the measures of the three angles in any triangle must be 180°. The triangle inequality says that the sum of the lengths of any two sides of a triangle must be strictly larger than the length of the third side.
- The Pythagorean theorem states that for a right triangle with legs a and b and hypotenuse c, $a^2 + b^2 = c^2$.
- Two triangles $\triangle ABC$ and $\triangle DEF$ are congruent if all three corresponding pairs of angles are congruent AND all three corresponding sides are congruent. Two triangles $\triangle ABC$ and $\triangle DEF$ are similar if the ratios of the three pairs of corresponding sides are the same; that is, $\dfrac{AB}{DE} = \dfrac{BC}{EF} = \dfrac{AC}{DF} = k$, where k is a positive number.
- The area formula for a triangle with base b and height h is $A = \dfrac{1}{2}b \cdot h$.
- There are some triangles with special relationships between sides and angles that, when recognized, can simplify your calculations: 3-4-5 and 5-12-13 right triangles, as well as 30-60-90 and 45-45-90 right triangles.
- The circumference of a circle with radius r (or diameter $d = 2r$) is $C = 2\pi r = \pi d$. The area of a circle with radius r is $A = \pi r^2$.
- Part of a circle's circumference is called an arc; the length of an arc can be found with the following formula: $P = \dfrac{\theta}{360°}\pi 2r$, where θ represents the measure of the central angle of the arc and r is the radius of the circle.
- Part of a circle's area is called a sector; the area of a sector can be found with the following formula: $A = \dfrac{\theta}{360°}\pi r^2$, where θ represents the measure of the central angle of the sector and r is the radius of the circle.
- To graph a circle in the coordinate plane, use the following formula: $(x - h)^2 + (y - k)^2 = r^2$, where (h, k) is the center of the circle.

- Ellipses in a coordinate plane are represented by the following formula: $\dfrac{(x-h)^2}{a^2}+\dfrac{(y-k)^2}{b^2}=1$, where a is half the major axis and b is half the minor axis. When the ellipse is taller than it is wide, a and b are switched in the formula.

- Trigonometric ratios are used to identify the lengths of sides of a right triangle when one side and one angle (instead of two sides) are known. There are six trigonometric ratios: cosine (cos), sine (sin), tangent (tan), secant (sec), cosecant (csc), and cotangent (cot).

- Trigonometric ratios for right triangles are defined as follows:

$$\sin\theta = \frac{\text{opposite}}{\text{hypotenuse}} \text{ and } \csc\theta = \frac{\text{hypotenuse}}{\text{opposite}} = \frac{1}{\sin\theta}$$

$$\cos\theta = \frac{\text{adjacent}}{\text{hypotenuse}} \text{ and } \sec\theta = \frac{\text{hypotenuse}}{\text{adjacent}} = \frac{1}{\cos\theta}$$

$$\tan\theta = \frac{\text{opposite}}{\text{adjacent}} \text{ and } \cot\theta = \frac{\text{adjacent}}{\text{opposite}} = \frac{1}{\tan\theta}$$

- Angles can be measured in two ways: degrees and radians. Radians often arise when dealing with circles and trigonometry. You can convert between degree and radian measures using the following formula: $\text{Radians} = \dfrac{\text{Degrees}}{180°} \cdot \pi$.

- When graphing lines and inequalities, you'll need to know the slope of the line and at least one point on the line or two points on the line. This information can be retrieved from graphs, equations in standard form, or equations in slope-intercept form.

- Parallel lines have the same slope while perpendicular lines have slopes that are negative reciprocals.

- When working with points, lines, and shapes in the coordinate plane, you can apply a variety of transformations: translations, reflections, rotations, and dilations.

TEST YOURSELF

PREPARING FOR HIGHER MATH – GEOMETRY

10 Questions—10 Minutes

Directions: Solve each problem and choose the correct answer.

Do not dwell on problems that take too long. First, solve as many as you can; then, you can return to others you have left.

You are permitted to use a calculator. You may use your calculator for any problem you like, but some of the problems may best be completed without a calculator.

Note: Unless otherwise stated, all of the following should be assumed:

1. Illustrative figures are NOT necessarily drawn to scale.

2. Geometric figures lie in a plane.

3. The word *line* indicates a straight line.

---

1. A rectangle of length (w + 6) inches and width (w − 1) inches is shaded, except for a square region of side length (w − 3) inches. What is the area of the shaded region, in terms of w?

   A. $w^2 + 5w - 6$

   B. $w^2 + 4w - 9$

   C. $2w^2 + 11w + 3$

   D. $11w - 15$

   E. $-w - 7$

2. Consider the following triangle:

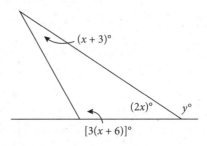

   What is the value of $x + y$?

   F. 29

   G. 58

   H. 122

   J. 151

   K. 180

3. Which of these expressions represents the height of triangle *ABC*?

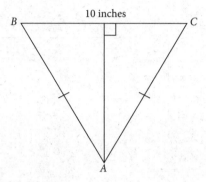

10 inches

A. $\sqrt{y^2 + 25}$ inches

B. $\sqrt{y^2 - 25}$ inches

C. $y + 5$ inches

D. $y^2 + 25$ inches

E. $y - 5$ inches

4. A family builds three tree houses in the backyard and connects them with bridges, as shown:

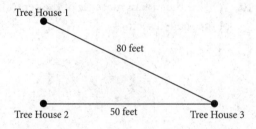

Assuming Tree House 1 is directly across from Tree House 2, which of these expressions represents the length of the bridge connecting these two tree houses?

F. $80^2 - 50^2$ feet

G. $80 - 50$ feet

H. $\sqrt{50^2 + 80^2}$ feet

J. $50 + 80$ feet

K. $\sqrt{80^2 - 50^2}$ feet

5. What is the length, *S*, of the arc of the circle corresponding to the shaded sector?

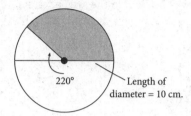

220° Length of diameter = 10 cm.

A. $\dfrac{9}{35}\pi$ cm.

B. $\dfrac{\pi}{4}$ cm.

C. $\dfrac{11}{9}\pi$ cm.

D. $\dfrac{35}{18}\pi$ cm.

E. $\dfrac{35}{9}\pi$ cm.

6. What is the area of the shaded region?

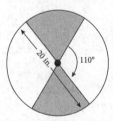

20 in.   110°

F. $\dfrac{175}{9}\pi$ square inches

G. $\dfrac{275}{9}\pi$ square inches

H. $\dfrac{350}{9}\pi$ square inches

J. $\dfrac{550}{9}\pi$ square inches

K. $\dfrac{700}{9}\pi$ square inches

7. The circumference of circle A is three times the circumference of circle B. What is the ratio of the area of circle B to the area of circle A?

   A. 1:3

   B. 3:1

   C. 1:9

   D. 1:6

   E. 9:1

8. Compute $\csc(2\theta)$ for the following triangle:

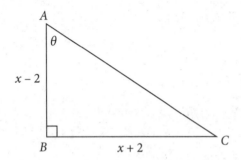

   F. -1

   G. $\dfrac{2x^2+8}{2x^2-8}$

   H. $\dfrac{2\sqrt{x^2+8}}{x+2}$

   J. $\dfrac{2x}{x^2-4}$

   K. $\dfrac{1}{2x^2-8}$

9. Let $0 < x < \dfrac{1}{2}$. Compute $\sec(B) + \csc(C)$ for the following triangle:

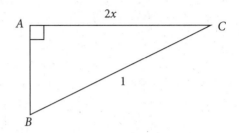

   A. $\dfrac{2}{\sqrt{1-4x^2}}$

   B. $\dfrac{1}{x}$

   C. $\dfrac{1}{2x} + \dfrac{1}{\sqrt{1-4x^2}}$

   D. $2\sqrt{1-4x^2}$

   E. $2x + \sqrt{1-4x^2}$

10. What is the radian measure of the central angle of the shaded sector?

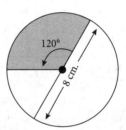

   F. $\dfrac{\pi}{3}$

   G. $\dfrac{5\pi}{6}$

   H. $\dfrac{2\pi}{3}$

   J. $\dfrac{3\pi}{4}$

   K. $\dfrac{3\pi}{4}$

ANSWER KEY AND EXPLANATIONS

1. D	**3.** B	**5.** E	**7.** C	**9.** A
2. J	**4.** K	**6.** H	**8.** G	**10.** H

1. **The correct answer is D.** First label all the dimensions in the figure:

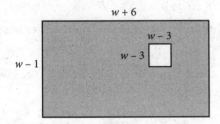

In order to find the shaded area, we need to subtract the area of the inner square from the area of the outer rectangle. The area of the outer rectangle is:

$$(w + 6)(w - 1) = w^2 + 5w - 6$$

and the area of the inner square is:

$$(w - 3)^2 = w^2 - 6w + 9$$

Subtracting these, we get:

$$w^2 + 5w - 6 - (w^2 - 6w + 9)$$
$$w^2 + 5w - 6 - w^2 + 6w - 9$$
$$11w - 15$$

2. **The correct answer is J.** This problem involves two main notions—the triangle sum law and the notion of supplementary angles. To begin, the sum of the measures of the three angles inside the triangle is 180°. This leads to the equation $(x + 3) + 3(x + 1) + 2x = 180$. Solve for x as follows:

$$(x+3)+3(x+1)+2x=180$$
$$x+3+3x+3+2x=180$$
$$6x+6=180$$
$$6x=174$$
$$x=29$$

Next, you need to find y. To do so, note that the adjacent angles with measures $2x$ and y are supplementary. Since $2x = 2(29) = 58$, it follows that $y = 180 - 58 = 122$. Hence, $x + y = 29 + 122 = 151$.

Pay attention to the goal of the question. Choice F is the value of x, and choice H is the value of y. Choice G is $2x$, and choice K is $2x + y$.

3. **The correct answer is B.** First note that ABC is an isosceles triangle. As such, the bisector from vertex A to side BC must be perpendicular. So we have the following updated diagram:

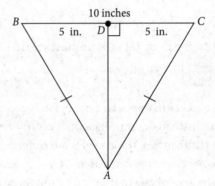

The height of triangle ABC is the length of segment AD. Use the Pythagorean theorem to find:

$$\left(AD\right)^2 + 5^2 = y^2$$
$$\left(AD\right)^2 = y^2 - 25$$
$$AD = \sqrt{y^2 - 25}$$

4. **The correct answer is K.** First, you should complete the given drawing by connecting Tree House 1 to Tree House 2; this forms a right triangle, as shown:

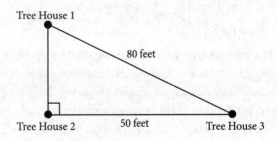

Use the Pythagorean theorem to find its length, s. Keep in mind that this side is a leg of the triangle, not the hypotenuse. As such, we see that $s^2 + 50^2 = 80^2$, so that $s = \sqrt{80^2 - 50^2}$ feet.

5. **The correct answer is E.** This problem asks you to plug in given values, but it requires that you know the formula for arc length and can identify the parts. The formula is $S = \left(\dfrac{\theta}{180°}\right)\pi(r)$, where θ is the central angle across from the arc and r is the radius of the circle.

$$\theta = 360° - 220° = 140°$$
$$r = \frac{1}{2}(10 \text{ cm}) = 5 \text{ cm}$$

Substituting these into the formula yields
$$S = \left(\frac{140°}{180°}\right)\pi(5) \text{ cm., or } \frac{35}{9}\pi.$$

6. **The correct answer is H.** The region is comprised of two distinct sectors. Since their central angles are vertical angles, these angles are congruent, so the sectors have the same area. You only need to find the area of one of the sectors and then double it. To find the area of one of these sectors, you need the radius and the central angle. Notice that the angle corresponding to one of the two congruent unshaded sectors is 110°. Since the combination of one unshaded sector and one shaded sector comprises half the circle, it follows that the central angle for a shaded sector is 180° – 110° = 70°. Since the diameter is 20 inches, the radius is 10 inches. The area of one shaded sector is $(10)^2 \pi \left(\dfrac{70°}{360°}\right)$ square inches. Doubling this yields the area of the shaded region as $200\pi\left(\dfrac{70°}{360°}\right)$ square inches, or $\dfrac{350}{9}\pi$ square inches.

7. **The correct answer is C.** Here again, this problem requires the use of knowledge from two different subjects: number systems and geometry. To begin, you must find the relationship between the radii of the two circles. Use the given information about how the circumferences are related to do so.

The circumference of circle A is $2\pi r_A$, and the circumference of circle B is $2\pi r_B$. Using the first sentence of the problem yields $2\pi r_A = 3(2\pi r_B)$. Dividing both sides by 2π shows that $r_A = 3r_B$. To get the ratio of the areas in the correct form, you must express them using multiples of a single radius. To this end, observe the following:

Area of circle A $= \pi r_A^2 = \pi (3r_B)^2 = 9(\pi r_B^2) = 9 \cdot$ area of circle B

So the ratio of "area of circle B" to "area of circle A" is 1:9.

8. **The correct answer is G.** First, write the given expression in terms of $\sin\theta$ and $\cos\theta$:

$$\csc(2\theta) = \frac{1}{\sin(2\theta)} = \frac{1}{2\sin\theta\cos\theta}$$

To compute $\sin\theta$ and $\cos\theta$, you need the hypotenuse of ABC. Use the Pythagorean theorem to find it:

$$(x-2)^2 + (x+2)^2 = (AC)^2$$
$$x^2 - 4x + 4 + x^2 + 4x + 4 = (AC)^2$$
$$2x^2 + 8 = (AC)^2$$
$$\sqrt{2x^2 + 8} = AC$$

Hence:
$$\sin\theta = \frac{x+2}{\sqrt{2x^2+8}}$$
$$\cos\theta = \frac{x-2}{\sqrt{2x^2+8}}$$

So:
$$\csc(2\theta) = \frac{1}{2\sin\theta\cos\theta}$$
$$= \frac{1}{2}\cdot\frac{1}{\sin\theta}\cdot\frac{1}{\cos\theta}$$
$$= \frac{1}{2}\cdot\frac{\sqrt{2x^2+8}}{x+2}\cdot\frac{\sqrt{2x^2+8}}{x-2}$$
$$= \frac{\left(\sqrt{2x^2+8}\right)^2}{2(x+2)(x-2)}$$
$$= \frac{2x^2+8}{2(x^2-4)}$$
$$= \frac{2x^2+8}{2x^2-8}$$

9. **The correct answer is A.** You need all three sides of the triangle to compute these quantities. Use the Pythagorean theorem to find the missing side:

$$(AB)^2 + (AC)^2 = (BC)^2$$
$$(AB)^2 + (2x)^2 = 1$$
$$(AB)^2 = 1 - 4x^2$$
$$AB = \sqrt{1 - 4x^2}$$

Now, compute the two quantities in the given expression.

$$\sec B = \frac{1}{\cos B} = \frac{BC}{AB} = \frac{1}{\sqrt{1 - 4x^2}}$$
$$\csc C = \frac{1}{\sin C} = \frac{BC}{AB} = \frac{1}{\sqrt{1 - 4x^2}}$$

Then, add the two quantities:

$$\sec B + \csc C = \frac{2}{\sqrt{1 - 4x^2}}$$

10. **The correct answer is H.** The central angle of the shaded sector is 120 degrees. You want the angle units in radians. To convert the degree measure to radians, simply multiply 120 by $\frac{\pi}{180}$ which equals $\frac{2\pi}{3}$. Multiplying by $\frac{\pi}{360}$ would result in choice F.

CHAPTER

**Preparing for Higher Math:
Statistics & Probability**

PREPARING FOR HIGHER MATH:

OVERVIEW

Statistics

Probability

Summing It Up

Test Yourself: PHM—Statistics & Probability

The ACT Mathematics section will ask you to collect, describe, and analyze quantitative data in order to draw conclusions. A number of these questions will fall under the category of Preparing for High Math: Statistics & Probability. These six questions will build upon the principles found in Integrating Essential Skills questions while also touching upon more advanced concepts, such as standard deviation, counting principles, expected value, and set notation. While it is the case that PHM: Statistics and Probability questions amount to a relatively small portion of the mathematics test, depending on your goals, they can still play a vital role for your Mathematics section score. This chapter will prepare you for any of the possible subjects that could appear on test day. Use the Test Yourself at the end of the chapter to assess your understanding. Refer back to the Basic Statistics and Probability section in Chapter 9 as needed.

STATISTICS & PROBABILITY

STATISTICS

Statistics topics can arise in both the Integrating Essential Skills questions as well as for the six Preparing for Higher Math: Statistics & Probability questions. More than likely, the questions will reference some measure of central tendency (mean, median, or mode), perhaps even combining multiple concepts. For review of those items, revisit Chapter 9. Beyond those items, higher level statistics questions may also invoke concepts like range and standard deviation, along with various data representations.

Range

The range, or the spread, of a data set is the difference between the greatest and least data values. To find the range of a set of data, first write the values in ascending order to make sure that you have found the least and greatest values. Then, subtract the least data value from the greatest data value.

Example

Celia kept track of the average price of a gallon of gas over a period of 10 years. Her data is shown in the following table. What is the range in the average price of gas?

Year	Average price/gallon in US dollars
2006	2.00
2007	2.08
2008	2.44
2009	3.40
2010	2.85
2011	2.90
2012	3.50
2013	4.20
2014	3.80
2015	3.25

Solution

Write the data in order from least to greatest:

2.00. 2.08 2.44 2.85 2.90 3.25
3.40 3.50 3.80 4.20

Subtract the least value from the greatest value:

4.20 – 2.00 = 2.20

$2.20 is the range (or spread) of the data.

Standard Deviation

A more precise way to measure spread in a data set is by finding the standard deviation, a calculation of how far the actual observations fall from the mean. There are two ways of finding standard deviation. Their appropriateness depends on the situation.

If you're looking at a whole population, then you use the population standard deviation. Population standard deviation can be calculated with the following:

$$\sigma = \sqrt{\frac{\Sigma^n (x_i - \mu)^2}{n}}$$

Don't be afraid of the Greek letters. The one on the left, σ, is the lowercase sigma and stands for population standard deviation. The one the looks like an "E" under the radical is an uppercase sigma. It indicates sigma notation, telling you that you'll be summing the given terms—that you're going to perform the operation in parentheses n times, n being the number of data points there are. The right character, μ, is lowercase mu, which represents the mean of the data set.

Calculating Standard Deviation

You'll work through this formula in four steps:

1. First, subtract the mean, μ, from each data point, resulting in what's called a deviation.

2. Next, square each deviation and find the sum of all deviations.

3. Then, divide the sum of the deviations by the number of data points, n.

4. Finally, take the square root of that total value.

What you're doing mathematically is finding the average distance of the data points from the average of the whole data set. Let's see what this looks like for a small data set. Consider a data set with four values: 1, 2, 5, and 7. The mean, μ, is 3.75, found by adding the data points together and dividing by their total. The standard deviation for such a set would then be calculated as follows:

$$\sigma = \sqrt{\frac{\left((1-3.75)^2 + (2-3.75)^2 + (5-3.75)^2 + (7-3.75)^2\right)}{4}} \approx 2.3848$$

Each data point in that set, on average, is 2.3848 points away from the average of 3.75.

If you were told that the data you were looking at was only a sample of the overall data, then you would use the formula for sample standard deviation, denoted s.

$$s = \sqrt{\frac{\sum^n (x_1 - \overline{x})^2}{n-1}}$$

The only difference between these two formulae (other than replacing some of the Greek letters) comes down to the number of values in the denominator under the radical. In the sample standard deviation, one data point is subtracted from the total number of available data points.

The key feature of the standard deviation is that the smaller it is, the more tightly the observations are centered around the mean; the larger it is, the more spread out they are. The standard deviation is never negative, and it is only 0 when there is no spread at all—that is, when all observations are equal. The standard deviation should only be used together with the mean, not the median. Just like the mean, the standard deviation is easily influenced by outliers.

Graphing Data Sets

Numerical data sets can be visualized in various ways. Four common types of graphs are dot plots, histograms, box plots, and scatterplots. Let's take a look at the data set {1, 1, 1, 2, 3, 3, 6, 6, 6, 6, 6, 10} using a dot plot, histogram, and box plot.

Dot Plots

A dot plot is a type of plot obtained by illustrating each member of a data set as a point above the appropriate position on a number line, as follows:

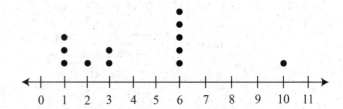

Histograms

In a histogram, bars appear above each value of the data set. The height of each bar represents the number of times that data value appears in the set. The appearance resembles a dot plot, but the bars replace the stacks of dots. The bars on a histogram always touch, may or may not appear on a number line, and will most often have labels that identify the horizontal (x) and vertical (y) axes.

Here is an example of a histogram:

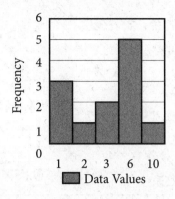

Box Plots

A box plot requires a bit more information to construct, but it tells you much more about the spread and center of a data set. Five numbers are needed to form a box plot:

- **Minimum:** This is the smallest number in the data set. Here, this number is 1.

- **First Quartile:** This is the 25th percentile, or number for which 25% of the data set is less than or equal to it. Assuming the data are arranged in increasing order, the position of the first quartile is obtained by finding the median of the lower half of the data set. The median of the lower half will fall between the third value and the fourth. Here, this number is 1.5.

- **Median:** This is the 50th percentile. Assuming the data are arranged in increasing order, the position of the median is obtained by averaging the middle two data values since there is an even number of data in this set. (If there is an odd number of data values, it is the single value in the middle of the data set.) The middle two values are those in the 6th and 7th positions, namely 3 and 6. When you calculate the median, you get 4.5.

- **Third Quartile:** This is the 75th percentile. Assuming the data are arranged in increasing order, the position of the third quartile is found by finding the median of the upper half of the data set. Because there are an even number of values, the Q3 would be the value between the

9th and 10th values. Both of those values are 6, so the third quartile is 6.

- **Maximum:** This is the largest number in the data set. Here, this number is 10.

- **Interquartile Range:** In order to compute the interquartile range (IQR), determine the quartiles, or data values in the 25th, 50th and 75th positions in the data set once it has been arranged in numerically increasing order. The IQR is Q3 – Q1. For this set, the IQR = 6 – 1.5 = 4.5.

The box plot obtained is as follows:

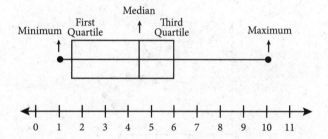

Scatterplots

A scatterplot is another type of visual presentation used to show relationships or trends in data. A scatterplot is a graph in which the x-axis represents the values of one variable and the y-axis represents the values of the other variable. Several values of one variable and the corresponding values of the other variable are measured and plotted on the graph.

If two variables have a relationship such that when one variable changes, the other changes in a predictable way, the two variables are correlated. There are typically three types of correlation: positive, negative, and no correlation.

- A **positive correlation** occurs when one variable increases and the other variable increases as well.

- A **negative correlation** occurs when one variable increases and the other decreases.

- **No correlation** occurs when there is no apparent relationship between the variables.

Generally, the more tightly packed the points are in a scatterplot, the stronger the relationship. If the data points rise from left to right, we say the relationship is positive, while if they fall from left to right, we say the trend is negative.

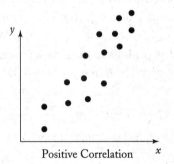

Positive Correlation

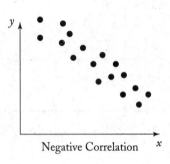

Negative Correlation

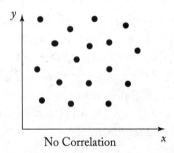

No Correlation

If there is a strong correlation in the data, it is likely that there will be a line that could be drawn on the scatterplot that comes close to all the points. This line is known as the "line of best fit." Without performing any computations, it is possible to visualize the location of the line of best fit, as the diagrams show.

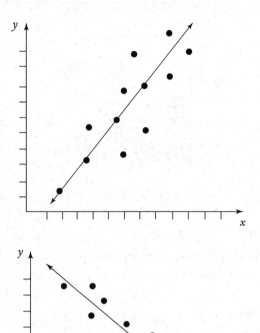

Comparing Data Sets Using Shape, Center, and Spread

Statistics questions may require you to know measures of central tendency, meaning the mean (average), median, and mode of a data set, but you will also need to be familiar with the shape, center, and spread of data. The shape of the data refers to the normal distribution curve. The center could be the average (arithmetic mean) or the median of the data values in the set. The spread is the range of the data, or the standard deviation of the data that describes the distance between values in a data set.

Data may be presented in tables, bar graphs, or via other methods, so it is important to be familiar with different types of data presentation.

Standard Deviation—Normal Distribution

A standard deviation describes how far the data values in a set are from the mean or how much they "deviate" from the mean. The graphs shown are both normal distribution curves.

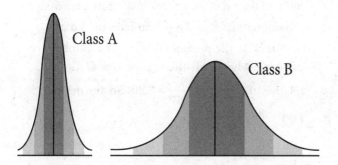

Class A

Class B

In the graph on the left, since much of the data clusters closely around the mean, there is a small standard deviation. In the graph on the right, since the data is more spread out, there is a larger standard deviation. If these were sets of test scores on a math exam for Class A and Class B, most of the scores in Class A would be very close to the average score, but, in Class B, the scores would be more varied.

PROBABILITY

Probability refers to the likelihood of an event occurring (or not occurring). As you saw in Chapter 9, basic probability can be calculated by dividing the number of desired outcomes by the number of possible outcomes. But not all probability can be determined this way. Sometimes finding the probability of a particular outcome requires using other concepts: sample space, relative frequency, counting principles, expected value, and more.

Sample Space

An outcome is the result of a single trial of a probability experiment, and the collection of all outcomes is the sample space, which is written as a set. For instance, if you roll a typical six-sided die and record the number of the face on which it comes to rest, the outcomes are the labels on the faces, namely $S = \{1, 2, 3, 4, 5, 6\}$. An event is a subset of the sample space and is usually described using one or more conditions. For instance,

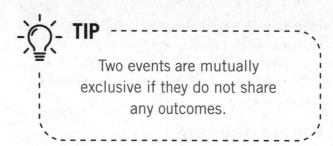

TIP

Two events are mutually exclusive if they do not share any outcomes.

the event that "the die lands on an even number" is the subset $E = \{2, 4, 6\}$. Suppose E and F represent events of some probability experiment. Some common events formed using them are as follows:

Event	Description in words
Complement of E	All outcomes NOT in E
E or F	All outcomes in E OR in F OR in both
E and F	All outcomes in common to E AND F

Set Notation

A set is a collection of objects. The objects in a particular set are called the members or the elements of the set. In mathematics, sets are usually represented by capital letters, and their members are represented by lower case letters. Braces, { and }, are usually used to enclose the members of a set. Thus, the set A, which has members a, b, c, d, and e and no other members, can be written as $A = \{a, b, c, d, e\}$. Note that the order in which the elements of a set are listed is not important—the set {1, 2, 3} and the set {2, 3, 1} represent identical sets.

The symbol used to indicate that an element belongs to a particular set is $\in$, and the symbol that indicates that an element does not belong to a set is $\notin$. Thus, if $B = \{2, 4, 6, 8\}$, we can say $6 \in B$ and $7 \notin B$. If a set is defined so that it does not contain any elements, it is called the empty set, or the null set, and can be written as { } or $\varnothing$.

The union of two sets A and B, written $A \cup B$, is the set of all elements that are in either A or B. The intersection of two sets, indicated $A \cap B$, is the set of all elements that are in both A and B. Thus, if $A = \{2, 4, 6, 8, 10\}$ and $B = \{1, 2, 3, 4\}$, we have $A \cup B = \{1, 2, 3, 4, 6, 8, 10\}$ and $A \cap B = \{2, 4\}$. If $A \cap B = \varnothing$, then A and B are said to be disjoint.

Relative Frequency

Sometimes, data from an experiment (like a survey) is in the form of frequencies. For instance, you ask a question of 120 people, all randomly chosen, and there are 1 of 5 possible responses. You tabulate the number of responses (that is, the frequencies) for each choice and divide that number by 120 (the total number of responses). This relative frequency can be used to make an educated guess about how the entire population from which the respondents were chosen would answer the question.

Hospital records indicated that 157 maternity parents stayed in the hospital for the number of days shown in the following distribution:

Number of days stayed	Frequency
3	15
4	32
5	56
6	49
7	5

Compute the probability that a maternity patient will stay at most 4 days.

    A. 0.20

    B. 0.25

    C. 0.30

    D. 0.50

    E. 0.75

The correct answer is C. We use the relative frequency to determine the percentage of people of those for whom we have information satisfy the condition. Then, we use that to assign the probability to the event for general maternity patients. "No more than four days" translates to "3 days or 4 days" in the present problem. The number of people who satisfy this is $15 + 32 = 47$. So, the relative frequency is $\frac{47}{157} \approx 0.30$. So, the desired probability is 0.30.

Counting Principles

Determining the *total* number of possible outcomes in an experiment, whether tossing a coin 5 times, rolling a die twice, or randomly selecting colored balls from a bin, is an important step to assessing the likelihood, or chance, of getting each possible outcome. Sometimes that process can be simple. In situations in which order doesn't matter and all the quantities are different, you can apply the fundamental counting principle. Let's look at an example:

Example

A deli offers a lunch special composed of a salad, a beverage, and a dessert. The deli serves 7 kinds of salads, 5 kinds of beverages, and 3 kinds of desserts. How many different lunch special combinations are possible?

Solution

There are 7 kinds of salads, 5 kinds of beverages, and 3 kinds of desserts, so there are a total of $7 \times 5 \times 3 = 105$ possible lunch combinations.

Sometimes order does matter, though, and all the quantities will be the same. In those cases, you'll need to apply two other counting concepts: permutations and combinations.

Permutations

A permutation of a set of objects is an arrangement of those objects in which each object is used once and only once. For example, if you have objects labeled *A*, *B*, *C*, *D*, and *E*, some permutations of these objects are *ABCDE* and *DECBA*. Any unique ordering of the letters produces a different permutation. The number of ways to arrange *n* objects in such a manner is *n*!. You can define *n*! as:

$$n! = n \times (n-1) \times (n-2) \times ... \times 3 \times 2 \times 1$$

For instance, $4! = 4 \times 3 \times 2 \times 1$.

In permutations, order often matters. Sometimes, we want to arrange only *some* of the objects in a given set. For instance, say we had *n* letters, but we only wanted to arrange *k* of them. This is a "permutation of *n* objects taken *k* at a time." The number of such arrangements is written as:

$$P(n,k) = \frac{n!}{(n-k)!}$$

PRACTICE

In how many ways can 4 books from a collection of 7 be arranged on a shelf?

- **A.** 120
- **B.** 210
- **C.** 720
- **D.** 840
- **E.** 900

The correct answer is D. We wish to arrange 4 of the 7 books, so we must calculate *P* (7, 4):

$$P(7,4) = \frac{7!}{(7-4)!}$$
$$= \frac{7!}{3!}$$
$$= \frac{7 \times 6 \times 5 \times 4 \times \cancel{3} \times \cancel{2} \times \cancel{1}}{\cancel{3} \times \cancel{2} \times \cancel{1}}$$
$$= 7 \times 6 \times 5 \times 4$$
$$= 840$$

There are 840 ways to arrange 4 of the 7 books.

Combinations

There are times when the order in which objects are arranged doesn't matter, like when forming a committee of 4 people from a group of 10 people in which all committee members have the same influence, or when simply selecting 5 cards randomly from a standard deck of 52 cards. To determine the number of such selections, a combination is required.

The number of ways of selecting *k* objects from a group of *n* objects in which order does NOT matter is called the "number of combinations of *n* objects taken *k* at a time." The formula is as follows:

$$C(n,k) = \frac{n!}{k!(n-k)!}$$

PRACTICE

Max found 10 used books that he likes equally well in a clearance bin, but he only has enough money to purchase 3 of them. In how many different ways can he select 3 books to purchase?

- **A.** 120
- **B.** 500
- **C.** 720
- **D.** 604,800
- **E.** 3,628,800

The correct answer is A. Order does not matter here because Max is simply purchasing a collection of unrelated books. (Max is not, as in the previous example, ordering them in a certain way on a shelf.) So, we use the combinations formula with *n* = 10 and *k* = 3:

$$C(10,3) = \frac{10!}{3!(7)!}$$

When simplified (or entered into a calculator), this equals 120.

Random Variables

Consider the experiment of rolling two fair dice and recording the values of Die 1 and Die 2 in an ordered pair. The sample space consists of 36 elements (including redundancies if we do not distinguish between Die 1 and Die 2), pictured below:

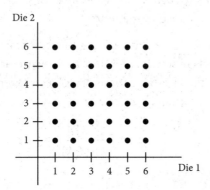

Suppose we are interested in how likely it is to get the various sums of the two dice when you roll the dice, but we are less interested in the actual outcomes that produce these sums. We could define a function that assigns the sum to each possible roll and then calculate the frequencies to answer our question. Such a function is called a random variable when discussing probability.

Let us define a random variable X to be the sum of the dots appearing on Die 1 and Die 2 when they've come to rest. The assignment of the values of X for the members of the sample space is as follows:

$X(1,1) = 2$

$X(1,2) = X(2,1) = 3$

$X(1,3) = X(2,2) = X(3,1) = 4$

$X(1,4) = X(2,3) = X(3,2) = X(4,1) = 5$

$X(1,5) = X(2,4) = X(3,3) = X(4,2) = X(5,1) = 6$

$X(1,6) = X(2,5) = X(3,4) = X(4,3) = X(5,2) = X(6,1) = 7$

$X(2,6) = X(3,5) = X(4,4) = X(5,3) = X(6,2) = 8$

$X(3,6) = X(4,5) = X(5,4) = X(6,3) = 9$

$X(4,6) = X(5,5) = X(6,4) = 10$

$X(5,6) = X(6,5) = 11$

$X(6,6) = 12$

Now, since the dice were both fair, all outcomes in the sample space are equally likely. As such, we are guided by classical probability and assign the probabilities to each value of X in a manner consistent with the relative frequency of the value. This is tabulated below—for ease of comparison, the fractions are not simplified:

Value x of X	Probability $P(X = x)$
2	$\frac{1}{36}$
3	$\frac{2}{36}$
4	$\frac{3}{36}$
5	$\frac{4}{36}$
6	$\frac{5}{36}$
7	$\frac{6}{36}$
8	$\frac{5}{36}$
9	$\frac{4}{36}$
10	$\frac{3}{36}$
11	$\frac{2}{36}$
12	$\frac{1}{36}$

This is an example of a probability distribution. We can pictorially represent it using a bar graph called a probability histogram:

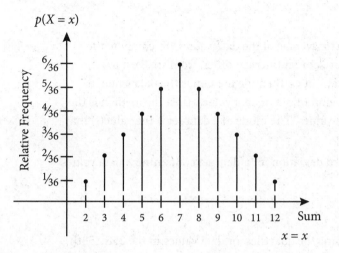

$p(X = x)$

Relative Frequency

$\frac{6}{36}$
$\frac{5}{36}$
$\frac{4}{36}$
$\frac{3}{36}$
$\frac{2}{36}$
$\frac{1}{36}$

2 3 4 5 6 7 8 9 10 11 12   Sum

$x = x$

PRACTICE

A survey of CheapBooks4U.com shoppers reveals the following probability distribution of the number of books purchased per visit.

x	0	1	2	3	4	5	6	7
$P(X=x)$	0.35	0.25	0.20	0.08	0.06	0.03	0.02	0.01

What is the probability that a shopper will buy between 3 and 5 books, inclusive?

A. 0.06

B. 0.09

C. 0.11

D. 0.14

E. 0.17

The correct answer is E. Using the given data, the event "between 3 and 5 books, inclusive" corresponds to buying 3, 4, or 5 books, all of which are mutually exclusive, written $3 \leq X \leq 5$. So, the probability of this event is $P(3 \leq X \leq 5) = P(X = 3) + P(X = 4) + P(X = 5) = 0.08 + 0.06 + 0.03 = 0.17$.

Expected Value

A weighted average of all possible values of a random variable X, computed using their probabilities, often provides insight on what to expect for events over time. It is called the expected value, denoted $E(X)$, and is computed using the formula $E(X) = \sum x \cdot P(X = x)$. The value you get will likely NOT be an outcome produced by X, but rather it is viewed as a typical value of that random variable.

The expected value, E, of a random variable X that takes on possible values $x_1, x_2, \ldots$ is

$$E = \sum x_i P(x_i)$$

To summarize that formula, each possible value is multiplied by its probability, and these products are summed.

If X is a binomial random variable, the expected value of X is $E = np$, where n is the number events, and p is the probability of a particular event. If you were to flip a coin, you would expect that of 50 flips that 25 would be heads. That expectation comes from the probability of flipping heads in a single event (.5) and the total number of events, 50.

Let's look at another example: suppose a bag contains one yellow marble and three black marbles. A marble is selected from the bag, and then replaced. This is repeated ten times. What is the expected value of how many times the chosen marble will be black? This is a binomial experiment with $n = 10$ and $p = \frac{3}{4}$. Therefore, the expected value is $10 \cdot \frac{3}{4} = 7.5$.

Note that the expected value is not necessarily even a possible outcome, as seen in the previous example.

The expected value of random variable X is also called its mean, and denoted by μ_x; for a binomial random variable, we have seen that $\mu_x = np$.

SUMMING IT UP

- The mean of a data set is the arithmetic average of the data values. To compute the median, arrange the values in the data set in numerical order, from smallest to largest. If there are an odd number of data values, then the median is the data value in the middle of the set. If there is an even number of data values, then the median is the arithmetic average of the middle two values. The mode of a data set is the value(s) that occur most frequently.

- The formula for a population standard deviation for a data set containing n data values is $s = \sqrt{\dfrac{\Sigma(x-\text{mean})^2}{n}}$.

- In order to compute the IQR, determine the quartiles, or data values in the 25th, 50th and 75th positions in the data set once it has been arranged in numerically increasing order. The IQR is Q3 – Q1.

- In a scatterplot, the relationship between x and y is linear if the trend between x and y can be described by a line. If there is another curve that more reasonably describes the relationship, the relationship is nonlinear.

- A set is a collection of objects. The union of two sets A and B, written $A \cup B$, is the set of all elements that are in either A or B. The intersection of two sets, indicated $A \cap B$, is the set of all elements that are in both A and B.

- For any positive integer n, $n! = n \times (n-1) \times (n-2) \times \ldots \times 3 \times 2 \times 1$. For example, $4! = 4 \times 3 \times 2 \times 1$.

- In permutations, order matters. The number of such arrangements is written as $P(n,k) = \dfrac{n!}{(n-k)!}$.

- In combinations, order does not matter. The number of ways of selecting k objects from a group of n objects is written as $C(n,k) = \dfrac{n!}{k!(n-k)!}$.

- If a sample space contains N outcomes, then the probability of any one of them occurring is $\dfrac{1}{N}$. This can be extended to events in the sense that if A contains k elements, then $P(A) = \dfrac{\text{Number of outcomes in } A}{\text{Number of possible outcomes}} = \dfrac{k}{N}$. To find the probability of a compound event, use $P(A \text{ or } B) = P(A) + P(B) - P(A \text{ and } B)$.

- The expected value of random variable X is also called its mean, and denoted by μ_x; for a binomial random variable: $\mu_x = np$.

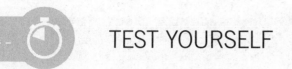
PREPARING FOR HIGHER MATH: STATISTICS & PROBABILITY

8 Questions—8 Minutes

Directions: Solve each problem and choose the correct answer.

Do not dwell on problems that take too long. First, solve as many as you can; then, you can return to others you have left.

You are permitted to use a calculator. You may use your calculator for any problem you like, but some of the problems may best be completed without a calculator.

---

1. A four-sided tetrahedral die has faces marked as A, 1, B, and 2. It is rolled twice, and the results are recorded as ordered pairs of the form (1st roll, 2nd roll). What is the probability that an ordered pair contains at least one 2?

   A. $\dfrac{1}{16}$

   B. $\dfrac{1}{4}$

   C. $\dfrac{3}{8}$

   D. $\dfrac{7}{16}$

   E. $\dfrac{9}{16}$

2. There are 13 contestants in a baking competition. Four ribbons will be awarded for first, second, third, and fourth place, and no contestant can receive more than one award. In how many ways can the ribbons be awarded?

   F. $13 + 12 + 11 + 10$

   G. $13 \times 12 \times 11 \times 10$

   H. $(13 + 12 + 11 + 10)!$

   J. $13! \times 12! \times 11! \times 10!$

   K. $13!$

3. Every data value in a data set composed of at least eighteen values is 40, except for one that has a value of 5. Which statement best describes the median of this data set?

   A. The median is greater than 40.

   B. The median equals 40.

   C. The median is less than 40.

   D. The median may be greater than or less than 40, depending on the size of the data set.

   E. This cannot be determined, irrespective of the size of the data set.

4. Let $a > 0$. Consider the following two data sets:

   Data Set I: $\{a, 2a, 3a, 4a, 5a\}$

   Data Set II: $\{2a, 4a, 6a, 8a, 10a\}$

   Which of the following measures, if any, are the same for Data Set I and Data Set II?

   F. Mean

   G. Median

   H. Mode

   J. Range

   K. None of these

5. The following scatter plot shows data relating the two variables X and Y:

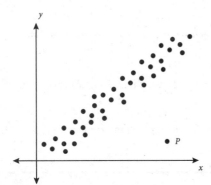

Which of the following is the most accurate description of the relationship between X and Y?

A. Moderate, negative linear relationship between X and Y

B. Strong, positive nonlinear relationship between X and Y

C. Strong, negative linear relationship between X and Y

D. Moderate, positive linear relationship between X and Y

E. No discernible relationship between X and Y because of the presence of the outlier

6. A department stores discounts all mattresses by $200 three days before the start of the Christmas holiday. If the store sells seventy-eight mattresses as a result, how does the discount affect the mean and standard deviation of the profit data from the sale mattresses had the discount never been applied to these seventy-eight mattresses?

F. The mean decreases and the standard deviation remains the same.

G. Both the mean and the standard deviation decrease.

H. The mean and standard deviation remain unchanged.

J. The mean and standard deviation both increase.

K. The mean increases and the standard deviation decreases.

7. A social psychologist conducts an experiment to assess the relationship between one's level of social media usage and one's level of self-confidence. She collected her data in the following table:

	High level of use of social media	Low-to-moderate level of use of social media
Normal-to-high level of self-confidence	50	88
Below-normal level of self-confidence	61	1

If one of the subjects of this study is selected at random, what is the probability that the person chosen has neither a high-level use of social media nor a below-normal level of self-confidence?

A. 0.25

B. 0.44

C. 0.64

D. 0.98

E. 2.27

8. You have 7 marbles—2 black, 3 white, and 2 red, but otherwise indistinguishable. How many different ways can the 7 marbles be ordered without repeating the same color sequence?

F. 5,040

G. 280

H. 210

J. 140

K. 84

14

ANSWER KEY AND EXPLANATIONS

1. D	**3.** B	**5.** D	**7.** B
2. G	**4.** K	**6.** F	**8.** H

1. **The correct answer is D.** The approach here is to write out the elements of the sample space. Then, identify each of the ones that satisfy the condition "contains at least one 2."

(A, A)	(B, A)	(1, A)	(2, A)
(A, B)	(B, B)	(1, B)	(2, B)
(A, 1)	(B, 1)	(1, 1)	(2, 1)
(A, 2)	(B, 2)	(1, 2)	(2, 2)

There are 16 possible outcomes in the sample space. Of these, 7 contain at least one 2. So, the probability of the desired event is $\frac{7}{16}$. A common error is to exclude the ordered pair (2, 2) from the list of those satisfying the condition "at least one 2." Here, "at least one 2" means that either one or both rolls can be a 2.

2. **The correct answer is G.** This is a variation of the typical "number of different arrangements" problem. Here, the entire group of objects—the 13 contestants—is not used. There are $13 \times 12 \times 11 \times 10$ ways to award the four ribbons.

3. **The correct answer is B.** If the values are placed in order, the first value will be 5 and then the remaining values will be 40. There would simply need to be three data values in the data set in order to ensure the median is 40. And so, since there are more than 18 total values, the middle value must be 40.

4. **The correct answer is K.** Each of these measures, except for mode (choice H), has double the value for Data Set II as compared to the values for Data Set I, so none of the measures can be equal (choice K).

5. **The correct answer is D.** The points are packed moderately close together (in that they are not all on the same line, but they are not so widely dispersed as to obscure the rising pattern that exists). The points rise from left to right, so the relationship is positive. A trend line reasonably describes the relationship between the variables as there is no curve evident.

6. **The correct answer is F.** The mean must decrease because all the data values being added have decreased. In fact, each will decrease by $200. The spread (or standard deviation) of the data remains unchanged because the same number is subtracted from all values in the data set.

7. **The correct answer is B.** Subjects in the upper-right cell of the table satisfy the criteria. Sincere there are 200 subjects (the sum of all four cells) and 88 of them satisfy the criteria, the probability is $\frac{88}{200} = 0.44$.

8. **The correct answer is H.** There are seven different places where a marble can be placed, so there are a total of 7! orderings (5,040). However, some orderings look exactly like each other. For example, if we denote the white marbles W1, W2, and W3; the black marbles as B1, B2; and the red marbles as R1 and R2, we see the following orderings: R1, R2, B1, B2, W1, W2, W3, which is the same as R2, R1, B1, B2, W1, W2, W3. But it is not the same as R2, R1, W1, B1, B2, W2, W3. We do not want to include the permutations of just the black marbles, just the red marbles, and just the white marbles. So to adjust the total possible number of permutations, divide by 2!(2!)(3!) = 24. So the answer is $\frac{7!}{24} = 210$.

CHAPTER

**Strategies for Approaching
the Mathematics Section**

STRATEGIES FOR APPROACHING THE

OVERVIEW

Reflecting on Your Diagnostic Test Score

Overall Section Strategies

Question Strategies

Test Yourself: Math Strategies

General Reminders and Advice

Strategy Roundup

Summing It Up

Knowledge Check: Mathematics

We've spent the last few chapters helping you review the math skills you'll need to perform your best on the ACT Mathematics test. Now, we'll fill you in on some strategies that can help you make the most of the time you're provided and maximize your score. This chapter contains lots of advice on how to approach the math section and save time as you work through it. You'll see some guided practice, a short Test Yourself, and at the end of the chapter, you'll find a full-length Knowledge Check for you to bring all your new skills and strategies together and assess your progress so far.

MATHEMATICS SECTION

REFLECTING ON YOUR DIAGNOSTIC TEST SCORE

Just as we had you do for English, start this section by revisiting your score charts from Chapter 2: Diagnostic Test and your reflections on your Mathematics test performance in Chapter 3. The process of reflecting on your diagnostic test performance is useful because it provides helpful information about who you are as a learner and test taker. With this information, you can make thoughtful decisions about how to select and apply strategies for the test section. Take a few moments to reflect on your performance when you first started studying for the Mathematics test. You can do so in your head, take notes on your own, or use this table to jot down some ideas.

DIAGNOSTIC TEST REFLECTION: MATHEMATICS	
Mathematics Diagnostic Test Score: _____	**Mathematics Scoring Goal:** _____
Reflection Question	**Notes**
What went well for you during the diagnostic test, and which skills were easiest for you to use?	
What did you struggle with during the diagnostic test, or which skills were harder for you to use?	
Did you feel rushed? Did you have left over time?	
How close were you to your goal?	
After reviewing math skills in the last few chapters, what are some things you might like to keep in mind as you study further?	
What are some aspects of approaching the ACT Mathematics test for which you are hoping to build strategies?	

Hopefully, reflecting on these questions gave you some useful feedback that you can now apply to determining your goals for the math section. Test takers hoping to achieve a perfect score will have to approach things differently than those who want to outperform the average score of ~20.

For ACT Mathematics, a scaled score of 20 is roughly equivalent to answering half of the questions correctly. From there, every two to three additional correct answers results in an additional point. Put another way, every 10 additional correct questions will increase your scaled score by about 5 points. Using those metrics, you can then determine how many questions you know you need to spend time with and the approximate number that you can guess on and still achieve your goal.

Your goal does not have to stay fixed and in fact should change as you continue to build your math knowledge and practice. Similar to the English test, Mathematics depends on what you know. Your goal and your past performance should direct what math subjects you study, how much you study, and how you approach the questions in the test section.

OVERALL SECTION STRATEGIES

We've said it before, and we will say it again before this book is through: The best way to do well on the ACT is to manage your time wisely. The better time management you exhibit, the more room you give yourself to carefully consider answers and review questions that require more of your effort. As such, you'll notice that most of the strategies in this section address how to use your time. As you study for your ACT Mathematics test, play with these strategies and experiment with different approaches until you land on an effective overall plan that works for you.

Divide Your Time According to Your Goals

As with any other section on the ACT, your score goals for the Mathematics test should inform your approach to the section. The Mathematics test requires you to answer 60 questions in 60 minutes. If you are aiming

for a perfect score, then you know that you need to carefully answer every single question. You won't want to spend more than a minute on any one question; furthermore, in this case, your goal is to not guess on any questions. Of course, if you do have to guess, you should mark that question and move on in hopes you'll have time to review it later.

However, if your aim is to exceed the average section scaled score of ~20 points, then you know that you can guess on about 25 questions before the guesses will negatively impact your goals. In this situation, you might choose to go through and answer as many easier questions as possible before returning to guesses you made on harder questions. Having that leeway for guessing means that you can take a bit more time on higher-level questions that you know you can solve with effort.

Make Choices That Support Time Management

On the ACT, any spare time you save will allow you the valuable opportunity to review questions you were forced to guess on or double check your math for your known areas of weakness. Consequently, saving time through thoughtful time management is one of the most important strategies you can adopt for your Mathematics test or any other section on the ACT. Here are a few strategies that can help you do so.

Evaluate Question Difficulty and Time Commitment

When you approach any math problem, your first task is to figure out its goal: What is being asked and what are you tasked with figuring out? When you evaluate the goal of a given question, what you're really doing is figuring out how difficult the question is and, by extension, how long that question is going to take you to complete. The more you practice evaluating the goals of different math questions, the easier it will be to determine the complexity of questions on your test. The following chart proposes some ways to evaluate question difficulty along with example questions that indicate situations of varying difficulty.

MATHEMATICS QUESTIONS BY DIFFICULTY

Difficulty	Identifying Characteristics	Example Question
"Simple" Questions	<ul><li>You understand the topic and goal of the question</li><li>You know how to do the math</li><li>You can solve it quickly (about 30 seconds)</li><li>Your calculator can speed up calculations</li><li>You can eliminate answers immediately</li></ul>	If $f(x) = -3x^3 + x - 1$, compute $f(-2)$. A. -24 B. 15 C. 25 D. 21 E. -11
"Moderate" Questions	<ul><li>You understand the goal of the question</li><li>You can do the math</li><li>You know it will take longer to answer</li><li>Your calculator will be of limited use</li><li>You may be able to apply a specific question strategy (working backwards, using numbers)</li><li>You'll have time to come back later</li></ul>	Which of the following expressions is equivalent to $\dfrac{z^a \left(z^2\right)^b}{z^{b-a}}$? F. z^b G. z^3 H. z^{a+b} J. z^{2a+3b} K. z^{2a+b}
"Challenging" Questions	<ul><li>You don't understand the goal</li><li>You don't know how to do the math</li><li>You don't know how long it will take to complete</li><li>You've never seen the topic before</li><li>Your calculator will be of limited to no use</li></ul>	For $90° < \theta < 180°$, if $\sin\theta = \dfrac{2}{3}$ then $\cot\theta$ is: A. $-\dfrac{\sqrt{5}}{2}$ B. $-2\sqrt{5}$ C. $-\dfrac{\sqrt{5}}{3}$ D. $\dfrac{\sqrt{5}}{3}$ E. $-\dfrac{2\sqrt{5}}{9}$

We put the adjectives describing each difficulty level in quotes because these difficulty levels will vary from student to student. However, these general guidelines can assist you in making sense of the questions you can address and how you move through the section. No question is worth more points than any other, so you're using your math knowledge, your goals, and what the question requires to decide where to spend your time. As you review math content, the goal is that more and more questions fall into the moderate and simple categories.

Focus First on the Simple Questions

When you come to a question you determine is "simple," answer it. Your goal is to answer as many questions correctly as you can and save time for harder questions later. Focus your time first on those that are easier for you to do and fast to complete. This should help you bank time for those harder questions you'll need to reach your goal and higher scaled scores, all without preventing you from getting to questions later in the section that you can answer but might not see otherwise.

Come Back to Moderate Questions

Once you've gone through and answered simpler questions, it's time to handle those you identified as higher difficulty. Remember, you don't want to spend more than a minute on these questions, so when you are

working on them, mark any that are taking too long for later review. Then, eliminate the incorrect answer choices you can identify and guess based on what you've calculated so far. Note your work in the margins of your text booklet so that you can pick up where you left off if you're able to return to the questions later. If time is running out before you have time to review, make sure you fill in a guess for any blank questions.

Mark But Also Guess on Complex Questions

For questions you deem as "complex," your best bet is to make quick guesses and then mark them for review later—if you have time after your moderate questions. With this method, you are ensuring that time does not run out while you still have some answers unmarked. The question difficulty notation system allows you to come back to those questions and make more considered answers with any review time that remains. Note that the higher your score goals, the more important it is to not guess—if you are aiming for a perfect score, you need to work that much harder to make sure you have time remaining at the end to review every "complex" question. Alternatively, your review of ACT math topics needs to be that much more intense so that no question (or very few) fall into the "complex" category.

Use Your Calculator Mindfully

Many students assume that because they have access to a calculator on an exam, they should use it as often as possible. For the ACT, this is not the case. No question will require the use of a calculator—though some calculations can be expedited with one. Instead, many questions (especially those that can be classified as "simple") can often be solved more quickly if you don't. When you can solve a question in your head or by doing simple calculations on paper, this will often be faster than taking the time to input multiple elements into a calculator. The calculator is there if you need it, but save yourself time by answering with your math skills whenever it makes sense to do so.

QUESTION STRATEGIES

In this section, we'll cover a series of strategies that can help you attack each question or which might be useful for certain types of questions.

Strategy #1: Approach Every Question with the Same Steps

Similar to what you saw for the ACT English test, having a general method for approaching questions can streamline how you move through the section to improve your time management. For ACT Mathematics questions, you always have a few things you're trying to determine: a question's goal, difficulty, and key information. From there, you'll either be doing straightforward math or using some other approach that works for the question. Once you've found an answer that matches your calculations, you need to make sure you answered the question and then move on.

How to Do It:

1. Read the question to determine the goal and assess the difficulty.

2. Identify key information from the question or mark the question and come back later.

3. Solve strategically and record your work.

4. Check your goal.

If $-2|3x + 1| \geq -8$, then $4x$ is at least:

A. $-\dfrac{20}{3}$

B. $-\dfrac{5}{3}$

C. 1

D. $\dfrac{17}{5}$

E. $\dfrac{20}{3}$

After reading the question, depending on your comfort with inequalities and absolute values, you will assess its difficulty. In the scope of the ACT Mathematics test's questions, this should fall into the "simple" or "moderate" category. For our purposes, let's say that it is a "simple" question and that you're going to answer now. In this case, let's also assume you know how to do the math, though perhaps you'd be able to work backwards (discussed later in this section). Regardless, your quick math would look like the following:

$$-2|3x + 1| \geq -8 = |3x + 1| \leq 4$$

You knew that you needed to flip the inequality sign when you divided by a negative. Next, you know that the absolute value signs create two different inequalities:

$$3x + 1 \leq 4 \text{ and } 3x + 1 \geq -4$$

In solving each inequality for x, you find that $x \leq 1$ and $x \geq -\dfrac{5}{3}$. You can see both of those values are among the answer choices (something the ACT likes to do). Instead of just guessing, though, you now refer back to the question to check your goal. The question asked what, with the initial inequality, "$4x$ is at least"? That phrasing not only tells you that you need to multiply a value by 4 but also that the value should be the lower of the inequality's boundaries. In this case, $4\left(-\dfrac{5}{3}\right) = -\dfrac{20}{3}$.

The steps for this question are simple and largely dependent on your ability to do the math, but notice how this question had you pursue a series of calculations while not having your work lead directly to the answer. Even after you solved for x, you still needed to perform an additional operation to get to the correct answer. This kind of multi-step approach is not uncommon for the ACT, and questions like these are why it is so important to work through questions in a focused step-by-step way, making sure you not only "did the math" but also did all the math you needed to do.

Strategy #2: Use the Question Form to Help You Solve

Just because the ACT might be expecting you to do the math for a question doesn't mean that you have to or that doing the math is necessarily the best way to get to the correct answer. The ACT presents questions in a variety of specific ways. Some of the test's design choices can be used to your advantage. In addition to just doing the math and recording your work, consider the following options in different situations.

Work Backwards

In certain situations on the ACT Mathematics test, you don't have to do the math the way the ACT might want you to. Because some questions on the ACT have numbers for answers, and because the ACT always puts them in order (unless there are also irrational values), you can use the answers to work backwards through the problem. There may be situations where you're not exactly sure how to get to a correct answer, but since you have values to work with, you can start plugging in numbers into simpler setups.

How to Do It:

1. Start with the answers and work backwards when answers are numbers.

2. Begin with C/H since the numerical choices are put in order of value.

3. If C/H is not the correct answer, determine if the answer you need should be higher or lower.

4. Repeat the process with one of the two choices that remain which are higher or lower, as appropriate.

A 1980s-style arcade charges each customer an admission fee of $8.50, and it costs just $0.25 per game. Mike and Stan, together, spent $35. If Stan played three fewer than twice the number of games Mike played, how many games did they play, total?

    A. 18

    B. 25

    C. 47

    D. 72

    E. 75

Here, you're trying to figure out how many games Stan and Mike were able to play with their $35. Because the numbers are numerical, you can start with choice C and multiply it by .25 to see how much was spent on games. Choice C multiplies to $11.75. That's not very much. But remember that you also have to account for the admission fees for both Mike and Stan, $8.50 each or $17. You would then calculate: $11.75 + $17 = $28.75. They could have played more games, so you can eliminate choices A through C. You now just need to do one more calculation for either choice D or E. You'll find the answer or eliminate another choice. In this case, if you check choice D, you find that 72 games multiplied by .25 cents is $18: $18 + $17 = $35. You found the correct answer, choice D. To solve that question another way, you could have modeled the situation using some basic algebra skills, but if you couldn't quite grasp how to do that, working backwards, as you saw, was a viable option.

Use Numbers for Variables

Some questions on the ACT may present answer choices that are exclusively comprised of variables. While you may be able to do the algebra or grasp the mathematical relationships at play, sometimes it is more efficient to select numbers that fit the question's conditions and plug them in instead. Such a presentation may be more common for Preparing for Higher Math: Number & Quantity questions.

How to Do It:

1. For problems that only have variables, choose numbers that fit the problem and that are easy to use.

2. Plug in your values consistently and evaluate the expressions or equations.

3. Based on the information you acquired when solving with substituted numbers, answer confidently or venture a guess.

GUIDED PRACTICE

A quantity X is directly proportional to Y and inversely proportional to Z^2. For which of the following equations is this true?

F. $X = \dfrac{k}{YZ^2}$

G. $X = \dfrac{kZ^2}{Y}$

H. $X = k(Y + Z^2)$

J. $X = \dfrac{kY}{Z^2}$

K. $X = kYZ^2$

Because the question and answers present only variables, you can consider picking some appropriate numbers to help you select the answer. Initially, this question hinges upon understanding of the terms "directly proportional" and "inversely proportional."

The first means that as Y increases, X also increases. The second means that as Z^2 increases, X decreases. If you still can't conceptualize that relationship mathematically, you can pick some values and start substituting them into the answer choices to see whether changing the value for Y or Z would cause X to increase or decrease, respectively.

Here, you're not too constrained by what values can be used, so pick easy-to-work-with with numbers. In this case, start with $k = 2$, $Y = 3$, and $Z = 4$. Then you could start to work down the list of choices and see what comes up.

For choice F, $\dfrac{2}{3(4^2)} = \dfrac{2}{48}$. If you were to increase either Y or Z, X would get smaller. That's not what we're looking for. Further, that's going to allow you to eliminate choice G as well, because any time Y gets bigger in the denominator, it will make X smaller, which is the opposite of what you want. Choices H and K are similar, so choose one and see what it reveals. Choice H would yield $2(3 + 4^2) = 38$. If Y increased in that expression, X would also increase. The same would be true for Z as well, which contradicts the given information. The same can be said for choice K. That leaves you with choice J.

This is a situation in which math knowledge is going to get you to the answer faster, but if you absolutely had to get this question right, plugging in numbers and evaluating what you see for each choice (and similar ones) is a viable option.

Draw It Out

Developing a mathematical mind takes time and practice, and even if you've built that skill, investing energy into doing everything in your head on the ACT can be draining. Instead, you should make use of the space in your test booklet to draw things out, recording not just your calculations but the models the questions present. This can be particularly true of questions that describe real-world scenarios related to geometry or statistics (think Modeling questions, PHM: Geometry, and PHM: Statistics and Probability). To simplify the information a question gives you, you can always draw it out or label any diagram that you may be given.

How to Do It:

1. Create a diagram based on the details of the question.

2. Label your diagram or any existing graphics/diagrams provided.

3. Update your diagram as you solve to track new relationships.

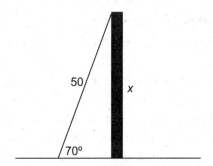

GUIDED PRACTICE

A 50-foot wire is attached to the top of an electric pole and is anchored on the ground. If the wire rises in a straight line at a 70° angle from the ground, how many feet tall is the pole?

   A. 50 sin 70°

   B. 50 cos 70°

   C. 50 tan 70°

   D. $\dfrac{\cos 70°}{50}$

   E. $\dfrac{50}{\cos 70°}$

In reading the question and scanning the answers, you see both an angle and some trigonometric ratios. You may be able to visualize the relationship described but tracking things in your test booklet is not only going to reduce the energy you spend on the question but perhaps render the situation a bit more clearly.

Based on the description in the question, you have a wire that goes from the ground to the top of an electric pole, also connected to the ground. And there's an angle opposite the electric pole that measures 70 degrees. Sketching that out results in the following:

That yields a triangle with a hypotenuse of length 50 and two unknown sides. You've been asked to find the height of the pole, so we'll label that x. Recall that the answers made it clear that you'll be dealing with some trigonometry. The expectation here is that you find the unknown side x using a trigonometric ratio. Based on the given information and your diagram, you'll be dealing with a sine ratio—because you know the hypotenuse and are looking for the side length opposite the 70° angle. Seeing that relationship, you can now eliminate every answer choice that doesn't use sine. That leaves you with choice A. That's a pretty ideal situation and likely won't happen that often on the ACT. Regardless, when a diagram isn't provided for geometry-related questions (and others), drawing things out can clarify and even shorten your path to a correct answer.

Eliminate Answers and Guess

Keep in mind that your ultimate goal is to understand the math on the test well enough that you can always work through a problem quickly and efficiently. But there are any number of situations that can arise that may make that difficult. You may be put in a position where you simply need to guess and move on so you can get to other questions you definitely know you can answer. However, even if you're guessing, with just a little bit of invested time, you may be able to significantly improve your odds of guessing correctly and achieving (even exceeding) your goal. For ACT Mathematics, you have a 1 in 5 (20%) chance of guessing correctly on a question. Those odds improve dramatically as you're able to eliminate 1, 2, or 3 answer choices. If you're able to combine information from the question with your knowledge of math and the ACT's design, you may be able to get to a place where you can accurately guess with minimal time investment.

How to Do It:

1. Determine if there are any unreasonable answers you can eliminate right away.

2. Pick numbers, solve backwards, or do partial calculations, if possible and time allows, to eliminate some answers.

3. Make your best guess from the answers that remain and move on.

If $w = \dfrac{2}{3}$ and $z = -\dfrac{1}{9}$, what is the value of $\dfrac{w+z}{2(w-z)}$?

F. $-\dfrac{1}{3}$

G. $-\dfrac{5}{14}$

H. $\dfrac{5}{14}$

J. $\dfrac{1}{2}$

K. $\dfrac{14}{5}$

If you were running out of time on the Mathematics test, you might consider skipping this question because of the fractions, the variables, or the number of calculations involved. If you were going to guess, though, you would want to see if you could increase your chances of guessing correctly.

In scanning the question, you see that you are being asked to plug two fractions into the algebraic expression. One value is positive, and one value is negative. Looking at the answer choices, all are fractions with two negative and three positive choices. Maybe you can eliminate some of those answers. In taking a quick look at the expression, you see that the negative sign for the

z term will only affect two places: the addition on top and the operation in parentheses on the bottom. On the top, it won't matter because z is smaller than w. On the bottom, the negatives will cancel, turning the negative into an addition sign. That means that the answer must be positive, letting you eliminate choices F and G. This leaves you with choices H, J, or K. While that's still three choices to choose between, your chance at guessing correctly just went from 1 out of 5 to 1 out of 3, a significant statistical jump.

Keep in mind that your ultimate goal is to be able to solve a question like this quickly and accurately, but you also have a lot of information (what the questions tell you and what the answer choices reveal) that can help you narrow your choices when you're not sure what to do or you just don't have the time you need to do the math.

Using the section strategies, question approach, and strategic solving techniques described earlier in the chapter, work through the following questions to see how such decisions impact how you move through the questions and affect your time and accuracy. It's entirely possible that you may know how to do the math without resorting to the strategies that we've described. In that case, practice identifying how long a question may take you and use those estimates to decide if you'll solve a question immediately or come back to it later on. One of your goals is to understand your strengths and weaknesses and use that information to make better decisions on the test.

TEST YOURSELF

MATH STRATEGIES

12 Questions—12 Minutes

Directions: Solve each problem and choose the correct answer. Do not dwell on problems that take too long. First, solve as many as you can; then, you can return to others you have left. You are permitted to use a calculator. You may use your calculator for any problem you like, but some of the problems may best be completed without a calculator.

Note: Unless otherwise stated, all of the following should be assumed:

1. Illustrative figures are NOT necessarily drawn to scale.

2. Geometric figures lie in a plane.

3. The word *line* indicates a straight line.

4. The word *average* indicates arithmetic mean.

---

1. 1. Let $h(x) = 1 - \dfrac{2}{3x}$. Compute $h\left(-\dfrac{4}{x}\right)$.

A. x

B. $\dfrac{x + 24}{x}$

C. $\dfrac{2x + 1}{12}$

D. $\dfrac{8 - 12x}{3x^2}$

E. $\dfrac{x + 6}{6}$

2. What is the least possible value for the product xy, if $x + y = 24$ and x and y are both prime numbers?

F. 23

G. 44

H. 95

J. 119

K. 143

3. A line passing through the point (–1, 4) is perpendicular to the line passing through (–3, 2) and (–3, –5). What is the equation of this line?

A. $y = x + 5$

B. $y = 4$

C. $9x + 2y = 5$

D. $x = -1$

E. $y = -x - 5$

4. The center of a circle is (–4, 3). If the point (2, –2) lies on this circle, what is the equation of this circle?

F. $(x - 4)^2 + (y + 3)^3 = 61$

G. $(x - 4)^2 + (y + 3)^3 = \sqrt{61}$

H. $(x + 4)^2 + (y - 3)^3 = 11$

J. $(x - 2)^2 + (y + 2)^2 = \sqrt{61}$

K. $(x + 4)^2 + (y - 3)^2 = 61$

5. What is the period of the graph of

$$y = 4\cos\left(3x - \frac{\pi}{2}\right) + 1 \text{ ?}$$

A. $\dfrac{\pi}{6}$

B. $\dfrac{2\pi}{3}$

C. 3

D. 4

E. 2π

6. What is the equation of the linear function shown in the graph below?

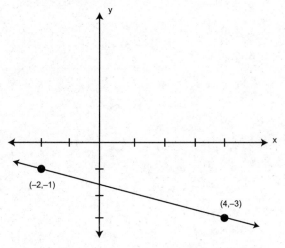

F. $f(x) = -3x - 7$

G. $f(x) = -\dfrac{1}{3}x - \dfrac{5}{3}$

H. $f(x) = -3x - 2$

J. $f(x) = -\dfrac{1}{3}x - 2$

K. $f(x) = \dfrac{1}{3}x + \dfrac{5}{3}$

7. The average of x numbers is 15. If two of the numbers are each increased by y, the new average will be increased by how much?

A. $2y$

B. y

C. $\dfrac{x}{2y}$

D. $\dfrac{y}{x}$

E. $\dfrac{2y}{x}$

8. Points A, B, and C lie on the circumference of a circle with center O. If the unshaded sectors AOB and BOC comprise $\dfrac{2}{5}$ and $\dfrac{1}{3}$ of the area of the circle, respectively, what is the measure of $\angle$AOC?

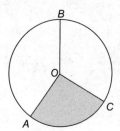

F. 48°

G. 90°

H. 92°

J. 96°

K. 264°

9. There are 3 teaspoons in 1 tablespoon. A bottle of cough medicine contains 24 tablespoon-sized servings and costs $4.50. What is the approximate cost per teaspoon?

A. $0.06

B. $0.15

C. $0.19

D. $0.60

E. $1.50

10. In the isosceles right triangle below, what is the value of tan x°?

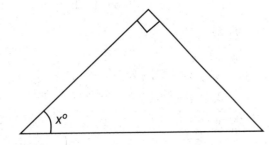

F. $\dfrac{\sqrt{2}}{2}$

G. 1

H. $\sqrt{2}$

J. $\dfrac{\sqrt{3}}{2}$

K. $\sqrt{3}$

11. What is the value of $\log_5\left(\dfrac{1}{625}\right)$?

A. −4

B. −3

C. $\dfrac{1}{4}$

D. 4

E. 125

12. If $0.3z - 0.24 = 1.2(0.3 - z)$, what is the value of $z \cdot 10^{-3}$?

F. 0.0004

G. 0.004

H. 0.4

J. 400

K. 4,000

15

Answer Explanations

1. **The correct answer is E.** Calculate as follows:

$$h\left(-\frac{4}{x}\right) = 1 - \frac{2}{3\left(-\frac{4}{x}\right)}$$

$$= 1 - \frac{2}{-\frac{12}{x}}$$

$$= 1 + 2\left(\frac{x}{12}\right)$$

$$= 1 + \frac{x}{6}$$

$$= \frac{x+6}{6}$$

2. **The correct answer is H.** Three pairs of prime numbers add to 24: 5 + 19, 7 + 17, and 11 + 13. The smallest resulting product is 5 × 19 = 95, so 95 is the least possible value of xy.

3. **The correct answer is B.** The given line is vertical since it passes through two points having the same x-coordinate. So, the desired line must be horizontal. Since it passes through the point (−1, 4), its equation must be $y = 4$.

4. **The correct answer is K.** The radius is the length of the segment connecting the two given points:

$$\sqrt{(2-(-4))^2 + (-2-3)^2} = \sqrt{6^2 + (-5)^2} = \sqrt{36+25} = \sqrt{61}$$

Using the center $(h, k) = (-4, 3)$ and radius $r = \sqrt{61}$ in the standard form for the equation of a circle $(x - h)^2 + (y - k)^2 = r^2$ yields the equation $(x-(-4))^2 + (y-3)^2 = \sqrt{61}$, which simplifies to $(x + 4)^2 + (y - 3)^2 = 61$.

5. **The correct answer is B.** The period of a graph of the form $y = A\cos(Bx + C) + D$ is $\frac{2\pi}{B}$. So the period of the graph of $y = 4\cos\left(3x - \frac{\pi}{2}\right) + 1$ is $\frac{2\pi}{3}$.

6. **The correct answer is G.** Use the two labeled points to determine the slope of the line:

$$m = \frac{-3-(-1)}{4-(-2)} = -\frac{2}{6} = -\frac{1}{3}$$

Using point-slope form with the point (−2, −1) yields the following equation:

$$y-(-1) = -\frac{1}{3}(x+2)$$

$$y+1 = -\frac{1}{3}x - \frac{2}{3}$$

$$y = -\frac{1}{3}x - \frac{5}{3}$$

7. **The correct answer is E.** If the average of x numbers is 15, then the total of these numbers is 15x. When two numbers are increased by y, 2y will be added to this total. The value of x does not change, so the new average will be $\frac{15x+2y}{x} = 15 + \frac{2y}{x}$. This is an increase of $\frac{2y}{x}$ over the original average.

8. **The correct answer is J.** The unshaded sectors AOB and BOC comprise a total of $\frac{2}{5} + \frac{1}{3} = \frac{11}{15}$ of the circle. This means that the shaded region, sector AOC, takes up the remaining $\frac{4}{15}$ of the circle. A circle has 360 total degrees, so set up a proportion to find the measure of $\angle AOC$:

$$\frac{4}{15} = \frac{m\angle AOC}{360°}$$

$$15(m\angle AOC) = 1,440°$$

$$m\angle AOC = 96°$$

9. **The correct answer is A.** There are 3(24) = 72 teaspoons in the jar of cough medicine. Divide the total cost by 72 to get the cost per teaspoon: $\frac{\$4.50}{72} \approx \$0.06$.

10. **The correct answer is G.** Tangent equals opposite divided by adjacent. In an isosceles right triangle, the legs are equal. In this case, that means the opposite and adjacent sides are equal, so $\tan x° = 1$.

11. **The correct answer is A.** Since $\frac{1}{625} = \frac{1}{5^4} = 5^{-4}$, it follows that $\log_5\left(\frac{1}{625}\right) = \log_5\left(5^{-4}\right) = -4$.

12. **The correct answer is F.** Solve for z:

$$0.3z - 0.24 = 1.2(0.3 - z)$$

$$0.3z - 0.24 = 0.35 - 1.2z$$

$$1.5z = 0.60$$

$$z = \frac{0.60}{1.5} = 0.4$$

So $z \cdot 10^{-3} = (0.4) \cdot 10^{-3} = 0.0004$.

Now that you have had an opportunity to practice, consider the strategies you used to answer questions. Ask yourself the following:

- Which strategies seemed to help you most?
- Did any strategy prove to be unhelpful for you? If so, could you modify it to make it helpful?
- After practicing, how might you like to change your overall approach to the Mathematics section? What would you like to keep the same about your approach?

Engaging in this kind of reflection is helpful in its own right, as it helps you make sense of what to expect on exam day and how best to plan for it.

GENERAL REMINDERS AND ADVICE

Here are a few other things to keep in mind as you prepare for the ACT Mathematics test. Please also refer back to Chapter 3 for additional test-taking advice.

The ACT May Use Partial Answers as Answer Options

For multi-step problems, the ACT may include as answer choices the steps used to reach the correct answer. The numbers that the ACT chooses for answer choices aren't random. They represent the results of common miscalculations and values that arise during your work to get the correct answer. If you have good number sense and an idea of what you're looking

for, you may be able to use certain answer choices to shorten your own work. Similarly, if you recognize those values for what they are, you may be able to eliminate answer choices and improve your chances of guessing correctly.

Prioritize Getting to More Questions

Don't let one question be a barrier to getting to other questions. If it is pushing you past a minute, it's taking time away from every question that you have yet to answer. Know your limits and don't be afraid to move on.

If You're Going to Guess, Do It Quickly

Ideally, you're guessing on very few questions because you've learned the math and can apply it quickly, thus pushing your score as high as you can. But if you do have to guess and you see no way to eliminate answers, pick a letter (even the same letter) and move on.

Understand Your Mistakes When You Practice

When you practice, you need to understand why you're making mistakes. Because the Mathematics section is so content-driven, you need to pay close attention to the kinds of errors you're making. Are you making simple mistakes in calculations? Perhaps you need to practice more or make better use of your calculator. Are you missing certain kinds of questions (either in setup or subject)? Then you need to study more. Are you simply running out of time? You need to refine your skills and make better time management decisions. Regardless of your specific mistakes, knowing what they are will help you formulate a plan of action.

Personalize Your Approach

Everything we've laid out here is a basic template for how to approach the Mathematics test, but you might need to adapt these strategies to suit your own needs as a test taker. Practicing like you are now is the best way to develop a personalized strategy, so you're already halfway there! In the next section, we'll lay out a base level approach that can help you bring all these skills together, but remember that you can adapt it to account for your own strengths, weaknesses, and scoring goals.

STRATEGY ROUNDUP

As with other test sections, you can personalize your approach to the Mathematics test. That said, the following plan will help you address all the strategies covered here. Use this plan as a starting point for any personal adjustments you might need to make to suit your unique needs as a test taker.

Step 1: Establish the Question Goal and Difficulty Level

Figure out what the test makers want you to do with the question and any related information given. Depending on that goal, you may recognize that the question is "simple" to complete or of a higher difficulty level. From there, you then decide to complete the question now or come back to it later. For "complex" questions, make a guess in case you don't have time to return later.

Step 2: Determine What Information You've Been Given

Math questions are designed for you to be able to answer them based on the information you have in combination with your math knowledge. Figuring out which pieces of information are provided for you is a key step to solving questions accurately. Not everything will be explicitly stated, but some things will be true because of inherent mathematical relationships.

Step 3: Do the Math or Use a Question Strategy

Whether you do the math, pick numbers, work backwards, draw things out, or eliminate answers and guess will depend largely on the question and its difficulty level. If you can answer a question quickly and accurately, do so. Otherwise, you need to be mindful of how long it will take so you don't prevent yourself from getting to easier questions that you need for your scoring goals. If you must answer a question to hit your score target, remember that you may have multiple ways to get to the correct answer.

Step 4: Check the Question and Your Math

Remember how the ACT designs some of its questions? Make sure you did all the math you needed to and didn't stop too soon. This is also an opportunity to check for any simple mistakes in your math (missed signs, etc.). Before you move on, take a few seconds to reread the question.

SUMMING IT UP

- Use your scores from Chapter 2: Diagnostic Test as well as your reflections on your diagnostic test performance at the beginning of this chapter to help you set a score goal and then divide your study time according to your goals.

- Determine in advance how many answers you can safely guess based on your score goals. Keep this number in mind as you formulate a personalized math section plan.

- Time management is key, especially on the Mathematics test, so make choices that support time management such as:

  - Evaluating questions and sorting them based on difficulty
  - Answering simple and quick to answer questions (i.e. those that require around 30 seconds to complete) first
  - Answering moderate difficulty questions after you've completed easier questions
  - Making initial guesses on complex questions and then revisit them as time allows

- Be thoughtful about when you use a calculator—you probably won't need it for most questions and can often answer faster by working it out on paper or using mental math.

- Remember to always evaluate the goal of the question being asked and determine what the test takers want you to figure out. Then, based on the goal for that given question, use a question-solving strategy such as:

  - Working backwards
  - Using numbers for variables
  - Drawing things out
  - Eliminating answers and guessing

- As a general strategy plan for the Mathematics test, complete the following steps in the following order. Remember, the order of steps or overall approach can be modified to match your personal needs as a test taker.

  - Step 1: Establish the question goal and difficulty level.
  - Step 2: Determine what information you've been given.
  - Step 3: Do the math or use a question strategy.
  - Step 4: Check the question and your math.

KNOWLEDGE CHECK: MATHEMATICS

60 Questions—60 Minutes

Directions: Solve each problem and choose the correct answer. Do not dwell on problems that take too long. First, solve as many as you can; then, you can return to others you have left. You are permitted to use a calculator. You may use your calculator for any problem you like, but some of the problems may best be completed without a calculator.

Note: Unless otherwise stated, all of the following should be assumed:

    1. Illustrative figures are NOT necessarily drawn to scale.

    2. Geometric figures lie in a plane.

    3. The word *line* indicates a straight line.

    4. The word *average* indicates arithmetic mean.

---

1. On the final project in Mr. Herrera's art class, 14 students earned a grade of B. Those 14 students were exactly 20% of the total number of students in the class. How many students were in the class?

   A. 28
   B. 34
   C. 56
   D. 70
   E. 84

2. What is the value of $-3^2 |-6 - (-4)|$?

   F. −90
   G. −18
   H. −12
   J. 18
   K. 90

3. The perimeter of a rectangle is 60 units. If the width of the rectangle is 12 units, what is the area of the rectangle, in square units?

   A. 18
   B. 34
   C. 216
   D. 432
   E. 576

4. Two numbers have a greatest common factor of 6 and a least common multiple of 36. Which of the following could be the pair of numbers?

   F. 6 and 12
   G. 6 and 18
   H. 12 and 18
   J. 12 and 24
   K. 18 and 24

5. An amateur bowler keeps track of the number of times per game (in a series of 10 games) she makes a spare (that is, she clears all 10 pins in two rolls of the ball). What is the median number of spares that she makes?

TABLE 1	
Game	Number of Spares
1	2
2	4
3	0
4	2
5	1
6	1
7	0
8	4
9	4
10	3

A. 1

B. 2

C. 2.1

D. 2.5

E. 4

6. In the figure below, points G, H, and I are on the same line. What is the measure of ∠GHK ?

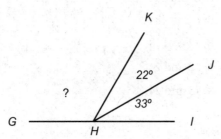

F. 35°

G. 55°

H. 75°

J. 125°

K. 147°

7. Which of the following triples are the sides of a right triangle?

A. 2, 3, 13

B. 4, 5, 6

C. 10, 20, 30

D. 6, 8, 11

E. 1, 1, √2

8. If $2a - 38 = -26$, then what is the value of $3a$?

F. −96

G. −18

H. 6

J. 18

K. 72

9. Data suggests that three of every five tomato seeds planted will germinate. If you plant 120 seeds, how many should germinate?

A. 24

B. 48

C. 60

D. 72

E. 90

10. The discounted price of a framed print of a lunar landscape is $75.50. If this is a 30% reduction of the original price, what was the original price?

F. $\dfrac{75.50}{0.70}$ dollars

G. $\dfrac{75.50}{0.30}$ dollars

H. 0.70(75.50) dollars

J. 75.50 − 0.30(75.50) dollars

K. 75.50 + 0.70 dollars

11. If three jazz CDs are added to a box of only classical CDs, the probability of randomly drawing a classical CD from the box becomes $\frac{4}{5}$. How many classical CDs are in the box?

   A. 6

   B. 9

   C. 12

   D. 15

   E. 18

12. A tin of candy contains three flavors. There are twice as many grape candies in a tin as there are cherry candies. There are three times as many lemon candies as grape candies. If a number of apple candies, equal to the number of cherry candies already in the tin, is added to the tin, what is the probability of randomly selecting a lemon candy from the tin?

   F. $\frac{1}{20}$

   G. $\frac{1}{10}$

   H. $\frac{1}{5}$

   J. $\frac{3}{5}$

   K. $\frac{2}{3}$

13. Which of the following has the largest value?

   A. $\sqrt{2}$

   B. 36^0

   C. 1^{200}

   D. 3^{-2}

   E. $\left(\frac{1}{4}\right)^3$

14. Among the points on the number line below, which is closest to $\sqrt{6}$?

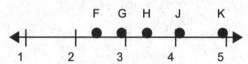

   F. Point F

   G. Point G

   H. Point H

   J. Point J

   K. Point K

15. If $1 - \frac{3x}{2} = \frac{x+1}{6}$, what is the value of x^3?

   A. $\frac{1}{8}$

   B. $\frac{1}{2}$

   C. $\frac{3}{2}$

   D. 2

   E. 8

16. Which of the following is equivalent to $\sqrt{\frac{7}{30}} \div \sqrt{\frac{21}{80}}$?

   F. $\frac{7\sqrt{2}}{40}$

   G. $\frac{20\sqrt{2}}{7}$

   H. $\frac{2\sqrt{2}}{3}$

   J. $\frac{2\sqrt{6}}{\sqrt{3}}$

   K. $\frac{3\sqrt{2}}{4}$

17. Which of the following equals (2,021.10)(0.0002)?

A. 0.40422×10^1

B. 4.0422×10^1

C. 0.40422×10^{-1}

D. 404.22×10^3

E. 4.0422×10^{-1}

18. Joel is 8 years older than Karen, and Karen is twice as old as Lina. If Lina is x years old, how old is Joel in terms of x?

F. $x + 8$

G. $2x$

H. $x - 8$

J. $-2x$

K. $2x + 8$

19. A large group of food tasters was asked to sample and rate a new cheesecake recipe. They were to use a scale of 1 to 5. 10% of the tasters gave the recipe a rating of 4. 15% gave a rating of 3. Half the tasters, 50%, gave the recipe a rating of 2. 25% gave the recipe a rating of 1. What was the average rating for the cheesecake recipe, rounded to the nearest tenth?

A. 2

B. 2.1

C. 2.2

D. 2.3

E. 2.4

20. The ratio of Elaine's weekly salary to Carl's weekly salary is 3:2. If Elaine gets a 20% raise and Carl gets a $200 raise, the ratio of their salaries will drop to 6:5. What is Elaine's salary?

F. $200

G. $400

H. $480

J. $600

K. $720

21. In succession, a fair coin is flipped and a standard 6-sided die is rolled. What is the probability that the coin shows heads and the die shows 3?

A. 0

B. $\dfrac{1}{12}$

C. $\dfrac{1}{3}$

D. $\dfrac{2}{3}$

E. $\dfrac{5}{6}$

22. What is the x-intercept of the line $4y + 3x = 12$?

F. 3

G. 4

H. 9

J. 12

K. 15

23. Which of the following is equal to $4 \begin{bmatrix} -2 & 0 \\ 2 & 3 \end{bmatrix}$?

A. $\begin{bmatrix} 2 & 4 \\ 6 & 7 \end{bmatrix}$

B. $\begin{bmatrix} -8 & 0 \\ 2 & 3 \end{bmatrix}$

C. $\begin{bmatrix} -8 & 0 \\ 8 & 12 \end{bmatrix}$

D. $\begin{bmatrix} -8 & 4 \\ 8 & 12 \end{bmatrix}$

E. $\begin{bmatrix} -8 & 0 \\ 2 & 12 \end{bmatrix}$

24. It took Renee exactly 4 minutes and 26 seconds to download a file from the internet to her computer. At that same rate, how long would it take Renee to download a file that is $2\frac{1}{2}$ times as large as the first file?

F. 10 minutes and 5 seconds

G. 10 minutes and 26 seconds

H. 10 minutes and 52 seconds

J. 11 minutes and 5 seconds

K. 11 minutes and 15 seconds

25. To which of the following expressions is $2(4y - 3z) - 4(2z - 3y)$ equal?

A. $5y - 11z$

B. $20y - 14z$

C. $6yz$

D. $25yz$

E. $-4y - 14z$

26. 120 amusement park patrons were asked to identify their favorite type of ride. The results are tabulated in the table shown:

Type of Ride	Number
Roller Coasters	43
Water Rides	31
Spinning Rides	27
Other	19

What is the probability that a patron chosen randomly from this group did NOT identify water rides as their favorite type of ride?

F. $\frac{19}{120}$

G. $\frac{31}{120}$

H. $\frac{40}{120}$

J. $\frac{89}{120}$

K. $\frac{101}{120}$

27. What is the solution set for the inequality $|4x + 1| < 5$?

A. $x < 1$

B. $-\frac{3}{2} < x < 1$

C. $-1 < x < \frac{3}{2}$

D. $-\frac{3}{2} < x$

E. $-\frac{5}{4} < x < \frac{5}{4}$

28. What is the value of $\left(\frac{2x+1}{2x-1}\right)^{-2}$ if $x = \frac{2}{3}$?

F. -14

G. $\frac{14}{19}$

H. $\frac{1}{49}$

J. $\frac{81}{49}$

K. 49

29. A garden needs to be covered with grass sod. The garden has the dimensions shown below. How many square feet of sod are required to cover the garden?

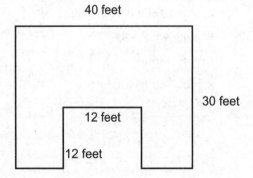

A. 656

B. 912

C. 984

D. 1,056

E. 1,200

30. Mae calculates that one gallon of paint can cover a 400 square foot wall with no paint left over. A house has four walls that are 20 feet tall. Two of the walls are 30 feet long, and two of the walls are 40 feet long. How many gallons of paint will Mae need to cover all four walls?

F. $3\frac{1}{2}$

G. $5\frac{1}{2}$

H. 6

J. 7

K. 30

31. What is the length of a line segment with endpoints (–3, 2) and (5, –1)?

A. $\sqrt{11}$

B. $\sqrt{61}$

C. 11

D. $\sqrt{73}$

E. 73

32. Which of the following is equal to $(p^2q - 2pq^3)^2$?

F. $p^4q^2 + 4p^2q^6$

G. $p^4q^2 - 2p^3q^4 + 4p^2q^6$

H. $p^4q - 4p^2q^3 + 4pq^9$

J. $p^4q^2 - 4p^2q^6$

K. $p^4q^2 - 4p^3q^4 + 4p^2q^6$

33. Consider the diagram shown.

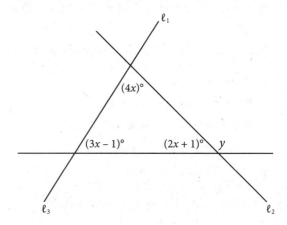

What is the value of y?

A. 41

B. 49

C. 80

D. 20

E. 139

34. If the surface area of a cube is 108 square centimeters, what is its volume (in cubic centimeters)?

F. $3\sqrt{2}$

G. 18

H. $27\sqrt{2}$

J. 54

K. $54\sqrt{2}$

35. A standard 6-sided die is rolled. What is the probability that it lands on either an even number or a 5?

A. $\frac{1}{12}$

B. $\frac{1}{6}$

C. $\frac{1}{2}$

D. $\frac{2}{3}$

E. $\frac{5}{6}$

36. What are the solutions of the equation $(3x + 1)^2 + 9 = 0$?

F. $x = -\dfrac{4}{3}$

G. $x = -\dfrac{4}{3},\ x = \dfrac{2}{3}$

H. $x = -\dfrac{\sqrt{10}}{3},\ x = \dfrac{\sqrt{10}}{3}$

J. $x = -\dfrac{1}{3} - i,\ x = -\dfrac{1}{3} + i$

K. $x = -\dfrac{i\sqrt{10}}{3},\ x = \dfrac{i\sqrt{10}}{3}$

37. If $f(x) = 1 - 2x$, which of the following equals $f(2x + 3)$?

A. $-5 - 4x$

B. $1 - 8 \bullet 4x$

C. $1 - 162x$

D. $1 - 32x$

E. $-4x - 9$

38. In tossing a fair coin three consecutive times, what is the probability of getting heads on two consecutive tosses but NOT on three consecutive tosses? (A fair coin has an equal likelihood of a heads or tails outcome.)

F. $\dfrac{1}{4}$

G. $\dfrac{3}{8}$

H. $\dfrac{1}{8}$

J. $\dfrac{1}{2}$

K. $\dfrac{3}{4}$

39. What is the length of the arc associated with the shaded portion of the circle shown?

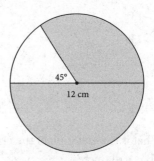

A. $\dfrac{21\pi}{2}$ cm

B. $\dfrac{3\pi}{2}$ cm

C. 3π cm

D. 21π cm

E. 12π cm

40. If a is a positive real number, what is the distance between the points $\left(\dfrac{1}{2}a, -\dfrac{1}{4}a\right)$ and $\left(-\dfrac{1}{4}a, -\dfrac{1}{2}a\right)$?

F. $\dfrac{\sqrt{10}}{4}a$

G. $\dfrac{\sqrt{2}}{2}a$

H. $\dfrac{5}{8}a^2$

J. $\dfrac{\sqrt{5}}{4}a$

K. $\sqrt{2}a$

41. If $x = 2y - 1$ and $y = 2x - 1$, what is the value of $3x + y$?

A. 1

B. 2

C. 6

D. 8

E. 9

42. Find the 21st term of the following sequence: 29, 21, 13, ...

   F. −131

   G. −139

   H. −123

   J. 181

   K. 189

43. What is the equation of the circle shown, where AB is a diameter?

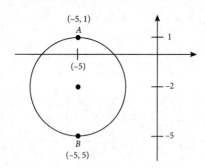

   A. $(x + 2)^2 + (y + 5)^2 = 9$

   B. $(x + 5)^2 + (y + 2)^2 = 9$

   C. $(x - 2)^2 + (y - 5)^2 = 3$

   D. $(x + 5)^2 + (y + 2)^2 = 3$

   E. $(x - 5)^2 + (y - 2)^2 = 9$

44. If $x^2 - 10x + 4 = 0$, what are the possible values of x?

   F. $5 \pm \sqrt{21}$

   G. $5 \pm 2\sqrt{21}$

   H. $-5 \pm \sqrt{21}$

   J. $10 \pm 2\sqrt{21}$

   K. $5 \pm i\sqrt{21}$

45. The graph of which of the following equations is parallel to the line shown?

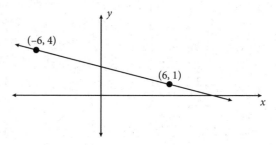

   A. $y = 4x - \dfrac{1}{4}$

   B. $4x - y = -2$

   C. $4y + x = 2$

   D. $2x - 8y = 1$

   E. $5x + 10y = 20$

46. O'Malley's Watch Factory has a failure rate of 2%. That is, every watch they produce has a 2% chance of being defective. In a shipment of 500 watches, what is the expected value of the number of defective watches?

   F. 250

   G. 100

   H. 10

   J. 5

   K. 2

47. Which of the following is the graph of
$f(x) = 2 + (x + 3)^2$?

A.

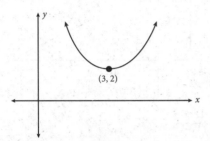

B.

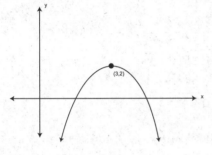

C.

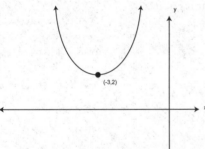

D.

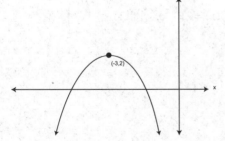

E.

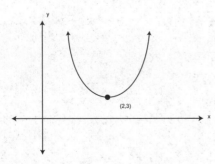

48. Which of the following is equal to $(3 - 2i)(4i - 1)$, where i stands for the $\sqrt{-1}$?

F. $-3 + 12i$

G. $5 + 14i$

H. $-11 + 14i$

J. $19i$

K. $14i$

49. If the surface area of a sphere is 100π square centimeters, what is the volume of the sphere?

A. 500π cubic centimeters

B. $\dfrac{250\pi}{3}$ cubic centimeters

C. $\dfrac{500\pi}{3}$ cubic centimeters

D. $\dfrac{125\pi}{3}$ cubic centimeters

E. 125π cubic centimeters

50. Consider the right circular cone shown:

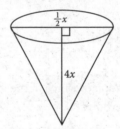

If you want to produce a cone whose dimensions are $\dfrac{1}{2}$ of the dimensions of the one shown, what would the DIFFERENCE in volume be between the pictured cone and the one you are producing?

F. $\dfrac{\pi}{3}x^3$

G. $\dfrac{\pi}{12}x^2$

H. $\dfrac{7\pi}{96}x^3$

J. $\dfrac{\pi}{96}x^3$

K. $\dfrac{\pi}{12}x^3$

KNOWLEDGE CHECK

51. What are the final coordinates of point *P* after a 180° rotation centered at point *C*?

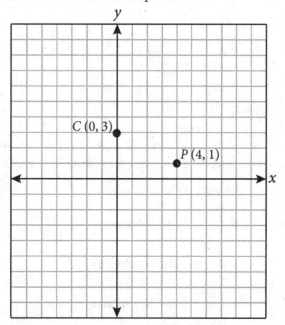

A. (−4, −1)

B. (2, 7)

C. (−2, −1)

D. (−4, 3)

E. (−4, 5)

52. The graph of which of the following equations is a hyperbola?

F. $x^2 - y^2 = 0$

G. $x^2 = 4 + y^2$

H. $y^2 + 2x = 0$

J. $x^2 + y^2 = 1$

K. $x + y = 1$

53. If the mean and standard deviation of a bell-shaped distribution are 2.0 and 0.75, respectively, what interval contains about 95% of the data?

A. (0.5, 3.5)

B. (1.25, 2.75)

C. (1.5, 2.5)

D. (1.0, 3.0)

E. (1.75, 3.75)

54. Consider the triangle shown:

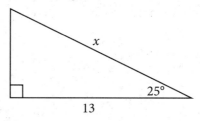

What is the value of *x*?

F. $\dfrac{13}{\sin 25°}$

G. $13 \sin 25°$

H. $13 \cos 25°$

J. $\dfrac{13}{\cos 25°}$

K. $\dfrac{\tan 25°}{13}$

55. Suppose $\sin\theta = -\dfrac{\sqrt{3}}{2}$ and $\cos\theta = -\dfrac{1}{2}$. What is $\cot\theta$?

A. $-\dfrac{2\sqrt{3}}{3}$

B. -2

C. $\sqrt{3}$

D. $-\sqrt{3}$

E. $\dfrac{\sqrt{3}}{3}$

56. If $f(x) = 2x - 6$, what is $f^{-1}\left(\dfrac{1}{2}\right)$?

F. -5

G. $-\dfrac{1}{5}$

H. $\dfrac{7}{2}$

J. $\dfrac{13}{4}$

K. $\dfrac{25}{4}$

57. The graph of the function $H(x)$ is shown below:

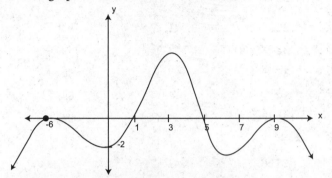

On what interval(s), if any, is $H(x)$ positive?

A. $(-\infty, -6) \cup (0, 3) \cup (7, 9)$

B. $(-\infty, -6) \cup (-6, 1) \cup (5, 9) \cup (9, \infty)$

C. $(-6, 0) \cup (3, 7) \cup (9, \infty)$

D. $(1, 5)$

E. No such interval

58. Let $f(x) = (2x + 1)^2 + 1$ and $g(x) = \sqrt{x-5}$. What are the x-intercept(s), if any, of $(g \circ f)(x)$?

F. $\left(-\dfrac{3}{2}, 0\right)$ and $\left(\dfrac{5}{2}, 0\right), \left(\dfrac{3}{2}, 0\right)$

G. $(5, 0)$

H. $(0, 2)$

J. $\left(\dfrac{1}{2}, 0\right)$ and $\left(-\dfrac{3}{2}, 0\right)$

K. No x-intercepts

59. What is the minimum y-value attained on the graph of $g(x) = 3\cos(2x) - 1$?

A. 0

B. -1

C. -3

D. -4

E. -7

60. What is the period of the graph of $y = 5\cos\dfrac{x}{2}$?

F. $\dfrac{\pi}{2}$

G. π

H. $\dfrac{3\pi}{2}$

J. 2π

K. 4π

ANSWER KEY AND EXPLANATIONS

1. D	11. C	21. B	31. D	41. E	51. E
2. G	12. J	22. G	32. K	42. F	52. G
3. C	13. A	23. C	33. E	43. B	53. A
4. H	14. F	24. J	34. K	44. G	54. J
5. B	15. A	25. B	35. D	45. C	55. E
6. J	16. H	26. J	36. J	46. H	56. J
7. E	17. E	27. B	37. B	47. C	57. D
8. J	18. K	28. H	38. F	48. G	58. J
9. D	19. B	29. D	39. A	49. C	59. D
10. F	20. J	30. J	40. F	50. H	60. K

1. **The correct answer is D.** If 20% equals 14 students, then 100% equals 70 students. 100% is five times 20%, so 100% of the class is 5 × 14, or 70 students.

2. **The correct answer is G.** Simplify using the order of operations:

$$-3^2\left|-6-(-4)\right|=-3^2\left|-6+4\right|$$
$$=-9\left|-2\right|$$
$$=-9(2)$$
$$=-18$$

3. **The correct answer is C.** Given the perimeter and the width of a rectangle, we can find the length by using the perimeter formula:

$$P=2l+2w$$
$$60=2l+2(12)$$
$$60=2l+24$$
$$36=2l$$
$$18=l$$

Therefore, the length is 18 units, and the area is $A=lw=(18)(12)=216$.

4. **The correct answer is H.** You know that the two numbers are both divisible by 6 and by no greater number. This eliminates choice J, as 12 is a common factor for 12 and 24. You also know that the least common multiple the two numbers share is

36. That knowledge eliminates choice F, as 12 is the least common multiple there. Choice B fails for the same reason, as 18 is a common multiple less than 36. Finally, choice K does not have 36 as a multiple of both numbers. Choice H has the only pair of numbers that fits the description.

5. **The correct answer is B.** Arrange the data in the second column in order:

$$0, 0, 1, 1, 2, 2, 3, 4, 4, 4$$

The average of the 5th and 6th data values is 2. So, the median is 2.

6. **The correct answer is J.** Since the three angles combine to form the straight line GI, the sum of the angles must equal 180°. You already know that $\angle\text{JHI} = 33°$ and $\angle\text{KHJ} = 22°$, so $\angle\text{GHK} = 180° - 33° - 22° = 125°$.

7. **The correct answer is E.** It is known that a, b, and c are the sides of a right triangle if and only if $a^2 + b^2 = c^2$, where c is the largest of the three numbers. The only triple that satisfies this relationship is the one in choice E.

8. **The correct answer is J.** Solve for a:

$$2a-38=-26$$
$$2a=12$$
$$a=6$$
$$3a = 3(6) = 18.$$

9. **The correct answer is D.** Let x denote the number that will germinate. Using the given ratio, we have $\frac{3}{5} = \frac{x}{120}$ Solving for x yields the equation $5x = 360$, so that $x = 72$.

10. **The correct answer is F.** Let x be the original price. Then, "70% of x is $75.50" translates to the equation $0.70x = 75.50$. So $x = \frac{75.50}{.0.70}$ dollars.

11. **The correct answer is C.** If the probability of drawing a classical CD is $\frac{4}{5}$, then the probability of drawing a jazz CD is $1 - \frac{4}{5} = \frac{1}{5}$. This means that there are 4 classical CDs for each jazz CD. Since there are 3 jazz CDs, there are $3 \times 4 = 12$ classical CDs in the box.

12. **The correct answer is J.** It's easiest to give numbers to the question, since none are provided. Let's make the tin have 1 cherry candy. We're told it has twice as many grape candies, so there are 2 grapes. There are three times as many lemon candies as grape, so that means the tin has $2 \times 3 = 6$ lemon candies. So, the bag has 1 cherry, 2 grape, and 6 lemon candies. Next, a number of apple candies equal to the number of cherry candies is added. That means 1 apple candy is added, and the tin has $1 + 2 + 6 + 1 = 10$ candies total. Six of the 10 are lemon, so the probability of selecting a lemon is $\frac{6}{10} = \frac{3}{5}$.

13. **The correct answer is A.** Compute the quantities in choices B, C, D, and E:

$$36^0 = 1$$
$$1^{200} = 1$$
$$3^{-2} = \frac{1}{3^2} = \frac{1}{9}$$
$$\left(\frac{1}{4}\right)^3 = \frac{1}{64}$$

Since $\sqrt{2} > 1$, it is the largest of the five quantities.

14. **The correct answer is F.** $\sqrt{6}$ is equal to approximately 2.449, so all the question is really asking is which point is closest to 2.449 on the number line. That number is just about halfway between 2 and 3,

so the closest point is F. Since choices G, H, J, and K are larger, they are not the correct answers.

15. **The correct answer is A.** Solve for x:

$$1 - \frac{3x}{2} = \frac{x+1}{6}$$
$$6 - 3(3x) = x + 1$$
$$6 - 9x = x + 1$$
$$5 = 10x$$
$$x = \frac{1}{2}$$

So, the value of x^3 is $\left(\frac{1}{2}\right)^3 = \frac{1}{2^3} = \frac{1}{8}$.

16. **The correct answer is H.** Use the properties of radicals and fractions to simplify, as follows:

$$\sqrt{\frac{7}{30}} \div \sqrt{\frac{21}{80}} = \frac{\sqrt{7}}{\sqrt{30}} \cdot \frac{\sqrt{80}}{\sqrt{21}}$$
$$= \frac{\sqrt{7}}{\sqrt{21}} \cdot \frac{\sqrt{80}}{\sqrt{30}}$$
$$= \sqrt{\frac{7}{21}} \cdot \sqrt{\frac{80}{30}}$$
$$= \sqrt{\frac{1}{3}} \cdot \sqrt{\frac{8}{3}}$$
$$= \frac{\sqrt{8}}{3}$$
$$= \frac{2\sqrt{2}}{3}$$

17. **The correct answer is E.** First, multiply the decimals as usual to get 0.40422. Then, convert to scientific notation by moving the decimal point one place to the right and multiplying by 10. This gives 4.0422×10^{-1}.

18. **The correct answer is K.** You can either solve algebraically or by choosing actual values for the ages. Algebraically, you know that Lina is x years old. Karen is twice as old, so Karen is $2x$ years old. Joel is 8 years older than Karen, so he is $2x + 8$ years old. Alternatively, you could choose a value for x. Let's say $x = 10$. Then Lina is 10, Karen is 20, and Joel is 28. Only choice K yields 28 when you substitute 10 for x, so this must be the correct answer.

19. The correct answer is B. The average is the sum of the terms divided by the number of terms—in this case, the sum of all the ratings divided by the number of tasters. You don't know how many tasters there were, but that's not a problem. Since you know all the percentages, simply pick a number for the number of tasters and use it. Since the percentages are in multiples of 5, you'll want a number that is easily divisible by 20, since 5% is one out of 20. Let's use 20 to keep things simple. (You could have used 100 or any other number divisible by 20.) 10% of 20 is 2, so 2 tasters gave a rating of 4. That's $2 \times 4 = 8$ points total. 15% gave a rating of 3. 15% of 20 is 3, so that is $3 \times 3 = 9$ points. Half the testers, 10 of them, gave a rating of 2, so that makes another $10 \times 2 = 20$ points. Finally, 25%, or 5 tasters, gave a rating of 1. That's $5 \times 1 = 5$ more points. Total points awarded = $8 + 9 + 20 + 5 = 42$ points. Divide that by the number of tasters used, 20, and the average rating is $\frac{42}{20} = 2.1$.

20. The correct answer is J. Let Elaine's salary be $3k$ and Carl's will be $2k$. A 20% salary raise for Elaine will bring her salary to $(1.2)(3k) = 3.6k$, while a $200 raise for Carl will bring his salary to $2k + 200$. Thus:

$$\frac{3.6k}{2k + 200} = \frac{6}{5}$$

After cross-multiplying, solve the proportion as follows:

$$18k = 12k + 1,200$$
$$6k = 1,200$$
$$k = 200$$

So, Elaine's salary is $3k = \$600$.

21. The correct answer is B. The probability of obtaining heads on a flip of a fair coin is $\frac{1}{2}$, and the probability of getting a 3 on a die is $\frac{1}{6}$. These events are independent, so we can simply multiply the probabilities to obtain $\frac{1}{2} \cdot \frac{1}{6} = \frac{1}{12}$.

22. The correct answer is G. Substitute $y = 0$ into the equation $4y + 3x = 12$ to get $3x = 12$. So $x = 4$. The x-intercept is 4.

23. The correct answer is C. In order to compute a scalar multiple of a matrix, multiply each entry of the matrix by that multiple. The result, in this case, will be a matrix of the same dimensions (2 by 2) with each value multiplied by 4. From left to right and top to bottom, the result would be -8, 0, 8, 12.

24. The correct answer is J. Since the second file is $2\frac{1}{2}$ times as large as the first, multiply the amount of time needed for the first file by $2\frac{1}{2}$. You can do this either by converting 4 minutes and 26 seconds to seconds, then converting back to minutes, or by multiplying both the minutes and seconds by $2\frac{1}{2}$, then combining the results:

$$4 \text{ minutes} \times 2\frac{1}{2} = 10 \text{ minutes}$$

$$26 \text{ seconds} \times 2\frac{1}{2} = 65 \text{ seconds}$$

10 minutes and 65 seconds = 11 minutes and 5 seconds

25. The correct answer is B. Use the distributive property and then combine like terms:

$$2(4y - 3z) - 4(2z - 3y) = 8y - 6z - 8z + 12y = 20y - 14z$$

26. The correct answer is J. Divide the total number of people who did NOT identify water rides as their favorite, namely $120 - 31 = 89$, by 120 to get the probability.

27. The correct answer is B. First, rewrite the absolute value inequality as the double inequality $-5 < 4x + 1 < 5$. To solve this inequality, subtract 1 from all parts to get $-6 < 4x < 4$ and then divide all parts by 4 to get $-\frac{3}{2} < x < 1$. This is the solution set.

28. The correct answer is H. Substitute $x = \frac{2}{3}$ into the given expression and simplify:

$$\left(\frac{2\left(\frac{2}{3}\right)+1}{2\left(\frac{2}{3}\right)-1} \right)^{-2} = \left(\frac{\frac{4}{3}+1}{\frac{4}{3}-1} \right)^{-2} = \left(\frac{\frac{7}{3}}{\frac{1}{3}} \right)^{-2} = 7^{-2} = \frac{1}{7^2} = \frac{1}{49}$$

29. The correct answer is D. The problem is asking you to determine the area of the figure. There are a few ways to do this. You could break the figure into 3 rectangles and add their areas. However, a quicker method is to consider the figure a solid rectangle by drawing a line from one of the bottom "legs" to the other. The area of that rectangle would be 30 feet × 40 feet = 1,200 square feet. But that's too big; you have to subtract from this the area of the 12 foot × 12 foot square that isn't really part of the garden. That square is 12 × 12 = 144 square feet. 1,200 square feet − 144 square feet = 1,056 square feet (choice D).

30. **The correct answer is J.** Each of the larger walls has an area of 20 × 40 = 800 square feet, which requires 2 gallons of paint. Each of the smaller walls has an area of 20 × 30 = 600 square feet, which requires $1\frac{1}{2}$ gallons of paint. The total area is 2,800 square feet, and the total number of gallons is $2 + 2 + 1\frac{1}{2} + 1\frac{1}{2} = 7$.

31. **The correct answer is D.** The x-coordinate of the midpoint of a line segment is the average of the x-coordinates of its endpoints; the same goes for the y-coordinate of the midpoint. So, the midpoint of this segment is $\left(\frac{2-6}{2}, \frac{-8+2}{2}\right) = (-2, -3)$.

32. **The correct answer is K.** FOIL the binomials to expand this expression:

$$\left(p^2q - 2pq^3\right)^2 = \left(p^2q - 2pq^3\right)\left(p^2q - 2pq^3\right)$$
$$= p^4q^2 - 2p^3q^4 - 2p^3q^4 + 4p^2q^6$$
$$= p^4q^2 - 4p^3q^4 + 4p^2q^6$$

33. **The correct answer is E.** First, since the sum of the angles in a triangle is 180°, we have $4x + (3x - 1) + (2x + 1) = 180$. Solving for x yields $9x = 180$ so that $x = 20$. Now, observe that $2x + 1 = 2(20) + 1 = 41$. Since this angle and the one labeled y are supplementary, we conclude that $y + 41 = 180$, so that $y = 139$.

34. **The correct answer is K.** Let e be an edge of a cube. The surface area formula is $6e^2$, so that setting this equal to 108, we see $6e^2 = 108$ and so $e^2 = 18$. Therefore, $e = \sqrt{18} = 3\sqrt{2}$ centimeters. Thus, its volume must be $e^3 = \left(3\sqrt{2}\right)^3 = 52\sqrt{2}$ cubic centimeters.

35. **The correct answer is D.** The even numbers are 2, 4, and 6, so the probability of rolling an even number is $\frac{3}{6}$. The probability of rolling a 5 is $\frac{1}{6}$. Since these are mutually exclusive events—that is, they cannot both occur together—we can simply add them. So, the probability of rolling either an even number or a 5 is $\frac{3}{6} + \frac{1}{6} = \frac{4}{6} = \frac{2}{3}$.

36. **The correct answer is J.** Solve for x using the radical method:

$$(3x+1)^2 + 9 = 0$$
$$(3x+1)^2 = -9$$
$$3x+1 = \pm 3i$$
$$3x = -1 \pm 3i$$
$$x = \frac{-1 \pm 3i}{3} = -\frac{1}{3} \pm i$$

37. **The correct answer is B.** Calculate as follows:

$$f(2x+3) = 1 - 2^{2x+3}$$
$$= 1 - 2^{2x} \cdot 2^3$$
$$= 1 - \left(2^2\right)x \cdot 8$$
$$= 1 - 4x \cdot 8$$
$$= 1 - 8 \cdot 4x$$

38. **The correct answer is F.** How can you have two consecutive heads but not three? The first two tosses could be heads and the third could be tails. Also, the last two tosses could be heads while the first is tails. Those are the only ways to achieve the desired outcome. For the first, you need heads, heads, tails. The probability of that outcome is $\frac{1}{2} \times \frac{1}{2} \times \frac{1}{2} = \frac{1}{8}$. There's a one out of two chance of getting the outcome we want on each toss, so the chance of getting all three outcomes in a row is $\frac{1}{2} \times \frac{1}{2} \times \frac{1}{2}$. That's not the answer though. You could also get the tails, heads, heads outcome. This too has a $\frac{1}{2} \times \frac{1}{2} \times \frac{1}{2} = \frac{1}{8}$ probability. Since either outcome is acceptable, you add the probabilities: $\frac{1}{8} + \frac{1}{8} = \frac{2}{8} = \frac{1}{4}$.

39. **The correct answer is A.** The length S of an arc of a circle with radius r and central angle θ expressed in

degrees is $S = r \cdot \left(\theta \cdot \dfrac{\pi}{180} \right)$.

Here, $r = \dfrac{1}{2}(12 \text{ cm}) = (6 \text{ cm})$ and $\theta = 360° - 45° = 315°$. Hence, the arc length is

$S = 6 \text{ cm} \cdot \left(315 \cdot \dfrac{\pi}{180} \right) = \dfrac{21\pi}{2} \text{ cm}$.

40. The correct answer is F. Use the distance formula:

$$\sqrt{ \left(\dfrac{1}{2}a, + \dfrac{1}{4}a \right)^2 + \left(-\dfrac{1}{4}a, + \dfrac{1}{2}a \right)^2 } = \sqrt{ \left(\dfrac{3}{4}a \right)^2 + \left(\dfrac{1}{4}a \right)^2 }$$

$$= \sqrt{ \dfrac{9}{16}a^2 + \dfrac{1}{16}a^2 }$$

$$= \sqrt{ \dfrac{10}{16}a^2 }$$

$$= \dfrac{\sqrt{10}}{\sqrt{16}} \cdot \sqrt{a^2}$$

$$= \dfrac{\sqrt{10}}{4} a$$

41. The correct answer is E. Solve the system using the substitution method. Substitute the expression for x given by the first equation into the second equation and solve for y:

$$y = 2(2y-1)-1$$
$$y = 4y-2-1$$
$$y = 4y-3$$
$$-3y = -3$$
$$y = 1$$

Substitute this value back into the first equation to determine the value of x: $x = 2(1) - 1 = 1$. Hence, $3x + y = 31 + 1 = 32 = 9$.

42. The correct answer is F. This is an arithmetic sequence in which a term is obtained by subtracting 8 from the previous term. So, the nth term of the sequence can be expressed using the formula $29 - 8(n - 1)$, where $n \geq 1$. So, when $n = 21$, the term is $29 - 8(20) = -131$.

43. The correct answer is B. The line segment connecting the points $(-5, 1)$ and $(-5, -5)$ is given to be a diameter. Hence, half of its length is the radius. Since its length is 6 units, the radius of the circle is 3. The midpoint of any diameter is the center of the circle. The midpoint of AB is

$\left(\dfrac{-5-5}{2}, \dfrac{1-5}{2} \right) = (-5, -2)$. So, the equation of the circle is $(x - (-5))^2 + (y - (-2))^2 = 32$, which simplifies to $(x + 5)^2 + (y + 2)^2 = 9$.

44. The correct answer is G. Use the quadratic formula directly to get:

$$x = \dfrac{-(-1) \pm \sqrt{(-1)^2 - 4(2)(3)}}{2(2)} = \dfrac{1 \pm \sqrt{-23}}{4} = \dfrac{1 \pm i\sqrt{-23}}{4} = \dfrac{1}{4} \pm \dfrac{i\sqrt{23}}{4}$$

45. The correct answer is C. The slope of the line shown is $m = \dfrac{4-1}{6-6} = \dfrac{1}{4}$ Any line with this same slope must be parallel to the one shown. Note that the equation in choice C can be written as $y = -\dfrac{1}{4}x + \dfrac{1}{2}$ and so must be parallel to the one shown.

46. The correct answer is H. This situation can be modeled by the binomial distribution $B(500, 0.02)$ The expected value of a binomial distribution $B(n,p)$ is np, so here it is $500 \times 0.02 = 10$. The other choices either use incorrect values of p (20% in choice G) or simply perform the calculation incorrectly (choices F and J).

47. The correct answer is C. The graph of $f(x)$ is a parabola opening upward (because the coefficient of x^2 is positive) with vertex $(-3, 2)$. The only graph that possesses these characteristics is the one in choice C.

48. The correct answer is G. FOIL the two binomials:

$$12i - 8i^2 - 3 + 2i = 14i - 8(-1) - 3$$
$$= 14i + 5$$
$$= 5 + 14i$$

49. The correct answer is C. First, solve the surface area equation $4\pi r^2 = 100\pi$ for r: $r^2 = 25$, so that $r = 5$ cm. Now, compute the volume for a sphere with this radius: $\dfrac{4}{3}\pi (5)^3 = \dfrac{500\pi}{3}$ cubic centimeters.

50. The correct answer is H. The radius of the given cone is $\dfrac{1}{2}\left(\dfrac{1}{2}x \right) = \dfrac{1}{4}x$ and the height is $4x$. So, the volume of the given cone is $\dfrac{1}{3}\pi \left(\dfrac{1}{4}x \right)^2 \cdot (4x) = \dfrac{\pi}{12}x^3$.

The radius of the cone you are producing is $\frac{1}{2}\left(\frac{1}{4}x\right)=\frac{1}{8}x$ and the height is $\frac{1}{2}(4x)$. So, the volume of the cone you are producing is $\frac{1}{3}\pi\left(\frac{1}{8}x\right)^2\cdot(2x)=\frac{\pi}{96}x^3$.

Therefore, the difference in their volumes is $\frac{\pi}{12}x^3-\frac{\pi}{96}x^3=\frac{8\pi}{96}x^3-\frac{\pi}{96}x^3=\frac{7\pi}{96}x^3$.

51. **The correct answer is E.** One way to visualize a rotation is by drawing a rectangle with one vertex at the center of rotation and the opposite vertex at the point to be rotated. Then rotate the entire rectangle to find the final location of the point P, as shown below.

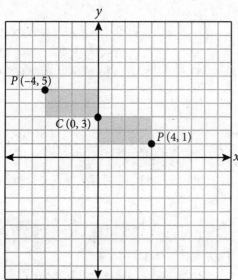

52. **The correct answer is G.** This equation can be written equivalently as $\frac{x^2}{4}-\frac{y^2}{4}=1$, which is in the standard form for a hyperbola.

53. **The correct answer is A.** For a bell-shaped curve, 95% of the data occurs within two standard deviations of the mean. Here, this is 2.0: 2(0.75) = 0.5 to 2.0 + 2(0.75) = 3.5. So, the interval (0.5, 3.5) is the desired answer.

54. **The correct answer is J.** By definition, $\cos\theta=\dfrac{\text{side adjacent to the angle }\theta}{\text{hypotenuse}}$. So, from the triangle, we have $\cos 25°=\dfrac{13}{x}$. Solving for x yields $x=\dfrac{13}{\cos 25°}$.

55. **The correct answer is E.** By definition,
$$cot\theta=\frac{\cos\theta}{\sin\theta}=\frac{-\frac{1}{2}}{-\frac{\sqrt{3}}{2}}=\frac{1}{\sqrt{3}}=\frac{\sqrt{3}}{3}$$

56. **The correct answer is J.** Let $y=2x-6$. To find the inverse, switch the x and y and solve for y:
$$y=2x-6$$
$$x=2y-6$$
$$x+6=2y$$
$$y=\frac{x+6}{2}$$
So $f^{-1}(x)=\dfrac{x+6}{2}$. Thus, $f^{-1}\left(\dfrac{1}{2}\right)=\dfrac{\frac{1}{2}+6}{2}=\dfrac{\frac{13}{2}}{2}=\dfrac{13}{4}$.

57. **The correct answer is D.** For a function to be positive, its graph must be above the x-axis. This is true only on the interval (1, 5).

58. **The correct answer is J.** Observe the following:
$$(g\circ f)(x)=g(f(x))=\sqrt{(2x+1)^2+1-5}=\sqrt{(2x+1)^2-4}$$

The x-intercept(s) are the solutions of the equation $\sqrt{(2x+1)^2-4}=0$. Solve for x, as follows:
$$\sqrt{(2x+1)^2-4}=0$$
$$(2x+1)^2-4=0$$
$$(2x+1)^2=4$$
$$2x+1=\pm\sqrt{4}=\pm 2$$
$$2x+1=2$$
$$or$$
$$2x+1=-2$$
$$x=\frac{1}{2}\text{ or }x=-\frac{3}{2}$$

So, the x-intercepts are $\left(\dfrac{1}{2},0\right)$ and $\left(-\dfrac{3}{2},0\right)$.

59. The correct answer is D. Analyze the range of the graph in stages:

$$-1 \leq \cos(2x) \leq 1$$
$$-3 \leq 3\cos(2x) \leq 3$$
$$-3-1 \leq 3\cos(2x)-1 \leq 3-1$$
$$-4 \leq 4\cos(2x)-1 \leq 2$$

Therefore, the smallest y-value attained on the graph is -4.

60. The correct answer is K. The graph of $y = \cos x$ has a period of 2π. However, if you graph $y = 5\cos\dfrac{x}{2}$, the period doubles in length to 4π. Note that the coefficient of the cosine, 5, affects only the amplitude—not the period. All of the other choices are incorrect because the period for $y = A \cos Bx$ is $\dfrac{2\pi}{B}$. Each of these choices is the result of not remembering this fact correctly.

Scoring Chart

Mark missed questions and calculate your total for each question category and the test as a whole. Then convert your raw score to a scaled score using the chart on page 287 in Chapter 8.

Question Types		Question Numbers	Score
Integrating Essential Skills (IES)		1, 2, 3, 4, 5, 6, 8, 9, 10, 11, 13, 14, 15, 18, 19, 20, 22, 24, 25, 26, 29, 30, 31, 33, 34	_____/25
Preparing for Higher Math (PHM)*			_____/35
	Number and Quantity	16, 23, 28, 48	_____/4
	Algebra	17, 27, 32, 36, 40, 41, 44, 52	_____/8
	Functions	37, 42, 47, 56, 57, 58, 59, 60	_____/8
	Geometry	7, 39, 43, 45, 49, 50, 51, 54, 55	_____/9
	Statistics and Probability	12, 21, 35, 38, 46, 53	_____/6
Modeling**		1, 5, 7, 9, 10, 11, 12, 18, 19, 20, 24, 26, 29, 30, 33, 34, 38, 39, 43, 45, 46, 47, 50, 51, 52, 57	_____/26**
			Raw Score: _____/60
			Scaled Score:

*Combine all subcategories of PHM questions for this score and add to your IES total to find your Raw Score.

**Modeling overlaps other scoring categories and is not added to your raw score.

PART IV
THE READING TEST ON THE ACT®

16 | Introduction to ACT® Reading

17 | Key Concepts in Reading Comprehension

18 | Strategies for Approaching the Reading Section

CHAPTER

Introduction to ACT® Reading

INTRODUCTION TO ACT® READING

OVERVIEW

How to Study with Part IV

All about the Reading Section

Scoring Table

Types of Reading Passages

Sample Questions

Common Challenges

Summing It Up

The ACT Reading Test evaluates your ability to read a given passage and then answer questions based on its content. Questions will task you with identifying things like the main idea, author's purpose, supporting details, and the meaning of vocabulary terms used in context. They will also test your ability to make inferences, summarize information, identify relationships between ideas, and more. Doing well in this section is about not only understanding how to read for comprehension but also developing critical strategies that will help you answer your questions within the time constraints of the exam. The chapters included in this part of the book are designed to help you with both of these tasks.

HOW TO STUDY WITH PART IV

This chapter provides a brief overview of the Reading section of the ACT exam, including test specifications, the types of reading questions you'll encounter, example questions, and common challenges test takers experience with this section. In Chapter 17, we'll cover reading comprehension as a skill set, including giving you the opportunity to hone your skills using example passages. If you are already an ace at reading, you may only need to skim Chapter 17 as a refresher. However, if you struggle with reading, it will give you a helpful primer on the different types of reading skills you'll be tested on by the ACT. Then, in Chapter 18, we'll lay out an array of tools and strategies to help you put your comprehension skills to work in a timed setting. We'll also provide more in-depth information on the types of questions you can expect to find on the Reading section of the ACT. By applying these tools and strategies, you should be better prepared for the specific kinds of tasks you'll need to complete in the Reading section. Even if you excel at reading skills already, our tips on managing your time and using strategic shortcuts to get through the test will help you tackle this section like a pro. At the end of Chapter 18, we'll have a Knowledge Check that replicates test conditions. That way, you can put all your new tools and strategies to work right away and measure your improvement so far.

As with each new part in this book, we encourage you to begin your studies by engaging in some self-reflection. You should consider how you'd evaluate yourself as a reader and determine if there are any particular reading skills that you'd like to focus on practicing more than others. You may find it helpful to periodically return to these questions while you work on reading, such as pondering them again between chapters. Doing so will help you process the information you take in and personalize it for your own test prep needs. In short, self-reflection helps you make the most of your study time.

Here are some self-reflection questions to consider as you begin studying for the reading test.

Self-Reflection: Reading

- Which of your high school courses helped you with your reading skills, and what strategies did you learn in those courses?

- Which aspects of reading have historically been easier for you?

- Which aspects of reading have historically been harder for you?

- Did you experience any conditions during your high school experience (remote learning, recovering from surgery, etc.) that could have created gaps in your learning around reading? If so, what topics were covered during those gaps?

- Which reading skills require the most time and effort for you?

- What do you like to read, and what do you enjoy about doing that type of reading?

- Do you find it easier to complete reading when it's on certain subjects, like art vs. science? What makes you prefer that subject, or why is it easier for you to read about?

ALL ABOUT THE READING SECTION

The ACT Reading test measures a test taker's ability to comprehend written material and draw conclusions from it. The section consists of 40 questions, and test takers are given 35 minutes to complete it. The questions are split between four passages, each of approximately 800 words, drawn from different subjects and genres, including social sciences, natural sciences, humanities, and literary narratives. One of the passages will be split into a set of two paired passages that add up to the same approximate word count as the single passage entries. Each passage is followed by 10 multiple-choice questions that assess the test taker's comprehension of the text. They cover topics such as identifying the main idea, making inferences, analyzing the author's tone or purpose, and evaluating arguments or evidence. A paired passage set will have questions specific to each passage and then questions that ask about both passages.

The Reading section comprises three types of questions.

KEY IDEAS AND DETAILS (55–60% OF QUESTIONS)

You'll be asked to identify key ideas and themes; summarize information; understand sequential, comparative, and cause-and-effect relationships; make logical inferences; and draw conclusions.

CRAFT AND STRUCTURE (25–30% OF QUESTIONS)

You'll be asked to analyze the organization and structure of a passage; pinpoint an author's perspective and purpose for writing; determine the meanings of certain words and phrases; rhetorically analyze the author's diction; and analyze characters' points of view.

INTEGRATION OF KNOWLEDGE AND IDEAS (13–18% OF QUESTIONS)

You'll be asked to break down an author's argument and identify key claims; evaluate the validity of both reasoning and evidence used in a text; distinguish between opinion and fact; and use evidence to compare and contrast different but topically related texts. These questions typically accompany the paired passages set.

SCORING TABLE

Your performance with the diagnostic test in Chapter 2 gave you a sense of what kind of scaled score you might receive on the ACT Reading section with your current knowledge, skills, and strategies. While working through this part of the book, you'll want to keep that performance in mind along with your desired scores for your college application process. While the raw-to-scaled score conversion is different for every test so the ACT can maintain standardization across different versions of the test, we've supplied a table here to help you approximate what your raw score (0–40 questions) should be for the Reading section in order to achieve your desired scaled score (1–36). This information represents an estimate and is thus not a precise reflection of official ACT scoring metrics.

SCORING TABLE—READING	
Raw Score	Scaled Score
40	36
39	35
38	34
37	33
35–36	32
34	31
33	30
32	29
31	28
30	27
29	26
28	25

SCORING TABLE—READING	
Raw Score	Scaled Score
27	24
26	23
24–25	22
22	21
20–21	20
19	19
18	18
17	17
15–16	16
14	15
12–13	14
11	13

SCORING TABLE—READING	
Raw Score	Scaled Score
9–10	12
8	11
7	10
6	9
5	8
4	7
3	6
–	5
2	4
–	3
1	2
0	1

TYPES OF READING PASSAGES

The ACT Reading test includes four passages, each drawn from a different genre or field of study: social sciences, natural sciences, humanities, or literary narratives, which is usually an excerpt from either prose fiction or a nonfiction narrative, such as a memoir or essay. The passages may cover a variety of topics and themes, such as history, economics, psychology, biology, literature, or current events. While the passages span a range of topics, you don't need to have any prior knowledge or expertise in the subjects. Reading passages will represent the complexity of texts you can expect to see in your first year of college coursework.

The four Reading passages are presented in a fixed order, as shown. The paired passage set may be presented in any one of the four genres.

 Prose Fiction or Literary Narrative: This passage will usually be from a short story, novel, or other piece of fiction. You may also be presented with narratives excerpted from literary nonfiction. You will be tested on your ability to understand and analyze literary texts.

 Social Sciences: This passage covers topics related to social sciences, such as sociology, anthropology, or psychology. It may present data, statistics, or arguments related to a social issue or trend.

 Humanities: This passage covers topics related to the humanities, such as history, philosophy, or art. For example, potential topics may include a historical event, a philosophical argument, or an analysis of a work of art.

 Natural Sciences: This passage covers topics related to natural sciences, such as biology, chemistry, physics, astronomy, or Earth science. It may present a scientific concept, a research study, or an analysis of a natural phenomenon.

SAMPLE QUESTIONS

Questions on the Reading section of the ACT will fit into one of three categories: Key Ideas and Details, Craft and Structure, and Integration of Knowledge and Ideas. We'll cover these in more depth throughout this part of the book.

Here, we've provided examples of questions you might encounter on the exam. Question 1 tests your understanding of Integration of Knowledge and Ideas by asking you to differentiate between a fact and opinion. Question 2 tests your ability to identify Key Ideas and Details by asking you about the main point of a paragraph in the passage. Question 3 tests your ability to assess Craft and Structure by asking you more about the author's use of a metaphor in the passage.

EXAMPLE

> **Directions:** Questions 1–3 refer to the following passage.

SOCIAL SCIENCES: This passage is adapted from a text about Far Eastern cultures and history.

The indigenous Ainu people of northern Japan are something of a mystery to those who try to trace their roots. Physically, they appear to embody a mix of both Asian and
5   European traits; they do not resemble other indigenous peoples in Asia. Some people believe that the Ainu are of Caucasian descent. Another theory holds that the Ainu are of the same descent as other Japanese peoples,
10   but their physical isolation on an island kept them from undergoing the changes that the larger population experienced over many years. Still others believe them to be descendants of an ancient people called Emishi. The
15   term *Ainu* is used today in reference mostly to the population of Hokkaido, Japan's northern-most island; there are also Ainu living on the Sakhalin and Kuril Islands in Russia.

20   Ainu culture, after struggling against centuries of oppression, is perilously close to extinction. The culture flourished in the 13th and 14th centuries. At that time, the Ainu lived in village communities alongside river
25   banks and supported themselves by hunting, fishing, and gathering. Their religious beliefs reflected their close existence with nature; their gods took the forms of animals, particularly the bear. They worshipped through
30   song, dance, and ritual. Notably, although the Ainu had no written language until the modern era, they had a rich literary culture based around an oral tradition of stories and songs.

35   Ainu oral literature served as a means of translating history, values, legends, and stories from one generation to the next. One type of Ainu tale is called "yukar," an epic tale in which the protagonist hero is
40   an orphan boy. In other stories, the heroes are gods who descend from the heavens and interact with people. Sometimes, the heroes of Ainu stories are gods in animal form; many of these tales are morality tales, much

like fables. The oral literature also includes stories that recount the experiences of the ancestors, either as history or as legends.

Women have a traditional place in Ainu oral literature. Emotional songs called "yaysama" are sung by women, who pass the songs down through the generations. Women also sing "upopo," a festival song that they perform in repeated choruses while sitting in a circle beating drums.

That any Ainu oral literature has survived for hundreds of years would itself be a remarkable achievement. It is even more remarkable in light of the Ainu culture's historic struggle to survive. Threats to the Ainu culture began in the 15th century, when the island of Hokkaido came under Japanese control and trade policies that disadvantaged the Ainu were established. A series of battles followed over the next few hundred years, each of which resulted in defeat for the Ainu and increasing control by the Japanese. Moreover, in the early to mid-1800s, the Ainu population was decimated by infectious diseases such as measles and tuberculosis.

During the period from 1868 to 1912, called the Meiji Era, the Japanese government pronounced claim to Ainu land and declared rule of the Ainu people. The Japanese government parceled out much of the land and offered it to Japanese settlers. As a result, the Ainu people became a minority. The Meiji government began a reign of enforced assimilation, requiring the Ainu to abandon their traditional way of life. They were forbidden to hunt and fish—their traditional livelihood—and were forced to farm the land. They were prohibited from speaking their language and from practicing their customs. Their children were forced to attend Japanese schools where they spoke only Japanese. The culture, language, and customs of the Ainu were rapidly disappearing

After the second World War, however, changes began to arise. The post-war government recognized the Ainu people as Japanese nationals who were entitled to equal protection under Japanese law. In 1997, a court ruling recognized the Ainu as indigenous people of Japan and entitled their culture to protection. Shortly thereafter, the Japanese Congress passed the "Act on the Encouragement of Ainu Culture and the Diffusion and Enlightenment of Knowledge on Ainu Tradition." The Act provides financial support for traditional Ainu dance, crafts, and language; provides research opportunities to study the language; and supports the preservation of Ainu culture and traditions.

Still, the culture is struggling to stay alive. Scholars are recording the stories and songs of the oral tradition so that their messages and lessons are not lost. Most Ainu now speak Japanese; the number of native Ainu speakers is extremely small. While it is important that the stories be preserved, there is a world of difference between a tradition preserved under glass—or, more literally, on paper—and one that is alive. While future generations will certainly be able to read translations of Ainu tales, the question remains as to whether the living, breathing literature itself, spoken in the Ainu language and accompanied by Ainu rituals, will survive.

GO ON TO THE NEXT PAGE.

1. In the author's view, would the assertion that the Ainu are of Caucasian descent be an expression of fact or opinion, and why?

   A. Opinion, because it is one of several viable theories

   B. Opinion, because the author clearly asserts that the Ainu are descendants of the Emishi

   C. Fact, because there is indisputable scientific proof that the Ainu are of Caucasian descent

   D. Fact, because Ainu culture is so clearly distinct from Japanese culture

The correct answer is A. Even if you are unsure about whether the statement is a fact or opinion, you can eliminate answer choices based on the "why" component. The first paragraph lists several theories about Ainu descent, so choice A is possible. Choice B is incorrect because the author lists the Emishi as just one possible origin of the Ainu people. Choice C is incorrect because there is no indisputable proof for any of the theories. While much of the article is about the distinction between Ainu and Japanese cultures (choice D), this does not make the case for Caucasian descent as a fact.

2. In Paragraph 6 (lines 70–87), the author's main point is that:

   F. the Japanese did not understand the traditional Ainu way of life.

   G. Ainu children wanted to assimilate into Japanese culture.

   H. the Japanese and Ainu cultures blended to form a new culture.

   J. the forced assimilation of the Ainu put their culture at risk of extinction.

The correct answer is J. The point of the sixth paragraph is to show the harshness of the Japanese government during the Meiji period and demonstrate how its policies almost eradicated the Ainu people. Choice F may be true, but cultural understanding is not the point of the paragraph. There is no evidence for choice G. Choice H is off-base because the two cultures did not blend to form a new one—the Ainu were forced to accept Japanese culture.

3. In the last paragraph, the narrator describes a language "that is alive" (line 113) as one that:

   A. is preserved on paper.

   B. has existed for many generations.

   C. is in current use.

   D. can be understood through translation.

The correct answer is C. The author's main point in the last paragraph is that even though the Ainu culture and language are now being preserved, this does not mean that the culture and language are alive. To be alive, it must currently be in use. Choices A, B, and D are distortions of the information in the last paragraph.

STOP.

**If you finish before time is up, you may check your work on this section only.
Do not turn to any other section in the test.**

Common Challenges

There are some common challenges that test takers often encounter on the ACT Reading test.

Time pressure

You have four passages and 40 questions to get through in 35 minutes. That means that you have less than 9 minutes for each passage and question set. That time crunch can create significant stress and lead you to make choices that can hurt your score. So, it's important to learn the appropriate strategies for managing your time effectively and to prioritize the passages you can get through the fastest with the greatest accuracy.

Complex vocabulary

The passages on the ACT Reading test often contain advanced vocabulary and technical terms that may be unfamiliar to you. This can make it challenging to comprehend the text and answer questions accurately. Throughout this part of the book, we'll discuss how to expand your vocabulary leading up to the test as well as strategies for approaching questions where you don't know the meaning of a specific word or phrase.

Dense passages

The passages on the ACT Reading test are dense, which can make them seem overwhelming and difficult to read. Some passages may contain complex sentence structures, which can make it harder to extract important ideas and details. In the chapters that follow, we'll cover strategies that can help you locate the most important information to answer each question about a given passage quickly and effectively.

Multiple viewpoints

Passages on the ACT Reading test may present multiple viewpoints, which can be confusing at times. As you read the passages you are given, be sure to identify the author's perspective and distinguish it from the viewpoints of other sources presented in the text.

Information overload

The passages on the ACT Reading test contain a lot of information. Trying to process everything under the harsh time constraints can be overwhelming. But knowing what to look for, where to find it, and how to use it can help you sidestep some of the pitfalls of the section. You'll learn to determine what information is relevant to the question at hand and what's only going to bog you down.

Throughout this part of the book, we'll address strategies for dealing with these challenges to help you do your best on the Reading section. We'll focus on things like active reading, time management, and understanding the structure of a text in order to locate essential ideas and details. If any of the previously mentioned challenges apply to you, make a make a mental note (or even jot it down) so that as you work through this section, you can hone the strategies that will make the biggest difference for you.

SUMMING IT UP

- The Reading section of the ACT exam is designed to measure your ability to understand complex texts. You'll have 35 minutes to read four passages and answer 40 questions.

- The Reading section includes four passages covering four different subjects, which are always presented in the following order: Literary Narrative, Social Sciences, Humanities, and Natural Sciences.

- Each passage is followed by 10 multiple-choice questions that assess your comprehension of the text. Questions will require you to identify the main idea, make inferences, analyze the author's tone or purpose, and evaluate arguments or evidence.

- You can expect to see three types of Reading questions: Key Ideas and Details, Craft and Structure, and Integration of Knowledge and Ideas.

- Because passages included in the Reading section of the ACT exam are meant to match the complexity of texts you'll see in your first year of college coursework, the prospect of answering 40 multiple-choice questions about four reading passages in 35 minutes can seem daunting. As you go through this part of the book, we'll cover strategies for active reading, expanding your vocabulary, and using the structure of a text to locate important information.

CHAPTER

**Key Concepts in
Reading Comprehension**

KEY CONCEPTS IN READING COMPREHENSION

OVERVIEW

**Understanding the ACT®
Reading Section**

**ACT® Reading Question
Types (with Practice!)**

**Building Vocabulary to
Increase Comprehension**

**Test Yourself:
Reading Comprehension**

Summing It Up

On the ACT Reading test, you'll be presented with
passages and questions that test your ability to understand what you read. The questions examine not only
how well you comprehend what you read on the surface
but also how well you can interpret a given passage's
meaning and the author's intent. In this chapter, we'll
discuss key skills related to reading comprehension and
reading actively based on the questions you are given.
We'll also spend some time discussing how to expand
your vocabulary for this and other sections of the ACT.
This chapter covers nine different categories of common reading comprehension questions, all of which are
likely to show up on your ACT Reading test.

UNDERSTANDING THE ACT® READING SECTION

As we outlined in the last chapter, the Reading test covers four passages, each with 10 questions. The passages are taken from Prose Fiction/Literary Narrative, Social Sciences, Humanities, and Natural Sciences. On your exam, one of these readings will be split into two related passages. Additionally, there are three categories of Reading questions: Key Ideas and Details (KID), Craft and Structure (CS), and Integration of Knowledge and Ideas (IKI). The first two types are the most prevalent on the test, and KID questions cover a range of different question forms (main idea, inference, details, etc.).

You only have 35 minutes to complete all 40 questions, all of which depend on the information in the passages, so reading actively and deploying the strategies we discuss in Chapter 18 will be critical to your success. In this chapter, we'll focus on the actual reading skills you'll need to succeed. In Chapter 18, we'll teach you how to deploy those skills using strategies that help you manage your limited time to maximize your score.

Here is an excerpt of a reading passage and an example question that reflects what you're likely to find on the ACT. Since we haven't provided you with an explanation of the answer, consider this your first practice question. What would be your justification for the indicated correct answer, and how might you arrive at it if you weren't sure?

> **EXAMPLE**

SOCIAL SCIENCES: The following passage is taken from a sociology journal.

In the US, enduring customs around weddings include purchasing an engagement ring, tossing the bouquet, cutting the cake as a couple, having a first dance, or even making sure you have "something old, something new, something borrowed, and something blue" for good luck. Outside the US, there are myriad other cultural wedding traditions. One common type involves rituals to ward off evil
5   spirits. In Germany, ahead of a wedding, guests will throw porcelain dishes on the ground to scare off spirits during what's called a "Polterabend." In Norway, brides believe that sporting elaborate gold and silver crowns with tinkling accessories and reflective charms does the trick. Armenian couples place lavash flatbread on their shoulders to keep the spirits at bay. Meanwhile in Scotland, newlyweds are covered in molasses, feathers, grass, or anything else that's messy to make them less attractive to
10 nefarious forces. It's also said that if an Irish bride wants to avoid being kidnapped by evil faeries, she must keep one foot on the dance floor during her entire first dance.

1. From this passage, it can be reasonably inferred that:

   A. Norwegians are more traditional about weddings than Americans are.

   B. numerous world cultures have traditionally believed in evil spirits.

   C. the most common reason for observing a wedding tradition involves bringing the couple good luck.

   D. wedding traditions are outdated.

Reading Passages on the ACT

Passages on the ACT Reading test typically follow one of three writing modes.

NARRATIVE

The purpose of the text is to tell a story, often by narrating an experience. It may focus on providing a play-by-play of how certain actions took place; describing an object, place, person, or time period in detail; relaying information about events that have already occurred; or some combination of all three. This is by far most common in the Literary Narrative/Prose Fiction passage, but could come up elsewhere too (such as a passage in which someone narrates an experiment for Social Sciences or Natural Sciences).

INFORMATIVE/EXPLANATORY

The purpose of the text is to explain a concept or inform the reader on a topic. It may focus on explaining key details of a concept or event, defining terms, or providing the reader with information. Passages that tend to summarize or provide overviews are most often of this type.

ARGUMENTATIVE

The purpose of the text is to make an argument. The author might focus on making a specific argument, persuading the reader to agree with their point of view, or convincing the reader to consider their analysis sound. The author will often provide claims, address counterclaims, and support their argument with examples and analysis.

Since the focus of this book is familiarizing you with the ACT, we've made every effort to replicate the formatting of reading passages as they appear on the official test. However, since test makers often change their approach from year to year, be aware that the reading passages on your exam day may look slightly different than how they are presented here. If this is the case, don't worry! The key to preparing for a reading test is recognizing how to address certain question types when they come up and learning to pull necessary information from a given reading passage. By practicing with this book, you will be well on your way to tackling any reading passage that might come up on the ACT, no matter how it is formatted.

Reading Question Categories on the ACT

The questions that follow your passages are multiple-choice with four answer choices each. There are 10 questions per reading passage or passage set. As a reminder, these questions will fall into one of three categories.

KEY IDEAS AND DETAILS (55–60% OF QUESTIONS)

You'll be asked to identify key ideas and themes; summarize information; understand sequential, comparative, and cause-and-effect relationships; make logical inferences; and draw conclusions.

CRAFT AND STRUCTURE (25–30% OF QUESTIONS)

You'll be asked to analyze the organization and structure of a passage; pinpoint an author's perspective and purpose for writing; determine the meanings of certain words and phrases; rhetorically analyze the author's diction, syntax, and use of figurative language; and analyze characters' points of view.

INTEGRATION OF KNOWLEDGE AND IDEAS (13–18% OF QUESTIONS)

You'll be asked to break down an author's argument and identify key claims; evaluate the validity of both reasoning and evidence used in a text; distinguish between opinion and fact; and use evidence to compare and contrast different but topically related texts.

One thing you'll notice as you work through this chapter is that certain types of skills, like identifying supporting details or making inferences, may pop up in questions from any one of these categories, though some are more likely than others. Therefore, while it is useful to know what these categories are, and it may even sometimes be helpful to pinpoint which kind of question you're looking at, your study time is usually better served breaking down reading comprehension into explicit skills that you can practice, as we do later in this chapter. Recognize the question categories by which you'll be evaluated, certainly, but remember that each category usually requires you to use a combination of reading skills simultaneously.

ACT® READING QUESTION TYPES (WITH PRACTICE!)

This section covers the nine most common types of questions that come up on reading exams. We have separated them into various study categories below but, as mentioned, certain question types will map more often to certain ACT question categories than others. We've identified the correspondence between question type and the ACT question category in which it is most likely to appear using the ACT's acronyms for each question type:

- Key Ideas & Details: KID
- Craft & Structure: CS
- Integration of Knowledge & Ideas: IKI

Common Question Types by ACT® Category

The most common types of reading exam questions address test takers' reading abilities along nine categories.

1 **Main Idea Questions (KID):** These questions test the reader's ability to identify the main idea of a text, including central themes or arguments and an author's overall purpose, as well as the ability to summarize either.

2 **Supporting Detail Questions (KID):** These questions test the reader's comprehension of supporting details in the passage and the ability to identify contextual information related to those details through effective reading.

3 **Inference Questions (KID):** These questions test the reader's ability to draw logical inferences and conclusions from ideas and details presented in the passage.

4 **Author and Passage Purpose Questions (CS):** These questions assess a reader's ability to determine the reasoning behind why a passage was written, thus indicating not only what a passage or paragraph is about but why it is presented in a particular way.

5 **Vocabulary Questions (CS):** These questions test a reader's word comprehension and the ability to define vocabulary words or phrases based on the context in which they are used within a passage or sentence.

6 **Tone, Style, and Language Use Questions (CS):** These questions test the reader's ability to identify the author's tone, style, and use of language to accomplish an explicit purpose, as well as other rhetorical choices they make including word choice, writing mode, and structure of claims and counterclaims.

7 **Organization and Logic Questions (CS):** These questions test the reader's ability to identify and evaluate how a passage's organization and logic help an author meet their purpose, including determining how a passage is structured and why.

8 **Opinion and Argument Questions (IKI):** These questions ask readers to evaluate the rhetorical choices authors make to express opinions and arguments, including how that rhetoric relates to an author's point of view and mode of writing, as well as their ability to support claims and counterclaims.

9 **Synthesis Questions (IKI):** These questions ask readers to synthesize information between two passages, including recognizing the relationship between two texts and where two authors converge and contrast in their claims. Additionally, a reader may need to summarize both individual texts and their combined impact or message.

In the sections that follow, we'll discuss each of these question types in terms of their most commonly associated ACT question categories, offer tips on how to address the different questions, and give you a chance to practice your skills with shortened excerpts from ACT passages. At the end of this section, you'll find a graphic model demonstrating how multiple question types relate to details from a single informational passage.

Key Idea and Detail Questions

Key Idea and Detail questions represent the majority of questions on the ACT Reading test, accounting for more than half of the questions. In each passage, you can expect to see 4–8 KID questions. For the 20+ questions throughout the section, you'll be expected to complete a variety of tasks. You'll need to determine main ideas and themes, summarize details and relationships from the passage, and make strong logical inferences. All of these tasks require you to understand the key elements of a passage and find information (in the reading) to support your answers. The information you'll need to find can vary significantly, but KID questions will always focus exclusively on what the passage says and, because of that, what can be understood after reading.

Main Idea Questions

The main idea of a passage is the primary point the text is trying to convey to readers. In argumentative writing, it will be the author's main opinion or argument. You can think of the main idea as the overall message an author is trying to send by writing a passage. Often, the quickest way to identify the main point is to read the first and last sentences of the first and last paragraphs of a passage. Otherwise, the main point should be evident after you complete your reading.

> ## Questions to Ask Yourself: Main Idea
>
> - What is the author telling me?
> - What does the author want me to take away from the passage?
> - What would be a good title for this passage?
> - Why did the author write this passage?
> - If I had to summarize this passage in one sentence, what would it be?

Main idea questions will sometimes be explicit, asking "What is the main idea of this passage?" Others involve identifying the passage's overall purpose or the purpose of a paragraph (or multiple paragraphs). No matter the approach, you can be prepared for any main idea question if you summarize the most important "takeaway" from the passage whenever you finish reading. Try and do so in a single statement, such as by completing sentences like "This passage was about _____." or "The author wants the reader to know that _____." Having this main idea in mind should make it easier to identify correct answers to both main idea questions and those that are related to them, such as supporting detail questions and questions about organization and logic.

 FYI -

Even if a test question doesn't use the words "main idea," it might still be asking for the main idea. If you have identified the main idea for yourself, then you shouldn't be caught off guard, no matter how the question is phrased.

Addressing Main Idea Questions

One of the fastest ways to eliminate incorrect answers to main idea questions is by looking for choices that are either too specific or too general. To demonstrate, let's say you read a passage, and when you finish, you mentally summarize the main idea as follows: "This passage was about how squid develop over the course of their entire life." Then, you are faced with the following common type of main idea question.

EXAMPLE

1. Which of the following best summarizes the main idea of the passage?

   A. The mating habits of squid

   B. The life cycle of squid

   C. Animals of the deep ocean

   D. The evolutionary biology of squid

Summaries of the main idea should properly encompass the scope of an entire passage. In this case, "the life cycle of squid" does the trick. If you've already identified the main idea after reading a passage, the correct answer should hopefully stand out the second you read it. If it doesn't, remember to check for answers that are too vague or too specific. For instance, "squid mating habits" (choice A) relate to the life cycle of squid and may even have been addressed in part of the passage; however, this choice represents only a detail and is too specific to address the main idea you identified, which included the stages of a squid's entire life. Meanwhile, "animals of the deep ocean" (choice C) is far too vague to summarize a passage that focuses on squid specifically.

Once you have eliminated options that are too specific or vague, the remaining incorrect option(s) will usually address something that either wasn't mentioned in the passage or that is slightly off topic from the passage. In this case, the evolutionary biology of squid (choice D) is related to the main idea you identified, but not directly so, since the evolution of a species is different than its life cycle. That distractor may be trying to capitalize on a reader's association between those two topics. This leaves you with only one choice.

Practice Set 1: Main Idea

Directions: Read the passage below and then answer the main idea question that follows. After you've selected your answer, read the answer explanation to check yourself.

NATURAL SCIENCES: The following is adapted from a textbook for pre-med students.

Selective serotonin reuptake inhibitors, or SSRIs, are commonly known simply as "antidepressants," though they are not the only kind of antidepressant that exists. Compared with other antidepressants, SSRIs are more commonly prescribed because they tend to cause fewer overall side effects in the general population. Most people who take SSRIs do so as treatment for depression, though others may do so in combination with forms of talk therapy related to generalized anxiety disorder, post-traumatic stress disorder (PTSD), obsessive-compulsive disorder (OCD), or other mental health afflictions.

Serotonin is a neurotransmitter found in serum and blood platelets. Common thinking around serotonin is that it's a "good mood" chemical that plays a vital role in regulating emotions, focus, and sleep—if you're feeling calm, happy, or at ease, it's probably because your serotonin levels are stable. In people with depression or other mental health concerns, it can be difficult to keep serotonin levels stable. When coupled with the fact that mental health disorders can also affect hormones, other neurotransmitters, and the body's physical sensations, it's

clear why a medication that can help regulate serotonin would be beneficial. This is where SSRIs come in.

SSRIs work by ensuring the brain has enough serotonin even in individuals who have trouble keeping levels stable. According to the United Kingdom National Health Service (NHS), "After carrying a message, serotonin is usually reabsorbed by the nerve cells (known as 'reuptake'). SSRIs work by blocking ('inhibiting') reuptake, meaning more serotonin is available to pass further messages between nearby nerve cells." This explains the "R" and "I" in the term SSRIs; these types of drugs are reuptake inhibitors. Since there is less serotonin reuptake, more serotonin sticks around, making it easier to combat issues caused by decreased serotonin. While low serotonin isn't necessarily the cause of all mental health concerns treated by SSRIs, studies show that increasing serotonin levels is a positive therapeutic intervention for many. Though SSRIs aren't without their side effects, which the NHS notes include gastrointestinal issues, feelings of dizziness or blurred vision, and a suite of side effects related to reproductive wellness, for many who suffer from mental health struggles, the benefits of this type of therapy outweigh potential side effects.

Adapted from UK National Health Service, 2021. "Overview - SSRI Antidepressants." *NHS*. February 15, 2021. https://www.nhs.uk/mental-health/talking-therapies-medicine-treatments/medicines-and-psychiatry/ssri-antidepressants/overview/.

1. The main idea of this passage is that SSRIs:

   A. are safe for most individuals to take daily.

   B. work by inhibiting serotonin reuptake, thereby helping the brain retain more serotonin.

   C. produce numerous side effects, including gastrointestinal issues and dizziness.

   D. can be used to treat OCD, PTSD, and anxiety as well as depression.

Answer

1. **The correct answer is B.** This passage is focused on how SSRIs work, so you need only identify which response concerns how SSRIs work.

Supporting Detail Questions

Supporting details, or supporting ideas, are pieces of information that help the reader understand the author's main idea or argument. Generally, they offer background or necessary context. These sentences might provide examples, facts, statistics, quotations, related stories, descriptions, or other information to support the main idea and purpose of a passage.

Quite often, questions about supporting details won't look like reading questions at all. Remember, though, these questions are on a reading exam, so they will never ask about anything you can't answer using the details of the reading passage(s) alone. Don't be thrown off if you get a question that looks like it's from history, science, math, or any other subject besides reading. Instead, assume the question is asking about something you can answer by finding the relevant sentence(s) in the passage.

Supporting detail questions will look wildly different depending on the topic of the reading passage; in other words, don't expect to see something like "What are the supporting details in this passage?" Instead, detail questions will ask you about the passage's content. For example, if the passage is informing you about different cultural theories prominent in the field of sociology, a detail question might ask, "According to the passage, tenets of postcolonial theory derive from:" Or "In this passage, the author compares structuralist theories of power to…" It's your job to scan

Questions to Ask Yourself: Supporting Details

- What information does the author provide?

- How is that information used to support and explain the main idea and purpose?

- Are there any important names, concepts, or words repeated multiple times?

- How do smaller details in the passage add up to a bigger picture?

- What claims and counterclaims does the author make to support their main argument?

back through the passage and choose the right answer based on the details provided. Incorrect choices can offer statements that capitalize on similarities to the passage's description but will, in some way, misrepresent details.

Practice Set 2: Supporting Details

Directions: Read the passage below and then answer the three supporting detail questions that follow. After you've selected each answer, read the answer explanations to check yourself.

HUMANITIES: The following passage is taken from a compendium on Slavic folklore.

There are few figures from Slavic folklore considered as formidable or intriguing as Baba Yaga. Loosely translated, her name is said to mean something like
5 "Grandmother Witch," though this only partially encompasses her being. Baba Yaga is also a cannibal, goddess figure, fairy godmother, trickster, and villain, popping up in stories to terrorize he-
10 roes only to inadvertently provide them with the skills or items they require to complete their journey. Perhaps most importantly, Baba Yaga is a figure who symbolizes transformation, affording her
15 further associations with birth, death, and transitional life phases like puberty.

There are numerous telltale characteristics that let you know Baba Yaga is in a story, even when she is not mentioned
20 by name. For one, she lives in a hut in the woods that rests on chicken legs, which act like moveable stilts to hold the hut aloft. Because the house can move around the forest and turn itself in any
25 direction, Baba Yaga is thought to always potentially be around the corner. This status gives her a frightening mystique. Her hut is not her only means of transport, however, as she can also fly around
30 using a mortar and pestle. Because she

is associated with fertility, the mortar and pestle are said to symbolize her male and female sides. When traveling this way, she uses a broom to sweep away the
35 tracks left behind; some scholars believe this is partially why we associate brooms with witches today. The primary way she threatens people is by kidnapping them and planning to eat them, though in most
40 stories, they escape before she can feast.

1. According to the passage, Baba Yaga can be described as:

   A. a vampire of western European origins.

   B. a trickster figure from Slavic culture.

   C. a young goddess embodying fertility and spring in European folklore.

   D. a historical figure accused of witchcraft in medieval Europe.

2. According to the passage, Baba Yaga travels by:

   F. flying broomstick.

   G. mortar and pestle.

   H. teleportation.

   J. floating.

3. According to the passage, Slavic folklore associates Baba Yaga with:

   A. a hero's doomed journey.

   B. depictions of witches in popular culture.

   C. periods of transition.

   D. successful marriages.

Answers

1. **The correct answer is B.** According to the first paragraph of the passage, Baba Yaga fulfills many diverse roles within Slavic folklore. While the incorrect choices reference some of these terms and phrases, they misrepresent the specific details associated with those terms or invent relationships neither explicit nor implied. No mention is made of vampires (choice A), and though an argument could be made because of the term *cannibal*, western Europe is not mentioned as an origin for Baba Yaga. Choices C and D distort the details of the passage, misrepresenting Baba Yaga's status as goddess and witch in Slavic folklore. Only choice B accurately represents the passage.

2. **The correct answer is G.** As Paragraph 2 states, in addition to having a moving hut that walks on chicken feet, "[Baba Yaga] can also fly around using a mortar and pestle" (29–30).

3. **The correct answer is C.** At the end of the first paragraph, it is stated that "Baba Yaga is a figure who symbolizes transformation" (lines 13–14). Before that point, the passage describes Baba Yaga's inclusion in stories of heroes (choice A); however, it is stated that she ultimately assists the heroes in their quests, intentionally or not. While Paragraph 2 mentions that Baba Yaga's means of transportation might have influenced modern conceptions of witches (choice B), such a conclusion derives from contemporary perspectives rather than the stories from Slavic folklore. The passage never mentions Baba Yaga being associated with marriage (choice D).

Inference Questions

You make an inference when you reach a conclusion based on information available in the passage. Generally, the answer won't be stated directly in the passage. Instead, you are looking for a reasonable conclusion that could be drawn from the information given. For instance, if the passage mentioned that field geologists must often spend long periods of time camping alone or in small groups, you could infer that camping skills are *most likely* a job requirement for field geologists even if the passage doesn't say so directly. You don't have enough information to know if this is definitely the case, but it's a logical conclusion you could draw from what you read.

Inference questions are therefore asking you to "do something" with what you've just read. For example, you might be asked to make a prediction about what happens next. Similarly, you may also be asked to give an interpretation of what you've read or to identify a situation that is most like the one described in the passage. Additionally, questions might ask you to infer the author's attitude or why characters within a narrative make the choices they make.

Questions to Ask Yourself: Making Inferences

- What do I know and what can I predict?

- How are ideas in the passage(s) alike and different?

- What do I know about the characters present in the story and how they feel about the situation presented?

- What am I supposed to "get" that the author isn't saying directly?

- What might I understand to be true or false after reading this passage?

Inference questions will sometimes be blunt and ask you "From the passage, you can reasonably infer that…" But these questions might also ask you things like "With which of these statements would the author of this passage most likely agree?" or "Based on this passage, what is the protagonist likely to do next?" They may also resemble supporting detail questions, such as by asking you to identify which statement *might* be true in light of another detail from the passage. All of these questions are asking you to infer since the answer is not stated directly in the passage—you can only make a logical prediction. Of all the reading comprehension abilities the ACT tests, this one relies the most on your critical thinking skills. You may have to think a little to find your answer, but remember that at their core, inference questions are asking you what you can figure out from the information you've been given. You shouldn't have to work too hard to make your answer fit.

Practice Set 3: Inferences

Directions: Read the passage below and then answer the three inference questions that follow. After you've selected each answer, read the answer explanations to check yourself.

SOCIAL SCIENCES: The following is taken from a cultural sociology journal.

Essentially all children are naturally endowed with curiosity, a sense of wonder about the world, and a need for nurturing and play. Similarly, almost all
5 children around the world greet the first day of school with a mix of anticipation and trepidation. To ease these concerns and make the transition to schooling a little easier, different countries engage in
10 a panoply of back-to-school traditions.

If you were a 6-year-old headed to your first day of school in Germany, you would likely do so with a giant paper cone in tow. These cones, called *Kinder-*
15 *tüte*, are fun-filled goodie bags containing candy, toys, school supplies, and anything else a child might need to have a joyful first day. Even though the treats are nice, the Kindertüte are more about
20 celebrating and communicating to children that they are entering a new stage of life. Japanese parents do something similar, gifting their children a new backpack and sometimes a new desk to use at
25 home to mark the first day of school. As in Germany, these presents are intended to help the child understand that they are embarking on a new chapter in their development.
30 Many cultures mark the first day of school with a celebration. In Kazakhstan, children start school at the age of 7.

Their first day is called Tyl Ishtar, which means "Initiation into Education," and
35 to celebrate it, parents will invite family and friends to a giant feast at their home. During this feast, the school-bound child is expected to recite the names of their grandfathers going back seven generations
40 to honor their ancestry. Other first-day celebrations are more about giving children an opportunity to get to know one another. In Saudi Arabia, the first few days of school contain no lessons, instead
45 giving children a chance to share food and play games. In parts of Indonesia, the first day is treated as an orientation to help children intentionally develop friendships meaningful enough to last through their
50 schooling years.

1. From this passage, it can reasonably be inferred that:

   A. children do not start school until after age 7 in Japan.

   B. there are no back-to-school traditions in the United States.

   C. Japanese and German children are culturally considered more mature once they start school.

   D. children in Japan are commonly homeschooled.

2. It can reasonably be inferred from the final paragraph (lines 30–50) that:

    F. children's friendships aren't considered meaningful in Kazakhstan.

    G. children's friendships aren't considered meaningful in Indonesia.

    H. families in Kazakhstan have traditionally followed a patriarchal structure.

    J. families in Indonesia have traditionally followed a matriarchal structure.

3. The passage most strongly suggests that:

    A. around the world, children do not always start school at the same age.

    B. around the world, children always start school at the same age.

    C. German families take the first day of school more seriously than families in other countries do.

    D. Indonesian students have more respect for their teachers than students in other places do.

Answers

1. **The correct answer is C.** Paragraph 2 mentions how both Germany and Japan consider the start of school an important life-stage transition for children. Consequently, it would be logical to infer that the start of school is considered an advancement in a child's maturity in these cultures.

2. **The correct answer is H.** On the first day of school, children in Kazakhstan are expected to honor their ancestors by reciting the names of their grandfathers going back seven generations. Since they are expected to recite the names of grand*fathers*, we can infer that families in Kazakhstan have traditionally followed a patriarchal structure.

3. **The correct answer is A.** In different parts of the passage, you are told that German children start school at 6 while children in Kazakhstan start at 7. Therefore, you can infer that around the world, children do *not* always start school at the same age.

Craft and Structure Questions

Craft and Structure questions represent the second largest category of questions on the ACT Reading test. They account for about 10–15 questions in the section and will likely represent 2–4 questions for each passage. While Key Idea and Detail questions focus on what's in a passage, Craft and Structure questions focus on the reasons behind how a passage is written, asking you to think about why an author made certain decisions and how those choices support the author's purpose.

Generally, you'll be asked to identify the purpose of a passage or paragraph, define words based on their context, think about an author's language and rhetorical choices, and discuss a text's structure.

Author and Passage Purpose Questions

One common subset of main idea questions specifically addresses the author's purpose for writing the text. In ACT Reading, these questions will likely fall under the Craft and Structure category. In short, the author's purpose is the reason the author has written the passage and thus made certain choices. While the main idea is about *what* is in the passage—the information the author wants you to know—the purpose is about *how* the author is presenting that information and *why* they've chosen to express it how they did. For the latter, the ACT will include a verb before the summary statements, suggesting the question is asking about what action the author is trying to achieve rather than what they're trying to say.

Questions that deal with the author's purpose are easy to spot because they usually contain the word *purpose*. The question might appear as "The author's main purpose in this passage is to…" and ask you to choose the answer that best matches how the author communicates the passage's main idea. An author's purpose can generally be expressed as a *to* + verb expression, with common purposes being to inform, explain, or argue. The following table provides a list of verbs commonly used to describe an author's purpose.

Questions to Ask Yourself: Author's Purpose

- Why did the author write the information they did in the way they did?

- What verbs would I use to describe what the author is doing in this passage?

- Is the author trying to convince me to believe something?

- Is the author making an argument for or against a particular idea or course of action?

- Is the author sticking to factual information?

- Is the author using any sources or pointing to any expert information to appeal to credibility or provide evidence?

- Is this passage written for a particular audience?

- Is the author telling me a story?

- Why has the author chosen the words they used or phrased things the way they did?

COMMON VERBS TO DESCRIBE AN AUTHOR'S PURPOSE

Purpose Verbs	In a reading passage, this looks like the author…
inform educate teach	providing information to educate a reader on a topic, often (but not always) while gesturing to credible support.
persuade argue convince	convincing the reader to agree with an opinion or point of view.
amuse entertain	entertaining the reader with an interesting, inventive, or humorous topic.
compare contrast	showing the similarities or differences between ideas or known facts.
describe	using the five senses or other descriptive details to portray the characteristics or qualities of a topic.
explain (information) clarify break down	making an idea or issue clearer through description, details, or a breakdown of how something works or occurred.
discuss examine consider	examining different angles or perspectives of a topic or argument.

Purpose Verbs	In a reading passage, this looks like the author…
analyze evaluate assess	conducting a detailed analysis of numerous facts, quantities, or perspectives impacting an issue or topic, most often using credible support.
critique criticize	expressing disapproval for a topic, issue, or the perspective of another person.
praise celebrate	expressing approval for a topic, issue, or the perspective of another person.
tell narrate explain (as a story)	using a narrative (storytelling) approach to entertain, relay ideas, or explain a topic using figurative details.
quantify	employing statistics, facts, and other quantifiable data to "place a number" on something that is otherwise a concept.
summarize	providing a summary of a topic.

As with main idea questions, state for yourself what the author's purpose is whenever you finish reading a passage. Whatever verb you choose to describe the author's purpose (or a synonym for it) is likely to pop up in your answer options later.

To illustrate, let's say you finish reading a passage and decide that the author's purpose was to compare an alligator's typical diet with a crocodile's typical diet. Consequently, you know you're looking for an answer that includes the word *compare* or a synonym for it. You are then given the following question:

> **EXAMPLE**
>
> 1. The primary purpose of the passage is to:
>   A. praise the historical conservation efforts of Australian regional governments in preserving saltwater crocodiles.
>   B. criticize the US Department of Fish and Wildlife for their response to poachers in the Florida Everglades.
>   C. contrast the dietary requirements of alligators and crocodiles as related to their habitats.
>   D. illustrate the evolutionary trajectory of large reptiles' diets.

If you have already determined that the author's purpose is to compare, you will easily spot that choice C is the correct answer, since *contrast* is used as a synonym for *compare* when discussing an author's purpose. Sometimes, two answers may seem plausible. For instance, you might convince yourself that such a comparison illustrates (choice D) the animals' diets. However, always choose the answer that *best* expresses the author's purpose. *Contrast* is a more specific description of the author's purpose, which you determined was to compare the diets of two similar but different species.

Now we'll revisit a passage from earlier in this chapter. However, instead of looking at a main idea question, this time we'll look at the passage for the author's purpose.

 TIP

If a question asks about the author's purpose, focus on the active verbs in the answer choices. Sometimes, you can automatically eliminate some incorrect choices by noting what the passage *didn't* do.

Practice Set 4: Purpose

Directions: Read the passage below and then answer the two purpose questions that follow. After you've selected each answer, read the answer explanations to check yourself.

NATURAL SCIENCES: The following is adapted from a textbook for pre-med students.

Selective serotonin reuptake inhibitors, or SSRIs, are commonly known simply as "antidepressants," though they are not the only kind of antidepressant that
5 exists. Compared with other antidepressants, SSRIs are more commonly prescribed because they tend to cause fewer overall side effects in the general population. Most people who take SSRIs do so as
10 treatment for depression, though others may do so in combination with forms of talk therapy related to generalized anxiety disorder, post-traumatic stress disorder (PTSD), obsessive-compulsive
15 disorder (OCD), or other mental health afflictions.

Serotonin is a neurotransmitter found in serum and blood platelets. Common thinking around serotonin is that
20 it's a "good mood" chemical that plays a vital role in regulating emotions, focus, and sleep—if you're feeling calm, happy, or at ease, it's probably because your serotonin levels are stable. In people with de-
25 pression or other mental health concerns, it can be difficult to keep serotonin levels stable. When coupled with the fact that mental health disorders can also affect hormones, other neurotransmitters, and
30 the body's physical sensations, it's clear why a medication that can help regulate

serotonin would be beneficial. This is where SSRIs come in.

SSRIs work by ensuring the brain has
35 enough serotonin even in individuals who have trouble keeping levels stable. According to the United Kingdom National Health Service (NHS), "After carrying a message, serotonin is usually reabsorbed
40 by the nerve cells (known as 'reuptake'). SSRIs work by blocking ('inhibiting') reuptake, meaning more serotonin is available to pass further messages between nearby nerve cells." This explains the "R" and "I"
45 in the term SSRIs; these types of drugs are reuptake inhibitors. Since there is less serotonin reuptake, more serotonin sticks around, making it easier to combat issues caused by decreased serotonin. While low
50 serotonin isn't necessarily the cause of all mental health concerns treated by SSRIs, studies show that increasing serotonin levels is a positive therapeutic intervention for many. Though SSRIs aren't without their
55 side effects, which the NHS notes include gastrointestinal issues, feelings of dizziness or blurred vision, and a suite of side effects related to reproductive wellness, for many who suffer from mental health struggles,
60 the benefits of this type of therapy outweigh potential side effects.

Adapted from UK National Health Service, 2021. "Overview - SSRI Antidepressants." *NHS.* February 15, 2021. https://www.nhs.uk/mental-health/talking-therapies-medicine-treatments/medicines-and-psychiatry/ssri-antidepressants/overview/.

1. The primary purpose of this passage is to:

   A. narrate an experience of taking SSRIs.

   B. praise SSRIs for their effectiveness.

   C. educate the reader about what SSRIs are and how they work.

   D. summarize scientific studies about the efficacy of SSRIs.

2. The author's purpose in the Paragraph 2 (lines 17–33) is to:

   F. debate the validity of SSRI research and determine if they are in fact safe.

   G. define *serotonin* and explain the serotonin reuptake process in order to introduce SSRIs.

   H. consider new ways that doctors might use SSRIs to make them even more effective for patients.

   J. explain what SSRIs are and how they function in therapeutic settings.

Answers

1. **The correct answer is C.** The author's purpose in this passage is to educate the reader about what SSRIs are and how they work. Note how the answer focuses not only on what the author is discussing but also how they're discussing it—with the desire to "educate."

2. **The correct answer is G.** In this question, you must consider the purpose of a particular paragraph. In this case, the author's purpose in the second paragraph is to define *serotonin* and explain the serotonin reuptake process. They do so in order to introduce SSRIs and explain how they help with mental health issues that relate to low serotonin, which is the topic of the third paragraph.

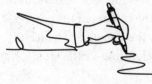

NOTES

Vocabulary Questions

When vocabulary questions come up after passages, you usually won't have to identify word definitions directly, as is common on other vocabulary tests. Instead, you'll be asked to identify a synonym for a word or phrase from the passage that matches the context in which it was used. Remember that a synonym is a word with the same meaning. You must consider how the word is used in the passage and then choose the answer that most nearly matches that same contextual meaning.

Questions to Ask Yourself: Vocabulary

- What does this word mean?

- If I don't know this word, can I figure out its definition based on what the passage tells me?

- Which of these answer options means the same thing or something close?

- Can I eliminate answer options that I know the meaning of and which I know are incorrect answers?

Sometimes, a question or answer option will present you with a short phrase instead of a single word, so don't be thrown off if you see this. For instance, "in a little bit" is a perfectly suitable synonym for *soon*, even if one is a phrase and the other a word. Remember, too, that building vocabulary and studying word parts can help you tackle unknown words when you encounter them. Knowing word parts can also help you eliminate answer choices that are less likely to be correct (see the "Building Vocabulary to Increase Comprehension" section later in this chapter).

When you encounter a vocabulary question, you will be provided with the word or phrase and the line number of the passage in which the indicated language can be found. Because the passage is seeking your understanding of that word or phrase in the context of the passage, you will want to read not only the sentence in which the word occurs but also a little before and a little after.

 ALERT -

Vocabulary-in-context questions don't always ask for the most common meaning of a word. Instead of choosing the most common definition, look for the meaning that best fits the context in which the word was used in the passage.

Practice Set 5: Vocabulary

Directions: Read the passage below and then answer the three vocabulary questions that follow. After you've selected each answer, read the answer explanations to check yourself.

NATURAL SCIENCES: The following passage is taken from a biology magazine.

The biggest of all species within the genus *Bathynomus* is the giant isopod, or *B. giganteus*. They may look like bugs, but giant isopods are not ocean insects.

5 Rather, like crabs and shrimp, they're crustaceans. You might not expect a somewhat scary looking bottom dweller crustacean to get much love, but it seems the internet at large has given the giant

10 isopod a new reputation. Thanks to the popularity of digital forms of communication like memes, the giant isopod has become recognizable to a wider swath of the general population, including a

15 dedicated subset of isopod fans who insist these little guys are quite cute.

Giant isopods truly are sizable; their average length is between 7.5 and 14.2 inches, but scientists have found speci-

20 mens as long as 2.5 feet! Their outer shells are usually brown or a pale lilac. Some researchers speculate that isopods evolved to be so massive to withstand the ocean's immense pressure. These carnivorous

25 scavengers typically gorge themselves on the corpses of dead animals that fall to the ocean floor but are also adapted to forgo eating for long periods of time. One interesting adaptation isopods share with

30 felines is what's called a tapeum, meaning a reflective layer toward the back of

the eye that increases their ability to see in the dark. However, this helps giant isopods only so much—they have weak eyesight

35 and often must depend on their antennae to augment their navigational abilities.

1. As used in line 15, the word *subset* most nearly means:

   A. team.

   B. portion.

   C. neighborhood.

   D. company.

2. When the author says that giant isopods "typically gorge themselves" (line 25), they mean that:

   F. certain subspecies of giant isopod are prone to overeating.

   G. most giant isopods can go a long time without eating.

   H. generally, giant isopods tend to eat a lot at once.

   J. generally, giant isopods tend to take a long time to digest their food.

3. As used in line 36, the word *augment* most nearly means:

   A. agree with.

   B. negate.

   C. camouflage.

   D. amplify.

Answers

1. **The correct answer is B.** In Paragraph 1, the term *subset* is used to refer to a portion of people from within a larger group (fans of giant isopods).

2. **The correct answer is H.** In saying that the giant isopods "typically gorge themselves," the author means that generally, giant isopods tend to eat a lot of food at once. The key term here is *gorge*, which means "to completely fill oneself with food or eat in a greedy manner."

3. **The correct answer is D.** In this context, the verb *augment* means "to amplify, strengthen, reinforce, or expand."

Tone, Style, and Language Use Questions

Tone, style, and language use are all related in that they are tools authors use to best fulfill their purpose. Questions on these topics tend to focus especially closely on rhetoric (meaning "the act of writing"), including word choice, style, tone, mood, mode of writing, genre, and use of figurative language. However, note that you may see such terms and references invoked for main idea and detail questions as well. The following sections cover some of the most common topics that tend to come up in questions on style, tone, and language use as related to Craft and Structure questions.

Author's Tone or Mood Questions

The term *tone* describes both an author's attitude toward the topic and the attitude they assume in writing about it. In fictional or literary narratives, questions may instead ask about mood. The concept of mood is

Questions to Ask Yourself: Style, Tone, and Language Use

- How does the author feel about this topic?
- What would I say the genre or style of this passage is?
- What does the author's word choice communicate to the reader about their stance on the topic or their tone?
- What position is the author taking in this passage?
- How does the author use language for comparisons, descriptions, or meaning?
- What sort of nonliteral language exists in the passage to communicate figurative ideas?
- What are the different methods the author uses to make their ideas and point of view clear?

similar to tone, but it relates to the mood the author wishes to convey to a reader. It is generally a combination of the author's tone as well as the word choices they make to describe the plot, characters, and setting. Questions about mood or tone might provide you with a few adjectives and ask you to pick which best describes the passage, or they might ask you to make a conclusion based on the tone. As with the author's purpose, taking a moment to determine the tone or mood of the passage while reading will make it easier to answer direct questions like "What is the author's tone?" If in doubt, eliminate the answer options that seem least correct first.

Point of View Questions

An author's point of view is their position, opinion, belief, or angle regarding a topic. For example, an author might be for or against an idea, or an author might be stating ideas from personal experience. They may also be taking a position or making an argument from a particular perspective. These questions can sometimes look like main idea questions since they also concern the primary argument or idea an author is trying to get across. Therefore, you can use the same techniques you use with main idea questions to address most questions about an author's point of view. Alternatively, in narrative passages, questions about point of view might refer to the narrator's point of view, such as first person vs. third person. A point of view question might ask "What position does the author take in this debate?" or "From whose perspective is this story narrated?" It might also ask you to complete a sentence, such as "We can assume that the author of this passage agrees that . . ."

Figurative Language Questions

An author uses figurative language to draw comparisons, enhance descriptions, or create deeper meaning. In short, the term "figurative language" describes language that is meant to communicate without being taken literally. It often makes a comparison, creates an image, or otherwise highlights a fundamental quality about a being, object, or situation. Questions about figurative language can pop up anywhere, but they are common following literary passages. Here are some common types of figurative language you might encounter.

COMMON TYPES OF FIGURATIVE LANGUAGE & FIGURES OF SPEECH		
Term	**Definition**	**Examples**
Simile	A comparison between two things using *like* or *as*	The lighthouse beacon was **as** bright **as** the sun. My bedroom looks **like** a landfill.
Metaphor	A comparison in which the literal use of a phrase about an object or idea stands in as an analogy for another object or idea; usually uses a form of *is*	My math teacher **is** a monster! Some say I **am** a shark in the courtroom. This restaurant has always **been** a ghost town.
Hyperbole	An overtly exaggerated statement for figurative effect	I'm so hungry that I could **eat a horse**! The **entire galaxy** stops to listen to her stories.
Imagery	Using vivid descriptions to create an image in a reader's mind, often involving adjectives, adverbs, and references to the five senses	The sun's **warm, bright** rays came **bursting** through the window as she **quickly** drew the **heavy velvet** curtain. I **felt goosebumps** as a **biting cold whooshed across my skin**—my **clumsy** brother had left the door open for the **blustering winter wind** to **whip back in**.

COMMON TYPES OF FIGURATIVE LANGUAGE & FIGURES OF SPEECH

Term	Definition	Examples
Irony	When an author says something that is the opposite of what they mean or that involves a contradiction between expectation and reality; in literary texts, it can also be situations that create irony for a character	• A character in a play tells their new friend Morgan that they wish they could speak to their brother, but the audience knows that Morgan is their brother in disguise. • A marriage counselor files for divorce. • A character in a story freezes to death in the desert.
Personification	When an object or animal is given human-like characteristics or abilities	• I'm so tired that my **bed is calling** me. • The **ocean swallowed** the tiny ship whole. • My **cat always flirts** with visitors.
Aphorism	A witty statement or saying that highlights a general truth	• Pride comes before a fall. • Finders keepers, losers weepers. • She's her mother's daughter.
Idiom	A group of words that make sense together because of their association with a common saying	• Getting to my house is a **piece of cake**. • Tim finally **saw the light** about that ugly paint color. • I'm sure you'll find a job with so many skills **under your belt!**
Analogy	A comparison between two things made for the purpose of adding clarity or offering an example; they often use similes, metaphors, or idioms to do so	• Finding a good dentist **is like finding a needle in a haystack.** • This summer **has been a rollercoaster of emotions.** • My puppy **is a wrecking ball,** crashing into everything.

A question about language use might point out one of these figures of speech and ask you about it, or it might point to a sentence and ask you to identify the purpose of the author's use of figurative language.

Practice Set 6: Style, Tone, and Language Use

> **Directions:** Read the passage below and then answer the two questions that follow, which address the author's tone/mood, style, word choice, or use of language. After you've selected each answer, read the answer explanations to check yourself.

LITERARY NARRATIVE: The following excerpt is adapted from a short story by Willa Cather entitled "The Sculptor's Funeral" (1905).

The coffin was got out of its rough box and down on the snowy platform. The townspeople drew back enough to make room for it and then formed a close
5 semicircle about it, looking curiously at the palm leaf which lay across the black cover. No one said anything. The baggage man stood by his truck, waiting to get at the trunks. The engine panted heav-
10 ily, and the fireman dodged in and out among the wheels with his yellow torch and long oilcan, snapping the spindle boxes. The young Bostonian, one of the dead sculptor's pupils who had come with
15 the body, looked about him helplessly. He turned to the banker, the only one of that black, uneasy, stoop-shouldered group who seemed enough of an individual to be addressed.
20 "None of Mr. Merrick's brothers are here?" he asked uncertainly.
The man with the red beard for the first time stepped up and joined the group. "No, they have not come yet; the
25 family is scattered. The body will be taken directly to the house." He stooped and took hold of one of the handles of the coffin.

"Take the long hill road up, Thompson
30 —it will be easier on the horses," called the liveryman as the undertaker snapped the door of the hearse and prepared to mount to the driver's seat.
Laird, the red-bearded lawyer, turned
35 again to the stranger: "We didn't know whether there would be anyone with him or not," he explained. "It's a long walk, so you'd better go up in the hack." He pointed to a single, battered conveyance, but the
40 young man replied stiffly: "Thank you, but I think I will go up with the hearse. If you don't object," turning to the undertaker, "I'll ride with you."
They clambered up over the wheels
45 and drove off in the starlight up the long, white hill toward the town. The lamps in the still village were shining from under the low, snow-burdened roofs; and beyond, on every side, the plains reached out into
50 emptiness, peaceful and wide as the soft sky itself, and wrapped in a tangible, white silence.

1. In the final paragraph (lines 44–52) of the passage, the author's description of the setting primarily emphasizes the:

   A. whimsical nature of the narrator.
   B. excitation for the imminent return of spring.
   C. desolate environment in which the story is set.
   D. somberness of the story.

2. The author states that the family of the sculptor is "scattered" (line 25) in order to imply that they are:

   F. too depressed to complete the task.
   G. in different places far from the town.
   H. mostly dead already.
   J. estranged from the dead sculptor.

Answers

1. **The correct answer is D.** Context clues like "driving up a long, white hill" in starlight," "snow-burdened roofs," and plains that reach "out into emptiness" and are "wrapped in a tangible, white silence" highlight the cold and solemn atmosphere in which this story unfolds.

2. **The correct answer is G.** Saying that the sculptor's family is "scattered" is a figurative way of saying that they are living in different places far from the town.

Organization and Logic Questions

A passage's organization includes how the information in the passage is arranged and whether that arrangement is logical. It is also about the transition between ideas and how smoothly those transitions are executed. An organized passage will follow a logical train of thought, using transitions and topic sentences when moving between ideas to guide the reader and show how all are related to an overall purpose or main idea. Disorganized passages, on the other hand, tend to jump around between topics without providing adequate transitions or integrating new topics into the context of older ones. You can trust that each of the passages you read on the ACT will be well organized, but you should be prepared to answer questions about *how* the author chose to organize the passage. You should also be prepared to identify a reasonable summary of a passage, which usually involves not just recognizing the main idea of the passage but also the sequence and structure through which the author has conveyed their message.

The term *logic* refers to reasoning that occurs in such a way as to lead to valid thinking. It's a rational way of thinking about things. In essence, logical ideas are organized, direct, ordered, and readily accessible to a reader with reasonable knowledge of the topic. By contrast, ideas are illogical if they are disorganized, jumbled, confusing, or unreasonable. All the reading passages you'll see should be logical, understandable, and clear. As with questions about organization, you will be tested less on whether the passage is logical or not and more on what logic it uses to justify its claims or ideas. It's up to you to decipher how each passage is organized, how the author has arranged their ideas, and how the author might logically build on what is already written if they were to do so.

Questions to Ask Yourself: Organization and Logic

- How are the ideas in this passage arranged—are they in order of importance, time, or a different pattern?

- How does the organization of the passage affect its logic?

- If the passage were to continue, what might logically come next?

- If the passage is an excerpt, what might have logically come before it?

- Has the author cited credible sources or otherwise demonstrated the credibility of their research or argument?

- How does the author use (or fail to use) evidence to support claims and counterclaims?

- Does the passage as presented follow a logical train of thought?

Organization and logic questions might ask you to choose how a particular section is organized. Questions might read something like "Which option best describes the organization of lines 6–12?" or "Why does the author begin the third paragraph with the example in line 21?" Questions might also ask you to describe the organizational strategy of an entire passage: "This passage is organized in _____ order." The passage might be presented in order of time (known as chronological or sequential order), in a step-by-step order, in order of importance, in physical order (known as spatial order), or something else. Or, for instance, it may ask you something like "Which of the following events from the passage happened first chronologically?" Still other questions might ask you about hypothetical writing that isn't included, such as "Which of the following would make a logical topic for a hypothetical Paragraph 5?" Or, as we mentioned before, you may be asked about the author's purpose in a particular paragraph as an extension of their overall organization. In each case, you're being asked to identify why the author constructed their passage the way they did, what that organization is, and how they might expand on it, if they were to do so.

Practice Set 7: Organization and Logic

Directions: Read the passage below and then answer the three questions that follow, which address the author's organization and logic. After you've selected each answer, read the answer explanations to check yourself.

HUMANITIES: The following excerpt is taken from a musicology textbook.

Sometimes referred to as the God-mother of Rock n' Roll, Sister Rosetta Tharpe is an example of a Black woman who shaped history but didn't end up as
5 famous as most of her male contemporaries. Born in Cotton Plant, Arkansas, she was the daughter of Willis Atkins and Katie Bell Nubin Atkins, a mandolin-playing singer who was also an evangelist
10 for the Church of God in Christ. As a result of her mother's influence, Tharpe's early musical inspiration came primarily from gospel music. To aid in her mother's efforts, Tharpe began singing and playing
15 the guitar as young as four years old.

By the time Tharpe was six years old, she was performing regularly with her mother and was adept at combining secular music styles with the gospel styles
20 popular in religious music. While she was a gifted singer, it was Tharpe's virtuoso skill on the guitar that from such a young age paved her path to fame. Not only could Tharpe easily find various chords and
25 tones, but she was also able to manipulate the strings to produce individual notes, melodies, and riffs, as well as combine chords unexpectedly to produce new sounds. Very few women played guitar at
30 the time, let alone young Black women, so

Tharpe was something of an anomaly. Her experimentation with the capabilities of the guitar as an instrument proved founda-tional to rock n' roll music as a genre.
35 Over the years, Tharpe gathered new influences from sources like blues and jazz, then integrated aspects of those sounds and styles into her own work, creating a hybrid sound that would set the stage for later de-
40 velopments in rock n' roll and other musical genres. When Tharpe was eventually signed to Decca Records in 1938, it didn't take long for her to become a sensation. To avoid alienating her divergent fan bases, Tharpe
45 would record gospel music for the religious crowd and more up-tempo songs for her growing (and largely white) secular audi-ence. She continued to find success this way for the rest of her career, which ended with
50 her death in 1973.

1. The author uses Paragraph 1 to discuss Sister Rosetta Tharpe's early childhood in order to:

A. begin the exploration of the lifelong role gospel music would play in Tharpe's career.

B. allude to Tharpe's later career by explain-ing her early influence on gospel music.

C. imply the key role experimentation with different genres would play in Tharpe's career.

D. establish context for Tharpe's remarkable musical talent and rapid growth in skill.

2. The author wants to add a fourth paragraph. What would be a logical topic for this hypothetical Paragraph 4?

   F. Distinctive guitar sounds of Sister Rosetta Tharpe's era

   G. How Sister Rosetta Tharpe influenced music before her death

   H. How Sister Rosetta Tharpe continued to influence music after her death

   J. The long-term influence of gospel music on popular music

3. This passage is organized:

   A. to provide step-by-step information.

   B. according to relevance of topic.

   C. in spatial order.

   D. in chronological order.

Answers

1. **The correct answer is D.** With the first paragraph, the author establishes the presence of music in Tharpe's life from a young age and signals, with the last sentence, the continued development of Tharpe's musical ability as discussed in Paragraph 2. This represents a logical progression to establish the trajectory that led Tharpe to be called the "Godmother of Rock n' Roll."

2. **The correct answer is H.** Since Paragraph 3 ends by mentioning Sister Rosetta Tharpe's death in 1973, the most logical next move would be to discuss how she continued to influence music after her death. All the other topics would be better suited to other sections of the passage if they were to be inserted.

3. **The correct answer is D.** Since the passage starts with Sister Rosetta Tharpe's birth and ends with her death, it is organized in chronological order.

Integration of Knowledge and Ideas Questions

Integration of Knowledge and Ideas questions represent a minor category of questions on the ACT Reading section. They account for only 3–5 questions in the section, and for the majority of the tests, they are associated almost exclusively with the paired passage set. These questions ask you to determine fact from opinion, consider multiple authors' claims, and express relationships between different texts.

Opinion and Argument Questions

When an author clarifies their own beliefs, viewpoints, or judgments, they are expressing an opinion. When an author takes a side in a debate, presents a plausible perspective on a researched subject, or tries to convince you to agree with their opinion, they are making an argument. If an author is making an argument, you should be able to identify the argument and how it's organized as well as any support given for that argument, such as related facts or examples. You should also be able to identify any claims the author makes and counterclaims they address.

ALERT -

> A statement being true doesn't necessarily mean it's a correct answer.
> Make sure that the answer choice you mark answers the question that is asked
> and is supported by the passage. Several answer choices might be true,
> but only one will be the answer to the question.

Questions to Ask Yourself: Opinion and Argument

- Is this passage fact or opinion?

- What is the author's opinion and why?

- What is the author's argument?

- What strategies does the author use to convince me to agree with their argument?

- Is the author sticking to their own ideas, or are they supporting their thoughts with outside information or sources?

- From whose perspective is the author speaking and to which intended audience?

- Does the author seem to have any bias that might cloud the logic of their argument?

A question dealing with opinion might take the form "Which of these choices best expresses the author's opinion?" For argument questions, you might be presented with several arguments and asked to consider "Which of these statements best summarizes the author's argument in this passage?"

Practice Set 8: Opinion and Argument

Directions: Read the passage below and then answer the two questions that follow, which address the author's argument. After you've selected each answer, read the answer explanations to check yourself.

SOCIAL SCIENCES: The following excerpt is adapted from the foreword to an economics book.

Teenagers today are not receiving adequate educations in financial literacy, and it is having an undue impact on their adult lives. On top of that, common ad-
5 vice given to teenagers encourages them to embark on risky financial endeavors that they are too young to fully under- stand. An 18-year-old is not even con- sidered responsible enough to purchase
10 alcohol, yet our culture believes they have the wherewithal to make a sound and informed decision concerning five-figure student loans. If the culture isn't going to change to be less financially predatory to-
15 ward young people, then school curricula must change to incorporate a far greater degree of financial literacy training be- fore students graduate high school.

Besides it simply being the ethi-
20 cal thing to do in today's world, there are numerous benefits for young people who learn financial literacy starting in high school or earlier. Knowing how to make money, save money, and make wise
25 financial decisions is empowering for teens, allowing them to feel like they're in control of their financial futures. Furthermore, not providing this type of education leaves young people anxious
30 and ill-equipped. As Geoffrey Bellamy

notes in his book *Guiding Teens Toward Financial Success*, when young people don't receive financial literacy education, "they struggle to maintain good credit
35 scores, are unable to save enough money to buy a home or prepare for retirement, and have no idea how to invest." Equipping teens with financial literacy ensures they enter the world with more confidence and
40 avoid falling into bad habits that will be harder to break when they're in a financial hole later. This can protect them, too, such as by making it easier for them to keep a savings fund for emergencies and making
45 them aware of common financial pitfalls, such as gambling and pyramid schemes.

1. The author's main argument in this pas- sage is that:

   A. financial literacy training should begin in early adulthood.

   B. young people deserve more financial literacy training before they graduate high school.

   C. teenagers are usually bad with money.

   D. it's becoming harder and harder to save money.

2. With which of the following statements would the author likely agree?

    F. No one should ever take out student loans.

    G. Credit scores are an unfair way to determine who deserves loans.

    H. Teenagers should not have to pay taxes until age 18.

    J. High school students should be taught how to financially plan for their retirement.

Answers

1. **The correct answer is B.** As is often the case with argumentative passages like this one, the author summarizes their argument in the final sentence of the first paragraph: "If the culture isn't going to change to be less financially predatory toward young people, then school curricula must change to incorporate a far greater degree of financial literacy training before students graduate high school."

2. **The correct answer is J.** Since the author's main idea is that young people should get more financial literacy education before they graduate high school, you can infer that the author would agree with the idea of teaching high school students how to start planning for their eventual retirement.

Synthesis Questions

When you are asked to address more than one passage at a time, such as in the paired set of passages you'll encounter in the ACT Reading section, you must use all the skills you've deployed in the prior sections simultaneously. Paired passages are about synthesizing information. The verb *synthesize* in this context means "to combine a number of elements into a coherent whole." Thus, your task with synthesis questions is to figure out how the passages make sense together rather than just on their own.

The good news is that when synthesizing information from multiple passages simultaneously, you're not actually reading any differently. You should approach reading the paired passages in the same way youwould solo passages in any other section.

If you can identify the main idea, purpose, and supporting details of each passage, you should have what you need to synthesize information between the two.

Questions to Ask Yourself: Synthesizing Information from Multiple Passages

- How would I summarize each passage individually?

- How would I summarize both passages together?

- In which ways do the authors agree and disagree?

- What are some key concepts or ideas that come up in both passages?

- How might looking at both passages give me deeper understanding than just looking at one or the other?

- If the authors of both passages were to debate each other, what topics might come up?

- How do the passages represent two different perspectives on the same topic?

Practice Set 9: Synthesis

Directions: Read the passages below and then answer the three questions that follow, which address your ability to synthesize information from two related passages. After you've selected each answer, read the answer explanations to check yourself.

HUMANITIES: Passage A is adapted from "When Modern Eurasia Was Born," published by the University of Copenhagen. Passage B is adapted from "European invasion: DNA reveals the origins of modern Europeans," by Alan Cooper and Wolfgang Haak.

PASSAGE A

The rewriting of the genetic map began in the early Bronze Age, about 5,000 years ago. From the steppes in the Caucasus, the Yamnaya Culture migrated
5   principally westward into North and Central Europe, and to a lesser degree, into western Siberia. Yamnaya was characterized by a new system of family and property. In northern Europe
10   the Yamnaya mixed with the Stone Age people who inhabited this region and along the way established the Corded Ware Culture, which genetically speaking resembles present-day Europeans living
15   north of the Alps today.

Later, about 4,000 years ago, the Sintashta Culture evolved in the Caucasus. This culture's sophisticated new weapons and chariots were rapidly
20   expanding across Europe. The area east of the Urals and far into Central Asia was colonized around 3,800 years ago by the Andronovo Culture. The researchers' investigation shows that this culture had
25   a European DNA background.

During the last part of the Bronze Age, and at the beginning of the Iron Age, East Asian peoples arrived in Central Asia. Here it is not genetic admixture we see, but
30   rather a replacement of genes. The European genes in the area disappear.

These new results derive from DNA analyses of skeletons excavated across large areas of Europe and Central Asia,
35   thus enabling these crucial glimpses into the dynamics of the Bronze Age. In addition to the population movement insights, the data also held other surprises. For example, contrary to the research team's
40   expectations, the data revealed that lactose tolerance rose to high frequency in Europeans, in comparison to prior belief that it evolved earlier in time (5,000–7,000 years ago).

PASSAGE B

45   What we have found is that, in addition to the original European hunter-gatherers and a heavy dose of Near Eastern farmers, we can now add a third major population: steppe pastoralists. These
50   nomads appear to have "invaded" central Europe in a previously unknown wave during the early Bronze Age (about 4,500 years ago).

This event saw the introduction of
55   two very significant new technologies to

western Europe: domestic horses and
the wheel. It also reveals the mysterious
source for the Indo-European languages.

60 The genetic results have answered
several contentious and long-standing
questions in European history. The first
big issue was whether the first farmers in
Europe were hunter-gatherers who had
65 learnt farming techniques from neigh-
bours in southeast Europe, or did they
instead come from the Near East, where
farming was invented? The genetic results
are clear: farming was introduced widely
70 across Europe in one or two rapid waves
around 8,000 years ago by populations
from the Near East—effectively the very
first skilled migrants.

At first the original hunter-gatherer
75 populations appear to have retreated to
the fringes of Europe: to Britain, Scandi-
navia and Finland. But the genetics show
that within a few thousand years they
had returned, and significant amounts of
80 hunter-gatherer genomic DNA was mixed
in with the farmers', 7,000 to 5,000 years
ago across many parts of Europe.

But there was still a major outstanding mystery. Apart from these
85 two groups, the genomic signals clearly
showed that a third—previously unsus-
pected—large contribution had been
made sometime before the Iron Age,
around 2,000 years ago. But by whom?
90 We have finally been able to identify
the mystery culprit, using a clever new
system invented by our colleagues at Har-
vard University. Instead of sequencing the
entire genome from a very small number
95 of well-preserved skeletons, we analyzed

400,000 small genetic markers right across
the genome. This made it possible to
rapidly survey large numbers of skeletons
from all across Europe and Eurasia.
100 This process revealed the solution
to the mystery. Our survey showed that
skeletons of the Yamnaya culture from the
Russian/Ukrainian grasslands north of the
Black Sea buried in large mounds known
105 as *kurgans* turned out to be the genetic
source we were missing.

1. Which choice best describes the relationship between Passage A and Passage B?

   A. Both passages show conflicting claims
      about the migrations.
   B. Both passages describe different scien-
      tific methodologies.
   C. Passage B provides supplementary
      information to Passage A.
   D. Passage B is written from a different
      perspective than Passage A.

2. Based on information in both passages,
   which of the following statements could be
   made about scientific inquiry?

   F. DNA evidence showed why many Euro-
      peans are lactose intolerant.
   G. Genetic research can provide valid his-
      torical information.
   H. Evidence showed that the steppe pasto-
      ralists introduced horses and the wheel
      to Western Europe.
   J. Scientific investigation can provide evi-
      dence about human history not obtain-
      able through other means.

3. How do the passages illustrate the contributions of DNA evidence to scientific inquiry?

   A. Both passages provide examples of how DNA evidence enabled scientists to fill in gaps in their knowledge about human migrations.

   B. Both passages describe how DNA analysis is used in scientific investigations.

   C. Both passages imply that DNA evidence can solve evolutionary questions.

   D. Both passages show how scientists solved the mysteries of DNA evidence.

Answers

1. **The correct answer is C.** When reading paired passages, you will encounter questions that ask you to examine the relationship between the passages. On your first reading, you probably noticed that the two passages do not contradict one another, nor do they show different points of view. This means you can eliminate choices A and D. Since both passages describe scientific studies and what scientists were able to learn from them, and both describe using DNA as the methodology, choice B cannot be correct. By process of elimination, choice C must be the best answer. The second passage adds to the information in the first, which makes the information in Passage B supplementary to the information shown in Passage A.

2. **The correct answer is J.** This question asks you to compare the two passages and look for a topic that is not directly discussed but that is implicit within it—the nature of scientific inquiry. While choices F and H are true, neither one answers the question. Choice G is also true, but it doesn't address the nature of scientific investigations; it is simply a general statement that could apply to many texts. Choice J, however, states a fact about scientific inquiry that can be gleaned from the texts: Both passages describe how scientists were able to use DNA data to answer questions they were unable to address before the use of DNA testing was available.

3. **The correct answer is A.** In paired passages, you will encounter questions that ask you to compare or contrast information presented explicitly in the passages. Both passages illustrate how DNA has been used to answer questions about human migration patterns—questions that had been unresolved before the ability to use DNA as evidence for such studies. Neither passage gives details about the actual scientific methodology as both are focused on the results, so you can eliminate choice B as a possible correct answer. Choices C and D are incorrect interpretations of the passages, so you can eliminate these choices as well.

Bringing Your Reading Comprehension Skills Together

You now know the most important reading comprehension topics and skills that are likely to be assessed by the ACT. As a reminder, these include the following:

- Main Idea (KID)
- Supporting Details (KID)
- Inferences (KID)
- Author and Passage Purpose (CS)
- Vocabulary in Context (CS)
- Author's Style, Tone/Mood, Language Use, and Word Choice (CS)
- Organization and Logic of Passage (CS)
- Opinion and/or Argument (IKI)
- Synthesis of Information from Multiple Passages (IKI)

In the "Example Reading Passage with Sample Questions" section that follows, you'll find a sample reading passage with a graphic illustration of how different parts of a passage relate to multiple question types we have discussed here. Keep in mind that you might get a question on the exam that doesn't seem to fall into any of these categories, but don't panic! Rest assured that the information you need to answer a question will always be found in the passage, so rely on the reading comprehension abilities you've built to find the right answer. If you're reading closely and actively for understanding, you can tackle any reading comprehension question that is thrown at you. On top of that, we'll spend the next chapter discussing all the different techniques you can use to save yourself time when using these skills on the reading exam, so don't worry—you're building a strong reading toolkit!

At the end of this chapter, you'll find a Test Yourself with a passage and ten practice questions to help you review what you've learned.

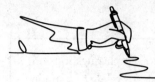

Example Reading Passage with Sample Questions

Directions: Read the passage and note how the numbered sections relate to the numbered sample questions on the opposite page. The numbers are there to help you identify how different types of questions relate to a single passage and where in the passage you would find the answer. Try to answer the questions for yourself. Then, check your answers against the answer key. As a challenge, imagine yourself in the role of an editor for this book. What sort of explanations would you write to show how and why the correct answers are correct?

Michelangelo Buonarroti's *David* is arguably the most famous statue in the world. Michelangelo sculpted the 17-foot biblical figure from marble be-

1 tween 1501 and 1504 to grace the Pallazo Vecchio, a public square near some government buildings. Today, a replica stands in its initial location and

2 Michelangelo's original is featured at the Galleria dell'Academia in Florence, Italy.

In his left hand, David carries a sling reminiscent of the biblical story

3 in which he slays a giant. This detail means that Michelangelo was likely picturing David as a left-handed person. However, art historians note that

4 it is David's right hand that presents a bigger mystery. First, it seems oversized compared to the otherwise proportionate statue. Second, the fingers appear to be curled around a mystery object. Art historians note that the veins in the right hand are prominent, suggesting that whatever David is holding, he's clutching it tightly.

There is some speculation that the oversized structure of the right hand is purely symbolic and meant to remind viewers of David having a "strong

5 hand" in his later years as a king. Others suggest it could be as simple as David holding the stone that he will use to slay a foe with his sling. Still others suggest he could be holding a second weapon entirely. Whatever the case may be, there is no way of knowing what exactly Michelangelo imag-

6 ined David gripping in his right hand, so the answer remains one of the art world's greatest mysteries.

Sometimes, you can knock a vocabulary question out before you even begin reading by previewing the sentence that contains it.

Note that previewing the first and last sentence of the first and last paragraphs would allow you to answer at least two questions before even reading the full passage!

1 INFERENCES

From Paragraph 1, we can infer that:

A. in the 16th century, all Italian art was required to have a religious context.

B. it took more than a decade to sculpt *David*.

C. *David* was not considered a masterpiece of sculpture until it was moved to a museum.

D. the government in Michelangelo's time was at least somewhat tied to the Christian church.

2 SUPPORTING DETAILS

Where is the original *David* located today?

F. Museo di Michelangelo

G. Pallazo Vecchio

H. Galleria dell'Academia

J. Sistine Chapel

3 VOCABULARY

As used in the first sentence of the second paragraph, the word *reminiscent* most nearly means:

A. bashful.

B. elusive.

C. mindful.

D. remindful.

4 ORGANIZATION AND LOGIC

The author's purpose in Paragraph 2 is to:

F. critique Michelangelo's artistic execution.

G. narrate Michelangelo's creative process.

H. clarify a prominent reason that art historians still speculate about the statue.

J. summarize recent findings about the importance of the statue.

5 TONE, STYLE, AND LANGUAGE USE

The author's use of the phrase "strong hand" in Paragraph 3 figuratively references the idea that David might have been a(n):

A. firm, decisive leader.

B. renowned athlete.

C. impulsive, hot-headed warrior.

D. celebrated artist.

6 MAIN IDEA

The main idea of this passage is that:

F. *David* is the most important statue of all time.

G. art historians remain divided as to what the David figure is holding in his right hand.

H. art historians determined that the David figure is holding a weapon in his left hand.

J. *David* is a proportionately oversized work, and its size reflects its symbolic meanings.

ANSWER KEY

1. D	2. H	3. D	4. H	5. A	6. G

BUILDING VOCABULARY TO INCREASE COMPREHENSION

Before we move on to practicing the different reading comprehension skills we've laid out here, let's take a moment to address vocabulary as it relates to reading comprehension. You can't grow your vocabulary without reading, and you can't comprehend a text without a firm grasp of the words the author is using. Both for the Reading section and other parts of the ACT, such as the English test or the optional Writing test, you'll need a strong vocabulary. Here are some ways you can build vocabulary expansion into your overall exam prep in order to be better prepared for the ACT as a whole.

Keep a Word Log

First off, read material that is more challenging. The key is to find material with words that are new or unfamiliar to you.

Next, write down the words that you don't understand. Once you have a good list of unfamiliar words, look up the definitions in a dictionary and write them down for future reference. Focus on learning a few words at a time so that you can learn them well.

Third, try to use the word in a sentence or in conversation. Practice using the word by creating your own sentences and writing them down in a notebook. This will help you get a sense of how to use the word in different contexts while cementing the word and its meaning into your vocabulary. Take note of the contexts in which you often see or use a word. Getting familiar with the topics and situations in which certain words are used will help you feel more confident when you integrate new words into your vocabulary.

Study Root Words, Prefixes, and Suffixes

You can increase your vocabulary by learning about the structure of words. This will help you figure out the meanings of unfamiliar words when you encounter them.

English words have recognizable parts that often come from Latin or Greek. Generally, there are three basic types of word parts:

1 **Roots** are the basic elements of a word that determine its meaning. Many derive from Latin and Greek and must be combined with prefixes, suffixes, or both.

2 **Prefixes** attach to the beginning of a root word to alter its meaning or to create a new word.

3 **Suffixes** attach to the end of a root word to change its meaning, help make it grammatically correct in context, or form a new word. Suffixes often indicate whether a word is a noun, verb, adjective, or adverb.

Sometimes, depending on the word, it can be difficult to determine if it is a prefix or a root word. However, the key takeaway here is that certain word parts carry meaning that is recognizable no matter what the word is. Knowing the meaning of part of a word can help you infer the meaning of the word.

To aid you in your vocabulary building, we've compiled some frequently used root words, prefixes, and suffixes. These tables are by no means comprehensive, but they should help you get started on breaking down the words you see often or encounter when reading, including while preparing for your exam.

COMMON PREFIXES

Prefix	Meaning	Example
Anti-	Against	Antifreeze, antibacterial
Bene-	Good	Benefit, benevolent
De-	Opposite	Deactivate, derail
Dis- Dys-	Not	Disagree, dysfunctional
En- Em-	Cover	Encode, embrace
Extra-	Beyond	Extraterrestrial, extracurricular
Fore-	Before	Forecast, forehead
Il- Im- In- Ir- Non- Un-	Not	Illegitimate, impossible, inexcusable, irregular, nonstop, nonsense, unable, undefined
Inter-	Between	Intergalactic, interpret, intermediary
Mal-	Bad, badly	Malicious, malnourished, malfunction
Mis-	Wrongly	Mistake, misinterpret, misnomer
Over-	Over, more, too much	Overlook, oversee, overachieve, overcast
Pre-	Before	Prefix, prevent, predict, prehistoric, prejudice
Re-	Again	Revision, reimagine, return
Trans-	Across	Transatlantic, transverse, transport

COMMON ROOTS

Root	Meaning	Example
Aqu Hydr	Water	Aqueous, aquarium, hydrate, hydrotherapy
Aud	Hear	Auditory, audio, audible
Biblio	Book	Bibliophile, bibliography
Chrono	Time	Chronological, chronology
Chrom	Color	Monochromatic, chromosome
Circ	Round	Circle, circus
Geo	Earth	Geography, geomagnetic
Juris	Law	Jurisdiction, jurisprudence
Junct	Join	Conjunction, juncture
Log Logue	Speaking, speech	Epilogue, eulogy, dialogue
Photo	Light	Photosynthesis, photography, photon
Scribe	Write	Describe, prescribe, inscribe
Sect	Cut	Dissect, sector
Volve	Roll, turn	Involve, evolve, revolve

COMMON SUFFIXES

Suffix	Meaning	Example
-able -ible	Capable	Agreeable, collectible
-al	Pertaining to	Logical, magical, criminal
-ance -ence	Indicating a state or condition; indicating a process or action	Clearance, ignorance, evidence, patience
-ent	Causing, promoting, or doing an action; one who causes or does something	Different, absorbent, student, agent, deterrent
-fy -ize -ate -en	Cause to be	Classify, diversify, realize, contextualize, create, communicate, awaken, sharpen
-ious -ous	Characterized by; full of	Nutritious, delicious, simultaneous, nervous
-ism	Belief, act	Catholicism, plagiarism
-ity	State or quality of being	Enmity, ability, responsibility
-less	Without	Homeless, restless, countless
-let	Small	Booklet, piglet
-or -er -ist	A person or object who is or does something	Benefactor, investigator, driver, teacher, chemist, narcissist, container
-ship	Position held	Friendship, citizenship, allyship, ownership
-tion -sion -ment	Action or instance of something	Liberation, concentration, admission, decision, achievement, bereavement
-y	Quality of	Thirsty, wintry

SUMMING IT UP

- The questions you will encounter on the reading comprehension section involve the following:

    ○ Identifying Main Idea

    ○ Finding Supporting Details

    ○ Making Inferences

    ○ Determining the Author's Purpose

    ○ Analyzing Vocabulary in Context

    ○ Explaining Author's Style, Tone, Mood, Use of Language, and Word Choice

    ○ Indicating Author's Organization and Logic

    ○ Determining Opinions and Arguments

    ○ Synthesizing Information from Multiple Passages

- The information you seek out to support your answer will depend on the goals and style of the question.

- Pay close attention to the specific wording of the question to inform your selection and elimination of answer choices.

- Answer choices on the test may be true statements, but the correct answer will always be supported by the passage.

- Incorrect answer choices may misrepresent the information provided by the passage. They may also be overly specific or too general in relation to what is stated.

- Building vocabulary as you prepare for the ACT will help with Reading as well as the English, Science, and optional Writing tests.

READING COMPREHENSION

10 Questions—9 Minutes

Directions: There are multiple passages in this test. Each passage is accompanied by multiple questions. After you finish reading a passage, choose the best answer to each question and fill in the corresponding oval on your answer sheet. You may refer to the passages as often as necessary.

HUMANITIES: This following excerpt is adapted from *The Science of Human Nature* by William Henry Pyle.

Science is knowledge; it is what we know. But mere knowledge is not science. For a bit of knowledge to become a part of science, its relation to other bits of knowledge must be found. In botany,
5　for example, bits of knowledge about plants do not make a science of botany. To have a science of botany, we must not only know about leaves, roots, flowers, seeds, etc., but we must know the relations of these parts and of all the parts of a
10　plant to one another. In other words, in science, we must not only know, we must not only have knowledge, but we must know the significance of the knowledge, must know its meaning. This is only another way of saying that we must
15　have knowledge and know its relation to other knowledge. A scientist is one who has learned to organize his knowledge. The main difference between a scientist and one who is not a scientist is that the scientist sees the significance of facts,
20　while the non-scientific person sees facts as more or less unrelated things. As one comes to hunt for causes and inquire into the significance of things, one becomes a scientist. A thing or an event always points beyond itself to something else. This
25　something else is what goes before it or comes after it—is its cause or its effect. This causal relationship that exists between events enables a scientist to prophesy.
　　By carefully determining what always
30　precedes a certain event, a certain type of

happening, a scientist is able to predict the event. All that is necessary to be able to predict an event is to have a clear knowledge of its true causes. Whenever, beyond any doubt, these causes are
35　found to be present, the scientist knows the event will follow. Of course, all that he really knows is that such results have always followed similar causes in the past. But he has come to have faith in the uniformity and regularity of nature. The
40　chemist does not find sulfur, or oxygen, or any other element acting one way one day under a certain set of conditions and acting another way the next day under exactly the same conditions. Nor does the physicist find the laws of mechanics
45　holding good one day and not the next.
　　The scientist, therefore, in his thinking brings order out of chaos in the world. If we do not know the causes and relations of things and events, the world seems a very mixed-up,
50　chaotic place, where anything and everything is happening. But as we come to know causes and relations, the world turns out to be a very orderly and systematic place. It is a lawful world; it is not a world of chance. Everything is related to
55　everything else.
　　Now, the non-scientific mind sees things as more or less unrelated. The far-reaching causal relations are only imperfectly seen by it, while the scientific mind not only sees things
60　but inquires into their causes and effects or consequences. The non-scientific person, walking over the top of a mountain and noticing a stone there, is likely to see in it only a stone and

think nothing of how it came to be there; but
65 the scientific person sees quite an interesting
bit of history in the stone. That person reads in
the stone that millions of years ago the place
where the rock now lies was under the sea. Many
marine animals left their remains in the mud
70 underneath the sea. The mud was afterward
converted into rock. Later, the shrinking and
warping earth-crust lifted the rock far above the
level of the sea, and it may now be found at the
top of the mountain. The one bit of rock tells its
75 story to one who inquires into its causes. The
scientific person, then, sees more significance,
more meaning, in things and events than does
the non-scientific person.
        Each science has its own particular field.
80 Zoology undertakes to answer every reasonable
question about animals; botany, about plants;
physics, about motion and forces; chemistry,
about the composition of matter; astronomy,
about the heavenly bodies, etc. The world has
85 many aspects. Each science undertakes to describe and explain some particular aspect. To
understand all the aspects of the world, we must
study all the sciences.

1. The primary purpose of Paragraph 1 (lines 1–28)
   is to:

   A. disprove certain beliefs about non-scientific
      thinking.

   B. illustrate the unpredictability of the scientific
      method.

   C. assert that a relationship exists between all
      scientific facts.

   D. categorize scientific thinking and various
      areas of study.

2. It can be inferred from the passage that observations in geology may offer insights in zoology as:

   F. rock formations may contain bite marks that
      convey information about the animals
      currently in the region.

   G. marine animal behaviors impact
      geological events.

   H. the remains of marine animals can be found
      preserved in rocks found beyond existing seas.

   J. geology as a science is older and thus can
      inform appropriate practices in zoology.

3. According to Paragraph 3 (lines 46–55),
   the world:

   A. is understood through science.

   B. follows orderly rules.

   C. is extremely chaotic.

   D. often seems chaotic.

4. As used in line 79, the word *field* refers to the
   fact that:

   F. botanists do most of their work outdoors.

   G. there are several scientific categories.

   H. studying science can be a rigorous and intense
      endeavor.

   J. scientists must be prepared to answer many
      questions.

5. As it is defined in the passage, the scientist:

   I. organizes knowledge.

   II. sees facts as unrelated.

   III. hunts for causes.

   A. I only

   B. II only

   C. I and III

   D. I, II, and III

6. It can be reasonably inferred from the passage that physics:

F. is unrelated to other scientific areas of study.

G. is inextricably linked to the study of probability.

H. is impossible to understand by non-scientists.

J. may reveal vital information about astronomy.

7. As used in line 66, the word *reads* refers to the idea that a stone:

A. presents information that can be analyzed.

B. often contains markings that look like words.

C. offers data beyond our technical ability to understand.

D. can be easily gathered by the scientist and non-scientist alike for observation.

8. The passage points to which of the following as justification for the idea that the world is not a chaotic place?

F. Information acquired through the scientific method is inconsistently applied from one day to the next.

G. Science has come to elucidate answers for humanity's oldest questions.

H. Understanding causes and relations yields predictability for related outcomes.

J. Even the non-scientific mind is able to use stories to explain physical phenomena.

9. As described in lines 26–31, the author implies that a scientist is in some way similar to a(n):

A. non-scientist.

B. fortune teller.

C. mechanic.

D. event planner.

10. According to the passage, in which order did the following events occur?

I. Rock was lifted above sea level.

II. The earth's crust shrank.

III. Mud was converted into rock.

F. I, II, III

G. III, II, I

H. II, I, III

J. I, III, II

ANSWER KEY AND EXPLANATIONS

1. C	3. B	5. C	7. A	9. B
2. H	4. G	6. J	8. H	10. G

1. **The correct answer is C.** The author uses the first paragraph to establish the premise that science and knowledge possess a specific relationship, asserting that within science, facts are always related to one another.

2. **The correct answer is H.** Support for this question appears in lines 68–74. There is no information in the passage that supports the conclusions of choices F or H. Choice G misrepresents the relationship between animals and geology as geological events, according to the passage, occur at a large enough scale to be independent of the actions of animals.

3. **The correct answer is B.** The third paragraph is mainly about how the world may seem chaotic but is actually very orderly. Choice B summarizes this idea well. You can eliminate choice C since it contradicts the paragraph's main idea. Choice A may be true, but it is too general to summarize the third paragraph effectively. Choice D is limited to a single detail in Paragraph 3.

4. **The correct answer is G.** The word *field* has a number of meanings, and each answer choice in this question refers to one of those meanings. However, only choice G matches the context in which the term is used in the passage.

5. **The correct answer is C.** Read lines 16–23. This information supports statements I and III and shows that statement II refers to a non-scientific person and not a scientist.

6. **The correct answer is J.** The author explains that all categories of science are related to each other, so it is logical to conclude that the category of physics may teach us vital information about astronomy. The fact that the sciences are all related contradicts the conclusion in choice F. Although all sciences are related to each other, and are also related to mathematics, no mention of probability occurs in the passage beyond allusions to the likelihood of events in the world. This

does not offer enough information to validate the conclusion in choice G. Choice H is an extreme statement. No such claims are made by the author.

7. **The correct answer is A.** The word *read* has several meanings, and each answer choice refers to one of these meanings. However, only one choice matches the context from the passage. Here, *reads* refers to the fact that scientists may understand information by observing the properties of stones.

8. **The correct answer is H.** The idea that the world is orderly and follows rigid laws receives specific attention in the second and third paragraphs. Therein, the author discusses that, regardless of the field of science, understanding the causes and relations between events affords predictability in that what happened one day for a particular reason would happen again under the same circumstances. Choices F and J distort the details of the passage, and no mention is made of "humanity's oldest questions" (choice G).

9. **The correct answer is B.** Lines 26–31 refer to how a scientist makes a "prophesy" or a "prediction." These are things that fortune tellers do, so choice B is the best answer. The passage points out several differences between non-scientific people and scientists (choice A) but never indicates how they might be similar. The author mentions the "laws of mechanics" in line 44 but not in any way that indicates a similarity between scientists and mechanics (choice C). An event planner (choice D) is someone who plans parties professionally, so even though lines 29–31 mention how scientists study events, they do not make scientists seem similar to event planners.

10. **The correct answer is G.** This question refers to the fourth paragraph's explanation of how a sea rock might end up atop a mountain. That paragraph reveals that mud is first converted into rock, and then the shrinking of the earth's crust lifts that rock far above the level of the sea. This order of events supports choice G.

CHAPTER

**Strategies for Approaching
the Reading Section**

STRATEGIES FOR APPROACHING

OVERVIEW

Reflecting on Your Diagnostic Test Score

Overall Section Strategies

Passage Strategies

Test Yourself: Reading Strategies

General Reminders and Advice

Strategy Roundup

Summing It Up

Knowledge Check: Reading

So far in this part of the book, we've discussed what you can expect from the ACT Reading test and provided an in-depth overview of the skills you'll be tested on and how. Now, we'll pivot to discuss the best ways to combine and apply your reading skills using strategies that can specifically help you manage your time and maximize your score. These strategies include general tips to help with the section as a whole as well as strategies for working through the passages. The goal of learning and practicing these strategies is to make the most of the parameters given to you by the ACT so as to improve your speed, accuracy, and score.

REFLECTING ON YOUR DIAGNOSTIC TEST SCORE

Now is a good time to flip back to the diagnostic test in Chapter 2 and your analysis of it in Chapter 3. Take a few moments to reflect on your score and performance when you started studying. You can do so in your head, take notes on your own, or use this table to jot down some ideas.

DIAGNOSTIC TEST REFLECTION: READING	
Reading Diagnostic Test Score: _____	**Reading Scoring Goal:** _____
Reflection Question	**Notes**
What went well for you during the diagnostic test and which skills were easiest for you to use?	
What did you struggle with during the diagnostic test or which skills were harder for you to use?	
Did you feel rushed? Did you have left over time?	
How close were you to your goal?	
After reviewing reading skills in the last chapter, what are some things you might like to keep in mind as you study further?	
What are some aspects of approaching the reading test for which you are hoping to build strategies?	

Now, take a moment to consider your goals for the ACT Reading test. If you are hoping to land a spot at a top university, then you should be shooting for the highest score possible. That said, not everyone has the lofty goal of achieving a perfect score. Instead, you may be simply hoping to raise your score a few points over a prior attempt or attain a score above the average for a given university. Whatever your goal, keep it in mind as you explore strategies to help you achieve it.

The basic rule for the ACT Reading section is that each question you answer correctly leads to an additional point for your score. Because there are 40 questions and a perfect score is 36, that system doesn't align perfectly, but it's good enough so that you can make some estimates. Your goal should reflect a score that makes you competitive for your desired school. At the same time, your goal also tells you how many questions you can guess on (how many questions you can feel uncertain about) and still achieve that goal. If you want a 36, then you can't guess on any questions. You have to be absolutely certain that your answer choice is the correct answer (by finding support, eliminating other answers, etc.). Otherwise, you're rolling the dice. If you're aiming for a 20, then you can guess on 18-20 questions and still feel confident you reached your goal.

That doesn't mean you're stuck with your goal after you select it. It should evolve as you continue to build your skills and practice. Just make sure, for Reading in particular, that you're using your goal to direct how you approach the section and develop your personal strategies for reading passages and answering questions.

OVERALL SECTION STRATEGIES

The strategies in this section can help you with your overall approach to the ACT Reading section. They have been selected, designed, and tested by experts to help increase your general accuracy and assist you with effective time management. You might notice that these strategies are likely to help you demonstrate the specific skills the ACT tests rather than ensure your mastery of a given passage's content. That's becausethe questions on the ACT Reading test offer plenty of signposts that can guide you to the information you need to answer

accurately. Because the questions can help point you in the right direction, you can make choices about how you approach the passage. With the options we'll present, you'll see that mastery of the passage's content is, more often than not, unnecessary to perform well.

You don't get points for reading the passage—you only get points for answering questions. Of course, you will still have to read at least some part of each passage. ACT questions simply cannot be answered accurately otherwise. However, how you approach extracting information from the passage can vary greatly depending on your reading skills, abilities, and reasoning.

As you prepare for your ACT Reading test, we encourage you to experiment with the different strategies outlined here and in the sections that follow. Experimentation is necessary to craft an overall approach that will help you capitalize on your personal strengths and get the best score you can.

Use Your Goals to Determine How You Divide Your Time

If you are aiming for as close to a perfect score as possible, then you'll need to divide your time in a way that allows you to evaluate all four passages and answer the 40 total questions in the 35 minutes you're allotted. That could mean spending equal time in each passage. Or, you could get through each passage as quickly as possible, then spend any remaining time on areas where you know you might have some weaknesses or guesses.

However, let's say you struggled with finishing the section in the past and were scoring below the national average (~20). Your approach doesn't need to look like that of someone who's seeking a perfect score; you have lots of options for how you spend your time in a way that supports your goals. For instance, it might be better to focus the bulk of your time on the two or three passages that are easier for you and try to ace their questions rather than spread your time evenly across all four passages. Then, with whatever time you have remaining, you can direct that to the one or two harder (for you) passage types, eliminating answers and guessing on remaining questions (and/or prioritizing questions that can be answered easily because of line references to the passage). Statistically, guessing should yield about two correct answers per every 10 guesses; this number only goes up if you are logically eliminating answers that you know are incorrect. Therefore, you are likely to get a few correct answers from the passage(s) you save for the end, even if you have to guess on every question.

That approach will keep you far from a perfect score, but it is a perfectly suitable method if you are aiming to score 20 or better, especially since you would likely still be able to answer some of the easier questions on the remaining passages rather than just guessing.

Consider which approach will help you make the most of your time in accordance with your goals and then practice bringing those strategies together before the big day.

Determine Your Passage Order

During your diagnostic test in Chapter 2, you might have found that certain passage types came easier to you, required less time and effort, or at the very least interested you more than others. You may have also noted a positive correlation between a certain passage type and your performance. For instance, maybe you noticed that you consistently got your highest scores on the Social Sciences passages or, perhaps, that no matter the subject matter, you tend to perform well on a set of two paired readings. That data isn't a lot to go off of, but it can help you evaluate whether the passage type impacts your performance. Whatever the case may be, the important thing to recognize is that you can work through the passages in any order, so it makes sense to do so in an order that capitalizes on your strengths, making the best use of your time to answer as many questions correctly as possible.

If you went in order on your diagnostic test and found that you weren't able to spend very much time on Passage IV: Natural Sciences, you need to evaluate which passage(s) slowed you down and if it might make sense to save any such passages for later (especially if it took a lot of time and didn't get you any additional accuracy).

In general, start with the passage with which you tend to perform the best and which you can do quickly. If you tend to perform similarly in multiple passage types, determine which type you normally complete

the quickest (while still maintaining accuracy) and start there. Then, you can conduct your reading of each passage in order from easiest for you (or most accurate or fastest to complete) to hardest for you (or least accurate or slowest to complete). Doing so ensures that the passages on which you are likely to perform best come at the start of your efforts, thereby maximizing your overall score and leaving any last-minute guessing for the passages and questions on which you were more likely to lose points anyway.

One suggested passage order is Passage II: Social Sciences, Passage IV: Natural Sciences, Passage III: Humanities, Passage I: Literary Narrative. This order prioritizes what are usually the more concrete passages (II and IV) while saving the more abstract passages (III and I) for later. Keep in mind, though, that your rder should emphasize your strengths. Analyze your diagnostic test performance, try a passage order for the Knowledge Check at the end of this part, and reflect on your approach afterward to refine your strategy.

In the space that follows, record a passage order to try with your Knowledge Check.

 NOTES

Develop and Practice an Active Reading Strategy

If you were to evenly divide your time between passages, you would have 8–9 minutes for each passage and its accompanying set of 10 questions. For each passage, that timeline needs to be broken down into time spent reading and time spent actually answering questions. For a test taker who is trying to distribute their time evenly across the section, that breakdown could be 3 minutes for reading and 30 seconds (on average) for each question. Those can be difficult time limits to maintain.

When you're strategizing for a passage, you're trying to answer one question: How do I extract enough information to answer the questions and still have plenty of time to answer as many as possible? To accurately answer each question, you have to read the question, read each answer choice, eliminate answer choices, find support in the passage for or against other choices that can't be eliminated easily, and then narrow it down to one choice and fill in your answer sheet. That's a significant number of steps to complete in roughly 30 seconds.

Given the section's strict time constraints and everything you need to do to answer questions accurately, your goal is to maximize what you know about the passage and maximize the time you spend thinking through the questions and their answer choices. Put another way, your goal is to spend as little time as possible not answering questions (a.k.a. reading the passage).

Given the complexity of managing your time, what will actually help you efficiently read the passage and answer the questions?

When it comes to reading the passages in the ACT Reading section, you have two goals. After reading the passages, you should be able to:

1	2
STATE THE MAIN IDEA OF THE PASSAGE	**POINT TO WHERE DIFFERENT IDEAS ARE LOCATED IN THE PASSAGE**

Firstly, that's because you don't know what details are important (unless you preview the questions—which can work for some people but be a drain for others). Since you don't know exactly what will be asked about, and because you should always find support for your answers (when it helps you meet your goals), it's more important to understand where things are in the passage so you can find them when you need to.

Secondly, you should always refer back to the passage or recall information to support your answers so as to maximize your accuracy. The ACT Reading questions make great use of certain traps in their answer choices that can easily lure test takers into making a mistake. Reading questions provide answers that have nuanced differences, so you'll always want to make sure your answer choice is supported by what the passage states (when doing so helps you meet your goals). If you can't find support for your answer choice, then you can't be certain that you're right. If you're not certain, you're guessing, and that has to align with your goals for the section.

As long as you know the main idea of the passage and where different ideas are discussed, you have what you need. What you need to determine, then, is how your reading skills can best help you identify that information.

Your objective is to gather as much information from the passage as quickly as you can to best support your quest to answer as many questions correctly as you're able. Doing so means pushing yourself to extract and process information from the passage quickly yet effectively. A lot of the choices you'll make when working with the passage will depend on your skills and abilities. But, regardless of your skills, you can practice some form of active reading to make your reading process more efficient.

Active reading is all about maximizing your engagement with the passage—thinking about what is being said and how it is being said while you're reading—to meet your needs. In a timed environment, active reading is an intense process, requiring you to inject as much energy into reading as you can, actively summarizing as you read and making critical, but brief, notes. But that doesn't mean that you have to be thorough when reading. Reading thoroughly would mean taking your time, figuring out all the supporting details and nuances of the argument as a whole, and revisiting sections that were complicated. Maybe

your goals can accommodate that thoroughness, but if you're striving for the highest score you can achieve, you don't have time for that (nor do you necessarily need it), so a strategic form of active reading will serve you best.

There are a few different ways to read actively and engage with the passage and questions. We've outlined one possible approach in the following section. This is not a universal approach, nor even a recommended method for most test takers. Instead, it is one approach to consider when approaching the Reading section. Later in this chapter, we offer multiple strategies for "reading" the passages and identifying the key information that will help you perform well. But remember that your individual strategy will depend on your strengths and challenges with the section, as well as your scoring goals. As you prepare for your test date, you should experiment, alter, and adapt your strategies for the section to align with your ever-growing reading and comprehension abilities.

Active Reading Strategy Example

For a test taker who can scan a passage quickly, preview questions and retain their topics quickly, and strategically read a passage to pinpoint main ideas, your time in an ACT Reading passage (8-9 minutes) could be spent on the following steps:

1 Preview the Passage and Scan the Questions

Read the passage intro text and then quickly scan through the passage (30 seconds or less) to get the gist of what it's about. Look for main ideas in topic sentences and repeated terms. Read the first and last sentence of the introductory paragraph, and see if there are any concepts or terms that stand out. Then, glance through the questions to see if there are any keywords that stand out or questions that you could answer right away (look for line numbers) before reading more rigorously.

2 Read Through the Passage Once, Then Answer Questions

You might have been able to answer some questions from your preview. Regardless, now you need to read actively but quickly through your passage one time. Later in this chapter, we'll discuss a few different techniques for how you might do this, but as discussed earlier, focus less on reading every single word and more on identifying main ideas, which means catching keywords, important ideas, and the purpose of each paragraph. Make sure you understand the main idea as having to reread for understanding, and not just supporting answers, will be costly for time. Remember, your goal isn't to memorize every single fact in the passage; it will contain much more information than what you directly need. Instead, you are reading to pinpoint the topic of each paragraph as that will guide you when answering questions.

3 Eliminate Distractors and Guess

You have so little time on the reading section that wasting too much of it trying to decide on the answer to a single question won't benefit you much. Your priority is to spend as much strategic time with as many questions as you can. And while one question is about equal to one point, it won't be worth it if it keeps you from spending time with multiple other questions. On the ACT, guesses don't count against you, so plan to make a guess and move on for any question that takes you longer than 45 seconds to answer. Whenever possible, use what you know from the passage to eliminate incorrect answers first before guessing as this will increase the likelihood of guessing correctly considerably.

TIP

When scanning and reading, make notes in your test booklet about the key idea of each paragraph. As soon as you see a question that references that idea, you know exactly where you can look to support your answer choice.

Complete a Passage before Moving On

Many test takers think the best move is to answer all the questions they can and move on to the next passage, assuming they'll have time to review again before time expires. However, if you do this for the first passage you read and then have to return to it after reading three more, you will likely have forgotten the details of the passage, which would force you to reread to be able to answer any remaining questions effectively. Similarly, you may find that you run out of time and forget to return to questions you didn't at least guess on. Those empty bubbles will only hurt your score. Instead of jumping around between passages, answer every question for a given passage before moving on.

Make Note of Guesses for Review

It's entirely possible that after working hard to manage your time, you find yourself with a few minutes to review the section. Remember that every second counts when you want to raise your score. In a section like Reading, that time can be used to turn a guess into a certainty. In order to make the most of that time, you need to have tracked which questions you guessed on so you can easily jump to them in the final moments of the section.

While moving through the section, notate in some way questions for which you were uncertain in your answer. You can even use multiple notation marks for different types of guesses. This way, you can prioritize reviewing questions you might be able to figure out with extra time over those which will require too much time and energy—or those for which you simply have no clue. Then, try to maximize the number of questions that you review to build certainty in your answers. One more correct question, in most situations, can net you an additional point on your scaled score, so make every second count.

PASSAGE STRATEGIES

So far, the strategies we've covered provide you with a general approach to the ACT Reading test. In this section, we'll discuss some of the ways to deal with passages on the ACT.

Strategy #1: Plan Out Your Reading Technique

There is more than one way to approach reading a passage in the ACT Reading section. Earlier in this chapter, we laid out some basic goals for active reading, and even one particular approach for extracting information from a passage and working through questions. But there are multiple ways to read actively. It all depends on the goals for the section and your own strengths and weaknesses as a reader.

The following list outlines just that. We've sequenced these reading techniques based on a combination of factors: impacts on speed and understanding, ease of implementation, and applicability. The first technique, reading first and last sentences, cuts down on reading time, emphasizes information questions will address, is relatively easy to do, and is applicable to most situations for most students. The last technique, scanning the passage, is fast but may reduce understanding and can work better for some students (and in only some situations) over others.

It's also important to keep in mind that, some passages are resistant to certain approaches. For instance, Passage I: Literary Narrative will not make the same structural choices that the other passages will, meaning that first and last sentences or scanning may not reveal much. In general, don't be afraid to alter your approach based on the passage type or mix and match in the moment to find your own approach.

- Read first and last sentences of each paragraph
- Read the first and last paragraphs
- Read the questions first
- Read the whole passage
- Read a paragraph, search for relevant questions, repeat
- Scan the whole passage

Strategy #2: Use Annotations to Mark Passage Ideas

One of the best ways to support your active reading strategy is to make notes on the passages in your test booklet. You can underline important information, circle keywords, use margin symbols to signal different types of reminders, or jot down a few words next to each paragraph to save you time when answering questions. Annotations have the added benefit of actually improving your retention of what you note as well. Even if you don't actively refer back to your notes, that extra interaction with the text will help reinforce your memory of what you have marked.

To guide you through this practice, here is a short passage. Notice the different types of notes the example test taker has made to remember what might be important about each paragraph.

[1]

Invasive species wreak havoc on ecosystems, and the emerald ash borer is no exception. Emerald ash borers are brightly colored wood boring beetles that only attack ash trees. Native to Asia, the emerald ash borer was first located in the United States in 2002 when it was spotted in Michigan. The

5　insect likely made its way over to the US by hitching a ride on a shipping crate or in wooden packing materials, one of many ways that foreign species can travel.

Emerald ash borer = invasive species

[2]

Emerald ash borers can now be found in the US and Canada, killing up to 99% of ash trees in their path. While adult emerald ash borers don't do

10　much damage, the larvae feed on the inner bark of the ash, making it difficult for the trees to get the proper nutrients. Signs of an emerald ash borer infesta- **!** tion include D-shaped exit holes, woodpecker feeding holes, bark deformities, yellowing foliage, and more.

Ash borer basics

[3]

The most recent data suggests that emerald ash borers have been spotted

15　in at least 35 states. In states where emerald ash borers are widespread, there are often restrictions on the transport of firewood between counties since this is how the insects are likely to spread. Residents with ash trees are encouraged to vaccinate their trees against emerald ash borer infestation or else risk losing their trees to the invasive beetle. In areas where infestation is likely or

20　even inevitable, some cities and counties are taking preemptive action by either vaccinating trees or replacing ash trees with more resilient native species. It's important that residents in affected areas look out for emerald ash borers or other invasive species and notify the proper authorities of any sightings.

Preventing EAB spread

What did you notice about the different types of notes this test taker made? They've labeled paragraph purposes, circled keys words and phrases, and marked some critical sentences. Perhaps not all of these annotation types would be useful to you personally, but each can be made quickly and easily when reading actively.

The goal is to use a system that helps you quickly navigate the passage after reading a question. You don't want to waste time and energy trying to remember everything from the passage or where things are. You want to create labels that you can follow after a question identifies the topic you're supposed to be thinking about. The question will identify the topic you need to consider (sometimes even the relevant line or sentence). From there, you can use your labels and symbols like a map to identify the paragraph with the relevant info, scan through, and find support for your prediction. The real secret is that by reading more actively (by summarizing and thinking about things while you read), you'll actually remember things from the passage better. And if you don't, that's okay, because you've still got your passage notes to support you.

TIP

Without previewing questions before reading the passage, you won't know what details will be important and thus what to mark in the passage. However, even if you lack that information, you do know that each paragraph in the passage serves a purpose. Even a basic label for each paragraph can be enough of an annotation to point you in the right direction after reading a question. How you annotate should align with your reading technique, your approach to the section, and your overall goal.

Now, consider the following two questions with the annotated version of the passage in mind:

1. According to the passage, signs of an emerald ash borer infestation are:

   A. signage for tree vaccination operations and new tree plantings.

   B. 99% death rates among ash tree populations.

   C. shipping crates and wooden packing materials from Asia.

   D. D-shaped holes and yellowing foliage.

2. Based on the passage, authorities are often motivated to replace ash trees with other native species because:

   F. it is easier to replace vast swaths of damaged trees with native species.

   G. other native trees are more resilient against emerald ash borer infestation than ash trees are.

   H. ash trees that have been subject to emerald ash borers are more susceptible to forest fires.

   J. it is impossible to vaccinate ash trees against diseases caused by emerald ash borer infestations.

So far in this book when you've been given examples questions like these, we've provided an explanation for the answer. In this case, look at the indicated correct answers instead and ask yourself how the notations this test taker made would have helped them quickly find the answer. As added practice, imagine yourself in the role of an editor for this book and try to write an explanation for each answer based on the annotated passage.

Strategy #3: Evaluate Question Difficulty and Respond Accordingly

Just like you have a choice about the order in which you approach passages, you also have a choice about the order in which you address questions. Some questions are "harder" than others not just because they require more complex thinking but also because they require more time to answer. For some questions, you may need to find more information in the passage or have information from both of the paired passages. Your reading technique and annotations should have helped you at least pinpoint where to find the information you'll need, but even then, you'll need to assess whether a question is worth the time it will take to answer and how guessing on said question can affect your goals. Generally speaking, you can divide questions into three categories of difficulty: easy, medium, and hard, with a special consideration for questions you may be able to answer prior to reading.

CATEGORIZING QUESTIONS BY DIFFICULTY

Question Difficulty	Explanation	Example Question
Easy (Pre-Reading)	These questions provide enough information that you can answer them before you even read the passage. Vocabulary questions and those that ask about particular lines can fall into this category. You may need to confirm your answer after reading.	2. According to its use in line 24, the phrase "backed into a corner" most nearly means:
Easy (Post-Reading)	These questions are relatively easy to answer based on a basic understanding of the text (such as an initial review of first and last sentences for each paragraph). You may be able to venture a guess for them before reading but must confirm your answer after reading.	24. The tone of this passage can most accurately be described as:
Medium	These questions require some reading before you can answer. However, once you read the passage, they are usually straightforward and can be verified with in-text information. Annotations often help you find answers for them faster.	32. The scientists identified that the change in acidity noted during the citrus experiment was most likely caused by which of the following factors?
Hard	These questions require you to engage in critical thinking beyond what is stated directly in the passage. You may need to make inferences, recognize relationships and patterns in the text(s) as a whole, synthesize, or draw conclusions based on incomplete information. If you have to guess the answer to a question, it can automatically be classified as hard.	17. Based on the information in both passages, with which of the following statements would the authors of both passages most likely agree?

Of course, only you can determine which of these four categories a question falls in for you. However, keeping these four stages of difficulty in mind will help you determine whether you should spend the time answering a question or whether you should save it for later—if you have time.

In terms of order, you could try the following: you could start by trying to answer the "Easy" questions before you read the entire passage. Then, once you've deployed your reading technique of choice, you could verify that the answers you already made are correct. At that point, you can tackle the medium questions before leaving any hard questions for the end. If a hard question is going to require multiple looks at the passage to complete (about 45 seconds to a minute), you can eliminate any incorrect answers you can, guess, note the guess in case you have time to review, and move on.

As a guided practice, let's look at a shortened excerpt from an example ACT Reading passage as well as four related questions. If you were to take the approach of evaluating the questions before reading the passage, which, if any, of the four questions could you answer in advance? What order would you answer the questions in if you were moving from easiest to hardest?

HUMANITIES: The following is excerpted from a compendium on the history of contemporary art since 1979.

Most people think of an image when they hear the word *art*. Whether it's an elaborate oil painting, a thoughtful photograph, an intricate drawing, or even a sculpture, art is
5 often considered the realm of the visual. This does not mean, of course, that no art exists beyond traditional visual art media and discourses. It does mean that conceptual artists like Jenny Holzer have free reign to inter-
10 rogate the idea of what art is by introducing elements that others might not initially think of as visual.

In Holzer's case, the two elements she plays with most in her conceptual artworks are
15 text and the built environment. Specifically, Holzer is known for projecting written statements in a bold font onto buildings, posting messages as neon signage, integrating poetry into places where more direct communication
20 usually appears, or otherwise finding ways to introduce text into the spaces of everyday life. Holzer has also been known to display her signature alongside these works, creating an additional thoughtful play on the idea of the
25 artist's signature as a type of visual representation that is both text and personal doodle.

1. The author's main purpose in this passage is to:

  A. examine how contemporary artists arrive at new ideas.

  B. offer a critical perspective on the work of Jenny Holzer.

  C. provide an overview of Jenny Holzer as an artist.

  D. analyze the evolution of contemporary art since 1979.

2. Holzer prefers to show her work in non-traditional spaces primarily because:

  F. it creates a thoughtful play on the idea of the artist's signature.

  G. alternative locations make it harder for collectors to purchase her art.

  H. she wants viewers to examine her art in the context of the messages they usually see when going about everyday life.

  J. her goal is to challenge the idea of what an art museum is.

3. In saying that "conceptual artists like Jenny Holzer have free range to interrogate the idea of what art is" (line 8–10), the author most likely means that conceptual artists:

  A. are not constrained by the same rules that govern more traditional forms of art.

  B. do not believe that art has to have meaning.

  C. adhere to traditional views about what art is and how it should be presented.

  D. use art primarily as a way to critique the world.

4. Based on the passage, we can most logically infer that:

  F. Jenny Holzer has never had a traditional museum show.

  G. the content of the messages Holzer creates is as important to her work as the appearance of the words themselves.

  H. people are not as interested in conceptual works like Holzer's as they are more traditional art.

  J. art critics are unimpressed by Holzer's works since they do not adhere to the rules governing visual media.

If we follow the technique for ranking questions based on their difficulty, we'll note that question 3 contains a specific line reference, making it a potential "Easy" question. We may be able to answer it before reading, provided we look at the line in question and determine the context in which the given phrase was used. Here, the context for the given line reveals that the answer to question 3 is choice A since the cited phrase implies that conceptual artists are not constrained by the same rules that govern more traditional forms of art.

You may also have noticed that question 1 is an "Easy" question. While you will have to at least glance at the first paragraph to determine a correct answer, you should be able to recognize from that little bit of information that the purpose of the passage is to provide an overview of Jenny Holzer as an artist (choice C). At this point, you've spent very little time reading but have already answered two questions!

Following the technique we've provided, you could then preview the questions that remain. You'd notice that question 2 is a potential "Medium" question (as it asks about something mentioned directly in the passage) and that question 4 could qualify as "Hard" (because it requires you to draw a logical conclusion based on something not stated directly). Now, you could apply your preferred reading technique to tackle the passage and review the questions again.

Once you've read, take a moment to verify that the questions you already answered are indeed correct, then move on to your "Medium" question. Since you hopefully annotated the passage and mapped where information occurs, you should be able to quickly find the lines (15-21) that help you identify the correct response. Choice H correctly summarizes the second paragraph of the given passage by asserting that Holzer prefers to display her work in non-traditional spaces because she wants viewers to examine her art in the context of the messages they usually see in everyday life. Having answered all the other questions, you can then focus any remaining time for that passage on answering the "Hard" question. If any hard question takes more than 45 seconds to answer, eliminate what

you can and make a guess so you can move on. You can always mark guesses to return to later if you end up having time. For question 4, the context of the entire second paragraph reveals that the answer is choice G, which states that the content of the messages Holzer creates is as important to her work as the appearance of the words themselves.

Strategy #4: Divide and Conquer Paired Passages

Paired passages present a unique challenge to test takers because some of the questions will require knowledge of both passages while others will only focus on one passage at a time. One of the best things a test taker can do is start with passage A and then answer all questions for that passage. Then, the test taker can do the same for passage B. Finally, they can answer the questions that relate to both passages, having completed both readings.

To practice, let's look at a shortened version of an ACT paired passage set. These passages are only a paragraph long so they don't completely reflect the passages you'll see on your ACT test, but we can still use them to practice this strategy.

NATURAL SCIENCES: Both of the following passages were taken from a special edition of a scientific journal on ecology.

PASSAGE A

Thailand's tropical rainforests are a treasure trove of biodiversity, with over 15,000 species of plants, 500 species of birds, and 300 species of mammals call-
5 ing them home. These lush forests provide critical ecosystem services, such as purifying air and water, preventing soil erosion, and regulating climate. However, these forests are under severe threat
10 from human activities such as deforestation, logging, and agricultural expansion. Between 1973 and 2009, Thailand lost more than 43 percent of its forest cover, which has resulted in the loss of habi-
15 tat for countless species. For example, the Siamese crocodile, one of the rarest crocodile species in the world, is now critically endangered due to habitat loss and hunting. Similarly, the Javan rhinoc-
20 eros, once common in Thailand, is now extinct due to habitat loss and poaching. Moreover, climate change exacerbates these threats by causing more frequent and severe droughts and floods, which
25 can destroy forests and wipe out entire animal populations. It is essential that we take immediate action to protect these rainforests. Only by preserving these vital ecosystems can we ensure that future
30 generations will have the opportunity to experience the wonder and beauty of Thailand's natural heritage.

PASSAGE B

Thailand is taking significant steps to fight climate change and protect
35 its rich biodiversity. The country has committed to reducing greenhouse gas emissions by 20 to 25 percent by 2030 and has launched several initiatives to promote renewable energy, such as the
40 Siam Green City project, which aims to make the city of Bangkok a hub for green technology. Additionally, Thailand has made significant efforts to protect its endangered species, such as the Siamese
45 crocodile. The Department of National Parks, Wildlife and Plant Conservation has established breeding programs and protected areas for the species, and there have been successful reintroduction
50 efforts in several parts of the country. Furthermore, the Elephant Nature Park in Chiang Mai is a well-known example of how ecotourism can support conservation efforts. The park provides a safe ha-
55 ven for abused and orphaned elephants and educates visitors about the importance of protecting the country's natural heritage. While there is still much work to be done, Thailand is making progress
60 in addressing the pressing challenges of climate change and biodiversity loss, efforts which activists hope will be redoubled as public support for species conservation expands.

Following the paired passage strategy, you would first read Passage A and then address questions that relate exclusively to it. Don't even worry about Passage B until these questions are addressed since doing so will help you stick to the details of Passage A. Any distractors lifted from Passage B won't affect you since you're only dealing with the first passage for now.

1. According to Passage A, one primary way that rainforests help the ecosystem is that they:

   A. provide a safe haven for elephants.

   B. regulate the climate while purifying the air and water.

   C. support the development of ecotourism opportunities.

   D. create opportunities for agricultural expansion.

If you have read Passage A before reading this question, you'd likely recognize that choice B is the correct answer right away since the passage states as much only in different words. You'd also have been less likely to get thrown off by choices A and C, which borrow details from Passage B to distract the reader. Alternatively, had you read both passages before getting to this question, it would be harder to remember which information came from which passage. Dealing with each passage in a paired set separately may only save you a few seconds of deliberation time per question, but those seconds can add up to serve your overall time management goals.

Once you've finished the questions that relate exclusively to Passage A, you should have a decent

understanding of the passage. This will help you as you read through passage B because you'll be better able to spot the relationships between the passages, including where they align and diverge. You can then address the questions that relate exclusively to passage B.

2. Passage B most strongly suggests that organizations like the Siam Green City project are important because they:

   F. are under severe threat from human activities.

   G. educate tourists about how Thailand is protecting the country's natural heritage.

   H. reduce greenhouse gas emissions by 20 to 25 percent.

   J. propose initiatives that support long-term conservation efforts.

Focusing on Passage B, you likely noticed that it provides more concrete examples than Passage A regarding conservation efforts currently being made in Thailand. File this information away for later when we address the synthesis questions. Here, the question that focuses on Passage B also gives the key term "Siam Green City project." That phrase can guide you towards the location in the text for the supporting details and context you need to answer the question with certainty. From there, you should be able to infer that the author of Passage B considers organizations like Siam Green City project important because they propose ideas that support long-term conservation efforts (choice J). The other answer choices are mentioned in either Passage A or Passage B, but only the correct answer is mentioned in the context of the Siam Green City project.

Once you've addressed all the questions that pertain to one passage or another, you'll have a better chance of remembering which ideas and examples came up in text, making it easier to eliminate distractors that which are only true for one passage and not the other, instead of addressing both.

3. Compared to the author of Passage A, the author of Passage B provides more information about:

   A. how the Javan rhinoceros became extinct as a result of human activity.

   B. individual organizations committed to addressing specific issues that relate to climate change in Thai rainforests.

   C. the number and types of species that inhabit the Thai rainforests.

   D. what Thai residents think about various types of conservation efforts.

Having already dealt with each passage in isolation, you should be able to recognize that choices A and C address topics that only came up in Passage A, making it impossible for them to be the correct answer to this question. Furthermore, since you've already reviewed both passages, you'll notice that neither author spent time addressing what Thai residents think about various types of conservation efforts (choice D). By this process of elimination, you are left with the correct answer, choice B. This demonstrates how saving the Integration of Knowledge and Ideas questions until after you've reviewed questions for each passage individually allows you to isolate correct answers and eliminate distractors, all without having to return to the passages. If you do need to review passages, this method will also ensure you have a decent sense of where to look for your answer, particularly if you made sure to annotate while you read.

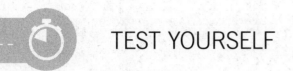
READING STRATEGIES

10 Questions—9 Minutes

Now that we have covered some of the critical strategies for the ACT Reading section, use the following practice passage to formulate and test out an approach. Make sure to choose a reading strategy you think will work best for you on this passage type, annotate the passage as you read, evaluate the questions for difficulty and time, and apply the paired reading strategy. Revisit what you saw for approaching different question types and stick to a strict time limit of 9 minutes to complete the question set.

SOCIAL SCIENCES: Passage A is taken from a peer-reviewed sociology journal. Passage B is excerpted from an academic lecture.

PASSAGE A

In recent years, there has been increasing debate in the social sciences about the role of cultural relativism in the interpretation of human rights. In theory, cultural relativism
5 argues that morality and ethical standards are culturally determined and cannot be judged objectively from one culture to another. Thus, as proponents state, human rights should be interpreted within the cultural context in which
10 they are practiced. However, there are also those that argue that across cultures there are indeed universal values that can be used to assess whether something is harmful or helpful to the well-being of humanity. Such thinkers allege
15 that cultural relativism can lead to the justification of human rights violations. While cultural context is important for understanding human rights, multiple western philosophers have also asserted that there are certain universal values
20 that should be upheld regardless of cultural differences, particularly those that relate to the dignity of human life.

American philosopher Martha Nussbaum argues that human rights are based on a set
25 of universal capabilities that are necessary for so-called human flourishing, such as the ability to reason, the ability to love, and the ability to form relationships. According to Nussbaum, this capabilities approach provides a basis for
30 evaluating different cultural practices and determining whether they promote or hinder human flourishing irrespective of variations between cultures. Any cultural practice that violates the capabilities necessary for a human to live a
35 flourishing life is therefore an objective violation of human rights. Regardless of how an activity may be justified by a given culture's beliefs and traditions, in Nussbaum's view, human flourishing is paramount.

40 Canadian philosopher Charles Taylor also holds a prominent role in the discussion, arguing that cultural relativism is an important perspective that can help us better understand and appreciate different cultures. However, he
45 also recognizes that there are certain values, such as human dignity, that are universal and should be respected in all cultures. Taylor suggests that rather than imposing Western values on non-Western cultures, we should engage in a
50 dialogue that allows us to better understand the values and beliefs of different cultures while also recognizing and upholding universal human rights.

That balancing act is less important to
55 Indian philosopher Amartya Sen who contends that cultural relativism can be dangerous. Human rights, Sen argues, should be understood

in terms of the capabilities and freedoms that individuals need to live a full and meaningful life. Cultural relativism can be used to justify oppressive practices and deny individuals what they need to flourish. Sen does state that we can recognize the importance of cultural diversity while also acknowledging that certain universal values and capabilities are essential for human well-being.

Passage B

In 1948, the United Nations adopted the Universal Declaration of Human Rights, recognizing the inherent dignity and equal rights of all human beings, regardless of race, class, gender, or culture. The 30 articles ratified by the general assembly describe a form of natural law, a concept that places the declaration firmly within Western culture, namely classical Greek philosophy, Christian theology, and Enlightenment political thought. Such an attempt to define and support human rights has led to nuanced discussions around the value of cultural relativism in a globalized world as well as the validity of universal rights. As the discussion goes, cultural relativism can help us understand the diversity of cultural practices; however, it cannot, critics state, be used to justify practices that harm individuals or groups. Then, there are those who argue that the work of Nussbaum and others represents a form of cultural imperialism, wherein Western values are privileged over non-Western cultural structures and traditions. In question is the balance between practicing cultural acceptance and identifying cultural activities that may harm humanity.

In response to Martha Nussbaum's capabilities approach, cultural relativists argue that there is no universal agreement on what constitutes human flourishing. Nussbaum's approach represents, in their minds, the imposition of Western values on non-Western cultures. For example, some cultures (like those in Japan, China, and other Asian countries) may place a higher value on collectivism than individualism, which could lead to different interpretations of the capabilities necessary for human flourishing. Additionally, critics argue that the capabilities approach may overlook the importance of community and social relationships in certain cultures, which could lead to a narrow and individualistic understanding of human flourishing that places primacy on the cultural perspectives of the richest and most developed (and primarily Western) nations.

In contrast, critics of a culturally relativistic approach suggest the notion of cultural homogeneity is overstated. Even within a single culture, there can be significant differences in values and beliefs. For example, in the United States, cultural attitudes can vary greatly between rural and urban populations, regions, ethnic and racial groups, even neighborhoods. Therefore, it may be difficult to identify a single set of cultural values and practices that can be used to justify or condemn human rights practices.

Multiple collectivist cultural practices are cited by both sides in the debate over the value of cultural relativism. For instance, in some cultures, arranged marriages are considered a social norm and are therefore not seen as a violation of human rights. Similarly, the practice of caste discrimination in India has been justified on the basis of cultural tradition. The complexity of the discussion arises from the notion that such practices may be deeply ingrained in a cultural tradition while, for some, being used to perpetuate oppression and deny individuals rights that are common in other parts of the world.

As the debate continues, it is clear that there are a variety of factors and theories that require assessment of the value of both cultural relativism and social science paradigms such as

Nussbaum's capabilities approach. Both sides of the debate seek to distinguish between cultural practices that promote human flourishing and those that violate what can be agreed upon as fundamental human rights.

1. Passage A makes which of the following claims about cultural relativism?

   A. Those who believe in cultural relativism believe there is never a circumstance in which cultural differences affect morality.

   B. Ethics and morality depend on the culture in which they are conceived so it is hard to judge cultures by a universal standard.

   C. Cultural relativists espouse the idea that all cultural behaviors can be judged according to a universal standard.

   D. What one culture defines as cultural relativism another might define as collectivism.

2. As used in line 39, the term *paramount* most nearly means:

   F. enduring.

   G. fragile.

   H. of least importance.

   J. of highest importance.

3. The author of Passage A most likely includes information on Amartya Sen in order to:

   A. illustrate why contemporary critics tend to disagree with Nussbaum.

   B. extend the debate to include a classical thinker.

   C. provide a counterclaim to the perspective Nussbaum represents.

   D. offer an example of a thinker whose ideas are similar to but not the same as Nussbaum's.

4. The example offered in paragraph 4 (lines 121–133) of Passage B serves to emphasize which of the following points?

   F. Contemporary critics no longer value the contributions of traditional thinkers like Charles Taylor and Amartya Sen.

   G. Even within a given culture, it can be difficult to justify or dismiss a given practice based on the notion of cultural relativism alone.

   H. Arranged marriage is an example of a collectivist practice that challenges the notion of cultural relativism as a black and white measure for human flourishing.

   J. Critics of cultural relativism suggest that it imposes Western values on non-Western cultures.

5. It can be most reasonably inferred from Passage B that:

   A. the UN affirmed the Declaration of Human Rights to develop a standard that could be used to evaluate human rights issues across cultures.

   B. those who oppose Martha Nussbaum's ideas believe that all humans rights issues can be evaluated by the same standard.

   C. there needs to be a balance between collectivism and individualism in any culture.

   D. Nussbaum's capabilities approach centers non-Western cultural values.

6. The author's tone in Passage B can be described as:

   F. skeptical.

   G. laudatory.

   H. explanatory.

   J. colloquial.

7. Which of the following statements best summarizes a shared purpose of Passage A and Passage B?

   A. While Passage A focuses more on specific cultural practices, both passages focus on how the idea of human flourishing can be applied to cultural relativism.

   B. While Passage A provides fewer examples, both authors are interested in enumerating the different ways cultural relativism is influenced by Nussbaum's ideas.

   C. Both authors critique Martha Nussbaum's approach to developing cultural relativism.

   D. Both authors aim to provide examples of how the concept of cultural relativism relates to Martha Nussbaum's ideas.

8. In Passage A, the author notes that Nussbaum's approach "provides a basis for evaluating different cultural practices and determining whether they promote or hinder human flourishing irrespective of variations between cultures" (lines 29–33). The author of Passage B counters this assertion by noting that:

   F. it doesn't apply to cultural practices that violate human flourishing.

   G. her approach is not actually universal if it can't account for important cultural differences like those between collectivistic and individualistic cultures.

   H. Nussbaum's theory is only applicable to Western societies.

   J. modern-day thinkers have largely rejected Nussbaum's ideas.

9. Both passages could be used to support the claim that:

   A. individualistic cultures are less likely to justify cultural practices that violate human rights than collectivist cultures are.

   B. Charles Taylor's ideas on cultural relativism are no longer relevant to fields in the social sciences.

   C. there is no such thing as a practice which cannot be justified by cultural relativism.

   D. practices which hinder a person's fundamental human rights and dignity should not be justified by cultural relativism.

10. Compared to the author of Passage A, the author of Passage B provides more details about:

   F. specific cultural practices that require examination within the debate around cultural relativism.

   G. different thinkers whose ideas regarding cultural relativism mirror Nussbaum's.

   H. the specific cultural practices that informed the formation of Nussbaum's theory.

   J. how Nussbaum's theories have been used to justify the existence of cultural practices that violate human dignity.

Answers and Explanations

1. **The correct answer is B.** Choice B is an elegant summary of the main idea behind Passage A. All the other answers are phrased to either contradict or overstate aspects of the passage.

2. **The correct answer is J.** The answer options present you with two pairs of antonyms. Contextually, neither *enduring* (choice F) nor *fragile* (choice G) make sense. Context suggests that human flourishing is important to Nussbaum's ideas, so it's far more likely to be of highest importance (choice J) to her than of least importance (choice H).

3. **The correct answer is D.** As with the author's discussion of Charles Taylor in the paragraph prior, the purpose of the author's discussion of Amartya Sen is to provide an example of another thinker whose thoughts on cultural relativism share some similarities with Nussbaum's but which are not identical.

4. **The correct answer is G.** The paragraph in question uses the example of the United States and its numerous regional cultural differences to underscore the point that cultures are not homogenous, which makes it difficult to discuss cultural relativism without recognizing the differences that exist even within a given parent culture.

5. **The correct answer is A.** Both the use of the term *universal* and the assertion that the Universal Declaration of Human Rights was affirmed by the UN to "[recognize] the inherent dignity and equal rights of all human beings, regardless of race, gender, or culture" (line 69–71) support the inference that the Declaration of Human Rights was intended to provide a universal standard regarding human rights.

6. **The correct answer is H.** The author of passage B uses an explanatory tone, which could also be described as academic, informative, or neutral. The author expresses neither skepticism (choice F) nor praise (choice G, as *laudatory* is a synonym for *praising*). The term *colloquial* (choice J) describes writing that is familiar, informal, or casual, which is the opposite of the case here.

7. **The correct answer is D.** Choices B and C both incorrectly define the relationship between Nussbaum's ideas and cultural relativism. Of the remaining options, choice A inaccurately describes Passage A—it focuses less on specific cultural practices. Choice D speaks to how both authors invoke Nussbaum's ideas to, in Passage A, present advocates of the capabilities approach and, in Passage B, represent criticisms and support on both sides of the universal human rights debate.

8. **The correct answer is G.** The author of Passage B notes that Nussbaum's approach "may overlook the importance of community and social relationships in certain cultures" (line 103–105) and mentions the difference between collectivist and individualist cultures in particular. Choice F pulls an unrelated assertion from Passage A. Choice H exaggerates the author's statements. Choice J is not supported by either passage.

9. **The correct answer is D.** Both passages offer statements that indicate that any discussion of cultural relativism must be tempered by the acknowledgement that the concepts should not be used to justify practices that violate human rights. Passage A states, "we can recognize the importance of cultural diversity while also acknowledging that certain universal values and capabilities are essential for human well-being" (lines 62–66). Meanwhile, Passage B concludes, "Both sides of the debate seek to distinguish between cultural practices that promote human flourishing and those that violate what can be agreed upon as fundamental human rights" (lines 138–142).

10. **The correct answer is F.** The author of Passage B includes examples of both arranged marriages and the Indian caste systems. These are represented as cultural practices which complicate the idea of cultural relativism since their relative ethics or morality are subjective and depend on the culture that evaluates them. This is the only answer that accurately represents the relationship between details from both passages.

Now that you have practiced with the passage, reflect on the strategies you used to complete it. You might even try reading the passage again using different techniques to see how each affects your time and energy. When you're finished, answer the following questions for yourself:

- Which strategies seemed to help you most?

- Did any strategy prove to be unhelpful for you? If so, could you modify it to make it helpful?

- After practicing, how might you like to change your overall strategy toolkit going forward? What would you like to keep the same about your strategy?

As you reflect on what works well for you and when, you'll likely find that you also feel more prepared and confident each time you practice your newly personalized approach.

GENERAL REMINDERS AND ADVICE

Here are a few other things to keep in mind if you want to tackle ACT Reading passages like a pro. You can also refer back to Chapter 3 for more ACT test-taking advice.

Read All Your Answer Choices

Don't just automatically mark down the first answer that seems correct. Instead, make sure you read each answer choice and eliminate those you know are wrong before choosing the *best* answer.

Stick to the Passage

Avoid involving personal or emotional judgments when finding your answers. Even if you disagree with the author, or spot a factual error in the passage, you must answer based on what's stated or implied in the text. Similarly, even if you have outside knowledge of a topic, you should only answer based on what's written in front of you. Just because an answer is true in a general sense does not mean that it is supported by the passage.

Don't Worry If You Don't Know the Topic

To put all test-takers on a level playing field, test-writers choose approachable reading passages on a variety of topics. Some will be a little harder than others, but all are designed to be understandable to a general audience. You probably have not seen the reading material before, but you're not being tested on your knowledge

of the topic. Instead, you're being tested on how well you can comprehend what you read and answer the questions accordingly.

Passages Stay Positive

Keep in mind that passage topics and author opinions in the ACT passages tend to be positive in nature. It's unlikely that you'll encounter a passage that wades into grim topics or that presents a vicious critique without offering any redeeming qualities or constructive feedback for how to improve a dire situation. At worst, the passage will be a neutral description of a particular phenomenon, which at least amounts to an "enthusiastic discussion" or "exploration" of a potentially interesting topic. Takedowns and radical polemics are few and far between if ever present.

Trust Yourself

Don't spend too long going back and forth about a correct answer simply because you can convince yourself that more than one is plausible. Find support for your choice. Remember, only one answer is right, so you just need to understand why the other answers are wrong. If you can still make an argument for two answers being correct, save your time and go with your gut instinct. If you end up with some remaining time, you can come back to check it.

Personalize Your Approach

Everything we've laid out here is a basic template for how to approach reading questions, but no one knows you better than you. If a certain aspect of reading is harder for you, such as understanding questions or getting through the passages in time, figure out which of the strategies here you need to prioritize. Maybe you're the type of person who needs to closely read the questions first before reading a single word of the passage. This is a fine strategy, but it can also cost time. If the greater time investment isn't yielding greater accuracy, you need a different strategy. Whatever choices you make, you're weighing how long your approach will take, how it impacts your accuracy, and how all of your choices come together to help you achieve your scoring goal. See what feels good and make sure to time yourself when practicing so you can identify where you might need improvement before exam day.

STRATEGY ROUNDUP

As we've said before, it's important to personalize your approach to ensure you are using the strategies that make the most sense for you (your time, your accuracy, your goals). That said, it's possible to follow a predetermined plan for how to bring all these strategies together and perform your best. As a starting point for all test takers, we recommend the following path to success. From here, you can make adjustments that suit your needs based on the specific strategies and advice we provided earlier in the chapter.

Use a Passage Order that Works for You

Whether you establish an order in advance or determine one based on quickly glancing through the topics of the passages, decide the order in which you will approach the four passages on the test. When evaluating day of, you can adjust your order based on things like density, structure, and topic difficulty. Remember, work with the passages you feel most confident with first and progress towards those that present the greatest struggle.

Read Actively and Annotate the Passage

Use an active reading technique, such as reading first and last sentences of paragraphs or previewing questions and skimming for relevant information. How you read can vary based on the passage type or structure. Your choice of reading technique should align with your goals—let your goals determine how much time you spend with each passage. Remember, though, that you're reading for main ideas and understanding. Whatever method you choose, annotate the passage to pinpoint the key ideas for easy reference later.

Come Back to Harder Questions

When looking through your questions, figure out which can be addressed quickly or easily. Address all the easy questions before moving onto the harder questions. Whenever you have to guess, make a note in your booklet.

Answer Questions Strategically

There are a few common multiple-choice techniques you can apply to every question. When you read a question, use what you know about the passage to predict an answer. That can direct you to an answer choice that aligns with your prediction and helps you avoid some question traps. However, even though you have made a prediction, you should still look at all the answer choices and eliminate those you know are wrong. If you still have multiple answers left, refer to the passage to confirm your prediction or eliminate the remaining choices. If this is taking a lot of time without giving you an answer you know is right, fill in your best guess and move on.

Move to the Next Passage

Once you have answered all 10 questions for a given passage and noted any for which you had to guess, move on to the next passage. As a general rule, try not to spend more than 9 minutes on any one passage and answer set unless doing so matches your personal goals.

As Time Allows, Review Guesses

After finishing your last passage, use any remaining time before the section ends to review questions you guessed on. If you find yourself running out of time and still haven't answered all of the questions, spend your last remaining minute filling in answers rather than leaving questions blank.

SUMMING IT UP

- Use your diagnostic score to determine the best way to practice for your ACT exam. As you learn different reading strategies that work for you, feel free to practice them using news articles, textbook entries, or any other readings that are sufficient to a first-year college student's level. Know that you can practice your reading comprehension skills with just about anything!

- Since you have 35 minutes to complete 40 questions across 4 passages, to reach every passage and question, you should plan to spend 8–9 minutes per passage and question set unless dictated otherwise by your personal strategy.

- Plan to spend no more than 45 seconds on any one question—unless your section goals allow for more. If you can't find the answer in that time, eliminate the distractors you can and guess. Mark guesses to review later if time allows.

- Use overall section strategies to help with the ACT Reading test as a whole:

  ○ Divide your time according to your personal score goals.

  ○ Determine the order in which you'd like to tackle passages (whether before the test or in a brief preview of the section).

  ○ Practice active reading strategies such as reading first and last sentences, skimming and scanning, previewing questions, and annotating passages to find information later.

  ○ Complete all the questions for a given passage before moving on to the next passage.

  ○ Note questions you guess on in case you have time to review them at the end.

- Deploy passage strategies that suit your needs:

  ○ Plan out a reading technique (or combination of techniques) that suits your needs as a test taker. Each technique may be suited to certain types of test takers or certain types of passages. Different reading techniques include:

    ▪ Reading the first & last sentences of every paragraph

    ▪ Reading the entire introduction and conclusion, as well as the first and last sentences of each body paragraph

    ▪ Reading questions before reading the passage

    ▪ Reading the entire passage

    ▪ Read a paragraph, search for relevant questions, repeat

    ▪ Skimming the entire passage

- Use annotations to map reading passages as you read them and assist you with recalling important information later.
- Evaluate the difficulty of the questions for a given passage and then start with the easiest questions first. You may be able to answer "Easy" questions before even completing a passage reading.
- When handling paired passages, focus entirely on Passage A and then entirely on Passage B before moving on to synthesis questions.

- Keep some general reminders for Reading test success in mind, such as:

  - Read all your answer choices
  - Stick to what's in the passage
  - Focus on reading comprehension rather than topic knowledge
  - Avoid tricking yourself and follow your gut instinct if two answers seem plausible
  - Personalize your overall reading test strategy

- As a basic strategy for bringing all these skills together, consider the following approach:

  1. Use a passage order that works for you(generally easiest to hardest)
  2. Read actively and annotate the passage
  3. Analyze questions for difficulty and purpose
  4. Answer questions strategically
  5. Move to next passage after guessing on any remaining questions
  6. If time allows, review guesses

KNOWLEDGE CHECK: READING

40 Questions—35 Minutes

> **Directions:** There are multiple passages in this test. Each passage is accompanied by multiple questions. After you finish reading a passage, choose the best answer to each question and fill in the corresponding oval on your answer sheet. You may refer to the passages as often as necessary.

PASSAGE I

PROSE FICTION: The following excerpt is taken from the novel *Twilight Sleep* (1927) by Edith Wharton.

The marriage of her half-brother had been Nona Manford's first real sorrow. Not that she had disapproved of his choice: how could anyone take that funny irresponsible little Lita Cliffe
5 seriously enough to disapprove of her? The sisters-in-law were soon the best of friends; if Nona had a fault to find with Lita, it was that she didn't worship the incomparable Jim as blindly as his sister did. But then Lita was made to be
10 worshipped, not to worship; that was manifest in the calm gaze of her long narrow nut-colored eyes, in the hieratic fixity of her lovely smile, in the very shape of her hands, so slim yet dimpled, hands which had never grown up, and which
15 drooped from her wrists as if listlessly waiting to be kissed, or lay like rare or upcurved magnolia-petals on the cushions luxuriously piled about her indolent body.

The Jim Wyants had been married for nearly
20 two years now; the baby was six months old; the pair were beginning to be regarded as one of the "old couples" of their set, one of the settled landmarks in the matrimonial quicksands of New York. Nona's love for her brother was too
25 disinterested for her not to rejoice in this: above all things she wanted her old Jim to be happy, and happy she was sure he was—or had been until lately. The mere getting away from Mrs. Manford's iron rule had been a greater relief
30 than he himself perhaps guessed. And then he was still the foremost of Lita's worshippers; still

enchanted by the childish whims, the unpunctuality, the irresponsibility, which made life with her such a thrillingly unsettled business after
35 the clock-work routine of his mother's perfect establishment.

All this Nona rejoiced in; but she ached at times with the loneliness of the perfect establishment, now that Jim, its one disturbing element,
40 had left. Jim guessed her loneliness, she was sure: it was he who encouraged the growing intimacy between his wife and his half-sister, and tried to make the latter feel that his house was another home to her.

45 Lita had always been amiably disposed toward Nona. The two, though so fundamentally different, were nearly of an age, and united by the prevailing passion for every form of sport. Lita, in spite of her soft curled-up attitudes, was not
50 only a tireless dancer but a brilliant if uncertain tennis-player, and an adventurous rider to hounds. Between her hours of lolling, and smoking amber-scented cigarettes, every moment of her life was crammed with dancing, riding, or
55 games. During the two or three months before the baby's birth, when Lita had been reduced to partial inactivity, Nona had rather feared that her perpetual craving for new "thrills" might lead to some insidious form of time-killing—some of
60 the drinking or drugging that went on among the young women of their set; but Lita had sunk into a state of smiling animal patience, as if the mysterious work going on in her tender young body had a sacred significance for her, and it was
65 enough to lie still and let it happen. All she asked was that nothing should "hurt" her: she had the

blind dread of physical pain common also to most of the young women of her set. But all that was so easily managed nowadays: Mrs. Manford (who took charge
70 of the business, Lita being an orphan) of course knew the most perfect "Twilight Sleep" establishment in the country, installed Lita in its most luxurious suite, and filled her room with spring flowers, hot-house fruits, new novels and all the latest picture-papers—
75 and Lita drifted into motherhood as lightly and unperceivingly as if the wax doll which suddenly appeared in the cradle at her bedside had been brought there in one of the big bunches of hot-house roses that she found every morning on her pillow.
80   "Of course there ought to be no Pain…nothing but Beauty…It ought to be one of the loveliest, most poetic things in the world to have a baby," Mrs. Manford declared, in the bright efficient voice which made loveliness and poetry sound like the attributes
85 of an advanced industrialism, and babies something to be turned out in series like Fords. And Jim's joy in his son had been unbounded; and Lita really hadn't minded in the least.

1. The mood of this passage can best be described as:

   A. melancholy.

   B. reflective.

   C. humorous.

   D. lonely.

2. What is the main reason for Nona's loneliness after Jim gets married?

   F. She misses having her brother around at the house all the time.

   G. She is unhappy with the new addition to her family.

   H. She is jealous of her brother's relationship with Lita.

   J. She is struggling to find happiness in her own life.

3. What does the passage suggest about Mrs. Manford?

   A. She is wealthy and influential in New York society.

   B. She values a traditional, close-knit family life.

   C. She has unreasonable expectations for her grandchildren.

   D. She can be controlling and overbearing towards family members.

4. What is the significance of the phrase "the matrimonial quicksands of New York" (line 23–24) in the passage?

   F. It emphasizes the stable nature of relationships in New York society.

   G. It suggests that New York is a place where many marriages fail.

   H. It underscores the challenges that young people face when getting married.

   J. It implies that people in New York are too focused on their careers to prioritize their relationships.

5. It can be reasonably inferred from the passage that:

   A. the novel's title refers to a form of medical treatment related to childbirth.

   B. Nona and Lita will grow much closer by the end of the novel.

   C. Jim wants a divorce from Lita.

   D. Lita dislikes Nona, but Nona doesn't realize it.

6. Which of the following statements best summarizes Lita's approach to her pregnancy?

   F. As a thrill seeker, Lita spent much of her pregnancy engaged in risky behaviors.

   G. Lita had no interest in becoming a mother and was miserable while pregnant.

   H. Lita became calmer and more patient as a result of her pregnancy, as if mindfully admiring the process.

   J. Lita spent the entire pregnancy gripped by terror at the thought of the pain she would experience.

7. According to the passage, a trait that Lita and Nona share is a:

A. fear of pain.

B. shy personality and a tendency to be introspective.

C. distaste for reckless behaviors.

D. love for playing sports.

8. As used in line 10, the word *manifest* most nearly means:

F. demonstrate.

G. incite.

H. obvious.

J. documented.

9. Which character is described as spending large amounts of time partying, dancing, and smoking?

A. Lita

B. Nona

C. Jim

D. Mrs. Mansford

10. Which of the following is NOT likely to happen in the remainder of the novel?

F. Mrs. Manford and Jim will have a falling out and never speak to each other again.

G. Nona and Lita will get into a feud over something trivial.

H. Nona will get married to Lita's older brother.

J. Lita will die giving birth to her first child.

PASSAGE II

SOCIAL SCIENCE: The following passage is taken from an academic guide to the field of cultural geography.

In the mid-twentieth century, many American cities were in a state of decay and decline. Suburbanization and the white flight that accompanied it had decentralized the power and resources once
5 consolidated in the urban milieu, leaving urban neighborhoods with fewer options for renewal than suburban communities. Across the country, once populous urban neighborhoods were often left to decay while their remaining residents suf-
10 fered through crumbling infrastructure, decreased property values, and increased crime rates. Urban planners and politicians, seeking to revitalize these cities, often turned to large-scale demolition and redevelopment projects. Recognizing how this
15 so-called "urban renewal" failed to take the needs of residents into account, Jane Jacobs argued that the best way to improve cities was to focus on their existing communities and the intricate connections that make them thrive. This was the topic
20 of Jacobs' 1961 book *The Death and Life of Great American Cities*, a key work in the fields of urban studies and cultural geography which continues to make a profound impact to this day.

Jacobs was a journalist and activist who
25 devoted her life to understanding the urban fabric of New York City. In *The Death and Life of Great American Cities*, she argued that healthy cities were those that had a diverse mix of people, buildings, and uses. She also advocated for a pedestrian-
30 friendly built environment, with small blocks, short streets, and mixed-use development. Jacobs believed that urban renewal, which at the time involved razing entire neighborhoods and replacing them with new construction, was a flawed
35 approach that destroyed the social and economic fabric of cities. These approaches rarely considered the needs of existing urban residents, instead focusing on theoretical ideals of what a modern city could look like rather than how it could func-
40 tion for those who would inhabit it. This type of development also tended to cater to the needs of wealthier classes above those with less money, despite the fact these neighborhoods were often already inhabited by lower income residents. Jacobs
45 argued that for urban planners to renew cities in ways that actually serve residents, they would have to better understand what makes communities thrive and plan spaces to better suit existing community needs.

50 One of Jacobs' key contributions to urban studies was the concept of social capital. This refers to the networks of relationships and trust that exist within communities. Jacobs believed that social capital was essential for creating vibrant
55 and resilient cities. When people know and trust each other, they are more likely to work together to solve problems and build strong local economies. Jacobs envisioned cities wherein neighbors felt connected to one another and their neighborhood
60 as a whole. She argued that social capital allows people to feel a sense of belonging and connection to their neighborhoods, which can lead to greater civic engagement and participation.

Another concept that Jacobs emphasized was
65 the importance of "eyes on the street." She believed that having a diverse mix of people and uses in a neighborhood led to more eyes on the street, which in turn made the streets safer and livelier. When people are out and about in their neighbor-
70 hoods, they are more likely to notice and report crime, and to interact with each other in positive ways. This creates a sense of collective ownership over public spaces and the social dynamics they support, which is essential for building strong
communities.

75 Some of Jacobs' ideas were considered controversial at the time, but they have since been widely adopted by urban planners and scholars. Today, many cities are focused on creating walkable, mixed-use neighborhoods that promote social capital and community engagement. However,
80 the challenges of gentrification and displacement remain prominent, particularly as relates to racial and socioeconomic divisions. In some cases, the very communities that Jacobs sought to protect

have been pushed out by rising rents and prop-
85 erty values. This highlights the continued need
for thoughtful and equitable urban planning that
prioritizes the needs of existing residents.

It's worth acknowledging that Jacobs' critics
both then and now have noted these exact con-
90 cerns by saying that her theories are dismissive
of racial issues and lean too heavily on solutions
that create gentrification rather than preventing
it. These critics often argued that Jacobs got the
big picture right by understanding that communi-
95 ties needed to be centered during urban planning;
however, they claimed that Jacobs overlooked critical issues about the demographics of communities
themselves, such as by not mentioning how issues
like race and social class add nuance to the topics
100 she highlighted. Contemporary urban theorists
recognize these faults in Jacobs' body of work
while still generally agreeing that, overall, her
contributions to the field have nonetheless proven
invaluable.
105 In conclusion, Jane Jacobs' legacy in urban
studies is profound. Her work challenged the dominant paradigm of urban renewal and highlighted
the importance of social capital and community
engagement in building healthy cities. While there
110 is still much work to be done to ensure that all residents can benefit from the urban renaissance that
is taking place in many American cities, Jacobs'
ideas remain relevant and inspiring. As Jacobs says
in *The Death and Life of Great American Cities*,
115 "Cities have the capability of providing something
for everybody, only because, and only when, they
are created by everybody."

11. According to the passage, which of the following
was a major contributing factor to the declin-
ing state of American cities in the mid-twentieth
century?

A. Neoliberal economic policies

B. Gentrification

C. Urban renewal

D. Suburbanization

12. According to its use in the passage, "urban
renewal" can best be defined as:

F. investing time and money into repairing a city's
physical infrastructure.

G. demolishing older neighborhoods and developing new infrastructure atop them.

H. welcoming community input on how to improve
the urban environment.

J. centering the needs of the wealthy over those of
the poorer classes.

13. Jane Jacobs' primary critique of mid-twentieth
century urban renewal was that it:

A. did not consider existing resident communities
or their unique needs and collective resources.

B. required too much demolition and disturbed
daily life.

C. didn't take racial issues into account.

D. was too costly and required too much of a time
and labor investment from struggling cities.

14. Julio needs his bike repaired so he goes to the corner bodega to talk to the owner, Marilyn, who he
heard has a cousin in the neighborhood who fixes
bikes. Marilyn gives Julio her cousin's number, and
the cousin fixes the bike for a discount since Julio
knows Marilyn. According to Jane Jacobs, this
scenario is an example of:

F. white flight.

G. social capital.

H. eyes on the street.

J. community engagement.

15. The author's purpose in writing this passage is to:

    A. provide an overview of Jane Jacobs and discuss her contributions to urban studies and cultural geography.

    B. define numerous terms first coined by Jane Jacobs.

    C. critique Jacobs' theories for being incomplete and neglecting issues related to race.

    D. analyze Jacobs' impact on a variety of fields of study within cultural geography.

16. The author most likely included the sixth paragraph (lines 88–103) in order to:

    F. summarize how Jacobs's book was reviewed by book critics when it was first published.

    G. offer specific details about why Jacobs was wrong in her evaluation of mid-twentieth century urban renewal.

    H. balance the otherwise laudatory evaluation of Jacobs by including information on what some of her critics have said.

    J. offer counterclaims to Jacobs' critics to show that Jacobs' analysis is indisputable.

17. As used in line 106, the word *paradigm* most nearly means:

    A. perspective.

    B. model.

    C. theory.

    D. shift.

18. The author most likely included the quote in the final sentence of the passage (lines 114–116) primarily to:

    F. provide a counterclaim from a critic of Jacobs' work.

    G. lend credibility to their passage by showing that they've read Jacobs' book.

    H. show that Jacobs was considered a controversial and radical thinker in her time.

    J. provide an example of something Jacobs said in her book that matches the author's summary of her work.

19. The main idea of the concept of "eyes on the street" is that:

    A. the more attractive the aesthetic of a neighborhood is, the more likely people are to want to invest in it.

    B. official and unofficial networks and relationships exist between individuals who share communities.

    C. the more diverse a mix of people going about daily life on the street there is, the more involved in the community individuals tend to be.

    D. whenever one is in public space, they are likely being watched by far more people than they realize.

20. It can reasonably be inferred from this passage that:

    F. cities today face much more complicated problems than they did in Jacobs's time.

    G. Jane Jacobs has largely been forgotten in the history of cultural geography.

    H. students don't enjoy reading *The Death and Life of Great American Cities* because it is now considered outdated.

    J. a college-level class entitled "Introduction to Urban Studies" would likely include at least one reference to Jacobs' work.

PASSAGE III

HUMANITIES: Passage A is taken from a philosophy textbook entry. Passage B is taken from an essay in a philosophy journal.

PASSAGE A

Georg Wilhelm Friedrich Hegel (1770-1831) is one of the most prominent German philosophers of all time. Though his dense works are notorious for giving today's philosophy students headaches,
5 his complex ideas were so revolutionary that they founded the basis of most modern philosophy, including serving as inspiration to prominent thinkers like Karl Marx, Søren Kierkegaard, and Michel Foucault. Hegel developed a way of thinking known
10 as the dialectic which involved investigating how contradictions between two seemingly true things, termed a thesis and antithesis, can reveal an even higher level of truth. The process of thinking through the contradiction between thesis and antithesis and
15 its implications was known as the "Hegelian dialectic" and the idea was that engaging in dialectical thinking helped advance knowledge over time.

Hegel's most illustrative example of the dialectic involves the idea of power. The concept is often
20 termed the "master/slave" dialectic and it describes a dialectical thought process which imagines the power dynamic that would exist between an enslaved person and the person who enslaves them. Sometimes also referred to as the "Lordship and
25 Bondage" dialectic, the concept is essentially that the two cannot exist without the other. Let's call the thesis the idea that a person cannot be enslaved without another person forcing them to do so. No one would choose to be enslaved, most likely, so
30 they can only become so if someone else exerts power over them. Meanwhile, the antithesis is the idea that the person who forces another person to be their slave cannot feel that sense of power over another without a person to force into slavery. Their
35 existence as "master" over a slave only happens so long as the slave exists. Therefore, the power of one does not exist without the antithetical power of the other. This master/slave dialectic is thus meant to reveal a greater truth about the nature of power and
40 how it is supported by contradictions.

PASSAGE B

There can be no doubt that much of modern philosophy has been shaped by the foundations set by Hegel's philosophical endeavors. Hegel's philosophy, particularly his concept of the dialectic, in-
45 fluenced a number of prominent philosophers who came after him, including Karl Marx and Simone de Beauvoir. In the case of Marx, his materialist interpretation of history was built upon Hegelian dialectics. Marx posited that economic and social
50 conditions were the primary drivers of historical change, and that class struggle was the mechanism by which this change occurred. In doing so, Marx used the dialectic to uncover contradictions and conflicts in human society, particularly those
55 related to power and exploitation.

Similarly, de Beauvoir used Hegelian dialectics in her feminist philosophy. In her influential book, *The Second Sex*, de Beauvoir used the dialectic to critique the oppressive patriarchal structure
60 of society. She argued that, like Hegel's master/ slave dialectic, the relationship between men and women was one of power and subordination. De Beauvoir used the dialectic to reveal the contradictions inherent in gender roles and to call for
65 the liberation of women from oppressive societal structures.

While Marx and de Beauvoir are perhaps the most well-known philosophers to have been influenced by Hegel, a number of others have also
70 drawn upon his ideas. Friedrich Nietzsche, for example, used the dialectic to explore the nature of power and morality, and Jean-Paul Sartre used Hegelian concepts to develop his existentialist philosophy. Martin Heidegger, meanwhile, focused on
75 the idea of being and its relation to time, building upon Hegelian ideas about history and the self.

One can be certain that the legacy of Hegel's philosophy lies not only in his original ideas, but in the rich tradition of philosophical inquiry that
80 his work inspired. By encouraging a focus on the contradictions and conflicts that arise in human society and thought, Hegel paved the way for later philosophers to use the dialectic to uncover new insights and refine existing ones.

21. In Passage A, the purpose of the first paragraph (lines 1–17) is to:

A. explain the master/slave dialectic.

B. introduce Hegel and the concept of dialectical thinking.

C. criticize Michel Foucault and other philosophers who followed Hegel.

D. give a background on Hegel's early years.

22. Based on passage A, the reader can reasonably infer that:

F. no one read Hegel anymore after the 19th century.

G. power dynamics, such as those between master and slave, do not contain contradictions.

H. Michel Foucault used dialectical thinking when developing his philosophical writings.

J. people find Hegel to be a very approachable philosopher to read.

23. When the author of passage A says that Hegel's works "[give] today's philosophy students headaches" (line 4), they are implying that:

A. Hegel is notorious for being difficult to read and understand.

B. Hegel can only be read in old tomes written in tiny script.

C. people find Hegel exceptionally boring and aren't interested in him.

D. many find Hegel's philosophical ideas offensive.

24. How might you characterize the primary contradiction of the master/slave dialectic?

F. Power can be both given and taken away.

G. No one wants to be a slave, yet some people are enslaved.

H. Power is also weakness.

J. Neither the slave nor the master can exist without the other.

25. Karl Marx used dialectical thinking to ponder the nature of:

A. race.

B. gender.

C. government.

D. class structures.

26. Based on Passage B, Simone de Beauvoir would likely argue that the master/slave dialectic relates to:

F. the dynamic of power and subordination that exists between men and women.

G. the nature of time in relationship to human existence.

H. how exploitation is inherent in most power dynamics.

J. human conceptions of morality as concerns power.

27. Both passages define Hegel's dialectic as a(n):

A. outdated approach to philosophy that has been mostly abandoned by modern thinkers.

B. key tenet in the development of existentialist philosophy.

C. way of thinking about the world that highlights contradictions and conflicts in society.

D. useful way to engage in philosophical debate with those who think differently.

28. Which statement best summarizes the differences and similarities between the passages?

    F. Both passages provide specific examples of how Hegel influenced other philosophers, but only passage B provides a working definition of the dialectic.

    G. Both passages summarize how Hegel contributed to the history of philosophy, but passage B provides more specific examples of how his ideas influenced later thinkers.

    H. Neither passage considers Hegel's personal biography, but Passage A gives some details about how Hegel was received by critics.

    J. Neither passage gives examples of Hegel's impact, but Passage A provides an example of a specific concept with which he is associated.

29. The authors of both passages would likely agree that:

    A. Hegel's philosophy suffered because it failed to account for things like class and gender, forcing later thinkers to correct him.

    B. Hegel's work was full of irreconcilable contradictions that make it less valuable to modern society.

    C. the thinkers who came after Hegel made better use of dialectical thinking than Hegel himself did.

    D. to have a full understanding of the history of philosophical thinking, a student would need to study Hegel's dialectic.

30. The authors of both passages share a primary purpose, which is to:

    F. define the dialectic and provide an example to support that definition.

    G. critique those who came after Hegel for their interpretations of the dialectic.

    H. increase a reader's understanding of Hegel's contributions to philosophical history.

    J. ensure the reader has a clear understanding of the master/slave dialectic.

PASSAGE IV

NATURAL SCIENCES: This is an excerpt from *The Outline of Science, Vol. 1* (1921) by J. Arthur Thomson.

It is highly probable that for long ages the waters covered the earth, and that all the primeval vegetation consisted of simple Flagellates in the universal Open Sea. But contraction of the earth's
5 crust brought about elevations and depressions of the sea-floor, and in places the solid substratum was brought near enough the surface to allow the floating plants to begin to settle down without getting out of the light. This is how Professor
10 Church pictures the beginning of a fixed vegetation - a very momentous step in evolution. It was perhaps among this early vegetation that animals had their first successes. As the floor of the sea in these shallow areas was raised higher and higher
15 there was a beginning of dry land. The sedentary plants already spoken of were the ancestors of the shore seaweeds, and there is no doubt that when we go down at the lowest tide and wade cautiously out among the jungle of vegetation only exposed
20 on such occasions we are getting a glimpse of very ancient days. This is the forest primeval.

Animals below the level of zoophytes and sponges are called Protozoa. The word obviously means "First Animals," but all that we can say is
25 that the very simplest of them may give us some hint of the simplicity of the original first animals. For it is quite certain that the vast majority of the Protozoa today are far too complicated to be thought of as primitive. Though most of them are
30 microscopic, each is an animal complete in itself, with the same fundamental bodily attributes as are manifested in ourselves. They differ from animals of higher degree in not being built up of the unit areas or corpuscles called cells. They have no cells,
35 no tissues, no organs, in the ordinary acceptation of these words, but many of them show a great complexity of internal structure, far exceeding that of the ordinary cells that build up the tissues of higher animals. They are complete living creatures
40 which have not gone in for body-making.

In the dim and distant past there was a time when the only animals were of the nature of Protozoa, and it is safe to say that one of the great steps in evolution was the establishment of three
45 great types of Protozoa: (a) Some were very active, the Infusorians, like the slipper animalcule, the night-light (Noctiluca), which makes the seas phosphorescent at night, and the deadly Trypanosome, which causes Sleeping Sickness. (b) Others
50 were very sluggish, the parasitic Sporozoa, like the malaria organism which the mosquito introduces into man's body. (c) Others were neither very active nor very passive, the Rhizopods, with out-flowing processes of living matter. This amœboid line of
55 evolution has been very successful; it is represented by the Rhizopods, such as Amœbæ and the chalk-forming Foraminifera and the exquisitely beautiful flint-shelled Radiolarians of the open sea. They have their counterparts in the amœboid cells of
60 most multicellular animals, such as the phagocytes which migrate about in the body, engulfing and digesting intruding bacteria, serving as sappers and miners when something has to be broken down and built up again, and performing other useful
65 offices.

The great naturalist Louis Agassiz once said that the biggest gulf in Organic Nature was that between the unicellular and the multicellular animals (Protozoa and Metazoa). But the gulf was
70 bridged very long ago when sponges, stinging animals, and simple worms were evolved, and showed, for the first time, a "body." What would one not give to be able to account for the making of a body, one of the great steps in evolution! No one knows,
75 but the problem is not altogether obscure.

When an ordinary Protozoon or one-celled animal divides into two or more, which is its way of multiplying, the daughter-units thus formed float apart and live independent lives. But there are
80 a few Protozoa in which the daughter-units are not quite separated off from one another, but remain coherent. Thus Volvox, a beautiful green ball, found in some canals and the like, is a colony of a

thousand or even ten thousand cells. It has almost
85 formed a body! But in this "colony-making" Protozoon, and in others like it, the component cells
are all of one kind, whereas in true multicellular
animals there are different kinds of cells, showing
division of labour. There are some other Protozoa
90 in which the nucleus or kernel divides into many
nuclei within the cell. This is seen in the Giant
Amœba (Pelomyxa), sometimes found in duck-
ponds, or the beautiful Opalina, which always lives
in the hind part of the frog's food-canal. If a por-
95 tion of the living matter of these Protozoa should
gather round each of the nuclei, then that would be
the beginning of a body. It would be still nearer the
beginning of a body if division of labour set in, and
if there was a setting apart of egg-cells and sperm-
100 cells distinct from body-cells.

31. The author claims that Protozoa cannot be
"thought of as primitive" (line 29) because:

A. they are living creatures but do not have bodies.

B. they are not made up of cells.

C. their bodies have many of the same attributes as
human bodies.

D. scientists still do not fully understand them.

32. The passage defines a Noctiluca as:

F. any animal without cells, tissues, or organs.

G. a deadly Protozoa that causes Sleeping Sickness.

H. a multicellular animal defined as a Metazoa.

J. an active form of Protozoa that produces
phosphorescence.

33. The passage explains that Protozoa include:

I. Rhizopods

II. Sporozoa

III. Flagellates

A. I only

B. I and III only

C. II and III only

D. I and II only

34. The author's statement that "when we go down at
the lowest tide and wade cautiously out among the
jungle of vegetation only exposed on such occasions we are getting a glimpse of very ancient days"
(lines 17–21) means that:

F. ancient treasures can be found on the floor of
the ocean.

G. plant life on the sea floor is reflective of plant
life as it was in ancient times.

H. opening one's eyes underwater creates the illu-
sion of time travel.

J. very small traces of ancient vegetation are found
in the sea occasionally.

35. It can be inferred from the passage that the word
Protozoa:

A. is a synonym for sponge.

B. contains elements that mean "first" and
"animal."

C. means "too complicated" in Latin.

D. existed before the term Metazoa.

36. The passage states that Rhizopods:

I. have out-flowing processes of living matter.

II. include Amoebae and Foraminifera.

III. are neither very active nor very passive.

F. I only

G. I and III only

H. II and III only

J. I, II, and III

37. According to the fourth paragraph (lines 66–75),
naturalist Louis Agassiz:

A. is the greatest naturalist in the history of organic
nature.

B. is considered laughable among more contemporary naturalists.

C. knew exactly how bodies were made.

D. mischaracterized a crucial element of organic
nature.

38. The passage claims that Earth:

- **F.** is not nearly as old as scientists believe.
- **G.** has a crust that contracts without affecting the sea floor.
- **H.** was likely once covered with water.
- **J.** no longer possesses the vegetation it did in ancient times.

39. When Protozoa split into two parts, those parts:

- **A.** die immediately.
- **B.** live independently.
- **C.** cease to divide.
- **D.** become incoherent.

40. What is the main idea of the third paragraph (lines 41–65)?

- **F.** Protozoa were once Earth's only animals.
- **G.** Infusorian Protozoa are very active.
- **H.** There are three distinct types of Protozoa.
- **J.** Phagocytes migrate about in the body.

ANSWER KEY AND EXPLANATIONS

1. B	9. A	17. B	25. D	33. D
2. F	10. J	18. J	26. F	34. G
3. D	11. D	19. C	27. C	35. B
4. G	12. G	20. J	28. G	36. J
5. A	13. A	21. B	29. D	37. D
6. H	14. G	22. H	30. H	38. H
7. D	15. A	23. A	31. C	39. B
8. H	16. H	24. J	32. J	40. H

1. **The correct answer is B.** In this passage, the tone is reflective. Even though the story is communicated through a third-person omniscient narrator, the passage still communicates that Nona is reflecting on and has thought a lot about her relationships with her brother, Jim, and his wife, Lita.

2. **The correct answer is F.** The passage states that Nona and Jim were very close, and Nona "ached" with "loneliness" (lines 37–38) in her mother's home after Jim got married and moved away. She missed having her brother around and sharing experiences together. The passage also implies that Lita is taking more of Jim's attention that used to be devoted to his sibling. There is no indication that Nona is unhappy with Lita joining the family (choice G); in fact, the narrator says she "rejoiced" (line 37) that Jim felt so happy in his marriage. While the reader may infer that Nona was jealous of Lita (choice H), there is less direct support for this conclusion than there is for the idea that Nona missed spending time with her brother. Though the passage mentions Nona's loneliness, there is no indication she is unhappy with her own life (choice J).

3. **The correct answer is D.** The passage implies that Mrs. Manford is controlling and overbearing to at least one family member—her son, Jim. The narrator states that Jim had been relieved to get away from Mrs. Manford's "iron rule" (line 29) and her attempts to maintain the household as a "perfect establishment" (lines 35–36). She is also shown in the final paragraphs taking charge of all the arrangements for Lita's birth experience.

4. **The correct answer is G.** The phrase "the matrimonial quicksands of New York" suggests that New York is a place where many marriages fail. The use of the term "quicksands" metaphorically implies that marriages in New York can be hazardous or difficult to navigate and may even lead to sinking, failure, or a sense of being trapped. None of the other options are supported by the passage.

5. **The correct answer is A.** The only inference that can be corroborated by the text itself is choice A. The title of the novel is given in the passage introduction, "Twilight Sleep." The passage states that Lita wishes that nothing would hurt her (line 66) during her pregnancy. She has a "blind dread of physical pain" (line 67), but, the passage states, "that was so easily managed nowadays" (lines 68–69). The passage then goes on to describe the "'Twilight Sleep' establishment," which will let Lita "[drift] into motherhood [. . .] lightly and unperceivingly" (lines 75–76). All of this can be taken to imply that "Twilight Sleep" alludes, at least, to a medical treatment that dulls or alters the pain or experience of childbirth.

6. **The correct answer is H.** Choice H provides the best summary of what is stated in the passage about Lita's pregnancy; namely, that after becoming pregnant, "Lita had sunk into a state of smiling animal patience, as if the mysterious work going on in her tender young body had a sacred significance for her, and it was enough to lie still and let it happen" (lines 61–65). The passage contradicts choice F and there is no support for choice G. While the author does mention that Lita feared the pain of childbirth, the statement in choice

J that she was "gripped with terror" for the "entire pregnancy" does not accurately reflect the degree of worry expressed in the passage.

7. **The correct answer is D.** The answer to this question can be found in lines 47–48 when the narrator notes that the two women were similar ages and "united by the prevailing passion for every form of sport."

8. **The correct answer is H.** Each of these words could be a definition for the word *manifest* in different contexts; however, only *obvious* makes sense in the context from lines 10–12. If you weren't sure, you could use a process of elimination by noticing that the grammatical context of the sentence requires an adjective rather than a verb, eliminating choices F and G right away. Of those that remain, choice H more logically completes the sentence.

9. **The correct answer is A.** Lita is the person who the narrator describes as being a party animal. She is described as "a tireless dancer" (lines 52–53) who spent hours of her life having fun, playing games, and "smoking amber-scented cigarettes" (line 53). She is the only person described this way in the narrative.

10. **The correct answer is J.** This question is tricky if you don't recognize that you're not making a prediction so much as determining which possibility is actually impossible given the information in the passage. Since line 20 states that "the baby was six months old" and the events of her childbirth experience are referenced in the past tense throughout, it would be impossible for Lita to die giving birth to her first child in the remainder of the novel.

11. **The correct answer is D.** The author opens the first paragraph by stating "In the mid-twentieth century, many American cities were in a state of decay and decline. Suburbanization and the white flight that accompanied it had decentralized the power and resources once consolidated in the urban milieu, leaving urban neighborhoods with fewer options for renewal than suburban communities" (lines 1–7). Gentrification (choice B) and urban renewal (choice C) are mentioned elsewhere

in the passage. There is no mention of neoliberal economic policies (choice A).

12. **The correct answer is G.** All of the statements given offer different concepts of the term "urban renewal" as understood in different contexts or by different thinkers. However, only choice G correctly reflects the way Jacobs would have defined it, which the author of this passage summarizes by stating: "Jacobs believed that urban renewal, which at the time involved razing entire neighborhoods and replacing them with new construction, was a flawed approach that destroyed the social and economic fabric of cities" (lines 31–36).

13. **The correct answer is A.** To answer this question, you need to identify the statement that best matches how the author summarizes Jane Jacobs' ideas. Since Jacobs believed that mid-twentieth century approaches to urban renewal "rarely considered the needs of existing urban residents" (lines 36–37) or the social capital they collectively possess, choice A is the best summary of her critique as communicated by the author.

14. **The correct answer is G.** All four of the given terms are mentioned in the passage, but only one correctly matches this scenario. To arrive at this answer, you first need to recognize that the author defines Jacobs' concept of social capital as "the networks of relationships and trust that exist within communities" (lines 52–53). In the scenario described, someone (Julio) goes to a local shop owner they know and trust (Marilyn) to get help with a matter (fixing a bike) that requires help from someone that they, in turn, know and trust (Marilyn's cousin). Therefore, the network of relationships described in the scenario is a good representation of how social capital helps strengthen community bonds, such as by allowing Julio to get in touch with someone local who can fix his bike and even offers him a discount due to his network of neighborhood connections.

15. **The correct answer is A.** If you recognize that the content, structure, and occasion for this passage all point to it being an informative overview, then you'll recognize that the best summary of the

author's purpose is choice A. While the author defines some of Jacobs's terms (choice B), mentions that some of her critics thought she neglected race issues (choice C), and analyzes her contributions to various fields of study within cultural geography (choice D), none of these alone encompasses the author's purpose for the passage as a whole.

16. **The correct answer is H.** The author spends most of the passage discussing Jane Jacobs' work, but they pivot in the sixth paragraph to include some of the critiques that Jacobs' work received. The answer that best summarizes this pivot is choice H since the author likely offers these critiques to bring balance to their analysis. Choice F is a misreading of the type of "critic" to which the author refers, whereas choices G and J are contradicted by the content of the passage as a whole.

17. **The correct answer is B.** The term *paradigm* is defined as "an example, pattern, or model, especially one that becomes typical." Contextually, this sentence suggests that Jacobs challenged the dominant model of urban renewal that was commonly deployed in the early 1960s, when her book was first published.

18. **The correct answer is J.** Both the fact that the author states that the quote is from *The Death and Life of Great American Cities* as well as the author's choice to position it at the end of the concluding paragraph is evidence that the quote was included to provide a summative example of Jacobs ideas in her own words.

19. **The correct answer is C.** In lines 65–73, the author states that "[Jacobs] believed that having a diverse mix of people and uses in a neighborhood led to more eyes on the street, which in turn made the streets safer and livelier" because it created "a sense of collective ownership over public spaces and the social dynamics they support." This evaluation is best summarized by choice C. Choice B is a summary of social capital rather than the concept of "eyes on the street." Choices A and D are not mentioned in the passage.

20. **The correct answer is J.** The author states multiple times that *The Death and Life of Great American Cities* was pivotal to the development of contemporary urban studies as a field and that Jacobs was a highly influential thinker within the subject. As a result, you

can reasonably infer that an intro level college course on urban studies would include at least one reference to her work. None of the other assertions can be supported directly by the passage.

21. **The correct answer is B.** The purpose of paragraph 1 is to introduce Hegel and the concept of dialectical thinking so that in paragraph 2, the author can go on to explain the master/slave dialectic (choice A). None of the other answers appear in the passage.

22. **The correct answer is H.** The passage states that Hegel's ideas were a big influence on Michel Foucault. The passage also states that dialectical thinking was central to Hegelian philosophy. Therefore, one can infer that if Foucault was drawing on Hegel's philosophy, he must have also been engaged in dialectical thinking. Don't get distracted by answers that seem true simply because they reference things from the passage; choice F is never implied, and choices G and J are contradicted by the passage.

23. **The correct answer is A.** Saying that the works give students headaches is a figurative way of saying that Hegel is difficult to read and comprehend.

24. **The correct answer is J.** As Passage A states in lines 24–25, "Sometimes also referred to as the 'Lordship and Bondage' dialectic, the concept is essentially that the two cannot exist without the other."

25. **The correct answer is D.** Passage B notes that "Marx posited that economic and social conditions were the primary drivers of historical change, and that class struggle was the mechanism by which this change occurred" (lines 49–52). Therefore, you can reasonably infer that Marx used dialectical thinking to ponder the nature of class structures.

26. **The correct answer is F.** Each of the answers represents a different way that later philosophers took up dialectical thinking (as covered in passage B), but only choice F correctly matches what the passage says about how Simone de Beauvoir used the master/slave dialectic to consider gender-based power dynamics. Choice G relates to Heidegger's use of the dialectic, choice H to Marx's, and choice J to Nietzsche's.

27. **The correct answer is C.** Choice C is a succinct summary of how both passages describe the dialectic. There is no support for choice A. Choice B relates to

a small detail in Passage B rather than a definition for the term *dialectic*. Choice D represents an inference one might make about the dialectic rather than a definition for the term.

28. **The correct answer is G.** If you understand the main idea of both passages, you should be able to identify choice G as the correct summary; both passages summarize Hegel's dialectic while only Passage B connects specific thinkers to the philosophies they generated as a result of Hegel's concepts.

29. **The correct answer is D.** Both authors make it clear that Hegel is a landmark thinker in the history of philosophy. Passage A states that "his complex ideas were so revolutionary that they founded the basis of most modern philosophy" (lines 5–6), while Passage B notes that "modern philosophy has been shaped by the foundations set by Hegel's philosophical endeavors" (lines 41–43). Consequently, it's reasonable to infer that any student who wants to have a full understanding of the history of philosophical thinking would need to study Hegel's dialectic. The other assertions, meanwhile, cannot be supported by content from the passage.

30. **The correct answer is H.** Notice the key word *primary* in the question. While some options (choices F and J) point to secondary purposes the authors had at points in their writing, only choice H points to their shared primary purpose. There is no attempt to critique in either passage (choice G).

31. **The correct answer is C.** In the second sentence of the second paragraph, the author explains that "Protozoa today are far too complicated to be thought of as primitive" (lines 28–29) before explaining that "Though most of them are microscopic, each is an animal complete in itself, with the same fundamental bodily attributes as are manifested in ourselves" (lines 29–32). This supports the conclusion in choice C.

32. **The correct answer is J.** This question tests your ability to locate specific details in the passage. This particular information can be found in the third paragraph, which states that there are three great

types of Protozoa, and "Some were very active, the Infusorians, like . . . night-light (Noctiluca), which makes the seas phosphorescent at night" (lines 45–48), which supports the description in choice J.

33. **The correct answer is D.** The first paragraph of the passage is the only one that mentions Flagellates, and it mentions them before even defining Protozoa. It also defines them as "primeval vegetation" (lines 2–3), which means they were plants, not animals like Protozoa. Therefore, you can conclude that Flagellates were not Protozoa. The third paragraph defines both Sporozoa and Rhizopods as types of Protozoa. Therefore, statements I and II are true while statement III is false. Choice A makes the mistake of including only one of the true statements, and choices B and C both include the false statement.

34. **The correct answer is G.** Consider the main idea of the paragraph; the author is discussing ancient vegetation. Therefore, it is unlikely he would conclude the paragraph with tangents about ancient treasures (choice F) or optical illusions (choice H). The answer that is most relevant to the topic is choice G, which captures the author's meaning well. Choice J distorts the details of the passage to suggest the literal presence of ancient vegetation, rather than indicating the semblance of the vegetation to ancient conditions.

35. **The correct answer is B.** In the second sentence of the second paragraph, the author writes that Protozoa "obviously means 'First Animals. . .'" (lines 23–24). Therefore, it is reasonable to conclude that the word contains elements meaning "first" and "animal" (and it does, as proto means "first" and zoa means "animals").

36. **The correct answer is J.** According to the third paragraph of the passage, all three statements are true. This means the correct answer must be the one that includes all three statements.

37. **The correct answer is D.** Although the author defines Louis Agassiz as "great" (line 66), the author also states that the naturalist's statement about the gulf between unicellular and multicellular animals was "bridged" when "sponges, stinging

animals, and simple worms [. . .] showed, for the first time, a 'body'" (lines 70–72). This implies that Louis Agassiz mischaracterized a crucial element of organic nature, and choice D is the best answer.

38. **The correct answer is H.** The very first sentence of the passage supports choice H as it discusses the "universal Open Sea." The passage contains no evidence that supports choice F. The author states the opposite of choice G, explaining that the "contraction of the earth's crust brought about elevations and depressions of the sea-floor." The final sentence of the first paragraph also suggests that much of the vegetation on the sea floor is reflective of vegetation from ancient times.

39. **The correct answer is B.** In the first sentence of the final paragraph, the author writes that "When an ordinary Protozoon or one-celled animal divides into two or more, which is its way of multiplying, the daughter-units thus formed float apart and live independent lives" (lines 76–79). This supports choice B and contradicts choice A. There is no information as to whether the daughter Protozoa cease to divide once they are fully separated, so choice C is not the best answer. The author also writes that the daughter-units "remain coherent" (lines 81–82) even if they do not separate completely, which contradicts choice D.

40. **The correct answer is H.** Choice H captures the main idea of the paragraph, which states that there are "three great types of Protozoa" and goes on to define and provide examples of those types. Choices F, G, and J are all true, but they are mere details in the paragraph. None of them capture the paragraph's main idea.

Scoring Chart

Mark missed questions and calculate your total for each question category and the test as a whole. Then convert your raw score to a scaled score using the chart on page 529 in Chapter 16.

Question Types	Question Numbers	Score
Key Ideas and Details (KID)	2, 3, 5, 6, 7, 9, 10, 11, 12, 13, 14, 19, 20, 22, 23, 24, 25, 26, 31, 32, 33, 34, 36, 37, 38, 39, 40	_____/27
Craft and Structure (CS)	1, 4, 8, 15, 16, 17, 18, 21, 35	_____/9
Integration of Knowledge and Ideas (IKI)	27, 28, 29, 30	_____/4

Raw Score: ____ /40

Scaled Score:

PART V

THE SCIENCE TEST ON THE ACT®

19 | Introduction to ACT® Science

20 | Key Concepts in Science

21 | Strategies for Approaching
     the Science Section

CHAPTER

Introduction to ACT® Science

INTRODUCTION TO ACT® SCIENCE

OVERVIEW

- **How to Study with Part V**
- **All about the Science Section**
- **Scoring Table**
- **Types of Passages**
- **Sample Questions**
- **Common Challenges**
- **Summing It Up**

As you approach the ACT Science test, it's important for you to know how the section is structured, what to expect from the questions you'll be asked to answer, and what common challenges test takers encounter. In this chapter, we'll give a quick overview of the Science test as well as information on how to approach this part of the book. In the chapters that follow, we'll cover the structure of the test in more depth along with specific strategies you can use to approach questions and passages on the Science test.

HOW TO STUDY WITH PART V

This chapter covers the structure of the Science test and provides information on the types of passages and questions you'll be given. In Chapter 20, we'll talk about the major skills necessary for success in the Science section and give you an opportunity to review significant scientific concepts while brushing up on your data analysis skills. If you are a science whiz with limited study time, you may find that you are best suited skimming this section for review and moving on to the next chapter right away. Conversely, if you have a lot of study time, are someone who struggles with science, or just want an extra-detailed review, then we recommend studying Chapter 20 very closely. There are bound to be some concepts you haven't learned or skills you haven't developed. Focus first on reviewing and improving upon skills you've built in the past. Once you feel confident in those, then you can devote time to building competence in new skills. Finally, in Chapter 21, we'll provide you with expert guidance on proven strategies that will help you approach the Science section of the ACT. When you finish learning the strategies, you'll be able to put them to the test with an test-length Knowledge Check at the end of the chapter.

ALL ABOUT THE SCIENCE SECTION

On the ACT Science test, you'll be given 35 minutes to answer 40 multiple-choice questions designed to assess your understanding of the scientific method and your ability to analyze and interpret scientific information presented in passages, graphs, and tables. The Science section covers biology, chemistry, and physics, as well as Earth and space sciences like geology, astronomy, and meteorology. While these topics will be covered, you don't need to have any advanced knowledge of them to do well on the Science section, which tests your proficiency in essential science skills and practices as opposed to specific content or subject knowledge. Essentially, you can think of the Science section as an extension of the Reading section, since it tests your ability to read scientific information and data and interpret that information successfully.

Self-Reflection: Science

- Which science courses did you take in high school, and which have you not taken (yet)?

- Which science concepts have historically been easier for you to understand?

- Which science concepts have historically been harder for you to understand?

- Did you experience any conditions during your high school experience (remote learning, recovering from surgery, etc.) that could have created gaps in your science learning? If so, what topics were covered during those gaps?

- Which science skills require more effort for you?

The ACT Science test comprises three types of questions.

INTERPRETATION OF DATA (45–55% OF QUESTIONS)

You'll be asked to analyze scientific data presented to you in a variety of formats, including tables, graphs, diagrams, etc.

SCIENTIFIC INVESTIGATION (20–30% OF QUESTIONS)

You'll be asked about experimental tools, procedures, and design, including independent and dependent variables.

EVALUATION OF MODELS, INFERENCES, AND EXPERIMENTAL RESULTS (25–35% OF QUESTIONS)

You'll be asked to evaluate the validity of scientific information in order to draw conclusions and make predictions.

SCORING TABLE

Your performance with the diagnostic test in Chapter 2 gave you a sense of the scaled score you might receive on the ACT Science section with your current knowledge, skills, and strategies. While working through this part of the book, you'll want to keep that performance in mind along with your desired scores for your college application process. While the raw-to-scaled score conversion is different for every test so the ACT can maintain standardization across different versions of the test, we've supplied a table here to help you approximate what your raw score (0–40 questions) should be for the Science section in order to achieve your desired scaled score (1–36). This information represents an estimate and is thus not a precise reflection of official ACT scoring metrics.

SCORING TABLE—SCIENCE	
Raw Score	**Scaled Score**
40	36
39	35
38	34
37	33
–	32
36	31
35	30
–	29
34	28
33	27
31-32	26
30	25
28–29	24
25–27	23
23–24	22
21–22	21
20	20
18-19	19
17	18
15–16	17
14	16
13	15
11–12	14
10	13
9	12
8	11
7	10
6	9

SCORING TABLE—SCIENCE	
Raw Score	Scaled Score
5	8
4	7
3	6
–	5
2	4
1	3
–	2
0	1

CONFLICTING VIEWPOINTS (15–20% OF QUESTIONS)

You will be given two or more passages that describe different perspectives on a scientific issue or phenomenon. You'll be asked to compare and contrast the viewpoints by identifying areas of agreement and disagreement and evaluating the strengths and weaknesses of each perspective.

In the chapters to come in this part of the book, we'll provide you with numerous examples and strategies for how to approach and answer each type of question.

TYPES OF PASSAGES

Passages in the Science section of the ACT will be presented in one of three formats.

DATA REPRESENTATION (30–40% OF QUESTIONS)

For these passages, you will be given a graph, table, chart, or other visual representation of scientific data and asked to interpret the information presented. Depending on the information presented, you may be asked to identify trends, make predictions, or draw conclusions based on the data.

RESEARCH SUMMARIES (45–55% OF QUESTIONS)

This type of passage describes a scientific study, experiment, or observation. You will be asked to understand and evaluate the methods, results, and conclusions of the research.

SAMPLE QUESTIONS

Here, we've provided three examples of questions you might encounter on the exam presented alongside passages in one of three formats. Oftentimes, certain question types appear in conjunction with certain types of passages. For example, Research Summaries are often paired with Scientific Investigation questions; Data Representation passages are often paired with Interpretation of Data questions; and Conflicting Viewpoints passages are often paired with questions on Evaluating Models, Inferences, and Experimental Results. However, keep in mind that these passages and question types may not always appear together.

A Scientific Investigation Question about a Research Summaries Passage

This is a Research Summaries passage with a Scientific Investigation question. Passages that provide you with visual representations of data require you to understand how graphs and other figures convey important scientific data. Because this question is also evaluating your knowledge of Scientific Investigation, it's important that you are familiar with key concepts pertaining to the scientific method and the design and implementation of a scientific experiment. Specifically, this question addresses controls and variables as well as how the results of an experiment might be modified, extended, or applied.

Directions: Question 1 refers to the following passage.

A student wanted to test the permeability of four different soil types in order to decide which will be best to use for her plant that requires a lot of water from the soil to survive. Permeability is the rate at which fluid flows through the pores of a solid. A soil type with high permeability will easily soak up water, while a soil type with low permeability will tend to accumulate water on its surface rather than soak it up.

To test Soils A, B, C, and D, found in various locations throughout her yard, the student took four identical metal cylinders, each of which had a height of 20.0 cm and a radius of 5.0 cm, and hammered them into the ground in the various soils so that 10.0 cm of each can was underground and 10.0 cm was above the soil surface. She then filled each cylinder with water to a depth of 18.0 cm, as measured with a ruler. Every 10 minutes for one hour, she returned and remeasured each water depth. Her data is shown in Figure 1.

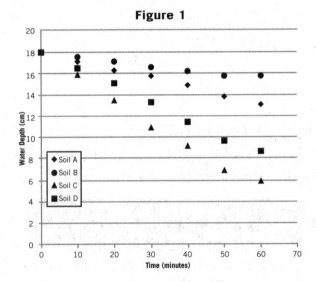

Figure 1

1. A constant in this experiment is the:

   A. soil type.
   B. cylinder size.
   C. change in water depth over time.
   D. soil density.

The correct answer is B. The cylinder size is the same for all trials, so it is a constant. The soil type is different for every trial, so choice A is incorrect. The change in water depth over time is the dependent variable, so choice C is incorrect. The soil density (choice D) may be related to soil type, but it is not a direct variable in this experiment, and it is not a constant among the trials.

An Interpretation of Data Question about a Data Representation Passage

This is an Interpretation of Data question on a Data Representation passage. For this question, you're given a report of some data collection and asked to zero in on the data presented in one of the tables that complements the description of the study. As such, you'll need to closely analyze the data presented and interpret its significance in light of the context presented.

Directions: Question 2 refers to the following passage.

The heat released in a combustion reaction can be measured using a bomb calorimeter. The reactants are encased in an explosion-proof bomb cell whose volume does not change during a reaction. The bomb cell is submerged in water. The water absorbs any heat released by the reaction, and this heat of reaction can be calculated based on the temperature change measured for the water using the following equation:

$$\text{heat of reaction} = -\text{Ccal} \times (\text{final temperature} - \text{initial temperature})$$

The variable Ccal refers to the heat capacity of the calorimeter, which is the amount of temperature required to raise its temperature by 1°C. The setup for a bomb calorimeter is shown in Figure 1.

Figure 1

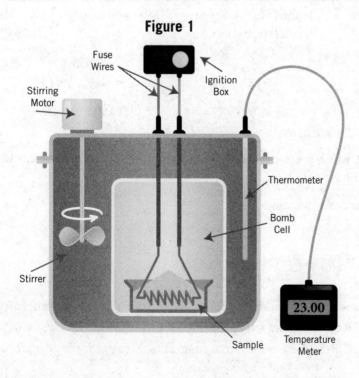

A group of scientists wanted to test the effect of reactant mass on the amount of heat produced by the combustion reaction using a bomb calorimeter. For each reaction, the scientists decided to burn an unknown organic compound in excess oxygen, guaranteeing that the unknown compound will be the limiting reactant. The scientists performed the same combustion reaction in the same calorimeter using three different masses of the unknown compound, and they measured the initial and final temperatures in each reaction. The results are shown in Table 1.

TABLE 1			
Mass of Unknown Compound (g)	Initial Temperature (°C)	Final Temperature (°C)	Temperature Change (Final–Initial) (°C)
0.100	30.5	67.5	37.0
0.200	25.2	100.4	75.2
0.300	31.2	142.1	110.9

Past experiments found that the heat of the bomb calorimeter is 1,000 J/°C. Based on this information, and using the equation above, the heat released by each reaction was calculated. Then, each heat was converted from joules to kilojoules and divided by the mass to calculate the heat per gram for each reaction. The data are shown in Table 2.

TABLE 2			
Mass of Unknown Compound (g)	Temperature Change (Final–Initial) (°C)	Heat of Reaction (J)	Heat of Reaction per Gram (kJ/g)
0.100	37.0	−37,000	−370
0.200	75.2	−75,200	−376
0.300	110.9	−110,900	−370

2. Based on Table 2, which organic compound mass provided the least precise calculated heat of reaction per gram?

F. All three were equally precise.

G. 0.100 g

H. 0.200 g

J. 0.300 g

The correct answer is H. Precision refers to how close a trial value is to the others. Two of the trial values for heat of reaction per gram were identical, –370 kJ/g, while the value for 0.200 g was a bit different, –376 kJ/g. This is, therefore, the trial among the three that is the least precise.

An Evaluation of Models, Inferences, and Experimental Results Question about a Conflicting Viewpoints Passage

This example involves a Conflicting Viewpoints passage paired with an Evaluation of Models, Inferences, and Experimental Results question. These questions ask you to determine the validity of a finding and use it to draw conclusions or make predictions. At the same time, because this is a Conflicting Viewpoints passage, you will also be tasked with considering if a given perspective is corroborated by a new piece of evidence.

Directions: Question 3 refers to the following passage.

The degree to which two species are related is measured by the number of shared homologous traits, or similar traits inherited from a common ancestral species. Such measurements, combined with genetic testing, have been frequently applied to solving the debate over the classification of the giant panda, the common name for a mammal found in the provinces of western China. Two scientists present their views on how to classify the giant panda.

Scientist 1

The giant panda is best classified not as a bear, but as a raccoon. The giant panda is related to the red panda (cat bear), which is a member of the raccoon family. Both the giant and red pandas have an additional bone protruding from their wrists, which serves as a sixth finger used to strip bamboo. Other morphological similarities include their skull shapes, teeth, foot bones, and digestive tracts. In addition to the similarities between the giant panda and red panda, modern genetic studies show that both the giant panda and the raccoon have 42 chromosomes. By contrast, except for the spotted bear with 56 chromosomes, members of the bear family have 72 chromosomes.

Scientist 2

When one looks at a giant panda, it is easy to see how its body shape and movements are very similar to those of bears. Panda cubs and bear cubs have a striking resemblance. Blood tests also show greater similarity between pandas and members of the bear family than pandas and members of the raccoon family.

Genetic tests further confirm that giant pandas have closer genetic ties to bears. Although the giant panda has fewer chromosomes than the bear, some of the modern panda's chromosomes comprise pairs of bear chromosomes that became fused together in the giant panda's ancestry. In addition, the banding patterns within giant panda chromosomes have been scientifically linked to those of bears and are almost identical. By contrast, the chromosomes of the giant panda share few similarities with those of red pandas or raccoons. The genetic link between giant pandas and bears is further upheld by three studies that utilized gene sequencing techniques to help classify pandas. The majority of the scientific evidence shows that pandas fit most clearly into the bear family, with raccoons as their "next-of-kin."

GO ON TO THE NEXT PAGE.

3. Based on the information given in the passage, with which of the following statements would both Scientists 1 and 2 be most likely to agree?

   A. Genetic evidence is valuable in determining how to classify an animal within a particular species.

   B. The existence of the giant panda's sixth finger is irrelevant to classification of the panda within an animal species.

   C. Blood tests on animals tend to produce less reliable results than do blood tests on humans.

   D. Giant pandas resemble red pandas more closely than they resemble other types of pandas.

   The correct answer is A. Both scientists use genetic evidence to support their respective claims about the classification of the giant panda within the raccoon or bear families. Scientist 1 discusses the number of chromosomes in the animals, while Scientist 2 discusses the banding patterns on chromosomes and genetic sequencing tests. Therefore, both scientists would most likely agree that genetic evidence is valuable in determining how to classify an animal within a particular species (choice A). Choice B is incorrect because Scientist 1 uses the sixth finger of the giant panda as evidence to support the resemblance between the giant panda and the red panda. Therefore, Scientist 1 likely believes that the existence of the finger is relevant. Choice C is incorrect because a comparison between blood tests on animals and humans is not mentioned in the passage. Choice D is incorrect because the passage never discusses pandas besides the red panda and the giant panda, as they are the only two species of panda.

COMMON CHALLENGES

There are some common challenges that test takers often encounter on the ACT Science test.

- **Interpreting scientific graphs and data:** For some test takers, it can be difficult learning to read and interpret visual models of scientific data and information. Familiarizing yourself with some types of visuals, including bar graphs, line graphs, etc. can help you feel more confident and prepared for these questions.

- **Understanding complex scientific concepts and theories:** Sometimes, the subject matter itself is the hardest part for test takers. If science isn't your best subject, that's okay—a lot of what you're tested on depends on your ability to apply the scientific method and draw conclusions based on data that is presented to you. Since you won't explicitly be tested on your ability to recall key concepts in science, focus on improving your strategies for interpreting and analyzing data.

- **Applying scientific information to real-world scenarios:** For the ACT Science test, it's not enough to just understand scientific procedures and processes in theory. You'll need to know how to apply those procedures to real-world scenarios in order to draw conclusions about the data, its usefulness and generalizability, and its limitations as well as how it might inform or shape future experiments and studies. We'll cover sample questions so you can get a handle on how to practically apply what you've learned about scientific concepts and theories.

- **Analyzing and evaluating scientific arguments:** Test takers will need to be familiar with the structure of academic arguments in order to break down and evaluate scientific arguments specifically. If you aren't familiar with how academic arguments are structured and supported, then you'll need to brush up on important concepts like thesis statements, claims, evidence, and warrants.

- **Distinguishing between observations and inferences:** Differentiating between observations and inferences is a critical skill you'll need for the Science test. An observation is a factual statement that can be verified by another person. For example, if you see that a pot of water is boiling, another person can look at the pot and confirm that it is indeed boiling. In other words, an observation is objective and can be verified by others. An inference, on the other hand, is a conclusion drawn from an observation or set of observations. It requires the use of background knowledge and critical thinking skills to interpret the observation and make a determination about what it means. For example, if you were to look at the pot and conclude that the water is 212° Fahrenheit, you would be making an inference because you're considering your observation in light of your additional knowledge about the boiling point of water.

- **Reading comprehension:** Because you'll be given short passages to read, analyze, and synthesize, it's important that you brush up on your reading comprehension skills. As you prepare for the Reading section of the ACT, keep in mind that those strategies and tips will also help you on the Science test.

- **Synthesizing information from multiple sources:** On the Science section of the ACT, you'll be given passages that express conflicting viewpoints. As such, it's your job to figure out how the viewpoints relate to one another and how they differ. In synthesizing multiple perspectives on a given topic, you should be able to identify the central arguments made in each passage and communicate where they overlap, how they are supported, the overall significance of each argument, and where the authors may overtly or implicitly disagree.

Think back to the self-reflection you were asked to do at the beginning of this chapter. Do any of the challenges mentioned here resonate with your experiences as a high school student? How might you need to approach studying for this section in light of your own strengths and challenges? As you proceed through the remainder of this part of the book, keep these challenges in mind and identify any that you feel apply to you as a test taker. Then, consider which of the strategies we offer might help you best work with your own unique skill set.

SUMMING IT UP

- On the ACT Science test, you'll be given 35 minutes to answer 40 multiple-choice questions.
- The questions fit into three categories: Interpretation of Data, Scientific Investigation, and Evaluation of Models, Inferences, and Experimental Results.
- Passages will appear in one of three formats: Research Summaries, Data Representation, and Conflicting Viewpoints.
- Depending on your comfort level with science as a subject and your familiarity with the process of scientific design and experimentation, you may encounter different challenges on this part of the exam. While the Science section of the ACT doesn't directly test your knowledge of scientific subjects like biology, chemistry, physics, and more, these may be the topics of passages or figures you are expected to interpret, analyze, and evaluate. As such, it's important to have strong reading comprehension skills; to be familiar with various types of graphs, figures, and other visuals; and to have a strong grasp of how to design and carry out a scientific experiment.

CHAPTER

Key Concepts in Science

KEY CONCEPTS IN SCIENCE

OVERVIEW

**Science Passages
and Question Types**

Research Summaries

Data Representation

Conflicting Viewpoints

Summing It Up

**Test Yourself:
Science Concepts**

Each section of the ACT exam tests a wide array of knowledge and problem-solving skills, and the Science test is no different. The ACT Science test focuses on your ability to use information from science-based passages and come to reasoned conclusions. Your general knowledge of the scientific process and the basics of biology, chemistry, physics, and Earth and space sciences will support you along the way, but by and large, your performance is tied to your ability to think critically using the information you're given. Across the passages, you will need to read critically, analyze data thoroughly, and apply the information you glean to different situations. And with only 35 minutes to get through 6–7 passages with 40 total questions, you must do all of this rather quickly. Success, then, depends on understanding the kinds of situations presented by the three types of ACT

Science passages and how questions will draw on that information to assess your reasoning abilities. This chapter will take a closer look at attributes of each passage type and related questions—with ample examples and a Test Yourself at the end of the chapter. For more specific strategies for working within each passage type and with different question types, see Chapter 21.

SCIENCE PASSAGES AND QUESTION TYPES

So how will the ACT Science test assess your ability to think analytically? As mentioned in Chapter 19, recall there are three types of passages that you will encounter as you make your way through the test.

RESEARCH SUMMARIES

Research Summaries focus on experimental design and the results of experiments. This is where you will come across questions that ask you to think about science procedures and reason through the results of experiments to come to valid conclusions. These passages will vary in length and are the most prevalent type in the Science section, usually appearing 3 times.

DATA REPRESENTATION

Data Representation passages will provide you with tables or graphs that contain scientific data, just like you would find if you were to read a science journal. These passages will require you to examine the data, identify key components of the data, and draw conclusions based on this information. These passages are often shortest in length. There are 2–3 Data Representation passages per Science section.

CONFLICTING VIEWPOINTS

Conflicting Viewpoints passages establish multiple viewpoints or hypotheses that are inconsistent in some way with one another. Questions will have you compare these viewpoints and analyze how situations may align with different viewpoints. Conflicting Viewpoints passages vary in length (sometimes having 2 or 3 different viewpoints presented), but there will be only one such passage in the section.

These passages can be accompanied by three different question types, as follows:

1. Interpretation of Data (IOD): This subcategory makes up 45–55% of the test and asks you to manipulate and analyze scientific data presented in tables, graphs, and diagrams (e.g., recognize trends in data, translate tabular data into graphs, interpolate and extrapolate, and reason mathematically). These questions are most commonly found with Data Representation passages but may appear elsewhere.

2. Scientific Investigation (SIN): This subcategory makes up 20–30% of the test, and asks you to understand experimental tools, procedures, and design (e.g., identify variables and controls) and compare, extend, and modify experiments. These questions see their highest prevalence alongside Research Summaries.

3. Evaluation of Models, Inferences, and Experimental Results (EMI): This subcategory makes up 25–35% of the test and asks you to judge the validity of scientific information and formulate conclusions and predictions based on that information. These questions are found in high numbers alongside Conflicting Viewpoints passages but can also be found attached to Data Representation passages and Research Summaries.

RESEARCH SUMMARIES

Research Summaries are the most frequently featured passages in the ACT Science section. These passages will present you with questions that fall under all three ACT Science question categories.

The challenge of Research Summary passages is that you are often given more background information about the experiment and the thought that went into its design. As such, questions for Research Summaries might ask you to identify the purpose of an experiment, identify differences between experiments, or propose a possible conclusion for the question the experiment is addressing. You might need to identify independent, dependent, or control variables (covered more in

depth in the following sections) or suggest methods or alternative techniques that will help answer the scientific question. The similarity to questions for Data Representation passages lies in the fact that they will also present you with data, which you will be expected to analyze to draw conclusions.

What to Expect

Research Summaries typically begin with a written introduction that provides background information about a scientific topic before introducing the experiment. Included in this background information may be important vocabulary words, reminders about principles and topics you may have learned about in the past, and specific details about the featured topic.

After the background information is provided, the passage will then give a description of the experiment that was performed. The written parts of Research Summaries will almost certainly be longer and more in-depth than the written parts of Data Representation passages. The goal of Data Representation passages is to present you with data to analyze, whereas Research Summaries place a far greater emphasis on experimental design and elements of the scientific method. Experimental descriptions may include images to help you visualize the setup described in the passage. Following the experimental description is data of some kind. This can include a table, a graph, or sometimes a written description of the results obtained.

Because these passages focus equally on both the experiment and the results (rather than just the results as seen in Data Representation passages), the questions that accompany Research Summaries cover more ground than the questions that accompany Data Representation passages. The questions that follow Research Summaries will test you on a number of important skills: identifying the purpose of a research project, formulating hypotheses to make predictions, proposing experiments or alternative experimental methods, analyzing data, and drawing conclusions based on experimental data. Keep these skills in mind as you read through Research Summaries because it is very likely you will have to answer relevant questions that test your proficiency in some or all of these areas.

Key Actions for Research Summaries

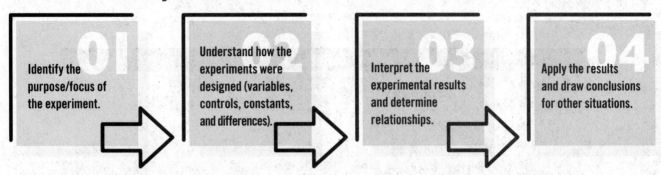

In essence, questions for Research Summaries will have you, in some way, demonstrate four unique analytical skills (as seen above).

To give you an idea of how each of these skills may be tested within the context of Research Summaries, consider the following topics, each of which is followed by a sample question so that you know what to expect when you come across them on the exam.

Understanding the Experiment's Purpose

For ACT Science section Research Summaries, your ability to answer questions effectively hinges on your understanding of the purpose of the experiment(s) in question. Here are some rhetorical questions that can aid your understanding of this element of Research Summaries:

- Why did anyone bother doing this experiment?
- Why was this particular topic chosen?
- What will this experiment test?
- Why will the results of this experiment be important?

If the purpose of the experiment is not clearly identified, then it will be very difficult to design (or understand the design of) the experiment because it may not be exactly clear what the scientist is trying to accomplish.

When you are trying to state the purpose of an experiment, you'll need to be able to identify elements of the experimental design. Most importantly, you need to be able to point to the independent variable and the dependent variable. The independent variable is the condition that the experimenter is altering throughout

the experiment, while the dependent variable is the condition that the experimenter is measuring throughout the experiment. Any conditions that do not change throughout the experiment, regardless of changes made in the independent variable, are called constants. Experiments may also include a control, which is an experimental trial that minimizes the effect of whatever the independent variable is testing.

For example, if an experiment is testing the effect of five different temperatures on the growth rate of pea plants, then:

- The independent variable is temperature.
- The dependent variable is the change in pea plant height.
- Constants might include amount of sunlight and amount of water provided because all pea plants receive the same amounts of each.
- A control could be a pea plant grown under the same conditions as the others but at standard room temperature.

These components are important in that they may be invoked by a question about purpose of the experiment (you'll also need to understand them for questions about experimental design, discussed later in this section). For example, you might be asked to choose a relevant scientific question or statement of purpose from four choices, or you could be asked to formulate a different but related question about the topic of interest.

Let's look at a test-style question in action. We will use this passage and data throughout the first few examples in this chapter, so make sure you can easily access it later.

EXAMPLE

TABLE 1						
Stonewort Sample	Measurement	Time (Hours)				
		0	6	12	18	24
Light	Dissolved O_2 (ppm)	2.35	2.81	4.61	5.02	5.30
	Volume 0.04 M NaOH (µL)	21.0	18.3	14.0	13.3	12.8
Dark	Dissolved O_2 (ppm)	2.36	2.37	2.01	1.84	1.79
	Volume 0.04 M NaOH (µL)	22.2	23.0	26.1	28.7	30.0

PASSAGE I

Photosynthesis is a biological process that generates stored energy through the formation of glucose from carbon dioxide and water, according to the following chemical reaction:

$$6 CO_2 + 6 H_2O \rightarrow C_6H_{12}O_6 + 6 O_2$$

Cellular respiration works in opposition, using oxygen to break down the sugar and release that energy to form ATP:

$$C_6H_{12}O_6 + 6 O_2 \rightarrow 6 CO_2 + 6 H_2O$$

Carbon dioxide reacts with water to form carbonic acid. Phenolphthalein is an indicator that remains colorless in acid and turns pink in base. Three drops of phenolphthalein can be added to a small water sample, and the amount of NaOH needed to turn a clear sample pink (its neutralization point) gives an indication of the concentration of carbonic acid in the sample.

Many plants and algae are capable of both photosynthesis and respiration. Among these is an algal species called stonewort, of the genus *Chara*. Stonewort grows well in lime-rich waters, which results in the formation of calcium carbonate deposits on the algae.

Study

A group of students wants to test the rates of photosynthesis and respiration in stonewort in different light conditions. The students acquire two 6.00 g stonewort samples and place each in a beaker containing 250 mL of spring water. One beaker was incubated in the dark at 25°C, while the other beaker was incubated in the light at 25°C. Over the course of one day, two 1 mL water samples were removed from each beaker every six hours. One of each pair of water samples was used to detect dissolved oxygen concentration using an oxygen electrode, which measures O_2 concentration in units of parts per million (ppm). The second water sample per pair was used to test carbon dioxide levels using phenolphthalein and 0.04 M NaOH. Both tests were performed immediately after sample extraction to avoid sample disruption. The results can be seen in Table 1.

Which of the following questions best captures the purpose of this study?

A. How do the concentrations of O and CO in water affect stonewort survival in dark and light conditions?

B. How do O_2 concentrations impact CO_2 production in stonewort submerged in water?

C. How do light and dark conditions impact net O_2 and CO_2 concentrations in water due to stonewort energy cycles?

D. What is the effect of acidic and basic water conditions on stonewort O_2 and CO_2 production in dark and light conditions?

The correct answer is C. This question requires you to read the passage, recognize precisely what the scientists are trying to discover, and understand the kind of data that was collected. The passage itself gives you most of your answer in one sentence: "A group of students wants to test the rates of photosynthesis and respiration in stonewort in different light conditions." However, this must be altered to include the kind of data collected. In this experiment, the net production or loss of CO and O was measured in the dark and light as a means of determining whether the rate of photosynthesis surpasses the rate of its reverse, respiration, or vice versa. The only answer choice among the four provided options that correctly identifies dark/light conditions as the independent variable and net CO_2/O_2 concentrations as the dependent variable is choice C.

Determining an Appropriate Hypothesis

A hypothesis is an educated prediction about the outcome of a particular experiment. When developing a hypothesis, a scientist must consider cause and effect and rely on both logic and background research. For example, if you had to hypothesize whether a ball will reach a higher speed when dropped from 20 inches or 20 feet, it is perfectly fine to rely on logic. A reasonable prediction might be that the ball dropped from 20 feet will reach a higher speed because it has a longer distance along which to accelerate due to gravitational acceleration.

On the other hand, if you had to predict the effect of different buffers on the stability of a specific protein in solution, you would need more background information about the protein and its amino acid content to make a reasonable prediction.

Hypotheses are often framed in the "if... then" format, where the first clause provides the reasoning for the prediction (the cause) and the second clause provides the prediction itself (the predicted effect). An example could be: "If a greater drop distance provides a falling object with more distance over which to accelerate, then the ball dropped from 20 feet will reach a higher maximal speed than the ball dropped from 20 inches." Hypotheses are not absolutely required to take on the "if... then" format, but it is a helpful way to frame predictions and is quite widely used. On the ACT Science test, your ability to develop hypotheses may be tested. Such questions fall into two conceptual subcategories.

1. Choose a hypothesis. The more straightforward question type might ask you to select which of the given choices is the most suitable hypothesis for an experiment. In this case, you would have to choose the answer that makes a logical prediction based on the background information you've been given. You should double-check that your answer also satisfies the correct independent and dependent variables described in the passage. For example, if your experiment is measuring the speed of a ball dropped from two different heights, your chosen hypothesis must also relate to speed as the dependent variable. In this example, your hypothesis should not be about, for instance, which ball will make the most noise or which ball will create the bigger crater when it hits the sand below.

2. Make a prediction. Another question type might ask you to make a prediction based on the background information provided. In a question like this, you might be given four choices that are all valid complements to an initial statement related to the given experiment, but based on the background information, there may be one choice that makes logical sense where the others do not.

Based on the provided information, which of the following might be a logical hypothesis to predict what will happen in the phenolphthalein/NaOH tests?

A. If light drives photosynthesis but not respiration, then the light samples should exhibit higher O_2 levels than the dark samples over the course of 24 hours.

B. If light drives photosynthesis but not respiration, then the light samples should exhibit lower O_2 levels than the dark samples over the course of 24 hours.

C. If light drives photosynthesis but not respiration, then the light samples should exhibit higher CO_2 levels than the dark samples over the course of 24 hours.

D. If light drives photosynthesis but not respiration, then the light samples should exhibit lower CO_2 levels than the dark samples over the course of 24 hours.

The correct answer is D. This question asks you to choose a valid hypothesis from four choices. All four choices have the same "cause" stem: "If light drives photosynthesis but not respiration…" That means that, based on the background information, we should choose a logical conclusion based on this stem. We can immediately eliminate choices A and B because the "effect" portions of these hypotheses refer to O_2 levels, and the passage indicates that the phenolphthalein/NaOH test detects CO_2 levels. Now we can home in on choices C and D. To come up with a reasonable hypothesis, we should focus on the chemical equations for photosynthesis and respiration. According to the passage, the chemical equation for photosynthesis is $6\,CO_2 + 6\,H_2O \rightarrow C_6H_{12}O_6 + 6\,O_2$. The chemical equation for respiration is $C_6H_{12}O_6 + 6\,O_2 \rightarrow 6\,CO_2 + 6\,H_2O$. If the "cause" stem of the hypothesis predicts that light will drive photosynthesis but not respiration, then the predictions for CO_2 levels in the light versus dark samples should reflect this. Per this stem, the light samples should promote photosynthesis and decrease CO_2 levels, while respiration should not be affected. Therefore, the light samples should exhibit lower CO_2 levels than the dark samples over 24 hours, based on the "cause" portion of the stem.

Understanding Experimental Design

After you've developed some skill identifying the purpose of a research project and formulating a hypothesis to predict the outcome, the next to focus on for Research Summaries is the experimental design. The experiment describes the methods and techniques used in the laboratory to explore the question of interest. Sometimes the experiment will be based on techniques you've seen before, but at other times you'll likely come across techniques you've never heard of. Fortunately, experimental descriptions in Research Summaries provide enough detail about the experimental design itself, as well as the independent and dependent variables, that you can figure out what's going on.

Since all ACT Science passages fit onto one page, the experimental methods and techniques will not be overly complicated—in many cases, they will be simple and straightforward. But if you do ever come across a technique with which you are unfamiliar, the passage will provide you with the background information you need; you won't ever be left completely in the dark about what a particular method does or how it relates to other elements of the design.

When it comes to ACT Science questions that ask about an experimental design, there are a few different ways you might be tested:

1. Recognize and identify. Some questions might simply ask you to recognize the basics of the experiment; for example, you may need to identify variables and controls, understand how the technique works based on the information provided, and recognize how the experiment correlates with a particular scientific question.

2. Compare and contrast. You might be asked to identify the key differences between experiments in a Research Summary. From there, you may need to decide which method would be more appropriate given new circumstances or conditions.

3. Provide alternative methods or changes. You could also come across a question that asks you to suggest an alternative experimental method to achieve a specific result. If, for example, a passage describes a study to investigate the rate of a chemical reaction and the scientist measures product formation, an alternative method might be to track reactant disappearance; both are valid ways to acquire data about reaction rate, but they are different ways to study the reaction rate.

4. Consider future experiments. EMI questions may have you consider additional future experiments. Questions that ask about future experiments require you to think beyond what is in front of you. Most often, you will be asked to build off what has been provided and your interpretation of the experimental results to recommend the logical next step in the research. For example, if an experiment discovers that plants grow better in the light than in the dark, logical follow-up experiments might be to test optimal light intensity, duration of light exposure, or light color, in relation to the same dependent variable or something new. Again, with this type of question, you won't be expected to know about any specialized techniques off the top of your head; the correct answer will be based on the application of the logic of the original experiment.

EXAMPLES

Researchers want to repeat the experiment, this time modifying the design to assess, in addition to the presence of light, the impact of temperature variation on the photosynthetic and cellular respiration reactions of the stonewort. In order to assess the impact of such a variable, the researchers could:

    A. use light sources of varying wattage to increase the temperature.

    B. adjust the pH of the water samples.

    C. increase the size of the water samples.

    D. vary the temperature of the water in the beakers.

The correct answer is D. Here, you must apply what you understand from the original experiment to suggest a change to measure the impact of an additional variable, temperature. As such, the suggested change must maintain the design of the original experiment but also effectively introduce the new criteria. In evaluating the choices, you can ask yourself two questions: 1. Does this choice maintain the efficacy of the original experimental design? And 2. Does this choice reflect the researchers' desire to assess the impact of temperature? In using those two questions, both embedded in the question stem, you can start eliminating answers. Both choices A and D introduce the concept of temperature. Let's hold on to those and examine choices B and C. Choice B, if one was unsure how pH could impact temperature, can be eliminated as changing the pH levels will effect the measurement of the carbon dioxide levels in the water samples. Choice C increases the size of the water samples, a choice that does not have a direct relationship with temperature. In looking back at choices A and D, we see that choice D offers direct control over the temperature of the water in the beakers, indicating a variable that will be adjusted by the researchers while still maintaining other

experimental conditions. Meanwhile, choice A, while offering a method to increase temperature (by using lights of different strengths), can only be applied to the light trials with the stonewort, as no light can be present for the dark trials—thus preventing consistent manipulation of temperature and failing to establish the researchers' new variable.

All of the following steps could significantly improve the reliability of the experiment EXCEPT:

    F. using a magnetic stir bar to ensure constant gas composition throughout the beakers.

    G. decreasing the concentration of NaOH used in the phenolphthalein test to more efficiently detect acidity.

    H. increasing the number of samples taken from each beaker at each time point.

    J. decreasing the number of time points over 24 hours to minimize disruption of the beakers.

The correct answer is J. This question asks you to suggest improvements to the experiment to increase the reliability of the results. You must decide which of the given suggestions would be least likely to improve the experiment. Choice F provides a method of ensuring that the dissolved gas composition is consistent throughout the beaker, which is something that was not addressed in the original experiment. This is certainly an improvement, so it is not the correct answer here.

Choice G suggests decreasing the concentration of NaOH added during the phenolphthalein test. While this would involve adding a greater volume of NaOH to the test sample, this step improves the reliability of the experiment because it allows for smaller concentration increment increases in the NaOH base, allowing the students to more

closely estimate the solution acidity rather than overshooting it. This is also an improvement. Increasing the number of experimental trials (choice H) is always an improvement because increasing the number of trials means you are basing your average numbers on a greater sample size, which improves reliability.

That leaves choice J. While minimizing beaker disruption would be ideal, decreasing the number of time points decreases the number of data points you obtain, and it decreases your chances of seeing more subtle changes. In terms of the data acquired in this particular experiment, there were certain time periods (e.g., 6–12 hours) that experienced more dramatic changes in dissolved gases relative to others, and this would all be missed if the number of time points were decreased.

Analyzing Data

To review, the principles of data analysis as they apply to the ACT Science section are as follows:

- Understand the provided data, identifying variables, units, etc.
- Draw conclusions based on the data.
- Analyze or construct graphs.
- Consider future work based on the data.

We'll focus on drawing conclusions in the next section, but the rest of these data analysis skills are relevant here. Understanding the data means identifying the variables and controls, and then determining how the data express these variables and controls. In examining the variables, you need to be able to determine whether variables possess direct or inverse relationships along with the ranges in which those relationships are maintained. Direct relationships exist in situations in which the independent variable increases and the dependent variable also increases. The relationship is also direct if both variables decrease. If the independent variable

either increases or decreases and the dependent variables does the opposite, then the relationship is inverse. Such relationships may not always exist over the entirety of the measurements of the independent variable, however. Certain thresholds (for instance, too high or low of a temperature) may cause the relationship to reverse or lose any clear correlation. When reviewing the results of the experiment, identifying these implicit relationships can support you for many of the Interpretation of Data questions associated with Research Summaries (and Data Representation passages too).

Analyzing and constructing graphs becomes essential in data analysis because you have to be able to read data provided in graphical form, but you also might be asked to interpret trends in tabulated data and present that data in graphical form as well.

Finally, considering future work based on data is a bit different than what we just discussed in the previous section, though only slightly. While the previous section focused on the experimental side of considering future work, here the future work is more idea- and data-based. In other words, this aspect of future work is geared more toward building new hypotheses based on data rather than just focusing on experimental variations. Still, the two go hand-in-hand and overlap in many respects.

For our purposes, the following examples fall under the category of considering characteristics of data and possible trends for the future, but in the context of the sample passage we've been working with throughout this section.

Which of the following graphs best represents the trend in dissolved oxygen as a function of time for the stonewort grown in the light?

A.

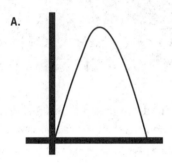

B.

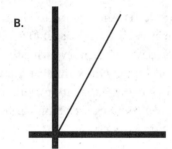

C.

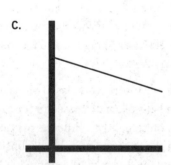

D.

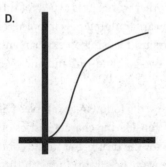

The correct answer is D. This question asks you to construct a chart based on the data provided in the table. Whenever you're asked to construct a graph based on a set of numerical data, the first thing you should do is identify the independent and dependent variables. Based on our data table, as well as the description of the experiment, the independent variable is *time*, and the dependent variable is the *concentration of dissolved oxygen*, as measured by an oxygen electrode.

The next step is to look for the general trend in the numbers. This requires you to examine whether the data increase, decrease, or fluctuate throughout the experiment—in other words, look for the presence of direct and inverse relationships, or even the presence of no correlation. In this case, we're looking at the dissolved oxygen data for stonewort grown in the light; this would be the first row of data in the data table. As time increases, the concentration of dissolved oxygen also increases—a direct relationship. There is never a decrease in oxygen concentration, so we can immediately rule out choices A and C because both exhibit some kind of a decrease in dissolved oxygen concentration over the measured time period. To distinguish between choices B and D, we must now determine whether or not the increase in dissolved oxygen is linear. To test this out, check out the increase in dissolved oxygen concentration over a few equivalent time periods; if the increase is the same, the increase is linear.

For this example, let's look at the 0–6 hour and 6–12 hour time periods. From 0 to 6 hours, the dissolved oxygen concentration increases by 0.46 ppm, but from 6 to 12 hours, the dissolved oxygen concentration increases by 1.80 ppm. These are clearly not the same, and if we check out each time point, we can confirm that we are not looking at a linear trend. The answer, then, cannot be choice B. The correct answer, which displays a graph that fits our trend, is choice D.

Based on the results of the study, the relationship between dissolved oxygen and carbon dioxide levels can be characterized as:

F. inverse, with dissolved oxygen levels decreasing and carbon dioxide levels increasing for stonewort samples exposed to light.

G. inverse, with carbon dioxide levels increasing and dissolved oxygen levels decreasing for stonewort examples in the dark.

H. direct, with dissolved oxygen levels increasing and carbon dioxide levels increasing for stonewort samples exposed to light.

J. direct, with carbon dioxide levels decreasing and dissolved oxygen levels decreasing for stonewort samples in the dark.

The correct answer is G. This question requires you to analyze the gas measurements resulting from the experiment and determine the relationship between them. In this case, the gas measurements are both dependent on the context of the stonewort (light or darkness) and the time interval after the study began. The dissolved oxygen and the carbon dioxide levels, when examined, present a clear relationship. From examining the table, you can see that stonewort in light has increased oxygen levels and decreased carbon dioxide levels, suggesting a greater presence of the photosynthetic reaction. Meanwhile, the stonewort in the dark has, over the 24-hour period, higher carbon dioxide levels and lower oxygen levels, indicating a higher incidence of cellular respiration. In both situations, the relationship between the two gas measurements is reciprocal, or inverse. As one increases, the other decreases, thus eliminating choices H and J. From the background information of the passage, we can verify that this is the case as we can see that the formulae for photosynthetic and cellular respiration reactions are inversions of one another. An increase in the output of one decreases the output of the other—allowing you to infer some additional relationship with light and darkness that triggers a greater presence of one reaction over the other. In deciding between choices F and G, you must accurately describe the results of the experiment. Choice F describes the opposite of what is observed for the stonewort in the light.

Drawing Conclusions

Once you've progressed through the question, hypothesis, experiment, and data, the final feature of Research Summaries on which you may be tested is your ability to draw conclusions based on the data. The goal of drawing conclusions is to answer the posed scientific question by interpreting the results and identifying trends and patterns in the data. Applying an observed pattern or trend to answer a scientific question is really the main point of doing scientific research. The ACT Science section therefore assesses you in this area by asking you to look at the data, identify trends, and apply these trends in a relevant way to a scientific question. It's with questions like these that you demonstrate your critical thinking abilities.

Let's see how you might be tested on this skill.

Based on the data, which of the following conclusions can be drawn about the effect of light and dark conditions on photosynthesis and respiration in stonewort?

A. The rates of photosynthesis and respiration increase under light conditions relative to dark conditions.

B. The rates of photosynthesis and respiration decrease under light conditions relative to dark conditions.

C. The rate of photosynthesis exceeds the rate of respiration in the light, but the rate of respiration exceeds the rate of photosynthesis in the dark.

D. The rate of respiration exceeds the rate of photosynthesis in the light, but the rate of photosynthesis exceeds the rate of respiration in the dark.

The correct answer is C. This question asks you to examine the data and draw a conclusion to answer the scientific question based on the data. The answer choices for this question refer to both photosynthesis and respiration under light and dark conditions, so it is important that we examine the data to include all of these relevant variables.

Based on the data, we can immediately rule out choices A and B, because the trends observed for carbon dioxide and oxygen, respectively, are not the same under light and dark conditions. We must now distinguish between choices C and D. To begin, look at the dissolved oxygen data. Under light conditions, the concentration of oxygen increases over time, but under dark conditions, the concentration of oxygen decreases over time. Oxygen is a product of photosynthesis and a reactant in respiration, so these data indicate that photosynthesis occurs more rapidly than respiration under light conditions and more slowly than respiration under dark conditions. The carbon dioxide data leads us to the same conclusion. Under light conditions, the carbon dioxide concentration decreases, but under dark conditions, the carbon dioxide concentration increases. Carbon dioxide is a reactant in photosynthesis and a product of respiration, so the same conclusion can be drawn from the carbon dioxide data. Based on these trends, the correct answer is choice C. To see these net gas increases and decreases, photosynthesis must be stimulated under light conditions, while respiration prevails under dark conditions. If you have any background knowledge of photosynthesis, this conclusion may be obvious, as photosynthesis depends on light absorption.

DATA REPRESENTATION

Now that we've reviewed Research Summaries and some of their question forms, we will move on to look at Data Representations. In many ways, questions based on Data Representation will require some of the same skills you used when answering questions for Research Summaries because both passage types require you to analyze data. Information from the same natural science disciplines (biology, chemistry, physics, and astronomy/Earth sciences) provides the passage source material. For questions that involve analyzing data and drawing conclusions, you will certainly be able to apply many of the same skills we've already discussed, but we will still talk about how to use these skills in the context of questions for Data Representation. Recognizing Data Representation passages should come easily because you will usually see short intro text and some kind of a graph, scatterplot, figure, or table that you will be required to understand and interpret. Measurement is the goal of these passages, without explicit focus on experimental design. Data Representation passages—which comprise 30 to 40 percent of the

data analysis: understanding the data, drawing conclusions from the data, analyzing graphical figures, and thinking about future work based on the data. To tackle Data Representation passages and their associated questions, you will have to consider the following topics, each of which is accompanied by an example to give you an idea of how the questions might appear when you're working within the ACT Science section.

Information in Tables and Figures

This question type is the launching point of your data analysis. To answer any of the questions in a set, you have to be able to look at the provided figure and determine what it is telling you. Once you are able to read a figure and extract information from it, you can start to draw conclusions and think about the data critically.

When you are attempting to read a figure, the best way to start is to read the introductory and surrounding paragraphs and determine the question the data is supposed to answer; in other words, what is the purpose of the experiment being conducted or the focus of the observations being made? The introductory and surrounding paragraphs may also provide details about the variables being measured.

If a figure is a diagram or picture, examine it closely, focusing on what is actually happening in the experiment and what is being measured. If the figure is a table, look at the headers along the top of the table to see which variables are being changed or measured. Usually, the headers in a table will include the independent and dependent variables. If the figure is a graph or scatterplot, look at the axes; the y-axis (the vertical axis) will usually be the dependent variable, while the x-axis (the horizontal axis) will usually be the independent variable. Understanding the passages will definitely help you to understand the specifics of the experiment more easily, but most of the time, you can figure out what is happening in the experiment based on the diagrams and figures alone.

Take a look at the following passage and practice question. We'll refer to this passage multiple times throughout this section, so make sure you can easily reference it.

ACT Science test, or 2–3 passages—tend to be rather straightforward conceptually, so the key to answering questions associated with these passages is figuring out how the data is presented, what the data actually means, and what relationships can be observed between the different elements under observation. This type of material will most often be associated with Interpretation of Data questions.

A Data Representation passage always begins with a written introduction that presents the scientific topic covered or question that is being asked, provides some key terminology, and introduces the data you will have to analyze. The introduction paragraph is usually no longer than a few sentences or so; this is because the most important part of a Data Representation passage is the diagram, figure, or chart. In addition to the introduction paragraph, most passages will include an additional written paragraph (or a few paragraphs) to provide details about the topic and the data.

Each Data Representation passage can be accompanied by 5–7 questions that test you on several key skills in

PASSAGE II

Five pea plants were planted in identical pots containing the same amount and type of soil. Each plant was placed in temperature-controlled boxes at different temperatures ranging from 0 to 80°C. Each plant was provided with the same sunlight exposure and volume of water at the same times each day. The height of each plant was measured and recorded every eighth day at 12 p.m.

Pea Plant Air Temperature (°C)	Pea Plant Height (cm) After x Days				
	0	8	16	24	32
0°	0	5.2	20.2	26.0	34.3
20°	0	5.3	23.4	28.2	35.0
40°	0	3.2	17.5	22.4	25.7
60°	0	2.7	13.0	15.2	19.0
80°	0	1.2	8.8	12.3	14.2

Within which temperature range did the pea plants experience the greatest amount of growth?

A. 0–20°

B. 20–40°

C. 40–60°

D. 60–80°

The correct answer is A. The introduction tells us that the five plants are grown under identical conditions, with the exception of varying temperatures, and that plant height was measured every eight days. That means that the independent variable is temperature, because temperature is the condition that the experimenter is changing. We can also see that the dependent variable is plant height, because this is the variable that the experimenter is measuring. Both of these variables appear in the table; the independent variable is the header of the first column, while the dependent variable is the header of the remaining columns.

The question stem has you consider both variables, asking you to search for the greatest amount of growth among the pea plants and connect that with the corresponding temperature range. In assessing the overall trends in the data, growth peaks at 20°, suggesting either choice A or B. Choice C could be plausible given the relatively high growth (when compared with 60° and 80°), but is still less than the 0° and 20° ranges. As pea plants appear to grow less at higher temperatures, choice D can be eliminated. Looking back at choices A and B, the total growth is greatest at 20°; however, growth begins decreasing at 40° (perhaps it accelerates between 20° and 40°, but not enough information is provided to support such a conclusion). Given the information from the table, this would eliminate choice B and indicate choice A (0–20°) as best supported by the passage. Whether you interpret "greatest amount of growth" to mean highest overall growth or highest growth rate between measurements won't affect your answer, but making sure you're assessing the correct metric will prove critical on the test itself.

Drawing Conclusions from the Data

Once you've successfully read a figure and determined its purpose, you will almost always be asked to use the figure to answer questions or draw conclusions. When examining a data set, you will probably notice patterns and trends. Recognizing these trends will be extremely helpful when you're trying to draw conclusions because the conclusions will usually be based on these observations. Questions that ask you to draw conclusions from the data might ask you to describe a pattern from the data, to predict a result that is not displayed in the figure, or to apply the data to a different but relevant scenario. Patterns and trends in the data will usually be fairly straightforward; for instance, if a few different conditions are tested for a particular independent variable, the results for each condition will be distinctive enough for you to tell them apart and draw conclusions.

If you're a visual thinker, you will probably have an easier time seeing trends and patterns in graphs or scatterplots. These kinds of figures show rather than tell—you will be able to see a line with a positive slope on a graph, or a progressive decrease in magnitude of a variable on a scatterplot. If you're better with numbers, you might prefer tables, on which you can compare values for different conditions. Regardless, you can always convert tables to graphs and vice versa. For example, if you're struggling to understand a scatterplot, you can write up your own small table with numerical estimates of the values from the scatterplot. Or if you're given a table and prefer a graph, you can always sketch a small graphical version of the numbers you've been given.

Once you've figured out the pattern or trend specified in the question, you can apply that trend to answer the question. If a question asks you directly about the trend, choose the answer that most accurately describes the pattern you found. If a question asks you to predict a result that is not given in the figure, you can apply the trend accordingly and predict how the new condition will compare to the conditions provided. If you're asked to apply that trend to a new situation altogether, simply imagine the use of that trend in the new situation and predict how it will apply.

Let's take a look at an example in action.

EXAMPLE

If you were to grow a pea plant under the same conditions at 50°C, during which time period would you expect to see the most rapid growth rate?

A. 0–8 days

B. 8–16 days

C. 16–24 days

D. 24–32 days

The correct answer is B. This question asks us to make a prediction about the growth rate of a plant grown at 50°C based on the data provided for these five other temperatures. For each of the five plants described in the table, the most rapid increase in height occurs between 8 days and 16 days. For example, the pea plant grown at 0°C grows 5.2 cm between Day 0 and Day 8, 15.0 cm between Day 8 and Day 16, 5.8 cm between Day 16 and Day 24, and 8.3 cm between Day 24 and 32. The largest difference in height over the course of eight days occurs between Day 8 and Day 16. For confirmation, you could repeat this procedure for the plants at the other temperatures. Since this trend is consistent for all five plants, which includes plants grown at temperatures above and below 50°C, it would be reasonable to predict that a plant grown at 50°C would also experience its most rapid growth rate between Day 8 and Day 16.

Analyzing Data Graphically

Graphs are an extremely useful way to convey scientific data. You will almost certainly be asked to graph data or interpret graphs on the ACT Science test, particularly in Interpretation of Data questions. Therefore, it is important to understand the various types of graphs and how they are used.

On a coordinate plane, graphs consist of points that are plotted based on their location along the x and y axes. Graphs in the ACT Science section will likely be 2D, but they may make use of multiple y-axes (one on the left and right), along with multiple different plotted variables (with multiple lines and symbols overlapping and intersecting). These more advanced presentations are one of the many reasons you need to inspect figures carefully, looking at labels on axes and units carefully. (3D graphs may also appear, making use of a z-axis, directed out of the page at you, but you will rarely, if ever, see these on the ACT Science test.)

Graphs that are straight lines indicate linear functions, while curved lines represent exponential functions. In linear functions, lines that increase from left to right have positive slopes, while lines that decrease from left to right have negative slopes. A perfectly horizontal line has a slope of zero, while a perfectly vertical line is usually described as "undefined" or "infinite." In exponential functions, the line can also increase or decrease; however, in exponential functions, the line is curved, which means that the slope is not constant. In a positive exponential function, the curve approaches zero (or a minimum) to the left and infinity to the right. In a negative exponential function, the curve approaches zero (or a minimum) to the right and infinity to the left.

The key difference between linear and exponential functions is that linear functions have a constant slope, which means that the change in y value per x value is the same for all intervals, while exponential functions have a slope that either increases (positive exponential function) or decreases (negative exponential function) from left to right.

There are other types of graphs, including parabolas (U-shaped graphs) and hyperbolas (curved graphs that approach, but never quite reach, invisible lines called asymptotes). However, linear and exponential functions are far and away the most common graphs you'll find on the ACT Science test and are the two types you should focus on when reviewing.

When interpreting a graph, it is important to determine which variable is represented by each axis. If you are given a graph as your figure, this will be quite obvious because the axes will be labeled. However, if you are given a table and asked to predict the shape of a graph, it may be a bit trickier. As a general rule, the x-axis is usually the independent variable, or the variable that the experimenter alters, while the y-axis is usually the dependent variable, or the variable that is being measured in the experiment. Once you recognize which variable is which on a table, converting the values into a graphical form is not so difficult. Questions that ask you to analyze graphs might ask you about graph types and shapes, patterns and trends, or axes and variables.

EXAMPLE

Over the course of the first 16 days of height measurement, the growth rate for the pea plants can best be described as:

A. increasing linearly.

B. decreasing linearly.

C. increasing exponentially.

D. decreasing exponentially.

The correct answer is C. This question asks for a graphical type/shape interpretation based on the numbers provided in a table. You can tell if a graph is linear if the measured dependent variable value increases or decreases by the same amount over the same given independent variable interval.

This particular question asks us to look at the shape over the first 16 days. First, let's take a look at Day 0 through Day 8 for the first plant. The height increases by 5.2 cm. Now let's look at Day 8 through Day 16. The height increases by 15.0 cm. Both of these time intervals are eight days, so if this were a linear trend, the height increases should be the same. They are not the same, however, so this must be an exponential trend. We can therefore rule out choice A and choice B because these answers both refer to linear changes. The difference between choice C and choice D is whether the change in height over time is an increase or decrease. Logically, plants don't decrease in height over time, but as always, we just have to look at the numbers for confirmation. The height of each plant increases over time—therefore, we can rule out choice D.

Using the Data to Infer Additional Experiments or Applications

In scientific research, one experiment usually leads to another experiment; when you learn something new from one experiment, you can do additional experiments to learn more about the topic of interest, make further observations, or even attempt to apply your results to a seemingly unrelated study. Additional experiments can be based on what was learned in the initial observations, or they can test a new variable that was not the focus of the original experiment.

Questions that ask you to suggest additional experiments will often state a goal, and you will have to select the response that would most successfully achieve that goal. To answer these questions, identifying the independent and dependent variables will be key. Given a particular goal, you can figure out what you are varying and what you are measuring. Once you have identified these variables, you can look at the answer choices and pick the one that uses these variables. At the same time, you will need to maintain the relationships revealed by the initial data but do so in the new context.

EXAMPLE

A scientist wants to focus on which temperature provides the most rapid germination period of pea plant growth. Germination is the process by which a plant sprouts from a seed. This can best be accomplished by:

A. repeating the experiment at 20°C only, varying the soil type between plants.

B. repeating the experiment at all temperatures, measuring plant heights after much smaller time increments.

C. repeating the experiment at all temperatures, using a variety of plant types.

D. repeating the experiment at all temperatures, extending the eight-day measurements to 40 days rather than 32 days.

The correct answer is B. Remember, with the questions that ask you to suggest additional experiments, it is important to identify the independent and dependent variables right away. This question asks you to suggest an experiment that will measure germination rate, or the rate at which the plant sprouts from the seed, at different temperatures. That means that the independent variable will again be temperature, and that the dependent variable will again be plant height. You can therefore rule out choice A, because if you use only one temperature, you cannot compare germination rates between plants at different temperatures. Choice A does not satisfy the desired independent variable. Based on the question alone, you can also rule out choice C. The goal is to look at germination growth rates in pea plants only, so using different plant types at different temperatures will not help to accomplish this goal.

Choices B and D both have temperature as the independent variable and plant height as the dependent variable, so you must choose the better answer between the two. Since germination refers to the sprouting of a plant from its seed, the new experiment should focus on the earliest stages of pea plant growth. Based on the original data provided, the plants reach heights of 3–5 centimeters after eight days, so the initial germination process is not included in the original experiment. Extending the overall measurement time to 40 days, as described in choice D, will not accomplish the goal of focusing on germination. Choice B, on the other hand, involves measuring after shorter time periods. The experiment described in choice B involves taking more measurements between 0 and 8 days, which will give a much better sense of how quickly each plant at the different temperatures emerges from its seed.

CONFLICTING VIEWPOINTS

Together, the passages in the Research Summaries and Data Representation categories make up the majority of the ACT Science test. The last 15–20 percent of the test that we have not yet discussed consists of a Conflicting Viewpoints passage. Conflicting Viewpoints passages are important because they test your ability to read about different views on the same topic and then analyze the distinctions and overlapping elements between them. While the Data Representation and Research Summaries passages have a lot in common with research articles and complex data, Conflicting Viewpoints passages are more similar to perspective pieces, commentaries, or short communications. These passages briefly convey at least two viewpoints about a particular topic, and it is your job to answer questions based on these views. Conflicting Viewpoints questions can cover all three ACT Science question categories: Scientific Investigation, Interpretation of Data, and Evaluation of Models, Inferences, and Experimental Results, with the greatest emphasis being placed on the latter.

Reading Comprehension in ACT Science

When it comes down to it, the ACT Science test is simply a test of reading comprehension with science-based passages. The Conflicting Viewpoints passage embodies this notion well because these passages are most similar to the passages from ACT Reading, particularly Passage IV: Natural Sciences. You will also use synthesis skills that are similarly tested through the paired passage of the ACT Reading test. Consequently, it may be useful to periodically return to Chapter 17 if you find yourself needing a refresher on reading comprehension skills.

Conflicting Viewpoints passages will usually pose two or three short viewpoints, theories, or hypotheses about the same science topic or about related science topics. The questions will then test your understanding of the viewpoints as individual pieces and in light of one another, with some questions asking you to apply what you know of the viewpoints to different situations. In other words, it will be important to understand each of the viewpoints on their own, but you will then be asked to compare and contrast the viewpoints or draw

connections between them to show how one might affect or align with the other.

As a reminder, a hypothesis is an educated guess about the outcome of a particular experiment or scientific phenomenon. Hypotheses are constantly posed to try to explain observations in nature and may be based on collected data, comparisons to similar phenomena, or basic logic, but they are considered hypotheses because they are still predictions rather than well-supported conclusions. The term *theory* is often used as a synonym for *hypothesis*, but a theory is usually based on a more substantial number of experiments and observations, constituting a well-accepted explanation for a particular phenomenon.

Both hypotheses and theories are often based on general principles of a scientific topic that are commonly regarded as correct or true, but they are still considered proposed explanations rather than incontrovertible fact. When it comes to Conflicting Viewpoints passages, you will often be presented with two hypotheses or theories that either differ or focus on different features of a scientific topic.

However, not all of the passages will be based on well-known scientific theories or hypotheses. You will also see passages in which hypothetical students tackle simpler questions by performing research and presenting their findings.

Each Conflicting Viewpoints passage will begin with a brief paragraph that introduces the topic of interest. After identifying the topic of interest, you can move on to the viewpoints themselves. Each viewpoint will be discussed in a paragraph or two and will usually be accompanied by supporting data in its explanation. When reading the viewpoints, it is important to figure out the opinions expressed. Underline key words and use the margin to write down the basic theory provided by each viewpoint in a clear and succinct way, so that when you have to start answering questions, you'll know where to look for the correct answers.

After you've identified the basic hypothesis or theory provided by the speakers, look for the provided evidence that supports each viewpoint. By identifying supporting data for each viewpoint, you can see whether the evidence for one viewpoint might support or refute the other viewpoint, and vice versa. Picking out the key pieces of evidence will also help you to compare and contrast the viewpoints as each supporting detail will likely support one theory more strongly than the other; otherwise, it would not be included.

To summarize, the basic strategy to employ when reading Conflicting Viewpoints passages is as follows.

Key Actions for Conflicting Viewpoints Passages

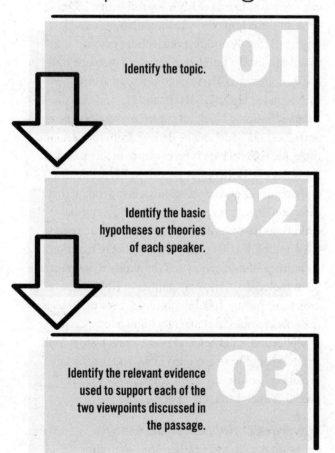

01 Identify the topic.

02 Identify the basic hypotheses or theories of each speaker.

03 Identify the relevant evidence used to support each of the two viewpoints discussed in the passage.

When you are presented with a set of Conflicting Viewpoints, you will likely be posed questions that test your ability to understand details, compare the conflicting viewpoints, contrast the conflicting viewpoints, and make inferences either to relate the viewpoints to one another, or to use data (real or hypothetical) to support or refute the conflicting viewpoints. These are the areas we will focus on in our preparation for these passage types.

Understanding Details

In some way, Conflicting Viewpoints passages will ask you to recall details from the passages. Questions may ask you about statements found explicitly in the passages or about the implications of statements found in the passage. For example, if a passage describes the short-term and long-term effects of mutations on human evolution, a question might ask you to choose the event that would most immediately follow a mutation; while all four answer choices may be correct based on the passage, you would have to choose the short-term effect rather than any of the long-term effects based on the use of the word *immediately* in the question. When you're reading a question, make sure you understand what you are being asked so that you don't simply choose what appears to be the first correct statement you see, when in fact the question is asking you about something entirely different.

As a general rule, you won't have to bring an abundance of background information to the situation when it comes to understanding details in Conflicting Viewpoints passages. Of course, having background knowledge about a particular topic won't hurt; for instance, if you know a lot about oceanography, that background knowledge will certainly be helpful to you if you encounter a Conflicting Viewpoints passage that introduces vocabulary related to a topic like deep-sea vents. However, you won't be expected to be an expert on any of the topics presented. Reading comprehension is all about understanding what you read, and the vast majority of information you'll need to answer questions about Conflicting Viewpoints passages can be found in the passages themselves. Occasionally you'll need to figure out a vocabulary definition based on the information provided, but everything you need to answer accurately will be in the passage.

There are usually one to three detail-oriented recall questions per question set for Conflicting Viewpoints questions, and they usually refer to just one viewpoint at a time.

Let's look at how the ACT Science test will present these questions. As in the other sections, we will use one passage and data set for the majority of practice questions. Mark the following for ease of access later.

EXAMPLE

PASSAGE III

There are numerous theories concerning the origin of life on Earth, focusing on how primitive Earth was able to chemically create biomolecules essential for biological life to arise. Two hypotheses for how those biomolecules came to be are presented below.

Hypothesis 1

Lightning and gases from volcanic eruptions may have given rise to the very first life on Earth. The Miller-Urey experiment, performed in 1952, simulated the conditions of primitive Earth. In this experiment, a mixture of gases thought to have been present in the primitive atmosphere (most prominently, H_2O, CH_4, NH_3, and H_2) was stored in a vial connected by a pipe to a heated water tank that simulated the evaporation of the ocean. In that vial, electrodes created a spark, simulating lightning, and reaction products were collected by reliquefying the water vapor. The Miller-Urey experiment showed that simple organic compounds, namely amino acids and various sugars, including ribose, can be produced from the gases in the atmosphere of primitive Earth with the addition of energy.

More recently, scientists performed a similar experiment with CO_2, CO, and N, an updated conception of Earth's early atmosphere, and these gases allowed for the production of an even wider array of biomolecules. The addition of volcanic gases like H_2 and CH_4 increased variety and supplied hydrogen, and follow-up experiments have shown that a simple volcanic gas called carbonyl sulfide (COS) helps free-floating amino acids to form peptides, the precursors to proteins, under various conditions, and that metal ions help to intensify this reaction by up to 80 percent. However, since carbonyl sulfide decomposes rather quickly, it is unlikely to be present in large quantities in the atmosphere. Instead, this gas would be most predominant at hydrothermal vents on the seafloor, forming peptide chains that would stick to rocks and continue to lengthen.

Hypothesis 2

RNA has the unique ability to act as both genes and enzymes, which makes RNA a sensible first biomolecule in the origin of life. Lab simulations have demonstrated that pyrimidine nucleotides cytosine and uracil can form a number of plausible prebiotic molecules under early-Earth conditions, an atmosphere that included H_2O, CH_4, NH_3, and H_2, and that the simplest building blocks of sugars, glycolaldehyde and glyceraldehyde, can be derived from the prebiotic molecule HCN. There is no evidence of formation of the other two nucleotides present in RNA, adenine and guanine, but current research is moving in that direction. In vitro experiments under primordial conditions have demonstrated the ability to produce RNA molecules that perform a number of functions, including self-replication and the ability to copy other RNA molecules. These capabilities of RNA make it a very promising "first biomolecule" because RNA is the only biomolecule currently known to be capable of replication, catalysis, and possession of genes itself, so RNA could have preceded DNA and proteins in evolution because RNA can self-catalyze to make protein, which can then replicate DNA.

Why were CO_2, CO, and N added to later experiments after the Miller-Urey experiment?

A. To simulate the evaporation of the ocean

B. To better simulate the conditions of the early-Earth atmosphere

C. To produce carbonyl sulfide (COS)

D. To produce sparks without the use of electrodes

The correct answer is B. This passage presents two different views on the origin of life. The first viewpoint describes the theory that atmospheric and volcanic gases, using energy from volcanic lightning, were capable of forming amino acids and simple sugars. The second viewpoint describes the hypothesis that RNA was the first biomolecule because there is some evidence that some of its nucleotides can be formed by the prebiotic atmosphere, and because RNA is genetic, self-replicates, and can act as a catalyst.

This is a recall question that asks you to look back at the viewpoints and identify the relevant information. As stated in Hypothesis 1, the addition of gases CO_2, CO, and N offered a better simulation of Earth's early atmosphere, resulting in production of a greater variety of organic compounds. Choice A explains the purpose of the heated water tank in the Miller-Urey experiment. Choice C represents another gas added to the later experiments that ended up acting as a key component in helping amino acids form peptide chains. Choice D distorts details of the passage, attempting to confuse more recent experiments with the Miller-Urey design.

Comparing Viewpoints

Each passage will present you with at least two conflicting viewpoints; by definition, *conflicting* seems to indicate that the viewpoints are in opposition to one another. However, in Conflicting Viewpoints passages, this doesn't necessarily mean that the two viewpoints are arguing in favor of completely opposite ideas; in some cases, the viewpoints are simply arguing in favor of different approaches, sometimes nuanced in their discrepancies, to a shared concept. They are considered to be "conflicting" only insofar as the arguments are not one and the same. In the previous example passage, both viewpoints could technically be correct, as both ideas seem to be valid based on experiments done thus far.

However, they are Conflicting Viewpoints because they are arguing that their theory or hypothesis is the key first step that ignited the development of life on Earth.

When different viewpoints are presented (and even if they are in direct opposition to one another), it is almost always possible to find commonalities between the two. Sometimes, the viewpoints will describe the same effect, but they will propose different causes for that effect. In other cases, viewpoints may be nearly identical, except for a detail or two that leads to a completely different conclusion. In still other situations, two viewpoints may propose entirely different theories about a particular phenomenon, but they could have a feature or two in common. Regardless of the viewpoints you encounter, there will always be some kind of parallel you can draw between them, and more often than not, one of the questions accompanying the passage will draw attention to one of those parallels.

Let's look at this type of question in action.

EXAMPLE

Supporters of Hypothesis 1 and supporters of Hypothesis 2 would both agree that:

F. RNA was the first biomolecule that led to the development of life.

G. the atmosphere of primitive Earth contained H_2O, CH_4, NH_3, and H_2.

H. RNA preceded DNA and proteins in evolution.

J. the first biomolecule formed near deep-sea vents.

The correct answer is G. This question asks you to find a feature that the two viewpoints have in common with one another. Since the question stem itself does not specify a particular feature of the viewpoints on which to focus, the easiest way to go about answering this question is to go through each answer choice and decide whether each is true.

Choice F indicates that both viewpoints point to the same biomolecule as the "first biomolecule" in the origin of life, which is not the case. This is the major point of contention between the two viewpoints as Hypothesis 1 proposes amino acids as the first biomolecule while Hypothesis 2 proposes RNA. Choice F only aligns with Hypothesis 2. Choice G indicates that both viewpoints agree on the prebiotic atmospheric content. Based on some of the listed gases in the passage, this is definitely a possibility. Choice H indicates that both viewpoints express that RNA preceded DNA and proteins in the evolution of lifeforms on Earth. Only Hypothesis 2 aligns with this perspective. Choice J indicates that the viewpoints agree that the formation of the "first biomolecule" occurred in deep-sea vents; this is really only specified in the first viewpoint in reference to carbonyl sulfide, so this cannot be correct. The correct answer, therefore, is choice G.

Identifying Key Differences

If you're going to be asked to compare the viewpoints, it makes sense that you would also be asked to contrast the viewpoints. You can approach the contrast question types in exactly the same way you would approach the comparison questions. If a question asks you to contrast the viewpoints with respect to a particular topic mentioned in the question stem, look through your notes or underlined words and phrases to find that topic within each viewpoint. If a question asks you to find differences between the viewpoints in general, you might need to take the same approach we took with the last example, by going through each answer choice and eliminating incorrect answers until you determine the correct answer.

When Conflicting Viewpoints differ dramatically in approach to the subject at hand, it may be a little more difficult to pinpoint differences between the viewpoints. However, you can always use the questions to your advantage. The ACT Science section consists

entirely of multiple-choice questions, and it is a perfectly valid strategy to look at the answers if you aren't sure about what exactly the question is asking you to determine from the viewpoints.

As described by Hypothesis 1 and Hypothesis 2, the key difference in biomolecule formation from the atmosphere is the experimental evidence that:

A. the prebiotic atmosphere can form the full array of amino acid monomers, but not all of the RNA nucleotide monomers.

B. the prebiotic atmosphere can form the full array of RNA nucleotide monomers, but not all of the amino acids.

C. indicates the prebiotic atmosphere directly forms peptides and proteins, bypassing amino acid formation, while RNA nucleotide monomers must be formed first.

D. indicates the prebiotic atmosphere directly forms RNA, bypassing nucleotide formation, while protein monomers, amino acids, must be formed first.

The correct answer is A. This question asks you to focus on differences in the modes of biomolecule formation. The question relates to experimental evidence, so if you took the time to identify and understand the experimental data while reading, it would pay off heavily here.

The answer choices are paired answers; choices A and B represent opposite ideas, and choices C and D represent opposite ideas. This means that one of these answer pairs is completely wrong altogether, while the other answer pair contains the correct answer. Choice A states that there is experimental evidence that shows that prebiotic atmosphere can form all of the amino acids, but not all of the nucleotides; this is true, according to the viewpoints, because the first viewpoint indicates that all amino acids have been formed experimentally, while the second passage indicates that only cytosine and uracil have currently been formed experimentally, with research making progress toward forming the others. This evidence indicates that choice A is correct, and that choice B is effectively incorrect.

To confirm our answer, let's check out choices C and D. Choice C indicates that peptide and protein formation bypasses the formation of amino acid monomers, while choice D indicates that RNA formation bypasses the formation of nucleotide monomers. The aforementioned experimental data appears to refute both of these statements, as the experimental evidence shows formation of amino acids and nucleotides rather than direct formation of full-fledged peptides and RNA. This makes sense, as it is much easier to form a smaller subunit of a bio-molecule than a more complex one. Therefore, we can rule out choices B, C, and D.

Inference Question Purposes

To connect or relate the two viewpoints in some way

To introduce real or hypothetical data that might affect one or both of the viewpoints

To apply the conclusions of one or more of the viewpoints to a new context

Making Inferences

So far, the question types we've discussed have been fairly straightforward reading comprehension questions for which you can find the answers simply by reading and understanding the passages. The last category of questions you might encounter will ask you to make inferences or to determine implied information, for one of three purposes:

Inference-based questions are still reading comprehension questions, but they require that you go beyond simply what is written in the text. In general, though, the process is much the same. Regardless of their form, inference questions can be answered correctly by selecting answers that are consistent with the information presented in the relevant viewpoints.

One inference question type might ask you to tweak one viewpoint so that it might work in collaboration with the second viewpoint or to indicate whether the two viewpoints are mutually exclusive. Another inference question could ask you to consider new information beyond the passage. You may be given a particular piece of real or hypothetical data and then determine how this new information will impact the two theories. For instance, a new hypothetical discovery might refute one viewpoint and support the other, refute both viewpoints, or might even be unrelated to either. This kind of question requires that you fully understand both perspectives, because you may have to apply new information to both to determine its effect on the two viewpoints.

The other version of this question type works in the reverse, in that you may be asked to choose a particular piece of information that supports or refutes one or both of the viewpoints. This question type may ask you to relate data to both viewpoints or to focus on only one; in either case, you'll have to have a thorough understanding of what each approach is conveying so that you know how new data could support or refute it.

The following examples will cover different types of inference-based questions so you can get a sense of how they work.

EXAMPLE

Which of the following pieces of data, if accurate, would best support Hypothesis 1?

- **A.** It is thermodynamically favorable for water to break down peptide chains via hydrolysis reactions.
- **B.** Nucleic acids cannot be converted to proteins without cell machinery already in existence.
- **C.** Pumice, the porous rock that forms when a volcano cools rapidly, can trap gas and nutrients to support microbe growth.
- **D.** There were no metal ions present in the deep-sea vent environment.

The correct answer is C. This question asks you to choose a piece of data that best supports one of the two viewpoints; in this case, the question asks you to choose the piece of data that best supports Hypothesis 1. To answer this question, we must go through each piece of data to determine how it affects the specified viewpoint.

Choice A is incorrect. In fact, this piece of data would contradict Hypothesis 1. Since amino acid polymerization requires dehydration synthesis, the thermodynamically favorable breakdown of peptides by water would refute the hypothesis, which indicates that the origin of life occurred at the deep-sea vents, located in water. Choice B is incorrect because Hypothesis 1 does not indicate that nucleic acids are converted into protein. Choice D is incorrect because, if anything, this piece of data would decrease support for Hypothesis 1. Therefore, the correct answer is choice C. Pumice is a volcanic rock that could potentially support microbe life by trapping gas and nutrients in its pores, which would be extremely important in the deep-sea environment.

If continued research indicates that the prebiotic atmosphere is unlikely to have been able to synthesize adenine and guanine, which of the following statements is likely correct?

- **F.** All described components of Hypothesis 1 should be regarded as inaccurate.
- **G.** Proteins could be confirmed as the "first biomolecules" per Hypothesis 1.
- **H.** All described components of Hypothesis 2 should be regarded as inaccurate.
- **J.** RNA may still be a key early biomolecule, but its synthesis requires non-RNA catalysts.

The correct answer is J. This question asks you to use a piece of hypothetical data, the inability of the prebiotic atmosphere to synthesize adenine and guanine, to draw a conclusion about the viewpoints. This piece of hypothetical data seems to clearly impact Hypothesis 2 more so than Hypothesis 1, but it is important to make sure by reasoning through each of the answer choices.

Choice F indicates that this new piece of data refutes entirely Hypothesis 1. This is incorrect because this particular finding would not impact this hypothesis since it does not propose that RNA is the "first biomolecule." Choice G indicates that this piece of data confirms proteins as the "first biomolecule." The need for a new catalyst to make RNA might strongly suggest that proteins are required for its synthesis, but this is a bit of a leap, as nothing about this piece of data specifically confirms that proteins are required for RNA synthesis. Therefore, choice G is incorrect. Choice H indicates that all components of Hypothesis 2 can be rejected with the introduction of this piece of data. This is not correct—Hypothesis 2 may indicate that RNA was likely the "first biomolecule," which this piece of data seems to reject, but the description of RNA's ability to contain genetic material, self-replicate, and act as a catalyst for propagation are all still true. Therefore, the correct answer is choice J, which indicates that this piece of data rejects RNA as the "first biomolecule," but RNA still performs important functions, particularly in self-propagation, that could make it an important early biomolecule.

Therefore, only the "first biomolecule" aspect of Hypothesis 2 would be refuted; the rest is still valid.

Suppose that a discovery was made that there exist enzymes that are capable of catalyzing the synthesis of nucleotides from basic precursor molecules. If true, this information would strengthen:

- **A.** Hypothesis 1
- **B.** Hypothesis 2
- **C.** both Hypothesis 1 and 2
- **D.** neither Hypothesis 1 nor 2

The correct answer is B. The discovery that enzymes can catalyze the synthesis of nucleotides from basic precursor molecules would support Hypothesis 2. It is stated that there "is no evidence of formation of the other two nucleotides present in RNA, adenine and guanine." However, with new information regarding the existence of enzymes that can lead to the synthesis of nucleotides, perhaps filling a gap in the RNA hypothesis, then Hypothesis 2, which proposes that RNA was the first biomolecule, would be strengthened. Choices A and C are thus incorrect as Hypothesis 1 does not rely on the presence of nucleotides to assert the early presence of amino acids to form peptide chains. Choice D is incorrect because of the discovery's connection with Hypothesis 2.

SUMMING IT UP

- Research Summaries pose a scientific question and describe an experiment or set of experiments to answer that question. They will also include the experimental results obtained, in the form of a table, graph, and/or chart.

- Identify the scientific question or purpose of the experiment first whenever you encounter a scientific experiment in an ACT Science passage. Ask yourself why the experiment is being conducted and what it's testing. Research Summaries provide you with all the background information you will need to identify the purpose of the given experiment.

- Some ACT exam questions might ask you to choose the most suitable hypothesis for an experiment. Your hypothesis must always correctly address the appropriate independent and dependent variables. Hypotheses are predictions, and a hypothesis will not always correctly predict the outcome of an experiment.

- Some ACT exam questions will ask you to identify variables and controls and recognize how and why the experiment was designed a certain way and how it answers the scientific question posed. Research Summaries always provide enough detail so that you can figure out what's going on. The techniques will not be overly complicated—the passage will provide you with the background you need.

- Drawing conclusions about data presented to you means finding trends and patterns in the data. When reading over an experiment and its accompanying data, take note of any obvious trends—you are sure to be asked about them and how they relate to the experiment's hypothesis.

- Data Representation passages present you with a graph, table, and/or figure that describes some kind of scientific observation or phenomenon.

- Read the introductory and surrounding paragraphs to determine the questions the data is supposed to answer. Even if you don't understand the terminology or vocabulary used, the figure itself can usually tell you all you need to know.

- Recognizing patterns and trends in data sets will be helpful when you're trying to draw conclusions—questions accompanying data sets will usually ask about these types of observations.

- If you need to change data from a table into a graph, remember that the *x*-axis is usually the independent variable (the variable that the experimenter alters), and the *y*-axis is usually the dependent variable (the variable being measured in the experiment).

- Identifying the dependent and independent variables is key to answering questions that ask you to suggest additional experiments or apply findings to other situations—you can look at the answer choices and pick the one that uses these variables. A good strategy for these questions is process of elimination. You can rule out answers describing experiments that obviously vary the wrong conditions or take the wrong measurement.

- Conflicting Viewpoints passages provide two (or sometimes three) arguments that each put forth a hypothesis or theory, along with supporting evidence, that are related to a shared topic.

- Follow these steps when you encounter a Conflicting Viewpoints passage on the ACT Science test:

  1. Identify the topic.
  2. Identify the basic hypotheses or theories of the scientists.
  3. Identify the relevant data used to support each of the two viewpoints discussed in the passage.

- Look for commonalities between viewpoints. There will always be some kind of parallel you can draw, and one of the questions accompanying the passage will draw attention to one of those parallels.

TEST YOURSELF

SCIENCE CONCEPTS

16 Questions—18 Minutes

> **Directions:** There are multiple passages in this test. Each passage is followed by several questions. After you read a passage, choose the best answer for each question. After you've selected each answer, read the answer explanations to check yourself. You may refer to the passages as often as necessary. Calculators are NOT permitted for this test.

PASSAGE I

In geology, rocks can be characterized by fractional porosity and dry density. Fractional porosity is defined as the volume of pore space in a rock divided by the total volume of a rock. It is essentially the fraction of void space that exists within a rock, and there are many factors that can influence porosity. Dry density is defined as the mass of dry solid per unit volume of dry solid.

A student wanted to examine rock porosity and dry density in order to determine whether or not the two are correlated with one another. The student used four different sandstone rock samples, cut in perfect rectangular prisms for simple volume measurement.

Experiment 1

Each dry rock sample was weighed and then vacuum-saturated with water. The water-saturated sample was then weighed. The difference between these two weights provided the mass of water within the pores. Since the density of water is known at the given temperature, the volume of water occupying the rock's pores, the void volume, can be

determined based on the measured mass. Using the void volume and total rock volume, The student determined the porosities of the four rocks (see Table 1).

Experiment 2

Each of the four rock samples was then weighed on a balance, and its mass was recorded. Dividing the mass by the volume of each rock allowed for the calculation of its dry density (see Table 2).

TABLE 2			
Rock Sample	Dry Mass (g)	Total Volume (mL)	Dry Density (g/mL)
A	147	60	2.45
B	143	64	2.23
C	87	60	1.45
D	109	56	1.95

1. Which of the following best summarizes the scientific question posed by the student?

   A. How does sandstone mass correlate with volume?

   B. How does the fractional porosity of sandstone vary with rock depth?

   C. What is the relationship between sandstone fractional porosity and dry density?

   D. What is the correlation between wet and dry densities of sandstone samples?

TABLE 1			
Rock Sample	Void Volume (mL)	Total Volume (mL)	Fractional Porosity
A	8.4	60	0.14
B	12.8	64	0.20
C	25.2	60	0.42
D	15.7	56	0.28

2. Measuring the temperature during fractional porosity determination is important for the measurement of the:

F. total rock volume.

G. void volume.

H. dry mass.

J. dry density.

3. The sandstone densities were plotted as a function of the measured fractional porosities. Which of the following graphs best depicts this relationship?

A.

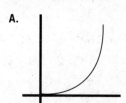

B.

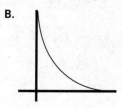

C.

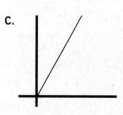

D.

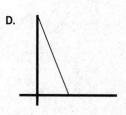

4. Which of the following measurement pairs would result in a dry density that is lower than 1.00 g/mL?

F. The void volume (mL) is lower than the total rock volume (mL).

G. The total rock volume (mL) is lower than the void volume (mL).

H. The mass of the rock (g) is lower than the total rock volume (mL).

J. The total rock volume (mL) is lower than the mass of the rock (g).

5. Which of the following procedures would NOT be useful to verify the determined correlation between the variables of interest?

A. Confirming the fractional porosities using a different technique to determine void volume

B. Decreasing the range of tested sandstone densities

C. Using samples of a different type of rock

D. Increasing the number of measured trials per rock sample

Passage II

A student noticed that at room temperature, she could not dissolve nearly as much sodium chloride (NaCl) or potassium chloride (KCl) in 100 mL of water as she could lead (II) nitrate ($Pb(NO_3)_2$). The student decided to test the solubilities of these three salts at different temperatures. For each trial, she measured out 100 mL of water and 100 g of the salt of interest. She then added salt to the water, stirring constantly, until the solution was completely saturated and no more salt would dissolve in the water. To determine the mass added, the student measured the mass of salt remaining from her original 100 g stock and subtracted the new mass from the original mass. This mass difference represents the mass of salt that she could dissolve in 100 g of water. She proceeded to perform this protocol for three salts at five different temperatures ranging from 0°C to 40°C. Her data are shown below:

Salts	Salt Solubility (g salt per 100 mL water) at Various Temperatures				
	0°C	10°C	20°C	30°C	40°C
NaCl	34.2	34.6	35.0	35.4	35.8
KCl	27.0	29.9	32.8	35.7	38.6
$Pb(NO_3)_2$	36.9	46.1	55.3	64.5	73.7

6. Which salt exhibited the lowest solubility at 30°C?

   F. NaCl

   G. KCl

   H. $Pb(NO_3)_2$

   J. All three salts exhibited identical solubilities.

7. At approximately which temperature do sodium chloride and potassium chloride have the same solubility?

   A. 0°C

   B. 17°C

   C. 28°C

   D. 35°C

8. If the solubility of KCl is plotted as a function of temperature, which of the following best represents how this graph would look?

   F.
   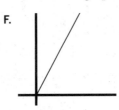

   G.
   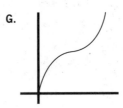

   H.
   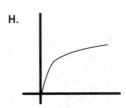

   J.
   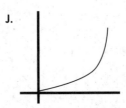

9. Based on the collected data, what mass of $Pb(NO_3)_2$ would you expect to be able to dissolve in 100 mL of water at 60°C?

A. 36.9 g

B. 73.7 g

C. 82.9 g

D. 92.1 g

10. What can be concluded about the effect of temperature on salt solubility?

F. Increasing the temperature increases the solubilities of KCl and $Pb(NO_3)_2$, but decreases the solubility of NaCl.

G. Decreasing the temperature increases the solubilities of KCl and $Pb(NO_3)_2$, but decreases the solubility of NaCl.

H. Increasing the temperature increases the solubilities of KCl, NaCl, and $Pb(NO_3)_2$.

J. Decreasing the temperature increases the solubilities of KCl, NaCl, and $Pb(NO_3)_2$.

PASSAGE III

There are a number of theories of personality, but only a few are based on biological evidence. Two such theories of personality based on biology are presented below.

Scientist 1

The relationship between personality and sensitivity to reinforcement relies on three brain systems, each of which responds in a different manner to stimuli that reward or punish. The behavioral activation system (BAS) includes the parts of the brain involved in controlling arousal, namely the thalamus, striatum, and cerebral cortex. This system responds to reward cues and is accordingly known as the reward system. When people have a more active BAS, they tend to be more

impulsive and behaviorally outgoing upon approaching a goal. The behavioral inhibition system (BIS), which includes the brain stem and the neocortical projections to the frontal lobe of the brain, acts in the opposite way. BIS responds to punishment and non-rewarding stimuli, and people with a more active BIS are more prone to experience negative emotions like fear, anxiety, and sadness. The third system is the fight/flight/freeze system (FFFS), also called the threat system, which regulates reactions of fight vs. flight and rage vs. panic. This system is sensitive to new, punishing stimuli.

Scientist 2

Personality traits are determined by a complex combination of genes, not a single gene. Most of the evidence linking genetics and the environment to personality is based on studies with genetically identical twins. The Minnesota Study of Twins Reared Apart examined 350 pairs of twins, both fraternal and identical, from 1979 to 1999. This study found not only that identical twins raised together have very similar personalities, but also that identical twins raised apart had very similar personalities. This finding indicates that some aspects of personality are controlled by genetics, and that some personality traits are heritable. Other twin studies have shown that there are higher correlations of personality traits in identical twins than in fraternal twins, which supports this link between genetics and personality. Still, the studies all indicate that while identical twins have similar personality traits, they also have distinct personalities overall, indicating that genetics alone do not determine personality. Another study that looked at twins in five different countries found 50% of personality traits in common among identical twins and 20% of traits in common for fraternal twins. Recent studies in genetics and personality have focused on single nucleotide polymorphisms (SNPs), which are specific, small repeating sections of genes found in certain versions of the gene, usually noncoding regions more so than coding regions. Well-studied SNPs include the APOE4 genetic polymorphism, which has been found to be linked to increased risk for Alzheimer's disease, and the

GG variant of the oxytocin receptor gene rs53576 has been found to be associated with intimacy and social bonds. Other SNPs related to dopamine are related to Parkinson's disease, attention deficit hyperactivity disorder (ADHD), and drug addiction.

11. According to Scientist 1, a student's level of nervousness before an exam for which he has not prepared can most nearly be attributed to a more active:

   A. SNPs.

   B. BAS.

   C. BIS.

   D. FFFS.

12. In 1848, a 25-year-old named Phineas Gage survived an iron rod penetrating his skull and damaging his frontal cortex. After the accident, it was noted that his personality changed, namely in social cognition and decision making. This case would serve as evidence for:

   F. Scientist 1.

   G. Scientist 2.

   H. both Scientist 1 and Scientist 2.

   J. neither Scientist 1 nor Scientist 2.

13. A similarity between the two viewpoints is that both:

   A. include a fight/flight/freeze personality component.

   B. use evidence from twin studies as support.

   C. attribute personality differences between siblings to SNPs.

   D. point to human biology as the basis for personality rather than environment.

14. Which viewpoint, if any, directly predicts sources for personality disorders?

   F. Scientist 1 only

   G. Scientist 2 only

   H. Both Scientist 1 and Scientist 2

   J. Neither Scientist 1 nor Scientist 2

15. A hypothetical genetic disorder causes a defect in the striatum of the forebrain. This genetic disorder is accompanied by a personality disorder. This evidence supports:

   A. Scientist 1 only.

   B. Scientist 2 only.

   C. both Scientist 1 and Scientist 2.

   D. neither Scientist 1 nor Scientist 2.

16. According to the two viewpoints, what is the significance of the environment with respect to personality?

   F. The first viewpoint proposes that the environment does not affect personality, while the second viewpoint proposes that human personality is based on biological responses to the environment.

   G. The first viewpoint proposes that human personality is based on biological responses to the environment, while the second viewpoint proposes that the environment does not affect personality.

   H. The first viewpoint proposes that the environment plays a role in personality separate from biology, while the second viewpoint proposes that human personality is based on biological responses to the environment.

   J. The first viewpoint proposes that human personality is based on biological responses to the environment, while the second viewpoint proposes that the environment plays a role in personality separate from biology.

ANSWER KEY AND EXPLANATIONS

1. C	4. H	7. C	10. H	13. D	16. J
2. G	5. B	8. F	11. C	14. G	
3. D	6. F	9. D	12. F	15. C	

1. **The correct answer is C.** As indicated in the passage, the student wishes to look for a correlation between fractional porosity and dry density, so both of these variables should be included in the scientific question. Choice A is incorrect because while it does incorporate relevant measurements, it does not focus on the variables of interest to the student. Choice B is incorrect because rock depth is not a relevant variable in this experiment. Choice D is incorrect because wet density is not a relevant variable in this experiment.

2. **The correct answer is G.** According to the passage, the temperature measurement was needed to find the proper water density, which was in turn used to calculate the void volume based on the mass of water from the pores. Choice F is incorrect because temperature does not affect total rock volume, and choices H and J are incorrect because they were measured in the dry density experiment, not the fractional porosity experiment.

3. **The correct answer is D.** Based on the data, dry density decreases as fractional porosity increases, which means that the correct graph will show decrease from left to right. This allows for choices A and C to be ruled out immediately. Focusing on Rocks A, C, and D, increasing the fractional porosity by 0.14 in. in each case results in a 0.50 g/mL decline in dry density. This indicates a linear decrease, which allows for the elimination of choice B. Choice D is correct because it is the only graph that shows a linear decrease.

4. **The correct answer is H.** According to the passage and the data, dry density is determined by dividing the mass of the rock by the total rock volume. Choices F and G are incorrect because the noted volumes are relevant to fractional porosity, not density. Between choices H and J, the choice that will give a density lower than 1.00 g/mL is the one that

indicates that the rock mass is lower than the rock volume. The correct answer is choice H, not choice J.

5. **The correct answer is B.** Decreasing the range of tested sandstone densities only limits the scope of the experiment. Choice A is incorrect because using a different mode of void volume determination would help to confirm the results. Choice C is incorrect because using a different type of rock would allow the student to see if this same pattern holds beyond sandstone. Choice D is incorrect because increasing the number of trials per rock sample will only help to verify the results if the same results are obtained per trial.

6. **The correct answer is F.** According to the table, the solubilities of NaCl, KCl, and $Pb(NO_3)_2$ at 30°C were 35.4 g, 35.7 g, and 64.5 g salt per 100 mL water. The lowest number of the group is 35.4 g, which corresponds with NaCl, so NaCl exhibited the lowest solubility at 30°C.

7. **The correct answer is C.** Choice A, the only answer choice directly represented on the data table, is incorrect because the data show that NaCl and KCl have different solubilities at 0°C. Based on the data, the solubilities of both salts increase with temperature, but the rate of increase is higher for KCl than NaCl. Therefore, even though KCl has a lower solubility than NaCl at lower temperatures, it has a higher solubility than NaCl at higher temperatures. Based on the data table, the solubility of KCl is lower than that of NaCl up to 20°C, and then higher than that of NaCl over 30°C. Therefore, the correct answer must be between 20°C and 30°C. Choice C is the only one that falls in this range.

8. **The correct answer is F.** KCl, as well as the other two salts, exhibits a linear increase in solubility as a function of temperature. For KCl, the solubility increases by 2.9 g salt per 100 mL water for every 10°C change in temperature. This constant increase

in solubility relative to temperature indicates a linear increase, and choice F is the only graph that displays a linear increase.

9. **The correct answer is D.** The data show a linear change in $Pb(NO_3)_2$ solubility as a function of temperature, and based on the provided data, there is an increase in solubility of 9.2 g salt per 100 mL water with every 10°C increase in temperature. The highest temperature provided on the table is 73.7 g at 40°C. To get to 60°C, two consecutive 10°C temperature increases are needed, so 9.2 g must be added twice to 73.7 g to get the mass of $Pb(NO_3)_2$ that will dissolve in 100 mL of water at 60°C: 73.7 + (2)(9.2) = 92.1 g.

10. **The correct answer is H.** According to the data in the table, all three salts exhibit increases in solubility as temperature increases. Choice F is incorrect because even though NaCl exhibits a smaller increase in solubility with temperature than the other salts, it is still an increase and not a decrease. Choice G is incorrect because the trend is incorrect with regard to KCl and $Pb(NO_3)_2$. Choice J is incorrect because it describes a trend that is completely opposite to what the data actually show.

11. **The correct answer is C.** A more active BIS contributes to anxiety and nervousness due to a negative stimulus, in this case an exam for which the student has not prepared. Choice A is incorrect because SNPs are relevant to the second viewpoint, not the first viewpoint. Choice B is incorrect because a more active BAS contributes to impulsiveness and behavior leading to a positive stimulus or end goal. Choice D is incorrect because an exam is not a new or unexpected stimulus that would require a fight/flight/freeze response.

12. **The correct answer is F.** Gage's injury does not correlate with DNA mutation, hormone imbalance, or a genetic disorder. Gage's trauma was the result of an environmental event and demonstrated that damage to a particular brain region, a region expressed by Scientist 1 to correspond with certain behavioral patterns, resulted in a change of personality. Such evidence would directly support Scientist 1 (choices F and H) and challenge

Scientist 2's viewpoint, thus allowing you to eliminate choices G, H, and J.

13. **The correct answer is D.** Both viewpoints indicate that human biology is the basis for personality; the introduction before the passages states this outright, but one can draw the same conclusion from the viewpoints themselves because the first viewpoint discusses the nervous system and the second viewpoint discusses genetics. Choice A is incorrect because the fight/flight/freeze personality component is discussed only in the first viewpoint. Choice B is incorrect because twin studies are discussed only in the second viewpoint. Choice C is incorrect because SNPs are mentioned only in the second viewpoint, though not specifically in the manner described by this choice.

14. **The correct answer is G.** Scientist 2 seeks sources for personality disorders in genes, while Scientist 1 focuses more on types of behaviors rather than specific personality disorders. Choices F and H are incorrect because they indicate that Scientist 1 seeks such sources, while choice J is incorrect because it indicates that Scientist 2 does not address this.

15. **The correct answer is C.** This disorder involves a genetic defect that affects the nervous system, which in turn causes a personality disorder. Therefore, this disorder is consistent with both viewpoints. Choices A and B are incorrect because they each indicate that only one viewpoint is consistent with this hypothetical piece of data. Choice D is incorrect because it indicates that the hypothetical piece of data supports neither viewpoint.

16. **The correct answer is J.** The first viewpoint is based on reward/punishment responses to the environment, while the second viewpoint concedes that the environment affects personality where genetics do not. Choices F and G are incorrect because each indicates that one of the viewpoints discounts the significance of environment on personality, which is untrue. Choice H is incorrect because it swaps the roles of the environment in each viewpoint.

CHAPTER

**Strategies for Approaching
the Science Section**

STRATEGIES FOR APPROACHING THE

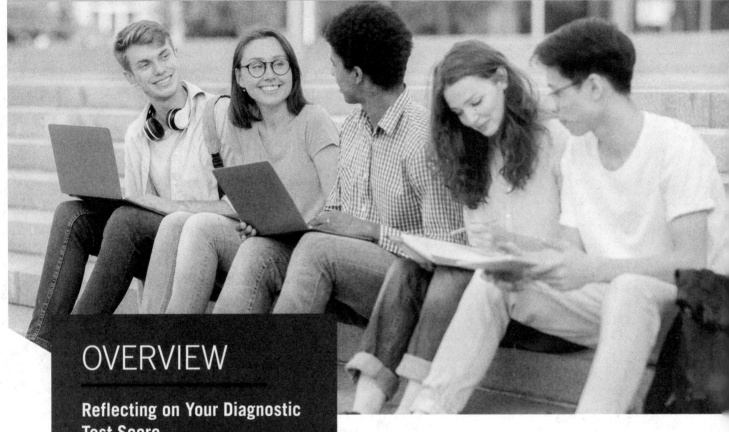

OVERVIEW

Reflecting on Your Diagnostic Test Score

Overall Section Strategies

Question and Passage Strategies

Test Yourself: Science Passages and Questions

General Advice and Reminders

Strategy Roundup

Summing It Up

Knowledge Check: Science

So far in this part of the book, we've discussed what you can expect from the ACT Science test and provided an in-depth overview of the skills you'll be tested on and how. Now, we'll pivot to discuss the best ways to combine and apply that knowledge of the test with strategies that can help you manage your time and increase your score. These strategies include an approach for the section as a whole as well as how to target different aspects of specific passage and question types. Throughout this chapter, you'll reflect on your diagnostic performance and practice strategies using a Test Yourself and a full-length Knowledge Check to see what problems you need to address and how certain strategies help you improve. You'll see some similarities to Chapter 18 here as the ACT Reading test assesses comparable skills, just in different ways.

REFLECTING ON YOUR DIAGNOSTIC TEST SCORE

Take some time to turn back to your diagnostic test in Chapter 2 and your analysis of it in Chapter 3. Reflect on your score and performance when you started studying. Think about it, write about it, and use this table to jot down some ideas.

DIAGNOSTIC TEST REFLECTION: SCIENCE	
Science Diagnostic Test Score: _____	**Science Scoring Goal:** _____
Reflection Question	**Notes**
What went well for you during the diagnostic test, and which skills were easiest for you to use?	
What did you struggle with during the diagnostic test, or which skills were harder for you to use?	
Did you feel rushed? Did you have left over time?	
How close were you to your goal?	
After reviewing science skills and methods in the last chapter, what are some things you might like to keep in mind as you study further?	
What are some aspects of approaching the science test for which you are hoping to build strategies?	

Take a moment to think about your goals for the ACT Science test. What kind of score are you looking to achieve? Whether you're looking for a perfect score or just to gain a few points, that goal should influence how you prepare for the test and the kinds of choices you make when working in the test section. To reach the highest scores, you need to work quickly and accurately, so you'll need to find ways to maximize your time and minimize your mistakes. To raise your score a few points, you may just need to improve time management or focus your time in different ways.

As you saw with the Reading test, each question you answer correctly in the Science section leads to approximately one additional point for your scaled score. If you analyze scoring charts from the ACT, this pattern holds up until the 20-30 scoring band. From there, you may find that you need two questions correct to increase your scaled score. Thus, you would need around 30 correct questions to achieve a 25-26. You can use that information to make some estimates for how many questions you can guess on. Keep in mind that your goal should reflect the score that makes you competitive for your desired school. It should also represent how far you can push yourself with the time you have before your test date. You should try to score as high as you can, but you can make some strategic decisions for how you spend your time as well. The choice is yours.

Make sure that your goal changes as you continue to build your skills and practice. Take some notes so you can check back to see how closely your testing outcome aligned with your goals. This will help you build a framework for future studying.

OVERALL SECTION STRATEGIES

Similar to the ACT Reading test, one of the most important skills to develop for the Science test is time management. This section will give you tips for how you can control your time, along with strategies for working through passages in an order that makes sense for you, reading actively for the priorities of different passage types, and thinking about how to guess effectively.

While it's true that the Science test will draw on some science terminology you would have encountered in your academic career, the questions have relatively limited priorities, as you saw in Chapter 20. You'll analyze data, demonstrate understanding of experimental design and results, and apply information from the passage to a variety of situations. All of those goals depend on understanding the information presented by the passage and using your reasoning skills to come to valid conclusions quickly.

The goal is to use your time to focus on what you know the questions care about and not let yourself get hung up anywhere in particular. You're trying to get to as many questions as you can and spend enough time with each question so that you can apply what you know from the passage and what you know about the test to get to a correct answer.

However, how you approach extracting information from the passage can vary greatly depending on your reading skills and reasoning abilities. As you prepare for your ACT Science test, we encourage you to experiment with the different strategies outlined here and in the sections that follow. Experimentation is necessary to craft an overall approach that will help you capitalize on your personal strengths and get the best score possible.

Divide Your Time According to Your Goals

Your scoring goals should reflect what you need for college admissions and what you're capable of with the time you have to prepare before your ACT test day. Just like with the Reading section, if you are aiming for as close to a perfect score as possible, then you'll need to divide your time in a way that allows you to evaluate all of the passages and answer the 40 total questions in the 35 minutes you're allotted. That means spending equal time in each passage (5-6 minutes) or getting through each passage and spending any remaining time where you know you might have some weaknesses or uncertainty. With practice, that is entirely possible.

However, let's say you struggled with finishing the section in the past and were scoring below the national average (~20). Your approach doesn't need to look like that of someone who's seeking a perfect score (though it can). You have lots of options for how you spend your time.

For instance, it might be better to focus the bulk of your time on two particular passage types (e.g., Data Representations and Research Summaries) that are easier for you to try to ace rather than spread your time evenly across all six (or seven) passages. Then, with whatever time you have remaining, you can direct that to the one or two harder (for you) passage types, eliminating answers and guessing on remaining questions (and/or prioritizing questions that can be answered easily because of their signposts for particular perspectives or sections of the passages). Statistically, guessing should yield about two correct answers per every 10 guesses; this number only goes up if you logically eliminate answers that you know are incorrect. Therefore, you are likely to get a few correct answers from the passage(s) you save for the end, even if you have to guess on every question.

Consider which approach will help you make the most of your time in accordance with your goals. From there, practice bringing those strategies together before the big day. You should use everything in your arsenal to push yourself and your score as much as you can.

Determine Your Passage Order

During your diagnostic test, you might have found that certain passage types came easier to you, required less time and effort, or at the very least interested (or bored) you more than others. You may have also noted a positive correlation between a certain passage type and your performance. For instance, in reflecting on your diagnostic score, you may have seen that you excelled with Data Representation passages, struggled with Research Summaries, and/or didn't get to spend much time with the Conflicting Viewpoints passage but did answer all the questions correctly that you looked at. Perhaps you saw that the topics were an issue since you missed all the questions related to a chemistry passage but got most questions correct for one related to physics.

That is not a lot of data to go off of, but analyzing your performance in those terms can help you evaluate how, if at all, different passage types impact your timing and, thus, your scoring. Just like with Reading, you can work through the passages in whatever order you prefer. However, unlike Reading, there is no predictable order to the passages, nor will there necessarily be the same number of each passage type on each test. Because of this unpredictability, you won't be able to say that you'll do the last passage first or the first passage last until you're on the test. What you can do, however, is select a passage order that prioritizes, for example, Data Representations and Research Summaries, or you could consider which topics might feel more digestible.

If something looks difficult to interpret, perhaps it is worth saving until you've worked through the passages with which you feel more comfortable. The goal should be to be able to work through every passage quickly and competently, but there's any number of reasons that something might become an obstacle rather than a boon.

Deciding your passage order is all about analyzing how well you've done in the past, how you've improved, and where you want to be on test day. Use what you know about yourself—and what your test results are telling you—to make this decision strategically.

Develop and Practice an Active Reading Strategy

Much of what was true for the Reading test is true for the Science test: you have limited time to get through multiple passages and 40 questions, all in 35 minutes. The details are different (6-7 passages each with 6-7 questions), but the priorities are largely the same. Can you read through each passage quickly, understand the purpose of the passage, and then accurately answer related questions?

If you're trying to evenly distribute your time throughout the section, you have 5-6 minutes per passage and question set (only 5 minutes if you have 7 passages). That time has to be divided between reading, in some way, and answering questions. You don't get points for reading the passages, only for answering questions correctly. And just like with Reading, you need information from the passage to eliminate answers and answer accurately. To gather that information efficiently, you should read actively.

Active reading is all about maximizing your engagement with the passage—thinking about what is being said and how it is being said while you're reading—to meet your needs. In a timed environment, active reading is an intense process, requiring you to inject as much energy into reading as you can, actively summarizing as you read and making critical, but brief, notes. You don't have to be thorough when reading. The chance of you recalling all the details from each passage is low. You would have to account for all the values given for an experiment's design, the data points in tables and figures, and more. Spare yourself that effort and focus on what you need. It may be helpful to review active reading strategies in Chapter 18.

You do know that the passages on the Science test are relatively short, but they can be quite dense. As you're reading through them, based on the passage type, you can be thinking about specific things. You can be active and make mental or physical note of the things that the questions will prioritize so you can try to save time. We discussed these elements in Chapter 20, but let's review now to consider how they affect your strategy:

DATA REPRESENTATIONS

What was measured, how it was measured, how measurements are presented (figure keys and axes), the relationships between measurements

RESEARCH SUMMARIES

Background information and experimental constants, variables, and procedure; changes between experiments; relationships and patterns in the data; changes between figures or tables

CONFLICTING VIEWPOINTS

The topic, the focus of each viewpoint, the differences between the viewpoints

How you memorize or label these things is up to you and your skills and how much you practice. Your priority is to be active, and your individual strategy will depend on your strengths and challenges with the section, as well as your scoring goals. As you prepare for your test date, you should experiment, alter, and adapt your strategies for the section to align with your increasing comfort with the Science section's passages, questions, and presentation.

Complete a Passage before Moving On

Many test takers think the best move is to answer all the questions they can and move on to the next passage, assuming they'll have time to review again before time expires. However, if you do this for the first passage you read and then have to return to it after reading five or six more, it's possible you will have forgotten the details of the passage. This would force you to reread a significant amount to be able to answer any remaining questions effectively. Similarly, you may find that you run out of time and forget to return to questions you didn't at least guess on. Those empty bubbles will only hurt your score. Instead of jumping around between passages, answer every question for a given passage before moving on, even if you just supply a guess.

Make Note of Guesses for Review

It's entirely possible that after working hard to manage your time, you find yourself with a few minutes to review the section. Remember that every second counts when you want to raise your score. In a section like Science, that time can be used to turn a guess into a certainty. In order to make the most of that time, you need to have tracked which questions you guessed on so you can easily jump to them in the final moments of the test.

While moving through the test, notate in some way questions for which you were uncertain in your answer. You can even use multiple notation marks for different types of guesses. That way you can prioritize reviewing questions you might be able to figure out with extra time over those which will require too much time and energy, or those for which you simply have no clue. Then, try to maximize the number of questions that you review to build to certainty in your answers. One more correct question may net you an additional point on your scaled score, so make every second count.

QUESTION AND PASSAGE STRATEGIES

So far, the strategies we've covered provide you with a general approach to the ACT Science test. Now, we'll turn to more specific strategies based on the three question and passage types—along with example situations and applications.

Question Strategies

How you approach a question in the Science section depends on the kind of question you're dealing with. Each question has different priorities, referring to different parts of the passages in different ways. The following strategies are a combination of the general priorities of each question type along with some minor steps you can take to help you avoid errors in reasoning or misreadings of information in the passages.

Interpretation of Data

Interpretation of Data questions will appear predominantly alongside Data Representations and Research Summaries. In other words, if there are tables and figures associated with a passage, you'll encounter this question type. Knowing that they'll appear then, there are things that you can do not only to prime yourself for their appearance but also work through them more effectively.

When reading the passage:

1. **Identify what is being measured and how:** The basic premise for an Interpretation of Data question is whether you understand the data as it is presented and what conclusions it allows you to draw. To get to that point, you need to understand what was measured and how it was measured. This can be as simple as actively reading the background paragraph and experimental procedure or closely inspecting the figures or tables to see what is measured and with what units.

2. **Summarize the relationships in the data:** The questions will in some way ask about the relationships between variables or the trends in the data. If you understand such things prior to wading into the questions, you'll be that much more prepared to answer them without being drawn into some of the distractions created by the incorrect answer choices.

3. **Pinpoint outliers in the data:** If an element of a figure or table contradicts the general trends depicted, it's likely that a question will inquire about it. You don't need to immediately understand why that outlier is present, but understanding where it is can prime you for any related questions.

When answering questions:

1. **Use question phrasing to guide you to the right figures and data points:** The question will either include clues for what data you should be interpreting or will point you directly to the correct data by saying "Figure 1" or "Study 2 for 30°C," sending you to a specific part of the figure that is connected to the study cited. You'll then look at, for instance, the corresponding figure and the indicated temperature and see how it connects to another variable.

2. **Interact with the figures, tables, and diagrams to support accuracy:** The complex presentation of some of the graphics on the Science test can easily lead your eye astray. Use your pencil to direct your eye. If a question says, "volume at 200 minutes for Substance A," then draw a line at 200 mins from the *x*-axis and then use your pencil to follow the intersection of Substance A to the corresponding volume on the *y*-axis.

3. **Double-check units and other labels:** A question may have you looking at one piece of data but present answers that have different units (something explained by the passage or contingent on your basic scientific knowledge). Make sure you compare the units and labels on figures and tables to what is desired by the question and adjust accordingly.

4. **Look at the axis indicated by the passage, not just the one on the left:** The ACT can present some truly wild charts and graphs. Sometimes a figure will have a horizontal axis and two vertical axes. It can be easy to find the point on the *x*-axis referenced by the question and instinctively follow it up and then to the left. In reality, what the question wants is the variable on another axis. Such figures may even have the same scales on both vertical axes, making it easier to look at the wrong variable.

Scientific Investigation

Scientific Investigation questions appear most commonly with Research Summary passages as the questions primarily interrogate how and why an experiment was performed. Your ability to answer correctly hinges on your understanding of the experimental design and choices the researchers made.

When reading the passage:

1. **Identify the elements of the scientific method:** Scientific Investigation questions will require you to demonstrate your understanding of an experiment's independent and dependent variables, its constants, and the steps in the procedure used to conduct the study. If you identify that information when reading a passage, you'll have what you need to answer the questions.

2. **Identify the changes between experiments:** Each experiment, study, or trial will change what was being measured from the last experiment. It may measure something similar, but the method or target will change. That change can be the subject of a question or impact your answer. Try to lock the purpose of each numbered experiment in mind so that you can quickly eliminate choices that contradict those purposes. Additionally, understanding that purpose will help direct your attention to the appropriate place when a question references said purpose or design rather than a specific experiment.

3. **Draw a conclusion from the results of the studies:** Even as a Research Summary attempts to encompass the scientific method, the ACT doesn't include conclusions for the experiments. The test makers want you to demonstrate your understanding of the results of the experiments. The questions are asking for relevant information that allows you to form a proper conclusion for the methods and data presented. You are acting as a researcher by interpreting the results.

When answering questions:

1. **Stay consistent with the experimental design:** Refer to the passage to check details of the experimental design. The descriptions can be dense, and it can be easy to forget the minor details (controlled temperatures, amounts, etc.). It's likely that you'll be able to eliminate answers based on the apparent contradictions they present when compared to what you know of the experiments.

2. **Apply your scientific knowledge:** Vocabulary and basic science facts (things like the freezing point of water, how to calculate density, the meaning of *diffusion*) can come up in these questions. Any terms and concepts that appear will be applied in the context of the passage. The researchers made choices that support effective experimental design. Your scientific knowledge will be applied in a way that supports the purpose of the experiments, unless the question directs you otherwise.

Evaluation of Models, Inferences, and Experimental Results

Evaluation of Models, Inferences, and Experimental Results questions are all about applying what you learned from the passage (how an experiment was designed, the results that it got, the impact of different variables and factors, the nature of different viewpoints, etc.) to new situations. If you've taken the proper steps to prepare for the other question types, then you should have what you need to answer these questions. Let's review your different priorities when reading the passage and consider what you can do while answering.

When reading the passage:

1. **Understand the purpose and lessons from the passage:** Just as you've sought out certain kinds of information in passages to prepare yourself for Interpretation of Data and Scientific Investigation questions, the same guidance applies for Evaluation of Models, Inferences, and Experimental Results (EMI) questions. Since EMI questions can be present for any passage type, you're reading every passage to determine the following:

   - Procedures for the experiment
   - Purpose of each experiment
   - Summary of each viewpoint
   - Nature of measurements
   - Patterns in the data

When answering questions:

1. **Eliminate answers that contradict what you see in the passage:** EMI questions will have you apply what can be inferred from the passage in different situations, asking what would occur under different circumstances given what you know. Any choice you make not only has to align with the conditions expressed by the question but must also align with what you observed in the passage.

2. **Analyze any new data in the questions:** EMI questions can sometimes look just like Interpretation of Data questions. The primary difference will be that they'll have you apply what you know about the data from the passage to new figures or tables the question introduces. You'll want to analyze any new data with the same attention and rigor you applied to the passage. Your goal would then be to determine how this new data impacts or is influenced by what you saw in the passage.

Passage Strategies

Beyond tips that are specific to certain question types, there are a few passage strategies that can help you achieve your goals. These strategies work in tandem to support your efforts for preparing and answering individual questions.

Strategy #1: Plan Out Your Reading Technique

There is more than one way to approach reading a passage in the ACT Science section. Earlier in this chapter, we laid out some basic goals for active reading for the different passage types, but there are multiple ways to read actively. It all depends on your goals for the section and your own strengths and weaknesses as a reader.

Unlike passages in the Reading test, the structures of the Science passages are rigid. They will have clear labels for the different experiments, viewpoints, figures and tables. While the Reading section questions provide line numbers, the Science questions will often provide references to figure or table numbers, elements of the experiment, variables on the axes of figures, or columns and rows of tables. Those are all signposts directing you to what you need to think about. Since you know the different kinds of things the questions will focus on and you've read actively in some way, you should be able to flow easily from the question to the passage to find the details you need.

If that process of reading the passage is throttling your time and keeping you from later passages and questions you need for your score, you can experiment with what you're reading in the passage. Ideally, you're able to read the whole passage and understand what you need in order to quickly answer questions. However, you can also focus on or ignore different elements of the passages and perform different steps to try to save yourself time without sacrificing accuracy.

Your reading of the passage could include any one of or a combination of the following steps:

- Read the passage
- Start with questions and refer back to the passage
- Read questions and then read the passage
- Jump to questions related to data
- Examine the figures and tables and infer experimental design
- Analyze data
- Read the experimental steps
- Read each experiment
- Read each viewpoint and ignore background information
- Skip the experimental procedures

How you decide to move through the passage depends on your current performance and how far it is from where you want to be. Your biggest consideration here is whether you have time to read the full passage. For most students, understanding will best be aided by reading the entire passage. If that is a struggle, experiment with what you read and when. As you gain comfort with the different passage and question types, see if you can read the whole passage and maintain (or improve) your timing and accuracy.

Strategy #2: Annotate the Passage Based on Passage Priorities

The helpfulness of annotations for Science passages depends on the level of specificity with which you annotate. Whether you have a set of symbols you're accustomed to using or if you jot quick notes in the margins, that effort should directly lend itself to supporting you when you answer questions. Because of the length and labeling of things in Science passages, a glance at the passage can often tell you where something is. Instead of identifying the location of information, you should focus on developing incisive summaries that will directly help you answer the questions. Consider the following passage examples and sample annotations.

Data Representation Annotations

Recall that for Data Representation passages, you'll be looking at the background information to determine what was measured and how. From there, you're looking at the data itself to understand the different measurements and their relationships.

EXAMPLE

To determine the relationship, if any, between a mass placed on the end of a spring and the force exerted by the mass on the spring, various weights were placed on the end of a spring and the force exerted on the spring was measured in newtons (N). The maximum displacement of the weight, called the amplitude, was measured by recording the extension of the spring. The time needed for one oscillation back and forth for the weight to return to its original position was also recorded. The results are shown in Table 1.

TABLE 1				
Mass (kg)	Square (root of mass)	Force (N)	Extension (cm)	Time (sec)
1	1.0	9.8	5	1.20
2	1.4	19.6	15	1.68
3	1.7	29.4	25	2.04
4	2.0	39.2	35	2.40

The intro paragraph reveals that the data displayed will depict a variety of measurements resulting from what happens when a mass is attached to the end of a spring. You could summarize quickly with "mass on spring." Additionally, you could underline or mark "time = oscillation," if you didn't feel comfortable with that terminology and wanted to activate that information for yourself.

In examining Table 1, you see that as mass increases, the square, force, extension, and time of oscillation also increase. There is a direct relationship between the independent variable (the mass) and all of the dependent variables. Therefore, a higher mass = higher dependent variables.

After finishing the passage and noting those different elements of the passage, you might see a question like the following:

EXAMPLE

If a weight with mass 2.7 kg were placed on the end of the spring, the force exerted on the spring would be approximately:

A. 9 N

B. 13 N

C. 26 N

D. 33 N

From your active reading and annotation, you discerned that there is a positive direct relationship between mass and the measured variables. A mass of 2.7 kg would obey this relationship and have values between the measurements for the 2 and 3 kg masses. You know that Table 1 represents this information. You would look there, follow the line between 2 and 3 kg and travel to the Force (N) column. The value would be between 19.6 and 29.4 N. This leads you to choice C.

Research Summary Annotations

For Research Summaries, you know you're trying to understand the experiment, how it was conducted, the differences between trials (if there are multiple), and the results so as to form a conclusion.

When two objects are placed near or next to one another and they are at different temperatures, energy is transferred to the cooler object. As a result of this energy transfer, the temperature of the cooler object rises. The ratio of the amount of energy transferred to the temperature change is called heat capacity. Table 1 summarizes the specific heat for various substances.

TABLE 1	
Substance	**Specific Heat Capacity (kJ/kgK)**
Aluminum	0.898
Steel	0.447
Lead	0.130

An experiment was done to illustrate the temperature changes that are observed when substances with different heat capacities are subjected to the same procedures. First, 1 kg of water at 27°C was placed in an insulated container. A 0.2 kg piece of metal was placed in the water after the metal was heated to a particular temperature. The final temperature of the metal was then recorded after the same time interval, as seen in Table 2.

TABLE 2				
Initial Temperature (°Celsius)	Final Temperature (°Celsius)			
	Aluminum	**Lead**	**Steel**	**Unknown**
50	27.95	27.14	27.48	27.25
75	28.98	27.29	28.01	27.53
100	30.01	27.45	28.53	27.81
150	32.08	27.76	29.58	28.36
200	34.14	28.07	30.63	28.92

While reading the passage, you could have labeled the following:

- Background paragraph: heat capacity = ratio of heat transferred to temp change
- Table 1: highest (aluminum) to lowest (lead) heat capacity
- Second paragraph: Experiment = water at 27°C; 0.2 kg of metal at particular temp
- Table 2: higher HC has higher temp relative to the initial temp

That's a lot to record, so you would want to minimize the amount of time you're spending to write those things, finding shorthand for those ideas or just actively thinking through those ideas; what's important is that you process the passage information and record or mark something on the page.

Let's look at a question associated with the passage to see how it may or may not tap into what we annotated:

EXAMPLE

As the specific heat capacity for a substance increases, what observable effect is there on the range of final temperature readings?

   F. There is little to no observable difference in the range of temperatures.

   G. There is a greater range of final temperature readings.

   H. There is a smaller range of final temperature readings.

   J. The range of final temperature readings is constant for all heat capacities.

Your analysis and annotation of the different elements of the passage, namely Table 2, has given you the answer to this question. Since aluminum has the highest heat capacity and the highest temperatures in the table, higher heat capacity has lead to a greater range of final temperature readings (choice G).

Conflicting Viewpoints Annotations

For Conflicting Viewpoints, the passage tells you where information related to each hypothesis or student or researcher is. What you want to know at a glance is what Hypothesis 2 is or what Student 3 thinks, in as concise but complete a way as possible so that you don't have to reread that paragraph when you get a related question. Your goal is to understand the passage topic and be able to accurately compare and contrast each viewpoint after reading.

EXAMPLE

Although astronomers have a general outline for the steps that lead up to the formation of the wide-ranging interplanetary bodies called comets, there remain as yet many questions of where and exactly how comets were formed. Three astronomers describe their views on this process.

Astronomer 1

The flattened, rotating disk of the nebula out of which our sun and its companion planets were formed is the ideal place for comets to have been born. The long, slow collapse of a nebula that evolved into a planetary system included the type of compression that would facilitate the accretion of the icy specks of matter into comet pellets. At a certain concentration level, these pellets began to clump into cometesimals and later aggregated into larger bodies. When our Solar System was formed, the bodies that formed in the outskirts became the population of comets known as the Oort cloud. Those comets that formed among the planets likely collided with the giant members of the sun's family, coalescing into them.

For the topic paragraph, your annotation should be brief. Here, "formation of comets" appears to capture the focus. Now, you can start wading into the first viewpoint. You can infer that this viewpoint and any others will focus their discussion on different ways that comets were formed (perhaps discussing how, when, or where). In reading and annotating the paragraph for Astronomer 1, you may have recorded something like the following:

- Solar system nebula > planets and pellets > cometesimals in solar system > outskirts comets to Oort
- Gradual, comets within and at edge of solar system nebula
- Oort cloud comets formed at edge of solar system nebula

Regardless of your specific verbiage, if your annotation (or even just your understanding) of the Astronomer 1 paragraph captures these ideas, then you've effectively identified the "where and how" cited by the introductory paragraph.

Let's take a look at a question from this passage and see how, even without looking at another viewpoint, your active reading and annotation impacts your ability to answer:

EXAMPLE

Which of the following statements about the formation of comets would be most consistent with the views of Astronomer 1 and not Astronomer 2?

- **A.** Gravity from other stars is a crucial factor in the birth of comets.
- **B.** Comets were not originally members of our solar system.
- **C.** The sun, planets, and comets formed out of the same nebula.
- **D.** Comets previously existed in the same region as the planets.

When you get a question similar to what's shown, you have a decent sense of what you're looking for. In this circumstance, your answer will depend on what you see

for Astronomer 2. But even without that information, you know from the Astronomer 1 passage that no mention of other stars was made, eliminating choice A. You also know that Astronomer 1 describes how comets were formed within and at the outskirts of our solar system, eliminating choice B. That leaves choices C and D. To answer with certainty, you would need to know the primary difference between Astronomer 2 and 1. Perhaps Astronomer 2 doesn't think the bodies formed from the same nebula, or they could think comets only formed beyond the planets. Such a distinction would be clear after some active reading and annotations of the next paragraph in the passage.

Strategy #3: Evaluate and React to Question Difficulty

Across the ACT, making judgments about what questions you can answer effectively and/or quickly can have a significant impact on your score. Deciding whether to answer a Science question or come back to it later can depend on your answers to a few questions:

- How comfortable are you with different question types?
- How clearly does the question point to specific places in the passage?
- How much time will it take you to answer accurately?
- How much time do you have left?

Alongside answers to those questions, you can also consider the following for the different question types:

- Many questions are Interpretation of Data questions, which will direct you to the data.
  - Sometimes you'll know exactly where to look.
  - Sometimes the figures and tables present complicated information.
- Scientific Investigation questions require you to understand the experimental design.
  - Sometimes the passages are shorter and easier to extract information from.
  - Sometimes the passages are dense and there are multiple experiments to understand.

- Evaluation of Models, Inferences, and Experimental Results questions require you to synthesize the information from the passage and new information.

  o Sometimes you'll have a good grasp of passage details and can apply new information quickly.

  o Sometimes perspectives are dense and challenging to distinguish.

As you've seen for the other Science strategies, the variability of the passages and questions can lead to some complex decision-making for test takers. In the end, though, you're trying to establish some rules for yourself so that you don't fall into the ACT's various time traps.

Consider the following questions:

1. A hiker plans to take an overnight camping trip in the mountains in the middle of winter. If the hiker is uncertain about the wind speed on the mountain but knows that it does not exceed 50 km/hr, what is the lowest that the actual temperature can be without the hiker risking exposure at moderately or extremely dangerous effective temperatures?

   A. 0°C

   B. –10°C

   C. –20°C

   D. –30°C

2. According to Figure 1, the volume of carbon dioxide in the Test Tube 1 at 23°C after 6 hours is:

   F. 5.7 ml

   G. 8.9 ml

   H. 11.6 ml

   J. 18.1 ml

For question 1, not only is the stem longer, but there are also numerous opaque references in the question. It mentions *wind speed*, *actual temperature*, and *moderately or extremely dangerous effective temperatures*. Each of those terms will have a referent in the passage, either embodied in a paragraph or depicted in a table or figure. More than likely, you're going to be connecting multiple pieces of information spread throughout the passage to answer one EMI question. If you remember where those details are or made annotations that can direct you, then you have what you need to work quickly. Otherwise, such a question can lead to considerable rereading and may be worth revisiting later after you've gotten to the passage's other questions.

For question 2, the question is shorter, but more importantly, contains many signposts in its phrasing. You know that you'll be looking at Figure 1 to find the volume of carbon dioxide in Test Tube 1 at 23°C after 6 hours. That gives you a precise set of directions that will take you directly to the correct answer.

SCIENCE STRATEGIES

6 Questions—6 Minutes

Now that we've discussed some strategies for the ACT Science test, use the following practice passage to formulate and test out an approach. Make sure you read actively and strategically for the passage type, annotate the passage, and evaluate question difficulty. Revisit what you saw for approaching different question types. Try to stick to a strict time limit of 6 minutes to complete the question set. Take note of the time needed to finish if you go over and make adjustments to your process before starting the Knowledge Check at the end of this part.

PASSAGE I

A chemical reaction is a process during which one set of substances, known as the reactants, are changed into new substances with different properties, known as the products. Chemical reactions can be described by equations. The reactants and products are separated by an arrow. The direction of the arrow indicates which substances are the reactants and which substances are the products. According to the equation below, A and B react to form C and D.

$$A + B \rightarrow C + D$$

Experiment 1

In order to understand how biochemical catalysts called enzymes influence the rate of chemical reactions in an organism, researchers measured chemical reactions that produced a product (P) in a substrate (S) without adding an enzyme. They then repeated the experiment under the same conditions, this time with the addition of an enzyme (E). The results of the experiment are shown in Figure 1.

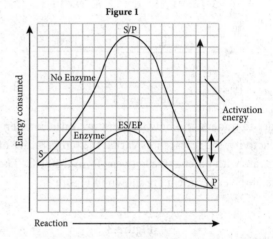

Figure 1

Experiment 2

In order to understand how pH level influences enzyme activity, the researchers measured chemical reactions using two different enzymes in substrates ranging in pH levels. The results of the experiment are shown in Figure 2.

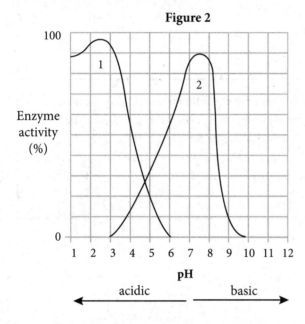

Figure 2

Enzyme activity (%)

pH

← acidic   basic →

Experiment 3

In order to understand how temperature influences enzyme activity, the researchers varied the temperature of a substrate with an enzyme between 0° and 100°C. The results of the experiment are shown in Figure 3.

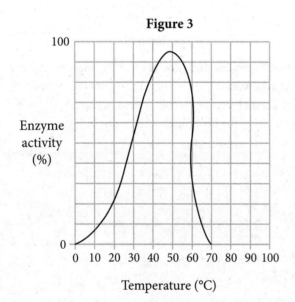

Figure 3

Enzyme activity (%)

Temperature (°C)

1. Which experiments produced data that show the differences in chemical reactions between a substrate with an enzyme and a substrate without an enzyme?

   A. Experiment 1 only

   B. Experiments 2 and 3 only

   C. Experiments 1, 2, and 3

   D. None of the experiments

2. According to Figure 1, how does an enzyme affect activation energy?

   F. It decreases activation energy.

   G. It increases activation energy.

   H. It has no effect on activation energy.

   J. It decreases the rate at which products are formed.

3. According to the data in Figure 1, what is the factor that initiates decreases in energy consumption during chemical reactions?

   A. Adding an enzyme

   B. Increasing the activation energy

   C. Decreasing the temperature

   D. Reaching the state S/P or ES/EP

4. In Experiment 2, one of the enzymes was pepsin, which is secreted in the stomach and helps in the reaction that breaks down proteins. Which enzyme do you think represents pepsin and why?

   F. Enzyme 1, because the enzyme activity is highest in a basic substrate

   G. Enzyme 1, because the enzyme activity is highest in an acidic substrate

   H. Enzyme 2, because the enzyme activity is highest in a basic substrate

   J. Enzyme 2, because the enzyme activity is highest in an acidic substrate

5. How might researchers account for the sharp drop in enzyme activity after 50°C?

   A. As temperatures fall, enzyme activity decreases.

   B. As temperatures increase, enzyme activity increases.

   C. High temperatures destroy enzymes.

   D. Above 50°C, the pH level is altered.

6. To further investigate how temperature influences enzyme activity, the researchers could alter Experiment 3 in which of the following ways?

   F. Run a trial with a substrate without an enzyme.

   G. Reduce the temperature range to 0°–50°C.

   H. Increase the temperature range to 0°–120°C.

   J. Run trials with several different types of enzymes.

Answer Explanations

1. **The correct answer is A.** The passage states that, in Experiment 1, the researchers measured chemical reactions that produced a product in a substrate without adding an enzyme. They then repeated the same conditions, except this time they added an enzyme. In Experiment 2, enzymes were used in all trials. In Experiment 3, there was only one substrate, and it did contain an enzyme.

2. **The correct answer is F.** Compare the length of the vertical arrows for each curve. The one for the enzyme-catalyzed reaction is shorter than the one for the reaction in which an enzyme is not involved. A shorter arrow means less energy was required to "activate" the reaction.

3. **The correct answer is D.** The y-axis of Figure 1 is labeled "energy consumed." Notice that the curves of both lines related to the chemical reactions descend at the points "S/P" and "ES/EP." Therefore, when the reactions reach the state S/P or ES/EP, the energy consumed decreases, leading to choice D.

4. **The correct answer is G.** The question tells you that the process in which pepsin is involved occurs in the stomach. You're expected to know that digestion in the stomach is aided by the presence of acid. Therefore, the enzyme representing pepsin should be the one that is most active in an acidic setting—Enzyme 1.

5. **The correct answer is C.** Enzyme activity on the upward slope increases more or less gradually. But on the downward slope, it decreases abruptly and rapidly falls to zero. The explanation that heat destroys enzymes fits the data best.

6. **The correct answer is J.** By repeating the experiment with several different types of enzymes, researchers would learn whether temperature affects different enzymes in different ways. Choice F would not be fruitful because the question asks about a further investigation of enzyme activity. A substrate without an enzyme would show no enzyme activity whatsoever.

GENERAL REMINDERS AND ADVICE

Here are a few other things to keep in mind if you want to tackle ACT Science passages like a pro. You can also refer back to Chapter 3 for more ACT test-taking advice.

Read All Your Answer Choices

Don't just automatically mark down the first answer that seems correct. Instead, make sure you read each answer choice and eliminate those you know are wrong before choosing the *best* answer.

Stick to the Passage

Short of some fundamental science vocabulary and concepts you likely already know, everything you need to answer the questions is in the passages. The information may be obscured by a complex graph or buried in a table or dense paragraph, but far more often than not, you'll have what you need. Use all the information you were able to glean from the passage and stick to it when answering, even if you don't' agree.

Trust Yourself

Don't spend too long going back and forth about a correct answer simply because you can convince yourself that more than one is plausible. Find support for your choice. Remember, only one answer is right, so you just need to understand why the other answers are wrong. If you can still make an argument for two answers being correct, save your time and go with your gut instinct. If you end up with some remaining time, you can come back to check it.

Personalize Your Approach

Everything we've laid out here can be used to develop an approach to the Science test's passages and questions, but no one knows you better than you. If a certain aspect of the Science section is harder for you, such as understanding questions or getting through the passages in time, figure out which of the strategies here you need to prioritize.

Whatever choices you make, you're weighing how long your approach will take, how it impacts your accuracy, and how all of your choices come together to help you achieve your scoring goal. Part of the benefit of practice is that you can figure out an approach that accounts for your strengths and weaknesses. See what feels good and make sure to time yourself when practicing so you can identify where you might need improvement before exam day.

STRATEGY ROUNDUP

As a starting point for test takers, we have put together the following set of steps. From here, you can make adjustments that suit your needs based on the specific strategies and advice we provided earlier in the chapter.

Choose a Passage Order

Whether you establish an order in advance or determine one based on quickly glancing through the formats and topics of the passages, decide the order in which you'd like to approach the Science passages first thing. When evaluating the day of, you can adjust your order based on things like density, structure, and topic difficulty. Consider working on the Data Representation passages first and then moving through the Research Summaries and Conflicting Viewpoints passage. Regardless of your order, remember to work with the passages you feel most confident with first and progress towards those that present the greater challenge.

Read Actively for the Passage Priorities and Annotate

Use an active reading technique and mark on the passages, annotating what you know will help you for the passage type in question. How you read and annotate should align with your goals to maximize the time you spend on questions while still giving you the details you need to answer effectively.

Come Back to Harder Questions

When you are ready to look at the questions, start with those that you can address quickly and easily. Address all the easier questions for a passage before moving on to others. If you're coming up to your passage time limit, make a guess and note it for later.

Answer Questions Strategically

There are a few common multiple-choice techniques you can apply to every question. When you read a question, use what you know about the passage to predict an answer. That can direct you to an answer choice that aligns with your prediction and help you avoid some question traps. However, even though you have made a prediction, you should still look at all the answer choices and eliminate those you know are wrong. If you still have multiple answers left, refer to the passage to confirm your prediction or eliminate the remaining choices. If this is taking a lot of time without giving you an answer you know is right, fill in your guess and move on.

Move to the Next Passage

Once you have answered all the questions for a given passage (whether by eliminating answers or guessing), move on to the next passage and repeat the same steps—applying your reading and question strategies as appropriate. As a general rule, you're trying to limit your time on any one passage to 6 minutes, unless more time matches your personal goals.

As Time Allows, Review Guesses

After finishing your last passage, use any remaining time before the section ends to review questions you guessed on. If you find yourself running out of time and still haven't answered all of the questions, spend your last remaining minute filling in answers rather than leaving questions blank.

SUMMING IT UP

- Since you have 35 minutes to complete 40 questions across 6 to 7 passages, to reach every passage and question, you should plan to spend 5-6 minutes per passage and question set unless otherwise dictated by your personal strategy.

- Plan to spend no more than 45 seconds on any one question—unless your section goals allow for more. If you can't find the answer in that time, eliminate the distractors you can and guess. Mark guesses to review later if time allows.

- Use overall section strategies to help with the ACT Science test as a whole:

  o Divide your time according to your personal score goals.

  o Determine the order in which you'd like to tackle passages (whether before the test or in a brief preview of the section).

  o Practice active reading strategies and annotate passages to review or find information more easily later.

  o Complete all the questions for a given passage before moving on to the next passage.

  o Note questions you guess on in case you have time to review them at the end.

- If as you're studying you notice that you consistently struggle with a given question type, use the Question Strategies section in this chapter to add useful tips and strategies to your overall section strategy.

- Deploy question and passage-specific strategies that suit your needs:

  o Plan out a reading technique (or combination of techniques) that suits your needs as a test taker.

  o Use annotations to map passages as you read them, pinpointing and summarizing different kinds of information relative to the passage type.

  o Evaluate the difficulty of the questions for a given passage and then start with the easiest questions first.

- Keep some general reminders for Science test success in mind, such as:

  o Read all your answer choices

  o Stick to what's in the passage

  o Trust yourself when you have two competing answers

  o Personalize your overall ACT Science test strategy

- As a basic strategy for bringing all these skills together, consider the following approach:

  1. Use a passage order (generally easiest to hardest)
  2. Apply your active reading strategy and annotate the passage
  3. Save harder questions for later
  4. Answer questions strategically
  5. Move to the next passage
  6. If time allows, review guesses

NOTES

KNOWLEDGE CHECK: SCIENCE

40 Questions—35 Minutes

Directions: There are several passages in this test. Each passage is followed by several questions. After reading a passage, choose the best answer to each question and fill in the corresponding oval on your answer document. You may refer to the passages as often as necessary.

You are NOT permitted to use a calculator on this test.

PASSAGE I

As power is supplied to a circuit, current flows through the circuit. An ammeter is the device used to measure the current, and many ammeters measure current in milliamperes (mA). The voltage responsible for the current can be measured by a voltmeter and is measured in volts. When a resistor is placed in a circuit, it dampens the current flowing through a circuit at a given voltage.

If there is a linear relationship between current and voltage when a resistor is placed in the circuit, the resistor is considered an ohmic device. If the temperature of the resistor changes, then it is not considered an ohmic device. Some resistors are sensitive to small external temperature changes and will show a change in resistance as a result of these temperature changes. These resistors are called thermistors. The change in resistance exhibited by a thermistor can be detected by a change in the observed current at a given voltage.

The following procedure was performed to investigate whether different resistors acted as ohmic devices in a circuit. The circuit was constructed as shown in Figure 1.

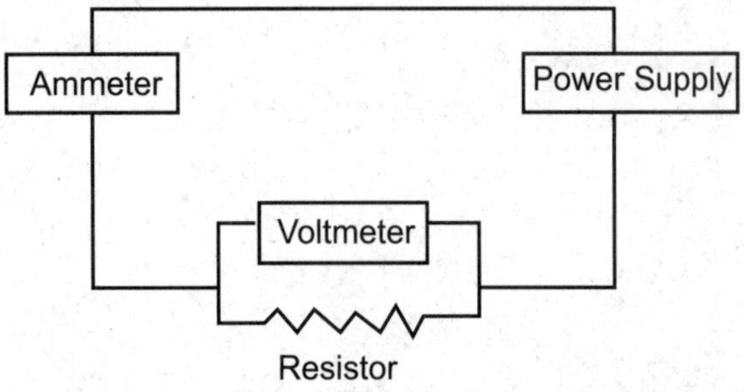

Figure I

After each resistor was connected to the circuit, the resistor was submerged in water to detect any changes in temperature as well as its sensitivity to different beginning temperatures. The power source was turned on and the voltages of the power source and the resulting current were recorded. The voltage was changed several times, and the corresponding current was noted.

Table 1 summarizes the results when three different resistors were tested at two different temperatures. In all cases, no change in water temperature was observed.

Table 1		
Voltage (V)	**Current (mA)**	**Current (mA)**
Resistor A		
	23°C	**25°C**
0.25	25	25
0.50	50	50
1.00	100	100
2.00	200	200
3.00	300	300
4.00	400	400
4.50	450	450
5.00	500	500

Table 1 (cont'd.)		
Voltage (V)	Current (mA)	Current (mA)
Resistor B		
	23°C	25°C
0.25	150	150
0.50	195	195
1.00	230	230
2.00	295	295
3.00	345	345
4.00	405	405
4.50	420	420
5.00	445	445
Resistor C		
	23°C	25°C
0.25	5	4.5
0.50	10	9.0
1.00	20	18.0
2.00	40	36.0
3.00	60	54.0
4.00	80	72.0
4.50	90	81.0
5.00	100	90.0

1. When the temperature is 25°C and the voltage is 4.5 volts, what is the current of the circuit when Resistor B is used?

   A. 81 mA

   B. 90 mA

   C. 420 mA

   D. 450 mA

2. If 3.5 volts were used with Resistor A at 27°C, approximately what would the current have read?

   F. 63 mA

   G. 70 m A

   H. 350 mA

   J. 375 mA

3. Based on Table 1, which of the following resistors respond linearly to a change in voltage?

   A. Resistor A only

   B. Resistor B only

   C. Resistors A and C

   D. Resistors B and C

4. Resistor B does NOT appear to be a thermistor because:

   F. at low voltages, Resistor B produces higher currents than either of the other resistors.

   G. at higher temperatures, Resistor B produces lower currents than either of the other resistors.

   H. there is a change in resistance at different voltages.

   J. there is no change in resistance at different temperatures.

5. What additional information would be necessary to conclude whether Resistor C is a thermistor?

   A. The current-voltage response of Resistor C at a third temperature

   B. The temperature of Resistor C at various voltages

   C. Whether the current of Resistor C responds linearly with temperature

   D. There is enough information to determine whether Resistor C is a thermistor.

6. Which of the following hypotheses would be disproved if there had been a noted temperature change in the water for all six trials?

   F. Resistor A is an ohmic device because of its linear relationship between voltage and current.

   G. Resistor B is affected by different starting temperatures.

   H. Resistor C is not an ohmic device because it does not have a linear relationship between voltage and current.

   J. Resistor C is not affected by different starting temperatures.

Passage II

Seagrasses are plants that grow along the coasts of warm, shallow seas. They form underwater meadows that improve water quality, help prevent erosion of sand and sediment during storms, and provide shelter and food for fish and other aquatic animals. Ecologists have discovered that they also store a large amount of carbon and other nutrients in the sediment. The ecologists were interested in how much.

Ecologists selected an area that was undergoing restoration after its original seagrass meadow was wiped out during a severe hurricane. Seagrass had been seeded onto two separate meadows; one meadow had been reseeded four years ago, and the other had been reseeded ten years ago. From each meadow, the ecologists took four 20-cm deep, 10-cm diameter sediment cores. They also took four similar cores from the unplanted sediment immediately around each of the meadows. They removed shells, rocks, and large roots from the sediment, weighed them wet and again after drying to determine bulk density, and determined the percentages of organic matter, carbon, and nitrogen in the sediment. The averages of their results are summarized in Table 1.

Table 1

Site	Meadow Age (years)	Seagrass Density (shoots /m²)	% Carbon	% Nitrogen	% Organic Matter	Bulk Density (g/cm³)
Site 1	0	0	0.4	0.2	1.6	1.53
Site 1	4	123	0.39	0.2	1.6	1.44
Site 2	0	0	0.36	0.86	1.4	1.61
Site 2	10	429	0.52	3.75	1.9	1.30

After examining nutrient accumulation, the ecologists wanted to determine which physical characteristics of the seagrass meadow are most helpful in stabilizing sediment to prevent erosion. They placed four sediment traps within the 10-year old meadow, and recorded the characteristics of the seagrass around the sediment trap: the shoot density (in shoots/m^2 of seabed), leaf mass (grams of seagrass leaves/m^2 of seabed), seagrass height (cm), and leaf surface area (m^2 leaf surface/m^2 of seabed). After each day, they weighed the amount of sediment collected in each sediment trap (g/m^2 of trap area, per day). They compared the average of six days of sediment results with each of the seagrass characteristics in Table 2.

Table 2

Trapped Sediment Weight (g/m²/day)	Seagrass Density (shoots/m²)	Seagrass Mass (g/m²)	Seagrass Surface Area (m²/m²)	Seagrass Height
3.3	200	6.0	1.8	29
3.8	170	10.2	2.8	56
4.1	260	6.8	3.0	33
4.8	230	10.0	4.1	52

7. According to the data in Table 1, the greatest difference in sediment bulk density was found between:

   A. years 0 and 4 at Site 1.

   B. years 0 and 10 at Site 2.

   C. the two sites without seagrass.

   D. the two sites with seagrass.

8. Based on Table 1, the biggest relative change between 0 and 10 years was found in:

   F. % carbon.

   G. % nitrogen.

   H. % organic matter.

   J. bulk density.

9. Which of the following best explains why the scientists collected sediment from an unplanted area at each site?

   A. To control for differences in original sediment composition between the two sites

   B. To control for differences in water depth between the two sites

   C. To determine the most effective seagrass density for nutrient sequestration

   D. To determine the rate of nutrient loss in unvegetated seabeds

10. Which hypothesis is supported by the data in Table 2?

    F. Taller seagrass plants reduce turbulence in a larger portion of the water column, resulting in greater sediment deposition.

    G. More densely planted seagrass meadows prevent sand from settling to the seabed, resulting in reduced sediment deposition.

    H. Greater seagrass mass increases turbulence in the water column, resulting in reduced sediment deposition.

    J. Greater seagrass surface area more effectively dissipates the energy of ocean currents, resulting in greater sediment deposition.

11. Suppose that a local company wants to dredge a nearby seagrass meadow to collect sand for a public beach. To decrease the negative impacts of the dredging, they would like to replant seagrass afterwards. What is the most likely outcome of replanting?

    A. After 10 years, the replanted seagrass meadow would have a higher shoot density than the original one.

    B. The percentage of organic matter found in the sediment would be unchanged by dredging and replanting.

    C. There would be immediate storage of carbon and nitrogen in the sediment, similar to that in the original meadow.

    D. There would be a lag of more than four years before carbon and nitrogen storage reached that of the original meadow.

12. How do the results of the second experiment support continued research efforts?

    F. By showing that seagrass has a positive effect on carbon capture

    G. By showing that higher densities and increased leaf surface area of seagrass had a positive effect in stabilizing sediment and preventing erosion

    H. By showing that higher densities and increased leaf surface area of seagrass had a negative effect in stabilizing sediment and preventing erosion

    J. The results do not support further research, because seagrass does not have any effect on sediment stability and erosion

PASSAGE III

A crystal is a solid whose molecules are arranged in an ordered, repeating pattern extending in all three spatial dimensions. In nature, crystalline solids usually form when molten materials cool and solidify. A key stage of the crystallization process is crystal growth. When a "seed" crystal is provided, crystal growth spreads outward from this site. As the crystal grows, an arranged system called a crystal lattice begins to form. Perfect crystals grow rather slowly, but real crystals grow more quickly because they contain defects that provide growth points, which catalyze further crystal formation.

After visiting a local underground cavern, a group of students became interested in crystal formation after seeing the stalactites and stalagmites. They decided to test the effect of pressure on crystal growth rate by using potassium ferricyanide, a compound that is red in color. The students prepared a single 70-mL solution of potassium ferricyanide in water at 99°C, keeping it well-mixed to ensure even salt dispersion in the solution. They split this volume into two equal 35-mL portions, pouring the portions into separate flasks. Each flask was sealed with a rubber stopper and hooked up to pressure pumps to control the pressure inside the flask. A pressure gauge provided a pressure reading, allowing the students to make sure that the pressure remained constant. Flask #1 was kept at a pressure of 1 atm, which is normal atmospheric pressure, while Flask #2 was kept at a pressure of 9 atm. Both flasks were then cooled down to room temperature, and the salts came out of solution for crystal growth to begin. The students used a caliper to measure crystal size over the course of three days. The students then measured the percent increase in crystal size and graphed their results as as seen in Figure 1.

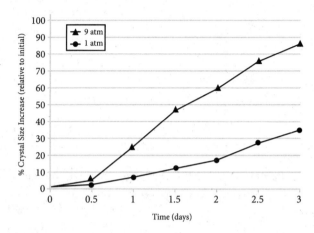

Figure 1

13. The dependent variable in this experiment is:

   A. temperature.

   B. pressure.

   C. crystal size.

   D. time.

14. The purpose of preparing one solution for both trials rather than two separate solutions of equal concentration was to:

   F. equilibrate the solutions to their appropriate tested pressures in each trial.

   G. ensure that the concentration of starting salt "seed" is equal for both trials.

   H. serve as a temperature control for the experiment.

   J. provide a second trial for the crystals grown at 1 atmosphere.

15. The initial salt solution was prepared at 99°C because:

   A. potassium ferricyanide crystals can only grow at the higher temperature.

   B. potassium ferricyanide will dissolve in solution at the higher temperature.

   C. the higher temperature is required to maintain the 1 atmosphere and 9 atmosphere pressures.

   D. the water in the solution will evaporate to increase the concentration of the solution.

16. One way to improve the reliability of the results in this experiment would be to:

   F. increase the number of trials at each tested pressure.

   G. perform the experiment at 99°C rather than room temperature.

   H. perform the experiment using smaller solution volumes and flasks.

   J. use different starting "seed" solution concentrations for each pressure trial.

17. Which of the following conclusions can be drawn from this experiment?

   A. Potassium ferricyanide crystals grow more rapidly than other crystal types.

   B. Potassium ferricyanide crystals grow more slowly than other crystal types.

   C. Potassium ferricyanide crystals grow more rapidly at low pressure than at high pressure.

   D. Potassium ferricyanide crystals grow more rapidly at high pressure than at low pressure.

PASSAGE IV

Sedimentary rocks are formed when sediment—sand, dirt, minerals, and organic particles—settle into place and are gradually compressed and cemented together. The relatively mild conditions of this rock-forming process make it ideal for the preservation of fossils. Geologists can use sedimentary rocks to determine an area's geologic history, including the different environments that an area experienced over time. Figure 1 shows different layers of sedimentary rock exposed at the edge of a canyon. The composition of rock, approximate age, thickness, and depth of each layer are listed in Table 1.

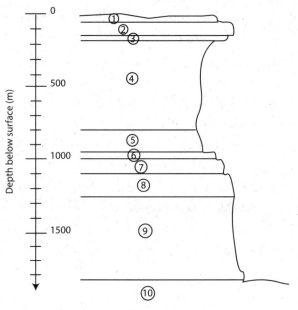

Figure 1

Table 1				
Layer	**Rock/Layer Composition**	**Age (Mill yrs)**	**Thickness (m)**	**Depth (m)**
1	Conglomerate, Sandstone	100	30	10.0
2	Limestone, Mudstone, Sandstone, Gypsum	130	80	0–30
3	Sandstone	160	30	30–110
4	Sandstone	170	670	110–140
5	Siltstone, Sandstone, Mudstone	180	150	140–810
6	Sandstone, Freshwater Fish Fossils	190	40	810–960
7	Siltstone, Sandstone, Mudstone, Shale	200	110	960–1,000
8	Shale, Conglomerate, Gypsum, Limestone, Sandstone, Quartz, Petrified Wood	220	160	1,110–1,270
9	Shale, Sandstone, Limestone, Siltstone, Mudstone, Gypsum	230	550	1,270–1,820
10	Limestone, Chert	260	*	1,820

*There is no thickness listed for Layer 10 because the thickness cannot be measured without excavating.

18. What is the relationship between thickness and depth of the rock layers?

   F. Thicker layers are typically found at greater depths.

   G. Thicker layers are typically found at shallower depths.

   H. Rock layers less than 50 m thick are only found at depths of less than 500 m.

   J. There is no relationship between thickness and depth of rock layers.

19. Limestone is composed mainly of compressed skeletal fragments from sea organisms such as coral, forams, and mollusks. It is high in calcium carbonate-containing minerals like calcite and aragonite. Given this information, during which of the following time periods is it most likely that the given region of the canyon was covered by a shallow sea?

   A. 60 million years ago

   B. 100 million years ago

   C. 130 million years ago

   D. 200 million years ago

20. Which measurement is shown on the vertical axis of Figure 1?

   F. Temperature

   G. Age of rock

   H. Depth below the canyon surface

   J. Thickness of rock layers

21. Carnotite is a bright greenish-yellow mineral found around petrified wood. It is a uranium ore and is radioactive. Assuming the sedimentary rock layers are uniform as they extend away from the canyon, approximately how deep would miners have to excavate in the surrounding area in order to obtain uranium?

   A. 160 m

   B. 500 m

   C. 1,200 m

   D. 2,000 m

22. Which conclusion is NOT supported in the data?

   F. The age of the rock layers increases with depth.

   G. The most common rock type in the canyon is sandstone.

   H. Thicker rock layers correspond to longer time periods.

   J. Gypsum is found only in layers that also contain limestone.

23. Geologists have found small remnants of a rock called welded tuff exposed at the surface (above layer 1) near the canyon. Welded tuff forms when rock and dust is exposed to temperatures over 1,000°C, hot enough that the rock welds together. What does this suggest about the area near the canyon?

   A. The area experienced a hot, tropical climate around 100 million years ago.

   B. A volcano erupted in the area less than 100 million years ago.

   C. The area was covered by sea at least twice in the last 260 million years.

   D. A volcano erupted in the area more than 260 million years ago and then went extinct.

PASSAGE V

The apparent bird-dinosaur evolutionary connection has been a source of considerable debate among paleontologists during the second half of the twentieth century. This association was proposed on the basis of numerous anatomical similarities and has been supported by the discovery of fossils of a small number of seeming transitional forms uncovered in Europe and Asia. Yet scientists differ in their interpretation of the significance of these similarities and the nature of the fossil evidence as well.

Paleontologist A

The discovery of fossil reptiles equipped with feathers, wings, and beak-like snouts may be significant but more likely provides only limited support for the dinosaurs-into-birds hypothesis. Convergent evolution often provides animals of very distant lineages with similar appendages—witness, for example, the similarities in the body shape and presence of fins in fish and cetaceans such as whales and dolphins. We would never put forth the idea that orcas evolved from sharks based on the morphological similarities of these creatures; it would be immediately deemed absurd.

It is more likely the case that birds and dinosaurs share a very distant common ancestor, perhaps from among the thecodonts. These prototypical reptiles of the late Permian survived the largest mass extinction recorded in the planet's history to bring forth many more recent lines; crocodiles, dinosaurs, pterosaurs, and birds are the most notable among these.

Paleontologist B

In our studies of numerous dinosaur fossils, it has become obvious that the lifestyles of dinosaurs were amazingly varied. No longer is it acceptable to view dinosaurs only as lumbering, cold-blooded monsters; indeed, the most frightening dinosaurs did not lumber at all. They were agile, swift, and deadly predators who could run, leap, kick, and shred to pieces an animal they were intent upon consuming. Lightweight muscular body structure would be crucial to the success of this type of predator.

Based upon this observation, along with a number of obvious physical similarities and evidence from the fossil record, we are convinced that birds evolved from small, carnivorous dinosaurs called theropods. A mere examination of the forelimb, hindlimb, and feet of a theropod fossil, and a comparison to one of the five available specimens of *Archaeopteryx**, will bear this out. In addition, more recent discoveries of fossil dinosaurs with bird-like traits and habits, particularly the finds uncovered in the Liaoning province of China, lend further credible support for our position that birds are for all intents and purposes actual members of the lineage Dinosauria living and thriving in our midst.

Archaeopteryx was a feathered reptile of the late Jurassic Era thought to represent an intermediate form between dinosaurs and birds.

24. According to Paleontologist A, similarities in the body forms of dinosaurs and birds:

    F. represent a failed experiment of evolution.

    G. are the products of convergent evolution.

    H. are completely without significance.

    J. helped both types of organism survive a large mass extinction.

25. Which of the following types of evidence, if found, would lend strong support to the position of Paleontologist A?

    A. Discovery of thecodont fossils with characteristics of modern birds and existing dinosaur fossils

    B. Discovery of another possible intermediate form between dinosaurs and birds from the Jurassic Era

    C. Discovery of an avian prototype dating back to before the beginning of the era of dinosaur dominance

    D. A careful examination of several sets of theropod fossil remains

26. Which of the following is a criticism that Paleontologist A would make of the avian evolutionary hypothesis posited by Paleontologist B?

    F. It ignores the possibility of the existence of transitional forms.

    G. It ignores the impact of a very large mass extinction.

    H. It assumes that morphological similarities are a result of a direct lineage.

    J. It proposes that dinosaurs and birds arose from distant lineages.

27. Which of the following perspectives would be consistent with the views of Paleontologist B?

    A. Convergent evolution produces similar forms in diverse lineages.

    B. Dinosaurs and birds may be related via a common ancestor.

    C. Birds and dinosaurs arose from completely separate lineages.

    D. Birds arose from a lineage of dinosaurs.

28. If genetic evidence were established to date the avian lineage 85 million years prior to the rise of *Archaeopteryx*, this finding would tend to:

    F. support the theory of Paleontologist A.

    G. support the theory of Paleontologist B.

    H. support the theories of both paleontologists.

    J. refute the theories of both paleontologists.

29. If Paleontologist B could confirm that birds appeared much later in evolutionary history than any dinosaurs, which of the following statements would reconcile this fact with the theory of Paleontologist A?

    A. The ancestors of birds and the ancestors of dinosaurs were exposed to specific environmental conditions at the same time, and this caused the development of similar characteristics.

    B. The ancestors of birds and the ancestors of dinosaurs were exposed to specific environmental conditions that caused the development of similar characteristics, but the dinosaur ancestors were exposed to these environmental conditions later than the bird ancestors were.

    C. The rate of evolutionary change from the thecodont ancestor was much slower for the lineage that resulted in birds than for the lineage that resulted in dinosaurs.

    D. The rate of evolutionary change from the thecodont ancestor was much faster for the lineage that resulted in birds than for the lineage that resulted in dinosaurs.

Passage VI

Ecology graduate students wished to experiment with levels of diversity in a simple community to observe the relationship between increasing complexity and stability of populations. In particular, they were interested in the impact of changing certain conditions in a community on populations of two species of *Paramecium*, a common ciliated protozoan.

A *trophic* level is the number of steps a species is away from the producer species in a community. Producers are organisms that synthesize energy out of chemical products into nutrients. Table 1 shows the trophic level occupied by each type of organism involved in the experiments and the number of species that would be used on each level.

Table 1		
Trophic Level	**Organism**	**Number of Species Studied**
First	Bacteria	3
Second	Paramecia	2
Third	Amoebae (predator of protozoa)	2

Experiment 1

The graduate students wished to study the relationship between one species of *Paramecium* and the number of species of bacteria available for consumption in the community. They created 300 "microcosms"—100 cultures each populated with communities of one, two, or three species of bacteria and one of the *Paramecium* species. After 20 days, they examined the cultures individually. The results are displayed in Table 2.

Table 2	
Number of Bacterium Species	**Number of Cultures in Which Paramecia Survived**
1	32/100
2	61/100
3	70/100

Experiment 2

The students then decided to study how two species of *Paramecium* would be affected when different combinations of *Paramecium* and bacteria were mixed in the cultures. They created 100 dishes each of six separate types of communities—600 cultures with different combinations of the *Paramecium* and the three bacteria species. After 20 days, they examined the cultures and recorded their results. These results are reproduced in Table 3.

Table 3	
Number of Bacterium/ *Paramecium* Species	**Number of Cultures in Which Paramecia Survived**
1/1	35/100
2/1	58/100
3/1	65/100
1/2	20/100
2/2	26/100
3/2	31/100

Experiment 3

The last condition that the graduate students studied was the addition of a third trophic level to their microcosms. They introduced two different species of *Amoebae* that feed on *Paramecium*. They decided to use five different versions in 100 culture dishes each, creating 500 communities for this last experiment. They allowed them to grow undisturbed for 20 days, and then examined the cultures and recorded their results in Table 4 displayed below.

Table 4

Number of Bacterium/ *Paramecium*/ Amoeba Species	Number of Cultures in Which Paramecia Survived
1/1/1	22/100
2/1/1	15/100
2/2/1	8/100
2/2/2	6/100
3/2/2	2/100

30. What was the dependent variable in Experiment 2?

    F. The number of species of bacteria

    G. The number of species of *Paramecium*

    H. The length of time after which cultures were examined

    J. The number of cultures with surviving *Paramecium*

31. According to the results of Experiments 1 and 2, increasing the number of bacteria species present in the community:

    A. decreased the survival rates of the paramecia in the community.

    B. increased the survival rates of the paramecia in the community.

    C. had no effect on any species in the community.

    D. decreased the survival rates of one type of bacteria in the community.

32. The ecologists most likely used 20 days for the testing time in the experiments to:

    F. allow enough time for the populations to reach equilibrium and for any effects of changing conditions on the populations to become apparent.

    G. test whether the populations would reach their maximum size within that time frame.

    H. see if the populations would all die out before that time frame.

    J. see if the populations would change their behavior in response to the length of the experiment.

33. What new factor was introduced in Experiment 3?

    A. An additional species of bacteria

    B. A longer time for incubation of the experimental cultures

    C. A new method for culturing the experimental microbes

    D. An additional trophic level

34. After examining the results of Experiment 3, it would be reasonable to conclude that increased diversity in the experimental communities:

    F. was beneficial to all species present in the communities.

    G. had no effect on any species in the communities.

    H. had a detrimental effect on the survival rate of one species of Amoeba only.

    J. had a detrimental effect on the survival rates of both species of *Paramecium* under study.

Passage VII

Classification of planets in our solar system has been a controversial issue, especially in the last decade. Advanced telescopes have allowed scientists to see more celestial objects in space, so scientists have observed characteristics among the objects that have caused them to reconsider whether certain planets should retain their "planet" status. Some of the characteristics that make these objects distinct include size, mass, and shape, as well as orbital characteristics. Two orbital characteristics of planets astronomers often compare are orbital inclination and orbital eccentricity. Orbital inclination is the amount an object's orbit is tilted with respect to the plane of the solar system. Orbital eccentricity refers to the amount that an object's orbit deviates from a circular orbit.

In 2006, the International Astronomical Union (IAU) officially defined what a planet is and established a system of classification for celestial bodies other than satellites (moons). According to the definition, a planet is a celestial body that orbits the sun, has sufficient mass to be rounded in shape by its own gravity, and has cleared out other large rocks and bodies from its orbital path. The other classifications established were *dwarf planets* and *small solar system bodies*. Based on these new definitions, Pluto was reclassified from a planet to a dwarf planet.

The table below summarizes many of the qualities of the eight planets in our solar system.

Table 1

Celestial Body	Inner Planets				Outer Planets			
	Mercury	Venus	Earth	Mars	Jupiter	Saturn	Uranus	Neptune
Mass (kg)	3.3×10^{23}	4.9×10^{24}	6.0×10^{24}	6.4×10^{23}	1.9×10^{27}	5.7×10^{26}	8.7×10^{25}	1.0×10^{26}
Mean Density (kg/m^3)	5,427	5,204	5,520	3,933	1,326	687	1,318	1,638
Black-body Temp. (°K)	442.5	238.9	247.3	216.6	90.6	63.9	35.9	33.2
Orbital Inclination (°)	7.000	3.390	0.000	1.850	1.305	2.484	0.770	1.769
Orbital Eccentricity (°)	0.2056	0.0068	0.0167	0.0934	0.0484	0.0542	0.0472	0.0086
Rotation Period (hrs.)	1,407.60	5,832.50	23.93	24.62	9.93	10.50	17.24	16.11

35. Uranus has a mass greater than which of the following planets?

    A. Mars, Jupiter, and Saturn
    B. Neptune, Mercury, and Earth
    C. Venus, Mars, and Saturn
    D. Mercury, Earth, and Mars

36. Black-body temperature is the temperature that would result from a planet absorbing all received electromagnetic radiation without reflection. If black-body temperatures are higher for objects closer to the sun, which of the following would be considered farthest from the sun based on the data presented?

    F. Mercury
    G. Uranus
    H. Jupiter
    J. Neptune

37. If an astronomer proposed that a celestial body does not qualify as a planet based solely on having an orbital inclination greater than 5 degrees and orbital eccentricity greater than 0.2, how many of the current planets would lose their planet classification?

    A. Four
    B. Three
    C. Two
    D. One

38. The orbital eccentricity of a celestial body refers to the amount that its orbit deviates from a perfectly circular orbit. A value of 0 is a circular orbit. The higher the eccentricity value, the more distorted the orbit, which can result in objects displaying elliptical, parabolic, and hyperbolic orbits. Which pair lists the planet with an orbit that deviates the least from a perfect circle and the one that deviates the most?

    F. Earth; Mercury
    G. Mercury; Neptune
    H. Venus; Mercury
    J. Neptune; Venus

39. It was hypothesized that Jupiter, Saturn, Neptune, and Uranus were gaseous planets, whereas the others were composed of solid material. Which of the following statements best supports this hypothesis?

    A. Jupiter, Saturn, Neptune, and Uranus have lower temperatures than most of the other planets.
    B. Jupiter, Saturn, Neptune, and Uranus have densities much smaller than the densities of the other planets.
    C. Jupiter, Saturn, Neptune, and Uranus have greater masses than the other planets.
    D. Jupiter, Saturn, Neptune, and Uranus have rotation periods that are much shorter than the other planets.

40. Which of the following statements is supported by the data?

    F. Rotational period increases as mass increases.
    G. The two planets with the highest mass also have the lowest densities.
    H. The two planets closest in mass are also closest in rotational period.
    J. The planet with the lowest mass has the highest orbital eccentricity.

ANSWER KEY AND EXPLANATIONS

1. C	8. G	15. B	22. H	29. C	36. J
2. H	9. A	16. F	23. B	30. J	37. D
3. C	10. J	17. D	24. G	31. B	38. H
4. J	11. D	18. J	25. A	32. F	39. B
5. D	12. G	19. C	26. H	33. D	40. J
6. F	13. C	20. H	27. D	34. J	
7. B	14. G	21. C	28. F	35. D	

1. **The correct answer is C.** From the table, at 4.5 V the current for Resistor B is 420 mA at either temperature.

2. **The correct answer is H.** Resistor A does not appear to be affected by external temperature. While 27°C is not within the tested temperatures, it is a small change, and it's reasonable to assume that Resistor A would show a similar current compared to the other tested temperatures. The current of Resistor A is linear with response to voltage, with 100 mA/volt. Therefore, 350 mA is the expected current at 3.5 V.

3. **The correct answer is C.** Both Resistor A and C behave linearly, while Resistor B does not. The amount to which the current of Resistor C depends on voltage is different at different temperatures, but in a linear fashion in both cases.

4. **The correct answer is J.** At a given applied voltage, a thermistor produces different currents at different external temperatures.

5. **The correct answer is D.** For a thermistor, a change in current is observed when external temperature is changed. At a given voltage with Resistor C, the observed current at 25°C is lower than that at 23°C.

6. **The correct answer is F.** Resistor A seems to be an ohmic device because there is a linear relationship between voltage and current. If Resistor A released heat into the water, it would not be considered an ohmic device.

7. **The correct answer is B.** The difference in sediment bulk density between years 0 and 10 at Site 2 is 1.61−1.30 = 0.31g/cm³.

8. **The correct answer is G.** The % nitrogen at the 10-year mark is more than 4 times greater than what was measured in the seagrass-free control. The greatest change in Table 1 between years 0 and 10 is the seagrass density; however, that is not one of the choices.

9. **The correct answer is A.** The ecologists cannot go back in time to test the original sediment composition before seagrass planting, nor can they go back to test the sediment of each replanted meadow over time. The original sediment composition under each of the two meadows may have been different, so it is important to collect a separate "year zero" for each of the meadows.

10. **The correct answer is J.** Larger amounts of trapped sediment were found in areas with greater seagrass surface area. The ecologists did not experimentally change one physical characteristic at a time, so Table 2 looks at correlations, not causations. For the data to support each hypothesis, there should be a clear trend between increasing sediment weight and an increase or decrease of the seagrass characteristic.

11. **The correct answer is D.** The data in Table 1 shows little or no change in % carbon and % nitrogen between 0 and 4 years, followed by significant change by 10 years.

12. **The correct answer is G.** The results of the second experiment showed that higher densities and increased leaf surface area of seagrass have a positive effect in stabilizing sediment and preventing erosion. This suggests that the density and leaf surface area of the seagrass have the most impact on

sediment stabilization, which supports continued research efforts in this area.

13. **The correct answer is C.** Since crystal size is the variable that is being measured, crystal size is the dependent variable.

14. **The correct answer is G.** Using the same starting solution guarantees that both trials will use the same starting "seed" concentration.

15. **The correct answer is B.** Since cooling down the solution results in crystal formation, the higher temperature is required to keep the ferricyanide dissolved in solution until after the solution has been aliquoted for use in the two trials. Here, it's easiest to arrive at your answer using a process of elimination. Choice A is incorrect because the crystals grew only when the flasks were cooled down to room temperature, according to the passage. Choice C is incorrect because the pressures were maintained at room temperature, so the 99°C temperature was not required to keep these pressures constant. Choice D is incorrect because water evaporation would disturb the carefully controlled salt concentration; plus, the boiling point of water is 100°C.

16. **The correct answer is F.** Increasing the number of trials in an experiment always increases reliability because you are collecting more data, making it easier to see trends and recognize outliers.

17. **The correct answer is D.** Choices A and B are incorrect because potassium ferricyanide was the only tested crystal, so no comparisons can be made with other crystal types. Choice C is incorrect because the 9-atmosphere line increased more rapidly over time than the 1-atmosphere line, and this trend is also the reason why choice D is correct.

18. **The correct answer is J.** There is no systematic relationship between thickness and depth of rock layers—the thickest layer (4) is found at less than 800 m, and one of the thinnest layers (6) is below that. Based on this information, you can eliminate choices F and G. Choice H is incorrect because layer 6 is 40 m thick, at depths of 960–1,000 m.

19. **The correct answer is C.** Limestone is formed in marine environments, so the layers containing

limestone give the age at which the region of the canyon was covered by sea. The time periods 130 million years and 220–260 million years contain limestone, but the latter time period is not one of the choices.

20. **The correct answer is H.** The vertical axis on the figure indicates that it refers to depth below a surface, which from the reading you know is the canyon surface.

21. **The correct answer is C.** The uranium ore (carnotite) is found around petrified wood, which is found in layer 8. That is at a depth of 1,110–1,270 m, which includes 1,200 m.

22. **The correct answer is H.** The data does not show what range of ages are found in each layer, only the approximate age difference between the different layers. The thickest layer (4) occurs between a separation of less than 20 million years, while one of the thinnest ones (3) occurs between a separation of 40 million years. In reality, the thickness of a layer depends on a number of factors, including the rate of sedimentation, the length of time the region experienced a particular environment, and the amount of weathering the rock layer experienced before being covered by a new layer.

23. **The correct answer is B.** Layers found at the top of the canyon are youngest, so rocks at the surface were deposited there at a time earlier than indicated by the age of the highest layer—100 million years. The extreme temperatures necessary to form welded tuff are indicative of a volcano. Choice A could be true, but a tropical climate is not hot enough by itself to produce welded tuff. Choice C is true based on the data in Table 1 but is not related to the existence of welded tuff. Choice D would be correct if the welded tuff was found at the lowest layer of the canyon, not the very surface.

24. **The correct answer is G.** Paleontologist A believes that morphological (body) similarities can just as reasonably be assumed to represent the effects of convergent evolution on distant lineages inhabiting similar environments.

25. **The correct answer is A.** Paleontologist A believes that dinosaurs and birds share a common ancestor.

A fossil find from before the age of the dinosaurs with common features would support this view.

26. **The correct answer is H.** Paleontologist B assumes that the body similarities between dinosaurs and early birds must be evidence that birds came forth from the dinosaur lineage. This view affirms the idea of transitional forms, meaning mass extinction is not relevant to this view.

27. **The correct answer is D.** Paleontologist B believes that birds arose from a lineage of dinosaurs, which makes choice C incorrect. Choice A is incorrect—Paleontologist B does not believe in convergent evolution. Choice B is the view of Paleontologist A.

28. **The correct answer is F.** This contradicts the theory of Paleontologist B, who suggests that birds arose from dinosaurs (making choices G and H incorrect). Paleontologist A suggests that the two arose from an extremely distant ancestor, and the theory of convergent evolution is not inconsistent with birds appearing before dinosaurs. Paleontologist A's view is present, so choice J is incorrect.

29. **The correct answer is C.** Paleontologist A postulates the existence of a very distant common ancestor for birds and dinosaurs. The development of birds much later than that of dinosaurs might seem to refute this argument. However, the rate of evolutionary change is not constant across different lineages. Dinosaurs may have developed relatively rapidly from thecodonts, for example, whereas birds did not evolve until much later.

30. **The correct answer is J.** The dependent variable is the condition the experimenter is measuring throughout the experiment—in this case, that is the number of cultures with surviving paramecia.

31. **The correct answer is B.** Examining the results in Tables 2 and 3 shows that increasing the number of species of their food sources, the bacteria, did produce a relative increase in the survival rate of paramecia.

32. **The correct answer is F.** The ecologists most likely used 20 days for the testing time in the experiments to allow enough time for the populations to reach equilibrium and for any effects of changing conditions on the populations to become apparent.

33. **The correct answer is D.** Experiment 3 added a predator of paramecia.

34. **The correct answer is J.** The results of this experiment suggest that increasing diversity in terms of trophic levels was ultimately harmful to the survival of the *Paramecium* species under study.

35. **The correct answer is D.** At 8.7×10^{25} kg, Uranus has the fourth greatest mass of the planets in the solar system. Jupiter, Saturn, and Neptune all have greater masses; therefore, choices A, B, and C are incorrect. It is important to note the size of the exponent; otherwise, any of the choices could appear correct.

36. **The correct answer is J.** Neptune has the lowest temperature; based on that measure, it would seem to be the farthest from the sun.

37. **The correct answer is D.** Mercury has an orbital inclination of 7.000 degrees and an orbital eccentricity of 0.2056. Therefore, Mercury would be reclassified.

38. **The correct answer is H.** The orbital eccentricity of Venus is 0.0068; its orbit is the most circular in the solar system. Mercury has an orbital eccentricity of 0.2056; its egg-shaped orbit exhibits the greatest eccentricity in the solar system and thus deviates the most from a circular orbit.

39. **The correct answer is B.** The gaseous planets would be expected to be less dense than the ones made of solid material. Choices A and D are incorrect—temperature and rotation period should not be affected whether a planet is a solid or a gas. Choice C is incorrect; even though these planets do have greater masses than the inner planets, such information does not support a claim about their gaseous composition.

40. **The correct answer is J.** Mercury has the lowest mass (3.3×10^{23} kg) and the highest orbital eccentricity (0.2056°).

Scoring Chart

Mark missed questions and calculate your total for each question category and the test as a whole. Then convert your raw score to a scaled score using the chart on page 636 in Chapter 19.

Question Types	Question Numbers	Score
Interpretation of Data (IOD)	1, 2, 3, 4, 6, 7, 8, 10, 17, 18, 19, 20, 21, 22, 23, 31, 34, 35, 36, 37, 39, 40	_____ /22
Scientific Investigation (SIN)	9, 13, 14, 15, 16, 30, 32, 33	_____ /8
Evaluation of Models, Inferences, and Experimental Results (EMI)	5, 11, 12, 24, 25, 26, 27, 28, 29, 38	_____ /10

Raw Score: _____ /40

Scaled Score:

PART VI

THE WRITING TEST ON THE ACT®

22 | Introduction to ACT® Writing

23 | Writing Skills and Strategies

CHAPTER

Introduction to ACT® Writing

INTRODUCTION TO ACT® WRITING

OVERVIEW

How to Study with Part VI

All about the Writing Test

Rubric for the Writing Test

Sample Prompt

Common Challenges

Summing It Up

The ACT Writing test is an optional section that assesses a test taker's ability to produce a clear and organized argumentative essay. The test consists of a single writing prompt, and test takers are given 40 minutes to complete the task. In this part, we'll focus on the tools and strategies you'll need to ace the Writing test. This chapter provides a brief summary of what to expect on the Writing test in addition to an overview of how you can use this part of the book to prepare. In the next chapter, we'll provide more guidance on the strategies for approaching timed writing and what the ACT is looking for when evaluating your Writing test.

HOW TO STUDY WITH PART VI

As you begin this section of the book, reflect on your experience and comfort level with writing. What have you learned about writing during your high school career? How would you characterize your interest in writing or different writing skills? For instance, do you excel at brainstorming ideas, doing research, and outlining your essay but struggle with creating a strong and concise thesis statement? Or are you the kind of person who can easily think of an argument and how you want to make it but struggle to organize your thoughts? As with all the previous parts of this book, begin this one by taking a moment to reflect on your writing skills.

In this chapter, we'll go over what to expect from the optional Writing test on the ACT. We'll talk about the requirements and expectations, provide the rubric the ACT uses to score your essay, look at a sample prompt, and cover the common challenges test takers

experience with this part of the ACT. Then, in Chapter 23, we'll discuss helpful strategies for how to approach planning your essay and drafting a well-supported argument. We'll focus on using your time effectively to both plan and proofread your essay. We'll also discuss how to draft an argument supported by claims, evidence, and analysis. Finally, we'll discuss synthesis and the best ways to incorporate and address the different perspectives provided as part of the prompt.

ALL ABOUT THE WRITING TEST

The Writing test on the ACT is an optional section that assesses a test taker's ability to produce a clear and organized argumentative essay. The test consists of a single writing prompt, which will describe a complex issue and present three different perspectives on that issue. You must analyze the given perspectives and provide examples and evidence for your argument, which should take a clear position on the topic and address,

Self-Reflection: Writing

- Which writing courses did you take in high school, and which have you not taken (yet)?

- Did you take courses in subjects outside of English that still required writing-intensive assignments?

- What do you know about the writing process?

- How do you usually approach the writing process?

- What do you enjoy about writing, and what do you dislike about writing?

- Did you experience any conditions during your high school experience (remote learning, recovering from surgery, etc.) that could have created gaps in your writing practice? If so, what topics were covered during those gaps?

- Is English your first language, or is it an additional language you've learned? What benefits and challenges, if any, have you experienced if English is a second or third language for you?

- How do you approach the editing process when evaluating your writing?

- How do you typically approach writing when it is timed on an exam?

if not incorporate, each of the different perspectives. You'll have 40 minutes to complete the essay. When taking the Writing test, you'll need to write your essay in pencil using the lined paper provided. Students who are not able to write the essay by hand can request accommodations.

Deciding whether or not to take the Writing test will depend on your goals for college or university admissions and how confident you feel showcasing your writing skills. Because this part of the ACT is optional, don't feel obligated to take it. That said, if you feel that it would help you demonstrate your readiness for college composition, then it can be a valuable complement to your college applications and help set you apart from applicants who did not take the optional Writing test.

To prepare for the Writing section of the ACT, it's important to familiarize yourself with the format of an ACT writing prompt and to practice outlining and writing essays within the given timeframe. This will help you build the necessary skills and confidence to perform well on test day.

RUBRIC FOR THE WRITING TEST

Here, we've provided the rubric that the ACT uses to score submissions for the Writing portion of the exam. Your entire essay will be considered by two raters who will use the criteria outlined here to evaluate and score your essay. Each rater will give you a score from 1 to 6 for each of the four rubric domains: Ideas and Analysis, Development and Support, Organization, and Language Use. The scores from the two raters are then added together to yield four domain scores. Then, those scores are averaged to yield a Writing Subject Score on a scale of 2 to 12 for your entire essay, with 12 being the highest possible score. Study this rubric closely, as it's intended to be a guide to what the ACT expects your essay to look like. To approximate your score, pick the appropriate score band for your essay and double the number provided.

Consider reviewing the rubric and identifying at which categories you excel and those with which you struggle. Work to replicate these expectations in your own practice essays while focusing your prep time on the areas of the writing process where you need the most improvement.

THE ACT® WRITING TEST SCORING RUBRIC

	Ideas and Analysis	Development and Support	Organization	Language Use
Score 6: Responses at this scorepoint demonstrate effective skill in writing an argumentative essay.	The writer generates an argument that critically engages with multiple perspectives on the given issue. The argument's thesis reflects nuance and precision in thought and purpose. The argument establishes and employs an insightful context for analysis of the issue and its perspectives. The analysis examines implications, complexities and tensions, and/or underlying values and assumptions.	Development of ideas and support for claims deepen insight and broaden context. An integrated line of skillful reasoning and illustration effectively conveys the significance of the argument. Qualifications and complications enrich and bolster ideas and analysis.	The response exhibits a skillful organizational strategy. The response is unified by a controlling idea or purpose, and a logical progression of ideas increases the effectiveness of the writer's argument. Transitions between and within paragraphs strengthen the relationships among ideas.	The use of language enhances the argument. Word choice is skillful and precise. Sentence structures are consistently varied and clear. Stylistic and register choices, including voice and tone, are strategic and effective. While a few minor errors in grammar, usage, and mechanics may be present, they do not impede understanding.
Score 5: Responses at this scorepoint demonstrate well-developed skill in writing an argumentative essay.	The writer generates an argument that productively engages with multiple perspectives on the given issue. The argument's thesis reflects precision in thought and purpose. The argument establishes and employs a thoughtful context for analysis of the issue and its perspectives. The analysis addresses implications, complexities and tensions, and/or underlying values and assumptions.	Development of ideas and support for claims deepen understanding. A mostly integrated line of purposeful reasoning and illustration capably conveys the significance of the argument. Qualifications and complications enrich ideas and analysis.	The response exhibits a productive organizational strategy. The response is mostly unified by a controlling idea or purpose, and a logical sequencing of ideas contributes to the effectiveness of the argument. Transitions between and within paragraphs consistently clarify the relationships among ideas.	The use of language works in service of the argument. Word choice is precise. Sentence structures are clear and varied often. Stylistic and register choices, including voice and tone, are purposeful and productive. While minor errors in grammar, usage, and mechanics may be present, they do not impede understanding.

THE ACT® WRITING TEST SCORING RUBRIC

	Ideas and Analysis	Development and Support	Organization	Language Use
Score 4: **Responses at this scorepoint demonstrate adequate skill in writing an argumentative essay.**	The writer generates an argument that engages with multiple perspectives on the given issue. The argument's thesis reflects clarity in thought and purpose. The argument establishes and employs a relevant context for analysis of the issue and its perspectives. The analysis recognizes implications, complexities and tensions, and/or underlying values and assumptions.	Development of ideas and support for claims clarify meaning and purpose. Lines of clear reasoning and illustration adequately convey the significance of the argument. Qualifications and complications extend ideas and analysis.	The response exhibits a clear organizational strategy. The overall shape of the response reflects an emergent controlling idea or purpose. Ideas are logically grouped and sequenced. Transitions between and within paragraphs clarify the relationships among ideas.	The use of language conveys the argument with clarity. Word choice is adequate and sometimes precise. Sentence structures are clear and demonstrate some variety. Stylistic and register choices, including voice and tone, are appropriate for the rhetorical purpose. While errors in grammar, usage, and mechanics are present, they rarely impede understanding.
Score 3: **Responses at this scorepoint demonstrate some developing skill in writing an argumentative essay.**	The writer generates an argument that responds to multiple perspectives on the given issue. The argument's thesis reflects some clarity in thought and purpose. The argument establishes a limited or tangential context for analysis of the issue and its perspectives. Analysis is simplistic or somewhat unclear.	Development of ideas and support for claims are mostly relevant but are overly general or simplistic. Reasoning and illustration largely clarify the argument but may be somewhat repetitious or imprecise.	The response exhibits a basic organizational structure. The response largely coheres, with most ideas logically grouped. Transitions between and within paragraphs sometimes clarify the relationships among ideas.	The use of language is basic and only somewhat clear. Word choice is general and occasionally imprecise. Sentence structures are usually clear but show little variety. Stylistic and register choices, including voice and tone, are not always appropriate for the rhetorical purpose. Distracting errors in grammar, usage, and mechanics may be present, but they generally do not impede understanding.

THE ACT® WRITING TEST SCORING RUBRIC

	Ideas and Analysis	Development and Support	Organization	Language Use
Score 2: **Responses at this scorepoint demonstrate weak or inconsistent skill in writing an argumentative essay.**	The writer generates an argument that weakly responds to multiple perspectives on the given issue. The argument's thesis, if evident, reflects little clarity in thought and purpose. Attempts at analysis are incomplete, largely irrelevant, or consist primarily of restatement of the issue and its perspectives.	Development of ideas and support for claims are weak, confused, or disjointed. Reasoning and illustration are inadequate, illogical, or circular, and fail to fully clarify the argument.	The response exhibits a rudimentary organizational structure. Grouping of ideas is inconsistent and often unclear. Transitions between and within paragraphs are misleading or poorly formed.	The use of language is inconsistent and often unclear. Word choice is rudimentary and frequently imprecise. Sentence structures are sometimes unclear. Stylistic and register choices, including voice and tone, are inconsistent and are not always appropriate for the rhetorical purpose. Distracting errors in grammar, usage, and mechanics are present, and they sometimes impede understanding.
Score 1: **Responses at this scorepoint demonstrate little or no skill in writing an argumentative essay.**	The writer fails to generate an argument that responds intelligibly to the task. The writer's intentions are difficult to discern. Attempts at analysis are unclear or irrelevant.	Ideas lack development, and claims lack support. Reasoning and illustration are unclear, incoherent, or largely absent.	The response does not exhibit an organizational structure. There is little grouping of ideas. When present, transitional devices fail to connect ideas.	The use of language fails to demonstrate skill in responding to the task. Word choice is imprecise and often difficult to comprehend. Sentence structures are often unclear. Stylistic and register choices are difficult to identify. Errors in grammar, usage, and mechanics are pervasive and often impede understanding.

SAMPLE PROMPT

Here, we've provided a sample prompt just like the ones you can expect to see on the ACT Writing test. Feel free to use this prompt for a spare practice essay of your own if you like.

EXAMPLE

The Effects of Social Media

Prompt: Social media has been an integral part of modern society for more than 20 years, influencing various aspects of people's lives, including news, politics, commerce, and entertainment. With more than 300 million social media users in the United States alone, the impact of the technology on individuals and society as a whole has been the subject of much debate. While proponents tout its benefits, such as increased connectivity and access to information, critics argue that social media is a source of addiction, mental health problems, and the spread of misinformation. In light of these competing perspectives, it is crucial to examine the potential benefits and harms of social media to determine whether it is a net positive or negative influence on society.

Read and carefully consider these perspectives. Each suggests a particular way of thinking about the effects of social media.

Perspective One	Perspective Two	Perspective Three
Social media has had a largely negative effect on our lives, contributing to increased feelings of loneliness, anxiety, and depression, as well as decreased attention spans and difficulty with interpersonal communication.	Social media has had a largely positive effect on our lives, enabling us to connect with others, share ideas and experiences, and mobilize for social and political causes.	The impact of social media is complex and depends on how it is used and by whom. While social media can have negative effects on some, it can also have positive effects on others, depending on factors such as age, personality, and social context.

Essay Task

Directions: Write a unified, coherent essay about the effects of using social media. In your essay, be sure to:

- clearly state your own perspective on the issue and analyze the relationship between your perspective and at least one other perspective

- develop and support your ideas with reasoning and examples

- organize your ideas clearly and logically

- communicate your ideas effectively in standard written English

Your perspective may be in full agreement with any of those given, in partial agreement, or completely different.

Common Challenges

Here are some of the common challenges test takers face on the optional ACT Writing test.

Time management

With only 40 minutes to complete the essay, it's essential to plan and organize the writing process effectively. Test takers need to allocate enough time to analyze the prompt, develop a clear thesis statement, outline the essay on their prewriting pages, write the body paragraphs on their lined pages, conclude the essay in a timely manner, and ideally leave time for at least one read through to edit and proofread.

Organizing your thoughts

Another common challenge is writing a well-organized and coherent essay. To address this, test takers should take the time to plan their essay before they start writing. A clear and concise thesis statement should guide the entire essay, and each body paragraph should have a specific focus and follow a logical train of thought from one paragraph to the next.

Common Challenges

Here are some of the common challenges test takers face on the optional ACT Writing test.

Analyzing and incorporating the different perspectives	Additionally, test takers may find it challenging to analyze the given perspectives and incorporate them effectively into their essay. To address this, it's essential to carefully read and understand the different perspectives provided in the prompt and use them to strengthen your argument.
Providing evidence and examples	Test takers may struggle with generating sufficient and appropriate examples and evidence to support their argument. It's important to use relevant and specific examples that effectively confirm the argument's validity while also demonstrating a clear understanding of the topic. Because you won't be able to do research while you're taking the ACT, you'll need to rely on things you've learned in class as well as your own personal experience to support your claim.
Proofreading and editing your work	It's important to save a few minutes to edit and proofread your essay. By doing this, you'll ensure that you catch grammatical errors and other mistakes. It'll be helpful to brush up on the conventions of standard English (see Chapter 6) so that you'll know what to look for when you review your own work on the Writing section.

Throughout this part of the book, we'll provide you with the tools and strategies you need to master the Writing test on the ACT. In preparation for the Writing section of the ACT, you'll want to brush up on your composition skills, including brainstorming, planning, and outlining your essay; drafting a thesis statement; supporting your claims with evidence and analysis; writing a compelling introduction and conclusion; utilizing effective paragraph structure; and creating purposeful transitions between your ideas. Luckily, we'll cover all of these skills in the next chapter.

SUMMING IT UP

- The Writing test on the ACT is an optional section that assesses your ability to produce a clear and organized essay. The test consists of a single writing prompt, which will describe a complex issue and present three different perspectives on that issue. You'll have 40 minutes to complete the essay.

- Two raters score the essay on a scale of 6 for each of the four rubric domains. The scores from the two raters are then added together to yield four domain scores. Then, those scores are averaged to yield a Writing Subject Score on a scale of 2 to 12 for your entire essay, with 12 being the highest possible score.

- Common challenges on the Writing section of the ACT include time management; organizing your thoughts; analyzing and incorporating the different perspectives provided; using evidence and examples; and taking the necessary time to edit and proofread your work.

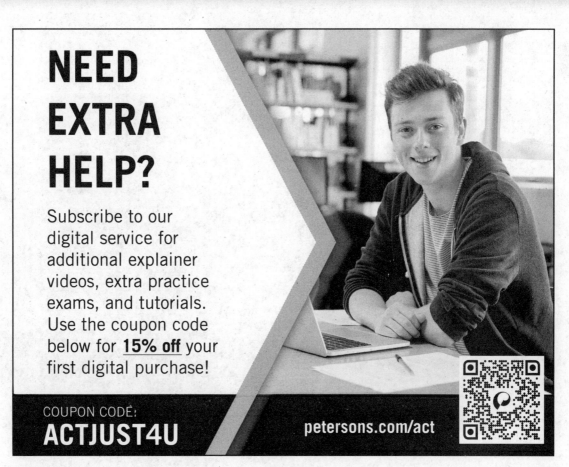

CHAPTER

Writing Skills and Strategies

WRITING SKILLS AND STRATEGIES

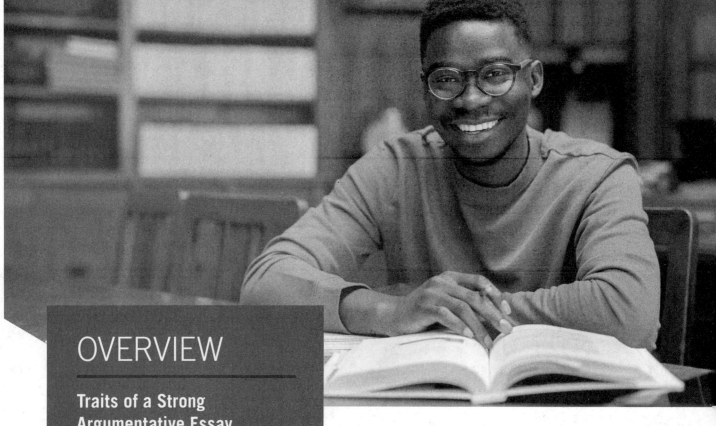

OVERVIEW

Traits of a Strong Argumentative Essay

Improving Your Writing Skills

Strategies for the ACT® Writing Test

Summing It Up

Sample Essay and Practice Writing Prompts

In the last chapter, we covered what you can expect on the optional ACT Writing test and some of the common pitfalls that trip up test takers. In this chapter, we'll first cover what a good argumentative essay looks like and then discuss the various writing skills you'll need to succeed on the ACT Writing section. Then we'll look at strategies that can help you maximize your score. As you work through this chapter, pay attention to which strategies best help you capitalize on your strengths and improve upon your weaknesses. Remember, the Writing test is timed, so you'll have to complete every part of the writing process within the time allotted. The tips we provide here will help you from the prewriting process all the way through to editing your essay before time is up. In place of a standard Knowledge Check, we'll end this chapter by giving you the opportunity to practice writing with multiple example prompts.

TRAITS OF A STRONG ARGUMENTATIVE ESSAY

To think about the writing skills you need to practice and the strategies you'll want to use in the ACT Writing section, consider the following points regarding what makes a strong argumentative essay.

A strong essay . . . .

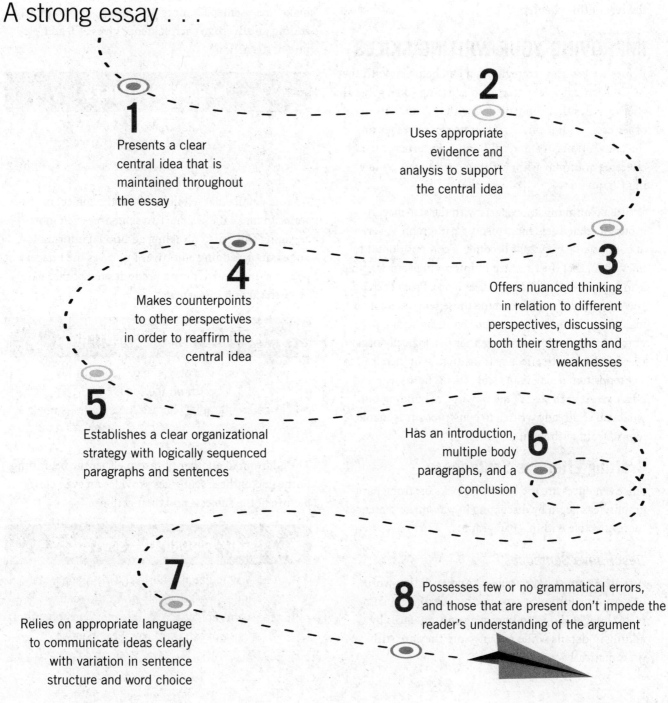

1 Presents a clear central idea that is maintained throughout the essay

2 Uses appropriate evidence and analysis to support the central idea

3 Offers nuanced thinking in relation to different perspectives, discussing both their strengths and weaknesses

4 Makes counterpoints to other perspectives in order to reaffirm the central idea

5 Establishes a clear organizational strategy with logically sequenced paragraphs and sentences

6 Has an introduction, multiple body paragraphs, and a conclusion

7 Relies on appropriate language to communicate ideas clearly with variation in sentence structure and word choice

8 Possesses few or no grammatical errors, and those that are present don't impede the reader's understanding of the argument

When scorers evaluate your essay for the ACT Writing section, these standards are at the forefront of their minds as they determine whether your writing represents college-level thought and argumentation. Consider your performance on the ACT diagnostic test Writing section in Chapter 2. Take some time to identify which skills you excelled in and where you struggled. Use that information to inform how you use the rest of this chapter.

IMPROVING YOUR WRITING SKILLS

Before we get into strategies that can help you with the ACT specifically, let's start by discussing some general writing rules that can help you with this and any other essay. Additionally, if you need a refresher on the conventions of standard English in terms of using effective grammar while writing, we suggest reviewing Chapter 6.

Written communication starts with the sentence. A group of related sentences forms a paragraph. A series of connected paragraphs becomes a composition. It follows, then, that the first step in improving your writing is to know what makes a good sentence. From there, you can decide how to combine those sentences into a logical and complete paragraph. Forming strong paragraphs and bringing them together in a logically organized fashion with effective transitions will then lead to a composition (such as an essay) that is both clear and effective. At each step of the way, you're building onto what you've already written to construct a reasonable, logical train of thought.

Crafting Effective Sentences

Since sentences are the building blocks of strong paragraphs, let's begin by discussing how to make sentences more effective within a paragraph.

Descriptive Sentences

A sentence must have a subject and an action word or verb. In addition, a sentence must express a complete thought. You can improve your sentences by adding in details while making sure they are still grammatically correct.

SHORT SENTENCES

My cat walks.
Erica swam.

Each of the sentences above are complete because they have a subject who completes a verb. Add details to make these sentences more descriptive. For example, adding an adverb to each sentence gives a clearer picture of the action.

IMPROVED SENTENCES

My cat walks briskly.
Erica swam rapidly.

Adding details that tell more about the subject or the verb can make these same two sentences even more engaging while also revealing additional information. For example, adding adjectives improves the imagery of your writing, and adding a prepositional phrase helps place the action in context.

MORE DESCRIPTIVE SENTENCES

My orange cat, Giorgio, walks briskly down the road.
Erica swam rapidly across the enormous pool.

The addition of another phrase at either the beginning or the end of these sentences provides an even clearer picture of the subjects and their actions.

HIGHLY DESCRIPTIVE SENTENCES

In a hurry to catch a butterfly, my orange cat, Giorgio, walks briskly down the road.
Erica swam rapidly across the enormous pool in an attempt to overtake her opponent.

The more you practice writing clear, descriptive sentences, the better you will become at writing them. Expanding your vocabulary so that you have a wide range of word choices will enrich your descriptive powers as well. More complex sentences (using dependent clauses and other modifying phrases) can represent more nuanced and complex ideas. Making use of different kinds of modifying words and phrases can bring clarity and additional context to your ideas. Consider the following example:

SIMPLE SENTENCE
We need greater regulation of railroad infrastructure.

COMPLEX SENTENCE
When we analyze recent railway incidents, we uncover an urgent need for significant changes to how railroad infrastructure is regulated in the United States.

Using a Thesis Statement to Preview Your Argument

In an essay, writers use a thesis statement to organize and ground their writing. The purpose of a thesis statement is to express up front what you plan to argue in your essay. Typically, a thesis statement is a single sentence that effectively summarizes your argument. While you can put it in a few different places, it often makes the most sense to place it at the end of your introductory paragraph. A reader should be able to tell what the main idea and purpose of your essay is just by reading the thesis statement.

Here are three examples of thesis statements on a similar topic:

- Despite the high costs associated, more cities need to invest in high-speed rails and other forms of transportation infrastructure that aren't centered on individual vehicles.

- Investing in high-speed rail systems and the development of rail infrastructure will lead to fewer emissions, increased public transportation revenue, and reduced traffic.

- It is imperative that cities invest in high-speed rail infrastructure to reduce both traffic congestion and vehicle-based emissions.

While each of these thesis statements is similar, each points to a different organizational structure. For instance, the first one sets the writer up to discuss "other forms of transportation infrastructure" besides just high-speed rail, while the latter two set the writer up to discuss the specific issues mentioned in the thesis, like reduced traffic and emissions.

TIP

Write your thesis statement first when planning your essay.
Then, when your essay is finished, revisit your thesis statement to make sure it
reflects the actual argument you wrote. If it doesn't, modify it so it does
(rather than trying to change the entire essay to fit the old thesis statement.)

A good thesis statement is specific, concise, and argumentative. To be specific, a thesis statement must not leave the reader with any questions as to what will be discussed. Consider these example statements:

NOT SPECIFIC

Albert Einstein is an important figure because of his many discoveries.

SPECIFIC

Albert Einstein revolutionized the field of physics with three key discoveries: the general theory of relativity, the photoelectric effect, and Brownian motion.

The first statement is too vague and leaves the reader with questions such as "an important figure to whom or in what?" and "which discoveries?" The second, more specific thesis makes it clear that the argument will be about three particular scientific discoveries Einstein made in the field of physics. Furthermore, because this specific thesis statement is also divided into three parts, it previews the organization an essay might follow. In this case, the first body paragraph could be about the general theory of relativity, the second about the photoelectric effect, and the third about Brownian motion, allowing the writer to conclude by showing the relationship between the three.

To be concise, a thesis statement should say exactly what it needs to say in as few words as possible without sacrificing meaning. Wordy thesis statements can typically be reduced by eliminating any details that are not necessary to understanding the overarching argument. Consider these example thesis statements.

TIP

Using a "divided" statement in parallel structure is a good way to preview
the topics of your body paragraphs within your thesis statement.

NOT CONCISE

Because many people, especially children who are unable to vaccinate as well as those who have compromised immune systems such as cancer patients, cannot get vaccinations on their own in order to have their own immunity, it is necessary for other members of the community, especially healthy adults who do not have a host of health concerns to worry about, to make sure they are vaccinated in hopes that a great enough percentage of the population is vaccinated and herd immunity can happen.

CONCISE

Because some portions of the population are unable to vaccinate, it is important that those who can vaccinate follow through so that communities can achieve herd immunity.

The statement that is too wordy offers a lot of extra information that is not necessary for understanding the basic premise of the argument. Yes, the writer will want to address many of those ideas in their body paragraphs, but in the introduction, where a thesis statement is usually found, it's best to stick to the most important tenets of the overall argument.

To be argumentative, a thesis statement must offer the reader the ability to agree or disagree with what is said. That doesn't necessarily mean that a reader is likely to react one way or another, only that it is possible for them to do so. If the thesis statement simply states an already known fact or reiterates common knowledge, it is not making an argument. Consider these example statements:

NOT ARGUMENTATIVE

In this novel, the author tells a fictional story about a young athlete.

ARGUMENTATIVE

In this novel, the author uses the fictional story of a young athlete's journey to overcome an injury as an allegory for adolescence.

In the nonargumentative statement, there is nothing to agree or disagree with—you can assume that a fictional novel about a young athlete does, in fact, tell a fictional story about a young athlete. Notice that the nonargumentative thesis also fails to be specific. There is nothing the author is arguing except for that which is already known, so the vague thesis statement does nothing to set up the argument that should follow. In the argumentative example, you get a clear picture of what the writer plans to argue, which is that the novel's discussion of a young athlete's post-injury experience can be considered an allegory for adolescence.

Using Topic Sentences and Transitions

Transitions are necessary to guide your reader through your writing. In essays, topic sentences are a particular type of transition that can help signal for your reader how different elements of your argument are thematically knit together. Think of a topic sentence as a mini thesis statement that occurs at the start of each body paragraph. The purpose of the topic sentence is to offer a clear picture of what will be argued in that paragraph, often by gesturing to what came before to show how the topics are linked. Consider the following example topic sentence:

> While some believe that hemp plants should be grown for medicinal and industrial uses, others believe that the potential negatives from drug-related abuses of the crop outweigh the benefits of mass cultivation.

This topic sentence gestures to what was likely discussed in the paragraph before (the medicinal and industrial uses of hemp as related to why some support cultivating the crop), while also showing what is likely to come in the new paragraph (information on why hemp critics are concerned about drug-related abuse of the plant). When writing an essay, you'll want to have a topic sentence at the beginning of each new body paragraph to help you transition between topics and ideas.

Most often, topic sentences and transitions between ideas within a paragraph require using some kind of transition word or phrase. Transition words and phrases are those that help you effectively transition between concepts, signaling the relationship between ideas before and after. Often, these words or phrases will come at the start of a sentence, but that is not always the case. Here is a list of common transition words with examples of how they might be used.

COMMON TRANSITION WORDS AND PHRASES

Purpose of Transition	Example Words	Example Sentences
To introduce new ideas or add to/agree with topics that have already been introduced	• additionally • coupled with • equally important • first, second, third, etc. • further • furthermore • in addition (to) • likewise • moreover • similarly	• **First**, one must understand how the structure of DNA affects genetics. • **Furthermore**, these same observations were noted at another dig site 20 km away. • The question of municipal water usage is **equally important** to the discussion of local conservation efforts.
To communicate the writer's opposition to or a limit placed upon a given idea or phrase	• as much as • by contrast • conversely • despite • however • notwithstanding • on the contrary • on the other hand • that said • while	• **Despite** new evidence, the theory remains the most prevalent in the field. • The question of parental input is, **conversely,** overemphasized in research on childhood literacy development. • **As much as** Sushmita had hoped to sleep in, the birds noisily nesting outside her window had other plans.
To show a cause-and-effect relationship or communicate the conditions that influence a circumstance or idea	• as a result • as long as • because (of) • consequently • due to • hence • in case • in effect • since • then • therefore • unless • whenever • while	• I am going fishing later, **hence** the tackle box and gear. • **Consequently**, commuters were unable to reliably predict what time the trains would arrive. • Tina was upset **because of** the letters she'd found in her brother's drawer. • **Therefore**, it's important for schools to invest adequate funds into arts and music programs.

COMMON TRANSITION WORDS AND PHRASES

Purpose of Transition	Example Words	Example Sentences
To set up an example, fact, piece of evidence, or other form of support for another concept	<ul><li>by all means</li><li>especially</li><li>explicitly</li><li>for this reason</li><li>indeed</li><li>in fact</li><li>in other words</li><li>markedly</li><li>notably</li><li>significantly</li><li>to clarify</li><li>to reiterate</li></ul>	<ul><li>The new model of the car is **by all means** a notable improvement on prior models.</li><li>**In other words**, those who wish to master a new skill should expect to devote numerous hours to being amateurish at first.</li><li>**Indeed**, Portugal was the first European nation to get actively involved in the transatlantic slave trade.</li></ul>
To communicate the time at which an event occurred or the timing of one event in relation to another	<ul><li>after</li><li>at the present moment</li><li>frequently</li><li>in the meantime</li><li>momentarily</li><li>now</li><li>occasionally</li><li>often</li><li>once</li><li>suddenly</li><li>then</li><li>today</li></ul>	<ul><li>I was distracted, **momentarily**, by a high-pitched shriek emitting from the far-off woods.</li><li>**Today**, the James Webb Space Telescope is known for producing the clearest images of far-off galaxies.</li><li>**Suddenly**, the doorbell rang.</li></ul>
To help the writer communicate a conclusion or final idea on a topic	<ul><li>altogether</li><li>effectively</li><li>in any event</li><li>in conclusion</li><li>in either case</li><li>in essence</li><li>in summary</li><li>nonetheless</li><li>to conclude</li><li>to summarize</li><li>to sum up</li></ul>	<ul><li>**In any event**, the festival proved a success despite the weather issues and a series of unfortunate technical mishaps.</li><li>**Altogether**, there are numerous factors that contribute to a feeling of loneliness, not all of them psychological.</li><li>This means that the industry as it once was is, **effectively**, over.</li></ul>

 TIP

Recognizing transition words helps a lot with reading comprehension questions on the Reading and Science tests too!

Varying Sentence Structure

Effective writing tends to have a natural flow and rhythm that makes it easier for a reader to follow. This happens not only at the content level, such as through the use of transitions, but also at the syntax level, such as when varying the length and complexity of sentences. You don't want to write only short, telegraphic sentences, as your writing will lack detail and start to sound robotic and elementary. Similarly, you don't want every single sentence to be long, compound, complex, and/or bursting with descriptive detail. Occasionally, short sentences are effective. Other times, a more detailed sentence will suit you better; for instance, consider how the longer sentence you're reading right now interplays with the short sentence that came before it. Varying your sentence structure helps guide your reader and keep their interest.

Paragraph Development

A paragraph is a group of sentences that develops one main idea. As we mentioned, this main idea is usually stated in a topic sentence at the start of the paragraph. The rest of the paragraph provides details about the topic or clarifies ideas by providing specific examples and warrants—explanations of how the evidence supports the main idea.

Developing Effective Paragraphs

There are no rules for determining the length of a paragraph; however, it is a good idea to make most paragraphs in an essay at least three sentences long. Generally, a paragraph should maintain its focus on a single key idea. Additionally, you don't want any paragraph to be so long that the reader may lose track of your train of thought or get muddled in the details. The key is to make sure that the idea of a given paragraph is clear from start to finish.

Most often, developing effective paragraphs means following many of the same rules we've already discussed for crafting effective sentences. Consider the two examples that follow. This first example is a very basic paragraph. As you read it, think to yourself what it is missing that could help make it more developed and effective.

EXAMPLE OF A POORLY DEVELOPED PARAGRAPH

Basically, there are lots of reasons to be a vegetarian. Some scientists think vegetarianism is good. It helps animals. They are in better conditions because of it. Scientists think that it is better for human health. They eat more vegetables and get more fiber than meat eaters. Vegetarians consume less saturated fat. So, they have lower cholesterol and live longer. Vegetarians have lower cancer rates. They have a lower risk of chronic diseases too.

What did you notice about this paragraph?

The paragraph has a topic sentence, albeit vague, as well as multiple facts that relate to the stated idea: "there are lots of reasons to be a vegetarian." However, the sequence, grouping, and lack of analysis of these ideas leads to a paragraph that feels disjointed and is, ultimately, less effective in conveying a position.

In examining the structure, you may have recognized that the writer didn't keep their sentence construction in mind as they wrote. They treated their ideas individually, rather than considering how the ideas work together to serve the topic of the paragraph. Additionally, you may have noticed that most of the sentences aren't wrong on their own, yet they still don't add up to an effective paragraph. For example, the sentence "Vegetarians consume less saturated fat" is neither grammatically nor logically incorrect, but because it's poorly integrated with the sentences that come before and after it, it lacks impact. This paragraph is a good example of what happens when combining multiple short sentences without varying sentence structure, using transitions, providing a specific topic sentence, or adding descriptive details and thoughtful word choices.

By contrast, good paragraph structure requires paying attention to the types of sentences you're using, how you're combining them, and where in the paragraph you include each sentence to express your reasoning in a logical train of thought. In the example we just gave, the writer provided the basic components of their argument, but the paragraph as written still fails to help the reader understand the topic better because the sentences don't come together in a way that develops the argument as a cohesive whole.

Now, let's consider how this paragraph might look if developed more effectively. This version covers the same basic information as before; however, it is vastly improved by a topic sentence, transitions, a clearer order and arrangement of sentences, variations in sentence structure, more effective word choices, and greater specificity in the details and explanations provided.

EXAMPLE OF A PARAGRAPH DEVELOPED BY DETAILS AND EXAMPLES

There are numerous reasons that scientists consider vegetarianism a smart choice. For one, vegetarianism both reduces the number of animals slaughtered and improves conditions for those that are raised to be consumed, leading to a smaller environmental impact. Humans, too, benefit from practicing vegetarianism. For instance, recent studies have noted that vegetarians tend to consume less saturated fat, which lowers their cholesterol compared to omnivores. Vegetarians also tend to consume more fiber, an important dietary regulator, and have lower blood pressure, improving heart health and life expectancy. Similar health benefits have been noted by additional research, wherein a correlation has been found between vegetarian diets and decreased risk of cancer and other chronic diseases. Taken together, these factors suggest that a vegetarian diet can lead to a longer, fuller life.

This is in no way a perfect argument; however, the structure of the paragraph and the presentation of topic, evidence, and analysis with varying sentence structures and transitions leads to an effective presentation of the argument.

Connecting Paragraphs

When you end a paragraph and start a new one, this indicates a change in focus. In an argumentative essay, start a new paragraph to show a change in:

- The perspective or topic of an argument
- The mood or point of view in a description
- Ideas or steps in an explanation

Just as you must provide for an orderly flow of sentences within a paragraph, you must also provide for a logical transition from paragraph to paragraph in any composition or report. A topic sentence is usually an effective transition, but there are times when you may need to connect paragraphs that deal with similar or adjacent topics.

The three most common ways of connecting paragraphs are:

- **Repetition of a key word or phrase** introduced in one paragraph and expanded upon in the next paragraph.

- **Use of pronouns** that refer to a person or an idea mentioned in the previous paragraph.

- **Use of transitional words and phrases** to illustrate the relationship of one topic to another, as discussed earlier in this chapter.

EXAMPLE OF PARAGRAPHS CONNECTED BY REPETITION OF A KEY WORD

While the scientists were initially skeptical about the results, they **expected** that replicating the experiment would yield similar findings.

When the lab repeated the experiments, the wild variations in the results exceeded all **expectations**.

The end of one paragraph is connected to the topic sentence of the next through variations on the word *expect*. *Expected* in paragraph 1 is repeated as *expectations* in paragraph 2, allowing one thought to flow from the first paragraph to the second. The second paragraph will continue with specific details on the variations the lab uncovered in further experiments. A similar effect could be achieved using pronouns, as in the following example:

EXAMPLE OF PARAGRAPHS CONNECTED BY USE OF PRONOUNS

While **the scientists** were initially skeptical about the results, they expected that replicating the experiment would yield similar findings.

However, when **they** repeated the experiments, **they** were flabbergasted by the results.

Here, the end of one paragraph is connected to the topic sentence of the next through the use of pronouns. *The scientists* in paragraph 1 is replaced by *they* at the start of paragraph 2, signaling to the reader that the scientists (and the results that flabbergasted them) will be the topic of the next paragraph.

EXAMPLE OF PARAGRAPHS CONNECTED BY TRANSITIONAL WORDS

While the scientists were initially skeptical about the results, they expected that replicating the experiment would yield similar findings.

Yet when the lab repeated the experiment, scientists found that there were actually a number of variables unaccounted for in the original experiment.

These paragraphs are connected by the use of the transitional word *yet* as well as repetition of key terms like *scientists* and *experiment*. The second paragraph will continue by elaborating on the unexpected variables the scientists discovered when replicating the experiment.

Development, Support, and Critical Thinking

On the ACT Writing test, you will be evaluated for how well you present, develop, and support your ideas. In argumentative writing, which is what is required on the ACT Writing test, this refers to how well you support your claims with evidence and analysis in your body paragraphs. It also relates to how well you address and offer counterarguments for perspectives other than your own. Because you'll be writing on the fly, you can't do research to support your claims, but you can use personal experience and things you've read or learned in class as evidence in your essay. You should also reference ideas from the given prompt and perspectives to support your thinking; just make sure to put those ideas in your own words instead of copying phrasing from the given material directly.

Your essay also needs to exhibit critical thinking, which refers to your ability to analyze the issue at hand, argue your point of view, and illustrate logical relationships among ideas, offering nuance and well-reasoned thought. You demonstrate critical thinking when you select appropriate evidence to support your claims and then engage in analysis to show how that evidence relates to your argument. Similarly, you can demonstrate critical thinking by responding effectively to perspectives with which you disagree, especially if you can discuss their strengths and weaknesses and explain your disagreement with counterarguments.

Structuring Body Paragraphs to Support Development

It's important to craft well-developed body paragraphs to demonstrate that you can organize your ideas logically, build and support your argument, and think critically. Body paragraphs should be structured in a way that helps advance the thesis statement of your essay. The sentences in a paragraph generally go in the following order, with adjustments made as needed for certain types of paragraphs, such as introductory and concluding paragraphs. Keep in mind that while a main idea/topic sentence and the summary are often one sentence each in a given paragraph, a writer can include multiple sentences of evidence and analysis to make the main idea stronger and thoroughly develop the paragraph.

How to Develop a Body Paragraph

1. MAIN IDEA/TOPIC SENTENCE (MI):

The first sentence should state the main idea, claim, or purpose of your paragraph. The topic sentence should tell your reader what the paragraph is about so that they know what to expect as they read. Think of topic sentences as signposts that guide the reader and tell them what's coming next. In pieces of writing with multiple body paragraphs, the topic sentence helps to develop the central argument, known as the thesis statement.

- -

2. EVIDENCE (E):

To develop the idea outlined in the topic sentence, you should provide supporting evidence like examples, anecdotes, facts, statistics, and more. Think of supporting details as proof of your main idea and purpose. Sometimes, you'll need to present evidence followed by analysis, and then more evidence followed by more analysis.

- -

3. ANALYSIS (A):

This is where you explain the evidence itself, why the evidence is important, and how it proves your point. Here, you should try to anticipate additional explanation and context the reader might need to understand how the evidence supports the main idea of the paragraph.

- -

4. SUMMARY (S):

Paragraphs often end with a summary of what was just discussed. This is where you reiterate the main idea to remind the reader of the most important takeaway from the paragraph. In a passage with several paragraphs, the last sentence of a paragraph usually summarizes what was just discussed while also functioning as a transition that prepares the reader for the next paragraph.

Let's look at a sample paragraph and break it down into parts, which we have labeled with the categories we just outlined:

If consumed too frequently, soda pop can be detrimental to one's dental health, especially if you don't practice good oral hygiene (**MI**). In fact, people who drink soda on a daily basis and only brush their teeth once a day are far more likely to experience tooth decay (**E**). This is because the sugar in soda interacts with the bacteria in your mouth and becomes highly acidic, causing cavities, erosion of enamel, and gum disease (**A**). To combat the harmful effects of soda, practice good dental hygiene: rinse your mouth out with water after drinking a soda, brush your teeth twice a day, and floss (**E**). These healthy habits can remove the bacteria on and in between your teeth while protecting your teeth from decay (**A**). That way, you can still enjoy the carbonation and syrupy sweetness of soda in moderation while keeping your teeth clean and healthy (**S**).

The first sentence in this sample paragraph is the main idea. It introduces the topic and focus of the paragraph. From this sentence, we know that we'll be reading about the effect of soda on dental health. In the next sentence, we're presented with evidence of a detrimental effect that soda can have on one's dental health, which is that those who drink soda daily are more likely to have cavities. The following sentence presents analysis to explain why this is the case: The ingredients in soda can damage teeth. The fourth sentence provides examples of good dental hygiene (Evidence), and the fifth sentence explains how these habits can mitigate

the damage done by soda (Analysis). Notice that in this one paragraph, there are two pieces of evidence each followed by their own analysis. Finally, the last sentence summarizes the main point of the paragraph, which is that while soda can harm dental health, it is nonetheless possible to use good oral hygiene practices to mitigate the risks of soda consumption.

Delivering an Effective Composition

Once you've developed and combined the individual paragraphs in your composition, your final task is to make sure you have delivered your ideas effectively in the essay as a whole. Remember, the Writing test is timed, so you'll ideally need to reserve a little bit of time before the end of the exam to proofread and determine if you've included all necessary components, presented your argument without any major gaps in logic, and concluded effectively. No one expects perfection on a timed exam, but you do yourself a disservice if you never take the time to review what you wrote before the end of the test. As we'll mention in the strategies section, we recommend reserving at least 5 minutes for proofing and improvement at the end of your initial writing.

Self-Reflection for Editing

When evaluating what you've written, start by considering these basic reflection questions.

- Did you clearly state your argument in response to the given prompt?
- Did you address other perspectives besides just your own?
- Did you provide relevant examples and details to support your argument?
- Does your essay follow a clear train of thought from beginning to end, or does it jump around?
- Are you missing any key details or contextual information that a reader needs to understand your argument?
- Have you provided an introduction, multiple body paragraphs, and a conclusion?
- Is your handwriting clear enough for a reader to evaluate, or are there some words you might need to rewrite more carefully?

ALERT

Since your essay is handwritten, make sure you are writing legibly enough for an evaluator to read what you've written. If they cannot read it, they cannot score it! This includes when editing what you wrote—a simple line to cross out unwanted words is much easier to read than chaotic scribbles.

Quickly pondering these questions should give you a clear path for polishing your essay before the test ends. Considering similar questions during the prewriting process can also help you preemptively structure your essay appropriately.

Proofreading Timed Essays

It may seem silly to spend time proofreading when you have so little time for writing as is, but if you can manage to read through your essay one time, you will likely find opportunities to improve the clarity of your writing. Here are some things you should look for when proofreading a timed essay:

- Spelling errors
- Grammar issues
- Missing words and sentences
- Capitalization issues
- End punctuation issues
- Missing transitions

It may be that you do not spot any errors. If so, you can use your proofreading time to consider if you've been repetitive and might need to alter phrasing, insert more effective word choices, or develop a fuller conclusion. Try to use simple editing marks, like a single line through unwanted words or a caret (^), which can be used to add a word or phrase. If you need to add more than a couple of words, consider using a caret plus a number within a circle. That way, instead of trying to shove a bunch of new words into the line using your tiniest, hardest-to-read handwriting, you can instead add the new information at the bottom of your writing space, as in the following example:

EXAMPLE

At the time, critics of the radical political (1) movement ^ suggested that the group's tactics were too violent. They believed that the group should have opted for more peaceful forms of social intervention instead as well.

(1), such as the opposition party and the clergy,

Adjusting Your Thesis Statement

As we mentioned before, you should always start your writing by developing a thesis statement that expresses your argument. That said, it's extremely common for a person's argument to shift and change as they develop an essay. Consequently, you will need to revisit your thesis statement at the end of your writing and make sure it still reflects the essay you actually wrote. If it needs to change, modify it or replace it with a new one that better matches the actual argument you ended up making.

Make Sure You Conclude

A common issue for test takers on timed essay exams is the failure to include a conclusion. Even if you find yourself struggling to finish before your time is up, make sure you wrap things up with at least a concluding sentence. A short conclusion is better than no ending at all, and you can often create a quick concluding sentence by simply restating your thesis statement in different words. If you have time to develop your conclusion more, we suggest starting with a restated thesis statement and then sharing some strong ideas for questions or topics that might help someone explore the given topic further in the future.

STRATEGIES FOR THE ACT® WRITING TEST

Up to this point, we've discussed techniques and strategies that are important for timed writing generally. Now, we'll discuss some of the ways you can work within the specific expectations of the ACT to present the best essay possible.

Understand the Rubric

In the last chapter, we discussed the rubric the ACT uses to evaluate test takers' writing. It may be helpful at this time to return to Chapter 22 and look over the rubric closely one more time. For general reference purposes, here's a simplified version of the four key skills addressed by each rubric section and what evaluators look for with each.

ACT® WRITING RUBRIC SIMPLIFIED	
Skill Category	**Test takers are evaluated on…**
Ideas and Analysis	• …how effectively they critically engage multiple perspectives. • …how nuanced, clear, and precise their thesis statement is and how effectively it encapsulates their argument. • …the efficacy of the context the writer provides for their perspective. • …the complexity and thoroughness used to examine implications and tensions within the topic and given perspectives.
Development and Support	• …whether or not the depth of their analysis helps a reader broaden their understanding of a topic. • …how effectively claims are supported and developed in terms of the writer's argument. • …the depth of reasoning deployed to support the argument and how logically claims fit together. • …how clearly analysis is communicated and supported by the evidence.
Organization	• …the strategy they've used to organize their essay and whether it presents the information in a clear, linear fashion. • …how logically ideas progress and build over the course of analysis. • …how clear the purpose of each paragraph is and how effectively the order of paragraphs serves the writer's overall purpose. • …their use of topic sentences and transitions to effectively guide the reader through the argument.

ACT® WRITING RUBRIC SIMPLIFIED	
Skill Category	**Test takers are evaluated on…**
Language Use	• …whether word choice, syntax, grammar, and sentence structures enhance the writer's argument or hinder it. • …the effectiveness of sentence structures for communicating ideas, including how varied sentences are and how effectively they flow together. • …the effectiveness of the writer's choices regarding style, voice, tone, and rhetoric. • …how many grammar, usage, and mechanics errors there are and whether they impede the reader's understanding. Note that a few minor errors are okay as long as they do not impede communication.

You'll notice that much of what evaluators are looking for can be addressed by engaging in meaningful prewriting; ensuring you have a clear, specific argument; developing your ideas with thoughtful, concrete examples; addressing perspectives beyond your own by analyzing strengths and weaknesses and providing counterclaims; and presenting your ideas in an organized fashion. In other words, if you bring together all the skills we've discussed to this point, you should be in good shape for your essay. The more you practice with the given time limit and evaluating your writing based on the ACT rubric, the easier it will be to do well on exam day since you'll know what you can do in that time and can plan accordingly. Keep the rubric in mind as you write, since it's exactly what you'll be scored on.

Analyze Prompts

Your first task when prewriting should be to dissect the different parts of the writing prompt to determine what kind of argument you need to develop. Once you know the kind of task the prompt requires, you will be better prepared to create a plan that responds to it properly.

After completing these tasks, you should be able to quickly develop a tentative thesis statement and begin outlining your argument.

Strategies for Time Management

Test takers will have 40 minutes to complete an essay. You should plan to spend 3–6 minutes prewriting (including analyzing the prompt), 24-30 minutes

After looking closely at a prompt, you should be able to do the following four tasks:

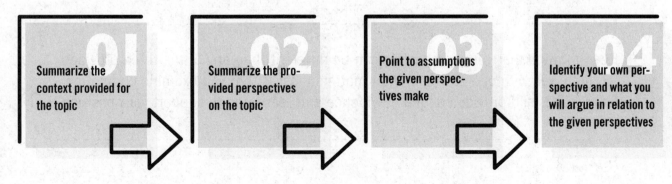

01 Summarize the context provided for the topic

02 Summarize the provided perspectives on the topic

03 Point to assumptions the given perspectives make

04 Identify your own perspective and what you will argue in relation to the given perspectives

able to accomplish in the given time. This may seem overwhelming at first, but it's actually a good thing; clear expectations allow you to keep a mental checklist of what you must include.

Consider Your Objectives

An objective is a goal made in accordance with what you hope to accomplish. When writing your essay for the ACT, your objectives include the following:

- Assert your position and craft a compelling argument to support it.
- Analyze the competing perspectives and present critiques.
- Deploy critical reasoning and thoughtful, concrete examples.
- Exhibit effective analysis of all evidence and connect that analysis to your argument.
- Organize your argument logically.
- Exhibit sophisticated sentence structure, vocabulary, and transitions while using effective, high-level written English.

It's impossible to tend to all of these objectives simultaneously at every moment while writing, but if you are familiar with them, it should help you keep them at the forefront of your mind while deciding how to write the sentences you draft.

Prioritize Must-Do Items

The tasks you need to complete in your essay can be divided into tasks you must do, tasks that you should do, and tasks that you can ignore. We've separated tasks according to their priority level as follows:

writing, and 5–8 minutes proofreading your essay. Many test takers think that skipping the prewriting and proofreading stages will save them time to draft better, but as you'll likely notice while practicing, those steps are critical if you want to deliver a logical and polished essay within the strict time limit. If you plan your essay well during the prewriting stage, it will be easier to quickly draft an essay that includes all necessary components, leaving you time enough to proofread at least once through.

Plan in Terms of Purpose and Goals

On the ACT, you have a very explicit purpose for writing and must achieve a measurable set of goals. In other words, the evaluators who read your essay will have a certain set of expectations about what you should be

TIP

Keep in mind that your perspective can be different than any of the three provided or align well with one of them. What matters most is that you examine competing perspectives and provide adequate evidence and reasoning to support your position.

PRIORITIZING WRITING TASKS	
Test takers must…	• Include an introduction and conclusion. • Use specific examples and provide concrete analysis to support evidence and claims. • Address all of the given perspectives, including analyzing the strengths and weaknesses of each and providing counterclaims. • Include a thesis statement that expresses their argument.
It's a good idea for test takers to…	• Take time to plan their writing. • Take time to proofread and make revisions. • Write with an academic style, such as by including the thesis statement at the end of an introduction paragraph that provides context for the topic and using topic sentences at the start of body paragraphs to guide the reader.
Test takers can ignore…	• Fact checking: The scorers will not be fact-checking, so while you shouldn't make totally unreasonable claims or use outrageous evidence, you can hedge and not fixate on inaccuracies of fact, as what matters most is how you make and present your argument. • Writing in an excessively formal style: It's okay to include personal perspectives and experience mixed in with academic perspectives. You can also use personal pronouns, such as by saying things like "I think that…" The important thing is to use a consistent tone and high-level language throughout.

Since you know which tasks are most important and which are a good idea to fit in, you can start with those high-priority tasks and include the others as time allows.

Personalize Your Prewriting Time

How much time you spend prewriting will depend on your personal strengths as a writer and whether you struggle with creating organized drafts. There

are certainly some test takers who are good at keeping multiple thoughts in their head simultaneously. This type of test taker will often jot down a few ideas when prewriting, connect the ideas in their head, and then be able to begin drafting after just a few minutes. However, some test takers benefit from using more time while prewriting so they can quickly outline their ideas and determine the order in which they'd like to write them. These test takers may spend a little more time than others in the planning stage, as much as 10 minutes, but they are then usually able to write their essay according to the plan much more quickly than someone who did not plan so thoroughly, since their outline acts like a map for what they will write. Still others prefer to quickly write down their ideas graphically, such as by using a brainstorm web, so that they can visually connect keywords and organize ideas in their mind as they write. There is no one right way to prewrite so long as you are planning out your essay in a way that makes sense to you, and which will allow you to write an effective, full essay in the time you're given.

Five Major Prewriting Tasks

As a general rule, there are five major tasks you want to accomplish while prewriting, no matter your personal approach.

- Create some kind of outline, web of claims, or organizing graphic to quickly note the key ideas and evidence you'll use in your argument.

- Select multiple concrete examples you can use in your argument.

- Determine the strengths and weaknesses of each given perspective and how you'll address them, including counterclaims you plan to make.

- Decide how the essay should be structured to support your argument, including the order in which you'll write your paragraphs and what should be in each.

- Create a tentative thesis statement that reflects the planned structure and argument.

As you prepare for your ACT Writing test, try planning essays a few different ways to see which kind of balance helps you most when prewriting for the given time limit.

Strategies to Improve Logic and Organization

In addition to communicating a clear, specific argument that effectively responds to the prompt, you'll want to account for the logic and organization of your essay from the beginning of your prewriting process through to your proofreading after you've completed your draft.

Recognize the Structure of the ACT Writing Prompt

The prompt itself gives you a lot of information that can help you organize your writing logically. If you are someone who struggles with logical organization, consider structuring your essay in such a way that it mimics some of the organization from the given prompt without copying it outright. For example, imagine that a prompt includes a sentence like the following:

EXAMPLE

While some people believe that organic foods are healthier, others suggest that what's more important is to produce a greater volume of food to feed more people.

The prompt itself is telling you that there are at least two perspectives you'll want to address: (1) those who believe its important to produce food organically for health reasons, and (2) those who believe that the benefits of organic farming are not as compelling as the benefits of producing more food for more people with other methods. The prompt will also be accompanied by three explicit perspectives with which you can choose to agree or disagree. This means that the prompt is automatically giving you multiple perspectives with which to engage, allowing you to organize your essay to address them one by one in the order the prompt offers them. The prompt

and perspectives give you very clear messages about what needs to be included in your argument and the competing claims you may need to counter. Feel free to make notes on the prompt itself as part of your prewriting process.

Use a Structured Template

As a general rule, use a five-paragraph structure with an introduction and conclusion sandwiching three body paragraphs. There are a few different ways to approach the organization of your body paragraphs, depending on your perspective for the prompt and ideas you have for pointing out the weaknesses of others. We suggest using one of three essay structures to guide your writing, as seen on the next page.

Structures A and B place different levels of emphasis on other perspectives or your own perspective. Both structures meet the rubric's criteria for high-scoring essays. Structure C is a shorter version of B. If you are struggling to come up with ideas for a topic or just need a "worst case scenario" option for when you're running low on time or energy and aren't sure you can develop a full five-paragraph essay, consider Structure C. This might not be enough for the highest scoring bands but it's enough to lay out a basic argument.

Alternatively, you may find that you routinely have time and energy to develop your essay beyond the basic five-paragraph structure. If you are wanting to develop a more in-depth essay or just want to make sure you stand out at the highest scoring bands, you can expand Essay Structures A and B by simply adding more paragraphs that either develop your argument or address further alternate perspectives.

Memorizing these structures gives you an easy template that you can apply to virtually any argument you want to make, thereby taking the guesswork out of how to organize your essay. As you practice, try out each structure to see if one comes easier for you when drafting. Consider also that one may be better suited to certain types of prompts or arguments than others, so it's a good idea to practice with multiple.

ESSAY STRUCTURE

Paragraph	Purpose			
Introduction (2–5 sentences)	Summarize the topic and outline your argument with a thesis statement.			
Body Paragraphs (5–7 sentences)		Structure A	Structure B	Structure C
	#1	Discuss one perspective different from yours. Describe its strengths and weaknesses as supported by examples and reasoning.	State a key idea that supports your thesis. Provide examples with analysis of how they relate to your claim.	Describe your perspective on the issue and provide evidence and analysis to support it.
	#2	Discuss another perspective that differs from yours. Discuss its strengths and weaknesses as supported by examples and reasoning.	State another key idea that supports your thesis. Provide examples with analysis of how they relate to your claim.	Address at least two other perspectives and their weaknesses. Include evidence and examples to support your counterclaims.
	#3	State your perspective along with evidence to support why you believe it is stronger than other perspectives. Use examples and reasoning to support your claims.	Address the other perspectives and their weaknesses while providing evidence and examples to support your counterclaims.	
Conclusion (1–3 sentences)	Restate your thesis in new words and summarize your argument.			

 TIP

You can use more than three body paragraphs if you have time and need them. Simply expand on the five-paragraph structure accordingly.

SUMMING IT UP

- The ACT Writing test is a 40-minute essay that requires you to respond with your own perspective on a topic for which there are multiple perspectives. Your essay will be evaluated by two different readers using four rubric categories:

  - Ideas and Analysis
  - Development and Support
  - Organization
  - Language Use

- When approaching the ACT Writing test, follow these five basic steps:

  - Step 1: Analyze and understand the task required by the prompt.
  - Step 2: Brainstorm ideas for what you want to say.
  - Step 3: Plan and outline your essay.
  - Step 4: Write your essay.
  - Step 5: Proofread your essay.

- Use a thesis statement to establish the central argument of your essay and to give your essay a sense of purpose and focus.

- Use topic sentences and transitions to clearly guide the reader through your ideas and to develop the argument over the course of your essay.

- Create well-developed body paragraphs by including topic sentences, evidence, analysis, and a transition. This gives your essay a sense of structure while developing the claims and ideas that support your central argument.

- Vary your sentence structure and use of punctuation to illustrate your mastery of various conventions in English. However, make sure to avoid common grammatical and mechanical errors in the process.

- Include an introduction and conclusion in your essay, as well as body paragraphs that address multiple perspectives on the topic, including your own. You must provide evidence and examples accompanied by sound analysis to score at the highest level.

- Follow strategies such as using a structured template, analyzing prompts, managing time, writing for the rubric, and personalizing prewriting time to maximize your essay score.

- Use timed practice tests to familiarize yourself with how it "feels" to write a timed essay according to the ACT specifications.

SAMPLE ESSAY AND PRACTICE WRITING PROMPTS

In this section, we've included a sample essay on a given prompt. We've also included two further practice writing prompts. If you've been using the Knowledge Checks throughout this book, use one of the writing prompts to complete the full practice test created by adding the Knowledge Checks together. Then, after evaluating your writing, you can practice the different strategies outlined in this chapter using the remaining prompts. Write your essay on lined paper, but complete your prewriting within your allotted time on the page adjacent to the prompt. Always use a timer when practicing your essay so you are replicating test conditions. When you are ready to evaluate your writing, consult the ACT rubric and self-scoring guide in Chapter 2.

Sample Prompt and Essay

Here, we've included a sample prompt along with a high-scoring sample essay response that follows Essay Structure B, as outlined earlier in this chapter. Pay attention to the use of a thesis statement along with the paragraph structure, topic sentences, and transitions.

EXAMPLE

Suffrage at 16

Voting is just one of many privileges that Americans cannot access until they are legally considered adults at age 18. However, in an effort to increase civic participation, there is a movement to reduce the voting age from 18 years old to 16 years old. Politics impact 16- and 17-year-olds just as much as 18-year-olds, and many 16- and 17-year-olds are ready and eager to vote, especially because in presidential elections, the leaders they choose will still be serving when they begin adulthood. Most have received civics education in school and demonstrate interest in civic engagement. By establishing voting habits earlier, lowering the voting age to 16 will increase the likelihood that people will become lifelong voters, thereby improving voter turnout and making government more representative.

Perspective One	Perspective Two	Perspective Three
Most students in the US have had civic education by age 16 and are ready to vote. Politics affects their future in important ways, so they should be allowed to take part in the democratic conversation.	There is no way teenagers have learned enough before graduating high school to meaningfully consider civic issues, so there is no need to raise the voting age. Voting rights can come at a later time when voters are more mature.	It doesn't seem reasonable to allow teenagers to vote on every topic, but they should at least be able to take part in major elections, like those for president and senators, since both serve longer terms.

Essay Task

Write a unified, coherent essay on the topic of potentially lowering the US voting age to 16. In your essay, be sure to:

- clearly state your own perspective on the issue and analyze the relationship between your perspective and at least one other perspective
- develop and support your ideas with reasoning and examples
- organize your ideas clearly and logically
- communicate your ideas effectively in standard written English

Your perspective may be in full agreement with any of those given, in partial agreement, or completely different.

Sample Essay (Score Level: 6)

Voting is an important act in American society. It's how you make your opinion on important issues known. While voting has always been limited to those who are 18 years of age and older, it's time that we as a country consider lowering the voting age to 16 years of age. Because 16-year-olds must bear the consequences of increasingly alarming political issues, such as gun violence and climate change, I believe they should be able to exercise the right to vote to elect candidates who will advocate on their behalf.

Sixteen-year-olds today have never known a world without school shooter drills, and they have a right to make their voice heard through voting in order to effect change when it comes to reducing gun violence. For example, after the school shooting in Parkland, many Parkland students turned their trauma into action, and they arranged to meet with local officials to talk about policies that could have prevented the shooting. Younger voters would be in a unique position to advocate for what does and doesn't work when it comes to preventing gun violence in schools because they are closer to the issue, and they are the ones at risk if policies fail. As such, it's important that 16-year-olds and 17-year-olds who want to vote are given the opportunity to do so, especially when it comes to the issues that matter most to them.

In addition to gun violence, 16- and 17-year-olds also bear the greatest burden, compared to older generations, when it comes to the effects of climate change, so they should be able to have a say when it comes to potential solutions. The effects of the climate crisis are already being experienced today: my family was forced to evacuate during the Marshall Fire in Colorado. Colorado doesn't usually get wildfires in December, but warm temperatures and strong winds quickly fueled the spread of the fire, which ultimately destroyed over 1,000 homes. I learned that day that climate change is real, and it is here, and it is everyone's responsibility to do whatever we can to mitigate it. Numerous reports suggest that 2030 is the tipping point at which the damage caused by climate change will become irreversible. By then, current 16- and 17-year-olds will be in their mid-twenties, facing unknown and potentially disastrous repercussions. Lowering the voting age to 16 years of age would bring those who are most impacted by this issue into the conversation while encouraging immediate action on climate change.

While some argue that teenagers are not mature enough to make decisions about politics, I would counter that politics affect teenagers just as much as anyone else, and any person of any age is motivated to be informed about things that affect their lives. 16- and 17-year-olds certainly have enough maturity to recognize that voting is a responsibility that shouldn't be taken lightly or without being informed. The perspective that they should only be allowed to participate in big elections like those for president and congressional representatives is also flawed because it fails to account for the fact that local and state political issues and new laws affect teenagers too. If we are going to extend the right to vote to younger generations, we need to grant them access to the full spectrum of civic participation.

Voting is essential to the preservation and well-being of our democracy. When 16-year-olds and 17-year-olds are so deeply impacted by political issues like gun violence and climate change, it's unfair that they do not have a say in how these issues are handled by the politicians who represent them. Therefore, it is critical that we consider lowering the voting age to 16 to ensure that more people are fairly represented and have the ability to contribute to the solutions to the most pressing issues of our time.

Practice Writing Prompts

We have included two practice writing prompts. Choose one to use as your Knowledge Check for this chapter. The other is included for you to practice with at your convenience. You may also practice using the sample prompt.

Practice Writing Prompt 1: Alternative Energy

The United States—and the entire world—is at a crossroads when it comes to our sources of energy. Traditional fossil fuels, including coal, petroleum, and natural gas, are our primary fuel sources, and are responsible for everything from powering our vehicles to warming our homes and providing electricity for our favorite gadgets. However, fossil fuels are also responsible for emitting carbon dioxide into the atmosphere, which most climate scientists feel adversely impacts the environment and contributes to global warming. As a result, some have called for increased exploration and investment in renewable, non-fossil sources of energy, including hydroelectric, solar, nuclear, and wind power, which are better for the environment and would also help reduce our dependence on foreign oil supplies. Efforts to find new, more efficient, and more cost-effective methods for harnessing the power of these alternative energy sources is already underway. As we continue to march through the 21st century, the question of how much to invest in alternative sources of energy becomes ever more prominent.

Read and carefully consider these perspectives. Each suggests a particular way of thinking about alternative energy exploration.

Perspective One	Perspective Two	Perspective Three
The United States has sufficient fuel from coal, oil, and gas, and we should continue to use these fossil fuels for all of our energy needs. Their negative effects are not fully understood, and the science isn't definitive.	A serious and committed investment in alternative energy is long overdue. Our reliance on fossil fuels has kept us dependent on energy sources that impact our planet, and we cannot afford any further apathy to their costs.	Continued long-term reliance on fossil fuels isn't sustainable, but quitting "cold turkey" or without a clear plan also isn't realistic. Our nation needs a long-term plan that includes tapering off from fossil fuels and increasing use of alternative, renewable energy sources.

Essay Task

Write a unified, coherent essay on the topic of exploring alternative sources of energy. In your essay, be sure to:

- clearly state your own perspective on the issue and analyze the relationship between your perspective and at least one other perspective
- develop and support your ideas with reasoning and examples
- organize your ideas clearly and logically
- communicate your ideas effectively in standard written English

Your perspective may be in full agreement with any of those given, in partial agreement, or completely different.

NOTES

Practice Writing Prompt 2: Abolishing Letter Grades

For many years, the standard for academic success was an A+ grade. However, in recent years, many educators and psychologists have been questioning the value of assigning letter grades to students. Supporters of the letter-grading system argue that it remains necessary to indicate how well students are performing using a readily understandable scale that is transferable between schools. Others contend that since recent psychological studies suggest effort and time spent learning is more important than the outcomes themselves, there is no need to continue grading students on a scale that places some above others simply for making fewer mistakes. Some suggest that we use alternative scales that measure student effort and improvement over raw achievement, while others believe that we should no longer assign students any kind of grades whatsoever. Individual schools tend to opt into whatever fits their personal education model.

Read and carefully consider these perspectives. Each suggests a particular way of thinking about the issue of abolishing letter grading systems.

Perspective One

The letter grading system works fine as it is. Some students might not like when they get a D, but those letter grades help them understand where they stand and what they need to do to improve.

Perspective Two

We should eliminate letter grading as it needlessly creates hierarchies among students. If someone is known as a "C student," their teachers might not value their efforts as much as if they weren't ranked. Students should be evaluated individually rather than by a totalizing system.

Perspective Three

We can't get rid of grades altogether since we do need some way of determining which students are learning and which are struggling, but a more holistic system that considers students' improvement over time would better serve students and educators than our existing letter system.

Essay Task

Write a unified, coherent essay on the topic of abolishing letter grades. In your essay, be sure to:

- clearly state your own perspective on the issue and analyze the relationship between your perspective and at least one other perspective

- develop and support your ideas with reasoning and examples

- organize your ideas clearly and logically

- communicate your ideas effectively in standard written English

Your perspective may be in full agreement with any of those given, in partial agreement, or completely different.

 NOTES

PART VII

PRACTICE TEST

24 | ACT® Practice Test

CHAPTER

ACT® Practice Test

ACT® PRACTICE TEST

PRACTICE TEST

This practice test is designed to help you recognize your strengths and weaknesses. The questions cover information from all the different sections of the ACT. Use the results to help guide and direct your study time and to measure your progress since the diagnostic test.

>>

PRACTICE TEST ANSWER SHEET

Section 1: English Test

1. Ⓐ Ⓑ Ⓒ Ⓓ
2. Ⓕ Ⓖ Ⓗ Ⓙ
3. Ⓐ Ⓑ Ⓒ Ⓓ
4. Ⓕ Ⓖ Ⓗ Ⓙ
5. Ⓐ Ⓑ Ⓒ Ⓓ
6. Ⓕ Ⓖ Ⓗ Ⓙ
7. Ⓐ Ⓑ Ⓒ Ⓓ
8. Ⓕ Ⓖ Ⓗ Ⓙ
9. Ⓐ Ⓑ Ⓒ Ⓓ
10. Ⓕ Ⓖ Ⓗ Ⓙ
11. Ⓐ Ⓑ Ⓒ Ⓓ
12. Ⓕ Ⓖ Ⓗ Ⓙ
13. Ⓐ Ⓑ Ⓒ Ⓓ
14. Ⓕ Ⓖ Ⓗ Ⓙ
15. Ⓐ Ⓑ Ⓒ Ⓓ

16. Ⓕ Ⓖ Ⓗ Ⓙ
17. Ⓐ Ⓑ Ⓒ Ⓓ
18. Ⓕ Ⓖ Ⓗ Ⓙ
19. Ⓐ Ⓑ Ⓒ Ⓓ
20. Ⓕ Ⓖ Ⓗ Ⓙ
21. Ⓐ Ⓑ Ⓒ Ⓓ
22. Ⓕ Ⓖ Ⓗ Ⓙ
23. Ⓐ Ⓑ Ⓒ Ⓓ
24. Ⓕ Ⓖ Ⓗ Ⓙ
25. Ⓐ Ⓑ Ⓒ Ⓓ
26. Ⓕ Ⓖ Ⓗ Ⓙ
27. Ⓐ Ⓑ Ⓒ Ⓓ
28. Ⓕ Ⓖ Ⓗ Ⓙ
29. Ⓐ Ⓑ Ⓒ Ⓓ
30. Ⓕ Ⓖ Ⓗ Ⓙ

31. Ⓐ Ⓑ Ⓒ Ⓓ
32. Ⓕ Ⓖ Ⓗ Ⓙ
33. Ⓐ Ⓑ Ⓒ Ⓓ
34. Ⓕ Ⓖ Ⓗ Ⓙ
35. Ⓐ Ⓑ Ⓒ Ⓓ
36. Ⓕ Ⓖ Ⓗ Ⓙ
37. Ⓐ Ⓑ Ⓒ Ⓓ
38. Ⓕ Ⓖ Ⓗ Ⓙ
39. Ⓐ Ⓑ Ⓒ Ⓓ
40. Ⓕ Ⓖ Ⓗ Ⓙ
41. Ⓐ Ⓑ Ⓒ Ⓓ
42. Ⓕ Ⓖ Ⓗ Ⓙ
43. Ⓐ Ⓑ Ⓒ Ⓓ
44. Ⓕ Ⓖ Ⓗ Ⓙ
45. Ⓐ Ⓑ Ⓒ Ⓓ

46. Ⓕ Ⓖ Ⓗ Ⓙ
47. Ⓐ Ⓑ Ⓒ Ⓓ
48. Ⓕ Ⓖ Ⓗ Ⓙ
49. Ⓐ Ⓑ Ⓒ Ⓓ
50. Ⓕ Ⓖ Ⓗ Ⓙ
51. Ⓐ Ⓑ Ⓒ Ⓓ
52. Ⓕ Ⓖ Ⓗ Ⓙ
53. Ⓐ Ⓑ Ⓒ Ⓓ
54. Ⓕ Ⓖ Ⓗ Ⓙ
55. Ⓐ Ⓑ Ⓒ Ⓓ
56. Ⓕ Ⓖ Ⓗ Ⓙ
57. Ⓐ Ⓑ Ⓒ Ⓓ
58. Ⓕ Ⓖ Ⓗ Ⓙ
59. Ⓐ Ⓑ Ⓒ Ⓓ
60. Ⓕ Ⓖ Ⓗ Ⓙ

61. Ⓐ Ⓑ Ⓒ Ⓓ
62. Ⓕ Ⓖ Ⓗ Ⓙ
63. Ⓐ Ⓑ Ⓒ Ⓓ
64. Ⓕ Ⓖ Ⓗ Ⓙ
65. Ⓐ Ⓑ Ⓒ Ⓓ
66. Ⓕ Ⓖ Ⓗ Ⓙ
67. Ⓐ Ⓑ Ⓒ Ⓓ
68. Ⓕ Ⓖ Ⓗ Ⓙ
69. Ⓐ Ⓑ Ⓒ Ⓓ
70. Ⓕ Ⓖ Ⓗ Ⓙ
71. Ⓐ Ⓑ Ⓒ Ⓓ
72. Ⓕ Ⓖ Ⓗ Ⓙ
73. Ⓐ Ⓑ Ⓒ Ⓓ
74. Ⓕ Ⓖ Ⓗ Ⓙ
75. Ⓐ Ⓑ Ⓒ Ⓓ

Section 2: Mathematics Test

1. Ⓐ Ⓑ Ⓒ Ⓓ Ⓔ
2. Ⓕ Ⓖ Ⓗ Ⓙ Ⓚ
3. Ⓐ Ⓑ Ⓒ Ⓓ Ⓔ
4. Ⓕ Ⓖ Ⓗ Ⓙ Ⓚ
5. Ⓐ Ⓑ Ⓒ Ⓓ Ⓔ
6. Ⓕ Ⓖ Ⓗ Ⓙ Ⓚ
7. Ⓐ Ⓑ Ⓒ Ⓓ Ⓔ
8. Ⓕ Ⓖ Ⓗ Ⓙ Ⓚ
9. Ⓐ Ⓑ Ⓒ Ⓓ Ⓔ
10. Ⓕ Ⓖ Ⓗ Ⓙ Ⓚ
11. Ⓐ Ⓑ Ⓒ Ⓓ Ⓔ
12. Ⓕ Ⓖ Ⓗ Ⓙ Ⓚ

13. Ⓐ Ⓑ Ⓒ Ⓓ Ⓔ
14. Ⓕ Ⓖ Ⓗ Ⓙ Ⓚ
15. Ⓐ Ⓑ Ⓒ Ⓓ Ⓔ
16. Ⓕ Ⓖ Ⓗ Ⓙ Ⓚ
17. Ⓐ Ⓑ Ⓒ Ⓓ Ⓔ
18. Ⓕ Ⓖ Ⓗ Ⓙ Ⓚ
19. Ⓐ Ⓑ Ⓒ Ⓓ Ⓔ
20. Ⓕ Ⓖ Ⓗ Ⓙ Ⓚ
21. Ⓐ Ⓑ Ⓒ Ⓓ Ⓔ
22. Ⓕ Ⓖ Ⓗ Ⓙ Ⓚ
23. Ⓐ Ⓑ Ⓒ Ⓓ Ⓔ
24. Ⓕ Ⓖ Ⓗ Ⓙ Ⓚ

25. Ⓐ Ⓑ Ⓒ Ⓓ Ⓔ
26. Ⓕ Ⓖ Ⓗ Ⓙ Ⓚ
27. Ⓐ Ⓑ Ⓒ Ⓓ Ⓔ
28. Ⓕ Ⓖ Ⓗ Ⓙ Ⓚ
29. Ⓐ Ⓑ Ⓒ Ⓓ Ⓔ
30. Ⓕ Ⓖ Ⓗ Ⓙ Ⓚ
31. Ⓐ Ⓑ Ⓒ Ⓓ Ⓔ
32. Ⓕ Ⓖ Ⓗ Ⓙ Ⓚ
33. Ⓐ Ⓑ Ⓒ Ⓓ Ⓔ
34. Ⓕ Ⓖ Ⓗ Ⓙ Ⓚ
35. Ⓐ Ⓑ Ⓒ Ⓓ Ⓔ
36. Ⓕ Ⓖ Ⓗ Ⓙ Ⓚ

37. Ⓐ Ⓑ Ⓒ Ⓓ Ⓔ
38. Ⓕ Ⓖ Ⓗ Ⓙ Ⓚ
39. Ⓐ Ⓑ Ⓒ Ⓓ Ⓔ
40. Ⓕ Ⓖ Ⓗ Ⓙ Ⓚ
41. Ⓐ Ⓑ Ⓒ Ⓓ Ⓔ
42. Ⓕ Ⓖ Ⓗ Ⓙ Ⓚ
43. Ⓐ Ⓑ Ⓒ Ⓓ Ⓔ
44. Ⓕ Ⓖ Ⓗ Ⓙ Ⓚ
45. Ⓐ Ⓑ Ⓒ Ⓓ Ⓔ
46. Ⓕ Ⓖ Ⓗ Ⓙ Ⓚ
47. Ⓐ Ⓑ Ⓒ Ⓓ Ⓔ
48. Ⓕ Ⓖ Ⓗ Ⓙ Ⓚ

49. Ⓐ Ⓑ Ⓒ Ⓓ Ⓔ
50. Ⓕ Ⓖ Ⓗ Ⓙ Ⓚ
51. Ⓐ Ⓑ Ⓒ Ⓓ Ⓔ
52. Ⓕ Ⓖ Ⓗ Ⓙ Ⓚ
53. Ⓐ Ⓑ Ⓒ Ⓓ Ⓔ
54. Ⓕ Ⓖ Ⓗ Ⓙ Ⓚ
55. Ⓐ Ⓑ Ⓒ Ⓓ Ⓔ
56. Ⓕ Ⓖ Ⓗ Ⓙ Ⓚ
57. Ⓐ Ⓑ Ⓒ Ⓓ Ⓔ
58. Ⓕ Ⓖ Ⓗ Ⓙ Ⓚ
59. Ⓐ Ⓑ Ⓒ Ⓓ Ⓔ
60. Ⓕ Ⓖ Ⓗ Ⓙ Ⓚ

Section 3: Reading Test

1. Ⓐ Ⓑ Ⓒ Ⓓ
2. Ⓕ Ⓖ Ⓗ Ⓙ
3. Ⓐ Ⓑ Ⓒ Ⓓ
4. Ⓕ Ⓖ Ⓗ Ⓙ
5. Ⓐ Ⓑ Ⓒ Ⓓ
6. Ⓕ Ⓖ Ⓗ Ⓙ
7. Ⓐ Ⓑ Ⓒ Ⓓ
8. Ⓕ Ⓖ Ⓗ Ⓙ

9. Ⓐ Ⓑ Ⓒ Ⓓ
10. Ⓕ Ⓖ Ⓗ Ⓙ
11. Ⓐ Ⓑ Ⓒ Ⓓ
12. Ⓕ Ⓖ Ⓗ Ⓙ
13. Ⓐ Ⓑ Ⓒ Ⓓ
14. Ⓕ Ⓖ Ⓗ Ⓙ
15. Ⓐ Ⓑ Ⓒ Ⓓ
16. Ⓕ Ⓖ Ⓗ Ⓙ

17. Ⓐ Ⓑ Ⓒ Ⓓ
18. Ⓕ Ⓖ Ⓗ Ⓙ
19. Ⓐ Ⓑ Ⓒ Ⓓ
20. Ⓕ Ⓖ Ⓗ Ⓙ
21. Ⓐ Ⓑ Ⓒ Ⓓ
22. Ⓕ Ⓖ Ⓗ Ⓙ
23. Ⓐ Ⓑ Ⓒ Ⓓ
24. Ⓕ Ⓖ Ⓗ Ⓙ

25. Ⓐ Ⓑ Ⓒ Ⓓ
26. Ⓕ Ⓖ Ⓗ Ⓙ
27. Ⓐ Ⓑ Ⓒ Ⓓ
28. Ⓕ Ⓖ Ⓗ Ⓙ
29. Ⓐ Ⓑ Ⓒ Ⓓ
30. Ⓕ Ⓖ Ⓗ Ⓙ
31. Ⓐ Ⓑ Ⓒ Ⓓ
32. Ⓕ Ⓖ Ⓗ Ⓙ

33. Ⓐ Ⓑ Ⓒ Ⓓ
34. Ⓕ Ⓖ Ⓗ Ⓙ
35. Ⓐ Ⓑ Ⓒ Ⓓ
36. Ⓕ Ⓖ Ⓗ Ⓙ
37. Ⓐ Ⓑ Ⓒ Ⓓ
38. Ⓕ Ⓖ Ⓗ Ⓙ
39. Ⓐ Ⓑ Ⓒ Ⓓ
40. Ⓕ Ⓖ Ⓗ Ⓙ

Section 4: Science Test

1. Ⓐ Ⓑ Ⓒ Ⓓ	9. Ⓐ Ⓑ Ⓒ Ⓓ	17. Ⓐ Ⓑ Ⓒ Ⓓ	25. Ⓐ Ⓑ Ⓒ Ⓓ	33. Ⓐ Ⓑ Ⓒ Ⓓ
2. Ⓕ Ⓖ Ⓗ Ⓙ	10. Ⓕ Ⓖ Ⓗ Ⓙ	18. Ⓕ Ⓖ Ⓗ Ⓙ	26. Ⓕ Ⓖ Ⓗ Ⓙ	34. Ⓕ Ⓖ Ⓗ Ⓙ
3. Ⓐ Ⓑ Ⓒ Ⓓ	11. Ⓐ Ⓑ Ⓒ Ⓓ	19. Ⓐ Ⓑ Ⓒ Ⓓ	27. Ⓐ Ⓑ Ⓒ Ⓓ	35. Ⓐ Ⓑ Ⓒ Ⓓ
4. Ⓕ Ⓖ Ⓗ Ⓙ	12. Ⓕ Ⓖ Ⓗ Ⓙ	20. Ⓕ Ⓖ Ⓗ Ⓙ	28. Ⓕ Ⓖ Ⓗ Ⓙ	36. Ⓕ Ⓖ Ⓗ Ⓙ
5. Ⓐ Ⓑ Ⓒ Ⓓ	13. Ⓐ Ⓑ Ⓒ Ⓓ	21. Ⓐ Ⓑ Ⓒ Ⓓ	29. Ⓐ Ⓑ Ⓒ Ⓓ	37. Ⓐ Ⓑ Ⓒ Ⓓ
6. Ⓕ Ⓖ Ⓗ Ⓙ	14. Ⓕ Ⓖ Ⓗ Ⓙ	22. Ⓕ Ⓖ Ⓗ Ⓙ	30. Ⓕ Ⓖ Ⓗ Ⓙ	38. Ⓕ Ⓖ Ⓗ Ⓙ
7. Ⓐ Ⓑ Ⓒ Ⓓ	15. Ⓐ Ⓑ Ⓒ Ⓓ	23. Ⓐ Ⓑ Ⓒ Ⓓ	31. Ⓐ Ⓑ Ⓒ Ⓓ	39. Ⓐ Ⓑ Ⓒ Ⓓ
8. Ⓕ Ⓖ Ⓗ Ⓙ	16. Ⓕ Ⓖ Ⓗ Ⓙ	24. Ⓕ Ⓖ Ⓗ Ⓙ	32. Ⓕ Ⓖ Ⓗ Ⓙ	40. Ⓕ Ⓖ Ⓗ Ⓙ

Section 5: Writing Test

Essay Instructions for Self-Scoring on page 866

SECTION 1: ENGLISH TEST

75 Questions—45 Minutes

Directions: In the following five passages, certain words and phrases are underlined and numbered. In the right-hand column, you will find alternatives for the part that is underlined. In most cases, you are to choose which alternative best expresses the idea, makes the statement appropriate in standard written English, or is worded to best reflect the style and tone of the whole passage. If you think the original version is best, choose "NO CHANGE." Sometimes, you may also find a question in the right-hand column about the underlined part. Here, you should choose the best answer to the question.

You may also find questions about a section of a passage, or a passage in its entirety. These questions do not refer to specific underlined portions of the passage, but rather are identified by a number or numbers in a box.

For each question, choose the answer you consider best. Read each passage through once before you begin to answer the questions that accompany it. For many of the questions, you must read several sentences beyond the questions to determine the answer. Be sure that you have read far enough ahead each time you choose an alternative.

PASSAGE I

FOSSEY'S QUEST

Dian Fossey was a <u>researcher, a visionary and a pioneer</u> in the field of animal conservation. More specifically, Fossey dedicated her life to preserving the endangered mountain gorilla in Africa.

<u>She was born in San Francisco, Fossey made her first trip to Africa in 1963.</u>

At the time, she was 31 years old. In the course of her trip, she met <u>Dr. Louis Leakey. A prominent</u> archaeologist and anthropologist.

1. **A.** NO CHANGE
   B. a researcher visionary and pioneer
   C. a researcher, a visionary, and a pioneer
   D. a researcher and a visionary, pioneer

2. **F.** NO CHANGE
   G. Fossey was born in San Francisco, and made her first trip to Africa, in 1963.
   H. Fossey was born in San Francisco and made her first trip to Africa in 1963.
   J. Born in San Francisco, in 1963 Fossey made her first trip, to Africa.

3. **A.** NO CHANGE
   B. Dr. Louis Leakey. Who was a prominent
   C. Dr. Louis Leakey; prominent
   D. Dr. Louis Leakey, a prominent

GO ON TO THE NEXT PAGE.

Dr. Leakey believed in the importance of research on

large apes, and he <u>encourages</u> Fossey to undertake it.
  ₄

Fossey took up the <u>challenge. Deciding</u> to study
  ₅
mountain gorillas.

    Fossey began her work in the African country of

Zaire, but was forced to <u>leaf</u> because of political unrest.
  ₆
She moved to another African country, Rwanda, where

she established a research camp in a national park.

There, she spent thousands of hours observing the

behavior of gorillas. Her steadfast patience won the trust

of the animals, and they <u>began to accept</u> her presence
  ₇
among them. As a result, she was able to observe

gorillas' behavior that had previously never been seen

by humans.

    <u>Spending so much time to observe the gorillas,</u>
  ₈

<u>Fossey naturally distinguished</u> among them and had
  ₉
particular favorites.

One of these favorites was a young male gorilla <u>name</u>
  ₁₀
Digit.

4. **F.** NO CHANGE
   G. was encouraging
   H. will encourage
   J. encouraged

5. **A.** NO CHANGE
   B. challenge; deciding
   C. challenge deciding
   D. challenge, deciding

6. **F.** NO CHANGE
   G. leave
   H. relieve
   J. reprieve

7. **A.** NO CHANGE
   B. began to accept and also tolerate
   C. began to show an acceptance, even, and also
      a tolerance
   D. began to show that they would be accepting

8. **F.** NO CHANGE
   G. Because she spent so much time observing
      the gorillas
   H. Spending much time in the observation of
      the gorillas
   J. To observe the gorillas

9. **A.** NO CHANGE
   B. Fossey must have distinguished
   C. Fossey did eventually have to distinguish
   D. Fossey was eventually distinguished

10. **F.** NO CHANGE
    G. named
    H. naming
    J. nameable

<u>Still</u>, Digit was killed by a poacher, an illegal hunter of
protected animals. Fossey was stunned and saddened.
She began a public campaign to raise awareness of
the problem of gorilla poaching, a practice that
threatened the continued existence of mountain gorillas.
<u>The rhinoceros, too, from poach has faced grave danger.</u>
Fossey's campaign earned worldwide attention and
support, and she continued to live and work in Africa
for many years thereafter.

[1] In 1980, Fossey took a teaching position at Cornell
University and wrote a book, *Gorillas in the Mist*, that
brought further attention to the crisis of diminishing
numbers of mountain gorillas. [2] Afterward, Fossey
returned to Rwanda and spent the rest of her life working
to protect the mountain gorilla. [3] <u>She continues
working even after her death.</u> [14]

Today, the population of mountain gorillas in
Rwanda is rising, thanks to the legacy of Dian Fossey.

11. **A.** NO CHANGE
    B. Unfortunately
    C. In fact
    D. Because

12. **F.** NO CHANGE
    G. The rhinoceros, too, has faced grave danger
    from poaching.
    H. The rhinoceros faced grave danger. From
    poaching.
    J. OMIT the underlined portion.

13. **A.** NO CHANGE
    B. Her works even after her death continued.
    C. Even after her death, her work continues.
    D. Her works live on even after her death.

14. Which of the following sentences, when inserted
    after Sentence 2 in this paragraph, would provide
    a concrete example to support a statement made
    by the author?

    F. She loved gorillas very much.
    G. She remains well known among
    conservationists.
    H. Her efforts included organizing patrols to
    protect gorillas from poachers.
    J. Another primate conservationist who was
    influenced by Louis Leakey was Jane Goodall.

GO ON TO THE NEXT PAGE.

Question 15 addresses the passage as a whole.

15. Suppose the author of this passage had been assigned to write an essay that discussed whether Fossey's goals justified her very controversial methods. Would this essay successfully address that topic?

A. Yes, because the author details the controversy Fossey inspired.

B. Yes, because the author describes Fossey's important legacy in the field of conservation.

C. No, because the author never offers an opinion as to whether Fossey's work was of any benefit to the mountain gorilla.

D. No, because the author does not mention that any of Fossey's methods were controversial.

PASSAGE II

THE SMOKE THAT THUNDERS

[1]

The Zambezi River is rushing through the border of
                        16
the African countries of Zambia and Zimbabwe.

It is home to one of the most stunning achievements of nature: a spectacular waterfall that is bigger and twice as
                                                        17
large as North America's Niagara Falls. The Kololo tribe,
17
who lived in the area in the 1800s, called the falls "Mosi-oa-Tunya," or "The Smoke That Thunders." Around the same time, British explorers who saw the falls for the
                                                    18
first time dubbed them "The Victoria Falls," after their queen.

16. F. NO CHANGE
    G. The Zambezi River rushes through
    H. The Zambezi River rushed along
    J. The Zambezi River rushes along

17. A. NO CHANGE
    B. twice as large and bigger
    C. bigger
    D. twice as large

18. F. NO CHANGE
    G. who seen the falls
    H. who will have seen the falls
    J. who had been seeing

[2]

The waterfall, <u>which is composed of five actually separate falls</u>, is considered to be one of the seven
₁₉
wonders of the natural world—

and <u>for good reason</u>. Visitors to the falls can spot
₂₀
columns of spray from up to 25 miles away, as millions of cubic meters of water per minute plunge 100 meters over a cliff.

Anyone <u>observing who witnesses</u> this wonder will
₂₁
understand the name "Smoke That Thunders."

The roaring, <u>crashing fall's</u> send up soaking billows
₂₂

of <u>spray. Imagine</u> —a rushing, two-kilometer-wide river
₂₃
makes a sudden plunge downward for over 100 meters, slamming into the gorge below.

[3]

Opposite the cliff, across the gorge, stands a spectacular stretch of <u>rain forest? This</u>
₂₄

forest provides another perspective on the

<u>grandiosity</u> of the falls.
₂₅

19. A. NO CHANGE

B. which is actually five separate composed falls

C. which is actually composed of five separate falls

D. it is actually composed of five separate falls

20. F. NO CHANGE

G. one of the others is the Grand Canyon

H. some people don't think it's that spectacular

J. Africa contains many wonders

21. A. NO CHANGE

B. who witnesses

C. who looks and observes

D. who sees and witnesses

22. F. NO CHANGE

G. crashing's falls

H. crashing falls'

J. crashing falls

23. A. NO CHANGE

B. spray, imagine

C. spray. To imagine

D. spray imagining

24. F. NO CHANGE

G. rain forest this

H. rain forest. This

J. rain forest, this

25. A. NO CHANGE

B. generosity

C. fruitfulness

D. peacefulness

GO ON TO THE NEXT PAGE.

Visitors can enjoy, a walk along a path through the
                    26
lush forest and a breathtaking, spray-soaked vision of

the falls. The Knife Edge Bridge provides a particu-

larly spectacular view of the falls and of the Boiling

Pot, a dramatic turn in the river. As some would say, "a
                                                    27
watched pot never boils." Many visitors choose to view
              27
the sights from above, taking advantage of the services

of pilots who fly small planes filled with tourists over

the falls.

[4]

While the waterfall is the attention-grabbing

attraction of the area, the surrounding Mosi-oa-Tunya

National Park is full of wonders as well. The natural
                                            28
beauty of the local wildlife is to be admired by visitors.
                          28
Among the animals who make their homes at the Mosi-

oa-Tunya National Park are zebras, giraffes, several

species of antelope, wildebeests, a dazzling array of

birds, and rare white rhinos.

[5]

Whichever attractions visitors choose to view

during their time at the Mosi-oa-Tunya National Park,

they will surely never forget the striking power and

beauty of the falls. The image of the massive wall of

water is one that lasts a lifetime.

26. **F.** NO CHANGE
    G. enjoy a walk,
    H. enjoy a walk
    J. enjoy, walking

27. **A.** NO CHANGE
    B. Some say a watched pot never boils.
    C. As the saying goes, "a watched pot never boils."
    D. OMIT the underlined portion.

28. **F.** NO CHANGE
    G. Visitors can admire the natural beauty of the local wildlife.
    H. But the natural beauty of the local wildlife can certainly be admired by visitors and those who come to see it.
    J. OMIT the underlined portion.

Questions 29 and 30 ask about the passage as a whole.

29. Suppose the author had been asked to write an essay describing why it is more worthwhile to see Victoria Falls than the other six wonders of the natural world. Would this essay meet the assignment?
    A. Yes, because it describes in detail how marvelous Victoria Falls is.
    B. Yes, because it does not mention most of the other wonders of the natural world.
    C. No, because it does not attempt to compare Victoria Falls to any other attractions.
    D. No, because the author does not seem to think that Victoria Falls is a very interesting place to visit.

30. The writer wishes to insert a paragraph about a place where visitors can buy locally made crafts. This paragraph would most logically be inserted between:

    F. Paragraph 1 and Paragraph 2.
    G. Paragraph 2 and Paragraph 3.
    H. Paragraph 3 and Paragraph 4.
    J. Paragraph 4 and Paragraph 5.

PASSAGE III

THE REAL VALUE OF MONEY

[31] Although I always considered myself a relatively responsible person, I can honestly say that I didn't understand the real value of money until the

winter of my senior year in high <u>school. During</u> which I
₃₂
learned valuable lessons—about money and the value of friendship.

I've always been a somewhat bookish kid, and ever since I could read, I had my face buried in one book after another. The tons of family photos that show me sitting and reading will <u>contest</u> to this fact. In truth, I
₃₃
haven't found a genre that I don't like, but my favorite is adventure. Tales of bravery and daring in the face of seemingly certain danger in exotic locations have captured and held my imagination for as long as I can remember.

31. The author would like to add an introductory sentence to this passage. Which of the following would be the most effective?

    A. Are you a fan of adventure stories and comic books?
    B. Do you know the real value of money in your life?
    C. How did you earn money when you were in high school?
    D. How much do you know about your best friend?

32. F. NO CHANGE
    G. school; during
    H. school, during
    J. school: during

33. A. NO CHANGE
    B. attest
    C. regress
    D. egress

GO ON TO THE NEXT PAGE.

My earliest exposure to adventure stories was from my dad, <u>who read me classic tales like *Treasure Island*</u>
34
and *The Count of Monte Cristo*, one chapter at a time, while I lay in bed each night before falling asleep.

It was late in the middle of my final year in junior high school that I discovered my latest obsession—comic books—and I've been hooked ever since. Having amazing illustrations alongside stories of action and adventure with characters with fantastic powers and abilities <u>was like catnip to me and really attracted me</u>.
35
Everything about them, from the smell of the paper to the bold and colorful artwork and the fantastical tales,

<u>kidnapped</u> my imagination and attention, along with
36
any spare money I had.

It's fair to say that building a respectable comic book collection was the early major initiative of my adolescence. I spent countless hours—and whatever meager savings <u>we could</u> cobble together—to gather together as
37
many of the comic books I wanted as possible.

My favorite character was, and still is, Spider-Man—the notion of a socially awkward and bookish young adult suddenly having these incredible superpowers and struggling with how to use them responsibly while finding his way in the world really resonated <u>with me? Ever since</u> I
38
discovered my arachnid-like role model,

34. F. NO CHANGE

   G. who read me classic tales

   H. who was reading classic tales like *Treasure Island*

   J. who would be reading classic tales like *Treasure Island*

35. A. NO CHANGE

   B. was attractive to me, like catnip

   C. was as attractive to me as catnip would be to a cat

   D. was like catnip to me

36. F. NO CHANGE

   G. captured

   H. hijacked

   J. attacked

37. A. NO CHANGE

   B. they could

   C. she could

   D. I could

38. F. NO CHANGE

   G. with me ever since

   H. with me. Ever since

   J. with me, ever since

it was, as I possibly could acquire, as many Spider-Man
<u>comics as I could—my mission.</u>
39

My parents always said that <u>when I set my mind on something</u>, there was absolutely no stopping me, and
40
that notion certainly applied to my comic-collecting
passion. Every extra dollar I received—from birthdays
and holidays to the money I made during my first
summer job, <u>making pizza boxes cleaning tables and
washing dishes</u> at the pizzeria a few blocks from my
41
house—went to buying comic books. Gino, my boss at
the pizzeria, jokingly asked me if he should just send my
paycheck to the comic book store to save me the trouble.
I actually considered his offer, believe it or not.

A few years passed and my collection grew. And so
did my friendship with Simon, my next-door neighbor
and classmate. He shared my love of comics, and it
really became something we bonded over, although his
favorite character was <u>Batman (there's no accounting for
taste).</u> We spent countless hours in the tree house at the
42
northeast corner of my family's yard reading, discussing,
and trading comic books. We even created a small
comic book club, which we affectionately dubbed "The
Adventurers' Realm," where other like-minded kids in
the neighborhood could join and share in our love of
comic books. Life was great—until everything changed,
seemingly overnight.

39. A. NO CHANGE

   B. it was my mission to acquire as many
   Spider-Man comics as I possibly could.

   C. to me, acquiring as many Spider-Man comics
   as I possibly could was a mission.

   D. as many as I possibly could, it was my mission
   to acquire Spider-Man comics.

40. F. NO CHANGE

   G. when I set up my mind on something

   H. when I set my mind with something

   J. when I set up my mind with something

41. A. NO CHANGE

   B. making pizza boxes, cleaning tables, and
   washing dishes

   C. making pizza boxes; cleaning tables, and
   washing dishes

   D. making pizza, boxes cleaning, tables and
   washing, dishes

42. F. NO CHANGE

   G. Batman, there's no accounting for taste.

   H. Batman. There's no accounting for taste.

   J. there's no accounting for taste, Batman.

I remember being in the tree house one afternoon when Simon came over. He didn't look like himself. His face was pale and he looked sullen beyond belief—I knew something was wrong, and I asked him if everything was ok.

"I just spoke to my parents," he said. He just lost it—he started crying, and I knew that whatever he told me next was going to be serious. "My dad...he has cancer."

The new reality of his <u>dads illness</u> was hard on
                                     43
him and his whole family, and I did my best to support my friend after that, in any way that I could. Our high school did what it could as well, and even decided to hold a silent raffle to help raise money for Simon's dad's medical bills. When I heard that this raffle was happening, I knew what I had to do.

I thought about the things that I owned that I could donate to the raffle. But the truth is, I knew what I was going to do already. I was prepared to say goodbye to my comic book collection, and I never once second-guessed my decision. Why? Because there are things more important than money or the possessions we own and cherish—and they are the connections we have and nurture with our families, friends, and loved ones.

43. **A.** NO CHANGE
    B. dads' illness
    C. dad's illness
    D. dad's illness's

Questions 44 and 45 ask about the passage as a whole.

---

44. The author of this essay is thinking of submitting their work to a school contest, which is calling for writing about an experience of emotional growth during adolescence. Does the essay fulfill this requirement?

    F. No, because the essay is mainly about comic book collecting.

    G. No, because the essay was written when the author was an adult.

    H. Yes, because the author discusses learning the value of money and friendship.

    J. Yes, because the author tells a story that we all could relate to.

45. The author would like to add a concluding sentence to this passage. Which of the following would be the most effective?

   A. As I learned that winter, those bonds beat any adventure story I've ever come across and ever will.

   B. I eventually lost interest in comic books after high school, and really got into skateboarding.

   C. My friend Simon and I both went to different colleges, but we still kept in close contact.

   D. After graduating from college, I bought the pizzeria that I worked in as a youth.

PASSAGE IV

CONSERVING A NATURAL RESOURCE

[1]

The Great Smoky Mountains National Park is created of over half a million acres of the Appalachian Mountains, straddling the border between Tennessee and North Carolina. It attracts more visitors each year than any other national park. This may be in large part due to its central location—it is within a day's drive for more than half of the American population—but surely most wouldn't make the trip if the mountains were not so majestic. The blue mist that gives the mountains their name rise above its peaks. The mountains are rich with streams, waterfalls, vegetation, and wildlife.

Hikers choose among many trails, ranging from a brisk, uphill walk, a truly challenging three-hour hike to the dramatic view from a mountain peak. However, it's likely that many of the visitors who enjoy the scenery

46. **F.** NO CHANGE
   G. is owned by
   H. consists of
   J. establishes

47. **A.** NO CHANGE
   B. rising above
   C. rises above
   D. rose above

48. **F.** NO CHANGE
   G. walk to a truly
   H. walk and a truly
   J. walk, truly a

GO ON TO THE NEXT PAGE.

are unaware of how this stunning stretch of land came
to be preserved as a national park.

[2]

The idea of establishing a national park in the
mountains of the Southeastern United States first
emerged in the 1880s, when conservationists wished to
protect the vast acres of forest area. The decision was
a politically tricky one that required balancing logging
interests with conservation concerns. Recognizing that
trying to ban logging was <u>unrealistic</u>, conservationists
suggested that in a national park area, the government
49

could regulate the logging <u>that, unchecked;</u> threatened
to destroy the entire forest. 51
50

[3]

[1] In 1926, Congress approved the idea of a national
park in the Southeast. [2] Next, it had to determine what
the location of this park would be. [3] This was no easy
task; initially, about sixty different sites were proposed
for the park. [4] After the decision was made, the United
States Geological <u>Survey an organization</u> that explored
and mapped land in the United States, created a
52

49. A. NO CHANGE
   B. unrealistically
   C. unreal
   D. not real

50. F. NO CHANGE
   G. that unchecked
   H. that, unchecked
   J. that, unchecked,

51. The purpose of Paragraph 2, as it relates to the
rest of the essay, is primarily to:

   A. give us a feeling for the motives behind the
   establishment of the park.
   B. encourage us to conserve endangered land by
   creating more national parks.
   C. argue that logging is a threat to America's
   national parks.
   D. provide background for further discussion of
   the conflict between environmentalists and
   loggers.

52. F. NO CHANGE
   G. Survey, an organization
   H. surveyed an organization
   J. surveys an organization

topographical chart of a proposed park stretching from western North Carolina to eastern Tennessee. [53]

[4]

To make this plan become a reality, it would be no easy task.
54

Unlike the vast stretches of land in the American West that had been preserved as national parks, much of the designated land was owned in privacy. It would
55
have to be purchased and then deeded to the federal government.

This, of course, meant that an enormous amount of
56
dollars would have to be raised to purchase land from
56
private owners and lumber companies, some of whom recognized their leverage and hiked their prices. [57]

[5]

Fundraisers in North Carolina and Tennessee collected over two million dollars from private citizens. Each of the two states' legislatures provided over a million dollars, and—just as the park's supporters feared—they had fallen short; they hadn't raised enough money. Just
58
as it appeared that the conservationists had failed, the Rockefeller family rushed to the rescue by donating an additional five million dollars. The federal government

53. Suppose the writer wanted to add the following sentence to Paragraph 3:

After much debate, the Smoky Mountains region emerged as the winner.

This sentence would most logically be added:

A. before Sentence 1.
B. between Sentence 1 and Sentence 2.
C. between Sentence 3 and Sentence 4.
D. after Sentence 4.

54. F. NO CHANGE
G. It would not be an easy task, to make this plan reality.
H. No, it would not be an easy task to make this plan a reality.
J. Making this plan a reality would be no easy task.

55. A. NO CHANGE
B. privately owned
C. owned by privacy
D. owned by private

56. F. NO CHANGE
G. amount of money
H. number of money
J. dollar

57. The writer's description of the landowners who hiked their prices makes the acquisition of the land seem even more:

A. challenging.
B. heroic.
C. foolish.
D. immoral.

58. F. NO CHANGE
G. short—they hadn't raised enough money.
H. short: they hadn't raised enough money.
J. short.

GO ON TO THE NEXT PAGE.

PRACTICE TEST

provided the final one and a half million dollars needed to complete the purchase. On June 15, 1934, over 800 majestic square miles of forested peaks were designated a national park.

Questions 59 and 60 ask about the passage as a whole.

59. Suppose the writer wanted to examine the conflict between loggers and environmentalists more closely. In order to expand upon material already present, this information would most logically be added to:

   A. Paragraph 1.
   B. Paragraph 2.
   C. Paragraph 3.
   D. Paragraph 4.

60. Suppose that the author had been asked to write an essay detailing the attractions that tourists can enjoy when they visit the Great Smoky Mountains National Park. Would this essay successfully fulfill that assignment?

   F. Yes, because it describes the park's beauty.
   G. Yes, because it mentions the park's popularity with visitors.
   H. No, because it concentrates on how the park was established.
   J. No, because it does not describe the park as being a place that tourists would want to visit.

PASSAGE V

A MAYAN WORLDVIEW

The ancient Mayans inhabited the area that now consists of Mexico, Guatemala, Belize, Honduras, and El Salvador. Their <u>rich civilization flourished</u> from the third through the ninth centuries.
61

61. A. NO CHANGE
   B. civilization flourished and was rich
   C. civilization flourished, richly,
   D. civilization was rich and flourished

Plus the many notable achievements of this society was the
62
Mayan understanding of astronomy, which was manifest

not only in Mayan science but in every aspect of the culture.

Ancient Mayans kept meticulous records of the

movements of the sun and moon, the planets, and the

stars that were visible to the naked eye. Based on the

solar year, they created a calendar, which they used to

keep track of time. So were astute the Mayans' observa-
63
tions that they could predict such events as solar and
63
lunar eclipses, and the movement of the planets.

For the ancient Mayans, astronomy was not just a
64
science; it was a combination of science, religion,

and philosophy that was found into many aspects of
65
their lives, including architecture. Mayan ceremonial

buildings, for example, were aligned exact with compass
66
points, so that at the fall and spring equinoxes, light

would flood the interior of the building. These buildings

were designed and built as acts of worship to the Mayan
67
gods: science, architecture, and religion, then, were all
67
intricately and beautifully blended. [68]

Government, too, was inextricably linked with

astronomy. The beginning and ending of the reigns of

Mayan leaders appear to have been timed to coincide

with astronomical events.

---

62. **F.** NO CHANGE
   G. Despite
   H. Among
   J. Between

63. **A.** NO CHANGE
   B. So astute were the Mayans' observations
   C. So were the astute Mayans' observations
   D. So were the Mayans' astute observations

64. **F.** NO CHANGE
   G. merely
   H. just
   J. not

65. **A.** NO CHANGE
   B. had to find
   C. found its way
   D. could be found

66. **F.** NO CHANGE
   G. exactly
   H. to be exact
   J. exacting

67. **A.** NO CHANGE
   B. Mayan gods,
   C. Mayan gods;
   D. Mayan gods

68. Which of the following words best expresses the writer's tone in this paragraph?
   F. Gleeful
   G. Indifferent
   H. Resentful
   J. Neutral

GO ON TO THE NEXT PAGE.

Ancient Mayan <u>artwork, carvings and murals—show</u>
[69] royalty wearing symbols relating to the sun, moon, and sky.
The Mayans believed that the sun and moon were guided
across the sky by benevolent gods and that these gods
needed human help to thwart the evil gods <u>and wanted</u> to
[70] stop them. Human intervention took the form of different rituals, including sacrifice. It was considered an
honor to die for this cause, and those who were sacri-
ficed were believed <u>to have</u> gained eternal life.
[71]

The planet Venus, which can often be seen by the
unaided eye, played a large role in Mayan life. <u>Mayans</u>
<u>appeared to Venus</u> in the sky as a means of timing when
[72] they attacked enemies. The night sky, then, among its
other duties, served as a call to war.

<u>In short, the</u> ancient Mayans, in looking to the night
[73] sky for <u>guidance; discovered</u> a natural order around
[74] which they were able to base a rich and textured civilization. [75]

69. A. NO CHANGE
　　B. artwork, carvings, and murals, show
　　C. artwork, including carvings and
　　　　murals—shows
　　D. artwork shows

70. F. NO CHANGE
　　G. who wanted
　　H. which are wanting
　　J. they want

71. A. NO CHANGE
　　B. and felt they
　　C. that they would soon have
　　D. one day they would have

72. F. NO CHANGE
　　G. Venus, to all appearances,
　　H. The Mayans used the appearance of Venus
　　J. Venus appeared to be to the Mayans

73. A. NO CHANGE
　　B. Shortly, the
　　C. To sum up the
　　D. Lastly, the

74. F. NO CHANGE
　　G. guidance, discovered
　　H. guidance discovering
　　J. guidance: discovered

75. The writer wants to add a sentence to the end
　　of the last paragraph describing the remarkable
　　astronomical accomplishments of the ancient
　　Babylonians. What effect would this have?

　　A. It would make the paragraph into a more
　　　　effective conclusion.
　　B. It would make the paragraph serve as a transi-
　　　　tion to another topic.
　　C. It would provide an illustrative detail.
　　D. It would contradict the information in the rest
　　　　of the passage.

STOP.

**If you finish before time is up, you may check your work on
this section only. Do not turn to any other section in the test.**

SECTION 2: MATHEMATICS TEST

60 Questions—60 Minutes

Directions: Solve each problem, choose the correct answer, and then fill in the corresponding oval on your answer sheet.

Do not dwell on problems that take too long. First, solve as many as you can; then, you can return to others you have left.

You are permitted to use a calculator on this test. You may use your calculator for any problem you like, but some of the problems may best be completed without a calculator.

Note: Unless otherwise stated, all of the following should be assumed:

1. Illustrative figures are NOT necessarily drawn to scale.

2. Geometric figures lie in a plane.

3. The word *line* indicates a straight line.

4. The word *average* indicates arithmetic mean.

---

1. It takes Leah 7 minutes 20 seconds to complete a segment of a workout. This is 20% less time than it took her to complete the same segment one month ago. What was her original time one month ago?

   A. 1 minute, 28 seconds

   B. 3 minutes, 40 seconds

   C. 5 minutes, 52 seconds

   D. 9 minutes, 10 seconds

   E. 36 minutes, 40 seconds

2. If $a = 5$, what value of b solves the proportion below?

$$\frac{a}{6} = \frac{b}{15}$$

   F. 15

   G. $12\frac{1}{2}$

   H. 10

   J. $2\frac{1}{2}$

   K. 2

3. In the figure below, points X, Y, and Z lie on the same line. What is the measure of $\angle WYZ$?

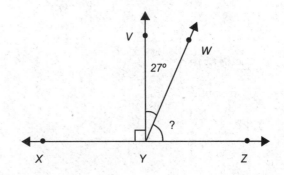

   A. 63°

   B. 73°

   C. 90°

   D. 117°

   E. 153°

GO ON TO THE NEXT PAGE.

4. Determine the fifth term of the sequence
$$\frac{3}{4}, \frac{4}{9}, \frac{5}{16}, \ldots$$

   F. $\dfrac{4}{25}$

   G. $\dfrac{8}{49}$

   H. $\dfrac{7}{37}$

   J. $\dfrac{7}{36}$

   K. $\dfrac{6}{25}$

5. Marta cuts four pieces of ribbon, each 1.5 feet long, from a spool of ribbon. If 27.5 feet of ribbon are now left on the spool, how many feet of ribbon did it originally contain?

   A. 21.5

   B. 26

   C. 29

   D. 33.5

   E. 39.5

6. Let $f(x) = \begin{cases} \sqrt{2x-3} - x, & x > 5 \\ 1 - 2x, & x \le 5 \end{cases}$.

   Compute $f(6)$.

   F. −11

   G. −6

   H. −3

   J. 3

   K. 9

7. If $\sqrt{w}$ is greater than 8, which of the following could be the value of w?

   A. 9

   B. 16

   C. 49

   D. 64

   E. 81

8. Line segment $\overline{AB}$ in the coordinate plane has endpoint A located at (3, −2). If the midpoint of the line segment is (−3, −1), what are the coordinates of endpoint B?

   F. (0, −1.5)

   G. (9, −3)

   H. (−9, 0)

   J. (−15, 1)

   K. (−3, 0)

9. Which of these does NOT describe y as a function of x?

   A. $y = 6$

   B.

x	1	2	4	8	9	10
y	−2	1	−2	0	−2	3

   C.

x	15	10	5	0	−5	−10
y	3	3	3	3	3	3

   D. $f(x) = x(1 - 2x)(3x + 1)$

   E.

x	−3	2	1	5	−1	2
y	0	2	4	6	8	10

10. A bag contains only red, blue, and green marbles. There are a total of 20 marbles in the bag, and the probability of NOT selecting a blue marble is $\dfrac{1}{4}$. How many blue marbles are in the bag?

   F. 4

   G. 5

   H. 8

   J. 10

   K. 15

11. Which of the following pairs of lines are parallel?

A. $3y = 2x - 1$ and $y = -\dfrac{3}{2}x + 1$

B. $y = 2x + 1$ and $y = 1 - 2x$

C. $\dfrac{1}{2}x - y = 2$ and $2y = x - 1$

D. $2y = 5x$ and $5y = 2x$

E. $x = 3$ and $y = 1$

12. A nutritionist prescribes a client two supplements, vitamin D and a turmeric blend, to be administered in a ratio of 4:3. If $2\dfrac{1}{4}$ teaspoons of the turmeric blend is the prescribed dose, what is the dose of vitamin D?

F. $2\dfrac{3}{4}$ teaspoons

G. 3 teaspoons

H. $3\dfrac{3}{4}$ teaspoons

J. 4 teaspoons

K. 9 teaspoons

13. In an experiment, the data Kenan collected strongly supports the conclusion that as the percentage of nutrient solution applied to lima bean seeds increases, the number of hours needed for the seed to germinate decreases. Which of these scatterplots could represent Kenan's data?

A.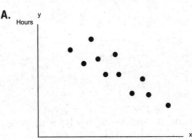

B.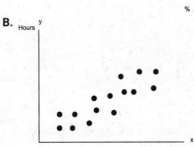

C.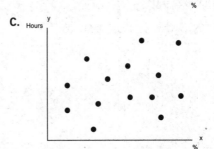

D.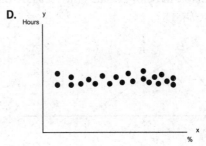

E.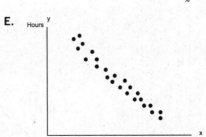

GO ON TO THE NEXT PAGE.

14. Michelle posted a dining room set for sale for $800 using an online auction store. Following weeks of receiving no bids on the set, she reduced the price by 15%. What is the new asking price for the dining room set?

    F. $120

    G. $680

    H. $785

    J. $815

    K. $920

15. For all m and n, $-m(n - m) + n(m - n) =$

    A. $m^2 + n^2$

    B. $(m - n)^2$

    C. $(m + n)^2$

    D. $n^2 - m^2$

    E. $m^2 - n^2$

16. Which number is a root of the equation $5(x - 4)(x + 2) = 0$?

    F. -4

    G. -2

    H. 0

    J. 2

    K. 5

17. In the diagram below, what is the measure of angle BCD?

    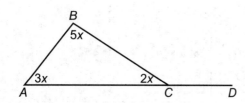

    A. $18°$

    B. $36°$

    C. $90°$

    D. $126°$

    E. $144°$

18. A jacket that normally sells for $75 is on sale for $50. By what percent is the original price discounted for this sale?

    F. 20%

    G. 25%

    H. $33\dfrac{1}{3}$%

    J. 50%

    K. 75%

19. If the point $(-3, 2)$ is on the graph of $y = f(x)$, what is the corresponding point on the graph of $g(x) = f(x + 1) - 4$?

    A. $(-7, 1)$

    B. $(-4, 6)$

    C. $(-2, 6)$

    D. $(-4, -2)$

    E. $(-2, -2)$

20. If an inch of wire costs $0.20, how much will 5.25 feet of wire cost?

    F. $1.05

    G. $2.40

    H. $12.60

    J. $63

    K. $315

21. $\dfrac{1}{3x-1} - \dfrac{2-9x}{1-3x} = $ _____

    A. -3

    B. 0

    C. $\dfrac{9x-1}{6x-2}$

    D. $-\dfrac{9x+1}{6x-2}$

    E. Undefined

22. A rectangle has a length of 8 inches and a width of 3 inches. What is the width, in inches, of a rectangle whose length and width are in the same proportion and whose perimeter is 44 inches?

F. 6

G. 11

H. 12

J. 16

K. 22

23. Hobarth Used Books charges a flat fee of $8.50 per shipment plus $2.25 for each book. If Joon orders b books, what is the cost of his order?

A. 2.25b dollars

B. 2.25 + 8.50b dollars

C. 8.50 + 2.25b dollars

D. (2.25 + 8.50)b dollars

E. 8.50 + 2.25 + b dollars

24. The garden in the figure below was created by adding equal semicircles to the four faces of a square. If the perimeter of this garden is 16π feet, what is its area in square feet?

F. 64 + 8π

G. 64 + 32π

H. 64 + 64π

J. 256 + 32π

K. 256 + 64π

25. Which of the following best describes the graph on the number line below?

A. $-2 \leq x < 2$

B. $-2 < x \leq 2$

C. $-2 \leq x \leq 2$

D. $-2 < x < 2$

E. $x > 2$

26. Suppose n is an odd integer. Which of the following must be an odd integer?

F. $n + 3$

G. $2n$

H. $n - 1$

J. n^2

K. $\dfrac{1}{3}n$

27. If the area of a square is 144 square inches, what is the length of a diagonal of this square?

A. $2\sqrt{12}$ inches

B. $2\sqrt{6}$ inches

C. 12 inches

D. $12\sqrt{2}$ inches

E. 24 inches

GO ON TO THE NEXT PAGE.

28. The graph of $g(x)$ on the interval $[-5, 5]$ is shown below:

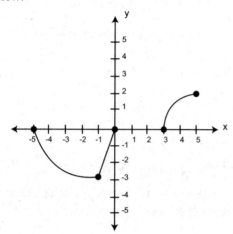

On what interval(s) is the graph of $g(x)$ decreasing?

F. $(-3, 0)$

G. $(-5, -1)$

H. $(-1, 0) \cup (3, 5)$

J. $(-1, 3)$

K. It is never decreasing.

29. Two sides of a triangle have lengths 7 and 2. Which of the following could be the perimeter of this triangle?

A. 9

B. 11

C. 14

D. 16

E. 18

30. Consider the circle whose equation is $(x - 1)^2 + (y - 1)^2 = 4$. Which of these lines intersects the circle at exactly one point?

F. $x = -1$

G. $y = x$

H. $y = -x$

J. $y = 3 - x$

K. $y = 3$

31. Jeff tracks the number of times various exercises or movements appear in his daily X-Fit workouts over a period. The data he compiles is illustrated in the following figure.

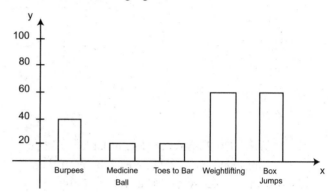

Based on Jeff's data, what is the probability that a workout contains either box jumps or weightlifting?

A. 0.12

B. 0.3

C. 0.4

D. 0.6

E. 0.7

32. In right triangle TRI, $TR = 8$ and $RI = 6$. What is the length of line segment IT?

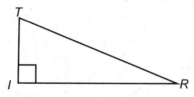

F. 10

G. $2\sqrt{7}$

H. 28

J. $\sqrt{2}$

K. Cannot be determined from the given information

33. The length of a square is increased by 5, and its width is decreased by 2 to create a rectangle. If the perimeter of the square is 4s, what is the area of the rectangle, in terms of s?

A. $4s + 6$

B. $2s + 3$

C. $s^2 - 10$

D. $s^2 + 3s - 10$

E. $s^2 + 7s + 10$

34. In the right triangle XYZ below, $\cos \angle YXZ = \dfrac{4}{5}$. What is the value of $\tan \angle ZYX$?

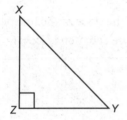

F. $\dfrac{3}{5}$

G. $\dfrac{3}{4}$

H. $\dfrac{4}{5}$

J. $\dfrac{5}{4}$

K. $\dfrac{4}{3}$

35. There are twice as many boys as girls in Mr. Botti's math class. The class's average grade on a recent test was 84. If the girls' average grade was 91, what was the boys' average grade?

A. 70

B. 77

C. 80.5

D. 87.5

E. 98

36. Which of the following is the graph of the solution set of $3x - 9 \leq 15$?

37. The figure below was formed by combining two equal squares, such that a vertex of one square is at the center of the other square. The area of the shaded region is x. In terms of x, what is the area of the unshaded region?

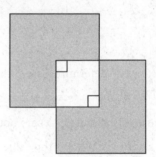

A. $\dfrac{6x}{7}$

B. $\dfrac{3x}{4}$

C. $\dfrac{x}{6}$

D. $\dfrac{x}{7}$

E. $\dfrac{x}{8}$

GO ON TO THE NEXT PAGE.

38. The average of three different positive integers is 99. What is the greatest possible value for one of these integers?

   F. 33

   G. 96

   H. 294

   J. 295

   K. 296

39. In right triangle ABC, what is the measure of angle BCA?

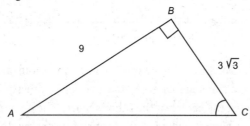

   A. 90°

   B. 60°

   C. 45°

   D. 30°

   E. Cannot be determined from the given information

40. Suppose $(-1, 2)$ and $(3, -x)$ are points on a line with slope $-\frac{1}{4}$. What is the value of $\frac{1}{2}x$?

   F. -1

   G. $\frac{-1}{2}$

   H. $\frac{1}{2}$

   J. 1

   K. 2

41. In the figure below, lines l_1 and l_2 are parallel. What is the value of n?

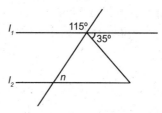

   A. 35°

   B. 65°

   C. 80°

   D. 100°

   E. 115°

42. What is the slope of the line perpendicular to a line whose equation is $3x = 4y - 1$?

   F. -4

   G. $-\frac{4}{3}$

   H. $\frac{3}{4}$

   J. 3

   K. 4

43. Which of the following numbers is equivalent to 0.000000301 on a number line?

   A. 3.16×10^6

   B. 3.21×10^{-6}

   C. 3.01×10^{-7}

   D. 2.01×10^{-8}

   E. 2.99×10^{-9}

44. In triangle *XYZ* below, what is the length of segment *XZ*?

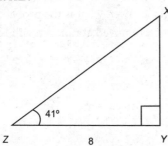

F. 8 cos 41°

G. 8 sin 41°

H. $\dfrac{8}{\cos 41°}$

J. $\dfrac{8}{\sin 41°}$

K. 8 tan(41)

45. If $f(x) = \dfrac{x}{2x-1}$ and $g(x) = \dfrac{2}{x}$, what is $(f \circ g)(x)$?

A. 1

B. $\dfrac{4x-2}{x}$

C. $\dfrac{2}{2x-1}$

D. $\dfrac{2}{x(2x-1)}$

E. $\dfrac{2}{4-x}$

46. A student has a 20-section spinner. She is going to color each section red, yellow, or blue. She wants the probability of landing on a blue section to be $\dfrac{1}{4}$, and she wants the probability of landing on a yellow section to be $\dfrac{1}{4}$ of the probability of landing on a red section. How many sections should she color red?

F. 3

G. 4

H. 5

J. 8

K. 12

47. Of the 24 guests who attended a barbecue, 8 guests ate hot dogs and 12 guests ate chicken. If 4 people ate both hot dogs and chicken, what fraction of the guests ate neither?

A. $\dfrac{2}{3}$

B. $\dfrac{1}{2}$

C. $\dfrac{1}{3}$

D. $\dfrac{1}{5}$

E. $\dfrac{1}{6}$

48. For all nonzero values of *a* and *b*, $\dfrac{\dfrac{1}{a}-\dfrac{1}{b}}{\dfrac{1}{a}+\dfrac{1}{b}} =$

F. 0

G. $b^2 - a^2$

H. $\dfrac{a+b}{a-b}$

J. $\dfrac{b-a}{b+a}$

K. $\dfrac{a-b}{a+b}$

PRACTICE TEST

GO ON TO THE NEXT PAGE.

49. In a right triangle ABC, the measure of angle C is 30°. If the length of BC is 4 meters, what is the length of the leg AB?

    A. $\dfrac{4\sqrt{3}}{3}$ meters

    B. $4\sqrt{3}$ meters

    C. 2 meters

    D. 4 meters

    E. 8 meters

50. $\dfrac{\left(\sin x - \cos x\right)^2}{\left(\sin x + \cos x\right)^2} =$

    F. $\sin^2 x - \cos^2 x$

    G. $\left(\sin x - \cos x\right)^2$

    H. $\dfrac{1 - \sin 2x}{1 + \sin 2x}$

    J. $1 - \sin 2x$

    K. -1

51. If $m(x) = -2x(1 - x)$ and $n(x) = x^3$, compute $(n \circ m)(-1)$.

    A. 0

    B. 4

    C. 16

    D. 36

    E. 64

52. A drawer contains 7 black socks, 5 white socks, and 4 green socks. If 1 black sock is removed from the drawer, what is the probability that the next sock removed at random will NOT be black?

    F. $\dfrac{1}{15}$

    G. $\dfrac{3}{8}$

    H. $\dfrac{2}{5}$

    J. $\dfrac{9}{16}$

    K. $\dfrac{3}{5}$

53. If line 1 is defined by the equation $2y + x = 4$, and line 2 is defined by the equation $3y + 6x = 6$, then which of the following statements must be true?

    A. Line 1 is parallel to line 2.

    B. Line 1 is perpendicular to line 2.

    C. Line 1 and line 2 both have positive slopes.

    D. Line 1 and line 2 both pass through the origin.

    E. Line 1 and line 2 intersect at (0, 2).

54. A group of science fictions fans was asked to indicate (1) if they prefer reading science fiction novels or watching science fiction movies/television programs, and (2) their preferred subgenre: alien invasion, alternate history, cyberpunk, or time travel. The summary of the data is summarized below:

	Alien Invasion	Alternate History	Cyber-punk	Time Travel
Prefers reading novels	50	20	65	30
Prefers watching movies/ TV	25	15	40	55

Based on this data, what is the probability that a science fiction fan who prefers to read novels identifies cyberpunk as their preferred subgenre?

F. $\dfrac{13}{60}$

G. $\dfrac{8}{21}$

H. $\dfrac{13}{33}$

J. $\dfrac{27}{60}$

K. $\dfrac{13}{21}$

55. Suppose $a < b$ and that a and b are not equal to zero. Which of the following must be true?

A. $\dfrac{1}{a} > \dfrac{1}{b}$

B. $a^2 < b^2$

C. $a \bullet c < b \bullet d$ for any nonzero real numbers c and d

D. $\dfrac{1}{a} < \dfrac{1}{b}$

E. $a - c < b - c$, for any real number c

56. Janey goes to the movies with 5 friends. They decide to sit in a row that contains exactly 7 seats. In how many different ways can they arrange themselves if Janey insists on sitting in the middle seat?

F. 24

G. 35

H. 120

J. 720

K. 5,040

57. The dimensions of a rectangular solid are in the ratio 2:4:8. If the volume of the solid is 512 cubic meters, what is the length of the longest edge of the solid?

A. 2 meters

B. 4 meters

C. 8 meters

D. 16 meters

E. 64 meters

GO ON TO THE NEXT PAGE.

58. Greg buys a stock on Monday. The price of the stock holds steady on Monday, remaining at the price Greg paid for it. On Tuesday, the price of the stock increases by 20%. On Wednesday, the price of the stock falls by 25%. By what percentage must the stock price rise on Thursday to regain the original price Greg paid for it on Monday?

F. 45%

G. $22\dfrac{2}{9}$%

H. $11\dfrac{1}{9}$%

J. 10%

K. 5%

59. Square *WXYZ* is inscribed within circle *O* as shown in the figure below.

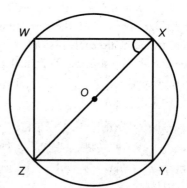

If the sine of $\angle WXZ = \dfrac{a}{b}$, which of the following represents the area of the circle?

A. $a^2\pi$

B. $b^2\pi$

C. $b\pi$

D. $\dfrac{b^2\pi}{4}$

E. $\dfrac{b\pi}{2}$

60. What is the units digit of 338^{340}?

F. 8

G. 6

H. 4

J. 2

K. 0

STOP.

If you finish before time is up, you may check your work on this section only.
Do not turn to any other section in the test.

SECTION 3: READING TEST

40 Questions—35 Minutes

Directions: There are multiple passages in this test. Each passage is accompanied by multiple questions. After you finish reading a passage, choose the best answer to each question and fill in the corresponding oval on your answer sheet. You may refer to the passages as often as necessary.

PASSAGE I

LITERARY NARRATIVE: The following excerpt is taken from the memoir *A Daughter of the Samurai* (1925) by Etsu Inagaki Sugimoto.

The standards of my own and my adopted country differed so widely in some ways, and my love for both lands was so sincere, that sometimes I had an odd feeling of standing upon a
5   cloud in space and gazing with measuring eyes upon two separate worlds. At first I was continually trying to explain, by Japanese standards, all the queer things that came every day before my surprised eyes; for no one seemed to know the
10 origin or significance of even the most familiar customs, nor why they existed and were followed. To me, coming from a land where there is an unforgotten reason for every fashion of dress, for every motion in etiquette—indeed, for almost ev-
15 ery trivial act of life—this indifference of Americans seemed very singular.

Mother was a wonderful source of information, but I felt a hesitation about asking too many questions, for my curiosity was so frequently
20 about odd, trifling, unimportant things, such as why ladies kept on their hats in church while men took theirs off; what was the use of the china plates which I saw hanging on the walls of some beautiful houses; why guests are taken to
25 the privacy of a bedroom and asked to put their hats and cloaks on the *bed*—a place that suggested sleep or sickness; why people make social calls in the *evening*—the time of leisure in Japan; what originated the merriment and nonsense of
30 Hallowe'en and April Fool's days, and why such

a curious custom exists as the putting of gifts in stockings—*stockings*, the very humblest of all the garments that are worn.

It seemed strange to me that there should
35 never be any hint or allusion to these customs in conversation, in books, or in newspapers. In Japan, tradition, folklore, and symbolism are before one all the time. The dress of the people on the streets; the trade-mark on the swinging
40 curtains of the shops; the decorations on chinaware; the call of the street vender; the cap of the soldier; the pleated skirt of the schoolgirl: each points back to some well-known tale of how or why. Even the narrow blue-and white towel
45 of the jinrikisha man and the layer lunch-box of the workman bear designs suggesting an ancient poem or a bit of folklore, as familiar to every Japanese child as are the melodies of Mother Goose to the children of America.

50 One afternoon, at a small reception, a lady spoke pleasantly to me on the healthfulness to the foot of a shoe like my sandal and then referred with disapproval to the high heels and pointed toes then in vogue.

55 "Why are these shapes worn?" I asked. "What started them?"

"Oh, for no reason," she replied. "Just a fashion; like—well, like you folding your dress over left-handed."

60 "But there is a reason for that," I said. "It is only a corpse that the kimono is folded over from the right."

That interested her, and we had a short talk on the peculiarity of Japanese always honouring

GO ON TO THE NEXT PAGE.

65 the left above the right in everything, from the
Imperial throne to the tying of a knot. Then,
lightly touching the back of my sash, she asked,
"Would you mind telling me what this bundle is
for? Is it to carry the babies on?"

70   "Oh, no," I replied, "it is my sash, and is only
an ornament. A baby is carried in a hammock-
like scarf swung from the nurse's shoulders."

        "This material of your sash is very beauti-
ful," she said. "May I ask you why you arrange it
75 in that flat pad instead of spreading it out, so that
the design can be seen?"

        Since she seemed really interested, I will-
ingly explained the various styles of tying a sash
for persons differing in rank, age, and occupa-
80 tion; and for different occasions. Then came the
final question, "Why do you have so much goods
in it?"

        That pleased me, for to a Japanese the mate-
rial beauty of an article is always secondary to
85 its symbolism. I told her of the original meaning
of the twelve-inch width and twelve-foot length,
and explained how it represented much of the
mythology and astrology of ancient Oriental
belief.

90   "This is very interesting," she said as she
turned to go, "especially about the signs of the
zodiac and all that; but it's a shame to hide so
much of that magnificent brocade by folding it
in. And don't you think, yourself, little lady," and
95 she gave me a merry smile, "that it's positively
wicked to buy so many yards of lovely goods just
to be wasted and useless?"

        And she walked away with a long train of
expensive velvet trailing behind her on the floor.

1. According to the passage, the narrator hesitated
to ask her mother too many questions about
American customs because:

A. her mother did not know the answers.

B. the narrator figured that her questions weren't
significant since they were often about unimportant matters.

C. the narrator did not want to appear disre-
spectful to her mother.

D. in Japanese culture, it's frowned upon for children to be too curious.

2. In what ways do Japanese customs differ from
American customs, according to the author?

F. Japanese customs are more traditional and
symbolic, while American customs are more
casual and indifferently observed.

G. American customs are more formal and
respectful, while Japanese customs are more
relaxed and friendly.

H. Japanese customs are more religious and
spiritual, while American customs are more
secular and materialistic.

J. American customs are more diverse and
colorful, while Japanese customs are more
uniform and monochromatic.

3. What is the significance of the way the narrator's
sash is tied?

A. It represents much of the mythology and
astrology of ancient Japanese belief.

B. The ornamental tie can be used to carry a
baby.

C. It is a symbol of the wearer's rank, age, and
occupation.

D. It is a fashion statement with no particular
meaning.

4. Of the following statements, which best describes the author's purpose in the passage?

   F. To provide a detailed comparison of Japanese and American customs.

   G. To describe her emotional state as she adjusted to living in America.

   H. To highlight how much more important religion is to Japanese customs than American customs.

   J. To describe her confusion and curiosity when she was first adjusting to American customs.

5. The primary purpose of the third paragraph (lines 34–49) is that it allows the author to:

   A. provide evidence for her belief that the symbolism of customs is part of everyday life in Japan.

   B. support her assertion that Americans have a secular attachment to their customs.

   C. describe her emotional state when confronted with confusing American customs.

   D. nostalgically ponder what she misses most about her childhood in feudal Japan.

6. It can reasonably be inferred from the passage that:

   F. religious customs are the primary source of long-standing traditions globally.

   G. the author did not enjoy her childhood in Japan compared with her life in the United States.

   H. the author did not enjoy her time in the United States compared with her childhood in Japan.

   J. traditions and customs in the United States are often closely linked with holidays.

7. As used in line 16, the word *singular* most nearly means:

   A. peculiar.

   B. solitary.

   C. lonesome.

   D. outstanding.

8. The contrast the author sets up between feudal Japan and suburban America can best be described as one of:

   F. old traditions vs. new traditions.

   G. awareness of the history of traditions vs. lack of awareness about the origin of traditions.

   H. adherence to traditions vs. refusal of traditions.

   J. indifference to traditions vs. meticulous observation of traditions.

9. The author most likely included the sentiment "I had an odd feeling of standing upon a cloud in space and gazing with measuring eyes upon two separate worlds" (line 4) in this personal narrative in order to:

   A. help the reader understand what it felt like to balance existing in two cultural paradigms simultaneously.

   B. allude to the frustration the author felt about not understanding American customs.

   C. question the purpose of engaging in certain American customs, such as removing one's hat in church.

   D. explain the cultural significance of her decision to wear a traditional sash to an American reception.

10. The author most likely included the final sentence in the passage (lines 98–99) in order to:

   F. question the narrator's recollection of events.

   G. emphasize that the woman's analysis of the narrator's cultural practices was biased and contradicted her own behavior.

   H. critique the woman for asking the narrator so many questions that could be considered insensitive or impolite.

   J. highlight how language barriers can contribute to misunderstandings around cultural customs.

GO ON TO THE NEXT PAGE.

PASSAGE II

SOCIAL SCIENCES: Passages A and B are both taken from academic journals focused on issues in psychology.

PASSAGE A

Ever since the federal government classified psychedelic drugs as schedule I substances in 1973, meaning it was illegal to possess them, it has been difficult for the scientific community to
5   engage in meaningful clinical research about the potential efficacy of these substances in treating a wide range of physical and psychological conditions. This policy was put in place in the wake of the countercultural movement of the 1960s,
10 which saw widespread recreational use of psychedelics like LSD and psilocybin among young people. While some scientists had been exploring the therapeutic potential of these substances before they were criminalized, the scheduling of
15 these drugs effectively put a halt to most of this research.

For decades, the use of psychedelics in clinical settings was largely confined to a small group of researchers, including pioneers like Timothy
20 Leary and Richard Alpert, who were largely ostracized from the scientific community due to their advocacy for the medicinal use of psychedelics. Luckily, sentiments seem to be shifting in favor of valuing scientific inquiry over outdated
25 notions of propriety regarding what is and is not suitable for therapeutic use. In recent years, there has been a growing recognition of the potential therapeutic benefits of these substances, and an increasing number of researchers are beginning
30 to explore this area.

One of the most promising areas of research is the use of psilocybin, the active ingredient in so-called "magic mushrooms," for the treatment of a variety of mental health conditions. Studies
35 have shown that in clinical settings, psilocybin can be effective in reducing symptoms of depression and anxiety and can also help people with addiction issues to break free from their habitual

patterns of behavior. Researchers like Roland
40 Griffiths at Johns Hopkins University have been at the forefront of this work, conducting studies that have shown promising results in terms of the potential therapeutic benefits of psilocybin.

Another area of research that is gaining
45 momentum is the use of psychedelic-assisted therapy for the treatment of posttraumatic stress disorder (PTSD). A number of studies have shown that substances like MDMA and ketamine can be effective in reducing symptoms
50 of PTSD when used in conjunction with psychotherapy. Some researchers believe that psilocybin could also be a useful tool in the treatment of PTSD, although more research is needed to fully explore this possibility.

55 Despite the challenges posed by restrictive drug policies, there are a growing number of researchers who are committed to exploring the potential therapeutic benefits of psychedelics. As more research is conducted, it is likely that
60 we will continue to discover new ways in which these substances can be used to treat numerous physical and psychological conditions. While there is still much to learn, it is clear that psychedelics have the potential to revolutionize the field
65 of mental health treatment, providing new options for people who are struggling with a variety of conditions.

PASSAGE B

As the public conversation around the potential therapeutic benefits of psilocybin and
70 other psychedelics gains momentum, it is becoming increasingly important to consider the risks associated with these substances. Although researchers have already made promising strides in the treatment of a variety of psychological issues,
75 including PTSD and addiction, it is important to note that any drug with the potential for habit-forming behavior must be treated with caution.

This is particularly true when it comes to schedule I psychedelics like psilocybin. While
80 the therapeutic benefits of these substances may

be numerous, they are not without risk. Even patients who are using the drugs in a controlled therapeutic setting may be susceptible to addictive behavior. Schedule II drugs like dextroam-
85 phetamine (more commonly known as Adderall) are widely available and have been linked not only with habit-forming behavior in patients who take them legally but also with addictive behavior in those for whom the drug is not prescribed,
90 meaning substances like these sometimes gain "street value" upon becoming widely available to patients. The takeaway is that even proper therapeutic applications of schedule I psychedelics are not without dangers of abuse by patients and
95 non-patients alike. In short, any potential benefits of psilocybin must be weighed against the risk of addiction and other negative side effects.

Furthermore, even when used in a therapeutic setting, these drugs can produce powerful
100 hallucinatory experiences that may be traumatic for some patients. This is particularly true for patients who have a history of mental illness or who are otherwise predisposed to negative reactions to psychoactive substances. As such, any clini-
105 cal investigation into the therapeutic benefits of psilocybin must be conducted with great care and attention to patient safety.

Despite these risks, there is no doubt that the potential benefits of psilocybin are signifi-
110 cant and that further clinical studies of their potential therapeutic benefits must be conducted. For patients who are struggling with conditions like PTSD or addiction, the prospect of a new and potentially more effective treatment is truly
115 exciting. At the same time, it is important to remember that the road to widespread acceptance of psilocybin and other psychedelics as a therapeutic intervention is likely to be a long and challenging one. In order to maximize the benefits
120 of these substances while minimizing their risks, researchers must proceed with caution and rigor, always prioritizing regulation and patient safety above all else.

11. Based on its use in line 21, the word *ostracized* most nearly means:

   A. included.

   B. excluded.

   C. forgotten.

   D. remembered.

12. The rhetorical stance the author takes in Passage A suggests that they are:

   F. against the legalization of schedule I psychedelics for possession in clinical research settings.

   G. perplexed as to why scientists have not bothered to investigate therapeutic uses of psilocybin in the past.

   H. enthusiastic about the potential benefits of allowing clinical researchers to conduct further experiments on psychedelics.

   J. wary of the potential pitfalls that might come from conducting clinical experiments using psilocybin.

13. Passage A states that the psychedelic substance known as ketamine has shown promising clinical results related to the treatment of:

   A. depression.

   B. anxiety.

   C. PTSD.

   D. MDMA.

GO ON TO THE NEXT PAGE.

14. What is the main idea of Passage A?

   F. Though restrictive drug policies have limited research on the topic in the past, psychedelics have the potential to revolutionize numerous areas of mental health treatment.

   G. The use of psychedelics in clinical settings was largely confined to a small group of researchers who were criticized by the scientific community for their efforts.

   H. The potential therapeutic benefits of psilocybin have been explored in recent years and have revealed promising results for patients with anxiety.

   J. There is growing recognition of the potential therapeutic benefits of psychedelic-assisted therapy in the treatment of posttraumatic stress disorder (PTSD).

15. As used in line 103, the phrase *predisposed to* most nearly means:

   A. persuaded by.

   B. more likely to encounter.

   C. ignorant of.

   D. prejudiced about.

16. It can be reasonably inferred from Passage B that:

   F. female patients are more likely to incur negative effects from psychedelics than male patients.

   G. increasingly, fewer scientists are willing to take on the risk of conducting research using schedule I psychedelics like psilocybin.

   H. Timothy Leary's work was instrumental in laying the foundation for a modern understanding of psychedelic drugs.

   J. even if therapeutic use of psilocybin use becomes prevalent, it won't necessarily be the best treatment for everyone with conditions like anxiety and PTSD.

17. The author of Passage B includes the example about dextroamphetamine to:

   A. name an instance of another scheduled substance that, when legalized for medical use, increased addiction issues among patients and non-patients alike.

   B. show the similarities between dextroamphetamine and psilocybin since both affect chemicals in the brain.

   C. question the validity of psilocybin treatment for psychiatric conditions since dextroamphetamine proved to be of limited therapeutic value.

   D. offer an example of an existing drug that should be on the list of schedule I substances so that it can be better regulated.

18. Which summary best describes the relationship between the two passages?

   F. Passage A is in favor of clinical research on schedule I psychedelics, while Passage B is opposed to clinical research on schedule I psychedelics.

   G. Passage A is in favor of clinical research on all psychedelics, while Passage B argues that some psychedelics (such as psilocybin) are too dangerous to be deserving of reclassification for research settings.

   H. Passage A primarily considers the potential benefits of clinical research on psychedelics for therapeutic purposes, while Passage B focuses exclusively on the potential negative impact of using such substances therapeutically.

   J. While the authors of both passages recognize that research into the therapeutic benefits of psychedelics is necessary, the author of Passage B cautions that research needs to be thorough, controlled, and accountable to patient safety concerns.

19. Given the claims made in the passages, both authors would most likely agree that:

    A. there is no way to conduct research on schedule I substances safely.

    B. the potential negative side effects of psilocybin and other schedule I substances would likely outweigh any potential therapeutic benefit the drugs might hold.

    C. psilocybin and other schedule I psychedelics should be clinically researched for potential therapeutic benefits.

    D. psilocybin and other schedule I psychedelics should not be clinically researched for potential therapeutic benefits.

20. Compared to the author of Passage B, the author of Passage A provides more information about:

    F. the psychedelic effects caused by psilocybin.

    G. specific scientists who have made important contributions to the study of psychedelic substances.

    H. why people are concerned about the negative effects of clinical psychedelic use.

    J. the chemical composition of psychedelic substances.

GO ON TO THE NEXT PAGE.

PASSAGE II

HUMANITIES: The following passage is adapted from "The French Impressionists" (1903) by noted art critic Severin Faust, who wrote under the pseudonym Camille Mauclair.

Now I must speak at some length of a painter who, together with the luminous and sparkling landscapist Félix Ziem, was the most direct initiator of Impressionist technique. Monticelli is
5 one of those singular men of genius who are not connected with any school, and whose work is an inexhaustible source of applications. He lived at Marseilles, where he was born, made a short appearance at the Salons, and then returned to
10 his native town, where he died poor, ignored, paralyzed and mad. In order to live he sold his small pictures at the cafés, where they fetched ten or twenty francs at the most. Today they sell for considerable prices, although the government
15 has not yet acquired any work by Monticelli for the public galleries. The mysterious power alone of these paintings secures him a fame which is, alas! posthumous. Many Monticellis have been sold by dealers as Diaz's; now they are more
20 eagerly looked for than Diaz, and collectors have made fortunes with these small canvases bought formerly, to use a colloquial expression which is here only too literally true, "for a piece of bread."
Monticelli painted landscapes, romantic
25 scenes, "*fêtes galantes*" in the spirit of Watteau, and still-life pictures: one could not imagine a more inspired sense of color than shown by these works which seem to be painted with crushed jewels, with powerful harmony, and beyond all
30 with an unheard-of delicacy in the perception of fine shades. There are tones which nobody had ever invented yet, a richness, a profusion, a subtlety which almost vie with the resources of music. The fairyland atmosphere of these works
35 surrounds a very firm design of charming style, but, to use the words of the artist himself, "in these canvases the objects are the decoration, the

touches are the scales, and the light is the tenor." Monticelli has created for himself an entirely
40 personal technique which can only be compared with that of Turner; he painted with a brush so full, fat and rich, that some of the details are often truly modeled in relief, in a substance as precious as enamels, jewels, ceramics—a substance
45 which is a delight in itself. Every picture by Monticelli provokes astonishment; constructed upon one color as upon a musical theme, it rises to intensities, which one would have thought impossible. His pictures are magnificent bou-
50 quets, bursts of joy and color, where nothing is ever crude, and where everything is ruled by a supreme sense of harmony.
Claude Lorrain, Watteau, Turner and Monti-celli constitute really the descent of a landscapist
55 like Claude Monet. In all matters concerning technique, they form the direct chain of Impres-sionism. As regards design, subject, realism, the study of modern life, the conception of beauty and the portrait, the Impressionist movement
60 is based upon the old French masters, princi-pally upon Chardin, Watteau, Latour, Largil-lière, Fragonard, Debucourt, Saint-Aubin, Moreau, and Eisen. It has resolutely held aloof from mythology, academic allegory, histori-
65 cal painting, and from the neo-Greek elements of Classicism as well as from the German and Spanish elements of Romanticism. This reac-tionary movement is therefore entirely French, and surely if it deserves reproach, the one least
70 deserved is that leveled upon it by the official painters: disobedience to the national spirit. Impressionism is an art which does not give much scope to intellectuality, an art whose fol-lowers admit scarcely anything but immediate
75 vision, rejecting philosophy and symbols and occupying themselves only with the consider-ation of light, picturesqueness, keen and clever observation, and antipathy to abstraction, as the innate qualities of French art. We shall see later on, when considering separately its principal

80 masters, that each of them has based his art upon some masters of pure French blood.

Impressionism has, then, hitherto been very badly judged. It is contained in two chief points: search after a new technique, and expression of
85 modern reality. Its birth has not been a spontaneous phenomenon. Manet, who, by his spirit and by the chance of his friendships, grouped around him the principal members, commenced by being classed in the ranks of the Realists of the
90 second Romanticism by the side of Courbet; and during the whole first period of his work he only endeavored to describe contemporary scenes, at a time when the laws of the new technique were already dawning upon Claude Monet. Gradually
95 the grouping of the Impressionists took place. Claude Monet is really the first initiator: in a parallel line with his ideas and his works Manet passed into the second period of his artistic life, and with him Renoir, Degas and Pissarro. But
100 Manet had already during his first period been the topic of far-echoing polemics, caused by his realism and by the marked influence of the Spaniards and of Hals upon his style; his temperament, too, was that of the head of a school; and
105 for these reasons legend has attached to his name the title of head of the Impressionist school, but this legend is incorrect.

21. As it is used in line 27, the word *inspired* most likely means:

A. incited.
B. encouraged.
C. exceptional.
D. educated.

22. The author of the passage would most likely agree with which of the following statements?

F. The use of symbols is not necessarily an integral element of good art.
G. Romantic and Classical art is worthless.
H. The finest art depicts imagery from mythology.
J. The Impressionists were the most technically advanced artists.

23. The imagery in lines 32–38 functions figuratively to suggest that:

A. music had a direct influence on Monticelli's paintings.
B. Monticelli never used more than one color in his paintings.
C. Monticelli was a great musical composer as well as a great artist.
D. the basic elements in Monticelli's paintings have great emotional impact.

24. According to the second paragraph (lines 24–52), Monticelli:

I. used a thick brush.
II. often painted jewels.
III. was influenced by music.

F. I only
G. I and II only
H. II and III only
J. I, II, and III

25. It can be inferred from the second paragraph (lines 24–52) that:

A. Impressionistic art can provoke strong emotions.
B. no artist can be compared to Monticelli.
C. landscape art was too mundane for the Impressionists.
D. Monticelli was not appreciated during his lifetime.

GO ON TO THE NEXT PAGE.

26. The passage suggests that Manet was considered a Realist because:

   F. of his peculiar temperament.

   G. he tended to paint contemporary scenes.

   H. he was friends with many Realists.

   J. he was often confused with Monet.

27. The main idea of the passage is that:

   A. Monticelli is one of the key artists of Impressionism, though his work was not appreciated until after his death.

   B. Impressionism is an exciting art form that took some time to develop and it has often been unfairly judged.

   C. in terms of subject, realism, modernity, beauty, and portraiture, Impressionism is based on the old French masters.

   D. Manet was often considered the head of the Impressionist school, but this is inaccurate.

28. According to the third paragraph (lines 53–81), Impressionistic art involves:

   I. abstract imagery.

   II. the consideration of light.

   III. picturesqueness.

   F. I only

   G. III only

   H. II and III only

   J. I, II, and III

29. Based on the information in the passage, which of the following is a fact rather than an opinion?

   A. Monticelli's use of color was inspired.

   B. Monticelli's style was entirely personal.

   C. All of Monticelli's pictures provoke astonishment.

   D. Monticelli painted landscapes and "fêtes galantes."

30. The phrase "an art whose followers admit scarcely anything but immediate vision" (line 72) implies that:

   F. the Impressionists refuse to discuss their work.

   G. spontaneity is the main quality of Impressionist art.

   H. the Impressionists are not honest about their work processes.

   J. the Impressionists are only influenced by artists of French heritage.

PASSAGE IV

NATURAL SCIENCE: The following is taken from a college physics textbook.

Quantum mechanics is an intriguing and complex field that explores the behavior of particles on a microscopic scale. It describes the fundamental nature of matter and energy
5 and how they interact with one another, including how those interactions affect our ability to measure and analyze particle behavior. Despite its complexity, quantum mechanics remains one of the most fascinating fields within physics
10 because it has led to groundbreaking discoveries and applications, from the development of the laser to the creation of new materials with extraordinary properties. Understanding some of the most important landmark discoveries in
15 quantum mechanics can help one recognize the great impact of the field as a whole.

One of the most important discoveries in quantum mechanics is the uncertainty principle, which was first proposed by Werner Heisenberg
20 in 1927. The principle states that it is impossible to precisely measure certain properties of particles, such as their position and momentum, at the same time. This means that the act of measurement itself changes the state of the par-
25 ticle, making it impossible to predict with certainty where a particle will be or how it will behave. The uncertainty principle has far-reaching implications for our understanding of the world, challenging our intuition about how things work.
30 Another fascinating concept in quantum mechanics is quantum entanglement, which was first described by Erwin Schrödinger in 1935. It occurs when two particles become linked in such a way that the state of one particle is dependent
35 on the state of the other, even when they are separated by great distances. This phenomenon has been demonstrated in laboratory experiments and has implications for technologies such as quantum computing and cryptography. For
40 example, quantum entanglement allows for the

creation of unbreakable codes, which are essential for secure communication.

Yet another important concept, the theory of wave-particle duality, describes the fact that par-
45 ticles can exhibit both wave-like and particle-like behavior, just as waves can do the same. It was first proposed by Louis de Broglie in 1924. This theory has led to the development of technologies such as electron microscopes and the discovery
50 of new materials with unique properties, such as graphene. The wave-particle duality of particles also underlies the fundamental behavior of subatomic particles and is essential to our understanding of quantum mechanics.
55 One of the more fascinating discoveries within quantum mechanics is that of quantum tunneling, which describes the ability of particles to pass through barriers that, classically speaking, they shouldn't be able to. This has been
60 demonstrated in many laboratory experiments, and it has significant implications for technologies such as transistors and scanning tunneling microscopes. For example, transistors use quantum tunneling to control the flow of electrons,
65 allowing for faster and more efficient electronic devices.

Similarly fascinating is the concept of superposition, which describes the ability of particles to exist in multiple states simultane-
70 ously. This was a particularly important discovery within the field of quantum computing since in quantum computing, information is encoded in the superposition of quantum states, allowing for the creation of exponentially more powerful
75 computers than classic computers.

The study of quantum mechanics has also led to the development of new fields such as quantum field theory, which seeks to describe the behavior of subatomic particles in terms of
80 fields that permeate space and time. This theory has led to the discovery of new particles and the development of the Standard Model of particle physics, which describes the fundamental building blocks of matter. The Standard Model
85 describes three of the four fundamental forces

GO ON TO THE NEXT PAGE.

of nature: electromagnetism, the strong nuclear force, and the weak nuclear force. However, it does not include gravity, which remains one of the biggest challenges in physics.

90   Quantum mechanics is a fascinating and complex field of physics that has led to ground-breaking discoveries and applications. It would not be a stretch to say that much of what has made the modern era such a technically ad-

95 vanced age owes a great deal to quantum mechanics. The study of quantum mechanics is not only essential to our understanding of the fundamental nature of matter and energy but also has significant implications for technolo-

100 gies such as quantum computing, cryptography, and the development of new materials. As our understanding of quantum mechanics continues to evolve, we can expect even more exciting breakthroughs and discoveries to come about,

105 which will undoubtedly change the way we view the world in ways we can't yet imagine.

31. The Standard Model of particle physics describes all of the fundamental forces of nature EXCEPT:

    A. gravity.

    B. electromagnetism.

    C. strong nuclear force.

    D. weak nuclear force.

32. Louis de Broglie is credited with the discovery of:

    F. quantum computing.

    G. superposition.

    H. the uncertainty principle.

    J. wave-particle duality.

33. The author's purpose in writing this passage was most likely to:

    A. explain the history of quantum mechanics as a field of study.

    B. determine why students of physics find the study of quantum mechanics so fascinating.

    C. analyze why quantum mechanics is such a complex subject within the natural sciences.

    D. provide an overview of different landmark concepts from quantum mechanics.

34. Based on the passage, which of the following was NOT a consequence of the development of quantum mechanics as a field of study?

    F. Scientists invented new types of computing technology.

    G. The field of study known as quantum field theory came into being.

    H. Scientists were able to develop new materials that behave in unique ways.

    J. Concepts from the field of chemistry were expanded upon and formalized.

35. As used in line 27, the word *implications* most nearly means:

    A. assumptions.

    B. reflections.

    C. significance.

    D. danger.

36. What evidence does the author give to support their claim that superposition was a particularly important discovery?

   F. It led to advancements in computing since it allows computers to encode far more information.

   G. It led to the development of new types of transistors and scanning tunnelling microscopes.

   H. It allowed scientists to make unbreakable codes, kickstarting the field of cryptography.

   J. It helped scientists develop the Standard Model of particle physics.

37. Which of the following is an accurate summary of quantum entanglement?

   A. Quantum entanglement occurs when the number of particles in a given space is so profuse that they cannot be separated from one another.

   B. The term describes a phenomenon wherein a pair of particles become so linked that their states become dependent on each other, even when separated.

   C. It describes a type of computing that utilizes the quantum states of subatomic particles to store information.

   D. It is a theory that states that waves and particles can behave like themselves or one another.

38. If you wanted to create a transistor that could control the flow of electrons, then according to the passage, you'd need a solid understanding of:

   F. the uncertainty principal.

   G. gravity.

   H. quantum tunnelling.

   J. wave-particle duality.

39. Which of the following is associated with the idea that it's impossible to simultaneously define certain properties of particles, like their location or speed?

   A. Cryptography

   B. The uncertainty principle

   C. The Standard Model of particle physics

   D. Quantum computing

40. The author most likely includes the line "it would not be a stretch to say that much of what has made the modern era such a technically advanced age owes a great deal to quantum mechanics" (lines 92–96) in order to:

   F. make a bold claim that quantum mechanics is the most important field within the natural sciences.

   G. emphasize how many modern technological innovations wouldn't exist if it weren't for quantum mechanics.

   H. critique those who don't see the value in studying quantum mechanics.

   J. argue that more educational funding should go toward encouraging students to study quantum mechanics.

PRACTICE TEST

STOP.

If you finish before time is up, you may check your work on this section only.
Do not turn to any other section in the test.

SECTION 4: SCIENCE TEST

40 Questions—35 Minutes

Directions: There are multiple passages in this test. Each passage is followed by several questions. After you read a passage, choose the best answer for each question and fill in the corresponding oval on your answer sheet. You may refer to the passages as often as necessary. Calculators are NOT permitted for this test.

PASSAGE I

Diabetes, a disease in which the body does not produce or properly use insulin to convert sugar into usable energy, is marked by elevated blood sugar levels. A glycated hemoglobin test reveals a person's average blood sugar level for the past three months. A result of 5% or more is considered high. A glycated hemoglobin reading above 7% is a strong indicator of diabetes.

Table 1 indicates the breakdown of glycated hemoglobin levels among 100 non-diabetics tested.

Table 1	
Glycated Hemoglobin Reading	Number of Test Subjects
3%	12
4%	21
5%	19
6%	29
7%	17
8%	2
9%	0

Scientists estimated the risk of developing cardiovascular disease associated with various glycated hemoglobin levels, first among a group of non-diabetics, and then among a group of diabetics. The results are represented in Figure 1.

FIGURE 1

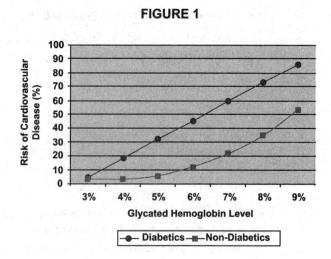

1. According to the data in Figure 1, as glycated hemoglobin levels increase, the risk of cardiovascular disease generally increases for:

   A. diabetics but not for non-diabetics.

   B. non-diabetics but not for diabetics.

   C. both diabetics and non-diabetics.

   D. neither diabetics nor non-diabetics.

2. Based on the data in Figure 1, is the risk of cardiovascular disease ever the same for both diabetics and non-diabetics?

   F. No, the lines representing risk of cardiovascular disease for the two groups do not intersect.

   G. No, the risk of cardiovascular disease for diabetics is always higher for each glycated hemoglobin level measured.

   H. Yes, the lines representing risk of cardiovascular disease for the two groups will eventually intersect at a 10% glycated hemoglobin level.

   J. Yes, the risk of cardiovascular disease is the same for both groups at the lowest glycated hemoglobin level measured.

3. If the data in Table 1 is representative of non-diabetics in general, what can be concluded about non-diabetics compared to diabetics?

   A. More than 90% of non-diabetics have less than a 50% risk of developing cardiovascular disease.

   B. Around 30% of non-diabetics have the same risk of developing cardiovascular disease as diabetics.

   C. Around 20% of non-diabetics have glycated hemoglobin levels indicative of diabetes.

   D. Fewer than 5% of non-diabetics have the same risk as diabetics of developing cardiovascular disease.

4. Figure 1 indicates that the change in the risk of cardiovascular disease associated with each 1% increase in glycated hemoglobin level is:

   F. always greater for non-diabetics than for diabetics.

   G. more consistent for diabetics than for non-diabetics.

   H. positive for diabetics and negative for non-diabetics.

   J. most similar for diabetics and non-diabetics at the 6% glycated hemoglobin level and below.

5. The information in Table 1 suggests that:

   A. non-diabetics are at a lower risk for cardiovascular disease than are diabetics.

   B. a glycated hemoglobin test is not a perfectly reliable predictor of diabetes.

   C. none of the subjects tested has a risk of developing diabetes in the near future.

   D. cardiovascular disease has a positive correlation with glycated hemoglobin levels.

PRACTICE TEST

GO ON TO THE NEXT PAGE.

PASSAGE II

At the end of the Cretaceous Period 66 million years ago, all dinosaurs except birds went extinct. Dinosaurs were not the only organisms that died out—more than half of all plant and animal species on Earth, both on land and in the oceans, went extinct at that time as well. The two most likely hypotheses for the cause of this catastrophic mass extinction are described below.

Hypothesis 1

Around 66 million years ago, a huge asteroid struck Earth just off the coast of what is now Mexico. The impact would have super-heated the atmosphere, generated an earthquake 1 million times stronger than the strongest ever recorded, blasted 5,000 cubic miles of dust into the atmosphere, and released huge amounts of carbon dioxide (CO_2) into the air. Over the next few months, dust would blot out the sun, causing freezing temperatures and complete darkness. Highly acidic rain, formed from reactions in the heated atmosphere, would have fallen into the seas, killing marine organisms. After the dust cleared, the released CO_2 would have caused extreme global warming for as long as tens of thousands of years. All of these environmental effects could have caused organisms to go extinct relatively quickly in geological terms, over thousands of years.

Hypothesis 2

Between 68 to 65 million years ago, about 480,000 cubic miles of molten lava seeped out of cracks in the earth's crust in present-day India. The lava erupted in many separate episodes, each lasting from a few days to a year or more, and each expelling tremendous amounts of ash and toxic gases into the air. In the short term, the ash would decrease the amount of sunlight reaching the earth's surface, decreasing temperatures, inhibiting photosynthesis, and disrupting the food chain. Sulfur dioxide (SO_2) gas from the eruptions would form super-acid rain that would poison marine organisms. In the long term, after the ash settled, the carbon dioxide (CO_2) released would cause global warming. These continuing environmental stresses would have caused a gradual extinction of organisms lasting from tens to hundreds of thousands of years.

6. The main difference between Hypothesis 1 and Hypothesis 2 is the:

   F. way that carbon dioxide affects the climate.

   G. length of time it takes for extinction to occur.

   H. effect of highly acidic rain on marine organisms.

   J. effect of dust or ash on sunlight.

7. According to the passage, which statement would be accepted by proponents of both hypotheses?

   A. Long-term effects on global temperatures were caused by carbon dioxide.

   B. Carbon dioxide caused a short-term decrease in the amount of sunlight reaching Earth's surface.

   C. The extinction-triggering event happened in an instant.

   D. Environmental stresses occurred over hundreds of thousands of years.

8. Which of the following pieces of evidence would help support Hypothesis 1 but not Hypothesis 2?

   F. Isotope data from rock layers at the end of the Cretaceous show warmer temperatures than earlier in the Cretaceous.

   G. Large amounts of volcanic ash are found in rock layers that are 68 to 65 million years old.

   H. Shells of marine organisms from the end of the Cretaceous show acid damage.

   J. Fossils of Cretaceous organisms disappear quickly over a few thousand years just before the end of the Cretaceous.

9. According to Hypothesis 1, what substance in the atmosphere caused super-acid rain to fall at the end of the Cretaceous?

   A. Carbon dioxide gas

   B. Sulfur dioxide gas

   C. Volcanic ash

   D. Dust

10. Hypothesis 1 proposes that which event occurred at the moment of asteroid impact?

  F. Freezing temperatures over all of Earth

  G. An exceptionally powerful earthquake

  H. Extreme global warming over all of Earth

  J. Highly acidic rain falling into the oceans

11. With which of the following statements would proponents of both hypotheses agree? The mass extinction at the end of the Cretaceous was caused by:

  A. an object from outer space.

  B. lava flows that buried organisms.

  C. strong earthquakes.

  D. environmental stresses.

12. Mount Tambora, in what is now Indonesia, exploded in a massive volcanic eruption in 1815. The following year, 1816, has been called "The Year without a Summer" as average global temperatures fell by about 0.5°C (1.0°F) that year. What part of Hypothesis 1 does "The Year without a Summer" support?

  F. Short-term effects of SO_2

  G. Long-term effects of CO_2

  H. Short-term effects of ash

  J. Long-term effects of acid rain

GO ON TO THE NEXT PAGE.

PASSAGE III

Heart rate, a measure of the number of heart beats per minute, rises as the body strives to meet the demands of physical activity. Fitness generally increases as one's resting heart rate decreases and as the degree of change in heart rate during exercise increases. Recovery rate is the decrease in the number of beats per minute calculated for each minute following the cessation of physical activity until heart rate returns to normal resting levels. Greater fitness correlates with higher recovery rates.

Scientists conducted three studies to investigate how heart rate fluctuates during and after two kinds of physical activity.

Study 1

A high school swimmer and a high school basketball player participated for 10 continuous minutes in their respective sports while an electronic device measured their heart rates in beats per minute (bpm) over the course of their exertions. Both began with their heart rate at normal resting levels. Both athletes ceased physical activity after 10 minutes, whereupon the devices continued to monitor their heart rates during 5 minutes of subsequent inactivity. The results are indicated in Figure 1.

FIGURE 1

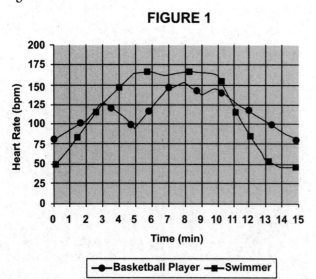

Study 2

Next, researchers analyzed a videotape of the basketball player's recorded activities during Study 1 and classified their movements into the following categories: walking, jogging, sprinting, shuffling (slight intense movements back and forth or side to side), and jumping. Figure 2 shows the percentage of time that the basketball player performed each kind of movement.

FIGURE 2

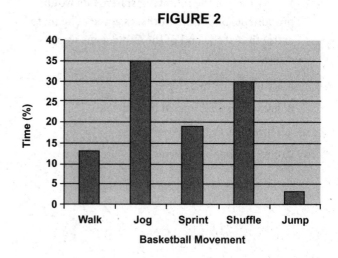

Study 3

Researchers then instructed the athletes to repeat the exercise according to the same parameters observed in Study 1, except this time with the swimmer playing basketball and the basketball player swimming. The athletes' heart rates after 10 minutes, and the decreases in their heart rates during the 5 minutes following that, are recorded in Table 1.

Table 1		
	Basket-ball Player Swimming	**Swimmer Playing Basketball**
Heart rate after 10 minutes	145	150
Decrease in heart rate between 10 and 11 minutes	15	40
Decrease in heart rate between 11 and 12 minutes	15	35
Decrease in heart rate between 12 and 13 minutes	11	30
Decrease in heart rate between 13 and 14 minutes	10	0
Decrease in heart rate between 14 and 15 minutes	10	0

13. Based on the results of Study 2, what can the researchers conclude about Figure 1?

   A. The highest heart rates on the graph correspond to the times that the basketball player was jogging.

   B. The lowest heart rates on the graph correspond to the times that the basketball player was jumping.

   C. The basketball player's heart rate fluctuates based on the type of movement performed.

   D. The basketball player first jumped, then walked, then sprinted, then shuffled, and finally jogged.

14. The results of Study 1 suggest that:

   F. the swimmer is more fit than the basketball player.

   G. the basketball player is more fit than the swimmer.

   H. swimming is a more strenuous activity than basketball.

   J. basketball is a more strenuous activity than swimming.

15. The researchers most likely designed Study 3 to investigate whether:

   A. swimmers are generally more fit than basketball players.

   B. swimmers are better at basketball than basketball players are at swimming.

   C. recovery rates are influenced by the type of physical activity in which one engages.

   D. the degree of change in heart rate during exercise is related to overall fitness.

16. After they stopped swimming, the swimmer's heart rate first returned to normal resting levels:

   F. by minute 12.

   G. 5 minutes after they stopped swimming.

   H. after the basketball player's heart rate returned to normal resting levels.

   J. before the basketball player's heart rate returned to normal resting levels.

GO ON TO THE NEXT PAGE.

17. The zeros in Table 1 indicate that the:

   A. swimmer is in worse physical condition than the basketball player.

   B. swimmer's heart stopped three minutes after they had stopped playing basketball.

   C. swimmer disobeyed instructions and played basketball for 13 minutes instead of 10 minutes.

   D. swimmer's heart rate had returned to normal resting levels by 3 minutes after they finished playing basketball.

18. The breathing rate, or number of breaths taken per minute (bpm), is another way to gauge the demands placed on the heart by physical activity. If breathing rate was also measured during Study 1, which of the following graphs best shows the breathing rate for the swimmer over the time of Study 1?

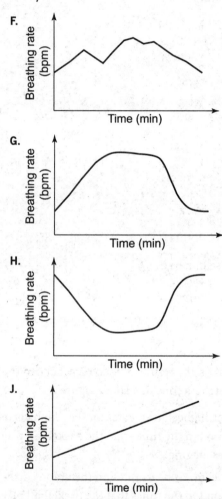

PASSAGE IV

Mitochondria are the source of energy within every living cell. Scientists conducted studies on a wasp species known as the European beewolf to investigate the mitochondria's role in species survival.

Study 1

Upon observing beewolf behavior, researchers noted that beewolves attack larger honeybees, which they sting, paralyze, and then feed to their young. The researchers tracked the breeding and hunting activities of six beewolves and compiled their findings in Table 1.

Table 1		
Beewolf	**Number of Offspring**	**Average number of honeybees fed to each offspring**
A	22	3
B	7	1
C	35	4
D	12	2
E	5	1
F	29	4

Study 2

The researchers then calculated, for 100 beewolves, the density of folded membranes inside the mitochondria of flight muscles. They were able to establish a general relationship between the density of these membranes and mitochondrial energy output (see Figure 1).

FIGURE 1

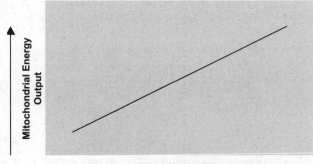

Density of Flight Muscle Mitochondrial Membranes

Study 3

Next the researchers measured the density of flight muscle mitochondrial membranes, expressed in folds per cubic centimeter (f/cc), of the original six beewolves observed in Study 1. The results are depicted in Table 2.

Table 2	
Beewolf	**Density of Flight Muscle Mitochondrial Membranes (f/cc)**
A	78
B	9
C	168
D	30
E	6
F	140

19. Based on the data from Study 1, an observed trend is that:

   A. beewolves with more offspring tend to provide fewer honeybees to each.

   B. beewolves with more offspring tend to provide more honeybees to each.

   C. the output of mitochondrial energy tends to correlate positively with the density of flight muscle mitochondrial membranes.

   D. the output of mitochondrial energy tends to correlate negatively with the density of flight muscle mitochondrial membranes.

20. The results of the studies suggest that mitochondrial energy output is directly related to:

   F. the honeybee-hunting proficiency of beewolves.

   G. the number of flight muscles a beewolf possesses.

   H. a beewolf's risk of being killed by a honeybee.

   J. the mortality rate of beewolf offspring.

GO ON TO THE NEXT PAGE.

21. Scientists tracked the hunting and breeding activities of an additional four beewolves: G, H, I, and J. Which beewolf's activities do NOT follow the trends of the beewolves in Study 1?

    A. Beewolf G: 18 offspring, 2 honeybees fed to each offspring

    B. Beewolf H: 6 offspring, 4 honeybees fed to each offspring

    C. Beewolf I: 31 offspring, 4 honeybees fed to each offspring

    D. Beewolf J: 8 offspring, 1 honeybee fed to each offspring

22. Using only the data from Studies 1 and 3, and without the data from Study 2, the scientists would only be able to directly observe the relationship between which two variables?

    F. Mitochondrial energy output and density of flight muscle mitochondrial membranes

    G. Average number of honeybees fed to each offspring and mitochondrial energy output

    H. Density of flight muscle mitochondrial membranes and average number of honeybees fed to each offspring

    J. Total number of honeybees killed and mitochondrial energy output

23. If the researchers conclude from the studies' results that mitochondrial energy output is directly related to species survival, this conclusion would be most strengthened by a further study showing that:

    A. the density of flight muscle mitochondrial membranes is directly related to mitochondrial energy output.

    B. beewolf species survival is enhanced in proportion to the volume and nourishment of offspring.

    C. the density of honeybee mitochondrial membranes is equal to or greater than that of beewolves.

    D. beewolves with higher mitochondrial energy output tend to have fewer offspring than beewolves with lower mitochondrial energy output.

24. Another beewolf, Beewolf K, is found to have a flight muscle mitochondrial membrane density of 92 f/cc. If Beewolf K is consistent with the other beewolves in this study, it is likely that:

    F. its mitochondrial energy output is greater than that of Beewolf F.

    G. it fed fewer than 60 honeybees total to its offspring.

    H. its mitochondrial energy output is less than that of Beewolf D.

    J. it fed more than 60 honeybees total to its offspring.

PASSAGE V

A mineral is a naturally occurring inorganic solid with a definite chemical composition and an ordered atomic arrangement. Minerals with the same chemical composition but different atomic arrangements can form under different temperature and pressure conditions. These minerals are called polymorphs. There are three polymorphs with the formula Al_2SiO_5 : andalusite, kyanite, and sillimanite. Scientists have experimentally determined the conditions under which these three polymorphs form, and their results are shown in Figure 1. Figure 1 is a phase diagram in which each shaded area includes all the temperature and pressures under which the labeled polymorph forms. Pressures are shown in gigapascals (GPa); one billion pascals (Pa) = one GPa. The average pressure at Earth's surface is about 100,000 Pa, or only 0.0001 GPa. Temperatures are shown in degrees Celsius.

FIGURE 1

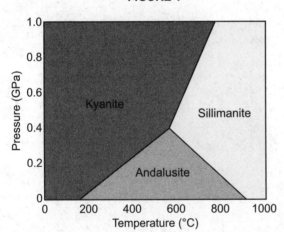

Scientists have also studied the temperature and pressure conditions in different geologic settings around the Earth, including those at different depths in the earth's interior. Figure 2 shows the range of temperature and pressure conditions in different geologic settings. Each shaded triangle includes the temperature, pressure, and depth range of its geologic setting.

FIGURE 2

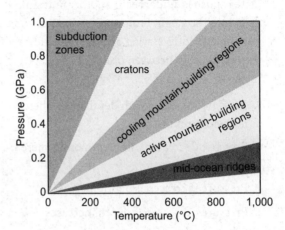

25. The lines between the shaded areas in Figure 1 represent conditions where two polymorphs are in equilibrium. One can conclude along these lines that:

   A. the two polymorphs can transform into the third polymorph.

   B. only the more stable polymorph can exist.

   C. the two polymorphs can both exist.

   D. the temperature and pressure stay the same.

26. Based on the information in Figures 1 and 2, sillimanite is most likely to form in:

   F. the lowest-pressure part (0–0.05 GPa) of a midocean ridge.

   G. the hottest part (800–1,000°C) of a mountain-building region.

   H. cratons.

   J. subduction zones.

27. According to Figure 1, which mineral(s) are most likely to form on the earth's surface, where temperatures and pressures are low?

   A. Kyanite

   B. Andalusite

   C. Sillimanite

   D. Both kyanite and sillimanite

GO ON TO THE NEXT PAGE.

PRACTICE TEST

28. A subduction zone is a region where one tectonic plate is pushed underneath another and sinks deep into the earth. From the subduction zone portion of Figure 2, what can one conclude about the relationship between pressure and depth inside the earth?

   F. Pressure increases with depth only where temperatures are high.

   G. Pressure decreases with depth only where temperatures are low.

   H. Pressure increases as depth increases.

   J. Pressure decreases as depth increases.

29. According to Figure 2, a rock from the hottest part (800–1,000°C) of an active mountain-building region would most likely contain:

   A. andalusite only.

   B. both kyanite and andalusite.

   C. both andalusite and sillimanite.

   D. sillimanite only.

PASSAGE VI

The rubbing between solid objects is called friction, while the rubbing between a solid object and a liquid or gas is called drag. Each produces a resistance force, measured in newtons (N), that works against the momentum of moving objects subjected to these forces. Both friction and drag produce heat. Researchers performed the following experiments to investigate the various properties of and relationships between these phenomena.

Experiment 1

A 20 kg box was placed on top of a long, inclined ramp and released such that it slid down the ramp, ranging in velocity from 0 km/hr at the top of the ramp to 30 km/hr at the bottom. A monitoring device was positioned to record the friction resistance force slowing the box's descent at five different velocities during five different trials. A boat on a river also accelerated from 0 km/hr to 30 km/hr, and the drag resistance force impeding its progress was measured during the course of five trials at the same five velocities at which the box friction was measured. The results are depicted in Figure 1.

FIGURE 1

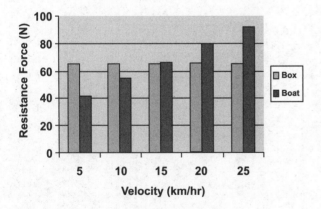

Experiment 2

Researchers repeated the ramp and box experiment, replacing the original box with a 10 kg box, a 30 kg box, and a 40 kg box. The friction resistance force working against each box was recorded at the point each attained a velocity of 20 km/hr. Moreover, the level of heat generated at that point was measured. The results are noted in Table 1.

Table 1		
Box	Friction Resistance Force	Heat Generated
10 kg	55 N	3.5°C
30 kg	75 N	10.5°C
40 kg	85 N	14°C

Experiment 3

The ramp used in Experiment 1 was coated with a layer of sand and the original 20 kg box was released from the same spot, reaching a velocity of 18 km/hr at the bottom of the ramp. The sand was then fully cleared away, and running water was sprayed down the ramp as the same box was again released from the same spot, this time achieving a velocity of 39 km/hr at the bottom.

30. Based on the results of Experiment 1, approximately what friction resistance force would you expect the 20 kg box to experience when it reached 30 km/hr at the bottom of the ramp?

    F. 40 N

    G. 65 N

    H. 90 N

    J. 105 N

31. Experiment 2 demonstrates a positive correlation between:

    A. velocity and drag.

    B. weight and drag.

    C. heat and weight.

    D. friction and velocity.

32. It can be concluded from the investigation that friction differs from drag in that friction:

    F. produces a resistance force.

    G. produces heat.

    H. varies with weight.

    J. does not vary with velocity.

GO ON TO THE NEXT PAGE.

33. The results of Experiment 3 are best explained by the hypothesis that:

   A. both water and sand decrease the resistance force between the ramp and the box.

   B. both water and sand increase the resistance force between the ramp and the box.

   C. sand decreases the resistance force between the ramp and the box while water increases it.

   D. water decreases the resistance force between the ramp and the box while sand increases it.

34. When the 20 kg box was released down the ramp that was coated with sand in Experiment 3, what can you conclude about the heat that was generated by the block at the bottom of the ramp?

   F. It is lower than the heat generated by a 10 kg box sliding down the original ramp in Experiment 1.

   G. It is higher than the heat generated by the same box sliding down the original ramp in Experiment 1.

   H. It is lower than the heat generated by the same box sliding down the ramp when it was sprayed with running water.

   J. It is higher than the heat generated by a 30 kg box sliding down the sand-coated ramp.

35. The best way for researchers to build on the results of Experiment 1 to test the effects of different fluids on drag resistance force is to measure the drag resistance force while they:

   A. accelerate the boat from Experiment 1 through different bodies of water.

   B. accelerate a heavier and lighter boat than the original boat from Experiment 1 through the same river.

   C. accelerate the boat from Experiment 1 through the same river while towing different-sized loads.

   D. accelerate a heavier and lighter boat than the original boat from Experiment 1 through different bodies of water.

PASSAGE VII

Wind speed is influenced by the obstacles the wind confronts on Earth's surface. Scientists have classified various types of Earth's terrain into roughness classes: the higher the roughness class, the rougher the terrain. Roughness Class 0 represents water surfaces, roughness Class 2 represents sparsely populated agricultural land, and roughness Class 4 represents very large cities with tall buildings.

Table 1 shows mean wind speeds observed at three different heights above Earth's surface, in three different roughness classes. Observation heights are represented in meters (m), and wind speed is represented in meters per second (m/s).

Table 1

Height Above Ground (m)	Roughness Class	Wind Speed (m/s)
50	0	13.73
50	2	10.7
50	4	8.1
100	0	14.4
100	2	11.7
100	4	9.39
150	0	14.8
150	2	12.29
150	4	10.14

Wind turbines convert wind power into electricity. The power generated from wind is expressed in watts per square meter, according to the formula $W/m^2 = (0.5)(1.225)(v^3)$, where v is wind speed in meters per second. Table 2 indicates the power of the wind at various wind speeds.

Table 2

Wind Speed (m/s)	Wind Power (W/m²)	Wind Speed (m/s)	Wind Power (W/m²)
0	0	8	313.6
1	0.6	9	446.5
2	4.9	10	612.5
3	16.5	11	815.2
4	39.2	12	1,058.4
5	76.2	13	1,345.7
6	132.3	14	1,680.7
7	210.1	15	2,067.2

36. For a given height above the ground, the data indicate that as the roughness of the terrain increases, wind speed:

   F. decreases.

   G. decreases, then increases.

   H. increases.

   J. increases, then decreases.

37. Table 1 indicates that as the height above the ground decreases, wind speed:

   A. increases more rapidly in rougher terrain.

   B. declines more rapidly in rougher terrain.

   C. increases more rapidly in smoother terrain.

   D. declines more rapidly in smoother terrain.

38. A wind turbine 100 m tall is built at the edge of a farm field to provide electricity for the farm. Using the data in Tables 1 and 2, what is the expected power generation of this turbine?

   F. 446 W/m²

   G. 815 W/m²

   H. 1,050 W/m²

   J. 1,680 W/m²

GO ON TO THE NEXT PAGE.

39. Based on the information in Table 1, which of the following locations exhibits the greatest mean wind speed?

    A. 50 meters above sparsely populated agricultural land

    B. 150 meters above a very large city with tall buildings

    C. 50 meters above a very large city with tall buildings

    D. 100 meters above sparsely populated agricultural land

40. A large coastal city wants to at least triple the power generation of its 50-meter wind turbine, which is currently located in the city center. Which of the following changes would provide the necessary boost in power generation?

    F. Double the height of the turbine to 100 m.

    G. Triple the height of the turbine to 150 m.

    H. Move the turbine to a farm field on the outskirts of the city.

    J. Move the turbine offshore onto the ocean.

STOP.

If you finish before time is up, you may check your work on this section only.
Do not turn to any other section in the test.

SECTION 5: WRITING TEST

1 Essay—40 Minutes

Directions: This is a test of your writing skills. You have forty (40) minutes to read the prompt, plan out how you'll respond, and write an essay in English. Before you start, read all material in the prompt carefully to make sure you know exactly what you are being asked to do.

You will write your essay on the lined pages provided with your answer sheet. On the official ACT exam, any work on the lined pages of your test booklet will be scored. You will also be permitted to use the unlined pages in your test booklet to plan your essay. Your work on the unlined pages will not be scored.

Your essay will be evaluated based on the evidence it provides of your ability to:

- clearly state your own perspective on a complex issue and analyze the relationship between your perspective and at least one other perspective

- develop and support your ideas with reasoning and examples

- organize your ideas clearly and logically

- communicate your ideas effectively in standard written English.

On test day, you are expected to lay your pencil down immediately when time is called.

Are 3D Printers Dangerous?

As humankind marches bravely through the current era of rapid technological innovation, we continue to create wondrous new inventions that help us live easier, work faster, and enhance our collective and individual experiences. A curious new gadget that has arisen in recent years is the 3D printer, which allows users to "print" solid three-dimensional objects through a complex shaping and molding process. 3D printing technology, which will continue to evolve and improve over time and become more accessible to the average consumer, also brings with it a growing concern—that 3D printers will be used to create potentially dangerous weapons, like guns for criminal use, or counterfeit objects. With that in mind, some feel that the sale of such technology should be subject to government oversight and regulation.

Read and carefully consider these perspectives. Each suggests a particular way of thinking about how to address the potential dangers of 3D printers.

Perspective One	Perspective Two	Perspective Three
The potential dangers of 3D printers are too great to allow private citizens to be able to own this new technology. It's hard enough for the government to deal with the volume of dangerous and illegal weapons now; how would it handle a society where we can create them at will from our own homes?	3D printers are exciting new outlets for creative thinking and innovation, so people should be able to use them freely. Just because something has the potential for danger or misuse doesn't mean that it should be made illegal.	We can't discard this intriguing new technology just because of a possible risk for misuse, but it would be unwise to just let individuals "run free" and use 3D printers however they see fit. Careful and pragmatic product regulation is not a new concept; extending it to 3D printers would help ensure that they are used responsibly.

Essay Task

Write a unified, cohesive essay about the potential pros and cons of allowing consumers to purchase and use 3D printers. In your essay, be sure to:

- clearly state your personal perspective on the issue and analyze the relationship between your own and at least one other perspective

- develop and support you ideas with examples and reasoning

- organize your ideas clearly and logically

- use standard written English to effectively communicate your ideas

Your perspective may be in full or partial agreement with any of those given, or it may be completely different.

Planning Your Essay

To mimic the ACT, we have provided you with some blank prewriting pages. On the ACT exam, your work on these prewriting pages will not be scored.

Use the indicated prewriting space to generate ideas and plan your essay. You may wish to consider the following as you think critically about the task:

- Strengths and weaknesses of different perspectives on the issue
- What insights do they offer, and what have they failed to consider?
- Why might they successfully persuade others, or why might they fail to be persuasive?
- Your own knowledge, experience, and values
- What is your perspective on the issue, and what are its strengths and weaknesses?
- How will you support your perspective in your essay?

NOTES

Prewriting Page

The prewriting page is provided to simulate the space the ACT gives test takers to plan their writing. Work on the prewriting pages will NOT be graded. On the ACT exam, you will be graded on anything you write into the lined pages of your booklet. Please write your essay on the lined pages provided.

ANSWER KEY AND EXPLANATIONS
Section 1: English Test

1. C	16. J	31. B	46. H	61. A
2. H	17. D	32. H	47. C	62. H
3. D	18. F	33. B	48. G	63. B
4. J	19. C	34. F	49. A	64. F
5. D	20. F	35. D	50. D	65. C
6. G	21. B	36. G	51. A	66. G
7. A	22. J	37. D	52. G	67. C
8. G	23. A	38. H	53. C	68. J
9. A	24. H	39. B	54. J	69. D
10. G	25. A	40. F	55. B	70. G
11. B	26. H	41. B	56. G	71. A
12. J	27. D	42. F	57. A	72. H
13. D	28. G	43. C	58. J	73. A
14. H	29. C	44. H	59. B	74. G
15. D	30. J	45. A	60. H	75. B

1. **The correct answer is C.** Items in a list, like those in this sentence, should be separated by commas. As written, the items are not correctly separated by commas. Choice C effectively inserts commas into the list in this sentence.

2. **The correct answer is H.** As it appears in the passage, this sentence is confusing and contains a comma splice (a comma separating two complete sentences). Choice H correctly separates the two parts of the sentence with a conjunction, and it is the most logical and straightforward of all of the choices.

3. **The correct answer is D.** As it appears in the passage, the full sentence, "A prominent archaeologist and anthropologist" is a sentence fragment because it contains no verb. To recognize this, you must contextualize beyond the underlined portion of the sentence. Choice D is correct because it connects the two phrases together into a complete sentence, with a comma between "Dr. Louis Leakey" and the descriptive phrase that follows. Choice B leaves the second sentence a fragment, so it does not correct

the issue. Choice C places a semicolon and drops the article. This does not correct the sentence fragment.

4. **The correct answer is J.** This is a verb tense question. The sentence describes something that happened in the past (Dr. Fossey met Dr. Leakey, and because of his influence, she decided to study the apes), so you need the past tense form of *encourage*. The correct answer is *encouraged*.

5. **The correct answer is D.** As written, we have a sentence fragment that needs to be fixed. Choice D correctly fixes the error, joining the independent clause (Fossey took up the challenge) and the fragment (Deciding to study mountain gorillas) with a comma. Choice B incorrectly uses a semicolon, which should only be used to join two independent clauses. Choice C removes the period but doesn't supply any punctuation to separate the nonessential information from the independent clause.

6. **The correct answer is G.** Here, we must determine the correct word choice given the context of the sentence. Fossey is facing political unrest in Zaire, and

although she began her work here, she must leave in order to maintain her safety. The other word choices are inappropriate given the context.

7. **The correct answer is A.** The sentence is correct as it is written. Choice B is redundant because *tolerate*, in this sentence, means approximately the same thing as *accept*. Choice C features the same issue of redundancy but is even more verbose. Choice D needlessly uses *would* as an auxiliary verb.

8. **The correct answer is G.** "Spending so much time to observe the gorillas" is incorrect because the infinitival form "to observe" does not agree with the rest of the sentence; the proper verb form is *observing*. This becomes clearer if you cut the "spending so much time" modifier (choice J): saying "To observe the gorillas, Fossey naturally distinguished among them" would imply that Fossey distinguished among the gorillas in order to observe them, not that she distinguished among them by observing them. The only option that contains the correct verb form is choice G. Choice H would be too wordy in any context.

9. **The correct answer is A.** The sentence is correct as it is written in the passage. The past tense fits well with the rest of the passage, which discusses Fossey's actions while she was studying the gorillas in Rwanda. All the other options create verb situations that would change the meaning or logic of the complete sentence.

10. **The correct answer is G.** As written, the form of "to name" used is incorrect. As the gorilla was already named in the past, *named* is the correct choice here.

11. **The correct answer is B.** This question asks you to pick the best introductory phrase for the sentence. Since the sentence describes an unhappy turn of events, *Unfortunately* is the best choice.

12. **The correct answer is J.** This awkward sentence should be eliminated rather than rewritten because there is no reason to include information about the rhinoceros in a passage that is about Dian Fossey's life, research, and conservation efforts among mountain gorillas in Africa. Choice G does not improve upon this problem in the original sentence,

and choice H introduces the additional problem of sentence fragments.

13. **The correct answer is D.** Here we can see that subtle shifts in word placement and use can drastically alter meaning. As written, the sentence implies that Fossey continued working after her death, which is impossible, and choice C fails to correct this error. Choice B introduces odd or unclear phrasing. Only choice D correctly fixes all grammatical errors and makes logical sense.

14. **The correct answer is H.** The author says that Fossey spent the rest of her life "working to protect the mountain gorilla." A concrete example would be a specific description of some sort of action she took to protect the mountain gorilla, which is provided by choice H.

15. **The correct answer is D.** The author simply does not discuss the controversial nature of Fossey's methods and, therefore, would not successfully meet the assignment described in the question. The author of this essay does not discuss any controversy surrounding Fossey, so eliminate choice A. While the author does describe Fossey's important legacy in the field of conservation (choice B), this has nothing to do with whether the author fulfilled the assignment of writing an essay about Fossey's controversial methods. The author clearly states that Fossey's work was of benefit to the mountain gorilla, so eliminate choice C.

16. **The correct answer is J.** First, you need to determine whether *through* or *along* better fits the sentence's construction and context in standard written English. Since a river typically rushes along a border rather than through it, you can eliminate choices F and G. Of the two that remain, only choice J correctly uses the present tense rather than the past tense.

17. **The correct answer is D.** As written, this sentence contains a redundancy—the phrase "twice as large" implies that the waterfall is bigger, so it doesn't need to be repeated. Choice D fixes this redundancy while maintaining the flow of the sentence as written,

since the word *as* follows the underlined portion. Choice B swaps the word order rather than fixing the error and, like choice C, creates the incorrect phrasing "is bigger as North America's Niagara Falls."

18. **The correct answer is F.** In this question, we're seeking to determine the appropriate verb form of "to see." The sentence is correct as written; the British explorers who named the falls most likely have already seen it, so the past tense form *saw* is correct.

19. **The correct answer is C.** The sentence as written seems to emphasize how separate the five falls are from each other, as though readers already understand that there are five of them. The sentence should instead use the word *actually* to emphasize that, rather than being one waterfall, Victoria Falls is a collection of five separate falls. Choice C does the best job at clarifying this.

20. **The correct answer is F.** The underlined phrase should be a bridge into the description of why Victoria Falls is considered one of the seven wonders of the natural world. Of all the answer choices, choice F provides the best transition from the fact that the falls is one of the seven wonders of the natural world to the reasons why it is on this list. The others introduce separate subjects—the Grand Canyon (choice G), people's differing opinions (choice H), the other wonders of Africa (choice J)—that are not directly relevant to why the waterfall is considered one of the world's natural wonders.

21. **The correct answer is B.** The words *observing* and *witnessing* are describing the same action, so you need to choose an option that eliminates one of these words as redundant. Choice B is the only option that does.

22. **The correct answer is J.** As written, *falls* is in its possessive form and is incorrect, as there is no possession indicated in this sentence. Choice J fixes this error. Choice G incorrectly sets *crashing* in possessive form. Choice H incorrectly sets *falls* in a plural possessive form.

23. **The correct answer is A.** The sentences are correctly separated. Choices B and D would create run-on sentences. In the second sentence, the word

imagine is used as a command to the reader and does not need the *to* added in choice C.

24. **The correct answer is H.** This question asks you to determine whether the sentences should be linked together or kept separate and, if the latter, which end punctuation does so properly for the context. The sentence is incorrect as written, as it is not a question. This declarative sentence should end in a period, so choice H is correct.

25. **The correct answer is A.** This word choice question asks you to understand the point that the author is trying to make about the falls. Contextual clues indicate that the author is trying to describe the size and splendor of the falls. In that case, neither *generosity* (choice B) nor *fruitfulness* (choice C) fits the description. Likewise, *peacefulness* (choice D) is a bad fit with the rest of the passage: words such as *crashing* and *roaring* in the previous paragraph do not imply that the falls are particularly peaceful. *Grandiosity*, however, aligns with earlier descriptions of the falls as spectacular and massive.

26. **The correct answer is H.** The phrase "enjoy a walk" should not be split by any commas, which eliminates choice F. Choice G needlessly adds a comma after the phrase, and choice J needlessly changes the form of the word *walk* from a noun to a verb.

27. **The correct answer is D.** Other than echoing the words *pot* and *boil* from the previous sentence, this sentence has no relevance to the passage and should be eliminated.

28. **The correct answer is G.** The subject matter of this sentence fits into the rest of the paragraph, which is about the additional natural attractions of the park. It should not be eliminated (choice J), just rewritten with the active voice—"is to be admired by" (choice F) is an example of the passive voice, which typically adds a phrase like "can be" or "will be" to a verb that should stand on its own. Choice H uses the passive voice and also introduces wordy redundancy.

29. **The correct answer is C.** Choices A and B can be eliminated since the essay does not fulfill the assignment described in the question. Considering the remaining options, choice C is correct because the writer *does* think Victoria Falls is interesting, so

choice D misidentifies the reason the essay would fail to meet the assignment.

30. **The correct answer is J.** A paragraph about buying locally made crafts would have to come after the introduction of the idea that there are other non-falls attractions in the park. Since that idea is introduced in Paragraph 4, a paragraph about crafts would most logically come between Paragraphs 4 and 5.

31. **The correct answer is B.** An introductory sentence grabs a reader's attention and introduces the topic of the piece. Choice B most effectively performs these tasks. Choices A, C, and D reference minor details of the essay and would not serve as appropriate introductory sentences.

32. **The correct answer is H.** As written, the final sentence of the paragraph is a fragment, and it needs to be combined with the previous independent clause. Choice H correctly combines the two clauses with a comma.

33. **The correct answer is B.** Context is the most important tool in determining appropriate word choice in a sentence. Here, *attest*, which means "to serve as clear evidence of," is the correct word choice; the family photos of the author reading serve as evidence of him being a bookworm.

34. **The correct answer is F.** As written, the underlined phrase describes the father reading to the writer and one of the books that he read. No other choice provides both pieces of information.

35. **The correct answer is D.** As written, the sentence contains an awkward redundancy—the phrase "like catnip" uses a simile to imply that the thing being discussed is attractive, so there is no need to reiterate that it is attractive. Choice D correctly fixes the redundancy. Choices B and C simply shift the words in the redundancy around and fail to eliminate it.

36. **The correct answer is G.** In order to figure out the correct word choice, an understanding of common language usage and context is essential. Here, *captured* is the most recognized and appropriate word choice.

37. **The correct answer is D.** In order to determine the correct pronoun choice here, we need to examine the antecedent. The pronoun here must refer to the author, who refers to himself in the first person; therefore, "I could" is the correct choice.

38. **The correct answer is H.** The correct punctuation to end this declarative sentence is a period, so choice H is correct.

39. **The correct answer is B.** A strong knowledge of standard English will help you determine the correct flow of words and ideas within sentences. As written, the word flow is awkward and confusing. Choice B fixes the error and provides a logical flow of thoughts. Choices C and D simply shuffle around the words in the sentence without repairing the confusion or awkwardness.

40. **The correct answer is F.** "When I set my mind on something" may sound strange if you're unfamiliar with the phrase and take it literally, but it is a commonly accepted idiom, so the sentence is correct as written. Choices G, H, and J provide incorrect variations of the phrase and would only add confusion to the sentence.

41. **The correct answer is B.** Items in a simple list, like the ones presented in this sentence, should be separated by commas, so choice B is correct.

42. **The correct answer is F.** Additional information that is relevant to the ideas expressed in a sentence but which could potentially interrupt the sentence flow are typically set in parentheses, as written here. Without parentheses (choice G), the additional information becomes an awkward and illogical addendum. Choice H needlessly makes the additional information its own sentence, and choice J misuses the phrase "there's no accounting for taste."

43. **The correct answer is C.** Apostrophes are used to create possessive word forms to show ownership. As written, *dads* is incorrectly in the plural form rather than the possessive form. Choice C correctly shows that it is the dad's illness. (That is, the illness that belongs to or is part of the dad.)

44. **The correct answer is H.** We are trying to determine if the essay effectively achieves a particular

goal; here, it is whether the essay is suitable for a contest that's asking for writing about an experience of emotional growth during adolescence. After a careful, holistic analysis of the essay, we can say that choice H is correct—the author discusses learning the value of money and friendship in the essay, so it is appropriate for the contest.

45. **The correct answer is A.** An effective concluding sentence ties up the key themes of the piece; choice A most effectively achieves this goal. Choices B, C, and D contain information and assumptions that are not supported by the information in the passage.

46. **The correct answer is H.** Based on the rest of the sentence, the underlined word or words should mean something like "is made up of," as in "over half a million acres make up the Great Smoky Mountains National Park." "Is created of" (choice F) is awkward because the verb *create* generally does not take the preposition *of*. *Consists*, on the other hand, is frequently paired with *of* and communicates the same meaning as "is made up of," so choice H is correct.

47. **The correct answer is C.** The sentence as written is incorrect because the verb phrase "rise above" should have a plural subject. In this sentence, however, the subject is "the blue mist," not "the mountains." Choice C uses the appropriate singular form, "rises above." Choice B creates a sentence fragment, and choice D creates a sentence that uses both present and past tenses.

48. **The correct answer is G.** This is a complex sentence that lists several options for the hiker. Since the sentence begins by saying that hikers can choose walks "ranging from a brisk, uphill walk…," you can predict that the rest of the sentence will tell you the other end of the range of choices: "ranging from a brisk, uphill walk to a truly challenging three-hour hike." The "from… to" construction is common in a sentence that tries to provide a brief sketch of different extremes; that is exactly what this sentence attempts to do, and choice G is the only answer that fits the demand.

49. **The correct answer is A.** *Unrealistic* is the adjective that conveys that conservationists knew a ban on logging was not likely to happen. This is the author's meaning in the context. Slightly rephrased, the author is trying to say that because the conservationists knew that a full ban on logging was not likely to be effective, they suggested a compromise. *Unrealistic* implies that they recognized that a ban was unlikely.

50. **The correct answer is D.** In this sentence, *unchecked* is extra information that needs to be set off by commas. In other words, you could eliminate *unchecked* and the sentence would have a similar meaning, but *unchecked* helps make the author's meaning clearer. A semicolon (choice F) is used to separate two independent clauses, so it isn't a good choice here. Choice G is missing all necessary commas, while choice H is missing one.

51. **The correct answer is A.** This question asks you what function the second paragraph serves in the passage. The essay as a whole is about the establishment of the Great Smoky Mountains National Park, so this paragraph should further that point. Paragraph 2 describes the initial reason for the establishment of the park—it was a compromise struck by conservationists and loggers. This idea is best described by choice A.

52. **The correct answer is G.** A phrase that contains extra information about the subject, in this case "an organization that explored and mapped land in the United States," must be set off by commas. The phrase modifies "United States Geological Survey," so the comma comes between Survey and "an organization…" As originally written, the phrase lacks the necessary comma. Choices H and J turn a word in an organization's title into a verb.

53. **The correct answer is C.** Logically, a sentence saying that the Smoky Mountains region emerged as a winner would have to come after a sentence explaining what the competition was, but before a sentence detailing what happened next. Sentences 2 and 3 explain the competition: the location of the park had to be determined, and there were sixty proposed sites. The logical place to describe the decision

would come next, right before Sentence 4 begins, "After the decision was made…"

54. The correct answer is J. As it is written, the sentence contains an unnecessary pronoun, *it*. Since you already know that the object in this sentence is "the plan," there is no need for the additional *it* to clarify matters. The option that uses the fewest words and eliminates redundancy is usually your best bet, and that is choice J.

55. The correct answer is B. All of these choices have different shades of meaning. *Privacy* (choice A) means "seclusion or lack of exposure," implying that the ownership carries a certain secrecy; this is different from "private ownership," which indicates that something is not common or public property. "Privately owned" (choice B) conveys the correct meaning: that this land would be difficult to acquire because it belonged to many private individuals. Neither of the constructions in choices C and D clarifies that the land is owned privately.

56. The correct answer is G. This question tests the fine distinction between *amount* and *number*. The underlined phrase, "amount of dollars," tries to describe countable items (dollars) with an indefinite quantifier (amount). *Amount* describes things that cannot be counted (e.g., the amount of rain that fell), whereas *number* describes things that can be specifically counted (e.g., the number of inches that fell). What is needed here, therefore, is either "number of dollars," which is not listed, or "amount of money" (choice G).

57. The correct answer is A. The detail about the landowners hiking their prices is intended to show the reader that purchasing the land was a challenging task. *Heroic* (choice B) might provide an alternative, since the author clearly approves of the purchasing of the land; however, *challenging* is the better choice because the author is trying to give a straightforward account of the difficulties of establishing the park.

58. The correct answer is J. "They had fallen short" is the same thing as "they hadn't raised enough money." To write both is redundant, so you should

omit the phrase "they hadn't raised enough money" entirely.

59. The correct answer is B. This question requires you to go back to the passage and find a paragraph that already contains material about the conflict between loggers and conservationists. Paragraph 2 discusses how compromises between conservation interests and logging interests led to the founding of the park, so this would be the best place to add this information.

60. The correct answer is H. While the first paragraph does mention a few of the park's attractions, it serves only as an introduction to an essay about the establishment of the park. Because only a small fraction of the essay discusses this theme, and someone who would want to know more about visiting the park would probably prefer knowing about the park's features rather than its history, the passage would not successfully respond to the assignment.

61. The correct answer is A. In this sentence, the simplest version works best, so the phrase does not need to be changed. Choice B has the same meaning, but it is unnecessarily awkward. Choice C changes the meaning of the sentence by using *richly* as an adverb to describe *flourished*. Choice D is needlessly wordy.

62. The correct answer is H. *Among* is the correct choice because it indicates that the Mayan understanding of astronomy was one of many notable achievements.

63. The correct answer is B. The description *astute* must appear before the verb *were* because *astute* here describes "the Mayans' observations," which follows the verb (*were*). Choices A, C, and D all result in poor syntax that changes the meaning of the sentence.

64. The correct answer is F. The underlined words are correct as written. The sentence intends to convey that astronomy is more than a science. *Merely* (choice G) and *just* (choice H) make the sentence mean that astronomy is nothing more than a science; this is not the author's argument. Choice J claims that astronomy is not a science at all, which clearly contradicts what follows the semicolon.

65. The correct answer is C. *Found* (or *find*) and *into* as a combination of words doesn't work in standard written English, so choice A is incorrect. Since *found* must have an object paired with it, you can choose the one option that pairs *found* with an object. "Found its way" provides this pairing.

66. The correct answer is G. Because *exact* modifies the verb *aligned*, it must be an adverb. Choices F, H, and J do not use the adverb form of *exact*.

67. The correct answer is C. A semicolon connects two related clauses that could stand on their own as sentences. A colon, on the other hand, indicates that the author is about to make a list without a subject. Since *were* is the verb in the second part of the sentence, a semicolon is a better choice, despite the list that appears at the beginning of the clause.

68. The correct answer is J. The author's tone is neutral and informative. *Gleeful* (choice F) expresses too positive a relationship between the writer and their subject matter, while *resentful* (choice H) expresses too negative a relationship. *Indifferent* (choice G) is similar to *neutral*, but it implies that the writer does not care about their subject matter; you do not have evidence that the writer doesn't care about the topic they're writing on.

69. The correct answer is D. Carvings and murals are examples of artwork, so choice D simplifies the sentence by eliminating redundancy. Choices A, B, and C retain the redundant words *carvings* and *murals*. They all contain unnecessary punctuation between *murals* and *shows* too.

70. The correct answer is G. The pronoun *who* is generally used when referring to people (or even gods with human characteristics). *Which* (choice H) refers to non-human subjects. A relative pronoun is needed in this case to make clear that it is the evil gods who wanted to stop the benevolent gods, and *they* (choice J) is a personal pronoun. As the sentence reads in the original, the verb appears

to refer to the benevolent gods, which does not fit the context of the sentence. The evil gods, not the benevolent gods, are the ones attempting to stop the progress of the sun and moon.

71. The correct answer is A. "Believed to have gained" correctly indicates that those who died were assumed to have gained eternal life. "And felt they" (choice B) makes the sentence redundant because *believed* and *felt* mean approximately the same thing in this context. While "they soon would have" (choice C) and "one day they would have" (choice D) express similar ideas, they do so awkwardly and with more words.

72. The correct answer is H. Word order is very important here. To determine it, you need to look at the context. The Mayans did not appear in the sky; Venus did. Therefore, you can eliminate the original sentence. The Mayans were using Venus to make a decision; choice H is the only choice that indicates this fact.

73. The correct answer is A. The phrase "In short" accurately indicates that this paragraph will serve as a summary for the rest of the passage.

74. The correct answer is G. The phrase "in looking to the night sky for guidance" is extra information that should be set off by commas. The two halves of the sentence cannot stand on their own as sentences, so the punctuation mark cannot be a semicolon (choice F) or a colon (choice J). Choice H fails to use any punctuation at all.

75. The correct answer is B. Since the passage is not about the ancient Babylonians, mentioning them would signal a transition to another topic. A new topic or supporting detail would not be introduced as part of a conclusion, which is meant to summarize the information already presented, so choice A is incorrect. The sentence does not illustrate (choice C) or contradict (choice D) any of the passage's information either.

ANSWER KEY AND EXPLANATIONS
Section 2: Mathematics Test

1. D	**11.** C	**21.** A	**31.** D	**41.** B	**51.** E
2. G	**12.** G	**22.** F	**32.** G	**42.** G	**52.** K
3. A	**13.** E	**23.** C	**33.** D	**43.** C	**53.** E
4. J	**14.** G	**24.** G	**34.** K	**44.** H	**54.** H
5. D	**15.** E	**25.** B	**35.** C	**45.** E	**55.** E
6. H	**16.** G	**26.** J	**36.** G	**46.** K	**56.** J
7. E	**17.** E	**27.** D	**37.** C	**47.** C	**57.** D
8. H	**18.** H	**28.** G	**38.** H	**48.** J	**58.** H
9. E	**19.** D	**29.** D	**39.** B	**49.** A	**59.** D
10. K	**20.** H	**30.** K	**40.** G	**50.** H	**60.** G

1. **The correct answer is D.** Using 1 minute = 60 seconds, convert the total time to seconds: 7 minutes 20 seconds = 7(60) + 20 seconds = 440 seconds. Let x be the number of seconds it took to complete the original workout. Then, $0.80x = 440$. Dividing by 0.80 yields $x = \dfrac{440}{0.80} = 550$ seconds. Now, convert back to minutes by dividing by 60. This yields 9 minutes, 10 seconds.

2. **The correct answer is G.** Plugging in $a = 5$ gives you $\dfrac{5}{6} = \dfrac{b}{15}$. Cross-multiply to solve for b:

$$(5)(15) = 6b$$
$$75 = 6b$$
$$b = \frac{75}{6}$$
$$b = 12\frac{1}{2}$$

3. **The correct answer is A.** Since $\overleftrightarrow{XYZ}$ is a straight line, angles VYX, VYW, and WYZ must total 180°. Therefore:

$$90° + 27° + \angle WYZ = 180°$$
$$\angle WYZ = 180° - 90° - 27°$$
$$\angle WYZ = 63°$$

4. **The correct answer is J.** The pattern for the numerator is to add 1 each time. The pattern for the denominator is to take the previous numerator and square it. Doing so yields the fourth term as $\dfrac{6}{5^2} = \dfrac{6}{25}$ and the fifth term as $\dfrac{7}{6^2} = \dfrac{7}{36}$.

5. **The correct answer is D.** Marta cuts 4(1.5 feet) = 6 feet of ribbon from the spool. If 27.5 feet remain, then originally there were 6 + 27.5 = 33.5 feet of ribbon.

6. **The correct answer is H.** Since we are evaluating for $f(6)$, only the first of the two expressions applies in this situation. Note that the first expression contains the condition $x > 5$, and since $6 > 5$, it means that we only evaluate for this expression.

$$f(6) = \sqrt{2(6) - 3} - 6$$
$$= \sqrt{12 - 3} - 6$$
$$= \sqrt{9} - 6$$
$$= 3 - 6$$
$$= -3$$

7. **The correct answer is E.** Squaring both sides of the inequality $\sqrt{w} > 8$ yields $w > 64$. The only choice that satisfies this inequality is 81.

8. **The correct answer is H.** Find the changes in the x and y coordinates between endpoint A and the midpoint, then repeat those changes starting at the midpoint to find endpoint B. Moving from A (3, –2) to the midpoint (–3, –1), x decreases by 6, and y increases by 1. Therefore, the coordinates of B are $(-3 - 6, -1 + 1) = (-9, 0)$.

9. **The correct answer is E.** A function will have only one output for every input. The input 2 has two different y-values associated with it.

10. **The correct answer is K.** If the probability of NOT selecting a blue marble is $\dfrac{1}{4}$, then the probability of selecting a blue marble is $\dfrac{3}{4} : \dfrac{3}{4}(20) = 15$; therefore, there are 15 blue marbles in the bag.

11. **The correct answer is C.** Convert both lines to slope-intercept form:
$\dfrac{1}{2}x - y = 2$ is equivalent to $\dfrac{1}{2}x - 2 = y$ and

$2y = x - 1$ is equivalent to $y = \dfrac{1}{2}x - \dfrac{1}{2}$.

Since the lines have the same slope, they are parallel.

12. **The correct answer is G.** Let x be the dose of vitamin D (in teaspoons). Set up and solve the following proportion:

$$\frac{4}{3} = \frac{x}{2\frac{1}{4}}$$

$$4\left(2\frac{1}{4}\right) = 3x$$

$$4\left(\frac{9}{4}\right) = 3x$$

$$9 = 3x$$

$$3 = x$$

13. **The correct answer is E.** The points fall from left to right and are tightly packed. This represents the fact that the number of hours decreases as the percentage of nutrient solution increases and that this conclusion is strong.

14. **The correct answer is G.** The reduced price is $800 – 0.15($800) = $800 – $120 = $680.

15. **The correct answer is E.** Use the distributive property and combine like terms:

$$-m(n-m) + n(m-n)$$
$$= -mn + m^2 + nm - n^2$$
$$= m^2 - n^2$$

16. **The correct answer is G.** Since the right side of the equation is 0, the zero product property tells us that at least one factor on the left side must equal 0. So either $5 = 0$, $x - 4 = 0$, or $x + 2 = 0$. We know that 5 cannot be 0, so either $x - 4 = 0$ or $x + 2 = 0$. Therefore, x must be either 4 or –2.

17. **The correct answer is E.** The interior angles of a triangle add up to 180°. Therefore:

$$2x + 3x + 5x = 180$$
$$10x = 180$$
$$x = 18$$

The measure of angle ACB is $2x$, so plugging in $x = 18$ gives you $2(18) = 36$. Since angle BCD is supplementary to angle ACB, their measures add up to 180°. Therefore, the measure of angle BCD is $180° - 36° = 144°$.

18. **The correct answer is H.** The jacket is discounted by $75 – $50 = $25.

Use percent $= \dfrac{\text{part}}{\text{whole}} \times 100\%$ to solve, keeping in mind that the whole must be the original price of $75. So this is a discount of

$$\frac{\$25}{\$75} \times 100\% = \frac{1}{3} \times 100\% = 33\frac{1}{3}\% \cdot$$

19. **The correct answer is D.** Shift the point 1 unit to the left by subtracting 1 from the x-coordinate and shift the point 4 units downward by subtracting 4 from the y-coordinate. This yields the point $(-3 - 1, 2 - 4) = (-4, -2)$.

20. **The correct answer is H.** If 1 inch of wire costs $0.20, 1 foot costs 12($0.20) = $2.40. Therefore, 5.25 feet of wire cost ($2.40)(5.25) = $12.60.

21. **The correct answer is A.** There are many methods to simplify this expression. In general, you need to find the least common denominator. See the following steps for one such option.

$$\frac{1}{3x-1} - \frac{2-9x}{1-3x} = \frac{1}{3x-1} - \frac{2-9x}{-1(3x-1)}$$

$$= \frac{1(-1)}{-1(3x-1)} - \frac{2-9x}{-1(3x-1)}$$

$$= \frac{-1-(2-9x)}{-1(3x-1)}$$

$$= \frac{-3+9x}{-1(3x-1)}$$

$$= \frac{3(3x-1)}{-1(3x-1)}$$

$$= -3$$

22. **The correct answer is F.** The lengths of the sides of the two rectangles are proportional. The perimeter of a rectangle is $2(l + w)$, where l and w are the length and width, respectively. Therefore, the perimeter of the original rectangle is $2(8 + 3) = 2(11) = 22$. The perimeter of the similar figure is 44, so each of its dimensions must be twice that of the original rectangle. Since the width of the original rectangle is 3, the width of the similar rectangle must be $2(3) = 6$.

23. **The correct answer is C.** The cost of b books is $2.25b$ dollars. Adding the flat fee to this yields the cost $8.50 + 2.25b$ dollars.

24. **The correct answer is G.** The perimeter is composed of four equal semicircles, so each must have a circumference of $16\pi \div 4 = 4\pi$. That means that the circumference of an entire circle would be 8π, and its diameter would be 8. Since the diameter of each semicircle lies on a face of the center square, each side of the square is also 8. The area of a square is equal to a side length squared, or 64 square feet. Since the diameter of each semicircle is 8, its radius is 4. The area of a circle is πr^2, where r is a radius of a circle, so the area of an entire circle is 16π. This makes the area of each semicircle 8π, so the combined area of all four semicircles is 32π. Therefore, the area in square feet of the entire garden is $64 + 32\pi$.

25. **The correct answer is B.** The closed circle at 2 indicates that the solution set to the inequality includes 2; eliminate choices A, D, and E since they do not include 2. The open circle at –2 indicates that the

solution set does not include –2; eliminate choice C since it includes –2. This leaves only choice B, which says that x is greater than –2 and less than or equal to 2.

26. **The correct answer is J.** Note that $n^2 = n \cdot n$. The product of two odd integers is always an odd integer. So n^2 is an odd integer. Choice F can be even, as seen by taking $n = 3$. Choices G and H are always even. Choice K might not even be an integer, as seen by taking $n = 5$.

27. **The correct answer is D.** Let x be the length of a side of the square. Then, the area formula yields the equation $x^2 = 144$. So $x = 12$. The diagonal of a square can be viewed as the hypotenuse of a right triangle with two adjacent legs having lengths 12 inches. Using the Pythagorean theorem then yields the length of the diagonal, d, as satisfying the equation $12^2 + 12^2 = d^2$. This is equivalent to $d^2 = 2 \cdot 12^2$, so that $d = 12\sqrt{2}$ inches.

28. **The correct answer is G.** The graph falls from left to right on this interval, so it is decreasing here.

29. **The correct answer is D.** The third side of a triangle must be greater than the positive difference of its other two sides and less than their sum. In this triangle:

$$(7 - 2) < \text{third side} < (7 + 2)$$

$$5 < \text{third side} < 9$$

If the third side must be between 5 and 9, then:

$$(7 + 2 + 5) < \text{perimeter} < (7 + 2 + 9)$$

$$14 < \text{perimeter} < 18$$

The only choice within this range is 16, so choice D must be correct.

30. **The correct answer is K.** The center of the circle is (1, 1), and its radius is 2. Remember that the equation of a circle "equals" the circle's radius squared. Since the square root of 4 is 2, this is how we arrive at the radius. The topmost point of the circle occurs when $x = 1$ and $y = 3$. The horizontal line $y = 3$, therefore, intersects the circle in exactly one point. Choices F and H do not intersect the circle. Choice G and J intersect the circle in two points.

31. **The correct answer is D.** First, compute the total frequency by adding the heights of the bars:

$$40 + 20 + 20 + 60 + 60 = 200$$

Now, the probability of a workout containing either box jumps or weightlifting is as follows:

$$\frac{60+60}{200} = \frac{120}{200} = 0.6$$

32. **The correct answer is G.** Apply the Pythagorean theorem. Note that TR is the hypotenuse, so $c = 8$.

$$a^2 + b^2 = c^2$$
$$a^2 + 6^2 = 8^2$$
$$a = \sqrt{64 - 36}$$
$$a = \sqrt{28}$$
$$a = 2\sqrt{7}$$

33. **The correct answer is D.** A square has four equal sides, so each side of the square has a length of $4s \div 4 = s$. Adding 5 makes its length $s + 5$; subtracting 2 makes its width $s - 2$. The area of a rectangle is equal to length times width, or $(s + 5)$ $(s - 2)$. Using FOIL, you find that the area of this rectangle is $s^2 - 2s + 5s - 10 = s^2 + 3s - 10$.

34. **The correct answer is K.** Use the information provided to label the side lengths of the triangle. Since the cosine of $\angle YXZ$ is $\frac{4}{5}$, the leg adjacent to that angle, XZ, is 4, and the hypotenuse is 5. Note that these are not the exact lengths, but that the ratios between side lengths are what matter here. With a leg of length 4 and a hypotenuse of 5, this is a 3-4-5 right triangle, so ZY has a side length of 3. Now we can find the tangent of ZYX: $\tan = \frac{\text{opposite}}{\text{adjacent}}$, so $\tan \angle ZYX = \frac{4}{3}$.

35. **The correct answer is C.** There are twice as many boys as girls in the class, so let x equal the number of girls and $2x$ equal the number of boys. This means that there are $3x$ total students in the class. Given a class average of 84, calculate the total of all students' grades.

$$\text{average} = \frac{\text{sum of values}}{\text{number of values}}$$

$$\text{sum of grades} = \text{average grade} \times \text{number of students}$$
$$= 84(3x) = 252x$$

You're also given that the girls' average is 91, so:

$$\text{sum of girls' grades} = \text{average grade}$$
$$\times \text{number of girls}$$
$$= 91x$$

If the total score for the class is $252x$ and the girls' total score is $91x$, then the boys' total score must be their difference, $161x$. Therefore, the boys' average is $\frac{161x}{2x} = 80.5$.

36. **The correct answer is G.** Solve the inequality as you would solve an equation:

$$3x - 9 \leq 15$$
$$3x \leq 15 + 9$$
$$3x \leq 24$$
$$x \leq 8$$

The graph of the solution set of the inequality should include 8 and all values less than 8. Choice G is correct because the point on 8 is shaded, as are all the values less than 8.

37. **The correct answer is C.** Based on the given description and figure, the unshaded square is exactly one fourth of either larger square, so within one of the larger squares the ratio of shaded area to unshaded area is 3:1. However, there is a second square that has an identical shaded region but no additional unshaded region, so over both squares the ratio of shaded area to unshaded area becomes 6:1. Therefore, if the shaded area is x, the unshaded area must be $\frac{x}{6}$.

38. **The correct answer is H.** Since average = $\frac{\text{sum of terms}}{\text{number of terms}}$, it follows that the sum of terms is equal to the product of the average and the number of terms. Therefore, the sum of these three positive integers is $3(99) = 297$. You can find the greatest possible value for one number by setting the other two numbers equal to their smallest possible values.

Since each term is a different positive integer, the smallest integer is 1, and the next smallest is 2. That makes the greatest possible value for one of the numbers $297 - 1 - 2 = 294$.

39. **The correct answer is B.** The key to this question is recognizing that triangle ABC is a 30-60-90 right triangle. In such a triangle the sides are related in a ratio of $1 : \sqrt{3} : 2$. Since $BC = 3\sqrt{3}$, it follows that $AB = (\sqrt{3})(3\sqrt{3}) = 9$. Therefore, angle BCA, the angle opposite segment AB, must measure $60°$.

40. **The correct answer is G.** Use the slope formula to obtain the equation:

$$\frac{2-(-x)}{-1-3} = -\frac{1}{4}$$
$$\frac{2+x}{-4} = -\frac{1}{4}$$
$$4(2+x) = (-1)(-4)$$
$$\frac{4(2+x)}{4} = \frac{4}{4}$$
$$2+x = 1$$
$$x = -1$$

So the value of $\frac{1}{2}x$ is $\frac{1}{2}(-1) = -\frac{1}{2}$.

41. **The correct answer is B.** You may use angle relationships in many ways to find the measures of all the angles in the diagram, including supplementary angles and the relationships between angles formed by parallel lines and a transversal. Note that the base of the triangle in the diagram is part of l_2 and is therefore parallel to l_1. As such, the other two sides of the triangle are both transversals.

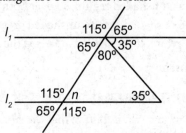

42. **The correct answer is G.** The slope-intercept of the line $3x = 4y - 1$ is $y = \frac{3}{4}x + \frac{1}{4}$. So its slope is $\frac{3}{4}$. Thus, any line perpendicular to it must have a slope of $-\frac{4}{3}$.

43. **The correct answer is C.** Each choice represents a number in scientific notation by raising a numerical value between 1 and 10 to a power of 10. Rewriting the given value of 0.000000301 in this way yields 3.01×10^{-7}. Since changing the power of 10 would most significantly change the overall value, the answer choice with the same power of 10 (choice C) will be equivalent.

44. **The correct answer is H.** You're given the side of the triangle adjacent to the angle marked 41° and asked about its hypotenuse. The cosine of an angle is equal to $\dfrac{\text{adjacent side}}{\text{hypotenuse}}$, so:

$$\cos 41° = \frac{8}{XZ}$$
$$(XZ)(\cos 41°) = \frac{8}{XZ}(XZ)$$
$$XZ(\cos 41°) = 8$$
$$\frac{XZ(\cos 41°)}{\cos 41°} = \frac{8}{\cos 41°}$$
$$XZ = \frac{8}{\cos 41°}$$

45. **The correct answer is E.** Compute the composition as follows:

$$(f \circ g)(x) = f(g(x))$$
$$= \frac{\dfrac{2}{x}}{2\left(\dfrac{2}{x}\right) - 1}$$
$$= \frac{\dfrac{2}{x}}{\dfrac{4}{x} - 1}$$
$$= \frac{\dfrac{2}{x}}{\dfrac{4-x}{x}}$$
$$= \frac{2}{4-x}$$

46. **The correct answer is K.** In order for the probability of landing on a blue section to be $\frac{1}{4}$, there must be 5 blue sections, since $\frac{5}{20} = \frac{1}{4}$. That leaves 15 sections

to divide between red and yellow. If yellow will be $\frac{1}{4}$ as likely as red, then red must be 4 times as likely as yellow, so we need two numbers that add up to 15 where one of the numbers is 4 times the other number: 3 and 12. Therefore, there must be 12 red sections.

47. **The correct answer is C.** You have multiple options for representing the different sets referenced by the question. For ease, you could create a Venn diagram showing what the guests ate:

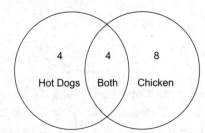

Now you can see that the number of people who ate hot dogs, chicken, or both is 4 + 4 + 8 = 16. That means that 24 – 16 = 8 guests ate neither, which is $\frac{8}{24} = \frac{1}{3}$ of the guests.

48. **The correct answer is J.** Get a common denominator in the numerator and denominator of the complex fraction. Then, simplify:

$$\frac{\dfrac{1}{a}-\dfrac{1}{b}}{\dfrac{1}{a}+\dfrac{1}{b}} = \frac{\dfrac{b}{ab}-\dfrac{a}{ab}}{\dfrac{b}{ab}+\dfrac{a}{ab}}$$

$$= \frac{\dfrac{b-a}{ab}}{\dfrac{b+a}{ab}}$$

$$= \frac{b-a}{ab} \div \frac{b+a}{ab}$$

$$= \frac{b-a}{\cancel{ab}} \cdot \frac{\cancel{ab}}{b+a}$$

$$= \frac{b-a}{b+a}$$

49. **The correct answer is A.** Let x be the length of AB. From the given information, it follows that $\tan 30° = \frac{x}{4}$. Also, $\tan 30° = \frac{\sin 30°}{\cos 30°} = \frac{\frac{1}{2}}{\frac{\sqrt{3}}{2}} = \frac{1}{\sqrt{3}}$

Substituting this into the left side of the equation yields $\frac{1}{\sqrt{3}} = \frac{x}{4}$. Cross-multiplying yields $4 = \sqrt{3}x$, so that $x = \frac{4}{\sqrt{3}} = \frac{4\sqrt{3}}{3} m$.

50. **The correct answer is H.** FOIL the numerator and denominator and then simplify using the identities $\sin^2 \theta + \cos^2 \theta = 1$ and $\sin 2\theta = 2\sin\theta\cos\theta$:

$$\frac{(\sin x - \cos x)^2}{(\sin x + \cos x)^2} = \frac{\sin^2 x - 2\sin x \cos x + \cos^2 x}{\sin^2 x + 2\sin x \cos x + \cos^2 x}$$

$$= \frac{(\sin^2 x + \cos^2 x) - 2\sin x \cos x}{(\sin^2 x + \cos^2 x) - 2\sin x \cos x}$$

$$= \frac{1 - \sin 2x}{1 + \sin 2x}$$

51. **The correct answer is E.**

$$(n \circ m)(x) = n(m(x)) = \left[-2x(1-x)\right]^3$$
$$= (-2)^3 x^3 (1-x)^3$$
$$= -8x^3(1-x)^3$$

$$(n \circ m)(-1) = n(m(-1))$$
$$= -8(-1)^3 (1-(-1))^3$$
$$= -8(-1)(2)^3$$
$$= -8(-1)(8)$$
$$= 64$$

52. **The correct answer is K.** After 1 black sock is removed, there are 6 black, 5 white, and 4 green socks, for a total of 15 socks. The probability of NOT selecting a black sock is equal to the probability of selecting a white or green sock, or $\frac{5+4}{15} = \frac{9}{15} = \frac{3}{5}$.

53. The correct answer is E. Putting both equations into slope-intercept form will make them easier to work with:

$$2y + x = 4 \text{ and } 3y + 6x = 6$$

$$2y = -x + 4 \text{ and } 3y = -6x + 6$$

$$y = -\frac{1}{2}x + 2 \text{ and } y = -2x + 2$$

When a line is in slope-intercept form, $y = mx + b$, its slope is m and its y-intercept is b. Lines 1 and 2 both have y-intercepts of 2, which means that they both pass through point $(0, 2)$, so choice E is correct.

54. The correct answer is H. Restrict your attention to the first row for the new sample space. Of these 165, 65 indicate a preference for the cyberpunk subgenre. The desired probability is then $\frac{65}{165} = \frac{13}{33}$.

55. The correct answer is E. Subtracting the same number from both sides of an inequality always results in an inequality in the same direction. Choices A, B, C, and D need not be true if a and b have opposite signs.

56. The correct answer is J. Janey must sit in the middle, so one of the 7 seats is taken. This leaves 6 choices for the first friend, then 5 choices for the second friend, 4 choices for the third friend, 3 choices for the fourth friend, and 2 choices for the fifth friend. The total number of possible arrangements of the 6 people is $1 \times 6 \times 5 \times 4 \times 3 \times 2 = 720$.

57. The correct answer is D. Let $2x$ be the length of the shortest edge. Then, the other two edges have lengths $4x$ and $8x$. So the volume is $(2x)(4x)(8x) = 512$. This is equivalent to $64x^3 = 512$, so that $x^3 = 8$. Thus, $x = 2$. Therefore, the three edges have lengths 4 m, 8 m, and 16 m. As such, the longest edge has a length of 16 meters.

58. The correct answer is H. Pick a number for the original price of the stock. Choose 100, since it's the easiest number to use with percentages. On Tuesday, the price increases by 20%, so the price increases to $100 + $20 = $120. On Wednesday, the price falls by 25%; 25% of 120 is 30, so the price drops to $120 – $30 = $90. The original price was $100, so the price

of the stock must increase by $10. As a percent of the stock price, this is:

$$\frac{10}{90} \times 100\% = \frac{1}{9} \times 100\% = \frac{100\%}{9} = 11\frac{1}{9}\%$$

59. The correct answer is D. The sine of an angle is $\frac{\text{opposite side}}{\text{hypotenuse}}$. Since the sine of $\angle WXZ = \frac{a}{b}$, $WZ = a$ and $XZ = b$.

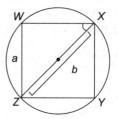

Since segment XZ passes through the center of the circle, it is a diameter of the circle. The area of a circle is equal to πr^2, where r is a radius of the circle.

The diameter of the circle is b, so its radius is half of this, or $\frac{b}{2}$. Plugging this into the area formula gives you:

$$\pi \left(\frac{b}{2}\right)^2 = \pi \cdot \frac{b^2}{4} = \frac{b^2 \pi}{4}$$

60. The correct answer is G. Since the unit digit of 338 is 8, the unit digit of its powers will follow the pattern of powers of 8. You can use your calculator to figure the first few powers of 8 and find this pattern:

$$8^1 = \underline{8}$$
$$8^2 = 6\underline{4}$$
$$8^3 = 51\underline{2}$$
$$8^4 = 4,09\underline{6}$$
$$8^5 = 32,76\underline{8}$$
$$8^6 = 262,14\underline{4}$$
etc.

The pattern here is 8, 4, 2, 6. That means that every fourth power of 8 (and, in turn, of 338) will have a unit digit of 6. In this question, the number is raised to the 340th power; since 340 is evenly divisible by 4 with no remainder, the 340th power corresponds to the 4th term in the pattern, 6.

ANSWER KEY AND EXPLANATIONS

Section 3: Reading Test

1. B	9. A	17. A	25. A	33. D
2. F	10. G	18. J	26. H	34. J
3. C	11. B	19. C	27. C	35. C
4. J	12. H	20. G	28. H	36. F
5. A	13. C	21. C	29. D	37. B
6. J	14. F	22. F	30. G	38. H
7. A	15. B	23. D	31. A	39. B
8. B	16. J	24. F	32. J	40. G

1. **The correct answer is B.** In line 17, the narrator states, "I felt a hesitation about asking too many questions, for my curiosity was so frequently about odd, trifling, unimportant things." There is no support in the passage for choices A and C. Choice D is both unsupported and factually inaccurate.

2. **The correct answer is F.** The author describes how Japanese customs, such as gift-giving and bowing, carry significant cultural meanings and require strict adherence to traditional practices, whereas American customs are often more relaxed and informally communicated. People in the US are also more indifferent to their customs, according to the narrator, since few know their origins or symbolic significance. The author notes that in Japan, even seemingly small gestures carry a great deal of cultural significance and are taken very seriously.

3. **The correct answer is C.** The narrator's sash, or obi, is described in line 79 as being tied to indicate the wearer's rank, age, and occupation. The design of the sash is not merely a fashion statement (choice D) since it serves a practical and symbolic purpose in Japanese culture. She mentions astrology or mythology (choice A) being significant to the pattern, but not to how the sash is tied, which is what the question asks. The passage also mentions a scarf-tying technique used to carry babies (choice B), but the narrator makes it clear in line 71 that that's not what the sash is for.

4. **The correct answer is J.** Throughout the passage, the author describes her experiences adjusting to American customs and culture, highlighting her initial confusion and curiosity as well as how that curiosity was sometimes shared by those she encountered. She does discuss a number of specific differences between customs in the two cultures (choice F), but her main focus is on her own reactions to these differences, not laying out the details of the differences themselves. While a reader might be able to infer how this all affected the narrator emotionally (choice G), describing her emotions is not the main purpose of the passage. The author does not highlight the religious importance of Japanese customs explicitly (choice H).

5. **The correct answer is A.** The author begins this paragraph by noting that Americans seem indifferent to their customs and traditions. She suggests that Japan, by contrast, has symbolic meaning for traditions ranging from formal to "the layer lunch-box of the workman" (line 45) and how custom in Japan is "before one all the time" (line 38). You can therefore assume that the primary purpose of the paragraph is to make this claim and support it with examples.

6. **The correct answer is J.** The only inference that can be supported by the text is that holidays in the United States are closely linked with traditions and customs. This is because a fair amount of time is spent in lines 29–33 questioning why Americans engage in certain holidays (Halloween, April Fool's Day) or holiday traditions (hanging stockings at Christmas).

7. **The correct answer is A.** All the answer options represent potential definitions for the word *singular*, but only *peculiar* is synonymous with its use in the passage.

8. **The correct answer is B.** The author makes it clear that Americans do have and keep traditions and customs since she spends most of the second paragraph listing American traditions she has observed being carried out. However, she also notes in lines 36–38 that "In Japan, tradition, folklore, and symbolism are before one all the time," whereas in the US, people don't seem to be as aware of where their traditions and customs come from or why they observe them. While the author does mention "indifference" in line 15 (choice J), contextual clues reveal that the indifference to which the author refers is that of knowing the history and purpose of traditions and customs, not indifference to the traditions themselves.

9. **The correct answer is A.** In this sentence, the author uses a metaphor to describe the experience of feeling caught between two cultures and the difficulty of navigating two different worlds simultaneously. The image of standing on a cloud and gazing upon two separate worlds emphasizes the disorienting nature of this experience. This line helps the reader understand the author's personal struggle of being an immigrant and the difficulties she must have faced when first trying to navigate her new life in the United States.

10. **The correct answer is G.** The final sentence emphasizes that the woman who is questioning the narrator's cultural custom involving using long bolts of fabric as ornamental fashion is being hypocritical. This is because she herself is wearing a great deal of fabric as a train on her dress and doing so for purely ornamental fashion purposes. The author included the sentence to highlight the woman's American bias toward the narrator's customs by showing how her behaviors contradicted her words. Since the story is told in first-person narration, there is no attempt to question the narrator (choice F). The narrator also makes no indication that the woman's questions were themselves insensitive (choice H), nor is there evidence that a language barrier hindered the conversation (choice J).

11. **The correct answer is B.** Synonyms for the word *ostracized* include *excluded*, *shunned*, *banished*, and *blacklisted*.

12. **The correct answer is H.** Different context clues support the inference that the author's rhetorical stance is one of enthusiasm for the potential benefits that could come from allowing clinical researchers to conduct experiments on schedule I psychedelics. Consider, for instance, this quotation: "Luckily, sentiments seem to be shifting in favor of valuing scientific inquiry over outdated notions of propriety regarding what is and is not suitable for therapeutic use" (lines 23–26). Both the use of the word *luckily* as well as the contrast between "scientific inquiry" and "outdated notions of propriety" reveal the author's perspective that the government's choice to limit researchers' access to schedule I psychedelics was not only a mistake but also an example of old-fashioned thinking. Their tone and rhetorical position throughout the passage is one of enthusiasm for the potential new routes for patient treatment opened up by increased clinical research on medicinal psychedelics.

13. **The correct answer is C.** Lines 47–51 state that when combined with psychotherapy, ketamine has shown promising results in reducing the negative effects of posttraumatic stress disorder (PTSD). While the passage does mention depression (choice A) and anxiety (choice B), these are not mentioned in the context of ketamine. MDMA (choice D) is not a psychological condition requiring treatment but rather another type of psychedelic substance that, like ketamine, the author says is being studied as a potential future treatment for PTSD.

14. **The correct answer is F.** The passage discusses the difficulties researchers have historically faced in studying the potential therapeutic benefits of psychedelic drugs due to their classification as schedule I substances. It then goes on to discuss the different ways that psychedelics might revolutionize treatment for things like anxiety and severe depression. While choices G, H, and J all point to critical elements of the author's argument, only choice F summarizes the main idea of the entire passage.

15. The correct answer is B. The sentence in question reads "This is particularly true for patients who have a history of mental illness or who are otherwise predisposed to negative reactions to psychoactive substances" (lines 101–104). Contextually, the author is suggesting that those who have a history of negative reactions to psychoactive substances would therefore be more likely to encounter negative effects from psychedelic treatment as well. If you used a process of elimination, you'd notice that choice A does not make grammatical sense in context. Choices C and D make grammatical sense but contextually do not match the logic of the sentence.

16. The correct answer is J. Passage B notes that "Even when used in a therapeutic setting, these drugs can produce powerful hallucinatory experiences that may be traumatic for some patients. This is particularly true for patients who have a history of mental illness or who are otherwise predisposed to negative reactions to psychoactive substances" (Lines 98–101). Therefore, it can be reasonably inferred that even if these types of treatments become available, they won't be suitable for all patients, as some may have medical histories or conditions that make it hard to use psychedelics even in proper therapeutic applications. Furthermore, if you didn't spot the right answer immediately, you could have used a process of elimination since choice F is never mentioned, choice G directly contradicts the passage, and choice H refers to an inference from Passage A rather than Passage B.

17. The correct answer is A. The author of passage 2 discusses dextroamphetamine as an example of an existing legal scheduled substance that has been shown to be habit-forming and that increased addiction issues among patients and the general population alike when it became available for therapeutic use. This example helps the author set up their concerns about what might happen should research of schedule I psychedelics be rushed or uncontrolled or if clinicians were to not consider a patient's specific medical history regarding psychoactive substances.

18. The correct answer is J. The summary that best synthesizes information from both passages is the one that states that while both authors recognize that research into the therapeutic benefits of psychedelics is necessary, the author of Passage B cautions that research on schedule I psychedelics like psilocybin needs to be thorough, controlled, and accountable to patient safety concerns.

19. The correct answer is C. The key to answering this question lies in lines 108–110, when the author of Passage B states: "Despite these risks, there is no doubt that the potential benefits of psilocybin are significant and that further clinical studies of their potential therapeutic benefits must be conducted." While the passage as a whole does focus on the potential problems that could come from therapeutic use of psychedelics, this sentence makes it clear that the author does still agree with researchers (like the author of Passage A) who argue that psychedelics should be researched further, meaning this belief is one shared by the authors of both passages.

20. The correct answer is G. Passage A provides more details on the history of psychedelic research, including the work of specific scientists like Timothy Leary and Richard Alpert, as well as more recent researchers like Roland Griffiths at Johns Hopkins University. In contrast, Passage B focuses more on the risks associated with psilocybin and other psychedelics, rather than the specific individuals who have contributed to the study of these substances.

21. The correct answer is C. Each answer choice can be used as a synonym for *inspired*, but choice C makes the most sense in this particular context.

22. The correct answer is F. The author clearly appreciates Impressionism, and in the third paragraph, he writes that Impressionism rejects symbols. Therefore, choice F is a logical conclusion.

23. The correct answer is D. The author compares Monticelli's use of color to a musical theme to indicate that such basic elements of art and music can still have great emotional impact. Choices A and C take the comparison between Monticelli's use of color and musical themes too literally. There is no evidence that Monticelli actually used music as an inspiration for his art (choice A) or that he actually composed music (choice C). Choice B is too extreme; while Monticelli may have emphasized one particular color in each of his paintings, there is no evidence that he never used more than one color in his paintings.

24. **The correct answer is F.** The author describes Monticelli's brush as "full, fat and rich" (line 42), which supports statement I. However, the author only compares Monticelli's reliefs to jewels and his construction of color to musical themes; he does not actually suggest that Monticelli painted jewels (statement II) or was directly influenced by music (statement III).

25. **The correct answer is A.** The author's use of strong, emotional words such as *delight, astonishment*, and *joy* supports the inference in choice A. While the author states that Monticelli has an entirely personal technique, he immediately follows this by stating that Monticelli's work can be "compared with that of Turner," so choice B is not the best answer. The author explains in that same paragraph that Monticelli painted landscapes, so choice C is incorrect. Choice D is a conclusion that can be reached after reading the first paragraph, not the second one.

26. **The correct answer is H.** In the fourth paragraph (lines 86–89), the author writes, "Manet, who, by his spirit and by the chance of his friendships, grouped around him the principal members, commenced by being classed in the ranks of the Realists . . .," which supports choice H.

27. **The correct answer is C.** The first three paragraphs deal with the gradual development of Impressionism, while the fourth paragraph deals with how it has been unfairly judged. The author's own descriptions of Impressionist art indicates that it is an exciting form, so this supports choice C. Choice A only describes the first two paragraphs, so it is not a very complete explanation of the primary purpose of the passage as a whole. Choices B and D each reflect specific details in the passage but both fail to capture the purpose of the entire passage.

28. **The correct answer is H.** In the third paragraph, the author writes that the Impressionists occupy themselves with consideration of light (statement II) and picturesqueness (statement III), but have an antipathy to abstraction, which means that they rejected abstract imagery (statement I).

29. **The correct answer is D.** A fact is a statement with which no one can argue, and this can be said only of choice D.

30. **The correct answer is G.** Choice G is the best interpretation of this line, especially since the author emphasizes the role of spontaneity in creating Impressionistic art. While the phrase does imply that Impressionists were reluctant to discuss their art, it does not support the extreme conclusion in choice F. Since the author discusses the role of spontaneity in Impressionism, choice H is not true. Choice J is a statement the author makes in the paragraph, but it has nothing to do with the phrase in question.

31. **The correct answer is A.** The author states this directly in lines 84–87, which read, "The Standard Model describes three of the four fundamental forces of nature: electromagnetism, the strong nuclear force, and the weak nuclear force. However, it does not include gravity, which remains one of the biggest challenges in physics."

32. **The correct answer is J.** Detail questions like this are testing your ability to locate relevant information within the passage and accurately represent it. Here, you need only find the name Louis de Broglie in the text and then determine the discovery associated with him. Looking at paragraph 4 (lines 43–47), you'll see that Louis de Broglie was credited with the discovery of wave-particle duality.

33. **The correct answer is D.** Since the passage mentions multiple concepts from quantum mechanics and provides basic overviews about them, you can conclude that the author's purpose was indeed to provide an overview of different landmark concepts from the field. Here, it can be helpful to analyze your answer options for degrees of accuracy. For instance, the author does provide some details that help you understand the history of quantum mechanics (choice A), and they also engage in a limited amount of analysis about why quantum mechanics is fascinating (choice B) and complex (choice C). However, only choice D provides an answer that encompasses the purpose of the entire passage.

34. The correct answer is J. Since you can only answer based on what's included in the passage, and since the question asks about something that is reflected in the passage's main purpose (communicating the consequences of quantum mechanics developing as a field of study), your only task is to determine which of the answer options was not mentioned in the passage. The passage talks about scientists developing new computing technology (choice F) in lines 69–75, the development of quantum field theory (choice G) in lines 76–80, and the creation of new materials like graphene (choice H) in lines 47–51. It may be possible that discoveries from quantum mechanics did, in fact, impact the field of chemistry; however, your task is to answer based on the passage alone and nowhere in the passage is there mention of chemistry.

35. The correct answer is C. In this context, the word *implications* means something like "consequences" or "meaning." Of the options you are given, the closest synonym is *significance*. Note also that the word *significance* would make conceptual sense if inserted into the given line in place of *implications*, even though one word appears plural and the other singular.

36. The correct answer is F. All of the answers describe evidence the author gives to support why quantum mechanics as a field is important, but only choice F describes the support the author gives for their claims about superposition specifically.

37. The correct answer is B. You are looking for the answer that most closely resembles the definition of quantum entanglement given in the passage, which reads, "[Quantum entanglement] occurs when two particles become linked in such a way that the state of one particle is dependent on the state of the other, even when they are separated by great distances" (lines 32–36).

38. The correct answer is H. The author states that "transistors use quantum tunneling to control the flow of electrons" (lines 63–64), so you can reasonably infer that you'd need a solid understanding of quantum tunnelling to create a transistor that could control the flow of electrons.

39. The correct answer is B. In the second paragraph (lines 17–29), the author describes how Werner Heisenberg is credited with the discovery of the uncertainty principle, which "states that it is impossible to precisely measure certain properties of particles, such as their position and momentum, at the same time" (lines 20–23).

40. The correct answer is G. First, notice that this sentence is part of the final paragraph, which here serves as a conclusion summarizing what the author has argued. Within the paragraph, the author makes the claim that the modern world owes much to quantum mechanics in order to summarize what they've discussed before in pointing to specific inventions that resulted from the discovery of certain quantum mechanics concepts. Therefore, you can reasonably conclude that the author included this line to emphasize that numerous modern technological innovations wouldn't exist if it weren't for quantum mechanics.

ANSWER KEY AND EXPLANATIONS
Section 4: Science Test

1. C	9. B	17. D	25. C	33. D
2. J	10. G	18. G	26. G	34. G
3. A	11. D	19. B	27. A	35. A
4. G	12. H	20. F	28. H	36. F
5. B	13. C	21. B	29. D	37. B
6. G	14. F	22. H	30. G	38. H
7. A	15. C	23. B	31. C	39. D
8. J	16. J	24. J	32. J	40. J

1. **The correct answer is C.** While the risk of cardio-vascular disease increases at a generally steeper and more consistent pace for diabetics than for non-diabetics, it nonetheless increases for both groups as glycated hemoglobin levels increase. The upward slope of both lines attests to this fact. Choices A, B, and D all claim one or both groups do not show an increase.

2. **The correct answer is J.** In Figure 1, the lines repre-senting the risk of cardiovascular disease intersect at a glycated hemoglobin level of 3%, the lowest level measured, indicating that both diabetics and non-diabetics have the same risk of cardiovascular disease with a 3% glycated hemoglobin level. Thus, choices F and G are incorrect because the lines do intersect and the risk for diabetics is not always higher. Choice H is incorrect because Figure 1 does not show the risk for glycated hemoglobin levels above 9%.

3. **The correct answer is A.** Based on the data in Figure 1, a 50% chance of developing cardiovascu-lar disease does not occur for non-diabetics until glycated hemoglobin levels reach 9%. According to Table 1, none of the non-diabetics has a glycated hemoglobin level above 8%, so it is true that more than 90% of non-diabetics have less than a 50% risk of developing cardiovascular disease. Non-diabetics and diabetics have the same risk of developing cardiovascular disease when both have a glycated hemoglobin level of 3%.

4. **The correct answer is G.** Choice G can be arrived at by noticing the difference in the shapes of the two upward lines on the graph. The diabetics' line is very nearly straight, indicating a steady and consis-tent rise in cardiovascular disease risk for each 1% increase in glycated hemoglobin. The non-diabetics' line, however, does not increase at all between 3% and 4% glycated hemoglobin and barely increases between 4% and 5%. After that, the rise in risk for each 1% increase gets larger and larger until by the end, between 8% and 9%, it approximates the risk increase for diabetics. The risk associated with each 1% increase in glycated hemoglobin level is much more consistent across the graph for diabet-ics than for non-diabetics. Choice F is incorrect, as evidenced by the fact that there appears to be no increase at all in risk for non-diabetics between the 3% and 4% hemoglobin levels, while diabetic risk increases significantly at this level. Choice H is incorrect because there is no decrease in risk for non-diabetics indicated anywhere in the graph. As glycated hemoglobin levels rise, the increase in cardiovascular risk appears to be 0 between 3% and 4% and then is positive from there on. Choice J is incorrect, for at 6% and below, the two lines in the graph are most dissimilar. The lines appear to better resemble one another between the 6% and 9% levels.

5. **The correct answer is B.** You can deduce choice B from a combination of the table figures and infor-mation provided in the passage's introduction.

We're told that a glycated hemoglobin reading above 7% is a strong indicator of diabetes. Yet Table 1 indicates two non-diabetics with a glycated hemoglobin level of 8%. Knowing that these people do not have diabetes allows us to conclude that one cannot infallibly predict diabetes via a glycated hemoglobin test, since a person with a reading that might normally point toward the existence of the disease may not, in fact, have diabetes.

6. **The correct answer is G.** The two hypotheses are fairly similar in how the environmental effects they cause would make life difficult for organisms on Earth, causing the extinction of over half of Earth's species. The main difference is how long the triggering event takes and thus how long it would take for that event to cause extinction. In the case of asteroid impact, the impact is an instantaneous one-time event; an asteroid can only hit Earth once and then it breaks apart. Its effects take place right after the impact, and so it took only a few thousand years for extinction to take place. In the case of volcanic eruptions, lava was erupting in many separate episodes over 3 million years, causing continued environmental stresses that would have caused a gradual extinction over tens to hundreds of thousands of years.

7. **The correct answer is A.** In Hypothesis 1, large amounts of carbon dioxide (CO_2) were blasted into the atmosphere by the impact of an asteroid. In hypothesis 2, large amounts of CO_2 were released by repeated volcanic eruptions. In both hypotheses, the CO_2 caused long-term global warming, or a long-term global temperature increase.

8. **The correct answer is J.** According to Hypothesis 1, extinction occurred relatively quickly, over a few thousand years at the end of the Cretaceous. Therefore, fossil evidence of Cretaceous organisms disappearing over only a few thousand years just before the end of the Cretaceous would support Hypothesis 1.

9. **The correct answer is B.** According to the passage, sulfur dioxide gas expelled by each volcanic eruption would form super-acid rain.

10. **The correct answer is G.** From the information in the passage, at the moment of asteroid impact, an earthquake 1 million times stronger than the strongest ever recorded was generated. In addition, the atmosphere was superheated, 5,000 cubic miles of dust was blasted into the atmosphere, and huge amounts of carbon dioxide (CO_2) were released into the air at the moment of impact.

11. **The correct answer is D.** In the passage, the last sentence of each hypothesis states that environmental effects or stresses caused the extinction of organisms. The only difference between the two hypotheses is the length of time it took for the extinctions to occur. Therefore, proponents of both hypotheses would agree that environmental stresses caused the mass extinction at the end of the Cretaceous.

12. **The correct answer is H.** According to the passage, the short-term effect of a volcanic eruption is decreased temperatures as volcanic ash decreases the amount of sunlight reaching Earth's surface. The decreased global temperatures in the year after the massive eruption of Mount Tambora would be a short-term effect that supports the short-term effects of ash proposed by Hypothesis 1.

13. **The correct answer is C.** While swimming is inferably a fairly constant activity, Figure 2 indicates that basketball is a sport consisting of numerous types of physical motions, some very strenuous (e.g., sprinting) and some not (e.g., walking). This helps explain why the heart rate curve of the basketball player depicted in Figure 1 shows sudden and dramatic dips while the swimmer's curve does not. However, Figure 2 does not indicate which of these movements is most strenuous (leading to the highest heart rate) or least strenuous (leading to the lowest heart rate), nor does it provide information about when each of these movements was performed. Figure 2 only provides information about what percentage of time each type of movement was performed, so heart rate cannot be matched to any specific movement at any specific time.

14. **The correct answer is F.** The passage's introduction indicates that, as a general rule, increasing fitness correlates with lower resting heart rates, a greater degree of change in heart rate during exercise, and greater recovery rates. The swimmer wins on all three counts. The swimmer's resting heart rate is under 50, while the basketball player's is over 75. The swimmer's heart rate increases faster during exercise than does the basketball player's (note the swimmer's steeper curve as their heart rate shoots from under 50 to around 160 at the 5-minute mark). Finally, the swimmer's steep downward curve from 10 to around 13 minutes when their heart rate is back to normal indicates a higher recovery rate than that of the basketball player. All of these clues allow us to deduce that the swimmer is fitter, which both confirms choice F and eliminates choice G. Choices H and J are incorrect because Study 1 provides data only on the heart rates of these two individuals. That, by itself, is not enough to state that one sport is more demanding overall.

15. **The correct answer is C.** Study 3 deals exclusively with minutes 10–15, which constitute the resting period following the end of physical activity. This study was, therefore, designed to explore some aspect of recovery rates. Having the athletes switch activities allows one to compare the recovery rates observed in Study 3 with those observed in Study 1 and, thus, to hypothesize whether the kind of activity one engages in changes one's recovery rate.

16. **The correct answer is J.** Study 1 is the only one that measures the swimmer's heart rate before and after swimming, so we need to refer to Figure 1 to answer this question. According to the introduction, each athlete began Study 1 with their heart rate at normal resting levels, so the heart rate at 0 minutes is each athlete's resting heart rate. The swimmer's heart rate first returned to normal resting levels at minute 13, not minute 12, so choice F is incorrect. The basketball player's heart rate first returned to normal resting levels at minute 15, so the heart rate of the swimmer returned to normal resting levels before that of the basketball player, which is why choice J is correct and choice H is incorrect. Choice

G is incorrect because it only took 3 minutes after ceasing swimming for the swimmer's heart rate to return to normal resting levels.

17. **The correct answer is D.** The numbers in Table 1 represent the decrease in heart rate at each 1-minute interval following the end of activity. The fact that the swimmer who had just played basketball has zeros as their final two entries shows that their heart rate is no longer decreasing following the 13-minute mark. This indicates that their heart rate returned to normal resting levels 3 minutes after they stopped playing.

18. **The correct answer is G.** If breathing rate is also a way to judge the demands on the heart during physical activity, then it should show a pattern similar to heart rate, which is another way to judge the demands on the heart. The swimmer shows a steady increase in heart rate to a more or less stable level, followed by a steady decrease in heart rate. Breathing rate should follow the same pattern, which is seen in choice G.

19. **The correct answer is B.** The three beewolves with significantly more offspring fed a larger average number of honeybees to their offspring while the opposite was true for the two beewolves with significantly fewer offspring.

20. **The correct answer is F.** Study 2 shows that the denser the flight muscle mitochondrial membranes, the more energy is produced by the mitochondria. Using information from Studies 1 and 3, we see that the beewolves with the highest density of flight muscle mitochondrial membranes (and, therefore, the highest mitochondrial energy output) are the same ones with the highest honeybee kill rates noted in Study 1. As such, it is reasonable to infer that mitochondrial energy output is directly related to beewolves' skill at procuring honeybees for their young.

21. **The correct answer is B.** In Study 1, beewolves that have a high number of offspring (greater than 20) also feed a relatively high number of honeybees to each offspring (3 or 4). Conversely, beewolves with a low number of offspring (fewer than 20) also feed a relatively low number of honeybees to each

offspring (1 or 2). Beewolf H does not follow this trend, having a low number of offspring but feeding a high number of honeybees to each offspring.

22. **The correct answer is H.** The introduction states that the scientists wanted to investigate the mitochondria's role in species survival. Study 1 measured the number of offspring and average number of honeybees fed to each offspring for six beewolves, from which the total number of honeybees killed can be calculated (by multiplying the number of offspring and average number of honeybees fed). Study 3 measured the density of flight muscle mitochondrial membranes of the same beewolves. So without Study 2, the scientists can only directly observe the relationship between the four variables just mentioned: number of offspring, average number of honeybees fed to each offspring, total number of honeybees killed, and density of flight muscle mitochondrial membranes. Choice H is correct because it is the only choice that includes two of the variables from this list.

23. **The correct answer is B.** The three studies, taken together, seem to imply that the higher the mitochondrial energy output of an individual beewolf, the more offspring it has and the more food it provides to each. Comparing the numbers in Study 3 with the results of Study 1, one finds a positive linear correlation to that effect, considering Study 2's indication that greater flight muscle mitochondrial density means more mitochondrial energy output. However, even with this implicit correlation in place, we still haven't gotten to the original point of the study—that is, to connect mitochondrial energy output with species survival. The way to do this would be to find a connection between species survival and the thing we have found correlated with mitochondrial energy output—namely, the volume of beewolf offspring and their nourishment. If beewolf species survival is enhanced in proportion to these things—a reasonable inference, but one never stated anywhere in the passage—then the conclusion that mitochondrial energy output is related to species survival would be more tenable. Choice B fills in this missing link, connecting the

implications of the studies to the investigation's original speculation.

24. **The correct answer is J.** Beewolf K has a higher mitochondrial membrane density than Beewolves A, B, D, and E, which, according to the results of Study 2, means that it has a higher mitochondrial energy output than these beewolves as well. Thus, choice H is incorrect. Beewolf K has a lower mitochondrial membrane density and lower mitochondrial energy output than Beewolves C and F, so choice F is incorrect. Beewolf A fed a total of 66 honeybees to its offspring, so we can use Beewolf A as a rough guide to the mitochondrial membrane density expected for a beewolf that can kill 60 honeybees. Beewolf A has a flight muscle mitochondrial membrane density of 78 f/cc, while Beewolf K has a density of 92 f/cc, so we can predict that it can kill more than 60 honeybees. Thus, choice G is incorrect and choice J is correct.

25. **The correct answer is C.** In a phase diagram like Figure 1, the lines between shaded areas represent conditions in which the two substances on either side of the line are in equilibrium. This means that both substances can exist under these conditions, and the rate of formation of one substance equals the rate of formation of the other substance. Even if you did not remember the exact definition of *equilibrium*, by looking at Figure 1 you could reason that on the boundary between two polymorphs' areas, both polymorphs would be able to exist because both areas make up that boundary—they intersect at that line and so those points are part of both shaded areas.

26. **The correct answer is G.** Based on Figure 1, sillimanite is most likely to form at high temperatures and a range of pressures. The hottest parts of both cooling and active mountain-building regions, between 800– 1,000°C, are both squarely in the sillimanite area of Figure 1, so sillimanite will form here.

27. **The correct answer is A.** You can estimate the temperature of Earth's surface by thinking about familiar temperatures, such as the boiling point of water, which is 100°C. You can reason that it is too cool on

Earth's surface for water to spontaneously boil, so it is safe to assume that Earth's surface temperature is always below 100°C. (The hottest temperature ever recorded on Earth's surface is actually only 54°C.) The introduction tells you that Earth's surface pressure is about 0.0001 GPa. The scale of the pressure axis in Figure 2 is so large that you can just estimate the surface pressure to be around 0 GPa on the figure. So below 100°C and around 0 GPa on Figure 1, kyanite is the only mineral that forms.

28. **The correct answer is H.** From Figure 2, you can see that the shaded area for a subduction zone extends all the way from 0 to 1.0 GPa. Temperatures stay relatively cool, not going above 400°C. The question stem tells you that in a subduction zone, a tectonic plate sinks deep into the earth. You know from the introduction that surface pressures are close to 0 GPa, so the higher pressures in the subduction zone must be occurring deeper within the earth. Therefore, you can conclude that pressure increases as depth increases.

29. **The correct answer is D.** According to Figure 2, the hottest part of an active mountain-building region, from 800–1,000°C, is between about 0.2–0.6 GPa. On Figure 1, this falls completely within the sillimanite area, so only sillimanite will form in the hottest part of an active mountain-building region.

30. **The correct answer is G.** The results of Experiment 1, graphed in Figure 1, show that friction resistance force does not change for the 20 kg box as its velocity changes. The friction resistance force stays constant at about 65 N for all five velocities measured. Thus, at a different velocity than the ones shown, such as 30 km/hr, the friction resistance force can be predicted to remain at 65 N.

31. **The correct answer is C.** The table indicates that as the weight of the boxes observed increases from 10 to 30 to 40 kg, the heat generated at the point the box reaches a speed of 20 km/hr increases as well. That constitutes a positive correlation between weight and heat.

32. **The correct answer is J.** The bars in Figure 1 representing the friction between the box and the ramp are constant at every velocity, roughly 65 N.

In contrast, the drag on the boat increases at every velocity listed. These results indicate that unlike drag, friction does not vary with velocity. Choices F and G contradict the passage's introduction, which states that both friction and drag produce a resistance force and heat. Choice H is incorrect because nothing in any of the experiments suggests that drag is unaffected by weight. While we know from Experiment 2 that friction does indeed vary with weight, we cannot conclude from the information given that drag does not.

33. **The correct answer is D.** In Experiment 1, the original 20-kg box reached a velocity of 30 km/hr at the bottom of the untreated ramp. Experiment 3 shows that the same box on a sandy ramp hits the bottom of the ramp at 18 km/hr. On a wet ramp, the box reaches the bottom moving at 39 km/hr. This means that the box moves slower than normal on a ramp covered with sand and faster than normal on a ramp covered with water. The most logical explanation is that sand provides greater resistance to the box's movement and water provides less resistance, making all the other choices incorrect.

34. **The correct answer is G.** In Table 1, we can see that there is a positive correlation between weight and heat, but we can also see a positive correlation between friction resistance force and heat. The higher the friction resistance force, the more heat generated. From Experiment 3, we see that sand increases the resistance force between the box and the ramp while water decreases the resistance force. Since the resistance force between the box and the ramp is greater when there is sand on the ramp, the heat generated by the box will be greater on a sand-covered ramp than on the original ramp.

35. **The correct answer is A.** To build on the results of Experiment 1 to test the effects of different fluids on drag resistance force, the researchers should try to keep one of the variables the same and only change the variable they are interested in studying. Studying the effects of different fluids on drag resistance force is similar to what the researchers did in Experiment 3, in which they studied the effects of different surfaces on friction resistance force. In

that case, they kept the box the same and changed the surfaces. Similarly, to study the effect of fluid on drag, the researchers should keep the boat the same and change the fluids through which it accelerates.

36. **The correct answer is F.** At all three heights listed in Table 1, as roughness increases from 0 to 2 to 4, wind speed decreases. Using 50 meters above ground as an example, the wind speed at roughness Class 0 is 13.73, at Class 2 is 10.7, and at Class 4 is 8.1. The figures corresponding to 100 and 150 meters above ground exhibit the same pattern of consistently decreasing wind speeds as roughness increases. Since there is this constant decrease, all the other choices are incorrect.

37. **The correct answer is B.** There are two important things to notice that help answer this question. First, we're asked to notice something about what happens when height above the ground decreases, and second, we're looking to compare the magnitude of wind speed changes in various kinds of terrain. In all three terrains, wind speed decreases as height above the ground decreases. For example, follow the numbers for Class 4 at 150 meters, then 100 meters, then 50 meters; you'll see that the wind speeds decrease. That observation eliminates choices A and C from consideration. The issue is now the rate of the decrease—do the numbers drop more quickly in rougher terrain or in smoother terrain? Let's use the figures in the table to determine this. In the roughest terrain, Class 4, wind speed drops from 10.14 at 150 meters above ground to 9.39 at 100 meters and 8.1 at 50 meters. This is a drop of approximately 0.7

and 1.3, respectively. In a less rough terrain, Class 2, the corresponding decrease is from 12.29 to 11.7 to 10.7, which represents a drop of roughly 0.6 and 1.0. This drop is less dramatic, and the decrease in roughness Class 0 even less so—from 14.8 to 14.4 (a drop of 0.4) to 13.73 (a drop of 0.67). Therefore, the drop-off in wind speed as height above ground decreases is more rapid in rougher terrains.

38. **The correct answer is H.** A farm field is an example of sparsely populated agricultural land and thus represents roughness Class 2. According to Table 1, wind speed 100 m above the ground over land of roughness Class 2 is 11.7 m/s, or just under 12 m/s. Looking at Table 2, a wind speed of 12 m/s will generate 1,058.4 W/m² of wind power, or just over 1,050 W/m².

39. **The correct answer is D.** Table 1 indicates that 100 meters above ground at roughness Class 2, the level that corresponds to sparsely populated agricultural land, the mean wind speed is 11.7 m/s.

40. **The correct answer is J.** Based on the information in Tables 1 and 2, wind speed in a large city, a roughness class of 4, at 50 m above the ground is about 8 m/s, which will generate around 314 W/m² of wind power. Triple that amount is 942 W/m². Looking at Table 2, wind speeds of 11 m/s will generate 815 W/m² of wind power, while speeds of 12 m/s will generate 1058 W/m² of wind power. So to get 942 W/m² of power, any change must lead to the turbine experiencing wind speeds of around 11.5 m/s or more.

ANSWER KEY AND EXPLANATIONS

Section 5: Writing Test

Essay Instructions for Self-Scoring

Now that you have completed your exam, it's time to figure out your score. On the actual exam, your essay will be scored across four different domains by two unique graders, on a scale from 1-6. The scores from each domain and each grader will then be added together for a final domain score. All domain final scores are then averaged together to give you your final ACT score, which will range from 2 to 12.

Because this is a practice exam, we have provided you with tools to evaluate and score your own writing. This should help you approximate where you stand according to the ACT's grading standards. The elements you should be considering when deciding your score are:

Ideas and Analysis: Did you build an argument that engages with the multiple perspectives given, reflecting precision in thought and purpose? Did you take a clear position on the issue while establishing insightful analysis of the issue and its perspectives?

Development and Support: Did you use sound reasoning and illustration to convey fully developed ideas and support for your perspective? Does your reasoning enhance your analysis of the issue and the perspectives while strengthening your own perspective?

Organization: Does the structure of your essay make sense? Is it logical, does it communicate a purpose, and does it increase the effectiveness of your argument? Is it in paragraphs made up of complete sentences? Do the transitions between paragraphs strengthen the relationships among ideas?

Language Use: Did you write in Standard English? Did you use a variety of words, including more difficult vocabulary? Was your grammar and syntax correct; e.g., do your subjects agree with your verbs, and did you use proper punctuation?

For more detailed information on how to self-score your essay, please refer to the Essay Scoring Rubric at the end of Chapter 2: Diagnostic Test. Here, we have included sample essays at the lowest and high scoring levels to help you compare your own writing. Give yourself a 0 only if you absolutely did not complete the assignment: you left it blank, you wrote about something completely unrelated to the question, or you just complained about the assignment. Give yourself a 6 only if you really think your essay was perfect based on every criterion listed above. For everything in between, use your own judgment.

Sample Essay: Score 1

Ideas and Analysis:	Score = 1
Development and Support:	Score = 1
Organization:	Score = 1
Language Use and Conventions:	Score = 1

Well, this is a good question because there is some different ways to think about it so I would have to say it's a complicated topical. Like I have never seen or even heard of one so I don't' know what to think about the issue but maybe I would say that they can't be that dangerous? It's a printer and printers aren't. Maybe it could make things easier for some people like in their jobs or school or even at home. I think they should be able to decide for themselves. People can do. It would be really creapy to find out someone uses a 3d printer to make a weapon thought because how does it even work and also why they would want to do that. criminals can always get weapons if they need them I don't think they need 3d printers for that so maybe it's not that big a deal even though it does yes sound creapy. I think people can make rules about how to get 3d prints or what people are doing. With the printers. Second, would you want for your neighbor to be able to make whatever they want? I don't think so. So I think maybe there should be rules but also people can defiantly think for themself and figure it out. I know I would.

Another reason would be that we don't know about new technological and what will happen from it until it has been here a long time. So it is probably too soon to say for this isshue. They are exiting new outlets for creative thinking and innovation so people should be able to use them freely for their creativity and innovations.

Scoring Explanation

Ideas and Analysis: Score = 1

The writer of this essay attempts to address the question provided by saying "it is probably too soon to say for this issue," but their stance is unclear from start to finish. It's difficult to figure out what, exactly, the writer wanted to communicate, except for the very last sentence, which they copied word for word from perspective two and did not expand on. There are some attempts to engage in analysis, such as the discussion about how people making weapons with 3D printers is a concern, but the writer fails to connect that analysis in a way that communicates a clear argument or stance to the reader.

Development and Support: Score = 1

The writer of this essay does share a few different thoughts on 3D printers, such as how they might help people complete certain school, work, or home tasks as well as the idea that they might support someone's "creativity and innovation," but their thoughts on these topics are scattered and unconnected to each other. The writer fails to provide the necessary context to develop their ideas further, making their ideas seems disjointed.

Organization: Score = 1

There is little attempt to organize thoughts in this brief essay. The few claims the writer does make are weak and non-specific. Additionally, the only way they address the perspectives they're supposed to is by copying word for word from the prompt. Each of their thoughts is disconnected from each other and they tend to jump back and forth between implying 3d printers are good and saying they cause harm. A reader would not be able to tell from what is written what the writer was trying to argue

Language Use and Conventions: Score = 1

While the basic grammar of this essay is not bad and in fact might land this essay closer to a 2 in this category, many of the errors made do still end up hindering understanding. There are a few spelling errors, some of which are easier to interpret (isshue, creapy) than others (defiantly). There are also word choices that don't work, such as the choice to use "second" as a transition when no first point has been introduced. The sentence structure throughout is not varied much, including sentence fragments ("People can do.") and a lot of telegraphic sentence structure, meaning lots of short sentences that could be made more complex by adding relevant details. Many of the pronouns are ambiguous, such as the frequently unclear use of "them" in place of 3d printers, and there are improper verb tenses distributed throughout ("there is some different ways"). Misused words are an issue, such as the use of *topical* in place of *topic*, and inexact spelling errors create confusion ("not that big a deal even thought"). Copying sentences directly from the prompt also signals a failure to use one's own words to express ideas.

Sample Essay: Score 6

Ideas and Analysis:	Score = 6
Development and Support:	Score = 6
Organization:	Score = 6
Language Use and Conventions:	Score = 6

In our current era of technological innovation, we have been fortunate enough to witness an explosion of new ideas, gadgets, and processes, which are reshaping how we work, live, and interact. Many of these technological marvels have ushered in dramatic, lasting, and positive impacts (imagine going back to a world without smartphones). Others have, thus far, shown themselves to be little more than opportunities to show off the creativity and skill of their creators (sorry, Segway). There's also another category of innovation that deserves our attention—those that come with an unexpected social cost, namely the potential for serious misuse and abuse.

It can be argued that 3D printers have earned this dubious distinction. However, that doesn't mean that we should try and stuff this exciting new technology back into Pandora's Box. It is worth our collective time to explore the potential societal hazards and benefits of the 3D printer and make a carefully considered, responsible decision regarding its use.

Although still in its relative technological infancy, 3D printing offers a great deal of promise in nearly every field of endeavor—art, medicine, and architecture are just a few examples. Imagine a world in which advanced 3D printers create artificial limbs or braces, produce amazing and creative sculptures, and even help reduce the costs and labor involved in new construction projects. Like all new technology, the best way to refine it, improve it, and make it evolve is by putting it in the hands of the people. As a society, and as individuals, we think of fantastic new ways to enhance gadgets and ideas by using them. Taking 3D printers out of the hands of average citizens would be a big mistake and would not be in the best interests of the technology or society as a whole.

However, as previously stated, 3D printers do possess the potential for misuse. They can be used to create dangerous, untraceable weapons, and even make counterfeit items. And, unfortunately, as the technology evolves, the ability to misuse it will expand and improve as well. This wouldn't be the first innovation with a negative social cost. Nuclear technology and automobiles can be added to this list—both of these have led to unfortunate accidents and deaths, but as the technology improves and we better understand and adopt new ways to use them responsibly, the social benefits clearly begin to outweigh the costs.

The evolution of 3D printing technology can follow a similar trajectory—exploring new safety features and allowing responsible levels of government regulation and oversight—all designed to protect users and society at large as we enjoy and make the most of this new innovation. An avenue of research regarding 3D printing should be to explore ways that possible template or molding limits can be implemented for certain dangerous objects like guns, as well as items where there's a counterfeiting concern. Perhaps we can adjust 3D printing technology so that all items created in each machine is marked with the appropriate registration number, which can be traced to the owner.

There should be a mandatory registration process for individuals who purchase 3D printers, which can be done quickly online or through an application process. Having people register or even obtain licensure in order to purchase potentially dangerous items is not a new concept, and its purpose is a noble one—to make us all safer. Furthermore, the way we approach, react, and respond to a new invention often evolves alongside the technology; as we gain increased exposure to 3D printers, and learn more about them and how they're used, our strategies for ensuring their responsible use will continue to become refined. Societies and cultures often follow a trajectory similar to new products—moving forward, sometimes in leaps and bounds and other times in small, cautious steps, occasionally with fits and starts through trial and error, but confidently and assuredly heading in a positive direction. When we're bolstered and supported by creative new ideas and wondrous, innovative marvels like 3D printing, we're truly putting our best foot forward.

Scoring Explanation

Ideas and Analysis: Score = 6

This essay response contains a wealth of ideas on how we could address the potential dangers of 3D printing ("exploring new safety features and allowing responsible levels of government regulation and oversight"), as well as how to react to the potential for misuse that many new innovations bring ("I think that the way we approach, react, and respond to a new invention often evolves alongside the technology"). Ideas are explored deeply and responsibly weighed, both for this instance as well as the larger social context ("as the technology improves and we better understand and adopt new ways to use them responsibility, the social benefits clearly begin to outweigh the costs"). The end result is a carefully considered and multi-faceted response to the essay task, with a confident, clear, and convincing perspective.

Development and Support: Score = 6

The writer of this essay clearly gave careful thought to the topic, and developed a compelling response that serves their perspective quite well. They provide a clear point of view ("taking 3D printers out of the hands of average citizens would be a big mistake, and would not be in the best interests of the technology or society as a whole," while acknowledging the need to find "new ways to use them responsibly"), takes the time to consider the perils of restrictive use of technology, and wisely offers other innovations for comparison (automobiles and nuclear technology) to bolster the position. The essay concludes with a stirring call for an acceptance of the risky yet potentially wonderful outcomes that can result from bold and innovative technological exploration and discovery.

Organization: Score = 6

From its engaging introduction to its memorable conclusion, this essay is a strong example of persuasive, impassioned writing, all of which supports a central unifying notion ("I feel that it is worth our collective time to explore the potential societal hazards and benefits of the 3D printer, and make a carefully considered, responsible decision regarding its use"). Although verbose, the writing is crisp, on target, and well organized, and the writer delivers a successful argument.

Language Use and Conventions: Score = 6

The author of this essay has a strong command of English language conventions and deploys them effectively throughout this piece of writing. The piece is largely free from errors in grammar and spelling, and a rich and varied word choice is on display, as are well-developed and interesting sentences and transitions. The result is a compelling essay that successfully responds to the task provided.

Determining Your Final Score

To self-score your essay, on a piece of paper, grade yourself a 1–6 for each domain, according to the detailed rubric given at the end of Chapter 2: Diagnostic Test. Next, double each score to represent the two unique graders' scores. Lastly, find the average by adding all four scores together and dividing by 4.

NOTES

SCORING CHARTS

Mark missed questions and calculate your total for each question category and each test as a whole. Then convert your individual test scores to scaled scores and calculate your composite score.

ENGLISH		
Question Types	**Question Numbers**	**Score**
Conventions of Standard English (CSE)	1, 2, 3, 4, 5, 8, 9, 10, 12, 13, 16, 18, 19, 22, 23, 24, 26, 32, 34, 37, 38, 39, 40, 41, 42, 43, 46, 47, 48, 49, 50, 52, 54, 56, 58, 63, 65, 66, 67, 69, 70, 71, 72, 74	_____/44
Production of Writing (POW)	11, 14, 15, 20, 27, 29, 30, 31, 44, 45, 51, 53, 57, 59, 60, 62, 73, 75	_____/18
Knowledge of Language (KLA)	6, 7, 17, 21, 25, 28, 33, 35, 36, 55, 61, 64, 68	_____/13
		Raw Score: _____/75

MATHEMATICS		
Question Types	**Question Numbers**	**Score**
Integrating Essential Skills (IES)	1, 2, 3, 4, 5, 8, 10, 12, 14, 15, 17, 18, 20, 22, 27, 29, 33, 35, 37, 41, 47, 56, 57, 58, 59	_____/25
Preparing for Higher Math (PHM)*		_____/35
Number and Quantity	7, 26, 48, 55, 60	_____/5
Algebra	9, 11, 16, 21, 23, 25, 36, 43	_____/8
Functions	6, 19, 28, 40, 42, 45, 50, 51	_____/8
Geometry	24, 30, 32, 34, 39, 44, 49, 53	_____/8
Statistics and Probability	13, 31, 38, 46, 52, 54	_____/6
Modeling**	1, 5, 8, 10, 12, 13, 19, 22, 23, 24, 27, 28, 29, 30, 31, 33, 35, 36, 37, 38, 46, 47, 49, 53, 54, 56, 57, 58	_____/28**
		Raw Score: _____/60

*Combine all subcategories of PHM questions for this score and add to your IES total to find your Raw Score.

**Modeling overlaps other scoring categories and is not added to your raw score.

READING

Question Types	Question Numbers	Score
Key Ideas and Details (KID)	1, 2, 3, 6, 8, 13, 14, 16, 17, 22, 24, 25, 26, 27, 28, 30, 31, 32, 34, 36, 37, 38, 39	_____/23
Craft and Structure (CS)	4, 5, 7, 9, 10, 11, 12, 15, 21, 23, 33, 35, 40	_____/13
Integration of Knowledge and Ideas (IKI)	18, 19, 20, 29	_____/4
		Raw Score: _____/40

SCIENCE

Question Types	Question Numbers	Score
Interpretation of Data (IOD)	1, 2, 3, 4, 5, 14, 16, 17, 19, 25, 26, 27, 28, 29, 30, 31, 36, 37, 38, 39	_____/20
Scientific Investigation (SIN)	13, 15, 20, 22, 23, 32, 33, 34, 35	_____/9
Evaluation of Models, Inferences, and Experimental Results (EMI)	6, 7, 8, 9, 10, 11, 12, 18, 21, 24, 40	_____/11
		Raw Score: _____/40

WRITING

Domain	Rubric Score	Domain Score*
Ideas and Analysis	_____/6	
Development and Support	_____/6	
Organization	_____/6	
Language Use	_____/6	
		Writing Score**:_____ /12

*Multiply Rubric Score by 2

**Sum Domain Scores and divide by 4; round to nearest whole number

Section	Raw Score	Scaled Score*
English	_____/75	
Mathematics	_____/60	
Reading	_____/40	
Science	_____/40	
	Composite Score**:	

*See p. 154 for English Score Conversion, p. 287 for Math Score Conversion, p. 529 for Reading Score Conversion, p. 636 for Science Score Conversion.

**Sum Scaled Scores and divide by 4; round to nearest whole number.